THE LIBRARIANS'
GLOSSARY

of terms used in librarianship, documentation
and the book crafts

AND REFERENCE BOOK

THE LIBRARIANS' GLOSSARY

of terms used in librarianship, documentation
and the book crafts

AND REFERENCE BOOK

Fourth Revised Edition

Leonard Montague Harrod

FELLOW OF THE LIBRARY ASSOCIATION

ANDRE DEUTSCH

A GRAFTON BOOK

THE THIRD (REVISED) EDITION
PUBLISHED IN JUNE 1971 BY
ANDRE DEUTSCH LIMITED
105 GREAT RUSSELL STREET LONDON WC1
FOURTH (REVISED) EDITION 1977

PRINTED IN GREAT BRITAIN
BY EBENEZER BAYLIS AND SON LTD
THE TRINITY PRESS
WORCESTER AND LONDON

ISBN 0 233 96744 3

The Librarians' Glossary was originally published
in 1938 and the 2nd (revised) edition in 1959 by
Grafton & Co.

Contents

Preface to First Edition

The need for an adequate glossary of terms used in librarianship has been felt by students of library work and by librarians in the performance of their duties for a long time. This work is an attempt to meet that need. It is primarily a glossary of *library* terms, but includes such subjects as printing, paper-making, publishing, binding, and illustrating, with which a librarian must be familiar, not only for the satisfactory performance of his professional duties, but also to meet the requirements of the Library Association's examinations. These other subjects have, therefore, been included, but only partially, because complete glossaries of these subsidiary subjects would not only be of immense size and beyond the purse of the average library assistant, but would be duplicating material which can be found in other books. The terms associated with these subjects have, therefore, been selected with the needs of the examination student and the practising librarian in mind.

This work has been compiled primarily for the use of students of librarianship who have always needed such a book at hand during their studies, and was intended to be of more immediate value for those preparing for the new Library Association syllabus, which included a section on terminology. The postponement of the adoption of this syllabus for a couple of years will not make the need for the book any the less.

It is anticipated that not only will the book be useful to public, university, county and school librarians, but that it will also find a place on the open shelves in reference libraries.

In certain subjects connected with librarianship, terms are used with different meanings by different people. In some cases it has been possible to give several definitions, in others the more usual definition and the one generally accepted has been used.

The classified lists of terms at the end of the book have been provided as a check-list for students, but they will also be useful as a reminder when trying to remember a term which is temporarily evasive.

I am indebted to my former Chief, W. C. Berwick Sayers, to my former colleague, Henry A. Sharp, and to Kenneth G. Hunt, for their valuable suggestions made when looking through the Classification, Cataloguing and Bibliography sections, respectively. Mr. Sharp has, in addition, permitted me to use the definitions which form an appendix to his *Cataloguing*. I am indebted also to Miss Helen M. Briggs for compiling the definitions of the terms used in palæography and archives.

I am grateful to the following publishers for permission to use definitions from certain books published by them: R. R. Bowker & Co. (Holden's *Bookman's Glossary*); G. E. Stechert & Co. (Hitchler's *Cataloguing for Small Libraries*); Spalding and Hodge, Ltd. (*Paper Terminology*); Allen and Unwin, Ltd. (Knight's *Business Man's Guide to Printing*); The Library Association (*A. A. Code*); United Typothetæ of America (*Dictionary of Graphic Arts Terms*); Grafton & Co. (Coutts and Stephen's *Library Bookbinding, Library Economics*).

Preface to Second Edition

Not until one compares the Library Association's examination papers of 1938 with those of 1956, or makes a systematic review of post-war library literature, does one realize the enormous progress that has taken place in the field of librarianship during this period.

When the first edition of the *Glossary* became out of print it was obvious that it would be unsatisfactory to reprint it. Complete revision was necessary, not only because of the development of the theory of librarianship and of library techniques, but also because of changes in the constitution and activities which library and bibliographical organizations have undergone.

The purpose and coverage of this edition of the *Glossary* are still the same but the scope has been very slightly widened to include some terms which, though not strictly limited to librarianship and the book crafts, are frequently met with by librarians in the course of their daily work. To find a satisfactory, or comprehensive definition of such is sometimes not easy.

This edition contains about 1,200 (75%) more entries than the first edition.

I am again grateful to friends for assistance with terms on certain subjects, and should like to express my great appreciation to the following for definitions of a few terms in fields in which they are specialists: Mr. W. Turner Berry for elucidating some printing terms; Mr. P. McGrath for definitions concerning British Government publications; Mr. B. Palmer for definitions of some terms used by Ranganathan; and Mr. F. A. Sharr for clarification of terms concerning county library work.

Singapore, November, 1958.

Preface to Third Edition

The second edition quickly went out of print but rather than re-print it, the publisher agreed that owing to the enormous development which had taken place since this edition had been prepared in the traditional field of librarianship and the new fields of knowledge which librarians have nowadays to be concerned with it, would be preferable once again to revise the work completely.

The extent of revision required was so great that it took much more time than was anticipated. The whole field covered has been gone over again to make the work more complete, and new subjects have been included.

In order that the book should be even more useful than in the past a number of headings are now included which do not lend themselves to 'definition'.

It was also found desirable to give more information than was necessary for a definition, and in many cases a 'definition' in the limited sense of the word either could not be used or would be totally inadequate. It is for these reasons that the title has been extended.

Librarianship has developed enormously in the last ten years, not only in its traditional areas, but has had to absorb new areas involving completely new techniques and the uses of equipment which has been developed to enable more work to be achieved with the minimum of extra manpower. This expansion is continuing. The whole field of librarianship and information services is now so wide that some areas are quite foreign to others, and in many cases specialization has become so great that one librarian or information officer is completely unfamiliar with the work and terminology of another.

Writings in English, wherever they originated, have been examined, and special attention has been given to American organizations, ideas and terminology as these are less familiar to English librarians.

This work could not have been revised without the assistance of numerous specialists, former colleagues at the School of librarianship, North-Western Polytechnic (especially John Morris with help on historical bookbinding and book-decoration terms), librarians of special and public libraries, and the secretaries of professional and learned societies all over the world, all of whom have readily given information on which definitions have been based. Their help is greatly appreciated.

A number of definitions in print have been included. I am grateful to Dr. Erhard Ühlein for permission to reproduce those marked (*Concepts . . .*) from his *Concepts of reprography*; to IBM United Kingdom Limited for those marked (*IBM*) from their *Reference manual*; to the late H. R. Verry for those marked (*Verry*) from his *Document copying and reproduction processes*, and to the Editor of the *Library Association Record* for those marked (*County libraries*) which appeared in the issue of that publication for August 1960.

June 1970

Preface to Fourth Edition

The third edition of the *Glossary* went out of print sooner than was expected, and it was intended to prepare an updated edition. But the whole conspectus of librarianship and information science has continued to develop so rapidly and extensively in recent years that it soon became evident that what was needed was a revised, rather than an updated, edition.

New techniques in publishing, mechanization of library methods, technological changes in information retrieval, the increasing use of computers in many aspects of library and information science activities, administrative changes in the provision of services, increased co-operation between organizations in local and national areas and also internationally, and the many new organizations which have been formed, have all had their effect on the contents of this book. A number of entries for organizations have had to be considerably altered, some have had to be deleted and many added.

The basic content of this book is still the *Glossary*, and a rough count indicates that 690 more terms have been defined and 310 expanded. Other types of entry account for about 400 additions and 130 amendments; minor alterations have been made to many other entries. In order to include the additional entries without making the volume too bulky, the three appendices in the third edition (Latin names of towns, classified lists of entries, and a precis of the provisions of the Public Libraries and Museums Act 1964) have been omitted.

The practice of referring to organizations by the acronyms of their names has become increasingly common; people nowadays usually use the acronyms, both in speech and in writing, rather than the full names (in fact these are often so lengthy and involved that this is to be expected). It was therefore decided to enter most of the new organizations under their acronyms. The full names are included in the main sequence but refer to the acronyms.

Much information has been gleaned from periodicals, specialized subject glossaries and publications of official bodies. Many chairmen, directors or secretaries of organizations have given up-to-date information. I have received much assistance from many people who have helped with definitions and information, and where it has been possible to use their information exactly as received, credit has been given, but often it has been slightly adapted or used to form part of an entry; in such cases there is no attribution. The list of such persons is lengthy – too long unfortunately for publication, but to all I express my great appreciation. I would however, specifically mention the staffs of the Information Department of the Library Association and of the British Library (Library Association Library) and express to them my grateful thanks for their resourceful help given over the past twenty months.

Harpenden, March 1976.

SUPPLEMENT

There is a Supplement at the end of the main sequence consisting of acronyms and definitions of developments which have taken place since the *Librarians' Glossary* was prepared for the printer. † by an entry in the main sequence indicates that there is additional material in the Supplement.

Acronyms and Abbreviations in general use

Abbreviations other than of organizations are in the main sequence of definitions. Entries will usually be found in the main sequence under acronyms and sometimes under unpronounceable abbreviations (arranged at the beginning of each letter sequence), where these are easily remembered; where a full name appears to be more familiar, or more appropriate, entry is made under it. Entries in this list with a * do not have an entry in the main sequence; they are included here solely for the purposes of identification. † indicates a further entry in the Supplement.

AACOBS Australian Advisory Council on Bibliographical Services.

AACR *Anglo-American Cataloguing Rules. See Anglo-American Code.*

AAL Association of Assistant Librarians.

AALL American Association of Law Libraries.

AALS Association of American Library Schools.

AAP Association of American Publishers, Inc.

AASL American Association of School Librarians.

ABLISS Association of British Library and Information Studies Schools.

ABTAPL Association of British Theological and Philosophical Libraries.

ACA Association of Canadian Archivists.

ACLO Association of Co-operative Library Organizations. *See entry under* ACLO.

ACM Association for Computing Machinery.

ACONDA Activities Committee of New Directions for ALA.*

ACRL Association of College and Research Libraries.

ACSI Association Canadienne des Sciences de l'Information. *See entry under* CANADIAN ASSOCIATION FOR INFORMATION SCIENCE.

ACURIL Association of Caribbean University and Research Libraries.*

ADBPA Association pour le Développement des Bibliothèques Publiques en Afrique. *See entry under* ASSOCIATION FOR THE DEVELOPMENT OF PUBLIC LIBRARIES IN AFRICA.

ADC Association of District Councils.

ADI American Documentation Institute.

ADP Automatic Data Processing.*

ADRIS Association for the Development of Religious Information Systems. *See entry under* ADRIS.

AFIPS   American Federation of Information Processing Societies.

AFR   Automatic Format Recognition.*

AGARD   Advisory Group for Aerospace Research and Development. *See entry under* AGARD.

AGRA   Association of Genealogists and Record Agents.

AHIL   Association of Hospital and Institution Libraries.

AID   Association Internationale des Documentalists et Techniciens de l'Information. *See entry under* INTERNATIONAL ASSOCIATION OF DOCUMENTALISTS AND INFORMATION OFFICERS.

AIDBA   Association Internationale pour le Développement de la Documentation des Bibliothèques et des Archives en Afrique. *See entry under* INTERNATIONAL ASSOCIATION FOR THE DEVELOPMENT OF DOCUMENTATION, LIBRARIES AND ARCHIVES IN AFRICA.

AIInfSc   Associate of the Institute of Information Scientists.

AIL   Association of International Libraries.

AJL   Association of Jewish Libraries.

ALA   American Library Association. Associate of the (British) Library Association.

ALAA   Associate of the Library Association of Australia.*

ALBIS   Australian Library-Based Information System. *See entry under* ALBIS.

ALCL   Association of London Chief Librarians.

ALEBCI   Asociación Latinamericana de Escuelas de Bibliotecalogia y Ciencias de la Información. *See entry under* ALEBCI.

ALIS   Association of Librarians in Schools. *See entry under* ALIS.

ALJH   Association of Libraries of Judaica and Hebraica in Europe.

ALTA   American Library Trustee Association.

AMA   Association of Metropolitan Authorities. *See entry under* AMA.

AMCL   Association of Metropolitan Chief Librarians.

AMLS   Master of Arts in Library Science.*

AMMLA   American Merchant Marine Library Association.

ANDBP   Association Nationale pour le Développement des Bibliothèques Publiques. *See entry under* ANDBP.

ANRT   Association Nationale de la Recherche Technique.

ANSI   American National Standards Institute.

ANSTEL   Australian National Scientific and Technological Library. *See entry under* ANSTEL.

APLA   Authors' and Publishers' Lending Right Association Committee. *See entry under* PUBLIC LENDING RIGHT.

ARBICA Arab Regional Branch of the International Council on Archives. *See entry under* INTERNATIONAL COUNCIL ON ARCHIVES.

ARL Association of Research Libraries.

ARLIS Art Libraries Society. *See entry under* ARLIS.

ASA American Standards Association. *See entry under* AMERICAN NATIONAL STANDARDS INSTITUTE, INC.

ASCII American Standard Code for Information Interchange. *See entry under* ASCII.

ASD Association Suisse de Documentation.

ASFEC The Arab States Fundamental Education Centre.

ASI American Society of Indexers.

ASIDIC Association of Scientific Information Dissemination Centers. *See entry under* ASIDIC.

ASIS American Society for Information Science.

ASL American Association of State Libraries.

ASLA Association of State Library Agencies.

ASTED l'Association pour l'Avancement des Sciences et des Techniques de la Documentation. *See entry under* ASTED.

ASTIA Armed Services Technical Information Agency; now the Defense Documentation Center.

ATALA Association pour l'Etude et de la Linguistique Appliquée.

ATLA American Theological Library Association.

BALLOTS Bibliographic Automation of Large Library Operations using a Time-sharing System. *See entry under* BALLOTS.

BASc Bachelor of Applied Science.*

BASIC Biological Abstracts Subjects In Context.†

BB&O Berkshire, Buckinghamshire & Oxfordshire Branch (of the Library Association).

B.BIBL Bachelier en Bibliotheconomie et en Bibliographie.

BC Borough Council.

BCM British Catalogue of Music.

BHI British Humanities Index.

BIALL British and Irish Association of Law Librarians. *See entry under* British and Irish Association of Law Librarians.

BIB Biennale of Illustrations Bratislava.

BIOSIS Bio-Sciences Information Service of Biological Abstracts. *See entry under* BIOSIS.

BIRS British Institute of Recorded Sound Ltd.

BIS Biological Information Service. *See entry under* BIS.

BL The British Library.

BLCMP Birmingham Libraries Co-operative Mechanization Project. *See entry under* BLCMP.

BLET Bureau of Libraries and Educational Technology. *See entry under* BLLR.

BLLR Bureau of Libraries and Learning Resources. *See entry under* BLLR.

BLSc Bachelor of Library Science.*

BM British Museum.

BML British Museum Library.

BN Bibliothèque Nationale.

BNB British National Bibliography.

BNBC British National Book Centre.

BRA British Records Association.

BRIMARC Brighton/MARC. *See entry under* BRIMARC.

BS British Standard. *See entry under* BRITISH STANDARDS INSTITUTION.

BSA Bibliographical Society of America.

BScB Bachelier ès Science Bibliothéconomie.*

BSI British Standards Institution.

BSIB British Society for International Bibliography.

BSO Broad System of Ordering.

BTI British Technology Index.

BUCCS Bath University Comparative Catalogue Study. *See entry under* BUCCS.

BUCOP British Union Catalogue of Periodicals.

CAB Commonwealth Agricultural Bureaux.

CACL Canadian Association of Children's Librarians (a Section of the Canadian Association of Public Libraries).

CACUL Canadian Association of College and University Libraries (a Division of the Canadian Library Association).

CAG Computer Applications Group (of Aslib).*

CAIN CAtaloguing and INdexing system. *See entry under* CAIN.

CAIS Canadian Association for Information Science.

CALL Canadian Association of Law Libraries.

CAN/SDI Canadian Selective Dissemination of Information. *See entry under* CAN/SDI.

CANSIM Canadian Socio-Economic Information Management System. *See entry under* CANSIM.

CAPL Canadian Association of Public Libraries (a Division of the Canadian Library Association).

CASLIS Canadian Association of Special Libraries and Information Services (a Division of the Canadian Library Association).

CBC Children's Book Council.

*CBI Cumulative Book Index.**

CC County Council.

CCC Central Classification Committee of the FID.

CDCR Center for Documentation and Communication Research.

CDS Computerized Documentation Service. *See entry under* CDS.

CEDI European Documentation and Information Centre.

CEN Comité Européen de Coordination des Normes. *See entry under* EUROPEAN COMMITTEE FOR CO-ORDINATION OF STANDARDS.

CERN European Organization for Nuclear Research.

CETIS Centre Européen pour le Traitement de l'Information Scientifique. *See entry under* CETIS.

CFSTI Clearinghouse for Federal Scientific and Technical Information.

CIA Conseil International des Archives. *See entry under* INTERNATIONAL COUNCIL ON ARCHIVES.

CIB Conseil Internationale du Batiment pour la Recherche, l'Etude et la Documentation. International Council for Building Research, Studies and Documentation.

CICRED Committee for International Co-ordination of National Research in Demography. *See entry under* CICRED.

CICRIS Co-operative Industrial and Commercial Reference and Information Service. *See entry under* CICRIS.

CIDB International Council for Building Documentation. *See entry under* INTERNATIONAL COUNCIL FOR BUILDING RESEARCH STUDIES AND DOCUMENTATION.

CIDESA The International Centre for African Social and Economic Documentation. *See entry under* CIDESA.

CIG Catalogue and Indexing Group (of the Library Association). Co-ordinate Indexing Group (of Aslib).*

CIP Cataloguing in publication.

CIS Cataloguing in Source.

CISE Colleges, Institutes and Schools of Education (a Group of the Library Association).

CISTI Canada Institute for Scientific and Technical Information. *See entry under* CISTI.

CISTIP Committee on International Scientific and Technical Information Programs. *See entry under* CISTIP.

CLA Canadian Library Association – L'Association Canadienne des Bibliothèques. The form CLA–ACB is also used.

CLA   Catholic Library Association.

CLR   Council on Library Resources, Inc.

CLTA   Canadian Library Trustees' Association (a Division of the Canadian Library Association).

CML   Central Music Library.

CNLA   Council of National Library Associations.

CNRS   Centre National de la Recherche Scientifique et Technique. *See entry under* CNRS.

CODATA   Committee on Data for Science and Technology. *See entry under* CODATA.

COM   Computer output on to microfilm/microforms.*

COMLA   Commonwealth Library Association.

COMPENDEX   COMPuterized ENgineering InDEX. *See entry under* COMPENDEX.

CONSAL   Conference on Southeast Asian Librarians. *See entry under* CONSAL.

CONSER   Co-operative CONversion of SERials. *See entry under* CONSER.

COPANT   Pan American Standards Commission. *See entry under* COPANT.

COPIC   Computer Information Centre. *See entry under* COPIC.

COSATI   Committee on Scientific and Technical Information. *See entry under* COSATI.

COSMIC   Computer Software Management Information Center. *See entry under* COSMIC.

CPL   Council of Planning Librarians.

CRG   Classification Research Group.

CRIS   Command Retrieval Information System.

CRL   Center for Research Libraries.

CROSS   Computerized Rearrangement of Special Subjects. *See entry under* CROSS.

CRSG   Classification Research Study Group.

CSD   Children's Services Division (of the American Library Association).

CSIRO   Commonwealth Scientific and Research Organization.

CSL   Circle of State Librarians.

CSLA   Church and Synagogue Library Association. Canadian School Library Association (a Division of the Canadian Library Association).

CTFE   Colleges of Technology and Further Education. A Group of the Library Association.

DC   Decimal Classification.

DDC Defense Documentation Center. Dewey Decimal Classification.

DLSEF Division of Library Services and Educational Facilities, U.S. Office of Education.*

DOCA Section Documentation Automatique (Automatic Documentation Section). A working party of CETIS (*q.v.*).

DP Data processing.

DRIC Defence Research Information Centre. *See entry under* DRIC.

EALA East African Library Association.

ECARBICA East and Central Africa Regional Branch (of the International Council on Archives). *See entry under* ECARBICA.

EDP Electronic data processing.*

EDUCOM Interuniversity Communications Council.

EFLA Educational Film Library Association.

ELBS English Language Book Society.

EMBLA East Midlands Branch (of the Library Association).

ERIC Educational Resources Reading Center. *See entry under* ERIC.

ERIC/IR ERIC Clearinghouse on Information Resources. *See entry under* ERIC/CLIS.

ESEA Elementary and Secondary Education Act.*

ETC European Translations Centre.

EUDISED European Documentation and Information System for Education. *See entry under* EUDISED.

EUSIDIC European Association of Scientific Information Dissemination Centres. *See entry under* EUSIDIC.

FGMC Federal Micrographics Council. *See entry under* FGMC.

FIAB Fédération Internationale des Associations de Bibliothécaires. *See entry under* INTERNATIONAL FEDERATION OF LIBRARY ASSOCIATIONS.

FIAF Fédération Internationale des Archives du Film. *See entry under* FIAF.

FID Fédération Internationale de Documentation. *See entries also under* INTERNATIONAL FEDERATION FOR DOCUMENTATION, and UNIVERSAL DECIMAL CLASSIFICATION.

FIInfSc Fellow of the Institute of Information Scientists.*

FIP Fédération Internationale des Phonothèque. *See entry under* INTERNATIONAL FEDERATION OF RECORD LIBRARIES.

FIT Fédération Internationale des Traducteurs. *See entry under* INTERNATIONAL FEDERATION OF TRANSLATORS.

FLA Fellow of the Library Association.* Federal Librarians Association.

FLAA Fellow of the Library Association of Australia.*

FLAI Fellow of the Library Association of Ireland.*

FLC   Federal Library Committee.
FLECC   Federal Libraries Experiment in Cooperative Cataloging. *See entry under* FEDERAL LIBRARIES EXPERIMENT IN COOPERATIVE CATALOGING.
FLIC   Film Library Information Council.
FLIP   Film Library Instantaneous Presentation.
FLIRT   Federal Librarians Round Table.
FNIC   Food and Nutrition Information and Educational Materials Center.
FNZLA   Fellow of the New Zealand Library Association.*
FORATOM   European Atomic Forum. *See entry under* FORATOM.
FSALA   Fellow of the South African Library Association.*
FTRF   Freedom to Read Foundation.
GLCLG   Greater London College Librarians' Group. *See entry under* GLCLG.
HALDIS   Halifax and District Information Service. *See entry under* HALDIS.
HATRICS   Hampshire Technical Research Industrial and Commercial Service. *See entry under* HATRICS.
HELPIS   Higher Education Learning Programmes Information Service. *See entry under* HELPIS.
HERTIS   Hertfordshire County Council Technical Information Service. *See entry under* HERTIS.
HILC   Hampshire Inter-Library Center.
HMSO   Her Majesty's Stationery Office. *See entry under* PARLIAMENTARY PUBLICATIONS also.
HRLSD   Health and Rehabilitative Library Services Division (of the American Library Association). *See entry under* HRLSD.
HTFS   Heat Transfer and Fluid Flow Service Information Centre. *See entry under* HTFS.
HULTIS   Hull Technical Interloan Scheme. *See entry under* HULTIS.
IAALD   International Association of Agricultural Librarians and Documentalists.
IABLA   Inter-American Bibliographical and Library Association.
IACODLA   International Advisory Committee on Documentation, Libraries and Archives. *See entry under* IACODLA.
IADIS   Irish Association for Documentation and Information Services. *See entry under* IADIS.
IALL   International Association of Law Libraries.
IAMCR   International Association for Mass Communication Research.

IAML   International Association of Music Librarians.
IAOL   International Association of Orientalist Librarians. *See entry under* IAOL.
IASA   International Association of Sound Archives.
IASL   International Association of School Librarianship.
IASLIC   Indian Association of Special Libraries and Information Centres.
IATL   International Association of Theological Libraries.
IATUL   International Association of Technological University Libraries.
IBBD   Instituto Brasileño de Bibliografía e Documentaçao. Brazilian Institute of Bibliography and Documentation. *See entry under* IBBD.
IBBY   International Board on Books for Young People. *See entry under* IBBY.
IBE   International Bureau of Education.
IBFD   International Bureau of Fiscal Documentation.
IBI–ICC   Intergovernmental Bureau for Informatics-International Computer Centre. *See entry under* IBI–ICC.
IBY   International Book Year. *See entry under* IBY.
IC   Implementation Committee.*
ICA   International Council on Archives.
ICAE   International Council for Adult Education. *See entry under* ICAE.
ICBA   International Community of Booksellers Associations. *See entry under* ICBA.
ICBD   International Children's Book Day. *See entry under* INTERNATIONAL BOARD ON BOOKS FOR YOUNG PEOPLE.
ICC   International Children's Centre.
ICC–IBI   International Computer Centre – Intergovernmental Bureau for Informatics. *See entry under* IBI–ICC.
ICCP   International Conference on Cataloguing Principles.
ICIC   International Copyright Information Centre. *See entry under* ICIC.
ICIREPAT   International Co-operation in Information Retrieval among Patent Offices. *See entry under* ICIREPAT.
ICLG   International and Comparative Librarianship Group (of the Library Association). *See entry under* ICLG.
ICLS   Irish Central Library for Students.
ICOGRADA   International Council of Graphic Design Associations. *See entry under* ICOGRADA.
ICOM   International Council of Museums.
ICRSC   International Council for Research in the Sociology of Co-operation.

ICSI   International Conference on Scientific Information.
ICSSD   International Committee for Social Sciences Documentation.
ICSU   International Council of Scientific Unions.
ICSUAB International Council of Scientific Unions Abstracting Board.*
IDC   International Documentation Centre.
IDRC   International Development Research Centre.*

IEAB   Internacia Esperanto-Asocio de Bibliotekistoj (International Association for Esperanto-Speaking Librarians). *See entry under* IEAB.
IEC   International Electrotechnical Commission.*
IFA   International Fiscal Association.*
IFD   International Federation for Documentation.
IFIP   International Federation for Information Processing.
IFLA   International Federation of Library Associations.
IGC   Intergovernmental Copyright Committee. *See entry under* IGC.
IGO   Inter-governmental Organizations.
IIB   Institut International des Brevets. *See entry under* International Patent Institute.
IICA–CIDIA   Inter-American Center for Agricultural Documentation and Information.
ILA   Indian Library Association. Israel Library Association.
ILAS   Inter-related Logic-Accumulating Scanner.
ILLINET   Illinois Library and Information Network. *See entry under* ILLINET.
IMC   International Micrographic Congress. Irish Manuscripts Commission.
IMCE   International Meeting of Cataloguing Experts. *See entry under* IMCE.
IMS   International Musicological Society.
INCIRS   International Communication Information Retrieval System. *See entry under* INCIRS.
INFOTERM   International Information Centre for Terminology. *See entry under* INFOTERM.
INIS   International Nuclear Information System. *See entry under* INIS.
INPADOC   International Patent Documentation Centre. *See entry under* INPADOC.
INSCOPE   Information System for Coffee and Other Product Economics. *See entry under* INSCOPE.
INSPEC   International Information Services for the Physics and Engineering Communities. *See entry under* INSPEC.

INTREX   Information Transfer Exchange.
IOL   Institute of Librarians.
IPA   International Publishers Association.
IR   Information retrieval.
IRA   International Reading Association.
IRCIHE   International Referral Centre for Information Handling Equipment.
IRLA   Independent Research Libraries Association. *See entry under* IRLA.
IRO   International Relations Office (of the American Library Association).*
IRS   International Referral System for Sources of Environmental Information. *See entry under* IRS.
IRT   Institute of Reprographic Technology.
ISA†   International Federation of National Standardizing Associations. *See entry under* INTERNATIONAL ORGANIZATION FOR STANDARDIZATION.
ISAD   Information Science and Automation Division (of the American Library Association).
ISBD   International Standard Bibliographic Description. *See entry under* ISBD.
ISBN   International Standard Book Number. *See entry under* ISBN.
ISCED   International Standard Classification of Education. *See entry under* ISCED.
ISDS   International Serials Data System. *See entry under* ISDS.
ISFL   International Scientific Film Library.
ISIS   Integrated Set of Information Systems. *See entry under* ISIS.
ISLIC   Israel Society of Special Libraries and Information Centres.
ISMEC   Information Services in Mechanical Engineering. *See entry under* ISMEC.
ISO   International Organization for Standardization.
ISODOC   International Information Centre for Standards in Information and Documentation. *See entry under* ISODOC.
ISORID   International Information System on Research in Documentation. *See entry under* ISORID.
ISSN   International Standard Serial Number. *See entry under* ISSN.
ITU   International Telecommunications Union.*
IYL   International Youth Library.
JFR   Joint Fiction Reserve
JLA   Jewish Librarians Association.
JMRT   Junior Members Round Table (of the ALA).*

KC The Kyle Classification. *See entry under* CLASSIFICATION FOR SOCIAL SCIENCES.

KWAC Keyword-and-Context. *See entry under* KWAC.

KWIC Keyword-in-Context. *See entry under* KWIC.

KWOC Keyword-out-of-Context. *See entry under* KWOC.

KWOT Keyword-out-of-Title. *See entry under* KWOT.

LA Library Association. Library automation.

LAA Library Association of Australia.

LACAP Latin American Cooperative Acquisitions Project. *See entry under* LACAP.

LACIRS Latin American Information Retrieval System. *See entry under* INCIRS.

LAD Library Administration Division of the American Library Association.

LADSIRLAC Liverpool and District Scientific, Industrial and Research Advisory Council. *See entry under* LADSIRLAC.

L&HCB London and Home Counties Branch (of the Library Association).

LAI Library Association of Ireland.

LAMSAC Local Authorities Management Services and Computer Committee. *See entry under* LAMSAC.

LARC Association. The Association for Library Automation Research Communications. *See entry under* LARC ASSOCIATION.

LAS Library Association of Singapore.

LASER London & South Eastern Library Region.

LBI Library Binding Institute.

LC Library of Congress.

L of C Library of Congress.

LCF Librarians' Christian Fellowship. *See entry under* LCF.

LCLA Lutheran Church Library Association.

LEC London Education Classification.

LED Library Education Division (of the ALA).

LEG Library Education Group (of the Library Association).

LIBER Ligue des Bibliothèques Européennes de Recherche. League of European Research Libraries. *See entry under* LIBER.

LIBTRAD Working Party on Library and Book Trade Relations. *See entry under* LIBTRAD.

LINOSCO Libraries of North Staffordshire in Co-operation. *See entry under* LINOSCO.

LISA   Library & Information Science Abstracts.

LISE   Librarians of Institutes and Schools of Education. *See entry under* LISE.

LIST   Library Information Service for Teesside. *See entry under* LIST. *Library and Information Services Today.**

LMRU   Library Management Research Unit.

LPRC   Library Publications Relations Council.

LRC   Library Research Center.

LSA   Library Science Abstracts.

LSCA   Library Services and Construction Act.

LTP   Library Technology Program. (*Formerly* Library Technology Project.)

LULOP   London Union List of Periodicals.

MAGB   Microfilm Association of Great Britain.

MAinLS   Master of Arts in Library Science.*

MALS   Master of Arts in Library Science.*

MANTIS   Manchester Technical and Commercial Information Services. *See entry under* Manchester Technical Information Services.

MARC   Machine Readable Catalogue.

MARLF   Middle Atlantic Regional Library Federation. *See entry under* MARLF.

MBSJC   Metropolitan Boroughs Standing Joint Committee. *See entry under* ASSOCIATION OF METROPOLITAN CHIEF LIBRARIANS.

MELA   Middle East Librarians' Association. *See entry under* MELA.

MIDLNET   Midwest Regional Library Network. *See entry under* MIDLNET.

MILC   Midwest Inter-Library Center. *See entry under* CENTER FOR RESEARCH LIBRARIES.

MINICS   Minimal-Input Cataloguing System. *See entry under* MINICS.

MISLIC   Mid and South Staffordshire Libraries in Co-operation. *See entry under* MISLIC.

MLA   Medical Library Association. Music Library Association.

MSC   Metropolitan Special Collection. *See entry under* ASSOCIATION OF METROPOLITAN CHIEF LIBRARIANS.

MSinLS   Master of Science in Library Science.*

MSLS   Master of Science in Library Science.*

MSLSc   Master of Science in Library Science.*

NACL   National Advisory Commission on Libraries.

NAEST   National Archive for Electrical Science and Technology. *See entry under* NAEST.

NAL   National Agricultural Library.

NALGO   National and Local Government Officers Association.

NANTIS   Nottingham and Nottinghamshire Technical Information Service. *See entry under* NANTIS.

NAS – NRC   National Academy of Sciences – National Research Council.

NASIC   Northeast Academic Science Information Center.*

NATIS   National Information Systems. *See entry under* NATIS.

NBA   National Braille Association. *See entry under* NBA.

NBC   National Book Committee (America). National Book Council (Australia. UK).

NBL   National Book League.

NBM   Non-book Materials.

NBN   National Book Number.

NBS   National Bureau of Standards.

NCALI   National Clearinghouse for Alcohol Information. *See entry under* NCALI.

NCES   National Center for Educational Statistics.

NCET   National Council for Educational Technology. *See entry under* NCET.

NCL   National Central Library.

NCLIS   National Commission on Libraries and Information Science. *See entry under* NCLIS.

NCRLC   National Committee on Regional Library Co-operation.

NEDL   New England Deposit Library.

NELINET   New England Library Information Network. *See entry under* NELINET.

NEMROC   Newcastle Media Resources Organizing Committee.

NERC   Natural Environment Research Council. *See entry under* NERC.

NFAIS   National Federation of Abstracting and Indexing Services.

NGO   Non-governmental Organizations.*

NIC   Neighbourhood Information Centers.

NIDER   The Netherlands Institute of Documentation and Filing (Nederlands Instituut voor Documentatie en Registratuur).

NIE   National Institute of Education. *See entry under* NIE.

NITCs   National Information Transfer Centres. *See entry under* ISORID.

NJFR   National Joint Fiction Reserve. *See entry under* JOINT FICTION RESERVE.

NLA   National Libraries Authority. National Librarians Association. *See entry under* NLA.

NLB   National Library for the Blind.

NLC   National Library of Canada.

NLL   National Lending Library for Science and Technology.

NLLST   National Lending Library for Science and Technology.

NLM   National Library of Medicine.

NLS   National Library of Scotland.

NLSLS   National Library of Scotland Lending Services. *See entry under* NATIONAL LIBRARY OF SCOTLAND.

NMA   National Microfilm Association. National Micrographics Association.

NORDFORSK   Scandinavian Council for Applied Research. *See entry under* NORDFORSK.

NPAC   National Program for Acquisitions and Cataloging.

NRC   National Referral Center for Science and Technology.

NRCD   National Reprographic Centre for Documentation.

NRLSI   National Reference Library of Science and Invention.

NSDP   National Serials Data Program.

NSF   National Science Foundation.

NSL   National Science Library (of Canada).

NSRDS   National Standard Reference Data System. *See entry under* NSRDS.

NTBL   Nuffield Talking Book Library for the Blind.

NTIS   National Technical Information Service. *See entry under* NTIS.

NUCMC   National Union Catalog of Manuscript Collections.

NVBF   Scandinavian Association of Scientific Librarians.*

OCLC   Ohio College Library Center.†

OCR   Optical Character Recognition.

OFR   Office for Research (ALA).

OLE   Office for Library Education (ALA).

ONULP   Ontario New Universities Library Project. *See entry under* ONULP.

OS   Ordnance Survey.

OSIS   Office of Science Information Service. *See entry under* OSIS.

OSRD   Office for Standard Reference Data. *See entry under* OSRD.

OST   Office for Science and Technology.*

OULMS   Office of University Library Management Studies.

PANSDOC   The Pakistan National Scientific and Technical Documentation Centre.

PIC   Publishers Information Card.

PIRA   Research Association for the Paper and Board, Printing and Packaging Industries. *See entry under* PIRA.

PLA   Private Libraries Association. Public Library Association.

PLR   Public lending right.

PNLA   Pacific Northwest Library Association.*

PRECIS   PREserved Context Index System. *See entry under* PRECIS.

PRO   Public Record Office.

PROI   Public Record Office of Ireland.

PRONI   Public Record Office of Northern Ireland.

PROSPO   Public Record Office of Ireland.

RAS   Readers Advisory Service. *See entry under* RAS.

RASD   Acronym of Reference and Adult Services Division of the American Library Association.

RDC   Rural District Council.

RILM   Répertoire Internationale de Littérature Musicale. *See entry under* RILM.

RLG   Research Library Group. *See entry under* RLG.

RMIS   Rock Mechanics Information Service.

RRIS   Railroad Research Information Service. *See entry under* RRIS.

RSIS   Reference, Special and Information Section of the Library Association.

RTSD   Resources and Technical Services Division (of the American Library Association).

SAA   Society of American Archivists.

SAALIC   Swindon Area Association of Libraries for Industry and Commerce.

SALALM   Seminars on the Acquisition of Latin American Library Materials. *See entry under* SALALM.

SARBICA   Southeast Asian Regional Branch of the International Council of Archives. *See entry under* SARBICA.

SASLIC   Surrey and Sussex Libraries in Co-operation. *See entry under* SASLIC.

SATCOM   Committee on Scientific and Technical Communication. *See entry under* SATCOM.

SBN   Standard Book Number.

SCAMP   Scottish Association of Magazine Publishers. *See entry under* SCAMP.

SCANDOC   Scandinavian Documentation Center. *See entry under* SCANDOC.

SCAUL   Standing Conference of African University Librarians. *See entry under* SCAUL.

SCAULEA   Standing Conference of African University Libraries: Eastern Area. *See entry under* SCAULEA.

SCEL   Standing Committee on Education in Librarianship.*

SCICON   SCIentific CONtrol Systems Ltd.*

SCI-TECH   Science-Technology Division of the Special Libraries Association.

SCL   Scottish Central Library.

SCOCLIS   Standing Conference of Co-operative Library and Information Services.

SCOLCAP   Scottish Libraries Cataloguing Automation Project. *See entry under* SCOLCAP.

SCOLLUL   Standing Conference of Librarians of Libraries of the University of London. *See entry under* SCOLLUL.

SCOLMA   Standing Conference on Library Materials on Africa. *See entry under* SCOLMA.

SCONUL   Standing Conference of National and University Libraries. *See entry under* SCONUL.

SCOPAS   Standing Conference on Professional Activities in Scotland. *See entry under* SCOPAS.

SCOTAPLL   Standing Conference on Theological and Philosophical Libraries in London. *See entry under* SCOTAPLL.

SDI   Selective dissemination of information.

SDM   Selective dissemination of microfiche. *See entry under* SDM.

SDS   Space Documentation Service. *See entry under* SDS.

SEAL   South East Area Libraries Information Service. *See entry under* SEAL.

SED   South East Division of the Association of Assistant Librarians.*

SIBMAS   Société Internationale des Bibliothèques – Musées des Arts du Spectacle. *See entry under* SIBMAS.

SIG–LOGIS   Special Interest Group – Local Government Information Service. *See entry under* SIG–LOGIS.

SINTO   Sheffield Interchange Organisation. *See entry under* SINTO.

SLA   School Library Association. Scottish Library Association. Special Libraries Association.

SLIC   Selective Listing In Combination. *See entry under* SLIC INDEX.

SM   Master of Science.*

SMART   Salton's Magical Automatic Retriever of Texts. *See entry under* SMART.

SMCCL   Society of Municipal and County Chief Librarians.*

SOLINET   Southeastern Library Network. *See entry under* SOLINET.

SPEC   Systems and Procedures Exchange Centre. *See entry under* ASSOCIATION OF RESEARCH LIBRARIES.

SPECOL   SPE Customer Oriented Language. *See entry under* SPECOL.

SPEL   Selected Publications in European Languages. *See entry under* SPEL.

SPEX   Specialist Publishers Exhibition. *See entry under* SPEX.

SPINES   Science and Technology Policies Information Exchange System. *See entry under* SPINES.

SRC   Subject-field Reference Code. *See* UNISIST.

SRL   Science Reference Library. *See entry under* NATIONAL REFERENCE LIBRARY OF SCIENCE AND INVENTION.

STISEC   Scientific and Technological Information Services Enquiry Committee. *See entry under* STISEC.

SVD   Schweizerische Vereinigung für Dokumentation. *See entry under* ASD.

TALIC   Tyneside Association of Libraries for Industry and Commerce. *See entry under* TALIC.

TESLA   Technical Standards for Library Automation.

TRC   Technology Reports Centre (of the Department of Trade). *See entry under* TRC.

TTS   Teletypesetting.

UBC   Universal Bibliographic Control. *See entry under* UBC.

UCC   Universal Copyright Convention. *See entry under* COPYRIGHT INTERNATIONAL.

UCRS   University, College & Research Section (of the Library Association).

UDC   Universal Decimal Classification. Urban District Council.

UKCIS   United Kingdom Chemical Information Service.

UKRA   United Kingdom Reading Association.

UNDIS   United Nations Documentation Information System. *See entry under* UNDIS.

UNESCO   United Nations Educational, Scientific and Cultural Organization. *See entry under* UNESCO.

UNIDO   United Nations Industrial Development Organization. *See entry under* UNIDO.

UNISIST   United Nations Information System in Science and Technology. *See entry under* UNISIST.

URISA   Urban and Regional Information Systems Association. *See entry under* URISA.

USASI   United States of America Standards Institute.

USBE   Universal Serials and Book Exchange, Inc. *See entry under* USBE.

USGPO   United States Government Printing Office.

USIA   United States Information Agency.

USIS   United States Information Service.

VDU   Visual display unit.

VINITI   Vsesoyuznyi Institut Nauchnoi Tekhnicheskoi Informatsii (All-Union Institute of Scientific and Technical Information). *See entry under* VINITI.

VOLS   Voluntary Overseas Libraries Service.

WAITRO   World Association of Industrial and Technological Research Organizations. *See entry under* WAITRO.

WALIC   Wiltshire Association of Libraries of Industry and Commerce.

WANDPETLS   Wandsworth Public, Educational and Technical Library Services.

WESLINK   West Midlands Library and Information Network. *See entry under* WESLINK.

WIPO   World Intellectual Property Organization. *See entry under* WIPO.

WISI   World Information System on Informatics. *See entry under* WISI.

WMBLA   West Midland Branch (of the Library Association).

WNBA   Women's National Book Association.

YASD   Young Adult Services Division of the American Library Association.

Glossary

The word-by-word method is used.

Hyphenated words are arranged as if separate words if the part preceding the hyphen has a separate meaning; in cases where words with hyphens are sometimes spelt as one word without the hyphen, the practice has been to arrange these as one word.

Abbreviations consisting of letters separated by points, and unpronounceable acronyms whether so punctuated or not, are arranged at the beginning of each letter sequence. Those consisting of two or more letters, and pronounceable acronyms, are arranged as if whole words in their normal place in the letter sequence.

★   ★   ★

36-LINE BIBLE.   Printed in Latin anonymously at Bamberg *c.* 1460, probably by Heinrich Keffer. It has 882 printed leaves, two columns to a page, 36 lines in each column, and is usually bound in three volumes.

42-LINE BIBLE.   *See* MAZARIN BIBLE.

48-LINE BIBLE.   The Bible printed by Johann Fust and Peter Schöffer at Mainz on 14th August 1462. The type, a medium gothic of humanistic design, was probably cut specially for this work in which it first appears. Many copies were printed on vellum.

A4 SIZE.   A European standard size of paper, 210 × 297 mm (8·27 × 11·69 inches). *See also* DIN, PAPER SIZES for a complete table of sizes.

A5 SIZE.   A European standard size of paper, 148 × 210 mm (5·83 × 8·27 inches). *See also* DIN, PAPER SIZES for a complete table of sizes.

A7 LIBRARY CARD.   Standard size card of 74 × 105 mm (2·91 × 4·13 inches), eight of which can be cut from a DIN A4 sheet of 210 × 297 mm (8·27 × 11·69 inches). Also called 'A7 size card'. *See also* CARD, DIN, PAPER SIZES for a complete table of sizes, STANDARD SIZE CARD.

A.B.C. Abridged building classification for architects, builders and civil engineers. See INTERNATIONAL COUNCIL FOR BUILDING RESEARCH, STUDIES AND DOCUMENTATION.

ABHB. Abbreviation for *Annual bibliography of the printed book and libraries* which began publication by Nijhoff, The Hague, in 1973. The first volume included publications issued in 1970; the second volume (also published in 1973) included publications issued in 1971. It is issued under the auspices of the Committee on Rare and Precious Books and Documents.

ABTAPL. Abbreviation for Association of British Theological and Philosophical Libraries. Founded in October 1956 on the recommendation of the International Association of Theological Libraries to promote the interests of libraries, scholars and librarians in these fields and to foster co-operation between them. One of its main objects is to make the bibliographical resources of constituent members as widely known as possible. Publishes *Bulletin* (q.). *See also* SCOTAPLL.

A.C.S. (*Pl.* A.Cs.S.) (autograph card signed). A card wholly in the handwriting of the signer.

A.D.S. (autograph document signed). A document entirely in the handwriting of the signer.

A.L. *See* A.L.S.

A.L.S. (autograph letter signed). A letter entirely in the handwriting of the signer. If unsigned it is referred to by the letters 'A.L.'; if written by someone else but signed, by 'L.S.'; if typed and signed by hand, by 'T.L.S.'.

A.Ms.S. (*Pl.* A.Mss.S.) (autograph manuscript signed). A manuscript wholly in the handwriting of the signer.

ANDBP. Acronym of the Association Nationale pour le Développement des Bibliothèques Publiques, which was formed in July 1971 to give all French people easier access to information, culture and life-long education by promoting the development of networks of modern public libraries.

ANRT Acronym for Association Nationale de la Recherche Technique. A French association which is particularly concerned with problems of technical information.

A.N.S. (*Pl.* A.Ns.S.) (autograph note signed). A note wholly in the handwriting of the signer.

AP Abbreviation for AUTHOR'S PROOF (*q.v.*).

ASD Acronym for Association Suisse de Documentation. The Swiss Association for Documentation; it was formed in 1939 after having been in existence as a study group since 1930. Publishes *Kleine Mitteilungen/Petites Communications* (irr.).

A.T.S. Abbreviation for Animal Tub-sized. *See* TUB-SIZING.

AACOBS. Acronym for the AUSTRALIAN ADVISORY COUNCIL ON BIBLIOGRAPHICAL SERVICES (*q.v.*).

ABACUS *See* KWOT.

ABBREVIATED CARD. A catalogue card which gives an abbreviated entry.

ABBREVIATED CATALOGUE ENTRY. A catalogue entry (title, subject, translator, etc.) which does not give as much information as the main entry card. *See also* ADDED ENTRY.

ABERRANT COPY. One in which binding or machining errors, and not merely defects, occur, and the correct state of which can be recognized.

ABRIDGED DECIMAL CLASSIFICATION. An abridgement of Dewey's *Decimal Classification* intended for use in small and slowly growing libraries.

ABRIDGED EDITION. An edition in which the author's text is reduced in length, or which summarizes the original text of a work. *See also* EXPURGATED EDITION.

ABRIDGEMENT. *Synonymous with* EPITOME (*q.v.*).

ABSOLUTE LOCATION. *See* FIXED LOCATION.

ABSOLUTE SIZE. *See* EXACT SIZE.

ABSORBENCY. The ability of paper to absorb printing ink. This quality varies widely between different papers.

ABSORBENT PAPER. Paper having the quality of absorbing and retaining ink or other liquid.

ABSTRACT. 1. A form of current bibliography in which sometimes books, but mainly contributions to periodicals, are summarized: they are accompanied by adequate bibliographical descriptions to enable the publications or articles to be traced, and are frequently arranged in classified order. They may be in the language of the original or be translated into English or some other language. Periodicals which contain only abstracts are known as journals of abstracts or abstract journals. Abstracts may be *indicative*, mainly directing to the original, *informative*, giving much information about the original, summarizing the principal arguments and giving the principal data, or *evaluative*, when they comment on the worth of the original. A *general* abstract is one which covers all essential points in an article, and is provided where the interests of readers are varied and known to the abstractor only in general terms. A *selective* abstract contains a condensation of such parts of an article known to be pertinent to the needs of the clientele and is prepared by a librarian (a) for the executives, research workers and specialists within his organization or those normally making use of his library services, (b) in response to a request for a literature search, or (c) to keep the staff of the organization or users of the services informed of developments in their field as revealed in the daily or periodical press, documents or reports. An *author* abstract is one written by the author of the original article. A *comprehensive abstracting service* endeavours to abstract every publication and article appearing in its subject field, whereas a *selective abstracting service* selects for abstracting only those publications and articles which it considers are likely to be of use to a specific class of reader. 2. The individual entry. 3. In documentary literature, three types of abstracts are found, (a) *traditional abstract*, a literary-style statement of the essential qualities of a work such as a book or periodical, and which may be descriptive or informative; (b) an *extract* from the original which is intended to provide its important subject matter; (c) a *telegraphic abstract*, a detailed index composed of (i) significant words selected from the document, (ii) code symbols called 'role indicators' which supply a context for the selected words, and (iii) punctuation symbols which separate and group the words and role indicators in various units as does conventional punctuation. An *auto-abstract* is an extract made by a machine. 4. (*n.*) An epitome or summary of a document. An abstract may be locative, illative, indicative or informative. A *locative abstract* (used solely in a few legal libraries) specifies the place where the original document may be found. An *illative abstract* (used solely in a few legal libraries) specifies the general nature of the material in the document. An *informative abstract* includes and specifies all pertinent material in the original document, summarizing all relevant arguments, data and conclusions. An *indicative abstract* points out what is in the original document, but usually does not include any of the material; from this the user determines whether or not to consult the original. 5. Printers' type, the design of the face of which is based on mechanical drawing, with more or less straight edges and lines of uniform thickness, having no serifs (sans-serif) or square serifs of the same weight as the letter (block-serif). Futura, Lydian and Optima are examples of sans-serif, and Beton, Cairo, Karnak and Memphis of block-serif. *See also* PSEUDO ABSTRACT, SYNOPSIS, TYPE FACE.

ABSTRACT BULLETIN. A publication, produced by any duplication, printing, or other means, which consists of abstracts. Also called 'Abstract journal'.

ABSTRACT CARD. A card, usually the standard 5 × 3 inch size, on which is entered an abstract of a document or of an article in a periodical.

ABSTRACT JOURNAL. *See* ABSTRACT.

ABSTRACTING SERVICE. The preparation of abstracts, usually in a limited field, by an individual, an industrial organization for restricted use, or a commercial organization; the abstracts being published and supplied regularly to subscribers. Also the organization producing the abstracts. Such services may be either comprehensive or selective. Also called 'Secondary service'.

ABSTRACTION. The mental process of dividing and grouping which is involved in classifying.

ABTICS. Acronym for Abstract and Book Title Card Index Service, which is provided by the Iron and Steel Institute; books, pamphlets, periodicals and reports are represented in this weekly service. Each card provides a UDC number and full biographical information.

ACADEMIC LIBRARIES. Those of universities, university colleges, and all other institutions forming part of, or associated with, institutions of higher education.

ACANTHUS. An ornament, representing two acanthus leaves pointing different ways, used in tooling book-bindings.

ACCESS. In information retrieval (i) a device or method whereby a document may be found; (ii) permission and opportunity to use a document (*IBM*); (iii) the approach to any means of storing information, e.g. index, bibliography, catalogue, electronic computer.

ACCESS. (*Archives*) Availability of government archives to the general public; such documents are subject to restrictions of confidentiality for a specified number of years. Similar restrictions are also sometimes applied to donations or bequests of other kinds of documents to archive depositories or libraries. Such documents are said to be 'closed' until their access date is reached and 'open' when the period of restriction has expired.

ACCESS POINT. (*Indexing*) Any unique heading, or heading with its QUALIFIER (*q.v.*) in an index.

ACCESS TIME. The time interval between the call for a specified item of data to be transferred to or from a selected address in computer storage, and (a) the completion of the transfer, or (b) the commencement of the transfer.

ACCESSION. 1. To enter in an ACCESSIONS REGISTER (*q.v.*) particulars of each book in the order of its acquisition. 2. (*Archives*) The act of taking documents into physical custody in an archival agency, records centre, or manuscript repository, and recording same. In some cases transfer of legal title may also be involved.

ACCESSION BOOK. *See* ACCESSIONS REGISTER.

ACCESSION CARD. *See* ACCESSIONS REGISTER.

ACCESSION DATE. The date on which a publication is entered in the ACCESSIONS REGISTER (*q.v.*).

ACCESSION DEPARTMENT. *See* CATALOGUING DEPARTMENT.

ACCESSION NUMBER. The number given a book from the ACCESSIONS REGISTER (*q.v.*). It may also be a number given to an article in a periodical, or other document, which is indexed by the Uniterm Concept Co-ordination System. *See also* UNITERM CONCEPT CO-ORDINATION INDEXING.

ACCESSION ORDER. The arrangement of books on the shelves according to the order of their addition to a class; a numerical and chronological, as distinguished from a classified, arrangement.

ACCESSION PART OF THE CRITICISM NUMBER. *See* ASSOCIATED BOOK.

ACCESSION RECORD. *See* ACCESSIONS REGISTER.

ACCESSION SLIP. *See* PROCESS SLIP.

ACCESSION STAMP. A rubber stamp which is impressed on the back of a title-page; when the information is written in the appropriate panels of which the stamp is comprised, it gives much information concerning the records, and processing, of the individual book.

ACCESSIONS. A group term indicating additions to the stock of a library.

ACCESSIONS CATALOGUE. *Synonymous with* ACCESSIONS REGISTER (*q.v.*).

ACCESSIONS LIST. *See* ACCESSIONS REGISTER.

ACCESSIONS REGISTER. The chief record of the books added to a library. Books are numbered progressively as they are added to stock and entered in the register. It may be in book form or on cards, and may give a condensed description of the acquisition and history of each book from its reception to its withdrawal. Materials other than books which are added permanently to stock and of which records should be kept are similarly recorded. Not to be confused with ACQUISITION RECORD (*q.v.*).

ACCESSIONS SECTION. A section of a cataloguing or processing department which is concerned with accessioning library materials.

ACCIDENT. *See* PREDICABLES, FIVE.

ACCOMPANYING MATERIAL. (*Cataloguing*) Material such as an atlas, portfolio of plates, gramophone record, etc., which is intended to be kept in physical conjunction with a publication, and to be used with it.

ACHROMATIC LENS. One which is corrected for black and white photography.

ACID BLAST. The spraying of half-tone and zinc plates with acid as part of the etching process. This results in a sharper image.

ACID-FREE PAPER. In principle, paper which contains no free acid or having a pH value (when determined by the standard method) of 7 or more. Commercial practice permits a limited amount of acid under this designation. *See also* pH VALUE.

ACID RESIST. An acid-proof protective coating which is applied to metal plates before etching.

ACLO. Acronym of the Association of Co-operative Library Organizations. During the June 1968 American Library Association Convention, twenty representatives of library co-operative organizations were invited to discuss the need for a stable group devoted to shared interests. Membership was open to all directors of library co-operative associations. No association headquarters is maintained; the group meets at the conventions of the ALA only by consent and is not an affiliate. There are two categories of membership: individual and organizational. The *Acquainter*, an international Newsletter for academic consortia for higher education (published by the American Association for Higher Education) carries announcements and summaries of ACLO's meetings.

ACQUISITION. The processes of obtaining books and other documents for a library, documentation centre or archive. *See also* FARMINGTON PLAN, SCANDIA PLAN.

ACQUISITION DEPARTMENT. The department of a library concerned with the ordering of books and possibly their cataloguing and processing also. Often other functions such as obtaining books by exchange or gift, administration of serials and binding are undertaken. One in which ACQUISITION WORK (*q.v.*) is performed (American). *See also* CATALOGUING DEPARTMENT, ORDER DEPARTMENT, TECHNICAL SERVICES DEPARTMENT.

ACQUISITION RECORD. A record of all books and other material added or in process of being added; it is usually kept in alphabetical order. It may be (1) in two parts consisting of (a) a file of orders completed and of orders outstanding, and (b) a register of periodicals – including government publications – received, or (2) separate files for each of these records. If a DEAD FILE (*q.v.*) is kept this would also be considered a part of the acquisition record (American).

ACQUISITION WORK. The work of book selection, ordering, obtaining by gift or exchange, serials control, and rebinding (American).

ACQUISITIONS OFFICER. An assistant who undertakes the duties necessary for acquiring new books for a library.

ACROGRAPHY. A method of producing relief surfaces on metal or stone by means of tracing with chalk, for making electrotype or stereotype plates.

ACRONYM. A word formed from the initial letter or letters of each of the successive parts of the name of an organization, group or term, e.g. IMCE (International Meeting of Cataloguing Experts), Unesco (United Nations Educational Scientific and Cultural Organization), Asfec (The Arab States Fundamental Education Centre), FLIP (Film Library Instantaneous Presentation), WISI (World Information System on Informatics).

ACROPHONY. In pictographic writing, the principle that the value of each consonant is the value of the first letter of its name, as the *b* of *beth*, the *g* of *gimel*, and the *d* of *daleth*.

ACTING EDITION. An edition of a play which gives directions concerning exits, entrances, properties, etc. It is intended for actors and is often published in a limp cover, usually of paper.

ACTIVE RECORDS. *See* CURRENT RECORDS.

ACTIVITY. (*Information Retrieval*) A term which indicates that a record in a MASTER FILE (*q.v.*) is used, referred to or altered.

ACTIVITY RATIO. (*Information Retrieval*) The ratio of the number of records in a file which have ACTIVITY (*q.v.*) to the total number of records in that file.

ACTS. *See* PUBLIC LIBRARIES ACTS.

ACTUAL ARRANGEMENT. *See* IDEAL ARRANGEMENT.

Ad loc. Abbreviation for *ad locum* (*Lat.* 'At the place cited').

ADAPTATION. 1. A book that has been re-written or edited, wholly or in part, for a particular purpose such as for reading by children when the original was intended for adults, or a novel adapted for dramatic presentation. Not to be confused with an abridgement or EPITOME (*q.v.*). 2. A work re-written or presented in another intellectual form to serve a different purpose from the original version, or converted into a different literary form (IFLA).

ADAPTER. One who adapts a literary work by simplifying the text, omitting passages, or changing its form, e.g. novel into play.

ADD INSTRUCTIONS. In the 18th ed. of Dewey's Decimal Classification, 'add instructions' which specify exactly what digits should be added to what base number, replaced the 'divide-like' notes. *See also* DIVIDE LIKE THE CLASSIFICATION.

ADD-TO-CARDS WORK. Data which is to be added to cards already in a catalogue. Elements which are subject to change, such as a statement of holdings, are usually entered in pencil. This work is usually performed by clerical assistants.

ADDAMS AWARD, JANE. Awarded annually by the Jane Addams Peace Association and the Women's International League for Peace and Freedom to the children's book of the year best combining literary merit, themes of brotherhood, and creative solutions to problems.

ADDED COPIES. Duplicate copies of titles already in stock. Not to be confused with ADDED EDITION (*q.v.*).

ADDED EDITION. A different edition from the one already in the library.

ADDED ENTRY. 1. A secondary catalogue entry, i.e. any other than the MAIN ENTRY (*q.v.*). Where printed cards are used, it is a duplicate of the main entry, with the addition of a heading for subject, title, editor, series, or translator. When printed cards are not used, the added entry is formed from the main entry by the omission of all or part of the imprint and collation, and sometimes of sub-titles, and the addition of an appropriate heading. It must not be confused with a CROSS REFERENCE (*q.v.*). Added entries may be made for editor, translator, title, subjects, series, illustrator, translator, etc., and in the case of music, for arranger, librettist, title, medium, form, etc. additionally. *See also* GENERAL SECONDARY. 2. The heading chosen for an added entry.

ADDED TITLE ENTRY. An entry, not being a main entry, made under the title for books with distinctive titles or in cases where title entries would be an advantage, such as anonymous works.

ADDED TITLE-PAGE. A title-page additional to the one from which a main entry for a catalogue entry is made. It may precede or follow the one chosen and may be more general, such as a series title-page, or may be equally general, as a title-page in another language, and placed either at the beginning or end of a book. The revision of Chapter 6 of *AACR: North American Text* provides that in the case of a facsimile edition or a reprint edition with a new title-page, a reproduction of the original title-page is not treated as an added title-page. *See also* PARALLEL TITLE.

ADDENDUM (*Pl.* ADDENDA). 1. Matter included in a book after the text has been set. It is printed separately and is inserted at the beginning or end of the text; it is less extensive than a SUPPLEMENT (*q.v.*).

2. A slip added to a printed book. *See also* CORRIGENDA. *Synonymous with* APPENDIX.

ADDITION. (*Classification*) The simple extension of an existing ARRAY (*q.v.*), either by interpolation or extrapolation.

ADDITION. (*Noun.*) A book or other item that has been obtained for addition to the stock of the library. This term is sometimes used to refer to such items before they have been accessioned; this is, strictly, incorrect. *See also* ADDITIONS, LIST OF.

ADDITIONAL DESIGNATION. (*Cataloguing*) Explanatory information, e.g. dates, place of birth or residence or a HONORIFIC TITLE (*q.v.*) added to a name for purposes of distinguishing it from other identical names. *See also* DESCRIPTOR.

ADDITIONS, LIST OF. A list of recent books added to a library's stock. It may be in alphabetical, classified, or accession order.

ADDRESS. 1. A label, name or number which designates a register, a location, or a device in a computer where information is stored. 2. That part of an instruction in a computer programme which specifies the register, location or device upon which the operation is to be performed (*IBM*).

ADDRESS TABLE. (*Information retrieval*) A list that links the leading term of each entry to the location, or address, of an entry made in connection with a RANDOM ACCESS SYSTEM (*q.v.*) in which a fixed location is assigned to each entry.

ADEQUATE DESCRIPTION, PRINCIPLE OF. The provision of enough information in a catalogue entry to enable a reader to make a right choice of books. *See also* CATALOGUING, PRINCIPLES OF.

ADJUSTABLE CLASSIFICATION. A scheme of classification designed by James Duff Brown in 1897. It was of little value, as the provision for new subjects was by leaving blank certain numbers in the notation. It was superseded by his SUBJECT CLASSIFICATION (*q.v.*).

ADJUSTABLE PERIODICALS LISTS. A list, consisting of the titles of periodicals typed or printed on small strips of card which are kept in position by xylonite strips attached to a wooden backing and framed, or in a visible index.

ADJUSTABLE SHELF. A shelf whose position may be adjusted to accommodate books of varying heights. *See also* LUNDIA SHELVING, TONKS FITTINGS.

ADJUSTABLE SHELVING. Shelves which may be raised or lowered at will. Shelving which enables this to be done while the books are still on them are the most useful in libraries. STORAGE SHELVING (*q.v.*), requiring the use of nuts and bolts, is not normally used because of the inconvenience of adjusting the shelves, which go into slots cut in the ends of the shelves as the latter are pushed into position. Although most modern shelving restricts adjustability to one inch there are some kinds which make closer intervals of adjustment possible. The most convenient form of adjustable steel shelving to operate, and which also gives unrestricted adjustability, is the bracket type where the position of the shelves can be altered by moving a small spring lever built into the bracket. Wooden shelving is rendered adjustable by using Tonks fittings consisting of slotted strips inserted in the shelf uprights, into the slots of which studs are placed to support the shelves, by resting shelves on wooden pegs inserted in holes in the uprights, or by using the Lundia shelving which consists of thin metal rods with turned ends which are inserted into holes in the uprights and the grooved ends of the shelves sliding over the projecting part of the rods. *See also* BRACKET SHELVING, CANTILEVER SHELVING, SLOTTED SHELVING.

ADMINISTRATIVE BOARD. *Synonymous with* ADMINISTRATIVE COUNCIL (*q.v.*).

ADMINISTRATIVE COUNCIL. A committee of the officers and faculty of an American college whose function is largely legislative and policy-making. It is appointed and elected by the president and faculty, and is usually advisory to the president in administrative matters, but it may exercise considerable authority in its own right. Also called 'Administrative board', 'Prudential committee'.

ADMINISTRATIVE OFFICE ASSISTANT. In American libraries, a person, such as a business manager or secretary to the Chief Librarian or Director, who performs work of a specialized nature but does not require to have a library training.

ADOLESCENT LIBRARY. One which is provided for the use of adolescents, usually as a bridge between the children's department and the adult department of a public library.

ADOPTION OF THE PUBLIC LIBRARIES ACTS. The decision of the local authority to take the necessary administrative and legal steps to provide library facilities as permitted by law.

ADRIS. Acronym of Association for the Development of Religious Information Systems which was founded to promote co-ordination and co-operation among existing and new information systems pertinent to religion by sharing relevant information, identifying needs, considering proposed projects, and developing co-operative ventures. Functions from Marquette University, Milwaukee, Wisconsin, U.S.A. Publishes *ADRIS Newsletter*.

ADULT DEPARTMENT. The department of a library which provides books for the use of adults.

ADULT LITERARY RESOURCE AGENCY. Formed under the aegis of the (British) National Institute of Adult Education to administer a one-year grant of £1 million made by the Government in 1974 for the Department of Education and Science and the Scottish Education Department to help local education authorities and voluntary organizations tackle the problem of adult illiteracy, it having been estimated that two million adults in Great Britain were unable to read.

ADULT SERVICES DIVISION. This Division of the ALA was combined in 1972 with the Reference Services Division to form the REFERENCE AND ADULT SERVICES DIVISION (*q.v.*).

ADVANCE COPY (SHEET). A copy of a book, usually bound, but sometimes in sheets, to serve as a proof of the binder's work, for review, notice, advertising or other purposes.

ADVERTISEMENT FILE. A file of advertisements, usually arranged by the name of firm or of product. Such files are most often maintained in a firm's library or advertising agency.

ADVISER, READERS'. *See* READERS' ADVISER.

ADVISORY COUNCIL. *See* LIBRARY ADVISORY COUNCIL.

ADVISORY GROUP FOR AEROSPACE RESEARCH AND DE-VELOPMENT. *See* AGARD.

ADVOCATES' LIBRARY, EDINBURGH. *See* NATIONAL LIBRARY OF SCOTLAND.

AERIAL MAP. A map made from one or more photographs taken from above the surface of the earth.

AEROGRAPH. An instrument, used for blowing, by means of compressed air, a fine spray of liquid colour on to a lithograph stone or drawing, or when re-touching photographs.

AFFECTIVE RELATION. One of the ten analytical relations used in the SEMANTIC CODE (*q.v.*) developed at the Western Reserve University, in which one concept is influenced or determined by another.

AFFILIATED LIBRARY. One which is part of a library system, but has its own board of management and is not administered as part of the system.

AFNOR. Acronym for Association Française de Normalisation, the French equivalent of the BRITISH STANDARDS INSTITUTION (*q.v.*).

AGAINST THE GRAIN. Said of paper which has been folded at right angles to the direction in which the fibres tend to lie. In a well-printed book the back fold of the paper is never 'against the grain'; the grain direction should run from head to tail in the finished book in order that the pages will lie flat when the book is opened. *See also* CROSS DIRECTION, GRAIN DIRECTION, WITH THE GRAIN.

AGARD. Acronym of the Advisory Group for Aerospace Research & Development, an organization within the North Atlantic Treaty Organization (NATO), which exists to bring together the leading personalities of the NATO nations in the fields of science and technology relating to aerospace for the following purposes, amongst others: (a) exchange scientific and technical information; (b) continuously stimulate advances in the aerospace sciences relevant to strengthening the common defence posture; (c) provide assistance to member nations for the purpose of increasing their scientific and technical potential; (d) recommend effective ways for member nations to use their research and development capabilities for the common benefit of the NATO community. A number of AGARD publications are useful in the field of general documentation and librarianship.

AGATE. (*Binding*) A bloodstone or agate used in hand binding to burnish gold or coloured edges. (*Printing*) Used to denote $5\frac{1}{2}$ point type.

AGATE LINE. An American standard of measurements for the depth of columns of advertising space in a newspaper. Fourteen agate lines make one column inch.

AGENT. In the U.S.A., an individual or firm acting as a middleman between librarian and publisher in the acquisition of material. An agent is commonly used in connection with periodical subscriptions, back numbers of periodicals, and foreign publications. *See also* LITERARY AGENT.

AGGLUTINATIVE SYMBOL. A symbol, in a system of NOTATION (*q.v.*) in a scheme of classification, two or more parts of which have a constant and inflexible symbol.

AIGLONNE. Trademark of a microfilm processor made by the Andre Debrie Corporation.

AIR BRUSH. *Synonymous with* AEROGRAPH (*q.v.*).

AIR-DRIED. Hand-made, or good machine-made, paper, or brown paper which is hung over lines and dried slowly in air at a uniform temperature, as distinct from paper which is machine-dried in heat.

AISLE. The passageway between two parallel bookcases.

AJOURÉ BINDING. A style of binding practised in the last third of the fifteenth century at Venice. It was in the traditional Eastern manner with arabesques, gilding, and cut-out leather, over a coloured background.

ALASKA SEAL.   Sheepskin or cowhide made to imitate sealskin.

ALBEMARLE REPORT.   *The youth service in England and Wales,* 1960. Known as the Albemarle Report from the fact that the Countess of Albemarle was chairman of the committee which had been set up in November 1958 by the Minister of Education to enquire into the youth service.

ALBERTYPE.   A process of making pictures with a gelatine-covered plate, the printing being a variety of photogravure (*United Typothetae*).

ALBION PRESS.   Invented in 1823 by R. W. Cope of London; it was an improvement on the STANHOPE PRESS (*q.v.*) and enabled sufficient pressure for printing to be achieved with a single pull on the spindle bar. It was simple in construction, durable, cheap, and easy to work. Its American counterpart was the Washington Press, and its German one, the Hagar Press. The Albion and COLUMBIAN (*q.v.*) presses were used commercially well into the twentieth century; several British private presses used the Albion.

ALBIS.   Acronym of the Australian Library-Based Information System, the practical objectives of its studies being: (a) the compilation of a directory of libraries and information services; (b) the encouragement of a much wider range of computer-based services for the public in Australia by voluntary co-operation between the National Library and other agencies; (c) the determination of the National Library's computer requirements to implement its normal development as a National Library, particularly in connection with an Australian library information service or bibliographical and shared cataloguing network and the provision of agreed computer-based information services. ALBIS depends on voluntary co-operation between Federal, State, Municipal and many specialist subject organizations able and willing to contribute to a library-based information system to meet the needs of the community by developing traditional and computer-based services in the most effective way. *See also* ANSTEL.

ALBUM.   1. A book of envelopes or jackets for holding gramophone records, usually with a decorative cover and sometimes with descriptive notes. 2. A book of blank leaves in which literary extracts, quotations, poems, drawings, photographs, autographs, newspaper cuttings, stamps, etc. are written, inserted or fixed.

ALBUM LETTER (NUMBER).   A serial letter or number allocated by the producers to an album of gramophone records.

ALBUM TITLE.   The title appearing on the cover or the inside of a gramophone record album. It is sometimes based on the original title of the composition but is often a title assigned by the producing company and differing from the title appearing on the record itself.

ALBUMEN PROCESS. The most commonly used sensitizer for coating photo offset plates (*Verry*).

ALCOPHOTO. A photo-mechanical process for making zinc, aluminium or other litho plates which has been developed in England. It has standardized the deep-etching process for all kinds of plates.

ALCOVE. A recess formed by placing two presses at right angles to a wall, and touching it at one end. Also called a CELL (*q.v.*).

ALCOVE MARK. In an old library, the mark used to indicate in which alcove any particular book may be found. Books in such libraries are arranged according to location and not classification. *See also* FIXED LOCATION.

ALDINE (ITALIAN) STYLE. (*Printing*) Ornaments of solid face without any shading whatever, used by Aldus and other early Italian printers. The ornaments are Arabic in character, and are suitable for early printed books. (*Binding*) Late fifteenth and early sixteenth century Venetian bindings in brown or red morocco which were carried out for Aldus Manutius. They had the title, or the author's name in a simple panel in the middle of the front cover of a book so that it could be seen when the book lay on a shelf or table. Early examples were decorated in blind with an outer frame and a central device. It is assumed that as Aldus was the leading printer in Venice he would supervise the binding of his books which was done by the Greek binders he employed.

ALDINE LEAVES. Small binders' stamps bearing a leaf and stem design; used on books bound for ALDUS (*q.v.*) *c.* 1510.

ALDINE PRESS. The Italian press which achieved fame for introducing italic type in 1501. The Press was founded by Aldus Pius Manutius. *See also* ALDUS, ITALIC.

ALDUS. An Italian publishing firm founded at Venice in 1495 by Teobaldo Manucci (Aldus Pius Manutius; Aldo Manuzio) 1450–1515. Aldus specialized in small-size editions of Greek and Latin classics which were published between 1494 and 1515, and the first ITALIC (*q.v.*) type, which was cut for Aldus by Griffi, was first used for a small format edition of the classics. Aldus's printer's device of anchor and dolphin has frequently been used by other printers, e.g. William Pickering for the Chiswick Press in the late nineteenth century. Between 1515 and 1533 the press was managed by his brothers-in-law, the Asolani, during which time the work of the press deteriorated.

In 1533 his youngest son Paulius Manutius (1512–74) took over the press and concentrated on Latin classics.

ALEBCI. Acronym of Asociación Latinamericana de Escuelas de Bibliotecologia y Ciencias de la Información. Established in 1970 at Buenos Aires to further library education in Latin America. Membership is open to individuals and institutions who support the aims of the Association. Financed by members' dues.

ALFA. An alternative name for esparto grass. *See* ESPARTO.

ALGOL. Acronym for Algorithmic Language, an international algebraic, procedure-oriented language which is similar in concept and content to FORTRAN the most-used programming language.

ALGORITHM. (*Indexing*) Instructions for carrying out a series of logical procedural steps in a specified order when compiling an index, such as the KWIC (*q.v.*) type of index, by machine methods.

ALGORITHMIC CODE. One that has rules for converting source (i.e. common language) words into code equivalents.

ALGRAPHY. The process of printing from aluminium plates by lithographic and offset printing. Also called 'Aluminography'.

ALIENATION. (*Archives*) The act of transferring, or losing, custody or ownership of documents to an agency or person not officially connected with the organization whose documents are involved.

ALIGNMENT. 1. The exact correspondence in a straight line of the top and bottom of the letters and characters in a fount. 2. The arrangement of type in straight lines. 3. The setting of lines of type so that the ends appear even at the margins.

ALIS Acronym of the Association of Librarians in Schools. Formed in April 1973 'To promote professional interests . . . (and) to provide a channel through which recommendations from school librarians may be communicated to the appropriate authorities.' Membership is open to all chartered librarians and their professional assistants employed in secondary schools. Membership is open to others at the discretion of the Committee. Membership is at present predominantly from the County of Nottinghamshire. Financed by subscriptions.

ALL ALONG. The method of sewing by hand the sections (usually on cords or tapes) of a book, when the thread goes 'all along' or from KETTLE STITCH (*q.v.*) to kettle stitch of each section. Also used to describe machine book-sewing when each section is sewn with the full number of stitches. *See also* TWO SHEETS ON.

ALL-OVER STYLE. The style of book decoration which covers the whole of the side of a binding, as distinct from a corner, centre or border design, whether made up of a single motif, different motifs, or a repeated motif.

ALL PUBLISHED. Used in a catalogue entry and in other connotations, concerning a work, the publication of which has been started but is not completed. Also relates to all the issues of a periodical, publication of which has ceased. *See also* CEASED PUBLICATION.

ALL-PURPOSE LINOTYPE. A machine similar to the LUDLOW (*q.v.*) in that the matrices are hand-set in a special stick. Matrices from Intertype, Linotype and Ludlow machines may be used. The casting mechanism of the machine is similar to that of the ordinary Linotype machine except that the slugs are ejected into a water-cooled compartment before being dropped into a galley. Blanks and ornaments, etc., can be cast as well as type. The machine is made by the American Linotype Company.

ALL RIGHTS RESERVED. A phrase placed in a book usually on the back of the title-page, signifying that the copyright is reserved, and that proceedings may be taken against any person doing anything which infringes that copyright.

'ALL THROUGH'. *Synonymous with* 'Letter by Letter' alphabetization. *See* ALPHABETIZATION.

ALL-UNION INSTITUTE OF SCIENTIFIC AND TECHNICAL INFORMATION. *See* VINITI.

ALLOCATE, TO. The process of deciding into which department or library of a library system books and other material shall be allocated.

ALLOCATION. The act of allocating books. *See also* ALLOCATE, TO.

ALLONYM. A false name, especially the name of some person assumed by an author to conceal identity or gain credit; an alias; a pseudonym.

ALLUSION BOOK. A collection of contemporary allusions to a famous writer.

ALMANAC(K). A publication, usually an annual, containing a variety of useful facts of a miscellaneous nature, and statistical information. It was originally a projection of the coming year by days, months, holidays, etc.

ALPHABET LENGTH. (*Printing*) The length, usually stated in points, of the twenty-six letters of the alphabet. The relative compactness of a type face is determined by the comparison of alphabet lengths. The alphabet length in points, divided into 341, gives the number of 'characters per pica'. *See also* TYPE FACE.

ALPHABET MARK. A mark, such as the CUTTER AUTHOR MARK (*q.v.*), which is incorporated in the call number of a book to enable alphabetic order to be maintained on the shelves without the use of abnormally long symbols.

ALPHABET OF SYMBOLS. A set of distinct recognizable and repeatable characters or symbols which are used for identifying documents, as the notation used in a scheme of classification, e.g. the figures, capital letters and lower case letters used in Bliss's Bibliographic Classification, or the 10 numerals, 26 capital letters, 26 lower case letters, 8 Greek letters and 9 punctuation marks used in the Colon Classification. Also called 'Base of Symbolism'.

ALPHABETIC SUBJECT CATALOGUE. One arranged alphabetically by subjects, usually without subdivisions.

ALPHABETIC WRITING. The third, and final, stage in the development of writing, in which a single symbol was used to represent a single distinctive sound feature in the spoken language, rather than ideas or syllables. *See also* PHONETIC WRITING, PICTOGRAPHY.

ALPHABETICAL ARRANGEMENT. The systematic arrangement of entries in a catalogue, index, bibliography or other list of items, or of books on the shelves of a library in alphabetical order of authors, subjects, titles or other distinguishing characteristics. The British Standards Institution has published a Standard, *Alphabetical arrangement* (BS 1749 : 1969).

ALPHABETICAL CATALOGUE. One in which the author, title, and/or subject entries are arranged alphabetically.

ALPHABETICAL COLLATERAL SEARCH. An examination of entries under headings alphabetically adjacent to, or near to, the headings covered in a HIERARCHICAL SEARCH (*q.v.*). *See also* SUBSTITUTION GENERIC, SYSTEMATIC COLLATERAL SEARCH.

ALPHABETICAL DEVICE. One of the principles used in the Colon Classification for determining the sequence of subjects. It is used only when no better systematic order is apparent, e.g. to proper names, trade names, etc.

ALPHABETICAL SUBJECT INDEX. An alphabetical list of all subjects named, or dealt with, in a book classification scheme, or classified catalogue, together with reference to the place(s) where each subject occurs.

ALPHABETICO-CLASSED CATALOGUE. An alphabetical subject catalogue, in which entries are not made under specific subjects, as in the dictionary form, but under broad subjects arranged alphabetically, and each sub-divided alphabetically by subject to cite more specific sub-divisions. Author and title entries may be included in the same alphabet under the appropriate subject headings.

ALPHABETICO-DIRECT CATALOGUE. One in which 'direct' headings, i.e. consisting of natural language and the natural form of phrases, as 'stamp collecting', 'subject cataloguing', are used, the headings being arranged in alphabetical order. *Synonymous with* ALPHABETICO-SPECIFIC CATALOGUE

ALPHABETICO-SPECIFIC CATALOGUE. *Synonymous with* ALPHABETICO-DIRECT CATALOGUE (*q.v.*).

ALPHABETICO-SPECIFIC SUBJECT CATALOGUE. One in which alphabetically arranged headings state precisely the subject of the literary unit indexed, whether it is a whole document or only a portion such as a chapter, section or paragraph of it. Also called 'Dictionary index'. *See also* BASIC ANALYSIS, COLLATERAL REFERENCE, DOWNWARD REFERENCE, QUALIFIED LIST, UPWARD REFERENCE.

ALPHABETIZATION. Arranging a list of words, names, or phrases according to the letters of the alphabet. In the main there are two methods in use: 1, 'word by word,' or 'nothing before something'; 2, 'letter by letter' strictly according to the letters irrespective of their division into words, or of punctuation. This may also be called the 'solid' method. In 1969 the British Standards Institution issued a Standard (no. 1749) on *Alphabetical arrangement* in which it recommends the 'word by word' or 'nothing-before-something' method (which is used in this book) whereby items which have the same first or second words are arranged in the alphabetical order of the subsequent word, e.g.

Black Acts	Blackberry
Black Book	Blackburn
Black Earth	

N.S.W.	Newark
New Castle (Pa., U.S.A.)	Newcastle (N.S.W., Australia)
New Haven (Conn., U.S.A.)	Newels
New Testament	Newhaven (England)
New York	News-room
	Newton

If the 'letter-by-letter' or 'follow-through' method were used these words would be arranged

Black Acts	Blackburn
Blackberry	Black Earth
Black Book	

Newark	News-room
Newcastle (N.S.W. Australia)	New Testament
New Castle (Pa., U.S.A.)	Newton
Newels	New York
New Haven (Conn., U.S.A.)	N.S.W.
Newhaven (England)	

By 1976, the impact of computerization and machine sorting resulted in the BSI Sub-Committee acknowledging the fact that the 'letter-by-letter' was more appropriate to machine sorting when it revised BS 3700 *The preparation of indexes to books, periodicals and other publications* by not making a recommendation for either method.

The British Standards 1749 and 3700 also recommend that words joined by a hyphen shall be arranged as separate words, the hyphens being treated as spaces for filing purposes, e.g.

Letter-by-letter	*Word-by-word*
Stockerau	Stock Exchange
Stock Exchange	Stock-jobber
Stockholm	Stock market
Stock-jobber	Stock-room
Stock market	Stockerau
Stockport	Stockholm
Stock-room	Stockport
Switch	Pre-impregnated
Switch-plug	Precipitation
Switch starter	Prefabrication
Switchboard	Pressure

Apostrophes are similarly treated. Hyphenated proper names, proper names containing apostrophes, and words incorporating hyphenated prefixes all come under this ruling, e.g.

> Jack, E. and L., Ltd.
> Jack's Café
> Jack, T.
> Jacks, A. B.
> Jacks-Bateson, M. L.

This is according to BS 1749. The Standard BS 3700, however, states that the apostrophe is to be disregarded and the word in which it occurs treated as one word.

ALPHABETOLOGY. The study of the development of ALPHABETIC WRITING (*q.v.*).

ALPHAMERIC. *Synonymous with* ALPHANUMERIC (*q.v.*). *See also* ALPHA-NUMERICAL INDEXING.

ALPHANUMERIC. A contraction of 'alphabetic-numeric'; a sequence of characters which may be letters of the alphabet, or numerals, or their symbols, punctuation or mathematical symbols.

ALPHA-NUMERICAL INDEXING. An indexing scheme which uses a combination of the alphabet and numbers, broad subjects being listed in alphabetical order and the subdivisions under them being given numbers. No attention need be paid to the first letter of the first word, and there may or may not be a hierarchical significance. The documents are identified with the number and filed according to it.

ALTERATIONS. (*Printing*) Changes made in a PROOF (*q.v.*).

ALTERNATIVE LOCATIONS. Bliss considers that one of the principles of classification is to provide alternative locations for certain studies or sciences regarded from different points of view or preferred in other allocations.

ALTERNATIVE TITLE. 1. A secondary title following the words 'or', 'a' or 'an'. More commonly known as the SUB-TITLE (*q.v.*). 2. One of several titles, which in particular circumstances (e.g. in multi-language publications with titles in the languages of the text) could be used as the MAIN TITLE (*q.v.*).

ALUMINIUM PLATES. Extremely flexible plates used in OFFSET PRINTING (*q.v.*).

ALUMINOGRAPHY. *Synonymous with* ALGRAPHY (*q.v.*).

AMA. Acronym of the (British) Association of Metropolitan Authorities which was formed on 31st July 1973 to watch over, protect and promote the interests, rights, powers and duties of its member authorities; also to provide a forum for the discussion of common concern, and to provide such central services for its member authorities as it may consider appropriate. Members are the Greater London Council, the Inner London Education Authority, the City of London Corporation, the 32 London Borough Councils, the 6 Metropolitan County Councils and the 36 Metropolitan District Councils. The Association is financed by subscriptions of the member authorities. Publishes *Municipal Review* (m.). *See also* ASSOCIATION OF DISTRICT COUNCILS.

AMBIGUOUS TITLE. One which is so vague that it may be misunderstood. In a catalogue, amplification may be made in brackets immediately following the title, or in a note.

AMBROGAL PRINTING. An offset printing process invented by

Ambrosius Galetzka; it is reminiscent of American aquatone printing. Sheets of celluloid are prepared for lithographic printing. *See also* AQUATONE.

AMERICAN ASSOCIATION OF LAW LIBRARIES. Established 1906. Aims 'to promote librarianship, to develop and increase the usefulness of law libraries, to cultivate the science of law librarianship and to foster a spirit of co-operation among members of the profession'. Abbreviated AALL. Publishes *Law Library journal* (q.), *Index to legal periodicals* (m. and cum.), *Index to foreign legal periodicals* (q., 4th. q. cum.), *Current legal publications* (9 a year), *Law libraries in the U.S. and Canada* (bi. an.), *AALL publication series.*

AMERICAN ASSOCIATION OF SCHOOL LIBRARIANS. A Division of the American Library Association since 1st January 1951; became an associated organization of the National Education Association in 1969. Founded in 1951, it is concerned with the improvement and extension of library services in elementary and secondary schools. It is the second largest of the divisions of the ALA. Abbreviated AASL. Publishes *School Media Quarterly* (q.) – formerly *School Libraries* until Fall 1972.

AMERICAN ASSOCIATION OF STATE LIBRARIES. *See* ASSOCIATION OF STATE LIBRARY AGENCIES.

AMERICAN BRAILLE. An obsolete variation of BRAILLE (*q.v.*).

AMERICAN DOCUMENTATION INSTITUTE. *See* AMERICAN SOCIETY FOR INFORMATION SCIENCE.

AMERICAN FEDERATION OF INFORMATION PROCESSING SOCIETIES. Founded in the U.S.A. in 1961 to serve as a national voice for the computing field; to advance knowledge of the information processing sciences. Formerly the National Joint Computer Committee. There are two membership classifications: member societies – those constituent societies whose primary interest is in computers and information processing as determined by the Board of Directors of AFIPS, and affiliated societies – those societies which, although they are not primarily concerned with computers and information processing, do have a major interest in this field. Abbreviated AFIPS.

AMERICAN FINISH. *See* PAPER FINISHES.

AMERICAN LIBRARY ASSOCIATION. Founded 1876 'to promote library service of excellent quality freely available to all.' The Association caters for special needs through thirteen divisions as follows, each division acting for the Association within its field of responsibility: *Type-of-library* divisions concerned with all activities that affect their types of library, American Association of School Librarians, Association of State Library Agencies, Association of College and Research Libraries, Association of Hospital and Institution Libraries, Public Library Association; *Type-of-activity* divisions concerned with the functional, technical, and resource fields which are related to their designated interests, Adult Services Division, American Library Trustee Association, Children's Services Division, Information Science and Automation Division, Library Administration Division, Library Education Division, Reference and Adult Services Division, Resources and Technical Services Division, Young Adult Services Division. Brief entries appear under each division name. Abbreviated ALA. Publishes *American Libraries* (11 p.a. to membs.) – formerly *ALA Bulletin* until December 1969, *Membership directory* (a.), *Library Technology Reports* (6 p.a.); *Washington Newsletter* (irreg.); *The Booklist* (23 p.a.); *ALA Handbook of Organization* (a.); a number of periodicals are published by divisions, departments and 'round tables'. *See also* DIVISION.

AMERICAN LIBRARY TRUSTEE ASSOCIATION. A Division of the American Library Association since 1 September 1961; founded in 1890 to study and encourage the development of libraries in all types of community and all types of library services in the U.S.A. and Canada; to study the library programmes of the several states and of Canada, and to disseminate the information gained from such study; to strengthen state trustee organizations. Abbreviated ALTA. Publishes *The Public Library Trustee* (4 p.a.).

AMERICAN MERCHANT MARINE LIBRARY ASSOCIATION. Founded in 1921 to maintain a library for the free use of the officers and crews of American ocean-going vessels of passenger, freight, tramp and tanker fleets, Great Lakes fleets, Coast Guard personnel and other members of the armed forces, lighthouses, lightships, etc. More than a million volumes are in circulation in American ships; eleven shore libraries are maintained. Collects books and other materials on nautical subjects for reference and research. Abbreviated AMMLA.

AMERICAN NATIONAL STANDARDS INSTITUTE, INC. The U.S.A. organization for issuing recommendations as to the production, distribution and consumption of goods and services; it is the American equivalent to the BRITISH STANDARDS INSTITUTION (*q.v.*) and is the United States member of the INTERNATIONAL ORGANIZATION FOR STANDARDIZATION (*q.v.*). Standards issued by the Institute are known as American National Standards. From 1918, when it was founded, until 1966 it was known as the American Standards Association (ASA) and from then until October 1969 as the United States of America Standards Institute (USASI) its Standards being known as U.S.A. Standards. Abbreviated ANSI. *See also* INTERNATIONAL STANDARDS, Z 39.

AMERICAN RUSSIA.   Cowhide used for bookbinding.

AMERICAN SOCIETY FOR INFORMATION SCIENCE.   Founded in 1937 to undertake the 'discussion, publication and critical analysis of work dealing with the theory, practice, research and development of all elements involved in the communication of recorded specialized information'. Known as the American Documentation Institute (ADI) until 1967. This non-profit national association is dedicated to the improvement of the information-transfer process through research, development, application and education. Membership includes information specialists from all fields of information processing. There are about twenty Special Interest Groups which give scope and focus to the divergent interest of members; they are in effect small professional organizations within the Society. The Special Interest Group Foundations (*SIG-FIS*) of ASIS commenced to publish *Foundations* (6 p.a.) in June 1974; its primary purpose is to foster a feeling of community among those interested in studying the foundations of information science. Abbreviated ASIS. Publishes *Journal of the American Society for Information Science* (6 p.a.), *Information Science Abstracts* (formerly *Documentation Abstracts*) in conjunction with the Chemical Literature Division of the American Chemical Society and the SLA (q.), *Annual Review of Information Science and Technology, Proceedings of the ASIS annual meetings, ASIS Newsletter* (bi-monthly), *Cable Libraries* (bi-monthly). Publication of a membership magazine, *Bulletin of the American Society for Information Science* (10 p.a.), began during 1974.

AMERICAN SOCIETY OF INDEXERS.   Founded 1968 with the following objectives: to (a) improve the quality of indexing and to secure useful standards for the field; (b) act as an advisory body on the qualification and remuneration of indexers to which authors, editors, publishers and others may apply for guidance; (c) issue from time to time books, articles and other material on the subject of indexing and to co-operate with other societies and organizations in such publication; (d) defend and safeguard the professional interests of indexers; (e) co-operate with other societies and organizations in the field of indexing and information science and especially with The Society of Indexers (Great Britain). It is affiliated to the Society of Indexers, whose journal, *The Indexer* (2 p.a.), serves as the journal of both societies. Abbreviated ASI. Publishes *Newsletter* (irreg. membs.).

AMERICAN STANDARD CODE FOR INFORMATION INTER-CHANGE. *See* ASCII.

AMERICAN THEOLOGICAL LIBRARY ASSOCIATION. Founded 1947 to bring its members into closer working relations with each other and with the American Association of Theological Schools; to study the distinctive problems of theological seminary libraries; to increase the professional competence of the membership; and to improve the library service to theological education. Abbreviated ATLA. Publishes *Proceedings* (a.), *Newsletter* (q. to membs.), *Index to Religious Periodicals Literature*, 1949 to date.

AMERICANA. Material relating to the Americas, whether printed about or in, the Americas, or written by Americans or not.

AMIGOS. In the American Southwest, the network of fifty-eight libraries in Texas, Arkansas, Oklahoma, New Mexico and Arizona which co-operate in such matters as using Ohio College Library Center (OCLC) system for on-line shared cataloguing, serials check-in and acquisition; regional catalogue card production, the generation of micro-image catalogues, user studies, on-line searching of other data bases, and facsimile reproduction transmission are other possible co-operative projects.

AMMONIA PROCESS. (*Reprography*) A two-component diazo process in which both the diazo and the coupler are on the base. Development is achieved by neutralizing the acidic stabilizers by evaporating aqueous ammonia. *See also* DIAZO.

AMPERSAND. The abbreviation, sign or character for the word 'and', thus: &. Also called 'Short and'.

-ANA (often with the euphonic *i* added: IANA). A suffix to names of persons or places, denoting a collection of books, anecdotes, literary gossip, or other facts or pieces of information, e.g. Americana, Johnsoniana, Lincolniana.

ANAGRAM. A transposition of the letters of a word or sentence resulting in some new word or sentence.

ANALECTS. A collection of literary fragments, gleanings or other miscellaneous written passages.

ANALET. A 'small analysis' or statement of the (*classification*) steps taken to analyse a complex subject.

ANALPHABET. A person who did not have the opportunity to learn to read (for whatever reason) but would be able to learn to read if the opportunity were given. One who is totally illiterate.

ANALOG COMPUTER. A computer which operates by directly representing changes in one phenomenon by changes in another. *See also* DIGITAL COMPUTER.

ANALYSIS. (*Cataloguing*) A book is said to be 'analysed' when any part of it is recorded separately in a catalogue by means of an ANALYTICAL ENTRY (*q.v.*). (*Classification*) Breaking down a subject into its facets. *See* FACET. (*Information retrieval*) 1. The perusal of source materials and the selection of analytics (e.g. index entries, subject headings, keywords and descriptors) that are considered to be of sufficient probable importance to justify the effort of rendering them searchable in an information-retrieval system. 2. A detailed examination of a document to determine and state its characteristics, including abstracting, classifying and indexing.

ANALYTIC. *See* ANALYTICAL ENTRY.

ANALYTICAL BIBLIOGRAPHY. The kind of bibliography which determines facts and data concerning a publication by examining the signatures, catchwords, cancels and watermarks, and making a record in an approved form of the results. Also called 'critical' or 'historical bibliography'. *See also* BIBLIOGRAPHY.

ANALYTICAL BOOKLET. A booklet of descriptive or bibliographical notes accompanying a gramophone record album or an individual record. *See also* LAID IN.

ANALYTICAL CATALOGUING. The branch of cataloguing which is concerned with making analytical entries. *See* ANALYTICAL ENTRY.

ANALYTICAL ENTRY. An entry in a catalogue for part of a book, periodical or other publication, article or contribution of separate authorship in a collection (volume of essays, festschrift, serial, volume of musical compositions, etc.). The entry includes a reference to the work containing it. The entry is supplementary to the comprehensive, or MAIN ENTRY (*q.v.*), for the whole work. Such entries, called 'Analytics', may be made under authors, subjects or titles. In special libraries they are often made for significant paragraphs, sections, tables, etc., and occasionally for particular facts or figures, in addition to parts or chapters of books, units of a series and of a collection.

ANALYTICAL INDEX. 1. An index in which the entries are not arranged in one straightforward alphabetical sequence, but the subject of the work is divided into a number of main headings and these in turn are sub-divided as necessary, each sequence of entries being arranged alphabetically. The abstracts (or papers) included in the volume to be indexed are then classified according to these main headings and so placed in their appropriate places in the analytical index.

2. An alphabetical subject index to information in articles of broader connotation than the subject index headings, as in an encyclopaedia. 3. A classified index to material under specific subjects, as in a reference book. (*ALA Gloss.*)

ANALYTICAL METHOD. In classification, the breaking down of a specific subject into constituent elements according to a given formula, these elements then being reassembled in a pre-determined order designed to give the most useful arrangement.

ANALYTICAL NOTE. 1. That part of an analytical entry containing the reference to the document for which the entry has been made. 2. A note following a MAIN ENTRY (*q.v.*) detailing the separate items which comprise the whole document.

ANALYTICAL RELATIONS. The ten relations used in the SEMANTIC CODE (*q.v.*) developed by the Center for Documentation and Communication at Western Reserve University, to link words to descriptors (here called semantic factors), to control the descriptor language. They are: categorical, intrinsic, inclusive, comprehensive, productive, affective, instrumental, negative, attributive, and simulative relation. *See also* SEMANTIC FACTOR.

ANALYTICO-SYNTHETIC CLASSIFICATION. A scheme which gives the classifier the maximum autonomy in constructing numbers for new specific subjects not enumerated in the schedules. Ranganathan's *Colon Classification* was the first scheme of this kind. A FACETED CLASSIFICATION (*q.v.*).

ANASTATIC PRINTING. A process or method of obtaining facsimile impressions of any printed design or engraving by transferring it to a plate of zinc, which, on being subjected to the action of an acid, is etched or eaten away, with the exception of the parts covered with ink. These parts are left in relief and can be printed from readily.

ANASTATIC REPRINT. An unaltered reprint made in the mid-nineteenth century, especially in France, by making an inked offset of the type on metal plates which were etched in relief.

AND OTHERS. When there are more than three joint authors, collaborators, etc., a catalogue entry may be made only under the first to be mentioned followed by *and others*, or by *et al* (*q.v.*).

ANDERSEN AWARD, HANS CHRISTIAN. In full, the International Hans Christian Andersen Youth Book Award. First awarded in 1956 (to Eleanor Farjeon for *The little book room*), it is now awarded to a living author, and to an illustrator as well, whose complete work has made 'a lasting contribution to literature for children and young people'. The Award takes the form of a medal and is made every two years by the INTERNATIONAL BOARD ON BOOKS FOR YOUNG PEOPLE. *See* IBBY.

ANEPIGRAPHON.   A publication whose title-page is missing.

ANGLE BRACKETS.   *See* BRACKETS.

ANGLO-AMERICAN CODE.†   The cataloguing code devised by the Library Association and the American Library Association, and published in 1908. It consists of definitions, 174 substantive rules (with variations where the two committees could not agree, and where some recognized authority such as the Library of Congress differed from the rule recommended), appendices of abbreviations, transliterations, and sample catalogue cards illustrating the rules. In 1949 the American Library Association published the *ALA Cataloguing Rules for Author and Title Entries* which incorporated the Library of Congress rules printed as 'supplementary rules' in the 1908 edition and ignored the English variations of certain rules which appeared in this edition. Considerable clarification took place, and better, and more numerous, examples were given. Committees of the ALA and of the LA met concurrently to prepare revised codes, and close co-operation was maintained by the exchange of minutes and working papers; later members of each committee met the other committees. The result was the publication in 1966 of the *Anglo-American cataloguing rules: North American text* and in 1967 of the *British text*. These rules are based on the PARIS PRINCIPLES (*q.v.*) which were adopted by the International Conference on Cataloguing Principles held in 1961. Some of the rules differ materially in the two texts. Manuscripts, incunabula, maps, music, motion pictures, filmstrips, phonorecords, pictures, designs and other two-dimensional representations are all provided for. This is not an internationally agreed, or adopted code, but it is the most widely used of the multi-national codes, being used in countries in which library development has stemmed almost entirely from the practices of the U.S.A. or the U.K. as well as in English language speaking countries. *See also* ISBD. *Examples illustrating Anglo-American cataloguing rules: British text, 1967,* edited and compiled by Eric J. Hunter, was published by the Library Association in 1973. *Anglo-American cataloguing rules: British text. Chapter 6 revised* (dealing with separately published monographs and other non-serial publications) was published in 1974, also by the Library Association, and a revision of Chapter 6 of the North American Text was published in 1974 by the American Library Association. These revisions have been undertaken to incorporate the provisions of *ISBD(M). The Anglo-American catologuing rules (AACR)* is under complete revision by its four 'authors' (Library Association, the American Library Association, the Canadian Library Association, and the Library of Congress) who are being joined by the British Library. The 2nd edition is expected to be published in 1977. Royalties from the sale of the new *AACR* will be placed in a common fund to support future activities associated with *AACR*. The revised code will use a newly-formulated General International Standard Bibliographical Description (*See* ISBD(G)) as the basis for its rules of description.

ANGSTROM. A unit of measurement, equal to one ten-millionth of a millimetre, used to express the length of light waves. In colorimetry, the millimicron (ten angstrom units) is used more frequently.

ANGULAR MARKS. *See* BRACKETS.

ANHYDROUS. Water-free. Normally used with reference to chemical salts and solvents. (*Verry.*)

ANIMAL TUB-SIZED. *See* TUB-SIZING.

ANIMALS IN FOLIAGE PANEL. A panel in a book-binding decoration which is divided vertically into two, each half containing curving foliage with an animal within each curve. It is the characteristic Netherlands design.

ANNAL. An entry in a record of events in their chronological order year by year.

ANNALISTIC ARRANGEMENT. A bibliography of an author's writings arranged in order of publication.

ANNALS. A record of events arranged in chronological order.

ANNEXE. 1. Supporting contributions to a main report, thesis, or other work. 2. A document usually attached to, but not physically a part of, that to which it is attached.

ANNOTATE. To make an annotation.

ANNOTATED. Said of a catalogue or bibliography entry which has been provided with an ANNOTATION (*q.v.*).

ANNOTATING. The act of preparing an ANNOTATION (*q.v.*).

ANNOTATION. A note added to an entry in a catalogue, reading list or bibliography, to elucidate, evaluate or describe the subject and contents of a book; it sometimes gives particulars of the author. The term originally embraced notes of all kinds which followed the collation, but modern practice provides bibliographical notes as the fifth part of a MAIN ENTRY (*q.v.*) and the annotation as the sixth and final part.

ANNUAL. A serial publication, e.g. a report, year book or directory issued once a year. *See also* BI-ANNUAL, YEAR BOOK.

ANNUAL BIBLIOGRAPHY OF THE PRINTED BOOK AND LIBRARIES. See ABHB.

ANONYM. 1. An anonymous publication. 2. An anonymous person or writer. 3. A pseudonym.

ANONYMOUS. A publication is said to be anonymous when the author's name does not appear anywhere in it, either on the title-page or cover, or in the preface, introduction or foreword. According to some authorities, if the authorship can be traced in catalogues or bibliographies it may be considered not to be anonymous. The opposite of onymous.

ANONYMOUS CLASSIC. A work of unknown or doubtful authorship, commonly designated by title, which may have appeared in the course of time in many editions, versions, and/or translations.

ANONYMOUS ENTRY. An entry in a catalogue for a book the author of which is not mentioned on the title-page.

ANOPISTHOGRAPHIC BLOCK BOOK. One that is printed on only one side of the paper.

ANOPISTHOGRAPHIC PRINTING. The manner of printing early block books, using writing ink and printing on only one side of the leaf. *See also* BLOCK BOOKS, OPISTHOGRAPHIC.

ANSAPHONE. Trade name for a telephone answering machine which records on a tape telephone messages when a line is engaged or the staff not in attendance. Somewhat similar machines are RECORDACALL and TEL-STOR (*qq.v.*). In libraries they are intended mainly to deal with the renewal of books after the library has closed but they will, of course, record all messages.

ANSTEL. Abbreviation for the Australian National Scientific and Technological Library, a subject unit of the National Library of Australia; it was set up late in 1974 in accordance with the STISEC (*q.v.*) report. *See also* ALBIS.

ANTE-DATED. A book which bears a date of publication which is earlier than the actual date. The opposite of 'Post-dated'.

ANTERIOR NUMERAL CLASSES. The first group of the main classes of Bliss's *Bibliographic Classification*. They are bibliothetic in character and conform to the generalia classes of other schemes. Three of the nine divisions accommodate general works (2 bibliography, 6 periodicals, 7 miscellanea); the remainder provide for special collections of books which for some reason it is preferred to shelve apart from the main collection. *See also* SYSTEMATIC AUXILIARY SCHEDULES.

ANTERIORIZING DIGIT. (*Classification*) The digit which, when added to a class number, causes the resulting class number to have precedence over the number to which it was added. For example the *a* in the class number X*a* is the anteriorizing digit. Also called 'Anteriorizing common isolates'. *See also* ANTERIORIZING VALUE.

ANTERIORIZING VALUE. (*Classification*) Said to be possessed by a digit which, when added to a class number (and which is then said to be the 'host class number'), causes the resulting class number to have precedence over the host number. For example, in the Colon classification, class numbers containing lower case roman letters, or arrows, have precedence over class numbers without them, as: X*a* precedes X, B63*a* precedes B63, L23: 45*a* precedes L23: 45, N ← M precedes N.

ANTHOLOGY. A collection of choice extracts, usually of poetry, or on one subject, from the writings of one author, or various authors, and having a common characteristic such as subject matter or literary form.

ANTIPHONARY. A liturgical book intended for use in a choir. Generically it includes antiphons and antiphonal chants sung at Mass and at the canonical Hours, but now refers only to the sung portions of the BREVIARY (*q.v.*).

ANTIQUA. A German name for Roman types. A small book hand based on the Caroline minuscule, called *lettera rotonda* or *lettre ronde* (round letter) in Italy and France. Type based on this writing is now known as Roman, and is the usual kind of type (as distinct from *italic*) used for book work.

ANTIQUARIAN BOOKSELLER. One who deals with very old books, many of which may have had several owners, and which are rare enough to command higher prices than ordinary second-hand books.

ANTIQUE. (*Paper*) The name given to printing papers made from esparto grass. They usually have a rough surface, and the poorer qualities are called *featherweight*, so loosely woven that 75 per cent of the bulk is air space. The term originally referred to machine-made paper made in imitation of hand-made paper. Antique papers have a matt or dull finish and are neither calendered nor coated. They are suitable for printing type and line engravings, but not for half-tones, and are used for most books without blocks. (*Binding*) Designates blind tooling. *See* TOOLING.

ANTIQUE FINISH. (*Paper*) A rough surface, suggestive of old hand-made printing paper. Generally used to indicate an 'unfinished' paper, i.e. one not calendered, and usually of the FEATHERWEIGHT PAPER (*q.v.*) class.

ANTIQUE GOLD EDGES. *See* GILT EDGES.

ANTIQUE LAID. Originally, paper made on moulds of which the

3

chain wires were laced or sewn direct to the wooden ribs or supports of the mould, thus causing the pulp to lie thicker along each side of every chain line in the sheet of paper. Now, any rough-surfaced laid paper. *See also* MOULD.

ANTIQUE TOOLING. A form of blind tooling.

ANTONYM. A word having the opposite meaning of another. The opposite of synonym.

ANTONYMOUS CATCHWORDS. Headings used in an index, which are exactly opposite in meaning.

APERTURE. The area of the hole available for light rays of an axial beam traversing the lens of a camera, or reproducer, to form an image on the sensitized film behind the lens. The lens is equipped with a diaphragm or stop which restricts the area to control the brilliance of the image (the larger the aperture, the more light passes through, and the greater the exposure) and to control the depth of field of the lens (the smaller the aperture, the greater the depth of field). The size of the aperture is indicated by its f- number, i.e. the ratio of the diameter of the opening to the focal length of the lens; a low f- number indicates a large aperture.

APERTURE CARD. A card with one or more openings (the number depending on the amount of space required for identifying stored document images) into each of which is mounted a 'frame' cut from a strip of microfilm. The identification on the card can consist of written information, punched holes, or characters on film. Also called IMAGE CARD, PEEPHOLE CARD (*q.v.*).

APOCALYPSE OF ST. JOHN. See BLOCK BOOKS.

APOCONYM. A name changed by the cutting off or elision of letters or syllables.

APOCRYPHAL. Of unknown authorship or doubtful authenticity.

APOGRAPH. A copy of an original manuscript.

APOSTIL (APOSTILLE). An annotation, or marginal note (archaic).

app. Abbreviation for APPENDIX (*q.v.*).

APPARATUS CRITICUS. The sources of information and the existence of manuscripts, letters and other material used by an author, and enumerated by him in footnotes, marginalia and commentary in support of his text, and thus associated with the preparation of the definitive edition of a work. Includes particularly, information concerning variant readings, doubtful texts and obscurities.

APPENDIX. Matter which comes at the end of the text of a book and contains notes which are too long for footnotes, tables of statistics, or other items for which there is no room in the body of the book, or which, from the nature of the information, is more suitably placed at the end of the text.

APPLICATION BLANK. *Synonymous with* APPLICATION FORM (*q.v.*).

APPLICATION FORM (VOUCHER). The form, usually a card size 5 × 3 inches, on which persons wishing to join the children's or adult lending libraries, or to obtain books for use in (or away from) a reference library, make their application. In many libraries, applicants for lending library tickets have to obtain the signature of a ratepayer as guarantor, but more often as recommender. In some libraries, applicants whose names appear in the current list of electors are permitted to borrow without obtaining the signature of another person but the practice is increasing of not requiring *any* counter-signature as verification of the applicant.

APPLIED BIBLIOGRAPHY. *Synonymous with* HISTORICAL BIBLIOGRAPHY (*q.v.*).

APPRAISAL. An estimate of the value of a book as a contribution to a subject.

APPRAISAL. (*Archives*) 1. The process of determining the value, and so the disposition, of documents, based upon: (a) their current legal fiscal or administrative use; (b) their research or information use; (c) their arrangement; or (d) their relationship to other records. Also called 'Selective retention'. 2. The monetary value of gifts of manuscripts. *See also* INTRINSIC VALUE.

APPROACH TERM. The word which a catalogue-user seeks in a catalogue, in anticipation that it will lead him to a statement in SUBJECT HEADING LANGUAGE (*q.v.*) of a required compound subject.

AQUATINT. 1. A process of etching on copper or steel plates by means of nitric acid, producing an effect resembling a fine drawing in water colours, sepia or India ink. It is used to render tonal effects rather than lines. Now supplanted commercially by lithography. 2. A print made by this method.

AQUATONE. A photographic printing process which is similar to collotype, but is used with offset presses.

ARAB STATES CENTRE FOR FUNCTIONAL LITERACY. *See* ARAB STATES TRAINING CENTRE FOR EDUCATION FOR COMMUNITY DEVELOPMENT.

ARAB STATES TRAINING CENTRE FOR EDUCATION FOR COMMUNITY DEVELOPMENT. Established late in 1952 as the Arab States Fundamental Education Centre (ASFEC) – a regional project for the whole of the Arab states. It was subsequently named the Arab States Centre for Functional Literacy, the name being again changed to the present one in 1969. It is sponsored mainly by UNESCO, although it derives part of its finances from the host government, the United Arab Republic. Its main purposes are: (a) training fundamental education workers from the Arab states; (b) conducting research in topics related to socio-economic development; (c) producing prototype materials in such fields as literacy teaching, health education, agriculture extension, home economics with a view to calling the attention of the participating governments to the importance of such materials. Since 1953 batches of students have been accepted from most of the Arab states for courses in varying subjects and for different periods.

ARABESQUE. A species of decoration consisting of interlaced lines and convoluted curves arranged in more or less geometrical patterns; so-called because it was brought to its highest perfection by Arabian or kindred artists. Also applied to a fanciful mixture of animals, birds, and insects, and of plants, fruit and foliage, involved and twisted; but pure arabesque has in it no representation of living forms, as this is forbidden by the Koran.

ARABIC FIGURES. The numerical characters 1, 2, 3, etc., as distinct from roman numerals I, II, III, etc., so called from having been introduced into European from Arab use: they have been used for foliation since the last quarter of the fifteenth century. Arabic numerals first appeared in European MSS. in the twelfth century, although the Arabs probably brought them from India in the eighth century. Arabic is used for numbering the text pages of books. 'Old Style' numerals are as follows 1, 2, 3, 4, 5, 6, 7, 8, 9, 0 and have ascenders and descenders, although tabular work makes it desirable to have 'lining figures' (1, 2, 3, 4, 5, 6, 7, 8, 9, 0) as an alternative. These are also known as 'Modern'. It is the presence or absence of ascenders and descenders which indicates whether the figures are 'Old Style' or 'Modern'. This distinction applies to italic as well as to roman: Old Style – *1, 2, 3, 4, 5, 6, 7, 8, 9, 0*. Modern – *1, 2, 3, 4, 5, 6, 7, 8, 9, 0*. *See also* FOLIATION, HANGING FIGURES, LINING FIGURES, PAGINATION, ROMAN NUMERALS.

ARBICA. Acronym of the Arab Regional Branch of the International Council on Archives. *See* INTERNATIONAL COUNCIL ON ARCHIVES.

ARBITRARY CODE. *Synonymous with* TABULATED CODE (*q.v.*).

ARBITRARY SYMBOL. (*Classification*) A symbol, e.g. a punctuation mark, used in a NOTATION as a FACET INDICATOR (*qq.v.*).

ARBUTHNOT HONOR LECTURE, MAY HILL. An endowed annual lecture, established by Scott, Foresman and Company in tribute to May Hill Arbuthnot, one of the foremost authorities on literature for children, for her outstanding (and in many ways pioneer) contribution to children's literature. The Children's Services Division of the ALA administers the selection of the lecture series. An outstanding author, critic, librarian, historian, or teacher of children's literature will be selected to prepare a paper which shall be a significant contribution to the field of children's literature; it will afterwards be published in the June issue of *Top of the News*. An honorarium of $1,000 is paid to each lecturer. First delivered in 1970, by the English author and editor of *Growing Point*, Margery Fisher who, in her lecture, surveyed the past ten years of children's literature in Britain. The lecture is printed in *Top of the News*, **26** (4) June 1970 pp. 374–91. *See also* CHILDREN'S BOOK CIRCLE.

ARC LAMP. A powerful source of artificial light obtained from an incandescent arc of light formed between two electrodes.

ARCHBISHOP PARKER'S BIBLE. *See* BISHOPS' BIBLE.

ARCHETYPAL NOVEL. Commonly used to describe the earliest romances, tales and works of fiction; the fore-runner of the modern novel.

ARCHITECTURAL BINDING. A sixteenth-century style of book cover decoration which consisted of columns supporting an arch under which was a panel to contain the title. The contents of the books so decorated seldom related to architecture.

ARCHIVAL DOCUMENT. A document which it is expected will be kept permanently, as near as possible in its original form, for the evidence which it might afford both in itself and within its context.

ARCHIVAL INTEGRITY. The standard of administration and preservation that requires that archive holdings are identified and arranged as originally compiled, assembled and administered, kept in their original filing sequence, and preserved in their entirety without mutilation, alteration or destruction of any portion of them.

ARCHIVAL QUALITY. (*Reprography*) The degree to which a processed film or print will retain its characteristics without loss of quality over an indefinite period of storage under controlled conditions.

ARCHIVAL VALUE. The decision, after appraisal, that documents are worthy of indefinite or permanent depository.

ARCHIVE ADMINISTRATION. The collection and conservation of ARCHIVES (*q.v.*), their organization for use, and the theoretical and practical studies of such procedures.

ARCHIVES. 1. Public records or historical documents kept in a recognized repository. 2. Documents which formed part of an official transaction and were preserved for official reference; these include documents specially made for, and those included in, an official transaction (*Jenkinson*). 3. The repository itself. 4. Colloquially a collection of old books or documents. 5. Written documents, or annexures to them, compiled for the purposes of, or used during, a public or private business transaction of which they themselves form a part; and which are preserved by the persons concerned with the transaction, or their successors, in their own custody for their own use. Similarly, any records of the activities of societies or groups. 6. A collection of original records assembled in the course of the normal activities of a person or persons, or of a public or private organization; or such records from a number of different sources, and kept together to ensure their preservation. 7. In 1973 the publication of the only national, or international, standards on the care of archive material was begun by the British Standard Institution which issued Part 1 *Treatment of sheets, membranes and seals* of BS 4971 *Recommendations for repair and allied processes for the conservation of documents.* Part 2 will deal more specifically with the make-up and binding of archival documents. A separate standard is being prepared for the storage and exhibition of such documents. Part 1 deals with the destruction by microbiological and insect infestation, mechanical and liquid cleaning, de-acidification, repair and joining, lamination, and various other processes. In January 1974, the Association of College and Research Libraries approved Statements on (a) Access to Original Research Materials in Libraries, Archives and Manuscript Repositories, and (b) The Reproduction of Manuscripts and Archives for Noncommercial purposes. *See also* INTERNATIONAL COUNCIL ON ARCHIVES, RECORDS.

ARCHIVIST. A person who has the care of archives, and also makes them available under proper safeguards to historians and researchers.

AREA (*County Libraries*) A part of the County Library area, not as extensive as a region, served by a number of branches and/or centres, and forming a library unit for administrative purposes. It will normally comprise two or more county districts or parishes. (*Cataloguing*) A major section of a bibliographic description (forming a part of a catalogue entry) which comprises data of a particular category or set of categories.

AREA HEADQUARTERS (*County Libraries*) The premises from which the Libraries in an Area are administered, which may or may not be a library to which the public has access.

AREA LIBRARIAN. One who is in charge of a compact and limited portion of a county library area, and responsible for a small number of branches and other service points in that area.

AREA OF SERVICE. A term applied to a geographical area to the residents of which a public library provides a free service, and from which (or on behalf of which) the library receives an income.

AREA SEARCH. Examination of a large group of documents to segregate those documents pertaining to a general class, category or topic. Screening (*IBM*).

AREA TABLE. A common geographical facet based on the geographical numbers used in the Dewey Classification in order to provide geographical arrangement of material classified primarily by subject.

ARISTO PAPER. A photographic copying paper, the colloid being gelatine.

ARISTRONYM. A title of nobility converted into, or used as, a surname.

ARITHMETICAL NOTATION. *Synonymous with* INTEGRAL NOTATION (*q.v.*).

ARLIS Abbreviation for The Art Libraries Society founded in 1969, this Society exists to promote art librarianship, particularly by acting as a forum for the interchange of information and materials. Membership is open to individuals and institutions in the United Kingdom. ARLIS is affiliated to its American counterpart ARLIS/NA. It regularly organizes social functions and professional visits for its members and holds a conference every alternate year. The policy of the Society is determined by the ARLIS Council elected annually. It publishes the *Directory of Members* (a.); *Newsletter* (q.) which is more of a journal than a newsletter.

ARLIS/NA. (Art Libraries Society of North America) Formed in 1972 by a group of ten art librarians, with similar objectives to the British Society to which it is affiliated. *See also* ARLIS. Publishes *Newsletter* (6 p.a.).

ARM. The projecting, or unclosed, horizontal or upward-sloping stroke of a type letter.

ARMARIA. Used in the first centuries of the Christian era to indicate cupboards for keeping books.

ARMARIAN. A worker in a monastic library whose duty it was to prevent the books under his charge from being injured by insects, to look after bindings, and keep a correct catalogue. He presided over a SCRIPTORIUM (*q.v.*) and supplied the scribes with parchment, pens, ink, knives, awls and rulers. Also called an 'Armarius'.

ARMARIUM. A wardrobe, or cupboard, possibly a separate piece of furniture in which scrolls, or subsequently books, were kept. Closed armaria apparently developed in Imperial times and survived in monastic libraries until the Renaissance or later.

ARMARIUS.   *See* ARMARIAN.

ARMED SERVICES TECHNICAL INFORMATION AGENCY.   A United States governmental organization, now known as the DEFENSE DOCUMENTATION CENTER (*q.v.*). Abbreviated ASTIA.

ARMENIAN BOLE.   A bright-red clay which is used as a colouring material and also to dust on to the edges of books before gilding to act as a base for the gold, to which it gives a greater depth and lustre. It is obtained mainly from Bohemia, Italy and Silesia.

ARMING PRESS.   A hand blocking press used now only for short runs but originally for impressing armorial bearings.

ARMORIAL BINDING.   One decorated with the arms or other device of royalty or nobility. Generally applied to bindings earlier than the mid-nineteenth century.

ARMS BLOCK.   An engraved brass block or a binder's ZINCO 2 (*q.v.*) made by a line-block maker and used in an arming or blocking press to impress a coat of arms on leather bindings.

ARRANGEMENT.   The adaptation of a whole musical work, or an integral part of a musical work, to a medium of performance other than that for which it was originally written, e.g. the casting of a song as a piano piece, or of an orchestral overture as an organ piece. Sometimes also, a simplification or amplification, when the musical structure and the medium of performance remain the same.

ARRANGER.   One who transcribes a whole musical work, or a part of a work, for a medium of performance other than that intended by the composer. The arrangement may be a simplification or amplification, the medium of performance and the musical structure remaining the same.

ARRAY.   1. In classification, the series of co-ordinate sub-divisions which are obtained by dividing a class or a division according to a single characteristic: e.g. Literature divided according to character-istic *Form* gives the array Poetry, Drama, Novel, Essay. Each co-ordinate division in an array should exclude all of the others, and the whole array should be exhaustive of the contents of the class. The order of the divisions in an array should be that deemed most helpful to users. 2. A set of co-ordinate terms (i.e. terms subordinate to the same genus). Also used in information retrieval for a sequence of headings in a file (Taube) and as a set of search terms (Bernier). An ordinal arrangement of informational materials (*IBM*). 3. A set of mutually exclusive co-ordinate subclasses totally exhaustive of a class, derived by its division according to some one characteristic (*IBM*).

ARRESTER. (*Classification*) The second curve; used in the Colon Classification to enclose the Subject Device Number. The first, or opening, curve is called the 'Starter'. *See also* BRACKETS, CIRCULAR BRACKETS, CURVES.

ARS MEMORANDI. *See* BLOCK BOOKS.

ARS MORIENDI. A mediaeval block book setting forth by means of pictures and text the art of dying becomingly.

ART. The name given to papers coated on one or both sides after the paper is made by brushing on China clay, sulphate of barium, or sulphate of lime and alumina (the last for the 'satin-white' finish) and afterwards polished. In *imitation art* the paper is 'loaded' (i.e. the China clay is mixed in with the fibre) not 'coated'. *Matt art* is unglazed coated paper with a smooth, soft, egg-shell finish.

ART CANVAS. A cloth for bookbinding, also known as *light-weight buckram.*

ART LIBRARIES SOCIETY. *See* ARLIS.

ART PAPER. *See* ART.

ART PARCHMENT. *See* VELLUM PARCHMENT.

ART VELLUM. 1. A brand name for a lightweight book cloth. 2. A fabric used for classes of works which do not require a very strong cloth.

ART WORK. A term covering all forms of illustrative matter (line drawings, photographs, paintings, diagrams, hand lettering, etc.) used in a printed publication to distinguish it from type-set matter. In America the term is used to distinguish any material prepared by hand as camera copy.

ARTEFACTS. (*Classification*) A group of 'artificial' entities, i.e. those which do not occur naturally, and which are 'concrete', e.g. chairs, automobiles. The other group is known as MENTEFACTS (*q.v.*).

ARTICLE. A contribution written by one or more persons for publication in a PERIODICAL (*q.v.*); such a contribution when so published. *See also* WORK.

ARTIFICIAL CHARACTERISTIC. *See* CHARACTERISTIC OF A CLASSIFICATION.

ARTIFICIAL CLASSIFICATION. One in which some accidental thing is adopted as the 'difference'. *See* PREDICABLES, FIVE. Classification by analogy, i.e. by external or accidental likeness, unlikeness, or apparent purpose. *See* CHARACTERISTIC OF A CLASSIFICATION.

ARTIFICIAL INDEXING LANGUAGE. (*Information retrieval, Indexing*) A group of signs, symbols or digits (or of phrases, or words arranged in an inverted order according to rules and so becoming 'controlled' language) to represent facts and ideas. An index language. The opposite of NATURAL LANGUAGE (*q.v.*). *See also* INDEXING LANGUAGE.

ARTISTIC MANUSCRIPT. A record or document produced by hand, and decorated or illustrated in such a way as to achieve distinction as a work of artistic merit. Illuminated manuscripts are the most important examples. *See also* LITERARY MANUSCRIPT.

ARTISTIC MAP. One made by an artist rather than by a cartographer; such maps consequently appeal to the eye and are often not correct cartographically. They are used as illustrations, endpapers, and for advertisement.

ARTIST'S PROOF. A proof of an engraving or etching, usually with the signature of the artist in pencil, and sometimes with a small sketch, known as a remarque, in the margin. Used as a model or sample. Also called 'Remarque Proof'.

ARTOTEK. A picture and art library.

ARTOTYPE. A photo-engraved picture made by one of the gelatine processes (*United Typothetae*).

ARTYPE. Type letters which are printed on acetate sheets gummed on the back. Those required are cut out of the sheet and pressed in the required position to form 'copy' which is photographed for printing by the offset process.

ARUNDEL PSALTER. Two Psalters bound together, and each illuminated in a distinct style. The first, containing many miniature-filled initials was probably done by an early fourteenth-century court artist. The second is typical of the East Anglian School and is probably earlier. It has full-page scenes from the Passion and a large number of allegorical scenes. It is in the British Museum.

'AS IF' FILING. The filing alphabetically of abbreviations as if they were spelled out, e.g. St. as Saint, Mr. as Mister, 1001 as One thousand and one.

AS ISSUED. Indicates that a book offered for sale secondhand is in its original format.

AS NEW. Used in secondhand booksellers' catalogues to indicate that the physical condition of a book offered for sale is 'almost indistinguishable from the condition of newness'.

ASCENDER. The vertical ascending stem of lower-case letters such as b, d, k, etc.; that part which extends above the X-HEIGHT (*q.v.*). *See also* DESCENDER.

ASCENDER LINE. (*Printing*) The imaginary line which runs along the top of ascenders. This will be above the CAP LINE (*q.v.*) in the case of types the capitals of which are lower than the ascenders. *See also* ASCENDER, BASE LINE, CAP LINE, MEAN LINE.

ASCETONYM. The name of a saint used as a proper name.

ASCII. Acronym for American Standard Code for Information Interchange which is the official data interchange code of the federal government of the U.S.A.

ASFEC. *See* ARAB STATES TRAINING CENTRE FOR EDUCATION FOR COMMUNITY DEVELOPMENT.

ASHENDENE PRESS. One of the most distinguished British private presses. It was founded in 1895 by C. H. St. John Hornby, a partner in the firm of W. H. Smith & Son, and undertook fine printing at the instance of Sydney Cockerell in 1900.

ASIDIC. Abbreviation for the (American) Association of Scientific Information Dissemination Centers, the purposes of which are to share experiences, recommend greater efforts at standardization, and promote more efficient use of data resources. It is composed of organizations which offer two or more current awareness and/or retrospective searches processed by computer, for data bases from a variety of sources. A European counterpart is EUSIDIC (*q.v.*).

ASLIB. Founded 1926 as the Association of Special Libraries and Information Bureaux. Merged with the British Society for International Bibliography in 1949. Aims 'to facilitate the co-ordination and systematic use of sources of knowledge and information in all public affairs and in industry and commerce and in all the arts and sciences'. It has geographical branches and subject groups to which members may belong, provides an information service, maintains an index of translations into English of articles on scientific and technical subjects, keeps a register of translators, provides training courses and organizes conferences and meetings. Additionally, Aslib undertakes research into information management problems, and offers consultancy and advisory services in this field. It has members in 80 countries. Publishes *Aslib proceedings* (m.), *Aslib Book list* (m.), *Index to theses* (a.), *Journal of documentation* (q.), *Aslib Information* (m.), *Program: news of computers in libraries* (q.), *Newsletter* (q.) (Aslib Transport and Planning Group).

ASLIB CRANFIELD RESEARCH PROJECT. An investigation into the comparative efficiency of four indexing systems; it consisted of the preparation – and subsequent testing – of four separate indexes for which 18,000 documents were indexed by the Universal Decimal Classification (using conventional card catalogues), an alphabetical subject index, a special facet classification, and the Uniterm system of co-ordinate indexing (for which alphabetical and facet aspect cards posted with document numbers were used). The Project was undertaken by means of a National Science Foundation grant which was offered to Aslib in July 1957; it was undertaken at the College of Aeronautics, Cranfield, under the direction of the Librarian, Mr. Cyril Cleverdon.

ASOCIACIÓN LATINAMERICANA DE ESCUELAS DE BIBLIO-TECOLOGIA Y CIENCIAS DE LA INFORMACIÓN. *See* ALEBCI.

ASPECT CARD. A record used in an ASPECT SYSTEM (*q.v.*) of recording information for retrieval. A separate card is used for one subject or point of view and entered on it are the numbers or other identification symbols of each document which has this quality. The number is entered on as many cards as are necessary to record every aspect of the document.

ASPECT SYSTEM. A method of indexing which assumes that a DISCRETE RECORD (*q.v.*) represents a single subject (or aspect) and contains, in searchable form, information as to which documents in a file have this subject in common. Also called 'Inverted' or 'Term entry' system. *See also* DISCRETE RECORD, DOCUMENT SYSTEM, TERM ENTRY.

ASSEMBLER. (*Information retrieval*) The program which converts the symbolic language program, written by the programmer, to a machine-language program.

ASSOCIATE LIBRARIAN. American term for a deputy librarian.

ASSOCIATED BOOK. As used in connexion with the Colon Classification, a book which is written about another book, as e.g. a criticism of, or reply to, it. The book which is the subject of the criticism or reply is called a 'Host book'. The BOOK NUMBER (*q.v.*) of an Associated Book should consist of that of the Host Book followed by ':g'. The number so added is called the 'Criticism number'. Where there is more than one Associated Book of the same Host Book, a digit, 1, 2, etc., representing each additional Associated Book, may be added to the Book Number and so becomes part of it. The number added in this way may be called the 'Accession part of the Criticism number'.

ASSOCIATION. *See* LINKS.

ASSOCIATION BOOK. One having an autograph inscription or notes by the author, or which was in any way intimately connected with a prominent person who may have owned or presented it, or which had belonged to someone connected with its contents. Evidence in or on the book of the association is essential. If there is no signature or presentation inscription there should be a bookplate, or binding stamp, or marginal or other notes to indicate the association.

ASSOCIATION CANADIENNE DES SCIENCES DE L'INFORMA-TION. *See* CANADIAN ASSOCIATION FOR INFORMATION SCIENCE.

ASSOCIATION COPY. *Synonymous with* ASSOCIATION BOOK.

ASSOCIATION FOR COMPUTING MACHINERY. Founded in the U.S.A. in 1947 to advance the science, design, development, construction and application of modern machinery for performing operations in mathematics, logics, statistics, and kindred fields. Abbreviated ACM. Publishes *Communications* (m.), *Journal* (q.), *Computing Reviews* (bi-monthly).

ASSOCIATION FOR LIBRARY AUTOMATION RESEARCH COMMUNICATIONS. *See* LARC ASSOCIATION.

ASSOCIATION FOR THE DEVELOPMENT OF PUBLIC LIBRARIES IN AFRICA. Founded at Dakar, 13th September 1957 and renamed the INTERNATIONAL ASSOCIATION FOR THE DEVELOPMENT OF LIBRARIES IN AFRICA (AIDBA) in 1960 and the INTERNATIONAL ASSOCIATION FOR THE DEVELOPMENT OF DOCUMENTATION, LIBRARIES AND ARCHIVES IN AFRICA (*q.v.*) in 1967. Abbreviated ADBPA.

ASSOCIATION FOR THE DEVELOPMENT OF RELIGIOUS INFORMATION SYSTEMS. *See* ADRIS.

ASSOCIATION INTERNATIONALE DES DOCUMENTALISTS ET TECHNICIENS DE L'INFORMATION. *See* INTERNATIONAL ASSOCIATION OF DOCUMENTALISTS AND INFORMATION OFFICERS.

ASSOCIATION LIBRARY. A library in Canada which is financed by the members of an association and staffed by volunteers. So named to distinguish such libraries from rate-supported or free public libraries.

ASSOCIATION MAP. (*Information retrieval*) A technique for manual thesaurus compilation which has been adopted by Euratom.

ASSOCIATION NATIONALE DE LA RECHERCHE TECHNIQUE. *See* ANRT.

ASSOCIATION NATIONALE POUR LA DÉVELOPPMENT DES BIBLIOTHÈQUES PUBLIQUES. *See* ANDBP.

ASSOCIATION OF ACADEMIC LIBRARIANS. Founded in Germany in 1900 'to safeguard the professional interests of the German Librarians, to stimulate interrelations among them and among the academic libraries, and to promote the academic library system'. It was re-established on 28th April 1948.

ASSOCIATION OF AMERICAN LIBRARY SCHOOLS. Founded

1915 to advance education for librarianship. Abbreviated AALS. Publishes *Journal of education for librarianship* (q.).

ASSOCIATION OF AMERICAN PUBLISHERS, INC. Formed in May 1970 by a merger of the American Book Publishers Council and the American Educational Publishers Institute. This confederation of more than 260 publishing houses is the major voice of the publishing industry in the U.S.A. Its aims are to: (a) improve the status of intellectual products in the United States; (b) nurture and strengthen public understanding that books play a central role in the process by which society seeks both the stability and the evolution of its values and its culture; (c) provide member houses with useful and accurate information regarding trade conditions, government policies and attitudes, pending legislation, postal rates, taxes, copyright, censorship movements, and other matters of importance or concern to publishers; (d) provide a framework within which the several groups comprising the combined general trade and educational publishing industry can work together to advance their common interests, and can articulate their particular interests; (e) provide a single authoritative spokesman for the industry on matters of agreed policy. Categories of membership are: *regular* which is open to all American corporations, partnerships, and private persons who, for at least one year, have been actively engaged in the U.S.A. in the creation, production and publication of books or copyrightable types of print and audiovisual materials; *associate* which is available to American non-profit-making organizations similarly qualified for regular membership; *foreign associate* which may be granted to foreign publishers doing business in the U.S.A. There are six divisions catering for those engaged in particular branches of publishing. Financed by members' dues. Abbreviated AAP. Publishes *Washington Newsletter* (m.), division newsletters (bi-m.).

ASSOCIATION OF ASSISTANT LIBRARIANS. A Group of the Library Association; it caters for members of a particular status rather than, as in the case of other groups, for those engaged in a particular branch of librarianship. It is organized in Divisions which operate at local level. Originally known as the Library Assistants' Association, it was formed on 3rd July 1895 at a meeting convened by Mr. W. W. Fortune; the name was changed to the Association of Assistant Librarians in June 1922. It was an independent association until 1st January 1930 when it became a Section of the Library Association. Abbreviated AAL. Publishes *Assistant Librarian* (11 p.a.).

ASSOCIATION OF BRITISH LIBRARY AND INFORMATION

STUDIES SCHOOLS. Founded 1962 as the Association of British Library Schools to further the work of the full-time schools of librarianship by affording heads of such schools, and some representatives of the library and professional organizations opportunities of meeting to discuss education in librarianship. Abbreviated ABLISS.

ASSOCIATION OF BRITISH THEOLOGICAL AND PHILOSOPHICAL LIBRARIES. *See* ABTAPL.

ASSOCIATION OF CANADIAN ARCHIVISTS. Formed in June 1975 in Edmonton. Aims: to (a) promote academic programmes leading to professional qualification in archival science and to advance general education in the preservation and use of records; (b) prescribe the highest standards in the conduct of archives administration and develop a code of professional responsibility; (c) represent the needs of the archival profession before governments and other regulatory authorities; (d) co-operate with regional, national and international organizations and related professional disciplines; (e) promote public knowledge and appreciation of archives and the function of archival institutions in preserving cultural heritage and identity. Membership is open to all persons studying, or employed in, archival administration, or interested in the field of archives; also to institutions wishing to receive the publications of the Association on a regular basis, or who wish to give financial support. Financed by membership fees and from advertising in publications. Abbreviated ACA. Publishes *Archivaria* (2 p.a.), *Archives Bulletin* (q.).

ASSOCIATION OF COLLEGE AND RESEARCH LIBRARIES. A Division of the American Library Association since 1938; founded in 1889 to represent and promote 'libraries of higher education (institutions supporting formal education above the secondary school level), independent research libraries, and specialized libraries'. Has eleven sections. It is the largest of the divisions of the ALA. Abbreviated ACRL. Publishes *College and Research Libraries* (17 issues p.a., 11 being *C&RL News*); *Choice: books for college libraries* (11 issues p.a.).

ASSOCIATION OF CO-OPERATIVE LIBRARY ORGANIZATIONS. *See* ACLO.

ASSOCIATION OF DISTRICT COUNCILS. Formed on 30th November 1973, this Association became operative on 1st April 1974 to: '(a) protect and further the interests of the district councils as they may be affected by legislation or proposed legislation or otherwise and to promote a high standard of administration of the public services in the district; (b) join, where appropriate, with other local authority Associations; (i) promote the interests of local government in general and (ii) provide such central services for the district councils as may be considered to be appropriate.' The Association consists of the non-metropolitan district councils in England and the district councils in Wales; these range in size and character from authorities which are substantially rural to large cities and towns. Members of the Council of the Association are elected from the districts and from the counties by formulae based on population. Financed by members' subscriptions. The Association superseded the Rural District Councils Association and also the Urban District Councils Association when these ceased to exist on 1st April 1974 due to the alteration of local authority boundaries and the reorganization of local government in England and Wales. Abbreviated ADC. Publishes *The District Councils Review* (m.). *See also* AMA, LOCAL GOVERNMENT BOUNDARIES

ASSOCIATION OF GENEALOGISTS AND RECORD AGENTS. Founded in 1968 in England to: (a) promote the science and skill of genealogical, biographical and topographical research and the competent use of records, manuscripts and muniments; (b) establish and promote a scale of professional fees; (c) maintain and promote professional standards of ethics and the reputation of the profession; (d) publish a professional journal and such other literature as may further the objects of the Association; (e) receive and dispense funds for the promotion of genealogical research and allied sciences and skills; (f) organize and supervise examinations in the interests of the profession; (g) associate or amalgamate with other societies having objects similar to those of the Association. Membership is open to any person (being an individual but not a corporation or association) who is actively engaged in the practice of genealogy or record searching within the U.K. or the Republic of Ireland. Financed by members' subscriptions. Abbreviated AGRA. Publishes *Newsletter* (3 p.a. members only).

ASSOCIATION OF HOSPITAL AND INSTITUTION LIBRARIES. A Division of the American Library Association since June 1956 by amalgamating the former Division of Hospital Libraries and the Institution Libraries Committee; founded in 1944. This Association was merged in 1974 with the Library Services to the Blind Round Table to form the HEALTH AND REHABILITATIVE LIBRARY SERVICES DIVISION. *See* HRLS. Abbreviated AHIL.

ASSOCIATION OF INTERNATIONAL LIBRARIES. Founded in September 1963 at the Sofia meeting of the International Federation of Library Associations, of which it is a Section. Aims: to facilitate co-operation between international libraries. Membership is open to (a) individuals capable of promoting co-operation between international libraries, (b) libraries of international organizations, in particular the libraries of inter-governmental organizations, (c) all other libraries whose international character is recognized by the Executive Committee. It is financed by members' dues. Abbreviated AIL.

ASSOCIATION OF JEWISH LIBRARIES. Formed in June 1966 by the amalgamation of the Jewish Librarians Association and the Jewish Library Association 'to promote and improve library services and professional standards in all Jewish libraries; to serve as a centre of dissemination of Jewish library information and guidance; to encourage the establishment of Jewish libraries; to promote publication of literature which will be of assistance to Jewish librarianship; to encourage people to enter the field of librarianship. Abbreviated AJL. An American association. Publishes *Bulletin* (2 p.a.).

ASSOCIATION OF LIBRARIANS IN SCHOOLS. *See* ALIS.

ASSOCIATION OF LIBRARIES OF JUDAICA AND HEBRAICA IN EUROPE. Founded in Paris, 28th April 1955, to facilitate the use of literature on Judaica and Hebraica in European libraries; to create a catalogue of such literature in Europe; to give bibliographical and other help to affiliated libraries and others. Has an information bureau and arranges training courses in Jewish librarianship. Abbreviated ALJH.

ASSOCIATION OF LONDON CHIEF LIBRARIANS. The organization which was formed in succession to the ASSOCIATION OF METROPOLITAN CHIEF LIBRARIANS (*q.v.*) when the boroughs of greater London were reconstituted as from 1st April 1965. The London Boroughs now total thirty-two: the City of London is in addition and was not altered. Abbreviated ALCL.

ASSOCIATION OF METROPOLITAN AUTHORITIES. *See* AMA.

ASSOCIATION OF METROPOLITAN CHIEF LIBRARIANS. An advisory body to the Metropolitan Boroughs Standing Joint Committee (MBSJC) which was composed of representatives of the Metropolitan Borough Councils and the Corporation of the City of London until 31st March 1965. It consisted of the respective chief librarians who met regularly to consider mutual library problems, advised on library developments in the area and managed the LONDON UNION CATALOGUE (*q.v.*). It has been responsible for, amongst other matters, organizing interavailability of tickets, standardizing some Library materials and routines, setting up the Metropolitan Special

Collection (MSC) and the Metropolitan Joint Fiction Reserve (JFR) which includes play-reading sets. Abbreviated AMCL. This body continued the work of the Committee of Metropolitan Chief Librarians formed in 1934, and was so named on the adoption of a formal constitution early in 1945. It ceased to function after 1st April 1965 when the reorganization of the London boroughs became effective. *See also* ASSOCIATION OF LONDON CHIEF LIBRARIANS.

ASSOCIATION OF NORTHERN IRELAND EDUCATION AND LIBRARY BOARDS. Formed on 24th October 1973 to: (a) seek to achieve the highest standards in education and library services for all the people of Northern Ireland, and to co-ordinate the efforts of the Education and Library Boards to that end; (b) promote and encourage the interchange of ideas on questions relating to the education and library services and to provide a forum for debate on such matters; (c) supply information and advice to member Boards on education and library matters; (d) exercise vigilance in relation to all proposed legislation, regulations and administrative arrangements affecting education and library services and to take action, where deemed necessary, for the safeguarding or improvement of standards in the services affected; (e) provide a collective voice for the education and library services in relations with the government and the community. Financed by the annual contributions of the five Area Boards in membership.

ASSOCIATION OF RESEARCH LIBRARIES. Founded 1931 to develop and increase by co-operative effort, 'the resources and usefulness of the research collections in American libraries'. Membership is institutional, by invitation only, and is around ninety. The Association's activities are largely conducted through a number of commissions. An OFFICE OF UNIVERSITY LIBRARY MANAGEMENT STUDIES (*q.v.*) began operations in 1970 through the Association. Abbreviated ARL. Publishes *ARL Academic Library Statistics; Foreign Acquisition Newsletter* (2 p.a.); *Minutes* (2 p.a.). At the end of 1973 ARL announced that it had established the Systems and Procedures Exchange Center (SPEC) which collected information and data devoted to the acquisition, organization, analysis, storage, and dissemination of information related to specific areas of research library management. Publishes *Management Supplements*. Abbreviated ARL.

ASSOCIATION OF SCIENTIFIC INFORMATION DISSEMINATION CENTERS. *See* ASIDIC.

ASSOCIATION OF STATE LIBRARY AGENCIES. Formerly the

AMERICAN ASSOCIATION OF STATE LIBRARIES (*q.v.*) this Division of the ALA, which was originally founded in 1957, is concerned with the development and co-ordination of library resources and services of all types of library. Its responsibility covers those functions and services relating to statewide library development and those pertaining to library services performed at a state level, including specialized book and information resources and services in support of the work of state government. Abbreviated ASLA. Publishes *President's Newsletter* (3 p.a. members only). *List of State Library Agencies* (a.).

ASSOCIATION OF THE LIBRARIES OF INTERNATIONAL ORGANIZATIONS. *See* INTERNATIONAL FEDERATION OF LIBRARY ASSOCIATIONS.

ASSOCIATION OF VISUAL SCIENCE LIBRARIANS. Founded in the U.S.A. in 1968 to foster collective and individual acquisition and dissemination of visual science information, to improve services for all persons seeking such information, and to develop standards for libraries to which members are attached. Publishes *Visual Union List of Serials* (irreg.), *PhD Theses in Physiological Optics* (irreg.).

ASSOCIATION POUR L'AVANCEMENT DES SCIENCES ET DES TECHNIQUES DE LA DOCUMENTATION. *See* ASTED.

ASSOCIATION POUR L'ETUDE ET DE LA LINGUISTIQUE APPLIQUÉE. *See* ATALA.

ASSOCIATION SUISSE DE DOCUMENTATION. *See* ASD.

ASSOCIATIVE INDEXING. Automatic (i.e. computer) indexing, which records association between terms, or words in a text, without there necessarily being a specified functional relationship between them.

ASTED. Abbreviation for ASSOCIATION POUR L'AVANCEMENT DES SCIENCES ET DES TECHNIQUES DE LA DOCUMENT- ATION, a Montreal organization which replaced L'Association Canadienne des Bibliothécaires de Langue Française (ALBLF). Publishes *Documentation et Bibliothèques* (4 p.a.); *Nouvelles* (10 p.a.).

ASTERISK (*). The first and frequently most used reference mark for footnotes, technically known as a 'Star.' *See also* REFERENCE MARKS.

ASTERISM. 1. A group of asterisks, as in a triangle, $*_*^*$ or $_*^*{}_*$, draw- ing attention to a following remark, passage or paragraph. 2. The use of a number of asterisks instead of a proper name, as Mr. T******; a form of pseudonym.

ASTIA.   *See* Defense Documentation Center.

ASTRONOMICAL MAP.   One showing the stars. Also called a 'Star map'.

ASYNDETIC.   Without cross-references. The reverse of Syndetic (*q.v.*). *See also* Syndetic Catalogue.

ATALA.   Acronym for Association pour l'Etude et de la Linguistique Appliquée.   Founded in 1959 to act as a focus for experimental and research work in progress on the mechanization of information.

ATLAS.   A volume of maps, with or without descriptive letterpress. It may be issued to supplement or accompany a text, or be published independently. Also, a volume of plates, engravings, etc., illustrating any subject; a large size of drawing paper measuring $26\frac{1}{2} \times 34$ inches; a large folio volume, resembling a volume of maps, sometimes called 'Atlas folio'. The word 'atlas' was first used in the title of the first collection of maps – Gerardus Mercator's *Atlas sive cosmographicae meditationes de fabrica mundi*, Düsseldorf, [1585]–1595, which was composed in three parts in 1585, 1590 and 1594, and issued after his death by his son Rumold Mercator in 1595.

ATLAS FOLIO.   The largest size folio. About 25 inches by 16 inches. *See also* Elephant Folio.

ATLAS SIZE.   A large square folio book, size about 25×16 inches.

ATTACHING.   (*Binding*) The process of attaching the boards to the sewn sections after rounding and backing. The attaching joint is a strip of tough paper pasted to the outside of the end leaf to serve as a connecting link with the boards. Not to be confused with Casing (*q.v.*).

ATTENTION NOTE.   A note, sometimes combined with a Routing Slip (*q.v.*), attached to a periodical in order to draw the attention of users to specific articles or items of information in which they may be interested. It is individual with respect to items to which attention is drawn and the individual addressed.

ATTRIBUTE.   In co-ordinate indexing, a characteristic mentioned as subject-matter. *See also* Characteristics of a Classification.

ATTRIBUTED AUTHOR.   The person to whom a book is attributed, because of doubt as to the authorship. *See also* Supposed Author.

AUDIO CHARGING.   A form of Transaction Charging in which the loan serial number, and the essential details of the book and of the reader are spoken into a microphope and recorded on a tape or disc. When all the Transaction Cards representing returned books have been sorted into serial number order, any missing ones represent overdue books. The appropriate parts of the record are played back, and the details, recorded in respect of the missing cards, entered on overdue notices. *See also* CHARGING METHODS, TRANSACTION CARD CHARGING.

AUDIOTAPE. A generic term designating a sound recording on magnetic tape. Also called 'Phonotape'.

AUDIO-VISUAL AIDS. Material such as gramophone records, tape recordings and various VISUAL AIDS (*q.v.*) used as an adjunct to teaching.

AUDIO-VISUAL AREA. An area within a library building, or serving as an adjunct to a library, which is equipped with apparatus for screening or listening, and for storing materials used in connexion with the apparatus.

AUDIO-VISUAL GROUP. A Group of the Library Association, formerly known as the SOUND RECORDINGS GROUP (*q.v.*). Publishes *Audiovisual Librarian* (q.).

AUDIO-VISUAL MATERIALS. Non-book materials such as gramophone records, tapes, slides, transparencies, films and filmstrips which require apparatus to render them usable.

AUDIT. Checking accounts for accuracy and to see that expenditure is authorized by the appropriate authority. The Local Government Act, 1933, sect. 219, provides that in England and Wales the following accounts shall be subject to audit by a district auditor:

(a) the accounts of every county council, metropolitan borough council, urban district council, parish council and of every parish meeting not having a council;

(b) the accounts of any committee of any such council or parish meeting;

(c) the accounts of any joint committee appointed by combined authorities of which one or more of whose accounts are subject to district audit.

The accounts of boroughs may be audited by borough auditors or district auditors or by a PROFESSIONAL AUDITOR (*q.v.*) (in which case the above-mentioned provision of borough auditors does not apply), or by the district auditor. Auditing is undertaken by borough auditors unless the council resolves to adopt the systems of district, or of professional, audit. The system of borough auditors is little used except as a tradition in a few boroughs. In Scotland, accounts of county and town councils are audited by an auditor appointed by the Secretary of State. In Ireland, library accounts must be audited in the same way as the other accounts of a local authority. *See also* DISTRICT AUDIT, MUNICIPAL AUDIT.

AURIANNE AWARD. Established in 1956 by the Executive Board of the American Library Association, and made under the will of Miss Augustine Aurianne. Awarded annually 'to an author for a book published in the preceding year but one, which is considered the best book of the year on animal life which helps to develop a humane attitude in the young'. The Award is of $200 cash and a certificate designed by Valenti Angelo; it is administered by the Children's Services Division, and the selection of the book to receive the award is made by the Aurianne Award Committee of this Division. The first award was made in 1958 to John and Jean George for *Dipper of Copper Creek*.

AUSTRALIAN ADVISORY COUNCIL ON BIBLIOGRAPHICAL SERVICES. Founded in April 1956 to plan and recommend to appropriate authorities measures for the development and co-ordination of Australian bibliographical resources and to co-operate with the International Advisory Committee on Bibliography. Represented on it are the governing bodies and principal librarians of the National Library of Australia, State libraries and library boards, the universities, the Commonwealth Scientific and Industrial Research Organization; and representatives of colleges of advanced education, institutions of further education, public, school and special libraries. The Council's Secretariat is located within the National Library of Australia. Abbreviated AACOBS.

AUSTRALIAN BIBLIOGRAPHICAL CENTRE. The Centre, which was established in 1956, was administratively part of the National Library of Australia; all its functions have been taken over by the National Library and it has ceased to be administered as a separate unit.

AUSTRALIAN LIBRARY-BASED INFORMATION SYSTEM. *See* ALBIS.

AUSTRALIAN NATIONAL SCIENTIFIC AND TECHNOLOGICAL LIBRARY. *See* ANSTEL.

AUSTRIAN SOCIETY FOR DOCUMENTATION AND BIBLIOGRAPHY. *See* Österreichische Zeitschrift für Buch-und Bibliothekswesen, Dokumentation, Bibliographie und Bibliophilie.

AUTHENTICATION. (*Archives*) The act of determining that a document, or a reproduction of a document, is what it purports to be. *See also* Certification.

AUTHOR. The person, persons, or corporate body, responsible for the writing or compilation of a book or other publication not a periodical. Usually to be distinguished from an editor, translator, compiler, etc., although, failing any alternative, these may be regarded as authors for purposes of cataloguing. In a wider sense, an artist, a composer of a musical work, and a photographer are authors to whom would be attributed work which they had created.

AUTHOR ABSTRACT. *See* ABSTRACT.

AUTHOR AFFILIATION. The organizations with which an author is affiliated, as indicated on the title-page, or in a periodical article or proceedings, and appearing after the author's name in a library catalogue.

AUTHOR ANALYTIC. *See* ANALYTICAL ENTRY.

AUTHOR AUTHORITY LIST. *See* NAME AUTHORITY FILE.

AUTHOR BIBLIOGRAPHY. One listing books, articles, or other contributions to knowledge by, or by and about, a particular author. It may include biographies and criticisms of his work as well as works by him.

AUTHOR CARD. A catalogue card bearing an author entry; usually the main entry card. *See also* MAIN ENTRY.

AUTHOR CATALOGUE. A catalogue of author entries arranged alphabetically under authors' names; it usually includes entries under editors, translators, composite authors, corporate bodies, first words of titles, or any other words or names used as headings for the main entries.

AUTHOR ENTRY. A catalogue entry under the name of the person or body responsible for the writing, or compilation, of a published work. Failing one or more real names, the author entry may have to be made under a pseudonym, initials, or some other heading. For music, it is generally an added entry under the name of the author of the text accompanying a musical work, e.g. librettist, or author whose work served as the basis or inspiration for a musical work, the main entry being made under the composer's name. It is usually the MAIN ENTRY (*q.v.*).

AUTHOR HEADING. The heading under which an author entry is made.

AUTHOR INDENTION. *Synonymous with* FIRST INDENTION (*q.v.*).

AUTHOR INDEX. An index of authors' names.

AUTHOR MARK. Symbols (letters, figures, or other signs) used to represent authors and so individualise books having the same class, subject, or shelf number, in order to simplify the arrangement of books and catalogue entries. *See also* BOOK NUMBER, CUTTER AUTHOR MARKS, MERRILL ALPHABETING NUMBERS, THREE NUMBER AUTHOR TABLE.

AUTHOR NUMBER. *Synonymous with* AUTHOR MARK (*q.v.*).

AUTHOR ORDER. Said of books, or of entries relating to books, which are arranged in alphabetical order of authors' names.

AUTHOR-PUBLISHER. The writer of a work who is his own publisher.

AUTHOR STATEMENT. That part of a catalogue entry which mentions the author when transcribing the title. It is usually omitted unless it contributes data which is essential in some way to the entry, e.g. it would be given for joint authors, as by R. H. Mottram, John Easton *and* Eric Partridge.

AUTHOR STYLE. The usual combination of black capitals and lower-case letters which is used for author headings in a catalogue. *See also* SUBJECT STYLE.

AUTHOR TABLE. A printed list used in assigning author numbers, e.g. the CUTTER AUTHOR MARKS (*q.v.*), or the CUTTER-SANBORN THREE-FIGURE TABLE (*q.v.*).

AUTHOR-TITLE ADDED ENTRY. An added entry which involves two elements, placed in a TRACING (*q.v.*) and also at the top of a secondary entry. It would be given for the author's name followed by the title of a book when an adaptation, supplement, etc., is involved, or in a subject heading for a commentary on an individual work.

AUTHOR-TITLE INDEX. One which has entries under authors' names and under titles, either in one or in two alphabetical sequences.

AUTHORITATIVE EDITION. *See* DEFINITIVE EDITION.

AUTHORITIES. *See* PRIMARY SOURCES, SECONDARY SOURCES.

AUTHORITY CARD. 1. A card which gives the form selected for a heading in a catalogue. If a personal name is used as a heading, references to sources and records of variant forms are given; if a corporate name, sources, brief history and any changes of name are given. 2. A card which bears the classification number given by the classifiers to a subject, and also the subject index headings for entries made out for it. Where chain indexing is undertaken, a separate entry would be made for each step taken in determining the number. *See also* AUTHORITY LIST, CHAIN INDEX, NAME AUTHORITY FILE, SUBJECT AUTHORITY FILE. 3. In acquisition work, a term sometimes used to denote a request, requisition or recommendation card, so named because it bears the signature or authority for an acquisition transaction.

AUTHORITY ENTRY. An entry for a society or institution, giving such particulars as the date of founding, date of incorporation, changes of name, and affiliation or union with other societies.

AUTHORITY FILE. *Synonymous with* AUTHORITY LIST (*q.v.*).

AUTHORITY LIST. 1. A list of all personal and corporate names, names of anonymous classics and sacred books, the titles of anonymous books and the headings for series cards, which are used as headings in the catalogue; sometimes references are given to books in which each name and its variants were found, and in the case of corporate entries, sources, a brief history and particulars as to changes of name. The entries are made when a heading is first decided upon. It gives the cataloguer a record in the forms used in the public catalogues. If the list is kept on cards, one entry to a card, each card is known as an 'authority card'. 2. A list in classified order of classification symbols or numbers which have been allocated to books, with their corresponding index entries. Also called 'Authority file'. *See also* AUTHORITY CARD, CHAIN INDEX, NAME AUTHORITY FILE, SUBJECT AUTHORITY FILE. 3. Also called, in the context of indexing documents, CLOSED INDEXING SYSTEM; CONTROLLED TERM LIST (*q.v.*). *See also* OPEN-ENDED TERM LIST, TERM.

AUTHORIZED EDITION. An edition issued with the consent of the author, or of his representative to whom he may have delegated his rights and privileges.

AUTHOR'S AGENT. *See* LITERARY AGENT.

AUTHOR'S ALTERATIONS. *Synonymous with* AUTHOR'S CORRECTIONS (*q.v.*).

AUTHORS' AND PUBLISHERS' LENDING RIGHT ASSOCIATION COMMITTEE (APLA). *See* PUBLIC LENDING RIGHT.

AUTHOR'S BINDING. A superior binding used on a few copies of a book as presentation copies from the author.

AUTHOR'S COPIES. The complimentary copies of a book, usually six in number, presented on publication to its author by the publisher.

AUTHOR'S CORRECTIONS. Deviations from the original copy, as distinct from corrections by the author of printer's errors marked on a printer's proof. *See also* AUTHOR'S REVISE.

AUTHOR'S EDITION. 1. The collected or complete edition of an author's works, uniformly bound, and indicating on the title-page that it is the complete works of the author. 2. An edition the publication of which has been authorized by the author. *See also* DEFINITIVE EDITION.

AUTHOR'S PROOF. The clean proof sent to an author after the compositor's errors have been corrected. Abbreviated: AP

AUTHOR'S REVISE. A proof bearing the author's or editor's corrections as distinct from one corrected by the printer.

AUTHOR'S RIGHTS. Those secured to an author under a copyright act.

AUTHOR'S SIGNATURE. A quantity of 40,000 ems of type (about sixteen printed pages) used as a basis for calculating author's royalties in the Soviet Union. The number of roubles paid per 'author's signature' varies with the quality or importance of the work.

AUTO-ABSTRACT. 1. (*Noun*) The resulting product of a machine preparing an extract consisting of complete sentences from a document which is so abstracted. *See also* ABSTRACT 3 (b). 2. (*Verb*) To select an assemblage of keywords from a document, commonly by an automatic or machine method, in order to form an abstract of the document (*IBM*).

AUTO-ABSTRACTING. The art of abstracting automatically by machine. 'Auto-extracting' is the preferred term.

AUTO-BIAS DEVICE. The linking, when determining notation in the Colon Classification, of two foci within the same facet by the use of a hyphen. *See also* FACET, FOCUS.

AUTOBIOGRAPHY. The life of a person written by himself.

AUTO-ENCODE. To select keywords from a document, by a machine method, in order to develop search patterns for information retrieval (*IBM*).

AUTO-ENCODING. The process of producing either auto-abstracts or automatically generated index entries on the basis of word frequency.

AUTO-EXTRACTING. *See* AUTO-ABSTRACTING.

AUTOGRAPH. A person's signature. In the book trade, a description of cards, documents, letters, manuscripts, etc., written or signed with the writer's own hand.

AUTOGRAPHED EDITION. An edition of a work, copies of which are signed by the author. *See also* LIMITED EDITION.

AUTOGRAPHY. 1. The author's own handwriting. 2. Reproductions of the form or outline of anything by an impression from the thing itself. 3. A lithographic process of reproducing writing, drawing, etc., in facsimile. 4. That branch of diplomatics which is concerned with autographs.

AUTO-INDEX. To prepare an index by a mechanical method.

AUTO-LITHOGRAPHY. A lithographic method in which the artist draws in reverse directly on to the stone or other medium.

AUTOMATIC ABSTRACTING. The selection by machine of words and phrases from a document for quotation in order to describe its content. *See also* AUTOMATIC INDEXING.

AUTOMATIC ASSIGNMENT INDEXING. The process of using machines to assign index entries in respect of the text of a document, such entries being obtained from a standardized list such as a subject heading list, a thesaurus, or a dictionary which exists independently of the text of the document being indexed.

AUTOMATIC DERIVATIVE INDEXING. The process of using machines to extract, or derive, index entries from the text of a document without human intervention once procedural rules or programs have been formulated.

AUTOMATIC DICTIONARY. The component of a language translating machine which provides a word for word substitution from one language to another. In automatic searching systems, the automatic dictionary is the component which substitutes codes for words or phrases during the encoding operation.

AUTOMATIC FORMAT RECOGNITION. (*Information retrieval*) The automatic recognition by a computer of the structure of a record in terms of fields, elements, etc., without the need for tagging (*See* TAGGED (TAGGING) 2).

AUTOMATIC INDEXING. 1. The selection of keywords from a document by a machine method in order to develop index entries. 2. The use of machines to extract and assign index terms without human intervention once programmes or procedural rules have been established. *See also* AUTOMATIC ABSTRACTING, MECHANIZED INDEXING.

AUTOMATIC ROUTING. *See* ROUTING.

AUTOMATIC SELECTION. *Synonymous with* MECHANICAL SELECTION (*q.v.*).

AUTONYM. The real name of an author.

AUTOPOSITIVE. Trade name for a Kodak direct positive copying process and for certain types of film which yield a direct positive image. *See also* DIRECT POSITIVE PROCESS.

AUTOPOSITIVE PAPER. Trade name for a type of SILVER HALIDE PAPER (*q.v.*) which gives a positive image without the necessity for first making a negative when making copies by a Lensless Process. *See also* LENSLESS COPYING.

AUTOTYPE. To make a copy by a carbon process.

AUTOTYPE REPRODUCTION. One reproduced by the autotype process, which is a variety of the collotype process, in which the plate is coated with a light-sensitive resin instead of a gelatine.

AUTOTYPY. The process of making copies by the carbon process.

AUXILIARIES. *See* UNIVERSAL DECIMAL CLASSIFICATION.

AUXILIARY NUMBER. One placed after the class number in order to group the books by some method, such as alphabetically or chronologically. The OLIN BOOK NUMBER (*q.v.*) and CUTTER AUTHOR MARKS (*q.v.*) are auxiliary numbers.

AUXILIARY PUBLICATION. The process of making data available by means of specially ordered microfilm or photocopies. Auxiliary publication usually presupposes that the materials have not been published before, although it is sometimes applied to publication of microcard copies of out-of-print books (*IBM*).

AUXILIARY SCHEDULES AND TABLES. Tables of sub-divisions which are appended to schedules of all schemes of classification. They consist of items of relationship, time, locality, etc. and then symbols of the different items can be added to book classification numbers. Broadly, they fall into three groups: those which (a) are common and can be used with the same meaning throughout the classification, e.g., the common subdivisions of Dewey's Decimal Classification; (b) are common to, and may only be applied to, certain subjects, e.g. the Systematic and Auxiliary Schedules of Bliss's Bibliographic Classification; (c) can be applied in only one place as in most of the Library of Congress Classification Schedules. *See also* SYSTEMATIC AUXILIARY SCHEDULES.

AUXILIARY SYNDESIS. The accessory apparatus – e.g. cross reference – which is used to supplement indexing sequence so as to reveal other relations (*IBM*).

AUXILIARY TABLES. In the Universal Decimal Classification tables of secondary aspects of subjects which may be applied to primary aspects to qualify them, and are distinguished by a special symbol, or 'facet indicator'. For a synopsis of auxiliaries, *see* UNIVERSAL DECIMAL CLASSIFICATION.

AVERAGE SLOPE MAP. One which indicates the average steepness of land slopes.

AZOFLEX. Trade name for an Ilford process for making translucent masters on a reflex foil from which copies are made by the diazo, or dyeline, process. Another method is to allow carbon to be transferred to a translucent paper which is then used as a master. Known in Holland, where it was originally introduced, as Océ. *See also* DIAZOTYPE PROCESS.

AZURE TOOLING. (*Bookbinding*) Tooling in which horizontal lines are shown close together.

AZURED TOOL. A bookbinder's tool with close parallel lines running diagonally across its surface. Derived from the use of thin horizontal lines used in heraldry to indicate blue.

B.BIBL. Bachelier en Bibliotheconomie et en Bibliographie. A degree in librarianship awarded in Canada.

b.f. Abbreviation for BOLD FACE type.

BII-CIC. Abbreviation for Bureau Intergovernmental pour l'Informatique – Centre International de Calcul. *See* IBI-ICC.

BLCMP. Acronym of the Birmingham Libraries Co-operative Mechanization Project which has designed and implemented a computer system to utilize centrally-produced machine readable bibliographic records in the MARC format. Initially the libraries involved were those of the universities of Aston and Birmingham, and the Birmingham Public Libraries. The Project began to function in January 1972. A variety of catalogue formats can be provided, filed in different sequences, and the output can be provided in bookform, microform (computer output on microfilm) and on cards. The system can be used to cater for other basic library housekeeping functions. The filing rules are designed to be used for the alphabetical arrangement of records and are based on study of the rules of the ALA, BNB and Library of Congress and with the British Standard BS 1749: 1969 (with which they are compatible); Part A of the rules comprises a statement of name catalogue rules, and Part B interprets the rules in computer terms. *See also* MASS.

BLLR. Acronym of Bureau of Libraries and Learning Resources. Known as the (American) Bureau of Libraries and Educational Technology (BLET) until August 1972 when its name was changed to reflect better the nature of its component programmes concerned with child education, the Right to Read, and school library media and media resources.

B.P. Abbreviation for 'before the present'; used in prehistoric dates.

BSIB. *See* BRITISH SOCIETY FOR INTERNATIONAL BIBLIOGRAPHY.

BSO. Acronym of Broad System of Ordering, a system (within the UNISIST (*q.v.*) programme) being developed to serve as a switching mechanism, between individual classifications and thesauri in the process of information transfer, rather than as a new classification system. It will be an essential tool for systems interconnection and will play an essential part in ISDS (*q.v.*), the referral network and the operation of information systems.

BACK. 1. The 'back' or inside margins of pages. 2. *Synonymous with*

SPINE (*q.v.*). 3. The surface of a piece of movable type parallel to the BELLY (*q.v.*).

BACK BOARD. The piece of millboard or strawboard which is used for the back cover of a book.

BACK CORNERING. (*Binding*) The cutting off of a small portion of the inner corners of the boards near the headcaps in order to improve their setting.

BACK COVER. *Synonymous with* REVERSE COVER (*q.v.*).

BACK FILE. The file or 'back numbers' (i.e. those preceding the current issue) of a periodical.

BACK FOLD. *See* BOLT.

BACK ISSUE. *Synonymous with* BACK NUMBER (*q.v.*).

BACK LINING. A piece of material (paper, cloth, calf skin) glued to the back sections of a book after sewing, before securing the cover.

BACK LIST. The titles which a publisher keeps in print because of continuous demand.

BACK MARGIN. The margin of a printed page which is nearest the fold of the section. Also called: 'Gutter', 'Gutter margin', 'Inner margin', 'Inside margin'.

BACK MARK. A small oblong block or number printed in such a position on the sheet that when the sheets of a book are folded and placed together for casing, the oblongs or numbers will follow each other in a slanting and/or numerical sequence down the spine and thus show if any section has been duplicated, misplaced or omitted. Also called 'Collating mark', 'Quad mark'. *See also* BLACK STEP.

BACK MATTER. Matter which is published at the end of the text, e.g. addenda, appendix, author's notes, bibliography, glossary, index, reference matter. Also called 'End-matter,' 'Subsidiaries.' *See also* PRELIMINARIES.

BACK NUMBER. An issue of a periodical which precedes the current number.

BACK ORDER. An uncompleted order which is held back for future delivery.

BACK PAGE. The verso, even-numbered, side of a leaf of a book or sheet of printed paper or manuscript. The back of a page.

BACK-PROJECTION READER. A reader in which an enlargement of a microform image is projected on to the back of a translucent screen for reading from the front by transmitted light.

BACK TITLE. The title which is placed on the spine, or back, of a book. *See also* BINDER'S TITLE, COVER TITLE.

BACK-UP. To print the second side of a sheet after the first has been printed.

BACK-UP SERVICES. 1. The services provided by libraries in support of a central loan collection. 2. Those providing documents, or substitutes for documents, in support of a literature survey, reading list or some similar information service.

BACKBONE. *Synonymous with* SPINE (*q.v.*).

BACKED. 1. A damaged leaf of a book, whether text or plate, which has been 'laid down' on, or pasted on, to paper, gauze or linen. 2. The spine of a book which is covered with a different material to the sides, as 'marbled boards backed with leather'. 3. The spine of a book which has been recovered with a different material to the original, a 're-backed' one having been re-covered with similar material to the original.

BACKING. The bookbinding operation whereby the sewn sections of a book, after glueing, are placed securely between backing boards after ROUNDING (*q.v.*), and hammered to splay them outwards from the centre of the book. It adds permanence to the rounding, and forms an abutment, or ridge, into which to fit the boards: the ridge so formed is called a 'joint'. This operation is carried out in Britain and America after ROUNDING (*q.v.*): in most Western European countries Rounding only is done. *See also* FLAT BACK, ROUND BACK.

BACKING BOARDS. (*Binding*) Boards used when backing and forming the groove or joint. They are made of very hard wood and sometimes faced with iron. The edge intended to form the groove is thicker than that which goes towards the fore-edge, so that when placed on either side of the book in the lying press the power of the press is directed towards the back.

BACKING MACHINE. A machine for backing books, generally used for publishers' binding and cheap work.

BACKING UP. *See* PERFECTING.

BACKLESS BINDING. A volume which is bound in such a way that the spine is flat or concave, covered with paper and gilt, and probably tooled, so as to look like the fore-edge which is itself finished in a similar manner.

BACKLINING. The material, usually paper, pasted on the inside of the SPINE (*q.v.*) of a book.

BACKS. The back margins of pages, i.e. those nearest the fold of the section. *See also* BACK.

BACKSLIDE. The block which is placed behind the cards in a catalogue drawer, and is moved backwards and forwards according to the quantity of cards in the drawer to prevent them from falling out of an upright position. It is usually made with its front sloping back at the top to permit of easy consultation.

BACKSTRIP. *Synonymous with* SPINE (*q.v.*).

BACONIAN CLASSIFICATION. The scheme propounded by Francis Bacon in his *Advancement of Learning* (1605), which more than any other philosophical scheme of thought, or classification of knowledge, has had the greatest influence on library classification. It was based on the three faculties, Memory, Imagination, and Reason, and these produced the three main headings, History, Poetry and Philosophy. The scheme was used for the arrangement of books, and its inversion is the basis of Dewey's *Decimal Classification*.

BAD COPY. 'Copy' which is difficult to read. This reduces the speed, and increases the cost, of typesetting. *See also* COPY I.

BAD LETTER. *Synonymous with* DAMAGED LETTER (*q.v.*).

BAILIFF. 1. Official under a sheriff mainly concerned with serving writs and making arrests. 2. Manorial official, usually next in rank to the Steward, and standing in a similar relationship to him as (1) to the sheriff.

BAINS REPORT. *The new local authorities: management and structure.* The report of a study group appointed jointly by the Secretary of State for the Environment and local authority associations to examine principles and structures in local government at both elected member and officer levels. The Group was set up in May 1971, chaired by Mr M. A. Bains, Clerk of the Kent County Council, and its Report was published in 1972.

BAKER REPORT. The Report of the Working Party appointed by the Minister of Education in March 1961, *Inter-Library Co-operation in England and Wales*, 1962. Mr. E. B. H. Baker was Chairman of the Working Party. *See also* BOURDILLON REPORT.

BALL. *See* INK BALL.

BALL. In typography, the finishing element at the top of the strokes of the type letter *a* and *c*.

BALLOTS. Acronym of Bibliographic Automation of Large Library Operations using a Time-sharing System which is the on-line interactive library automation system that supports the acquisition and cataloguing functions of the Stanford University libraries' technical processing operations. A grant of $348,800 from the Council on Library Resources, Inc. in 1975, enabled new development tasks toward a California automation network to be undertaken. For a one-year period, seven major California public libraries in metropolitan and rural areas used the BALLOTS system for bibliographic searching and catalogue production.

BALOPTICON. An instrument for projecting opaque materials; originally a trade name. Usually now called an OPAQUE PROJECTOR (*q.v.*).

BANDS. The cords or strings whereon the sheets of a book are sewed. With FLEXIBLE SEWING (*q.v.*), the bands appear upon the back. When books are sewn so as to embed the cord in the back, or in modern books sewn on tapes, the appearance of raised bands is sometimes produced by narrow strips of leather or cardboard glued across the back before the volume is covered. The space between the bands is called 'between bands'.

BANK LETTER. A bulletin or other periodical publication issued by a bank primarily to give information on current industrial, business and financial conditions in general.

BANNED. Prohibited from sale by ecclesiastical or secular authority.

BAR. The horizontal stroke of letters; e.g. A, H and e.

BARNARD MEMORIAL PRIZE, CYRIL. This Prize was established by the Medical Section of the Library Association in 1960 to commemorate a great librarian and one of the founders of the Section. Barnard was killed in a traffic accident in 1959; he was Librarian of the School of Hygiene and Tropical Medicine, a post he had held since 1921. It is the most important award the Section may bestow on any of its members for an outstanding contribution to medical librarianship and takes the form of a silver salver. It was first awarded (posthumously) to William John Bishop in 1962 and there have been four recipients since – Dr Frank B. Rogers (1964), Brian Armitage (1968), Leslie T. Morton (1971) and William R. Le Fanu (1974).

BARRIER. 1. The fixture placed beside a staff enclosure to form a passage through which readers must pass to have their books charged or discharged. *See* CHARGE. 2. A fixed or movable structure placed to keep the public within bounds or to prevent access to a department or part of the building.

BARROW PROCESS. (*Archives*) A process of document repair and restoration which involves de-acidification, the use of tissue to strengthen the original, and thermoplastic lamination. It is named after William J. Barrow (1904–67).

BARYTA PAPER. A form of metallic paper, consisting of a suitable body paper coated with barium sulphate; marks can be made on this with a metal point or stylus. It is used in some types of automatic recording apparatus and also for text impressions on photo-composing machines.

4

BASAN SKIN. Sheepskin tanned with the bark of oak or larch.

BASE. The range of characters of a NOTATION 1, (*q.v.*). The total number of such characters is known as the BASE LENGTH.

BASE LINE. (*Printing*) The lowest limit of the body of a piece of type; the imaginary line on which the bases of capitals rest. *See also* CAP LINE, MEAN LINE.

BASE MAP. One on which additional information may be plotted for a particular purpose.

BASE OF A NOTATION. (*Classification*) The series of symbols used. Their number is the length of base, or its first dimension. In the Dewey *Decimal Classification* it is ten – the ten arabic numerals, in Bliss's *Bibliographic Classification* it is thirty-five – the twenty-six letters of the English arabic combined with the nine arabic numerals.

BASE OF SYMBOLISM. Used by B. C. Vickery synonymously with ALPHABET OF SYMBOLS (*q.v.*).

BASE OF TYPE. The feet, or lowest part, on which the base of a capital letter rests.

BASE PAPER. *Synonymous with* BODY PAPER (*q.v.*).

BASE STOCK. The material, such as plastic, paper or cloth, used as a carrier for a photosensitive emulsion.

BASIC.† Abbreviation for Biological Abstracts Subjects In Context, a computer-composed subject index to *Biological Abstracts* in which the titles are permuted and supplemented keywords added. *See also* BIOSIS, CROSS.

BASIC ANALYSIS. The citation in upward hierarchical order of the constituent elements of a composite subject. It is the first stage in converting a classification symbol into a verbal subject heading for an alphabetico-specific subject catalogue. The second stage is producing the QUALIFIED LIST (*q.v.*).

BASIC CLASS. (*Classification*) *Synonymous with* MAIN CLASS (*q.v.*).

BASIC LIST. (*Information retrieval*) An alphabetical or classified list of terms from which a thesaurus may be constructed.

BASIC STOCK. Standard books which it may be considered should form the basis of a well-balanced and authoritative book stock.

BASIC WEIGHT. (*Paper*) The substance of paper is expressed as the weight of a given superficial area, the units most commonly used being either pounds per ream or grammes per square metre. For example '20 × 30 inches 36 lb 480s' means that if the paper were cut into sheets measuring 20 × 30 inches, then 480 sheets would weigh 36 lb.

BASIL. A thin sheepskin not suitable for library bookbinding. It is mostly used for binding account books.

BASKERVILLE. A type face named after John Baskerville (1706–75) of Birmingham, famous printer and type-founder who was printer of Bibles and prayer books to the University of Cambridge 1758–68. His folio Bible of 1763 was his masterpiece. The type is a modification of Caslon. For a specimen alphabet, see TRANSITIONAL, TYPE FACE.

BAS-RELIEF PRINTING. Synonymous with EMBOSSING (q.v.).

BASSO CONTINUO. Italian for continued bass, or FIGURED BASS (q.v.).

BASTARD TITLE. Synonymous with HALF TITLE (q.v.).

BASTARD TYPE. Type having the face larger or smaller than the size proper to the body, as a nonpareil face on a brevier body, or 10 point face on 12 point body (as this book), used to give the appearance of being leaded. See also GOTHIC TYPE.

BASTARDA. See GOTHIC TYPE.

BATCH PROCESSING. A technique by which items to be processed in a data processing machine must be collected into groups prior to their processing; contrasted to in-line processing (IBM).

BATCHELDER AWARD, MILDRED L. Awarded, for the first time in 1968, to an American publisher for the most outstanding of those books originally published in a foreign language in a foreign country, and subsequently published in English in the United States during the calendar year preceding the appointment of the Mildred L. Batchelder Award Committee which is appointed annually. This Committee nominates from three to five books, the final choice is made by the membership of the Children's Services Division. The Award was first made to Alfred A. Knopf, Inc., publisher of the American edition of Eric Kästner's The little man.

BATH UNIVERSITY COMPARATIVE CATALOGUE STUDY. See BUCCS.

BATTELLE MEMORIAL INSTITUTE. Formed in 1929 under the will of Gordon Battelle as a memorial to the Battelle family who were among the first settlers in Ohio and were prominent in developing the Ohio iron and steel industry. The Institute contracts with industry and government by providing the physical plant, equipment and personnel for the conduct of research, the results of which are utilized to encourage progress in science and in other ways benefit the public welfare.

BATTEN CARDS. Those, used in the Batten retrieval system, which represent the presence or absence of each document by a hole or no-hole in a specific position on the record card. See also PEEK-A-BOO.

BATTEN SYSTEM.   A method of indexing, invented by W. E. Batten, utilizing the co-ordination of single attributes to identify specific documents. Sometimes called the 'peek-a-boo' system because of its method of comparing holes in cards by superimposing cards and checking the coincidence of holes (*IBM*).

BATTERED.   Type matter or electros when accidentally injured, or so worn that they give defective impressions, are said to be battered.

BATTERED LETTER   *Synonymous with* DAMAGED LETTER (*q.v.*).

BATTLEDORE.   *See* HORN BOOK.

BAY.   A U-shaped arrangement of shelving. *See also* PRESS, STACK, TIER.

BAY GUIDE.   A guide to the subjects of the books shelved in a BAY (*q.v.*).

BAY PSALM BOOK.   *The whole Book of Psalmes faithfully translated into English metre;* the first book printed in Cambridge, Mass., in what is now the U.S.A., in 1640 by Stephen Day, on the first press introduced into English-speaking America in 1638.

BEARD.   That part of the shoulder of a piece of movable type that slopes down from the 'face', or bottom of the printing surface of the letter to the front of the 'body', but more particularly that portion sloping from the bottom serifs of the face to the 'belly'. It consists of the BEVEL (*q.v.*) and the SHOULDER (*q.v.*).

BEARERS.   (*Printing*) Type-high strips of metal placed around pages of type when locked in formes from which electrotype plates are to be made. They appear as black borders on proofs. *See also* FORME.

BEATER.   *Synonymous with* BREAKER (*q.v.*).

BED.   The flat steel table of a printing machine or press on which the *forme* of type is placed for printing. When the forme has been secured, it is described as having been 'put to bed'. *See also* CHASE.

BEDFORD BINDINGS.   Bindings by Francis Bedford (1799–1883) an Englishman who succeeded to the business of Charles Lewis. He was the greatest English binder of his time, but his work has little artistic merit and little originality. He attained good results by imitating early Venetian work, with twisted or Saracenic ornament, as well as the later Veneto-Lyonese style, practised in England in Queen Elizabeth's time.

BEIRUT AGREEMENT.   The 'Agreement for facilitating the international circulation of visual and auditory materials of an educational, scientific and cultural character' was intended essentially to promote social and cultural progress in all countries. The purpose of the Agreement is to facilitate the despatch from country to country of 1. films, filmstrips and microfilms; 2. sound recordings; 3. glass slides, models, wall charts, maps and posters. At a meeting of international experts held at Geneva in 1967 (the Agreement had been adopted at the Third Session of Unesco held at Beirut in 1948 and came into force on 12th August 1954) it was agreed that the term 'audio-visual' should be liberally interpreted to include the various types of such equipment which had been introduced in the intervening years.

BELLES LETTRES. Polite literature, or works of literary art showing grace and imagination, as poetry, drama, criticism, fiction and essays. From the French; literally 'beautiful letters'.

BELLOWS PRESS. A small flat-bed platen press used for jobbing work, e.g. envelopes, broadsides, cards, hand bills, etc. The presses manufactured by the Adana Company, and often used by amateurs, are of this kind.

BELLY. The front of the part of a piece of movable type called the body.

BEMBO. A Roman type face cut originally by Francesco Griffi for Aldus and first used by him in Cardinal Pietro Bembo's *Aetna*, 1495–6. It was the model followed by GARAMOND (*q.v.*) and was re-cut by the Monotype Corporation in 1929. It is regarded by many as the most beautiful of the old-face designs; the modern 'Monotype' Bembo is one of the best book types available. It is relatively condensed, a good space saver, and having long ascenders, is legible and pleasant even when set solid. For a specimen, see TYPE FACE.

BEN DAY PROCESS. A process invented by Ben Day to produce shaded tints or mottled effects by transferring various inked designs in relief on a gelatine film to the metal plate which is later etched.

BENCH PRESS. A small press, resting on a work bench and used by bookbinders to press cased books. *See also* STANDING PRESS.

BENEVENTAN HANDWRITING. A beautiful minuscule handwriting used in Southern Italy and Dalmatia which survived a number of national varieties developed from the Italian semi-cursive minuscule, itself a descendant of the Roman cursive. *See also* CURSIVE, HANDWRITING.

BERGHOEFFER SYSTEM. A filing system first used by Prof. Dr. Christian W. Berghoeffer who compiled the Frankfurter Sammelkatalog in 1891. It has been accepted as workable by the Committee for Union Catalogues of the International Federation of Library Associations. *See also* FINDING LIST CATALOGUE.

BERKSHIRE, BUCKINGHAMSHIRE & OXFORDSHIRE BRANCH. A branch of the Library Association; formed on 1st January 1963, having been from 1956 a Sub-Branch of the London and Home Counties Branch. Aims: the furtherance of the objects of the LA within the Branch area. Membership is open to all members living or working in the area of the Branch. The Branch is financed by a capitation grant from the LA. Abbreviated BB&O.

BERNE CONVENTION.   In full, Berne Convention for the Protection of Literary and Artistic Works. *See* BERNE COPYRIGHT UNION.

BERNE COPYRIGHT UNION.   The International Convention for the Protection of Literary and Artistic Works, known as the 'Berne Convention', was adopted by an international conference held at Berne in 1886. Designed to protect effectively, and in as uniform a manner as possible, the rights of authors in their literary and artistic works, the Berne Convention was originally signed on 9th September 1886, and completed in Paris on 4th May 1896; it was revised in Berlin on 13th November 1908, completed at Berne on 20th March 1914, revised at Rome on 2nd June 1928, at Brussels on 26th June 1948, at Stockholm on 14th July 1967, and at Paris on 24th July 1971. The United Kingdom has been a party to the Convention from 5th December 1887, but the U.S.A., although bound by the Universal Copyright Convention since 16th September 1955, has not been able to join the Union because of the provisions of its domestic laws. The protection of the Berne Convention applies to authors who are nationals of one of the countries of the Union established by that Convention, for their works whether published or not, and to authors who are nationals of non-Union countries, for their works first published in one of those countries, or simultaneously in a country outside the Union and in a country of the Union. The duration of the protection provided by the 'Paris Act' of the Berne Convention is for the author's life and fifty years after his death. *See also* COPYRIGHT, INTERNATIONAL, IGC, WIPO.

BESPEAKING BOOKS.   *See* RESERVED BOOK.

BEST BOOKS.   A group of books considered to be the most authoritative on a subject or group of subjects.

BEST SELLER.   A book which is so popular that unusually large numbers are sold.

BETA PHI MU AWARD.   Donated by the Beta Phi Mu, an American national honorary library science fraternity, to a library school faculty member or anyone making an outstanding contribution to education for librarianship. The Award was established in 1954, and became an official ALA award in 1956; it is administered by the Library Education Division of the ALA and made annually. Only persons nominated by an ALA member are considered. The Award is of $500 cash and a citation of achievement. The first recipient was

Rudolph H. Gjelsness in 1954. The Award is not to be confused with the Beta Phi Mu Good Teaching Award, which has been given annually since 1959 to a library school instructor for excellence in teaching; this award is administered by the Beta Phi Mu Fraternity.

BETWEEN BANDS. *See* BANDS.

BEVEL. The part of the shoulder of a piece of movable type immediately sloping down from the 'face'. The distance from the face to the bottom of the bevel is known as the 'depth of strike'. Also called 'Neck'.

BEVELLED BOARDS. Heavy boards with bevelled edges principally used for large books in imitation of antique work.

BIACHRONOUS. In user and citation studies, referring to changes that occur with the passage of time as revealed by observations made on two or more separate occasions. *See also* SYNCHRONOUS.

BI-ANNUAL. A publication which is issued twice a year. This word is sometimes used synonymously with *Biennial* which strictly means 'published every two years'. To avoid misunderstanding, the terms 'Half-yearly' or 'Twice a year' are tending to be used instead of Bi-annual. *See also* Bi-monthly.

BIAS PHASE. 1. In classification, where one topic is described (usually in a relatively elementary manner) for the benefit of those working in, or concerned with, another field, a document is classified under the topic introduced, not under the persons for whom it is written, e.g. anatomy for speech therapists would go under anatomy, not speech therapists. 2. The treatment of a subject generally and fairly completely, if concisely, from the point of view of a class of users whose primary interest is in another subject. It is one of Ranganathan's three chief 'phase relations,' the other two being INFLUENCE PHASE and TOOL PHASE (*qq.v.*).

BIBELOT. An unusually small book, valuable as a curiosity because of its format or rarity. Also called 'Dwarf book,' 'Thumb book'.

BIBLE. *See* BISHOPS' BIBLE, COMPLUTENSIAN POLYGLOT, 40-LINE BIBLE, GENEVA BIBLE, MAZARIN BIBLE, POLYGLOT, 36-LINE BIBLE, VINEGAR BIBLE, VULGATE.

BIBLE PAPER. A very thin tough opaque paper used for Bibles or other lengthy books which are required to have little bulk. It is made from new cotton or linen rags. Often erroneously referred to as INDIA PAPER (*q.v.*). Also called 'Bible printing'. *See also* CAMBRIDGE INDIA PAPER, OXFORD INDIA PAPER.

BIBLE PRINTING. *See* BIBLE PAPER.

BIBLIA PAUPERUM. A type of mediaeval picture book of scriptural subjects, with descriptive vernacular text. Very popular among clergy and laity in continental countries before the Reformation. Many manuscript copies are preserved in different languages. It was one of the first books printed in the Netherlands and Germany, originally from blocks and then from type. It was reprinted several times in later years, most recently in 1884, with a preface by Dean Stanley.

BIBLIO. The bibliographical note and/or imprint which is placed on the back of the title-page. *See also* PRELIMINARIES.

BIBLIOCLASM. The destruction of books, or of the Bible.

BIBLIOCLAST. A destroyer of books.

BIBLIOFOON. *See* DELFT CIRCULATING SYSTEM.

BIBLIOGENESIS. The production of books.

BIBLIOGNOST. One versed in knowledge about books and in bibliography.

BIBLIOGONY. The production of books.

BIBLIOGRAPH. A bibliographer.

BIBLIOGRAPHEE. A person concerning whom a bibliography has been made.

BIBLIOGRAPHER. 1. A person who is able to describe the physical characteristics of books by recognized methods. 2. One able to prepare bibliographies by recognized principles.

BIBLIOGRAPHIC. *Synonymous with* BIBLIOGRAPHICAL (*q.v.*).

BIBLIOGRAPHIC AUTOMATION OF LARGE LIBRARY OPERATIONS USING A TIME-SHARING SYSTEM. *See* BALLOTS.

BIBLIOGRAPHIC CENTRE. An organization, often a department of a library, which maintains a collection of Reference books from which it is possible to give information concerning the availability of books. In the U.S.A., some of these centres, with financial assistance from LIBRARY SERVICES ACT (*q.v.*) funds, are providing general reference information services. Also, a centre which acts as a depository for books and an agency for organizing book exchanges.

BIBLIOGRAPHIC CLASSIFICATION. A scholarly and detailed scheme devised by H. E. Bliss and first applied in the College of the City of New York where the author was librarian in 1902. In addition to normal sub-division there are Systematic Auxiliary Schedules which are used on similar lines to Dewey's common sub-divisions: these provide for sub-division by form, geography, language, historical period, and of the philology of any language, of an author's works, etc. Apart from these schedules and the Anterior Numerical Classes, the notation is alphabetical, and although not extending beyond four letters, tends to be complete. The publication of a totally radical revision and expansion of the scheme was commenced in the summer of 1976 with the issue of three of eighteen subject classes and an introductory volume. Every class has been gutted and reconstructed but the basic structure remains intact. This new edition has been prepared by Jack Mills and published by Butterworth. *See also* BLISS CLASSIFICATION ASSOCIATION. It is usually referred to as the Bliss Classification. The Bliss Classification Working Party operates in England and has prepared *The Abridged Bliss Classification; the Bibliographic Classification of Henry Evelyn Bliss revised for school libraries* which was published by the School Library Association in 1967 (reprinted with minor corrections, 1970).

BIBLIOGRAPHIC INDEX. A subject index to current bibliographies, whether published separately as books, or pamphlets, or bibliographies appearing in books and pamphlets, or as periodical articles. Published semi-annually, with annual and three-year cumulations, by the H. W. Wilson Company.

BIBLIOGRAPHIC INDEX. 1. A systematic list of writings or publications (e.g. of books or periodical articles) with or without annotations. 2. An index of publications or articles which contains no material descriptive of their contents other than bibliographical references. Also called 'Bibliographical index'.

BIBLIOGRAPHIC INFORMATION. Details concerning a publication which are sufficient to identify it for the purpose of ordering. They may include the following: author, title, publisher, place of publication, edition, series note, number of volumes, parts and/or supplements, and price; editor, translator or illustrator may also be necessary in the case of certain books. Sometimes called 'trade information'.

BIBLIOGRAPHIC ITEM. An article in a periodical, a technical report, a patent, a monograph, or a chapter in a symposium, which is capable of being given a separate bibliographical entry in a catalogue or bibliography. *Also called* 'Bibliographical item'.

BIBLIOGRAPHIC PROCESSING. *See* PROCESSING.

BIBLIOGRAPHIC UNIT. 1. Any document, part of a document, or several documents, forming a bibliographic whole which is treated as a single entity in a system of bibliographical description. A BIBLIOGRAPHIC ITEM (*q.v.*). 2. More commonly, a group of people working together as a team in some bibliographic work.

BIBLIOGRAPHIC VOLUME. A unit of publication distinguishable from other units by having its own title-page, half title, cover title, or portfolio title. If a periodical, all the parts which comprise the publisher's volume. *Also called* 'Bibliographical volume'.

BIBLIOGRAPHICAL. Of, or relating to, or dealing with, bibliography.

BIBLIOGRAPHICAL CENTRE. A place where bibliographies and catalogues of libraries, and those issued by publishers, are assembled, and information on books is given. They are usually associated with book-lending agencies, co-operative book stores, or national libraries, and may or may not be intimately connected with the lending of books. In the U.S.A. they also serve as bureaux organizing the inter-lending of books between libraries.

BIBLIOGRAPHICAL CLASSIFICATION. One designed for the classification of books and other literary material, and for the entries in bibliographies and catalogues. *See also* KNOWLEDGE CLASSIFICATION.

BIBLIOGRAPHICAL DESCRIPTION. The description of a published work of literary or musical composition, giving particulars of authorship, of others who have contributed to the presentation of the text (editor, translator, illustrator, arranger, etc.), title, edition, date, particulars of publication (place and name of publisher and possibly of printer), format, etc. In the case of music it may relate to a single gramophone record or to an album of the same, as well as to printed music, and is concerned only with the publication as a 'record'; its physical representation, not its musical content. Not to be confused with MUSICAL DESCRIPTION (*q.v.*).

BIBLIOGRAPHICAL INDEX. *Synonymous with* BIBLIOGRAPHIC INDEX (*q.v.*).

BIBLIOGRAPHICAL INFORMATION IN PRINTED MUSIC. The presentation of bibliographical and related information in printed music, for the guidance of editors and publishers of music, is specified in BS 4754 : 1971.

BIBLIOGRAPHICAL ITEM. *Synonymous with* BIBLIOGRAPHIC ITEM (*q.v.*).

BIBLIOGRAPHICAL NOTE. 1. A note, often a footnote, containing a reference to one or more books or periodical articles, etc., as sources for the work. 2. A note in a catalogue or in a bibliography relating to the bibliographical history of, or describing, a book. 3. A note, often a footnote or annotation, in a catalogue, mentioning a bibliography contained in a book.

BIBLIOGRAPHICAL REFERENCES. References to books and parts of books (including articles in books), to periodicals and other serials, and to articles in periodicals. BS 1629 : 1976 *Bibliographical references* gives rules and examples for entries in bibliographical lists and for identifying works or parts of works, quoted or referred to, in reviews, abstracts, etc.

BIBLIOGRAPHICAL SCATTER. The appearance of an article on one subject in a periodical devoted to a totally different subject. Their oversight can be avoided by providing entries in KWIC (*q.v.*) and similar indexes, current awareness lists, subject indexes to periodical articles, etc., and by analytical subject entries in library catalogues.

BIBLIOGRAPHICAL SERVICE. The facilities, procedures and devices which are employed to produce a bibliography consisting of a continuing series of publications, or bibliographical information as requested.

BIBLIOGRAPHICAL SOCIETY. The leading bibliographical society in the United Kingdom. It was founded in 1892. Publishes *The Library* (q.).

BIBLIOGRAPHICAL SOCIETY OF AMERICA. The leading bibliographical society in America. It was founded in 1904 to promote bibliographical research and to issue bibliographical publications. Abbreviated BSA. Publishes *Papers* (q. to memb.).

BIBLIOGRAPHICAL SOCIETY OF CANADA. Founded in May 1946 to (a) promote bibliographical publication, (b) encourage the preservation of printed works and manuscripts, and extend knowledge of them, particularly those relating to Canada, and (c) facilitate the exchange of bibliographical information. Membership is open to individuals and to institutions. Publishes *Papers* (a.).

BIBLIOGRAPHICAL SOCIETY OF THE UNIVERSITY OF VIRGINIA. Founded in 1950, this Society represents the most advanced school of thought in modern bibliography.

BIBLIOGRAPHICAL TOOL. A publication, such as a list of books, which is used by a bibliographer in the course of his work.

BIBLIOGRAPHICAL UNIT. A document (*Fr.* ouvrage) [*see* DOCUMENT 2] which is an independent unit and described in a separate main entry in a catalogue (*IFLA*).

BIBLIOGRAPHICAL VOLUME. *Synonymous with* BIBLIOGRAPHIC VOLUME (*q.v.*).

BIBLIOGRAPHING. The action of consulting bibliographies.

BIBLIOGRAPHIZE. To make a bibliography concerning some person and/or his writings, or of some subject.

BIBLIOGRAPHY. The terminology of bibliography is complicated, largely because different terms have been used by different people for the same kind of bibliography, partly because a bibliography can be constructed in such a way that different kinds of bibliographical

description or arrangement can contribute to its make-up. Bibliographies can be arranged in two main groups: 1. *Critical bibliographies*
(describing the physical appearance of books) and 2. *Systematic* or
Enumerative bibliographies, the history of books, MSS and other
publications arranged in some logical order giving author, title, date
and place of publication, publisher, details of edition, pagination,
series and literary contents. The following definitions have been
obtained from a variety of sources: 1. A list of books, and sometimes of other material such as periodical articles and illustrations,
written by one author, or on one subject, or printed by one printer,
or in one place, or during one period: the literature of a subject.
Bibliographies may be (*a*) complete; (*b*) general or universal,
i.e. attempting to include books published in every country and
age, and on all subjects; (*c*) national, i.e. those printed or published
in a specific country; (*d*) select, usually 'best books', or books, suited
to a special purpose; (*e*) special, i.e. limited to one author or subject;
(*f*) trade, compiled primarily to facilitate the sale or purchase of
books. 2. The art or science of correctly describing books (their
literary contents, or their physical make-up); loosely, the science of
books, which Van Hoesen and Walter consider can be divided in
four parts. These are: *Historical*, dealing with the history of book
production and including the description of books as physical objects (also called 'Critical' or 'Analytical' bibliography); *Bibliothecal*,
concerned with the collection, preservation, and organization of books
in libraries; *Enumerative*, listing all kinds of books and periodical
articles by an author or about a subject, with annotations enumerating
their contents; *Practical*, dealing with the methods of work of student
and author in compiling bibliographies. 3. The preparation of lists of
books, the study of lists of literature; the lists themselves are generally
called bibliographies, and their use is termed bibliographing
(*Schneider*). 4. The art of recording books. The science of the making
of books and of their extant record (*Esdaile*). 5. A list of books arranged
according to some permanent principle. (*Besterman*). 6. An annotated
catalogue of documents (*IBM*). 7. The process of compiling catalogues
or lists (*IBM*). 8. The technique of compiling systematically descriptive lists of manuscripts or published records of different kinds which
are not in the possession of one library or owner. *See also* BIO-
BIBLIOGRAPHY, CARTOBIBLIOGRAPHY. Conrad Gesner (1516–65), also
known as Konrad von Gesner, a Swiss naturalist, compiled a series of
bibliographies which were the earliest systematic books about books
and are the beginnings of modern bibliography. His *Bibliotheca*

universalis, Zurich, 1545–9, contained the titles of all the books then known in Latin, Greek and Hebrew, with summaries and criticisms of each. *See also* TEXTUAL BIBLIOGRAPHY.

BIBLIOGRAPHY NOTE. *Synonymous with* BIBLIOGRAPHICAL NOTE (*q.v.*).

BIBLIOGRAPHY OF BIBLIOGRAPHIES. An extensive list of bibliographies.

BIBLIOKLEPTOMANIAC. A book-thief who is regarded as insane.

BIBLIOLATER. One who exercises BIBLIOLATRY (*q.v.*); one who has excessive admiration or reverence for books. Also called a 'Bibliolatrist'.

BIBLIOLATROUS. Given to, or characterized by, BIBLIOLATRY (*q.v.*).

BIBLIOLATRY. Book-worship.

BIBLIOLOGICAL. Pertaining to bibliology.

BIBLIOLOGIST. One versed in bibliology.

BIBLIOLOGY. The scientific description of books, dealing with their construction from the beginnings to the present day, including paper and other materials, typography, illustration and binding. Also called 'Analytical', 'Critical', 'Descriptive' or 'Historical' bibliography. *See also* Bibliography.

BIBLIOMANCY. Divination by books, generally by verses of the Bible.

BIBLIOMANE. An indiscriminate collector of books.

BIBLIOMANIA. A mania for collecting and possessing books. Also called 'Bibliomanianism', 'Bibliomanism'.

BIBLIOMANIAC. One affected with a mania for collecting books, particularly old or rare editions. Also called 'Bibliomanist'.

BIBLIOMANIST. A BIBLIOMANIAC (*q.v.*).

BIBLIOPEGIC. Relating to the binding of books.

BIBLIOPEGIST. A bookbinder.

BIBLIOPEGISTIC. Of, relating to, or befitting, a bookbinder. Also called 'BIBLIOPEGISTICAL'.

BIBLIOPEGY. The art of bookbinding.

BIBLIOPHAGIC. Of, or pertaining to, a BIBLIOPHAGIST (*q.v.*).

BIBLIOPHAGIST. One who 'devours' books.

BIBLIOPHEGUS. The name used in early Christian times for a bookbinder.

BIBLIOPHILE. A lover of books who knows how to discriminate between good and bad editions. Also called 'Bibliophilist'.

BIBLIOPHILE BINDING. A special binding such as might be used by a bibliophile.

BIBLIOPHILE EDITION. A specially printed and bound edition of a book which is published for sale to bibliophiles. *See also* FINE PAPER COPY.

BIBLIOPHILIC.　Of, or pertaining to, a BIBLIOPHILE (*q.v.*).

BIBLIOPHILISM.　The love of books.

BIBLIOPHILIST.　*Synonymous with* BIBLIOPHILE (*q.v.*).

BIBLIOPHILOUS.　Addicted to BIBLIOPHILY (*q.v.*).

BIBLIOPHILY.　A love of books; a taste for books.

BIBLIOPHOBIA.　A dislike, or dread, of books; an aversion to books.

BIBLIOPOESY.　The making of books.

BIBLIOPOLAR.　Of, or belonging to, booksellers. Also called 'Bibliopolic', 'Bibliopolical'.

BIBLIOPOLE.　One who deals in books, especially rare or curious ones.

BIBLIOPOLISM.　The principles, or trade, of bookselling.

BIBLIOPOLIST.　A bookseller.

BIBLIOPOLISTIC.　Of, pertaining to, or befitting, a bookseller.

BIBLIOPOLY.　The selling of books. Also called 'Bibliopolery'.

BIBLIOPSYCHOLOGY.　The study of books, readers and authors and their mutual relationships. It was formulated by Nicholas Rubakin in his Institute of Bibliopsychology in Switzerland, 1916–46.

BIBLIOSOPH.　One who knows, or knows about, books.

BIBLIOSOPHIST.　A BIBLIOPHILE (*q.v.*).

BIBLIOTAPH.　One who keeps his books under lock and key. Also called 'Bibliotaphist'.

BIBLIOTAPHIC.　Of, or belonging to, a bibliotaph.

BIBLIOTEKSTJANST.　The Swedish library supply agency (a company since 1960) which developed from a central selling agency founded in 1936 by the Swedish Library Association (Sveriges Allmauna Biblioteksforening). It publishes lists of recommended new publications and binds them when ordered by public and school libraries, supplying them through local booksellers. It also publishes indexes of newspapers and periodicals, publications including book lists and library guides on behalf of the Swedish Library Association, schedules of the Swedish Classification scheme, and printed catalogue cards. Other activities are designing and manufacturing furniture and giving advice on library planning.

BIBLIOTHEC.　Belonging to a library or librarian. A librarian.

BIBLIOTHECA.　1. A library. 2. A bibliographer's catalogue.

BIBLIOTHECAL.　Belonging to a library.

BIBLIOTHECAL CLASSIFICATION.　A classification scheme for the arrangement of books on the shelves of a library.

BIBLIOTHECAL SCHEMES.　*See* BIBLIOGRAPHICAL CLASSIFICATION.

BIBLIOTHECAR. A librarian. *See also* BIBLIOTHECARIAN.

BIBLIOTHECARIAN. 1. A librarian. 2. Of, or belonging to, a library, or a librarian.

BIBLIOTHECARY. 1. A librarian. 2. A library. 3. Of, or belonging to, a library.

BIBLIOTHÈQUE NATIONALE. The oldest of the European national libraries; it has existed in Paris since the fourteenth century, although in its early days as the personal library of the sovereigns. It possesses over 6,000,000 volumes of printed books, 5,000,000 prints and 175,000 mss. It is the French legal deposit library. Abbreviated BN.

BIBLIOTHERAPIST. A person skilled in BIBLIOTHERAPY (*q.v.*).

BIBLIOTHERAPY. The use of selected reading and related materials for therapeutic purposes in physical medicine and in mental health. As an aspect of hospital and institution librarianship it requires an acquaintance with a wide range of literature and a knowledge of the techniques of group leadership and individual guidance.

BIBLIOTHETIC. Pertaining to, or based on, the placing or arrangement of books.

BIBLIO-TRAIN. A railway coach fitted up as a mobile library.

BIENNIAL. *See* BI-ANNUAL.

BIENNALE OF ILLUSTRATIONS BRATISLAVA. An international exposition of children's book illustrations which, with the co-operation of the Unesco national commissions, seeks to develop this art-form by creating a suitable environment for their evaluation. The Grand Prix BIB (value Kcs 20,000=US $1250 approx.) and many other prizes are awarded on the recommendation of an international jury, which judges the illustrations alone without the text. The exposition is organized by the Slovak National Gallery and the Czechoslovak Committee for Co-operation with Unesco. The first BIB was held in Bratislava, Czechoslovakia, in September 1967, and the first recipient of the Grand Prix BIB was Yasuo Segawa of Japan for his illustrations for *Taro and the bamboo shoot* by Masako Matsuno. Abbreviated BIB.

BIFURCATE CLASSIFICATION. 1. A classification branching in pairs, positive and negative, such as the Tree of Porphyry. Also called classification by dichotomy. 2. The bifurcate division of a genus by a single significant difference into a species and a residuum, which may or may not be disregarded in further division.

BIFURCATION. A method of subdivision in classification whereby every class is divided into two only, a positive and a negative group. Also called 'Dichotomy'.

BIGRAM.   Any group of two successive letters.

BILL.   1. A written complaint at law. 2. A draft of a proposed law introduced in a legislative body. 3. A North American term for an account of money owing for goods supplied or services rendered. *See also* INVOICE.

BILL BOOK.   A book in which invoices or bills (accounts) are entered as received. The entries are usually arranged alphabetically under the suppliers' names (American).

BILL OF MIDDLESEX.   A precept having the same force as a writ, but with the formal opening omitted.

BILL OF TYPE.   1. A complete assortment of any fount of type. 2. The plan or ratio by which founts of type are made up by type founders in order to provide the correct proportion of each letter or character, as ascertained by experience as to probable requirements. Also called 'Fount Scheme', 'Scheme'.

BI-MONTHLY.   A serial publication issued in alternate months.

BINARY.   (*Information retrieval*) 1. A number system using only two symbols, the digits one and zero. 2. A number system where quantities are represented in base 2 rather than base 10.

BINARY CODE.   (*Information retrieval*) A code that makes use of only two characters, usually O and I.

BINARY NUMBER SYSTEM.   A system, used in many electronic computers and in information theory, which has only one digit, I, and a zero. Thus the first ten whole numbers of this system, together with their decimal equivalents, which consist of nine digits and a zero, in parentheses, are: o(o), 1(1), 10(2), 11(3), 100(4), 101(5), 110(6), 111(7), 1000(8), 1001(9), 1010(10).

BINARY SEARCH.   (*Information retrieval*) A search in which a set of items is divided into two parts, where one part being rejected, the process is repeated on the accepted part until the item having the required property is found. *See also* FRACTIONAL SCANNING.

BIND, TO.   To assemble and fasten securely printed or manuscript SHEETS (*q.v.*) within a cover which may be made of wood or board covered with leather or cloth, plastic, stiff card (board) or paper. *See also* BOARDS 1, SHEETS.

BIND IN.   To fasten supplementary material securely into a bound book.

BINDER.   1. A person who binds books. 2. A case, or detachable cover, for filing magazines, pamphlets, etc. usually on wires or cords, one for each publication.

BINDER'S BLOCK.   *See* BINDER'S BRASS.

BINDER'S BOARD.   *See* MILLBOARD, STRAWBOARD.

BINDER'S BRASS.   A design, or letters of the alphabet, cut in brass and used by a bookbinder's finisher in lettering book covers. When a BLOCK (*q.v.* –2) is used it is called a 'Binder's block'. *See also* ARMS BLOCK, ZINCO.

BINDER'S DIES.   (*Binding*) Lettering or designs cut in brass and used for decorating book covers by stamping or embossing them. Also called 'Panel stamps'.

BINDER'S TICKET.   A small engraved or printed label, usually fixed to the top outside corner of one of the front end papers between about 1750 and 1825, and giving the name of the binder. These tickets were superseded by the binder's name stamped in gilt, ink, or blind, on one of the inside boards, usually on the extreme lower edge: this is called a 'name pallet'.

BINDER'S TITLE.   The title lettered on the back of a book when re-bound, to distinguish it from the publisher's title on the cover or title-page. *See also* BACK TITLE, COVER TITLE.

BINDER'S WASTE.   Printed sheets which are surplus to a bookbinder's needs and which are sometimes used in bookbinding for lining purposes.

BINDERY.   A place in which books are bound or re-bound.

BINDING.   1. The cover of a volume. 2. The finished work resulting from the processes involved in binding a book. 3. Colloquially, a number of books in a library which are waiting to be re-bound, or those which have been re-bound. *See also* BOOKBINDING.

BINDING BOOK.   A book in which are entered particulars of books sent to a binder for re-binding. It may vary in information given, from a title list to full binding instructions.

BINDING CLOTH.   *See* BOOK CLOTH.

BINDING COPY.   A book which is so worn as to need rebinding.

BINDING DEPARTMENT.   The department of a library or printing establishment in which books are bound or re-bound.

BINDING EDGE.   A back edge of a volume, or the folded edge of a section; the edge opposite the FORE-EDGE (*q.v.*). *See also* RIDGE.

BINDING FROM SHEETS.   Purchasing books in unfolded sheets and having them bound by the library binder.

BINDING RECORD.   A record of books sent to the binder. This may consist of the book-cards, a duplicate of the binding slips, or a special record kept on a card or in a BINDING BOOK (*q.v.*).

BINDING SLIP (SHEET).   The form on which instructions for binding are written for the binders' guidance. A slip relates to one book only and is usually inserted in a book before it leaves the library and remains in it throughout all the binding processes.

BINDING VARIATIONS.   The bindings of books, which, although published in the same edition, vary in colour or type of book cloth, tooling, etc. This may arise through a number of manufacturing causes, especially if the whole of an edition is not bound at the same time, or through storage under unsatisfactory conditions, e.g. dampness.

BINOMIAL.   (*Classification*) A name which consists of two, and occasionally three, terms.

BIOBIBLIOGRAPHY.   A bibliography which contains brief biographical details about the authors.

BIOGRAPHEE.   A person who is the subject of biography.

BIOGRAPHEE ENTRY.   The entry in a catalogue (dictionary, name, or subject) under the name of the BIOGRAPHEE (*q.v.*); the subject entry for a biography.

BIOGRAPHER.   A person who writes a biography of another.

BIOGRAPHICAL DICTIONARY.   A collection of lives of people arranged in alphabetical order.

BIOGRAPHY.   1. A written account of a person's life. 2. The branch of literature concerned with the lives of people.

BIOGRAPHY FILE.   A file of records on standard size cards, or of cuttings, giving information about individuals. Also called a 'Who's who' file.

BIOLOGICAL INFORMATION SERVICE.   *See* BIS.

BIOSCIENCES INFORMATION SERVICE.   *See* BIOSIS.

BIOSIS.   Abbreviation for Biosciences Information Service of Biological Abstracts, the organization responsible for publishing the fortnightly *Biological Abstracts*, founded 1926, the world's leading abstracting journal for the life sciences, covering the entire literature; its four computer-generated indexes are provided in each issue: (1) *BASIC* (*q.v.*) a keyword-in-context subject index; (2) the *CROSS* (*q.v.*) index based on subject concept; (3) the *Biosystematic Index* consisting of taxonomic categories; (4) the Author Index. Other abstracting and indexing publications are also issued, including *Bioresearch Index* (m.) which provides citations to research reports which do not appear in *Biological Abstracts*, and a *Cumulative Index* to each volume of both these publications. Experimental services to evaluate the computerized current-awareness services based on the BIOSIS computer tapes, and carried out at Oxford and Nottingham Universities, have demonstrated that the BIOSIS computer files can be most effectively used to meet the growing needs for biological information in the U.K. scientific community. Consequently the (British) Institute of Biology and the British Library have sponsored the Biological Information Service (BIS *q.v.*), together with a research programme, which complements existing information services in the agricultural, chemical and medical fields. *See also* EXCERPTA MEDICA, UKCIS.

BIRMINGHAM AND DISTRICT LIBRARY ASSOCIATION. An autonomous Association founded in 1895, which became the Birmingham and District Branch of the Library Association on 1st April 1929. *See* WEST MIDLAND BRANCH to which the Birmingham and District Branch of the Library Association changed its name in 1964.

BIRMINGHAM AND DISTRICT PERIODICALS INTERCHANGE SCHEME. An organization for the interloan of periodicals. It has been operating since 1953, and is centred on the Technical Library, Ratcliff Place, Birmingham, 1, but the holdings of this Department are not available for loan.

BIRMINGHAM BIBLIOGRAPHICAL SOCIETY. Formed in March 1972 to: (a) promote and encourage bibliographical and allied studies; (b) promote friendly intercourse among book lovers and scholars and to further their common interests; (c) hold meetings and exhibitions. Membership is open to all persons interested in the objects of the Society. The University of Birmingham provides a base for the activities of the Society. The West Midland Book Trade project is in hand, and the resulting papers will eventually be published. This has as its aims the compilation from primary and secondary sources of a historical directory of the book trade until 1900 in Herefordshire, Shropshire, Staffordshire, Warwickshire and Worcestershire and the publication of a directory to serve as a work of reference. The Society publishes a *Newsletter*. The Birmingham and Midland Bibliographical Society functioned from 1963 to 1970, being affiliated to the Birmingham and Midland Institute. Its aims were the same as those of the Birmingham Bibliographical Society.

BIRMINGHAM LIBRARIES CO-OPERATIVE MECHANIZATION PROJECT. *See* BLCMP.

BIRMINGHAM NOTATION. *See* GKD NOTATION.

BIRMINGHAM PUBLIC LIBRARIES WORKS LIBRARIES LOAN SCHEME. Industrial libraries which are properly constituted and under the care of a designated librarian may become members and so borrow material for short periods from the Birmingham Reference

Library. The Scheme has been in operation since 1958 and is organized from the Technical Library, Paradise, Birmingham B3 3HQ.

BIRTH AND DEATH DATES. The years of birth, and possibly of death, given in personal name entries in catalogues.

BIS. Acronym of the Biological Information Service which began operation in April 1975 by the United Kingdom Chemical Information Service at Nottingham University, under a contract between the Institute of Biology and the Chemical Society. The service, which is available, for payment, to all, not only biologists, seeking information in the biological field, offers a variety of computerized current-awareness services, based on the *Biological Abstracts* and *Bioresearch Index* computer tapes provided by BIOSIS (*q.v.*) based in Philadelphia.

BISCOE TIME NUMBERS (BISCOE DATE TABLE). A table (designed by W. S. Biscoe) which allocates letters to year periods in order to arrange books in chronological, rather than alphabetical, order both on the shelves and in the catalogue. The full table is as follows:

A	B.C.	J	1830–1839	S	1920–1929
B	0–999	K	1840–1849	T	1930–1939
C	1000–1499	L	1850–1859	U	1940–1949
D	1500–1599	M	1860–1869	V	1950–1959
E	1600–1699	N	1870–1879	W	1960–1969
F	1700–1799	O	1880–1889	X	1970–1979
G	1800–1809	P	1890–1899	Y	1980–1989
H	1810–1819	Q	1900–1909	Z	1990–1999
I	1820–1829	R	1910–1919		

Examples of use: a book published in 1676 would be lettered E76, a book published in 1916 would be lettered R6.

BISHOPS' BIBLE. A Bible printed [1568] in London by Richard Jugge, senior Queen's Printer to Elizabeth I. Sometimes called 'Archbishop Parker's Bible'.

BISHOP'S RULES. A set of rules for abbreviating periodical titles: (1) if the journal title consists of a single word, the first four letters are taken; (2) if of two words, the first two letters of each word; (3) if of three words, the first letter of each of the first two words and the first two letters of the last word; (4) if of more than four words, usually the first letter of each of the first four words. *See also* CODEN.

BIT. A contraction of 'binary digit'. The smallest unit of information; a zero or a one; a 'yes' or 'no'.

BITE. The term given to the action of acid eating into metal in the process of block making or plate engraving.

BI-WEEKLY. *Synonymous with* FORTNIGHTLY (*q.v.*) and 'Semi-monthly'.

BLACK. A mark made unintentionally on a sheet of paper by a lead, space or piece of furniture which has risen. Also called 'Work up'.

BLACK FACE. *Synonymous with* BOLD FACE (*q.v.*).

'BLACK' HEADINGS. Headings, other than subject headings, in a dictionary catalogue. The term has its origin in the fact that it was the practice in many libraries to use red for the subject headings and black for all the others.

BLACK LETTER. A term used to indicate old English, text, or church type, which was based on the writing in mediaeval manuscripts. *Synonymous with* GOTHIC TYPE (*q.v.*).

BLACK-LIST. A list of readers who have lost books and not paid for them, or owe fines, and of guarantors who have not fulfilled their obligations in respect of readers they have guaranteed.

BLACK STEP. A rule about 6 points thick and up to 24 points long printed between the first and last pages of a section so as to show on the spine of the section when folded. In the first forme it is positioned opposite the top line of text, and about 24 points lower in each successive forme, so that when all the sections of a book have been gathered and placed together a diagonal line is seen across the spine. Any error in gathering is immediately apparent. Also called 'Back mark', 'Collating mark' (*qqv.*), 'Quad mark'.

BLANK. An unprinted page which is part of a SIGNATURE (*q.v.*) and is consequently recorded when making a bibliographical description of a book in the form 'bl.' following the unprinted signature or page number in [ ].

BLANK BOOK. A bound book consisting of blank leaves only; used for notes, records, accounts, etc.

BLANK COVER. The cover of a bound book which is devoid of lettering or ornamentation.

BLANK LEAVES. The unprinted leaves to be found at each end of a book. If these are conjugate with printed leaves they should be included in a bibliographical description of the book, but if only binder's fly-leaves, ignored.

BLANK PAGE. A page of a book on which nothing has been printed.

BLANKET. 1. The packing used on the impression cylinder of a printing machine; it may consist of cloth, rubber or paper. 2. The resilient rubber sheet attached to a cylinder on to which the image to be printed is transferred, or offset, from the inked lithographic plate, and then offset on to the paper.

BLANKET CYLINDER. *See* OFFSET PRINTING.

BLANKING. (*Binding*) An impression made on the cloth cover of a book with a heated brass stamp as a base for lettering or decorative stamping.

BLEACH. The process of whitening pulp or cellulose, usually with a solution of chlorine.

BLEACHED KRAFT. A white paper made from bleached sulphate wood pulp and used for a variety of purposes when strength is required, e.g. as a body paper for coating. *See also* KRAFT PAPER.

BLED. A book the letterpress or plates of which have been cut into by the binder is said to have been 'bled'. *See also* CROPPED.

BLED OFF. Said of a book when the illustrations have been intentionally printed across the normal margins so that the final trim has brought some of the illustrations to the outside edges of the page.

BLEED. 1. To trim printed matter so close that the text or plates are cut into. *See also* CROPPED, CUT, TRIMMED, UNCUT. 2. In the diazotype process of reproduction, the dye image which has run or spread.

BLEEDING. The diffusion of printing inks or colours into surrounding areas.

BLIND. Lettering on a book or other article without using gold leaf or colour.

BLIND-BLOCKED. Lettering on book covers not inked or gilt, only embossed or impressed.

BLIND EMBOSSING. Raising paper in a pattern, or in the shape of letters, by means of dies but not using ink on the raised (i.e. embossed) parts. *See also* EMBOSSING.

BLIND INDEX. A form of indexing equipment in which the headings on cards or slips cannot be seen until those immediately in front are turned over. The opposite of VISIBLE INDEX (*q.v.*).

BLIND P. The paragraph mark ¶. *See also* PARAGRAPH MARK, REFERENCE MARKS.

BLIND PAGE. An unnumbered, and usually blank, page which is included in the overall pagination. These usually occur in the PRE-LIMINARIES (*q.v.*).

BLIND REFERENCE. A reference in an index to a catchword which does not occur in the index, or a reference in a catalogue or bibliography to a heading under which no entry will be found.

BLIND STAMPING. Embossing lettering or a design on to book

covers, whether by hand or in a press, without using gold leaf or colour. Also called 'Antique', 'Blind blocking' and 'Blind tooling'.

BLIND TOOLING. *See* TOOLING.

BLINDED-IN. A design which is impressed on a book cover with heated tools but not coloured or gilt.

BLISS' BIBLIOGRAPHIC CLASSIFICATION. *See* BIBLIOGRAPHIC CLASSIFICATION.

BLISS CLASSIFICATION ASSOCIATION. Formed in May 1967 to replace the former British Committee for the Bliss Classification consequent upon the receipt of the copyright of the BC from the H. W. Wilson Company. Publishes *BC Bulletin* (a.).

BLOCK. 1. To print with a solid shading at the bottom or sides, as a second impression in a different colour and in a projecting position. 2. In bookbinding, to emboss or letter book covers with a block or frame containing the entire device, and at one operation, as distinguished from die stamping. 3. A large stamp without a handle used in a blocking press by bookbinders for impressing a design on a book cover. 4. A type-high piece of wood, plastic or metal, bearing a design from which an impression can be made. A general term which includes line-blocks, half-tones, electros, etc. 5. To secure a plate to its proper position for printing. 6. A piece of wood or metal on which a stereotype, electrotype or other plate is mounted to make it type high. 7. A piece of hard wood used by engravers. 8. The core of a roller on a lithographing press. 9. In photography, to paint over a part of a negative to prevent or modify its printing. 10. A stop in a catalogue drawer. *See also* BACKSLIDE.

BLOCK BOOKS. Those printed from engraved blocks of wood. Block books originated in the Netherlands and in Germany after about 1410; most are dateable from 1460 to 1480. They were printed on one side of the leaf in a thin brownish ink. Generally they may be divided into three groups; 1. those which have pictures and words descriptive of the pictures engraved at the foot of the picture or in cartouches proceeding from the mouths of the principal figures; 2, those which have pictures on one page and a full page of explanatory text opposite, or form distinct and separate units on the same page; 3, those with xylographic text only. The *Biblia pauperum* and *Apocalypse of St. John* are well-known examples of Group 1; *Ars memorandi, Ars moriendi* and *Speculum humanae salvationis* of Group 2; and the *Donatus de Octobus Partibus Orationis* of Group 3. Block books continued to be printed well into the sixteenth century and several of the later ones were printed on a press with printer's ink, in such instances often on both sides of the paper. Those printed on one side only of the paper are called 'anopisthographic'. Books printed from engraved wood blocks, are called 'xylographic' books. *See also* OPISTHOGRAPHIC, WOOD BLOCK, WOODCUT, XYLOGRAPHY.

BLOCK CALENDAR. A calendar with small pieces of paper bearing the date, one for each day, and pasted in a pile to form a block, the top one being torn off daily.

BLOCK INDEXING. 1. A system of indexing wherein 'blocks' of materials are collected, each block being small enough to permit easy manual search of the group contained therein. (*IBM*) 2. A system for separation of information on microfilm into groups or 'blocks' identified by readily distinguishable numbers to facilitate reference.

BLOCK PRINTING. Making an illustration, or printing a design on paper or material, from wood or metal blocks with the design in relief.

BLOCK-PULL. A proof of an illustration or text engraved on a block as distinct from type.

BLOCKING. The impressing of a gold leaf, metal foil, or other graphic medium into a book-cover by means of a stamp, 'brass' or BLOCK 3 (*q.v.*) having a raised surface. The term is also applied to the impressing of type, blocks, etc., without any intervening media, this operation being known as 'blind-stamping'. Called 'Stamping' in the U.S.A.

BLOCKING FOIL. A paper foil coated with gold, white metal or coloured pigment which is transferred to the leather or cloth cover of a book by means of a heated die used in a blocking press. The process using these materials is known as 'foil blocking'.

BLOCKING OUT. (*Reprography*) The use of opaque, or indian, ink to paint part of a negative to prevent areas from printing.

BLOCKING PRESS. A press using heated blocks to impress, or stamp, lettering, designs, etc., on the book covers and cases. In machine bookbinding, ribbons of blocking foil of varying widths are used; these contain their own glair or adhesive. The press is also used for blind or ink blocking, no heat being necessary for the latter process.

BLOTTING PAPER. Absorbent paper made from specially prepared rags, and unsized.

BLOW UP. 1. A photograph, jacket, book review, specimen page of a book, etc., greatly enlarged for exhibition or advertising purposes. *See also* GIANT BOOK. 2. In documentary reproduction a copy having a larger scale than the original; an enlargement or PROJECTION PRINT (*q.v.*).

BLUE BOOK. A more lengthy official publication of similar character to a WHITE PAPER (*q.v.*), printed with a blue paper cover. (The traditional blue cover is now used principally for Select Committee Reports and for certain Accounts and Papers presented to Parliament under statute). The French colour is yellow; German, white; Italian, green. *See also* GREEN PAPER, PARLIAMENTARY PUBLICATIONS, WHITE PAPER.

BLUE-LINE PRINT. 1. A positive print made by the DIAZOTYPE PROCESS (*q.v.*). 2. A blue-print with blue lines on a white field, made by printing from a negative master.

BLUEPRINT. A blue on white, or white on blue, print submitted by a blockmaker as a rough proof before blocks are supplied. Also, a print produced by the BLUEPRINT PROCESS (*q.v.*).

BLUE PRINT PROCESS. A method of reproducing documents whereby a sheet of paper, which has been treated with a preparation mainly consisting of ferro prussiate, together with the document are exposed to powerful arc lamps. The paper is then developed by placing it in running water. A blue and white negative results and this can be used to produce a blue and white positive. Only single-sided documents which are perfect (having no creases or alterations) are suitable for reproduction by this process.

BLURB. The publisher's description and recommendation of a book, usually found on the front flap of a book jacket. *See also* PUFF.

BOARD LABEL. The label pasted on the inside of the front board of a library book to show ownership, and usually bearing a few of the more important rules. Also called a 'Book plate' or 'Book label.'

BOARD OF DIRECTORS. *Synonymous with* BOARD OF LIBRARY TRUSTEES (*q.v.*).

BOARD OF LIBRARY TRUSTEES. The committee responsible for the control of an American library system. Also known as 'Library Board,' 'Board of Directors,' 'Library Trustees' and occasionally, 'Library Commission.'

BOARD PAPER. *Synonymous with* PASTE-DOWN (*q.v.*).

BOARDS. 1. The sheets of millboard, pasteboard or strawboard used for bookcovers. When covered with paper, a book so bound is said to be bound in 'paper boards,' when covered with cloth, in 'cloth boards.' 2. So named because wood was used originally. 3. A general term which includes pulp, index, paste, ivory and other forms of card used for printing. *See also* BRISTOL BOARD, IVORY BOARD. 4. The pieces of wooden board used by a binder to grip a book when pressing, cutting, backing, burnishing, etc.

BOAR'S HEAD PRESS. A private printing press founded in 1931 by Christopher Sandford who afterwards acquired the GOLDEN COCKEREL PRESS (*q.v.*).

BODONI. An early MODERN FACE roman type designed in 1790 by
Giambattista Bodoni (1740–1813) of Parma, the most celebrated
printer of his day. It was re-cut for contemporary printing in 1921.
Characteristics are mathematically vertical stress, long ascenders and
descenders, fine straight-line serifs, and thin hair lines. For a specimen
alphabet, see TYPE FACE.

BODY. (*Printing*) 1. The measurement (or thickness) from back to front
of a type letter, slug, rule, lead, etc. 2. The part of a piece of movable
type from the foot to the flat surface at the upper end, above which is
the 'SHOULDER' (*q.v.*) and from which the moulded letter rises. It
comprises the 'BELLY,' 'BACK,' 'FEET,' 'SIDES,' 'PIN-MARK,' 'NICK'
and 'GROOVES' (*qq.v.*). Also called the 'Shank' or 'Stem.' (*Paper*). The
apparent weight of a sheet of paper.

BODY MATTER. (*Printing*) The text, as distinct from display matter,
or illustrations.

BODY OF THE BOOK (WORK). The main part of the book, commencing at the first page of the text and including any illustrations or
foot-notes which may accompany it, and excluding any preliminary
or appended matter.

BODY OF THE ENTRY. The part of a catalogue entry which
describes a publication. It usually follows a heading (thus beginning
with the title) and ends with the imprint. See IMPRINT 1.

BODY PAPER, or BOARD. The foundation for art, chromo, coated,
blue print, gummed, photographic and other papers which are made
by coating or treating with a composition of any kind. Also called
'base' or 'raw' paper.

BODY SIZE. See TYPE SIZE.

BODY TYPE. Type, of 14 point or less, used for the main body of a
composition, as distinguished from the display type used in headings,
etc. It also includes sizes of type up to 24 point which may be used in
book work. Display type may begin at 18 point.

BOILER. The part of paper-making machinery in which the raw
material is boiled in water before it goes into the BREAKER (*q.v.*). Also
called 'Kier.' See also DIGESTER.

BOLD FACE. Heavy-faced type, also called 'Full face' and 'Black face.'
This is bold face, and is indicated in a MS. by wavy underlining
∿∿∿∿∿∿. Bold face is usually used to give emphasis to certain
words, and for headings. In machine setting, bold characters can
normally be set or tapped in the same line as the roman and italic.
Most FOUNTS (*q.v.*) have a bold face based on the same design as the
medium weight as well as the roman and italic. Bold face developed

from the CLARENDON (*q.v.*) face which has only slight contrast in the up and down strokes and was used, with other type faces, for emphasis. Clarendon grew out of the Antique face cut by Vincent Figgins prior to 1815 believed to be the earliest of the designs now generally known as Egyptian. It is peculiar in giving equal emphasis to the up and down strokes and serifs. *See also* EGYPTIAN, TYPE FACE.

BOLE. (*Printing*) To reduce the height of type by shaving the feet. *See also* ARMENIAN BOLE.

BOLOGNESE LETTERS. Manuscript lettering which originated at the legal school of the University of Bologna and was used as the basis for the Gothic types known as 'Rotunda.' It was introduced into Germany from Venice and was consequently often called 'Litterae Venetae' by the early German printers.

BOLT. The folded or doubled edge of paper at the head, tail or fore-edge of a sheet in an uncut or unopened book. These are known as head bolts, tail bolts or fore-edge bolts. The folded edge at the back of a sheet is referred to, not as a 'bolt,' but as the 'last fold' or 'back fold.' *See also* FOLD TO PAPER, FOLD TO PRINT, OPEN EDGE.

BOM PROOF. A proof which is specially printed and bound for submission to a book club.

BOMBAY LIBRARY ASSOCIATION. Founded on 9th December 1944 with the object of promoting the library service and librarianship mainly within the municipal limits of the city of Bombay and Greater Bombay. Any person or institution interested in library work may become a member.

BONE FOLDER. A flat piece of bone 6 to 9 inches long, about 1 inch wide and ⅛ inch thick with rounded corners and edges which is used for rubbing along the fold of a sheet of paper to bend the fibres of the paper firmly into position, and in book repairing. *See also* FOLDING STICK.

BONNANGE CARD CATALOGUE TRAY. An obsolete form of tray invented by M. F. Bonnange. The cards are hinged near the bottom, the lower piece (which is thicker than the upper) having shoulders which fit into grooves in the sides of the tray.

BOOK. 1. A set of blank sheets of paper bound along one edge and enclosed within protective covers to form a volume, especially a written or printed literary composition presented in this way. 2. A division of a literary work, which is separately published and has an independent physical existence, although its pagination may be continuous with other volumes. 3. At a UNESCO conference in 1964 a book was defined as 'a non-periodical printed publication of at least

forty-nine pages, exclusive of cover pages.' *See also* PAMPHLET.
4. A collection (*Fr.* assemblage) of manuscript or printed leaves fastened together to form a volume or volumes, forming a BIBLIOGRAPHICAL UNIT (*q.v.*). (It is distinct from periodicals, and from other forms of material, such as films, prints, maps, etc.) (*IFLA*). *See also* ADAPTATION, DOCUMENT, FASCICLE, PART, PRINTED BOOK, PUBLICATION, VERSION, VOLUME, WORK.

BOOK AUCTION SALE. A method of selling second-hand books; it dates from the early seventeenth century, and is the usual method of selling large libraries or individual copies of rare or valuable books. The prices realized are recorded in *Book auction records* or the American *Book prices current*.

BOOK BAND. A narrow strip, or band, of printed paper placed round a jacketed book to advertise it by drawing attention to it, e.g. its cheap price, an award which had been made in respect of it, the 'book of the film,' etc.

BOOK BARROW. A barrow from which books are sold, usually in a street market. The wheels of the barrow are intended to enable the display fitting and the books to be moved conveniently from the storage place to the sales position rather than from one sales position to another, although this is done in some cases.

BOOK BIN. An unenclosed receptacle in which books are placed, especially in a staff enclosure while awaiting attention such as discharging or shelving.

BOOK BOAT. A common means of providing a library service to residents on islands and land masses accessible only by boat. They are provided in Norway, Sweden and Denmark.

BOOK BOXES. Boxes in which books are transported.

BOOK CAPACITY. *Synonymous with* SHELF CAPACITY (*q.v.*).

BOOK CARD. A piece of card or plastic material on which are written the means of identifying a particular book (usually some or all of the following: charging symbol, accession number, class number, author, title) and which is used in charging (i.e. recording) the loan of the book. Book cards are usually made of manilla, of different colours for different departments or classes of books, but plastic is often used because of its better handling properties and greater durability. Also called 'Charging card,' and in America 'Book slip,' 'Charge slip' and 'Charging slip.'

BOOK CARRIER. *See* BOOK CONVEYOR.

BOOK CATALOGUE. A catalogue produced in book form. Also used as a synonym for PRINTED CATALOGUE (*q.v.*). Sometimes used synonymously for PAGE CATALOGUE (*q.v.*) and 'Book form catalogue'.

BOOK CHAMBER OF THE BYELORUSSIAN SSR. *See* LENIN STATE LIBRARY.

BOOK CLASSIFICATION. A general term covering bibliographical and bibliothecal classifications.

BOOK CLOTH. Cotton or linen cloth (usually coloured) used for book covers.

BOOK CLUB. A publishing activity issuing to subscribing members, specially, and cheaply, printed books of merit. The subjects of the books published may be restricted to one subject; the books have usually been published before, although in some cases very recently, and are limited in number in any one year.

BOOK CLUB EDITION. A book sold by a Book Club to its members. Such books may not be the same edition, reprint, issue or impression as are normally available through trade channels to the public; they are usually specially printed and bound, and except in the cases of clubs or societies whose purpose is to supply books of exceptional quality, of inferior materials.

BOOK COLLECTING. The assembling of books which because of their bibliographic interest, their contents (historic or factual), the history of the individual copies, or their rarity, have some permanent interest to the collector.

BOOK COLLECTION. *Synonymous with* BOOK STOCK (*q.v.*).

BOOK COLLECTOR. One who purchases books systematically often in a given field of knowledge or within the limits of some branch of historical bibliography.

BOOK CONVEYOR. A system of metal or other containers joined to an endless chain, or other device, which is capable of conveying books, correspondence, papers, etc., either horizontally or perpendicularly between the various parts of a large library on different floors. They are usually operated by electricity, and push button control ensures the automatic discharge of the containers' contents at specified service points. Also called 'Book carrier,' 'Book distributor.'

BOOK COUPON. *See* UNESCO COUPONS.

BOOK COVER. *See* COVER.

BOOK CRAFTS. The operations which are carried out in producing books and which require varying degrees of skill in their performance; these include paper-making, printing, design of books, design and production of illustrations, and binding.

BOOK DECORATION. The impressing of a design on the cover of a book, often by gold (but sometimes blind) tooling. The design so impressed.

BOOK DEVELOPMENT COUNCIL. The export division of the Publishers Association which provides a comprehensive information service to publishers on conditions in overseas markets. It also answers queries about British publishing from potential customers abroad.

BOOK DISPLAY. A small exhibition of books usually on one or several related subjects, in (and sometimes outside) a library.

BOOK DISTRIBUTOR. *See* BOOK CONVEYOR.

BOOK DRIVE. A campaign to secure gifts of books or of money for buying books. (American.)

BOOK DROP. A box or chute provided so that readers can return books when a library is closed or where drive-in facilities are available.

BOOK END. *See* BOOK SUPPORT.

BOOK FAIR. 1. An exhibition of books and of book-making, sometimes including talks by authors, illustrators, booksellers and publishers. 2. Trade exhibitions of books with the object of selling and exchanging books. Some, particularly those held at Frankfurt and Leipzig before the Second World War, became world famous. The Frankfurt Book Fair has in recent years developed into an important international means of selling books and encouraging translation of books into other languages.

BOOK FORM. Said of a work published as a book but which has been issued previously in serial form, usually in a periodical.

BOOK FUND. The fund, or amount of money, which is available for the purchase of books, and possibly of non-book materials.

BOOK HAND. A style of artificial, calligraphic handwriting used for books (as distinct from the cursive styles used by individuals for records, memoranda, correspondence, etc.), before the introduction of printing. Uncial, Caroline minuscule, Gothic, and Humanistic are book hands. Bastard, and Chancery are not.

BOOK HOIST. *See* BOOK LIFT.

BOOK HOLDER. (*Reprography*) A device for holding open a bound volume in a level or near-level plane so that all parts of the image are in focus during reproduction.

BOOK HUNTER. One whose occupation is the tracing of specific titles in the second-hand market, sometimes at the request of a would-be purchaser.

BOOK ILLUSTRATION. The making of drawings or paintings to illustrate the text of a book. The resulting illustration.

BOOK JACKET. The paper wrapping covering a book as issued by the publisher. It serves the purposes of protecting the book, and if illustrated (as it usually is), of attracting attention. It bears the name of the author, the title, and usually has a BLURB (*q.v.*) on the first flap, and elsewhere, particulars of other books by the same author or issued by the same publisher. Also called 'Dust cover,' 'Dust jacket,' 'Dust wrapper,' 'Jacket,' 'Wrapper.'

BOOK LABEL. *See* BOARD LABEL, BOOK PLATE.

BOOK LIFT. A small device for carrying not more than 1 cwt. of books perpendicularly from one floor to another. Usually operated by electricity, it may be hand-operated by hauling on a rope if the distance is not more than about 25 feet; this is a slow and tedious method. A hand-operated lift is sometimes called a book hoist.

BOOK LIST. A list of books, usually on some specific subject and arranged in classified or author order.

BOOK NUMBER. 1. The number, letter, or other symbol or combination of symbols used to distinguish an individual book from every other book in the same class, and at the same time to arrange books bearing the same class number in the desired order on the shelves, by author, title, edition, date of publication, etc. It usually consists of the (a) AUTHOR MARK, (b) WORK MARK, (c) VOLUME NUMBER. Also called 'Book mark.' *See also* CALL NUMBER. 2. In the Colon Classification it follows the class number and precedes the COLLECTION NUMBER (*q.v.*) to form the CALL NUMBER (*q.v.*); it is the symbol used to fix the position of a book in relation to other books having the same ULTIMATE CLASS (*q.v.*). The Book Number individualizes the document among the documents having the same class number, and is used to mechanize the position of a document among those having the same ultimate class. *See also* ASSOCIATED BOOK.

BOOK OF ARMAGH. Written by Ferdomnach, a scribe, who died in 844, this MS contains portions of the New Testament. It is the first example of the Irish pointed hand to which a definite date can be given, and resembles the English pointed hand of the period.

BOOK OF HOURS. The name given to books of private devotions designed for the laity; they were very popular and in general use throughout the Catholic Church from the fourteenth to the sixteenth centuries. Both before and after the discovery of printing they were often beautifully illuminated, and fine examples of them are today much coveted by collectors. Great personages were fond of having these books made specially for themselves, with decorations and illustrations of an individual appeal.

BOOK OF KELLS. See KELLS, BOOK OF.

'BOOK OF THE YEAR FOR CHILDREN' MEDAL. A bronze medal awarded by the Canadian Association of Children's Librarians for outstanding children's books, one in English and one in French, published in Canada during a calendar year and written by a Canadian or resident of Canada. The award is made only when an entry is worthy in quality; the first book in English to receive the award was Roderick Haig-Brown's *Starbrick Valley winter* (1947) and the first book in French was Emile S. J. Gervais' *Mgr. de Laval* (1954). The Medal was designed after the bas relief of Alfred Laliberté from the Hébert Memorial in Quebec City and shows the European mother, Marie Rollet Hébert, reading to her children.

BOOK PAPER. A name given to paper manufactured for books to distinguish it from newsprint, cover paper and writing paper.

BOOK PLATE. A label pasted in a book to mark its ownership and some-times to indicate its location in a library. Private book plates are often ornate or artistic: simpler and smaller ones bearing merely the owner's name are called 'book labels.'

BOOK POCKET. The strong paper receptacle like the corner of an envelope pasted on the inside of the board of a book to take the book card. The BOARD LABEL (*q.v.*) frequently serves this purpose.

BOOK POST. A postal rate applying to the carrying of books: it is usually cheaper than the ordinary parcel rate providing the packages are made up in such a way that the postal authorities may examine them at will without breaking any seals and without inconvenience.

BOOK PREPARATION. See PROCESSING.

BOOK PRESS. A press, usually of wood or steel, into which books are placed during binding or repairing processes. See also BOOK STACK, BOOKCASE, DOUBLE-FACED SHELF, DOUBLE SIDED STACK, PRESS, TIER.

BOOK PROCESSING. See PROCESSING.

BOOK PROCESSING CENTER. A co-operative organization operated for a group of libraries where the ordering and processing of books (cataloguing, preparation, catalogues for use of public) is undertaken for all the participants, whether as a separate service or as one of other services. (American.)

BOOK PRODUCTION. The art and craft of making books includnig designing, choice and use of materials, illustration, printing and binding.

BOOK RACK. A shelf or small group of shelves used for displaying books.

BOOK RAILBUS. A means of taking books to isolated residents in northern Sweden. The railbus stops at every house alongside the railway.

BOOK RARITIES. Books of which few copies are known to exist; scarce books.

BOOK REST. A portable fitting similar to the music rest of a piano which is placed at a convenient angle for reading on a table or desk to hold a book when notes are being made from it.

BOOK REVIEW. An evaluation of a book published in a periodical or newspaper.

BOOK SATCHEL. A bag used in mediaeval times for carrying books. It frequently hung from a cleric's habit cord or on a warrior's belt.

BOOK SELECTION. The process of choosing books for inclusion in a library with a view to providing a balanced increase to the stock.

BOOK SHRINE. A box or chest, usually ornamented, in which valuable books were placed in mediaeval times. *See also* CUMDACH.

BOOK SIZES.

	Octavos:	Quartos:
Pott	$6\frac{1}{4} \times 4$	$8 \times 6\frac{1}{4}$
Foolscap	$6\frac{3}{4} \times 4\frac{1}{4}$	$8\frac{1}{2} \times 6\frac{3}{4}$
Crown	$7\frac{1}{2} \times 5$	$10 \times 7\frac{1}{2}$
Large Crown	$8 \times 5\frac{1}{4}$	$10\frac{1}{2} \times 8$
Large Post	$8\frac{1}{4} \times 5\frac{1}{4}$	$10\frac{1}{2} \times 8\frac{1}{4}$
Demy	$8\frac{3}{4} \times 5\frac{5}{8}$	$11\frac{1}{4} \times 8\frac{3}{4}$
Post	8×5	10×8
Small Demy	$8\frac{1}{2} \times 5\frac{5}{8}$	$11\frac{1}{4} \times 8\frac{1}{2}$
Medium	$9 \times 5\frac{3}{4}$	$11\frac{1}{2} \times 9$
Small Royal	$9\frac{1}{4} \times 6\frac{1}{8}$	$12\frac{1}{4} \times 9\frac{1}{4}$
Royal	$10 \times 6\frac{1}{4}$	$12\frac{1}{2} \times 10$
Super Royal	$10\frac{1}{4} \times 6\frac{3}{4}$	$13\frac{1}{2} \times 10\frac{1}{4}$
Imperial	$11 \times 7\frac{1}{2}$	15×11

See also OCTAVO, PAPER SIZES, SIZE. American book sizes are given below: in several instances there are minor differences between these and the British sizes with a common name. The sizes are not absolute.

5

Name	inches	
Thirty-sixmo	4 ×	$3\frac{1}{3}$
Medium Thirty-twomo	$4\frac{3}{4}$ ×	3
Medium Twenty-fourmo	$5\frac{1}{2}$ ×	$3\frac{5}{8}$
Medium Eighteenmo	$6\frac{2}{3}$ ×	4
Medium Sixteenmo	$6\frac{3}{4}$ ×	$4\frac{1}{2}$
Cap Octavo	7 ×	$7\frac{1}{4}$
Duodecimo	$7\frac{1}{2}$ ×	$4\frac{1}{2}$
Crown Octavo	$7\frac{1}{2}$ ×	5
Post Octavo	$7\frac{1}{2}$ ×	$5\frac{1}{2}$
Medium Duodecimo	$7\frac{2}{3}$ ×	$5\frac{1}{8}$
Demy Octavo	8 ×	$5\frac{1}{2}$
Small Quarto (usually less)	$8\frac{1}{2}$ ×	7
Broad Quarto (varies up to 13 × 10)	$8\frac{1}{2}$ ×	7
Medium Octavo	$9\frac{1}{2}$ ×	6
Royal Octavo	10 ×	$6\frac{1}{2}$
Super Royal Octavo	$10\frac{1}{2}$ ×	7
Imperial Quarto	11 ×	15
Imperial Octavo	$11\frac{1}{2}$ ×	$8\frac{1}{4}$

(*The first column gives the vertical height.*)
For metric book sizes, *see* METRIC BOOK SIZES.

BOOK SLIDE. A coverglass used as a lantern slide and bearing in ink particulars of a book or books available for borrowing at the close of a library talk.

BOOK SLIP. *See* BOOK CARD.

BOOK STACK. A room closed to the public, which is equipped to shelve large numbers of little-used books in as small a space as possible. Stack rooms are usually built adjacent to the points of service, have narrow gangways and steel shelving, and do not require natural lighting. *See also* BOOK PRESS, BOOKCASE, DOUBLE-FACED SHELF, DOUBLE-SIDED STACK, PRESS, TIER.

BOOK STAMP. An ownership mark made by means of an ink impression from a metal or rubber stamp, embossed, on the title-page, cover or end-paper of a book.

BOOK STAND. A small portable stand for carrying or displaying a few books.

BOOK STOCK. The whole of the books comprising a library.

BOOK STORE. 1. A room or stack in which books are kept. 2. A book shop.

BOOK SUPPORT. An L or T shaped piece of iron or wood placed at the end of a row of books to keep them upright. Also called 'Book end.'

BOOK TALK. A talk about books, often given in a library by a librarian.

BOOK TRADE. The organized business of selling books. The term usually relates to the whole national organization involving booksellers and their organizations together with the publishers and their organizations.

BOOK TRAY. A tray for carrying books. It has three sides no more than about 4 inches high provided with slots or handles to facilitate carrying.

BOOK TROLLEY. *Synonymous with* BOOK TRUCK (*q.v.*).

BOOK TROUGH. A short V-shaped shelf for displaying books on a counter or desk.

BOOK TRUCK. A wheeled trolley about 3 feet long, with two or three shelves accessible from each side which is used for conveying books to different parts of a building. Special adaptations are made for taking books to patients in hospital wards.

BOOK VAN (WAGON). A large motor van fitted up with shelves so that readers in outlying areas where there is no library may choose their books. A vehicle used for delivering books to county branches. Also called a TRAVELLING LIBRARY (*q.v.*) or (in America) a 'Bookmobile.'

BOOK WEEK. A local or national event in which librarians, often with the co-operation of booksellers and publishers, arrange book displays and lectures, with the object of stimulating interest in books, particularly amongst children. These are arranged on a national scale less often in England than in America, where in addition to the general book week in November, others dealing with a particular type of book are arranged, as Religious Book Week, Catholic Book Week. The idea of a children's book week originated with Franklin K. Mathiews, who was Chief Librarian of the Boy Scouts of America. He enlisted the support of Frederick G. Melcher, President of the R. R. Bowker Co.; together they secured the help of booksellers and librarians with the result that the first Children's Book Week was held in 1919.

BOOKAMATIC. The trade name for a method of TRANSACTION CARD CHARGING (*q.v.*). An Addressograph-Multigraph recorder, which is much cheaper than any of the machines used in other such systems, records the details of loan on a pre-numbered TRANSACTION CARD. Embossed plastic book cards and readers' cards are used in the machine to print the name and address of the reader and the author and title of the book on a transaction card which is kept in the library.

A transaction card bearing the same number and the date due for return is placed in the book. The book-card is kept always in the book and is only taken out to place it in the recorder so as to print the details of loan on the transaction card. *See also* CHARGING METHODS.

BOOKBINDER.   A person whose occupation is the binding of books.

BOOKBINDING.   1. The act or process of binding a book, whereby the sheets are sewn or otherwise fastened into a permanent cover of bookbinder's board, the sides and back of which are covered with leather or cloth, or other suitable material. 2. The strong covering of the book.

BOOKBINDING BOARD.   A 'board' used as a component in making covers of hardback books.

BOOKBINDING STAMP.   A tool with an embossed design which is used to impress a design on the cover of a book.

BOOKCASE.   A case with shelves for books: it may or may not have doors. *See also* BOOK PRESS, BOOK STACK, DOUBLE-FACED SHELF, DOUBLE-SIDED STACK, PRESS, TIER.

BOOKETERIA.   A self-service library, mainly of novels, placed in a modern store in parts of American towns which are not served by branch libraries. Borrowers issue books to themselves, place returned books in special parts of book shelves for assistants who attend each morning to discharge them, and leave any fines due. As far as is known, this idea was pioneered by Stewart W. Smith in Lincoln, Nebraska, in about 1947.

BOOKFORM INDEX.   An index having the physical form of a book, the terms, or headings, followed by their appropriate references, being printed and bound up in the form of a book.

BOOKLET.   A small book in a paper cover or in very light binding.

BOOKMARK.   A piece of paper or other material placed between the leaves of a book to mark a place. Bookmarks are frequently used as a means of advertising. It may take the form of a piece of ribbon fastened in the 'hollow' back of a book, i.e. between the back folds of the sections and the spine. Also called 'Book marker.'

BOOKMARK LIST.   A list of books printed in the form of a bookmark.

BOOKMOBILE.   A large motor vehicle, equipped with shelves and a book-issuing desk, which the public may enter to select books for home reading. Also called a 'Mobile branch library' or TRAVELLING LIBRARY (*q.v.*). *See also* BOOK VAN.

BOOKS, USA, INC.   A private, non-profit, educational organization formed late in 1963 to provide a means for American citizens and organizations to buy and have sent abroad collections of 'meaningful paperback books.' USIS officers and Peace Corps Volunteers distribute the ten-book packets to overseas libraries, reading rooms, schools and individuals. Thirteen different packets of books enable foreigners to learn more about the U.S. through reading substantial works about its political and economic systems, its culture, people and aspirations. A similar organization, Law Books, U.S.A., is confined to books dealing with the philosophy and spirit of the American legal system.

BOOKSELLER. A dealer having a varied selection of books covering a wide range of subjects and of all types. Sometimes second-hand books are also stocked.

BOOKSELLERS' ASSOCIATION OF GREAT BRITAIN AND IRELAND. Founded in 1895, membership of this Association is open to all booksellers who are approved by the PUBLISHERS ASSOCIATION (*q.v.*). It exists to increase the sale of books, to protect the interests of booksellers, to provide classes and correspondence courses for the training of members and their assistants, to uphold the status of the trade, and to ensure adherence to the Net Book Agreement.

BOOKSHOP. *See* BOOKSTALL.

BOOKSTALL. A 'stand,' of temporary or permanent design, at which books are sold, the vendor usually being on the inside and the purchaser on the outside of the stand. A bookshop is a larger place which the purchaser enters.

BOOKWORK. The branch of the printing industry, particularly typesetting, which is concerned with book production.

BOOKWORM. 1. The larva of a moth or beetle which burrows into the covers and pages of books. 2. A person who reads voraciously.

BOOLEAN LOGIC. A technique of using the most basic conceivable forms of expression to represent any logical possibility. i.e. a thing either exists or does not exist, is either present or not present, operative or not operative, etc. It was first developed and codified by the English mathematician George Frederick Boole (1815–1864), who made a substantial contribution to current understanding of the relationship of one subject to another by demonstrating that such relationships are subject to algebraical laws.

BORDER. 1. (*Bibliography*) An ornamental enclosure of a title-page or a substantial part of it, or of a page of type, illuminated manuscript or body of printed matter; or merely an ornamental design placed on one or more sides of the above. *See also* BLOCK 4, COMPARTMENT, FRAME, RULE BORDER. 2. (*Binding*) Ornamentation placed close to the edges of the sides of a book-cover or the spine of a volume. To be distinguished from FRAME (*q.v.*). 3. (*Printing*) A continuous decorative design arranged around matter. It can consist of continuous cast strips of plain or patterned rule, or be made up of repeated units or FLOWERS (*q.v.*).

BOROUGH AUDITORS. In a few boroughs, accounts are audited by three persons none of whom need have professional qualifications or experience. Two of these, known as elective auditors, are elected by local government electors, the third, known as the mayor's auditor, is appointed from among the members of the council. Collectively they are known as 'Borough auditors.' The term of office for all borough auditors is three years. None of these has the power of disallowance or surcharge as does a district auditor. A borough council whose accounts are subject to borough audit may pass a resolution to adopt either district or professional audit. *See also* DISTRICT AUDIT, MUNICIPAL AUDIT, PROFESSIONAL AUDITOR.

BOROUGH COUNCIL. A statutory local authority which provided local government services within its geographical area. It was entitled to provide public library services under the Public Libraries Act, 1892. Councils which had not adopted this Act by the time the 1919 Act became operative lost their power to become library authorities. Abbreviated BC. Borough Councils ceased to exist as such when they were absorbed into District Councils or some other form of local authority under the Local Government reorganization which came into operation in England and Wales in 1974 and in Scotland in 1975. For powers to provide libraries, *see* LIBRARY AUTHORITY. *See also* LOCAL GOVERNMENT BOUNDARIES, NON-COUNTY BOROUGH.

BORROWER. *See* READER.

BORROWERS' INDEX. *See* BORROWERS' REGISTER I.

BORROWER'S NUMBER. The registration number assigned to a member of a library.

BORROWERS' REGISTER. 1. A list of members of a library entered in the order of joining and giving particulars as to name and address and the number (if any) of the tickets. This requires an index. 2. Borrowers' application forms filed in alphabetical order. This is the modern and more satisfactory method.

BORROWER'S TICKET (CARD). The membership card entitling the holder to borrow books from a library.

BOSS. A metal knob, often ornamented, fixed upon the covers of books, usually at the corners and centre, for protection and embellishment.

BOTTOM EDGE. The TAIL (*q.v.*) of a book. Also called 'Lower edge,' 'Tail edge.'

BOTTOM MARGIN. *Synonymous with* TAIL MARGIN (*q.v.*).

BOTTOM NOTE. *Synonymous with* FOOTNOTE (*q.v.*).

BOUND. 1. A book which is sewn or otherwise fastened into stiff boards. 2. (*Adj.*) In CO-ORDINATE INDEXING (*q.v.*) joined in modification of the meaning of a commonly used term; e.g. 'Free Energy' is a *bound* term (unit concept) while 'Free' and 'Energy' may be *free* terms in the same co-ordinate indexing system (*IBM*).

BOUND TERM. (*Indexing*) A heading, or term, consisting of more than one word. *See also* COLLATERAL TERM, GENERIC TERM.

BOUND VOLUME. Any book that is bound; usually a number of issues of a periodical comprising a volume and bound.

BOUND WITH. A term used by cataloguers when referring to books published separately but subsequently bound together. When such a volume has been supplied with a collective title-page the main catalogue entry may be made from this, the individual publications being entered in a contents note and given analytical entries. Otherwise each item would be given its own entry 'Bound with . . .' and the first item in the collection quoted. In each case there would be only one CALL NUMBER (*q.v.*).

BOUNDARY STRAPS. *Synonymous with* DECKLE STRAPS (*q.v.*).

BOURDILLON REPORT. The Report of the Working Party appointed by the Minister of Education in March 1961, *Standards of Public Library Service in England and Wales*, 1962. Mr. H. T. Bourdillon was Chairman of the Working Party. This, together with the BAKER REPORT (*q.v.*) formed the basis of parliamentary discussions and the framing of the Public Libraries and Museums Bill of 1964.

BOURGEOIS. An obsolete name for a size of type equal to 9 pt.

BOUSTROPHEDON WRITING. Derived from *boustrophedon*, Greek for 'as the ox ploughs'; refers to ancient Greek writing in which alternate lines run from left to right and then from right to left – the pattern that would be made by an ox ploughing a field. The letters in the lines commencing at the right are reversed as if mirrored.

BOW BRACKET. *Synonymous with* BRACE (*q.v.*).

BOWDLERIZED. A text which is altered by changing or omitting words or passages considered offensive or indelicate: after Thomas Bowdler who in 1818 published an expurgated edition of Shakespeare.

BOWKER BIBLIOGRAPHY PRIZE. Offered annually by the Bowker Publishing Company Ltd., beginning in 1975, to a student or a group of students, at the College of Librarianship Wales for an original work of scholarly bibliography. The Prize takes the form of a bursary of £100, plus subsequent grants of £750 towards books and travel to complete the work, which is later published by Bowker jointly with

the College in a series of College of Librarianship Wales Biblió-
graphies. The Prize was awarded first to Robert Gill for *Contemporary
conjuring : a bibliography of magic as a performing art.*

BOWL.   The full rounded and entirely enclosed portion of a type letter
as in O, B, D, b, a; the part enclosing a closed COUNTER (*q.v.*).

BOX.   (*Printing*) 1. An area within a larger type area, or within or
between type columns, formed by rules or white spaces with the object
of emphasizing what is printed within. 2. A rectangular or square
border of one or more lines placed around type matter, and made up
of rules which may be mitred or butted.

BOX FILE.   A container made to stand on a shelf, and intended primarily to contain flimsy material such as correspondence or newspaper
cuttings. The most durable kinds are those with wooden sides, board
base and hinged lid, the whole being covered with cloth and/or paper
and lined with paper. A spring clip is usually provided to keep the
contents in position. Unless the lid fits tightly, overlaps the box, and
does not warp, they are not dust-proof. *See also* PAMPHLET BOX.

BOX-IN.   To place rules around type matter so that the characters when
printed appear in a frame or box.

BOX LIBRARY.   Boxes containing standard sets of books catering for
different tastes and supplied in developing countries by community
development organizations to community centres in rural areas for
circulation from village to village.

BOXED.   A work in two or three volumes inserted into a container to
display them, keep them together, or protect them.

BOXHEAD.   1. A series of printed or ruled lines for headings in a ruled
table. 2. A cut-in head with a frame around it. Also called 'Box
heading.'

BOXHEAD RULING.   The space at the top of a ruled column for the
insertion of hand-written headings for each column.

BOYET STYLE.   A style of book decoration practised by Luc Antoine
Boyet, who worked in France in the eighteenth century for Count
Hoym. It is characterized by a plain border, ornamental corners and
edges, and a central monogram or device. Boyet is sometimes credited
with introducing DOUBLURES (*q.v.*).

BOYS AND GIRLS HOUSE, TORONTO.   Established in 1922 by
the Toronto Public Library as a library for children, it is now an
international centre for those concerned with library work for
children.

BRACE.   (*Printing*) A bracket ⌒ cast on its own body, usually to a
definite number of ems. Formerly called 'Vinculum.' A *sectional brace*

is made of several parts which can be assembled to the length required; the middle position is called a Cock (*q.v.*).

BRACKET SHELF. A shelf secured temporarily or permanently for display purposes at the end of a bookcase.

BRACKET SHELVING. Adjustable shelving where the shelves rest, or are fixed, on brackets, which are secured to the rear upright stanchions of steel shelving fixtures, and which also serve as book supports. Also called 'Suspension shelving.' Sometimes the brackets simply support the shelves from underneath; this type is also called 'Cantilever shelving.'

BRACKETS. Rectangular enclosing marks [ ]. Used in cataloguing to indicate something which does not appear in the original but is added by the cataloguer. To be distinguished from Curves ( ), (*q.v.*). Angle brackets ⟨ ⟩ are used to enclose matter which itself appears in [ ] on the title-page. Also called 'Angular marks,' 'Square brackets.' *See also* Circular Brackets, Curves.

BRADEL BINDING. A type of temporary binding said to have originated in Germany, and first adopted in France by a binder named Bradel.

BRADFORD SCIENTIFIC, TECHNICAL AND COMMERCIAL SERVICES. *See* Brastacs.

BRADFORD'S LAW OF SCATTERING. *See* Law of Scattering.

BRAILLE. A system of reading and writing for the blind in which the letters are formed by raised dots embossed into the paper in groups of six, three high and two wide. Named after the inventor Louis Braille (1809–52), a blind Frenchman.

BRAILLE BOOK BANK. *See* NBA.

BRANCH. 1. A section of the Library Association's membership admission to which is dependent on the place in which a librarian is resident or works. There are at present twelve branches. Membership of only one branch is permitted. Aslib also has geographical branches. *See also* Division, Group, Library Association, Section. 2. In a college or university, a collection of books and other materials on one subject, housed in a separate area and serviced by its own staff. It is centrally administered and is usually on the same campus as the main library.

BRANCH AND MOBILE LIBRARIES GROUP. A Group of the Library Association; it was formed in January 1966 and is concerned with the particular outlook and needs of such kinds of service point. Publishes *Service Point* (3 p.a.); *Occasional Paper Series* (irreg.); *Fiction Guides Series* (irreg.).

BRANCH LIBRARIAN.   The librarian in charge of a branch library. *See also* DEPARTMENTAL LIBRARY. (*County Libraries*). The librarian in charge of a branch library not covered by the definitions of AREA LIBRARIAN, DISTRICT LIBRARIAN, REGIONAL LIBRARIAN, REGIONAL OFFICER (*qq.v.*).

BRANCH LIBRARY.   A library other than the main one (called the 'Central') in a system. It usually comprises adult lending and children's departments, a quick-reference collection and possibly a news-room, and is intended to meet the library needs of the surrounding population, particularly in the matter of books for home-reading. It is housed in premises set aside for the purpose, is specially equipped and furnished, and staffed by trained assistants. The book stock is a permanent one. Sometimes called a 'District Library.' In English county libraries, a *full-time branch* is open not less than thirty hours a week: a *part-time branch*, less than thirty but more than ten hours per week in premises specially equipped and furnished. A *sub-branch* is one staffed, stocked and administered from a larger branch in the vicinity. 'Branch' is a general or collective term which includes more than one of the types of service points known as Full-time Branch Library, Library Centre or Part-time Branch Library (e.g. 'branch library policy', 'staffing of branches') but excludes those which are not administered by paid staff.

BRANCHING CLASSIFICATION.   A classification with two or more sub-classes, or main branches, each subdivided again, and perhaps again and again. It may be converted into a TABULAR CLASSIFICATION (*q.v.*). Also called a 'Ramifying classification.'

BRASS RULE.   *See* RULE.

BRASTACS. (BRADFORD SCIENTIFIC, TECHNICAL AND COMMERCIAL SERVICE.)   A scheme of library co-operation inaugurated in 1961 and centred on the Bradford Public Library, Darley St., Bradford, 1, with the co-operation of the Library of the Institute of Technology. It operates similarly to the Sheffield Interchange Organization (*see* SINTO) and aims to make industry more information-conscious and help to bring about the establishment of more libraries. Books and periodicals are lent, and there is an information service. Member organizations should have a minimum of twenty-five books and take current periodicals.

BRAYER.   Formerly a wooden pestle, round in shape and flat at one end with a handle on the other, used to spread ink on the block to an even depth and consistency before being taken up by the ink balls. Later, a hand-roller for distributing the ink before it is taken up by forme rollers. Also used when making a galley proof.

BRAZILIAN INSTITUTE OF BIBLIOGRAPHY AND DOCU-MENTATION. *See* IBBD.

BREAK (BREAK UP). *(Printing)* To dispose of a forme of printing matter by separating material to be re-melted from furniture, blocks, rules, foundry type, etc. *See also* DISTRIBUTING.

BREAK-LINE. The last line of a paragraph where quads are needed to fill out the last space. In good type-setting it does not begin a new page. *See also* END A BREAK, END EVEN, RUN ON.

BREAKER. A part of the machinery used to make paper; it is a tub-like vessel into which the raw material is placed after boiling in the 'boiler' or 'kier' in order that it may be washed and further broken to reduce and separate the fibres. Also called 'Beater' or 'Hollander.'

BREECHES BIBLE. *See* GENEVA BIBLE.

BREVIARY. The book of daily Divine Office used in the Roman Catholic Church. It contains: 1. Calendar; 2. Psalter; 3. Proprium de Tempore (collects and lessons); 4. Proprium Sanctorum (collects, etc., for Saints' Days); 5. Commune Sanctorum (collects, etc., for Saints without special services); 6. Hours of the Virgin, burial services, etc., i.e. Small Offices. It contains neither the Communion Service nor the Mass.

BREVIER. An obsolete name for a size of type equal to about 8 pt.

BRIEF. 1. A letter of authority. 2. A letter of the pope to a religious community, or an individual upon matters of discipline, and differing from a BULL *(q.v.)* by being less solemn and ample, and in the form in which it is written. 3. A letter patent which used to be issued by the sovereign as head of the church, licensing a collection to be made in churches for a specified object or charity. 4. A written description of the requirements for a building to be designed, and supplied to an architect so that he may prepare plans. It sets out the purpose of the building and its various rooms or departments, indicating their size, shape and juxtaposition, and any special features to be provided.

BRIEF CATALOGUING. Simplified cataloguing, especially in respect of details after the imprint and including the tracing, for books that are likely to go into a storage library, for pamphlets, and for other special categories. *See also* LIMITED CATALOGUING, SIMPLIFIED CATALOGUING.

BRIEFLISTING. *(Cataloguing)* A method of briefly cataloguing books which pose problems for the cataloguer, as a means of temporarily reducing a backlog of cataloguing arrears. The books are numbered and arranged numerically on the shelves of the cataloguing department, and an author entry (consisting of the author heading and a photograph of the book's title-page) is prepared for the catalogue. Once a brieflisted book is asked for it is catalogued fully; in the meantime, the service to readers is inadequate due to the absence of subject and added author and other entries. Inadequately catalogued books may tend to congest the cataloguing department unless other steps are taken to clear the backlog.

BRIGHTON/MARC. *See* BRIMARC.

BRILLIANT. An obsolete name for a size of type about 4 pt.

BRIMARC. Abbreviation for Brighton/MARC, 'an experiment in the use of a machine readable national data base and of national processing facilities for the production of a local book catalogue' carried out at the Brighton Public Libraries.

BRING-UP. To bring a block up to the correct printing height by using underlay or interlay.

BRIQUET. A conventional representation on a bookbinding of a steel used with tinder for striking a light.

BRISCH-VISTEM SYSTEM. A system of recording information on punched cards (called 'characteristics cards'), each of which has a thousand numbered squares and is reserved for a particular subject in accordance with a coded scheme of classification appropriate to the general subject area. Holes are punched to record information, each numbered square being allocated to a particular document or item of information; these are indexed alphabetically. Information is obtained by super-imposing cards allocated to the appropriate subjects, the co-incident holes indicating the items possessing the characteristics required. This system is now sold in Great Britain under the trade name VISIscan. *See also* PEEK-A-BOO.

BRISTOL BOARD. A fine quality board made from rags and used for drawings or paintings. It is made by pasting two or more sheets of paper together, the substance being determined by the number of sheets.

BRITISH AND IRISH ASSOCIATION OF LAW LIBRARIANS. Founded in 1969 'to: (a) provide a forum for meetings of all interested in law library work; (b) hold conferences and discussions on bibliographical questions affecting law libraries; (c) promote their better administration; (d) promote whatever may tend to the improvement of the status of law librarians; (e) encourage legal bibliographical study and research; (f) publish information of service or interest to the members of the Association; (g) support and co-operate with any other organizations or activities which tend to benefit the members or objects of the association.' Membership is open to any practising law librarian, government document or inter-governmental document librarian, lecturer in law librarianship, or any person who has held such a post for five years in the U.K., Isle of Man, Channel Islands or the Republic of Ireland. Institutional membership is open to any institutional or professional library in the same areas which has a legal collection or a collection of governmental or inter-governmental documents. Financed entirely from members' subscriptions. Co-operates with the Lord Chancellor's Department concerning libraries in the courts of England and Wales and with other groups of special librarians in the holding of meetings and providing specialist information involving law librarianship. Abbreviated BIALL. Publishes *Law Librarian* (3 p.a.); *Manual of law librarianship* ed. by E. M. Moys (Deutsch for BIALL); *Directory of British law libraries* in preparation.

BRITISH CATALOGUE OF MUSIC. A catalogue of music and books about music published in Great Britain and consisting of entries made from material deposited under the Copyright Acts at the Copyright Receipt Office at the British Museum. Publication, quarterly, began in 1957 under the auspices of the Council of the British National Bibliography. A faceted scheme of classification, drawn up by Mr. E. J. Coates, formerly Editor of the *Catalogue*, is used for arranging entries. This was published in 1960 by the Council of the British National Bibliography. The completion and publication of this catalogue was transferred to the BRITISH LIBRARY (*q.v.*) in 1974. Abbreviated *BCM*.

BRITISH CATALOGUE OF MUSIC CLASSIFICATION. The scheme, drawn up by Mr. E. J. Coates, which is used to classify the entries in the BRITISH CATALOGUE OF MUSIC (*q.v.*).

BRITISH COPYRIGHT COUNCIL. Founded in 1954 as the British Joint Copyright Council. The name was altered and the scope and membership greatly increased in 1965. The aims of the Council are briefly (a) to defend and foster the true principles of copyright; (b) to cherish as an ultimate aim the acceptance of those principles throughout the world; (c) to bring together the bodies who speak for authors, artists, composers, actors, musicians and all others who are partners in or justly interested in the protection of copyright; (d) to keep a vigilant watch on any changes in law, administration, social practice, or mechanical contrivance which may require an amendment to the law; (e) to give attention to any matter relating to copyright brought to notice by a member; (f) to increase public knowledge of the principles, problems and importance of copyright law and practice. The membership of the Council is composed of British societies of authors, artists, actors, musicians and others who are concerned with creative activity.

BRITISH EDUCATION INDEX. Formerly compiled by the Institute of Education in England but now centrally compiled by the BSD of the British Library; indexes articles on education in some fifty British periodicals. It is published four times a year by the Library and is intended to complement the American *Education Index.*

BRITISH HUMANITIES INDEX. A quarterly index, with annual cumulations, of articles appearing in nearly 400 British, and a few Dominion, periodicals; it is published by the Library Association. Prior to January 1962 it was known as the *Subject Index to Periodicals,* and first appeared in 1915; no volumes were issued in the years 1923 to 1925 inclusive. Abbreviated BHI.

BRITISH INSTITUTE OF RECORDED SOUND LTD. A non-profit-making company, registered as a charity, which exists to promote the study and use of recorded sound in all its aspects. A collection of records, international in scope, has been built up since June 1955; this includes music of all countries and periods, literature and drama, speeches and historical events, music hall and popular entertainment, language and dialect, bird song, and everyday sounds doomed to disappear with changing times. Donations of records are desired, private recordings are copied for preservation, and the Institute itself copies B.B.C. transmissions in order to prevent them from being lost to posterity. In addition to the record archive the Institute has a reference library of books, periodicals and record catalogues. Abbreviated BIRS. Publishes *Recorded Sound* (*q.*).

BRITISH LIBRARY. The proposal to set up The British Library was made in a WHITE PAPER (*q.v.*) *The British Library* (Cmnd. 4572) in January 1971. The decision accorded with the main recommendation of the National Libraries Committee, also familiarly known as the DAINTON COMMITTEE chaired by Dr. F. S. Dainton, which reported in June 1969 (Cmnd. 4028). The British Library Act 1972 authorized the establishment of the Library on 1st July 1973. A number of existing libraries were incorporated to provide a large national library, at the same time leaving some specialist national libraries (*See* NATIONAL LIBRARY) to function independently as heretofore. The library now consists of several sections. These are:
1. **The Reference Division** which incorporates the former library departments of the British Museum (the Department of Printed Books including the Map Room, the music and philatelic collections

and the Newspaper Library at Colindale, the Official Publications Library – formerly the State Paper Room, the Department of Manuscripts, the Department of Oriental Manuscripts and Printed Books, and the National Reference Library of Science and Invention which had previously been known until 1973 as the Patent Office Library and is now known as the Science Reference Library). 2. **The Lending Division** (BLLD) incorporating the National Central Library and the National Lending Library for Science and Technology, the largest lending library in the world. 3. **The Bibliographic Services Division** including the former British National Bibliography Ltd., the former acquisition and exchange functions of the British Museum Library, the *British Catalogue of Music*, Machine Readable Catalogue Services (MARC) and the *British Union Catalogue of Periodicals (BUCOP)*. The successors to the (British Museum) General Catalogue of Printed Books and to the Subject Index come under Bibliographical Services which is also the U.K. centre for the allocation of International Standard Serial Numbers (ISSN *q.v.*). 4. The Central Administration Branch, which comprises all the usual financial, administrative, staffing, accommodation and legal services and the Press and Public Relations Section; and the Research and Development Department which incorporates the functions of the former Office for Scientific and Technical Information (OSTI) and carries out, promotes and supports research and development related to library and information operations in the natural and social services and the humanities. The Department's work is directed to the benefit of library and information service as a whole and to this end it can award research grants and contracts to outside bodies.

Several changes of location have been, or are being, made and are as follows: The Reference Division is at the British Museum, Great Russell Street, London, WC1B 3DG, except for the Science Reference Library which is in two buildings, the Holborn Branch (the former Patent Office Library) at 25 Southampton Buildings, Chancery Lane, London, WC2A 1AW, and the Bayswater Branch which houses mainly life-science books and journals at 10 Porchester Gardens, Queensway, London, W2 4DE. The Lending Division is at Boston Spa, Wetherby, Yorkshire, LS23 7BQ. The Bibliographic Services Division is at Store Street, London WC1E 7DG. The Central Administration and the Research and Development Department are both located at Sheraton House, Great Chapel Street, London W1V 4BH. Eventually the parts of the Library which are scattered throughout London will be brought together in a single building to be erected near St. Pancras Station in the Euston Road.

All the libraries which have been absorbed to form the British Library will continue to carry out their functions as indicated under their former names in this *Glossary*. In addition, the Lending Division acts as the U.K. centre for any library wishing to dispose of publications, a function which was previously performed by the British National Book Centre at the National Central Library. It also acts as the national centre for MEDLARS (*q.v.*) searches, and is responsible for a translation service from Russian and Oriental languages.

The British Library is managed by a Board consisting of a part-time Chairman, a Chief Executive who is also Deputy Chairman, the heads of the three operational divisions, and nine part-time members, who are corporately responsible for all the activities of the Library. The policy-making and controlling bodies of the incorporated organizations have consequently ceased to exist, or to function, in respect of the incorporated organizations. The major objectives of the Board are: to (1) develop the best possible British Library library services; (2) promote reference and lending library networks in the U.K.; (3) ensure the provision of appropriate bibliographic services; (4) promote the development and use of a range of flexible information networks; (5) provide British Library information services, as appropriate. Each of the three Divisions has a Director-General, under whom are a number of Directors who are heads of major departments. The Head of the Central Administration Branch is Secretary to the Board. The British Library Act provides for the setting up of one or more Advisory Councils consisting of members nominated by the Secretary of State for Education and Science. These have not been formed but a less formal consultative-committee has been established to advise specifically on lending services. The Library of the Library Association has been incorporated within the Reference Division of the British Library. Publishes *Science Reference Library News* (irreg.), *BLL Review* (q.), *British Library R & D Newsletter* (previously *OSTI Newsletter*), *British Library Journal* (2 p.a.).

BRITISH MUSEUM LIBRARY. The chief British national library, consisting of four departments: Printed Books; Manuscripts; Oriental Printed Books and Manuscripts; Prints and Drawings. As the national deposit library, it receives and preserves for public record a copy of every piece of printed matter published in the United Kingdom, and has benefited under the Copyrights Acts in this way ever since the Royal Library (which had enjoyed the right since 1662) was transferred to the British Museum in 1757 although these rights were not enforced until the middle of the nineteenth century. The Library contains over 7,000,000 printed books, about 75,000 Western and 30,000 Oriental MSS., 121,000 charters and rolls, etc. There is an associated British Museum (Natural History) Library at the Natural History Museum; this does not benefit from the Copyright Act. These are both references libraries. This Library ceased to exist as a part of the British Museum on its incorporation as a major part of The Reference Division of the BRITISH LIBRARY (*q.v.*). The British Museum (Natural History) Library was not so transferred. Abbreviated BML.

BRITISH NATIONAL BIBLIOGRAPHY.† An organization which has issued since 4th January 1950 a weekly printed list of books published in Great Britain. Full catalogue entries are made from books received at the Copyright Office of the British Museum, classified by Dewey's *Decimal Classification* and published each week in classified order, but with appropriate subject headings. The last issue each month contains a monthly author index. Quarterly, half-annual, and annual and five-year cumulations are made. The publications are known as '*BNB*' or *British National Bibliography*. Entries are also available on international standard size cards (12.5 × 7.5 cms. or 5 × 3 inches). This organization was incorporated in the activities of the BRITISH LIBRARY (*q.v.*) in 1974, becoming a major part of the Bibliographic Services Division.

BRITISH NATIONAL BOOK CENTRE. This Centre and the National Central Library became a part of the Lending Division (BLLD) of the BRITISH LIBRARY (*q.v.*) when this was formed in 1974; the centre continues to function, but as the 'Gift and Exchange Section'.

BRITISH NATIONAL COMMITTEE ON PALAEOGRAPHY. A sub-committee on manuscripts of the Standing Conference of National and University Libraries (SCONUL). *See also* SCONUL.

BRITISH PAPER AND BOARD INDUSTRY RESEARCH ASSOCIATION. This Association was concerned with research on pulping, and paper-making processes, the assessment of raw materials, performance of paper-making machinery, performance testing of paper and effluent treatment. It was grant-aided through the Ministry of Technology. Abbreviated BPBIRA. But since the MINISTRY OF TECHNOLOGY (*q.v.*) was dissolved and its research responsibilities distributed, research in the field of printing, paper and board is being undertaken by PIRA. *See entry under* PRINTING AND ALLIED TRADES RESEARCH.

BRITISH RECORD SOCIETY. Formed in 1889 with the object of preserving records and making them accessible to scholars by the publication of indexes in a series known as the *Index Library*. Over 80 volumes have been published relating to various categories of record, and in the last few decades they have been concerned almost exclusively with indexing testamentary records.

BRITISH RECORDS ASSOCIATION. Inaugurated November 1932 to co-ordinate the work of the many individuals, authorities, institutions and societies interested in the conservation and use of archives in the United Kingdom. Its aims are (a) to serve as a link between all authorities, institutions or individuals concerned in the preservation, custody, study and publication of records; (b) to develop informed opinion on the necessity for preserving records of historical importance; (c) to provide a centre for the accumulation and dissemination of all kinds of technical information useful to individuals or institutions engaged in archive work, or in the publication of record sources; (d) to encourage the use of records as historical material, particularly as regards their publication. Abbreviated BRA. Publishes *Archives* (two p.a.).

BRITISH SOCIETY FOR INTERNATIONAL BIBLIOGRAPHY, THE. Founded in 1927 as the British section of the Institut de Bibliographie, known as BSIB, and amalgamated in 1948 with the Association of Special Libraries and Information Bureaux (ASLIB).

BRITISH STANDARDS INSTITUTION.† The approved British body for the preparation and promulgation of national standards covering, inter alia, methods of test; terms, definitions and symbols; standards of quality of performance or of dimensions; preferred ranges; codes of practice. A selection of Standards of interest to librarians, information officers and documentalists include the following:

1219 : 1958 *Recommendations for proof correction and copy presentation.*

1413 : 1970 *Page sizes for books.* [Five metric page sizes and sheet sizes . . . specifically for paperbacks.]

1629 : 1976 *Bibliographical references.*

1749 : 1969 *Alphabetical arrangement and the filing order of numerals and symbols.*

2509 : 1970 *Presentation of serial publications, including periodicals.* [Title page information, form of titles, numbering and dating, table of contents and indexes, presentation of articles, pagination, and format.]

2961 : 1967 *Typeface nomenclature and classification*. [Defines terms frequently used in catalogues and specimen sheets, and gives a system for the classification of typefaces.]

2979 : 1958 *Transliteration of Cyrillic and Greek characters*.

3203 : 1964 *Glossary of paper, stationery and allied terms*.

3700: 1976 *The preparation of indexes to books, periodicals and other publications*.

3814 : 1964 *Glossary of letterpress rotary printing terms used in connection with newspaper, magazine and similar machines*.

4000 : 1968 *Sizes of papers and boards*.

4148 : – *The abbreviation of titles of periodicals Part 1: 1970 Principles*. Principles for establishing title abbreviations for both serial and non-serial publications. Supplemented by *Part 2: 1975 Word-abbreviation list*.

4149 : 1967 *Glossary of paper/ink terms for letterpress printing*. [Defines commonly used terms.]

4277 : 1968 *Glossary of terms used in offset lithographic printing*.

4280 : 1968 *Transliteration of Arabic Characters*.

4719 : 1971 *Title leaves of a book*. [Information to be shown on them and the manner in which it should be presented.]

4748 : 1971 *Bibliographic information interchange format for magnetic tape*.

4754 : 1971 *Presentation of bibliographical information in printed music*.

4762 : 1971 *Book numbering*. [Describes the method of constructing an ISBN (*q.v.*).]

4785 : 1972 *Colour proof correction symbols*.

4811 : 1972 *Presentation of research and development reports*.

4812 : 1972 *The romantization of Japanese*.

4821 : 1972 *Presentation of Theses*.

5195 :   *Bibliographical references to maps and charts. Part 1: 1975 References in accession lists. Part 2: References in books and articles* is in process of publication.

5261 :   *Guide to copy preparation and proof correction. Part 1: 1975 Preparation of typescript copy for printing. Part 2: 1976 Specification for typographic requirements marks for copy preparation and proof correction, proofing procedure*.

Abbreviated BSI. *See also* STANDARDS, Z39.

BRITISH TALKING BOOK SERVICE FOR THE BLIND. *See* **NTBL.**

BRITISH TECHNOLOGY INDEX. A current subject guide to the major articles published in 400 British technical journals; published monthly since January 1962, each twelfth issue being an annual cumulation. Published by the Library Association. Abbreviated *BTI.*

BRITISH THEATRE INSTITUTE. A co-ordinating and information centre for all theatrical activities, which was opened in London early in 1976.

BRITISH UNION CATALOGUE OF PERIODICALS. A list of over 140,000 titles of periodicals of the world, from the seventeenth century to the present day, together with particulars of the holdings of over 440 British libraries. Compiled with funds made available by the Rockefeller Foundation, it was published in four volumes between 1955 and 1958. A *Supplement* to 1960 was published in 1962. It is being kept up-to-date by the Bibliographical Services Division of the BRITISH LIBRARY (*q.v.*), additions and amendments being recorded in the quarterly *BUCOP: new periodical titles* and annual cumulations. Familiarly called *BUCOP.*

BROAD. Applies to a sheet of paper which is divided by halving the long side (i.e. across the narrow way). This is the regular or common way of dividing a sheet. Hence a *broad folio,* quarto, or octavo. The opposite of OBLONG (*q.v.*). A *broad fold* is a sheet folded so that the longest dimension is horizontal; the grain then runs with the shorter dimension of the paper.

BROAD CLASSIFICATION. 1. Use of only the more inclusive classes of a classification scheme, omitting detailed subdivision. Also called 'Reduction of numbers'. 2. A classification scheme which does not provide for minute subdivision of topics. (Both from *Abridged Dewey Decimal Classification,* 10th ed. 1971). 3. An arrangement of books in main classes with little or no sub-division, instead of in their more minute sub-divisions. *See also* CLOSE CLASSIFICATION.

BROAD FOLIO. *See* FOLIO.

BROAD SYSTEM OF ORDERING. *See* BSO.

BROADER TERM. (*Information retrieval*) A term which denotes a concept which is broader than one with a more specific meaning, e.g. Science is broader than Anthropology. *See also* NARROWER TERM, RELATED TERM.

BROADSHEET. A long, narrow advertising leaflet; usually the long quarto of the sheet of paper from which it is cut. It may be printed on both sides. Sometimes used synonymously with BROADSIDE (*q.v.*).

BROADSIDE. A large sheet of paper printed on one side right across the sheet, for sheet distribution, and usually intended to be posted up, e.g. proclamations, ballad sheets, news-sheets, sheet calendars, etc. *See also* BROADSHEET. Also used of a poster of which the width is greater than the depth.

BROADSIDE PAGE. *Synonymous with* LANDSCAPE PAGE (*q.v.*).

BROCHURE. Literally 'a stitched work' (from the French 'brocher,' to stitch). A short printed work of a few leaves, merely stitched together, and not otherwise bound; a pamphlet.

BROKEN BACK. A book whose back has broken open from head to tail. Also called 'Broken binding.'

BROKEN LETTER. One, the face of which is damaged and cannot give a complete impression. Indicated in a proof by placing a small x in the margin. Also called 'Bad letter,' 'Battered letter,' 'Damaged letter,' 'Spoiled letter.'

BROKEN ORDER. The removal of a section, or sections, of the book stock from its proper sequence in the classification in order to facilitate use.

BROKEN-OVER. A PLATE (*q.v.*) or other separate sheet which is to be inserted in a book, and is given a narrow fold near the back, or binding, edge before sewing, etc., to ensure that it will lie flat and turn easily when the book is bound.

BROKERS' CIRCULAR. A circular published by a firm of stockbrokers, sometimes at regular intervals, containing particulars of securities.

BRONZING. Dusting with a fine metallic powder over a sheet freshly printed with ink, varnish or size to give a brilliant, lustrous effect.

BRONZING SIZE. A printing ink made specially for bronzing. The term is sometimes used for printing ink for subsequent printing with metallic ink.

BROTHERS OF THE COMMON LIFE. Monks who maintained monasteries in various parts of Germany and the Low Countries in the last quarter of the fifteenth century and set up printing presses in about sixty of them between 1475 and 1490. Their first dated book was issued in 1476 from the 'Nazareth' Monastery at Brussels.

BROWN CLASSIFICATION. The familiar name for James Duff Brown's *Subject Classification* (*q.v.*). *See also* ADJUSTABLE CLASSIFICATION.

BROWN LIBRARY, JOHN CARTER. A collection of 30,000 books dealing with the discovery and settlement of America to 1800; assembled by John Carter Brown (1797–1874) who was one of America's best-known book collectors. The library was passed on to Brown University, Providence, Rhode Island, U.S.A., in 1900, since when it has grown considerably and is one of the finest collections of Americana in existence.

BROWN MECHANICAL WOODPULP. A woodpulp for paper-making obtained by grinding steamed or boiled logs.

BROWNE BOOK CHARGING SYSTEM. A system of book charging which is attributed to Nina E. Browne, an American Librarian, who described it in 1895. It is, however, very little different from the method adopted about 1873 by Mr. L. G. Virgo, Librarian of Bradford Public Library. The reader has a limited number of tickets, each of which is available for one book only at a time, and which he gives up when books are borrowed and which are handed back when the books are returned. This simple, reliable and speedy method was replaced in America by the Newark and Detroit methods and others based on them, but, until photo-charging was introduced, was the most universally used method in Great Britain. 'Reverse Brown' uses a pocket book-card and a card ticket: this was described by Jacob Schwartz in 1897 and had been in use for a number of years. Since World War Two other methods have taken the place of Browne, but two modifications of this system have enabled it to meet the demands of busier public libraries; these are CHEQUE BOOK CHARGING METHOD and the ISLINGTON CHARGING SYSTEM (qq.v.). An adaptation with the object of reducing queues at the return counter was introduced at Gravesend in 1964 by the Librarian, Mr. E. N. Moore. All books issued within seven days are stamped with the same date for return, which is a Tuesday in order to spread the load from Saturday. The date stamp used also stamps a running number; the charges are not sorted but kept in the order of issue; guide cards bearing two figures are used between each ten charges and one bearing three figures is inserted for each hundredth book issued. In this way it is possible to find required charges without numbering them. A new sequence of numbers is begun each week. *See also* CHARGING METHODS, TOKEN CHARGING.

BROWSABILITY. The ability of an indexing system to lend itself to unsystematic or random searches. This ability is of interest or use to the searcher even though it may not produce a logical answer to the search question (*IBM*).

BROWSE. To investigate, without design, the contents of a collection of books or documents (*IBM*).

BROWSING ROOM. A room provided in an American college, university, or public library which contains novels and non-fiction books on all subjects, but no text books. It is intended for recreational reading and not for study, in order to help achieve which, furnishings are bright and informal. Books may or may not be borrowed for home reading. A development of the POPULAR LIBRARY (*q.v.*).

BRUSH COATED. (*Paper*). Paper given a smooth printing surface by applying the clay, or other, coating substance as a separate and later operation to the actual paper making, in order to make it perfectly smooth so as to take a high degree of finish. *See also* ART, COATED PAPER, MACHINE COATED.

BRUSH-PEN. A pen, with a fibrous point, made of reed, used for writing on papyrus.

BRUSSELS CONVENTION. Popular name for the revision (signed on 26th June 1948) of the BERNE COPYRIGHT UNION (*q.v.*). *See also* COPYRIGHT, INTERNATIONAL.

BRUSSELS EXPANSION. A familiar name for the UNIVERSAL DECIMAL CLASSIFICATION (*q.v.*).

BRYANT MEMORANDUM. The *Memorandum on the present program of the Library of Congress and related agencies*. It comments on the Federal and research library situation and the role of the Library of Congress. It was written in 1962, by Douglas Bryant, Associate Director of the Harvard Library, at the request of Senator Claiborne Pell of Rhode Island who introduced it into the *Congressional Record* for 24th May 1962. The reply by the Librarian of Congress, Mr. L. Quincy Mumford, appeared in the *Congressional Record* for 2nd October 1962.

BUCCS. Acronym of the Bath University Comparative Catalogue Study which was carried out with a grant from OSTI in 1972 – to determine which form (card, printout, COM., rollfilm, or fiche), and which order (name, title, classified, or KWOC) (a) best meets demands on the catalogue; (b) is easiest to use; (c) is most cost-effective.

BUCKET. A section in the memory of a computer. (*IBM*).

BUCKLE-FOLDER. A machine which folds printed sheets by passing them between two continuously revolving rollers placed one above the other until the leading edge touches a stop bar. The rollers continue to impel the rear half of the sheet until it is folded and so carried down between the lower revolving roller and a third one which is parallel to it. *See also* KNIFE-FOLDER.

BUCKLES. (*Binding*) Severe wrinkles near the head and back of the folded sections. *See also* SECTION.

BUCKRAM. A strong textile, either of linen or cotton, used for covering books. *See also* ART CANVAS.

BUCOP. Abbreviation for *British Union Catalogue of Periodicals* (*q.v.*).

BUDGET.   The total amount of money which is available for library purposes after the estimate of anticipated needs has been approved by the appropriate authority.

BUDS.   In bookbinding, an ornament filling a small panel on some rolls: it is a conventionalized form of a spray bearing buds.

BUFFER.   A substance, or mixture of substances, which in document preservation is used to control the acidity or alkalinity of a solution or paper at a pre-determined level, e.g. the use of chalk in the manufacture of paper.

BUILDING-IN MACHINE.   A machine which, in book production, dries cased books in a matter of seconds by means of several applications of heat and pressure. This is an alternative to the slower method of the STANDING PRESS (*q.v.*).

BULK.   1. The thickness of a book exclusive of its covers; this will be less after, than before, binding. Book papers are measured by the thickness of a number of pages. The extremes between which papers of the same weight, but of a different class, vary in bulk may be seen from the following figures, based on 320 pp. of quad crown 100 lb.

Featherweight	53/32 in.	Pure Super – calendered	22/32 in.
Esparto M.F.	29/32 in.	Coated Art	21/32 in.
Pure M.F.	24/32 in.	Imitation Art	20/32 in.

2. The thickness of a sheet of paper related to its weight and measured in thousandths of an inch. 3. To 'bulk' a book is to make it appear bigger than it need be by using a thick but light-weight paper.

BULL.   A formal papal letter under the leaden seal (Bulla).

BULLETIN.   1. A publication, generally a pamphlet, issued by a government, society or other organization at regular intervals and in serial form. 2. A periodical or occasional publication containing lists of books added to a library, and other library information.

BULLETIN BOARD.   A notice board in a library on which are exhibited lists of books, announcements of forthcoming events, jackets of new books added to the library, and miscellaneous library information.

BULLOCK REPORT.   *A language for life, report of the Committee of Inquiry appointed by the Secretary of State for Education and Science under the Chairmanship of Sir Alan Bullock* published in 1975. The Committee was set up by Mrs Thatcher in 1972 when Secretary of State for Education and Science, to inquire into the teaching of reading and the other uses of English in schools.

BUMPED OUT.   (*Printing*) 1. Matter which is widely leaded. 2. A line of characters in which extra spacing has been inserted to square it up with the measure of a longer line.

BUMPER. A machine used to compact the sections of a book after they have been sewn together. Also called a 'Nipper' or 'Smasher'.

BUREAU OF LIBRARIES AND LEARNING RESOURCES. *See* BLLR.

BURGH LIBRARIANS' ASSOCIATION. A Scottish association set up in 1970 to press the case for library powers to be retained in 'second-tier' local government authorities, whereas the Library Association and the Scottish Library Association wanted them to go to regional councils and the islands council, i.e. the 'top tier' authorities. *See also* LOCAL GOVERNMENT BOUNDARIES.

BURIN. An engraver's tool.

BURN-IN. (*Reprography*) The act of exposing sensitized material, or of increasing the exposure of a specific area of sensitized material.

BURN-OUT. (*Reprography*). The complete destruction of the diazo component through exposure to actinic lights.

BURNESS AWARD, JACK K. An award of $500, offered by the Newspaper Division of the Special Library Association and given by the Jack K. Burness Memorial Fund for distinguished newspaper librarianship.

BURNISHED EDGES. Coloured or gilt edges which have been made smooth and bright by a polishing tool.

BURSTING STRAIN. The measurement, expressed in pounds per square inch, of pressure required to rupture paper when being tested on a Mullen or Ashcroft machine.

BUSINESS ARCHIVES COUNCIL. A non-profit-making body supported by voluntary contributions from business firms, universities libraries and record offices, and managed by a committee representing all of these interests. Its objects are to preserve business records and encourage interest in business history. Publishes *Business Archives* (2 a year).

BUTT SPLICE. *See* SPLICE.

BUTTED. (*Printing*). Lines of type, or rules, placed end to end to make larger lines. Also called 'Butted slugs'.

BUTTED SLUGS. *See* BUTTED.

BUTTERFLY PLAN. An arrangement of bookstacks in a butterfly or fan shape. *See also* RADIATING STACKS.

BUTTING. 1. To produce a line of type in the form of a slug (using a Linotype, or similar machine,) which is longer than the machine normally makes (30 picas); the line is set on two slugs which are butted together – placed end to end. 2. To place two pieces of paper, cloth or leather with edges touching.

BYE-LAWS. Bye-laws may be made under the provisions of the Public Libraries and Museums Act 1964, s. 19, regulating the use of facilities provided by the authority under this Act and the conduct of persons in premises where those facilities are provided. Bye-laws may include provisions enabling officers of a local authority to exclude or remove from premises maintained by the authority any person who contravenes the bye-laws. A set of model bye-laws has been prepared at the Department of Education and Science. Before bye-laws can be effective they must be submitted by local authorities in England and Wales to the Secretary of State for confirmation. Bye-laws must be displayed in any premises maintained under the Act to which the public have access. The provisions in Northern Ireland and in Scotland are slightly different.

BYLINE. The line of type at the head of a newspaper or magazine article indicating its authorship. *See also* MASTHEAD.

BYNAME. *See* NICKNAME.

BYTE. (*Information retrieval*) 1. A generic term to indicate a measurable portion of consecutive binary digits, e.g. an eight-bit or six-bit byte. 2. A group of binary digits usually operated as a unit. 3. An element of data which consists of eight data bits plus a parity bit, and represents either one alphabetic, or special, character, two decimal digits, or eight binary bits; a sequence of binary digits which is handled as a unit.

BYZANTINE BINDINGS. Book covers, rather than true bindings, finely wrought in gold and silver, and often inlaid with precious stones. They date from the foundation of Byzantium by Constantine the Great in the fourth century.

c. Abbreviation for CHAPTER (*q.v.*), caput or *circa* (*q.v.*), although in the last instance 'ca' is preferable. Also for the word 'copyright' when used in descriptive notes, though not legally valid in a copyright notice when © should be used.

© The symbol claiming copyright under Article III (1) of the Universal Copyright Convention (*see* COPYRIGHT, INTERNATIONAL); it is required by law to be placed before the name of the copyright proprietor and the year of first publication. The Inter-governmental Copyright Committee, meeting in Washington in October 1957, recommended positions in various kinds of publication where the symbol might be placed: amongst these was the title-page or the page immediately following, or at the end of a book or pamphlet; under the main title or the MASTHEAD (*q.v.*) of a newspaper, magazine or other periodical;

on the face side of a map, print or photograph, either on the actual map or picture (but near the title or the margin) or on the margin.

CCC. Acronym for the Central Classification Committee of FID; it is responsible for the UNIVERSAL DECIMAL CLASSIFICATION (*q.v.*).

CDS. Acronym of the Computerized Documentation Service which was set up in 1971 within Unesco's Department of Documentation, Libraries and Archives to make effective use of the existing computer configuration of Unesco for the information and bibliographic control of the documents and publications from other sources but pertinent to the work of the organization. Beginning in 1973 it started to process information from Member States under the ISORID (*q.v.*) project, and later proceeded to process documents in the field of education to which Unesco devotes the major part of its efforts.

C.D. SYSTEM. Abbreviation for the CLASSIFICATION DECIMALE UNIVERSELLE now known as UNIVERSAL DECIMAL CLASSIFICATION (*q.v.*).

CFSTI. Abbreviation for Clearinghouse for Federal Scientific and Technical Information. A section of the U.S. Department of Commerce; its function is to make available particulars of unclassified (i.e. non-secret) reports in the U.S.A., which it does by publishing a list *United States Government research and development reports* (USGRDR). This clearinghouse was transferred to the National Technical Information Service (*See* NTIS) when this was formed in 1970, and its functions merged with the broader mission of NTIS.

C-LIBRARY. A 'circulating library' as distinct from a D-LIBRARY (*q.v.*).

CN AWARD. An Award made annually at the discretion of the Council of the North Western Branch of the LA on the acceptance by the LA of a Fellowship Thesis written by a member of the N.W. Branch. One or more awards may be made in any year, e.g. three, of £20 each, were made in 1973. Originally, the Award was made in respect of results in the Final Part II (Library Organization and Administration) examination, supplemented with reports from tutor and chief officer. The first recipient was Miss D. A. Harrop in 1957. The Award is financed from interest on a sum of money subscribed as a memorial to Charles Nowell soon after his death. Charles Nowell, an outstanding librarian, had been Chief Librarian of Manchester, President of the LA, and a firm supporter of the Manchester Library School which was accommodated for some years in the Manchester Central Library.

CNRS. Acronym for Centre National de la Recherche Scientifique et

Technique. The most important centre in France for scientific documentation; it was set up in 1939 under the aegis of the Ministry of Education, and maintains a library of periodicals only. It collaborates with a number of documentation centres in compiling a location index of translations and the *Bulletin Signalétique* (formerly *Bulletin Analytique*) which contains brief abstracts of articles on a wide range of scientific subjects. Abbreviated CNRS.

CTFE. Acronym for Colleges of Technology and Further Education, a Group of the Library Association.

ca. Abbreviation for *circa* (*q.v.*).

CABINET. 1. An enclosed rack or frame for holding type cases, galleys, etc.; made formerly of wood but now also of pressed sheet steel. 2. A standard size of card, $4\frac{1}{4} \times 6\frac{1}{2}$ inches.

CABINET EDITION. *See* LIBRARY EDITION.

CABINET SIZE. *See* OBLONG.

CADASTRAL MAP. One drawn on a large scale to show ownership, extent and value of land for purposes of taxation.

CADENZA. An ornamental solo passage towards the end of a piece of music or the end of a section; in a concerto, the cadenza is usually towards the end of the first, or the last, movement. Cadenzas were originally improvised by the soloist who was thus given an opportunity to demonstrate his brilliance as an executant, but are sometimes written by the original or a later, composer. Sometimes they are provided with an accompaniment.

CADIG. Abbreviation for Coventry and District Information Group which was commenced on an informal basis in 1953, with a membership of fifteen, a formal constitution being adopted in 1962 when the membership had reached thirty. The Group aims to promote the rapid and relatively informal exchange of both written and verbal information. It is organized from the City Reference Library, Bayley Lane, Coventry. A computer-produced list of periodical holdings (over 9,000 items) is provided for each member to facilitate rapid exchange of information. Members include educational institutions, industrial organizations, research associations and public libraries. There is no geographical limitation. An annual subscription is payable by members for which they receive a wide range of services.

CAESURA. A break in a line of verse, usually in the middle, or a pause in the reading aloud thereof (which is the intent of the break); rhythm greatly depends on the position of the caesura.

CAIN. Abbreviation for the CAtaloguing and INdexing system which provides comprehensive world-wide coverage of the published literature on agriculture and allied subjects as represented in the collections of the (American) NATIONAL AGRICULTURAL LIBRARY (*q.v.*). The information is issued in machine-readable form at the CAIN data base.

CALCOGRAPHY.   *See* CHALK DRAWING.

CALDEBERRY AWARD.   *See* NEWCOTT-CALDEBERRY LUNCHEON.

CALDECOTT MEDAL.   An award made annually in America for the most distinguished American picture book for children. Named after Randolph Caldecott, the nineteenth-century English artist and book illustrator. The Medal was donated by Frederic G. Melcher and the award is administered by the Children's Services Division of the ALA. The Newbery-Caldecott Awards Committee of the CSD, which numbers 22 plus the chairman, makes the selection. The Medal was designed by Rene Paul Chambellan and is named after the nineteenth-century English artist and book illustrator Randolph Caldecott (1846–1886). It was first awarded (in 1938) to Dorothy P. Lathrop for *Animals of the Bible*.

CALENDAR.   1. A chronological list of documents in a given collection, e.g. charters, state papers, rolls, etc., giving the date and with annotations indicating or summarizing the contents of each. 2. An almanack giving lists of days, months, saints' days, etc., for a given year, or a special list of important days for certain purposes throughout the year e.g. a university or gardening calendar.

CALENDER.   A machine consisting mainly of metal rollers between which paper is passed to give it a smooth surface. The degree of smoothness depends on the pressure of the rollers and the extent to which they close the pores.

CALENDERED PAPER.   Paper that is given a smooth surface by rolling, when newly-made, between smooth cylinders under pressure. Paper which receives a minimum of calendering emerges as an antique. With more calendering it acquires a machine finish, then an English finish, and it finally becomes a super-calendered, glossy sheet. *See also* SUPER-CALENDERED PAPER.

CALF.   A bookbinding leather made from calfskin and so used since at least 1450. It may have a rough or a smooth (the more usual) finish. Books which are full-bound can be further described as being diced, grained, marbled, mottled, scored, sprinkled, stained, or tree, according to the form of decoration used. Special styles are known as antique, divinity, law, reversed or roughened.

CALINET.   A programme created in 1974 by the University of Southern California, the California Institute of Technology and the University of California at Los Angeles to enable the three campuses to share their library facilities.

CALL. *Current Awareness Library Literature* (2 p.a.) presents the tables of contents of over 300 issues of more than 200 library and library-related periodicals.

CALL CARD. *Synonymous with* CALL SLIP (*q.v.*).

CALL NUMBER. As the term implies, the number by which a reader requisitions a book. Usually the classification number (or in fixed location, shelf number) followed by the BOOK NUMBER (*q.v.*) or simply the AUTHOR MARK (*q.v.*). It is used to identify a particular book, and to indicate both its position on the shelves and its position relative to other books; it is marked on the lower part of the spine of a book as well as on catalogue cards and other records. In the Colon Classification, the call number consists of the class number, book number and COLLECTION NUMBER (*q.v.*). The class number fixes the position of a book's specific subject relative to other subjects.

CALL SLIP. A printed blank on which are entered the author, title and call number for books required in a reference or university library. Also called 'Call card', 'Readers' slip'; 'Requisition form'.

CALLIGRAPHIC INITIAL. An initial in a mediaeval illuminated manuscript made by a scribe rather than an artist. Such initials are in ink, and rarely brushed with colour or touched with gold.

CALLIGRAPHY. The art of fine handwriting: penmanship. A calligrapher is a trained penman. Calligraphic types are those designed in close sympathy with the spirit of good handwriting.

CALOTYPE. An early photographic process invented (c. 1839) by W. H. F. Talbot. Paper sensitized with silver iodide was brushed over with a solution of silver nitrate, acetic acid or gallic acid and exposed while wet. Translucent paper permitted a positive to be printed and led to the use of the glass plate. Also called 'Talbotype'.

CAMBRIDGE INDIA PAPER. Trade name for a grade of paper used for Bibles; made by James R. Compton & Bros. Ltd., Bury, Lancashire. So named to distinguish it from OXFORD INDIA PAPER (*q.v.*). *See also* INDIA PAPER.

CAMBRIDGE STYLE. The English style of book decoration characterized by double panels with a flower tool at each of the outer four corners.

CAMEO. A die-stamping process which results in the design being in plain relief on a coloured background.

CAMEO BINDING. A binding having the centre of the boards stamped in relief, in imitation of antique gems or medals. Also called 'Plaquette binding'.

CAMEO-COATED PAPER. An American dull-finished coated paper suitable for printing half-tones with a non-lustrous surface: it is particularly suitable for artistic engravings. The English equivalent is matt-finished art paper. *See also* ART.

CAMEO STAMP. The earliest form of tool for blind tooling used between the eleventh and early sixteenth centuries. It was oval in shape and engraved with a pictorial design; when impressed on the side of a book it resembled a cameo.

CAMERA CARD. An electric accounting machine-size card containing unexposed and unprocessed microfilm in an aperture of the card, and which is to be exposed and processed while in the aperture of the card in order to create an image of a document on the microfilm. A 'copy card' is a similarly-made card used to make a microfilm copy from a camera card which has been exposed and processed (the exposure of the copy card and its processing being carried out with the microfilm in the aperture). *See also* IMAGE CARD.

CAMERA COPY. Material (e.g. table, diagram, photograph, etc.) which is ready for photographing for reproduction, usually by litho, in a publication.

CAMERA MICROFILM. The developed microfilm used in a camera to photograph a document; so used to distinguish the film from a microfilm copy made therefrom. Also called 'First generation microfilm'. *See also* FIRST REPRODUCTION MICROFILM.

CAMERA READY. Typescript which is ready to be photographed as part of a book production process.

CAMERAGRAPH. A similar machine to the photostat, but reproducing work on both sides of the sheet.

CAMPBELL CITATION, FRANCIS JOSEPH. A citation and medal awarded by the ALA for outstanding contributions to library services for the blind.

CAN. A circular metal can (a 'tin') used for storing film.

CAN/SDI. Abbreviation for Canadian Selective Dissemination of Information; a network of which the National Library of Canada operates an automated retrieval system that regularly scans thousands of publications, searching for titles in the fields of the social and behavioural sciences and the humanities of interest to the system's subscribers. CISTI (*q.v.*) is concerned with the scientific fields.

CANADA INSTITUTE FOR SCIENTIFIC AND TECHNICAL INFORMATION. *See* CISTI.

CANADIAN ASSOCIATION FOR INFORMATION SCIENCE. Association Canadienne des Sciences de l'Information. Formed in 1970 to promote the development of information science in Canada by bringing together persons in the many disciplines engaged in the production, storage, retrieval, and transmission of scientific and other information. Membership is open to persons interested in, and to organizations sympathetic to, the aims of the Association. Financed by membership dues, annual conferences of the Association, and publications. Abbreviated CAIS/ACSI. Publishes *Newsletter* (q.), *Journal of the Canadian Association for Information Science* (a.), *Proceedings* (a.).

CANADIAN ASSOCIATION OF CHILDREN'S LIBRARIANS. Formed 1939. Agreed, consequent upon the re-structuring of the Canadian Library Association, to become a Section of the CANADIAN ASSOCIATION OF PUBLIC LIBRARIES (*q.v.*) on certain conditions. Abbreviated CACL. Publishes *CACL Bulletin*.

CANADIAN ASSOCIATION OF COLLEGE AND UNIVERSITY LIBRARIES. A Division of the CANADIAN LIBRARY ASSOCIATION (*q.v.*). Exists to further the interests of librarians and libraries in institutions which offer formal education above the secondary level, and to support the highest aims of education and librarianship. There are three sections: Small Universities Libraries, Community and Technical Colleges and Canadian Academic Research Libraries (CARL); membership of the last is confined to Chief Librarians of academic institutions who have graduated doctoral in both arts and science. An affiliated member of the Association of Universities and Colleges of Canada to which it acts in an advisory capacity on matters relating to academic libraries. Abbreviated CACUL. Publishes *CACUL Newsletter* (6 p.a.) and reports.

CANADIAN ASSOCIATION OF LAW LIBRARIES. Founded in July 1962 as a Chapter of the American Association of Law Libraries with the objects of fostering a spirit of co-operation among Canadian law libraries and increasing their usefulness and efficiency. Any person engaged or interested in law library work may become a member; there are five classes of member: (a) Individual – any person officially connected with a law library or law book collection; (b) Institutional – any law library; (c) Associate – any person interested in a law library or law collection but not directly connected with it; (d) Honorary; (e) Life – persons retired from active work who were formerly individual members. Membership of classes (d) and (e) is by election; of the remainder by payment of appropriate fees.

Abbreviated CALL. Publishes *CALL newsletter, Index to Canadian legal periodical literature.*

CANADIAN ASSOCIATION OF PUBLIC LIBRARIES. A Division of the CANADIAN LIBRARY ASSOCIATION (*q.v.*). Founded in June 1972 at the Canadian Library Association's annual conference; it incorporates three former sections of the Canadian Library Association – Adult Services, Canadian Association of Children's Librarians and Young People's, and aims to further public library service to all Canadians. Provides sections and committees to encourage interchange among public librarians who serve various groups. Awards the annual 'Book of the Year for Children' Medal (*q.v.*). Abbreviated CAPL. Publishes a newsletter.

CANADIAN ASSOCIATION OF SPECIAL LIBRARIES AND INFORMATION SERVICES. A Division of the CANADIAN LIBRARY ASSOCIATION (*q.v.*). Membership is open to special librarians, librarians from subject divisions of academic and public libraries, and specialists in information science. Abbreviated CASLIS. Publishes a newsletter *Agona* (q.) and directories, etc.

CANADIAN BOOK EXCHANGE CENTRE. This Centre was created in 1973 to centralize and improve the surplus exchange services of the National Library of Canada.

CANADIAN LIBRARY ASSOCIATION. Formed in 1946, this Association exists (a) to promote education, science and culture within the nation through library service; (b) to promote high standards of librarianship and the welfare of librarians; (c) to co-operate with library associations both within and outside Canada and with other organizations interested in the promotion of education, science and culture. In 1972 a new structure for the Association was approved by the membership, amended at the Annual General Meeting on 19th June 1973 and became effective on 1st July 1973. The main structure is now based on five type-of-library Divisions: (1) the Canadian Association of College and University Libraries (CACUL); (2) the Canadian Association of Public Libraries (CAPL); (3) the Canadian Association of Special Libraries and Information Services (CASLIS); (4) the Canadian Library Trustees' Association (CLTA) and (5) the Canadian School Library Association (CSLA). Abbreviated CLA. Publishes *Canadian index to periodicals and documentary films* (m., 11 p.a.; annual cumulation); *Canadian Library Journal* (6 p.a); *Feliciter* (8 p.a. membs.) and books.

CANADIAN LIBRARY TRUSTEES' ASSOCIATION. A Division of the CANADIAN LIBRARY ASSOCIATION (*q.v.*). Its main objective is

6

to educate members in the principles of trusteeship; membership is open to all library trustees interested in promoting better public library services. Abbreviated CLTA. Publishes a *Newsletter* (4 p.a.).

CANADIAN MANUAL. *Nonbook materials: the organization of integrated materials. See NON-BOOK MATERIALS.*

CANADIAN NATIONAL SCIENCE LIBRARY. *See* NATIONAL SCIENCE LIBRARY (of Canada).

CANADIAN SCHOOL LIBRARY ASSOCIATION. Founded in 1961; became a Division of the Canadian Library Association in 1973. Aims: to improve the quality of school library service by stimulating interest at all levels of the education system. Abbreviated CSLA. Publishes a newsletter – *Moccasin Telegraph* (3 p.a.).

CANADIAN SOCIO-ECONOMIC INFORMATION MANAGEMENT SYSTEM. *See* CANSIM.

CANCEL. This term is loosely given to a part of a book (leaf, part of a leaf or leaves) on which there is a major error which cannot be allowed to remain, and to the leaf which is printed to take the place of the original. The original leaf, which would be more accurately described as the 'Cancelled leaf' (Cancellandum), is cut out by the binder and the corrected one (cancel, cancelling leaf, cancellans) pasted to its stub. Occasionally both leaves are found in a book, the binder having omitted to remove the cancelled leaf.

CANCEL A LOAN. To record the return of a borrowed book; to cancel the record of its loan.

CANCEL TITLE. A reprinted title-page to replace one cut out.

CANCELLAND. *Synonymous with* CANCELLANDUM (*q.v.*).

CANCELLANDUM. *See* CANCEL.

CANCELLANS. *See* CANCEL.

CANCELLATION. The removal of a leaf of a section of a book because of textual error, or for some other reason, leaving a portion of the leaf in the form of a stub. The portion left is known as a disjunct leaf. The portion of the leaf removed is known as the cancellandum and a leaf inserted to take its place is known as the cancellans. *See also* CANCEL.

CANCELLATION MARK. *Synonymous with* DELETION MARK (*q.v.*).

CANCELLED LEAF. *See* CANCEL.

CANCELLING LEAF. *See* CANCEL.

CANEVARI BINDING. A style of binding named after Demetrio Canevari (1539–1625), physician to Pope Urban VII, and usually consisting of a blind-tooled centre panel enclosing a sunken portion bearing a large cameo either glued to the leather or impressed on it.

CANON. An obsolete name for a size of type equal to about 48 pt. The name is probably derived from the use by early printers of this size of type for printing the Canon of the Mass.

CANONICAL CLASS. (*Classification*) Traditional sub-class of a main class, enumerated as such in a scheme of classification, and not derived on the basis of definite characteristics.

CANONICAL ORDER. (*Cataloguing*) An order for arranging a group of entries, other than by alphabetical sequence, which derives from a convention associated with the material to which the entries refer, as for example, the order of the books of the Bible. (*Classification*) A possible order for terms in an array forming a series of co-ordinate classes. Order by means of a notation. *Synonymous with* MATHEMATICAL ORDER (*q.v.*).

CANSIM. Abbreviation for the Canadian Socio-Economic Information Management System, a time-series data bank established, controlled and maintained by Statistics Canada, the central statistical office of the Federal Government of Canada.

CANTILEVER SHELVING. Shelving in which the shelves rest on cantilever brackets having lugs at the back which engage in slots in the upright. No uprights support the shelves at the front, all the weight being carried on the brackets. This provides a long line of shelving without the obstructions caused by the supporting brackets of the bracket type shelving. Deep shelving of this kind is excellent for bound volumes of newspapers or other large publications it is desired to shelve flat, but firmly secured book supports are essential for books which are to be stood up in the normal way. *See also* BRACKET SHEIVING, SHELVING.

CAOUTCHOUC BINDING. A method of binding which was introduced in about 1840 whereby the spine folds of a book were cut off and the resulting separate leaves attached to each other and to a backing strip by a coating of flexible rubber solution and cased in the ordinary way. The rubber solution eventually perished and the leaves fell out. The process was abandoned about 1870, the method being revived in the late 1940s when the so-called PERFECT (*q.v.*) method was used.

CAP. 1. Abbreviation for capital. 2. (*Binding*). Protection given to the leaves of a book while being tooled by hand, by wrapping and pasting brown paper around all the book except the boards. When so protected, the book is said to be capped.

CAP LINE. (*Printing*) 1. A line of type which is set in capital letters. 2. An imaginary line which runs along the top of capital letters. *See also* ASCENDER LINE, BASE LINE, MEAN LINE.

CAPITALES QUADRATA. *Synonymous with* SQUARE CAPITALS (*q.v.*).

CAPITALIZATION. The use of capital letters.

CAPITALS. The largest letters of any size of type: those kept in the upper of the two cases of printer's type. Sometimes called 'full capitals' to distinguish them from SMALL CAPITALS (*q.v.*). The headings used in this glossary are in capitals. The use of capitals is indicated in a MS. or proof by a treble underlining. Abbreviated caps. *See also* LOWER CASE LETTERS, SMALL CAPITALS, UPPER CASE LETTERS.

CAPPED. *See* CAP.

CAPSA. A cylindrical box used in Roman libraries to hold one or more rolls standing upright.

CAPSTAN. (*Binding*) An ornament, roughly resembling a capstan, which was common on English and French heads-in-medallions rolls.

CAPTION. 1. The heading at the beginning of the text or of a chapter, section, etc. 2. The wording which appears immediately underneath, or adjacent and relating to, an illustration. This is sometimes called 'Cut line', 'Legend', or 'Underline'.

CAPTION TITLE. The title printed at the beginning of a chapter or section, or at the top of a page. Where the title-page of a book is missing, this may be used to provide a title for the entry in a catalogue or bibliography; in such a case a note 'caption title' is normally used. Also called 'Head title', 'Drop-down title', 'Text title'.

CARAVAN LIBRARIES. Mobile libraries drawn by mechanical horses Landrovers or other vehicles which may perform other duties after taking the library to its site. They may be caravans or other trailers adapted for use as mobile libraries. Sometimes these libraries provide static library services in urban areas in emergency or until a permanent branch can be opened or erected. *See also* MOBILE LIBRARY.

CARBONIZED FORMS. Paper so coated with a pressure-transferable pigmented layer so that copies of all or part of original typescript or manuscript can be obtained without inserting separate sheets of carbon paper, and made up into unit books or used in sets or continuous forms. *See also* NCR.

CARBRO. A photographic colour print process (*Verry*).

CARD. A rectangular piece of card (*see* BOARDS 3) of international standard size, usually 5 × 3 inches, 12·5 cm × 7·5 cm (7·5 cm × 12·5 cm in continental countries), having a surface suitable for writing or typing on, and used for entries in catalogues and similar records. *See also* A7 LIBRARY CARD.

CARD CABINET. The case of drawers for accommodating a CARD CATALOGUE (*q.v.*). Also called a 'Card Catalogue Cabinet'.

CARD CATALOGUE. A catalogue, the entries of which are made on cards of uniform size and quality, and stored in any desired order on their edges in drawers or other form of container, each card being restricted to a single entry and with details of class number or call number to enable the item to be found. *See also* A7 LIBRARY CARD, MAIN ENTRY, STANDARD SIZE CARD.

CARD CHARGING. The recording of issues of books by means of book-cards associated with readers' tickets or identification cards.

CARD DRAWER. A drawer for holding cards in a CARD CABINET (*q.v.*). Also called 'Card tray'.

CARD FOUNT. The smallest complete fount of type stocked and sold by a typefounder.

CARD INDEX. An index made on cards usually of standard size (5 × 3 inches) and kept on their edges in a drawer. *See also* CARD, STANDARD SIZE CARD.

CARD NUMBER. A symbol consisting of numbers, or a combination of letters and numbers, and possibly the date, used to identify particular entries on centrally produced printed catalogue cards such as those of the British National Bibliography or the Library of Congress, mainly to facilitate ordering.

CARD-OPERATED TYPEWRITER. A typewriter into which is fed punched cards and which, when the electric current is switched on, automatically types on paper in the ordinary way. Some machines similarly type from punched paper tape.

CARD RANDOM ACTION MACHINE. *See* CRAM.

CARD STOCK. A 'board', or heavy weight paper, usually over ·006 inch in thickness made to withstand heavy wear in tabulating or punched card machines, or in catalogues.

CARD TO CARD PRINTER. A machine which produces, by contact printing, duplicate card mounted microfilm.

CARD TRAY. *Synonymous with* CARD DRAWER (*q.v.*).

CARD-A-LENT. A shared profit type of service which consists of the weekly despatch of abstracts which have appeared in *Engineering Index* on 5 × 3 inch cards. There are 167 technical specialities, or 'Divisions', for which subscriptions may be paid at choice.

CARDATYPE. Trade name for a card-operated typewriter which reads punched cards and causes a typewriter to transcribe the punching on to some form of record.

CARDING. A North American term for making out cards for books and other library materials, either from the materials themselves or from lists, to be used when checking records for ownership or for bibliographic accuracy, and possibly later as part of the acquisition record.

CARDMASTER. 1. Trade name for a simple duplicating device specially designed for producing catalogue cards. Stencils are cut from mimeograph machine stencils, inserted in a holder and inked on a card-size pad. Also called a 'Chiang Small Duplicator'. 2. Trade name for a make of rotary card filing cabinet. *See also* ROTARY CARD FILE.

CARET (*Lat.*: 'it needs'). The mark (ʌ) used in a MS. or proof to signify that something is omitted and indicate where an addition or insertion is to be made. Also called 'Insertion mark'.

CARNEGIE LIBRARY. A library built with the financial assistance of funds given by Andrew Carnegie.

CARNEGIE MEDAL. An award made by the Library Association to the writer of an outstanding book for children. The book must be written in English and have been published in the United Kingdom during the year preceding the presentation of the award. Named after Andrew Carnegie (1835–1918) the iron-master and philanthropist, it was first awarded in 1936 to Arthur Ransome for *Pigeon Post*. A list of the books awarded the Medal is published in the Library Association *Year book*.

CAROLINGIAN. A minuscule book hand developed in France in the eighth century from the Roman cursive, much influenced by the English half uncial. The Carolingian minuscule is the prototype of the modern styles of penmanship, and of lower case roman type. It belongs to the second dynasty of French Kings founded by Carl the Great (Charlemagne) and much of its success was due to Alcuin of York, a distinguished English scholar, churchman and poet, who took charge of the Abbey of St. Martin at Tours at the invitation of Charlemagne. It was the dominant book hand for nearly three centuries.

CARREL. A small room connected with a reference library, which is set aside for continuous research work by one reader and in which books, note-books, etc. may be securely locked during the temporary absence of the reader. This word is now used in America to indicate any table or other space reserved for one reader which provides by means of front and side screening a more or less secluded study and writing area, whether or not facilities are provided for locking up books. Such facilities for up to four readers are also called carrels. *Closed carrels* are cubicles which give complete seclusion. *Open carrels* give partial seclusion. *Suspended carrels* are those which are provided by fitting (suspending) writing areas similar to table tops into the uprights of steel shelving to give writing space in stack rooms. *See also* OASIS.

CARRIAGE. A flat frame bearing the guide rails on which the plank (supporting the stone on which rests the forme) of a hand printing machine moves to its printing position.

CART. A small book box, not on wheels, but divided into sections to display children's books face up. (American.) Called in Europe a KINDERBOX (*q.v.*).

CARTER G. WOODSON BOOK AWARD. *See* WOODSON BOOK AWARD, CARTER G.

CARTOBIBLIOGRAPHY. A bibliography of maps.

CARTOGRAM. A highly abstracted, simplified map the purpose of which is to demonstrate a single idea in a diagrammatic way. In order to do this outlines of land or the exact locations of other features are often altered.

CARTOGRAPHER. A maker of maps.

CARTOGRAPHER ENTRY. An entry under a cartographer's name.

CARTOGRAPHY. The science and art of making maps.

CARTOUCHE. 1. A frame, either simple or decorative, or a scroll, in which the title, name of the cartographer, and other particulars relating to a map are placed. The cartouche usually appears in a corner of the map, and in old maps was frequently adorned with country scenes, animals, human figures, armorial or architectural designs, etc. 2. A drawn framing of an engraving, etc. 3. (*Binding*) A small rectangular ornament formed on blind rolls by one or more lines, generally with a plain centre.

CARTOUCHE TITLE. The title which appears within the cartouche or scroll-like design on a map or engraving.

CARTRIDGE. A single-core container enclosing (a) processed microforms, for insertion into readers, reader-printers and retrieval devices, the film requiring no threading or rewinding; the cartridge containing the film is inserted in the projector and the machine turned on; (b) a plastic box containing a continuous loop of sound tape for insertion into a sound reproducing machine, thus providing continuous playback without rewinding.

CARTRIDGE PAPER. A hard, tough paper made with a rough surface and in a number of grades; used for drawing upon. Also a grade of paper used as an ENDPAPER (*q.v.*).

CARTULARY. *Synonymous with* CHARTULARY (*q.v.*).

CASE. (*Binding*) The cover for a book which is made completely before being attached to a book by means of the endpapers and sometimes tapes in addition. (*Printing*) In hand composition, a tray divided by 'bars' into compartments in which printer's individual letters, numerals and spaces are kept and which is placed on the FRAME (*q.v.*) when in use, and in a cabinet when idle. The arrangement of the compartments is the same for all types and sizes. Cases may be in pairs, an upper and a lower containing respectively the capitals and small letters (hence *upper* case (u.c.) and *lower* case (l.c.)) or the whole fount may be in a double unit. *See also* CASING.

CASE BINDING.　*See* CASE.

CASE BOOK.　A book bearing a cloth cover, as originally issued by the publisher. Thus 'cased'.

CASED.　*See* CASE BOOK.

CASING.　The operation of inserting a sewn book into its case, or cover, which is made separately from the book, and pasted to the book by means of endpapers.

CASLON.　A type face designed and cut in 1722 by William Caslon (1692–1766), England's first and greatest type-founder. It is an OLD FACE (*q.v.*) type and is one of the most widely used of all type faces in American and British printing. For a specimen alphabet, *see* TYPE FACE.

CASSETTE.　1. A double-core container enclosing processed roll microfilm for insertion into readers, micro-printers and retrieval devices. 2. A container for film or audiotape for insertion into a camera, projector, reader or tape-recorder.

CASSIE.　An old term, derived from the Fr. *cassé* (broken), for the outside and frequently damaged sheets of a ream of good paper. 'Cassie quires' are the two outside quires of a ream, also called 'Coding quires'.

CAST COATED PAPER.　A very expensive American art paper with an exceptionally soft, absorbent and uniformly flat surface. It was developed about 1950.

CAST-UP.　To calculate the cost of composing type.

CASTING BOX.　(*Printing*) A machine, or device, for casting stereos.

CASTING OFF.　The process of estimating the amount of space COPY (*q.v.*) will occupy when set up in a given size of type.

CASUAL MNEMONICS.　Characters used mnemonically in a scheme of classification where letters in the notation are used to indicate subjects, the notation letter being the same as the first letter of the name of the subject. They are used in particular circumstances and not as part of the normal method of notation. *See also* MNEMONICS.

CATALOGUE.　(*Noun*) A list of books, maps, or other items, arranged in some definite order. It records, describes and indexes (usually completely) the resources of a collection, a library or a group of libraries. To be distinguished from (1) a list, which may or may not be in any particular order and may be incomplete, and (2) a bibliography, which may not be confined to any one collection of books or to a particular group of libraries. Each entry bears details of class number or call number to enable the item to be found, as well as sufficient details (such as author, title, date of publication, editorship, illustrations, pagination and edition) to identify and describe the book. (*Verb*) To compile a list of documents according to a set of rules so as to enable the consulter to know what items are available, and from the class number, call number, or other means of identification, where they may be found. In a special library, in addition to entries under authors, subjects, and possibly titles, it may include (a) analytical entries; (b) abstracts – especially in scientific and technical libraries; (c) annotations indicating the treatment or coverage of the subject; (d) entries under subjects for work in progress and for individuals who are authoritative sources of information on specific subjects; (e) entries for pertinent information material in other parts of the organization or in other libraries.

CATALOGUE CARD. 1. A plain or ruled card on which catalogue entries may be made. 2. A card containing such an entry. *See also* STANDARD SIZE CARD.

CATALOGUE CODE. A set of rules for guidance of cataloguers in preparing entries for catalogues so as to ensure uniformity in treatment. Such codes may include rules for subject cataloguing, and for filing and arranging entries. Examples are: the *Anglo-American cataloguing rules*, *A.L.A. rules for filing catalog cards*, *Rules for a dictionary catalogue* by A. C. Cutter, and the Library of Congress *Rules for descriptive cataloging in the Library of Congress*. Examples of rules for cataloguing special materials are Music Library Association/American Library Association *Code for cataloguing music and phonorecords*, Guppy, H., *Rules for the cataloguing of incunabula*; Unesco, *International rules for the cataloguing of educational, scientific and cultural films and filmstrips*; Cataloguing Committee of the Aslib Film Production Librarians Group *Film cataloguing rules*; British Film Institute *Rules for use in the Cataloguing Department of the National Film Archive*. *See also* ANGLO-AMERICAN CODE NON-BOOK MATERIALS.

CATALOGUE DRAWER, CATALOGUE TRAY. One of the drawers of a card catalogue, in which catalogue cards are kept.

CATALOGUE RAISONNÉ. A catalogue of an author's work, especially of an artist's pictures, engravings, etc., usually arranged by subjects, with comments, elucidations, appraisals, and bibliographical details. Also called '*Classed catalogue*' and '*Classified catalogue*' (*qq.v.*).

CATALOGUER. A librarian who prepares an entry for a catalogue.

CATALOGUING. Strictly, the process of making entries for a catalogue; it may also cover all the processes involved in preparing books for the shelves, or simply the preparation of entries for the catalogue.

CATALOGUING, PRINCIPLES OF. There may be said to be seven basic principles of cataloguing, five (multiple approach, unique entry, inevitable association, probable association, specific entry) common to all types of entry, and two (adequate description, concise description) relating to book description. See under the names of the various principles.

CATALOGUING AND INDEXING GROUP. A Group of the Library Association. It was formed in 1964 and came into official existence on 1st January 1965. Aims: to unite members of the LA engaged in, or interested in, the planning, production or maintenance of library catalogues, and of bibliographies and indexes, and to promote the study and discussion of questions relating to those activities. Abbreviated CIG. Publishes *Catalogue and Index* (q.).

CATALOGUING DEPARTMENT. The department of a library which deals with the ordering, cataloguing and classification of books, together with their processing, i.e. preparation for issue to the library users. Where there is no ORDER DEPARTMENT (*q.v.*), the work of ordering and processing books is also done here. In some American libraries, the work of preparing the books for the shelves, other than cataloguing and classification, is carried out in a separate department.

CATALOGUING IN PUBLICATION. A resurrection of the Cataloguing in Source (CIS) scheme on 1st July 1971 was made possible by grants of $200,000 from both the National Endowment for the Humanities and the Council on Library Resources, Inc. for an experimental period of two years. During this period the number of books catalogued prior to publication and for which LC cards are printed on or before publication, increased rapidly. In 1974 about 65% of the current U.S. book trade output was being covered by this scheme. The Library of Congress cataloguers, on receipt of galley proofs from publishers, catalogue the books and send the publishers those elements of cataloguing that require professional decisions for incorporation in the books. Completed data contains details for catalogue entries – everything now on a LC printed card except for the information between the end of the title proper and the beginning of the series statement plus LC and DDC classification numbers, the

LC catalogue card number, and the ISBN number, if supplied by the publisher. This is returned to the publisher for printing on the back of the title-page. The complete cataloguing record (containing the full cataloguing information except the collation area and pagination in the notes area) is entered in the MARC system. On receipt of the published book, the collation and pagination area are added, and the complete MARC-CIP record is disseminated to all MARC subscribers. Several other countries have also developed, or are developing, similar programmes. In the U.K., a corresponding scheme was commenced in 1976, as part of the centralized cataloguing services provided by the British Library's Bibliographic Services Division, by inviting all publishers to print advance cataloguing information in the books themselves. Abbreviated CIP.

CATALOGUING IN SOURCE. Cataloguing books before they are published, the entries being compiled from proof copies made available by the publishers, and the work being carried out by a centralized agency so that full cataloguing information is printed in the books concerned, and also so that catalogue cards are available for purchase on the day of a book's publication. A grant was made by the Council on Library Resources, Inc. to the Library of Congress in 1958 to test the financial and technical feasibility and the utility of such cataloguing. The Library of Congress reported in 1960 that the experiment which had been carried out in conjunction with other bodies indicated that such cataloguing was not practicable because of the very high cost of the programme to both publishers and the Library of Congress, disruptions of publishing schedules, the high degree of unreliability of catalogue entries based on texts not in their final form, and the low degree of utility which would result from the copying of these entries. *See also* CATALOGUING-IN-PUBLICATION.

CATALOGUING RULES. *See* CATALOGUE CODE.

CATCH. A metal plate secured to a book cover and having a bar, over which the clasp fits. Sometimes a pin is used instead of there being a bar.

CATCH LETTERS. Groups of letters (usually three in a group) appearing in dictionaries, gazetteers, etc., at the tops of pages to indicate the first or last words of a page or column. Those on *verso* pages represent the first three letters of the first word on that page, those on the *recto* represent the first three of the last word on that page. Sometimes two groups of letters joined by a hyphen indicate the first and last words on a page.

CATCH STITCH. *Synonymous with* KETTLE STITCH (*q.v.*). Also a stitch made when sewing on tapes by passing the needle (after it comes out of the right side of the tape and before it goes across the tape) eye-end down under three or four threads below it and then into the loop so formed. The thread is then pulled up tight to form a knot in the centre of the tape before being drawn back into the middle of the section. This is done to avoid too great looseness.

CATCH TITLE. *Synonymous with* CATCHWORD TITLE (*q.v.*).

CATCHLINE. A line of type inserted temporarily at the top of matter by the compositor in order to identify it, and so printed on proofs. Also the name given to a short line of type in between two large displayed lines.

CATCHMENT AREA. (*County Libraries*). In library planning denotes the area from which readers may be expected to be drawn to a given library service point.

CATCHWORD. 1. The word occurring at the bottom of a page after the last line, such word being the first on the following page. Catch-words originally appeared at the last page of a quire of a MS. and served as a guide to the binder. Later, they appeared at the foot of every verso, sometimes every page, but in conjunction with the signa-ture served no useful purpose and were discontinued in the nineteenth century. Also called 'Direction word'. 2. A word at the top of a page or column in encyclopaedias and works of a similar nature, denoting the first or last heading dealt with on the page. 3. In indexing, the word or words which govern the position of an entry in the index.

CATCHWORD ENTRY. An entry in a catalogue, bibliography or index under some striking word in a book's title, other than the first, which is likely to be remembered, and so selected as entry word.

CATCHWORD INDEX. One which uses a significant word from a title or text to index an item (*IBM*).

CATCHWORD TITLE. A PARTIAL TITLE (*q.v.*) consisting of some striking or easily remembered word or phrase. It may be the same as a sub-title or the ALTERNATIVE TITLE (*q.v.*). Also called 'Catch title'.

CATEGORICAL TABLES. In J. D. Brown's *Subject classification*, tables representing forms, standpoints, qualifications and other modes of dividing subjects. Each term in the tables is given a number (0 to 975). These are added (after a point which is used as a separating device) to subject numbers in any part of the classification:

        e.g. .1   Bibliography.
            .2   Dictionaries.
           .10 History.
           .33 Travel.
           .57 Museums.

Examples of the application of numbers from the Categorical Tables:

Russia S 000.

- Bibliography of   S 000.1
- History of   S 000.10
- Travel in   S 000.33
- Museums in   S 000.57

London U 900.

- Bibliography of   U 900.1
- Dictionary of   U 900.2
- History of   U 900.10
- Travel in   U 900.33
- Museums in   U 900.57

CATEGORY. (*Classification*) A term with varying meanings. 1. A 'point of view' according to which a subject can be divided. (*Wildhack*). Considered by some to be synonymous with FACET (*q.v.*). 2. 'A concept of high generality and wide application which can be used to group other concepts' (*Glossary and subject index*). *See also* FUNDAMENTAL CATEGORIES. 3. A comprehensive class or description of things (*IBM*). 4. A logical grouping of associated documents (*IBM*). 5. A class or division formed for purposes of a given classification. In faceted classification, special distinctions are made between categories, classes, facets and phases (*IBM*). *See also* FUNDAMENTAL CATEGORIES.

CATENA. A series of extracts from the writings of the fathers, arranged with independent additions to eludicate scripture and provide a commentary thereon.

CATENATI. Chained books.

CATER-CORNERED. Paper which is cut diagonally, not square.

CATHEDRAL BINDING. One decorated with Gothic architectural motifs, often including a rose window, done between 1815 and 1840 in England and France. In England the decoration was sometimes built up of large single tools: in France it was normally stamped on the covers. This was a revival by the nineteenth century binder Thouvenin of the ARCHITECTURAL BINDING (*q.v.*) style.

CATHOLIC LIBRARY ASSOCIATION. Founded 1921 in the U.S.A. to initiate, foster, and encourage any movement toward the development of Catholic literature and Catholic library work. Abbreviated CLA. Publishes *Catholic library world* (10 p.a.); *Catholic periodical and literature index* (6 p.a.); *Handbook and membership directory* (a.).

CAT'S PAW CALF. (*Binding*). An acid strain pattern on a calf binding which resembles the paw marks of a cat.

CAWTHORNE PRIZE. An award instituted in memory of the late Mr. Albert Cawthorne, formerly Chief Librarian of Stepney as a result of a gift of £300 worth of shares by his son, Mr. B. A. Cawthorne. The interest on these shares is awarded each year to the candidate obtaining the highest marks in Part I of the Library Association's professional examinations, and was first awarded to Mr. G. K. Barnett in 1965.

CEASED PUBLICATION. A work in several volumes, the publication of which was not completed, or a periodical, the publication of which has been discontinued.

CEDILLA. The mark under the letter ç to indicate that it has a sound other than that of *k*; in French it has the sound of *s* and in Spanish of *th*.

CEL. Generally a sheet of transparent acetate on which letters, characters or objects are printed or painted. They are used as overlays on top of an opaque background, and can be exchanged for other cels over the same background.

CELL. An area in a library formed by placing two free-standing book-cases against wall shelving. This arrangement was used by Sir Christopher Wren at Trinity College, Cambridge, in 1676. Usually called 'Alcove'.

CELLO-CLIPS. Clips, two of which can be affixed to the top edges of maps, large or heavy drawings, or plastic relief models, for suspension from horizontal rods.

CELLULOSE. The common term for chemical wood pulp, the basic substance of paper manufacture. It is the predominating constituent of plant tissues from which it must be separated before it can be used.

CELLULOSE ACETATE. *See* FILM BASE.

CELLULOSE TRIACETATE. *See* FILM BASE.

CEN. *See* EUROPEAN COMMITTEE FOR CO-ORDINATION OF STANDARDS.

CENELEC. *See* EUROPEAN COMMITTEE FOR CO-ORDINATION OF STANDARDS.

CENSORSHIP. Prohibition of the production, distribution, circulation or sale of material considered to be objectionable for reasons of politics, religion, obscenity or blasphemy. This action is usually taken by persons empowered to act by federal, national, state or local laws, and takes the forms of preventing publications passing through the Customs or through the post, or of action in a law court to prevent their sale. *See also* INDEX LIBRORUM PROHIBITORUM.

CENTER FOR DOCUMENTATION AND COMMUNICATION RESEARCH. This organization is based on the School of Library

Science at Western Reserve University, Cleveland, Ohio, U.S.A., and is concerned with machine literature searching. Abbreviated CDCR.

CENTER FOR RESEARCH LIBRARIES. An American co-operative scheme to house little-used materials integrated into a collection in which duplicates are eliminated in order to sponsor broader co-operation including co-operative acquisition. Proposed in 1941, it started in 1951. Members (now nearly 140) share operating costs. It is situated in Chicago, and was known as the Midwest Inter-Library Center, abbreviated MILC until the Spring of 1965 when, because it served institutions in eleven States and the University of Toronto in Canada, it was decided to change its name. Its scope now extends to all research libraries in the U.S.A. and Canada, and potentially, Mexico. With a grant of $450,000 from the Carnegie Foundation, a national experiment was begun in January 1973 in lending infrequently-used journals such as those in foreign languages and in highly specialized subject fields. Over a five-year period the Center will acquire 6,000 titles in addition to the 7,000 already available for loan. The Center is to work in close co-operation with the Lending Division (at Boston Spa, England) of the British Library. Abbreviated CRL. *See also* LIBRARY RESEARCH CENTER.

CENTESIMAL DEVICE. A method used in the Universal Decimal Classification to lengthen arrays where nine divisions are inadequate; the digits 11–99 are used to represent co-ordinate subjects instead of 1–9.

CENTRAL ADVISORY COUNCIL FOR EDUCATION (ENGLAND). This organization developed from a Consultative Committee which existed prior to the Second World War and was responsible for enquiries which resulted in such reports as the Hadow Report; it ceased to function during the war but was known as the Central Advisory Council for Education from 1946 until it was reconstituted in August 1963. Enquiries which have been undertaken in recent years have been published as *Early leaving, 15 to 18* (the Crowther Report), *Half our future* (the Newsom Report) and *Children and their primary schools* (the Plowden Report). There is a separate Council for Wales.

CENTRAL CATALOGUE. 1. A catalogue placed in the central library of a library system but containing entries for books in all the libraries. 2. A catalogue of the central library of a library system.

CENTRAL LIBRARY. 1. The chief library in a system, containing the office of the chief librarian, the administrative department, and the largest collections of books. Sometimes called the 'Main Library'; if a public library it is usually situated in the centre or busiest part of a town, if a non-public library it would be at the most important or effective place in the organization, possibly at the headquarters. 2. The library which is provided in a primary school for all the children to use as distinct from the class library which is placed in each class room. Also called a 'General library.'

CENTRAL MUSIC LIBRARY. A limited company which is housed at the Buckingham Palace Road Branch of the Westminster City Public Libraries and administered by the Westminster City Council. Founded on 21 October 1948 by an original donation of £10,000 from Winifred Christie Moór, it includes the former collections of Gerald Cooper, Edwin Evans and his father, Charles Woodhouse and Eric Blom. The large collection of sheet and bound music, as well as the books, are available for loan through public libraries. Thematic indexes are published with the financial support of the Arts Council and the British Council. From 1st January 1974 this Library became a back-up library of the British Library Lending Division (BLLD), applications for the loan of books, scores and periodicals being made on BLLD forms. A catalogue of the Library's complete holdings of books about music (including opera libretti but not scores or periodical literature) is to be published; it will be a computer production on sale in both print-out and microfilm versions. Abbreviated CML.

CENTRAL PROCESSING UNIT. (*Information retrieval*) The centre of any digital computer system; it co-ordinates and controls the activities of all the other units and performs all the logical and arithmetic processes to be applied to data. All program instructions to be executed must be held within the central processing unit, and all data to be processed must first be loaded into this unit.

CENTRAL SHELF LIST. 1. A shelf list recording all the books in the central library of a system of libraries. 2. A combined shelf list, housed in the central library, but recording all books in all the libraries of a library system.

CENTRALIZED CATALOGUING. 1. The cataloguing of books by some central bureau, and the distribution therefrom, of printed entries on catalogue cards, or otherwise. Notably the Library of Congress scheme and the British National Bibliography. 2. The cataloguing at one library of all the books of a library system comprising more than one library, thus achieving uniformity throughout the system.

CENTRALIZED PROCESSING. In the U.S.A., the Library Services

Act has stimulated the setting up of processing centres for the purchase, cataloguing, classifying and processing of books, audio-visual and other material for a number of libraries. This has resulted in considerable economies and the freeing of professional staff for other duties.

CENTRALIZED REGISTRATION. The registering of readers at one library in a system, comprising several libraries, rather than at those at which the application forms are handed in.

CENTRE. 1. In an English county library, a small static library service point, provided in premises which may at times be used for other purposes, open less than ten hours a week, having a stock which is changed from time to time, and staffed by voluntary or paid librarians. 2. An organization, with or without a building for its exclusive use, which makes available at one central point a pool of specialized personnel and information, or services, for the benefit of other organizations or individuals. *See also* DOCUMENT CENTRE, REFERRAL CENTRE, INFORMATION EVALUATION CENTRE, RESEARCH LIBRARY.

CENTRE FOR EPISCOPAL ACTA. Established at the Borthwick Institute of the University of York; the Centre has taken over a central index of English episcopal *acta* relating to the twelfth and thirteenth centuries which had been established at the Institute, and with the assistance of The British Academy is publishing volumes of bishops' *acta*.

CENTRE FOR INFORMATION SCIENCE. A department of the City University, London, which runs a twelve months' full-time MSc in information science course and also a two-year day release Diploma course. These courses, long recognized by the INSTITUTE OF INFORMATION SCIENTISTS (*q.v.*), now give exemption from the Library Association's registration examinations. Their predecessors were the first courses in information science to be offered in the U.K. – *Dr. R. T. Bottle.*

CENTRE NATIONAL DE LA RECHERCHE SCIENTIFIQUE ET TECHNIQUE. *See* CNRS.

CENTRE NOTE. (*Printing*) A note, or reference, placed between columns of text as in a Bible. *See also* INCUT NOTE.

CENTRED DOT. (*Printing*) A period placed higher than the base line of a piece of type, as, c·e·n·t·r·e·d, to show multiplication ($1·2 = 2$), or to separate roman capitals in the classic form of inscriptions (M·A·R·C·V·S). Also called 'Space dot.'

CENTRED HEADING. (*Classification*) A typographical device used with the Dewey Decimal Classification. It consists of a range of notation numbers and a heading, which are centred on the page instead of the numbers being in the usual column, and represents a concept for which there is no specific number in the hierarchy of notation, and which therefore covers a span of numbers.

CENTREING ARROWS. Markings on a document to aid positioning of the document when filming, and of the microfilm when mounting.

CENTREPIECE. (*Binding*) An ornament, usually ARABESQUE (*q.v.*), placed in the centre of the cover of a bound book and often used with cornerpieces, or cornerstamps. It was a favourite style of binding in the late sixteenth and early seventeenth centuries. Also used of a piece of metal usually embossed and engraved, and fastened on to the cover. Also called 'Centrestamp.'

CENTRESTAMP. *Synonymous with* CENTREPIECE (*q.v.*).

CENTRO DE DOCUMENTAÇAO CIENTIFICA. The Portuguese Scientific Documentation Centre was formed to survey the country's library resources and to rationalize holdings.

CENTRO DE DOCUMENTACIÓN CIENTIFICA Y TÉCNICA. The Mexican Centre of Scientific and Technical Documentation.

CERNE, BOOK OF. An illuminated MS. of the Passion and Resurrection portions of the Gospels, written at Lichfield in the early 9th century, so named as it was formerly kept at Cerne Abbey, Dorset; it is now in the Library of Cambridge University. The style of decoration is severely calligraphic and the colours used are light shades with only occasional gold; some pages are enlivened with beasts.

CEROGRAPH. A wax engraving process usually used for making maps. A drawing is made direct on wax spread over a copper plate which is then used as a mould from which an electrotype is made. Also called 'Cerotype.'

CEROGRAPHY. The process used for making cerographic prints. *See also* CEROGRAPH.

CEROTYPE. A print made by the cerographic process. *See also* CEROGRAPH.

CERTIFICATE OF ISSUE. The statement, printed in a LIMITED EDITION (*q.v.*), certifying the number of copies printed and sometimes bearing the autograph of the author and/or illustrator.

CERTIFICATION. (*Archives*) 1. The act of attesting that a document, or a reproduction of a document, is what it purports to be. 2. The document containing such an attestation. *See also* AUTHENTICATION.

CETIS. Acronym for Centre Européen pour le Traitement de l'Information Scientifique; it was set up by EURATOM (Organisation

Atomique Européene) to standardize documentary method and establish a European network of information in the field of nuclear energy. *See also* COPIC.

cf. Abbreviation for *confer* (*q.v.*) (*Lat.*, meaning 'compare').

ch. Abbreviation for CHAPTER (*q.v.*).

CHAIN. (*Classification*) The succession of divisions subordinate one to another expressing the relation 'A includes B, which in turn includes C' (or, conversely, 'C is part of B, which is part of A'), e.g. Literature, English Literature, English Poetry, Shakespeare's Poetry, *Adonis*, constitute a chain of divisions in the class Literature. A hierarchy of terms, each containing or including all which follow it in the same series: a hierarchy of sub-classes of decreasing extension and increasing intension, devised by successive division. The chain of progression in a scheme of classification from general to specific may be:

    780 Music
      782 Dramatic music
        782·1 Opera
          782·154 Wagner *Die Meistersinger*

The indexer, using the principle of chain indexing, works his way back from the most specific step to more general terms, and in this case would provide these entries:

Operas by individual composers	782·154
Opera	782·1
Music: Dramatic	782
Music	780

CHAIN INDEX. An alphabetic index wherein a heading is provided for each term, or link for all the terms used in a subject heading or classification (*IBM*). Each term represented by a given part of the classification symbol, followed by the term for each other part, appears as a heading in the reverse order of the symbol, so that the last term in the symbol becomes the first. If the symbol is comprised of four parts, there will be four entries: the first consisting of four terms; the second, of three after the first term of the previous entry has been omitted; the third, of two, and so on. The final one is the heading for the symbol with the widest connotation, and the most extension, relating to the subject in question. *See also* CORRELATIVE INDEX, RELATIVE INDEX.

CHAIN INDEXING. *See* CHAIN.

CHAIN LINE. *See* LAID PAPER.

CHAIN MARK. *See* LAID PAPER.

CHAIN PROCEDURE. (*Cataloguing*) A method of constructing subject index entries, without permutation of components, by citing terms contained in particular chains. *See also* CHAIN. (*Classification*) The procedure for determining the class index entries, the specific subject entries, and the *see also* subject entries for a document from its class number and the class numbers of the cross-reference entries provided for it.

CHAIN STITCH. *See* KETTLE STITCH.

CHAINED BOOKS. Books chained to shelves or reading desks in libraries of the fifteenth to early eighteenth centuries to prevent theft. The practice began to die out by the middle of the seventeenth century when it became customary to shelve books upright.

CHAINED LIBRARY. One in which the books were chained to shelves or reading desks.

CHALCOGRAPHY. Engraving on copper or brass.

CHALK DRAWING. One executed in crayon or pastel. The art of drawing with chalks or pastels is called calcography.

CHALK ENGRAVING. *Synonymous with* CRAYON ENGRAVING (*q.v.*).

CHALK OVERLAY. A method of overlaying whereby an impression is taken on paper having a thin coating of chalk. This coating is then washed off the non-inked parts with diluted acid, thus leaving the inked design in relief. The resulting outline is then fitted as an overlay to the cylinder or platen so as to decrease or increase pressure. Also called 'Mechanical overlay.'

CHAMBER MUSIC. Seriously intended instrumental music for two or more instruments, played by one instrument to each 'part.' It excludes music for orchestra, chorus and other large combinations, vocal music and all instrumental music for one instrument. *See also* ORCHESTRAL MUSIC.

CHAMPLEVÉ. Enamelled bindings made by craftsmen between the eleventh and thirteenth centuries. Designs were cut into a thin sheet of gold or copper which formed the cover, the cavities being filled with enamel. On other bindings the enamel was limited to the decoration of borders and corners. This kind of binding was mainly carried out at Limoges. *See also* CLOISONNÉ.

CHANCERY. The department of the Lord Chancellor, from which issue documents under the Great Seal, such as Charters, Letters Patent, writs and the like, also the place where Charters, Letters Patent and documents of a like nature are enrolled.

CHANCERY LIBERATE. *See* LIBERATE ROLL.

CHANGED NAME. Used of a person who has written under a different name.

CHANGED TITLE. Used to describe a book that has been published under a different title to the one originally used.

Chap. Abbreviation for CHAPTER (*q.v.*).

CHAP-BOOK. A small, cheap book, in a paper binding, and of a popular, sensational, juvenile, moral or educational character. These were popular in the seventeenth and eighteenth centuries, and contained tales, ballads, historical incidents, biographies, tracts, interpretations of dreams, palmistry, astrology, etc. They were sold by chapmen, i.e., pedlars, hawkers. The word comes from the Anglo-Saxon root *ceap* (trade).

CHAPEL. An association of journeymen in the printing and binding trades. Chapels usually exist in printing works of medium and larger size. The secretary, or leader, called the Father of the Chapel, is appointed by the members and one of his duties is to collect and forward trade union dues. To 'call a chapel' is to hold a chapel meeting of the journeymen.

CHAPTER. A division of a book, usually being complete in itself in subject matter but related to the preceding and following ones.

CHAPTER HEADING (HEAD, HEADLINE). The heading placed at the text beginning a chapter. It is usually set below the normal top of the type area of the other pages; the type used is normally larger than that used for running titles, and is of a uniform size and position for each chapter.

CHARACTER. 1. A letter of the alphabet, numeral, punctuation mark, or any other symbol cast as a type. Also called 'Sort.' 2. A personage, real or fictitious, figuring in an opera or work of imaginative literature, especially a novel or play. 3. A style of handwriting. 4. (*Information retrieval*) A symbol which is used in a data processing system; it may be a numeral, a letter of the alphabet, punctuation mark or space.

CHARACTER COUNT. A count of every letter, number, punctuation mark, word or sentence space, etc., in a piece of prose copy.

CHARACTER READER. (*Information retrieval*) A specialized device which can convert data represented in a type fount or script read by human beings directly into machine language. Such a reader may operate optically or, if the characters are printed in magnetic ink, the device may operate either magnetically or optically.

CHARACTER RECOGNITION. (*Information retrieval*) The use of a machine to sense and encode into a machine language characters which are written or printed to be read by human beings.

CHARACTER SIGNIFICANCE SEQUENCE. An order applied to

symbols forming headings which are used as filing media and indicating the precedence each symbol is to have in the filing sequence. Thus the letters of the alphabet are normally arranged in their conventional order in the character significance sequence, but numerals and other non-alphabetic symbols may be arranged in their own conventional order (or if contractions or abbreviations, to be filed as if in full) or be arranged to precede or follow the alphabetic sequence.

CHARACTERISTIC OF A CLASSIFICATION.   A distinctive property, element, or feature, inherent in a character by which a class is defined. A *typical characteristic* is one by which an individual of a class is representative of that class. A *type* is a typical individual, one that has most distinctly the typical characteristic, or characteristics, distinctive of the class. A class may be a type, or *typical class*, if it is representative of a *class of classes* (*Bliss*). The attribute which forms the basis of division. Language, form, and historical period are common characteristics in the classification of literature. A term used to express the principles by which a group is divided (as, genus into species) e.g. the characteristic that divides the animal kingdom into two parts is the absence or presence of a backbone. The characteristic is said to be 'natural' when it exhibits the inherent properties of the things classified. When it does not affect the structure, purpose, or intrinsic character of the things to be divided, but separates according to an accidental quality it is said to be 'artificial.' Thus, in zoology, the presence of a backbone is a natural characteristic, while the habitat (land, sea, or air) is an artificial characteristic. The characteristics chosen as the basis of arrangement must be essential (i.e., the most useful) for the purpose of the classification. They must be used consistently, i.e. it is impossible to classify a subject by two characteristics at once. *See* CROSS CLASSIFICATION. Ranganathan's characteristics are: differentiation, concomitance, relevance, ascertainability, permanence, relevant sequence, consistency. Also called a 'Principle of division.'

CHARACTERS IN PICA.   *See* ALPHABET LENGTH.

CHARCOAL DRAWING.   One made with a charcoal crayon on paper with a rough surface. Such drawings are easily smudged, and to prevent this they are sprayed with a fixative.

CHARCOAL PAPER.   A soft, rough-surfaced paper used for making charcoal drawings.

CHARGE.   1. The record of a loan, giving particulars of the book lent and the reader's name and address. 2. To 'issue' a book; to record the loan of a book; to make a 'charge.' 3. An amount of money which is authorised by s.8 of the Public Libraries and Museums Act 1964 for a service provided by a public library. Charges, not exceeding such amount as may be specified by the Secretary of State, may be made (a) for notifying a person that a book or other article reserved by him has become available for borrowing, (b) in respect of failure to return a book or other article before the end of the period for which it was lent. The latter has always been known as a 'fine.' A library authority may make a charge for the borrowing of any article, except that where the authority is under a duty to make facilities for borrowing available to residents, non-resident students and non-resident employees, such a person shall not be charged for borrowing (a) a book, journal, pamphlet or similar article, or (b) a reproduction made by photographic or other means of the whole or a part of any such article s.8 (3). A charge may be made for supplying book catalogues or indexes, or any similar articles, where they become the property of the persons to whom they are supplied s.8 (4), and also for facilities which go beyond those ordinarily provided as part of the library service s.8 (5). Where premises are provided under the Public Libraries and Museums Act 1964, charges may be made for admission to any event of a cultural or educational nature (s.20).

CHARGE A BOOK. The action of recording the loan of a book, or making a 'charge.'

CHARGE SLIP. *See* BOOK CARD.

CHARGING CARD. *See* BOOK CARD.

CHARGING DESK. *Synonymous with* STAFF ENCLOSURE (*q.v.*).

CHARGING MACHINE. A machine used for recording the loan of books to readers.

CHARGING METHODS. The methods by which loans of books are recorded. *See* BOOKAMATIC, BROWNE BOOK CHARGING SYSTEM, CHEQUE BOOK CHARGING METHOD, DETROIT SELF-CHARGING SYSTEM, DICKMAN CHARGING SYSTEM, ISLINGTON CHARGING SYSTEM, NEWARK CHARGING SYSTEM, PHOTOCHARGING, PUNCHED CARD CHARGING, TOKEN CHARGING, TRANSACTION CARD CHARGING. In the early 1970s various experiments were carried out with photographic and data processing methods of recording the loan of books. *See also* COMPUTERIZED LIBRARIANSHIP.

CHARGING SLIP. *See* BOOK CARD.

CHARGING SYSTEM. The method used in keeping records of the loan of books. *See* CHARGING METHODS.

CHARGING TRAY. The steel or wooden tray which is used to hold the 'charges.'

CHART. 1. A map for the use of marine navigators showing the coast-line, the position of rocks, sandbanks, channels, anchorages, and the depths of water in different parts of the sea expressed in feet or fathoms. 2. A graphical representation by means of curves, or the like, of the fluctuation of statistical records of such items as population, prices, production, barometric pressure, temperature, etc. 3. Information of any kind arranged in tabular form, or graphically by means of curves. 4. A map designed for aeronautical navigation.

CHART PAPER. A hard, tub-sized paper which must be strong, tough, pliable and subject to folding without cracking. It should be liable to stretch as little as possible during printing in view of register, smooth without gloss, suitable for pen and ink charting and therefore able to withstand erasure. *See also* PLAN PAPER.

CHARTER. An instrument whereby a sovereign or legislature grants rights to a person or corporation.

CHARTER BOOKSELLER. A retail bookseller who satisfies certain conditions laid down by the Booksellers Association with regard to service to the public.

CHARTER OF THE BOOK. A declaration of the principles which should guide the treatment of books both nationally and inter-nationally, was approved in 1971 by the international professional organizations of authors, publishers, librarians, booksellers and documentalists, in association with Unesco and in connexion with International Book Year, 1972. The theme of each of the articles was: (1) everyone has the right to read; (2) books are essential to education; (3) society has a special obligation to establish the conditions in which authors can exercise their creative role; (4) a sound publishing industry is essential to national development; (5) book manufacturing facilities are necessary to the development of publishing; (6) book-sellers provide a fundamental service as a link between publishers and the reading public; (7) libraries are national resources for the transfer of information and knowledge, and for the enjoyment of wisdom and beauty; (8) documentation serves books by preserving and making available essential background material; (9) the free flow of books between countries is an essential supplement to national supplies and promotes international understanding; (10) books serve inter-national understanding and peaceful co-operation. The full text of each article is given in *Unesco Bulletin for Libraries*, **26** (5) Sept.–Oct. 1972 pp. 238–40.

CHARTER ROLL. A parchment roll upon which charters were enrolled at the Chancery.

CHARTULARY. 1. A keeper of archives. 2. A place in which records or charters relating to a religious, civil or private state are kept. 3. The book in which they are listed or copied. Also called 'Cartulary.'

CHASE. (*Printing*) A rectangular iron frame in which, by means of wedges, composed matter is secured and rendered portable. The wedges are called side- and foot-sticks and quoins. When they are adjusted, between the type matter and the chase, the whole becomes a forme, and is said to be 'locked up.' In SHEET WORK (*q.v.*) the forme which contains the text which will be on the inside pages of a printed sheet when folded, is called the 'inner forme' and that which contains those on the outside, the 'outer forme.'

CHASED EDGES. *Synonymous with* GAUFFERED EDGES (*q.v.*).

CHAUCER TYPE. A re-cutting, in 12-point, of the TROY TYPE (*q.v.*) designed by William Morris. It was first used in 1892. *See also* GOLDEN TYPE.

CHEAP EDITION. An edition of a book issued at a cheaper price. Usually it is a reprint of an earlier edition, printed on poorer paper and bound in a cheaper cover.

CHECK DIGIT. (*Information retrieval*) In computerization, a digit, usually the last, by which the accuracy of transcription of a number may be verified.

CHECK-LIST. 1. A record on which is noted each number, or part, of a work 'in progress' as it is received. 2. A list of items giving brief information sufficient only for identification. 3. An enumeration of documentary holdings with a minimum of organization and bibliographic information (*IBM*).

CHECK MARKS. Indications made by cataloguers on title-pages of books, as a guide to assistant cataloguers or typists, of items to be omitted in the entries, e.g. ( ) may mean, 'omit from all cards,' [ ] may mean 'omit from title card but include on subject cards.' They are pencilled on by the cataloguer as a guide to his assistants.

CHECKOUT ROUTINE. 1. A procedure used in machine documentation systems to determine the correctness of answers, involving the use of sample inquiries, the answers to which are known (*IBM*). 2. The necessary procedures demanded before removing a document from a collection (*IBM*).

CHECKPOINT. A library book, magazine and document security system developed by Checkpoint Systems, a subsidiary of Logistics Industries Corporation, through the efforts of the Free Library of Philadelphia.

CHELTENHAM. An unattractive type face designed by Bertram G. Goodhue (1869–1924) in 1896 and widely used by jobbing printers as it is a FOUNDERS' TYPE (*q.v*).

CHELTENHAM CLASSIFICATION. A system devised for the library of the Ladies' College, Cheltenham, and used in a number of schools. The tables were published under the editorship of Miss E. S. Fegan and Miss M. Cant who were successive librarians of the College. Being aligned closely with the school curriculum, the contents of the main classes correspond with the traditional coverage of subjects as taught.

CHEMAC. A kind of copper line block used for blocking. *See also* BLOCK 2.

CHEMICAL WOOD. Wood reduced to pulp by a chemical process, cooking in acid (sulphite process), or an alkaline liquor (soda process), for use in the manufacture of paper. This produces a purer pulp than that obtained by the MECHANICAL WOOD (*q.v*.) process. A combined chemical and mechanical wood process results in a paper which is intermediate in quality between the two.

CHEMISE. A loose cover for a book with pockets for boards. These were sometimes used in the Middle Ages instead of binding.

CHEQUE BOOK CHARGING METHOD. An adaptation of the BROWNE BOOK CHARGING SYSTEM (*q.v*.) to enable it to deal more rapidly with great pressure at the entrance side of staff enclosures, which it does most satisfactorily. This was the problem facing librarians when they were seeking methods of avoiding queues in the middle 1950's and which resulted in the introduction of TOKEN CHARGING (*q.v*.) and of transaction charging systems. With this system a reader is issued with a small book of fifty perforated slips of paper, similar to a small cheque book, and each bearing the same number. When a book is borrowed, a slip torn from the cheque book by an assistant is placed with the book card to form a CHARGE (*q.v*.). On discharging a book, the numbered cheque book slip is destroyed. When writing overdue notices, the name and address of the borrower is obtained by referring to the list of cheque book numbers against which names and addresses have been entered. Delayed discharging (i.e. cancelling the loan record at a less busy time) is possible with this method. *See also* CHARGING METHODS.

CHEQUERING. (*Binding*) To divide a surface into squares of alternately different ornament or colours, by equidistant vertical and horizontal lines like a chess-board.

chi. (*Bibliography*) The Greek letter χ used to denote an unsigned gathering or leaf in respect of which no signature can be inferred and which is not the first gathering. *See also* pi.

CHIANG SMALL DUPLICATOR. *See* CARDMASTER.

CHIAROSCURO. 1. A black and white sketch. 2. A method of printing engravings, usually wood-engravings, from blocks representing lighter and darker shades, used especially in the fifteenth and sixteenth centuries. 3. A print produced by this means. 4. The earliest form of colour printing. It was a woodcut method, the colours being successively printed in register from separate blocks after an impression from the master block had been made.

CHIEF ASSISTANT. The senior assistant librarian next to the deputy librarian.

CHIFFON SILK. A thin, strong and durable silk material which can be used for mending and strengthening paper, especially of valuable books.

CHILDREN'S BOOK CIRCLE. An informal group of children's book editors and those who work in publishers' children's book departments. It was started in 1962 to provide an opportunity for such persons to exchange ideas on the publication of, and publicity for, children's books. The Eleanor Farjeon Award 'for distinguished services to children's books in the past year' was first made in 1966 (to Mrs. Margery Fisher for her reviews of children's books in *Growing Point*) in memory of Eleanor Farjeon, one of the greatest children's writers, who died in 1965. Anyone doing outstanding work for children's books, whether librarian, teacher, author, artist, publisher, reviewer, television producer – in fact, anyone – is eligible for the award which is a monetary prize of at least fifty guineas. Nominations for the award may be made by members of the Circle only.

CHILDREN'S BOOK COUNCIL. A non-profit making organization, encouraging the reading and enjoyment of children's books. The Council consists of sixty-seven American publishers of trade books for children. It organized the first National Children's Book Week in 1945 and has continued to do so each year since; it is also concerned with projects involving the annual Children's Book Showcase. The Council acts as the U.S. section of the International Board on Books for Young People (IBBY) (*q.v.*) and participates in this connection by making an annual donation of a selection of children's books to twelve repositories throughout the world. Abbreviated CBC. *See also* BOOK WEEK, TRADE BOOK.

CHILDREN'S BOOK GROUP. A specialist publishers' group of the PUBLISHERS ASSOCIATION (*q.v.*); regular meetings of members are held for the common interest of the kind of publishing with which they are concerned. A fairly regular and close contact is maintained with the Youth Libraries Group of the Library Association.

CHILDREN'S BOOK GROUPS. Unofficial groups of persons concerned with furthering the use of books for children by means of story telling, children's activities, talks, book exhibitions and book sales, co-operation with public libraries and with schools and booksellers. The first such group was held at Weybridge in Surrey in 1965, others have been formed in many British towns (often based on public libraries) and in overseas countries. The usefulness of the group was recognized in the BULLOCK REPORT (*q.v.*). *See also* FEDERATION OF CHILDREN'S BOOK GROUPS.

CHILDREN'S BOOK TRUST. A non-profit-making Indian publishing venture inspired by Shankar Pillai, the Indian cartoonist. Situated in Delhi, it publishes books in English and Hindu which are sold at subsidised prices.

CHILDREN'S BOOK WEEK. *See* BOOK WEEK.

CHILDREN'S LIBRARY. The department reserved for the exclusive use of children. It usually contains lending and reference sections and periodicals.

CHILDREN'S SERVICES DIVISION. Became a Division of the American Library Association on 1 January 1957. It is concerned with the extension of library services to children in all types of library, and is responsible for evaluating and selecting book and non-book materials for, and improving the techniques of, library services to children from pre-school age through the eighth grade or junior high school age, when such materials or techniques are intended for use in more than one type of library. Abbreviated CSD. Publishes *Top of the News* (4 p.a. free to membs.) jointly with the Young Adult Services Division.

CHINA CLAY. A substance (Si O$_2$) found in large quantities in Cornwall and used in paper making to obtain finish, consistency and opacity, it is also used for coating papers.

CHINA PAPER. Very thin, silky and costly, waterleaf paper used for proofs for woodcuts and for woodcuts to be mounted on stronger paper. Also called 'Chinese paper' and 'Indian proof paper.'

CHINESE STYLE. A book printed on double leaves, i.e. with unopened folds at the fore-edges and the interior pages blank. In a catalogue entry double leaves would be indicated by, e.g. 18 *double* 1, or 36 pp. (*on double leaves*); if unnumbered, each double leaf is counted as two pages, e.g. [36] *pp.* (*on double leaves*). 'Japanese style' refers to a Japanese book printed in the same manner.

CHIP.   A unit of microfilm containing a micro-image, or images, and coded identification. Chips are used in automatic retrieval systems.

CHIP BOARD.   (*Binding*) A less expensive material than MILLBOARD or STRAWBOARD (*qq.v.*) used for covering books.

CHI-RHO.   Sacred monogram formed by the first two letters of the Greek word for Christ ☧.

CHIROGRAPH.   A formal handwritten document.

CHIROXYLOGRAPHIC.   A mediaeval block book in which the illustrations are printed from blocks and the text added by hand.

CHISWICK PRESS.   The printing press founded by Charles Whittingham the Elder (1767–1840) in 1811, and continued even more successfully by his nephew of the same name (1795–1876) who controlled the Press from 1840. The elder Whittingham was famous for his attractive, popularly priced classics and for his handling of woodcuts; the nephew was well known for his association with the publisher William Pickering, whose printing he did after 1830. The name of the Press was first used in an imprint in 1811 and persisted for 150 years.

CHLORIDE PAPER.   Sensitized photographic paper with an emulsion of gelatin-silver chloride of medium sensitivity. Mainly used for contact printing.

CHOROCHROMATIC MAP.   One in which areal distribution is shown by distinctive colours or tints. This method is used for most geological, soil or political maps.

CHOROGRAPHIC MAP.   One representing a large region, country, or continent, on a small scale.

CHOROPLETH MAP.   One showing 'quantity in area' calculated on a basis of average numbers per unit of area, such as population in a country, by tinting civil divisions by graduated lines or colours, the degree of darkness of which is proportionate to the value represented.

CHOROSCHEMATIC MAP.   One in which small semi-pictorial symbols such as dots or lines of various shapes, sizes and density are used over the area of the map to represent distribution without indication of quantity, of land utilization or vegetation.

CHORUS SCORE.   *See* SCORE.

CHRESTOMATHY.   A collection of excerpts and choice selections, especially from a foreign language, with notes of explanation and instruction.

CHROMIUM-FACED PLATES.   Printing plates upon which chromium has been deposited electrolytically.

CHROMO.   Pertaining to colours. 1. In colour printing there are many terms prefixed by this word, the combining word often giving the particular definition, such as chromo-collotype, chromo-lithography, chromo-xylography. 2. (*Paper*) A heavily coated paper used for chromo-lithography; it is more heavily coated than art paper.

CHROMOGRAPHY. A reproduction of a coloured illustration by lithography, or one of the many photo-mechanical processes.

CHROMO-LITHOGRAPHY. *See* COLOUR LITHOGRAPHY.

CHROMO-XYLOGRAPHY. Coloured woodcuts. *See also* CHIAROSCURO.

CHRONFILE. (Archives) *See* READING FILE.

CHRONICLES. These differ from annals in being more connected and full, though like annals, the events are treated in the order of time.

CHRONOGRAM. A phrase, sentence or inscription, in which certain letters (usually distinguished by size or otherwise from the rest) express by their numerical values a date or epoch, e.g. stVLtVM est DIffICILes habere nVgas, which is:

V	L	V	M	D	I	I	C	I	L	V
5	50	5	1000	500	1	1	100	1	50	5	$= 1718$.

See also ROMAN NUMERALS.

CHRONOLOGICAL DEVICE. One of the distinctive principles for determining the sequence of subjects in the Colon Classification. It is a notational device which ensures chronological order by using a symbol to represent a date or origin.

CHRONOLOGICAL FILE. (*Archives*) *See* READING FILE.

CHRONOLOGICAL ORDER. Arrangement in order of date. Applies to order of entries in a catalogue (date of publication – imprint or copyright) or of the material itself (books, pamphlets or cuttings).

CHRYSOGRAPHY. The art of writing in gold letters, as practised by mediaeval writers of manuscripts.

CHUNK. In automatic indexing, a string, or sequence of uninterrupted words forming a single title, phrase or sentence, and which serves to guide the arrangement or selection of entries.

CHURCH AND SYNAGOGUE LIBRARY ASSOCIATION. Formed on 11th July 1967 in Philadelphia to enable librarians of all church and synagogue libraries (which total more than all the public, college and special libraries combined) to encourage and aid the development of improved church library service. Membership is open to voluntary and professional librarians, to library committee members, ministers, priests, rabbis, directors of Christian education, principals of synagogue schools, Sunday school superintendents, churches, publishers, booksellers and others interested in church and synagogue libraries. It is an ecumenical association, having Chapters based on geographic areas. Abbreviated CSLA. Publishes *Church and Synagogue Libraries* (6 p.a.).

CICERO. A continental unit for measuring the width of a line of type. One Cicero equals 4·511 mm, or 12 Didot points. The name is said to be derived from the size of type used in Schoffer's edition of Cicero's *De Oratore* in the late fifteenth century. *See also* DIDOT SYSTEM, MEASURE, POINT.

CICRED. Abbreviation for the Committee for International Co-ordination of National Research in Demography which was set up in 1972 following a meeting, held at Lyon (France), of the directors of national institutes of demographic research. Its objects are: to (1) make, and distribute, an inventory of the activities concerning demographic research; (2) create an information system; (3) stimulate research in demographic fields. It functions from Paris. Publishes *CICRED* (2 p.a.) in English, French and Spanish editions.

CICRIS. Abbreviation for Co-operative Industrial and Commercial Reference and Information Service; a scheme started in 1951 at the instigation of Mr. R. D. Rates when Borough Librarian of Acton. It was set up to assist commerce and industry in West London by librarians co-ordinating their selection and purchase of books, periodicals and other printed material in agreed fields, and making it available to one another. The public libraries of eight London Boroughs, one university, fifteen colleges and over eighty firms and organizations co-operate, holding between them 1½ million books and over 3,000 technical periodicals. Members should have a library and be willing to lend; there is a nominal annual subscription.

CIDESA. The International Centre for African Social and Economic Documentation (Le Centre Internationale de Documentation Économique et Sociale Africaine). Set up in January 1961. Aims to collect and co-ordinate documentation on economic and social subjects concerning Africa with a view to furthering the progress of the continent in these fields. Membership is open to scientific and philanthropic institutions. Financed by members' dues. Publishes an annual bibliographic index; a bulletin of information on studies and theses in course of publication, or planned; bibliographical enquiries.

CIPHER. 1. The initials of a name, or the arrangement of its letters in an ornamental manner, but disposed in such a way that it becomes a kind of private mark. 2. In machine searching as part of information retrieval, the codes whose notations, whether alphabetic or other symbols, are intentionally scrambled so as to keep the system of rules, and thus the common or source language, a secret.

circa. (*Lat.* 'about') Used to indicate uncertainty in a date, as *c.* 1934, about 1934.

CIRCLE OF STATE LIBRARIANS. The organization to which those employed in British government libraries and information bureaux may belong. It had its beginnings in 1914 when the PANIZZI CLUB (*q.v.*), named after Sir Anthony (Antonio) Panizzi who was Director of the British Museum, was formed. In those early days government librarians were only a minority of the membership of the Club, the objects of which were 'to provide opportunities for social intercourse between the Senior Officers of Reference and Research Libraries and to promote all measures tending to their higher efficiency.' After the First World War, the then Treasurer of the Panizzi Club (*q.v.*), Mr. A. E. Twentyman, Librarian of the Board of Education, took the initiative of reviving the Club and associating State Librarians as such with it. The name 'Circle of State Librarians' was used; it was an informal organization limited to officers-in-charge of Government libraries; it had only two officers (Chairman and Secretary), there was no committee, and no subscription was collected. In general, its objects were to encourage and maintain personal acquaintance and contact between its members and so facilitate co-operation in the ordinary day-to-day business of their libraries. Three meetings a year were held but these and other activities of the Circle were brought to a stop by the Second World War. The circle was revived in 1946 and membership was widened to admit 'those employed in a State Library or Information Service, who possess such professional qualifications or experience as will satisfy the Committee,' and who were engaged in the storing and dissemination of knowledge, such as archivists, intelligence officers of research departments and others whose interests and problems were similar to those of librarians. In 1953 the function of the Circle was again widened 'to cultivate a common interest in bibliographical problems arising in Government service' and the membership opened 'to all members of the Government service who are interested in the activities of the Circle.' Abbreviated CSL. Publishes *State Librarian* (3 p.a.).

CIRCUIT EDGES. The edges of a book-cover which overlap the edges of the book. Used mostly for Bibles. Also called 'Divinity circuit,' 'Divinity edges,' 'Yapp edges.'

CIRCULAR BRACKETS. CURVES (*q.v.*), or Round Brackets, used in the

Colon Classification to enclose the SUBJECT DEVICE NUMBER (*q.v.*) which forms part of the CLASS NUMBER (*q.v.*). The first '(' is called 'Starter' and the second ')' 'Arrester.' *See also* BRACKETS.

CIRCULAR ROUTING. *See* ROUTING.

CIRCULATING LIBRARY. A library which lends books for use outside the building. In England, the term usually indicates a commercial library where payment has to be made for the use of the books. *See also* SUBSCRIPTION LIBRARY.

CIRCULATION. The total number of books issued from a library in a given period.

CIRCULATION DEPARTMENT. The American term for the department of a public library which lends books for home-reading. Called a 'Lending department' in England.

CIRCULATION DESK. The American equivalent of the English STAFF ENCLOSURE (*q.v.*). Also called 'Charging desk,' 'Delivery desk,' 'Discharging desk,' 'Issue desk,' 'Lending desk,' 'Loan desk,' 'Receiving desk,' 'Return desk,' 'Slipping desk.'

CIRCULATION RECORD. A record of the books issued for home-reading.

CIRCULATION STATISTICS. A record of the number of books circulated (issued) for home-reading.

CIRCULATION WORK. The American term indicating the work of a department issuing books for home-reading.

CISE. Colleges, Institutes and Schools of Education – a Group of the Library Association.

CISTI. Acronym of Canada Institute for Scientific and Technical Information which was formed in Ottawa on 16th October 1974 by combining the National Science Library (NSL) and the Technical Information Service (TIS) both of which were – and in their combined form still are – activities of the National Research Council. In CISTI, the NRC has concentrated its principal information transfer systems into a single point of focus for the use of the evolving Canadian network of STI services. The stock of nearly 1,000,000 volumes includes many documents in non-print forms; approximately 20,000 journal titles from all parts of the world are held. *See also* NATIONAL SCIENCE LIBRARY OF CANADA.

CISTIP. Acronym of the Committee on International Scientific and Technical Information Programs, which was established within the Commission on International Relations of the National Academy of Sciences – National Research Council. Its function is to provide continuing reviews, analyses and information to the Academy, the

7

National Science Foundation and other bodies on issues and activities relating to U.S. participation in the planning, development, co-ordination, operation and financing of international scientific and technical information programmes.

CITATION. A reference to a text or part of a text identifying the document in which it may be found. *See also* REFERENCES.

CITATION INDEX. A list of articles that, subsequent to the appearance of the original article, refer to, or cite, that article. This method has been used extensively in the legal profession and is particularly applicable to scientific literature. *See also* SCIENCE CITATION INDEX.

CITATION ORDER. The order of application of principles of division in determining an appropriate class number for a document. Also called 'Facet formula.'

CIVILITÉ. A group of gothic cursive printing type faces, the earliest and best of which was cut by Robert Granjon in the mid-sixteenth century. They were based on a relatively informal hand, closely related to the English 'secretary'.

CLAIM. Any communication sent to a bookseller or other supplier to hasten the delivery of overdue material.

CLANDESTINE LITERATURE. Publications which are printed, published, and circulated secretly. They are usually of a political nature and seek to overthrow the government, or in time of war, act against the power in authority. Also called 'Secret literature,' 'Underground literature.'

CLANDESTINE PRESS. A printing press which operates secretly.

CLAPP-JORDAN FORMULAE. Formulae devised by Verner Clapp and Robert T. Jordan, and stated in 'Quantitative criteria for adequacy of academic library collections' (*College and Research Libraries* **26** (5) September 1965). They attempt to identify the principal factors affecting the academic needs for books and to ascribe suitable weights to each.

CLARENDON. The name of a particular type face, and also of a group of faces characterized by little difference between thick and thin strokes, narrowness, and angular semi-Egyptian serifs. 'Consort' and 'Fortune' are of this kind. They were originally designed to give bold emphasis, particularly for dictionaries so that the word defined stood out clearly, and although still used for this purpose are now being used in their own right. For a specimen alphabet, *see* TYPE FACE.

CLARENDON PRESS. Edward Hyde, first Earl of Clarendon (1609–74), gave the profits of the copyright of his *History of the Rebellion* to the University of Oxford to erect the first building in which the University's business of printing was wholly carried on – hence the name Clarendon Press. The business was transferred from the Sheldonian Theatre to this new building in 1713.

CLASP. A metal fastening hinged to one board and made to clip or lock into a loop or bar on the other board of a bound book or album. *See also* CATCH.

CLASS. (*Classification*) (*Noun*) 1. A group of concepts, or of things, assembled by some likeness which unifies them. This likeness is called the 'characteristic of a classification.' A class consists of all the things that are alike in essentials, characters, properties and relations, by which it is defined. 2. A group having the same or similar characteristics (*IBM*). 3. A major division of a CATEGORY (*q.v.*). *See also* FORM CLASSES, MAIN CLASS, SUMMUM GENUS. (*Verb*) To classify books according to a scheme of classification. 4. (*Archives*) A self-contained unit within an archive group.

CLASS CATALOGUE. *Synonymous with* CLASSIFIED CATALOGUE (*q.v.*).

CLASS ENTRY. An entry in a catalogue under the name of a class, as distinct from one under a specific subject.

CLASS GUIDE. A guide to the shelves which gives the main class symbol and subject, and perhaps the same information for the main divisions of the class. It is usually placed at the end of a press or over the central tier.

CLASS LETTER. The first letter of a main class or division of a classification scheme the notation of which begins with a letter of the alphabet, it is used to designate a particular main class of the classification.

CLASS LIBRARY. The class room library in a primary school, so called to distinguish it from the 'general' or 'central' library provided in the same school for all to use.

CLASS LIST. A list of the books in a particular class, usually arranged in classified order. In archive administration, a list of the documents in a CLASS (*q.v.*), the entries being arranged in numerical order with enough detail to distinguish one document from another.

CLASS MARK. The classification symbol placed on the spine of the book, on the title-page and added to a catalogue entry to indicate the book's place in the classification and on the shelves.

CLASS NOTATION. *Synonymous with* CLASS MARK (*q.v.*).

CLASS NUMBER. One or more characters showing the class to which a book belongs in the scheme of classification in use. In a RELATIVE LOCATION (*q.v.*), this number also shows the place of the book on the shelves and in relation to other subjects. It translates the name of its specific subject into the artificial language of the notation of the scheme of classification. The class number may be compounded of a variety of symbols used in a specified sequence, and followed by certain signs or symbols the purpose of which is to separate the constituent parts of the Class Number and/or to indicate the characteristic of the following symbol. 'Relation marks' are used for this purpose in the UDC – see UNIVERSAL DECIMAL CLASSIFICATION. In the Colon Classification the Class Number consists of the ten Arabic numerals; the twenty-six capital letters of the Roman alphabet; twenty-three small letters of the Roman alphabet (*i*, *l*, and *o* being omitted); some Greek letters; the punctuation marks; circular, or round, brackets (the first '(' being called Starter and the second ')' Arrester) and horizontal arrows. The digit 'O', the punctuation marks and the arrows are called 'Connecting symbols' and occur only as connectives or conjunctions in the Colon language.

CLASS SYMBOL.   *Synonymous with* CLASS MARK (*q.v.*).

CLASSED CATALOGUE.   *Synonymous with* CLASSIFIED CATALOGUE (*q.v.*). Also called 'Class catalogue.'

CLASSED LIBRARY.   *Synonymous with* CLASSIFIED LIBRARY (*q.v.*).

CLASSER.   As used by Bliss and Savage, one who allocates class numbers to books according to an existing scheme of classification. *See also* CLASSING, CLASSIFIER.

CLASSIC.   An outstanding work, usually appearing in several versions and in translation, and sometimes adapted, being the subject of commentaries and other writings, and continuing in print even long after first publication. In classification it is often treated as if it were a class or a subject.

CLASSIC DEVICE.   (*Classification*) In the Colon Classification, the digit *x* which is put after the class number to which a CLASSIC (*q.v.*) should be assigned and which precedes a Work Facet or Author Facet. This is done to bring together the different editions of a classic in a class, also the different editions of each of its commentaries, and to keep a classic and the commentaries thereon in juxtaposition. Also to keep each classic and its associated commentaries in juxtaposition to other classics in the same class.

CLASSICAL AUTHOR.   For the purposes of the Colon Classification, an author, one at least of whose works is a classic. The Classic Device, consisting of the digit *x* placed after the number representing the ultimate class to which the classic should be otherwise assigned and adding after it an Author Facet, is employed to bring together the different editions of a classic in a class and also the different editions of commentaries on the classic.

CLASSIFICATION. 1. The arrangement of things in logical order according to their degrees of likeness, especially the assignment of books to their proper places in a scheme of book classification. 2. A scheme for the arrangement of books and other material in a logical sequence according to subject or form. 3. A 'coding' system within which the series of symbols indicating a concept, or semantemes, are subject to certain order relationships. *See also* BROAD CLASSIFICATION, CLOSE CLASSIFICATION, ENUMERATIVE CLASSIFICATION, HIERARCHICAL CLASSIFICATION, SUMMUM GENUS. 4. 'Any method of recognizing relations, generic or other, between items of information, regardless of the degree of hierarchy used and of whether those methods are applied in connection with traditional or computerized information systems' – the definition adopted in the terms of reference of the FID Committee on Classification Research (FID/CR) in 1973.

CLASSIFICATION CODE. A scheme of classification.

CLASSIFICATION DECIMALE UNIVERSELLE. *See* UNIVERSAL DECIMAL CLASSIFICATION.

CLASSIFICATION FOR SOCIAL SCIENCES. Compiled by Barbara Kyle for the Unesco Social Science bibliographies at the request of the INTERNATIONAL COMMITTEE FOR SOCIAL SCIENCES DOCUMENTATION (*q.v.*). Referred to as the KC.

CLASSIFICATION MARK. *See* CLASS MARK.

CLASSIFICATION OF LIBRARY SCIENCE. A faceted scheme which was prepared by the CLASSIFICATION RESEARCH GROUP (*q.v.*) and published by Aslib in 1965. The Scheme is in two sections; the first (sections A/Z) contains the 'core' subjects of library science, while the second (classes 1/8) contains 'fringe' subjects which are disciplines in their own right but are of concern to librarians and information scientists. This scheme is used for arranging entries in *Library and Information Science Abstracts.*

CLASSIFICATION RESEARCH. A Committee on Classification Research (FID/CR), based on the Documentation Research and Training Centre, Indian Statistical Institute, Bangalore, India, has classification matters constantly under review. Publishes *FID/CR Newsletter* (q.).

CLASSIFICATION RESEARCH GROUP. An unofficial group of British librarians who have been meeting since February 1952 to discuss the theory and practice of classification. Its bulletins are published in the *Journal of Documentation*. Abbreviated CRG. *A classification of library and information science,* an extensively revised version of the Group's *A classification of library science,* has been used since 1970 for the LA's publication *Library and Information Science Abstracts.*

CLASSIFICATION RESEARCH STUDY GROUP. Founded in the U.S.A. in 1959 to promote basic and applied research in classification without allegiance to any particular system; to afford members an opportunity to exchange information on classification; to encourage publication of papers of interest in classification. Abbreviated CRSG. Publishes *CRSG News Notes* (2 p.a. to membs.).

CLASSIFICATION SCHEDULE. The printed scheme of a system of classification.

CLASSIFICATION SCHEME. A scheme by which books are classified or arranged in systematic order. The following are some of the better known schemes, the author's names being given in brackets: Bibliographic Classification (Bliss); Colon Classification (Ranganathan); Decimal Classification (Dewey); Expansive Classification (Cutter); Library of Congress Classification; Subject Classification (Brown); Universal Decimal Classification. The above are all general schemes. Some schemes for narrower fields of literature are: Barnard, C. C., *A classification for medical and veterinary libraries;* Stewart, J. D., *A tabulation of librarianship;* Foskett, D. J., *The London education classification;* Glidden, S. H., *and* Marchus, D., *A library classification for public administration materials;* Coates, E. J., *British catalogue of music classification;* Vickery, B. C., *and* Farradane, J. E. L., *Cranfield classification for aeronautics and allied subjects; Faceted classification for engineering.*

CLASSIFICATION SYSTEM. A particular scheme of classification. *See also* CLASSIFICATION SCHEME.

CLASSIFICATIONIST. 1. One who makes a scheme of classification. Called by Bliss and Savage a 'classifier.' 2. A theorist who organizes and divides documents according to a specific criterion. *See also* CLASSIFIER.

CLASSIFIED ARRANGEMENT. The arrangement of books in a library according to some scheme of classification.

CLASSIFIED CATALOGUE. A catalogue in which the entries are arranged in classified order of subjects, whether logically, in systematic order, exhibiting hierarchical relationship between subjects as in the SYSTEMATIC CATALOGUE (*q.v.*) – the more usual, or alphabetically, as in the ALPHABETICO-CLASSED CATALOGUE (*q.v.*). It is usually in two parts: the classified file of entries in systematic order, and the alphabetical subject index to the classified file. Also called 'Classed catalogue,' 'Classified subject catalogue.'

CLASSIFIED FILE. The entries, in systematic order, of the CLASSIFIED CATALOGUE (*q.v.*). This is one (the main) part of this kind of catalogue, the other part being the alphabetical subject index. Also called 'Systematic file'. *See also* FEATURE HEADING.

CLASSIFIED INDEX. I. One in which entries are not arranged in one strict alphabetical sequence, but under general headings, e.g. the names of binders would be arranged alphabetically, under the heading 'binders' and not in their correct places in the alphabetical sequence. 2. An index characterized by sub-divisions of hierarchic structure. An index using or displaying genus-species (class-subclass) relationships (*IBM*). *See also* CLASSIFIED CATALOGUE, CORRELATIVE INDEX.

CLASSIFIED LIBRARY. A library in which the books are arranged according to a recognized scheme of classification. Also called a 'Classed library.'

CLASSIFIED MATERIAL. Memoranda, reports and other documents emanating from government departments, industrial and other corporations, research associations, etc., which are of a secret and confidential nature. They are classified as 'top secret,' 'secret,' 'confidential' and 'restricted' in a descending order of secrecy and are treated variously in libraries. Also called 'Classified information'.

CLASSIFIED ORDER. The arrangement of books and other materials, or of entries in a catalogue, in order according to a scheme of classification.

CLASSIFIED SUBJECT CATALOGUE. *See* CLASSIFIED CATALOGUE.

CLASSIFIER. As used by Bliss and Savage, one who names and defines classes and co-ordinates them into tables to form a scheme of book classification. The process of compiling the tables is called 'classifying.' These terms have generally related to the allocation of classification numbers to books, and are so used by Palmer and Wells. *See also* CLASSER, CLASSIFICATIONIST.

CLASSIFY. To classify is to bring individuals with the same or similar characteristics together actually, or mentally, that is, conceptually. Also, in a secondary sense, to arrange classes in a classification, and to allocate the appropriate CLASS NUMBER (*q.v.*) to a book or other document according to a scheme of classification. *See also* CLASS.

CLASSIFYING. The act of fitting books or other material into an existing scheme of classification. Called by Bliss, Savage and Sayers 'classing.' *See also* CLASSER, CLASSING, CLASSIFICATIONIST, CLASSIFIER, FACET, FOCUS, PHASE.

CLASSING. As used by Bliss, Savage and Sayers, allocating class numbers to books according to a scheme of classification. *See also* CLASSER, CLASSIFYING.

CLASSROOM COLLECTION. 1. A temporary, or semi-permanent, collection of books deposited in a schoolroom by a public, or a school, library. 2. A number of books sent by a college library to a classroom for use by students and teachers. (American.)

CLAY TABLETS. Cuneiform clay tablets were the earliest form of books, and were protected by an outer shell of clay which was inscribed with a copy, abstract, or title, of the contents.

CLEAN PROOF. One having very few, or no, printer's errors.

CLEAR BASE. *See* FILM BASE.

CLEARING HOUSE OF INFORMATION. Applied to an organization or special library which possesses only a small amount of published material but obtains information or provides a referral service, for users by means of the telephone and correspondence.

CLEARINGHOUSE. An organization that collects and maintains records of research, development, and engineering being planned, currently in progress, or completed; it provides documents derived from these activities, and provides referral services to other sources for information relating to these activities.

CLEARINGHOUSE FOR FEDERAL SCIENTIFIC AND TECHNICAL INFORMATION. *See* CFSTI.

CLEMENTS LIBRARY, WILLIAM L. In 1923 William L. Clements deposited the library of Americana which he had been collecting for over twenty years with the University of Michigan, Ann Arbor. It is primarily a 'collection of the sources of American history', and has been extended over the years by the addition of books and documents which promote that study. The stock totals 37,000 volumes, 25,000 maps and 200,000 MSS.

CLERICAL ASSISTANT. In America, a person who performs work requiring ability of a high order, but not knowledge of the theoretical or scientific aspects of library work.

CLICHÉ. 1. A common and stereotyped journalistic or literary phrase. 2. An electrotype or stereotype plate.

CLICHOGRAPH. *Synonymous with* KLISCHOGRAPH (*q.v.*).

CLINICAL LIBRARIAN. A person who, by aptitude, training and experience, is qualified to participate in the remedial, therapeutic and rehabilitative care of individuals in hospitals and institutions.

CLIP. The metal eye, of whatever form, fixed to one of the covers of a book in a medieval chained library, and to which the book's chain was fastened.

CLIPPING. A piece clipped, or cut from a newspaper or periodical. (American.) Called in England a 'Cutting,' 'Press cutting.'

CLIPPING BUREAU. A commercial organization which clips, or cuts, items from newspapers and periodicals on specific subjects and sends them to subscribers (American). Called in England a 'Cuttings bureau.'

CLIPPING SERVICE. The cutting of news items, etc. daily from newspapers and periodicals in an industrial, commercial or other organization, and sending them to officials who will find them useful. This is often undertaken in the library or information department.

CLIPPINGS FILE. A collection of cuttings from newspapers and periodicals, used to supplement the information to be found in books, and usually kept in classified or subject order in folders in a vertical file. Also called 'Cuttings file.'

CLOGGED. A half-tone, or line block, the impression from which has become smudged by the spaces between the dots or lines of the block becoming filled with ink. It may be due to dirty ink, dust, over-inking or the incorrect damping of a lithographic plate. Also known as 'filling in.'

CLOISONNÉ. Enamelled bindings made during the eleventh century, mainly by Greek and Italian craftsmen. The design was first outlined by soldering thin strips of metal on to a metal plate and then filling the compartments so formed with coloured enamels. *See also* CHAMPLEVÉ.

CLOSE. The second of a pair of punctuation marks, e.g. ')]. *See also* CIRCULAR BRACKETS, SQUARE BRACKETS.

CLOSE CLASSIFICATION. 1. The arrangement of books in a classification system in as minute sub-divisions as possible; i.e. the full application of a scheme. Also called 'Exact classification', 'Bibliographic classification'. 2. Arrangement of works in conformity with the provisions of such a scheme. (From *Abridged Dewey Decimal Classification.* 10th ed. 1971). *See also* BROAD CLASSIFICATION.

CLOSE MATTER. Lines of type set without leads, or thinly spaced.

CLOSE ROLL. A parchment roll upon which letters close were enrolled at the Chancery.

CLOSE SCORE. A musical score in which the music of more than one part or instrument is written on one stave. Also called 'Short score,' 'Compressed score,' 'Condensed score.'

CLOSE UP. (*Printing*) To place lines or characters together by removing spacing-out leads or intervening letters.

CLOSED ACCESS.   The now obsolete method of keeping readers from
the book shelves; this necessitated the provision in lending libraries of
printed catalogues and indicators to inform readers which books were
'in' or 'out.' Also called 'Closed shelves,' and 'Closed library.' In
archive administration, archives which are not available to the general
public due to the existence of a confidentiality restriction. They are
said to be 'open' when the period of restriction has expired. *See also*
ACCESS.

CLOSED BIBLIOGRAPHY.   One which has been completed. The
opposite of PERIODICAL BIBLIOGRAPHY (*q.v.*). *Synonymous with*
RETROSPECTIVE BIBLIOGRAPHY. SEE ALSO BIBLIOGRAPHY, CURRENT
BIBLIOGRAPHY.

CLOSED ENTRY. 1. The catalogue entry for all the parts or volumes of
a serial publication or work in several volumes, containing complete
bibliographical information. Until the library has acquired a complete set, the bibliographical details are recorded in an OPEN ENTRY
(*q.v.*). 2. A catalogue entry in which blank spaces are not left in the
body of the entry or in the collation so that additional particulars of
holdings may be entered subsequently. This is the normal form of
catalogue entry.

CLOSED FILE.   1. One containing documents on which action has been
finalized and to which further material is unlikely to be added. 2.
One to which access is limited or denied because of the confidential
nature of its contents.

CLOSED INDEXING SYSTEM.   One in which the terms comprising
the AUTHORITY LIST (*q.v.*) or File, or CONTROLLED TERM LIST (*q.v.*)
may not be added to when new knowledge, or the indexing of a new
document, would make the addition of new terms appear appropriate.
A new edition of the approved list or an amendment sheet must be
awaited. An Open Indexing System permits the addition of terms as
necessary. *See also* OPEN ENDED TERM LIST.

CLOSED JOINT.   (*Bookbinding*) The type of joint which is obtained
when cover boards are laced on. Also called 'Tight joint.' *See also*
FRENCH JOINT.

CLOSED LIBRARY.   *See* CLOSED ACCESS.

CLOSED SHELVES.   *See* CLOSED ACCESS.

CLOSED UP.   When typesetting is divided between several compositors and each has completed his allocation, the matter is closed
up.

CLOTH.   A generic term applied to material which is not leather or
obviously paper used for covering books. It was originally a material

made of natural fibres of some kind. It was first used for this purpose in about 1820. *See also* CLOTH BINDING.

CLOTH BINDING.   Used to describe a book which is bound entirely in cloth. A book so bound is called 'Cloth bound.'

CLOTH BOARDS.   *See* BOARDS.

CLOTH-CENTRED.   A duplex board or paper having a core, or centre, of muslin, linen or canvas (i.e. a cloth with paper on both sides), and used for maps, tables, membership tickets, envelopes, etc. Cloth-faced, -lined, or -mounted paper or card indicates that the cloth is not a core but is pasted on one side only, and is termed linen- or canvas-lined (-backed) according to the kind of cloth used.

CLOTH JOINT.   Piece of cloth used to cover the joints on the inside of very heavy or large books.

CLOTH-LINED PAPER (BOARD).   Paper or board which is re-inforced with muslin or cloth affixed to one side. *Cloth centred paper, or board*, is made up of two sheets or furnish layers with muslin or cloth between them.

CLOTH PRINT.   (*Reprography*) A print made on sensitized cloth. Prints are usually made on paper or film.

CLOTH SIDES.   A book which has cloth sides but leather at the spine and possibly at the corners as well.

CLUB LINE.   (*Printing*) The last line of type on a page when it begins a new paragraph. Printers try to avoid this, as they do a WIDOW (*q.v.*), because of its unsightliness.

CLUMP.   A thick piece of type metal, ranging in width from 5 pt. upwards, but usually 6 pt. or 12 pt., and of the height of leads. Clumps are used in whiting out, and as footlines at the bottoms of columns and pages.

CLUSTER.   (*Information retrieval*) A group of related documents.

COARSE SCREEN.   *See* SCREEN.

COATED PAPER.   1. A general term for papers such as chromo, art, enamel, which have been prepared for different printing processes by applying a mineral such as china clay after the body paper has been made. Also called 'Surface paper.' 2. Any paper whose surface is coated with a mixture of clay and glue made of casein to give it a smooth surface. The term is used to distinguish it from loaded papers in which the clay is mixed with the pulp during manufacture. *See also* ART.

COATING.   A thin layer of light-sensitive chemical applied to a base material such as cloth, paper, or transparent plastic, or a mineral such as china clay to a printing paper. *See also* COATED PAPER.

COBOL. Abbreviation for COmmon Business Oriented Language, or high-level programming language designed for commercial and business applications.

COCK. The middle portion of a Brace (*q.v.*). when cast in three pieces as ⌐ ᴧ ⌐.

COCK-UP INITIAL. An initial letter that extends above the first line of text but aligns with the foot of it.

COCKLE. (*Paper*) A puckered effect on paper, produced either naturally or artificially during the drying process. Paper and board will cockle and get out of shape with excessive heat or moisture; to prevent this these materials must be kept under temperature- and humidity-controlled conditions.

cod. Abbreviation for CODEX (*q.v.*).

CODATA. Abbreviation for Committee on Data for Science and Technology, an interdisciplinary committee of the International Council of Scientific Unions (ICSU), which deals with data of importance to science and technology, their compilation, critical evaluation, storage and retrieval. Formed in 1966, it seeks to provide co-ordination and guidance for worldwide data-computing projects. Its scope includes quantative data on the properties and behaviour of matter, characteristics of biological and geological systems, and other experimental and observational data. Publishes *Newsletter* (2 p.a.); *CODATA Bulletin.*

codd. Abbreviation for codices.

CODE. 1. A system of conventional signs which are used as abbreviations to represent information. Rules for their use may be incorporated. Such symbols may represent specific subjects and may be presented in the form of holes punched into cards for the retrieval of information. 2. Any system of symbols by which messages in the normal, common, or source language are transferred into a target, or code, language in order to achieve some desirable advantage over the normal language or numerical expression. 3. In information retrieval, (*noun*) information presented in the 'language' that a computer can understand and handle; (*verb*) to put into machine language. 4. A system of symbols used in transmitting or storing information (*IBM*). 5. A system of arbitrary signs and symbols used to represent words or concepts, as distinguished from a cipher wherein arbitrary signs and symbols are used to represent single letters or syllables (*IBM*). 6. A systematic body of laws, regulations or rules (*IBM*). 7. A communication system for information (*IBM*). 8. In connexion with information retrieval systems, 'a set of discriminable physical marks or signals such as holes, notches, magnetic dots, pulses, etc.' (*Taube*). 9. 'A set of unambiguous rules, whereby messages are converted from one representation to another' (*Verry*). 10. A code, or notation, consisting of configurations of 'marks' (or code elements), each distinctively recognizable configuration of which is called a 'sort.' Also called 'Code character.' 11. 'A determinant for the location of holes on a punched card' (*Scheele*). 12. 'The translation of names of specific subjects into written symbols suitable for presentation in the form of a series of perforations ... etc., permitting mechanical retrieval' (*Ranganathan*). 13. A set of rules for carrying out some such function as cataloguing. *See also* ALGORITHMIC CODE, CODE LANGUAGE, DESCRIPTOR, DIRECT CODING, INDIRECT CODING, NON-SEMANTIC CODE, SEMANTIC CODE, TABULATED CODE.

CODE CHARACTER. *See* CODE 10.

CODE COMPARISON. (*Information retrieval*) In human search, the matching of search words with words in a DESCRIPTOR FILE (*q.v.*).

CODE INDEX. (*Information retrieval*) Any list of headings which directs the searcher, by means of a code number, to information required.

CODE ELEMENTS. *See* CODE.

CODE LANGUAGE. The symbols used to represent words or numerals in a natural, or source, language.

CODE MARK. An indication of purchase made in code on the back of a title-page.

CODED TAPE. A strip of paper, film, or other material containing an electronic or punched code for the activation of typewriter, typesetter or other machinery.

CODELESS SCANNING. A system of retrieval which has been developed from the L'UNITÉ (*q.v.*) system.

CODEN. 1. A code classification assigned to a document or other library item consisting of four capital letters followed by two hyphenated groups of arabic numerals, or of two arabic numerals followed by two capital letters, or of some similar combination. 2. The combination of letters, numbers and symbols assigned as a result of applying coding rules in order to produce a bibliographical citation. *See also* BISHOP'S RULES. The *ASTM coden for periodical titles* uses five-letter codes for the titles of periodicals and serials; the first four letters of each coden have some mnemonic relation to the title, and the fifth letter is arbitrary and will assist in maintaining as many mnemonic relationships as possible for similar periodical titles. The ASTM CODEN system was transferred on 1st January 1975 by the American Society for Testing Materials (ASTM), which has sponsored the system since 1955, to Chemical Abstracts Service (CAS). The CODEN serves as a unique and unambiguous permanent identifier for a specific title, and is used in lieu of full or abbreviated titles of publications in processing and storing bibliographical data in many computer-based information handling systems.

CODEX (*Pl.* Codices). An ancient book composed of pieces of writing material fastened so as to open like a modern book as distinct from the SCROLL or VOLUMEN (*qq.v.*) which it superseded. The name was originally given to two or more tablets of metal, wood or ivory, hinged together with rings; the inner sides were covered with wax and these were written on with a stylus. Later 'Codex' was given to books of this type made of papyrus, vellum or parchment, and later still to volumes consisting of many leaves of parchment or vellum, e.g. *Codex Alexandrinus*. Codices became general for law-books in classical Rome, and were used largely for MS. copies of the scriptures and classics. Codex means a block of wood, probably from the wooden covers. When a codex of the original form consisted of two leaves, it was called a Diptych, of three, a Triptych, and of more, a Polytych. Abbreviated cod. (*Pl.* codd.). There are a number of codices of the Bible, and these are often named after the place of discovery. The four most important of these are *Codex Sinaiticus* (4th or beginning of the 5th century – in the British Museum), *Codex Vaticanus* (4th century – in the Vatican), *Codex Alexandrinus* (5th century – in the British Museum) and the palimpsest *Codex Ephraemi* (5th century Greek text overwritten in a 12th-century hand – in the Bibliothèque Nationale, Paris). These originally contained the whole Greek text of the Old and New Testaments, but are now incomplete. The *Codex Bezae* (5th or 6th century – at Cambridge) containing only the *Gospels* and *Acts* is another important early copy of the *Bible*. All were written in uncials (i.e. capitals) and without breaks between words. The term 'codex' was also used for a collection of Roman laws; these included *Codex Theodosianus* and *Codex Justinianeus*.

CODEX ALEXANDRINUS. This codex was given to Charles I in 1627 by the Patriarch of Constantinople, and formerly Patriarch of Alexandria. It has been in the British Museum since 1757. *See also* CODEX.

CODEX AMIATINUS. One of three codices written by order of Ceolfrid, who became Abbot of Jarrow in 690, and taken by him on a journey for presentation to Pope Gregory II in 716. It is written in

Latin uncials, and is one of the Vulgate. At one time it was preserved at Monte Amianta in the Abruzzi Mountains and is now in the Laurentian Library, Florence. *See also* CODEX.

CODEX ARGENTEUS. The remains of the fifth- and sixth-century MSS. of the translation of the Bible into the Gothic tongue by Wulfilas (or Ulfila), Bishop of the Visigoths. It is written mainly in Greek, but with some roman and runic characters, in gold and silver on purple-stained parchment. On 187 leaves, it contains most of the New Testament, and has been in the library of Uppsala University, Sweden, since 1669. Other fragments are in Milan and Wolfenbüttel.

CODEX BEZAE. On vellum, this codex was presented to Cambridge University Library by Theodorus Beza who acquired it from the Monastery of St. Iremaeus at Lyons. *See also* CODEX.

CODEX LAUDIANUS. This codex contains the Book of the Acts of the Apostles in Greek and Latin, and was brought from Italy to England in the seventh century, probably by Benedict Biscop. It is now in the Bodleian Library at Oxford. *See also* CODEX.

CODEX RESCRIPTUS APHRAËMI. A fifth century palimpsest MS. of the Bible with some works of Ephrem Syrus overwritten in the twelfth century. Fragments are in the Bibliothèque Nationale, Paris. Also known as *Codex Ephraemi*. *See also* CODEX.

CODEX SINAITICUS. The oldest extant Greek vellum codex, the text being written on 48-line columns. It was discovered in 1844, and the portion of 347 leaves (of an estimated total of 730) containing part of the Old Testament and all the New Testament was acquired by the British Museum in 1933. A further 43 leaves is in the Leipzig Library and is known as the *Codex Frederico-Augustaneus*. *See also* CODEX.

CODING. (*Information retrieval*) 1. The translation of the names of specific subjects or of recorded information into written symbols according to a pre-arranged system or code, which may if necessary be presented in the form of perforations; it must be legible to the eye or by machine and must have three characteristics: it must (1) suit the retrieving device used, (2) be capable of representing all likely subject descriptions, (3) be as compact as possible. 2. A list of successive computer operations in code for solving a given problem. Also, the act of writing a prepared list in code. *See also* CODE, MARGINAL HOLE-PUNCHED CARDS, NOTATION, SOUNDEX.

CODING QUIRES. *See* CASSIE.

CODING SHEET. (*Information retrieval*) A sheet of paper on which is listed, in the form of the symbols of a code, the results of the analysis of a document.

CODOT. Acronym for Classification of Occupations and Directory of Occupational Titles – a classification based on the work performed, of 3,500 separate occupations covering 11,000 different jobs. It is used within the (British) Department of Employment for vacancy classification and for improving manpower information.

CO-EXTENSIVENESS. Intensive classification to coincide with the specific nature of the subject of a book.

COFFIN. A square frame in a hand printing press in which is bedded a stone on which the FORME (*q.v.*) is placed.

COIL BINDING. *Synonymous with* SPIRAL BINDING (*q.v.*).

COILED BINDING. *Synonymous with* SPIRAL BINDING (*q.v.*).

COLD COMPOSITION. (*Printing*) Any method of composition which does not involve the casting of metal type. Typewriter, filmsetting and photographic methods are included. 'Cold type' is sometimes used to distinguish this method from 'hot metal' typesetting.

COLD TYPE. Composition by a composing machine which does not require hot metal, such as photographically or on a typewriter, JUSTOWRITER or VARITYPER (*qq.v.*).

COLE SIZE CARD. A graduated card for determining the sizes of books (not by measurement but by bibliographical description) when writing catalogue and bibliography entries. This size card, which was first issued in 1889 by the Library Bureau, was based on the size rules of the American Library Association, the more uniform and accurate use of which the size card was intended to achieve. The card was named after its designer, Dr. George Watson Cole (1850–1939), who was Librarian of the Henry E. Huntington Library from 1915 to 1924. *See also* HUNTINGTON LIBRARY. A description of the card may be read in *The Library Journal* 14, 1889, pp. 485–6.

COLLABORATOR. One who is associated with another, or others, especially in the writing of books, being responsible for some aspect of, or contribution to, a work, but not responsible for the content as a whole.

COLLAGE. A picture or visual arrangement made partly or entirely of pieces of paper, wallpaper, illustrations, photographs or any other textured or figured material.

COLLATE. 1. To examine a book, whether bound or in the process of being bound, to see if the sections are complete and in the right sequence and to make sure that no maps, illustrations, etc., are missing. 2. To collect, compare and examine minutely and critically books and manuscripts to determine whether or not two copies are identical or variants. 3. Used in connection with tabulation machines to indicate the combining or merging of record cards into a desired sequence. 4. To transfer corrections marked on one proof to another marked proof, e.g. from a proofreader's proof to an author's proof.

COLLATERAL ARRAYS. (*Classification*) Arrays of the same order. *See also* ARRAY.

COLLATERAL CLASSES. (*Classification*) Classes of the same order but not belonging to the same array. *See also* ARRAY.

COLLATERAL REFERENCE. One which in an alphabetico-specific subject catalogue links two headings belonging to the same hierarchical level under a common generic term, and which would stand side by side if arranged in a classification scheme.

COLLATERAL TERM. (*Indexing*) A word which forms a constituent part of a BOUND TERM (*q.v.*) and which is also found in association with another word, both being used as a heading in a subject index. *See also* GENERIC TERM.

COLLATING MARK. A quad mark having a printing surface about 12-point deep by 5-point wide, which is printed so that after folding and gathering, the marks appear in descending order on the back of each section in such a way that the omission or duplication of a section becomes immediately apparent. Also called BACK MARK, BLACK STEP (*qq.v.*), 'Quad mark'.

COLLATION. 1. That part of a description of a book, apart from the contents, which describes the book as a physical object by specifying the number of volumes, pages, columns, leaves, illustrations, photographs, maps, format, size, etc. In a bibliographical description of an old book the number, which is expressed by the signature letters (*see* SIGNATURE 2), and composition of the sections is important. A *collation by gatherings* records the make-up of a book by stating the signature letters, e.g. A⁴, *², B–2A⁴, etc.; a *collation by pagination* records the make-up by the page numbers, e.g. [1]–[12], 1–374, etc. 2. The process of examining a new book to check its completeness, presence of all the illustrations, etc. 3. To check that a book is complete before binding or re-binding. 4. To compare two or more texts, either (a) to ascertain which is the first edition of a printed work, or (b) to establish a definitive or standard text. 5. To merge and combine two or more similarly ordered sets of items to produce an ordered set (*IBM*).

COLLATOR. 1. A fitting consisting of trays or divisions into each of which is put a number of small printed or duplicated sheets of paper in a required order so that one of each may be arranged in sequence quickly when required. This saves the labour and table space involved in laying the sheets out in piles in order to take one from each. 2. In electric accounting machines, one which combines or emerges files of cards into any desired sequence.

COLLECTANEA. Passages selected from one or more authors, generally for instruction. A collection or miscellany.

COLLECTED EDITION. An edition of an author's works published in one volume or in a number of volumes in a uniform style of binding.

COLLECTED WORKS. All the writings of an author, including those which have not been printed previously, published in one volume or a number of volumes in a uniform style of binding, usually with an inclusive title.

COLLECTING DRUM. A revolving drum which is fitted to a high-speed printing press or paper-making machine to catch the sheets of paper coming out of the machine and collect them in groups of from five to ten so that final delivery can be at a slower speed. They are then delivered together as a group which can be passed on at only a fifth of the speed otherwise required.

COLLECTION. 1. A number of books or other items on one subject, or of one kind, or collected by one person or organization. 2. (*Bibliography*) A number of works, or parts of them, not forming a treatise or monograph on a single subject, and regarded as constituting a single whole, as a collection of plays, essays, etc. 3. (*Cataloguing*) If written by one author, three or more independent works, or parts of works, published together; if written by more than one author, two or more independent works, or parts of works, published together but not written for the same occasion or for the same publication.

COLLECTION NUMBER. In the Colon Classification, a suitable symbol to be determined by each individual library, and added to the CLASS NUMBER (*q.v.*) and BOOK NUMBER (*q.v.*) to indicate the collection to which the book belongs.

COLLECTIVE BIOGRAPHY. A volume, or volumes, consisting of separate accounts of the lives of people.

COLLECTIVE CATALOGUING. The cataloguing of minor and fugitive material by (a) assembling a group of such items and assigning it a heading and a collective title; (b) cataloguing it by form but stating the corporate or personal authorship and giving the class number or other retrieval identification. *See also* FORM ENTRY, FORM HEADING.

COLLECTIVE ENTRIES.   In selective cataloguing, several entries on one card for pamphlets on the same or related subjects. They may be either author or subject entries.

COLLECTIVE TITLE.   1. A title under which articles written separately by several authors are published together. If there is no recognized author, compiler, or editing body, the main catalogue entry appears under the title of the work. 2. The title given to a work as a whole when that work consists of several works, each with its own title (*IFLA*).

COLLECTOR.   One who puts together several works or parts of works. Usually called an editor.

COLLEGE LIBRARIES, STANDARDS FOR.   *See* STANDARDS FOR COLLEGE LIBRARIES.

COLLEGE LIBRARY.   A library established, maintained, and administered by a college to meet the needs of its students and faculty.

COLLEGES, INSTITUTES AND SCHOOLS OF EDUCATION.   Formerly a sub-section of the UNIVERSITY, COLLEGE AND RESEARCH SECTION (*q.v.*) of the LIBRARY ASSOCIATION (*q.v.*). Now an independent Group. Abbreviated CISE. Publishes *Newsletter* (3 p.a.).

COLLEGES OF TECHNOLOGY AND FURTHER EDUCATION.   Formerly a sub-section of the UNIVERSITY, COLLEGE AND RESEARCH SECTION (*q.v*) of the LIBRARY ASSOCIATION (*q.v.*). Since January 1970 it has been an independent Group. Abbreviated CTFE. Publishes *Bulletin* (3 p.a. irreg.).

COLLOCATION.   The arrangement of sub-classes of a classification by degrees of likeness.

COLLOCATIVE *v.* DIRECT CATALOGUING.   The principle of entering books written by one author using several pseudonyms under his real name (collocative) or under the name used for each individual title (direct).

COLLOGRAPHY.   A similar production process to collotype except that a film base wrapped around a cylinder is used instead of a flat glass plate.

COLLOPLAS.   Trade name for a process for making non-etched gravure cylinders in which a rubber surface on which the printing image is impressed hydraulically is substituted for the copper-coated etched cylinders used in photogravure. The method was announced in 1954 by Koch Processes Ltd., a member of the Photogravure and Allied Holdings Ltd. Group.

COLLOTYPE.   A variety of photogravure. A print which gives accurate gradation of tone; it is made by a photo-mechanical process directly from a hardened emulsion of bichromated gelatine on glass. Phototype, Albertype, Artotype, Heliotype and Lichtdruck are forms of collotype. William Henry Fox Talbot, an English pioneer of photography, discovered in 1852 that a chromate gelatine layer was case-hardened by exposure to light, and the first person to employ this process for the production of printing plates was Alphonse Louis Poitevin in 1855. By coating a plate with chromated gelatine and printing and developing a photographic image on it, a surface could be obtained which, when damped, responds to ink in the same way as a lithographic stone. Also called a 'Gelatine print'.

COLOMBIER.   Drawing and plate paper size 24 × 34½ inches. Also spelled 'Columbier'.

COLON.   1. A device used in the Universal Decimal Classification to link related class terms (*IBM*). 2. A device used in the Colon Classification to separate successive foci. Later, in the Colon Classification, a device to introduce the energy facet (*IBM*). 3. A punctuation symbol.

COLON ABBREVIATIONS.   A scheme devised by C. A. Cutter to save the writing out in full of authors' forenames. It consists of the initial letters of the most used Christian names in each letter of the alphabet followed by a colon (vertically for men, horizontally for women), e.g..

> H: (Henry)
> J: (John)
> M. .   (Mary).

COLON BOOK NUMBER.   A book number used in connection with the COLON CLASSIFICATION (*q.v.*). The numbers are based on the facet formula as follows: L the language of exposition (taken from the CC Language Schedule); F the number for the form of exposition (from the CC Form Schedule); T the number for the year of publication (from the CC Chronological Schedule); SN the serial number, used to distinguish the different books in the same ultimate class and having the same language and form numbers; V the volume number (from the book itself); S the number for the supplement (from the book itself); C the copy number, other than the first (made serially as for the SN); EVN the evaluation number for pseudo classics. Usually only three numbers are used to provide the Book Number: only the year of publication is used for individualizing each document, and the other provisions in the formula are seldom needed. *See also* BOOK NUMBER.

COLON CLASSIFICATION.   An elaborate, scholarly scheme designed by S. R. Ranganathan especially for Indian libraries. It is based on the classification of any subject by its uses and relations, which are indicated by numbers divided by the colon ':'. In this classification, ready-made class numbers are not provided for most topics, but are constructed by combining in assigned permutations and combinations the classes of the various unit schedules of which the scheme consists, colons separating the different units. Special schedules are provided for Geographical Divisions (a Local List), Language Divisions, and Chronological Divisions (Space Isolate, Language Isolate, and Time Isolate respectively). A schedule of common sub-divisions (Common Isolate), using the lower-case letters of the alphabet as its primary symbol is also provided. It was the first example of an analytico-synthetic classification, in which the subject field is first analysed into facets, and class numbers are then constructed by synthesis. *See* BOOK NUMBER 2, COLON BOOK NUMBER.

COLONIAL EDITION. An edition of a work, usually of fiction, often printed and bound at the same time as the ordinary edition, but usually on poorer paper, and bound in a poorer style. Issued for export to the Colonies.

COLOPHON (Gr. 'finishing, end'). 1. Particulars of printer, place and date of printing, title, name of author, and publisher's or printer's device, found at the end of early printed books. It was first used in printed books by Fust and Schoeffer in the 'Mainz Psalter' of 1457, and gradually became common, but was superseded towards 1600 by the Publisher's Imprint. Its use in MSS. was occasional; it then gave the scribe's name and the date. *See also* IMPRINT. 2. A current, but incorrect, meaning is the publisher's device, e.g. Benn's horse, Deutsch's bow and arrows, Hutchinson's bull, Heinemann's windmill or Thames and Hudson's dolphins.

COLOPHON DATE. The date give in the COLOPHON (*q.v.*), and so described when used in a catalogue or bibliography.

COLOUR CODING. The visual presentation, by means of coloured signals, of information in a conventional card catalogue, e.g. the colours indicating in a catalogue of periodicals the frequency, language, subject, etc., of each title.

COLOUR FILTER. Coloured gelatine, glass or plastic, used in front of a camera lens to absorb certain colours.

COLOUR GRAVURE. The process of producing coloured illustrations in colour by PHOTOGRAVURE (*q.v.*). This method is used principally for mass circulation colour magazines and packaging materials. The colour picture is usually of almost continuous tone, the dark and light shades being obtained by varying depths of the etched cells.

COLOUR LITHOGRAPHY. A method of printing in colour by lithography using separate stones or plates for each colour.

COLOUR PRINTING. The art of producing pictures, designs, etc., in a variety of colours, shades and tones by means of printing from plates, or by lithography; chromatic printing.

COLOUR PROCESS. A set of two or more half-tones made by colour separation. Half-tone colour printing is commonly called process colour work.

COLOUR SEPARATION. The process by which colours of an original work of art or colour print are analysed into the basic colours in such a way that printing plates may be prepared in order to print in succession and finally yield a print of correct colouring. This is done by placing filters in front of the camera lens when making negatives.

COLOUR SEPARATION NEGATIVE. A negative for use in colour printing which, by the use of a colour filter, has recorded a primary colour.

COLOUR TRANSPARENCY. A positive colour photograph on a transparent support, usually film.

COLOUR UNDER GILT. The edges of a book coloured (usually red) before gilding. Usually found in Bible binding. *See also* EDGES, RED UNDER GOLD EDGES.

COLOUR WORK. Printing processes used to print in two or more colours, such as two-, or four-colour half-tone; planographic and intaglio work in colour. Often called according to the number of plates used, 'Three-colour Process', 'Four-colour Process'.

COLOURED EDGES. *Synonymous with* SPRINKLED EDGES (*q.v.*).

COLOURED PLATE. A whole-page coloured illustration produced by any process.

COLOURED PRINTINGS. A cheap quality paper, having a high content of mechanical wood pulp; it is used, among other purposes, for the covers of pamphlets.

COLPORTEUR. A travelling bookseller or agent, usually of a religious group or society, who sells tracts and copies of the scriptures at low prices.

COLUMBIAN. An out-of-date name for a size of type equal to about 16 point.

COLUMBIAN PRESS. A printing press designed by George Clymer of Philadelphia and brought to England in 1817 where it became more successful than in the United States. The press derived its power from a system of levers which converted the lateral movement of the bar to the vertical movement of the iron beam from which the platen was suspended. The most conspicuous feature of the press was a cast-iron eagle which acted as an adjustable counter weight.

COLUMBIER. *See* COLOMBIER.

COLUMN. 1. A narrow division of a page of a book formed by vertical lines or spaces to form two or three columns of type. When such columns, instead of pages, are numbered, the revisions of Chapter 6 of the North American and British Texts of *AACR* provide that the publication shall be described in terms of the number of columns. 2. A narrow block of letterpress arranged in the form of a column. 3. (*Printing*) A vertical line or square bracket.

COLUMN INCH. (*Printing*) *See* AGATE LINE.

COLUMN PICTURE. Picture in a mediaeval illuminated manuscript the width of a column of text, whether at the head of a page, or interrupting the text at intervals.

COLUMN RULE. (*Printing*) A metal rule used to separate columns of type in the text or in tables. *See also* RULE.

COLUMNAR. A series or classification in which the terms, or classes, are arranged in a column. The classes may be co-ordinate, or they may be regarded as subordinate, each to that above it. (*Bliss*). *See* HORIZONTAL, TABULAR CLASSIFICATION.

COLUMNS. Some kinds of books such as encyclopaedias have the text printed in two or more parallel columns of type to the page. Where these, instead of the pages, are numbered, the collation in a cataloguing or bibliographical entry should make this clear, as: XI pp., 1480 columns.

COM. Acronym of Computer-Output Microfilm(ing). 1. A generic term embracing the processes – or the result – of transferring computer data on magnetic tape on to microfilm or microfiche at very high speed. 2. A unit of hardware which produces some form of microfilm record from a signal which has been created in a computer, regardless of whether the signal comes directly from the computer or from an auxiliary memory unit. The basic COM unit converts digital information from a computer either directly or from magnetic tapes to an image on a cathode ray tube. This image is photographed, thus producing the microfilm. In 1974 the British Standards Institution published quality requirements for COM, in the form of a draft for development, DD27, *Quality requirements for computer output on microfilm*. This has been produced to establish standards of quality for the resulting microfilm and the duplicates which can be made from it.

COMAC. Continuous Multiple Access Collator. A punched card collating system for the storage and retrieval of information prepared for the Air Force Office of Scientific Research, Directorate of Advanced Studies, Washington, D.C. It is a mechanized Uniterm index, codes punched on one card being matched against codes punched on another card, the codes for the logical product or sum being punched on a third card.

COMB PATTERN. A pattern produced on marbled papers or other surfaces from a vat in which colours have been combed to form a pattern. *See also* MARBLED PAPER.

COMBINATION CODING. *Synonymous with* INDIRECT CODING (*q.v.*). *See also* MARGINAL-HOLE PUNCHED CARDS.

COMBINATION ORDER. (*Cataloguing, Classification, Information retrieval*) The order in which facets in a compound subject heading are to be arranged, e.g. the order of DECREASING CONCRETENESS (*q.v.*). *See also* DESCRIPTOR SEQUENCE, DISTRIBUTED FACETS.

COMBINATION PLATE. One in which both half-tone and line methods have been used.

COMBINATION SYSTEM. *Synonymous with* CORRELATIVE SYSTEM (*q.v.*).

COMBINED NEGATIVE. Negative film carrying both sound and picture.

COMBINED POSITIVE PRINT. A positive print of a film carrying both sound and picture.

COMMA. A punctuation mark. *See also* QUOTES, TURNED COMMA.

COMMAND PAPERS. *See* PARLIAMENTARY PAPERS.

COMMAND RETRIEVAL INFORMATION SYSTEM. A system of images on scrolls of 16 mm or 35 mm microfilm, with 500,000 images on a scroll. Scrolls are placed in a special retrieving device having a keyboard selector and a screen where an enlargement can be viewed or copied as a micro image. Abbreviated CRIS.

COMMENTARY. 1. Explanatory or critical notes on an Act of Parliament, a literary text or some other work. It may accompany the text or be issued separately. 2. A spoken commentary to a film or filmstrip.

COMMERCIAL LIBRARY. Similar to a commercial section but on a much larger scale and housed in a separate room from the reference library, and sometimes in a separate building.

COMMERCIAL SECTION. The section of a reference library devoted to providing material and information of a commercial nature.

COMMITTEE FOR INTERNATIONAL CO-ORDINATION OF NATIONAL RESEARCH IN DEMOGRAPHY. *See* CICRED.

COMMITTEE ON DATA FOR SCIENCE AND TECHNOLOGY. *See* CODATA.

COMMITTEE ON INTERNATIONAL SCIENTIFIC AND TECHNICAL INFORMATION PROGRAMS. *See* CISTIP.

COMMITTEE ON SCIENTIFIC AND TECHNICAL COMMUNICATION. *See* SATCOM.

COMMITTEE ON SCIENTIFIC AND TECHNICAL INFORMATION. *See* COSATI.

COMMON AUXILIARIES. *See* UNIVERSAL DECIMAL CLASSIFICATION.

COMMON FACETS. Facets or terms which may occur in more than one field in a general classification.

COMMON FOLIO. *See* FOLIO.

COMMON ISOLATES. Symbols attached to many classes in the Colon Classification and indicating literary form, e.g. *a* bibliography; *c* concordance; *v* history; *y*2 syllabus; P*v* history of linguistics; Plll*v* history of English linguistics. When attached to a host class number without a connecting symbol, as in the examples given, they are called *Anteriorising Common Isolates*, but when needing a connecting symbol *Posteriorising Common Isolates*.

COMMON RULING. Term used to denote the vertical lines (rules) printed on account-book paper. *See also* FEINT RULING.

COMMON SUBDIVISIONS. Form divisions which are used throughout a classification to sub-divide any subject. These have distinctive names in different classifications, e.g. AUXILIARY TABLES (*q.v.*) in Dewey and the Universal Decimal Classification; CATEGORICAL TABLES (*q.v.*) in Brown's *Subject classification*, and SYSTEMATIC SCHEDULES (*q.v.*) in Bliss's *Bibliographic classification*.

COMMONWEALTH AGRICULTURAL BUREAUX. This organization was set up to act as a clearing-house for information for scientists and research workers in agriculture throughout the world. The organization covers all the agricultural sciences, including forestry and animal health, and operates three Institutes and ten Bureaux. Abbreviation CAB.

COMMONWEALTH LIBRARY ASSOCIATION. Arising from a suggestion first made by the Commonwealth Foundation, and its grant of £29,500 spread over a period of three years, representatives of over twenty Commonwealth library associations participated in a preliminary conference at the Library Association's headquarters in 1971, and in 1972 it was agreed to form the Commonwealth Library Association. This Association is intended to help to improve libraries in the Commonwealth; maintain and strengthen links between librarians of the various countries; support and encourage library associations in the individual countries; and concern itself with education for librarianship and common, reciprocal, standards of qualification. Abbreviated COMLA. Publishes *COMLA Newsletter* (q.).

COMMONWEALTH SCIENTIFIC AND RESEARCH ORGANIZA-TION. Established in Australia by the Science and Industry Act of 1949; it replaced the Council for Scientific and Industrial Research established in 1926 which itself replaced the Institute of Science and Industry which was formed in 1919. It is concerned with all fields of pure and applied science, excluding medicine, and operates through nearly forty subject divisions and sections. The functions are: carrying out scientific research for the promotion of primary and secondary industries in the Commonwealth and its Territories; training scientific research workers and awarding studentships; making grants in aid of scientific work; the recognition and support of research associations; maintaining Commonwealth standards of measurement; disseminating scientific and technical information, publishing scientific and technical reports. Compiles and publishes *Australian Science Index* (m.) and *CSIRO Abstracts* (m.). Most of the divisions and sections issue publications. Abbreviated CSIRO.

COMMUNITY LIBRARY. A major library unit containing an adequate, well-organized collection of books, serving a population of 55,000, open 48 to 66 hours a week, and having a professional and clerical staff. (American.)

COMPACT STORAGE. The storing of books on rolling or swinging stacks which have to be moved into another position to permit consultation, or of books or other material placed in drawers built into shelving and opening into a stack aisle. Such shelving is used normally in stack rooms, and increases capacity up to 114%. *See also* COMPACTUS, DRAW-OUT SHELVES, ROLLING BOOKCASE, ROLLING PRESS, STOR-MOR, SWINGING BOOKCASE.

COMPACTUS. Trade name for a particular design of shelving invented by Ingold, a Swiss engineer. Steel bookcases are placed against one another and are moved sideways for consultation of the books by operating a lever which activates a clutch which grips a revolving cable set in the floor, or by pressing a switch which operates the same mechanism by electricity. The books on one side of each of two cases are exposed to view by this means. Also called 'Ingold-Compactus'.

COMPANY FILE. A file, kept especially in commercial, industrial, research and learned or professional association libraries, containing information relating to individual firms. The type of information kept depends on the type of library and the needs of its users but may include reports, company reports, house journals, catalogues, booklets, cuttings, advertisements, stock exchange listings, etc. Also called 'Corporation file'.

COMPARATIVE LIBRARIANSHIP. 'The analysis of libraries, library systems, some aspects of librarianship, or library problems in two or more national, cultural, or societal environments, in terms of socio-political, economic, cultural, idealogical, and historical contexts. This analysis is for the purpose of understanding the underlying similarities and differences, and for determining explanations of the differences, with the ultimate aim of trying to arrive at valid generalizations and principles.' – *J. Periam Danton.*

COMPARTMENT. 1. In a book stack, sets of shelves arranged vertically between two uprights and placed back to back. (American.) 2. (*Bibliography*) A group of decorative borders comprising (a) a single carved or engraved piece with the centre portion cut out so as to resemble a picture frame into which the letterpress of a title or other matter is set; (b) a piece originally carved or engraved as (a) but later cut into four or more pieces; (c) four or more pieces cut or engraved separately but intended to form a single design when assembled; (d) such borders made from four pieces of cast type-ornaments but with ends cut obliquely to help form a border. *See also* FRAME.

COMPARTMENT PICTURE. An illumination, in a mediaeval illuminated manuscript, divided into sections each of which contains a picture.

COMPASS MAP. *See* PORTOLAN CHART.

COMPATIBILITY OF THESAURI. (*Information retrieval*) The quality of two or more thesauri which are compiled by the same methods and in which the descriptors can be interchanged, and which may be used to index, or for searching, in equivalent subject fields.

COMPEND. A subject treated briefly, or in outline only.

COMPENDEX. Abbreviation for COMPuterized ENgineering InDEX, the machine-readable version of *Engineering Index*, the principal abstracting and indexing periodical covering the broad field of engineering.

COMPENDIUM. A work containing in a small compass the substance or general principles of a larger work; a brief, comprehensive summary.

COMPENSATION GUARDS. Short stubs bound into a volume to balance the space taken up by folded maps or other bulky material so that this can be incorporated without distorting the shape of the book. Also called 'Filling-in guards'. *See also* GUARD, STUB.

COMPETITOR FILE.   A record on cards, or a file of cuttings, publications, reports about, or published by, competitor companies.

COMPILATION.   A work compiled by assembling material from other books.

COMPILER.   1. A collector or editor of written or printed material gleaned from various sources or from one or more authors; and who arranges it for publication. 2. One who produces a musical work by collecting and putting together written or printed matter from the work of several composers. Also, one who chooses and combines into one work selections and excerpts from one or more composers (*MLA/ALA Code*).

COMPILER ENTRY.   A catalogue entry for the compiler of a work.

COMPLETE BIBLIOGRAPHY.   *See* BIBLIOGRAPHY 1.

COMPLETE SPECIFICATION.   *See* PATENT, SPECIFICATION.

COMPLETION.   *See* CONTINUATION.

COMPLEX ARRAY ISOLATE.   (*Classification*) An array isolate which is found by combining two or more array isolates to form one array in order to express the relation between them.

COMPLEX CLASS.   (*Classification*) A class which is formed by combining two or more isolates to form one facet in order to express the relation between them.

COMPLEX ISOLATE.   (*Classification*) An isolate which is formed by the combination of two or more isolates to form one FACET (*q.v.*) in order to express the relationship between them.

COMPLEX SUBJECT.   In classification, one which reflects more than one distinct conventional class.

COMPLUTENSIAN POLYGLOT.   The polyglot *Bible* in six volumes printed between 1514 and 1517 at Alcalá de Henares, a small town near Madrid, by Arnald Guillen de Brocar. It was the first of the great multi-lingual Bibles, and is by far the most important landmark in Spanish printing. The text is in Hebrew, Aramaic, Greek and Latin. Called Complutensian Bible because Complutum is the Roman name for Alcalá de Henares. *See also* POLYGLOT.

COMPONENT.   An individual constituent word in a compound subject heading.

COMPOSE.   To set type-matter ready for printing.

COMPOSER.   One who composes, especially music.

COMPOSER ENTRY.   1. An entry in a catalogue for a musical composition under the name of the composer as the heading. Normally this is the main entry but it may be an added entry. 2. Sometimes used for the composer heading chosen for the entry, and not the entry itself.

COMPOSING ROOM.   A room in which printing type is set, or composed, and made up into formes for printing. *See also* COMPOSITOR.

COMPOSING RULE.   A flat strip of steel or brass placed by the compositor between each line of type in his composing stick when setting type. Rules provide a flat surface for each line of type and facilitate the handling of the composed type. Also called 'Setting rule'.

COMPOSING STICK.   *Also called* STICK (*q.v.*).

COMPOSITE AUTHORS.   Name given to the several authors contributing to one work. Not to be confused with JOINT AUTHOR (*q.v.*).

COMPOSITE BOOK.   1. A book of a composite nature, where an editor has brought together several works by different authors into one volume. 2. A book on more than one subject. 3. A COMPOSITE WORK (*q.v.*).

COMPOSITE CLASSIFICATION.   A method of classifying whereby specific subjects are represented by coupling two or more elementary terms from the classification schedules as indicated at COMPOSITE SUBJECT (*q.v.*).

COMPOSITE HEADING.   (*Cataloguing*) A heading consisting of more than one element each of which is to be distinguished by punctuation, or typographically, for filing purposes.

COMPOSITE SUBJECT.   (*Classification*). One which consists of more than one element, e.g. the design of furniture for children's libraries.

COMPOSITE WORK.   1. A literary production on a single subject written by two or more authors in collaboration, the contribution by each forming a distinct section or part of the complete work. 2. A musical composition in which two or more composers collaborate similarly, each contribution forming a distinct section or part of the complete work.

COMPOSITION.   Type setting: hence Compositor.

COMPOSITION FOUNT.   Loosely used to indicate any type-face of a size of 14-point or less, used for book printing and 'tapped' on a type-composing machine.

COMPOSITOR.   One who sets printer's type. A typesetter.

COMPOUND.   (*Information retrieval*) A pattern of data units showing all the features which are possessed in common by a given set of items.

COMPOUND CATCHWORD.   In indexing, a hyphenated word which must be treated as if the hyphen did not exist.

COMPOUND CLASS. In the Colon Classification, a class made of a Basic Class (i.e. Main, or Canonical, Class) and one or more Isolates.

COMPOUND HEADING. (*Information retrieval*) A number of general terms arranged together in a co-ordinate relationship to designate a complex idea. *See also* MAIN HEADING.

COMPOUND NAME. A name made of two or more proper names, generally connected by a hyphen, conjunction or preposition.

COMPOUND SUBJECT. (*Cataloguing*) One which requires more than one word in the subject heading to express its meaning. A compound subject may consist of a phrase or a combination, the separate words of which are divided by punctuation. (*Classification*) One which reflects more than one facet within a conventional class, for example, within the class Building, Wooden Floor is a compound, reflecting both a material and a part.

COMPOUND SUBJECT HEADING. A heading which consists of (a) two words joined by a conjunction, as 'Punch and Judy'; (b) a phrase, as 'Council of Trent'; (c) words which are always associated together; e.g. 'Capital Punishment'; 'Political Economy'.

COMPREHENSIVE BIBLIOGRAPHY. One which lists, as far as possible, everything published on the subject. *See also* CURRENT COMPREHENSIVE BIBLIOGRAPHY.

COMPRESENCE. A linked set of FEATURES (*q.v.*) describing a given ITEM (*q.v.*), or of items defining a given feature.

COMPRESSED FULL SCORE. *See* SCORE.

COMPRESSED SCORE. *Synonymous with* CLOSE SCORE (*q.v.*). *See also* SCORE.

COMPUTER INFORMATION CENTRE. *See* COPIC.

COMPUTER OUTPUT MICROFILM. (*Information retrieval*) Microfilm produced as direct computer output, without printout as an intermediary. The film is printed at approximately the same rate as the computer can transfer information internally.

COMPUTER SOFTWARE MANAGEMENT INFORMATION CENTER. *See* COSMIC.

COMPUTER TYPESETTING. A technique whereby text in machine-readable form can be printed out in graphic art quality without conventional typesetting.

COMPUTERIZED DOCUMENTATION SERVICE. *See* CDS.

COMPUTERIZED ENGINEERING INDEX. *See* COMPENDEX.

COMPUTERIZED LIBRARIANSHIP. Computer installations exist which will provide a book-ordering system, and then prepare catalogues and book lists, record the loan of books, and prepare overdue notices complete with book number, author and title, date due for return, etc. *See* R. J. Huse 'The West Sussex Libraries catalogue and information system', *Library Association Record* 75 (7) July 1973 pp. 127–130.

COMPUTERIZED REARRANGEMENT OF SPECIAL SUBJECTS. *See* CROSS.

CONCEPT CO-ORDINATION. 1. A system of multi-dimensional indexing with single concepts to define a document uniquely (*IBM*). 2. A system of co-ordinate indexing for information retrieval. *See also* CO-ORDINATE INDEXING, UNITERM CONCEPT CO-ORDINATE INDEXING, ZATOCODING.

CONCEPT INDEXING. 1. The process of deciding which are the concepts in a particular document that are of sufficient importance to be included in the SUBJECT INDEX (*q.v.*). 2. The use of a standard description for each concept (whether it has been used by the author of the text or not) and using it as a subject heading whenever appropriate.

CONCERTINA FOLD. A method of folding paper, first to the right and then to the left, so that it opens and closes in the manner of a concertina. Also called 'Zig-zag fold'.

CONCILIUM BIBLIOGRAPHICUM. A bibliographical work begun by Herbert Haviland Field at Zurich in 1895. Cards were printed and distributed as soon as published for all publications (primarily periodical articles, with some books and pamphlets) on zoology, palæontology, general biology, microscopy, anatomy, physiology and kindred subjects, from all countries. It thus formed a complete bibliography. After the death of the founder in 1921, the Rockefeller Foundation made a grant for five years, hoping that the organization would receive finance internationally. The enterprise continued on subscriptions alone until 1940 when it ceased to function. It is often referred to as the ZURICH INDEX.

CONCISE DESCRIPTION, PRINCIPLE OF. The avoidance of duplication or unessential information in a catalogue entry. *See also* CATALOGUING, PRINCIPLES OF.

CONCORDANCE. 1. A book arranged so as to form an alphabetical index of all passages, or of all the more important words, in any work, with indications of the context of such passages and phrases in the text. 2. In machine indexing, an alphabetical index of words in a document, each word present in the text being an index entry. As no discrimination is exercised in preparing this type of index, the decisions that must be made can be performed well by machines.

CONCRETENESS, PRINCIPLE OF DECREASING. *See* DECREAS-ING CONCRETENESS, PRINCIPLE OF.

CONCRETES AND PROCESSES. A method of indexing devised by K. Kaiser in which the main (first, or leading) word of the subject-entry is the main, 'concrete', subject, and the later one/s the secondary (or aspect) 'processes' sub-dividing it.

CONDENSED SCORE. *Synonymous with* CLOSE SCORE (*q.v.*). *See also* SCORE.

CONDENSED TYPE. Type which is narrow in proportion to its height. **This is an example.**

CONDITIONING. The maturing of paper, carried out in the paper mill by drying out or adding moisture to it so as to bring it 'into balance' with what is accepted as normal printing-room atmosphere and to enable it to be used on fast-running machines without danger of cockling. The process is carried out in a temperature of $60°-65°$ F. and a relative humidity of 65%; the paper will then contain about 7% moisture evenly distributed over the sheet, and the fibres will remain stable during printing.

CONDUCTOR'S PART. The printed music for an instrumentalist who also simultaneously conducts a concerted work. Also called 'Conductor's score'. *See also* SCORE.

CONDUCTOR'S SCORE. *Synonymous with* CONDUCTOR'S PART (*q.v.*). *See also* SCORE.

confer. (*Lat.* 'compare'.) To compare or refer to. Usually used in the abbreviated form (cf.).

CONFERENCE OF SOUTHEAST ASIAN LIBRARIANS. *See* CONSAL.

CONFIDENTIAL FILE. Material in a special library which is kept securely, and apart from other material, and is only used under certain conditions. *See also* CLASSIFIED MATERIAL.

CONFIGURATION. (*Information retrieval*) The general term given to a computer system; it is normally used to indicate the physical units of the system.

CONGER. A group of from ten to twenty wholesale booksellers who combined to share the publishing and selling of books, and to protect the sale of their books from undercutting and piracy. Congers were a feature of the London book trade in the late seventeenth and early eighteenth centuries.

CONGRESS, LIBRARY OF, CLASSIFICATION. *See* LIBRARY OF CONGRESS CLASSIFICATION.

CONJOINT AUTHORSHIP. *See* JOINT AUTHOR.

CONJUGATE. (*Bibliography*) This term is applied to two leaves which can be traced into and out of the back of a book and found to be one piece of paper.

CONJUNCTION. (*Classification*) In the Colon Classification, a symbol used to couple two substantives.

CONJUNCTIVE. Pertaining to the joining or coupling of two documents, words, phrases, or elements of information in order to express a unity. Being neither disjunctive nor collateral (*IBM*).

CONNECTING SYMBOLS. *See* CLASS NUMBER and FUNDAMENTAL CATEGORIES.

CONNECTIVE CATALOGUE. *Synonymous with* SYNDETIC CATALOGUE (*q.v.*).

CONNOTATION. A term in classification indicative of all the qualities conveyed by, or comprised in, a class name; e.g. 'man' in connotation means the qualities (mammalian structure, upright gait, reason, etc.) that go to make up man, as opposed to *detonation*, where the term merely marks down or indicates. The phrase: 'That man is really a man' shows the denotative followed by the connotative use of the word. Connotation and denotation may be considered synonymous with intension and EXTENSION (*q.v.*).

CONNOTATIVE. *See* CONNOTATION.

CONSAL. Abbreviation for Conference of Southeast Asian Librarians, a regional library association which was created on the initiative of the Malaysian and Singapore library associations and held its first conference at the University of Singapore in August 1970. CONSAL II was held in December 1973 at the University of the Philippines in Manila, and Consal III, jointly with the Third General Conference of SARBICA (*q.v.*) at Jakarta in December 1975.

CONSER.† Abbreviation for Co-operative CONversion of SERials, a U.S.-Canadian project for developing a machine-readable catalogue of some 300,000 titles of journals and periodicals held by libraries in the U.S.A. and Canada – the first approach towards a truly international serials bibliography, which can be used by the generators and maintainers of union lists of serials. The project was first discussed at the ALA annual conference at Las Vegas in 1973 and was to become operative in 1975. The file is available through the Library of Congress and the National Library of Canada. The Project is managed by the Council on Library Resources (CLR) and the Ohio College Library Center (OCLC) computer network is being used. Ten institutions (the American national libraries – *see* NATIONAL LIBRARY) the State University of New York/New York State Library, and the libraries of the Universities of California, Minnesota and of Yale and Cornell Universities, were involved initially.

CONSERVATION. (Archives) The use of chemical and physical procedures in treatment or storage to ensure the preservation of a document.

CONSERVATIVE LIBRARY ASSOCIATION. Founded in the U.S.A. in 1964. Is devoted to collections that emphasise educational books, and to a conception of the freedom to read that includes books of the right as well as the left.

CONSIDERATION FILE. The accumulation of current selections for purchase. (American.)

CONSISTENT CHARACTERISTICS. *See* CHARACTERISTIC OF A CLASSIFICATION.

CONSOLE. (*Information retrieval*) The unit of a computer which is used for all manual communication with the computer.

CONSOLIDATED INDEX. An index, in one sequence, to several volumes, a long run of a periodical or other serial publication, or to several independent works or serial publications.

CONSOLIDATED SYSTEM. A system of libraries established by the decision of several municipal governing bodies, or by the action of voters, and governed by the Board of Trustees of the system. The individual library units operate as branches of the system. (American.)

'CONSONANT' CODE. (*Information retrieval*) One of several systematic methods of abbreviating words.

CONSTANCE LINDSAY SKINNER AWARD. *See* WOMEN'S NATIONAL BOOK ASSOCIATION.

CONSTANT MNEMONICS. *See* MNEMONICS.

CONTACT. A copy of a photograph or document made in direct contact with the original.

CONTACT COPYING. A non-optical copying process whereby the original and the material of reproduction are brought into close contact during exposure. The resulting copy can be described as a 'contact copy' or 'contact print'. The opposite of OPTICAL COPYING (*q.v.*). *See also* CONTACT PRINTING, LENSLESS COPYING. REFLEX COPYING, TRANSMISSION COPYING.

CONTACT PHOTOGRAPHY. A method of making a photographic copy of a document on only one side of which the record appears, whereby the light shines through the document being copied on to the sensitized paper. The resulting black-on-white negative is then placed together with a sheet of sensitized paper and the process repeated to make a positive. *See also* REFLEX COPYING.

CONTACT PRINT. *See* CONTACT COPYING.

CONTACT PRINTER. A machine for making contact copies (i.e. transmission prints or reflex copies) which are the same size as the original. *See also* REFLEX COPYING, TRANSMISSION COPYING.

CONTACT PRINTING. Any form of photographic or other copying method in which a sheet of sensitized material is held in firm and even contact with the original photographic negative or original document during exposure. The copying may be done by the direct or transmission method, or by the reflex method; the resulting print may be termed a 'contact copy'. *See also* CONTACT COPYING, REFLEX COPYING, TRANSMISSION COPYING.

CONTAINER LIBRARY SERVICE. A service for providing library facilities in small urban communities as an alternative to a small static branch library or visits from mobile libraries or trailers. The containers are special portable buildings 36' 6" long and 8' wide which are built to International Container Standards to withstand frequent loading and unloading. They are moved from site to site on a trailer drawn by a tractor (being off-loaded by two lifting arms (cranes) working simultaneously) and stay at each site – a car park – for two days at a time; each container serves three communities a week. The system was first used by the Cornwall County Library in 1973. *See also* MOBILE LIBRARY.

CONTEMPORARY BINDING. One that is contemporary with the printing of the book.

CONTEMPORARY SCIENTIFIC ARCHIVES CENTRE. The aim of the Centre is to locate, preserve and make accessible the personal papers of contemporary scientists and technologists in all fields of work in science, engineering and medicine. A small management committee is concerned with administrative and financial control of the Centre, but its main task is to identify men of science who might have papers of historical importance and whose families might welcome a rescue service of this kind. Names are submitted to a Joint Committee on Scientific and Technological Records of the Royal Society and the Royal Commission on Historical Manuscripts which was formed in 1967 and which sponsored a pilot scheme for arranging and listing the personal papers of three distinguished Fellows of the Royal Society of widely different disciplines. Grants from a number of trusts enabled the Centre to function from 2nd April 1973 for, in the first instance, three years. Papers, drawings, notebooks, calculations, drafts of lectures, articles, etc., are sorted and listed at the Centre and later passed on to an appropriate depository as a permanent loan, or gift, or on deposit, according to the wishes of the scientist or his family. The Centre is situated at the Indian Institute, Broad Street, Oxford OX1 3BE.

CONTENTS.   Strictly, a 'table of contents' but seldom used in this form. 1. A list of the 'preliminaries' and chapter headings of a book in their correct order, or of articles in a periodical, with the numbers of the pages on which they begin. 2. A list of the musical works contained in a printed collection of music or in an album of gramophone records, or of those recorded on a single record.

CONTENTS-BOOK.   A loose-leaf book in which a list of the contents of a volume or of a continuation is kept if too lengthy for a catalogue card.

CONTENTS LIST.   1. The contents page of a periodical, or other publication. *See also* CURRENT CONTENTS. 2. *Synonymous with* CONTENTS (*q.v.*).

CONTENTS LIST BULLETIN.   A periodical bulletin consisting of reproductions of copies of the contents pages of selected periodicals, and assembled into some form of cover. *See also* CURRENT AWARENESS JOURNAL.

CONTENTS NOTE.   A note appearing after the catalogue entry giving the headings of the chapters, parts, or volumes. In a descriptive bibliography it will indicate what is printed on each page included in the collation by gatherings.

CONTENTS PAGE.   The page, usually in the PRELIMINARIES (*q.v.*) of a book on which the table of contents is printed.

CONTEXT.   (*Indexing*) The parts of a title or text that precede or follow the KEYWORD (*q.v.*), usually influencing its meaning.

CONTINUATION.   1. A book only partly written by the original author and continued by someone else. 2. A work issued as a supplement to one already published. 3. A part issued in continuance of a serial, series or book. An order to supply subsequent parts as issued is called a 'Continuation Order'.

CONTINUATION CARD.   1. A card used for ordering a CONTINUA-TION (*q.v.*). 2. A CONTINUATION LIST (*q.v.*). 3. An EXTENSION CARD (*q.v.*).

CONTINUATION LIST, CONTINUATION RECORD.   A list of all books such as annuals, series, and works issued in parts for which there are standing orders.

CONTINUATION ORDER.   An order to supply each succeeding issue of an annual or serial publication – a 'continuation' of an item already in stock. *See also* CONTINUATION.

CONTINUATION REGISTER. *Synonymous with* CONTINUATION
   LIST (*q.v.*).

CONTINUITY FILE. (*Archives*) *See* READING FILE.

CONTINUOUS FEED. The action of an automatic sheet feeder
   attached to a printing press, folding, or other machine, so that the
   supply of sheets can be replenished without interrupting the operation
   of the machine.

CONTINUOUS FLOW CAMERA. Apparatus for taking photographs,
   which automatically moves the originals and the film to be exposed
   after each exposure. Also called 'Flow camera', 'Rotary camera'.

CONTINUOUS-FORM LOAN RECORDS. Continuous stationery
   used in specially made writing cabinets called 'registers' where up to
   five copies of the records of loans are required in non-public libraries.
   A carbon, or self-carbon paper is used, and the sets of paper are supplied printed and perforated. After each loan is recorded the set of
   papers is torn off and the separate pieces of paper are filed in different
   sequences under author, borrower's name, accession number, date,
   etc. as desired. Each piece is usually of a distinct colour to enable
   insertion in the correct file to be done easily and without inserting in
   wrong files. Borrowers are permitted in some libraries to make out
   their own loan records.

CONTINUOUS PAGINATION. The use of one sequence of page
   numbering throughout a book or several parts or volumes.

CONTINUOUS PRINTER. A photographic printing apparatus for the
   reproduction of an original, from either a negative or positive on to
   sensitized film or paper, by a continuous movement of the material
   through the exposing and processing stages. During the exposing
   process, the film being copied and a roll of paper or film, are synchronized to move at the same speed past the printing aperture. *See
   also* OPTICAL PRINTER.

CONTINUOUS PROCESSING. Processing photographs or films in
   machines which automatically transport the photographic material
   through the required solutions, finally drying the product.

CONTINUOUS REVISION. A multi-volume work, such as an extensive encyclopaedia, which is not completely revised and published as a
   new edition. Minor alterations or extensive additions or revisions are
   carried out for each printing, replacement and additional pages being
   inserted within the existing pagination by the addition of 'A.B.C.'
   etc. to the page numbers.

CONTOUR LINE. One drawn on a map to connect points having the
   same elevation.

CONTOURS. Lines drawn on a map to join all places at the same height above sea level. The intervals between contours may represent height differences from 50′ to several thousand feet dependent on the scale of the map. On physical maps the areas between contours are often shown in different colours progressing from various shades of green for lowlands through browns to red and finally white. Depths of the sea bed are indicated by Isobaths (*q.v.*).

CONTRACT SERVICES. Items appearing in a library's statement of income and expenditure to record funds (a) received from a governmental, library, or other, agency for specific services rendered, or (b) for services rendered to the library by individuals or agencies on the basis of a specific contract. (American.)

CONTRARIES. Any impurities in the waste paper, rags or other materials such as silk, feathers, wool, string, bones, pins, rubber, etc., to be used for paper- or board-making, and which are likely to be injurious.

CONTRAST. The difference between the high and low densities in a print or negative. (*Concepts* . . .)

CONTROL FIELD. A FIELD (*q.v.*) in a machine-readable record which identifies a particular part of the date within that record. It may contain a TAG (*q.v.*).

CONTROLLED CIRCULATION. *See* ROUTING.

CONTROLLED CIRCULATION SERIAL. A serial publication which is usually issued without charge and is only available to those whom the author or those responsible for its publication specify.

CONTROLLED INDEXING. Implies a careful selection of terminology so as to avoid, as far as possible, the scattering of related subjects under different headings. *See also* WORD INDEXING.

CONTROLLED TERM LIST. A term used in the indexing aspects of information retrieval which is equivalent to the AUTHORITY LIST (*q.v.*) in cataloguing; it is a list of terms which have a fixed and unalterable meaning, and from which a selection is made when indexing data or items in documents. The list may not be altered or extended. *See also* CONTROLLED INDEXING, OPEN-ENDED TERM LIST, TERM.

CONVENIENCE COPY. (*Reprography*) A copy of a document made quickly and economically, but not necessarily of the highest standard of quality or permanence.

CONVENIENCE FILE. (*Archives*) Duplicates of documents, PERSONAL PAPERS (*q.v.*), or books, assembled for easy access and reference.

CONVENTION APPLICATION. A patent application filed within ten months of the first application, and made for protection of the invention in any one of the countries signatory to the Paris Convention of 1883, and claiming priority accordingly. *See also* PATENT OF ADDITION, PRIORITY DATE.

CONVENTION CONCERNING THE EXCHANGE OF OFFICIAL PUBLICATIONS AND GOVERNMENT DOCUMENTS BETWEEN STATES. A multilateral convention which was adopted by the General Conference of Unesco in December 1958, and came into force on 30th May 1961. It had been ratified or accepted by eighteen States by September 1963.

CONVENTION COUNTRY. A country which is a signatory to the 1883 Paris Convention for the Protection of Industrial Property, and which is thereby bound to observe the international rules for protecting patents.

CONVENTION DATE. The date on which disclosure is made in an application for patent protection in any CONVENTION COUNTRY (*q.v.*) and therefore the date for which priority can subsequently be claimed when application is made in any other of the convention countries.

CONVENTIONAL FOLIAGE. A bookbinding ornament which is often quite unrealistic but obviously suggested by foliage.

CONVENTIONAL NAME. A name, other than the real or official name, by which a person, corporate body, thing or place has come to be familiarly known.

CONVENTIONAL TITLE. A UNIFORM TITLE (*q.v.*) which is constructed from terms describing the form or subject of a work, and arranged in a generally accepted sequence. It is used mostly in cataloguing music, where, e.g. terms are arranged in the order given to describe the musical form of the composition, its instrumentation (sonata, concerto, trio, piano quartet, etc.), its position in a sequence of the composer's works, its key, its opus (or equivalent) number, and descriptive title or soubriquet.

CONVERSION. The process of changing the representation of information to a form which is usable by a computer, e.g. converting it to machine 'language' on paper tape.

CONVEYOR BELT. A moving continuous belt of rubber, webbing or similar material, used to carry goods from one place to another. Used in libraries to convey books when handed in by readers from the place of receipt to the 'transaction' or 'discharging' room where they are examined and checked with lists of 'reserves' before being returned to the shelves.

CO-OPERATION, LOCAL.   Amongst the numerous schemes providing various forms of co-operation among libraries in small geographical areas are the following, under which entries will be found:

BRASTACS	HULTIS	NANTIS
CADIG	KIS	SAALIC
CICRIS	LADSIRLAC	SINTO
HALDIS	LINOSCO	TALIC
HATRICS	LIST	WALIC
HERTIS	MANTIS	WANDPETELS
	MISLIC	WESLINK

CO-OPERATIVE ACQUISITION.   A system for organizing and co-ordinating acquisitions between two or more documentary organizations (library, archive or documentation centre) at a local, regional, national or international level to ensure that one copy of each publication is held in the geographical area concerned.

CO-OPERATIVE CATALOGUING.   The sharing by a number of libraries of the cost and/or labour of cataloguing to avoid the duplication of effort common to each. Not to be confused with CENTRALIZED CATALOGUING (q.v.).

CO-OPERATIVE CONVERSION OF SERIALS.   See CONSER.

CO-OPERATIVE, INDUSTRIAL AND COMMERCIAL REFERENCE AND INFORMATION SERVICE.   See CICRIS

CO-OPERATIVE PUBLISHERS.   See VANITY PUBLISHERS.

CO-OPERATIVE PURCHASING.   An arrangement between several libraries whereby one of them, or a separate organization, purchases books for all of them in order to obtain books at a cheaper rate than is possible for individual libraries, because of the smaller number of copies, and therefore the less-advantageous terms, which the small libraries obtain.

CO-OPERATIVE SYSTEM.   A group of independent and autonomous libraries co-operating by informal or formal agreements or contracts which stipulate the common services to be undertaken. (American.)

CO-OPTED MEMBER.   A member of a (libraries) committee who is not a member of the local council, but has special knowledge, or interest in social, educational, political, or public activities.

CO-ORDINATE.   (Classification) Specific terms subordinated to the same genus. See also CO-ORDINATE CLASSES.

CO-ORDINATE CLASSES.   (Classification) 1. Classes which are correlated so that classes leading up to a subject come before it and those which develop from it, or are next in likeness or character, come after it. 2. Classes which are of the same order of SPECIFICATION (*q.v.*) and grade of division in a classification. (*Bliss*). 3. Classes belonging to the same ARRAY (*q.v.*).

CO-ORDINATE INDEXING. 1. An indexing scheme whereby the inter-relations of terms are shown by coupling individual words (*IBM*). 2. A system of information retrieval in which the indexing or recording of information in, or characteristics of, a document are accomplished by entering a reference number (page number, report number, etc.) on a card (or a column of a card) which is reserved for, and bears the heading of, an individual term to which it is devoted. Scan-Column Index and Tabledex are forms of compact book-form co-ordinate indexes. Also called 'Concept Co-ordination', 'Correlative indexing', 'Enriched co-ordinate indexing', 'Mutiple aspect indexing', 'Synthetic indexing'. In 'grouped co-ordinate indexing', the accession number becomes the identifying number of a group of documents all of which are indexed by the same set of features. *See also* FREE INDEXING, MANIPULATIVE INDEX, UNITERM CONCEPT CO-ORDINATION INDEXING.

CO-ORDINATE RELATION. (*Information retrieval*) The relation between terms which are subordinate to the same term.

CO-ORDINATED DECENTRALIZATION. The management of a number of libraries as separate units, although they together form a library system (as faculty or departmental libraries within a university system), their varying activities being co-ordinated to provide a cohesive, efficient service to meet all the needs which may be made upon the library as a whole.

CO-ORDINATION OF TERMS. The modulation from one term to another by gradual steps in order that the process of evolving a classification may exhibit its hierarchy or schedule.

COPAL. A resinous substance obtained from various tropical trees, and used in the manufacture of varnish and printing inks.

COPANT. Abbreviation for the Pan American Standards Commission which was founded in 1961; it comprises national standards bodies in the U.S.A. and eleven Latin American countries. It is a co-ordinating organization concerned with the regional implementation of International Standards Organization and International Electrotechnical Commission recommendations.

COPIC. Abbreviation for Computer Information Centre for the Program Commission of the European Communities Joint Research Centre (CETIS *q.v.*). Publishes *Computer Program Index* (2 p.a.).

COPIER-DUPLICATOR. A machine for making automatically one or several copies of an original document by a photocopying method without the use of a special master.

COPPER ENGRAVING. *See* ENGRAVING.

COPPER PLATE. A plate used for ENGRAVING (*q.v.*) in which the drawing is incised with a burin.

COPPERPLATE. A carefully written cursive script often used when inscribing the captions under engravings and used until recent times by writing masters as models for their pupils to copy.

COPY. 1. Matter for the printer to set up in type. 2. A single specimen of a printed book. 3. The material to be reproduced by photographic or other means; also the result of a reproduction process.

COPY-BOARD. The board on which the copy is secured whilst being photographed.

COPY CARD. *See* CAMERA CARD.

COPY EDIT. The checking of a MS. by a publisher or printer before marking it up for the typesetter, for accuracy of facts, grammatical construction, possible libel, HOUSE-STYLE (*q.v.*), etc.

COPY FITTING. (*Printing*) Adjusting 'copy' to the space available by changing the space allotment, the length of copy, or the size of type. *See also* COPY 1.

COPY NUMBER (or COPY LETTER). A figure or letter added to the call number of a book to distinguish different copies of the same book, e.g. 821C46, 821C46s, 821C46 (cop. 2). *See also* BOOK NUMBER, VOLUME NUMBER, WORK MARK.

COPY PREPARATION. (*Printing*) The act of preparing for the compositor a MS. which has been 'copy edited', by making the MS. legible and accurate, indicating printing style, type to be used, etc.

COPY-PREPARER. (*Printing*) One who is employed by a printer to translate a publication designer's typographical specification into instructions on the typescript.

COPY READER. An employee at a printing works whose task is to prepare the copy for composition by marking the measure, sizes of type to be used for text, quotations, footnotes, etc. and check the author's consistency in the use of capitals, citation, spelling, punctuation and sentence structure.

COPY SLIP. *See* PROCESS SLIP.

COPY-TAX. *See also* LEGAL DEPOSIT.

COPYCAT. A trade name of a particular machine for reproducing photographically sheets of printed, written or drawn matter the same size as the original.

COPYFLO. Trade name for a xerographic continuous printer which will make fully automatic reproductions from roll or card-mounted micro-film. It is made by the Haloid Company, and a service unit has been installed in London by Rank Xerox Ltd. The machine prints on one side of the paper only and the paper is delivered flat up to 24 inches wide, or, in the case of a book, folded in such a way that the folds form the edges of each pair of printed pages as in Chinese books.

COPYHOLDER. 1. A device attached to composing machines or used in conjunction with a typewriter to hold a MS. or 'copy'. 2. An assistant who reads the 'copy' to a proof reader. 3. A device which may be a simple board or an elaborate vacuum frame designed to hold the copy before the camera (*Verry*).

COPYING PROCESS. A process for making copies of documents on sensitized material. *See also* CONTACT COPYING, DIAZOTYPE PROCESS, ELECTROPHOTOGRAPHIC PROCESSES, NEGATIVE 3, OPTICAL COPYING, PHOTOGRAPHIC PHOTOCOPYING, POSITIVE PROCESS, RAPID COPYING, REFLEX COPYING, THERMAL PROCESS, TRANSMISSION PRINTING.

COPYIST. A person who transcribed MSS. prior to the introduction of printing.

COPYRIGHT.† The exclusive right of an author or his heirs to produce and reproduce (e.g. to publish and receive royalties) in respect of a literary, musical or artistic work. It is valid for a limited number of years and the work must not be reproduced in whole or in part, without the copyright owner's permission. The Copyright Act, 1956, is the only source of copyright law in the United Kingdom and Northern Ireland. It repealed the Copyright Act, 1911, except sections 15, 34 and 37. Copyright differs in its meaning according to its usage in relation to the various works in which it can subsist, i.e. literary works, dramatic works, musical works, artistic works, sound recordings, cinematograph films, television broadcasts, sound broadcasts and published editions of works. The Act establishes separate codes of copyright in respect of these different types of work. In relation to literary, dramatic or musical works, copyright is the exclusive right to do certain 'acts restricted by the copyright'. These are set out in Section 2(5): (a) reproducing the work in any material form; (b) publishing it; (c) performing it in public; (d) broadcasting it; (e) causing it to be transmitted to subscribers to a diffusion service; (f) making any adaptation of it; (g) doing, in any adaptation of it, any of the acts specified in relation to it in paragraphs (a) to (e) above. Copyright subsists (1) in every unpublished work of which the author was a qualified person (defined in Section 1(5) as a British subject, a British protected person, a citizen of the Republic of Ireland, persons domiciled or resident in the United Kingdom, persons domiciled or resident in another country to which the provisions of the Act extend, or a body corporate); (2) in publication of the work. Copyright continues to subsist until fifty years from the end of the year in which the author died or in which a work was first posthumously published, performed, offered for sale to the public in record form, or broadcast. Section 15 makes new provision whereby copyright subsists in a 'published edition'; this protects the material form in which a work – even if it is not itself a copyright work – is presented to the public, and entitles the publisher to a copyright in a particular typographical arrangement. Copyright in this case subsists for twenty-five years from the end of the year in which the work was first published. If British publishers adopt the device of marking publications with the symbol © – which is usually done on the back of the title-page – and fulfilling the other requirements of the Universal Copyright Convention (i.e. the name of the copyright proprietor and the year of first publication), copyright in such publications is automatically secured in all countries which have ratified this Convention. *See also* BERNE COPYRIGHT UNION, COPYRIGHT, INTERNATIONAL.

COPYRIGHT, INTERNATIONAL.† International copyright relations are governed primarily by two multilateral conventions: the Universal Copyright Convention and the International Convention for the Protection of Literary and Artistic Works (the Berne Convention) for details of which, *see* BERNE COPYRIGHT UNION. The Universal Copyright Convention, adopted at Geneva on 6th September 1952 by an international conference convened under the auspices of Unesco, came into force in 1955. Its main features are: (a) the recognition of the principle of 'national treatment' according to which a state party to the Convention shall extend the same protection to works of nationals of any other contracting state and works first published in that state, as it accords to works of its own nationals; (b) the simplification of formalities; (c) the introduction of special provisions governing translation rights; and (d) the fixing of a minimum period of protection covering the life of the author and 25 years after his death. The U.S.S.R. acceded to the Universal Copyright Convention (1952) and became bound by the Convention on 27th May 1973; royalties and fees to a foreign copyright owner for a published work are not based on the cost of sold copies but on other factors and may be used by the author, if he so wishes, or his heirs, in the U.S.S.R. currency or freely transferred to his country in the currency of that country, accounts in foreign currency being settled by the Copyright Agency of the U.S.S.R. through the Vneshtorgbank of the U.S.S.R. Material published prior to 27th May 1973 remains permanently in the public domain, books and periodicals published from 27th May onwards, and in which copyright is claimed, can no longer be freely produced, or translations of them published. Both the Berne Convention and the Universal Copyright Convention were revised in Paris on 24th July 1971 to take into account the economic, social and cultural conditions obtaining in the developing countries. *See also* IGC, INTERNATIONAL COPYRIGHT INFORMATION CENTRE, WIPO.

COPYRIGHT DATE. The date copyright was granted for an individual work. This is usually printed on the verso of the title page of books. If several dates are given, they signify changes in the text, or renewals of copyright. The first copyright date indicates the date of the first edition of a book and corresponds to the imprint date of the original edition. *See also* BERNE CONVENTION, COPYRIGHT, COPYRIGHT, INTERNATIONAL.

COPYRIGHT DEPOSIT. The deposition of free copies of a book or musical composition in a COPYRIGHT LIBRARY (*q.v.*) according to law. *See also* LEGAL DEPOSIT.

COPYRIGHT FEE. Fee paid to the holder of a copyright for the right to use his material for a particular purpose, e.g. to include a poem in an anthology or to read it in public, or to play a piece of music, or a record of the same, in public.

COPYRIGHT LIBRARY. A library which is entitled under copyright laws to receive a free copy of any or every book published in the country. Section 15 of the Copyright Act, 1911 – which was not repealed by the Act of 1956 – provides that the publisher of every book (including 'sheet of letterpress, sheet of music, map . . .'), is, within one month after publication, to deliver, at his own expense, a copy of the book to the British Library, and also if written demand is made before the expiration of twelve months after publication, to send a copy to the Bodleian Library, Oxford; the University Library, Cambridge; the National Library of Scotland, Edinburgh – except that law books are to be transmitted to the Faculty of Advocates to be vested in their Law Library (National Library of Scotland Act, 1925); Trinity College, Dublin, and with certain exceptions specified by the Board of Trade, the National Library of Wales, Aberystwyth. These exceptions are designed to exclude books published in small editions unless they are written in Welsh or relate wholly or mainly to the Welsh or other Celtic peoples or to the natural history of Wales. In

October 1972 the British copyright libraries other than the BRITISH LIBRARY (*q.v.*) agreed in principle that they would attempt, as a last resort, to satisfy requests that the British Library Lending Division was unable to meet from its own and the other non-copyright library resources to which it had access.

COPYRIGHT LIST.   A list of the books deposited in a library under the copyright laws.

COPYTRON.   Trade name for an electrostatic reproduction machine made by the Charles Bruning Company, Inc.

COPYWRITER.   A writer of advertisements.

CORANTO.   1. The earliest form of newspaper, consisting of one leaf in small folio, the text being in two columns on each side of the leaf. Published first in Holland and Germany, and in England in 1620 and 1621, such publications were known by the name coranto, whether published in England or on the continent. They were issued at least once a week as a half-sheet in folio, and only foreign news was printed. 2. Sometimes the word Coranto is used to include Newsbooks which were published until 1642. *See also* NEWSBOOK, RELATION. Nathaniel Butter began a *Newes* on 2nd August 1622, and in October 1622 commenced publishing with Nicholas Bourne and William Sheffard *A Coranto;* these were numbered serially.

CORDING QUIRES.   *See* CASSIE.

CORDONNIER CARDS.   *See* PEEK-A-BOO.

CORDOVAN LEATHER.   Goatskin, originally tanned and dressed at Cordova, Spain. Used for MUDÉJAR BINDINGS (*q.v.*), and often dyed red. The English name is 'Cordwain.'

CORDS.   Heavy strings to which the sections of large and heavy books are bound. Sometimes called BANDS (*q.v.*). *See also* TAPES.

CORDWAIN.   *Synonymous with* CORDOVAN LEATHER (*q.v.*).

CORNER-MARKED CARD.   A catalogue card bearing in the top right-hand corner information such as language, date of publication, editor, or translator, or a combination of these where there are many entries under the same heading. The purpose is to facilitate rapid perusal of a number of cards at one reading. Sometimes the original title of a translated work is written in the upper right-hand corner so that original and translations may be filed together.

CORNER MARKING.   The original title of a translated work placed in the upper right-hand corner of a catalogue card so that the original and the translation will be filed together. A reference is required from the translation title to the original. Alternatively, translations may be entered on the same card as the original title, or in other words the original title may appear above the translation, a reference under the translation title being optional but desirable. In libraries, such as those of universities, where many books in translation are in stock, the supplying of original titles is a very expensive procedure.

CORNERPIECE. 1. (*Binding*) An ornament, usually arabesque, designed to be used at the corners of a bound book, usually to match a centre-piece or other decoration. Also used of metal corners attached to the binding. Also called 'Cornerstamp.' 2. (*Bibliography*) Interlacing bars, 'cusping,' or other separate ornament at the corner of a border around type, or lettering of an illuminated manuscript.

CORNERS. 1. The leather over the corners of a book in 'half' binding. *See also* LIBRARY CORNER, MITRED CORNER, SQUARE CORNER. 2. In printing, ornamental type metal connecting borders. 3. Pieces of metal or pasteboard to slip over the corners of a book to protect them in the post. Also called 'Cornerpieces.'

CORNERSTAMP. *Synonymous with* CORNERPIECE (*q.v.*).

CORPORATE AUTHOR. A corporate body such as a government or government department, a society (learned, social, etc.), or an institution which authorizes the publication of documents, and under the name of which, as the author, the documents will be entered in a catalogue. In certain kinds of corporate authorship, entries are made under the *place* followed by the *name* of the body.

CORPORATE BODY. An institution, organized body, or assembly of persons known by a corporate or collective name (*IFLA*).

CORPORATE ENTRY. A catalogue entry made under a government, government department, society or institution or other body, of a work issued by that body, or under its authority. It may be a main or an added entry.

CORPORATE NAME. The name by which a corporate body is known.

CORPORATION FILE. *See* COMPANY FILE.

CORRECTED EDITION. A new edition of a book in which errors, etc., have been corrected.

CORRECTED PROOF. A printer's proof on which errors in type-setting have been marked, using the generally accepted code of correction-marks. *See also* PROOF, PROOF CORRECTIONS.

CORRECTION MARKS. The signs used on a printer's proof to mark errors in typesetting. These are set out in British Standard 5261: Part 2: 1976 *Copy preparation and proof correction. See* PROOF CORRECTIONS.

CORRELATION. A systematic or reciprocal connexion – sometimes, the establishment of a mutual or reciprocal relation of or between (*IBM*).

CORRELATION OF PROPERTIES. In classification the likeness between the various qualities which are common to all the things comprised by a genus.

CORRELATIVE INDEX. An index enabling selection of documents or of references to them by correlation of words, numbers, or other symbols which are usually unrelated by hierarchic organization (*IBM*). *See also* CLASSIFIED INDEX, CO-ORDINATE INDEXING.

CORRELATIVE SYSTEM. A non-conventional indexing or retrieval system in which any descriptor can be combined with any other, to indicate the subject content of a document.

CORRESPONDENCE MANAGEMENT. (*Archives*) The application of the techniques of archive administration to correspondence. Called 'Treatment of correspondence' in Canada.

CORRIGENDA. (*Sing.* CORRIGENDUM). A printed list of corrections of errors which were noticed after matter was printed. It is usually printed on a slip and inserted among the PRELIMINARIES (*q.v.*) but sometimes a blank page is used. Also called 'Errata.' *See also* PASTE-IN.

CORRUPT A TEXT. To tamper with a text by omission, addition, or alteration in order to convey a meaning which was not intended by the original author. This is sometimes done to standard or modern works for political propaganda.

CORYMBE. A French system of information retrieval using continuous strips of 3 mm. film on which items of information are stored in the form of black on white images. There are identical images but white on black, and exact coincidence will cause a black-out and operate the selector.

COSATI. Acronym of the Committee on Scientific and Technical Information of the Federal Council for Science and Technology (FCST). *See also* SATCOM. It was set up by the U.S.A. Government as the principal mechanism by which the views of individual agencies can be obtained and a concensus reached on desirable Federal programmes. COSATI issued in 1966 a standard for the descriptive cataloguing of government scientific and technical reports. It aims at uniformity, its purposes being to: (a) provide rules appropriate to the needs of information and documentation centres, and reports depositories of libraries; (b) provide users with a consistent form of citation and index entries; (c) enable government agencies to use each others' descriptive catalogue entries with minimal editorial revision, thereby avoiding costly duplication of effort; (d) provide a guide to the other organizations and institutions which wish to formulate a compatible descriptive cataloguing practice.

COSMIC. Abbreviation for Computer Software Management Information Center which was established at the University of Georgia, Athens, Georgia 30601, U.S.A. in 1966 to collect and disseminate computer software developed by government agencies to the public. Computer programs in all areas of aerospace, engineering, mathematics, business and industry are distributed to companies and industries, normally to U.S.A. purchasers only.

COSTERIANA. Fragments of books, having the appearance of early printing and asserted to have been printed before 1473, and consisting mostly of editions of the *Donatus*, or the *Doctrinale*. These were supposed to have been printed by Laurens Janszoon Coster of Haarlem (1405-84) who was thought at one time to have invented printing with movable types in or about 1440.

COTTAGE BINDING. *Synonymous with* COTTAGE STYLE (*q.v.*).

COTTAGE STYLE. A decorative binding in which the centre panel was often given a gable at head and foot, and the spaces filled with a variety of interlacings, sprays, and small 'tools.' Although this style may have originated in France, it is most characteristic of English bindings of the late seventeenth century to 1710. Also called 'Cottage binding.' *See also* MEARNE STYLE.

COTTON LINTERS. The short fibres adhering to the cotton seed after ginning (separating the seeds from the fibre), and also obtained as 'recovered' fibres from the cotton seed oil and cake factories. When purified it is used for paper-making. It can be used to replace 5-35 per cent of the rag content of fine papers without lessening the strength of the paper; it improves uniformity and the colour properties of the paper, and provides a cleaner, bulkier sheet. It is also used in the cheaper kinds of blotting paper used for interleaving diaries and account books.

COUCH ROLL. That part of a Fourdrinier paper making machine which removes some of the moisture from the sheet of paper during manufacture.

COUNCIL FOR COMPUTERIZED LIBRARY NETWORKS. Formed in the U.S.A. in 1974 for co-operatives with electronic capabilities. It 'provides a forum in which colleagues may identify common problems relating to library network development and operation and co-ordinate solutions to them'. The charter members are listed in *RQ* 15 (2) Winter 1975.

COUNCIL FOR MICROPHOTOGRAPHY AND DOCUMENT REPRODUCTION. *See* MICROFILM ASSOCIATION OF GREAT BRITAIN.

COUNCIL OF NATIONAL LIBRARY ASSOCIATIONS. Founded

in 1942 'to promote a closer relationship among the national library associations of the United States and Canada by providing a central agency to foster co-operation in matters of mutual interest, by gathering and exchanging information among its member associations, and by co-operating with learned, professional and scientific societies in forwarding matters of common interest.' Membership is open to national associations of the U.S.A. and Canada as well as those in related fields. Abbreviated CNLA. Publishes *Library Placement Services. See also* Z–39.

COUNCIL OF PLANNING LIBRARIANS. Founded in the U.S.A. in 1960 by a group of planning librarians associated with schools of planning and planning agencies during the annual convention of the American Institute of Planners, to exchange information about professional practices in libraries with particular concern for those which are peculiar to planning libraries; to formulate and to administer projects which the Council decides are of service to the planning profession and librarianship; to advise on library organization for new planning programmes in institutions and agencies. Abbreviated CPL. Publishes *CPL Exchange Bibliographies* (irreg.), *CPL Newsletter.*

COUNCIL ON LIBRARY RESOURCES, INC. An independent, non-profit making corporation which was established in September 1956 with the aid of a five million dollar grant from the Ford Foundation which also made a second grant of eight million dollars in January 1961. Its function is 'to assist in solving the problems of libraries generally and of research libraries in particular, conducting research in, developing and demonstrating new techniques and methods, and disseminating through any means the results thereof, and for making grants to other institutions and persons for such purposes; and for providing leadership in and wherever appropriate, co-ordination of efforts (1) to develop the resources and services of libraries and (2) to improve relations between American and foreign libraries and archives.' It assists through research, development and demonstration, in solving problems that are common to libraries generally rather than to provide assistance toward library activities which normally constitute local responsibilities. The council works principally through grants or contracts to qualified individuals or institutions. Additional grants received from the Ford Foundation were: 1967—$5,000,000; 1971—$5,000,000; 1974—$6,000,000. In recent years the Council has begun to devote a larger portion of its efforts and funds to Council-administered programmes. Abbreviated CLR. Publishes *Recent Developments* (irreg.).

COUNTER. 1. *Synonymous with* STAFF ENCLOSURE (*q.v.*). 2. (*Printing*) The interior 'white' of a letter; it may be entirely enclosed by a bowl as in 'O' or it may be the sunken part of the face as 'M' 'E' 'n'. The angular corner is known as the 'crotch'. The distance from the face to the bottom of the counter is known as the 'depth of counter'.

COUNTER DUTY. Duties performed in the counter or staff enclosure in a public department of a library.

COUNTERMARK. A smaller and subsidiary WATERMARK (*q.v.*) found in antique papers, usually in the centre, or lower centre of the second half of a sheet and opposite the watermark. Border or corner positions are not uncommon. It usually comprises the name or initials of the maker (in the U.K., and in later times, the mill number) and the date (first in 1545) and place of making, although small devices such as a small post-horn or cabalistic signs have been found.

COUNTERSUNK. A binding having a panel sunk or depressed below the normal level of the binding to take a label, inlay or decoration.

COUNTY BIBLIOGRAPHY. A bibliography of books and other forms of written record relating to a county.

COUNTY BOROUGH COUNCIL. The council of a local authority known as a 'county borough'. A county borough, like a county council, could provide all the services which are permitted to be provided by a local authority. *See also* BOROUGH COUNCIL, COUNTY COUNCIL, LIBRARY AUTHORITY, LOCAL GOVERNMENT BOUNDARIES, NON-COUNTY BOROUGH.

COUNTY COUNCIL. A statutory LOCAL AUTHORITY (*q.v.*) with more powers than any other kind of authority except a Metropolitan District; these are exercised within a county's geographical area. Public Libraries were provided in county areas by the County Education Authority under the Public Libraries Act, 1919, but under the Public Libraries and Museums Act, 1964, county councils were enabled to set up library committees directly responsible to the county council if they wished. Abbreviated CC. There were fifty-two administrative counties in England and Wales but Middlesex County Council and the London County Council disappeared with the formation of the Greater London Council on 1st April 1965. The London County Council (now the Greater London Council) has never been a library authority, as all the metropolitan borough councils in the area had provided public libraries by adopting the Public Libraries Acts prior to the Public Libraries Act, 1919, which first authorized county councils to provide public libraries. *See also* LOCAL GOVERNMENT BOUNDARIES.

COUNTY DISTRICT. A generic term, first used in the Local Government Act, 1933, to indicate an urban district, rural district, or non-county borough forming part of a geographical and administrative county, but having its own form of local government for certain purposes. A distinct local government area within the area of a county council.

COUNTY HEADQUARTERS. The administrative centre for a county library system. It usually has the main book reserve, operates a postal service direct to readers, provides offices for the senior administrative librarians, and may house a lending library. It is usually situated in the county town or the one where the administrative headquarters of the county council is.

COUNTY LIBRARIES GROUP. A Group of the Library Association; it existed until January 1975 to unite the interests of those working in county libraries of the UK, to provide for the expression of opinion and for liaison with the parent body. It was formed in 1927 as the County Libraries Section, the name being changed when the present constitution of the Library Association came into operation in 1963. This Group combined with the newly formed PUBLIC LIBRARY GROUP (q.v.) from January 1975.

COUNTY LIBRARY. A library provided to supply the reading needs of people dwelling in the area. See also COUNTY COUNCIL. In America, a free public library service provided for county residents and financed from county tax funds; it may be administered as an independent agency or in co-operation with another library agency.

COUNTY RECORD OFFICE. A RECORD OFFICE (q.v.) which is required by law to be set up in England by every county council.

COUNTY REGIONAL BRANCH. A REGIONAL BRANCH (q.v.) in a county library system.

COUNTY SCHOOLS LIBRARY. An instructional materials library maintained in America by a county superintendent of schools who provides materials and services to contracting schools.

COURANTS. Dutch news publications, related but not numbered, known to have existed since the year 1607. See also CORANTO, NEWSBOOK.

COURT. A standard size for cards, $3\frac{1}{2} \times 4\frac{1}{2}$ inches; envelopes are $3\frac{3}{4} \times 4\frac{3}{4}$ inches.

COURT BARON. Court held by the Lord of a Manor in virtue of his right as a land holder, in which offences against the customs of the manor could be published but no punishments involving the life or limbs of the subject could be inflicted.

COURT HAND. 1. Style of writing used in legal and other public documents. Generally used of 'hands' from about 1100 to the end of the sixteenth century. 2. Sometimes used to mean legal hands of the same period only.

COURT LEET. Court of Record to punish all offences under High Treason, not incidental to a manor, but frequently held by a Lord of a Manor by virtue of a special grant.

COURT ROLL. A roll on which records of cases in private courts such as a Court Baron or Court Leet were kept.

COURTESY STORAGE. *See* DEPOSIT.

COVENTRY AND DISTRICT INFORMATION GROUP. *See* CADIG.

COVER. 1. That which is placed securely on a sewn or stapled publication to protect it in use; it may be of paper or cloth, or board covered with paper, cloth or leather. The cover of a 'hard cover' book (as distinct from a 'paperback') is known as a 'case' or 'publisher's case'. 2. The outside sheet of a pamphlet, or the case of a book, used to protect the body of the work. 'Front cover,' and 'back cover' relate to the side pieces or outsides of the boards of the cover.

COVER DATE. The date which appears on the cover of a publication, usually a pamphlet. Should this be different to another inside the book, it may appear in the imprint part of a catalogue or bibliography entry as [*cover* 1965]. Where all the cataloguing data is on the cover, this procedure is unnecessary.

COVER INCLUDED IN PAGING. Where the cover is included in the pagination of a pamphlet the collation portion of the catalogue or bibliography entry may be in the form '28 pp (incl. cover)'.

COVER PAPER. A generic term usually indicative of a strong, coloured paper with good folding qualities suitable for brochure, booklet, pamphlet and price-list covers. Cover papers are available in a variety of embossings as well as plain. Sizes:

	inches
Cover Double Crown	$20\frac{1}{2} \times 30\frac{1}{2}$
Cover Medium	$18\frac{1}{2} \times 23\frac{1}{2}$
Cover Royal	$20\frac{1}{2} \times 25\frac{1}{2}$
Double Crown	20×30
Double Medium	23×36
Double Royal	25×40
Imperial	22×30
Quad Crown	30×40

COVER POCKET. *Synonymous with* POCKET (*q.v.*).

COVER TITLE. The title of a book placed on a publisher's case, or as distinguished from that printed on the title-page. Not to be confused with the BINDER'S TITLE (*q.v.*). *See also* BACK TITLE.

COVER TO COVER TRANSLATION. A serial publication which contains in each issue a translation of the whole, or a major part, of an issue of a serial publication in another language.

COVERS BOUND IN. The original covers of a publication bound in, or to be bound in, when a book is re-bound.

CRABS. Books returned to a publisher by a bookseller because he had been unable to sell them. Also called 'Returns'.

CRACKLE. *See* RATTLE.

CRADLE BOOKS. *See* INCUNABULA.

CRAM. Abbreviation for Card Random Access Mechanism, a unitized magnetic card system developed by the National Cash Register Company for recording and retrieving data. Data are recorded on cards 14 inches long by $3\frac{1}{4}$ inches wide, there being fifty-six parallel channels divided into seven sets of eight channels. The total capacity of each card is 160,000 bits (at 250 to the inch).

CRANFIELD CLASSIFICATION FOR AERONAUTICS AND ALLIED SUBJECTS. A scheme devised by B. C. Vickery and J. E. L. Farradane to provide a faceted classification for the materials in the library of the College of Aeronautics at Cranfield.

CRANFIELD PROJECT. *See* Aslib Cranfield Research Project.

CRASH. *Synonymous with* MULL (*q.v.*).

CRASH FINISH. A cover paper which is similar to LINEN FINISH (*q.v.*) but has a coarser texture.

CRAYON DRAWING. A drawing made with a soft, black crayon, usually for strong or impressionistic effects. It is suitable for illustrations, portraits, etc., and may be reproduced by half-tone.

CRAYON ENGRAVING. A similar process to STIPPLE (*q.v.*) but aiming to produce the effect of a chalk drawing. Various specially grained roulettes, etching needles, and a *mattoir* (a form of miniature cudgel) are used through the etching ground to prepare the printing plate for biting with acid. The graver and roulette may be used afterwards directly on the surface of the plate. Stipple and crayon processes are sometimes used together in portrait work, stipple being used for the face and crayon for the body and clothing. Also called 'Chalk engraving'.

CREASING. 1. A linear indentation made by machine in a card or thick paper. By compressing the fibres it provides a hinge and increases the number of times the paper can be flexed at the crease before breaking. *See also* SCORING. 2. A printing fault, seen as deep creases; it may result from storing the paper at an incorrect humidity, or from other causes.

CREDIT. A statement of the authorship, cast, and those associated with the production of a radio, television or film programme.

CREDIT LINE. A statement giving the name of an artist, photographer, author, agency, or owner of an original or of copyright, and printed under a photograph, drawing, article or quotation which is reproduced or published.

CRESTING ROLL. A ROLL (*q.v.*) which has, on one side of the design, a series of crests or tufts, the other side being approximately straight. *See also* HERALDIC CRESTING.

CRIBLÉ INITIAL. A decorated initial used at the beginning of a chapter, specially by the sixteenth-century French printer Geoffrey Tory, in which the capital appears on an all-over ground of small dots, or sieve-like pattern.

CRIBLÉ METAL CUT. A soft metal used late in the fifteenth century for block printing instead of wood, the metal being punched with holes (criblé) to relieve the black mass. *See also* MANIÈRE CRIBLÉE.

CRIS. Abbreviation for Command Retrieval Information System. Trade name of the Information Retrieval Corporation for their mechanized storage and retrieval device which uses a scroll of microfilm as the information storage medium.

CRITICAL ANNOTATION. *Synonymous with* EVALUATION (*q.v.*).

CRITICAL APPARATUS. *Synonymous with* APPARATUS CRITICUS (*q.v.*).

CRITICAL BIBLIOGRAPHY. 1. The comparative and historical study of the make-up of books (*Besterman*). 2. The science of the material transmission of literary texts (*Greg.*). Also called 'Analytical' or 'Historical' bibliography. *See also* BIBLIOGRAPHY.

CRITICAL CLASSIFICATION. The exercise of the classifier's personal opinion when classifying a book; if care is not taken to avoid bias or prejudice, this may result in wrong placing.

CRITICAL EDITION. A scholarly text of a work, established by an editor after original research, and the comparison of manuscripts, documents, letters and earlier texts. This editorial work is considerable, especially in textual criticism. The edition is characterized by the APPARATUS CRITICUS (*q.v.*) included. *See also* STANDARD EDITION, VARIORUM EDITION, DEFINITIVE EDITION.

CRITICISM NUMBER. *See* ASSOCIATED BOOK.

CROCKETED CRESTING. (*Binding*) A frame formed by roughly rectangular stamps ornamented with crockets (small curved designs) or with roughly triangular stamps, which, placed together and pointing outwards, give a cresting effect.

CROPPED. 1. In bookbinding, a term applied to a book when too much of its margin, especially the head-margin, has been trimmed off and the type area mutilated. *See also* BLED, CUT, SHAVED, TRIMMED, UNCUT. 2. A photograph of which a part of the top, bottom or sides is omitted from its reproduction, in order to bring it into proper proportions for the space it is to occupy.

CROPPER. A small printing machine working on the platen principle; so named after the English manufacturer H. S. Cropper & Co. who produced the 'Minerva' machine in 1867; this was similar to the 'Franklin Press' manufactured by George Phineas Gordon, a small master printer of New York.

CROPPING. (*Printing*) Masking, or trimming off portions of an illustration to eliminate unimportant detail and to obtain desired proportion.

CROSS. Abbreviation for Computerized Rearrangements Of Special Subjects; one of four computer-composed indexes included in each fortnightly issue of *Biological Abstracts* (*See* BIOSIS). The others are: (a) BASIC (*q.v.*); (b) an author index for every author of papers abstracted or cited; and (c) *Bio-systematic Index* which co-ordinates all studies concerned, regardless of their methodology or purpose, according to the taxonomic position of the organisms investigated. It co-ordinates all abstracts pertinent to each of the major and subordinate subject headings used in arranging abstracts included in each issue of *BA*, the numbers of relevant abstracts being placed under each in ten columns as determined by the last figure of the abstract number.

CROSS-BARS. Metal bars used to divide a CHASE (*q.v.*) into sections of equal size, each of which contains the same number of pages. They enable the pages to be locked up more securely, and also make corrections in one section easier while not disturbing the others.

CROSS CLASSIFICATION. 1. The action of dividing when forming a scheme of classification by more than one characteristic in a single process of division, leading to confusion of ideas and terms and resulting in the parts having no real relationship to one another, and in placing related subjects in different divisions. 2. A TABULAR CLASSIFICATION (*q.v.*), or one that is reducible to tabular form, in which the classes or sub-classes of each series are crossed by the terms of a secondary series of specifications, so that the resulting sub-classes have the specifications of both series and are therefore common to both (*Bliss*).

CROSS DIRECTION. Said of paper which is cut across, that is, cut at right angles to the direction in which the web of a paper machine moves. The cross direction of the paper is much weaker, and expands more, than in the direction parallel to the flow of the pulp on the machine. *See also* AGAINST THE GRAIN, GRAIN DIRECTION, WITH THE GRAIN.

CROSS DIVISION. *Synonymous with* CROSS CLASSIFICATION (*q.v.*).

CROSS HATCHING. (*Binding*) Two sets of parallel lines executed in opposite directions so that the lines cross.

CROSS-HEAD. A short descriptive heading placed in the centre of a type line to divide the sections of a work, or the chapters of a book. Cross-heads are separated from the text by one or more lines of space, and normally indicate primary sub-divisions of a chapter. Subsequent sub-divisions are: shoulder-heads and side-heads. *See also* HEADING 4, SHOULDER-HEAD, SIDE-HEAD.

CROSS-INDEX. To make an index entry under several headings, where appropriate, for the same item.

CROSS-REFERENCE, GENERAL. *See* GENERAL REFERENCE.

CROSS-REFERENCE CARD. The catalogue card on which a cross-reference is entered.

CROSS-REFERENCE SHEET. A record on a pro forma sheet recording the filing of related material in other files. It may refer to (a) a specific publication, (b) part of a publication, (c) specific facts in a given publication.

CROSS-REFERENCES. In indexing and cataloguing, references or directions from one heading to another. 1. *Single* (*see* ——). An instruction to look elsewhere for *all* items relating to the subject matter which is sought. 2. *Reciprocal* (*see also* ——). An instruction to look elsewhere for *other* items relating to the subject matter sought. 3. *Multiple* (*see also* ——). An instruction to refer to several other places, usually to more specific entries. 4. References in the text of a book to other parts of the same book. *See also* GENERAL REFERENCE.

CROTCH. (*Printing*) The angular corner of the COUNTER (*q.v.*) of a type letter.

CROWN. A sheet of printing paper measuring 15 × 20 inches.

CROWN COPYRIGHT. Copyright that is vested in the Crown when any work, whether published or unpublished, has been made by, or under the direction or control of, the Sovereign or any Government department.

CROWN OCTAVO. A book size, $7\frac{1}{2} \times 5$ inches. *See also* BOOK SIZES.

CROWN QUARTO. A book size, 10 × $7\frac{1}{2}$ inches. *See also* BOOK SIZES.

CROWTHER REPORT. *15 to 18: a Report of the Central Advisory Council for Education (England)*, 1959. Known as the Crowther Report after the Chairman Sir Geoffrey Crowther. The report deals with the educational needs of young people between the ages of 15 and 18 and was the result of a comprehensive study of those needs since March 1956.

CRUSHED LEVANT. A large-grained LEVANT (*q.v.*) leather binding with a smooth, polished surface, caused by crushing down the natural grain.

CRUSHED MOROCCO. Morocco, the grain of which has been smoothed by hand. *See also* GLAZED MOROCCO.

CRYPTOGRAPHY. Writing in cipher.

CRYPTONYM. A secret name.

CRYPTONYMOUS BOOK. One in which the name of the author is concealed under an anagram or similar device, e.g. Mesrat Merligogels (Master George Mills).

CUBE UNIT BUILDING. *See* MODULAR CONSTRUCTION.

CUBOOK. The volume of space required to shelve books of average size and allowing for vacant space 10 per cent of each shelf. A tier 3 feet wide by 7 feet 6 inches high (seven shelves) contains 100 cubooks. For a full treatment, see the *Library Journal* 59: 865–8, Nov. 15, 1934; 61: 52–4, Jan. 15, 1936.

CUE SYSTEM. A system, proposed to be used in bibliography and indexing, consisting of alphabetical codes placed above an entry to indicate the chronological, topical, and geographic aspects of the article referred to.

CUIR BOUILLI. Book decoration in which the leather cover is soaked in hot water, modelled and hammered to raise the design in relief; it sets very hard, and in the ninth century it was found to be so hard that boards were unnecessary.

CUIR-CISELÉ BINDING. A binding with a design cut into dampened leather instead of being stamped or tooled on it. A relief effect was then obtained by punching the leather around the design. Hammering from the back gave an embossed effect. A widely-practised method in fifteenth-century Germany.

CUL-DE-LAMPE. A form of decorative printing practised in the sixteenth century which used arabesque title-borders and tail-pieces strongly suggestive of metal lantern-supports. A tail-piece. J. B. M. Papillon (1698–1776), the most distinguished member of a family of French wood-engravers, was renowned for the delicacy in his minute floral head- and tail-pieces (culs-de-lampe), which decorate many mid-eighteenth-century French books.

CUM LICENTIA. *Synonymous with* CUM PRIVILEGIO (*q.v.*).

CUM PRIVILEGIO. (*Lat.* 'with permission'). Printed by authority, either secular or ecclesiastical. Sole authority for printing.

CUMDACH. A rectangular box (usually of bronze, brass or wood, and plated with ornamented silver or gold), which was made for the preservation of precious books. Also called 'Book shrine'.

CUMULATED BOOK CATALOGUE. A compromise between the card and the book (printed) catalogue. Linotype slugs are preserved by the printer after a printing and subsequent entries are interpolated as necessary.

CUMULATED VOLUME. A publication consisting of entries for a bibliography, catalogue, index, etc., which have previously appeared in periodically published parts, and re-assembled into one sequence.

CUMULATION. The progressive inter-filing of items arranged in a predetermined order and usually published in periodical form, the same order of arrangement being maintained.

CUMULATIVE INDEX. One which is built up from time to time by combining separately published indexes into one sequence.

CUMULATIVE LIST. A list of books published separately and afterwards incorporated in other similar lists which in their turn may have been compiled in the same way.

CUNEIFORM WRITING. Wedge-shaped letters in which Old Persian and Babylonian inscriptions were written, so termed from their wedge-like appearance and made by pressing the end of a stick or reed into the soft clay of the tablet at an angle and continuing the stroke in a straight line with constantly diminishing pressure.

CURATOR. The superintendent of a museum, art gallery, etc.

CURATORS. Name given to boards of people responsible for managing the various institutions of Oxford University. The Curators of the Bodleian Library, for example, number eighteen, namely, the Vice-Chancellor, the Proctors or their deputies, seven members of Congregation elected by that House, six professors elected by the professors of the various faculties, and two members of Congregation elected by Council, one of whom must be a Curator of the Chest; these are elected to serve for ten years, and are entrusted with the general control of the affairs of the library, including the appointment of a librarian, and of other officers, subject to the approval of Convocation, and are responsible for the expenditure of all sums accruing to them through the University Chest or otherwise.

CURIA REGIS. Under feudal organization a court of justice, or administration was called a 'curia'; Curia Regis was the Court of the Norman Kings of England.

CURIOSA. Term used in describing books of curious and unusual subject matter. Sometimes used euphemistically as a classification for *erotica*.

CURL. A deformation of a sheet of paper or board over its whole surface so that it tends to roll up into the form of a cylinder.

CURRENT AWARENESS. A system, and often a publication, for notifying current documents to users of libraries and information services, e.g. selective dissemination of information, bulletin, indexing service, current literature. The term is sometimes used synonymously for SDI.

CURRENT AWARENESS JOURNAL. A periodical consisting of reproductions in facsimile of contents tables of many individual journals.

CURRENT BIBLIOGRAPHY. A list of books which is compiled at the same time as the books are published. It is usually published as a periodical. Sometimes called 'Open bibliography'.

CURRENT COMPLETE NATIONAL BIBLIOGRAPHY. A complete list of published or issued records of a nation; such a list can be complete only to a specified date. A current national bibliography is a listing of publications compiled at the time of publication and falling within the definition of a NATIONAL BIBLIOGRAPHY (*q.v.*).

CURRENT COMPREHENSIVE BIBLIOGRAPHY. The technique of making available, through current bibliographical services, informative lists of the totality of publications in particular catagories defined solely by (a) recency of publication; (b) type of issuing agency; (c) the geographical area or political jurisdiction within which they were produced; but not by their contents (e.g. literary form or subject-content) or distribution (e.g. location of copies). *See also* CURRENT SELECTIVE BIBLIOGRAPHY.

CURRENT CONTENTS. A registered trade mark of the Institute of Scientific Information; used in their publications which reproduce the contents pages of periodicals.

CURRENT NUMBER. The last-issued number of a newspaper or serial publication and bearing the most recent issue number and/or date. Also called 'Current issue'.

CURRENT PUBLICATION SURVEY. *See* LITERATURE SURVEY 2.

CURRENT RECORDS. The records which are necessary for conducting the day-to-day work of an office or business, and which must therefore be kept readily accessible. Called 'Active records' in Canada.

CURRENT SELECTIVE BIBLIOGRAPHY. The technique of making available, through current bibliographical services, informative lists of publications in particular catagories defined by (a) recency of publication, (b) some one or more characteristics of the publications. The usual characteristics are content (e.g. literary form, subject), distribution (e.g. location of copies), and value. *See also* CURRENT COMPREHENSIVE BIBLIOGRAPHY, SELECT BIBLIOGRAPHY.

CURRENTLY RECEIVED. Periodicals which are received on publication.

CURRICULUM MATERIALS CENTER. A centre, usually located in an American school central administration building, in which are kept professional books, current and back numbers of teaching professional periodicals, microfilms, recordings, supplementary textbooks, art prints mounted on cardboard, pamphlets, fabrics, filmstrips, models, and possibly high school and elementary school books (which may be borrowed for the children). The materials are issued to teachers only. The ALA *Standards* recommends that any district having over 10,000 students should have such a centre. Also called a 'District Materials Center'. *See also* INSTRUCTIONAL MATERIALS CENTER.

CURSIVE. 1. Running writing, letters within words being joined. 2. Sometimes used to differentiate smaller 'hands' from uncial. 3. A class of type face which is based on handwriting. It may be ITALIC (*q.v.*) in which there is a version of almost every named type face or script which is drawn to look as though handwritten. Kaufman Script, Trafton Script and Typo Script are names of script type faces. *See also* TYPE FACE.

CURVES. ( ) Signs used to denote inserted explanatory or qualifying words, phrases, clauses or remarks. To be distinguished from BRACKETS (*q.v.*). Also called 'Round brackets' and PARENTHESES (*q.v.*). *See also* BRACKETS, CIRCULAR BRACKETS.

CUSTODIAN. A person in charge of a special collection or of a building in which exhibits are displayed.

CUSTOM-BOUND. (*Binding*) A book which is bound to specific instructions, not in accordance with general instructions.

CUT. (*Noun*) 1. A design cut or engraved on wood, copper, or steel from which a print is made. 2. The impression from such a printing block.

3. An engraving, or plate, printed on the text page. 4. (*Verb*) To trim the edges of a book. 5. (*Adjective*) Of a book having cut edges. *See also* CUT EDGES, OPENED, PLATE.

CUT CORNER PAMPHLET FILE.   A free-standing box file which has the upper back corners of the sides cut away to half the height of the box; the upper half of the back as well as the top are unenclosed. Such boxes are used for containing pamphlets on the shelves. *See also* PRINCETON FILE.

CUT DUMMY.   Complete proofs of the illustrations of a book, arranged in proper sequence and containing the figure and galley numbers.

CUT EDGES.   (*Binding*) The top, fore, and tail edges of a book cut solid by a guillotine. When gilt they are known as 'gilt edges'. *See also* EDGES.

CUT FLUSH.   A book having its cover and edges quite even, the cutting operation having been done after the cover (usually paperboards or limp cloth) had been attached to the book. Also called 'Stiffened and cut flush.' A book so made is described as with 'flush boards.'

CUT IN-BOARDS.   A book which has had the head, tail and fore-edge trimmed after the boards have been secured. *See also* CUT OUT-OF-BOARDS.

CUT-IN HEADING.   A paragraph or section heading set in a bold or otherwise distinguishing type in a space made available against the outer margin but within the normal type area. Also called 'Incut heading'. *See also* INCUT NOTE.

CUT-IN INDEX.   *Synonymous with* THUMB INDEX (*q.v.*).

CUT-IN LETTER.   One of a large size, and occupying the depth of two or more lines of type as at the beginning of a chapter or paragraph. *See also* COCK-UP INITIAL, DROP LETTER.

CUT-IN NOTE.   *Synonymous with* INCUT NOTE (*q.v.*).

CUT-IN SIDE NOTE.   *Synonymous with* INCUT NOTE (*q.v.*).

CUT LINE.   Matter appearing below an illustration. More often called a 'Caption'.

CUT-OUT HALF-TONE.   *See* HALF-TONE.

CUT OUT-OF-BOARDS.   A book which has had its edges cut or trimmed before the boards are affixed. This method is used for books with a hollow back, the boards of which are not laced on but fit closely in the grooves. *See also* CUT IN-BOARDS, LACING-IN.

CUT TO REGISTER.   Watermarked paper which has been so cut that the watermark appears in the same position in each sheet.

CUTTER AUTHOR MARKS.   A system of author marks devised by Mr. C. A. Cutter, and consisting of from one to three letters at the beginning of an author's name, followed by numbers which increase as the names proceed along the alphabet. Author's names beginning with a consonant other than S have one letter, with S or a vowel have two letters, and Sc have three letters, followed in each case by a number, e.g.:

Ab2	Abbot	G42	Gilman	Sal	Saint
A12	Aldridge	Sch51	Schneider	Swl	Swain
G16	Gardiner	Sch86	Schwarts		

Their purpose is to enable books to be arranged alphabetically by using a relatively brief symbol. *See also* AUTHOR MARK, BOOK NUMBER, CUTTER-SANBORN THREE-FIGURE TABLE, THREE NUMBER AUTHOR TABLE.

CUTTER CLASSIFICATION. *See* EXPANSIVE CLASSIFICATION.

CUTTER NUMBERS. *See* CUTTER AUTHOR MARKS.

CUTTER-SANBORN THREE-FIGURE TABLE. An extension of the Cutter Author Marks for individualizing authors by using a combination of letters and three numbers (two for J, K, Y, Z, E, I, U, O; one for Q and X) in numerical order.

For example:

Rol	744	Roli	748	Roman	758
Role	745	Roll	749	Romani	759
Rolf	746	Rolle	751		
Rolfe	747	Rollo	755		

CUTTER'S OBJECTS. The 'objects' of a dictionary catalogue as adumbrated by Charles Amni Cutter in his *Rules for a dictionary catalogue*, 1875, are: 1. to enable a person to find a book of which either (a) the author, (b) the title, (c) the subject is known; 2. to show what the library has (d) by a given author, (e) on a given subject, (f) in a given kind of literature; 3. to assist in the choice of a book (g) as to its edition (bibliographically), (h) as to its character (literary or topical).

CUTTING. A piece cut from a newspaper or periodical. Also called 'Clipping' (American), 'Press cutting'.

CUTTINGS BUREAU. *See* CLIPPING BUREAU.

CUTTINGS FILE. *Synonymous with* CLIPPINGS FILE (*q.v.*).

CYANOGRAPHY. A blue-printing method of copying on only one side of the paper drawings and documents which do not include half-tone prints; the process is based on iron compounds and produces copies with white lines on a blue ground.

CYBERNETICS. The science of control and communication processes in animals and machines.

CYCLIC CLASSIFIED CATALOGUE.   *See* ROTATED CATALOGUE.

CYCLIC INDEX.   *Synonymous with* ROTATED INDEX (*q.v.*).

CYCLOPAEDIA.   *Synonymous with* ENCYCLOPAEDIA (*q.v.*).

CYLINDER DRIED.   Paper which has been dried on the paper-making machine by being passed over steam-heated cylinders, as distinct from other methods of drying. Also called 'Machine-dried'.

CYLINDER PRESS.   A printing press which makes the impression by a cylinder as opposed to a platen. It has a revolving impression cylinder under which is a flat bed containing the type or plates which moves backwards and forwards. These presses can be of two types; the Wharfedale or stop-cylinder press in which for every sheet printed, the cylinder makes almost one complete revolution and stops while the bed returns, an opening in the cylinder allowing the bed to return freely, and the Miehle or two-revolution press in which a smaller and continuously revolving cylinder revolves once to print one sheet then rises and revolves once more while the type bed slides back into position. This type of machine is the best letterpress machine for colour-printing and book-work. *See also* FLAT-BED PRESS, PLATEN PRESS, ROTARY PRESS.

CYRIL BARNARD MEMORIAL PRIZE.   *See* BARNARD MEMORIAL PRIZE, CYRIL.

d.c.   Abbreviation for a page of printed matter set in Double Column; Double Crown (paper 20 × 30 inches); Double Cap (i.e. double foolscap) printing paper, 17 × 27 inches.

DLAI.   Documentation, library and archives infrastructures—the subject of an inter-governmental conference held in September 1974 at Unesco in Paris.

D-LIBRARY.   A 'duplicating library', which processes and stores photo-reduced copies of books and other documents which are not lent for use outside the library. The objects are to save space in storing multiple copies, avoid loss through wear, mutilation, and theft, and avoid costs of, and wasted effort recording and discharging loans and binding books. *See also* C-LIBRARY.

D.M.C.   District Materials Center. *See* CURRICULUM MATERIALS CENTER.

D.S. (document signed).   A document of which only the signature is autographic.

d.w.   Abbreviation for dust wrapper. *See* BOOK JACKET.

DAGGER (†).   The second reference mark in footnotes, coming after the asterisk. When placed before an English, or after a German, person's name, it signifies 'dead' or 'died'. *See also* REFERENCE MARKS.

DAGUERREOTYPE. A means of making a photographic image on a copper plate coated with a light-sensitive layer of silver. The process was invented by Louis Jacques Mandé Daguerre (1789–1851) in 1833 following the death of J. N. Niepce, with whom he had been in partnership, but not made public until 1839. The earliest daguerreotypes are unique in that they cannot be copied, but the process was superseded in the 1850s by a negative positive process by which an unlimited number of copies may be made. The process is considered to be the first really practicable photographic method. Daguerre was a French scene-painter who became well known as a result of the diarama he built in Paris in 1822; after 1826 he devoted himself to developing photographic processes.

DAILY. A serial publication issued every day, except perhaps on Sunday.

DAINTON REPORT. The Report of the National Libraries Committee of which Dr. F. S. (now Sir Frederick) Dainton was chairman, was published in June 1969. The main recommendations were incorporated in a White Paper, entitled *The British Library*, and published on 13th January 1971; these are briefly enumerated in *Keesing's Contemporary Archives* for 27th March—3rd April 1971, p.24522A. The subsequent *British Library Bill* implemented these proposals, which were mainly: (1) a board comprising a chairman and up to 13 members, would be created to manage and develop the British Library resulting from the amalgamation of the library departments of the British Museum, including the National Reference Library of Science and Invention, with the National Central Library, the National Lending Library for Science and Technology, and the *British National Bibliography*; (2) councils would be appointed to advise on the needs of the Library's users. The Bill was enacted on 27th July 1971. *See also* BRITISH LIBRARY.

DAMAGED LETTER. A piece of type, the printing surface of which has been damaged. When appearing in a printer's proof it is marked by a X in the margin. Also called 'Bad letter', 'Battered letter', 'Broken letter', 'Spoiled letter'.

DAMPERS. The damping rollers which are an important part of lithographic printing presses; they damp the printing plate after each impression with a fluid, known as a damping mixture, the composition of which varies according to the material used for the forme (stone, zinc, steel, aluminium, etc.), in order to prevent the ink adhering to the plate, which it would do if the plate became too dry. In a hand-press damping is done with a sponge.

9

DANDY ROLL. A cylinder of wire gauze which presses upon the drained but still moist pulp just before it leaves the wire cloth of the paper-making machine for the rollers. The weaving of the wire of the dandy roll leaves its impression on the paper and determines whether it is to be wove paper (with the impression of fine, even gauze) or laid paper (with the impression of parallel lines). When devices or monograms are worked into the fine wire of the roll, 'watermarks' are produced.

DANIEL PRESS. A private printing press established by the Rev. C. H. O. Daniel at Frome in 1846, revived at Worcester College, Oxford, in 1874 and used until he died in 1919 for the private publication of family verses as well as small pamphlets and books. In 1877 he discovered the punches, matrices and types which had been used by Dr. Fell at the University Press between 1667–74 and used them at his press. *See also* FELL TYPES.

DANSK CENTRAL FÖR DOKUMENTATION. (Danish Centre for Documentation.) Exists to give advice on the use of the Universal Decimal Classification and on the organization of special libraries.

DARE. A computerized storage and retrieval system for data on the social and human sciences continuously being collected by the Social Science Documentation Centre (Department of Social Sciences, Unesco). The service, which became operational in September 1972, is primarily for internal programme use but is also offered through individual arrangements and a publication programme, to research institutes, etc.

DASH. A short strip of rule cast in the following lengths, and used for punctuation: the two-em dash——; the one-em dash—; the en rule –; and the hyphen - . These may be used for decoration or for the clearer laying out of printed matter, but usually longer rules or ornamental rules are more often used for these purposes. *See also* BORDER, FRENCH RULE, RULE, SWUNG DASH.

DASH ENTRY. Said of an entry for a book – following one or two long dashes (one for the author, the second for the title) – which continues, indexes, or supplements a monograph. Such an entry follows the entry for the main work in a printed bibliography or catalogue.

DATA. (*Information retrieval*) A general term for information. It is used to distinguish input and output information from instructions, and also to indicate the absence, or presence, of a certain condition, such as a magnetic field.

DATA BANK. Synonymous with DATA BASE (*q.v.*).

DATA BASE. A body of machine-readable records which is not created solely for a specific application, but may be regarded for some purposes as a homogeneous collection. Also called 'Data bank'.

DATA CENTRE. An organization for acquiring, processing, receiving, storing, retrieving and disseminating data. Evaluation is carried out at an INFORMATION EVALUATION CENTRE (*q.v.*). *See also* DOCUMENT CENTRE.

DATA COMPILATION. The regular and systematic recording on standard-size cards or record sheets, of facts as they are discovered in a variety of miscellaneous publications.

DATA PROCESSING. Recording information by some means whereby it (or only some of that stored on the same record) may be obtained immediately by some mechanical or semi-mechanical process. There are two basic modes of data processing: conventional and inverted. In the conventional mode, an 'item record' (which may be a punched card, section of a magnetic tape or magnetic disc) bears a number of codes representing characteristics describing the 'item of information' which may be a document, test, sale or employee. In the inverted data processing mode the process is reversed, 'items of information' being stored on records reserved for recognized characteristics.

DATA STORAGE AND RETRIEVAL SYSTEM. One which stores items for later re-use rather than modification, and which usually maintains the file items unaltered.

DATA VALIDATION ROUTINE. (*Information retrieval*) A program written to check the validity or the consistency of data.

DATAMATION. A shortened form of data automation; automatic data processing.

DATE. The statement in a book, either at the foot of the title-page, or on the reverse thereof, of the year in which the book was published. (*Cataloguing*) A filing element appearing in a heading and consisting of the date(s) of birth and/or death of a person whose name is the main element in the name heading. *See also* COLOPHON, COPYRIGHT DATE, DEDICATION DATE, FALSE DATE, IMPRINT DATE, MAINZ PSALTER.

DATE CARD. *See* DATE LABEL.

DATE DUE. The date on which a book is due for return to a library.

DATE GUIDE. A guide bearing numerals representing the dates on which books are due for return and placed in front of the appropriate charges in the issue trays.

DATE LABEL. The label placed in a lending library book and dated to indicate when it is due for return. In a few libraries dates of issue are used instead. Also called in America a 'Date slip' or 'Dating slip'.

Sometimes a loose card, called a 'Date card' is used. *See also* TRANS-
ACTION CARD.

DATE LINE.   The line in any paper or magazine on which the date of
issue appears.

DATE OF ISSUE.   The date on which a book was issued.

DATE OF PUBLICATION.   1. The year in which a book was published.
It is usually printed at the foot of, or on the back of, the title-page. In
old books a date often formed part of the colophon. 2. The day and/or
month and year of publication in the case of a newspaper or other
periodical. 3. The exact date a document was released to the public.
See also COPYRIGHT DATE.

DATE SLIP (DATING SLIP).   A DATE LABEL (*q.v.*).

DATE STAMP.   1. The date a library book is due for return (or of issue)
which is stamped on a transaction card or date label. 2. The machine
or dater used to make the impression.

DATUM.   (*Information retrieval*) The smallest element of information.
A BIT (*q.v.*).

DAY OF PUBLICATION.   *See* PUBLICATION DAY.

DE LUXE BINDING.   A fine leather binding, lettered and tooled by
hand. So-called de luxe bindings are often machine products.

DE LUXE EDITION.   An edition of a book in which especially good
materials and fine workmanship have been used.

DE VINNE.   A type face cut for Theodore Low De Vinne, 1828–
1914, a distinguished American printer. He was a co-founder with
Robert Hoe in 1884 of the Grolier Club and printed its first publication, a reprint of the *Star Chamber Decree*, 1637. He encouraged New
York printing house owners to form a union which, when combined
with similar groups from other cities, became known in 1887 as the
United Typothetae.

DE-ACIDIFICATION.   The process which raises the pH value of
paper documents to a minimum of 7.0 to assist in their preservation.
This process is usually carried out before thermoplastic lamination
of documents. *See also* pH VALUE.

DEAD FILE.   In acquisition work, a file containing (1) cards for books
received and catalogued, (2) cards for books not available as gifts or by
purchase despite considerable correspondence, (3) completed or filled
cards for serial publications.

DEAD MATTER.   (*Printing*) Type matter or plates which have been
used for printing but are not to be used again and may therefore be
distributed or melted. *See also* GOOD, KILLING, LIVE MATTER,
MATTER.

DECALCOMANIA. 1. A transfer or design printed on special paper for transfer to pottery or some other permanent base. 2. The paper for printing such transfers on. 3. The process of printing illustrations on glass, wood, pottery, etc. Abbreviated DECAL.

DECET. 1. A combination of ten singers or musicians. 2. The music for same.

DECIMAL CLASSIFICATION. There have been several schemes which have employed decimals in some way but the one usually referred to by this name is that compiled by Melvil Dewey and published in 1876, in which it is the notation that is used decimally. In this scheme it is possible to extend the printed scheme at any point to any desired extent. It divides knowledge into ten main classes and is the most used classification for general libraries. Abbreviated DC. *See also* ABRIDGED DECIMAL CLASSIFICATION, DEWEY DECIMAL CLASSIFICATION, UNIVERSAL DECIMAL CLASSIFICATION.

DECIMAL DIVISION. The expansion of a portion of a classification schedule and giving the resulting terms a numerical notation on the decimal principle.

DECIMAL NOTATION. A notation used to identify subjects in a scheme of classification; it consists of numerals used decimally so as to permit the logical subdivision of subjects, or a chain of classes, indefinitely. The notation of the Dewey Classification is of this kind. *See also* NOTATION.

DECIMAL NUMBER. The number of a book, or of a term, in a classification schedule, which is determined by the decimal principle. This method is used in both the Dewey Classification and the Universal Decimal Classification.

DECIMO-OCTAVO. *Synonymous with* Octodecimo, EIGHTEENMO (*q.v.*)

DECIMO-SEXTO. *Synonymous with* SEXTO-DECIMO.

DECK. 1. One floor of a stack containing book shelves, lifts, and workrooms (American). 2. The American term for a collection of cards, commonly a complete set of cards, which have been punched for a definite service (*IBM*). Often called in Britain a 'Pack'.

DECKLE. 1. Abbreviation for DECKLE EDGE (*q.v.*), and for deckle strap. 2. The frame or border, usually of wood, which confines the paper pulp to the mould when making paper by hand. 3. In the papermaking machine, the distance between the two deckle straps.

DECKLE EDGE. The feathery edge at the borders of a sheet of handmade or mould-made paper; it is caused by the deckle or frame which confines the paper pulp to the mould. It is also found in machine-made papers, being caused in these by the rubber deckle straps at the sides of the paper machine, or by artificial means such as a jet of water. Also called 'Feather-edge'.

DECKLE STRAPS.   Endless rubber bands which run on both sides of the wire cloth of a paper-making machine in order to keep the wet pulp within the desired limits of width. Also called 'Boundary straps'.

DECKLET.   A set of cards forming a single record (*IBM*).

DECLASSIFY.   To remove a secret or confidential document from a security classification under proper authorization. *See also* DOWN-GRADE.

DECODER.   In information retrieval, the locator which searches and extracts items from the DOCUMENT STORE (*q.v.*).

DECORATED COVER.   The front cover of a book which bears distinctive lettering or an illustration or design.

DECORATIVE.   A class of type faces which have exaggerated characteristics of the other three classes, ABSTRACT, CURSIVE and ROMAN (*qq.v.*), or distinctive features which preclude them from being included in those classes. They are usually fussily ornamental, but included in this group is OLD ENGLISH (*q.v.*).

DECREASING CONCRETENESS, PRINCIPLE OF.   A general principle for choosing an order of application of the characteristics of a classification. Ranganathan has developed a general facet formula which reflects this principle and is popularly known by the abbreviation PMEST standing for the five 'fundamental categories' Personality, Matter, Energy, Space and Time.

DEDICATED SPACE.   (*Information retrieval*) Physical space, provided on a punched card, for the representation of new documents integrated into an information retrieval system.

DEDICATION.   The author's inscription to a person or persons testifying respect, and often recommending the work to his (or their) special protection and favour, it usually appears on the recto of the leaf following the title-page. In sixteenth- and seventeenth-century books the dedication often took the form of a dedicatory letter written by the author to his patron.

DEDICATION COPY.   A copy of a book presented by the author, and so inscribed, to the person to whom the work is dedicated.

DEDICATION DATE.   The date given at the beginning or end of a dedication.

DEDICATORY LETTER.   *See* DEDICATION.

DEEP-ETCHED HALF-TONE.   *See* HALF-TONE.

DEEP ETCHING.   In photo-engraving, additional etching made necessary to secure proper printing depth where this cannot be accomplished by routing, as in places where dense black lines are used, or where line negatives and half-tone negatives are combined in the same place (*United Typothetae*). *See also* ETCHING.

DEFAULTER. A reader who fails to return a book or pay a fine. Such people are usually black-listed.

DEFENCE RESEARCH INFORMATION CENTRE. *See* DRIC.

DEFENSE DOCUMENTATION CENTER.† The U.S.A. centre which was commenced in 1951 as the Armed Services Technical Information Agency (ASTIA), the name being changed in 1963. Abbreviated DDC.

DEFERRED CATALOGUING. The postponement by a library of the full cataloguing of less important material, brief catalogue entries being made and possibly separately arranged temporarily to serve as a finding medium.

DEFINITION. (*Classification*) Concise description in distinct terms for essentials and characteristics (*Bliss*).

DEFINITIVE EDITION. The final authoritative text of the complete works of an author – the nearest possible approach to what the author intended – edited usually after the author's death. It is characterized by its editorial introduction, notes and sometimes APPARATUS CRITICUS (*q.v.*). Not to be confused with a VARIORUM EDITION (*q.v.*). Applies also to the works of a composer of music.

DEGRESSIVE BIBLIOGRAPHY. Varying the details of a bibliographical description according to the difference in the period treated or the importance of the publication described.

DEGRESSIVE DESCRIPTION. *Synonymous with* SELECTIVE CATALOGUING (*q.v.*).

del, delt. Abbreviation for delineavit (*Lat.* 'he or she drew it'). Used on engravings, maps, etc. and followed by the name of the artist or cartographer responsible for the original drawings. *See also* fecit, sculpt.

DELAYED DISCHARGING. Delaying the cancellation of a loan until after the reader returning a book has entered the library to choose another book. This is done as a normal part of the routine in some libraries, but in others discharging is only delayed during very busy periods, it being the usual practice to discharge books immediately they are returned. *See also* CHEQUE BOOK CHARGING METHOD, DISCHARGING BOOKS, ISLINGTON CHARGING SYSTEM, TRANSACTION CARD CHARGING.

dele. *See* DELETE.

deleatur (*Lat.* 'delete'). *See* DELETE.

DELEGATION OF POWERS. The handing over by a local authority, with or without restrictions, to the library committee, of all powers relating to the management of the library, except the power of levying, or issuing a precept for, a rate, or of borrowing money.

DELETE. To blot out, to erase, to omit. A mark, like the Greek letter δ, used in correcting proofs, is put in the margin to show that certain letters or words crossed through are to be deleted. Often abbreviated 'del', 'dele', or δ (representing the lower case initial letter of the Latin 'deleatur', delete).

DELETION MARK. The mark used in correcting a proof to indicate matter to be omitted. Also called 'Cancellation mark'. *See also* DELETE.

DELETION RECORD. (*Information retrieval*) A new record which will replace, or cause the removal of, an existing record in a MASTER FILE (*q.v.*).

DELFT CIRCULATION SYSTEM. A method for recording the loan of books from the closed access library of the Technical University at Delft. It uses a mechanized and partly automated book retrieval system called 'Bibliofoon'; books are then retrieved by call number.

DELIMITER. (*Information retrieval*) A symbol (1) separating data elements with a FIELD (*q.v.*) or (2) separating fields.

DELIQUESCENCE. Tendency to absorb atmospheric moisture (*Verry*).

DELIVERY DESK. *Synonymous with* CIRCULATION DESK (*q.v.*).

DELIVERY HALL. The centrally-placed focal point in a library where books may be issued and returned, and where the catalogue may be consulted.

DELIVERY ROOM. In American libraries, the room in which books are returned and issued.

DELIVERY STATION. A library service point at which no books are shelved but to which books requested by readers are sent to await collection.

DELIVERY VAN (*County Libraries*). A vehicle intended and adapted primarily for the transport of books in boxes or trays, and providing no facilities for the selection of books. Some delivery vans are designed to be used on occasion as DISPLAY VANS (*q.v.*), but this term is not now included in the County Libraries Section's list of definitions.

DELPHI. In contemporary operations research, a prophetic method of forecasting technique whereby experts solicit the opinions of a group of advisers through a series of carefully designed questionnaires. The experts reply to the questionnaires, receive statistical feedback and resubmit their estimates. The process is repeated more than once. This Delphi approach has been used to predict trends for periods as far as fifty years ahead, e.g. an environmental forecast for research libraries in Sweden. The name originates from the Delphic Oracle of classical times, presided over by Apollo, the god of the sun, prophecy, music, medicine and poetry.

DEMCO SELF-CHARGING SYSTEM. A simplification of the NEWARK CHARGING SYSTEM (*q.v.*) in which reader's tickets are not used. The borrower enters his ticket number on the next vacant line of the book card; this is checked by the assistant who stamps the date label.

DEMONYM. A popular or ordinary qualification used as a pseudonym, as 'An Amateur', 'A Bibliophile'.

DEMOPLETH MAP. A type of CHOROPLETH MAP (*q.v.*) which shows distribution by civil divisions.

DEMY. A standard size of printing paper, $17\frac{1}{2} \times 22\frac{1}{2}$ inches, and of writing and drawing paper (also called 'small demy') $15\frac{1}{2} \times 20$ inches. *See also* OCTAVO, PAPER SIZES.

DEMY OCTAVO. A book size, $8\frac{3}{4} \times 5\frac{5}{8}$ inches. *See also* BOOK SIZES.

DENOTATION. *See* CONNOTATION.

DENOTATIVE. *See* CONNOTATION.

DENSITOMETER. A photoelectric instrument for measuring the density, or degree of blackness, of a photographic image. A reflection-densitometer is used to measure the density of an opaque surface (print) before setting the camera and screen for half-tone exposure. Measuring the optical density of ink films during printing is done with a similar instrument.

DENSITY. In documentary reproduction, the degree of photographic opacity. (*Concepts* . . .) The degree of opacity of films and blackness of prints (the light-absorbing quality of a photographic image); it is usually expressed as the logarithm of opacity.

DENTELLE. Lace-like tooling on the borders of a book cover, placed near the edges and pointing towards the centre. The most notable binders working in this style were the Derome family and Pierre-Paul Dubuisson who was appointed binder to Louis XV in 1758.

DENTELLE A L'OISEAU. Dentelle bindings in which birds are introduced into the design of the borders; chief executant was N. D. Derome. *See also* DEROME STYLE.

DENUDATION. (*Classification*) The formation of a chain of classes by the application of successive characteristics of division.

DEPARTMENT. 1. A section of a library devoted to one subject as in a DEPARTMENTALIZED LIBRARY (*q.v.*), or to one kind of service, as a

'Reference library'. 2. An administrative section of a library which has one function or series of functions, such as 'Cataloguing department'. In America sometimes called a 'Division'.

DEPARTMENT HEAD. A member of the professional staff of an American library who is directly responsible to the Chief Librarian, or Director, for a division of the library organization having its own staff. In a library organized under the divisional system, a head of one of the divisions of the central library.

DEPARTMENT OF TECHNICAL PROCESSES. *See* PROCESSING DEPARTMENT.

DEPARTMENTAL CATALOGUE. A catalogue consisting of entries for books in one department only of a library.

DEPARTMENTAL LIBRARY. A library in a college or university which is apart from the main library and restricted to one subject or group of subjects. Also called 'Branch library', 'Faculty library', 'Laboratory collection', 'Office collection', 'Seminar collection'.

DEPARTMENTAL PUBLICATIONS. Those Non-Parliamentary Publications published and made available from the Departments of the British Central Government or through H.M. Stationery Office, whether printed by H.M. Stationery Office as the Government's printer or not.

DEPARTMENTALIZED LIBRARY. A large library in which all the material on each broad subject, whether for reference or lending, is kept in separate rooms or clearly defined sections. Also called SUBJECT DEPARTMENT (*q.v.*).

DEPENDENT WORK. A term used by cataloguers to indicate a work which is related in some way to a work by another author already published. It may be a modification, adaptation or amplification of the earlier work; the term includes such writings as abridgements, commentaries, continuations, dramatizations, librettos, parodies, revisions, selections, sequels and supplements.

DEPOSIT. Documents which have been placed in a record office, usually for reasons of security but also to make them more readily available for consultation, the depositor retaining ownership. Sometimes called 'courtesy storage'.

DEPOSIT COLLECTION. A collection of materials from a single publisher, or owner, placed in a library organization as a collection and so that they may be made available to the public. The depositor often prescribes regulations for access.

DEPOSIT COPY. A copy of a newly published book, pamphlet or periodical, etc., which is sent to one or more libraries, as required by law, and sometimes to complete copyright protection in the country. *See* DEPOSITORY LIBRARY.

DEPOSIT LIBRARY. 1. A library service point stocked with a small collection of books which is changed periodically, and which is open for a few hours only daily, or on selected days of the week. These are usually established in new housing areas to provide a temporary book service until a permanent library can be provided, and in factories and institutions. 2. (*Archives*). A library in which documents are deposited under special conditions. 3. A library to which books and other publications are sent by the publishers for permanent preservation under the provisions of national copyright or legal deposit legislation; also called a COPYRIGHT LIBRARY (*q.v.*).

DEPOSIT STATION. *Synonymous with* DEPOSIT LIBRARY (*q.v.*).

DEPOSITORS. Readers who pay a deposit, in lieu of obtaining a guarantee, to enable them to borrow books from a library.

DEPOSITORY CATALOGUE. A copy of a national library catalogue, such as that of the Library of Congress, which is deposited in selected libraries.

DEPOSITORY LIBRARY. In England, a library which is entitled by law to receive a free copy of every book published. In America, a library which is entitled to receive all, or selected, United States government publications, or designated to receive free a full list of Library of Congress catalogue cards. *See also* COPYRIGHT LIBRARY.

DEPTH CLASSIFICATION. 1. Classifying so minutely that the most specific subject in all its aspects is identified and dealt with fully and accurately. 2. Classification schedules that have been sufficiently worked out to meet the needs of MICRO-THOUGHT (*q.v.*), of libraries for specialist materials and users, and of documentation.

DEPTH INDEXING. Indexing as fully as possible by making specific entries for all the subjects, persons, places, books, etc. mentioned in the text.

DEPTH OF FIELD. The distance between the nearest and farthest objects from a camera which are acceptably sharp, at a given lens aperture.

DEPTH OF STRIKE. *See* BEVEL.

DEPUTY LIBRARIAN. The chief assistant librarian. One who becomes acting chief librarian in all absences of the principal. Formerly called 'Sub-librarian'. Sometimes called 'Associate librarian' in America.

DEQUEKER SYSTEM. (*Information retrieval*) The first information searching system to be introduced. It consisted of cards with rows of holes punched in the body of the cards and filed on their edges in a cabinet. Rods were inserted through the holes corresponding to the codes for the subject of an enquiry, and a half-turn of a handle operated a mechanism to raise slightly above the level of the remainder of the cards those bearing the codes required. *See also* EDGE-NOTCHED CARDS, MARGINAL-HOLE PUNCHED CARDS, PUNCHED CARD, SLOTTED CARDS.

DERIVATIVE BIBLIOGRAPHY. Used synonymously for selective or subject bibliographies of the secondary type, and sometimes for retrospective bibliographies. *See also* BIBLIOGRAPHY, PRIMARY BIBLIOGRAPHY, RETROSPECTIVE BIBLIOGRAPHY, SECONDARY BIBLIOGRAPHY.

DERIVATIVE WORK. A WORK (*q.v.*) e.g. extracts, anthology, abridgement, adaptation, translation, revision, compilation, arrangement of a musical work, which is the result of adapting, arranging, translating or transforming an INTELLECTUAL WORK (*q.v.*). The copyright of a derived work is protected without affecting the copyright of the original, provided that the choice, the presentation, or the form, represents the personal work of the author.

DEROME STYLE. A style of book decoration practised by the Derome family in France in the eighteenth century. It is mainly confined to symmetrical corner tooling of a very richly engraved floreated scroll work, pertaining very closely to the roccoco style of the Louis period. Nicholas Denis Derome (1731–88) who worked for Count Hoym is famous for his Dentelle borders. *See also* DENTELLE.

DESCENDER. The vertical descending stem of lower-case letters such as j, p, q, etc.; that part which extends below the 'X'-HEIGHT (*q.v.*). *See also* ASCENDER.

DESCRIPTIVE BIBLIOGRAPHY. The kind of bibliography which makes known precisely the material condition of books, that is, the full name of the author, the exact title of the work, the date and place of publication, the publisher's and printer's names, the format, the pagination, typographical particulars, illustrations and the price, and for old books, other characteristics such as the kind of paper, binding, etc. Also called 'Analytical bibliography'. *See also* HISTORICAL BIBLIOGRAPHY.

DESCRIPTIVE CATALOGUING. That part of the cataloguing process which is concerned with the choice and form of main and added entries, transcription of title-page details, collation, etc. The term was coined by the survey committee at the Library of Congress in 1940. *See also* SUBJECT CATALOGUING.

DESCRIPTIVE LIST. (*Archives*) A list of documents, with a brief description of the contents of each, sufficient to enable the researcher to determine whether it is likely to provide the information needed.

DESCRIPTOR. (*Information retrieval*) 1. An elementary term used to identify a subject. 2. A simple word or phrase used as a subject (*IBM*). 3. A word, translatable into a code, or symbol, which is given to a document to describe it and by means of which it can be discovered when required. Also called 'Code', 'Semantic factor'. It may be a subject heading or a class number. 4. (*Cataloguing. Indexing*) A descriptive designation added to a heading in a catalogue entry or index entry to distinguish otherwise identical headings. A type of ADDITIONAL DESIGNATION (*q.v.*). *See also* SUBJECT HEADING, THESAURUS, UNIT RECORD.

DESCRIPTOR ASSOCIATION LIST. (*Information retrieval*) A list of descriptors associated with a particular descriptor, or with a group of particular descriptors, in an information retrieval system.

DESCRIPTOR FIELD. (*Information retrieval*) The area of subject matter covered by descriptors. *See also* DESCRIPTOR GROUP.

DESCRIPTOR FILE. A file, or sequence, of UNIT RECORDS (*q.v.*), i.e. DESCRIPTORS (*q.v.*) followed by their relevant supplementary information.

DESCRIPTOR GROUP. (*Information retrieval*) A subdivision of a DESCRIPTOR FIELD (*q.v.*).

DESCRIPTOR LANGUAGE. A standardized indexing vocabulary comprising descriptors and used to describe documents, or their contents. A controlled descriptor language economizes on the number of symbols used in the descriptor file, standardizes subject description, maximizes the probability of retrieving all documents relative to an enquiry and none that are irrelevant, and provides for specific reference and generic survey to the extent needed by the users.

DESCRIPTOR NETWORK. (*Information retrieval*) A diagram illustrating the logical relations between descriptors.

DESCRIPTOR SEQUENCE (*Information retrieval*) A controlled COMBINATION ORDER (*q.v.*) of descriptors. *See also* DISTRIBUTED FACETS.

DESENSITIZATION. Applying a solution, called an 'etch', (of nitric acid and gum arabic for stone; gum arabic, chromic acid and phosphoric acid for zinc, gum arabic and phosphoric acid for aluminium) to a lithographic printing plate after an image has been transferred to it, to desensitize the non-image areas, remove stray traces of grease from them, and increase the moisture-retaining capacity.

DESIDERATA. 1. A list of subjects on which the author of a book requires information. If only one is required the singular form 'desideratum' is used. 2. A list of books required.

DESIGN. (*Verb*) To plan the entire format of a book. (*Noun*) The specification for the format of a book.

DESIGNATION MARK. Letters corresponding to the initial letters of the title of a book, and the volume number (if any), which are sometimes printed alongside the SIGNATURE MARK (*q.v.*) on each section to help the binder identify the sections belonging to a particular title. *See also* DIRECTION LINE.

DESK. *Synonymous with* STAFF ENCLOSURE (*q.v.*).

DESK SCHEDULE. A schedule arranged to show the assignments of staff to each desk or department in a library. (*American.*)

DESK-TOP LIBRARY. *See* PACKAGE LIBRARY.

DESTINATION SLIPS. Pieces of paper which project from books in the Order Department or Cataloguing Department to indicate by their colour or marking to which libraries they are allocated.

DESTRUCTION SCHEDULE. A list of documents, or of types of document, which may be destroyed as of no further value after the expiry of a specified term of years, the promulgation of the list being authority to destroy.

DETROIT SELF-CHARGING SYSTEM. A simplified form of the NEWARK CHARGING SYSTEM (*q.v.*), the borrowers themselves making some of the records.

DEVICE. An emblem or monogram used by a printer or publisher to identify his work. It is usually used as part of the printer's IMPRINT (*q.v.*) or publisher's name on the title-page or spine.

DEVIL. *See* WILLOW.

DEWEY DECIMAL CLASSIFICATION. The classification devised by Melvil Dewey (1851–1931) in 1873, and first published anonymously in 1876, since when it has been revised seventeen times. Knowledge is divided into the following main classes: O, General works; 1, Philosophy; 2, Religion, 3, Sociology; 4, Philology; 5, Natural Science; 6, Useful Arts; 7, Fine Arts; 8, Literature; 9, History. The notation is a pure one, being based on three figures and used decimally. Subdivision by form is facilitated by the use of a table of common subdivisions with a mnemonic notation; the linguistic numbers from 420–499 and the geographical numbers from 940–999 are used mnemonically to subdivide by language and place. The relative index is original, and shows the relation of each subject indexed to a larger subject (or class or division), or after the entry word the phase of the subject is indicated. This scheme is used in most public, school, and many non-public, libraries. The schedules were considerably extended in each successive edition until the fifteenth 'Standard' Edition (1951) which was published after Dewey's death and was a much attenuated edition, being designed for a small library. In this, the simplified spelling which Dewey had always used was discontinued. Since 1951 the revision of the schedules has been undertaken within the Library of Congress Library. Some major changes were made in the seventeenth edition. There were some re-locations and re-casting of schedules; form divisions were retitled 'standard sub-divisions' in recognition of the fact that many are modes of treatment rather than forms. The index is new in concept and execution. The scheme is kept up to date between editions by means of the bulletin issued by the revisers under the title *Decimal classification: additions, notes and decisions* (free to users from LC). The Dewey numbers have been printed on LC. catalogue cards since April 1930; they used also to appear on the cards supplied by the H. W. Wilson Company. The 18th edition was published in 3 volumes (1: Tables; 2: Schedules; 3: Index) in 1971. There are fewer re-locations than in the 17th edition but two divisions (340 Law; 510 Mathematics) have been entirely revised. This edition began to be used in January 1971 by the *British National Bibliography* and also by the Library of Congress. In use in 123 countries, a French edition of the Dewey Decimal Classification was first published when the 18th edition (which had been translated by librarians in Canada and France) was issued in January 1975. The schedules are under constant scrutiny in order to make them more relative to modern knowledge and national and international changes of various kinds. One example was the publication in 1974 of a new area table for Great Britain. *See also* ADD INSTRUCTIONS, DIVIDE LIKE THE CLASSIFICATION, DIVISION OF DDC, UNIVERSAL DECIMAL CLASSIFICATION.

DEWEY MEDAL, MELVIL. Donated by Forest Press, Inc., this annual award, consisting of a medal and citation of achievement, is made to an individual or a group for recent creative professional achievement of a high order, particularly in those fields in which Melvil Dewey was so actively interested, notably library management, library training, cataloguing and classification, and the tools and techniques of librarianship. The award is administered by the ALA Awards Committee which appoints a jury of five to make the selection. The Medal was first awarded (in 1953) to Ralph R. Shaw.

DIACRITICAL MARK. A mark, such as an accent, placed over or under a letter to express some special phonetic value.

DIAERESIS. Two dots placed over the second of two consecutive vowels to show that they are to be pronounced separately, as Chlöe, coöperate. In English it is now an obsolescent symbol, having been replaced by the hyphen (co-operate); the Americans now use neither.

DIAGONAL FRACTION. The separation of the numerator from the denominator by an oblique stroke instead of a horizontal one, e.g. 1/2.

diagr. (Pl. diagrs.) Abbreviation for DIAGRAM (q.v.).

DIAGRAM. As distinct from an illustration proper, a diagram gives only the general outline or plan of the thing represented. Abbreviated diagr.

DIAMOND. An out-of-date name for a size of type equal to about $4\frac{1}{2}$ point.

DIAPER. A binding pattern consisting of a simple figure constantly repeated in geometrical form: the pattern may consist of figures separated by the background only, or of compartments constantly succeeding one another, and filled with a design. The design is done with a 'diaper roll'.

DIAPHRAGM CONTROL. A device for indicating the correct aperture for any camera extension and screen ruling when using a PROCESS CAMERA (q.v.).

DIAPOSITIVE. A positive copy (of a document) made on transparent material. See also NEGATIVE, POSITIVE.

DIAZO. A contraction of diazonium, the chemical compound used in ammonia-developing reproduction papers, cloths and films which will reproduce anything printed, drawn, or written on a translucent or transparent material when exposed to ultra-violet light and developed in ammonia fumes. See also DIAZOTYPE PROCESS. Also used of a dye-coated paper which will produce a copy directly by exposure to a transparent or translucent original. The sensitive dye is bleached by exposure to light, the unbleached portions can be developed by a liquid developer or ammonia fumes, according to the type of paper used.

DIAZOTYPE PROCESS. A copying process whereby paper treated with a diazo compound is placed against the document to be copied and an exposure made by means of powerful arc lamps. The exposed paper is developed by passing it through a chamber containing ammonia fumes or over rollers damped with a specially prepared solution. It enables a positive black and white copy to be made in one operation but cannot reproduce facsimiles of double-sided documents. Blue, brown or red lines may be produced as well as black. A print made by this method may be called a 'Diazo print' or 'White print'. The base materials for diazo printing may be paper, film, or cloth. Before prints can be made by the diazo process, which can be done on the cheapest of sensitized papers, a translucent master must first be made. Non-reversible images are generally produced by this method, i.e. negative and positive images will produce the same kind of image. The process originated in 1923. Also called 'Dyeline'. *See also* AZOFLEX, OZALID.

DICED. Binding with tooling to resemble dice or small diamond squares.

DICHOTOMY, CLASSIFICATION BY. *See* BIFURCATE CLASSIFI-CATION.

DICKMAN CHARGING SYSTEM. A slightly simplified and mechanized development of the Newark system to obviate the necessity for making records in longhand, thus lessening the possibility of mistakes.

DICTIONARY. 1. A book explaining the words of a language, the words being arranged in alphabetical order; it usually gives the orthography, pronunciation and meaning of each word. A dictionary of the words in a restricted field of knowledge usually gives only the meaning. 2. In information retrieval, *synonymous with* THESAURUS (*q.v.*).

DICTIONARY CATALOGUE. A catalogue in which all the entries (author, title, subject, series, etc.) and references are arranged in a single alphabet – like a dictionary. As distinct from other alphabetical catalogues, subject entries are made under specific subjects. In some instances, the arrangement of sub-entries may depart from a strictly alphabetical order in order to provide a logical, or other convenient, arrangement, the main headings still retaining the alphabetical order. For the 'objects' of a dictionary catalogue, *see* CUTTER'S OBJECTS.

DICTIONARY CODE. The use, as a code, of words and terms in the alphabetical order of a dictionary.

DICTIONARY INDEX. A series of entries with verbal headings arranged in alphabetical order. Also called 'Alphabetico-specific subject catalogue'.

DIDONE. A category of type face having a sharp contrast between the thick and thin strokes. The axis of the curves is vertical, the serifs of the lower-case ascenders are horizontal and there are no brackets to the serifs. Of such are Bodoni, Corvinus, Extended and Modern. The term Didone has replaced MODERN FACE (*q.v.*).

DIDOT. A MODERN-FACE (*q.v.*) type cut in 1784 by Firmin Didot (1764–1836) the most famous of a French family which is important in the history of printing. Most eminent as a type-founder, he was mainly responsible for developing the type which is now familiar. He revived and developed the stereo-typing process, and produced singularly perfect editions of many classical English and French works. He and other members of his family fixed the standard for book types in France in the nineteenth century.

DIDOT NORMAL. The standard on the Continent of Europe for the height of type from the feet to the printing surface. It is 0·9278 inches. *See also* TYPE HEIGHT.

DIDOT POINT. *See* DIDOT SYSTEM.

DIDOT SYSTEM. A system of type measurement originated by François Ambroise Didot (1730–1804), the French typefounder, in 1775. One Didot point equals 0·0148 inches; one English point equals 0·013837 inches. The Didot System was generally adopted in France early in the nineteenth century and by German typefounders between 1840 and 1879. *See also* CICERO, POINT.

DIE. An engraved stamp used for stamping a design.

DIE SINKING. The process of making dies; die cutting.

DIE STAMPING. A printing process that gives a raised effect. Sometimes the die does not carry the ink, and the raised paper alone makes the letter discernible. *See also* EMBOSSING.

DIE SUNK. A depression produced by the application of a heated die or block.

DIFFERENCE. *See* PREDICABLES, FIVE.

DIFFERENTIAL FACET. A facet which applies only to the limited group of terms in the facet enumerated.

DIFFERENTIAL RATING. A local rate levied (in addition to the county rate) to provide staff and maintain a library building in order to satisfy the reading requirements of the area covered by the local rate. *See* FLAT RATE.

DIFFUSE FACETS. (*Information retrieval*) Facets representing very general and abstract subjects without specification of primary substance.

DIFFUSION TRANSFER. A photocopying method which produces a positive by chemical diffusion from the negative, e.g. Agfa rapid, Gevacopy (*Verry*).

DIFFUSION TRANSFER PROCESS. *See* TRANSFER PROCESS.

DIGEST. A methodically arranged compendium or summary of literary, historical, legal, scientific, or other written matter.

DIGESTER. (*Paper*) The vessel in which rags, esparto or wood are boiled, with chemicals, often caustic soda, to break down the fibres. *See also* BOILER.

DIGIT. 1. Each of the symbols comprising a BOOK NUMBER (*q.v.*) in the Colon classification. 2. In classification, a distinctively recognizable configuration of marks (e.g. letters – both capital and lower case – numbers, punctuation marks and any other symbols), or code elements, included in a notation, therefore synonymous with 'sort'. 3. In computer codes, each item comprising a symbol; in the symbol ABA553 there are six digits but only four 'sorts' or 'characters' (A, B, 3, 5). Each conventional set of sorts is called a 'species' (the capitals, the numerals). *See also* CODE. 4. The printers' symbol ☞. Also known as 'Fist', 'Hand' or 'Index'.

DIGITAL COMPUTER. A computer which operates symbolically, by reducing all its input to binary digits ('bits') and so giving it increased flexibility. *See also* BIT, DIGIT 3, ANALOG COMPUTER, BINARY CODE.

DIGRAPH. *Synonymous with* DIPTHONG (*q.v.*).

DIME NOVEL. An American term for a type of paper-covered fiction which was popular during the second half of the nineteenth century. A cheap, sensational, novel.

DIN. The characters used before figures to identify standards issued by the Deutscher Normenausschuss (DNA), the German standards institution. The DIN standards for sizes of paper were later adopted by the International Standards Organization.

DIPLOMATIC. The science of the critical study of official as opposed to literary sources of history, i.e. of charters, acts, treaties, contracts, judicial records, rolls, chartularies, registers and kindred documents.

DIPHTHONG. Two letters joined together and representing one sound, as æ, Æ, œ, Œ. Also called 'Digraph'.

DIPTYCH. *See* CODEX.

DIRECT CATALOGUING. *See* COLLOCATIVE v DIRECT CATALOGUING.

DIRECT CODING. The assignation of a separate meaning to each individual part of a search medium, as e.g. each hole in an edge-punched card or each individual punching position in a machine-punched card. *See also* INDIRECT CODING, MARGINAL-HOLE PUNCHED CARDS.

DIRECT CONTACT COPYING. A process for documentary copying which requires the action of light on a sensitized coating on paper. One method uses infra-red light waves acting on a heat sensitive coating which is placed in firm contact with the document to be copied. The infra-red rays are passed through the copy paper to the original and in so doing are absorbed by the text image, the resultant heat blackening the corresponding areas of the copy paper to produce a positive copy. This is called a THERMAL PROCESS (*q.v.*). The other method uses ultra-violet light waves and sensitive paper coated with diazo compounds. The original must have printing on one side only and must have opaque images on translucent paper capable of passing ultra-violet light. The original is placed, under pressure, on the paper with the image side up and ultra-violet light is played across the original with the result that the translucent portions of the original disintegrate the diazo compounds, making them incapable of acting as a colouring agent. The dry paper is then passed through gaseous ammonia, the dye remaining in the image area being brought out and resulting in a readable, dry positive. This is a DIAZOTYPE PROCESS (*q.v.*).

DIRECT COPYING. *See* LENSLESS COPYING.

DIRECT ENTRY. (Indexing) An entry for a multi-word subject in its normal word order, as opposed to inverted word sequence.

DIRECT HALF-TONE. A half-tone for which the screen negative is made directly from the subject, not from a photograph or drawing.

DIRECT IMAGE FILM. The type of film which produces a negative or positive copy from the same kind of original, in one step.

DIRECT POSITIVE. 1. A photographic paper which gives a positive copy by direct exposure to a positive original. 2. The positive print prepared without an intermediate negative. Also called 'Self positive'.

DIRECT POSITIVE PROCESS. One where the exposed film is developed to a positive, instead of to a negative, by using a reversal developing process.

DIRECT PRINTING. Printing in which the impression is made direct from forme to paper, as in letterpress, and is not offset on to the paper from another medium. *See also* LETTERPRESS, OFFSET.

DIRECT SUB-DIVISION. When determining subject headings for a dictionary catalogue in respect of a book limited to one locality, the heading is sub-divided by the name of a county, province, city or other locality without the interposition of the name of the country; e.g. GEOLOGY – SURREY. Indirect sub-division interposes the name of the country; e.g. GEOLOGY – ENGLAND – SURREY.

DIRECTION DES BIBLIOTHÈQUES DE FRANCE. This organization, which is under the control of Le Ministère de l'Éducation Nationale was founded in 1945 when it took over from the Ministry the responsibilities for the employment and training of professional librarians. It is responsible for the administration and functioning of the big French national libraries and the municipal libraries as well as the libraries of the University of Paris and 15 other universities.

The Direction provides instruction and issues certificates and diplomas to staff employed in libraries which come under its control.

DIRECTION LINE. Used to indicate the line of characters when the abbreviated title of a book called DESIGNATION MARK (*q.v.*) follows the signature mark, or letter, which is printed at the foot of the first page of each sheet, to guide the binder when gathering. Originally, the line on which a CATCHWORD (*q.v.*) was printed. Also called 'Signature line', 'Title signature'. *See also* DESIGNATION MARK, SIGNATURE AND CATCHWORD LINE.

DIRECTION NUMBER. The number which appears on the DIRECTION LINE (*q.v.*) at the bottom of a leaf of an old book, i.e. below the lowest line of type.

DIRECTION WORD. *See* CATCHWORD.

DIRECTOR OF CULTURAL SERVICES. One of the titles of local government positions which were used in England after the 1965 (in London), 1974 (rest of England) and 1975 (Scotland) re-organization of local authority boundaries, when the administration of libraries was combined with that of other departments under one committee and one chief officer. In some cases the chief officer was the librarian; sometimes not. Titles varied according to the kinds of departments which were grouped together; sometimes they were cultural, e.g. arts, sometimes entertainment, and the resulting name of the chief officer varied with the main interest of the committee or the largest department in the group.

DIRECTORY. A book containing lists of names of residents, organizations or business houses in a town, a group of towns or a country, in alphabetical order, and/or in order of situation in roads, or of firms in trade classifications arranged in alphabetical order; or of professional people, manufacturers or business houses in a particular trade or profession. *See also* TRADE DIRECTORY.

DIRTY PROOF. A proof containing many errors or typographical imperfections; a proof that has been returned to the printer with many corrections.

DIS. *See* DISTRIBUTING.

DISC. Popular name for a gramophone (in America, a 'phonograph') record. Also spelt 'Disk'. *See also* MAGNETIC DISC.

DISC INKING. The inking system which is found particularly in some platen printing machines. A round disc revolves on its own gearing at the head of the machine and the inking rollers pass over the disc before descending on the type-forme. *See also* PLATEN PRESS.

DISC NUMBER.   A symbol, consisting of letters and numbers allocated to a DISC (*q.v.*) by the manufacturer for purposes of identification. It is printed on the label on the disc and is used in lists and catalogues as a means of identification.

DISCARD.   A book that is withdrawn from circulation in a library because it is out-of-date or in too worn or dirty a condition.

DISCHARGE.   (*Verb*) The act of cancelling the record of the loan of a book or other item on its return to the library. *See also* CHARGE.

DISCHARGING BOOKS.   The act of cancelling the record of books on loan by re-inserting the book-cards in them on their return, or otherwise cancelling the loans to indicate that they have been returned. *See also* SLIP.

DISCHARGING COUNTER.   The staff enclosure which is set aside for the work of discharging books, i.e. cancelling the record of a loan.

DISCHARGING DESK.   *See* CIRCULATION DESK.

DISCIPLINE.   An organized field of study or branch of learning dealing with specific kinds of subjects and/or subjects considered from specific points of view.

DISCOBUS.   A vehicle which carries gramophone records for loan.

DISCOGRAPHY.   A list of gramophone records (popularly called 'discs') giving details of composer, title, performer/s, maker, and maker's catalogue number.

DISCONTINUED NUMBER.   (*Classification*) A number from the immediately preceding edition of a scheme of classification vacated because its content has been moved back to a more general number.

DISCOUNT.   The reduction from the list price of goods. With regard to English published books this is limited to 10% off the published price to those who sign the NET BOOK AGREEMENT (*q.v.*) although some booksellers who do not sign the agreement offer more. It is only available to libraries which provide a free service to the whole of a community. In the U.S.A. discounts are much greater; each publisher has his own discount schedule which is applicable to wholesalers, retailers, schools, libraries, etc. It is usually a sliding scale based on the quantity ordered.

DISCOURSE.   *Synonymous with* RELATION (*q.v.*).

DISCRETE RECORD.   A marginal-hole punched card, a machine sortable punched card, a piece of film, or a length of tape. If these records represent single documents and bear all the results of analysing a single document such records are said to result in a 'document system', whereas if they represent a single subject (or aspect) and contain information as to which documents in a file have this subject in common, the result is an 'aspect system'.

DISJOINED HAND. Handwriting in which the letters are not connected to one another. Also called 'Script writing'. The opposite of JOINED HAND (*q.v.*).

DISJUNCT LEAF. The stub which remains in a book after the removal of the remainder of the leaf because it contained matter which could not be allowed to remain. *See also* CANCELLATION.

DISPLAY STAND. A piece of furniture built to stand on the floor of a library on which to display books.

DISPLAY TYPE. Large or heavy-faced type used for headings, title-pages, posters or advertisements. They may include sizes between 18 and 24 point but usually comprise 30, 36, 42, 48, 60, 72 and more exceptionally 84 and 96 point.

DISPLAY VAN. A vehicle which may be used primarily or occasionally to display books either to persons within the van or to those passing along the outside of it. *See also* DELIVERY VAN.

DISPLAY WORK. The setting of short lines in varying faces and sizes of type, as distinct from a solid area of type. Advertisements, titles and headings are 'display' work.

DISPLAYED. (*Printing*) Matter which has been set on separate lines and distinguished from the remainder of the text by being set in a smaller or larger size of type, or by its position in relation to the margin (by being full out, indented or centred). Such matter is normally further emphasized by being preceded and followed by additional space. Long quotations, mathematical equations and headings are examples of displayed matter.

DISPOSAL LIST. In archives management, a list of types of document with instructions for their disposal, i.e. destruction or permanent preservation.

DISPOSITION. (*Archives*) The action taken after the APPRAISAL (*q.v.*) of non-current documents. This may include transfer to a records centre or archive depository for temporary or permanent storage, reproduction on microfilm, or destruction.

DISSECTION. (*Classification*) The formation of an array of co-ordinate classes.

DISSEMINATION OF INFORMATION. The distribution, or sending, of information whether specifically requested or not, to members of an organization by a librarian or information officer. The means used normally include news bulletins, abstracts, individual memoranda or letters, and personal interviews or telephone calls, but may also include notes accompanying articles, memoranda, cuttings or reports and the underlining of sentences or marking of paragraphs in same.

DISSERTATION, ACADEMIC. A thesis or treatise prepared as a condition for the award of a degree or diploma.

DISTINCTIVE TITLE. One that is peculiar to a particular publication.

DISTRIBUTED FACETS. (*Classification, Information retrieval*) In a compound subject, facets which are scattered throughout a classification consequent upon the COMBINATION ORDER (*q.v.*) applied. Also called 'Distributed terms'. *See also* DESCRIPTOR SEQUENCE.

DISTRIBUTED RELATIVES. A secondary aspect of a subject which is used to show a relationship when classifying a document, and which will not be used as the main, but as a subordinate, subject when determining the class number. The same sub-heading may be used to subdivide many headings.

DISTRIBUTED TERMS. *Synonymous with* DISTRIBUTED FACETS.

DISTRIBUTING. 1. Putting loose type back into their respective boxes and cases after use, or for melting, after use in the forme. This is done after machining and when type is not to be kept standing for reprints. Commonly called 'dissing'. Abbreviated 'dis'. *See also* BREAK. 2. In presswork, the uniform spreading of ink on the face of the printing forme.

DISTRIBUTION COPY. (*Reprography*) A microcopy from which further copies of equal legibility can be obtained.

DISTRIBUTION IMPRINT. The statement on the verso of the title-page of a book, which names the branches or representatives through which the publisher's books are distributed.

DISTRIBUTOR ROLLERS. The rollers on a printing press which spread ink on the ink slab, roll it to the correct consistency and transfer it to the rollers which ink the type-forme. They are made wholly of metal, or of rubber or composition on a metal core. Also called 'Distributing rollers'.

DISTRICT. (*County Libraries*) A part of the County Library area other than a REGION or AREA (*qq.v.*) and usually comprising a town and its adjacent rural area organized as a library unit.

DISTRICT AUDIT. The accounts of all local authorities other than boroughs are subject to District Audit, and certain accounts of boroughs are also subject statutorily to district audit. These are such accounts as the rate accounts and education accounts. District auditors are appointed by the Minister of Housing and Local Government, and their powers and duties are prescribed in the Local Government Act, 1933. *See also* AUDIT, MUNICIPAL AUDIT.

DISTRICT CENTRAL LIBRARY. (*County Libraries*) The principal library in a DISTRICT (*q.v.*), usually situated in the main centre of communications. If it has no branches or centres, it is a DISTRICT LIBRARY.

DISTRICT LIBRARIAN. One in charge of a county branch library serving directly residents in an area larger than the town in which it is situated, but possibly excluding residents of that town.

DISTRICT LIBRARY. 1. *Synonymous with* BRANCH LIBRARY (*q.v.*) in an urban library system. 2. In a British county library system, a branch situated in a market town or other focal area, at which books are not distributed or services provided to the service points in surrounding areas, but is used by residents in those areas, although possibly excluding the residents in the town itself if this is not within the county library area. *See also* REGIONAL BRANCH, REGIONAL HEAD-QUARTERS.

DISTRICT MATERIALS CENTER. *Synonymous with* CURRICULUM MATERIALS CENTER (*q.v.*).

DITTOED. Something that is duplicated on a spirit duplicator, strictly one produced on the American machine of this kind, called a Ditto. A generic name (as 'Roneoed' for items produced on a wax stencil duplicating machine).

DITTOGRAM. A printed character, or group of printed characters, repeated in error.

DIURNAL. A periodical which is published or issued every day.

DIURNALL. *See* NEWSBOOK.

DIVIDE LIKE THE CLASSIFICATION. The mnemonic use after the point (.) of symbols from various parts of a classification schedule in order to sub-divide a subject, as e.g. in 016 of Dewey's *Decimal Classification*:

016	Bibliography of special subjects	
016·1	„	of philosophy
016·17	„	of ethics
016·22	„	of the Bible
016·54	„	of chemistry

The 'divide-like' notes which were used in the 17th and earlier editions of the Dewey Decimal Classification were replaced in the 18th ed. by ADD INSTRUCTIONS (*q.v.*).

DIVIDED CATALOGUE. A catalogue in which the entries are

separated into two or more sequences in order to simplify filing and consultation, which may become complicated in a large dictionary catalogue. All subject and form entries and their necessary references may form an alphabetical subject catalogue and the remaining entries form an author-title catalogue. *See also* SPLIT CATALOGUE.

DIVIDING STROKE.   *Synonymous with* LINE DIVISION MARK (*q.v.*).

DIVINITY CALF.   A plain dark brown calf binding often used in the mid-nineteenth century for theological or devotional books. The boards were sometimes bevelled and the edges red.

DIVINITY CIRCUIT.   The American equivalent of Yapp, or CIRCUIT EDGES (*q.v.*).

DIVINITY EDGES.   *See* CIRCUIT EDGES.

DIVISION.   1. In some libraries, a section of a Department. 2. In some libraries, a Department. 3. A unit in a library system which is concerned with a particular function, as a 'Catalogue division', or with a definite subject, as 'Science division'. 4. In the American Library Association and the Special Libraries Association, sections of the membership which exist to further the work of libraries and librarianship and the well being of librarians within the limitations of each division. These divisions may represent a type of organization or a subject field; each has its own officers and organizational machinery. *See also* BRANCH, GROUP, SECTION.

DIVISION.   (*Classification*) 1. The process of dividing classes or groups of a classification scheme into their more minute parts. 2. The result so formed. 3. A subject or topic which is subordinate to a class. 4. Breaking down a FACET (*q.v.*) into its foci. *See* FOCUS. *See also* EXHAUSTIVE DIVISION, MAIN CLASS.

DIVISION HEAD.   In American libraries a member of the professional staff directly responsible to a department head, and in charge of a subdivision of a department.

DIVISION LIBRARY.   In an American university or college, a collection of books attached to, and administered by, a division or a group of related departments, usually with some form of co-operative arrangement with the general library, or as a part of the library system.

DIVISION OF DDC.   The second degree of subdivision in the Dewey Decimal Classification (the first degree of subdivision of one of the ten main classes), represented by the second digit in the notation, e.g. the 2 in 620. There are a hundred of these.

DIVISIONAL TITLE.   A page preceding a section or division of a book, and bearing the name or number of the section or division. The reverse is usually blank.

DIVISIONAL TITLE-PAGES. *See* GENERAL TITLE.

do. Abbreviation for ditto, the same.

DOCUMENT. 1. A record – made on a more or less flat surface or on a surface admitting of being spread flat when required, made of paper or other material fit for easy handling, transport across space, and preservation through time – of thought created by mind and expressed in language or symbols or in any other mode, and/or a record of natural or social phenomena made directly by an instrument without being passed through the human mind and woven into thought created and expressed by it. (*S. R. Ranganathan*.) 2. Material of any kind, regardless of its physical form and characteristics, on which information has been recorded. 3. A record, usually inscribed or written, which conveys information, and which is relied on to establish facts. It is now taken to include any form of graphic, acoustic or haptic record (book, cutting, map, manuscript, drawing, periodical, etc.). 4. A work recorded in language or symbols, or by other means (*IFLA*). 5. Any form of recorded information, whether indited, alphanumeric, pictorial or auditory. The tendency has developed in the last few years when referring to the contents of a library or documentation centre to consider all the individual items as 'documents' on the grounds that various kinds of record are included in the collections. By 'Document' is often meant any kind of record, whatever its data or form, and whether it is on paper, parchment or film or any other material. The result is that 'document' is being used when 'book' or any other form of record is meant. *See also* ARCHIVAL DOCUMENT, DOCUMENTS, WORK.

DOCUMENT ADDRESS. (*Information retrieval*) A class number or other symbol indicating the whereabouts of a document in a STORE (*q.v.*). *See also* UNIT RECORD.

DOCUMENT CARD. A UNIT CARD (*q.v.*). A card carrying all the bibliographic and index information for an item. Used in ZATOCODING (*q.v.*) and other edge-notched card systems as well as in serially searched files (*IBM*). Cards used in machine-sorting systems are also called document cards. Frequently each card represents a document or part of a document.

DOCUMENT CASE. A container, usually made of stout cardboard and approximately 15 × 10 × 3 inches, for the filing flat of archives or manuscripts.

DOCUMENT CATALOGUE. A catalogue of documents.

DOCUMENT CENTRE. An organization which has fewer functions than a DOCUMENTATION CENTRE (*q.v.*); they are mainly confined to selecting, acquiring, storing and retrieving specific documents. Such a centre disseminates the documents delivered to it, or facsimiles of them; other processes such as abstracting, extracting, etc. are carried out at a DOCUMENTATION CENTRE (*q.v.*). *See also* INFORMATION EVALUATION CENTRE, REFERRAL CENTRE.

DOCUMENT COPYING. *See* DOCUMENTARY REPRODUCTION.

DOCUMENT RETRIEVAL. The process of providing relevant documents on a specified subject when required. This cannot be done until (a) the documents have been classified or indexed in some way, (b) the classification or index decisions stored by some means, (c) these decisions have been searched.

DOCUMENT RETRIEVAL SYSTEM. One which provides a complete copy of a required document instead of merely a citation or reference. An aspect of INFORMATION RETRIEVAL (*q.v.*).

DOCUMENT STORE. In information retrieval, a place where documents are kept.

DOCUMENT SYSTEM. A method of machine indexing that presumes a discrete record, e.g. a marginal-hole punched card, a machine-sortable punched card, a piece of film, or a length of tape which represents a single document and contains, in searchable form, all of the results of an analysis of a single document. Also called 'Item entry system'. *See also* ASPECT SYSTEM, DISCRETE RECORD, ITEM ENTRY.

DOCUMENTALIST. One who practises documentation. An information officer or intelligence officer who is concerned with the collection and dissemination of knowledge, rather than the librarian who is concerned with the techniques of handling records of knowledge, making them available and possibly exploiting them. He is concerned with assembling information contained within documents together with data from other sources to form a new compilation.

DOCUMENTARY INFORMATION. Information about documents, or information recorded in documents. Either kind of information may be 'retrieved' according as to whether the purpose of the retrieval is to indicate where the needed information can be found, or what it is.

DOCUMENTARY REPRODUCTION. The copying of documents or pages of books by photographic or non-photographic means so that the copy has the appearance of the original, and without first of all copying the text letter by letter on a typewriter or by typesetting. *See also* DIAZOTYPE PROCESS, ELECTROPHOTOGRAPHIC PROCESSES, LENSLESS COPYING, PHOTOCOPY, PSEUDO-PHOTOGRAPHIC PHOTOCOPYING, REFLEX COPYING, SILVER PROCESSES, THERMAL PROCESS, TRANSFER PROCESS.

DOCUMENTATION. 1. The act of collecting, classifying and making readily accessible the records of all kinds of intellectual activity. 2. The recording of knowledge and the sources of knowledge, organizing such records systematically so that they may be found quickly, and disseminating by various means both the knowledge and the sources of the knowledge. 3. The recording, organization and dissemination of specialized knowledge (*Aslib*). 4. The science of collecting, storing and organizing recorded informational materials or documents for optimum access. 5. Includes the activities which constitute special librarianship plus the prior activities of preparing and reproducing materials and the subsequent activity of distribution. 6. The selection, classification and dissemination of information. 7. The science of ordered presentation and preservation of the records of knowledge serving to render their contents available for rapid reference and correlation. 8. The procedure by which the accumulated store of learning is made available for the further advancement of knowledge. 9. The art of facilitating the use of recorded, specialized knowledge through its presentation, reproduction, publication, dissemination, collection, storage, subject analysis, organization, and retrieval. 10. Collection and conservation, classification and selection, dissemination and utilization of all information (*IBM*). 11. The designation of the total complex of activities involved in the communication of . . . specialized information . . . including the activities which constitute special librarianship plus the prior activities of preparing and reproducing materials and the subsequent activity of distribution. (*Mortimer Taube*) 12. The group of techniques necessary for the ordered presentation, organization and communication of recorded specialized knowledge, in order to give maximum accessibility and utility to the information contained. (*J. D. Mark and R. S. Taylor*) 13. The identification, the investigation, the assembling and the use of documents (*French Union of Documentation Services*).

DOCUMENTATION, LIBRARY AND ARCHIVES INFRA-STRUCTURES. *See* DLAI.

DOCUMENTATION CENTRE. A place where publications are received, processed, preserved, summarized, abstracted and indexed; where bulletins relating to such material are prepared for distribution to those interested; where research is undertaken, bibliographies prepared, and copies or translations made.

DOCUMENTATION LIST. Bibliography with an emphasis on the inclusion of periodical articles and on the reader being served by a specialist engaged in research, business, deliberation or administration.

DOCUMENTATION WORK. The preparation of a DOCUMENTATION LIST (*q.v.*).

DOCUMENTOGRAPHY. Bibliography, but widened in scope in order to give details of materials included in mixed files containing printed matter, articles from reviews, manuscripts, typescripts, photographs, maps and plans such as are collected in documentation centres. A faster method of recording material, developed so that it may be more easily consulted as soon as the material is processed.

DOCUMENTS. Things admissible to archives (see ARCHIVES 2) being manuscripts made of any suitable materials, scripts produced by writing machines or by means of type, type-blocks, engraved plates or blocks, or film, together with all other material evidence whether they include alphabetical or numerical signs which form part of or are annexed to, or may reasonably be assumed to have formed part of, or been annexed to, a manuscript or script record, and which were drawn up or used in the course of an administrative or executive transaction (whether public or private) of which they formed part, and which were subsequently preserved in the custody of the person or persons responsible for that transaction and for their legitimate successors. For the preservation of documents, *see* ARCHIVES. *See also* DOCUMENT.

DOCUMENTS DEPOSITORY. In America, a library which is legally designated to receive without charge copies of all or selected U.S. government publications, or a library which is designated to receive without charge a full set of Library of Congress printed cards.

DOG-EARED. Said of a book, portfolio, or similar article having the corners of the leaves turned down and soiled by careless or long continued usage.

DONATION RECORD. A record of gifts; it may be kept in a book or on cards.

DONATUS DE OCTOBUS PARTIBUS ORATIONIS. *See* BLOCK BOOKS.

DONORS LIST. The record of donors arranged alphabetically and kept on cards, one card to each person. (American.)

DORKING CONFERENCE. *See* INTERNATIONAL CONFERENCE ON CLASSIFICATION FOR INFORMATION RETRIEVAL.

DORMITORY DISTRICT. The part of a town which is residential and in which no industry is carried on.

DORMITORY LIBRARY. A collection of books placed in a dormitory of an American college or university. The books are usually intended for recreational reading but may also be recommended texts.

DORSE. The reverse side of a MEMBRANE (*q.v.*).

DOS-A-DOS BINDING. Two or more books – usually small ones – bound back to back so that the back cover of one serves as the back cover of the other and the fore-edges of one are next to the fore-edges of the other.

DOT-ETCHING. *Synonymous with* RETOUCHING (*q.v.*).

DOT MAP. One which shows density of distribution by dots of uniform size, each dot representing a given quantity.

DOTTED RULE. A strip of metal of type height with a face showing a dotted line which may vary from fine dots close together to a sequence of short dashes. *See also* RULE.

DOTTING WHEELS. Small hand-tools of varying shapes used by artists when engraving metal plates.

DOUBLE. 1. In printing, a word, etc., erroneously repeated. 2. A sheet of paper twice the unit size, e.g. double crown (20 × 30 inches), ordinary crown being 15 × 20 inches. *See also* PAPER SIZES.

DOUBLE-BOOK. A book printed on half sheets.

DOUBLE COLUMNED. A page of printed matter set to half the width of a normal page line, with an em or more space, or a RULE (*q.v.*), between the columns. Abbreviated d.c. Also said to be set in 'Half-measure'. Double columns are used in such works as dictionaries, encyclopaedias and Bibles.

DOUBLE CROWN. A sheet of paper measuring 20 × 30 inches.

DOUBLE DAGGER (‡). The third reference mark for footnotes, coming after the DAGGER (*q.v.*). Sometimes called a 'Double obelisk'. *See also* REFERENCE MARKS.

DOUBLE DOCUMENT. A defect in microfilming whereby a rotary camera photographs simultaneously two documents in such a way that one covers or overlaps the other. Adjustment of the document stop will usually prevent this.

DOUBLE ELEPHANT. *See* ELEPHANT.

DOUBLE ENTRY. Entry in a catalogue under more than one subject, or under subject and place, and under the names of subordinate contributors such as joint authors, editors, illustrators, translators, etc., using the same form of entry with suitable headings added. Also, entry for a pseudonymous work under the real name of the author as well as under the pseudonym.

DOUBLE-FACED CATALOGUE CABINET. A catalogue in which drawers are placed to face both sides, or which, although made as one unit, is in effect two catalogues placed back to back.

DOUBLE-FACED SHELF. A shelf which is accessible on both sides.

DOUBLE HEADED. Two films, one for picture and one for sound, to be run in synchronization.

DOUBLE KWIC INDEXING. A variation of the KWIC (*q.v.*) indexing method whereby two words in the title (the entry word and another) instead of one are rotated. The effectiveness of the index is thus theoretically doubled but indexes compiled by this method are about four times as long as ordinary KWIC indexes.

DOUBLE LEADED. *See* LEADED MATTER.

DOUBLE LEAVES. The leaves of CHINESE STYLE (*q.v.*) books. These are recorded in a catalogue entry in the form '18 double l' or '36 pp. (on double leaves)'. Should the leaves be unnumbered, each is counted as two pages, as: [36] pp. (on double leaves).

DOUBLE LETTER. *Synonymous with* LIGATURE (*q.v.*).

DOUBLE NUMERATION. A system of numbering whereby illustrations, charts, etc., are related to the chapter, the numbers of which are the key numbers, e.g. Fig. 7.5 indicates the fifth figure in the seventh chapter.

DOUBLE OBELISK. *Synonymous with* DOUBLE DAGGER (*q.v.*).

DOUBLE PICA. An out-of-date name for a size of type equal to about 22 points.

DOUBLE PLATE. An illustration which stretches across two pages of a book when open. *See also* FOLDING PLATE.

DOUBLE PRINTING. Two impressions on the same sheet.

DOUBLE QUOTES. Pairs of superior commas " . . . " used to indicate quoted matter. *See also* SINGLE QUOTES, TURNED COMMA.

DOUBLE REGISTER. Two ribbons fastened in a book to serve as book-markers.

DOUBLE ROW CODING. (*Information retrieval*) A method using edge-notched cards which have a double row of holes at the edges.

DOUBLE RULE. A RULE (*q.v.*) having two lines of different thickness of face. *See also* PARALLEL RULE.

DOUBLE SETTING. A resetting of part of a book after some of the type had been distributed in order to print more copies than had at first been intended, the decision to print more having been made during machining.

DOUBLE-SIDED STACK. A book-case or stack with shelves on both sides.

DOUBLE-SPREAD. Two facing pages on which printed matter is spread across as if they were one page. When printing an illustration this way two blocks must be used unless the spread comes in the middle of a section. *See also* CONJUGATE, OPENING.

DOUBLE TITLE-PAGE. Used where a work has both a right-hand and a left-hand title-page. Usually one of these serves for the series or the complete volumes of a set, and the other is limited to the individual volume.

DOUBLE WEIGHT PAPER. Sensitized photographic paper between 0·0112 and 0·0190 inches inclusive. *See also* PHOTOGRAPHIC PAPERS.

DOUBLETTE. *See* REPLICA.

DOUBLURE. 1. An ornamental inside lining of a book cover of leather or silk, usually with a leather hinge, and often elaborately decorated. 2. Ornamental end-paper. Also called 'Ornamental inside lining'.

DOUBTFUL AUTHORSHIP. Authorship ascribed to one or more persons with no convincing proof. *See also* ATTRIBUTED AUTHOR.

DOVES PRESS. One of the most famous British private presses. It was directed by T. J. Cobden-Sanderson, who founded it with Sir Emery Walker, at Hammersmith, London, in 1900. Their partnership was dissolved in 1909 but Cobden-Sanderson continued to operate until 1916. The most important publication was the Doves Bible, published in five volumes between 1903–5. The name 'Doves' was taken from Doves Place, a passage off the Upper Mall, Hammersmith. The name was first used for the Doves Bindery which Cobden-Sanderson started in 1893 at 15 Upper Mall.

DOWNGRADE. To assign a secret or confidential document to a less restricted security classification under proper authorization. *See also* DECLASSIFY.

DOWNWARD REFERENCE. A direction from a more- to a less-comprehensive heading in an alphabetico-specific subject catalogue. The reverse of UPWARD REFERENCE (*q.v.*).

DRAGON'S BLOOD. Any of several resinous substances, mostly dark red in colour. It is used in powdered form in photo-engraving for etching line plates. Dragon's blood powder is brushed up against the slightly raised lines of the image or design on the metal plate from four sides, and 'burned in', thus protecting these lines against the action of the etching solution or acid (*United Typothetae*).

DRAMATIC WORK. An INTELLECTUAL WORK (*q.v.*) which expresses dramatic action. Copyright in performance arises when the work is staged for presentation before the public.

DRAW-OUT SHELVES. A form of compact storage consisting of shelves wide enough to take two rows of books, one facing each way, fixed across, or in place of, ordinary shelves. When it is desired to consult the books these shelves are drawn out, as if they were drawers, into the gangway. An example of this kind of shelf is 'Stor-mor', made by W. R. Ames of San Francisco, California.

DRAWER HANDLE.   A tool of a Corinthian volute which was commonly used in English Restoration book decoration. So called from its similarity to the handle of a small drawer.

DRAWN-ON COVERS.   The binding of square-backed magazines and paperbacks, the cover being attached by gluing to the spine of the book. When the end-papers are pasted down, it is said to be *drawn-on solid*.

DRESSED FORME.   A forme of pages of type with furniture between and around them, the page-cord having been removed. *See also* FORME, NAKED FORME.

DRESSING.   1. Fitting the FURNITURE (*q.v.*) between and around the pages in a chase prior to locking up the FORME (*q.v.*). 2. Fitting an illustration block into type so that text and illustration can be printed together.

DRIC.   Acronym of Defence Research Information Centre, which is the central facility of the Ministry of Defence for acquiring unpublished scientific and technical reports from the U.K. and overseas sources. Its primary function is to serve the Ministry of Defence establishments and branches and also defence contractors.

DRIVE OUT.   (*Printing*) 1. Said of type-matter which is spaced widely between the words so as to occupy more lines. 2. An instruction to the compositor to insert wide spaces between words. *See also* KEEP IN.

DROP.   (*Printing*) To unlock a forme and remove the furniture and chase after printing, the type then being either distributed or 'kept standing', i.e. tied up and stored.

DROP-DOWN TITLE.   The short title on the first page of text. It should be the same as the RUNNING TITLE (*q.v.*). *See also* CAPTION TITLE.

DROP FOLIO.   A folio number or page number at the bottom of a page.

DROP GUIDES.   *See* FEED GUIDES.

DROP INITIALS.   *See* DROP LETTER.

DROP LETTER.   Large initial used at the beginning of a chapter or article, and running down two lines or more. *See also* COCK-UP INITIAL, CUT-IN LETTER.

DROP-OUT.   (*Information retrieval*) The total number of documents identified by a retrieval system in answer to a search question. (*Printing*) A HALF-TONE from which all, or some, of the dots have been removed. Also called a 'Highlight'.

DROP SLIP. Publications ordered from a JOBBER (*q.v.*) but sent direct, at the jobber's request, by the publisher to the library. (American.)

DROPPED HEAD. The first page of a chapter or book where the first line commences a third or more down the page.

DROPPED LETTER. A character which becomes removed during the course of printing and drops out of the forme causing an omission in the matter when printed.

DROPPING FRACTION. (*Information retrieval*) The fraction of the file of records in an edge-notched card system which are delivered after needle-sorting.

DRUM. (*Information retrieval*) A magnetized drum which acts as a computer storage device, providing fast direct access to items stored on the film.

DRY AMMONIA PROCESS. The AMMONIA PROCESS (*q.v.*) of reprography. Also called DRY PROCESS (*q.v.*).

DRY END. The drying end of a paper-making machine. The other end is known as the WET END (*q.v.*).

DRY FLONG. *See* FLONG.

DRY OFFSET. 1. Printing by letterpress onto a rubber cylinder from which the impression is offset on to paper. The resulting advantages are reduced make-ready, the possibility of using uncoated paper for fine half-tones, etc. The process is not lithographic and no water need be used. 2. A printing process by which photo-engraved plates are printed by the offset transfer principle, the inked impression from a relief-etched magnesium plate being made on a rubber blanket cylinder and offset from this on to the paper as this is carried round the impression cylinder.

DRY-POINT ETCHING. An etching made directly on copper by means of a sharp needle called a point. In dry-point work, the etching is all done by hand and not by a mordant applied to a wax-covered plate in which the design has been cut, as is the rule in ordinary etching. Etchings often have dry-point lines, which have been added after the acid etching has taken place. The beauty of this method is due to the burr caused by the point on each side of the channel being left and not removed as in an engraving. The effect of this in printing is to produce the velvety line which is characteristic of a dry-point.

DRY PROCESS. A method for producing copies of documents which does not employ wet chemicals. Some diazotype prints are made by a dry process. The usual developing process used in electrophotography is dry. *See also* DOCUMENTARY REPRODUCTION, DUST DEVELOPMENT.

DRY SILVER. A silver halide process in which the latent image is made visible by the application of heat rather than the use of chemicals. *See also* SILVER PROCESSES.

DRYING END. The end of a paper-making machine where there are the steam-heated drying cylinders over which the damp web of paper (containing about 70 per cent of water) is passed before it reaches the calender rolls.

DUAL PROGRAMMING. *Synonymous with* MULTI-PROGRAMMING (*q.v.*).

DUAL-SPECTRUM. A two-stage copying process developed by the 3 M Company. The master is first made by the action of ultra-violet light, and the subsequent copy is produced from the master by infra-red light. Each stage may involve manual operations or the second may be done automatically.

DUCALI BINDINGS. Venetian bindings of the decrees of the Doges which are decorated with a combination of Oriental and Western techniques. The method was to cover the board with a paper composition, the centre and corners being recessed, then to paste on thinly pared leather and add a coating of coloured lacquer to complete the background. Gold-painted arabesques provided the final decoration.

DUCK-FOOT QUOTES. The common name for Continental quotes or inverted commas. The form « » is used by French printers, but the Swiss and German printers use them in reverse, i.e. » «. They were first used in 1546 by Guillaume Le Bé of Paris, and are consequently also known as 'Guillemets'.

DULL-COATED. Paper which is coated but not polished: it is suitable for fine half-tones, being smooth but having no gloss. The term 'dull finish' is sometimes applied to the low or natural finish of COATED PAPER (*q.v.*) or uncoated papers which have not been glazed; practically identical with 'matt art' paper. *See also* ART.

DULL FINISH. *See* DULL-COATED.

DUMMY. 1. A copy, generally made up of blank leaves, trimmed and sewn but not bound, to represent the actual bulk of a book about to be published. 2. A complete layout of a job showing the arrangement of matter to be printed on every page, and giving particulars of type, illustrations, etc. 3. A temporary catalogue card, usually handwritten and distinctively coloured, which serves as a substitute while a main or other entry, or a block of cards, are out of the catalogue for amendment. *See also* SHELF DUMMY.

DUMMY BANDS. Imitation RAISED BANDS (*q.v.*) on the spine of a book. Also called 'False bands'.

DUMMY MAKE-UP. A DUMMY (*q.v.*) with page proofs, or galley proofs cut up, and pasted in position.

DUO. A method of making microcopies on film in which the film makes two passages through the film printer, printing on one half of the film first, and then on the other.

DUODECIMO (12 mo.). 1. A sheet of paper folded four times to form a section of twelve leaves (24 pp.). As a sheet cannot be folded for binding without a portion being cut, the smaller cut-off portion has to be inserted after folding into the larger folded portion to provide the page sequence. Alternatively a sheet and a half sheet can be used. If the printer lays down two rows of six pages the result is known as 'Long twelves', but if three by four pages, 'short' or 'square' twelves. Where the width of the pages is greater than the height, the term 'broad twelves' is used. Also called 'Twelvemo'. 2. A book printed on paper folded to form sections of twelve leaves. *See also* OBLONG.

DUOSTAT. Trade name for the equipment made by Photostat Ltd., and the process for making copies of documents using direct positive paper.

DUOTONE. Two-colour half-tone printing.

DUOTYPE. Two half-tone plates of the same black and white original, both made from the same half-tone negative, but etched separately so as to give different colour values when superimposed during printing.

DUPLEX. 1. Photographic paper which has a coating of emulsion on both sides. 2. An image-positioning technique used in rotary camera microfilming, whereby the use of mirrors or prisms enables an image of the front side of a document to be photographed on one half of the film, while an image of the back side of the same document is photographed simultaneously on the other half of the film. 3. Any make of camera which will copy as described in 2.

DUPLEX HALF-TONE. A screen reproduction in two printings from half-tone blocks made from a monochrome original, one being used as a colour tone. The method is used in both letterpress and offset work to give the impression of a mellow monochrome picture, being richer and better toned than is possible from a single-colour half-tone block.

DUPLEX LEDGER. *See* LEDGER WEIGHT.

DUPLEX PAPER. 1. Paper having two different coloured surfaces. 2. Any paper composed of two sheets pasted together. Duplex papers are usually made by bringing the two layers, generally of different colours or quality, together in the wet state and pressing or rolling

them together, thus forming a homogeneous mass. *See also* TWIN
WIRE PAPER. If three papers are brought together in the way described the resulting paper is known as Triplex.

DUPLICATE.   A second, or subsequent, copy of a book already in stock.
Strictly it should be identical in edition, imprint, etc., but the kind of
library and the intrinsic value placed on variations of bibliographical
details or contents determines the exact meaning of 'duplicate' in
specific libraries. (*Reprography*) In microcopying, a copy-film usually
made from a master film negative or a printing master. Duplicators
may be either negative or positive in character.

DUPLICATE ENTRY.   Entry in an index or other form of record of the
same subject matter under two or more distinct aspects of it or under
two headings.

DUPLICATE PAGING.   Description of a book which has paging in
duplicate, as e.g. a book with the original text on the verso and the
translation on the recto. This would be recorded in the collation part
of a catalogue entry as: *148, 148 pp.*, possibly with the note: 'Opposite
pages numbered in duplicate'.

DUPLICATE PAY COLLECTION.   A selection of duplicate copies of
new novels which are available only on payment for each book
borrowed. After a time these books become part of the ordinary stock
and are lent without charge. Also called 'Rental collection'.

DUPLICATE TITLE.   Used of a reprint which has a reproduction of
the original title-page in addition to its own.

DUPLICATED SIGNATURES.   Two sets of signatures which are
identical.

DURABLE PAPER.   *Synonymous with* PERMANENT PAPER (*q.v.*).

DURHAM BOOK.   *See* LINDISFARNE GOSPELS.

DUST COVER.   *Synonymous with* BOOK JACKET (*q.v.*).

DUST DEVELOPMENT.   A development process used in document
copying by which latent electrostatic images are made visible by treatment with a developing powder. *See also* XEROGRAPHY.

DUST JACKET.   *Synonymous with* BOOK JACKET (*q.v.*).

DUST WRAPPER.   *Synonymous with* BOOK JACKET (*q.v.*).

DUSTER.   *See* WILLOW.

DUTCH GOLD.   *Synonymous with* DUTCH LEAF (*q.v.*).

DUTCH LEAF.   A thin sheet obtained by beating an alloy of copper and
zinc; it is sometimes used in tooling as a substitute for gold leaf. It
quickly discolours. Also called 'Dutch gold'.

DUTCH PAPER.   *Synonymous with* VAN GELDER PAPER (*q.v.*).

E. P. DUTTON – JOHN MACRAE AWARD. $1,000 offered by the

E. P. Dutton Co. for advanced study in serving the needs of culturally deprived children and youth.

DWARF BOOK.   *Synonymous with* BIBELOT (*q.v.*).

DYADIC ALPHABET.   A two-letter alphabet.

DYE-LINE FILM COPY.   A print made by the transmission process on diazo film. *See also* DIAZOTYPE PROCESS, TRANSMISSION PRINTING.

DYE-LINE PROCESS.   *Synonymous with* DIAZOTYPE PROCESS (*q.v.*).

DYFLEX.   Trade name for Remington Rand equipment for making diazo prints using a reversed copy on DIRECT POSITIVE (*q.v.*) paper.

DYNAMIC MAP.   One which expresses movement such as transport, migration, or military manoeuvres. The symbols used are mainly flow lines and arrows but change is sometimes expressed by isopleths or choropleths.

E.A.M.   Abbreviation for electronic accounting machine.

E.A.M. CARD.   An electric accounting machine card, i.e. a tabulating card, into which coded holes are punched. Often called a 'punched card'. When holes have been punched it is called a 'Master data card'.

EBCDIC.   Acronym of the Extended Binary Coded Decimal Interchange Code, which is the code in general use on IBM computers.

e.g.   Abbreviation for *exempli gratia* (*Lat.* 'for example'). Also for edges gilt.

E.S.   Abbreviation for engine-sized. *See* ENGINE-SIZING.

EARLY MAP.   *See* MAP.

EAST AFRICAN LIBRARY ASSOCIATION.   Founded in 1956 to encourage the promotion, establishment and improvement of libraries, library services, books and book production in East Africa; to improve the standard of librarianship and the status of the library profession; to bring together all who are interested in libraries and librarianship. Abbreviated EALA. Published *East African Library Association Bulletin* (2 p.a. membs. only). This Association was dissolved in September 1972 and in its place three national associations for Tanzania, Kenya and Uganda were formed. A standing conference was formed to encourage East African libraries to meet every two years on a rotation basis to discuss common problems.

EAST MIDLAND BRANCH (of the Library Association).   Previously known as the North Midland Library Association and later the North Midland Branch of the Library Association (1929–70). The area of the Branch is now the administrative counties of Derbyshire,

Leicestershire, Lincolnshire, Northamptonshire and Nottingham-shire. Abbreviated EMBLA. Publishes *Nemcon* (3 p.a.) in association with Groups of the L.A. in the area and *East Midlands Bibliography* (q.) (previously *North Midlands Bibliography*).

EAST PAKISTAN LIBRARY ASSOCIATION. Founded in 1958 to: (a) promote library services in East Pakistan; (b) provide and promote library training facilities and research in library science; (c) improve the status and conditions of service of library personnel; (d) co-operate with library organizations and associations with similar aims in and outside the country with a view to advancing the cause of library service. Membership is open to those engaged in library work and others interested in libraries and librarianship. Abbreviated EPLA. Publishes *The Eastern Librarian* (q.).

EASTERN BRANCH. A Branch of the Library Association; members of the Association living or working in the counties of Cambridge-shire, Norfolk and Suffolk are automatically members of the Branch. Publishes *The Easterner* (q.).

EASY BOOK. A book for the youngest readers; usually more illustrative than textual.

ECARBICA. Acronym of the East and Central Africa Regional Branch of the International Council on Archives. Publishes *ECARBICA Journal*. *See also* INTERNATIONAL COUNCIL ON ARCHIVES.

ÉCRASÉ LEATHER. Leather which has been crushed mechanically to give it a grained appearance.

Ed. (edit.). Abbreviation for EDITED, EDITION, EDITOR (*qq.v.*).

EDGE DECORATION. The application of ink, colour (sprayed, sprinkled or marbled), or gold leaf to the edges of a book.

EDGE FOG. Light or dark areas along the edge of a developed film or print, caused either by the unintentional admission of light to the sensitive material, or to the effects of age or unsatisfactory storage conditions.

EDGE-NOTCHED CARDS. Punched cards which have up to four rows of holes drilled around the edges. These are punched out to record information; the cards fall off the needle when it is inserted in the hole reserved for the information required. One edge-notched card is allocated to each document and each punchable position is reserved for one feature. This limits the usefulness of the system. Also called 'Edge-punched cards'. *See also* FEATURE CARD-SYSTEM, MARGINAL-HOLE PUNCHED CARDS, SLOTTED CARDS.

EDGE-PUNCHED CARDS. *Synonymous with* EDGE-NOTCHED CARDS (*q.v.*).

EDGE-ROLLED. Said of leather-bound books the broad edges of which have been tooled 'blind' or 'gold' with a FILLET (*q.v.*). *See also* TOOLING.

EDGES. (*Binding*) The three outer edges of the leaves of a book; they may be finished in a number of ways. *See also* CUT EDGES, EDGE-ROLLED, GAUFFERED EDGES, GILT EDGES, GILT TOP, MARBLED EDGES, RED EDGES, RED UNDER GOLD EDGES, SPRINKLED EDGES, TOOLED EDGES, TRIMMED 2, UNCUT, WHITE EDGES.

EDIAC. Acronym of Electronic Display of Indexing Association and Content. A device which displayed the logical sum of all other words used in indexing any document indexed by the first word entered in the device.

EDIT. To prepare or arrange the work of one or more authors for publication, whether in book form or as a periodical or newspaper.

EDITED. 1. A literary work by one author, or several authors, which has been prepared for publication by one or more persons other than the author of the whole work. 2. A work consisting of separate items, often written by different people, which has been assembled or prepared for publication by an EDITOR (*q.v.*).

EDITIO MINOR. A lesser, but important, edition of a book or work previously printed, but sometimes the first separate printing of a work previously included in a larger volume. *See also* EDITIO PRINCEPS.

EDITIO PRINCEPS. 1. The first edition of a book printed from the old manuscript, when printing first began. *See also* EDITIO MINOR. 2. The first edition of any new work, but for this the term 'first edition' is more commonly used.

EDITION. 1. The whole number of copies of a work printed from the same type or plates and issued at one time or at intervals. An edition may comprise a number of impressions. A statement of the edition of a book is often placed on the title-page or on the verso thereof, together with particulars of any previous editions on the verso. 2. A number of copies printed at any one time, when either the text has undergone some change, or the type has been partly or entirely reset, or the format has been altered. The term is applied also to the copies forming the original issue known as the 'first edition', as well as to subsequent editions. (B.S. 1413: 1947). 3. The embodiment of a work in a particular typographical form. Different editions may embody an identical text, or varying texts (*IFLA*). 4. One of the various editions of a newspaper printed at different times on the same day, or periodically summarizing the news of the period since the previous edition was issued, or to celebrate some particular event. 5. One of the successive forms in which a musical composition is issued and in which alterations have been incorporated either by the composer or by an editor. 6. Defined in BS 4719: 1971 as 'All those copies of a document produced from one unchanged type image whether by direct contact or photographic methods.' The Standard states, however, that in current publishing practice, reprints which are made a substantial number of years after the edition, are regarded as new editions, and that a new edition is created when the type is re-set even if the text remains the same as in the earlier edition, but that such cases are best described as '2nd (etc.) edition re-set'. *See also* ABRIDGED EDITION, AUTOGRAPHED EDITION, DEFINITIVE EDITION, EXPURGATED EDITION, FINE PAPER COPY, FIRST EDITION, GRANGERIZING, IMPRESSION, ISSUE, LARGE PAPER EDITION, LIBRARY EDITION, LIMITED EDITION, NEW EDITION, NUMBERED AND SIGNED EDITION, PARALLEL EDITION, POLYGLOT, REPRINT, REVISED EDITION, SUBSCRIBERS' EDITION, TITLE LEAF, UNEXPURGATED EDITION, VARIORUM EDITION.

EDITION BINDERY. A bindery in which books are bound for publishers; one in which EDITION BINDING (*q.v.*) is undertaken. *See also* CASE, PUBLISHER'S COVER.

EDITION BINDING. A binding, usually a casing, ordered and paid for by the publisher as a part of the normal publishing of trade editions, and used for all the copies of a title published by him, as distinct from individual binding carried out for the bookseller or purchaser. Also called 'Publisher's binding'.

EDITION DE LUXE. A special edition of a book containing extras not in ordinary editions, such as additional plates, or printed on large paper, etc.

EDITION STATEMENT. That part of a catalogue entry which relates to the edition of the book catalogued, as: 2nd rev. ed.

EDITIONS FILE. A list on cards of editions which a library wishes to purchase.

EDITOR. 1. A person, employed by a publisher, who prepares someone else's work for publication. The editorial work may be limited to mere preparation of the matter for printing, or may involve considerable revisionary and elucidatory work, including an introduction, notes and other critical matter. 2. A person who is responsible for the contents of a newspaper, journal, or periodical and sometimes its publication.

EDITOR REFERENCE. A reference in a catalogue from the name of an editor, or from an entry under an editor's name to another entry where more complete information is to be found.

EDITORIAL. An article expressing a paper's own policy and beliefs on current matters.

EDITORIAL COPIES. Copies of a new publication sent out by the publisher for review, notice, or record. *See also* ADVANCE COPY, REVIEW COPY.

EDUCATIONAL FILM LIBRARY ASSOCIATION. Founded in the U.S.A. in 1943 to promote the production, distribution and utilization of educational films and other audio-visual materials. Abbreviated EFLA. Publishes *EFLA Evaluations*, *Sightlines* (5 p.a.), *Film Evaluation Guide* (supplemented every 3 years).

EDUCATIONAL RESEARCH LIBRARY. *See* NIE.

EDUCATIONAL RESOURCES INFORMATION CENTER. *See* ERIC.

EDUCOM. Abbreviation for Interuniversity Communications Council. An American non-profit corporation started in mid-1965 with a five-year grant of $750,000 from the Kellogg Foundation to facilitate 'collaboration among institutions of higher learning in their efforts to utilize the emerging communications sciences'.

EDWARDS OF HALIFAX. *See* FORE-EDGE PAINTING.

EGGSHELL. A paper with a non-glossy, soft, smooth finish. Most antique papers have an eggshell finish.

EGMONT. A light-faced roman type-face designed by S. H. De Roos and available from Intertype since 1937. It has a very small x-height, with tall ascenders and short descenders; there is vertical stress, rather thin flat serifs extending both ways on the top of the ascenders. For a specimen alphabet, *see* TYPE FACE.

EGYPTIAN. A group of display faces having slab-serifs and little contrast in the thickness of the strokes. They developed from the Antique face cut by Vincent Figgins prior to 1815 and were extensively used by jobbing printers in the nineteenth century. Early sans serif types were also known as Egyptians but the name gradually became limited to slab-serif types, 'grotesque' being given to sans serifs. Modern Egyptian faces are Beton, Cairo, Karnak, Luxor, Playbill, Rockwell, etc. These are also called block-serif abstract faces. *See also* BOLD FACE, CLARENDON.

EICHNER DRY COPY. A method of producing facsimile copies of single-sheet documents by feeding them through an Eichner machine in contact with copying paper. It is an indirect thermographic process. *See also* THERMOGRAPHY.

EIGHTEEN-MO. 1. A book in which the sections are folded four times so that each leaf is an eighteenth of the sheet. Also called 'Octodecimo'. 2. A sheet of paper so folded.

EJECTOR. In the Linotype and Intertype casting machines, the mechanism for ejecting cast lines.

ELEANOR FARJEON AWARD. *See* CHILDREN'S BOOK CIRCLE.

ELECTIVE AUDITOR. *See* BOROUGH AUDITORS.

ELECTORS' ROLL. *Synonymous with* REGISTER OF ELECTORS (*q.v.*).

ELECTRIC STYLUS. An electrically heated stylus used over a strip of metallic foil to impress the CALL NUMBER (*q.v.*) on to the spine of a book.

ELECTRO. Abbreviation for ELECTROTYPE (*q.v.*).

ELECTROFAX. Trade name for an electrophotographic process which was developed by the Radio Corporation of America Laboratories in 1954. The chief difference between this method and xerography is that a sensitive zinc-oxide coating is applied to a paper base and forms the actual copy paper whereas xerography uses a sensitive plate as an intermediate from which the image is finally transferred. In the machines on the British market, development techniques are by liquid and brush development.

ELECTROGRAPHIC PROCESSES. *Synonymous with* ELECTRO-PHOTOGRAPHIC PROCESSES (*q.v.*).

ELECTRONIC PHOTO-ENGRAVING MACHINES. Machines which produce half-tone printing plates automatically. The engraving is done on metal or plastic by a cutting or burning stylus used in conjunction with a scanning device which traces the original by means of a photographic cell. They utilize the action of light to give instructions, through electronic apparatus, to a mechanical instrument which removes unwanted areas of the plate. Trade names of such machines are: Elgrama, Fairchild Scan-a-Graver, Luxographe, Klischograph, Photo-Lathe.

ELECTROPHOTOGRAPHIC PROCESSES. XEROX and ELECTROFAX (*qq.v.*) are electrophotographic processes used in documentary reproduction. Both produce dry permanent copies at high speeds and can also make masters for the diazo, hectographic and lithographic processes. Xerox uses selenium plates or drums, and the copy can be made on any kind of paper. Electrofax uses paper coated with zinc oxide in place of the drum and on this the print is made. Small table machines are made for using the Electrofax method, and this type of machine is being used to make printing masters for offset lithography from normal paper copies.

ELECTROPHOTOGRAPHY. A documentary copying process which uses layers of photosemiconductors on the base material. A print so made may be called an electrophotocopy. *See also* ELECTROPHOTO-GRAPHIC PROCESSES, PHOTOGRAPHY.

ELECTROSTATIC COPY. A copy of a document made by one of the ELECTROPHOTOGRAPHIC PROCESSES (*q.v.*).

ELECTROSTATIC PROCESSES. *Synonymous with* ELECTROPHOTO-GRAPHIC PROCESSES (*q.v.*).

ELECTROTYPE. A facsimile plate of a type forme or another plate, produced by taking an impression in wax, lead or plastic, depositing in this mould a thin shell of copper or other metal by an electro-plating process, backing it with type metal, and mounting it type high on wood. Half-tones (except the very coarsest) demand electros, which may also be made from line blocks and composed type. Abbreviated 'Electro'.

ELEMENT. (*Cataloguing*) 1. A unit of data appearing in a record which can be, or needs to be, distinguished for filing purposes, or which, representing a distinct item of bibliographic information, forms part of an area of a bibliographical description within a catalogue entry. *See also* AREA FILING CODE. 2. A portion of an AREA (*q.v.*) of a catalogue entry, e.g. a parallel title.

ELEPHANT. A size of paper varying from 28 × 23 inches to 34 × 28 inches. 'Double elephant' printing and writing papers vary from 36 × 24 inches to 46 × 31 inches; drawing papers are 26¾ × 40 inches (not an exact multiple of 'Elephant'). 'Long elephant' is a term employed for wallpaper 12 yards long and usually 22, 22½ or 30 inches wide.

ELEPHANT FOLIO. A folio volume larger than an ordinary folio but not so large as ATLAS FOLIO (*q.v.*). About 14 × 23 inches and formerly used for service books, maps, etc.

'ELIMINATE AND COUNT' CODE. (*Information retrieval*) One of several systematic methods of abbreviating words.

ELIOT PRIZE ESSAY AWARD, IDA AND GEORGE. $100 offered by the (American) Medical Library Association for the essay published in any journal during the previous year which has done most to further medical librarianship.

ELISION. The contraction of pairs of numbers, e.g. 93–98 becomes 93–8; 1974–1975 becomes 1974–5.

ELISION MARKS. *Synonymous with* OMISSION MARKS (*q.v.*).

ELITE. The smaller of the two common sizes of typewriter type, having twelve characters to the inch as against ten for the larger 'pica' size.

ELLIPSIS. *Synonymous with* OMISSION MARKS (*q.v.*).

ELROD. *See* LUDLOW.

ELZEVIER. Name of the house of Elzevier, Dutch booksellers and printers; founded by Lodewijck (Louis) Elzevier (1542–1617) at

Leyden in 1583 it continued until 1791, being directed by members of the Elzevier family. Of the books emanating from this firm, the most famous are the 32 mo. pocket-sized editions of the Latin classics begun in 1629. Books of this size printed elsewhere were known as 'Elzevirs'. Also spelled Elsevier and Elzevir. The distinctive type-face they used had a great influence on book design.

EM. The square of the body of any size of type; the printer's unit of square measure. A standard unit of typographic measurement, for which a 12 point em is the basis. This equals 0·166 inch, and there are approximately six 12-point ems to one inch. Sometimes called 'Pica.' This unit is used for computing the area of a printed page no matter what size of type is to be used for setting the text; thus if the area is 20 ems wide and 30 ems deep, the width is 240-point and the depth 360-point. It is also used to indicate the amount of indenting required. So called because the space taken up by the letter m is usually square. If the printer is instructed to indent paragraphs one, two or three ems, the indention will be approximately the width of one, two or three lower-case *m*'s of the type used. *See also* EN, PICA.

EM DASH. The dash—as here—used in punctuation. *See also* DASH.

EM QUADRAT. A square of metal used to fill out short lines of type to the required length; its width is equal to the BODY (*q.v.*). It is a type body cast less than type height, and is always the square of the size of type it accompanies, e.g. an em quadrat of 12-point type is 12 × 12 points. Em quadrats are often made in multiple. Used normally before the first word of a new paragraph. Usually called 'Em quad' or 'Mutton' (slang). The second and subsequent lines of these definitions are indented two ems. *See also* EN QUADRAT.

EMAGE. The area of a block of text, or of a text page, measured in terms of ems of its type size.

EMBLEM BOOK. A type of book in which designs or pictures called emblems, expressing some thought or moral idea, were printed with accompanying proverbs, mottoes, or explanatory writing; or in which verses are arranged in symbolic shapes such as crosses.

EMBOSSED. (*Binding*) A design which is raised in relief. (*Printing*) Lettering, or a design, which is raised above the surface of the paper.

EMBOSSED BOOK. A book in which the text is printed in embossed characters, such as Braille, for the use of the blind.

EMBOSSING. Relief printing by the use of a sunken die and a raised counterpart, called female and male, the surface of the paper being raised in relief. It may also be done by the use of certain substances dusted on the printed surface and caused to be raised by heating.

Also called 'Process embossing', 'Relief printing', 'Bas relief printing'. *See also* DIE STAMPING, THERMOGRAPHY.

EMBOSSING PLATE. A plate cut or etched below its surface and used for producing a design, usually lettering, in relief on a sheet of paper. *See also* EMBOSSING.

EMBOSSING PRESS. A machine used in binderies for impressing lettering and designs on book covers.

EMBROIDERED BINDING. Binding in which the covering material is embroidered cloth. Also called 'Needlework binding'.

EMPTY DIGITS. (*Classification*) 1. Symbols, e.g. punctuation marks used in a notation solely to separate meaningful characters (or groups of characters) forming part of a composite notation, which themselves have no meaning but merely convey structure. 2. A digit (*see* DIGIT 1) having ordinal value but without representing any specific idea.

EMPTYING DIGIT. A digit (*see* DIGIT 1) having ordinal value but depriving the preceding digit of its focal idea.

EMULSION. The chemicals with which a photographic film or paper is coated. In documentary reproduction the emulsion used on papers is usually silver halide suspended in a medium such as gelatine.

EN. A unit of printer's measurement that is half of the EM (*q.v.*) in width but the same as the em in depth; thus a 12-point en quad is 12 by 6 points, a 10-point en is 10 by 5 points, and an 8-point en is 8 by 4 points.

EN POINT. A point, i.e. dot, set midway along a piece of printer's type as wide as an en, so that when printed it will appear with space on either side of it. It may be on, or above, the BASE LINE (*q.v.*).

EN QUADRAT. A square of metal half the width of the body of a type, and half an EM QUADRAT (*q.v.*), usually inserted after a punctuation mark when not ending a sentence. Usually called 'En quad' or 'Nut' (slang).

EN RULE. A dash the width of an en space. *See also* DASH.

ENAMEL PAPER. A highly finished paper coated on one side.

ENAMELLED BINDINGS. *See* CHAMPLEVÉ, CLOISONNÉ.

ENCHIRIDION (*Pl.*, – ONS or – A.). A hand-book, specifically a manual of devotions.

ENCODE. 1. To put into symbolic form. 2. In information retrieval, to transform a document, message or abstract by means of a specific notation.

ENCODING. (*Information retrieval*) A process whereby a message is transformed into signals that can be carried by a communication channel.

ENCYCLOPAEDIA. A work containing information on all subjects, or limited to a special field or subject, arranged in systematic (usually alphabetical), order. Encyclopaedias may be in one volume, in which case very brief information will be given, or they may be in forty or more volumes in which the various matters will be comprehensive, usually written by experts, and sometimes containing bibliographies and illustrations. The term was first used in a book title in Johann Heinrich Alsted's *Encyclopaedia cursus philosophici*, Herborn, 1608. It was one of the last encyclopaedias written in Latin and compiled on a systematic plan; in future they were to be in the vernacular languages with the entries in alphabetical order. The first of this kind to be published in English was John Harris's *Lexicon technicum, or, An universal English dictionary of the arts and sciences*, London, 1704. One of the earliest encyclopaedias was the Spanish Archbishop Isidore of Seville's *Etymologiarum sivi originium libri XX* which was completed in 623. More than a thousand manuscripts of this have survived, and in printed form it had an undiminished appeal as late as the seventeenth century.

END A BREAK. An instruction to the compositor that the last line of a TAKE (*q.v.*) or section of copy is to be filled out with quad spacing after setting the last word. *See also* BREAK-LINE, END EVEN, RUN ON.

END EVEN. An instruction to the compositor that the last line of type in a TAKE (*q.v.*) or section of copy is to be spaced out so that the last word is at the end of a line. *See also* BREAK-LINE, END A BREAK, RUN ON.

END LEAF. The piece of paper covering the turned-in covering material and the joint, or hinge reinforcement, of a re-bound book. (American.)

END-MATTER. The items which follow the text of a printed book. These include appendices, bibliography, notes, supplements, indexes, glossary, imprint or collation, advertisements. *See also* BACK MATTER.

ENDNOTES. Notes printed at the end of a chapter or end of a book. In certain types of book such as those intended for the general reader, or printed lectures, endnotes are preferable to footnotes.

ENDPAPER. A sheet of paper at each end of a book which is inserted by the binder to help fasten the sewn sections to the cover. One half, the 'paste-down endpaper', is pasted on to a cover of the book (with the tapes between); the other, the 'free endpaper' or 'fly-leaf' is pasted with a narrow strip of paste at the fold to the end leaf of a section. Endpapers are best left plain but are frequently used for maps and tables. *See also* DOUBLURE, MAP ENDPAPERS.

ENGINE-SIZING. Hardening paper by adding a moisture-resistant substance as casein, starch or resin to the pulp before the stuff flows on to the machine wire. This is the usual method of sizing the cheaper papers and produces a weaker paper than TUB-SIZING (*q.v.*). Engine-sized paper is abbreviated ES. *See also* SURFACE SIZING.

ENGINEERING NOISE. (*Information retrieval*) False retrieval due to mistakes by human agents, or by errors in machine operation.

ENGLISH. An out-of-date name for a size of type equal to about 14 point.

ENGLISH FINISH PAPER. A calendered paper with a smooth but not highly glossy finish.

ENGLISH LANGUAGE BOOK SOCIETY. A non-profit-making publishing organization financed by the British Government through the Overseas Development Administration and administered by the British Council with the object of making books of an educational nature—provided both publisher and author are British—available through the usual trade channels. The titles are chosen by a Committee and are printed in very large quantities. Since 1960 when the scheme was launched more than 10,000,000 books have been sold at a third or sometimes less of their normal price in seventy-nine scheduled developing countries of Asia, Africa, the West Indies and the Pacific. These editions cannot be purchased except in the scheduled countries. Abbreviated ELBS.

ENGLISH STOCK. A group of publications of which the STATIONERS COMPANY (*q.v.*) held the sole rights of printing and distributing. Perpetual rights were given in a patent granted in 1603 by James I to the Master, Wardens and Assistants of the Company. The publications included almanacs, ABC primers, prognostications, psalters, psalms in metre and catechisms and were sold in large numbers.

ENGRAVED TITLE-PAGE. A supplementary title-page usually wholly engraved on copper which faces the usual printed title-page. These were popular in the seventeenth century and were frequently elaborate allegorical pictures or symbolic designs.

ENGRAVER'S PROOFS. Proofs of engravings used for verifying the quality of the work and for dummying up in pages.

ENGRAVING. 1. The art or process of making letters or designs on wood, metal or other substances, by cutting or etching, for the purpose of printing or stamping by an intaglio or recess process on paper or other material. 2. An engraved plate, or an impression made from an engraved plate. 3. An engraved inscription. 4. The act of taking an impression from an engraved plate. *See also* AQUATINT, ETCHING, LINE ENGRAVING, MEZZOTINT, WOOD ENGRAVING.

ENLARGED EDITION. *Synonymous with* REVISED EDITION (*q.v.*).

ENLARGEMENT. A copy, usually of a photograph or microphotograph, having a larger scale than the original. Also called 'Blow-up', 'Projection print'.

ENLARGER-PRINTER. An optical machine for producing images larger than the one being copied; it incorporates processing facilities for the rapid reproduction of copies, and can be operated under conditions of normal room-lighting.

ENRICHED CO-ORDINATE INDEXING. *Synonymous with* COORDINATE INDEXING (*q.v.*).

ENROLLED ACCOUNT. An account which has been entered on a roll, usually for audit.

ENROLMENT. Entry of a document upon a roll.

ENSLA. Eastern Nigeria Division School Libraries Association. *See* NIGERIAN LIBRARY ASSOCIATION.

ENTITY.† In co-ordinate indexing, a material thing mentioned as subject-matter.

ENTRANCE COUNTER. The side of a staff enclosure at which readers enter a library and return any books they have borrowed.

ENTROPY. The unavailable information in a group of documents. The degree of disorganization in an informational assemblage (*IBM*).

ENTRY. 1. The record of a book publication, or other item in a catalogue or other library record. In a catalogue it may be the main entry or an entry under subject, or an ADDED ENTRY (*q.v.*) or an INDEX ENTRY (*q.v.*). It may give a description of the item and also the location. 2. Sometimes used to indicate the cataloguing process which is concerned with determining the headings to be used for the BODY OF THE ENTRY (*q.v.*) or that part of the description of an item which follows a heading. 3. (*a*) A unit of an index consisting of a heading (and qualifying expression, if any) with at least one reference to the location of the item in the text or with a 'See' cross-reference. (*b*) In a complex entry, when references are numerous enough for systematic grouping, sub-headings are used to introduce sub-entries, each with the relevant reference(s). 4. An item in an index to a literary composition (MS., book, periodical, etc.) which refers to a single specific place in the text, and possibly indicates the nature of the material to be found there. 5. The physical form of record on which entries are made; in information retrieval sometimes called a TALLY (*q.v.*). 6. (*Classification*) In schedules and tables, a self-contained unit of the text consisting of a number or span of numbers, a heading, and often one or more notes. *See also* ADDED ENTRY, ANALYTICAL ENTRY,

GENERAL SECONDARY, HEADING, MAIN ENTRY, REFERENCE, SERIES ENTRY, TITLE ENTRY.

ENTRY-A-LINE INDEX. *See* LINE-BY-LINE INDEX.

ENTRY WORD. 1. The first word, other than an article, of a heading in a catalogue; the one by which the entry is arranged. *See also* HEADING. 2. The word determining the place of an entry or group of related entries in the catalogue (*IFLA*).

ENUMERATIVE BIBLIOGRAPHY. A list of recorded items compiled within limits set by the compiler; these may be geographical, chronological or topical.

ENUMERATIVE CLASSIFICATION. A classification which attempts to list specific subjects. Owing to the difficulty of enumerating all possible specific subjects, most of such classifications are necessarily selective. The Library of Congress Classification is of this kind.

ENUMERATIVE INDEXING LANGUAGE. Subject terms used as headings for both single and composite concepts and providing a closed system (i.e. a list of terms allowing of no insertions) which the classifier could use. *See also* SYNTHETIC INDEXING LANGUAGE.

ENUMERATIVE NOTATION. *Synonymous with* FENCED NOTATION (*q.v.*).

EPHEMERA. 1. Pamphlets, cuttings and other material, of ephemeral interest and value. 2. Such material of earlier periods which has acquired literary or historical importance.

EPHEMERIDES. *See* EPHEMERIS.

EPHEMERIS (*Pl.* EPHEMERIDES). 1. An almanac or calendar. 2. An obsolete term for a diary having been so used since the fourth century B.C. 3. A title-word of many seventeenth and eighteenth century periodicals. 4. An astronomical almanac giving the daily positions of stars and other heavenly bodies.

EPIGRAPH. A quotation in the preliminary pages or at the commencement of the chapter of a book to indicate the sentiment or idea.

EPISTEMOLOGY. The science of organized ideas in their exact correspondence with outward things, or knowledge.

EPISTOLARIA. A liturgical book containing the Epistles.

EPITHALAMIUM. A poem or song in honour of a wedding, or of a bride and bridegroom.

EPITHET. A descriptive, significant name; an additional name or title expressing an attribute of the person referred to, and used to distinguish him from others of the same name. In catalogue entries, the epithet follows the personal name under which the entry is made.

EPITOME. A work that has been abridged or summarized from some larger work for a particular purpose, the essential matter of the original being retained. To be distinguished from an ADAPTATION (*q.v.*).

EPONYM. 1. One who gives, or is supposed to give, his name to a people, place or institution; also the name of that personage. 2. A distinguishing title formed from the name of a person to designate a period, people or place, e.g. Victorian era.

EPOPEE. An epic poem. Epic poetry.

EQUIVALENCE RELATION. (*Information retrieval*) A horizontal relationship between descriptors having the same meaning.

ERA. Acronym for Electronic Reading Automation. A machine which will identify the numerals 0–9 and some fractions, the plus sign, and twelve specified capital letters at a speed of 200–300 characters a second. It is made by Solartron.

ERGOGRAPH. A graph which shows the amount and nature of seasonal human activities. An ordinary line graph may be used, or it may take the form of a circle with the circumference divided into 30° sections to represent each month, with concentric graphlines to show the proportions of time spent in each activity.

ERGONOMICS INFORMATION ANALYSIS CENTRE. Formed in 1968 to provide (a) a locus and clearinghouse for the international literature in ergonomics; (b) a service to British Industry which will allow the application of current ergonomics knowledge. It is a self-supporting organization providing a full enquiry service to any user and is centred at the Department of Engineering Production, University of Birmingham, England. Publishes *Ergonomics Abstracts* (*q.*).

ERIC. Acronym for Educational Resources (formerly Research) Information Center, a national organization, supported financially by the U.S. Office of Education, which acquires, abstracts, indexes, stores, retrieves, and disseminates the most significant educational research documents. The management responsibility and sponsorship of ERIC was moved from the U.S. Office of Education to the newly-formed NATIONAL INSTITUTE OF EDUCATION (*q.v.*) in 1972.

ERIC/CLIS. The Clearinghouse for Library and Information Sciences of the Educational Resources Information Center of the U.S. Department of Health, Education and Welfare. Established in March 1967 at the Library School of the University of Minnesota, Minneapolis, Minnesota, this organization has a field of responsibility defined as 'the operation of libraries and information centers, the technology used to improve their operations and the education and training of librarians and information specialists'. The American Society for Information Science (ASIS) became responsible for this organization in 1970. There are 18 'clearinghouses' concerned with particular aspects of education. On 1 January 1974, ERIC/CLIS was merged with the ERIC Clearinghouse on Educational Media and Technology (ERIC/EM) at Stanford University and these two became known as the ERIC Clearinghouse on Information Resources (ERIC/IR). The new clearinghouse covers the combined subject areas of library/ information science and educational media/technology. ERIC/IR is one of a number of clearinghouses comprising the Educational Resources Information Center (ERIC) sponsored by the National Institute of Education of the Department of Health, Education and Welfare. Each clearinghouse acquires, processes (abstracts and indexes) fugitive materials in their subject field of interest for announcement in *Resources in Education* (m.), and the journal literature for announcement in *Current Index to Journals in Education* (m.).

ERIC/IR.   *See* ERIC/CLIS.

EROTICA.   Indecent or obscene books. *See also* CURIOSA, FACETIAE.

ERRATA (*Sing.* ERRATUM).   *Synonymous with* CORRIGENDA (*q.v.*).

ESCAPIST LITERATURE.   Light literature such as thrillers, adventure stories and romances which are read for entertainment, as a relief from more serious reading, and as a distraction.

ESDAILE MEMORIAL FUND, ARUNDELL.   This Fund was opened in 1958 in memory of a former Secretary of the British Museum and a Past-President of the Library Association, in order to endow a lecture to be given periodically as a memorial to the late Dr. Arundell Esdaile in commemoration of his unique services to librarianship and bibliography. The English Association and the LA considered in 1972 that they should also be permitted to use the Fund on occasions to award a prize for a work of literary merit instead of providing a lecture. An application was made, and approved, to establish a scheme under the Charities Act 1960 for this purpose.

ESPARTO.   A coarse grass, also termed 'Alfa', growing in countries around the Mediterranean, particularly southern Spain and northern Africa, which is used for making the better (but not the best) grades of book paper, featherweight and coating papers. The best grade is known as 'Spanish', the cheaper grades as 'Tripoli'. Esparto papers are distinguished by their refined silky texture and bulk, and their close uniform surface or finish. Their finish is their chief characteristic; this together with their bulkiness makes them eminently suitable for fine printings and other papers required to take a good impression from plates.

ESSAY PERIODICAL. A periodical publication, prevalent in the fifteenth century, each issue of which usually consisted of a single essay. The *Spectator* and the *Rambler* are examples.

ESSENTIAL CHARACTERISTICS. *See* CHARACTERISTIC OF A CLASSIFICATION.

ESTABLISHED. Said of a catalogue heading when an authority card or catalogue entry of any kind is made for it.

ESTHER J. PIERCY AWARD. *See* PIERCY AWARD, ESTHER J.

ESTIENNE, ROBERT. Born 1503 and son of Henry Estienne who founded in 1501 the famous firm of Parisian scholar-printers. Founded his own business in 1524, and was appointed in 1539 and 1540 printer to the king in Latin, Greek and Hebrew. The fine press-work of his books matches the careful editing of the classical texts, dictionaries and translations. From 1550 until his death in 1559 he worked at Geneva, where he printed several of Calvin's works. The most important member of the greatest family of scholar-printers of all ages, his chief and most secure claim of many to immortality, is that based on his Thesaurus, *Dictionarius sive Latinae thesaurus*, Paris, 1531. He established the principle, contrary to his mediaeval predecessors, that a Latin dictionary must be based on classical authorities. He undertook the compilation of a series of Latin-French and French-Latin dictionaries which helped to create the classical French language: these were translated into German, Dutch and English, and were the progenitors of all bilingual dictionaries.

ESTIMATES. Annual calculations of amounts of money needed to provide a service. In the case of local authorities the estimates in respect of each committee are submitted to the financial officer who presents them to the finance committee which forwards complete estimates for the whole of the authority's activities to the council for adoption. *Special estimates* are those for completely new items which could not be anticipated when the annual estimates were prepared. *Supplemental estimates* (sometimes called *supplementary estimates*) are those made during the course of the financial year for amounts in excess of the figure which was included in the annual estimates and are due to a variety of causes such as an increase in the cost of materials or labour, or unanticipated difficulties in the carrying out of work, or urgent and unanticipated developments in the service. Increased expenditure cannot be incurred until supplemental estimates have been approved.

ESTRAY. (*Archives*) The legal term applying to a document not in the custody of the original records creator or its legal successor. *See also* REPLEVIN.

et al. Abbreviation for *et alii* (*Lat.* 'and other things (people)'). Used in footnotes in a second or subsequent reference to a work. It follows the name of the first of three or more collaborators whose work has previously been cited. Also for *et alia* 'and other things', *et alibi* 'and elsewhere'. In cataloguing, where authorship of a work consists of more than three named persons, the revision of Chapter 6 of *AACR* (both North American and British texts with slight variations), stipulated that, in the author statement, the name of the first is mentioned followed by the three-dot omission sign and 'et al' within square brackets, as: . . . [et al].

et infra. (*Lat.* 'and below'.) Used to indicate that something which follows may be of smaller size, as '24 vols., 8vo. *et infra*', meaning that the largest is 8vo. *See also infra.*

et seq. Abbreviation for *et sequens* (*Lat.* 'and the following one'). *Pl. et seqq.* abbreviation for *et sequentes, et sequentia* 'and those that follow'. *See also seq.*

etc. Abbreviation for *et cetera* (*Lat.* 'and the other, the rest'). Also abbreviated '&c.'

ETCHING. 1. The process of producing a design upon a plate of steel, copper, glass or zinc by means of drawing lines with an etching needle through an acid-resisting wax coating upon the polished surface of the plate, and then covering this surface with an acid which corrodes the metal in the lines thus laid bare. 2. A plate with an etched design upon its surface. 3. The art of producing impressions on paper or other material from an etched plate. 4. The impression produced by 3. *See also* DEEP ETCHING, DRY-POINT ETCHING.

ETHNIC NUMBERS. Numbers added to a classification symbol so as to arrange books by language or race. They are usually applicable throughout a classification scheme. Also called 'Linguistic numbers'.

ETHNOMUSICOLOGY. The study of the native music of a people or of a race.

ETRUSCAN ALPHABET. The most significant offshoot from the Greek alphabet and adapted to the language of the Etruscans. It developed, probably in the eighth century B.C. and lasted until the first century A.D. The Latin alphabet was derived from it.

ETRUSCAN STYLE. A calfskin binding style, so called because of the contrasting colours or shades of leather (light brown or terra-cotta) and decoration (dark brown or black tooling); the terra cotta shades and decoration combined represent Greek and Etruscan vases. Such bindings usually have a rectangular central panel on each cover, or occasionally a plain oval with a classical urn in the middle and are tooled in black, surrounded by a border of Greek palmated leaves in black, with outer borders of classical design (Grecian key or Doric entablature) tooled in gold. The spines also are decorated with classical ornaments. This style was used by and probably originated by William Edwards of Halifax towards the end of the eighteenth century, and was practised until about 1820.

EUDISED. Abbreviation for the European Documentation and Information System for Education, a programme of the Council of Europe. It has been in existence since 1970, and has produced a number of reports and technical studies. Two working parties have also produced reports: one on *Standards, format, character representation*, 1973; the other a *Multilingual EUDISED thesaurus* for indexing and searching educational documentation, published in English, French and German by Mouton, Paris and the Hague, 1974. All publications except the Thesaurus are available from the DOCUMENTATION CENTRE FOR EDUCATION IN EUROPE, the Council of Europe, Strasbourg.

EUNICE ROCKWELL OBERLY MEMORIAL AWARD. *See* OBERLY MEMORIAL AWARD, EUNICE ROCKWELL.

EURIM. Abbreviation for a European conference on research into the management of information services and libraries, the first being organized by Aslib and held at Unesco headquarters in Paris 20th–22nd November 1973. The second was held at Amsterdam 23rd–25th March 1976.

EUROPEAN ASSOCIATION OF RESEARCH LIBRARIES. *See* LIBER.

EUROPEAN ASSOCIATION OF SCIENTIFIC INFORMATION DISSEMINATION CENTRES. *See* EUSIDIC.

EUROPEAN ATOMIC FORUM. *See* FORATOM.

EUROPEAN COMMITTEE FOR COORDINATION OF STANDARDS. Founded in March 1961 in Paris in succession to a Common Market committee which had been set up in October 1957, also in Paris. Its aims are to establish standardization documents common to the countries of the European Economic Community and those of the European Free Trade Association for the purpose of harmonizing the standards of these countries so as to promote the development of trade and the exchange of services between them. National standardization organizations are members. Abbreviated CEN. Electrotechnical matters are dealt with by the parallel organization CENELEC.

EUROPEAN DOCUMENTATION AND INFORMATION CENTRE. Founded in 1952; registered under German law in 1957. Aims to group the active forces in all the European countries which are ready to defend in public the fundamental principles of European Christian culture, and to assist in the permanent co-operation of the personalities of the cultural, political and economic life of the European countries. Individuals and national centres may become members. Abbreviated CEDI (Centre Européen de Documentation et d'Information).

EUROPEAN DOCUMENTATION AND INFORMATION SYSTEM FOR EDUCATION. See EUDISED.

EUROPEAN ORGANIZATION FOR NUCLEAR RESEARCH. Established on 29th September 1954 'to provide for collaboration among European states in nuclear research of a pure scientific and fundamental character, and in research essentially related thereto'. Governments may become members. Abbreviated CERN. Publishes *CERN Courier* (m.).

EUROPEAN TRANSLATIONS CENTRE. Conceived in 1960, this information centre concentrates on East European scientific and technical literature with the following objectives: (a) to create a permanent link between national centres dealing with translations and to undertake studies connected with them, (b) to keep a title index of available translations and to issue a regular Translation List, (c) to collect non-commercial translations from countries that are willing to contribute such translations. It is based on the Technological University of Delft, Holland, and comprises sixteen national translations centres as well as the main centre. Publishes a quarterly comprehensive index of all existing translations (into chiefly English, French and German) which are processed at the Centre, the fourth issue being a yearly cumulation entitled *World index of scientific translations*, and *List of translations notified to ETC* (fortnightly). *Translations journals* containing lists of journals translated cover to cover, abstracted publications, etc. are issued annually. Abbreviated ETC.

EUSIDIC. Abbreviation for European Association of Scientific Information Dissemination Centres. Founded 20th April 1970 to: (a) promote applied technology of information storage and retrieval as related to large data bases; (b) share experiences and information; (c) promote and develop standards for data elements, formats, codes and coverage, and to recommend the adoption of such standards to standards organizations and data-base producers; (d) promote research and development for more efficient use of various data bases; (e) promote co-operation between members of the organization; (f) establish links with similar, specialized organizations. Membership is open to scientific information dissemination centres. Publishes *Newsidic* (q.). *See also* ASIDIC.

EVALUATION. An estimate of the value of a work as a contribution to the literature of a subject.

EVALUATIVE ABSTRACT. *See* ABSTRACT.

EVE STYLE. *See* FANFARE (FLOURISH) STYLE.

EVEN PAGE. A page of a book bearing an even number; usually the VERSO (*q.v.*).

EVEN RIGHT-HAND MARGIN. Said of type-written matter where the lines have been justified and all have the same length, thus giving an even right-hand margin as well as the usual even left-hand margin.

EVEN SMALL CAPS. An instruction to the compositor that all the copy so marked is to be set in small capitals without any large capitals as would be done in 'caps and smalls'. Abbreviated even s. caps, or even s.c. Also called 'Level small caps'.

EVEN WORKING. The setting of 'copy' so that it will occupy a full sheet of, say, 32 pages. If an additional portion of a sheet is required for completion, say eight pages, this is called 'uneven working'. *See also* ODDMENTS.

EVOLUTIONARY ORDER. (*Classification*) The method by which subjects are shown in the order of their history or development, 'in natural history putting the parts of each subject in the order which that theory assigns to their appearance in creation. As science proceeds from the molecular to the molar, from number and space through matter and force to matter and life, etc., etc.' (*Cutter*) Cutter's Expansive Classification follows this order, as also in a rough way does Brown's Subject Classification. No scheme is, or can be, evolutionary throughout.

ex libris. 1. Latin phrase, meaning *from the books of* (i.e. from the library of); frequently used on book plates, the owners' name being written or printed after 'ex libris'. 2. Surplus books from a subscription or other library.

EXACT CLASSIFICATION. *Synonymous with* CLOSE CLASSIFICATION (*q.v.*).

EXACT SIZE. The measured size of a book expressed by centimetres or inches rather than by a signature symbol. Also called 'Absolute size'.

EXCERPT. A verbatim extract from a book, or piece of music, whether printed or manuscript. An extract or selection.

EXCERPTA MEDICA. An automated retrieval system of medical information provided by the Excerpta Medica Foundation, an Amsterdam-based, non-profit-making organization. It covers the biomedical sciences including environmental health, and commenced in 1968. The data base comprised 3,400 biomedical journals and 15,000 technological, agricultural and scientific journals, and is the most complete medical literature research data base available on a worldwide basis. In June 1974, Informatics Inc., with its headquarters in Los Angeles, agreed with the Foundation to have the exclusive licence to market the EM Data Base on the N. American Continent. *See also* BIOSIS.

EXCHANGE. 1. The exchange by barter or trade of duplicate material with other libraries. 2. An arrangement whereby an organization exchanges its publications for those of another organization.

EXCHANGE CENTRE. An administrative office which negotiates the exchange of books between libraries, arranging for books to be sent from libraries where they are surplus to libraries where they are needed. *See also* BRITISH NATIONAL BOOK CENTRE.

EXCHANGE LIBRARIAN. One who is responsible for the exchange of the library's publications with those of another library or organization.

EXCHEQUER SERIES. *See* LIBERATE ROLL.

EXHAUSTED EDITION. An edition which has become out-of-print.

EXHAUSTIVE DIVISION. Dividing as exhaustively and minutely as possible in order to give specific places in a scheme of classification.

EXHIBITION CASE. A glass-fronted case built against a wall, possibly amongst wall shelving; or a glass-topped showcase on legs, in which selected books, documents, illustrations or other items are exhibited.

EXHIBITION VAN. (*County Libraries*) A vehicle fitted with shelving or other method of displaying books from which local librarians, teachers, etc., select the stocks for their centres, but which does not serve the public direct.

EXHIBITS ROUND TABLE AWARD. $500 offered by the Exhibits Round Table of the American Library Association to an individual or group for aiding or improving some aspect of librarianship or library service on the basis of need in the profession or in the operation of professional library associations. This award has been renamed the John R. Rowe Memorial Award.

EXIT COUNTER. The side of a staff enclosure at which readers leave a library and have books issued or 'charged' to them.

EX-LIBRARY COPY. A catalogue description of a book originally in a public or circulating library.

EXOTICS. A general name used in the printing industry for Cyrillic, Arabic and other non-latin letter-forms.

EXPANSION. (*Classification*) The development of a concept or series of concepts in the schedules or tables to provide for more minute subdivision.

EXPANSIVE CLASSIFICATION. The scheme of classification devised by C. A. Cutter, which began to appear in 1891, it is one of the most minute and scholarly of schemes for a general library, but it is now out-of-date. It consists of seven expansions (the seventh, uncompleted, being very detailed and suitable for a very large library) each of which covers the whole field of knowledge but in varying detail, and can be used according to the size of the library. Later expansions cannot be used in the same library, however, without re-classifying a number of the books, as the fundamental symbols had to be altered as the expansions progressed. The order of the schedules is evolutionary, the main classes being:

A	General Works.	R	Useful Arts, Technology.
B	Philosophy.	V	Athletic and Recreative Arts.
Br	Religion.	Vv	Fine Arts. Music.
D	Historical Sciences.	X	Arts of Communication by
H	Social Sciences.		Language.
L	Sciences and Arts.		

The intervening letters in the above schedule are given to the more important divisions. The notation is a pure alphabetical one, permitting sub-division at any point in the scheme by the use of the alphabet, but form divisions and the Local List for sub-dividing geographically have numerical notations which can be used mnemonically.

EXPLANATORY GUIDE CARDS. Guide cards giving an explanation of the arrangement of the catalogue cards and placed at the beginning of groups of cards for voluminous authors, anonymous classics, sacred books, etc.

EXPLICIT. The closing phrase of a manuscript or early printed book indicating its completion and sometimes giving the author's name and the title of the work. It is the author's or scribe's colophon taken over from the manuscript, and may appear instead of, or in conjunction with, the printer's colophon. It is a contraction for *explicitus est* 'it is unfolded'.

EXPRESSIVE NOTATION. One of Ranganathan's canons of notation – that the notation should be designed to show that two terms are in the same array, or the same chain.

EXPURGATED EDITION. An edition with those parts left out that might be objected to on moral or other grounds. *See also* ABRIDGED EDITION, BOWDLERIZED, UNEXPURGATED EDITION.

EXTENDED BINARY CODED DECIMAL INTERCHANGE CODE. *See* EBCDIC.

EXTENDED SCORE. *Synonymous with* OPEN SCORE (*q.v.*). *See also* SCORE.

EXTENDER. That part of a type letter which projects above or below the main body of the letter. Also called 'Extruder'. *See also* ASCENDER, DESCENDER.

EXTENSION. (*Classification*) The extension of a term or class indicates all the different items included in the term; in other words, the compass of the term. The intension indicates their *qualities*. Extension and intension vary conversely; when one is great the other is small.

EXTENSION AGENCIES. Activities of the library services which are undertaken outside the main library buildings. These include REGIONAL BRANCHES, COMMUNITY LIBRARIES, SUB-BRANCHES, DEPOSIT LIBRARIES and BOOKMOBILES. (*qq.v.*). (American.)

EXTENSION CARD. Second and subsequent catalogue cards used when the entry is too long to go on one card. It contains the classification number and the entry word from the first card, and is numbered 2, 3, etc. Also called a 'Continuation card', 'Run-on card'.

EXTENSION CENTRE LIBRARY. A branch library which is placed in an American University of college extension centre where college-level classes or other educational services are provided, usually through a specific division of an educational institution.

EXTENSION WORK. Activities which are undertaken with the object of reaching groups of people who might otherwise be unaware of the library, such as lecture societies, reading circles, discussion groups; and the provision of books for prisons, clubs, hospitals, literary societies, etc.

EXTENT. (*Publishing*) The length of a book expressed in terms of the number of pages.

EXTERNAL BIBLIOGRAPHY. *See* HISTORICAL BIBLIOGRAPHY.

EXTERNAL READER. A person who is permitted to use a library provided primarily for the use of privileged persons, such as the members of a professional body or association.

EXTRA BINDER. A craftsman who uses the best materials and employs the soundest methods of construction; he usually decorates each binding with a design specially made for it.

EXTRA BINDING. In binding, a trade term for the best work. Applicable to any book well 'forwarded', lined with marbled or other special paper, silk head-bands, and gilt with a narrow roll round the sides and inside the 'squares'.

EXTRA-ILLUSTRATED. A book which has had additional illustrations and printed matter inserted since publication. *See also* GRANGERIZING.

EXTRA LIGHTWEIGHT PAPER. Sensitized photographic paper between 0·0023 and 0·0031 inches inclusive. Also called 'Ultra thin paper'.

EXTRA THIN PAPER. Sensitized photographic paper between 0·0032 and 0·0037 inches inclusive. *See also* PHOTOGRAPHIC PAPERS.

EXTRA TICKET. *Synonymous with* SUPPLEMENTARY TICKET (*q.v.*).

EXTRACT. *See* ABSTRACT 5.

EXTRACT TYPE. Type which is different from that used for the text, normally being smaller, and used to enable quoted (or extracted) material such as poems, bibliographies, extracts, etc., to be easily distinguished from the text itself.

EXTRACTED ARTICLE. *Synonymous with* SEPARATE (*q.v.*).

EXTRAPOLATION. (*Classification*) The addition of new subjects to the end of an ARRAY (*q.v.*). This flexible aspect of notation is facilitated by the OCTAVE DEVICE (*q.c.*). *See also* INTERPOLATION.

EXTRUDER. *Synonymous with* EXTENDER (*q.v.*).

EXTRUDERS. The collective term for the ASCENDERS and DESCENDERS (*qq.v.*).

f. Abbreviation for 'following'. *Pl.* ff.

FGMC. Abbreviation for the Federal Micrographics Council which was formed under the sponsorship of the (American) General Services Administration, the National Archives, and the Records Service, to serve as a 'continuing forum for the interchange of information regarding micrographic systems and program management'. All full-time employees of the federal government and the District of Columbia government involved in the use of micrographics technology are eligible for membership.

FABRIANO PAPER. An Italian paper used for special and fine editions.

FABRIC BINDING. One in which a fabric has been used instead of leather and vellum. Velvet, silk, satin, and canvas have been the most popular materials, and have been used more frequently in England than elsewhere. Velvet, a most extensively used fabric, was plain, embroidered, or even gilt-tooled. Embroidered bindings, in a form of split-stitch work known as *opus anglicanum* on satin, were popular in the fifteenth century.

FABRIKOID. The trade name for the pyroxylin-coated book cloth made by du Pont.

FABROLEEN. Trade name for a cheaper variety of LINSON (*q.v.*), made of specially prepared paper and used for case-making. *See also* CASE.

fac. Abbreviation for FACSIMILE and FACTOTUM (*qq.v.*).

FACE. 1. The entire unbroken front of shelving on one side of a double case or on one side of a room or gallery. 2. (*Printing*) The printing surface of type. It comprises STEM, BOWL, SERIF, COUNTER, CROTCH and KERN (*qq.v.*). Measured set-wise, i.e. left to right, a face may be condensed (compressed) or extended (expanded); measured body-wise, it may be small, ordinary, medium or large, according to the actual size of the short and long letters. Also, the printing surface of any kind of printing plate. 3. (*Printing*) A particular design or style of a fount of type. *See also* TYPE FACE.

FACE UP. (*Printing*) Said of full-page illustrations which are printed on the right-hand side of an opening, i.e. on the recto of a leaf.

FACET. In classification, the whole group of divisions (*see* DIVISION 4), or foci (*see* FOCUS *noun*), produced when a subject is divided according to a single characteristic. Five kinds of facet are discernable in any class: these relate to personality, matter, energy, space and time. Facets may be divided into *subfacets* (called by Ranganathan 'arrays'). *Dependent facets* do not appear in the classification except as a further division of a more fundamental facet. Modifications of basic facets are called *differential facets*. Each division of a facet is said to be an Isolate Focus, or simply an Isolate. Sometimes used to denote any single ISOLATE (*q.v.*) or any basic class. Also called 'Category'. *See also* AUTO-BIAS DEVICE, CHARACTERISTIC OF A CLASSIFICATION, SUBORDINATION. 2. An aspect, or orientation, of a topic (*IBM*).

FACET ANALYSIS. (*Classification*) The analysis of any subject to determine what characteristics should be used to divide it, relating them to the five fundamentals. *See also* FACET, FUNDAMENTAL CATEGORIES.

FACET FORMULA. (*Classification*) A formula for the application of division; used so that the order of applying characteristics may be consistently maintained. *See also* CITATION ORDER.

FACET INDICATOR. A symbol which separates parts of a notation of a scheme of classification and indicates exactly what facet is to follow. Facet indicators were made possible in the Colon Classification by adopting the five FUNDAMENTAL CATEGORIES (*q.v.*), each of which is introduced by its own symbol. It may be a different kind of character in a mixed notation, e.g. a letter whereas other characters in the notation are figures, in which case every letter would indicate a facet. *See also* NOTATION.

FACET INTERPOLATION. (*Classification*) The insertion of a new facet into a MAIN CLASS (*q.v.*).

FACETED CLASSIFICATION. 1. A scheme of classification which reflects in its structure the analysis of subjects according to a number of fundamental concepts, particularly those denominated: personality, matter, energy, space, time. It lists constituent parts of specific subjects, which parts must be assembled in a predetermined order to express the specific subjects. All modern schemes of classification are faceted to a certain degree: e.g. they provide tables of constant numbers for divisions relating to time and to space. A classification scheme which allows the classifier to build up the notation for a particular book from various unit schedules is called a 'faceted', 'synthetic' or 'analytico-synthetic' classification. 2. Classification schemes whose terms are grouped by conceptual categories and ordered so as to display their generic relations. These categories or 'facets' are standard unit-schedules and the terms, or rather the notation for the terms from these various unit-schedules, are combined at will in accordance with a prescribed order of permutation or combination (*IBM*).

FACETED INITIAL. In a mediaeval illuminated manuscript, an initial letter given the appearance of being faceted.

FACETED NOTATION. (*Classification*) A NOTATION (*q.v.*) representing the classification of a book in which a distinctive symbol is used to separate the facets which comprise it.

FACETED SUBJECT CLASSIFICATION FOR ENGINEERING. A scheme constructed by Mrs. Jean Aitchison in 1957 at the Whetstone Library of the English Electric Group for use in the Central Reports Files of internally published reports and in the abstract bulletins published by the Library.

FACETIAE. Coarsely witty books; objectionable or indecent works collectively. *See also* CURIOSA, EROTICA.

FACING PAGES. The two pages which are visible when a book is open. An OPENING (*q.v.*).

facsim. Abbreviation for FACSIMILE (*q.v.*). Also abbreviated 'fs.', 'fac.'.

FACSIMILE. 1. A copy of an original, reproduced in its exact form and style. 2. Used in cataloguing to indicate that the book catalogued contains a facsimile. Abbreviated 'facsim.', 'facsims.' (pl.) and some-times 'fs', 'fac.' 3. An electronic system for transmitting pictures and graphic materials over very high frequency air waves.

FACSIMILE BINDING. A binding which closely resembles an older binding.

FACSIMILE CATALOGUE. One which incorporates facsimiles of maps, pictures, designs, etc., as part of each catalogue entry which is made on larger cards than the normal size, or in loose leaf binders.

FACSIMILE EDITION. An exact copy of a book made photographic-ally, by xerography, or by an offset process. Used to avoid the cost of setting up type in order to produce a new edition of an out-of-print book. Previously, a copy, as near the original as possible typographic-ally, published to make widely available a book which existed only as an incunabulum or as a manuscript.

FACSIMILE REPRINT.† A reproduction of a work, however printed, and reproducing exactly the appearance of the original.

FACSIMILE TRANSMISSION. The rapid transmission of printed pages from one point to another, using electronic devices. The process involves converting the original picture into an electrical impulse which is then transmitted over telephone lines, private lines, microwave, or a combination of these communication media. The receiving unit reconverts the electrical impulse into an exact duplicate of the original document on a screen or in the form of a hard copy.

FACT RETRIEVAL SYSTEM. One which yields specific information in response to a search request. An aspect of INFORMATION RETRIEVAL (*q.v.*).

FACTOTUM. An ornament of wood or metal having a space in the centre for the insertion of a capital letter of an ordinary fount of type; used to print ornamental initial letters at the commencement of a chapter. It is sometimes called a 'Factotum initial'. Abbreviated: fac.

FACTUM. 1. A statement of facts, or of the points in a case of contro-versy; a memorial (OED). 2. A statement of fact. A memorandum summarizing the chief facts of a case.

FACULTY LIBRARY. *Synonymous with* DEPARTMENTAL LIBRARY (*q.v.*).

FACULTY OF ADVOCATES, EDINBURGH. *See* NATIONAL LIBRARY OF SCOTLAND.

FAIR CALF. *Synonymous with* LAW CALF (*q.v.*).

FAIR COPY. A carefully made typescript or manuscript without mis-takes or corrections, made after examining a draft.

FAIR COPYING DECLARATION.† An agreement by over 140 pub-lishing organizations, including scientific societies under which the

11

reproduction of articles for use by individual research workers is permitted. It developed from The Royal Society's Scientific Information Conference, held in 1948. The signatories regard it as fair dealing for a non-profit making organization, such as a library, archives office, museum or information service, to make a *single* reproduction of a part of an issue of a periodical on behalf of a person who represents in writing that he desires it solely for the purpose of private study, research, criticism or review, and providing he undertakes not to sell or reproduce for publication the copy supplied. The declaration does not apply to books and other non-periodic or non-serial publications. It was rendered somewhat redundant by the Copyright (Libraries) Regulations 1957 (S.I. No. 868 1957) which came into force on 1st June 1957. These apply, *inter alia*, to the British Library, university and college libraries, libraries established under the public libraries acts, those established for further education, and government departmental libraries. These Regulations provide the conditions involved. The Society of Authors and the Publishers Association in a pamphlet *Photocopying and the law* have jointly suggested that 'they would not normally regard it as unfair if a single copy is made from a copyright work of a single extract not exceeding 4,000 words, or a series of extracts (of which none exceeds 3,000 words) to a total of 8,000 words, provided that in no case the total amount copied exceeds ten per cent of the whole work.' *See also* GENTLEMEN'S AGREEMENT; WILLIAMS AND WILKINS V. THE UNITED STATES.

'FAIR DEALING'.† A circumstance under which the copying of copyright material may be undertaken. This permits the making of a single copy for the purposes of research or private study. Sometimes referred to as 'fair use'. An important law suit has been heard in the U.S.A. *See* WILLIAMS AND WILKINS V. THE UNITED STATES.

FAIR USE. *See* FAIR COPYING DECLARATION.

FALL-OUT RATIO. (*Information retrieval*) In the testing of an information retrieval system, a measure expressing the ratio of the number of non-relevant documents retrieved to the total number of non-relevant documents in the file.

FALSE BANDS. *Synonymous with* DUMMY BANDS (*q.v.*).

FALSE COMBINATIONS. (*Information retrieval*) A NOISE (*q.v.*) which is produced by simple correlation of descriptors. Also called 'False sorts'. *See also* MARKER.

FALSE DATE. A date given wrongly, either intentionally or in error. In a catalogue entry the correct date is given in brackets following 'i.e.'.

FALSE DROP. (*Information retrieval*) 1. Citation that does not pertain to the subject sought. An alien, usually in a manipulative or co-ordinate index (*IBM*). 2. An irrelevant reference made in indexing documents for concept co-ordinate indexing. Also called 'False co-ordination'. *See also* UNITERM CONCEPT CO-ORDINATION INDEXING.

'FALSE FIRST' EDITION. An edition of a book said to be the first when in fact there had been an edition published previously by another publisher.

FALSE HYPHEN. One placed by the printer between two parts of a word which is broken at the line end.

FALSE IMPRINT. *Synonymous with* FICTITIOUS IMPRINT (*q.v.*).

FALSE LINK. (*Classification*). In chain indexing, a step in the notational hierarchy where the notational chain is lengthened by a symbol without an appropriate term being supplied. In the Dewey Decimal Classification, for example, where a zero is needed to introduce a standard sub-division or geographical table number, the zero having no verbal equivalent, but being merely an indicator that a form or geographical division is about to be employed. *See also* UNSOUGHT LINK.

FALSE RETRIEVALS. Library references which are not pertinent to, but are vaguely related to, the subject of a library search for information or documents.

FALSE SORT. The recalling, or retrieving, of information, especially with co-ordinate indexing, which is not required; this can be reduced by the careful choice of indexing terms when recording (indexing) documents. Also called in America 'False drops' and 'False reports'.

FALSE SORTS. Synonymous with FALSE COMBINATIONS (*q.v.*).

FALSTAFF. A fat face type. *See* FAT FACES.

FAMILY. The complete group or collection of all the sizes and styles of type of the same design: they have common characteristics and differ only in size, set or thickness of lines, e.g. the Gill Sans family, comprising: Gill Sans, **Gill Sans Bold,** Gill Sans Light, **Gill Sans Bold Condensed, Gill Sans Extra Bold.**

FAMILY NAME. A surname.

FAN. A book decoration style characteristic of Italian bindings in the seventeenth century, and of Scottish bindings, in which a design like a fan is tooled on the sides making a full circle in the centre, and often quarter circles in the corners. It is a development of the centre and cornerpiece bindings.

FANCY TYPE. Printing type of various sizes, ornamental in design; usually used for display purposes.

FANFARE STYLE.   The later Eve style of decorating bookcovers, being a complication of geometrical interlacings and a multitude of scrolls, wreaths, sprays and flowers, filling all available space on back and sides of the book. It was practised in the late sixteenth century. Also called 'Flourish style'.

FANZINES.   Uncommercial, non-professional, small-circulation magazines which deal with fantasy literature and art.

FARJEON AWARD, ELEANOR.   *See* CHILDREN'S BOOK CIRCLE.

FARMINGTON PLAN.   A scheme whereby over sixty American research libraries have agreed co-operatively to purchase books published in foreign countries in order to ensure that at least one copy of new books and pamphlets likely to interest research workers is acquired by an American library. Such books are promptly listed in the Union Catalogue at the Library of Congress and made available by inter-library loan or photographic reproduction. The plan was drawn up at Farmington, Connecticut, by K. D. Metcalf, J. P. Boyd and Archibald Macleish, and began to operate in January 1948.

FASCICLE.   Parts of a work which for convenience of publishing or printing, is issued in small instalments. They are usually incomplete in themselves and do not necessarily coincide with the formal division of the work into parts. They usually consist of sections, or groups of plates, protected by temporary wrappers, and may or may not be numbered or designated as a 'part', 'fascicule', 'lieferung', etc. Also called 'Fascicule', 'Fasciculus'.

FASCICULE.   *Synonymous with* FASCICLE (*q.v.*).

FASCICULUS.   *Synonymous with* FASCICLE (*q.v.*).

FAST BACK.   *Synonymous with* TIGHT BACK (*q.v.*).

FAT FACES.   Type faces which have extra thick perpendicular strokes whether straight or curved, such as Elephant, Ultra Bodoni, and Falstaff.

FAT MATTER.   'Copy' which can be set up in type easily since many lines of type will not be full. Novels which are largely dialogue are 'fat'. This is the opposite to difficult copy which is known as 'lean matter'. *See also* MATTER.

FAULTY MARGIN.   An unequal margin due to imperfect registering.

FAVOURED FOCUS.   Any simple or compound Focus (*q.v.*) which represents the subject of specialization of a library or the isolate in which its collection is more numerous than in other co-ordinate sub-classes.

FAVOURED LANGUAGE.   The language in which most of the books in a library are written.

FEATHER-EDGE. *Synonymous with* DECKLE EDGE.

FEATHER ORNAMENT. (*Binding*) Engraved ornament which resembles feathers, on clasps or catches.

FEATHERING. 1. A fault in printing which results in a feathering effect visible when ink spreads beyond the printed impression via the fibres of the paper. It is caused by an excess of solvent in the ink, or an unsuitable paper. 2. Thinning down the overlapping edges of two pieces of paper which are to be joined when repairing a book.

FEATHERWEIGHT PAPER. Light, bulky, printing paper with 75% air space; it is made largely from esparto and has little or no calendering. It is slightly porous and not easy to handle. *See also* ANTIQUE.

FEATHERWORK. A type of book decoration which originated in Irish eighteenth century bindings, in which curved lines formed freehand with a gouge radiate from one point to produce a delicate and very rich pattern resembling feathers.

FEATURE. A characteristic of a thing indexed. *See also* CHARACTERISTIC OF A CLASSIFICATION, COMPRESENCE, ITEM, TERM.

FEATURE CARD. A plain or punched card allocated to a 'feature' in CO-ORDINATE INDEXING (*q.v.*) – a characteristic of the document indexed – on which are recorded the different items in a SET OF DOCUMENTS (*q.v.*) which have this same characteristic. Also called 'Term card' because a feature referring to subject matter is known as a 'term'.

FEATURE CARD SYSTEM. A method of information retrieval in which a card is reserved for a feature (variously called 'aspect', 'dimension', 'facet'), characteristic, or piece of information. Each card is printed with the same grid of punchable positions, which are numbered, and each of these corresponds to a particular document. The document number is punched in each appropriate feature card. When it is required to know which document, or documents, possess certain features, or combination of features, the feature cards are withdrawn from the file and placed one on the other. Light shining through the holes will reveal the documents possessing the features required. The number of features can be increased indefinitely simply by adding an additional card but when the number of documents exceeds the number of punchable positions (numbering 10,000 on cards of manageable size) a new set of feature cards must be commenced. *See also* EDGE-NOTCHED CARDS, MARGINAL-HOLE PUNCHED CARDS, SLOTTED CARDS.

FEATURE FILM. A term used by exhibitors to define the principal film or films used in a cinema programme and filling over 3,000 feet of 35mm film. It is loosely used to describe a fictional film, and sometimes to describe documentaries on television.

FEATURE HEADING. The verbal part of a subject heading used in the systematic file of a CLASSIFIED CATALOGUE (*q.v.*), i.e. that part which is a translation into words of the last element of a classification symbol. The verbal part usually follows the symbol, and may be utilized to specify subjects for which no exact notation is provided in the scheme of classification.

FEATURING. The provision in a classified catalogue of the hierarchic 'chain', setting out the classificatory steps (class, number and heading) leading to the individual entries at any particular number. This practice has been adopted in both the *British National Bibliography* and the *British Catalogue of Music*, and should help in understanding and utilizing fully the construction of the class number and the arrangement of the catalogue.

fecit. (*Lat.* 'he or she made (did) this'). Frequently added after the artist's name on a drawing, engraving or sculpture. *See also* del., sculpt.

FEDERAL LIBRARIANS ASSOCIATION. A non-profit-making association which was formed in the U.S.A. in 1972. Aims: to (a) provide members with a variety of communication channels within and outside the library profession, including meetings and publications; (b) provide members with a service organization to help them in their professional development and advancement; (c) increase the usefulness and advance the standards, ideals, and welfare of the library profession. Membership is open to all persons retired from, or holding professional positions in U.S.A. federal libraries. Abbreviated FLA.

FEDERAL LIBRARIANS ROUND TABLE. Established by the Council of the A.L.A. on 28th February 1972 to: (1) promote library services and the library profession in the federal community; (2) promote the appropriate utilization of federal library resources and facilities; (3) provide an environment for the stimulation of resources and development relating to the planning, development and operation of federal libraries. Abbreviated FLIRT.

FEDERAL LIBRARIES EXPERIMENT IN COOPERATIVE CATALOGUING. A project begun late in 1972 under a contractual arrangement between the FEDERAL LIBRARY COMMITTEE (*q.v.*) and the Ohio College Library Center (OCLC) to experiment with the communication of cataloguing information on-line, inter-library loan and other technical processing among American federal libraries.

The experiment is administered by the FLC, and costs are divided amongst the participants. Abbreviated FLECC.

FEDERAL LIBRARY COMMITTEE. After consideration of a report of the survey of Federal libraries conducted for the Brookings Institution by Dr. Luther H. Evans the Committee was formed in March 1964 'for the purpose of concentrating the intellectual resources present in the federal library and library-related information community: to achieve better utilization of library resources and facilities; to provide more effective planning, development, and operation of federal libraries; to promote an optimum exchange of experience, skill and resources'. A number of 'task forces' concerned with specific aspects of federal libraries have been formed. The most important federal libraries have permanent membership; others have a rotating membership. Federal librarians who are also members, outnumber the libraries by four to three. Abbreviated FLC. Publishes *FLC News-letter* (m.), *Library Vacancy Roster* (m.), *Roster of Prospective Federal Librarians* (m.), *Advanced Technology/Libraries* (m.).

FEDERAL MICROGRAPHICS COUNCIL. *See* FGMC.

FEDERATION INTERNATIONALE DE DOCUMENTATION. The organization (formerly the Institut International de Documentation and the Institut International de Bibliographie) which publishes the UNIVERSAL DECIMAL CLASSIFICATION (*q.v.*) and many other publications in the field of information and documentation in which it is the major international non-governmental scientific organization. Abbreviated FID. *See also* INTERNATIONAL FEDERATION FOR DOCUMENTATION.

FEDERATION INTERNATIONALE DES ARCHIVES DU FILM. *See* FIAF.

FEDERATION OF ASIAN LIBRARY ASSOCIATIONS. Founded 9th November 1957 to promote the library movement and library co-operation in Asia. Its activities now appear to be in suspense. Abbreviated FALA. Published *FALA News Letter*.

FEDERATION OF CHILDREN'S BOOK GROUPS. Formed on 26th October 1968 at the headquarters of the NATIONAL BOOK LEAGUE (*q.v.*) to: (a) promote an awareness of the importance of children's literature, principally among parents and children; (b) encourage a wider distribution and availability of a large range of books for children; (c) facilitate negotiations with publishers, libraries and any other official body concerned with children's books. Membership is open to any society or other body operating as a non-political and non-profit-making organization with similar aims and to individuals. Financed by members' subscriptions and from profits from sale of publications. Publishes *Year Book* (a.), *Newsletter* (q.), booklists.

FEED BOARD. The platform on a printing machine on to which single sheets of paper are passed from the pile on the stock table and from which they are passed to the impression cylinder.

FEED GUIDES. One, or more, of several kinds of device for holding a sheet of paper in a uniformly straight position before it is taken, possibly by the grippers, to the place at which it will come into contact with the printing surface. On a cylinder press these are called 'Drop guides'.

FEEDBACK. 1. (*Information retrieval*) Partial reversion of the effects of a given process to its source. Control of a system by the output of the system—that is, a self-correcting or self-compensating control (*IBM*). 2. User or client response to, or opinion on, a service.

FEEDER. The various pieces of automatic apparatus by means of which sheets of paper are fed to, and positioned on, printing presses and paper processing machines of various kinds.

FEET. The base of a piece of movable type formed by the 'groove' or 'heel-nick' which runs set-wise across the bottom surface of the body. Type not standing squarely is said to be 'off its feet'.

FEET OF FINE. In law, the foot of a fine was that one of the parts of a tripartite indenture recording the particulars of a fine, which remained with the court, the other two being retained by the parties. When the undivided sheet was placed so that this counterfoil could be read, it was actually at the foot of the parchment.

FEINT RULING. Term used to indicate the horizontal lines (rules), or cross-rules, printed on account-book paper or exercise books. *See also* COMMON RULING.

FELL TYPES. Types cut by the Dutch typefounder Walpergen between 1667 and 1672 and introduced by Dr. John Fell to Oxford University Press during and after 1671 when this press was revived. Dr. Fell was Dean of Christ Church and later Bishop of Oxford. The beautiful Fell types which are used by the OUP for books requiring an OLD STYLE (*q.v.*) type are still cast from the collection of type-punches and matrices made by Dr. Fell, having been re-discovered by the Rev. C. H. O. Daniel in 1877, and used by him on his private press at Worcester College. Dr. Fell was the second of the Press's great patrons, the first being Archbishop Laud. He took charge of printing and publishing on behalf of the University from 1672 until his death in 1686.

FELT MARK. An imprint left on paper by the felt of the papermaking machine due to the pressure of the felt on it.

FELT SIDE. The side of a sheet or roll of paper which has not come in contact with the wire during manufacture; therefore the smooth side of a sheet instead of the WIRE SIDE (*q.v.*). Also known as the 'Top side'.

FELTBOARD. A piece of cardboard or thin wood covered with felt or similar cloth and used for displays. Letters or pictured symbols to be displayed are covered with similar materials and adhere to the board when pressed against it. When flannel is used instead of felt it is called a 'Flannelboard' or 'Flannelgraph'.

FENCE. (*Classification*) Part of the NOTATION (*q.v.*) which merely separates facets without indicating the type of facet which is to follow. These were replaced in the fourth edition of the Colon Classification with FACET INDICATORS (*q.v.*).

FENCED NOTATION. A type of notation which separates two or more terms by a connective symbol, or FENCE (*q.v.*) in order to combine them. Also called 'Enumerative notation'.

FERE-HUMANISTICA. *See* GOTHIC or BLACK LETTER, TYPE.

FERROPRUSSIATE PROCESS. *See* BLUEPRINT PROCESS.

FERROTYPE PROCESS. A method for making direct positive prints in the camera on black or chocolate-coloured enamelled iron plates, called ferrotype plates. This method was popular for while-you-wait photography but the image is in reverse, there being no intermediate negative. *See also* GLOSSY PRINT.

FESTOON DRYING. A method of drying paper in a drying chamber in which warm air is circulated. The paper is hung in loops over rods which travel slowly through the chamber.

FESTSCHRIFT. A memorial or complimentary volume usually consisting of a number of contributions by distinguished persons, often students and colleagues of a person and issued in his honour. The subject matter of the various contributions is usually concerned with the subject in which the individual distinguished himself. It may also honour an institution or society especially on the occasion of an anniversary. LC cards give the contents of Festschriften when there are fewer than twenty-six contributions. Also called 'Memorial volume'.

ff. Abbreviation for *folgende Seiten* (*Ger.* 'following pages'); for a proper name (e.g. ffolkes); for *fecerunt* (*Lat.* 'they made it'); for folios (e.g. 200ff., i.e. 200 leaves, not pages) and foliation.

FIAF. Acronym of the Fédération Internationale des Archives du Film (International Federation of Film Archives). Founded in 1938. Aims:

the collection, preservation and cataloguing of films, and the dissemination of film culture. Financed by contributions made by member organizations of which there are 53 in 39 countries. The International Commission for Documentation is a continuing activity of FIAF; it is concerned with problems of the documentation of books, magazines and other information material regarding films. It has developed a periodical indexing project and publishes the *International Index to Film Periodicals*. The International Commission also considers problems of film cataloguing and informs members accordingly. Publishes *FIAF-Bulletin* (irreg.).

FIBRES.   The plant cells, largely composed of cellulose, which are contained in the rag, grass, wood or other vegetable matter from which paper is made. The length and strength of these fibres, and the way in which they are interwoven, determine the quality and strength of the paper.

FICHE.   A card. *See also* MICROFICHE.

FICTION RESERVE.   *See* JOINT FICTION RESERVE.

FICTITIOUS IMPRINT.   An imprint that is misleading with the object of evading legal or other restrictions, concealing the anonymity of the author, or concealing a piracy publication, etc. Also called 'False imprint'. Fictitious and imaginary imprints may be given in catalogue entries (1) as given, or (2) in the conventional form. When the real imprint is known, it is given in [] after the fictitious one.

FID.   *See* INTERNATIONAL FEDERATION FOR DOCUMENTATION.

FIELD.   1. A fixed column or group of columns in a punched card allocated for punching specific information. The total area of a punched card available for information storage (*IBM*). 2. (*Cataloguing*) Normally considered to mean an ELEMENT (*q.v.*) or a group of elements. Used in some systems, e.g. MARC, to mean a group of one or more subfields. *See also* FILING CODE. 3. (*Classification*) A group of things, or concepts, or their representations, having one or more characteristics in common. Sometimes used in contradiction to CLASS (*q.v.*) when class is defined as a group formed by consideration of characteristics used in drawing up a strictly conventional hierarchy, then 'field' is defined as a group formed in ARRAY (*q.v.*) by consideration of secondary characteristics. In this sense, a field is a group formed by consideration of characteristics other than those used in drawing up a classification schedule. 4. A broad group of related subjects. 5. (*Information retrieval*) In machine-readable records, the position of a data element, or a set of data elements, regarded as a single descriptive element; it may be allocated a unique identification symbol in the record format. 6. A particular section of a computer record, e.g. in a bibliographic record, the author, or the publication date, of a document. Fields may be of fixed or of variable length.

FIELD VISIT.   A direct, personal, contact by a librarian or library consultant with a library agency, individual, group, organization, institution or governmental body, with the object of securing a better library service. (American.)

FIELD WORK.   In county library work, the visiting of local branches in order to maintain official contact between these and headquarters.

FIGURE.   1. An illustration, map, chart, graph, etc., forming part of a page of text with which it is printed from a block imposed with the type, as distinct from a PLATE (*q.v.*). Figures are usually numbered consecutively by means of Arabic numerals. 2. A graphic symbol or character to represent a number. *See also* MARGINAL FIGURE.

FIGURE INITIAL.   In a mediaeval illuminated manuscript, an initial letter which is made by representations of the bodies of human beings or animals.

FIGURED BASS.   On a music score, a line of bass notes with figures under or over them from which indications the player of a harpsichord or organ could tell what chords the composer intended to be used, and could construct his own accompaniment. This is known as realization. Also called 'Basso continuo', 'Thorough bass'.

FIGURES, OLD STYLE.   *See* HANGING FIGURES, OLD STYLE, RANGING FIGURES.

FILE.   (*Noun*) 1. A collection of written, typed or printed material or information arranged in some systematic order. 2. A holder or cabinet designed to hold such material. 3. A homogeneous collection of a single type of file items. *See also* ADVERTISEMENT FILE, BIOGRAPHY FILE, COMPANY FILE, COMPETITOR FILE, CONFIDENTIAL FILE, GEOGRAPHIC FILING METHOD, JOB FILE, LATERAL FILING, LEGAL FILE, MAP FILE, MEDIA FILE, OPEN BACK FILE, ORGANIZATION FILE, PATENT FILE, SUSPENSION FILE, TICKLER SYSTEM, TRANSFER FILE, VERTICAL FILE. 4. In information retrieval, a collection of entries on tallies. 5. (*Information retrieval*) A collection of written or printed records or documents arranged in some systematic order. *See* RECORD 4. (*Verb*) To arrange written, typed or printed material in order.

FILE-AS-IF.   An instruction to file an entry consisting of, or beginning with, a symbol, an abbreviation, or a numeral, as if that which is represented by the filing element were spelled out in the letters of the alphabet.

FILE ITEM. The smallest module or piece of information to be handled as a unit in a file.

FILESEARCH. A commercial system of information retrieval using 1,000-foot rolls of 35 mm film each containing approximately 32,000 pages with coded indexing beside each page. Coding of the film and retrieval of the documents utilize an intermediate FLEXOWRITER (*q.v.*). It is made by FMA Inc., and is a version of the RAPID SELECTOR (*q.v.*).

FILIGREE. Initials and borders decorated with fine lines around the edges.

FILIGREE LETTER. An initial letter with a decorated or filigree outline or background.

FILING. The action of arranging papers, non-book materials and other documents, and records of such, or other, items, into pre-determined sequences; also the subsequent insertion of additional items in their correct places.

FILING CARS. Desks on casters with a small table and a chair on a swivel, used when filing cards in catalogues. (*American.*)

FILING CHAIR. A chair used to reduce fatigue for a filing assistant working at a very large card catalogue. It, often together with a small table, is mounted on a light platform on wheels. The filing assistant while seated moves the chair along by pushing against the catalogue case. Also called 'Filing car'.

FILING CODE. A code of rules for arranging the entries in a catalogue: or other material in a file. *A.L.A. Rules for filing catalog cards* (Chicago, ALA, 1968) and *Filing rules for the dictionary catalogs of the Library of Congress* (Washington: U.S. *Government Printing Office*, 1956) are such codes. The provisional version of *Filing arrangements in the Library of Congress catalogs* prepared by the Library of Congress Technical Processes Research Office and published by LC in 1971 has been developed to ease the task of filers and users of LC catalogues. The rules have been used as a basis for developing a computer program to arrange MARC (*q.v.*) records and they will be applied to computer-produced book catalogues for motion pictures and filmstrips, the LC Main Reading Room collection, and the Science and Technology Division reference collection. They will also be used in connection with output from the machine-readable file of LC subject headings. No decision has yet been taken with regard to their use for the *National Union Catalog* in book form or the Library's card catalogues. The Provisional Version was published to encourage full discussion of the implications of the use of the rules for the

Library of Congress. The rules have been adopted for all computer-generated bibliographic products of the LC Processing Department, and they have been implemented by the LIBSKED (*q.v.*) programme. The terms used differ somewhat from those commonly used in arranging catalogue entries, and are given here in sequence, *Filing entry*. All of the fields that may be considered in determining the filing position of an item in a catalogue (e.g. an author heading, title and imprint date). *Field*. A major component of a filing entry that comprises one or more elements (e.g. a heading; a title). *Element*. One or more words that make up an integral part of a field (e.g. the surname in a personal name heading). An element and a field are identical when the field contains only one element (e.g. a title). The first element in a field is called the *leading element*, the others are called *subordinate elements*. For example, in a heading consisting of a surname, forename and birth and death dates, the surname is the leading element, the forename and the dates are subordinate elements. *Word*. One or more characters forming a meaningful group and separated from others by spaces and/or marks of significant punctuation. *Character*. A letter, digit, symbol, or mark of punctuation. Letters may be called alpha characters, and digits numeric characters. *Significant punctuation* is a mark of punctuation that marks the end of an element, e.g. (a) period after a direct order corporate name such as 'London University Library'; (b) the comma after a surname as 'Wilson, Woodrow'; (c) parentheses surrounding a qualifying term in a subject heading, as 'Mass (Physics)—Measurement'. Punctuation that does not indicate the end of an element is to be ignored.

FILING ENTRY. *See* FILING CODE.

FILING EPITHET. An EPITHET (*q.v.*) which is added to a personal name to assist in the filing sequence as well as to distinguish between persons whose names would otherwise be identical. A kind of DESCRIPTOR (*q.v.*). *See also* HONORIFIC EPITHET.

FILING MEDIUM. That part of the entry or an added heading-word, phrase or symbol under which a card is filed. Also called ENTRY WORD (*q.v.*), FILING TERM, FILING WORD.

FILING ORDER. The order (usually alphabetical, but also by classification notation, or some other appropriate sequence such as makers' catalogue number for, e.g. gramophone records) for arranging books, documents, records, and records of the same, including catalogue entries.

FILING PRACTICE. The sequential arrangement of entries in a

library catalogue. To ensure consistency, this is best carried out in accordance with a recognised code. *See also* FILING CODE.

FILING RULES.　Explicit directions, preferably based on a recognised code, and provided in written or printed form, for the filing of entries in catalogues. For the Library of Congress filing rules, *See* FILING CODE.

FILING SIGNIFICANCE.　(*Cataloguing*) 1. An attribute of an element of data which makes it necessary to take account of the data when filing entries. 2. The sum of the attributes of one or more elements of data, which determines the position in a filing order of the entry or record which contains them.

FILING TERM.　*Synonymous with* FILING MEDIUM (*q.v.*).

FILING TITLE.　1. The title under which are filed catalogue, or bibliography, entries for work known by a number of different titles. 2. The portion of a title which is longer than an essential part by which the book is well known, and under which the catalogue entry is filed, e.g. *David Copperfield*, the full title of which is *The personal history of David Copperfield*. The filing title is indicated by putting a small stroke under the filing letter – in this case the 'D'. Augmented headings, conventional titles in the entries for music scores, and corner markings, are all forms of filing title. *See also* UNIFORM TITLE.

FILING WORD.　*Synonymous with* ENTRY WORD (*q.v.*).

FILLET.　1. A plain line or lines impressed upon the back or side of a book-cover. A 'French fillet' is three gilt lines unevenly spaced. 2. The wheel-shaped tool, with which these lines are impressed. Also called 'Roulette' or 'ROLL' (*q.v.*). *See also* TOOLING.

FILLING IN.　A printing fault in which the spaces in type characters, or the spaces between the dots of a half-tone block, fill with ink. This may be caused by using too much, or an unsuitable, ink, the forme being too high or the rollers incorrectly set, or by using an unsuitable paper, especially one which gives off fluff. *See also* CLOGGED.

FILLING-IN GUARDS.　*Synonymous with* COMPENSATION GUARDS (*q.v.*).

FILM BASE.　The plastic material which is coated with chemicals to make it sensitive to light. Cellulose acetate and cellulose triacetate are widely used for this purpose because of their dimensional stability, transparency, and relative non-inflammability. These materials may be edge-printed 'safety'. Cellulose nitrate was once used almost universally as a film base, but because of its inflammability is seldom used nowadays. Called 'Clear base' before being coated with photographic emulsion. *See also* BASE STOCK.

FILM CLIP. A strip of film cut specially to illustrate something specific.

FILM JACKET. A transparent holder into which individual frames, or strips, of 16 or 32 mm. microfilm may be inserted for storage.

FILM LIBRARY. A collection of films. A few public libraries lend films to local societies and many preserve films of local interest as part of their local collection.

FILM LIBRARY INFORMATION COUNCIL. A national, professional organization of film librarians in public libraries in the U.S.A. and Canada. It was formed on 12th May 1967 during the American Film Festival in New York with the aim of promoting wider and better use of audio-visual materials in the communities served by public libraries. Abbreviated FLIC. Publishes *Film Library Quarterly*.

FILM LIBRARY INSTANTANEOUS PRESENTATION. *See* FLIP.

FILM PRODUCTION LIBRARIANS GROUP. A sub-committee of ASLIB (*q.v.*).

FILM SCRIPT. The story, dialogue and acting instructions for a film.

FILMAC. Trade name for microfilm reader-printers made by the Minnesota Mining and Manufacturing Co.

FILMOREX. 1. A system for the electronic selection of microfilm cards. Each card has a micro-reproduction of the document or abstract and a field of twenty 5-digit code numbers giving the bibliographic reference and the subjects treated (*IBM*). 2. A system devised in 1950 by Dr. Jacques Samain, Chef de Service of the Centre National de la Recherche Scientifique, Paris, for the storage and retrieval of micro-print with the relative coding on the same piece of microfiche size 72 × 45 mm. The Filmorex Selector sorts through the microfiches at the speed of 600 per minute; those selected can be read with a microfilm reader and enlarged prints can be made from them.

FILMSET. Matter which has been composed by using photographic film and a PHOTO-COMPOSING MACHINE (*q.v.*).

FILMSETTING. The setting of type by photographic means using film as a medium. Each key on a filmsetting machine operates the placing of a negative of a letter of the alphabet (or other character) in position to be printed photographically in its correct order on a sheet of film. This sheet of film represents whole pages which can then be imposed in the proper position and printed down on to the lithographic printing plate. *See also* COLD COMPOSITION, FOTOSETTER, LINOFILM, MONOPHOTO, PHOTON.

FILMSORT. Trade name for: 1. A microfilm system of information

retrieval including the punched cards used therewith and allied products; it consists of aperture punched cards to which a microfilm frame
is glued. Filmsort is produced by the Microfilm Products Division of
Minnesota Mining and Manufacturing Company. The system has
been applied primarily to the storage and retrieval of engineering
drawings. 2. Jacket cards for filing and storing microfilm cut into
strips.

FILMSTRIP.   A strip of 16 mm or 35 mm film varying in length up to
about fifty frames and bearing pictures, text or captions, and used as a
visual aid to teaching. The positive images, in black and white or in
colour, and usually on 35 mm film, are projected one at a time by
means of a film strip projector. Some film strips are equipped with a
tape or a recording that contains not only the narration but also a
subsonic signal that activates a solenoid to advance the filmstrip to the
next frame on being given a cue.

FILMSTRIP PROJECTOR.   An electrically operated machine designed
to accept filmstrips, usually 35 mm. Some also have slide holders to
take 35 mm and larger mounted single transparencies. They are
available with manual and/or remote control.

FILTER.   Coloured transparent material used to absorb certain colours
when taking black-and-white or colour photographs and in making
separation negatives for colour printing.

FINAL PROOF.   Also called 'Page proof'. *See* PROOF.

FINAL TITLE STRIP.   The wording at the end of a film which indicates its contents.

FINDEX.   Trade name for a system of punched cards used to record
information, and kept in a framework. Holes in the cards are joined
together by a punch to form slots of varying length and so record
information. To ascertain any information recorded, rods are inserted
into selected holes in the frame (corresponding to those in the cards)
which is then inverted by hand. This causes punched cards to fall out
of alignment. The framework is then turned to its original position
after inserting a rod to prevent cards from dropping back into
alignment; this permits the projecting cards to be examined.

FINDING AID.   In archives management, a document which provides
direction to information contained in other documents.

FINDING AIDS.   Classification schemes, catalogues, indexes of various
kinds and of different varieties of library materials, etc., which have
been devised to enable stored material, or information, to be obtained
(retrieved) when required.

FINDING LIST.   A very brief list of books and documents in a library system, usually limited to author, title and class mark or location symbol.

FINDING LIST CATALOGUE. A catalogue which contains only brief author entries consisting of author's surname, title (possibly abbreviated), date of publication, and possibly edition number if not the first. The absence of bibliographical particulars results in its use merely as a finding list of books, the authors of which are known. *See also* BERGHOEFFER SYSTEM.

FINDING UNIT. The catalogues, bibliographies and circulation and information desks, which are usually grouped together in a university library. *See also* LIBRARY KEYS.

FINE. A charge made for retaining a book longer than the time allowed. This is referred to as a 'charge' in s.8 of the Public Libraries and Museums Act, 1964. *See also* CHARGE.

FINE CALCULATOR. *Synonymous with* FINE COMPUTOR (*q.v.*).

FINE COMPUTOR. A simple device for calculating the amount of fine due on a book which has been retained longer than the period allowed.

FINE COPY. Used to describe a second-hand book the condition of which is better than 'good' but poorer than MINT (*q.v.*).

FINE EDITION. *Synonymous with* DE LUXE EDITION (*q.v.*).

FINE-FACE RULE. A printer's brass RULE (*q.v.*) of hair-line thickness.

FINE PAPER COPY. Name applied to a book printed on better and larger paper than the ordinary edition.

FINE SCREEN. A screen with ruling above 120 lines per inch. *See also* SCREEN.

FINIS. (*Lat.*). The end, conclusion. Frequently printed at the end of a book.

FINISH. (*Paper*) The degree of smoothness of the surface of paper; printing papers may be described as, e.g. antique or super-calendered, writing and drawing papers as vellum or rough. 'Hot pressed' (H.P.) means plate glazed finish. *See also* NOT, PAPER FINISHES. (*Block-making*) The treatment of the outer edges of blocks as e.g. squared up, vignetted. (*Binding*) Ornamenting and lettering a bound book.

FINISHER. 1. A bookbinding craftsman who performs the processes (polishing the leather, lettering, embellishing) which are carried out on a hand-bound book after the sections have been secured within the case. 2. A machine which applies varnish, lacquer, liquid plastic or other fluid to cover materials by spraying, by roller, or by a printing plate.

FINISHING. That branch of binding concerned with the book after it has been put into its cover. Includes tooling, lettering, polishing. The workman who does this is called a 'finisher'. *See also* FORWARDING.

FINISHING HOUSE. *Synonymous with* SALLE (*q.v.*).

FINISHING ROOM. *Synonymous with* SALLE (*q.v.*).

FIRM ORDER. In acquisition work, an order placed with a dealer specializing in material which is difficult to obtain, authorizing him to search for and supply certain items within fixed price limits, or to supply items at a cost not to exceed a stated amount. Generally an order which will not be withdrawn.

FIRST ASSISTANT. In American libraries, a member of the professional staff of a department, division or branch having a minimum staff of three professional persons.

FIRST EDITION. The whole number of copies first printed from the same type and issued at the same time. Later printings from the same type are known as Reprints. Sometimes small typographical errors in a first edition are corrected during the printing, qualifying the later printings for the classification 'Corrected Edition', 'New Edition' or 'Revised Edition', but described as 'First issue of the first edition'. *See also* EDITION, IMPRESSION, ISSUE, NEW EDITION, REPRINT, REVISED EDITION.

FIRST ENGLISH EDITION. The first edition published in England of a book written in English and which had already been published abroad.

FIRST GENERATION MICROFILM. *Synonymous with* CAMERA MICROFILM (*q.v.*).

FIRST IMPRESSION. All the copies of a book printed at the first printing and before any alterations or additions have been made to the text. Subsequent printings made soon after the first, and before a reprint is made after a lapse of time, are called 'Second impression', 'Third impression', etc.

FIRST INDENTION. The eighth typewriter space from the left edge of a catalogue card, or the first, or outer, vertical line on a catalogue card ruled for handwriting. It is at this position that the author heading begins; should it run over the line, it continues at the 'Third indention'. Also called 'Author indention' and 'Outer indention'. *See also* SECOND INDENTION, THIRD INDENTION.

FIRST-LINE INDEX. An index in which the first lines of poems, hymns, songs are arranged in alphabetical order.

FIRST LINING. The piece of mull which is glued with a flexible glue to a book after it is sewn and nipped; it extends to within $\frac{1}{4}$ in. from the head and tail of the book and projects $1\frac{1}{4}$ in. on either side for affixing to the end-papers to give strength and firmness to the book. A strip of brown paper, the full size of the spine, is then stuck over it; this is known as the 'second lining'. The purpose of this lining is to give strength and firmness to the back of the book.

FIRST NAME. The first of the forenames or Christian names; a personal name as distinct from family or clan name.

FIRST PRINTING. The first quantity of a book to be printed; equivalent to FIRST IMPRESSION (*q.v.*).

FIRST PROOF. A proof of type-set matter which is read by the printer's reader and corrected before the galley proof is made. *See also* PROOF.

FIRST PUBLISHED EDITION. The first edition published for sale to the public, and implying that it was preceded by an edition printed for private, official or otherwise restricted, circulation.

FIRST REPRODUCTION MICROFILM. A microfilm copy made from the CAMERA MICROFILM (*q.v.*). Also called 'Second generation microfilm'. *See also* GENERATION.

FIRST SEPARATE EDITION. The first edition to be printed within its own covers, of a publication which had previously been published with other matter.

FIRST VERTICAL. The left of the two vertical lines printed on a catalogue card intended for hand writing and serving as a guide to where the author heading and the second and subsequent lines of the entry should begin. *See also* FIRST INDENTION, SECOND VERTICAL.

FIRST WORD ENTRY. Entry under the first word of a book's title other than an article.

FIRSTS. First editions.

FIST. *Synonymous with* HAND (*q.v.*).

FIVE LAWS OF LIBRARY SCIENCE. 1. Books are for use. 2. Every reader his book. 3. Every book its reader. 4. Save the time of the reader. 5. A library is a growing organism. (*S. R. Ranganathan.*)

FIVE PREDICABLES. *See* PREDICABLES, FIVE.

FIXED FIELD CODING. (*Cataloguing. Information retrieval*) In computer cataloguing, the allocation of as many columns of a punched card as there are particular parts of a catalogue entry, including the classification notation. With 'fixed symbol', or 'variable field' coding each part of the entry is 'tagged' with a special symbol (e.g. a punctuation mark) to indicate which part of the entry is to follow. *See also* TAG.

FIXED FIELDS. In information retrieval, locations on a search medium, such as a punched card, that are reserved for information of a particular type, form or length. *See also* FREE FIELDS.

FIXED-FUNCTION PLANNING. Planning a building in such a way

that each room or department is designed and constructed for its specific purpose, thus giving the architect opportunities for displaying his architectural abilities. Walls dividing the rooms are permanent, and normally an essential part of the structure. The opposite of modular planning. *See also* MODULAR CONSTRUCTION.

FIXED LOCATION.   An antiquated method of arrangement by marking a book with shelf and other marks so that its position on a particular shelf should always be the same. The bookcases, tiers and shelves are each marked distinctly to make finding easy and these markings are often incorporated in the book number. Also called 'Absolute location'. The opposite of RELATIVE LOCATION (*q.v.*).

FIXED SHELF.   One which cannot be adjusted.

FIXED SYMBOL CODING.   *Synonymous with* Variable Field Coding. *See* FIXED FIELD CODING.

FIXING.   In photography and some documentary reproduction processes, the immersion of a film or paper after exposure to light, in a solution so as to remove any light-sensitive chemicals which have not been acted upon by exposure to light and 'fix' the film or paper to prevent further development.

fl.   Abbreviation for *flores* (*Lat.* 'flowers'), *floruit* (*q.v.*).

FLAG.   *Synonymous with* MASTHEAD (*q.v.*).

FLANGE.   The margin round a half-tone plate or line block to provide for fixing to the block.

FLANNELBOARD.   *See* FELTBOARD.

FLANNELGRAPH.   *See* FELTBOARD.

FLAT.   (*Printing*) The sheet containing offset negatives or positives in the proper arrangement, from which the printing plate is made. Also, a flat printing plate.

FLAT BACK.   A book which has not been rounded before being placed inside its CASE (*q.v.*), its back being at right angles to the sides. Also called 'Square back'. *See also* BACKING, ROUND BACK, ROUNDING.

FLAT-BED CAMERA.   *Synonymous with* PLANETARY CAMERA (*q.v.*).

FLAT-BED CYLINDER PRESS.   A printing machine with a flat bed on which the forme is placed under a rotating cylinder.

FLAT-BED PRESS.   A printing machine having the printing forme on a bed with a flat surface, as distinct from a press with a curved surface.

FLAT-BED WEB PRESS.   A machine for printing from a flat forme on to an endless roll of paper.

FLAT COPY.   A photograph having no contrast and therefore normally unsuitable for process work. *See also* PROCESS ENGRAVING.

FLAT DISPLAY. A book display which features the front covers rather than the spines of the books.

FLAT PROOF. A print made from each plate in a colour series, using the colour in which that plate is to be printed in the series. *See also* PROOF, PROGRESSIVE PROOF.

FLAT PULL (ROUGH PULL). The proof taken on the machine without UNDERLAY or OVERLAY (*qq.v.*).

FLAT RATE. A rate levied over the whole of a county area to provide an adequate library service in all parts without the levying of additional local rates. *See also* DIFFERENTIAL RATING.

FLAT STITCHED. A publication which is sewn by the FLAT STITCH-ING (*q.v.*) method.

FLAT STITCHING. Sewing a pamphlet or book, which must have a flat back, in such a way that the wire or linen thread used passes through the inner margins as close to the folds of the sections as possible from the front right through to the back. *See also* SADDLE STITCHING, SIDE-STITCH.

FLATNESS. A condition of paper or board when it has no COCKLE, CURL (*qq.v.*) or wave.

FLEUR-DE-LIS LOZENGE. A lozenge stamp consisting of a flower with fleur-de-lis, or a variation of this design, filling the corners.

FLEURON. A conventional flower or an anomalous type of ornament of floral or foliage character, generally of roughly lozenge shape, used in decorating book-bindings. *See also* FLOWERS.

FLEXIBILITY. *See* FLEXIBLE CLASSIFICATION.

FLEXIBLE BINDING. A binding that allows the book to lie flat when open. This is largely achieved by using a FLEXIBLE SEWING (*q.v.*) and flexible glue.

FLEXIBLE CLASSIFICATION. A classification which permits the insertion of new subjects without destroying the sequence or logic of the arrangement. Flexibility is mainly a function of the notation.

FLEXIBLE NOTATION. A NOTATION (*q.v.*) which has the quality of allowing, by the addition of one or more symbols, the insertion of any new subject into any place in the classification without dislocating the sequence of either the notation or the classification schedule. *See also* NOTATION.

FLEXIBLE PLATE. A plastic or rubber printing plate.

FLEXIBLE SEWING. Sewing a book on raised bands or cords, passing the thread entirely round all the bands which are then laced through the boards. It is the strongest form of sewing. A style of binding which allows the book to lie quite flat when open.

FLEXIONAL SYMBOL. A symbol in a notation system, in which the meaning of each component character is dependent on those which precede it.

FLEXOWRITER. Trade name for a machine, similar to a typewriter, which will punch holes in a roll of paper tape to represent type characters as well as provide a typed page. The rolls of tape can be stored, and if later fed into the machine will cause it to operate electrically and type characters on paper in the traditional way.

FLIP. Abbreviation for Film Library Instantaneous Presentation. Trade name for a mechanized storage and retrieval device which uses a reel of coded microfilm, made by the Benson-Lehner Corporation, and storing 72,000 pages on 1,200-foot rolls of film.

FLOATING LIBRARY. A mobile library accommodated on a boat which takes books to isolated residents or hamlets on islands and places which are inaccessible except by river or sea. Books are left in boxes and placed in the care of a responsible person, or readers are allowed to choose from those displayed on shelves in the boat.

FLONG. A pulp-like board used for making the moulds for casting stereotypes. *Wet flong* is made (usually in the foundry of a printing establishment) from layers of tissue paper and blotting paper pasted together with a special paste and beaten onto the type or blocks in the forme and then dried. *Dry flong* is a similar material which, either in a completely dry state, or damp, is placed together with the forme in a hydraulic press. The use of paper in place of plaster of paris for moulding was introduced by Genoux of Lyons in 1829; a British patent, based on this method, was taken out by Moses Poole in 1839.

FLOOR CASE. *Synonymous with* ISLAND STACK (*q.v.*).

FLOOR DUTY. Being available to readers in a library in order to assist them with their choice of books; this is made possible for senior librarians by freedom from routine duties at the staff enclosure, departmental librarian's desk, or readers' adviser's desk.

FLORENCE AGREEMENT. The 'Agreement on the importation of educational, scientific and cultural material' reduces tariff and trade obstacles to the international circulation of the following groups of materials, thereby permitting organizations and individuals to obtain them from abroad with less difficulty and at less cost: 1. books, publications and documents; 2. works of art and collectors' pieces of an educational, scientific or cultural character; 3. visual and auditory materials of an educational, scientific or cultural character; 4. scientific instruments or apparatus; 5. articles for the blind. Contracting states undertake not to apply customs duties on any of the materials covered by the Agreement; they also undertake, *unconditionally*, to grant licences and/or foreign exchange for a variety of categories of books and publications. The Agreement, which was adopted unanimously by the General Conference of Unesco at its Fifth Session held in Florence in July 1950, was brought into force on 21st May 1952. It is of major interest to libraries, making it easier to import such materials, reducing tariff and trade obstacles to the international circulation of these materials and permitting organizations and individuals to obtain them from abroad with less difficulty and at less cost. A guide to the operation of the Agreement may be obtained from the Division of Free Flow of Information, Unesco, 7 Place de Fontenoy, 75700 Paris.

FLORENTINE WOODCUTS. These are often characterized by the combination of black-line and white-line methods in the same block; e.g. black is used as the colour of the ground, any stones, plants or other objects being represented by white lines on a black ground, while the upper part of the illustration follows the Venetian style of black lines on a white ground.

FLORET. 1. A binder's finishing tool with a flower or leaf design. 2. A flower or leaf-shape type used to separate sentences or paragraphs.

floruit. (*Lat.* 'he flourished'). The period during which a person, whose birth and death dates were not exactly known, was believed to have been alive or flourished. Indicated by 'fl' before the dates or period.

FLOURISH. 1. A mark or flourish after a signature, often made as a protection against forgery. Also called a 'Paraph'. 2. A curved line or ornament, made of brass or cast metal, and used with lines of type.

FLOURISH STYLE. *Synonymous with* FANFARE STYLE (*q.v.*).

FLOW CAMERA. *Synonymous with* CONTINUOUS FLOW CAMERA (*q.v.*).

FLOW-LINE MAP. One which shows movement, the direction or route followed being indicated by a line representing the railway or waterway concerned, while the width of the line represents the quantity of material conveyed.

FLOWER-HEADED RIVET. (*Binding*) A rivet with an ornamental head with a design resembling a daisy.

FLOWERS. Printer's ornaments which can be made up into decorative borders, strips, head and tail pieces. They may be floral, arabesque, geometric or pictorial in design. The best of them derive from bookbinders' arabesque stamps. *See also* FLEURON, TYPE FLOWERS, TYPE ORNAMENTS.

FLUSH.   (*Printing*) Denotes the absence of INDENTION (*q.v.*). The instruction 'set flush on left' means that the matter is to be set evenly at the left margin, 'flush right' that all lines align at the right margin.

FLUSH BINDING.   A binding in which the covers do not project beyond the leaves, the whole having been placed in a guillotine and trimmed after the covers were secured.

FLUSH BOARDS.   A style of binding in which boards are glued to the paste-downs and a paper cover glued to the boards. The whole is then put into a guillotine and CUT FLUSH (*q.v.*). *See also* FLUSH TRIM.

FLUSH PARAGRAPH.   A paragraph having no indention, spacing being used to separate paragraphs.

FLUSH TRIM.   A style of binding in which the top, fore and bottom edges are cut after the paper, board or lining cloth covers have been put on. The covers are thus flush with the edges and do not overlap. Such books are said to be 'cut flush'. Also called 'Flush work'. *See also* FLUSH BOARDS.

FLUSH WORK.   *Synonymous with* FLUSH TRIM (*q.v.*).

FLY-LEAF.   A blank leaf at the beginning or end of a book, being the half of an ENDPAPER (*q.v.*), which is not stuck down to the board, or cover, of a book. Also called 'Free endpaper'. The half which is stuck down to the board, is called a PASTE-DOWN (*q.v.*). If there are other blank leaves, these are parts of the end sections—not fly-leaves although they are sometimes known as such.

FLY-SHEET.   1. A two- or four-page tract. 2. An endpaper.

FLY-TITLE.   *Synonymous with* HALF TITLE (*q.v.*).

fo.   Abbreviation for FOLIO (*q.v.*).

FOCUS.   (*Classification*) (*Noun*) 1. A generic term used to denote an ISOLATE (*q.v.*) or a class or any of its equivalents in the other PLANES (*q.v.*). 2. Any specific division (*see* DIVISION 4) of the subject according to one characteristic, i.e. any single division of a FACET (*q.v.*). (*Verb*) To decrease the EXTENSION (*q.v.*) and increase the intension within any facet, and so to arrive at a specific division of a facet. *See also* CLASSIFYING, FACET, PHASE.

FOIL.   1. Metal or pigment forming a very thin film on a thin backing material which is used with a stylus or a block when lettering or BLOCKING (*q.v.*) a book. 2. (*Reprography*) Diazo-sensitized plastic film.

FOIL BLOCKING. *See* BLOCKING FOIL.

fol.   Abbreviation for FOLIO (*q.v.*). Less usual than 'fo', or 'Fo'.

FOLD.   *Synonymous with* BOLT (*q.v.*).

FOLD SYMBOLS.   The symbols used to indicate the way the paper of which a book is made is folded, and consequently the number of leaves in the section. These are F., Fo (Folio); 4to (Quarto); 6to (Sexto); 8vo (Octavo); 12mo (Duodecimo, Twelvemo); 16mo (Sextodecimo, Sixteenmo); 18mo (Octodecimo, Eighteenmo); 24mo (Vicesimo-quarto, Twenty-fourmo); 32mo (Trigesimo-secundo, Thirty-twomo); 64mo (Sexagesimo-quarto, Sixty-fourmo). They are often used to indicate the size of modern books.

FOLD TO PAPER.   An instruction that a sheet of printed paper is to be folded so that the edges of the leaves and the bolts are all level. *See also* BOLT, FOLD TO PRINT.

FOLD TO PRINT.   An instruction that a printed sheet is to be folded in register, i.e. the edges of the printed areas are to be placed over one another exactly before the sheet is folded. *See also* FOLD TO PAPER.

FOLDED BOOK.   One consisting of a long strip of paper folded like a sheet map, concertina fashion, the ends being attached to stiff covers. Used commonly in the Orient, but in the rest of the world mainly for books of a pictorial character giving views of places or panoramas. Also called 'Folding book'.

FOLDED LEAF.   A leaf of a bound book which is so large that it has to be folded one or more times to keep it within the area of the page size. The abbreviation *fold.* is added to the appropriate term in the collation to indicate that illustrative matter is folded, as: 80 *l.* (3 *fold.*)*; fold. frontis; 2 fold. family trees; 60 maps (2 fold. in pocket). See also* FOLDING PLATE, GATEFOLD, THROW OUT.

FOLDER.   1. A publication consisting of one sheet of paper folded to make two or more leaves but neither stitched nor cut. 2. A large sheet of stout paper, usually manilla, folded once, and having a projection or tag for a heading at the top of the back portion, into which papers are placed for storage in a filing box or cabinet.

FOLDING.   The folding of flat printed sheets into sections. The number of pages in a folded sheet is always a multiple of four (i.e. two leaves). After the last folding all the sections are secured by SEWING (*q.v.*) or stapling.

FOLDING BOOK.   *Synonymous with* FOLDED BOOK (*q.v.*).

FOLDING GUIDES.   Short lines printed on imposed sheets to indicate where they are to be folded.

FOLDING MACHINE.   A machine for folding printed sheets to make sections for bookbinding. *See also* BUCKLE-FOLDER, KNIFE-FOLDER.

FOLDING PLATE.   An illustration bound into a book but folded so as not to project beyond the pages of the book. Called a 'folded plate' by cataloguers. *See also* DOUBLE PLATE.

FOLDING STICK.   A strip of white bone used when folding paper

by hand to crease the paper without damaging it. *See also* BONE
FOLDER.

FOLDINGS. A general term referring to printed sheets which have
been folded to form sections. The following table gives the usual
foldings.

Folio	(Fo)	folded once	giving	2 leaves	4 pages
Quarto	(4to)	„ twice	„	4 „	8 „
Sexto	(6to)	„ three times	„	6 „	12 „
Octavo	(8vo)	„ three „	„	8 „	16 „
Duodecimo (twelvemo)	(12mo)	„ four „	„	12 „	24 „
Sectodecimo (sixteenmo)	(16mo)	„ four „	„	16 „	32 „
Octodecimo (eighteenmo)	(18mo)	„ five „	„	18 „	36 „
Vicesimo-quarto (twenty-fourmo)	(24mo)	folded five times	giving	24 leaves	48 pages
Trigesimo-secundo (thirty-twomo)	(32mo)	„ five „	„	32 „	64 „
Trigesimo-sexto (thirty-sixmo)	(36mo)	„ six „	„	36 „	72 „
Quadrigesimo-octavo (forty-eightmo)	(48mo)	„ six „	„	48 „	96 „
Sexagesimo-quarto (sixty-fourmo)	(64mo)	„ six „	„	64 „	128 „

FOLDOUT. *Synonymous with* THROW OUT (*q.v.*).

FOLGER SHAKESPEARE LIBRARY. This research centre for
advanced scholars was opened in Washington, D.C., in 1932. It
contains the world's largest collection of research materials on William
Shakespeare and one of the Western Hemisphere's finest collections
of materials on the British civilization of the sixteenth and seventeenth
centuries. The stock numbers 250,000 volumes. Henry Clay Folger,
an American industrialist and his wife Emily Jordan Folger selected
the material forming the original collection. The collection was
bequeathed to the American people, together with an endowment
which was sufficient to maintain and expand it. The trust is administered by the Trustees of Amherst College, Folger's alma mater. The
library is a modern building on Capitol Hill although the interior
preserves the architectural conventions of the Tudor period.

FOLIAGED STAFF. A bookbinding ornament consisting of a staff or
branch entwined with foliage.

FOLIATE. To number the leaves of a book.

FOLIATE INITIAL. In a mediaeval illuminated manuscript, an initial letter decorated with, or composed of, foliage.

FOLIATED. Used to describe the marking of every leaf – not page – of a manuscript or printed book with a consecutive number, or foliation.

FOLIATION. (*Verb*) Allotting folio or section numbers or other markings to pages. (*Noun*) The numbering of leaves of a MS. or book. Foliation was comparatively rare until the last quarter of the fifteenth century: it consisted originally of the word 'Folio', or an abbreviation thereof, followed by a roman numeral. Arabic figures were used in Italy between 1475 and 1500, and outside Italy after 1500. Eventually the Arabic figures stood alone. Sometimes columns of print were numbered instead of leaves. The numbering of pages (pagination) began to replace foliation towards the end of the sixteenth century but was not finally established until the eighteenth century. Abbreviated ff.

FOLIO.† 1. Relates to the format of a book; a book printed on sheets of paper folded once, each sheet making two leaves or four pages. For an accurate indication, the paper size should also be stated, e.g. *crown folio*. In practice, a double-size sheet could be used and folded twice, or a quad-size sheet folded three times to give the same size page. *See* FOLDINGS. 2. The individual leaf of a book. A sheet is usually folded into two parallel with the narrow way (i.e. halving the long side) and when so folded is called 'regular', 'common', or 'broad' folio. 3. An indication of the size of a book, usually 30 cm. The actual size depends on the size of the sheet of paper and on the way it is folded. Abbreviated *Fo., fo., fol., or 2°*. *See also* BOOK SIZES, ELEPHANT FOLIO. 4. A sheet of paper in its full size, i.e. flat unfolded, hence a folio ream is a ream of paper supplied flat. 5. The number of a leaf written or printed at the top or more usually, the bottom of the RECTO (*q.v.*).

FOLIO EDITION. One issued in FOLIO (*q.v.*) form.

FOLLOW COPY. When written on a MS. this is a direction to the compositor to follow precisely the spelling and punctuation, however incorrect it may appear. When written on printed matter it indicates that the style and setting of the original are to be followed as closely as possible.

FOLLOW THROUGH. *Synonymous with* the 'letter-by-letter' system of ALPHABETIZATION (*q.v.*).

FOLLOW-UP FILE. An American term for a chronological file of cards, correspondence or copies of orders sent, to facilitate checking overdue orders or letters.

FOLLOW-UP NOTICES. The American term for second and subsequent overdue notices.

FONDS. The chief archive unit in the continental system and the basis of all rules as to arrangement of the contents of archives. An archive group consisting of archives resulting from the work on administration which was an organic whole, complete in itself, capable of dealing independently, without any added or external authority, with every side of any business which could normally be presented to it.

FONT. *See* FOUNT.

FOOD AND NUTRITION INFORMATION AND EDUCATIONAL MATERIALS CENTER. Designed primarily for use by U.S. Department of Agriculture personnel and those providing lunches in state schools, this centre became fully operational in September 1972 at the (American) NATIONAL AGRICULTURAL LIBRARY (*q.v.*). Its function is to assemble and maintain a repository of instructional materials relating to: (1) training and instruction of school food service personnel; (2) operational management of volume feeding services; (3) management and training research specifically pertinent to the Child Nutrition Program. Abbreviated FNIC.

FOOLSCAP. A sheet of printing paper measuring $13\frac{1}{2} \times 17$ inches, usually folded to give a size of $13\frac{1}{2} \times 8\frac{1}{2}$ inches. Formerly known as 'large foolscap.'

FOOLSCAP FOLIO. A book size $13\frac{1}{2} \times 8\frac{1}{2}$ inches. *See also* BOOK SIZES.

FOOLSCAP OCTAVO. A book size $6\frac{3}{4} \times 4\frac{1}{2}$ inches. *See also* BOOK SIZES.

FOOLSCAP QUARTO. A book size $8\frac{1}{2} \times 6\frac{3}{4}$ inches. *See also* BOOK SIZES.

FOOT. 1. The bottom edge of a book. *See also* HEAD. 2. The margin at the bottom of a page of type. 3. The under-surface of type. The plane, parallel to the face on which the BODY (*q.v.*) rests. *See also* FEET.

FOOTLINE. 1. The line at the bottom of a page, especially the blank line or DIRECTION LINE (*q.v.*) i.e. the line containing the folio, signature, or page number just below the lowest line of type. 2. The horizontal ruled line near the bottom of a ruled page or sheet. 3. Supplementary material at the bottom of a page to be used in connection with matter appearing above it.

FOOTNOTE. A note at the foot of a page, usually in smaller type than the text, giving a reference, an authority, or an elucidation of matter in the text above. Footnotes are usually referred to by SUPERIOR FIGURES (*q.v.*) or symbols in the text. *See also* REFERENCE MARKS. Also called 'Bottom note'.

FOOTSTICK. *See* CHASE.

FORATOM. Abbreviation for Forum Atomique Européen—European Atomic Forum. Founded 12th July 1960 in Paris to take joint action with a view to co-ordinating and promoting on an international level the activities of members. It has consultative status with IAEA (*q.v.*). Members are national associations or forums.

FORE-EDGE. The front edge of a sheet of paper or of the sections of a book opposite the folded edge through which the sewing passes. Also called 'Front edge'.

FORE-EDGE FOLD. *See* BOLT.

FORE-EDGE MARGIN. The space between the type matter and the fore-edge of a book or periodical. Also called 'Outside margin'. *See also* MARGIN.

FORE-EDGE PAINTING. A picture painted on the fore-edges of a book which is seen to the best advantage when the pages are splayed out. A 'double fore-edge' has two paintings which can be seen singly by fanning the leaves first one way, and then the other. Gold is usually applied after the paintings have been done. A 'triple fore-edge' has a visible painting in addition. This form of decoration is particularly associated with William Edwards of Halifax, a binder who opened a bookshop in London for his sons James and John in 1785, although the earliest known *dated* disappearing fore-edge painting is on a Bible dated 1651, where the painting of the Leigh arms is signed 'Lewis fecit, Anno Dom. 1653'. Edwards pioneered the idea of painting landscapes on fore-edges, first of all in brown or grey monochrome, and later in a full range of colours.

FORE-EDGE TITLE. A title hand-written on the fore-edge of a book so that it could be identified when standing on a shelf with its fore-edge outwards, the normal position in the sixteenth century.

FOREL. 1. Heavy, rough parchment used for covering old books. Also called 'Forrel', 'Forril'. 2. A case or cover in which a book or MS. is kept for protection, or into which it is sewn.

FOREL BINDING. English book-bindings in which oak boards were covered with roughly dressed deerskins. They were made by monks in the eighth and ninth centuries.

FORENAME. A name that precedes the family name, clan name, or surname. A Christian, or personal, name. It is a name or part of a name which designates a person as an individual and distinguishes him from others bearing the same family name, surname or clan name. Also called GIVEN NAME (*q.v.*), 'Personal name'.

FORENAME ENTRY. The entry in a catalogue for a book under the

author's forename or personal name instead of the surname or family
name as is usual. Books by the following are so entered: saints, popes,
persons known by the first name only, sovereigns, ruling princes and
members of the immediate families of sovereigns.

FOREWORD.   *Synonymous with* PREFACE (*q.v.*).

FORM.   1. A classification term applied to the manner in which the text
of a book is arranged, as a dictionary, or the literary form in which it
is written, as drama, poetry, etc. *See also* FORM CLASSES, FORM DIVI-
SIONS. 2. *Form in music* indicates the structure of a musical composition which may be indicated by 'sonata', 'symphony', etc. 3. American
spelling for FORME (*q.v.*).

FORM CLASSES.   Those parts of a classification in which the books are
arranged according to the form in which they are written, e.g. poetry,
drama, fiction, essays, etc., the subjects of the books being ignored.

FORM DIVISIONS.   Adjuncts to a classification which enable books to
be arranged (within their subject) according to the form in which they
are written. They usually have a mnemonic notation which can be
applied to any part of a scheme. There are two kinds of form division:
OUTER FORM indicates books of which the contents is arranged in a
particular way, such as in classified or alphabetical order as in dictionaries, or according to the form of writing or presentation, as
essay, bibliography, periodical. Subjective, or INNER FORM, indicates
modes of approach such as the theory, history, or philosophy of a
subject.

FORM ENTRY.   An entry in a catalogue under (1) the name of the form
in which a book is written, e.g. Poetry, Drama, Fiction, or (2) the
form in which the subject material is presented, e.g. Periodicals.

FORM HEADING.   1. A heading used in a catalogue for a FORM ENTRY
(*q.v.*), e.g. 'Encyclopaedias'. Also called 'Form subject heading'.
2. A heading derived from and describing the category of document
(*See* DOCUMENT 2) entered under it rather than its author, title or
subject, e.g. Encyclopaedias (*IFLA*).

FORM NUMBER.   (*Classification*) A symbol used to indicate the literary
form in which a work is written. It is obtained in connexion with the
Colon Classification by translating the name of the form of exposition
into appropriate symbols in accordance with the Scheme's Form
Schedule, and may be used as part of the BOOK NUMBER (*q.v.*).

FORM SUB-HEADING.   1. A sub-heading used for sub-arranging in a
catalogue entries for books on the same subject by their literary or
practical form, e.g. Electronics – Bibliography. 2. A sub-heading, not
consisting of an author's name or of a title, designed to delimit a group

of entries according to some common characteristic of form, e.g. Laws' Treaties, under the name of a country (*IFLA*).

FORM SUBJECT HEADING. *Synonymous with* FORM HEADING (*q.v.*).

FORMAL ANONYMA. Works, like periodicals, which do not involve the idea of concealed authorship. These are catalogued by Library of Congress and many other libraries in the style known as HANGING INDENTION (*q.v.*). *See also* TRUE ANONYMA.

FORMAT. 1. A term used to describe the appearance and make-up of a book; its size, shape, paper, type, binding, illustrations, etc. 2. Strictly, the number of times a sheet of paper has been folded to form a section of a book, e.g. quarto (folded twice giving four leaves). 3. The layout or presentation of items in machine-readable form or in a machine printout. 4. (*Indexing*) The general style, or makeup, or the general plan of physical organization, or arrangement, of an index. *See also* FOLDINGS, FOLIO.

FORME. The combination of chase, furniture and type when 'locked up' ready for machining; i.e. the pages imposed in a chase. The forme containing the text, which will be on the inside pages of a printed sheet when folded, is called the 'inner forme' and that which contains those on the outside, the 'outer forme'. Spelt in America without the 'e'. *See also* DRESSED FORME, NAKED FORME.

FORME GAUGE. *See* GAUGE.

FORREL. *Synonymous with* FOREL (*q.v.*).

FORRIL. *Synonymous with* FOREL (*q.v.*).

FORTNIGHTLY. A serial publication issued every second week. Also called 'Bi-weekly', 'Semi-monthly'.

FORTY-EIGHTMO (48mo). A sheet of paper folded six times to form a section of forty-eight leaves (96 pp.). Also called 'Quadrigesimo-octavo'.

FORWARDING. The processes of binding a book after it is sewn until it is about to be placed in its cover ready for FINISHING (*q.v.*). The workman doing this is called a 'Forwarder'.

FOSDIC. Acronym for Optical Scanning Device for Input to Computers, a storage and retrieval system using 16 mm. microfilm. It was developed by the (American) National Bureau of Standards for the National Weather Record Center.

FOTOSETTER. A machine for typesetting by photography, constructed by the Intertype company and used since 1947. It works mainly on the same principle of circulating matrices as the Intertype slug-casting machine. A keyboard releases matrices from the magazines in which they are stored. A matrix, known as a *Fotomat*, has a photographic negative character embedded in its side; otherwise it is similar to an ordinary toothed Intertype matrix. The type lines are made up separately photographed characters, justification being pre-arranged and automatic, and interlinear spacing obtained by adjusting the micrometer film feed dial as necessary. Four magazines, each with 114 characters, can be mounted on the machine at the same time; eight lenses enable the camera to set eight different sizes of type from each of these four magazines – 3,648 characters in all.

FOUL CASE.   A case of type in which some of the separate pieces of type have been put into wrong compartments.

FOUL PROOF.   One with many corrections marked on it. In America a proof pulled after corrections have been made.

FOUNDERS' TYPE.   Type cast by a type-founder as distinct from type cast by the printer on such machines as the Monotype, Linotype, Ludlow or Intertype.

FOUNDRY.   The department of a printing works where matrices are made from the type-formes and blocks, and where stereo plates are cast. Other operations concerned with the casting or fabricating of type and other printing surfaces are also carried out here; the casting and routing machines, type-metal, stereo-metal and similar materials and the necessary tools are to be found here.

FOUNDRY PROOF.   A proof pulled before the forme is sent to the foundry to be stereotyped.

FOUNDRY TYPE.   *Synonymous with* FOUNDERS' TYPE (*q.v.*).

FOUNT.   1. A full set of type of one style and size containing the correct number of the various characters, i.e. upper and lower case, numerals, punctuation marks, accents, ligatures, etc. A type family includes founts of roman, italic, semi-bold, semi-bold condensed, and sanserif. *See also* SORT, TYPE FACE 2. 2. The whole collection of tools used by a binder's finisher.

FOUNT SCHEME.   *See* BILL OF TYPE.

FOUR-COLOUR PROCESS.   An extension of the THREE-COLOUR PROCESS (*q.v.*), by adding black or grey to give greater depth or solidarity. Also called 'Full colour'.

FOURDRINIER MACHINE.   The first machine for making a continuous roll of printing paper. It was invented by Nicolas Louis Robert in 1797, developed in England by Bryan Donkin on behalf of Henry and Sealy Fourdrinier but not perfected until 1804. The principle of this machine is the basis for contemporary machines. The fluid pulp flows from a tank to a moving wire mesh belt during which it is strained and the fibres shaken into a web by agitation. This web of pulp then passes between couch rolls which give it enough strength to be transferred from the wire-cloth to an endless felt on which it passes through successive pairs of press rolls and so to drying cylinders. Thus all the separate processes carried out in the vat, mould, couch and press are combined in one machine. Originally the paper was then cut into sheets and loft-dried in the traditional way, but later additions to the Fourdrinier machine enabled the web of paper to be passed round a series of heated drums and so dried before being drawn through the rolls of a calender to impart the desired finish.

FOURNIER. A type face cut about 1730 by the French engraver and type-founder Pierre Simon Fournier *the younger* (1712–68). A MODERN FACE (*q.v.*) type which is characterized by its very fine hairline serifs. For a specimen alphabet, *see* TYPE FACE.

FOURNIER POINT. A unit of type measurement, one point being 0·0137 inch, established by P. S. Fournier in 1737. It was superseded by the Didot Point. *See also* DIDOT SYSTEM.

FOXED. 1. Prints and pages of old books with yellowish-brown spots caused by dampness. 2. A mechanical gluing technique sometimes used to make up shortrun multiple snap-apart forms.

FOXING. *See* FOXED.

FRACTIONAL SCANNING. (*Information retrieval*) Scanning a file by a series of stages. *See also* BINARY SEARCH.

FRAGMENTING. (*Information retrieval*) Determining a number of appropriate terms or descriptors, to indicate adequately the various aspects of a document.

FRAKTUR. (*Printing*) The group name for German blackface type or bold face type. *See also* BOLD FACE.

FRAME. 1. A wooden stand with a sloped top on which cases of type are placed for the compositor's use. 2. (*Binding*) Ornamentation consisting of a simple hollow rectangle placed some distance from the edges of the cover of a book. To be distinguished from BORDER (*q.v.*). 3. (*Bibliography*) The complete borders which are not COMPARTMENTS (*q.v.*). They comprise (a) enclosures made up of separate cuts or ornaments which show no evidence of having been carved or engraved for use together as a border; (b) those made up of separate cast type-ornaments, commonly used for book decoration. 4. (*Reprography*) An area containing an image in a film or microprint. 5. A geometric subdivision of the microfiche grid. A micro-image and its margins are contained within a frame. The standard size of a microfiche frame is 11.25 mm × 16 mm (single) or 23 mm × 16 mm (double). 6. In microcopying and cinematography, the portion of film

12

exposed to light through the camera optical system for one image.

FRAME MARGIN. (*Reprography*) The non-image area between the micro-image and the frame. *See also* FRAME 4.

FRAME SIZE. The size of the frame, or exposable area, of film.

FRAMED-CUT. A completely carved decorative full-page cut except for a small panel into which is set a letterpress title. Also called 'compartment', 'title-cut' or 'woodcut title-page with panel'.

FRANCIS J. THACKER SCHOLARSHIP. *See* WEST MIDLAND BRANCH.

FRANCIS JOSEPH CAMPBELL CITATION. *See* CAMPBELL CITATION, FRANCIS JOSEPH.

FRANKPLEDGE. In Old English, 1. The system by which every member of a 'tithing' – a company of ten householders – was answerable for the good conduct of, or damage done by, any one of the other members. 2. One of the mutually responsible members of a tithing. Occasionally, the tithing itself.

FRATERNITY LIBRARY. A library in a fraternity on an American college or university campus. It may be one of a circulating collection from the main library, or it may be owned by the fraternity.

FRED. Acronym for Figure Reading Electronic Device. A machine made by E.M.I. which can read a specially designed type-face consisting of the numerals and six letters, at the rate of 10,000 characters a second.

FREDERIKSBERG TYPE. The name given to a type of public library building, the main lending library of which consists of a large ground floor room with a gallery all round, and with reference and reading rooms and children's library on one side or the other of the lending library. The charging desk is placed in the entrance hall. So named after the Frederiksbergs kommunebiblioteker, Denmark, designed by the municipal architect, H. C. Andersen.

FREE. 1. In CO-ORDINATE INDEXING (*q.v.*), alone, not bound or joined to a separate modifier. *See also* BOUND 2. 2. (*Binding*) Said of a stamp, of whatever form, which has no boundary line, or frame, round it; such stamps may be in intaglio or relief.

FREE ACQUISITION. A procedure enabling an organization to acquire a publication or document, or a series of same, without buying them.

FREE ENDPAPER. That portion of an endpaper which is not pasted down to the cover but adhered to the end section of a book. Also called 'Fly-leaf'. *See also* ENDPAPER.

FREE FIELD CODING. (*Information retrieval*) The use of a complete coding field, the entry of codes not being restricted to fixed positions.

FREE FIELDS. In information retrieval, location on a search medium, such as a punched card, which is not reserved for information of a particular type, form or length. *See also* FIXED FIELDS.

FREE HAND. Writing of any period not conforming to definite rules, such as the regular use of set abbreviations.

FREE INDEXING. In CO-ORDINATE INDEXING (*q.v.*), the assignment as index terms for a given document, of words or phrases chosen from a set of words or phrases considered by the indexer to be appropriate indexing terms even though they may not appear in the document.

FREE LANCE. A journalist or photographer not holding a salaried position on the staff of any one particular paper but who contributes to several papers at will.

FREE TERM LIST. (*Information retrieval*) A list of terms or descriptors in which they are not rigidly defined, and to which other terms or descriptors can be freely added.

FREEDLEY MEMORIAL AWARD, GEORGE. Established in 1968 by the THEATRE LIBRARY ASSOCIATION (*q.v.*) to honour the late founder of the Association, theatre historian and first curator of the Theatre Collection of the New York Public Library. The award, in the form of a plaque, is made on the basis of scholarship, readability, and general contribution to knowledge. It was first awarded (in 1969) to Louis Sheaffer for his *O'Neill, son and playwright*.

FREEDOM TO READ FOUNDATION. Founded in 1969 by the A.L.A., the Foundation has a two-part objective: to (a) support and defend librarians whose jobs are jeopardized because they challenge violations of intellectual freedom; (b) provide a means through which librarians and others can set legal precedent for the freedom to read. As a non-profit group, it is supported entirely by membership contributions: there are no special criteria for membership. Abbreviated FTRF. Publishes *Freedom to Read Foundation News* (*q.* membs. only).

FRENCH FILLET. *See* Fillet.

FRENCH FOLD. A sheet printed on one side only and then folded into a section, the bolts being left uncut. *See also* ORIHON.

FRENCH JAPON. *See* JAPANESE PAPER.

FRENCH JOINT. A joint formed by keeping boards a short distance from the back, splitting the boards and placing tapes between, thus allowing greater play at the hinge and permitting the use of a much thicker leather or cloth than otherwise. *See also* CLOSED JOINT.

FRENCH RULE. (*Printing*) A rule made of brass or type metal and widening to a diamond shape in the middle.

FRENCH SEWING. (*Binding*) Sewing without TAPES (*q.v.*).

FRET. A continuous border pattern made up of interlaced bands or fillets. Such patterns may be used for the decoration of pages or tooled on book covers.

FRIAR. A light patch left on a forme or printed sheet due to imperfect inking. *See also* MONK.

FRIEDMAN-JEFFREYS REPORT. A survey of cataloguing and classification in fifty-one British university libraries and published by the University of Sheffield Postgraduate School of Librarianship, under the auspices of SCONUL in 1967, with the title *Cataloguing and classification in British University libraries: a survey of practices and procedures*.

FRINGED FOLIAGE ORNAMENT. (*Binding*) A finisher's ornament of roughly lozenge shape, with a design of conventional foliage, the characteristic feature of which is a shallow fringe round its edge.

FRISKET. A light rectangular iron frame about the size of a TYMPAN (*q.v.*) which is covered with brown paper and attached to the upper part of the tympan. The frisket sheet is folded over the tympan, the centre part of the brown paper which would otherwise cover the printing surface being cut out, before the tympan is turned over the forme. Its purpose is to prevent the sheet of paper being dirtied or blackened by the CHASE (*q.v.*), and FURNITURE (*q.v.*), to hold the sheet to the tympan and to lift the sheet from the FORME (*q.v.*) after printing.

front. (frontis.). Abbreviation for FRONTISPIECE (*q.v.*).

FRONT BOARD. The piece of millboard or strawboard which is used for the front cover of a book.

FRONT COVER. *Synonymous with* OBVERSE COVER (*q.v.*).

FRONT EDGE. *Synonymous with* FORE-EDGE (*q.v.*).

FRONT MATTER. *Synonymous with* PRELIMINARIES (*q.v.*).

FRONT-PROJECTION READER. A reader in which an enlargement of a microform is projected onto the front of an opaque screen and read by reflected light. *See also* BACK-PROJECTION READER.

FRONTISPIECE. Any pictorial representation at the front of a book, usually facing the title-page, and as a rule unnumbered and unpaged. In cataloguing, the abbreviation *front.* or *frontis.* was given in the collation only when there was no other illustrative material and the frontispiece could not be better described as *port*, *map*, etc., but the revision of Chapter 6 of *AACR* (North American and British Texts) eliminated the term 'frontispiece' from the collation statement. *See also* ILLUSTRATIONS.

fs. Abbreviation for FACSIMILE (*q.v.*).

FUGITIVE COLOURS. Coloured printing inks which change or fade when exposed to normal light. Reds, greens and blues are particularly susceptible to fading.

FUGITIVE FACTS FILE. A file of facts which it has been difficult to obtain in answer to readers' inquiries, and which are likely to be asked for again. (American.)

FUGITIVE MATERIAL. Such publications as pamphlets, programmes and duplicated material produced in small quantities and of immediate, transitory or local interest.

FULDA MS. A MS. of the Gospels and other books of the New Testament written in Latin uncials and dating from *c.* 546.

FULL BINDING. A binding in which the covering material covers back and sides. Usually applied to a leather bound book. A book so bound is described as 'full bound' or 'whole bound'. *See also* HALF LEATHER, QUARTER LEATHER, THREE-QUARTER LEATHER.

FULL BOUND. A book wholly covered with leather.

FULL CATALOGUING. The style of cataloguing in which the entries give all the information provided for by the rules of the code adopted. In 1951 the Library of Congress decided to catalogue fully only certain categories of books in order to speed up the cataloguing processes. The following illustrate the kinds of categories included although individual items within the groups are assigned to full, or limited, cataloguing on the basis of their individual value: (1) basic reference and research tools in all subjects, e.g. encyclopaedias, dictionaries, bibliographies, etc.; (2) scholarly works in all fields of knowledge, including records of research, scholarly editions and translations of classical writings, publications of learned societies, institutes, governments, etc., which embody the results of research; (3) incunabula, rare books, and other works valuable for their bibliographical interest; outstanding examples of the art of book-making; art books containing exceptionally valuable reproductions. Other categories of books are dealt with by a method of LIMITED CATALOGUING (*q.v.*). *See also* SHORT CATALOGUING.

FULL COLOUR. When an ample amount of ink has been used in printing; in distinction from grey colour, when only a small quantity of ink is used (*United Typothetae*).

FULL FACE. Sometimes used *synonymously with* BOLD FACE (*q.v.*). Also used to denote FULL ON THE BODY (*q.v.*).

FULL-GILT. A book with all edges gilded.

FULL LEATHER.　*See* FULL BINDING.

FULL MEASURE.　Type set throughout the whole length of a line, whether of type column or page. *See also* MEASURE.

FULL MUSIC EDITION.　*See* SCORE.

FULL NAME.　A name in which all the names of an individual are given in full.

FULL-NAME NOTE.　The full name of an author which is given in the bottom right-hand corner of Library of Congress catalogue cards when a short form of the name (e.g. omitting an indication of a Christian name or giving only the initials) is used for the heading. Similar notes are given in the same position for the name in religion, the original name, a pseudonym which covers joint authors, the real name, secular name, or stage name.

FULL ON THE BODY.　A fount of capitals designed to occupy the complete body area, AS THIS. Also called 'Full face'.

FULL OUT.　(*Printing*) To commence printed matter flush without indention.

FULL POINT.　The punctuation mark used at the end of a sentence, between figures to mark decimals, and elsewhere in typography. Also called a 'Full stop'.

FULL SCORE.　*See* SCORE.

FULL STOP.　*Synonymous with* FULL POINT (*q.v.*).

FULL-TERM CO-ORDINATION.　A PERMUTED TITLE INDEX (*q.v.*) in which all significant words in the title are co-ordinated with every other significant word.

FULL-TIME BRANCH LIBRARY.　(*County Libraries*) One housed in premises set aside for the purpose, and specially equipped and furnished, open not less than thirty hours a week. *See also* BRANCH LIBRARY.

FULL TITLE.　*Synonymous with* MAIN TITLE (*q.v.*).

FUNDAMENTAL CATEGORIES.　(*Classification*) Personality, Matter, Energy, Space, and Time (PMEST) are the five fundamental categories of facets which Ranganathan has developed into a general facet formula which represents the PRINCIPLE OF DECREASING CONCRETENESS Personality being regarded as the most concrete category and Time as the most abstract. *See also* CATEGORY. 'Each facet of any subject, as well as each division of a facet, is considered as a manifestation of one of the five fundamental categories' (*Ranganathan*). Placed in reverse order to that given above they would be in the order of increasing sequence of concreteness. The Connecting Symbols and Symbols of the Facet are given below.

Fundamental category (F.C.)	Connecting symbol (C.S.)	Symbol for the Facet
Personality	, (comma)	[P]
Matter	; (semicolon)	[M]
Energy	: (colon)	[E]
Space	. (dot)	[S]
Time	. (dot)	[T]

See also DECREASING CONCRETENESS, PRINCIPLE OF.

FURNISH. The materials from which a paper is made, e.g. the furnish of a litho paper might be: esparto, 60 per cent; chemical wood, 30 per cent; loading, 10 per cent.

FURNISH LAYER. Paper or board made up of one or more plies of the same furnish, combined while still moist, without the use of adhesive. Two, three, or more, furnish layers similarly combined are known as 'Two-layer, Three-layer, or Multi-layer paper or board' (in some countries as 'Biplex' or 'Duplex', 'Triplex', or 'Multiplex' respectively) according to the number of layers. The external furnish layers of the three-layer papers may be of the same composition, while the multi-layer papers may have two or more furnish layers of the same composition.

FURNITURE. The wood or metal material used by the printer to form margins and to fill in large gaps between the type matter especially where there is a small amount of type to a page as on a dedication or title-page, and to help secure the printing material in the CHASE (*q.v.*).

FUTHARK. *See* RUNES.

g.e. Abbreviation for GILT EDGES (*q.v.*).

GKD NOTATION. An abbreviation for the Gordon-Kendall-Davison notation which is used simply to describe structural formulae in chemistry. Also called the 'Birmingham notation'.

GLCLG. Acronym of the Greater London College Librarians' Group which was formed in December 1966 to facilitate the meeting of, and exchange of information with librarians working in further and higher education in the Greater London area.

G.S.G.S. SERIES OF MAPS. A series of maps published by the Directorate of Military Survey of the British War Office (formerly known as the General Staff, Geographical Section) covering Europe, Africa and Asia, and the East Indies.

g.t. (or g.t.e.). Abbreviation for GILT TOP (*q.v.*).

GALLEY. A long narrow and shallow steel tray about 22 inches long and open at one end, into which type is transferred from the compositor's stick or from the type-setting machine to await making up into pages. It is from the type in this galley that the galley proof (also called a 'galley') is taken. *See also* PROOF.

GALLEY PRESS. A printing press made for the pulling of galley proofs. *See also* PROOF.

GALLEY PROOF. *See* PROOF.

GAP. (*Information retrieval*) A hiatus in a collection, commonly of serials or regularly issued proceedings (*IBM*).

GARALDE. A category of type face in which the axis of the curves is inclined towards the left. There is generally more contrast between the relative thickness of the strokes than in the Humanist designs (*See* HUMANIST 1), the serifs are bracketed, the bar of the lower-case 'e' is horizontal, and the serifs of the lower-case ascenders are oblique. These designs are based on those of Aldus and Garamond, and were formerly called OLD FACE or OLD STYLE (*qq.v.*). Bembo, Caslon and Vendôme are garalde faces.

GARAMOND. An elegant OLD FACE (*q.v.*) type – and one of the most venerable – named after Claude Garamond (d. *circa* 1561), a pupil of Geoffroy Tory, and the first, and perhaps the finest, of the French letter-cutters and type-founders. His roman fonts were very beautiful; these and his italic, which he admits was based on the Aldine italic, have a delightfully unconventional design. They were cut about 1540. Garamond types are very legible and unusually pleasing; the face is of light and clean design, showing a very slight difference between the thick and thin strokes. For a specimen alphabet, *see* TYPE FACE.

GASCON. *See* LE GASCON STYLE.

GATEFOLD. An illustration, map, or other insert which is larger than the page of the publication into which it is bound, so that it must be unfolded for viewing. (American.) *See also* FOLDED LEAF, FOLDING PLATE, THROW OUT.

GATHERING. (*Verb*) The process of assembling and arranging in correct order the various sections which go to make up a book, preparatory to SEWING (*q.v.*). (*Noun*) *Synonymous with* SECTION 1 (*q.v.*).

GAUFFERED EDGES. The gilt edges of the leaves of a book which have been decorated by impressing heated engraved tools to indent a small repeating pattern. This style was popular in the sixteenth and seventeenth centuries. Also called 'Chased', 'Gauffred', 'Goffered'.

GAUFFERING. The decoration of the gilded edges of a bound book with heated finishing tools which indent a small repeating pattern. Also called 'Chased edges', 'Goffered edges'.

GAUGE. (*Printing*) A strip of metal or wood with a notch which is used by the make-up man to denote the exact lengths of pages or widths of margins. Also called 'Forme gauge'.

GAZETTE. A record of public events which is published periodically. A journal or newsheet. A publication issued by a government or university to convey official information, decisions or statements.

GAZETTEER. A geographical dictionary with a varying amount of descriptive, geographical, historical or statistical information.

GELATIN-DYE-TRANSFER. A range of processes in which dye -containing gelatine images produced photographically are physically transferred from a light sensitive matrix to a receiving sheet. *See also* TRANSFER PROCESS, VERIFAX.

GELATINE PRINT. Another name for COLLOTYPE (*q.v.*).

GENEALOGICAL TABLE. A representation of the lineage of a person or persons in tabular or diagrammatical form.

GENERAL ABSTRACT. *See* ABSTRACT.

GENERAL BIBLIOGRAPHY. *See* BIBLIOGRAPHY 1.

GENERAL CLASSIFICATION. A classification which arranges the whole field of knowledge – the visible and invisible universe – in logical order.

GENERAL CROSS-REFERENCE. *Synonymous with* GENERAL REFERENCE (*q.v.*).

GENERAL INFORMATION REFERENCE. A general reference in a catalogue from a specific subject on which there are no individual books to a more general subject which includes the specific subject.

GENERAL LIBRARY. 1. A library which is not limited to a particular field or subject. 2. The main library in a primary school. Also called CENTRAL LIBRARY (*q.v.*). 3. The main library of a university library system. (American.) 4. An agency, undertaking library functions at a state level, which administers a state library's general collections. (American.)

GENERAL REFERENCE. A *See also* reference in an index or catalogue which directs the user to a number of headings under which entries on specific subjects may be found. These are often used to avoid bulking out the catalogue with a number of specific references. Also called 'General cross-reference', 'Information entry', 'Multiple reference'. *See also* CROSS-REFERENCES, SPECIFIC REFERENCE.

GENERAL SEARCH. *Synonymous with* HIERARCHICAL SEARCH (*q.v.*).

GENERAL SECONDARY. An entry for a person or a corporate body whose connexion with the publication catalogued cannot be indicated in the heading by the use of some specific designation as arranger, editor, etc.

GENERAL SPECIAL CONCEPT. A subdivision of a topic according to a characteristic which has general applicability to other subdivisions that are based on different characteristics, e.g. the division of diseases by the process of diagnosis, which applies to kinds of diseases, such as liver diseases.

GENERAL TITLE. One which is provided for a book consisting of several works which have previously been published separately and whose title-pages are called 'Divisional title-pages'.

GENERAL WORKS. A group name, sometimes used as a heading in a scheme of classification, for books of a general nature, i.e. dealing with many different subjects. Sometimes called a GENERALIA CLASS (q.v.).

GENERALIA CLASS. The main class of a classification which is reserved for books on many subjects such as encyclopaedias.

GENERATION. (*Reprography*) An indication of the remoteness of a copy from the original document. The original picture of the document is called a 'first generation' microfilm (camera microfilm); copies made from this are called 'second generation', and copies made from this, 'third generation', etc.

GENERIC. Pertaining to a genus or class of related things (*IBM*).

GENERIC CODING. (*Classification*) The encoding of descriptors in such a way as to preserve generic relations, e.g. encoding by hierarchical class numbers, or with characteristics, replacing each descriptor by a compound of its characteristics.

GENERIC DESCRIPTOR. A DESCRIPTOR (q.v.) related to a genus or class of related things.

GENERIC RELATION. (*Classification*) 1. The relationship between GENUS and SPECIES (qq.v.). 2. The relationship between a class term and the members of that class, where all the members have certain characteristics defined by the class term. 3. The relation between classes in a chain of subordinate classes, where each foregoing member includes all the following members of the chain. 4. (*Information retrieval*) The relationship between two concepts or classes of a classification where one is the genus and one the species. *See also* RELATION.

GENERIC SEARCHING. (*Information retrieval*) In machine searching for indexed material, where the machine has a 'memory unit' which will hold references to allied ideas, then searching under broader headings than the more specific ones under which a document is indexed.

GENERIC TERM. (*Indexing*) A single word which is a constituent part of a BOUND TERM (*q.v.*). *See also* COLLATERAL TERM.

GENEVA BIBLE. A version of the English Bible, translated by William Whittingham, Anthony Gilby, Thomas Sampson and possibly others, and printed by Rouland Hall, Geneva, 1560. It was produced by Marian exiles and was never sanctioned by the Archbishop of Canterbury; after the death of Archbishop Matthew Parker in 1575, it was openly printed in London (first English edition, 1576) and was the Englishman's private Bible until Cromwellian times. The General Assembly of the Scots Kirk adopted the Geneva Bible (1579) as its official version. Being the first English Bible printed in roman type it did much to help the English reading public to become familiar with the roman face. It was the first Bible in English to be divided into verses. Because of the rendering of Genesis iii. 7, 'They sewed fig leaves together and made themselves breeches', it is sometimes referred to as the *Breeches Bible*. It is also called the *Whig Bible* because a printer's error causes Matt: 5:9 to read 'Blessed are the place makers, for they shall be called the children of God'.

GENEVA CONVENTION. Popular name for the Universal Copyright convention. *See* COPYRIGHT, INTERNATIONAL.

GENTLEMEN'S AGREEMENT.† Practices concerned with the duplication of copyright work which were agreed in the U.S.A. to be 'fair use' in an informal coalition between authors, publishers, and librarians. These have been codified in the pending revision of copyright legislation which it is anticipated will pass the Congress in 1976. In the meantime courts have used this criteria as a guideline in determining infringement cases. Reproduction in copies or phonorecords for purposes such as criticism, comment, news reporting, teaching, scholarship or research, is not considered to be an infringement of copyright. In determining whether the use made of a work in any particular case is a fair use, the factors to be considered are: (1) the purpose and character of the use; (2) the nature of the copyrighted work; (3) the amount and substantiality of the portion used in relation to the copyrighted work as a whole; (4) the effect of the use upon the potential market for, or value of, the copyrighted work. *See also* FAIR COPYING DECLARATION.

GENUS. *See* PREDICABLES, FIVE.

GEOGRAPHIC DIVISION. Sub-division in classification or in subject headings by country, region or locality. *See also* AREA TABLE.

GEOGRAPHIC FILING METHOD. Arranging material, or entries in a catalogue, list or bibliography, according to place, either by place-names or by a geographic classification scheme. Also sub-arrangement by place (either alphabetically by place-name or by classification) in any method of filing. Alphabetical filing may be by specific place.

GEOGRAPHICAL ENTRY. The name given to catalogue entries for topographical books and geographical guides, which go under the name of the district to which they refer.

GEOGRAPHICAL NUMBERS. Numbers added to a classification symbol to arrange the books geographically. They are usually applicable throughout a classification scheme. *See also* AREA TABLE.

GEOLOGICAL SURVEY. An organization which publishes geological maps of Britain through the ORDNANCE SURVEY (*q.v.*).

GEOMECHANICS INFORMATION CENTRE. *See* ROCK MECHANICS INFORMATION SERVICE.

GEOMETRIC. A group of LINEALE (*q.v.*) type faces which are based-on a circle, a triangle or on geometric shapes. They are usually MONO LINE (*q.v.*), and the 'a' is often single-storey.

GEO-REF. The machine-readable file of citations covering the world literature in the geosciences. It is developed and maintained by the American Geological Institute.

GEORGE FREEDLEY MEMORIAL AWARD. *See* FREEDLEY MEMORIAL AWARD, GEORGE.

GERMANIC HANDWRITING. A pre-Carolingian, or pre-Caroline handwriting, which was greatly limited in time and space (eighth to ninth centuries A.D.). A 'national' style of handwriting which developed after the dissolution of the Roman Empire, and was a development of the Latin cursive. *See also* CURSIVE, HANDWRITING.

GET EN MOL. *See* JETÉ EN MOULE.

GET IN. 1. To set 'copy' in less space than estimated. 2. To set type very close, or to set it so that it will fit within a required area by using thin spacing.

GHOST WRITER. One who writes or prepares a book such as an autobiography, or articles for, and in the name of, another (usually well-known) person.

GIANT BOOK. A three-dimensional cardboard blow-up of the outside of a book for purposes of display. *See also* BLOW-UP.

GIFT BINDING. Any book bound in leather for presentation such as a school prize, or part of an edition bound in leather at the publisher's order for the gift market.

GIFT BOOK. *See* KEEPSAKES.

GIFT CARD. A record made for each gift; it corresponds to an order card made for a purchased book.

GIGGERING. Polishing a blind impression on a leather binding by rubbing a small hot tool on it.

GILL. A type-face named after Eric Gill (1882–1940) the English sculptor, artist and type designer: it is characterized by the absence of serifs and is therefore known as 'Gill Sans'. Although excellent for display captions it is not wholly suitable for book work as it becomes tiring to read after a time. Gill designed two type faces which are excellent for this purpose: 'Joanna' (1930) and 'Perpetua' (1929–30), the last being his most widely-used type. This most pleasing type is used for display as well as for text. In 1934 he designed a special type for Sterne's *Sentimental Journey* published by the Limited Editions Club of New York. This was the basis for Linotype's 'Pilgrim' which appeared in 1953. For alphabet specimens, *see* TYPE FACE.

GILT EDGES. (*Binding*) The edges of a book which have been trimmed by a guillotine, covered with gold leaf and burnished. 'Antique gold edges' are those which have an unburnished gilt finish. Edges are sometimes tooled with a diapered pattern after binding. *See also* EDGES.

GILT EXTRA. (*Binding*) A binding with more than the normal amount of gilt ornamentation.

GILT IN THE ROUND. A book, the fore-edges of which have been gilded after rounding, the fore-edge appearing as a solid gilt surface.

GILT IN THE SQUARE. A book, the fore-edges of which have been gilded before rounding with the result that there is a tendency for the sections at the beginning and the end of the book to show a white edge.

GILT ON THE ROUGH. Gilding on the uncut edge of a book, or on one that has not been cut solid. It provides the elegance of gold without any sacrifice of margin but does not, like smooth gilt edges, keep the dust out. This was a popular style in France in the nineteenth century and continues popular there. *See also* MARBLING UNDER GILT, ROUGH GILT EDGES, SOLID GILT.

GILT TOP. The top edge of a book trimmed smooth and gilded, the remaining edges being trimmed only. Also called 'Top edges gilt'. Abbreviated g.t., g.t.e., or t.e.g. (top edges gilt). *See also* EDGES, GAUFFERED EDGES, SOLID GILT.

GIRDLE BOOK. A book used in the middle ages and early Renaissance which had secured to it an extra protective cover of soft leather made in such a way that the book could be hung from the girdle or habit cord of a cleric.

GIVEN NAME. The personal name (in Western races the 'Christian' name) given to an individual to distinguish him from other members of his family or clan. This name is given at baptism and/or inserted on a birth certificate.

GLAIRE. An adhesive substance (made by heating up the white of eggs and vinegar or water) used as a size to retain gold in 'finishing' and edge-gilding books.

GLASS. Acronym for the Greater London Audio Specialisation system, which is a subject specialisation scheme, with inter-lending facilities, for gramophone records and eventually, other audio materials. The scheme became operational on 1st April 1972, and embraces the thirty-two London Boroughs (excluding originally the City of London and the Upper Norwood Joint Library), which comprise the Greater London area. Aims: to (a) ensure that at least one copy of all issues within scheduled composer/jazz artist/subject fields is purchased and preserved for public lending within the region; (b) avoid over-purchase of records with low loan potential within the region; (c) make each specialising library within the region the discographical reference point for its particular subjects; (d) issue accessions lists, and where the subject warrants it, printed catalogues of holdings. Records of classical music, jazz and spoken word are covered by the Scheme. The purchase and collection of classical music is allocated to the libraries by composer, and of jazz by performer; records by these composers/performers withdrawn from stock in other libraries in the Scheme may be sent to the 'specialising' libraries for preservation.

GLASSINE. A transparent glossy-surfaced paper obtained by excessive beating of the stock, or by acid treatment. It is made in white and a variety of colours, and is used for panels for window-envelopes, as jackets to protect new books, and for general wrapping purposes.

GLAZED MOROCCO. Morocco, the grain of which has been smoothed by calendering to impart a polished appearance. *See also* CRUSHED MOROCCO.

GLOSS. In ancient MSS. an explanation or interpretation of a word or expression, placed in the margin or above the line, and often in a more familiar language. Also used for an explanation inserted in the margin or text of a book to clarify a foreign or difficult passage. *See also* SIDE NOTE.

GLOSS INK. A printing ink consisting of a synthetic resin base and drying oils; this composition ensures that penetration and absorption into the paper is retarded and that it dries with a brilliant, glossy surface. Specially suitable for use with coated papers and for printing by letterpress or lithographic methods.

GLOSSARIAL INDEX. An index to a book which gives a description or definition of the word indexed as well as its page number.

GLOSSARIST. *Synonymous with* GLOSSOGRAPHER (*q.v.*).

GLOSSARY. 1. An alphabetical list of abstruse, obsolete, unusual, technical, dialectical or other, terms concerned with a subject field, together with definitions. 2. A collection of equivalent synonyms in more than one language.

GLOSSATOR. A writer of glosses to texts; a commentator; especially a mediaeval commentator on the texts of civil and canon law. *See also* GLOSSOGRAPHER.

GLOSSIST. *Synonymous with* GLOSSOGRAPHER (*q.v.*).

GLOSSOGRAPHER. A writer of glosses to a text, or of commentaries on a text; an annotator. Also called a 'Glossarist', 'Glossist', 'Glottographer'. *See also* GLOSSATOR.

GLOSSOGRAPHY. The writing of glosses or commentaries; the compiling of glossaries (*OED*).

GLOSSY PRINT. A photographic print with a shiny surface. These are necessary for the making of satisfactory half-tone blocks. They are usually made on smooth bromide and contact paper that is glazed on a heated metal or ferrotype plate, highly polished chromium-plated steel, stainless steel or plastic which is now often in the form of an electrically heated drum that is kept constantly revolving during operation. Also called 'Ferrotype'.

GLOTTOGRAPHER. *Synonymous with* GLOSSOGRAPHER (*q.v.*).

GLUING OFF. The process of applying glue to the spine of a book, either after sewing, or instead of sewing, and just prior to placing it within its case.

GLYPHIC. Styles of type face which are chiselled, rather than calligraphic, in form. Of such are Albertus, Augustea and Latin.

GLYPHOGRAPHY. A process of making printing plates by engraving on a copper plate covered with a wax film, then dusting with powdered graphite, producing a surface that is used to make an electrotype (*United Typothetae*).

GO LIST. (*Indexing. Information retrieval*) A list of terms or characters which one wishes to include in a printout. A Go List makes it possible to select specific items from a very large number forming a group. The opposite of a STOP LIST (*q.v.*).

GOATSKIN. Leather manufactured from the skins of goats; the best skins come from the River Niger, the Levant or Morocco, and are named after the places from which they come.

GOFFERED EDGES. *Synonymous with* GAUFFERED EDGES (*q.v.*).

GOLD. Used in the form of thin leaves or foil for lettering or tooling books.

GOLD CUSHION. A pad, used by binders' finishers, to which a sheet of gold leaf adheres and from which the finisher takes the small pieces required for each book. The pad is usually filled with blotting paper, felt, or similar material, and covered with leather.

GOLD KNIFE. A knife used by binders' finishers to cut gold leaf while on the gold cushion. It has a long, flat blade, and is sharpened on both sides.

GOLD STAMPED. A book with a design stamped in gold on the binding by means of a stamp. *See also* BLOCK 3, PANEL STAMP, TOOLING.

GOLD TOOLING. *See* TOOLING.

GOLDEN COCKEREL PRESS. An English private press, founded in December 1920 by Harold Midgely Taylor at Waltham Saint Lawrence, Berkshire, to print and publish (in a co-operative manner, and under the conditions of a 'village industry') new works of literary significance by young authors; and to print and publish fine editions of books of established worth. When Mr. Taylor retired in January 1924 owing to illness, the Press was purchased by Robert Gibbings, illustrator and woodcutter who operated it until 1933. The press is still active. Most of the printing is done in Caslon Old Face.

GOLDEN TYPE. The first of three types cut by William Morris for his Kelmscott Press. It was a 14-point roman based on an early fount used by Nicholas Jenson and was first used in 1891. In 1891 he designed the TROY and, in 1892 the CHAUCER, types (*qq.v.*). *See also* KELMSCOTT PRESS.

GONE TO BED. *See* GONE TO PRESS.

GONE TO PRESS. A term used to indicate that formes or plates have been sent for machining and that it is too late to make any but vital corrections or alterations. Any which occur at this stage are often included in corrigenda. In a newspaper office the term 'Gone to bed' is generally used.

GOOD. Said of composed type which has been printed off and which, because it may be used at a later date, is not distributed but kept standing.

GORE. 1. The projection of an elongated narrow strip of the earth's surface usually comprising the zone between two meridians which have small angular separation and extending to the geographic poles. The principal scale is preserved along the central meridian of each gore. 2. A triangular piece of paper or thin card on which is printed a section of a map of the world, bounded by meridians and tapering to the Poles; twelve or twenty-four of these can be stuck to a sphere and so make a complete printed globe. 3. A triangular piece of land or of ploughland found in corners where the ploughland is not rectangular.

GOTHIC MINUSCULE. The style of handwriting which, by the end of the twelfth century, had degenerated from the Carolingian Minuscule into a hand consisting of long, angular, pointed letters. It was on this that most of the early European printers based their first types.

GOTHIC TYPE. Type resembling the Gothic script used as a book hand in the later middle ages. Gothic types are usually divided into four groups: (1) *Text*, *Lettre de forme* (Ger. *textura*), or (pointed) church type; (2) *Gothico-antiqua*, *lettre de somme* (Ger. *fere-human-istica*), the simple round gothic; (3) *Rotunda*, the ordinary round text-type; (4) *Bastard*, *lettre de bâtarde* (Ger. *bastarda*), or cursive type. It is now loosely used to include all bold sans serif and grotesque type faces. Also called 'Black letter type'.

GOTHICO-ANTIQUA. *See* GOTHIC TYPE.

GOTTLIEB PRIZE, MURRAY. $50 and publication offered by the (American) Medical Library Association for the best essay submitted on some phase of medical history.

GOUDY. A type face named after the American type-designer, Frederic W. Goudy who flourished in the early years of the present century. Probably his most famous type is Kennerley.

GOUFFERED. *See* GAUFFERED EDGES.

GOUGE. A bookbinder's finishing tool used for producing a curved line on a book cover at a single application. It has a set of arcs of concentric circles.

GOVERNMENT DOCUMENT. A publication issued at government expense or published by authority of a governmental body. As used in America, any publication in book, serial or non-book form bearing an imprint of a government, whether federal, state, local, or foreign, and of inter-governmental organizations, such as Unesco, etc. *See also* OFFICIAL PUBLICATION.

GOVERNMENT LIBRARY. A library maintained out of central government funds. Government libraries normally fall into three broad groups: National libraries, departmental libraries and the libraries of research stations.

GOVERNMENT PUBLICATIONS. Publications of an official character, or of an instructional, descriptive, or historical nature, which are published by the government publishing department for parliament or one of the government departments. *See also* PARLIAMENTARY PUBLICATIONS.

GRABHORN PRESS. Founded by the Grabhorn brothers, Edwin and Robert, of San Francisco, this press has established a leading reputation for gifted and original work since their first commission from the Book Club of California in 1921. The Grabhorns' work is lively and virile and they are particularly skilful in colour-printing, especially from wood-blocks.

GRACE. Abbreviation for the Graphic Arts Composing Equipment – a photocomposition machine that converts information from magnetic tape into latent typographical images on photosensitive film or paper. *See also* MEDLARS.

GRADATION IN SPECIALITY. Bliss's 'principle by which the several sciences and studies distinguished by their conceptional scope and their relations to the real order of nature, are arranged in serial order from the most general to the most special.' The modulation of more fundamental classes into their derivatives in the same way that special sciences depend on, and to some extent are derived from, the general sciences.

GRAIN. The direction in which the fibres lie in a sheet of paper. *See also* AGAINST THE GRAIN, MACHINE DIRECTION, WITH THE GRAIN.

GRAIN DIRECTION. The direction in which the majority of the fibres in a sheet of paper lie. The moving web of a paper-making machine causes the fibres in the pulp to lie parallel with one another in the direction of the web movement. Also called 'Machine direction'. It is important to determine the 'direction' of paper used for lithography, postage stamps, account books or close register work, to avoid differences in expansion. Hand-made papers expand or shrink equally in all directions due to the shaking which occurs during manufacture and which felts the fibres in all directions. *See also* AGAINST THE GRAIN, WITH THE GRAIN.

GRAINED LEATHER. A tanned skin on which the natural grain (visible on the side on which the hair grew) has been worked up to raise and accentuate it. Graining is also artificially produced by stamping a skin with engraved metal plates.

GRAINING. 1. The process of producing the natural grain markings of leather by boarding, i.e. the pushing or pulling of a fold in the skin with the aid of a board covered with cork, which grips that portion of the skin with which it is in contact. 2. The art of producing an artificial grain on leather by stamping it with metal plates or passing it through rollers on which the desired grain markings are engraved.

GRAMOPHONE LIBRARY. A collection of gramophone records. Such collections are maintained by public libraries, the records being lent to local gramophone or musical societies, clubs, schools, or private individuals. 'Record library' is also used in the U.K. *See also* GLASS.

GRAMOPHONE RECORD. A recording of sound on a thin, flat, circular plastic material which is placed on a machine to reproduce the sounds recorded. Called in America, a 'Phonograph record' and popularly, a 'disc'.

GRAMOPHONE RECORD NUMBER. A symbol, usually consisting of one or more letters and numbers, and allocated by the manufacturer to an individual recording for purposes of identification. It is printed on the label on the record.

GRANGERIZING. The practice of inserting in a bound volume illustrations, letters, documents, etc., not issued as part of the volume but referred to in the text. Such additional matter is mounted or inlaid on sheets of good quality paper and inserted in the appropriate parts of the book which is usually re-bound. The practice dates from 1769, when James Granger published a 'Bibliographical History of England' with blank leaves for the reception of illustrations. Such a volume is said to to be 'Extra-illustrated' or 'Grangerized'.

GRAPH. A pictorial representation of numerical data. Graphs may take various forms and are described as pictograms or as bar, line, broken-line or circular, graphs.

GRAPHIC. Styles of type faces which suggest that the characters have not been written but drawn. Of such are Cartoon, Libra and Old English (Monotype).

GRAPHIC LENGTH. A characteristic of the length of notation symbols used in a scheme of classification, whereby there is ability to remember easily a sequence because of their visual appearance. A pure notation (one consisting of the same kind of characters, as all figures or all letters) is easier to remember than a mixed notation comprising figures, letters or symbols. *See also* PHONIC LENGTH.

GRAPHICS. Non-verbal material, e.g. diagrams, drawings, photographs, graphs.

GRATICULE. A system of lines representing meridians and parallels on a map. Not to be confused with grid which is a network of parallel lines drawn at right angles on a map to represent fixed distances.

GRAVER. A BURIN (*q.v.*).

GRAVURE. A French word, meaning cutting or engraving; used as a continuing word, like photogravure, rotogravure, etc. (*United Typothetae*). An abbreviation for PHOTOGRAVURE (*q.v.*).

GREAT PRIMER. An out-of-date name for a size of type equal to about 18 point.

GREATER LONDON AUDIO SPECIALISATION SCHEME. *See* GLASS.

GREATER LONDON COLLEGE LIBRARIANS' GROUP. *See* GLCLG.

GREATER LONDON COUNCIL. The new administrative area comprising thirty-two London boroughs each with a population range of 169,000 to 340,000 and replacing as from 1st April 1965 the London County Council, the Middlesex County Council and eighty-five other local authorities. The status of the City of London remains but with the powers of a London Borough Council. The Middlesex County Libraries were transferred to the new boroughs in the former area of the Middlesex County Council. Boundary changes occurred in most boroughs.

GREEK FASHION. Book bindings with raised HEADBANDS (*q.v.*), i.e. those which project beyond the boards at the head and tail of the spine. The Greek technique of forwarding was used in the West only for Greek books.

GREEK LIBRARY ASSOCIATION OF CYPRUS. Founded in April 1962 for the purposes of uniting librarians and improving libraries and librarianship in Cyprus. Membership is open to all persons working in libraries in Cyprus.

GREEN BOOK. An official report published by the Italian government; so called because bound in a green paper cover. *See also* BLUE BOOK.

GREEN PAPER. A document issued by any Department or Ministry of the British Government. It has green covers, and sets out government propositions so that full consultation and public discussion may take place while policy is still in a formative stage. Green Papers are intended to meet the need for better communication between Government and public rather than to present proposals as in a White Paper. *See also* BLUE BOOK, PARLIAMENTARY PAPERS, WHITE PAPER.

GREENAWAY MEDAL, KATE. *See* KATE GREENAWAY MEDAL.

GRID. (*Binding*) An ornament which is frequently used on heads-in-medallions rolls, and consists of two horizontal lines with a few short vertical bars between them, the sides having a foliage character.

(*Cartography*) A referencing system using distances measured on a chosen projection. Not to be confused with GRATICULE (*q.v.*).

GRID REFERENCE. The position of a point on a map expressed in grid letters and co-ordinates, or co-ordinates alone. *See also* GRID.

GRIGG COMMITTEE. Popular name of the Committee on Departmental Records of which Sir James Grigg was Chairman. It was set up in 1952 by the Master of the Rolls and the Chancellor of the Exchequer to review the arrangements for the preservation of Government Department's records and to make recommendations. The Committee's report was presented in 1954; and the recommendations it contained were accepted by Government in principle; the Public Records Act 1958 which came into force on 1 January 1959 repealed the former acts of 1838, 1877 and 1898. This Act transferred the direction of the Public Record Office from the Master of the Rolls to a Minister of the Crown, the Lord Chancellor, who was given a general responsibility for public records.

GRIPPER EDGE. *See* LAY EDGES.

GRISA. Groupe de Recherche sur l'Information Scientifique (Scientific Information Processing Research Team). A working party of CETIS (*q.v.*).

GROLIER-AMERICANA SCHOLARSHIPS. Donated by the Grolier Foundation, and made to two library schools, one of which is a graduate library school and the other with a programme of library education at undergraduate level, for scholarships for a student in each institution who is in training for school librarianship. It is awarded annually in the form of $1,000 cash for each school, and administered by the American Association of School Librarians whose Grolier-Americana Scholarships Awards Committee considers applications received previously from directors of library schools. The schools selected choose the student to whom the scholarship is to be given. The Scholarship was first awarded in 1957 to the Department of Librarianship, Western Michigan University and to the School of Library Service, Columbia University.

GROLIER AWARD. Donated by Grolier Inc., and consisting of $1,000 cash and a citation of achievement, this award is made annually to a librarian in a community or in a school who has made an unusual contribution to the stimulation and guidance of reading by children and young people. It 'is usually given for outstanding work with children and young people through high school age, for continued service, or in recognition of one particular contribution of lasting value'. Selection of the recipient is made by a jury of five appointed by the ALA Awards Committee (which administers the Award), and representing the following ALA divisions: AASL, CSD, YASD and one member representing the ALA Awards Committee who serves as chairman. The Award was first made in 1954 to Siddie Joe Johnson.

GROLIER NATIONAL LIBRARY WEEK GRANT. $1,000 donated by Grolier Inc., and offered by the ALA Committee on National Library Week to the state library association sponsoring the most effective statewide Library Week programme.

GROLIERESQUE. The style of binding which is associated with Jean Grolier (1479–1565). It depends for its effect on light and graceful geometrical 'strapword' (interlaced double fillets), and influenced ornate binding for two centuries. *See also* MAIOLI STYLE.

GROOVE. The cut-out portion of the base of a piece of movable type. Also called 'Heel-nick'. It has no particular purpose in printing. *See also* FEET.

GROOVES. (*Binding*) 1. The shoulders formed on the sides of books in backing, to allow the boards to lie even with the back when secured. 2. Incisions in the back edge of a board to take the cords on which the sections are sewn.

GROSS SQUARE FOOTAGE. The sum of the areas of a library at each floor level included within the principal outside faces at exterior walls, but not including architectural setbacks, or projections. (American.)

GROTESQUE. Sans serif display types of unconventional design which are not usually pleasing to behold. A name given at the beginning of the nineteenth century to the earliest SANS SERIF (*q.v.*) types, which have been revived and come into favour for display work. During the 1920's and 1930's the following sans serif faces became popular: Futura, Gill, Granby, Vogue. These are a group of LINEALE (*q.v.*) type faces with nineteenth-century origins. Some contrast in the thickness of the strokes exists, and there is a squareness in the curves. The ends of the curved strokes are usually horizontal. The G is spurred and the R usually has a curled leg. *See also* NEO-GROTESQUE.

GROUND. An acid-resisting compound used on etching plates to protect the non-image-bearing portions from the action of the acid. It is composed of beeswax, asphaltum, gum mastic and pitch.

GROUNDWOOD PULP. *Synonymous with* MECHANICAL WOOD (*q.v.*).

GROUP. A section of the membership of the Library Association, and formally constituted in accordance with the bye-laws of the Association. Each group is concerned with a particular subject interest in librarianship. Members are entitled to join two groups: more on payment of small additional subscriptions. *See also* BRANCH, DIVISION, LIBRARY ASSOCIATION, SECTION. Aslib also has subject Groups.

GROUP NOTATION DEVICE. The device of using ordinal decimal fraction numbers of two or more digits (but the same number of significant digits) to represent a number of co-ordinate isolates or array-isolates, when they are too many to be represented economically by SECTOR DEVICE (*q.v.*) alone.

GROWING FLOWER. A common ornament on bookbinders' finishers' rolls, consisting usually of a flattened elliptical base from which springs a stem bearing leaves and at the top two flowers, the tops of which curl outwards.

GRUB STREET. According to Dr. Johnson, 'originally the name of a street near Moorfields, much inhabited by writers of small histories, dictionaries, and occasional poems. . . .'

GUARANTEE. The undertaking signed by a guarantor when undertaking to be responsible for any losses incurred as a result of the guaranteed person using the library.

GUARANTOR. A person who signs a voucher for a reader who is not a ratepayer, guaranteeing to make good any financial losses caused by the person guaranteed by reason of his using the library.

GUARD. 1. A strip of linen or paper pasted by a binder (1) on to or into the sections of a book to prevent the sewing tearing through the paper, (2) on the inner edge of an illustration, the guard being sewn through. 2. One or more pieces of paper or linen placed together to equalize the space taken by a folded map or other insert or by material pasted to the pages of a cuttings book. Also to enable additional illustrations, maps or leaves to be added after binding. Also called 'Stub'.

GUARD BOOK CATALOGUE. *See* PAGE CATALOGUE.

GUARD SHEET. A sheet of paper, usually thinner (and often transparent) than that on which the book is printed, bearing a letterpress description or an outline drawing to protect and/or elucidate the illustration which it accompanies. The guard sheet is not normally included in the pagination.

GUARDING. Fixing a guard to a section, map or illustration, etc. Strengthening the fold between two conjugate leaves with an adhesive, pasted, or glued-on strip of paper.

GUIDE BOOK. A handbook for travellers and visitors which gives information about a country, region, or building.

GUIDE CARD. A card with a projecting tab used in a card catalogue or file to indicate the arrangement and to facilitate reference.

GUIDE-LETTER. A letter printed in the space to be filled by the rubrisher or illuminator of an early printed book as a guide to prevent him inserting a wrong letter.

GUIDE SLIP. *See* PROCESS SLIP.

GUILLEMETS. *See* DUCK-FOOT QUOTES.

GUILLOTINE. A machine for cutting paper, with a knife having a perpendicular action.

GUM ARABIC. A solution used to preserve offset plates, and in lithographic printing. *See also* DESENSITIZATION.

GUMMING UP. Applying a solution of gum arabic to an offset plate to protect it from grease and oxidation.

GUTENBERG BIBLE. *See* MAZARIN BIBLE.

GUTTER. 1. The adjoining inner margins of two facing pages of type; the margins at the sewn fold of a section. 2. (*Binding*) The trough between the edge of the board and the backed spine of a bound book. *See also* BACKING, GROOVE, JOINT 3, SPINE. 3. In a permuted title, index, or similar mechanically-produced listing, a vertical column of one or more spaces at which point the index words are positioned to provide a readily-viewable alphabetical order.

GUTTER MARGIN. *Synonymous with* BACK MARGIN (*q.v.*).

GUTTERING. The ridges that sometimes occur (as a result of use) along the spine of a binding which has a tight or a flexible back.

GYPSOGRAPHIC PRINT. *Synonymous with* SEAL PRINT (*q.v.*).

HRLSD. Acronym of Health and Rehabilitative Library Services. This Division of the American Library Association was until 1974 the Association of Hospital and Institution Libraries (AHIL). 'The purpose and responsibility of this Division includes the educational, recreational, cultural and rehabilitative development of persons needing library materials and services of a unique nature because of visual, physical, health and/or behavioural problems, and the professional development of those providing these materials and services ... Those served ... are adults, young adults, and children who are handicapped, ill, infirm, homebound, confined, or receiving services through an institution.' Abbreviated HRLSD. Publishes HRLSD *Newsletter* (10 p.a.), HRSLD *Journal* (2 p.a.) (both membs. only) which superseded *AHIL Quarterly* as from March 1975.

h.t. Abbreviation for HALF-TITLE (*q.v.*).

HTFS. Acronym of the Heat Transfer and Fluid Flow Service Information Centre, the objectives of which are to provide access to selected technical information relevant to heat transfer and fluid flow and related topics, and to provide background information for HTFS Design Reports, for the confidential consultancy, and for the HTFS Research Programme. It is part of the Atomic Energy Research Establishment at Harwell.

HABILITATIONSSCHRIFTEN. A 'probationary treatise embodying the results of original research that is submitted to the faculty in order that its author be recognized as a Privatdozent at the university'. (*Cassell's New German and English Dictionary.*)

HACHURES. Vertical and horizontal lines used on a map to indicate by their length and closeness the direction and steepness of variations in height of the earth's surface, the lines being crowded together to represent the steepest slopes. *See also* HATCHING.

HADIS. A co-operative grouping of organizations, based on the Huddersfield Public Libraries, and which functioned after 1959 within a radius of ten miles from Huddersfield, was re-constituted in 1973. *See* KIS.

HAGAR PRESS. The German counterpart of the ALBION PRESS (*q.v.*).

HAGIONYM. The name of a saint taken as a proper name.

HAGUE SCHEME. A scheme of book classification compiled by Dr. Greve. *See also* SISO.

HAIR LINE. A thin stroke of a letter or type character.

HAIR SPACE. (*Printing*) The thinnest spacing material. It is cast less than type height and is used between letters or words. Hair spaces vary in thickness from eight to twelve to an em, according to body size, thus in 6 pt. the hair space is ½ pt.; in 12 pt. it is 1½ pts.; in 18 pt. it is 2 pts.; and in 24 pt. it is 3 pts. Thissentenceishairspaced.

HALDIS. The Halifax and District Information Service; formed in 1966 at the College Library, Percival Whitley College of Further Education, Francis Street, Halifax, Yorkshire, whereby organizations which have literature, and are willing to inter-lend and pay a nominal annual subscription, may co-operate with one another.

HALE AWARD, SARAH JOSEPHA. A medal awarded to a distinguished author whose work and life reflect the literary tradition of New England. Donated by the friends of the Richards Free Library.

HALF BANDS. Ridges on the spine of a bound book, at the top and bottom, smaller than bands. They usually mark the position of the KETTLE STITCH (*q.v.*).

HALF BINDING. *See* QUARTER BINDING.

HALF BOUND. *Synonymous with* HALF LEATHER (*q.v.*).

HALF CLOTH. A book with a cloth spine, usually with the title printed on a paper label, and having paper covered 'board' (i.e. strawboard) sides. May also be called 'Half linen'.

HALF-DARK TYPE. *Synonymous with* MEDIUM FACE (*q.v.*).

HALF FRAME. The use of a mask in the gate of a camera to reduce the image to half size, e.g. to 24 × 18 mm. from 24 × 36 mm.

HALF LEATHER. A term used to describe a book with a leather spine and corners, but with the rest of the sides covered in cloth. *See also* LEATHER BOUND, QUARTER LEATHER.

HALF-LINE BLOCK. A printing block made by interposing a half-line screen (i.e. parallel lines without cross-lines) between the original line drawing and the negative. The result is lighter in tone than the original.

HALF LINEN. *See* HALF CLOTH.

HALF-MEASURE. *See* DOUBLE COLUMNED.

HALF MONTHLY. A periodical issued twice a month, or fortnightly.

HALF SEE SAFE. An expression used by a bookseller when ordering copies of a book from a publisher to indicate that, while all copies will be paid for, he may ask the publisher to take back half of them in exchange for copies of another title. *See also* SEE SAFE.

HALF-SHEET IMPOSITION. *Synonymous with* HALF-SHEET WORK (*q.v.*).

HALF-SHEET WORK. Printing (with two machinings) a sheet of paper on both sides with the same forme. The paper is then cut in half to give two copies. *See also* SHEET WORK. Also called 'Half-sheet imposition'.

HALF-STAMP. (*Binding*) A finisher's stamp the design of which is the same as, or similar to, one half of a fleuron, pineapple, etc. It is generally used for the compartments at the edges of the frame in lozenge compartment bindings. Sometimes used back to back to form the lozenges in the centre.

HALF-STUFF. (*Paper*) Partially broken and washed STOCK (*q.v.*) which has been reduced to a fibrous pulp, usually before it is bleached. The finished pulp, ready for the vat or paper machine is termed 'whole-stuff'. *See also* PULP, STOCK, STUFF, WHOLE-STUFF.

HALF-TITLE. The brief title of a book appearing on the recto of the leaf preceding the title-page. It serves to protect the title-page and help the printer to identify the book to which the first sheet belongs. The wording of long titles is often abbreviated. The use of such a page dates from the latter half of the seventeenth century although a blank sheet had been used to protect title-pages for a very long time. It is often abbreviated h.t. Also called 'Bastard title', 'Fly-title'. *See also* SECOND HALF-TITLE.

HALF-TONE.   The name given to the process by means of which photographs, drawings, designs, etc., are reproduced in tone as opposed to solid black and white: also to the actual prints made by it. The printing plate is of copper or zinc and the image is reduced to a series of dots varying in intensity with the tone values of the original. This is done photographically in conjunction with a mechanically ruled screen which is coarse with few dots to the square inch for printing on coarse papers, and many to the square inch for fine, smooth papers. Etching removes the background, leaving the dots representing the image to be printed by relief process. A *Squared-up half-tone* is one finished with straight sides at right angles. Half-tones are also finished as Circles or Ovals. A *Vignetted half-tone* is one which has no sharp edge to the design, and 'fades' out. A *Cut-out half-tone* is one from which the background is entirely removed. A *Deep-etched half-tone* is one from the highlights of which the dots characteristic of a half-tone are entirely removed, leaving the paper virgin white in the reproduction. A *Highlight*, or *Drop-out*, is one from which the dots have been removed.

HALF-TONE PAPER.   An ART (*q.v.*), imitation art, or other supercalendered or coated paper suitable for the printing of half-tones.

HALF-TONE SCREENS.   Transparent plates of glass used for making half-tone blocks. They are ruled diagonally with opaque lines usually, but not necessarily, at right angles to each other, the thickness of the lines and of the intervening spaces being approximately equal. The number of lines to the inch varies, 'fine' screens having more than 'coarse' ones. The smoother the paper used, the finer must be the half-tone block. *See also* SCREEN.

HALF UNCIAL.   The last stage in the development of the Roman period of Latin manuscript handwriting, being a somewhat informal kind of letter based on minuscule forms and used from the fifth to the ninth centuries. It is specially associated with the calligraphic revival by Alcuin in the ninth century. Most of the letters were miniscules, only a few of the capitals, such as N and F, remaining.

HALF YEARLY.   A periodical which is issued at six-monthly intervals. Also called 'Semi-annual'. *See also* BI-ANNUAL.

HALIFAX AND DISTRICT INFORMATION SERVICE.   *See* HALDIS.

HALSEY W. WILSON LIBRARY RECRUITMENT AWARD.   *See* WILSON LIBRARY RECRUITMENT AWARD, HALSEY W.

HAMMOND INCORPORATED LIBRARY AWARD. An annual Award of $500 cash and a citation, donated by the C. S. Hammond Company, and made to a librarian who has effectively encouraged the use of maps and atlases or promoted an interest in cartography. The Award is administered by the ALA Awards Committee, the selection being made by a jury of five representing various divisions of the ALA. The first recipient was Mrs. Clara E. Le Gear in 1963.

HAMPSHIRE INTER-LIBRARY CENTER. *See* HILC.

HAND. The printers' symbol ☞. Used to attract attention. Also called 'Digit', 'Fist', 'Index'.

HAND COMPOSITION. The setting up of printer's type by hand as distinct from machine setting.

HAND GRAVURE. A method of copperplate printing. After inking and before each impression is taken, the surface is wiped by hand (*United Typothetae*).

HAND-MADE PAPER. Paper made by dipping a mould into the pulp vat and taking up sufficient 'stuff' to form a sheet of paper of the required substance. A shaking movement causes the fibres to mix together. The pulp is composed of rag fibres; when the best linen rags are used the resulting paper is the most durable obtainable. Also called 'Vat paper'.

HAND PRESS. A press in which the forme is inked, the paper fed and removed, and the pressure applied, by hand; used to distinguish it from one worked by power; often used in printing offices to pull proofs by hand and for short runs on small sheets of paper. It is the direct descendant of the earliest type of printing press.

HAND ROLLER. *See* Brayer.

HAND SET. Type which has been set by hand, as opposed to type set by machine.

HAND SEWING. The sewing by hand through the folds of sections of a book, using a sewing frame. *See also* Sewn.

HAND STAMP. A brass letter, or motif, set in a wooden handle, and used by a binder's finisher in lettering the cover of a hand-bound book.

HANDBILL. A poster, or placard, printed by hand.

HANDBOOK. A treatise on a special subject; often nowadays a simple but all-embracing treatment, containing concise information, and being small enough to be held in the hand; but strictly, a book of science or technology written primarily for practitioners and serving as a book for constant revision or reference. Also called a 'Manual'.

HANDWRITING. Books were produced by writing by hand before the use of wood blocks early in the fifteenth century (*see* BLOCK BOOK). After European countries had shaken off the political authority of the Roman empire, and the educated communities had been scattered and dissolved, the Latin 'cursive' or 'running' script changed and several 'national' hands, or styles of the Latin cursive minuscule developed. The five principal national hands are South Italian or Beneventan, Merovingian (in France), Visigothic (in Spain), Germanic pre-Carolingian, and Insular (in Ireland and England). The earliest of the five periods into which Latin manuscript handwriting can be divided is the Roman period (second to eighth centuries) and this can be divided into five groups: *Quadrata,* or *Square capital,* hand; *Rustic capital* hand; *Uncial* hand; *Later cursive* hand; and *Half uncial* hand (*qq.v.*).

HANGING FIGURES. The numerals of certain type-designs which range within the limits of the EXTRUDERS (*q.v.*), e.g. the Caslon figures 3456789 as distinct from the 12 and 0 of the same face. Old-face types usually have hanging figures, although in some, e.g. Plantin, RANGING FIGURES (*q.v.*) are available as an alternative. *See* OLD STYLE FIGURES.

HANGING INDENTION. 1. A paragraph of which the first line is set to the full width of the measure, the second and all subsequent lines of the paragraph being indented one or more ems from the left-hand margin as for this definition. *See also* EM, PARAGRAPH INDENTION. Also called 'Hanging paragraph'. 2. In cataloguing, the form of indention in which the first line begins at the 'author indention' ('first indention') and succeeding lines at the 'title indention' ('second indention'). This method is used by the Library of Congress and many other libraries for 'formal anonyma', i.e. works like periodicals which do not involve the idea of concealed authorship. It is a method which tends to emphasize the first word of the title.

HANGING PARAGRAPH. *Synonymous with* HANGING INDENTION (*q.v.*).

HANS CHRISTIAN ANDERSEN AWARD. *See* ANDERSEN AWARD, HANS CHRISTIAN.

'HANSARD'. *See* PARLIAMENTARY PAPERS.

HARD BOUND. Bound in cloth- or paper-covered boards. Also called 'Hard cover'.

HARD COPY. 1. A human-readable copy produced from information that has been transcribed to a form not easily readable by human beings (*IBM*). 2. A record on card or paper, to distinguish it from a record on microfilm or magnetic tape. It may be a contact copy or an enlargement. 3. A printed copy of machine output in readable form for human beings; e.g. reports, listings, catalogues, documents, summaries.

HARD COVER. *See* HARD BOUND.

HARD PACKING. Thin card, or hard or stiff paper, used to cover the cylinder of a printing press in order to obtain a sharp impression, with little indentation of the paper, when printing on smooth hard paper.

HARDBACK. A book published in stiff covers. The opposite of PAPERBACK (*q.v.*).

HARDWARE. Apparatus used in information retrieval, data processing, the audio-visual field, or required for the consultation of all non-book materials which are not readable by the unaided eye. *See also* SOFTWARE.

HARKNESS FELLOWSHIPS. Twenty fellowships for twelve–twenty-one months' study and travel in the United States are offered annually to candidates from the United Kingdom. Applicants may propose an American programme which best suits their personal and professional needs, with unrestricted choice of university or other institution at which to work. Competition for the fellowships is intense, and only those with outstanding records are considered. Fellowships are open to men and women in any profession or field of study between twenty-one and thirty years of age, whose education has been wholly or mainly in the United Kingdom. Nearly forty awards are made each year. 'The Harkness Fellowships of the Commonwealth Fund of New York' was incorporated in the State of New York, and the endowment derives entirely from the estates of the founder, Mrs Stephen V. Harkness, and of Mr & Mrs Edward S. Harkness.

HARLEIAN STYLE. An English style of book decoration with a centre motif composed of small tools usually arranged in a lozenge-shaped design, and having an elaborate if sometimes rather narrow border decorated by means of one or more rolls. These 'Harleian' bindings were made by Thomas Elliott for Robert and Edward Harley, the First and Second Earls of Oxford.

HARRIS AWARD, JOHN. Offered by the New Zealand Library Association 'for the written record of notable library work, whether in the bibliographical, critical, historical or administrative fields, which will be a contribution to New Zealand librarianship'. The work should be the result of original research. The Award consists of an 'appropriate diploma, plus the sum of £25'. It was first made to Mr. W. J. McEldowney, a former Honorary Secretary of the NZLA, in 1963.

HARVARD SYSTEM. A method of citing papers from scientific books and periodicals. The items making up a reference are as follows: (i) author's name and initials; (ii) year of publication, in parentheses, with a, b, etc. if more than one paper in the year is cited; (iii) full title of paper (roman type); (iv) name of periodical, contracted as in the *World List of Scientific Periodicals* (italic type); (v) volume number (in bold arabic figures); (vi) number of first page of paper; e.g.

> Gregory, P. H. (1940). The control of narcissus leaf disease. *Ann. appl. Biol.* **27**, 338.
> Jensen, H. L. & Betty, R. C. (1943). Nitrogen fixation in leguminous plants. *Proc. Linn. Soc.* N.S.W. **68**. I.

One of the chief advantages of this system is that footnotes can be dispensed with, a list of references being printed at the end of the article in alphabetical order of authors' names. In the text, references are given by printing the author's name and the date of publication in parentheses as (Gregory, 1940), (Jensen and Betty, 1943), but if the author's name is part of the text the date only is given in ( ). When three or more authors have collaborated in a paper, all the names are given in the first citation, but subsequently only the first name followed by '*et al.*' need be used.

HATCHING. A row of parallel, diagonal lines. Often found on the half bands or on the heads and tails of the spines of bindings from the sixteenth century onwards. Also used for the 'azured' shading on the centres of finishers' tools. *See also* CROSS HATCHING, HACHURES.

HATRICS. Abbreviation for Hampshire Technical Research Industrial and Commercial Service which was set up in 1964 and has its headquarters at the Commercial Library of the Central Library, Civic Centre, Southampton. It is the intention of the various institutions concerned with the acquisition and distribution of technical, scientific and commercial information in Hampshire to communicate directly with one another through the medium of a directory of resources. There are no membership limitations. An annual subscription of three pounds is payable.

HAWNT REPORT. The Report on *The Public library service in Northern Ireland*, 1966, (Belfast, H.M.S.O., Cmd. 494), so named after Dr. J. S. Hawnt, the Chairman of the Advisory Committee appointed in September 1964 by the Minister of Education, Government of Northern Ireland, 'to consider the public library service . . . and make recommendations for its development, having regard to the relationship of public libraries to other libraries'.

In many respects the Committee's recommendations follow closely those of the ROBERTS REPORT (*q.v.*), but there was the important difference that the Hawnt Committee considered that financial arrangements were altogether unable to meet the demands of a modern library service; proposals were therefore made for government grants. The powers and duties of local library authorities were enumerated. It was considered that a Provincial Library should be created and that the Belfast Central Library should become this Provincial Library and function under a Provincial Joint Committee, leaving the branch libraries under the control of the Belfast Corporation. A minority report, however, could not accept this dismembering of the Belfast Public Libraries as the price of establishing the Provincial Library. *See also* LIBRARY AUTHORITY.

HAYSTAQ. Name of an information searching procedure with electronic computers used by the U.S. Patent Office (*IBM*).

HEAD.   1. The margin at the top of a page. 2. The top of a book or of a page. 3. The top of the spine of a book where the headband is placed. 4. The top edge of a book. *See also* FOOT.

HEAD AND TAIL.   The top and bottom edges of a book.

HEAD MARGIN.   The blank space above the top line of printed matter. 'Heads' relates to the top margins.

HEAD ORNAMENT.   An ornament specially designed for the top of a page: it may incorporate the lettering of the chapter heading, or provide an *island space* in which to print it. It is sometimes called a 'Headband' or 'Head piece'. *See also* TAIL ORNAMENT.

HEAD PIECE.   *Synonymous with* HEAD ORNAMENT (*q.v.*).

HEAD TITLE.   The title, even in abbreviated form, given as a heading above a page of type or on the first page of a piece of music. *See also* HEADLINE.

HEADBAND.   (*Binding*) The band, usually of coloured silk threads, at the head of a book, sewn or glued to the folds of sections, placed between the sections and the cover, and projecting slightly beyond the head. Originally it was a cord or leather thong similar to the ordinary bands, around which the ends of the threads were twisted, and laced-in to the boards. Nowadays headbands are usually made of coloured silks and are sewn on after the book has been forwarded thus having no purpose other than decoration. The two were formerly distinguished as 'headband' and 'tailband' but both are now called 'headbands' or 'heads'. *See also* TAILBAND. 2. (*Printing*) A printed or engraved decorative band at the head of a page or chapter. Also called 'Head piece', 'Head ornament'.

HEADCAP.   The thickened end of the spine at head and tail of the leather spine of a book; this is caused by placing a piece of sized Italian hemp inside the turn-in at the head and tail of the spine after the leather has been fitted to the book. If headbands are used, they are left visible. *See also* HEADBAND, TAILCAP.

HEADING. 1. (*Cataloguing*) The first sequence of characters (forming a number, name, word or phrase) at the beginning of a catalogue entry – usually written or printed on a separate line and sometimes in larger type than the remainder of the entry – to (a) determine the exact position of an entry in a catalogue, (b) to keep group-related entries together in a catalogue. A third function of a heading is to display entries either singly or in groups. This function has become more important in the various forms of printed catalogues that have become common in recent years. The heading is generally the author, subject, or first word not an article, of the title, but may be the class number. *See also* ENTRY WORD, FORM HEADING, FORM SUB-HEADING, SUB-HEADING, UNIFORM HEADING. 2. (*Indexing*) The word(s) or symbol(s) selected from, or based on, an item in the text, used as an additional part of an entry; this includes any qualifying expression or epithet. Such words or symbols express the subject or idea to which reference is given and appear at the beginning of the entry. 3. The entry word followed by any other (or others) necessary for its meaning. 4. The word or words at the top of a page, chapter or section. 5. (*Book production, Printing*) Sub-headings which divide chapters and comprise CROSS-HEADS, INCUT NOTE, MARGINAL NOTES, SHOULDER-HEADS, SIDE-HEADS (*qq.v.*). 6. (*Information retrieval*) The word, name or phrase at the beginning of an entry to indicate some special aspect of the document (authorship, subject content, series, title, etc.) (*IBM*).

HEADLINE. The heading at the top of the page giving the title of the book (usually on the verso) or the subject of the chapter or of the page (usually on the recto). Also called 'Page head'. *See also* CAPTION TITLE, HALF TITLE, PAGE HEADLINE, RUNNING TITLE, SECTION HEADLINE. When giving the title of the book, even in abbreviated or different form, it may be called 'Head title'.

HEADQUARTERS. *See* COUNTY HEADQUARTERS.

HEADS. *See* HEAD MARGIN.

HEALTH AND REHABILITATIVE LIBRARY SERVICES. A Division of the American Library Association. *See* HRLSD.

HEAT COPYING. Making copies of documents by a heat process. *See also* THERMAL PROCESS, THERMOGRAPHY.

HEAT DEVELOPMENT PROCESS. A term sometimes applied to the

13

THERMAL DIAZO PROCESS (*q.v.*) and to processes using VESICULAR FILM (*q.v.*).

HEAT TRANSFER AND FLUID FLOW SERVICE INFORMATION CENTRE. *See* HTFS.

HECTOGRAPH PROCESS. A duplicating process in which the impression is transferred from a gelatine bed on to paper (gelatine hectograph), or from a master sheet on which the matter to be reproduced has been imprinted through a hectograph carbon and which is transferred to paper by means of a solvent such as industrial methylated spirit. This modern development is known as spirit duplicating.

HECTOGRAPHY. Reproducing an image by the hectograph process.

HEEL-NICK. *See* GROOVE.

HEIDELBERG. The name of a fully automatic printing press made by the Schnellpressenfabrik A.G., Heidelberg. The first press was a platen press made in 1914, in which the paper was fed by revolving wings. The Cylinder Heidelberg, first marketed in 1936, is a single-revolution machine in which the cylinder, moving at a constant speed, makes one revolution for each impression.

HEIGHT TO PAPER. The exact height of type from the bottom (or feet) of the type to the printing surface. Types of the exact height will print evenly; those which are too high receive too much pressure while those too low receive little or no pressure. Also called TYPE HEIGHT (*q.v.*).

HEILIGENBILDER. *See* HELGEN.

HELGEN. Woodcuts printed on paper at the end of the fourteenth century and beginning of the fifteenth. They were usually very simple black-line pictures, often hand-coloured, with little or no shading, and consisted of pictures of the saints or other religious subjects. They were intended to illustrate the teachings of the wandering monks who distributed them to the illiterate peasantry. Also called 'Heiligenbilder'.

HELIOGRAPH. A print made by Albrecht Breyer of Berlin who used the REFLEX COPYING (*q.v.*) process in 1839. He placed silver chloride papers in contact with the printed pages to be copied.

HELIOGRAPHIC MATERIALS. Those used to make a HELIOGRAPH (*q.v.*) print.

HELIOGRAPHY. 1. An obsolete name for photography. 2. In photo-engraving, the art of fixing the images produced by the *camera obscura*.

HELIOGRAVURE. Any photo-engraving process by which intaglio engravings are made.

HELLBOX. (*Printing*) The box into which damaged or broken type made on a casting machine is thrown for melting down and re-casting.

HELPFUL ORDER. The order of items in a classification schedule which displays the subjects in such a way that the order itself leads the user to the specific subject needed.

HELPIS. Acronym of Higher Education Learning Programmes Information Service, a British project which was begun in 1970 by the NATIONAL COUNCIL FOR EDUCATIONAL TECHNOLOGY (*q.v.*) at the request of the Department of Education and Science and the University Grants Committee to take responsibility for the exchange of information about teaching and learning materials produced in all sections of higher and further education. Published *Catalogue of some audio-visual materials made by institutions of higher and further education* the first comprehensive list of non-book materials to be processed, along book-format lines, by computer.

HEMI-CELLULOSES. (*Paper*) Impure forms of cellulose consisting of organic substances, comprising, in the main, sugars, starches and carbohydrates. These are associated with cellulose (which is formed from the elements carbon, hydrogen and oxygen, and obtained from the atmosphere by the process known as photosynthesis) in plant fibres. A high hemi-cellulose content in pulp is desirable as this provides a paper with good bonding and folding qualities.

HEMP. A fibre derived from the tissue of an annual plant which is grown extensively in America, Asia and many parts of Europe. Hemp, hemp refuse, twines and old ropes are used to make brown wrapping paper and cable insulating paper.

HER MAJESTY'S STATIONERY OFFICE. The government publisher in Britain, variously named 'Her Majesty's' or 'His Majesty's' according to whether the ruling monarch is a queen or king. The HMSO prints all parliamentary publications and many others but arranges with commercial printers to print much that is published. The printing of stationery and the purchase of books is undertaken for government departments and libraries as well as the publishing for all government departments. HMSO publishes more titles than any other British publisher. It is also the agency in the United Kingdom for publications of Unesco, the United Nations and some other international bodies and governments. *See also* NON-PARLIAMENTARY PUBLICATIONS, PARLIAMENTARY PAPERS, PARLIAMENTARY PUBLICATIONS.

HERALDIC CRESTING. Cresting on bindings, the projections of which terminate in heraldic (usually Tudor) emblems. *See also* CREST-ING ROLL.

HERTFORDSHIRE COUNTY COUNCIL TECHNICAL INFOR-MATION SERVICE. *See* HERTIS.

HERTIS. Abbreviation for Hertfordshire County Council Technical Information Service. A scheme, conceived in 1956, and based on the integrated resources of the Hatfield Polytechnic (on which it is centred – the library having the majority of the specialized resources) and fifteen Colleges of Technology and Further Education in the County. There is close collaboration with the public library sector in the Hertfordshire Library Service, and with the many industrial and research libraries in the area. Emphasis has been placed on exploiting library resources through an active information service available to local industry and the professions. Industrial members subscribe according to use. Books, periodicals and other material may be borrowed, and information obtained, by the members. With the aid of a grant from OSTI, a laboratory to study improved reprographic processes has been established under the name of the NATIONAL REPROGRAPHIC CENTRE FOR DOCUMENTATION (*q.v.*).

HEURES. *See* BOOK OF HOURS.

HEURISTIC SEARCHING. The searching for information or a document by the user of a library, the search being modified as it progresses, each piece of information or document found tending to influence the user's continuous search.

HEURISTIC TECHNIQUES. In machine indexing, simulations of human methods of learning and problem solving. Functionally heuristic programmes are designed to discover solutions to problems which they do by setting up goals and sub-goals, which are then put in order and tested to determine whether in fact any of the solution sequences fully satisfy the requirements of the problem.

HIERARCHIC. 1. Arranged in serial rank rather than ordinal position. 2. Pertaining to a generic classification or organization of materials (*IBM*).

HIERARCHICAL CLASSIFICATION. 1. A scheme of classification in which the schedules are developed systematically, every term, descriptor, or isolate (*See* ISOLATE 3) showing a logical relationship to each preceding and following term. 2. A scheme of classification in which the terms are arranged according to a hierarchical principle and are consequently arranged in subordination to other terms. The Dewey Classification is of this kind. The opposite of an ENUMERATIVE CLASSIFICATION (*q.v.*).

HIERARCHICAL FORCE. (*Classification*) The property by which headings and certain notes apply to all subdivisions of the topic described and defined.

HIERARCHICAL NOTATION. (*Classification*) A NOTATION (*q.v.*) which is designed to show that two terms are in the same array, chain, hierarchy or facet. The chains and arrays of symbols reflect the hierarchy of terms. All main classes are represented by symbols of equal length, and new main classes are inserted by the introduction of new digits. Also called 'Expressive notation', 'Structural notation'.

HIERARCHICAL RELATION. (*Information retrieval*) Relationship between two concepts or classes in a classification scheme in which one is subordinate to the other. *See also* RELATION.

HIERARCHICAL SEARCH. An examination of entries in a subject catalogue under heads which constitute a CHAIN (*q.v.*): it is conducted in an upward direction from the most, to the least, specific heading. Also called 'General search'. *See also* ALPHABETICAL COLLATERAL SEARCH, SUBSTITUTION GENERIC, SYSTEMATIC COLLATERAL SEARCH.

HIERARCHY. The order of precedence in which subjects are set out in the schedule of a scheme of classification. Where each element in a sequence of terms has a unique predecessor as in the traditional classificatory tree (*see* PORPHYRY, TREE OF), this is known as *strong hierarchy*; each given class is immediately subordinate only to a single genus. *Weak hierarchy* is where an element may have more than one predecessor; a given descriptor (e.g. plastic transparency tray) may be immediately subordinate to more than one generic descriptor (plastic tray, transparency tray).

HIEROGLYPH. A character, originally in the form of picture-writing engraved in stone by the ancient Egyptians, to convey thoughts or information. Any symbol or character used in any form of picture-writing. The meaning of the ancient Egyptian symbols was discovered in 1799 by Champollion when he deciphered the Rosetta Stone, now in the British Museum, on which was a parallel text in hieroglyphics, demotic script and Greek.

HIEROGLYPHICS. 1. Ancient Egyptian picture-writing; hence symbols or characters used in any picture-writing. 2. The form of communicating information or ideas by hieroglyphs.

HIEROGRAM. A sacred character or written symbol.

HIEROGRAPHIC. Pertaining to sacred writing.

HIERONYM. A sacred name used as a surname.

HIGHER EDUCATION LEARNING PROGRAMMES INFORMATION SERVICE. *See* HELPIS

HIGHLIGHT.   The white, or light, parts of a photograph, drawing or half-tone block. Also called 'Drop-out half-tone'.

HILC.   Abbreviation for Hampshire Inter-Library Center which originated at the end of 1951 as a joint enterprise between the three colleges of Amherst, Mt. Holyoke and Smith in western Massachusetts. The University of Massachusetts and Hampshire College now participate with the three mentioned. Aim: to provide a jointly-owned research collection to supplement the holdings of the participating institutions. Members contribute funds which, with money obtained from the sale of duplicates, provide for limited acquisition of rarely consulted serials and expensive sets. The Center also subscribes to 700 journals not in member libraries which are circulated to each college library for three months and then retained at the Center and are available on request. It is based at the campus of the University of Massachusetts. Publishes *Annual Report, Newsletter*.

HINGE.   (*Binding*) A strip of paper or fabric, placed between the two halves of an endpaper, where the body of the book is fixed to the covers, to give strength. In America this term is used to indicate the part of the book identified by the groove along the front and back covers when they join the back strip or spine, allowing the book to be opened easily. *See also* JOINT.

HINGED.   Plates, maps or other separate sheets to be inserted in a book, which have been given a narrow fold on the inner edges so that there is little chance of the sheets tearing away from those to which they are attached; also so that they will lie flat, and turn easily in use, when bound.

HINGED AND JOINTED PLATES.   Two adjoining plates from which a strip has been cut away at the binding edge and then joined together by means of a common strip of linen or paper to form a hinge and joints.

HISTORIATED INITIAL.   An initial, capital or border of a mediaeval MS. or early book decorated with figures of men and/or animals, rather than illuminated with flowers or conventional designs; a representation of a person or scene, illustrating the text it introduces. *See also* INHABITED INITIAL.

HISTORICAL BIBLIOGRAPHY.   Dealing with the history and methods of book production – printing, binding, paper making, illustrating and publishing. Also called 'analytical', 'applied', 'critical', 'descriptive', 'external', or 'material' bibliography.

HISTORICAL MANUSCRIPTS COMMISSION.   Founded 1869 to discover and publish papers of historical importance. Until recently its principal activity was the publication of printed Reports and

Calendars. Since 1945, and especially since the new warrant of 1959, its activities have proliferated: it maintains the NATIONAL REGISTER OF ARCHIVES (*q.v.*), new series of publications are appearing, including a list of *Record repositories in Great Britain*, (4th ed., 1971), joint publications in conjunction with record societies, publication of papers of nineteenth-century prime ministers, a guide to scientists' papers under a joint Royal Society/HMC committee, and a summary guide, list by list, to the contents of the National Register of Archives. *Reports to the Crown* now appear every five years and an Annual Report is published. *Sectional List 17* (*gratis* from HMSO) gives the Warrant and details of publications.

HISTORY CARD.   A card inserted in a catalogue and giving particulars, under the name of a corporate body, of dates of foundation, incorporation, changes of name, affiliation with other bodies, etc. Also called 'Information card'.

HISTORY ENTRY.   An entry in a catalogue which gives changes of name, affiliations, etc., concerning a person or corporate body, or in the wording of a title, together with significant dates. Such entries precede specific entries under the appropriate headings.

HISTORY FILE.   *Synonymous with* ORGANIZATION FILE.

HIT.   Term used in mechanized retrieval systems to represent an apparent answer found by the machine (*IBM*).

HOLDING AREA.   (*Archives*) Space assigned for storing semi-current records temporarily.

HOLDINGS.   1. The stock (books, pamphlets, periodicals, microrecords, and other material) possessed by a library. 2. Specifically, the volumes, or parts of serial publications, possessed by a library.

HOLDINGS CARD.   A catalogue card which shows the volumes or parts of a work which the library has. It is usually the main entry card.

HOLIDAY GUIDE.   A publication giving particulars of a town which caters for holiday makers.

HOLIDAY ISSUE.   Books issued in excess of the usual number and for a longer period than usual to persons going on holiday.

HOLING.   The drilling, or punching, of holes in the boards of a book to take the slips or cords ready for lacing. Also called 'Holing out.'

HOLING OUT.   *Synonymous with* HOLING (*q.v.*).

HOLKHAM BIBLE PICTURE BOOK.   A MS. probably made in London for a Dominican patron between 1326 and 1331 and now in the British Museum. It has no contemporary title and consists of forty-two leaves all but two of which are illustrated with 231 pictures.

HOLLANDER. *(Paper)* A beater or beating engine of the type made in Holland towards the end of the seventeenth century.

HOLLOW. The space between the back of a book itself (i.e. the folded and sewn sheets) and the spine of a HOLLOW BACK *(q.v.)* book.

HOLLOW BACK. A binding in which there is a space between the back of the book itself and the cover, caused by the leather, cloth or other material being attached at the joints, and not glued to the back of the book itself. Also called 'Loose back', 'Open back'. Sometimes a tube of thin card or paper is flattened and pasted between section folds and spine-covering. A publisher's case binding is of this type. *See also* CASE. When the cover is glued to the back it is known as a TIGHT BACK *(q.v.)*.

HOLLOW QUADS. Large quads which are cast with hollow parts to make them lighter and save metal. Also used of type which is occasionally cast similarly for the same reason.

HOLOGRAPH. 1. A document or manuscript wholly in the handwriting of its author. Hence, holograph reprint, a reproduction of a MS. by mechanical means. 2. A recording on photo-sensitive film, made without the use of lenses, by combining two or more laser beams of different colour to form a single beam. When the holograph is viewed in white light a three-dimensional, multi-colour picture is revealed.

HOLOGRAPHY. The process of making holographs. *See* HOLOGRAPH 2.

HOLOTHEME. All the notions (things or characteristics mentioned as subject matter) considered as subject-matter.

HOME BINDERY. 1. A binding department maintained by a library committee and under the control of the librarian. 2. A method of developing the book-buying habit in Asia. It is run by a single publisher who has a strong and varied list of publications, or by a wholesale bookseller, and incorporates features of book clubs in the West. New subscribers who undertake to purchase at a specially low price a specified number of books in a year from a large selection offered, are entitled to buy the season's best sellers at extremely low prices.

HOME READING DEPARTMENT. *Synonymous with* LENDING DEPARTMENT *(q.v.)*.

HOMO. *See* MARLIS.

HOMOGRAPH. One of several words having the same spelling but a different meaning, e.g. Birmingham (Alabama), Birmingham (England); skate (fish), skate (sport); game (sport), game (fowl). These should be avoided in subject headings and indexes where possible, but when unavoidable, a qualifying, or defining word or phrase should be added to each in order to clarify the meanings and to separate entries on different subjects. *See also* HOMONYM, HOMO-PHONE.

HOMOLOGY.   The principle used in forming schedules in a classification which uses the similarity of essential characteristics as a basis of division.

HOMONYM.   1. An identical name (surname and forenames) for two or more people. A namesake. Also an identical corporate, or other, name. 2. One of several words which may have a different origin and meaning but the same sound and possibly a different spelling, e.g. pail (bucket), pale (stake), pale (wan).

HOMONYMIC, HOMONYMOUS.   Having the same name.

HOMOPHONE.   A word with a different spelling and meaning as another but with the same pronunciation, e.g. rough, ruff.

HOMOTOPIC ABSTRACT.   An abstract of an article published in the same issue of a journal as the article abstracted.

HONORIFIC EPITHET.   (*Cataloguing. Indexing*) A title of honour or of rank which is appended to a heading (and so becomes part of it) for identification but which may or may not be used as a FILING EPITHET (*q.v.*).

HONORIFIC TITLE.   A title conferred on a person to indicate royalty, nobility, rank, or an honour. The whole name is sometimes incorporated with that of an organization or activity with which the person was associated. Examples: John XIV, *Pope*; Mountbatten, *Earl*, *Field-Marshal*; Princess Mary Home; Bishop Creighton House; Sir Halley Stewart Trust; Lord Roberts Workshops. A 'title of honour'.

HOOKED ON OWN GUARD.   The method of securing a single-leaf illustration by folding its binding edge, so as to form a guard, around the fold of the section before sewing. *See also* GUARD 1 (2), PLATE GUARDED AND HOOKED.

HORAE.   *See* BOOK OF HOURS.

HORIZONTAL.   A series or classification in which the terms, or classes, are arranged in a horizontal line. The several classes are then usually regarded as co-ordinate; but a series of successively subordinate classes and sub-classes might also be so arranged, instead of in a column (*Bliss*). *See also* COLUMNAR, TABULAR CLASSIFICATION.

HORN BOOK.   A children's primer which appeared towards the end of the sixteenth century. It consisted of a thin sheet of vellum or paper mounted on an oblong piece of wood and covered with transparent horn. The wooden frame had a handle by which it was hung from the child's girdle. The sheet bore the alphabet, the vowels in a line followed by the vowels combined with consonants in tabular form, the Roman numerals, the Lord's Prayer, and the exorcism 'in the name of the Father and of the Sonne and of the Holy Ghost, Amen!' A simpler and later form of Horn book, consisting of the tablet without the horn covering, or a piece of varnished cardboard, and resembling a horn book without the handle, was called a battledore.

Hors texte. Illustrations to a book which are without text matter. A plate. They are usually numbered with roman numerals to avoid confusion with numbered illustrations in the text (which are usually in line) and with the pagination of a book.

HOSPITAL LIBRARIES AND HANDICAPPED READERS GROUP. A Group of the Library Association which was formed in 1962 following the activities of the Guild of Hospital Librarians between 1934 and 1953 and sporadic meetings of hospital librarians subsequently. It seeks to provide facilities for librarians concerned with meeting the reading needs of those who are physically or mentally handicapped (whether in hospital or not), to meet and exchange views and impart information, and to arrange for reports and books of particular interest to members to be written and published. Publishes *Book Trolley* on and after March 1974 renamed *Health and Welfare Libraries Quarterly* (q.).

HOSPITAL LIBRARY. A library provided for the use of hospital patients and sometimes the staff, either by the hospital authority, a voluntary organization, or a public library. In England the Ministry of Health contributes a fixed sum per occupied bed towards the cost of the service.

HOSPITALITY. (*Classification*) The quality of a notation which enables new subjects to be inserted in their appropriate place. A feature of the notation of the Colon Classification in which it is virtually infinite, and is achieved by combining the decimal fraction principle with the faceted principle. *Hospitality in array,* i.e. the ability to accommodate co-ordinate topics, is achieved by (1) the octave device, (2) group notation, (3) the chronological device, (4) the subject device, and (5) the alphabetical device. *Hospitality in chain,* i.e. the simultaneous specification of all the facets of a subject, if necessary, and the ability to specify new facets in their correct sequence, is secured by (1) decimal fractions, (2) faceted notation, (3) the apportionment of 'sectors', or zones, of notation to different array within the same facet, (4) auto-bias, (5) intra-facet relation and (6) phase relations.

HOST BOOK. As used in connexion with the Colon Classification, a book about which another is written, as e.g. a criticism or a reply; the latter is called an ASSOCIATED BOOK (*q.v.*).

HOST DOCUMENT. A MACRO-DOCUMENT (*q.v.*) when considered from the point of view of a document forming part of it; e.g., a periodical would be considered a macro-document, and each article in it a micro-document; the periodical would then be the host document for each of the articles in it.

HOT MELT. In bookbinding, a glue which is applied hot and sets immediately when used on a cool surface.

HOT-METAL TYPESETTING. A method of typesetting which uses a process for casting type from molten metal (e.g. Intertype, Monotype, Linotype) as distinct from COLD COMPOSITION (*q.v.*).

HOT-PRESSED. Good quality rag paper which is given a glazed, smooth finish by being pressed with hot metal plates. Abbreviated H.P. *See also* FINISH, NOT, ROUGH.

HOUSE CORRECTIONS. Corrections, or alterations, made to a script or proof by the publisher or printer's proof reader, as distinct from those made by the author.

HOUSE JOURNAL. A periodical produced by a commercial or industrial organization, either for internal distribution amongst the staff and employees or externally to customers. Its purpose is to interest readers in the technical side of the organization's activities, rather than the social or personal side, which is more the concern of the 'House magazine'. Also called 'House organ'.

HOUSE MAGAZINE. *See* HOUSE JOURNAL.

HOUSE OF COMMONS BILLS. Public Bills, printed by HMSO on pale green paper for consideration in the House of Commons. *See also* PRIVATE BILLS.

HOUSE OF COMMONS PAPERS. Reports and returns which have to be presented to the House under the provisions of various Acts of Parliament, reports from government departments compiled by direct order of the House, and reports of the Standing Committees and Select Committees of the House.

HOUSE OF LORDS PAPERS AND BILLS. A series of publications consisting almost entirely of Public Bills but also a few Papers. Public Bills are printed by H.M.S.O. on pale green paper.

HOUSE OF LORDS RECORD OFFICE. Contains over 1,500,000 records of Parliament as a whole dating back to 1497. They are in the custody of the Clerk of the Parliaments. The Search Room is open to the public who may also be granted access to the Journals of the House of Commons (from 1547), and to the other surviving records of the Commons (from 1572). Records of Parliament prior to 1497 are preserved in the PUBLIC RECORD OFFICE (*q.v.*).

HOUSE ORGAN. *See* HOUSE JOURNAL.

'HOUSE' PAPERS. *See* PARLIAMENTARY PAPERS.

HOUSE STYLE. The typesetting style normally used in a printing establishment or publishing house. *See also* STYLE MANUAL, STYLE OF THE HOUSE, STYLE SHEET.

HOUSEKEEPING. Routine and continuing library operations, such as book ordering, accessioning, cataloguing, processing, and the circulation, etc. of documents and other library materials. In computer operations, it is generally contrasted with information retrieval.

HUDDERSFIELD AND DISTRICT INFORMATION SERVICE. *See* HADIS.

HULL SCHEME. *See* HULTIS.

HULTIS. The Humberside Libraries Technical Interloan Scheme, previous to April 1974 the Hull Technical Interloan Scheme, is centred on the Library of Science, Technology and Commerce in Hull Central Library. Industrial, academic and other specialized libraries in the area agree to lend to each other with certain safeguards and limits set out in the Rules and Constitution. Minimum qualifications for free membership are three current specialized periodicals and 25 specialized books. A computer-produced Checklist of Members Periodicals is revised annually (price £4 includes the Supplement). News and information is included in the monthly *Commercial and Technical Bulletin*. A *Members' Handbook and Directory* provides more detailed information on individual members with an index of their specialized interests.

HUMANIST. 1. A group of type faces, formerly known as 'Venetian' and derived from the fifteenth-century style of minuscule handwriting characterized by a varying stroke thickness achieved by means of an obliquely-held broad pen. In faces in this group the cross stroke of the lower case 'e' is oblique, the axis of the curves is inclined to the left, there is little contrast between thin and thick strokes, the serifs are bracketed, and the serifs of the ascenders of the lower case letters are oblique. Examples of this category of type faces are Verona, Centaur and Kennerley. *See also* TYPE FACE. 2. Also a group of LINEALE (*q.v.*) type faces based on the proportions of roman capitals and Humanist or GARALDE (*q.v.*) lower-case letters, rather than on the early grotesques which are another group of Lineales. They have some contrast between the thick and thin strokes, and the 'a' and 'g' are two-storey.

HUMANISTIC HAND. A mediaeval hand-writing less angular than Gothic, based on Old Roman capitals and the Carolingian minuscule. It was a result of the Renaissance in the fifteenth century which brought a general awakening of interest in classic, and pre-Christian literature. Also called 'Neo-Caroline'.

HUMBERSIDE LIBRARIES TECHNICAL INTERLOAN SCHEME. *See* HULTIS.

HUNDRED ROLLS, of A.D. 1274. Public records of great importance for local history, containing an inquisition into the state of every hundred (a division of a county) and answers, on oath, to questions relating to the public exchequer.

HUNTINGTON LIBRARY. One of the most famous of scholars' libraries of Americana and English literature. It is situated in San Marino, California, U.S.A., and is surpassed only by the British Museum and the Bodleian libraries, in the quality and importance of its British books. The library is in a building which was opened in 1920 and was especially designed to protect and preserve the valuable collection of books in the grounds of Huntington House (formerly the home of Henry Edwards Huntington, 1850–1927) which houses the Art Gallery containing some of the world's famous pictures. The stock totals 390,000 volumes and 3,000,000 MSS.

HYDROGRAPHIC CHART. A chart of coasts and harbours.

HYPHEN. The shortest rule used for punctuation. It is used to join compound words, or as the link at the end of a line to join the parts of a word which cannot be set in one line. *See also* DASH.

HYPHEN STRINGING. (*Indexing*) The process of using hyphens to bind terms in order to convey more information, as well as for filing purposes.

HYPO. Abbreviation for hyposulphite of soda (formerly known as sodium thiosulphate) which is used in photography for fixing prints.

HYPOSOMETRIC MAP. One on which the successive altitudes are indicated by the system of colour tints.

I & R. Information and referral service.

IAC. An INFORMATION ANALYSIS CENTRE (*q.v.*).

IBBD. Acronym of the Institute Brasileiro de Bibliografia a Documentação (Brazilian Institute of Bibliography and Documentation); situated in Rio de Janeiro, it is the country's national bibliographical information centre.

IBI – ICC. Abbreviation for the Intergovernmental Bureau for Informatics – International Computation Centre. Established as an intergovernmental institution by international treaty which became effective as from 11th November 1961. Aims: to promote research, education and utilization of informatics at government level. With this objective, the Bureau operates in a number of ways to further the use of informatics in economic and industrial planning and development. It operates from Rome. Publishes *IBI – ICC Newsletter* (6 p.a.), *International Directory of Computer and Information systems* (a).

IBY. Acronym of the International Book Year which was organized by Unesco and held on a worldwide basis in 1972 to promote books and encourage reading. *See also* INTERNATIONAL BOOK AWARD, INTERNATIONAL BOOK COMMITTEE.

ICAE. Acronym of the International Council for Adult Education, a non-governmental organization whose chief function is to facilitate development and exchange of experience in adult education, 'adult education' in this connection including those who are interested in many associated fields such as functional literacy, publishing and libraries, manpower training, labour education and 'learning at a distance'. The Council does not duplicate the work of existing institutions but works with and through them in order to build upon and support their activities. The Secretariat is in Toronto. Publishes *Convergence* (q.) *Newsletter* (irreg.).

ICIC. Acronym of the International Copyright Information Centre, and its establishment, at Unesco Headquarters, Paris, was approved at the 16th Session of Unesco in 1970. Functions: to: (a) collect copyright information on books that can be made available to developing countries on terms as favourable to them as possible; (b) arrange for the transfer to developing countries of rights ceded by copyright holders; (c) help in the development of simple model forms of contracts for translation, reprint and other rights required by developing countries; (d) study ways and means of securing copyright and other rights as well as methods of financing the rights required where foreign currency is not available; (e) promote arrangements for the adaptation and publication of works, particularly those of a technical and educational nature; (f) encourage the formation of national copyright information centres in both developed and developing countries, and act as a link between them; (g) provide assistance to developing countries for the organization of training courses for translators and covering all aspects of the publishing industry, for the provision of fellowships and equipment, for the joint publication of technical works, and for bringing together pedagogical authorities to develop adaptations of works. Publishes *Information Bulletin* (irreg.) which gives information on the centres and serves as a link for the exchange of information and ideas on copyright activities.

ICIREPAT. Abbreviation for the Paris Union Committee for International Co-operation in Information Retrieval among Patent Offices, which is part of the World Intellectual Property Organization (WIPO). Aim: to promote international co-operation in the field of storage and retrieval of technical information needed in connection with the search or examination of applications for patents, inventors' certificates or other similar documents. It was established in Munich in 1962 and became in 1968 a Committee of Experts of the Paris Union; membership was open to all members of that Union. It was visualized as an organization to help patent offices throughout the world solve their search problems co-operatively and to avoid duplication of effort. The Secretariat operates at WIPO in Geneva. *See also* INPADOC.

ICLG. Acronym of the International and Comparative Librarianship Group. A Group of the Library Association, formed in 1968 with the object of uniting librarians concerned with international and comparative librarianship and fostering relations with librarians abroad. The Group arranges meetings which are addressed by foreign librarians and at which problems of international librarianship may be discussed. Publishes *Focus on International and Comparative Librarianship* (3 p.a.).

ICOGRADA. Abbreviation for International Council of Graphic Design Associations which has (at the Bolton College of Art and Design, Bolton, U.K.) an Audio/Visual Library and Archive. The aims of this library are to establish and maintain a collection of magnetic tape recordings, films and photographic slides concerned with graphic communications, graphic techniques and educational matters. Publishes *Icographic* (*q.*).

IEAB. Acronym for the Internacia Esperanto-Asocio de Bibliotekistoj (International Association for Esperanto-Speaking Librarians) which was formed in 1972. Amongst its aims are: (a) the promotion of Esperanto for use in library affairs; (b) the building of Esperanto collections, both instructional and literary, in all major world libraries; (c) the promotion of Esperanto-language sections in the various national library associations; (d) the encouragement of bibliographical and literary projects, and the compilation of Esperanto bibliographies and translations of important technical literature (in the library field) into Esperanto.

i.e. Abbreviation for *id est* (*Lat.* 'that is').

IGC. Abbreviation for Intergovernmental Copyright Committee which was established in Geneva on 6th September 1952; it is administered by Unesco. Aims: to study the problems concerning the operation of the Universal Copyright Convention of 1952; make preparations for periodic revisions thereof; study any other problems concerning the international protection of copyright (or which may affect copyright) in co-operation with the various interested international organizations. It works jointly with the Berne Convention which is basically concerned with copyright. *See also* BERNE COPYRIGHT UNION, COPYRIGHT, INTERNATIONAL, WIPO.

IMCE. Acronym of the International Meeting of Cataloguing Experts which met in Copenhagen in 1969 (prior to the IFLA Conference) to examine closely *inter alia* an annotated edition, in a provisional form, of the *Statement of principles* with a view to the preparation of a definitive edition. Another working party was formed to prepare the International Standard Bibliographic Description to serve the needs of catalogues and national bibliographies, and which would include all the bibliographical data required for catalogues, bibliographies and other records, e.g. book orders. *See also* INTERNATIONAL CONFERENCE ON CATALOGUING PRINCIPLES, ISBD, PARIS PRINCIPLES.

i.q. Abbreviation for *idem quod* (*Lat.* 'the same as').

IRS. Abbreviation for International Referral System for Sources of Environmental Information which was set up at the June 1972 U.N. Conference. It functions as a switchboard mechanism between users and sources of information.

ISBD. Acronym for International Standard Bibliographical Description. A group of standards, the first of which was officially adopted by the International Federation of Library Association's Committee on Cataloguing at its meeting in Liverpool in 1971 and published by this Committee the same year. Its primary objective is to provide a standard for preparing the descriptive portion of bibliographic entries (including catalogue entries) prepared by the national bibliographic and cataloguing agencies of all countries. The Standard is being used by the *British National Bibliography*; it does not differ appreciably from the *Anglo-American cataloguing rules* although there are some significant departures. The first standard was confined to monographic publications; subsequent ones dealing with serials and audiovisual materials are referred to below. Abbreviated ISBD. *International standard bibliographic description (for single volume and multi-volume* *monographic publications*), which was recommended by the Working Group set up at the International Meeting of Cataloguing Experts, Copenhagen, 1969, was published by the IFLA Committee on Cataloguing in December 1971. The 'first standard edition' of *ISBD(M) International standard bibliographic description for monographic publications* was published in 1974, and superseded the 1971 text. Its purpose is to provide an internationally accepted framework for the presentation of descriptive information in bibliographic records of monographic, i.e. non-serial, publications. It is being used in a number of national bibliographies. This is referred to as ISBD(M) to distinguish it from later work on serials known as ISBD(S) which was published in January 1974 with the title *ISBD(S), International standard bibliographic description for serials*. This specifies requirements for the description and identification of printed serial publications. Work is being undertaken by others on the preparation of ISBD(A/V) for audio-visual materials. ISBD(G). – the General International Standard Bibliographical Description – was drawn up in 1975 and provides a single framework for the description of all types of publication in all types of media; it is to be used as the basis for the rules of the ANGLO-AMERICAN CODE (*q.v.*) and also for all specialised ISBDs in future, in order to ensure an optimum level of uniformity in IFLA's programme of ISBD development as a whole. ISBD(NBM) is a projected International Standard Bibliographical Description for Non-Book Materials which are included in the stock of libraries. This project was discussed by the Committee on Cataloguing of the International Federation of Library Associations (IFLA/FIAB). *See also* ANGLO-AMERICAN CODE, ISBD(G).

ISBD(A/V). *See* ISBD.

ISBD(G). The Joint Steering Committee for Revision of the Anglo-American Cataloguing Rules has stated that the second edition of the *Rules* (AACR) will be a newly formulated general international standard bibliographic description of all types of media, thus providing a single framework for all specialized types of ISBDs hereafter in order to ensure an optimum level of uniformity in IFLA's programme of ISBD development as a whole.

ISBD(M).† *See* ISBD.

ISBD(NBM).† *See* ISBD.

ISBD(S).† *See* ISBD.

ISBN. Acronym for International Standard Book Number. A number which is given to every book or edition of a book before publication to identify the publisher, the title, the edition and volume number.

The ISBN consists of ten digits (arabic o to 9) the first group of which is a group identifier and indicates a national geographical, language or other convenient group. The other digits comprising the ISBN are grouped to indicate the publisher and the title or edition of a title; the final digit serves as a check digit. Each group of numbers is separated by a space or a hyphen. The ISBN system was a development of the STANDARD BOOK NUMBER (*q.v.*) system and was recommended for international use by the International Organization for Standardization (ISO) in October 1969 being accepted by the delegates to the plenary session then and circulated to all member bodies in 1970. The numbers comprising the ISBN are the same as a national SBN plus a preceding group identifier, and are allocated by the appropriate national standard book numbering agency. *See also* ISSN, STANDARD BOOK NUMBERING AGENCY.

ISDS. Acronym for INTERNATIONAL SERIALS DATA SYSTEM. An international network of operational centres (established in 1973 within the framework of the UNISIST (*q.v.*) programme) which are jointly responsible for the creation and maintenance of computer-based data banks. Objects: to (a) develop and maintain an international register of serial publications containing all the necessary information for identifying the serials; (b) define and promote the use of a standard code (ISSN – *q.v.*) for identifying each serial; (c) facilitate retrieval of scientific and technical information in serials; (d) make this information currently available to all countries, organizations or individual users; (e) establish a network of communication between libraries, secondary information services, publishers of serial literature and international organizations; (f) promote international standards for bibliographic description, communication formats, and information exchange in the area of serial publications. The system has an International Centre (IC) in Paris and also national and regional centres; the International Centre delegates to the national and regional centres (when these have been formed) the allocation of ISSNs in respect of serials published in their respective areas. The British Library is the national centre for the U.K., and the Library of Congress for the U.S. The IC handles the input of ISDS from countries that do not yet have a national centre. *See also* ISSN. The IC publishes *ISDS Bulletin* (*q.*).

ISMD. Acronym for International Standard Materiagraphic Description for Library Materials which was devised by Malcolm Shifrin. It is now in use in the Inner London Education Authority's Media Resources Centre as a cataloguing tool for materials of all kinds as well as in the SCELMIS (Schools and Colleges of Education Learning Materials Information Service) catalogue published by the Centre.

ISSN. Acronym for International Standard Serial Number – an internationally accepted code for the identification of serial publications; it is precise, concise, unique and unambiguous. The ISSN consists of seven arabic digits with an eighth which serves to verify the number in computer processing. A letter code indicating the country of publication may precede 'ISSN' as an additional identifier; this is optional. The International Organization for Standardization Technical Committee 46 (ISO/TL 46) is the agency responsible for the development of the ISSN. The organization responsible for the administration and assignment of ISSN is the International Centre (IC) of the International Serials Data System (ISDS – q.v.); this is supported by the French government and Unesco, and is situated in Paris. National and regional centres of ISDS are assuming responsibility for the registration and numbering of serials, but where these have not yet been established, this function is being performed by the IC. An ISSN is the tool for communicating basic information about a serial title with a minimum of error, and may be used by subscription agencies and publishers for such processes as ordering, invoicing and inventory control; authors may use it for copyright. It can be used by librarians for a number of administrative purposes. A serial may have an ISBN (q.v.) as well as an ISSN if the publication is one of a monographic series (each work being issued separately under a common title, generally in a uniform format with numeric designation), an annual or other work is a separately edited written publication related only to other works by having some relationship in content and similarity in format. The ISSN is assigned to the serial title whether 'dead' or 'alive' while the ISBN is assigned to each individual title or monograph in the series. *See also* ISBN.

IACODLA. Acronym of the International Advisory Committee on Documentation, Libraries and Archives which was established in 1967 to advise the Director-General of Unesco at his request, on questions of documentation in general, and in particular on those related to subject fields of interest to Unesco.

IADIS. Acronym of the Irish Association for Documentation and Information Services which was originally founded as the Irish Association for Documentation (q.v.), the name being changed, and a new constitution adopted, in 1967. Aims: 'to promote in Ireland the recording, organization and dissemination of specialized knowledge and information by providing for: (a) the collaboration of all documentation, information and library services in the acquisition and availability of books and other material, and the preparation of bibliographies, abstracts, indexes, systems of classification and other activities of documentation and information; (b) the encouragement of all measures for the improvement of the dissemination of specialized knowledge and information in Ireland, and for promoting co-operation with similar bodies in other countries.' Financed mainly through members' subscriptions, also by special grants made by some bodies towards the cost of publishing the *Union list of periodicals*. Membership is open to institutions and corporate bodies. Publishes *Union list of periodicals and serials in Irish libraries* (periodically), *Irish publishing record* (a.).

IAOL. Acronym of the International Association of Orientalist Librarians. Founded in 1967 to: (a) promote better communication between Orientalist librarians and libraries throughout the world; (b) provide a forum for the discussion of problems of common concern; (c) improve international co-operation among institutions holding research resources for oriental studies. Members: librarians in oriental studies and others who have an interest in the activities of the Association. Operates from the Graduate School of Library Studies, University of Hawaii, Honolulu. Financed through members' dues. Publishes *IAOL Newsletter* (2 p.a.), *Proceedings of IAOL Conference* (triennial).

IASLIC. Acronym for Indian Association of Special Libraries and Information Centres. Founded in September 1955 with the following aims: to encourage and promote the systematic acquisition, organization and dissemination of knowledge; to improve the quality of library and information services and documentation work; to co-ordinate the activities of, and to foster mutual co-operation and assistance among, special libraries, scientific, technological and research institutions, learned societies, commercial organizations, industrial research establishments, as well as other information and documentation centres to the fullest extent; to provide contact for libraries, information bureaux, documentation centres, scientists, research workers, specialists and others having a common interest; to improve the technical efficiency of the workers in special libraries and information and documentation centres, and to look after their professional welfare; to act as a centre of research in special librarianship and documentation techniques; to act as a centre of information in scientific, technical and other fields. Various categories of membership exist. Publishes working papers irregularly, technical pamphlets and monographs; also *IASLIC Bulletin* (q.).

ib., *ibid.* Abbreviation for *ibidem* (*Lat.* 'in the same place', 'the same reference'). Used in a footnote reference to avoid repeating the title of a work referred to immediately above. It can be used in successive references to the same work.

IBBY. Abbreviation for INTERNATIONAL BOARD ON BOOKS FOR YOUNG PEOPLE. Founded by Jella Lepman in 1953 in Zurich to promote international understanding through children's books. Has informational and consultative relations with Unesco. It is composed of national Sections from many countries which work within their own countries to promote children's books. Awards the Hans Christian Andersen Medal for important contributions to children's literature. International Children's Book Day (ICBD), originated by Jella Lepman, is a well-known activity of the Board observed each year throughout the world on 2nd April which is Hans Christian Andersen's birth date. The Board's secretariat is at Basle, Switzerland. A British Section has been formed, its secretary being based on the NATIONAL BOOK LEAGUE (*q.v.*). Publishes *Bookbird* (*q.*) in co-operation with the INTERNATIONAL INSTITUTE FOR CHILDREN'S LITERATURE AND READING RESEARCH (*q.v.*).

ICONOGRAPHY. 1. The study of the portraits, statues, coins, and other illustrative material relating to a person, place or thing. 2. The detailed listing of such material. 3. The art of illustrating, or representing, by figures, images, diagrams, etc.

id. Abbreviation for *idem* (*Lat.* 'the same [author or publication]'). Used in footnotes to avoid repeating an author's name, or other identity of a book or periodical when being referred to successively.

id est. (*Lat.* 'that is to say'). Abbreviated i.e.

IDA AND GEORGE ELIOT PRIZE ESSAY. *See* ELIOT PRIZE ESSAY, IDA AND GEORGE.

IDEAL ARRANGEMENT. (*Classification*) The mental operation resulting in placing things in order corresponding to an idea, or series of ideas, in the mind and in accordance with the mental picture of the things to be arranged. *Actual arrangement* is the physical placing in order, of specimens which can be seen or touched, such as botanical specimens, postage stamps or books.

IDENTIFICATION. (*Bibliography*) The discovery of the date of an undated book, or the determination of the precise edition, impression, issue or state of a given copy or series of copies of a book. (*Information retrieval*) A classification number, code number or code name which identifies a record, file, document or other unit of information.

IDENTIFICATION CAPTION. (*Reprography*) The identification symbol or phrase, both on the document and on the frame of micro-film, which is visible to the unaided eye.

IDENTIFICATION CARD. Used in place of a borrower's ticket in the NEWARK CHARGING SYSTEM (*q.v.*) and TRANSACTION CARD (*q.v.*) systems generally.

IDENTIFIERS. (*Information retrieval*) Terms, such as acronyms, projects, proper names of persons, geographical locations, the number of a patents specification or of a national 'standard', or any part of a bibliographical description, test names, and trades name which provide subject indexing, in addition to descriptors. Also called 'Identifying factors'.

IDENTIFY. (*Information retrieval*) To allocate and attach a unique code, or code name, to a unit of information.

IDENTIFYING FACTORS. *See also* IDENTIFIERS.

IDEOGRAM. *Synonymous with* IDEOGRAPH 2 (*q.v.*).

IDEOGRAPH. 1. An individual signature or trade mark. 2. A symbol or picture used in writing, e.g. in Chinese, to represent an object or an idea, and not, as in the phonetic system, the sounds which make up the name of these.

IDEOGRAPHY. The representation of ideas by graphic symbols ('ideograms'). A highly developed form of picture-writing in which ideas are conveyed by pictorial representation.

IFLA. Acronym for INTERNATIONAL FEDERATION OF LIBRARY ASSOCIATIONS (*q.v.*).

ILL. Abbreviation for INTER-LIBRARY LOAN (*q.v.*).

ill. (illus.). Abbreviation for illustrated, ILLUSTRATION/S (*q.v.*). *ill* is the recommended form of the abbreviation for use in the collation area of a cataloguing entry – revision of Chapter 6 of *AACR* (North American and British Texts). This revision also provides that 'ill.' is to include frontispiece which is no longer included in the collation statement.

ILLATIVE ABSTRACT. *See* ABSTRACT.

ILLINET. Abbreviation for Illinois Library and Information Network. An affiliation of over 550 school, academic and special libraries, which, with an administrative grant of $400,800 under the LSCA for a two-year project designed primarily as a multimedia advertising campaign to inform Illinois residents of basic and special library services available to them. A central information clearinghouse for librarians to share ideas and materials being produced for system and library publicity, is also provided.

ILLINOIS LIBRARY AND INFORMATION NETWORK. *See* ILLINET.

ILLUMINATED BINDING. A term used for all bindings which included extra colours, but particularly to those where a design was blocked in blind and the outline afterwards filled in with colour. Originally a French innovation, this style was practised in Britain from about 1830 to 1860.

ILLUMINATED BOOK. A book or manuscript, usually on vellum, decorated by hand, with designs and pictures in gold, silver and bright colours, not primarily to illustrate the text, but to make with it a unified whole.

ILLUMINATED INITIAL. A first letter of a word or paragraph decorated with colours, especially gold.

ILLUMINATION. The painting of initial letters at the commencement of a chapter of a MS. in gold, silver, or colour.

illus. Abbreviation for illustrated, illustration, illustrator.

ILLUSTRATIONS. Photographs, drawings, portraits, maps, plans, plates, tables, facsimiles, diagrams, etc., placed in a book to elucidate the text. Abbreviated illus. In the revision of Chapter 6 of *AACR*, (North American and British Texts) the collation statement '*ill*', for illustrations, is used to describe all types of illustrative matter unless particular types in the work are considered important enough to be specifically designated.

ILLUSTRATIONS COLLECTION. A collection of photographs, prints, drawings or reproductions of pictures assembled either for general use in public libraries or in institutions as an aid to their work or an essential part of the organization's activities. Called 'picture collections' in America; in Britain this term usually relates to a collection of original pictures or to a collection of reproductions of same. *See also* PICTURE FILE, PICTURE COLLECTION.

ILLUSTRATOR. A person who makes drawings and designs to illustrate a book or periodical.

ILLUSTRATOR ENTRY. A catalogue entry for an illustrator whose work is of sufficient importance to be catalogued.

IMAGE. 1. A design or picture to be reproduced by a printing process as an illustration. 2. (*Reprography*). That area within the frame (*see also* FRAME 4) which, after exposure and processing, contains the whole of the representation of the original.

IMAGE CARD. An APERTURE CARD (*q.v.*) which contains an image on exposed and processed microfilm in an aperture of the card. *See also* APERTURE CARD, CAMERA CARD.

IMAGIC. A thermal document-copying process which is not yet a commercial process. Designed by Mr. A. Games, the process is operated through distillation.

IMBRICATION. A style of book decoration in which the pattern consists of overlapping leaves or scales.

IMITATION ART. *See* ART.

IMITATION BINDING. A modern binding made to represent an old style.

IMITATION EMBOSSING. *Synonymous with* THERMOGRAPHY (*q.v.*).

IMITATION LEATHER. Paper or cloth embossed or finished to represent leather.

IMITATION PARCHMENT. A variety of tough paper first made by W. E. Gaine in 1857. It may be (a) rendered transparent, strong, grease-proof, and sometimes water-proof, by prolonged beating of the pulp, or (b) passed through a bath of sulphuric acid which 'toughens' the fibres.

impensis (*Lat.* 'at the expense of'). Used in an IMPRINT (*q.v.*) or COLOPHON (*q.v.*) of an early printed book to indicate the publisher, or bookseller or patron who was financially responsible for its publication.

IMPERFECT. A book which is found to have pages or sections omitted, duplicated, misplaced or inserted upside down, damaged or missing.

IMPERFECTIONS. Printed sheets rejected by the binder on account of being in some respect imperfect, and for which others are required to make the work complete.

IMPERIAL. A sheet of printing and drawing paper measuring 22 × 30 inches.

IMPERIAL WAR MUSEUM LIBRARY. One of the national libraries maintained by the British government. It is concerned only with collecting material relating to the Great War and later military operations involving Great Britain and the Commonwealth. There are three separate collections – Reference, Film, Photographic.

IMPORT. A book published in one country and imported into another. The importer may act as one of several importers or may have sole distribution rights over a given area. He may or may not arrange to have his own name placed on the title page as distributor or publisher either in addition to or in place of the original publisher's name, and he may do this by means of a small label.

IMPOSING STONE. *See* STONE.

IMPOSITION. The arrangement of the pages of type in the chase so that they will read consecutively when the printed sheet is folded. On correct imposition depends not only the right order of the pages but also REGISTER 3 (*q.v.*).

IMPRESSED WATERMARK. A watermark produced, not by the usual method, but by placing a stereo, in bronze, rubber, or other substance, on the press roll of the paper-making machine, and so leaving a design in the paper where it was more compressed. *See also* WATERMARK.

IMPRESSION. 1. (*Printing*) The copies of a book printed at the same time from the same type or plates. A *new impression* is one taken from the same standing type, or stereotype, as the original. An edition may consist of several impressions providing no alterations are made. Also called a 'Printing'. 2. All those copies of an edition printed at one time. B.S. 1413:1947 recommends that when a book is reprinted or reproduced from the same setting of type, the word 'impression' should be used and not the word 'edition'. *See also* EDITION, FIRST EDITION, ISSUE, REPRINT, REVISED EDITION. 3. The pressure applied to a forme of type by the cylinder or platen. 4. (*Binding*) The effect of impressing a block or type into the cover of a book. 5. A single copy of a print or map. 6. (*Illustration*) A print taken, by means of the special engraving press, from an engraved plate. *See also* STATE.

IMPRESSION CYLINDER. The roller of an offset printing press which presses the paper into contact with the blanket cylinder; or any cylinder around which the paper is carried during its contact with type or plates.

imprimatur (*Lat.* 'let it be printed'). The licence for publication, granted by a secular or ecclesiastical authority, carrying the name of the licenser, and the date (which may differ from that of the imprint). Usually printed at the beginning of a book: when on a separate leaf this is called a 'licence leaf'. Now rarely found except in the form of the words 'permissu superiorum' on works by Roman Catholic priests. This is distinct from copyright. Where state or church censorship exists, the imprimatur becomes an approval of what has been published.

IMPRINT. 1. The statement in a book concerning the publication or printing of a book. Also called 'Biblio'. The PUBLISHER'S IMPRINT is the name of the publisher and the date and place of publication, it usually appears at the foot of the title-page, and sometimes more completely on the back. The PRINTER'S IMPRINT gives the printer's name and the place of printing, it usually appears on the back of the title-page, on the last page of text, or on the page following. It is compulsory in all books printed in the United Kingdom (2 & 3 Vict. c. 12 S2).

See also COLOPHON, DISTRIBUTION IMPRINT. 2. (*Cataloguing and bibliography*) That part of an entry which gives the above particulars, though it is customary to omit the *place* of publication if it is the capital city of the country. When the imprint is covered by a label (usually giving the name of a publisher or agent in a country other than that of origin) the data for the catalogue entry is taken from the label. 3. (*Binding*) The name of (a) the owner; (b) the publisher appearing at the bottom of the spine; (c) the binder stamped on the cover of a book, usually at the bottom of the inside of the back board. 4. (*Printing*) The name of an OLD FACE type which is much used for book work. For a specimen alphabet see TYPE FACE.

IMPRINT DATE. The year of publication as specified on the title-page. *See also* DATE OF PUBLICATION.

IN BOARDS. 1. When a book is cut after the mill-boards are attached, it is said to be cut in boards. *See also* BOARDS. 2. A cheap style of binding common in the eighteenth and early nineteenth centuries, consisting of pasteboards covered with paper (usually blue sides and white spine). It was superseded by cloth. Occasionally used in the early twentieth century.

IN GALLEY. Type which has been set and is in a galley awaiting correction and making up into pages.

IN PENDENTIVE. (*Printing*) Typesetting in which successive lines are set in decreasing width, the first (and possibly second) line being set to the full measure, the subsequent ones being indented left and right of a central axis so that the last line of a page or paragraph is only a single word. It has the effect of a triangle resting on its apex.

IN PRINT. Said of a book which is available from the publisher.

IN PROGRESS. A term used in catalogues and elsewhere to indicate that a work in several volumes is not complete but still in course of publication. *See also* CHECK-LIST.

IN QUIRES. A book in unbound sheets. *See also* IN SHEETS.

IN SHEETS. Printed sheets of a book, either flat or folded, but unbound. This term is gradually replacing 'in quires' with which it is synonymous. *See also* SHEETS.

IN SLIP. Matter set up and proof-pulled on galleys before being made up into pages.

IN STOCK. Said of a book, copies of which are held by a book-seller for sale.

IN THE PRESS. A book which is in the actual process of being printed.

IN THE TRADE. Books published by, and obtainable from, commercial publishing firms rather than from government or private presses. (*American*).

INCIDENTAL MUSIC. Music written for performance during the presentation of a theatrical play or film whether it has an essential connexion with the plot, or story, or not.

incipit (*Lat.* '(here) begins'). The commencement of a mediaeval MS. or early printed book. The identity of the work and of the author may be found here if it is not given on the title-page or in the colophon.

INCIRS. Abbreviation for International Communication Retrieval System, a bibliographic programme established in 1974 at the Communications Research College of Journalism and Communications, University of Florida at Gainesville. It features comprehensive coverage of references pertaining particularly to Latin America, called LACIRS (Latin American Communication Information Retrieval System).

INCLUSION NOTE. (*Classification*) An enumeration of subordinate topics under a heading (and which are not obviously part of it) that have not yet been given separate provision. Such notes do not have HIERARCHICAL FORCE (*q.v.*).

INCOMPLETE. Said of a book from which a part has been omitted during manufacture.

INCUNABULA (*Sing.*, INCUNABULUM; Anglicized, INCUNABLE). Books printed before 1500, this date limitation probably deriving from the earliest known catalogue of incunabula: an appendix to Johann Saubert's *Historia bibliothecae Noribergensis . . . catalogus librorum proximis ab inventione annis usque ad a. Chr.* 1500 *editorum*, 1643. 'Incunabula' derives from the Latin 'cunae' (cradle) and indicates books produced in the infancy of printing; more specifically those which were printed before the use of loose type was common. It is said that Philippe Labbé (1607-67), a Parisian bibliographer, was the first to use the term 'incunabula' for the act of printing, not for the books themselves. The word was not used with this latter meaning until the late eighteenth century. Before the use of movable type, books were handwritten, and later printed from engraved wooden blocks (xylographic books).

INCUNABULIST. One who is well versed in a knowledge of incunabula.

INCUT HEADING. *See* CUT-IN HEADING.

INCUT NOTE. A side note which is let into the outer edge of a paragraph of text instead of appearing in the margin. Usually set in smaller and heavier type than the text. Also called 'Cut-in note', 'Cut-in side note', 'Let-in note'. *See also* CENTRE NOTE.

INDENT.   To begin a line of type a little way in, as at the beginning of a fresh paragraph.

INDENTED STYLE.   In book indexes, the typographical setting which allows subheadings to be indented, usually one em, the main heading being set flush to the lefthand margin. Sub-subheadings are further indented. *See also* RUN-ON STYLE.

INDENTION.   1. (*Printing*) The leaving of a blank space at the beginning of a line or a new paragraph. *See also* EM, HANGING INDENTION. 2. (*Cataloguing*) The distances from the left edge of a catalogue card at which the various parts of the entry begin. The purpose is to ensure uniformity in setting out the various parts of an entry. The 'first indention', at which the author's surname begins, is normally the first vertical line, or eighth typewriter space from the left-hand edge of the card; the 'second indention', at which the title begins, is then the second vertical line, or the tenth typewriter space, and the 'third indention' – for the second (indented) line of a two-line analytic author and title heading on a UNIT CARD (*q.v.*), or for any other indented entry beyond the second indention – the twelfth typewriter space. Akers' *Simple Library Cataloging* recommends 12 and 14 as the spacing for the second and third indentions; this is satisfactory for simple entries, but 10 and 12 are better for catalogues in larger libraries. *See also* FIRST INDENTION, SECOND INDENTION, THIRD INDENTION.

INDENTURE.   A document drawn up in duplicate and divided so as to leave a tooth-like edge on each part.

INDEPENDENT RESEARCH LIBRARIES ASSOCIATION.   *See* IRLA.

INDEPENDENTS.   Books or pamphlets published separately and afterwards bound together.

INDEX.   1. A systematically arranged list giving enough information for each item to be traced by means of a page number or other symbol indicating its position in a sequence. 2. A detailed alphabetical list or table of topics, names of persons, places, etc., treated or mentioned in a book or series of books, pointing out their exact positions in the volume, usually by page number (sometimes with an additional symbol indicating a portion of a page) but often by section, or entry, number. 3. A systematic guide to the location of words, concepts and other items in publications, documents and other records. An index consists of a series of entries appearing in some logical order, usually alphabetical, which enables the user to find them easily, together with references to show where each item is located. In 1964 the B.S.I. issued *Recommendations for the Preparation of Indexes for Books, Periodicals and Other Publications* (BS 3700); a thoroughly revised edition of this was published in 1975. 4. 'A systematic guide to items contained in, or concepts derived from, a collection. These items, or derived concepts, are represented by entries arranged in a known, or stated, searchable order, such as alphabetical, chronological, or numerical'. (ANSI Z39.4–1968). 5. A much broader connotation is now given to this term due to contemporary practices of compiling finding-guides to the contents of, and shelved position of, material in a library collection, sometimes using mechanical methods (even computers) for this purpose. From many points of view an index is synonymous with a catalogue, the principles of analysis used being identical, but whereas an index entry merely locates a subject, a catalogue entry includes descriptive specification of a document concerned with the subject. 6. (*Information retrieval*) That which specifies, indicates or designates the information, contents or topics of a document or a group of documents. Also a list of the names or subjects referring to a document or group of documents (*IBM*). 7. (*Verb*) To prepare an organized or systematic list which specifies, indicates or designates the information, contents or topics in a document or group of documents (*IBM*). *See also* AUTO-ABSTRACT, CONTROLLED INDEXING, INDEX LIBRORUM PROHIBITORUM, KWIC INDEX, PERMUTATION INDEXING, SOCIETY OF INDEXERS, UNITERM CONCEPT CO-ORDINATION INDEXING, AMERICAN SOCIETY OF INDEXERS, WORD INDEXING. 8. The printers' symbol ☞. Also called 'Digit', 'Fist', 'Hand'.

INDEX BOARD. A quality of single- or twin-wire pulp board, white or coloured, used for cutting into standard sizes for index cards and record work generally. They may be described as pulp board with a good, even and well-finished surface suitable for writing. They are smooth, hard-sized and of even LOOK THROUGH (*q.v.*). Sizes: Index Royal $20\frac{1}{2} \times 25\frac{1}{2}$ inches. Index Royal and a half $25\frac{1}{2} \times 30\frac{1}{2}$ inches.

INDEX ENTRY. The entry which is included in an index.

INDEX EXPURGATORIUS. An index to passages to be expunged or altered in works which are otherwise permitted. This term is loosely used for the list of books that the Roman Catholic Church forbade its members to read, or permitted them to read only in expurgated form; this is the INDEX LIBRORUM PROHIBITORUM (*q.v.*).

INDEX LANGUAGE. The language that is used in the subject index which is part of an information retrieval system. It may be an alphabetical or classified arrangement of terms, or a variation of these. Each term or heading actually used in the index language, of whatever kind, is called an 'index term'. Also called 'Descriptor language'. Its 'vocabulary' is the complete collection of sought terms in the natural language.

INDEX LIBRORUM PROHIBITORUM. A list of books which Roman Catholics were prohibited by ecclesiastical authority from reading or keeping without permission. Such books could not be imported into countries where Roman Catholic control was considerable. The list was commonly called the 'Index' or 'Roman Index', and was also known as 'Index Expurgatorius'. The *Index* was printed first by Antonio Blado in Rome in 1559 and is the classic example of censorship. From late Roman times there had been censorship of books considered to be dangerous to religion and morals, and although bishops, universities and inquisitions had circulated lists of prohibited books this was the first really effective means of censorship. The 'Congregation' which was first set up in 1558 to prepare the *Index* continued to be responsible for its publication. The Index was last brought up to date in 1947; Cardinal Ottaviani, pro-prefect of the Doctrinal Congregation declared in April 1965 that no more books would be put on the Index. On 14 June 1966 the Vatican announced that it had been abolished; although it ceased to be legally binding, Roman Catholics were reminded of their duty to avoid reading books dangerous to faith and morals.

INDEX MAP. A small-scale key map to an atlas or series of maps, which shows how the total area has been divided up by the individual maps.

INDEX TAB. A small piece of paper, card or fabric attached to, and projecting from, the fore-edge of a leaf and bearing in progressive order from top to bottom letters or words. Its purpose is to assist the speedy finding of the information required. *See also* THUMB INDEX.

INDEX TERM. *See* INDEX LANGUAGE.

INDEX TRANSLATIONUM. A Unesco publication which lists translations of literary, scientific, educational and cultural works published in pamphlet or book form. Resumed as an annual in 1949, it continues a similar publication issued regularly from July 1932 to October 1940, as a quarterly publication (thirty-one issues being published) by the former International Institute of Intellectual Co-operation. The present ('New' Unesco) series began with a volume number No. 1, 1948, dated 1949 © 1950.

INDEXING. The art of compiling an INDEX (*q.v.*). *See also* AMERICAN SOCIETY OF INDEXERS, INDEX, SOCIETY OF INDEXERS.

INDEXING AT SOURCE. The publication of indexing data simultaneously with (often at the head of) a periodical article.

INDEXING BY EXCLUSION. A system of automatic indexing based on the isolation and exclusion of non-significant or meaningless words. All words which have not been so excluded are processed as indexing words.

INDEXING LANGUAGE. A set of indexing terms as used in a particular retrieval system. The 'language' can be 'natural' (the language of the documents indexed) or 'structured' or 'controlled' (classified or having classificatory features). Tests carried out on a number of vocabularies have shown that those based on natural language might give better results than a structured language. See also ARTIFICIAL INDEXING LANGUAGE, NATURAL LANGUAGE.

INDEXING SERVICE. A periodical publication which regularly and systematically indexes the contents of periodicals and sometimes other forms of publication, either of a general nature or within specified subject fields. They are usually cumulated at regular intervals.

INDIA PAPER. Originally a soft absorbent paper, cream or buff in colour, imported from China for proofs of engravings. In 1875 the name was used for a thin opaque paper made from hemp or rag. See also BIBLE PAPER, CAMBRIDGE INDIA PAPER, OXFORD INDIA PAPER.

INDIA PROOF. A proof of an engraving taken on India or other fine paper. Sometimes wrongly applied to the whole first edition.

INDIA PROOF PAPER. See also CHINA PAPER.

INDIAN ASSOCIATION FOR SPECIAL LIBRARIES AND INFORMATION CENTRES. See IASLIC.

INDIAN BIBLE. The first Bible printed in the American Colonies was a translation by John Eliot into the Indian language.

INDIAN INK. A very black waterproof writing and drawing fluid having great density, used for drawings designed for reproduction and for records where permanence is desired.

INDIAN LIBRARY ASSOCIATION. Founded in 1933, with the following objects: the furtherance of the library movement in India, the promotion of the training of librarians, and the improvement of the status of librarians. Published *Abgila* (=annals, bulletin and granthalaya of the Indian Library Association) (q.).

INDICATIVE ABSTRACT. See ABSTRACT.

INDICATOR. 1. A frame, glazed on the public side, which indicated the numbers of the books 'in' and 'out' in a closed access library. 2. A similar system, but without being in a glazed frame, is used currently

to indicate which gramophone records are 'in' or 'out'. 3. A dye used
to evaluate the active acidity of paper. 4. (*Printing*) A 'superior'
number or symbol in the text which indicates a footnote at the bottom
of the page (or at the end of the chapter, or at the end of the textual
matter) to the word or sentence. *See also* SUPERIOR FIGURES (LETTERS).

INDICATOR DIGIT.   A symbol used in the notation of a scheme of
classification to announce a change of method of division. *See also*
DIVISION 4.

INDICOGRAPHY.   The compilation of an index.

INDIRECT CODING.   The use of combinations of holes or of punching positions in edge-punched or machine-punched cards because of
the need to provide rotations for more subjects, or meanings, than
there are individual positions available. Also called 'Combination
coding'. *See also* DIRECT CODING.

INDIRECT SUBDIVISION.   *See* DIRECT SUBDIVISION.

INDIRECT SUBJECT HEADING.   (Indexing) A subject heading
which merely refers to another subject heading by means of a *See*
reference. *See also* MIXED SUBJECT HEADING.

INDIS.   Abbreviation of Industrial Information Service, a function of
UNISIST (*q.v.*).

INDIVIDUAL ENTRY.   Entry in a catalogue under a person or place as
subject.

INDUSTRIAL GROUP.   Formed in May 1971, this Group of the
Library Association aims to represent librarians and information
workers employed in industry and commerce. It is concerned with
the interests of its members as individuals and keeps a close watch
on working conditions. Publishes *Newsletter* (irreg).

INDUSTRIAL LIBRARIES.   Libraries provided by, and in, industrial
firms.

INEDITA.   Unpublished works.

INEDITED.   A work published without editorial changes; it may contain
indelicate passages which might have been altered or omitted in editing.

INEVITABLE ASSOCIATION, PRINCIPLE OF.   In descriptive
cataloguing, the principle that applies to any name, whether it be
of person, book (title), corporate body, periodical, etc., that contains
a word that will inevitably be remembered by anyone who asks for
that person, book, subject, corporate body or periodical. The
principle dictates that the entry chosen for that name will be the
word inevitably remembered. *See also* CATALOGUING, PRINCIPLES OF.

INFECTIOUS DISEASES.   Certain infectious diseases are 'notifiable
diseases'; these have been re-defined in Section 47 of the Health

Services and Public Health Act 1968 and comprise cholera, plague, relapsing fever, smallpox and typhus. The Secretary of State for Social Services is empowered to make other diseases notifiable by regulation and the Public Health (Infectious Diseases) Regulations 1968, which consolidated into one instrument, with amendments, all previous regulations relating to the notification and prevention of infectious diseases, provide for the notification of acute encephalitis, acute meningitis, acute poliomyelitis, amoebic dysentery, anthrax, bacillary dysentery, diphtheria, infective jaundice, leprosy, leptospirosis, malaria, measles, ophthalmia neonatorum, paratyphoid fever, scarlet fever, tetanus, tuberculosis, typhoid fever, whooping cough and yellow fever. A local authority may, with the approval of the Secretary of State, and after advertisement, extend the category of notifiable diseases in its area. Chickenpox and glandular fever have been made notifiable in this way from time to time. Notice of the occurrence of all these diseases must be sent by the medical practitioner to the medical officer of the local authority. A local authority may provide a disinfecting station and may, in certain circumstances, disinfect premises and articles likely to retain infection. Persons who have books known to have been exposed to infection from a notifiable disease must not return the books to the Library but must notify the appropriate local authority so that they may be disinfected. A person who knows he is suffering from a notifiable disease shall not take any book, or cause any book to be taken, from a public library. A person shall not permit any book which has been taken from a public library, and is under his control, to be used by any person whom he knows to be suffering from a notifiable disease.

INFERIOR CHARACTERS. Small figures and letters cast below the level of the base line, as in chemical formulae, thus: H_2SO_4. Also called 'Subscript'. *See also* BASE LINE, SUPERIOR FIGURES (LETTERS).

INFIMA SPECIES. The class with which the division of a classification ends. *See also* SUBALTERN GENERA and SUMMUM GENUS.

INFLUENCE PHASE. One of Ranganathan's three main 'phase relations'; it is the relationship of one subject influencing another. The other two are BIAS PHASE and TOOL PHASE (*qq.v.*). The process of determining the appropriate class for a document; where one thing influences another, the document is classified under the thing influenced. *See also* PHASE.

INFORMATICS. 1. The processes, methods and laws relating to the recording, analytical-synthetical processing, storage, retrieval and dissemination of scholarly information, but not the scholarly

14

information as such which is the attribute of the respective science or discipline. 2. The study of the structure of knowledge and of its embodiment in information-handling systems.

INFORMATION. The essential ingredient of any control system (*Edwards*).

INFORMATION ANALYSIS CENTRE. A formally structured organizational unit specifically (but not necessarily exclusively) established to acquire, select, store, retrieve, evaluate, analyse and synthetize a body of information and/or data in a clearly defined specialized field, or pertaining to a specific mission, with the intention of arranging and presenting the material in a most authoritative and useful form. Abbreviated IAC.

INFORMATION AND REFERRAL SERVICE. A service set up in five NEIGHBOURHOOD INFORMATION CENTRES (*q.v.*) in America which receives, mainly over the telephone, enquiries for information of all kinds and refers the enquirers instantly to a community or agency, or individual capable of providing the answer.

INFORMATION AREA. (*Reprography*) The printed, or written, area of a document or micro-print which contains the information; it usually excludes the margins.

INFORMATION CARD. *Synonymous with* HISTORY CARD (*q.v.*).

INFORMATION CENTRE. Usually an office, or a section of a bibliographical centre, research bureau or documentation centre, which gives information about books or on a subject with which the organization providing the facilities of the centre is concerned. Staffing varies, but may include any or all of the following: research officers, librarians, bibliographers or trained information officers. It may include the functions of a special library and extend its activities to include collateral functions such as: technical writing, functions performed by machine methods, and library research for clients.

INFORMATION CENTRE FOR TERMINOLOGY. *See* INFO-TERM.

INFORMATION CLEARING HOUSE. A name sometimes given to a special library possessing a limited amount of published material, but which collects and gives information by telephone, correspondence and the use of other libraries. (American.)

INFORMATION DEPARTMENT. The department of an organization, the primary function of which is to give information when requested.

INFORMATION DESK. A desk in a library or other building staffed by one or more persons whose function is to give information. This may vary from little more than directions to various parts of the building to a full information service (even if only of a quick-reference nature) based on an appropriate collection of reference books and other appropriate material.

INFORMATION ENTRY. *Synonymous with* GENERAL REFERENCE (*q.v.*).

INFORMATION EVALUATION CENTRE. An organization which exists primarily to judge the values, validity and completeness of the information derived from experiments, research, development, test and engineering; it also undertakes the summarizing and reporting on such evaluations. Also called an 'Information centre'. *See also* DATA CENTRE, DOCUMENT CENTRE.

INFORMATION FILE. 1. A list of sources of information which is not readily found and which may in the first instance have been difficult to obtain. 2. Extracts, illustrations, pamphlets, and articles torn from periodicals and other fugitive material filed, usually in a vertical file, in some systematic order for ready reference.

INFORMATION HANDLING. The storing, processing and retrieval of information from acquisition to user.

INFORMATION ITEM. *Synonymous with* TOPIC (*q.v.*).

INFORMATION LIBRARIAN. The librarian in charge of an INFORMATION LIBRARY (*q.v.*).

INFORMATION LIBRARY. A library which serves as the basis of an INFORMATION SERVICE (*q.v.*).

INFORMATION OFFICER. One whose function is to give information; he often works in close co-operation with a librarian, giving information from his own knowledge (often being a specialist in the field of knowledge concerned) and from published materials which are collected, administered and made available by a librarian.

INFORMATION PROCESSING. *See* PROCESSING 1.

INFORMATION RESOURCE. As defined for the purposes of the NATIONAL REFERRAL CENTER (*q.v.*): any organization, facility, or individual willing and able to give authoritative responses to scientific or technical inquiries out of an existing store of knowledge or expertise.

INFORMATION RETRIEVAL. Finding documents, or the information contained in documents, in a library or other collection, selectively recalling recorded information. Methods of retrieval vary from a simple index or catalogue to the documents, to some kind of punched card or microfilm record which requires large or expensive equipment for mechanically selecting the material required. Classification, indexing and machine searching are all systems of information retrieval.

See also DATA PROCESSING, RETRIEVAL, TERMATREX SYSTEM. Abbreviated IR.

INFORMATION SCIENCE. The study of the properties and behaviour of information, the forces governing the flow of information, and the means of processing it for optimum accessibility and usability. – *H. Borko.*

INFORMATION SCIENCE AND AUTOMATION DIVISION. A Division of the American Library Association since 28 January 1966. Is concerned with the application of electronic data processing techniques and the use of automated systems in all areas of library work; within this field it fosters research, promotes the development of appropriate standards, disseminates information, and provides a forum for the discussion of common problems. This Division is also concerned with educational psychology, and ideas and cable communications. In 1975, two sections were formed: one, the Video and Cable Communications Section, is concerned with the use of television in libraries; the other, the Audio-Visual Section, is concerned with the development and use of A-V media in use in libraries and the automation thereof. Abbreviated ISAD. Publishes *Jola Technical Communications* (6 p.a.), *Journal of Library Automation* (JOLA) (q.).

INFORMATION SCIENTIST. Originally an INFORMATION OFFICER (*q.v.*) who has a science degree and may be qualified in the administration of a library of scientific literature. Emphasis is now more on providing the science of an information service than with a knowledge of a science. His concern is therefore more with acquiring, processing and retrieving information than with the content of the information possessed. *See also* INSTITUTE OF INFORMATION SCIENTISTS.

INFORMATION SERVICE. A service provided by, or for, a special library which draws attention to information possessed in the library or information department in anticipation of demand; this is done by preparing and circulating news sheets, literature surveys, reading lists, abstracts, particulars of articles in current periodicals, etc. which it is anticipated will be of interest to potential users of the service.

INFORMATION SERVICES IN MECHANICAL ENGINEERING. *See* ISMEC.

INFORMATION SPECIALIST. A person who is primarily concerned with the processing of data in a particular area of knowledge rather than with the control of documents.

INFORMATION SYSTEM. An organized procedure for collecting, processing, storing, and retrieving documentary information to satisfy a variety of needs. – *H. Borko.*

INFORMATION SYSTEM FOR COFFEE AND OTHER PRODUCT ECONOMICS. *See* INSCOPE.

INFORMATION TRANSFER EXCHANGE. *See* PROJECT INTREX.

INFORMATION WORK. The collection, evaluation and organized dissemination of scientific and technical information. It includes (a) abstracting technical writings; (b) translating same; (c) editing the products of (a) and (b); (d) indexing, subject classification and retrieval of information; (e) searching literature, preparing bibliographies, reports, etc.; (f) obtaining, providing, and advising on scientific and technical information; (g) disseminating information; (h) research on problems in information work.

INFORMATIVE ABSTRACT. *See* ABSTRACT.

INFOTERM. Abbreviation for International Information Centre for Terminology. Established in 1971 within the framework of UNISIST (*q.v.*) with the assistance of Unesco, and affiliated to the Austrian Standards Institute in Vienna, this Centre has as its main objective to enhance and co-ordinate terminological work. As the co-ordinator of terminological activities carried out throughout the world, its documentation and information functions include: (a) collecting terminological publications from all over the world, particularly terminological standards and principles, and specialized dictionaries; (b) providing information on terminological libraries and their sources; (c) extensive dissemination of information on terminological publications in existence or in preparation; (d) providing information on terminological courses; (e) investigating the possibility of interconnection of terminological word banks. The collection of publications in the field of terminology had previously been undertaken by the Secretariat of ISO/TC 37 which had been held by Austria since 1952; these have served as essential sources for elaboration of ISO Standards and ISO Recommendations on terminological and lexicographical principles.

infra. (*Lat.* 'below'). Used in footnotes and sometimes in the text to refer to an item mentioned subsequently. *See also supra.*

INGO-PACT. Ingold's world patent for compact shelving. *See* COMPACTUS.

INGOLD-COMPACTUS. *See* COMPACTUS.

INGRAIN. A rough and shaggy quality of tinted paper used for pamphlet covers and wall hangings.

INHABITED INITIAL. In a mediaeval illuminated manuscript, an initial letter containing figures of human beings, beasts, or both. *See also* HISTORIATED INITIAL.

INIS. Acronym of the International Nuclear Information System which was established by the International Atomic Energy Agency (IAEA) – a U.N. Agency – in April 1970 with the release of *INIS Atomindex* in printed form (12 p.a.) and on magnetic tape. The System is fully decentralized, computer-based and mission-oriented, and covers the world's literature in nuclear science and allied fields. The operation of the Secretariat in Vienna is financed by the IAEA, and of the INIS centres (which provide the 'input') by the respective countries. Membership is open to any country which is a member of the IAEA.

INITIAL LETTER. A capital letter, being the first letter of a word, sentence or paragraph, larger than the subsequent letters, and so set to give emphasis or for decoration. In typography, its size is indicated by the number of lines of body type it occupies, as '3-line initial'. Sometimes called 'Ornamental initial'. *See also* FACTOTUM.

INITIALISM. *Synonymous with* ACRONYM (*q.v.*).

INK BALL. A large, round sheepskin or buckskin pad stuffed with wool, or horsehair and cotton, and fastened to a wooden handle. It was used from the fifteenth century until about 1820 (when superseded by rollers) for inking set-up type in the forme. The pressman used them in pairs holding one in each hand.

INK BLOCK. A piece of beech wood fastened to the hind-rail of a printing press and used for spreading the ink. *See also* INK SLAB.

INK SLAB. The part of some printing machines, consisting of a large, flat, steel bed, on to which the ink is placed and from which the distributing rollers take, mix and spread it, before transferring it to the forme. *See also* INK BLOCK.

INLAID. 1. A piece of printing, a MS., or an illustration, which is inset in a frame or border of paper, the overlapping edges having first been shaved thin in order to prevent bulkiness at the joins. 2. A leather binding with leather of another colour or kind set in the cover.

INLAY. 1. The paper used to stiffen the spine of a book when being re-bound. 2. A picture or decoration inlaid in the cover of a book. *See also* ONLAY. 3. A MS., letter, leaf, plate or document mounted in a cut-out frame to protect it and permit both sides to be read.

INLAYING. In bookbinding, pasting down a differently coloured leather to that of the cover as part of the decoration; usually within an outlined tool form, border or panel. *See also* ONLAY.

IN-LINE PROCESSING. (*Information retrieval*) A technique by which an item may be fully processed, with random access to all of the entries which that item may affect. The processing of data without sorting or any prior treatment other than storage (*IBM*).

INLINE LETTERS. Jobbing and display work letters in which hand-tooling of the main strokes results in a white line forming their central part when printed. This gives the effect of blackness relieved by white. *See also* OPEN LETTERS.

INNER FORM. *See* FORM DIVISIONS.

INNER FORME. A forme containing the pages of type which will, when printed, become the inside of a printed sheet in SHEET WORK (*q.v.*). The reverse of 'outer forme'.

INNER INDENTION. *Synonymous with* SECOND INDENTION (*q.v.*).

INNER LONDON LIBRARY COMMITTEE. The organization on which the Inner London Boroughs (formerly the Metropolitan Boroughs but reconstituted on 1 April 1965) are represented. It maintains from levies paid by these boroughs the catalogue previously known as the LONDON UNION CATALOGUE (*q.v.*).

INNER MARGIN. *Synonymous with* BACK MARGIN (*q.v.*).

INPADOC. Abbreviation for International Patent Documentation Centre. Established by the Austrian Government in collaboration with WIPO (*q.v.*) in 1972, and as a result of the signing (at a Diplomatic Conference held in Washington in 1970) of the Patent Co-operation Treaty (PCT). It aims to furnish to national or regional patent offices, and also to make available to industry, bibliographic data concerning patent documentation in machine-readable form, as well as services identifying patent documents relating to the same invention or to a given branch of technology. *See also* ICIREPAT.

INPUT. (*Information retrieval*) That which is put in – that is, the information transferred from external storage to the internal storage of the machines (*IBM*).

INPUT DEVICES. (*Information retrieval*) Equipment that provides the means by which data and programs are entered into a computer. It includes various devices employing a keyboard, optical character equipment, etc.

INSCOPE. Abbreviation for Information System for Coffee and Other Product Economics. This is a co-ordinate index in the field of applied economics which is used by the International Coffee Organization (ICO), an intergovernmental organization established to administer the provisions of the International Coffee Agreement. INSCOPE was first used to index the ICO Library in 1973.

INSCRIBED COPY. *See* PRESENTATION COPY.

INSDOC. The Indian National Science Documentation Centre was founded by the Indian Government in 1952 with the following objects: (1) to receive and retain all scientific periodicals; (2) to inform scientists and engineers of articles of interest by means of a monthly bulletin of abstracts; (3) to answer specific enquiries; (4) to supply photocopies or translations to individual workers; (5) to be a national depository for published and unpublished Indian scientific reports; (6) to be a channel through which Indian scientific work is made known and available to the rest of the world. The Centre comes under the Council for Scientific and Industrial Research and has been placed under the administrative control of the Director, National Physical Laboratory. Publishes *Insdoc list of current scientific literature* (*f.*), which serves to give information concerning articles published outside India before the publications are received by surface mail in India, and is compiled from microfilm copies of the tables of contents of scientific periodicals which are received by airmail.

INSERT.   An additional sentence or a paragraph added to a proof to be inserted in a revise or final proof.

INSERTION MARK.   *Synonymous with* CARET (*q.v.*).

INSERTION MOTIF.   An ornament such as a pillar or a bar, etc., dividing two columns of text, or one scene from another, in a mediaeval illuminated manuscript.

IN-SERVICE TRAINING.   A scheme consisting of practical work and a course of lectures given on one or more occasions every week or so, whereby trainees or the more junior members of a staff are given instruction in the routines carried out in the library and on wider and more general aspects of librarianship.

INSET.   1. An illustration, map or other item, not part of the printed sheets, included when binding a pamphlet or book. They may or may not be sewn in. 2. A folded sheet laid inside another. It may be part of a printed sheet cut off before folding and inserted in the middle of the folded sheet to complete the succession of the pages. If so, it is also called 'offcut'. 3. An advertisement or separate leaf, not an integral part of the publication inserted in a magazine or booklet. 4. An extra page or set of pages inserted in a proof, or a book. 5. A small map, illustration, etc., set within the border of a larger one.

INSET MAP.   A small map printed within the border of a larger one.

INSIDE LINING, ORNAMENTAL.   *Synonymous with* DOUBLURE 1 (*q.v.*).

INSIDE MARGIN.   *Synonymous with* BACK MARGIN (*q.v.*).

INSPEC.   Acronym for International Information Services for the Physics and Engineering Communities which is the information services division operated by the (English) Institution of Electrical Engineers. Originally *Science Abstracts*, the service now produces *Physics Abstracts and Electrical and Electronics Abstracts* (twice monthly) and *Computer and Control Abstracts* (monthly). INSPEC operates the world's largest computerized information service in the English language in the fields of physics, electrical engineering, electronics, computers and control; it also publishes current awareness journals, (*Current Papers in Electrical and Electronic Engineering*, . . . *in Physics*, . . . *on Computers and Control* and *Key Abstracts*—six subject information journals) and operates SDI services in the same disciplines. The INSPEC data base is available on computer readable magnetic tape, and part of the data base is available for on-line searching through the service RETROSPEC 1 (*q.v.*). In 1975, INSPEC co-operated with the Warwick Research Unit for the Blind at Warwick University on a pilot project to produce a monthly braille information service for blind computer programmers and analysts.

inst. Abbreviation for instant, and meaning 'of the current month' when following a date. *See also* ult.

INSTALMENT. A part of a literary work, published serially in a periodical; sometimes a portion of a work which is published in 'parts' or 'numbers'. This term is falling into disuse, largely because the publication of a work 'in parts' is becoming less common.

INSTITUT INTERNATIONAL DE DOCUMENTATION. Formerly the Institut International de Bibliographie. Now the Fédération Internationale de Documentation. *See* UNIVERSAL DECIMAL CLASSIFICATION.

INSTITUT INTERNATIONALE DES BREVETS. *See* INTERNATIONAL PATENTS INSTITUTE.

INSTITUTE FOR DOCUMENTATION (Institut für Dokumentationswesen). Established in Frankfurt-Niederrad, Federal Republic of Germany in 1961 as part of the Max Planck Gesellschaft zur Foerderung der Wissenschaften (Max Planck Society for the Advancement of Science), comprises forty-seven institutes and is the largest research organization in the Federal Republic of Germany. It is mainly a co-ordinating, advisory and financing body with planning and administrative functions in scientific and technical information. The Centre for Documentation at Frankfurt/Main, which is an agency of the Institute, is a training, advisory, equipment-testing, and information centre.

INSTITUTE OF ARAB MANUSCRIPTS. Founded in April 1946 by the Arab League to make more widely known the Arab contribution to universal culture which is to be found in more than three million volumes scattered in public and private libraries throughout the world. By the middle of 1958 microfilms and over 80,000 enlargements had been made of over 15,000 rare and valuable manuscripts. These are available for consultation at the Institute in Cairo, through inter-library loans or by providing enlargements.

INSTITUTE OF INFORMATION SCIENTISTS. A professional organization formed in 1958 to promote and maintain high standards in scientific and technical information work and to establish a professional qualification for graduates engaged therein. The Institute claims that there is a clear distinction between the work of a librarian and of an information officer, arising from the latter's use of specialized scientific knowledge in evaluating, interpreting and collating information. Outline membership conditions: a *Student Member* must have obtained a General Certificate of Education at two 'A' levels including an approved scientific subject and be employed in information work. An *Associate* must have a science or engineering degree or other approved qualification, obtained the Certificate of the Institute and have one year's approved experience in information work, or five years' experience in scientific or technical work other than in information work after 'A' levels. *Members* must have a degree or equivalent and have had at least two years' experience in information work and achieved distinction in this. Extensive experience in information work is often accepted in lieu of the certificates, etc. (Persons not meeting the qualifications required for Member or Associate grades may be elected Affiliates.) *Fellows* are elected at the discretion of the Council. – *Dr R. T. Bottle. See also* CENTRE FOR INFORMATION SCIENCE.

INSTITUTE OF LIBRARIANS. A national voluntary organization of professional librarians in India which was formed in 1975; the Institute is located at the Department of Library Science, University of Calcutta. Abbreviated IOL. Publishes *Indian Journal of Library Science* (q.).

INSTITUTE OF LIBRARY RESEARCH. Established in 1966 by the University of California to conduct research into library problems and develop methods for improving library work (using the numerous libraries of the University and campuses of the University as a laboratory) and advance education for librarianship.

INSTITUTE OF REPROGRAPHIC TECHNOLOGY. Inaugurated in England in 1961, the objects of this professional association are stated to be to provide for the professional and technical advancement of all those (whether users, suppliers or advisers) concerned with: (a) photocopying and duplicating; (b) the reproduction of engineering drawings; (c) inplant printing; (d) photography and visual aids; (e) micrographics and micropublishing; (f) office systems; (g) mechanized addressing and mailing. Apart from the central administration in London, there are fifteen regional units (to which members are automatically allocated) which organize meetings and visits to places of reprographic interest. The Institute is an examining body and awards the qualifications AMIRT and MIRT. There are five grades of membership. Abbreviated IRT. Text books are published as well as *Repro* (q.).

INSTITUTION. An organization or society established for some scientific or social purpose and supplying some public or educational need. For purposes of cataloguing it is distinguished from a society or an association by requiring for its efficient functioning a building with plant and equipment whereas a society may function without these, and as efficiently in one place as another.

INSTITUTO BRASILEÑO DE BIBLIOGRAFÍA E DOCUMENT-AÇAO. Founded in 1954 in Rio de Janeiro with the assistance of Unesco. It is a unit of the Conselho Nacional de Pesquisas, and provides a science reference library and documentation training courses. Abbreviated IBBD.

INSTITUTO DE DOCUMENTACIÓN E INFORMACIÓN CIENTIFICA Y TECNICA. A national documentation centre established in 1963, with the technical assistance of Unesco, at Havana, Cuba, being attached to the Comisión Nacional de la Academia de Ciencias de la República de Cuba. Publishes a *Boletín*.

INSTRUCTION. (*Information retrieval*) A machine word consisting of characters which are recognized by the computer and therefore capable of causing machine action. A set of characters which specifies an operation and usually indicates the location of the data to be processed.

INSTRUCTION NOTE. (*Classification*) A note directing the user to take some specific step which is not obvious from the heading and its context or from the general notes.

INSTRUCTIONAL MATERIALS CENTER. A room, in an American elementary or high school, in which all learning materials (books, periodicals, vertical file materials, slides, films, filmstrips, transparencies, gramophone records, tapes, models, art reproductions, 8 mm. loops, and any necessary machinery to operate them) are kept and from which they may be borrowed, or used, by teachers or

pupils. Also called 'Learning Resources Center'. *See also* CURRICULUM
MATERIALS CENTER.

INSTRUMENTAL CUES. Abbreviations and/or thematic indications
in a music score or PART (*q.v.*), and serving as a guide to the instrumentation, or as an entry signal, for the performer. These are common
in 'parts' of concerted music and essential in the scores for piano-
conductor. *See also* SCORE.

INSULAR HANDWRITING. The most beautiful of all national styles
of handwriting which developed from the semi-uncial book hand of the
early Christian missionaries to the British Isles and, unlike the Continental styles, from the cursive minuscule. The two principal varieties
of this script are (a) the Irish hand which was used from the sixth
century to the Middle Ages and developed into the modern Irish script,
and (b) the Anglo-Saxon semi-uncial style which developed from (a)
in the seventh and eighth centuries. *See also* CURSIVE, HANDWRITING.

INTAGLIO. 1. (*Printing*) A design engraved or incised in the surface
of a hard plate. An intaglio plate for printing is usually of copper and
has the design engraved with a graver or etched by acid. Photogravure
is an intaglio process. 2. (*Binding*) The impression of a ROLL (*q.v.*)
in which the sunk part of the leather forms the design.

INTAGLIO PRINTING. Printing done from an intaglio (incised)
plate, into which the design or image is countersunk or depressed;
after being inked and wiped, leaving ink only in the engraved parts,
it is placed with a damp sheet of printing paper on the press, layers of
felt are added, and pressure applied. The thickness of the ink transferred to the paper varies with the depth of the incisions on the plate;
this ink being layered on the plate can be felt on the resulting print (as
distinct from the planographic and letterpress methods) and is a means
of identifying the method of printing. Copperplate printing, steel die
embossing and impressions taken from dry-point plates are forms of
intaglio printing, as are etchings, line engravings, mezzotints, aqua-
tints, photogravures and dry-point etchings. The opposite of LETTER-
PRESS (*q.v.*) and RELIEF PRINTING (*q.v.*).

INTAMEL. The International Association of Metropolitan City
Libraries, a sub-section of IFLA (*q.v.*) which was formed in 1968
with the object of encouraging members (libraries in metropolitan
areas serving not less than 400,000 population) (a) to participate in
international co-operation; (b) to exchange books, staff, and information particularly in connection with deposits and collections of
international and foreign literature; (c) to participate in IFLA and
its Public Libraries Section.

INTEGER NOTATION. One in which the notation of a scheme of classification consists of whole numbers as opposed to decimal *fraction notation*. There is no method of allowing for interpolation of new subjects in an integer notation except by leaving gaps where it is estimated that future expansion might take place.

INTEGRAL. A leaf which is part of a section, as distinct from one which is printed independently from a section but inserted in it.

INTEGRAL NOTATION. The NOTATION (*q.v.*) of a scheme of classification which uses numbers arithmetically (as does the Library of Congress scheme) and not decimally. Also called an 'arithmetical' notation.

INTEGRATED SET OF INFORMATION SYSTEMS. *See* ISIS.

INTEGRATION. The bringing together in a conventional manner of the various details which comprise a catalogue entry.

INTEGRATIVE LEVEL. *See* LEVEL.

INTEGRATIVE LEVELS. A theory propounded by the biologist Joseph Needham who considers 'the existence of levels of organization in the universe, successive forms of order in a scale of complexity' and suggests that 'a sharp change in the organizational level often means that what were wholes on the lower level become parts on the new, e.g. protein crystals in cells, cells in metazoan organisms, and metazoan organisms in social units'. The theory tries to discover a logical and durable 'progressive' or 'developmental' order in the evolving structure of nature itself.

INTEGRITY OF NUMBERS. The view that the numbers or other symbols used to denote items in a scheme of classification should not be drastically altered in later revisions of the scheme.

INTELLECTUAL WORK. (*Copyright*) A creation resulting from intellectual activity covering all forms of expression, and possessing the characteristics of NOVELTY (*q.v.*) or ORIGINALITY (*q.v.*).

INTELLOFAX SYSTEM. An aperture card combined with a punched card system of recording information enabling a portion of the card to be used for index and selection purposes by EAM (*q.v.*) equipment. The installation of this system at the Central Intelligence Agency in America is possibly the largest single installation of such EAM aperture punched cards. The system was instituted in 1954. Each card contains a set of subject and area codes in punched form identifying the coverage of a document together with a pre-printed abstract to be copied for presentation to the requester.

INTENSION. *See* EXTENSION.

INTER-AMERICAN BIBLIOGRAPHICAL AND LIBRARY ASSO-CIATION. Founded on 3 October 1930 in Washington as the Inter-American Bibliographical Association. The present title and revised statutes were adopted on 21 December 1934. Its aims are to furnish information on bibliographical sources to investigators, research workers, students and writers; act as a clearing house for requests about organizations, libraries, or individuals known to have access to, possess, or know of, particular bibliographical resources; undertake bibliographical, library, archival work in co-operation with related agencies in all American countries and publish bibliographical and library aids. Abbreviated IABLA. Publishes conference proceedings, books, *Doors to Latin America* (q. to membs.) which is a guide to books published in the U.S.A.

INTER-AMERICAN CENTER FOR DOCUMENTATION AND AGRICULTURAL INFORMATION. A field centre in Costa Rica of the Inter-American Institute of Agricultural Sciences, a specialized agency of the Organization of American States which endeavours to promote economic and social development through graduate teaching, research, technical assistance, consultation services and communications in the field of agriculture and rural life. Abbreviated IICA-CIDIA.

INTER-AVAILABILITY OF TICKETS. Arrangements whereby the membership tickets of one library may be used to borrow books from another library.

INTERCALATION. The act of inserting a heading for a new subject between two existing headings of a classification.

INTERCALATION DEVICE. (*Classification*) The part of a NOTATION (*q.v.*) which indicates the incorporation of part of a notation from an entirely different scheme of classification, e.g. ( ) could be used in this way to embrace the figures 33 which in the U.D.C. scheme indicate economics.

INTEREST-PROFILE. A list of terms selected from a thesaurus indicating the area of interest of the user of an information service; it is used in the selection of documents in a Selective Dissemination of Information System. Also called USER-PROFILE. *See also* SDI.

INTERESTS RECORD. A record of the interests of individuals habitually using a library. It is compiled from statements made on their membership application forms, from requests for books or information, deliberate interviews, or contacts, and in an organization of fixed and limited numbers such as a firm or research laboratory, by reading correspondence. It is maintained, usually in subject order, to determine what current matter shall be routed or abstracted and to whom lists of additions and other information shall be disseminated.

INTERFIX. (*Information retrieval*) 1. A device to signal relationships between concepts. Thus for a series of compounds, A, B, C, . . . insertion of the interfixes 1 and 2 (for example A_1, B_1, B_2, C_2 . . .) signals that the compounds with the same numerical interfix are in one mixture and those with a different one are in a different mixture (*IBM*). *See also* LINKS, MODULANT, ROLES. 2. A neutral symbol attached to a DESCRIPTOR (*q.v.*) to indicate other descriptions with which it is interlocked.

INTERGOVERNMENTAL BUREAU FOR INFORMATICS – INTERNATIONAL COMPUTER CENTRE. *See* IBI – ICC.

INTERGOVERNMENTAL COMPUTATION CENTRE. *See* IBI – ICC.

INTERGOVERNMENTAL COPYRIGHT COMMITTEE. *See* IGC.

INTERLACING. Ornament composed of bands, etc., woven together.

INTERLAY. An UNDERLAY (*q.v.*) consisting of a sheet of paper or other material placed between a printing plate and its mount in order to raise the plate to its proper height for good printing.

INTERLEAF. An extra leaf, usually blank, inserted between the regular leaves of a book. The blank leaves may be provided for the writing of notes, or if they are thin tissues, to prevent the text and illustrations from rubbing. The latter may be pasted to the inner margins, or they may be loose. The plates so protected are known as tissued plates. Such a book is said to be interleaved.

INTERLEAVING. Tissue or blank paper used for interleaving illustrations and letterpress. Also thin blotting paper used for interleaving diaries.

INTERLENDING. The lending of books between libraries.

INTER-LIBRARY LOAN. A book lent between libraries of the same or different systems for a particular reader. *See also* REGIONAL BUREAUX.

INTERLIBRARY REFERENCE SERVICE. A form of co-operation whereby reference work is done by one library for patrons of another which is not an integral part of the same system. (American.)

INTERLINEAR BLANK. *Synonymous with* INTERLINEAR MATTER (*q.v.*).

INTERLINEAR MATTER. Characters providing explanations, translations or subsidiary matter, written or printed in smaller characters between the ordinary lines of text to which they relate.

INTERLINEAR SPACE. Space between lines of type. Also called 'Interlinear blank'.

INTERLINEAR TRANSLATION. A translation printed between the lines of the original text to which it relates.

INTERMEDIATE COPY. (*Reprography*) A copy of a document which serves as an intermediate stage in producing the final copy, as e.g. a readable negative (white on black) from which a black on white copy is made.

INTERMEDIATE FILE. *See* MARLIS.

INTERMEDIATE LIBRARY. A department containing specially selected books and duplicates of some of those in the adult and junior departments for the use of adolescents.

INTERN. In America, a graduate who works in a library full-time while attending part-time at a school of librarianship. *See also* INTERNE.

INTERNACIA ESPERANTO-ASOCIO DE BIBLIOTEKISTOJ. *See* IEAB.

INTERNATIONAL ADVISORY COMMITTEE ON BIBLIO-GRAPHY, DOCUMENTATION AND TERMINOLOGY. A Unesco Committee which as from 1 January 1961 succeeded the two Unesco international advisory committees on Bibliography and for Documentation and Terminology in Pure and Applied Science. Publishes *Bibliography, Documentation and Terminology*.

INTERNATIONAL ADVISORY COMMITTEE ON DOCUMEN-TATION, LIBRARIES AND ARCHIVES. *See* IACODLA.

INTERNATIONAL AND COMPARATIVE LIBRARIANSHIP GROUP. *See* ICLG.

INTERNATIONAL ASSOCIATION FOR ESPERANTO-SPEAK-ING LIBRARIANS. *See* IEAB.

INTERNATIONAL ASSOCIATION FOR RESEARCH IN CHILD-REN'S AND YOUTH LITERATURE. Founded 1970 at Frankfurt am Main to promote research in this field by exchange of specialist information, discussion of theoretical aspects, and by co-operation with specialists, institutions and organizations sharing its objectives. Membership is open to individuals only.

INTERNATIONAL ASSOCIATION FOR THE DEVELOPMENT OF DOCUMENTATION, LIBRARIES AND ARCHIVES IN AFRICA. Founded in 1960 and known as the International Association for the Development of Libraries in Africa until 1967 when the name was changed to indicate the expanded aims of: promoting and establishing in all African countries a public archives service, a national system of libraries, documentation centres and museums.

Membership is open to individuals. It has national sections in four countries. This Association was developed from the Association for the Development of Public Libraries in Africa which was founded in 1957. Abbreviated AIDBA (Association Internationale pour le Développement de la Documentation des Bibliothèques et des Archives en Afrique).

INTERNATIONAL ASSOCIATION FOR MASS COMMUNICA-TION RESEARCH. Established in Paris in 1957 to promote throughout the world the development of research on problems relating to the press, radio, television and films. It has amongst its objects the establishment of a list of research institutes, and the collection of data on current research projects and current bibliographical material. Abbreviated IAMCR.

INTERNATIONAL ASSOCIATION FOR THE DEVELOPMENT OF LIBRARIES IN AFRICA. *See* INTERNATIONAL ASSOCIATION FOR THE DEVELOPMENT OF DOCUMENTATION, LIBRARIES AND ARCHIVES IN AFRICA.

INTERNATIONAL ASSOCIATION OF AGRICULTURAL LI-BRARIANS AND DOCUMENTALISTS. Founded 1955 to promote internationally, and nationally, 'agricultural library science and documentation as well as the professional interest of agricultural librarians and documentalists'. It succeeded the International Committee of Agricultural Librarians (founded 1935). Abbreviated IAALD. Publishes *Quarterly Bulletin of the IAALD*.

INTERNATIONAL ASSOCIATION OF BIBLIOPHILES. Founded 10th October 1963 at Barcelona. Aims to establish permanent links between bibliophiles in all parts of the world. Membership is open to individuals, societies and libraries in any country. Publishes *Bulletin du bibliophile*.

INTERNATIONAL ASSOCIATION OF DOCUMENTALISTS AND INFORMATION OFFICERS. Founded 1962 in Paris to promote contacts between people of all nationalities whose work concerns the problems of documentation, and to defend their professional interests. Individuals may become members. Abbreviated AID (Association Internationale des Documentalistes et Techniciens de l'Information). Publishes *AID News* (m.), *AID Bulletin* (q.).

INTERNATIONAL ASSOCIATION OF LAW LIBRARIES. Founded in New York in 1959 'to promote on a co-operative, non-profit and fraternal basis the work of individuals, libraries, and other institutions and agencies concerned with the acquisition and bibliographic processing of legal materials collected on a multi-national basis, and to facilitate the research and other uses of such materials on a world-wide basis.' Abbreviated IALL. Publishes *International Journal of Law Libraries* (3 p.a.) formerly *IALL Bulletin*.

INTERNATIONAL ASSOCIATION OF METROPOLITAN CITY LIBRARIES. *See* INTAMEL.

INTERNATIONAL ASSOCIATION OF MUSIC LIBRARIES. Founded in Paris in 1951, the object of this Association is 'to constitute a representative international organization charged with stimulating and co-ordinating all the activities, national and international, of music libraries, and to study and facilitate the realization of all projects dealing with music bibliography and music library science.' It aims to arrange for co-operation in the compilation of music bibliographies, exchange material, and train music librarians. Abbreviated IAML. Publishes *Fontes artis musicae* (3 a year). It has a British branch which was founded in 1953 and was primarily responsible for inaugurating the *British catalogue of music* (1957); publishes *Brio* (q.).

INTERNATIONAL ASSOCIATION OF ORIENTALIST LIBRARIANS. *See* IAOL.

INTERNATIONAL ASSOCIATION OF SCHOLARLY PUBLISHERS. Formed at the International Conference on Scholarly Publishing, held in Toronto in 1972, to associate university presses with other publishers of scholarly works. Aims: to encourage the dissemination of the fruits of scholarship and research; to exchange ideas and advice relating to scholarly publishing. The headquarters of the Association was established at Toronto University Press. An Asian Group is based on the University of Tokyo Press, Tokyo, Japan.

INTERNATIONAL ASSOCIATION OF SCHOOL LIBRARIANSHIP. Founded in 1969 to promote school library provision all over the world. Financed by the subscriptions of individual members and associations. Abbreviated IASL. Publishes *Newsletter* (4 p.a.).

INTERNATIONAL ASSOCIATION OF SOUND ARCHIVES. Established in 1969, this Association functions as a medium for the exchange of information on such matters as the preservation, storage and cataloguing of sound recordings, the technique of oral history, interviewing, national discographies, the exchange of duplicates and the relationship between research and broadcasting archives. Membership is open to individuals concerned with aural phenomena, the preservation of which might be useful for research purposes. The

Association meets annually in conjunction with the International Association of Music Libraries; at these meetings there is close co-operation with the Record Library Committee of IAML (*q.v.*) which is concerned with archives and libraries of music recordings. Abbreviated IASA.

INTERNATIONAL ASSOCIATION OF TECHNOLOGICAL UNIVERSITY LIBRARIES. Founded in Brussels in May 1955 to act as an organ for international co-operation between member libraries and to stimulate and develop library projects of international and regional importance. It is a section of IFLA (*q.v.*). Abbreviated IATUL. Publishes *Reprints* (irr.) and *Newsletter* (6 p.a.).

INTERNATIONAL ASSOCIATION OF THEOLOGICAL LIBRARIES. Formed at a conference of the International Federation of Library Associations (IFLA) in Brussels in 1955 of which it was a subsidiary. Abbreviated IATL. It ceased to function in 1960.

INTERNATIONAL BOARD ON BOOKS FOR YOUNG PEOPLE. *See* IBBY.

INTERNATIONAL BOOK AWARD. Instituted at the first meeting of the International Book Committee (*q.v.*) held at Bogatá, Colombia, in 1973, the Award is designed to accord recognition for outstanding services rendered by a person or institution to the cause of books in such fields as authorship, publishing, production, translation, bookselling, encouragement of the reading habit and promotion of international co-operation. The Award is an honorary distinction bestowed in the form of a diploma or other means decided upon by the International Book Committee at regular intervals on the nomination of the Committee. It was first awarded to Mr Herman Liebaers, Royal Librarian of Belgium, President of IFLA, and Chairman of the Preparatory Meeting, the Planning Committee and the Support Committee which organized IBY (*q.v.*) 'in recognition of his outstanding contribution to International Book Year, 1972.'

INTERNATIONAL BOOK COMMITTEE. Arising out of the worldwide activities of International Book Year (*See* IBY), this Committee was formed, in 1973, of international non-governmental organizations of professionals in the world of books to continue the work of the Support Committee for IBY. *See also* INTERNATIONAL BOOK AWARD.

INTERNATIONAL BOOK YEAR. *See* IBY.

INTERNATIONAL BUREAU OF EDUCATION. A Co-operative

Abstracting Service of this, Unesco's specialized centre for comparative education, was put into full effect in 1971, and was later extended to cover all Member States, thus enabling participating centres to select and summarize important national documents on educational policy worthy of being communicated to other countries. The Bureau acts as an international centre of information and educational research, and provides for a wide exchange of data so that each country may be encouraged to profit by the experience of others. Abbreviated IBE.

INTERNATIONAL BUREAU OF FISCAL DOCUMENTATION. Created as a foundation of the International Fiscal Association (IFA) this Bureau aims at complete co-operation with the Association. The Bureau's objects include the foundation and maintenance of an international documentation bureau for the supply of information on fiscal legislation and the application of fiscal law, and particularly the study of fiscal science. It seeks to realize this by establishing a library on fiscal legislation, supplying both general and detailed information, providing research facilities, issuing a journal, and continuing co-operation with the publications of other interested bodies. Abbreviated IBFD. Publishes *Documentation service* (f.) a literary survey covering books and periodical articles, and other publications.

INTERNATIONAL CATALOGUE CARD. The size of card which has been adopted internationally for use in card catalogues: it is 5 × 3 inches (7·5 × 12·5 centimetres).

INTERNATIONAL CENTRE FOR AFRICAN ECONOMIC AND SOCIAL DOCUMENTATION. Founded January 1961 to gather together and co-ordinate documentation on economic and social material concerning Africa with a view to facilitating and promoting the progress of the Continent in these fields. Publishes *Bibliographical index* (a.).

INTERNATIONAL CHILDREN'S BOOK DAY. *See* IBBY.

INTERNATIONAL CHILDREN'S CENTRE. Founded in Paris in 1950 by the United Nations Children's Fund (UNICEF) and the French Government to study childhood problems in the various countries. A Centre of International Documentation on Pediatrics and Child Welfare was set up at the Chateau de Longchamp. The library has 5,000 books, 1,000 files of periodicals and about 10,000 files of reprints in addition to government and international organization documents. Catalogue cards, indexing not only books but periodical articles, etc., are supplied to other libraries and individual research workers on a subscription basis. Abbreviated ICC. Publishes *Le*

Courrier (6 p.a.), *Biologia Neonatorum* (*q.*), *L'Enfant au Milieu Tropical* (m.).

INTERNATIONAL CLASSIFICATION. The brief name for Fremont Rider's scheme of classification for a general library, *International classification for the arrangement of books on the shelves of general libraries*, first published in 1961. Its main outline is similar to the Library of Congress classification; form and geographical subdivisions are enumerated in each main class; the notation consists of three letters and can be extended by 'book numbers' which are a combination of letters from the BISCOE DATE TABLE (*q.v.*) plus the initial letter of the author's name; no auxiliary tables are provided, neither are alternative locations. The schedules have 14,000 places.

INTERNATIONAL COMMITTEE FOR AFRICAN SOCIAL AND ECONOMIC DOCUMENTATION. *See* CIDESA.

INTERNATIONAL COMMITTEE FOR SOCIAL SCIENCES DOCUMENTATION. Founded in November 1950 in Paris at a meeting called by Unesco following recommendations of two committees of experts in 1948 and 1949. Registered in accordance with French law. Collects, keeps up-to-date and disseminates information on the different documentation services in the social sciences, and helps establish bibliographies and documentary tools which its surveys show to be necessary. The Committee sponsors or undertakes the following categories of bibliography: those on inter-disciplinary problems within the social sciences; guides to bibliographical sources of use to social scientists, but not restricted to them; retrospective regional bibliographies in the social sciences. It also sponsors the regular publication by Unesco in English and French of separate bibliographies of sociology, of political science, of economics, of social and cultural anthropology. It initiated, with the help of the Nuffield Foundation, investigation into the need for, and production of, a scheme of classification for the four Unesco bibliographies dealing with sociology, political science, economics, and social anthropology. The Kyle Classification for Social Sciences is the result. The membership consists mainly of representatives of international associations specializing either in the social sciences or in documentation and bibliography. It is financed by a grant from Unesco, and its activities include the compilation of current bibliographies and directories. Abbreviated ICSSD. Publishes *International Political Science Abstracts* (q.), *Confluence* (2 p.a.), *International Bibliography of the Social Sciences* ... (annually).

INTERNATIONAL COMMUNICATION INFORMATION RE-
TRIEVAL SYSTEM. *See* INCIRS.

INTERNATIONAL COMMUNITY OF BOOKSELLERS ASSOCIA-
TIONS. Founded in 1956. Aims: co-operation between all book-
sellers and associations of booksellers of countries which enjoy
freedom of thought and expression with a view to the exchange of
experience and the discussion of common commercial problems.
Financed by members' dues. Has originated several conferences.
Membership is available to relevant associations. Abbreviated
ICBA.

INTERNATIONAL CONFERENCE ON CATALOGUING PRIN-
CIPLES. An outstanding conference of cataloguers, bibliographers
and library officers with cataloguing expertise was held in Paris, 9–18
October 1961, consequent upon a proposal made by the council of
IFLA in 1957 to seek agreement on certain basic cataloguing principles. It was sponsored by IFLA with the object of reaching 'agreement on basic principles governing the choice and form of entry in the
alphabetical catalogue of authors and titles'. The definitive annotated
edition of the *Statement of principles*, known as the PARIS PRINCIPLES
(*q.v.*), which was an outcome of this Conference and was mainly
written by Dr Eva Verona, was published by the IFLA Committee
on Cataloguing, London, in 1971. *See also* IMCE. Abbreviated
ICCP.

INTERNATIONAL CONFERENCE ON CHILDREN'S LITERA-
TURE. Annual conferences have been held in Austrian cities
beginning in 1965, and organized by the *International Institute
for Children's Literature and Reading Research* (*q.v.*). An international exhibition of children's books have been held on each
occasion.

INTERNATIONAL CONFERENCE ON CLASSIFICATION FOR
INFORMATION RETRIEVAL. Held at Dorking, England, 13–
17 May, 1957. The *Proceedings* of the Conference were published by
Aslib who organized it as the British member of FID in co-operation
with the Classification Research Group and the University of London
School of Librarianship and Archives.

INTERNATIONAL CONFERENCE ON INFORMATION PRO-
CESSING. Held 15–20 June 1959 in Paris; organized by Unesco
with the help of experts from various countries, with the object of
bringing experts together to share their knowledge and experience.
The conference was mainly concerned with the workings and
uses of computers. The International Federation of Information

Processing Societies was set up and was later known as the INTER-NATIONAL FEDERATION FOR INFORMATION PROCESSING (*q.v.*).

INTERNATIONAL CONFERENCE ON SCIENTIFIC INFORMA-TION. Held 16–21 November 1958 in Washington, under the general sponsorship of the American Documentation Institute, the U.S. National Science Foundation and the National Academy of Sciences in collaboration with Unesco and the International Federation for Documentation. It was designed to summarize the state of scientific information. Abbreviated ICSI.

INTERNATIONAL CONGRESS ON REPROGRAPHY. The first congress was held in Cologne 14–18 October 1963. It was organized by the German Society for Photography with the object of bringing together research workers and specialists who are engaged in the development of facsimile reproduction processes in order to discuss their experience and plans.

INTERNATIONAL CO-OPERATION IN INFORMATION RETRIEVAL AMONG PATENT OFFICES. *See* ICIREPAT.

INTERNATIONAL COPYRIGHT. *See* COPYRIGHT, INTERNATIONAL.

INTERNATIONAL COPYRIGHT ACT, 1886. This was passed to enable the original Berne Convention to be carried out in the Dominions. *See* COPYRIGHT, INTERNATIONAL.

INTERNATIONAL COPYRIGHT INFORMATION CENTRE. *See* ICIC.

INTERNATIONAL COUNCIL FOR ADULT EDUCATION. *See* ICAE.

INTERNATIONAL COUNCIL FOR BUILDING DOCUMENTA-TION. Abbreviated CIDB. *See* INTERNATIONAL COUNCIL FOR BUILDING RESEARCH STUDIES AND DOCUMENTATION.

INTERNATIONAL COUNCIL FOR BUILDING RESEARCH, STUDIES AND DOCUMENTATION. Founded in 1953. Superseded the International Council for Building Documentation (CIDB) which had been established in 1950. Aims to encourage, facilitate and develop international co-operation in building research, studies and documentation, covering technical, economic and social aspects of building. Abbreviated CIB. Has published *ABC: abridged building classification for architects, builders and civil engineers: a selection from the Universal Decimal Classification system by the International Building Classification Committee* in single language editions in English, Dutch, French, German, Hungarian, Italian, Norwegian, Serbo-Croatian, Swedish and Danish. Publishes also the 'CIB Directory' – in full: *Directory of building research and development organisations;*

Organisations in Europe; CIB member organisations outside Europe; International organizations, Rev. ed. 1971, and *Building Research and Practice* (bi-m.) bilingual English/French.

INTERNATIONAL COUNCIL FOR RESEARCH IN THE SOCIOLOGY OF CO-OPERATION. Established in 1953. Its aims embrace the development, encouragement and exchange of information concerning the work and research done in its field. Each of the national research centres affiliated to the Council pursues a triple policy of research, documentation and integrated consultation in the social and economic context of its country. Thus the second point comprises the setting up of co-operative libraries and documentation centres to aid research workers, the establishment of an International Library of the Sociology of Co-operation comprising works published in English, French, German and Italian, and giving aid in the publication of research work arising from these activities. Publishes amongst many works *International archives of sociology of co-operation.* Abbreviated ICRSC.

INTERNATIONAL COUNCIL OF GRAPHIC DESIGN ASSOCIATIONS. *See* ICOGRADA.

INTERNATIONAL COUNCIL OF MUSEUMS. Founded in Paris in 1946 on Unesco's initiative. The Council's aims include the establishment of an international organization representing museums and the museum profession, and the development of international co-operation between them. Maintains a Museum Documentation Centre which also acts in that capacity for the Museums Division of Unesco. Abbreviated ICOM. Publishes *ICOM News.*

INTERNATIONAL COUNCIL OF SCIENTIFIC UNIONS. Founded in 1919 in Brussels as the 'International Research Council'; re-named in 1931. Its aims are to co-ordinate and facilitate activities of international scientific unions in the field of natural sciences, encourage international scientific activity in subjects which do not fall within the purview of any existing organizations, maintain relations with the UN and its specialized agencies, and make contacts and mutual arrangements with other international councils or unions, where common interests exist. In 1952 the Council set up the ICSU Abstracting Board which, with a Unesco subvention, aims to assist scientific abstracting reviews to co-operate with one another. Additionally, Unesco makes a financial contribution to bibliographical publications issued by the Council and its members. Abbreviated ICSU.

INTERNATIONAL COUNCIL ON ARCHIVES. Founded in June

1948 by professional archivists meeting in Paris under the auspices of Unesco. Aims to hold periodical international congresses, establish and maintain relations among archivists of all nations, and among all professional agencies and institutions whose activities relate to the conservation, organization or administration of archives; to further technical and administrative aspects of public and private archives wherever located and to facilitate access to archives, their objective study and the knowledge of their contents. Financed by members' dues and by Unesco subvention. Membership is open to: (a) central archive directorates and other archival institutions having authority over the whole of state archives; (b) national or international regional associations of archivists; (c) all archival institutions; (d) all professional archivists. Three regional branches have been formed (SARBICA, ECARBICA and CARBICA *qq.v.*) and others are in process of being formed in Latin America, the Caribbean, and Southern and Central Asia. The Secretariat is in Paris. The continuous study of professional and technical problems and the initiation of important projects is entrusted to committees or working groups. Liaison committees with IFLA and FID were established in 1974. Guides to the sources of the history of nations are being published in three series: 1. Latin America; 2. Africa; 3. North Africa, Asia and Oceania. Abbreviated ICA. Publishes *Archivum* (a.), *Bulletin* (2 p.a.) in English and French editions.

INTERNATIONAL DOCUMENTATION CENTRE. Situated at Hogelby Hus, Tumba, Sweden, the function of this information centre is to microfilm books and periodicals both in-print and out-of-print in anticipation of demand and to order. Copies are made on 3 × 5 inches microfiche and on filmstrip. Abbreviated IDC.

INTERNATIONAL FEDERATION FOR DOCUMENTATION. The English name of the Fédération Internationale de Documentation (FID) by which the International Institute of Bibliography became known in 1938. This organization developed from the UDC and exists (a) to group on an international basis, organizations and individuals interested in the problems of DOCUMENTATION (*q.v.*) and to co-ordinate their efforts; (b) to promote the study and practice of documentation in all its branches and forms, and to create an international network of documentation; (c) to establish guiding principles for the member organizations in their work; (d) to organize the exchange of information relevant to the work of member organizations; (e) to convene conferences dealing with the problems of documentation; (f) to publish, sell and distribute periodical and non-periodical publications dealing with documentation; (g) to co-operate with other international organizations concerned with related subjects; (h) to take such other legal and appropriate measures as may be conducive to the attainment of the above objects. The development of the UNIVERSAL DECIMAL CLASSIFICATION (*q.v.*) is its major activity but it is concerned with other aspects of documentation especially since the Warsaw Conference in 1959. In addition to a number of committees concerned with the UDC schedules, FID also has committees and working groups considering particular aspects of librarianship. Since 1971 FID has published monthly *R & D projects in documentation and librarianship* as a current awareness service for on-going and projected research and development in the fields of library, documentation and information sciences and related areas of interest. Publishes *International Forum on Information and Documentation* (*q.*), *FID News Bulletin* (m.). *See also* STANDARD REFERENCE CODE.

INTERNATIONAL FEDERATION FOR INFORMATION PROCESSING. Formerly the International Federation of Information Processing Societies which was set up as a result of an international congress on information processing organized by Unesco and held in Paris in 1959. The members of the Federation are national societies, the adhering society in the United Kingdom being the British Computer Society. The Federation organized its first congress in Munich 1962, and a full report was published in 1963 by the North Holland Publishing Company under the title *Information processing*, 1962. Aims: to sponsor international conferences and symposia on information processing; to establish international committees to undertake special tasks falling within the scope of member societies; to advance the interests of member societies in international co-operation in the field of information processing. Has organized four congresses. Registered in accordance with Belgian law. Abbreviated IFIP. Publishes *IFIP Summary*.

INTERNATIONAL FEDERATION OF FILM ARCHIVES. *See* FIAF.

INTERNATIONAL FEDERATION OF INFORMATION PROCESSING SOCIETIES. Became known in 1962 as the INTERNATIONAL FEDERATION FOR INFORMATION PROCESSING (*q.v.*).

INTERNATIONAL FEDERATION OF LIBRARY ASSOCIATIONS. Founded June 1929 in Edinburgh to promote and facilitate international co-operation in librarianship and bibliography. Also known by the French name Fédération Internationale des Associations de Bibliothécaires (FIAB). The work of IFLA is done through annual Council meetings and a number of sections and committees studying practical questions of international librarianship such as union catalogues, international loans, exchange of publications, national and university libraries, public libraries, work with children, library buildings, library education, reprography, bibliographical work, etc. Its membership includes a number of international associations and national associations in seventy countries. Following the appointment of a full-time secretary in 1963 it now has its headquarters in the Netherlands. During the twenty-ninth session of the Council, held in Sofia (Bulgaria) in September 1963, an Association of the Libraries of International Organizations was formed within the framework of IFLA. Publishes *Libri* (q.), *IFLA Journal* (q.). *IFLA Yearbook* (a.), *Inspel* (2 or 3 times p.m. by the Special Libraries Section). IFLA developed from FIAB's International Library and Bibliographical Committee. *See also* ISBD. The IFLA Committee on Cataloguing was provided (for an initial period of three years from July 1971, with a grant from the Council on Library Resources, Washington) with a permanent Secretariat at the British Library, London, the executive responsibility resting with Mrs Dorothy Anderson. Its aim is particularly to carry out investigations and, in the field of cataloguing, make propositions concerning the international regulations between libraries, library associations, bibliographers, and other organized groups. The Committee has published the *Statement of principles* and the *International standard bibliographic description for monographs*, and since early 1972 *International cataloguing* (q.). It acts as a clearinghouse for cataloguing problems and as a centre for consultation. The completion of the project on monographs – ISBD(M) – has been followed by the creation of a new working party to draw up an ISBD for serials – ISBD(S).

INTERNATIONAL FEDERATION OF NATIONAL STANDARDIZATION ASSOCIATIONS (ISA). A body which was liquidated during the Second World War and superseded by the INTERNATIONAL ORGANIZATION FOR STANDARDIZATION (*q.v.*).

INTERNATIONAL FEDERATION OF RECORD LIBRARIES. Founded in Milan on 27th May 1963 and registered in accordance with French Law. It aims (a) to facilitate co-operation between gramophone record libraries and contribute to the development of their activities; (b) to contribute to the organization of the profession of record librarian. Membership is open to international associations and to national committees comprising institutions and individuals.

It is financed by members' dues. Abbreviated FIP (Fédération Internationale des Phonothèques).

INTERNATIONAL FEDERATION OF SOUND ARCHIVES. Founded in 1963 'to encourage co-operation between sound archives. To aid in the development of the activities of sound archives. To aid in establishing professional standards for librarians of recorded sound. To engage in any or all activities related to the field of recorded sound'.

INTERNATIONAL FEDERATION OF TRANSLATORS. Founded in Paris with Unesco support in December 1953 to bring together representative groups of translators in order to defend their material and moral interests, encourage the establishment of such groups in countries where they do not exist, represent translators at the international level, follow the development of theoretical and practical questions relating to translation, and contribute to the spread of culture. Organizes congresses and pursues various projects through committees relating to terminology, registers of specialist translators, copyright, training, etc. Registered in accordance with French law. Abbreviated FIT. Publishes *Babel* (q.).

INTERNATIONAL INFORMATION CENTRE FOR STANDARDS IN INFORMATION AND DOCUMENTATION. *See* ISO-DOC.

INTERNATIONAL INFORMATION CENTRE FOR TERMINO-LOGY. *See* INFOTERM.

INTERNATIONAL INFORMATION SERVICES FOR THE PHYSICS AND ENGINEERING COMMUNITIES. *See* INSPEC.

INTERNATIONAL INFORMATION SYSTEM ON RESEARCH IN DOCUMENTATION. *See* ISORID.

INTERNATIONAL INSTITUTE FOR ADULT LITERACY METHODS. Established by Unesco and the Government of Iran in Teheran, primarily to provide documentation and disseminate information. This is done by (a) providing for information centres and research workers, current relative bibliographical information in *Literacy Documentation* (q.) in French and in English editions; (b) by supplying, on request, detailed bibliographies on given aspects of literacy; (c) by the reproduction of specific documents. Publishes additionally *Literacy Work* (bi-m.), *Literacy Discussion* (q. text in English and French).

INTERNATIONAL INSTITUTE FOR CHILDREN'S LITERA-TURE AND READING RESEARCH. This Institute, which operates in Vienna, is a non-profit-making association; it also serves as the office of the Austrian Section of the International Board on Books for Young People (IBBY *q.v.*). Founded in 1965, it endeavours to create an international centre of work and co-ordination in the field of children's literature and to take over documentation in this area. Its aims are to: (a) promote international research and co-ordination in the fields of juvenile literature and reading; (b) collect and evaluate the results of research undertaken in various countries and provide a specialized technical library; (c) develop an international bibliography of technical literature on children's reading and make it available to anyone by means of a card index and publication in two periodicals, *Bookbird* and *Jugend und Buch*; (d) arrange conferences, exhibitions and seminars; (e) compile and publish lists of recommended books; (f) establish and develop a documentation and advisory centre for all areas of children's book work; (g) undertake studies in children's literature and the problems of reading; (h) collaborate with publishers by advising on, and promoting, translations and licences; (i) publish professional literature on children's books and reading; (j) collaborate with Austria's teacher training institutions to help awaken the interest of pre-service and in-service teachers for children's books. Publishes *Bookbird* (*q.*) in co-operation with the IBBY and *Jugend und Buch* (*q.* in German) in co-operation with the Austrian Children's Book Club, *Pa-Kontakte* (irreg.), *International Press Service*. Membership is available to individuals and groups (institutions, publishing houses, associations, etc.).

INTERNATIONAL INSTITUTE OF ARTS AND LETTERS. Founded on 20th December 1931 in Paris to achieve worldwide co-operation in the cultivation and promotion of arts, letters and sciences, with the object of increasing knowledge and of contributing in other ways to human progress. Members (Fellows, Corresponding and Associate) are selected from those qualified by outstanding achievements in the field of culture in forty countries.

INTERNATIONAL MEETING OF CATALOGUING EXPERTS. *See* IMCE.

INTERNATIONAL MICROGRAPHIC CONGRESS. Originally, the National Microfilm Association (U.S.A.) considered setting up foreign chapters but later decided to sponsor an international microfilm organization. Finance was provided and formal incorporation papers issued in the state of Michigan in September 1962. Officially, IMC dates from 30th April 1963. The first international meeting, however, was held during the NMA Convention in April 1964. An international federation of national societies of the world which are engaged in furthering the progress and application of the micro-recording and micro-reproduction art. The congresses are held annually. Aims to: promote understanding and co-operation among such societies; stimulate development of new methods and devices; provide an international clearinghouse for information of developments and facilities for exchange of publications and papers among member societies; promote and encourage the establishment and use of international standards; promote international exhibitions and conventions. National microfilm societies and individuals in countries without national societies may join. Abbreviated IMC. Publishes *IMC Journal* (q., distributed through national associations), and *The International Directory of Microreproduction Equipment*.

INTERNATIONAL MILLIONTH MAP. A 'map' of the world on a 1:1,000,000 scale; so far, about 300 of the projected 1,500 sheets have been completed.

INTERNATIONAL MUSICOLOGICAL SOCIETY. Founded in Basle, 1927, by amalgamating the *Internationale Musikgesellschaft* and the *Union Musicologique*. Reconstituted in 1949, the Society aims to establish relations between musicologists in different countries; serve as a central information and bibliographical office. Abbreviated IMS. Publishes *Acta musicologica* (q.). and congress reports.

INTERNATIONAL NUCLEAR INFORMATION SYSTEM. *See* INIS.

INTERNATIONAL ORGANIZATION FOR STANDARDIZATION. Constituted in London under its present statutes in October 1946 to replace the pre-war International Federation of National Standardizing Associations (ISA) and the United Nations Standards Coordinating Committee. Aims to promote development of standards in the world with a view to facilitating international exchange of goods and services, and to developing mutual co-operation in the sphere of intellectual, scientific, technological and economic activity. Over 100 technical committees of experts appointed by national standard bodies who are members formulate recommendations to national member associations. Abbreviated ISO. Publishes *ISO journal* (m.), *ISO memento* (a.), both for member bodies only.

INTERNATIONAL PAPER SIZES. The international 'A' series of paper sizes are now widely used throughout the world. In Britain many organizations have adopted them and there is both a British Standard (B.S. 4000) and an international recommendation (ISO/R 216) covering them.

'A' SERIES OF TRIMMED PAPER SIZES

Desig-nation	SIZE		Desig-nation	SIZE	
	mm	inches		mm	inches
4 A	1682 × 2378	66.22 × 93.62	A 5	148 × 210	5.83 × 8.27
2 A	1189 × 1682	46.81 × 66.22	A 6	105 × 148	4.13 × 5.83
A 0	841 × 1189	33.11 × 46.81	A 7	74 × 105	2.91 × 4.13
A 1	594 × 841	23.39 × 33.11	A 8	52 × 74	2.05 × 2.91
A 2	420 × 594	16.54 × 23.39	A 9	37 × 52	1.46 × 2.05
A 3	297 × 420	11.69 × 16.54	A 10	26 × 37	1.02 × 1.46
A 4	210 × 297	8.27 × 11.69			

INTERNATIONAL PATENT DOCUMENTATION CENTRE. *See* INPADOC.

INTERNATIONAL PATENT INSTITUTE. Aims to provide technical reports on novelty of inventions, undertake documentary research in all fields of science and technology. Financed by the eight member governments (Belgium, France, Luxemburg, Monaco, Netherlands, Switzerland, Turkey, U.K.) and by payment for services provided. Situated at The Hague. Abbreviated IIB (Institut Internationale des Brevets).

INTERNATIONAL PUBLISHERS ASSOCIATION. Founded in Paris in 1896 as International Publishers Congress to consider problems common to the publishing and bookselling trades, and to uphold and defend the right to publish and distribute the work of man's mind in complete freedom, both within the frontiers of each country and among the nations; to secure international co-operation among themselves and to overcome illiteracy, the lack of books and other means of education. Congresses are held periodically in different countries. A permanent office is maintained at Geneva. Membership is open to professional book and music publishers associations. Activities include help to secure signatories to the BERNE CONVENTION and UNIVERSAL COPYRIGHT CONVENTION (*qq.v.*) and to keep the flow of books between countries free of tariffs and other obstacles, provision of aid to emerging countries, and consideration of international copyright and translation rights. Publishes reports and congress proceedings. Abbreviated IPA. Publishes a newsletter (q.).

INTERNATIONAL READING ASSOCIATION. Founded in the

U.S.A. on 1st January 1956 to encourage the study of reading problems at all levels, and also to stimulate and promote research in developmental, corrective and remedial reading. There are 60,000 members in 65 countries. Abbreviated IRA. Publishes *The Reading Teacher*, *Journal of Reading* (both 8 p.a.), *Reading Research Quarterly* and about twenty different works annually. *See also* UNITED KINGDOM READING ASSOCIATION.

INTERNATIONAL REFERRAL CENTRE FOR INFORMATION HANDLING EQUIPMENT. One of the centres developed within the conceptual framework of the programme of UNISIST (*q.v.*), it was established in November 1974 at the University of Zagreb, Jugoslavia, with the object of promoting the exchange of information on recent developments in the field of information-handling equipment. Its functions in the area of referral activities are to collect data on: (a) institutions that deal with standards, regulations and procedures for information handling; (b) producers of information handling equipment; (c) organizations for research and development of networks and special activities in the area of information storage and retrieval; (d) specialists and special events (symposia, conferences, training courses) in the field of information handling equipment. Its functions in the area of information activities are to: (a) collect information related to information handling equipment as produced in periodicals, books, scientific papers, proceedings of conferences, reports, catalogues, etc; (b) provide bibliographic surveys for information under (a) in the form of special indexes; (c) organize a service for the information delivery on the user's request in the form of hard copies, of microfilm and of microfiche for the existing abstracts or for complete texts of publications and semi-publications; (d) publish annually or periodically cumulative indexes of the Centre's holdings. Abbreviated IRCIHE. Publishes *IRCIHE Bulletin*.

INTERNATIONAL REFERRAL SYSTEM FOR SOURCES OF ENVIRONMENTAL INFORMATION. *See* IRS.

INTERNATIONAL SCIENTIFIC FILM LIBRARY. Founded in 1961 in Brussels by the International Scientific Film Association (ISFA) and the Belgian Ministry of Education. Aims to: preserve outstanding scientific and technical films; promote the study, knowledge, widest possible dissemination, and the rationalization of the production of scientific films. It collects and preserves prints and sound tracks of films on research, higher and technical education and popularization of science produced in different countries, prepares sound versions in languages other than the original. Membership is open to individuals or representatives of corporate bodies. Abbreviated ISFL. Publishes *Bulletin*.

INTERNATIONAL SERIALS DATA SYSTEM. *See* ISDS.

INTERNATIONAL SOCIETY FOR PERFORMING ARTS LIBRARIES AND MUSEUMS. Founded in September 1954 at Zagreb with the object of developing co-operation among libraries, as well as museums, public, private and specialized collections concerned with the theatre, dance, cinema, marionettes, mime, festivals, son et lumière, radio and television. Membership is open to individuals and organizations. Eleven congresses have been held in different capital cities since 1960. Publishes *Spectacles-Documents* (bulletin) in *Theatre Documentation* (3 a year). Congress proceedings.

INTERNATIONAL STANDARD BIBLIOGRAPHIC DESCRIPTION. *See* ISBD.

INTERNATIONAL STANDARD BOOK NUMBER. *See* ISBN, STANDARD BOOK NUMBER.

INTERNATIONAL STANDARD CLASSIFICATION OF EDUCATION. *See* ISCED.

INTERNATIONAL STANDARD SERIAL NUMBER. *See* ISSN.

INTERNATIONAL STANDARDS. Of several international standards organizations the two most important are International Organization for Standardization (ISO) and International Electrotechnical Commission (IEC). ISO seeks to achieve worldwide agreement on international standards with a view to the expansion of trade, the improvement of quality, the increase of productivity and the lowering of prices. Some ISO recommendations of interest to librarians include:

ISO/R 4   International code for abbreviation of titles of periodicals

ISO/8   Layout of periodicals

ISO/R 18   Short contents list (of periodicals or other documents)

ISO/R 66   *Paper vocabulary. First series of terms.* (Subsequent series of terms are given in /R 135, /R 231, /R 372, /R 1295, /R 1912)

ISO/R 77   Bibliographical references (Essential elements)

ISO/R 169   Sizes of photocopies (on paper) readable with optical devices

ISO/R 193   Microcopies on transparent bases. Recommended bases, dimensions

ISO/R 214   Abstracts and synopses

ISO/R 215 Presentation of contributions to periodicals

ISO/R 216 Trimmed sizes of writing paper and certain classes of printed matter

ISO/R 218 Microcopies – scale of 35 mm microfilms for international exchange.

ISO/R 233 *International system for the transliteration of Arabic characters.*

ISO/R 259 *Transliteration of Hebrew.*

ISO/R 260 *Terms relating to microcopies and their bases.*

ISO/R 371 *Terms relating to microcopy apparatus.*

ISO/R 690 *Bibliographical references. Essential and supplementary elements.*

ISO/R 833 *Abbreviations of generic names in titles of periodicals*

ISO/R 999 *Index of a publication.*

ISO/R 1086 *Title leaves of a book.*

ISO 2108 *International standard book numbering (ISBN).*

ISO 2146 *Directories of libraries, information and documentation centres.*

ISO 2636 *Information processing. Conventions for incorporating flowchart symbols in flowcharts.*

ISO 2789 *International library statistics.*

ISO/DIS 3166.21 *Codes for the representation of names of countries.* The ISO Information Network came into operation officially on 1st January 1974 in order to link the ISO Information Centre at the Central Secretariat in Geneva with information centres nominated by the national standards organizations throughout the world, so as to create a fast and efficient technical information service for all questions relating to standardization. *See also* AMERICAN NATIONAL STANDARDS INSTITUTE, INC., BRITISH STANDARDS INSTITUTION, DIN, INTERNATIONAL ORGANIZATION FOR STANDARDIZATION, COPANT STANDARDS, Z39.

INTERNATIONAL UNION FOR THE PROTECTION OF LITERARY AND ARTISTIC WORKS. Founded 9th September 1886 to ensure effective protection to authors of literary and artistic works, and to ensure and develop the international protection of literary and artistic works. Membership is open to governments. Organizes diplomatic conferences. Has a specialized library of 12,000 vols. Publishes *Le droit d'auteur* (m.), *Copyright* (m.).

INTERNATIONAL YOUTH LIBRARY. An Associated Project of Unesco, founded in 1949 in Munich. It developed out of the first post war exhibition of international children's books organized in Munich by Mrs. Lepman in 1946. The stock totals over 100,000 books from more than fifty countries, about 80 per cent of the books being donated by the publishers. Abbreviated IYL.

INTERNE. An assistant librarian who, for a period of about a year, exchanges positions with someone holding a similar position in another country. Also spelt 'intern'.

INTERPOLATED NOTE. An explanation or description added to an entry by the compiler of a catalogue or bibliography to clarify the original material. Such information is inserted within SQUARE BRACKETS (*q.v.*).

INTERPOLATION. (*Classification*) The insertion of a new topic at any point in a scheme of classification. A non-structural type of notation renders this readily possible. *See also* EXTRAPOLATION.

INTERPRETER. An electric accounting machine which prints information recorded by holes punched on cards. The printing of such information is called 'interpreting'.

INTER-REGIONAL SUBJECT COVERAGE SCHEME. Under this scheme each of the Regional Bureaux became responsible on 1st January 1959 for seeing that one library in its area purchases every new book and pamphlet published in the United Kingdom, which is included in the *British National Bibliography*; the allocation of sections of the Dewey Classification is as follows:

000–099	Northern	400–499	East Midlands
100–199	Wales	800–899	„ „
200–299	South-Western	500–599	West Midlands
300–349	Yorkshire	600–699	North-Western
350–399	Scotland	700–799	London
		900–999	South-Eastern

These books are not recorded in the National Union Catalogue at the National Central Library as it is known that they are available in a particular region; requests for books are sent to the appropriate regional bureau. The books purchased under this scheme are intended to be provided primarily for preservation.

INTER-RELATED LOGIC-ACCUMULATING SCANNER. An atypical punching pattern used on punched cards, developed at the U.S. Patent Office. Abbreviated ILAS.

INTERROGATION MARK. A punctuation sign (?) placed at the end of a direct question. Also used between parentheses to indicate an author's questioning of the accuracy of a statement. Also called 'Interrogation point', 'Mark of interrogation', 'Question mark'.

INTERSECTING FRAME. (*Binding*) One or more decorative frames, the sides of which (or some of them) are extended, where they meet each other, to the edges of the cover.

INTERSPACING. *Synonymous with* LETTER SPACING (*q.v.*).

INTERTYPE. A typesetting machine casting type in a slug, similar to, but differing in detail from, the LINOTYPE (*q.v.*).

INTERUNIVERSITY COMMUNICATION COUNCIL. *See* EDU-COM.

INTRA-FACET RELATION. *See* PHASE.

INTREX. *See* PROJECT INTREX.

INTRINSIC VALUE. (Archives) In the appraisal of manuscripts, the worth in terms of money, of a document as affected by some unique factor such as its age, an attached seal, a signature or the handwriting of a distinguished person, or the circumstances regarding its creation. *See also* APPRAISAL.

INTRODUCTION. 1. A short essay or statement, usually being a general survey of the subject preparing the reader for the treatment to follow, of a commendatory nature, and written by an authority in the field with which the book deals. Its order in the PRELIMINARIES (*q.v.*), is after the Preface and immediately before the first page of text. Sometimes it is the first chapter. 2. Included in the title of a book, it indicates that it is an introductory book on the subject, intended for students, and possibly a popular treatment, but not as elementary as a PRIMER (*q.v.*). If dealing with a learned or highly scientific subject, it may be comprehensible only by specialists.

INTRODUCTION DATE. The date given at the beginning or end of an INTRODUCTION (*q.v.*).

INVERPOS PAPER. Trade name for a type of SILVER HALIDE PAPER (*q.v.*) which gives a positive image without the necessity for first making a negative when making copies by LENSLESS COPYING (*q.v.*).

INVERSION, PRINCIPLE OF. In classification, placing the facets in schedule order in such a way that the most concrete, intensive or significant is last.

INVERSION OF TITLE. The turning about of a title to bring a particular word to the front. This practice is frequently adopted in dictionary catalogues.

INVERTED BACONIAN SCHEME. A scheme of classification in which the order of the main classes in Francis Bacon's philosophical system outlined in his *The advancement of learning* (1605) – history poesy, philosophy – are inverted, as in the schemes of Dr. W. T. Harris and Melvil Dewey.

INVERTED COMMAS. Pairs of superior commas, or sometimes single commas, placed at the beginning and end of quotations. *See also* QUOTES. One inverted comma is sometimes used in the abbreviation for Mac, thus; M'.

INVERTED ENTRY. An index entry which has been re-arranged to bring the most important word or words to the front. For example, 'CO-EFFICIENT OF EXPANSION, APPARENT'. The opposite of DIRECT ENTRY (*q.v.*).

INVERTED HEADING. A catalogue heading which has had the order of the words inverted to bring the most important word to the front, as CHEMISTRY, ORGANIC. Also called 'Indirect heading'.

INVERTED TITLE. *See* INVERSION OF TITLE.

INVOICE. A list of items supplied, together with the prices charged for each. An itemized bill.

IONAMETER. *See* pH Value.

IRA. Acronym for INTERNATIONAL READING ASSOCIATION (*q.v.*).

IRISH ASSOCIATION FOR DOCUMENTATION. Founded 1947 with the aim of co-ordinating documentation services in Ireland. Most special and large public libraries have contributed to the *Union list of current periodicals and serials in Dublin libraries*, 1960 (Supplement 1962), which records more than 6,000 titles and gives locations.

IRISH ASSOCIATION FOR DOCUMENTATION AND INFORMATION SERVICES. *See* IADIS.

IRISH CENTRAL LIBRARY FOR STUDENTS. Founded by the Carnegie United Kingdom Trust in 1923; control was transferred to An Chomhairle Leabharlanna (The Library Council) in 1948. Supplements the regular library services of local authorities, educational institutions and learned societies, and the services of public and special libraries generally, by providing books for study and research both from its own stock and by means of inter-library loans. Abbreviated ICLS.

IRISH MANUSCRIPTS COMMISSION. Set up in October 1928 (under a warrant of the President of the Executive Council of Saorstát Éireann) to report on collections of manuscripts and papers of literary, historical and general interest, relating to Ireland, whether in private or public ownership, and also to arrange for and supervise the execution of programmes of publication. Since September 1970, the Commission has been responsible for a Survey of Business Records throughout the Republic of Ireland. Financed by government vote under the Department of Education. Abbreviated IMC. Publishes *Analecta Hibernica* (*irreg.*) and many books of calendars, abstracts, reports, etc.

IRISH STYLE. An eighteenth-century style of book decoration distinguished by a large centre lozenge of inlaid fawn leather.

IRLA. Acronym for Independent Research Libraries Association. Some fourteen American research libraries (including some of the best known libraries with worldwide reputations) and societies not affiliated to colleges or universities formed this association on 10th May 1972. It is concerned with the particular problems which independent American research libraries have in common and seeks to secure legislation which will establish the positions of such libraries as institutions of higher education.

IRON INFORMATION CENTER. Established in 1973 at the Columbus (Ohio) Laboratories of Battelle Memorial Institute, this Center is supported by groups related to the iron industry of U.S.A., Canada, Japan, Australia and Brazil. Membership is open to all companies in the Free World. The Center anticipates that published information written in about twenty languages will be processed.

ISAD. Acronym for INFORMATION SCIENCE AND AUTOMATION DIVISION (*q.v.*) of the American Library Association.

ISADORE GILBERT MUDGE CITATION. *See* MUDGE CITATION, ISADORE GILBERT.

ISARITHMS. *Synonymous with* ISOPLETHS (*q.v.*).

ISCED. Acronym of the International Standard Classification of Education. At an international governmental meeting of experts to review this Classification for statistics of education held in Paris from 3rd to 11th December 1974, a technical examination was made of it; after approving the general principles of ISCED and considering it to be an appropriate framework for international comparisons and a suitable basis for designing a national classification system, it was agreed, *inter alia*, that at the 1975 International Conference on Education it should be recommended to member States that ISCED should be used by statisticians and planners.

ISEPHODIC MAP. One which shows the equal cost of travel, places of equal freight rates being connected by isephodes similar to isochrones.

ISIS. Acronym of Integrated Set of Information Systems developed and implemented in the Central Library and Documentation Branch of the International Labour Office in Geneva. It is composed of three interdependent systems: (a) a bibliographic control system; (b) a serial system; (c) a loan system. A fourth evaluation and control system receives information from the other three to permit subsequent analysis.

ISLAND BOOKCASE. *See* ISLAND STACK.

ISLAND CASE. A bookcase (usually double-sided) which is so placed that readers can walk all around it.

ISLAND STACK. A book STACK (*q.v.*) which is placed away from the wall so that readers can walk all round it. Also called 'Island bookcase'.

ISLIC. *See* ISRAEL SOCIETY OF SPECIAL LIBRARIES AND INFORMATION CENTRES.

ISLINGTON CHARGING SYSTEM. A method of recording the loan of books introduced at the Islington Public Libraries in 1963. Readers are provided with plastic identity cards bearing their name and address in raised characters: these they insert in a machine called a Recorder to print their name and address on a small slip of paper. This is used together with a book-card to record a loan. Otherwise the system is exactly the same as the BROWNE BOOK CHARGING SYSTEM (*q.v.*). It has the advantage of permitting delayed discharging. *See also* CHARGING METHODS.

ISMEC. Abbreviation for Information Services in Mechanical Engineering. In July 1973 the Institution of Mechanical Engineers and INSPEC (*q.v.*) began providing an international information service covering all aspects of mechanical engineering including production engineering and engineering management. A technically-qualified team selects material from the world's mechanical engineering journals and conference publications. This material is classified, indexed, and processed for entry on to a computer data base from which all the ISMEC services are provided. Publishes *ISMEC Bulletin* (fortnightly) and provides a computer-readable magnetic tape service covering all items in the *ISMEC Bulletin* including subject indexing in depth.

ISOBARS. Lines on a map which connect places with the same barometric pressure.

ISOBATHS. Lines on a map joining points on the sea bed which have an equal depth. Such lines show the relief of the sea bed, just as CONTOURS (*q.v.*) show the relief of the land by joining places of equal altitude. Areas between isobaths are coloured in varying shades of blue.

ISOCHRONIC MAP. One which shows possible progress of travel in all directions from a given centre in certain specified time intervals.

ISOCRYMES. Lines on a map which connect places with the same degree of frost.

ISODOC. Abbreviation for International Information Centre for Standards in Information and Documentation which was established by agreement between Unesco and ISO and is located at the Secretariat of ISO/TC 46. The Centre is designed to facilitate and promote the availability and application of standards in the area of information and documentation and related fields by (a) collecting, evaluating and storing information on standards, (b) disseminating this information.

ISOGONES. Lines on a map which connect places with equal angles of magnetic variation. Also called 'Isogonic lines'.

ISOGONIC CHART. One which shows lines connecting places of equal magnetic declination or variation.

ISOGRAMS. *Synonymous with* ISOPLETHS.

ISOHALINES. Lines on a map joining points in the oceans which have equal salinity.

ISOHELS. Lines on a map which connect places with the same amount of sunshine over a certain period.

ISOHYETS. Lines on a map which connect places with the same amount of rainfall over a certain period.

ISOHYPSES. Lines on a map which connect places with the same elevation.

ISOLATE. (*Classification*) 1. A generic term applicable to all the three planes – Idea, Notation, Words – in the Colon Classification, and indicating a division of a FACET (*q.v.*). Also called 'Isolate focus'. In addition to COMMON ISOLATES (*q.v.*), there are Time, Space and Language isolates used to indicate periods of time, geographical division, and languages respectively. 2. The name of anything that can exist and behave as a unit or a word expressing its behaviour. Isolates are taken from the literature of a subject. 3. A single component ('ingredient') of a compound subject.

ISONEPHS. Lines on a map which connect places with the same amount of cloud over a certain period.

ISOPLETH MAP. A quantitative aerial map on which the geographical distribution of the elements is shown by lines of equal value, such as contours, isobars, isohyets and isotherms. *See also* ISOPLETHS.

ISOPLETHS. Lines on a map which connect places of equal density or value of distribution of any specific element. Also called 'Isorithms' and 'Isograms'. If they connect places of equal temperature they are called 'isotherms'; of equal rainfall, 'isohyets'; of barometric pressure, 'isobars'; of magnetic variation, 'isogones'; of sunshine, 'isohels'; of frost, 'isocrymes'; of clouds, 'isonephs'; of equal elevation, 'isohypses'. They connect an average number of individual units. Lines which connect a continuous value, such as temperature, are called 'isarithms'.

ISORID. Acronym of the International Information System on Research in Documentation which was started in 1972 by Unesco's Department of Documentation, Libraries and Archives to collect, organize, analyse and disseminate information on research projects and research reports in the field of documentation, libraries and archives, and to make this information available in a form allowing maximum use of these data by research workers, documentalists, librarians, etc. An international register of research projects and reports, which is being established by Unesco makes this information available to Member States, institutions and specialists through publication in *Bibliography, Documentation, Terminology* (6 p.a.). Member States have designated national institutions, called National Information Transfer Centres (NITCs) which regularly provide the Unesco Secretariat with relative information. *See also* CDS.

ISOSEISMAL LINES. Lines on a map joining places which have suffered an equal intensity of shock from an earthquake. Such lines usually form closed curves round their seismic focus.

ISOTHERMS. Lines on a map which connect places with the same temperature at a particular instant or having the same average temperature over a certain period.

ISRAEL LIBRARY ASSOCIATION. Founded in 1952 to raise professional standards of all types of libraries and improve the working conditions of librarians. Membership is open to anyone who has held a permanent position in a library for one year or who has graduated from the Graduate Library School of the Hebrew University in Jerusalem. Abbreviated ILA. Publishes *Yad-la-kore* (*The Reader's Aid*) – contains abstracts in English of the main articles.

ISRAEL SOCIETY OF SPECIAL LIBRARIES AND INFORMATION CENTRES. Registered in August 1966 to encourage and promote efficient utilization of knowledge through special libraries and information centres, to facilitate written and oral communication among its members, and to co-operate with other bodies with similar or allied interests in Israel and abroad. Abbreviated ISLIC. Publishes *Bulletin* (3 p.a.), *Contributions to information science* (irreg.).

ISSUE. 1. All the charges or other records representing books on loan. 2. The number of books so issued. 3. The copies of a book in which the original sheets are used but which differ in some respects from copies previously issued (e.g. a new title-page, an additional appendix, the inclusion of a list of publisher's announcements, or different format – paper edition). 4. The number of impressions (copies) of an old map or print made at a given time without any change being made in the plate. 5. A particular publication, complete in itself, of a serial or periodical which is issued at intervals or in parts. *See also* EDITION, FIRST EDITION, IMPRESSION, NEW EDITION, REPRINT, REVISED EDITION.

ISSUE DESK. *See* CIRCULATION DESK.

ISSUE GUIDES. Pieces of card, plastic or metal which project above the issue (the projection being numbered or lettered according to the method of arrangement) to facilitate the finding of records of books on loan. *See also* CHARGE.

ISSUE NUMBER. The number given to a separately issued part of a serial to distinguish it from other issues. Numbers may run consecutively from the first issue onwards, but if the issues are divided into volumes, a new sequence of issue numbers commences with each volume; in this case they are printed on the cover, and also in each issue immediately after the volume number.

ISSUE TRAY. A tray containing the ISSUE (*q.v.*).

ital. Abbreviation for italic.

ITALIAN STYLE. *See* ALDINE (ITALIAN) STYLE.

ITALIC. Sloping type, as distinguished from the normal, upright, Roman type, used to emphasize any special point, or for the names of publications, ships, etc. It was first used by Aldus Pius Manutius in 1501, and was originally called Aldine or Chancery, and was based on a humanistic Italian handwriting of a somewhat earlier period. *This is italic* and is indicated in a MS. prepared for the printer by a single underlining. Abbreviated ital.

ITALTYPE. A slug-composing machine which was made in Italy in the early 1950s. INTERTYPE (*q.v.*) and LINOTYPE (*q.v.*) matrices can be used as well as the maker's Italtype matrices.

ITEM. (*Information retrieval*) In an index, the reference to the document. Also the document itself, whether a book, serial, abstract, article, photograph or microform, etc. *See also* COMPRESENCE, FEATURE, TERM.

ITEM CARDS. Cards used to record information by means of coloured tabs, holes or notches in connexion with some form of CO-ORDINATE INDEXING (*q.v.*). *See also* FEATURE CARD.

ITEM ENTRY. In information retrieval, the entry of particulars of a document under a heading or symbol identifying the document. This is the traditional method used in library catalogues. It is also the method used on edge-slotted cards. Also called 'Document system'. *See also* TERM ENTRY.

ITERATIVE SEARCHING. The searching for information or a

document by a librarian for a user, the librarian finding such material as will meet the user's needs. A subsequent search, or searches, may be required, based on the use made of this material and the user's further request/s. This kind of search is modified at intervals and not continuously as with HEURISTIC SEARCHING (*q.v.*).

IVORY BOARD. A good quality card, made from wood, and used for printing.

J. D. STEWART TRAVELLING BURSARY. *See under* STEWART TRAVELLING BURSARY, J. D.

JACKET. *Synonymous with* BOOK JACKET (*q.v.*).

JACKET BAND. A strip of paper wrapped round a book-jacket to emphasize some sales aspect.

JACKETED FILM. Microfilm which has been inserted in a FILM JACKET (*q.v.*). *See also* MICROFILM JACKET.

JACONET. Cotton material, glazed on one side, and used to line and strengthen the spines of books.

JAMES REPORT. The Report of a Committee of Enquiry into Teacher Education and Training, of which Lord James of Rushden (Vice-Chancellor of the University of York) was Chairman, was published in January 1972. It produced recommendations which were incorporated in the White Paper published on 6th December 1972, entitled *Education: a framework for expansion* (Cmnd. 5174). This provided a ten-year programme for the expansion of education in England and Wales, including proposals for a great expansion of nursery education, an increased school building programme, more teachers and a new kind of higher education qualification.

JANE ADDAMS AWARD. *See* ADDAMS AWARD, JANE.

JANNON, JEAN. A master printer in Paris in 1610, who, due to his Protestant leanings, went to Sedan where he printed for the Calvinist Academy and issued one of the finest and earliest of French specimen books in 1621. His types were used solely for the Academy and the Prince of Sedan during the next twenty years at the end of which period he returned to Paris to set up a business, but went again to Sedan to print for the Academy because of oppression and the confiscation of some of his punches and some matrices; these were sent to the Imprimerie Royale which had recently been set up by Cardinal Richelieu. They remained there until 1898 when they were revived and used for various de luxe editions published by the Imprimerie Nationale, as the Imprimerie Royale became known after the Revolution, and which attributed their design to Claude Garamond whose style he undoubtedly used for his work. His types had a considerable influence because of their use at Sedan over many years, and much later, because of their revival at the end of the nineteenth century.

JANSENIST STYLE. A very simple binding named after Cornelius Jansen, the seventeenth century Bishop of Ypres, decorated only by a centre-piece (often armorial) and corner fleurons, or devoid of ornamentation on the outside of the covers, but with elaborate DOUBLURES (*q.v.*) tooled with DENTELLE (*q.v.*) borders.

JAPANESE PAPER. A paper, or tissue, in varying substances, having a silky texture; it is handbeaten from the bark fibres of the mulberry tree, or in imitation thereof. Used for printing, etchings, photogravures, books; also used for binding. 'French Japon' is a good imitation, it is less expensive but not so strong.

JAPANESE STYLE. *See* CHINESE STYLE.

JAPANESE VELLUM. An extremely costly, strong hand-made Japanese paper with a firm glossy surface, and a creamy tint. It is much used for engravings, and diplomas, or where a very durable paper is required. It will not withstand india-rubber, and must be handled very carefully. An imitation is made by treating thick ordinary paper with sulphuric acid.

JEFFREYS REPORT, FRIEDMAN-. *See* FRIEDMAN-JEFFREYS REPORT.

JENKINS BIBLIOGRAPHICAL AWARD, JOHN H. This award is offered annually by Union College, Schenectady, New York, for a bibliographical work of unusual merit bearing an imprint date two years before the year of the Award. It is named after John H. Jenkins, bookseller, of Austin, Texas, who returned to Union College the $2,000 reward given him for the recovery of J. J. Audubon's 'elephant folio' of the *Birds of America* which had been stolen from Schaffer Library, Union College, in June 1971, on condition that the College match it and establish a bibliographical prize. The book had been acquired by the College in the 1840s from Audubon himself. The Award was first made in 1973 to G. Thomas Tanselle for his *Guide to the study of United States imprints* (Harvard, 1971).

JENSON. A type face named after Nicolas Jenson (1420–80), a French printer who went to Venice in 1468 and had his own printing works there. 'The world's first great type designer, perhaps the greatest in all typographical history' – *McMurtrie*. He used his 'perfect roman letter' in *De praeparatione evangelica* by Eusebius, 1470; this served as the model for Morris's Golden type and for Benton's Cloister. Jenson was working in Venice, and his type became a pattern for all future type designs. The Monotype Centaur, designed by Bruce Rogers, is based on Jenson. The letters are open, dignified, clear and legible, of even colour and perfect harmony. The contrast between thick and thin strokes is slight; the serifs are blunt with very small brackets.

JETÉ EN MOULE. ('Cast in a mould'). Mould metal type for use in printing. Also called 'Get en mol'.

JEWETT'S CODE. A code of cataloguing rules prepared by Charles Coffin Jewett, Librarian of the Smithsonian Institution, Washington, and published as the second part of *The Smithsonian report on the construction of catalogues of libraries, and their publication by means of separate stereo-titles*, 1852. Jewett accepted most of Sir Anthony Panizzi's British Museum *Rules* ... with some minor modifications and at least one major difference.

JEWISH LIBRARIANS ASSOCIATION. FOUNDED in 1946 in the U.S.A. to advance the interests of Jewish libraries and the professional status of Jewish librarians; to promote publications of Jewish bibliographical interest. Abbreviated JLA. It was merged in June 1966 with the Jewish Library Association to form the ASSOCIATION OF JEWISH LIBRARIES (*q.v.*) of which it is an autonomous Division.

JEWISH LIBRARY ASSOCIATION. Founded in 1962 in the U.S.A. 'to promote and improve library service and standards in Jewish communities; to serve as a centre for the dissemination of Judaica, library information and guidance; to encourage the establishment of new Judaica libraries'. Published *Newsletter* (3 a year). It was merged in June 1966 with the Jewish Librarians Association to form the ASSOCIATION OF JEWISH LIBRARIES (*q.v.*) of which it is an autonomous Division.

JOANNA. A light roman type designed by Eric Gill in 1930. It is remarkable for its small capitals which do not reach the height of the ascenders, themselves not tall. It is eminently suited for book work.

JOB FILE. A collection of SEARCH RECORDS (*q.v.*). The record of the results of the enquiries may be kept separately from the search records. In either case they serve as a record of information and may save searching on a subsequent occasion when the enquiry is repeated.

JOB PRESS. A small platen printing press which is used for producing small items such as handbills.

JOB PRINTER. One who prints small items such as labels, leaflets, forms, stationery, handbills, etc., in small quantities.

JOBBER. In America, a wholesale bookseller who stocks many copies of various kinds of books issued by different publishers and supplies them to retailers and libraries. There are two types of jobber (1) those who stock mainly current text-books, trade, and technical books, and (2) those who stock only remainders.

JOHN CARTER BROWN LIBRARY. *See* BROWN LIBRARY, JOHN CARTER.

JOHN H. JENKINS BIBLIOGRAPHICAL AWARD. *See* JENKINS BIBLIOGRAPHICAL AWARD, JOHN H.

JOHN HARRIS AWARD. *See* HARRIS AWARD, JOHN.

JOHN NEWBERY MEDAL. *See* NEWBERY MEDAL, JOHN.

JOHN R. ROWE MEMORIAL AWARD. The new name of the EXHIBITS ROUND TABLE AWARD (*q.v.*).

JOHN RYLANDS UNIVERSITY LIBRARY OF MANCHESTER. The magnificently endowed John Rylands Library, Manchester, with its special collections of books including those of incunabula, manuscripts, and rare books, was merged administratively in 1972 with the existing large research library of the University to form the University Library with this title. The collection now comprises over 2,000,000 books; some 8,000 periodical titles are currently taken, and over 300,000 titles are on microfilm. The extensive holdings of MSS., early printed and rare books are housed in the superb Deansgate building, the home of the original John Rylands Library, and an additional building.

JOINED HAND. Handwriting in which the letters are all joined to one another. The opposite of DISJOINED HAND (*q.v.*).

JOINER'S PRESS. The name given to the earliest hand printing presses which were introduced about 1440. Made of wood, they were similar to wine presses, the pressure needed to press the paper on to type being applied by means of a screw turning on to a flat platen.

JOINT. 1. One of the two parts of the covering material that bend when the covers of a book are opened. 2. The strips of cloth, leather or other material that are used to reinforce the end-papers. 3. The grooves, formed by the backing process, which are made to receive the boards when binding a book. *See also* HINGE.

JOINT AUTHOR. One who writes in collaboration with another, or several other writers. The parts written by each are not always indicated; in fact, the contribution of each is usually not distinguishable.

JOINT AUTHORSHIP. (*Cataloguing*) Describes the authorship of books in which two or more persons collaborate, the parts written by each not being specified.

JOINT BOARD. Two or more library authorities which are authorized by an order of the Secretary of State made after consultation, and with the agreement of the authorities concerned, to be a library authority and provide a library service covering the areas of the separate library authorities before the formation of the joint board. Provision for their formation is made in Section 5 of the Public Libraries and Museums Act, 1964. *See also* LIBRARY AREA, LIBRARY AUTHORITY.

JOINT CATALOGUE. One containing entries for the books in two or more libraries.

JOINT CODE. The popular name for the code of cataloguing rules prepared by a joint committee of the British and American library associations. *See also* ANGLO-AMERICAN CODE.

JOINT COMMITTEE. A committee composed of representatives of two authorities and possibly co-opted members, which administers one or more libraries serving both areas. The committee has such of the powers of a library authority, except that of borrowing money, as the two authorities agree to confer upon it.

JOINT FICTION RESERVE. A scheme whereby a number of libraries agree to hold novels permanently. The authors are allocated according to alphabetical sequence amongst the co-operating libraries by agreement. The first scheme of this kind was started in Metropolitan London and included the keeping of all copies which were redundant in Metropolitan libraries as well as buying all new titles by the allocated authors. A similar scheme was adopted in the Northern Regional Bureau and on 1st January 1962 a National Joint Fiction Reserve scheme (abbreviated NJFR) which is a co-operative effort of all regional bureaux outside London and the South-Eastern began to operate. Each region is responsible for a certain section of the alphabet. This scheme provides only for the purchase and retention of new publications and is not retrospective. Allocation by author amongst the regions is as follows:

A–C	North-Western	K–M	West Midlands
D–F	Northern	N–S	Yorkshire
G–J	East Midlands	T–Z	South-Western

See also ASSOCIATION OF METROPOLITAN CHIEF LIBRARIANS, LIBRARY ASSOCIATION OF IRELAND.

JOINT REPORT. Familiar name for *School libraries in post-war reconstruction: a joint report* published in 1945. It was the result of co-operation between the School Library Association and the School Libraries Section of the Library Association. This section ceased to exist in 1945 in order to make possible a single association for school librarians.

JOINT WORK. A work by two or more authors in which the individual contributions are not distinguishable (*IFLA*).

JOSEPH W. LIPPINCOTT AWARD. *See* LIPPINCOTT AWARD, JOSEPH W.

JOURNAL. 1. A newspaper or periodical. Particularly a periodical issued by a society or institution and containing news, proceedings, transactions and reports of work carried out in a particular field. 2. A record of a person's activities day by day.

JOURNALESE. Words and phrases commonly used by journalists. Hackneyed phrases.

JOURNALISM. The profession of compiling, writing for and editing newspapers, periodicals, etc.

JOURNALIST. One who edits or contributes to a newspaper or periodical.

JOURNALS OF THE HOUSE OF COMMONS and of the HOUSE OF LORDS. *See* PARLIAMENTARY PAPERS.

JUDICIAL WRIT. One issuing from a Court of Law.

JUMBLED TYPE. *Synonymous with* PIE (*q.v.*).

JUNIOR ASSISTANT. A young assistant librarian who does not supervise the work of other assistants.

JUNIOR BOOK. A book for children.

JUNIOR DEPARTMENT. *Synonymous with* JUNIOR LIBRARY and CHILDREN'S LIBRARY (*q.v.*).

JUNIOR LIBRARIAN. One who works with children, or in a children's library.

JUNIOR LIBRARY. *Synonymous with* CHILDREN'S LIBRARY (*q.v.*).

JURIS. The information retrieval and inquiry system of the U.S. Department of Justice.

JUSTIFICATION. (*Cataloguing*) The provision of data, especially in the form of a note, introduced into an added entry, cross-reference, or subject heading for the sole purpose of making clear why the particular entry was provided. An entry treated in this way is said to be justified.

JUSTIFYING. (*Printing*) In typesetting, equally spacing out letters and words to a given measure, so that each line will be of the same length.

JUSTOWRITER. The trade name for an American machine for composing typewriter characters. Two electrically-driven machines are used, each having a typewriter keyboard. As words are typed on paper on the first machine, a moving tape is punched with a code for each character and the spacing needed to justify each line. When this tape is run through the second machine, interpretation of the punched code produces automatically typed and justified lines. The finished and corrected page is suitable for reproduction by photo offset or photogravure.

JUTE. A plant which contains weaker and less durable fibres than flax or hemp. and which are somewhat easily rotted by water. Jute paper was originally made from old rope, burlap, jute or manilla clippings, but is now usually made from sulphite stock (woodpulp used for making kraft paper) and is the material from which heavy wrapping paper and large bags for such materials as cement, coal and potatoes are made. 'Jute tissue' is made from old sacks and similar material and is used for tailors' patterns.

JUTE BOARD. A strong, light-weight board, made from jute fibres, and used for binding books.

JUVENILE BOOK. Trade name, now rarely used, for a book for children.

JUVENILE DEPARTMENT. *Synonymous with* CHILDREN'S LIBRARY (*q.v.*).

JUVENILE LIBRARY. *Synonymous with* CHILDREN'S LIBRARY (*q.v*).

K.C. Stands for the Kyle Classification, the familar name of the CLASSIFICATION FOR SOCIAL SCIENCES (*q.v.*) compiled by Barbara Kyle.

KAISER INDEX. *See* KAISER'S SYSTEM.

KAISER'S SYSTEM. A method of subject indexing propounded by J. Kaiser in his *Systematic indexing*, 1911. He emphasized that subject indexing policy must be entirely guided by the purpose for which the collection of documents had been formed. In determining subject headings, classificatory order has been introduced into the dictionary arrangement.

KALVAR. A dry copying process in which Kalvar materials are used in paper and film. It is used for the duplication of microfilm; being speedy in exposure and development it is the most conveniently processed commercially available film, and has great possibilities of further development and application. It uses a non-silver emulsion, has some characteristics similar to diazo, and does not require the wet processing or washing stages. A trade mark of the Kalvar Corporation. According to *American Libraries* (July–August 1973) Kalvar film was used for editions of the *New York Times* from 1967 through 1970, and where the manufacturer's storage conditions were not rigidly followed an ingredient in the film resulted in the destruction of storage boxes, cabinets, and shelves in which the film was kept, and harmed close-by materials as well. This ingredient emits hydrogen chloride gas which becomes hydrochloric acid. The film is expected to have an extremely long life and is impervious to its own havoc. The Microfilming Corporation of America (a subsidiary of the *New York Times*) which was manufacturing Kalvar microfilm, moved into a new factory in 1970 and then used silverhalide film instead.

KARD-A-FILM. Trade name for a Remington Rand system for filing strips of roll film. Slotted cards in three sizes have translucent protectors into which two or three strips of 16 mm or 35 mm film may be placed.

KARDVEYOR SYSTEM. A system (marketed by Remington Rand Ltd.) for containing a very large number of cards; they are kept on edge in a unit of metal trays placed side by side in twenty-one banks which rotate vertically by electronic operation. This system is used for accommodating a large central catalogue of books in stock and on order for a number of libraries, and being constantly staffed when the libraries are open, avoids the maintenance of catalogues at the individual libraries.

KATE GREENAWAY MEDAL. An award, made by the Library Association annually with the intention of recognizing the importance of illustrations in children's books, to the artist who in the opinion of the Library Association has produced the most distinguished work in the illustration of children's books during the year preceding the award. The work must have been originally published in the United Kingdom. It was first awarded in 1956 to Edward Ardizonne for *Tim all alone*. A list of books awarded the medal is published in the Library Association *Year book*.

KEEP DOWN. (*Printing*) To use capitals sparingly.

KEEP IN. (*Printing*) 1. To set matter closely so that it does not take up more space than necessary. 2. Type matter with narrow openings between the words. *See also* DRIVE OUT.

KEEP OUT. (*Printing*) To set matter widely spaced so that it takes up as many lines as possible.

KEEP STANDING. An order not to distribute the type after running off, pending possible reprinting.

KEEP UP. (*Printing*) To use capitals freely, even promiscuously.

KEEPSAKE. 1. A lavishly printed and ornately bound gift book, often consisting of poetry; many such books were issued annually in the first half of the nineteenth century. 2. Printed commemorative publications issued by clubs or other organizations for special occasions. 3. Before the end of the seventeenth century it was the custom in some English printing establishments to honour visitors by printing their names and the date in an ornamental style – usually in a framework of flowers and rules – and present it to them as a memento. The guest witnessed the setting of the type and pulled the press. The practice became more general during the eighteenth century but declined in the last quarter; it was reserved for distinguished persons in the nineteenth century, for the most exalted of whom the printing was done on silk or satin.

KELLS, BOOK OF.   An illuminated MS. of the Latin Gospels, found in the ruins of the Abbey of Kells, Ireland, and thought to date from the eighth or early ninth century. It has been in the Library of Trinity College, Dublin, since 1661. It is an important example of Hiberno-Saxon art.

KELMSCOTT PRESS.   A private press founded and directed by William Morris between 1891 and his death in 1896, although the Press continued until 1898. The three founts of type used (Golden, 1890; Troy, 1891; Chaucer, 1892) were designed by Morris and cut by E. P. Prince in the years stated but not used until 1892. The books issued were excellent examples of book production. The Golden Type face was named after Caxton's *Golden Legend* in which it was to have been used first. It was, however, first used in 1891, and for six books, before the *Golden Legend* was printed in 1892. *See also* JENSON.

KEPT BOOK.   *Synonymous with* RESERVED BOOK (*q.v.*).

KERFS.   Shallow saw-cuts, about $\frac{1}{32}$ inch deep, made between $\frac{1}{4}$ and $\frac{1}{2}$ inch from the ends of the gathered sections of a book. The loops of the kettle stitches formed by the sewing of the sections, or the cords, fit snugly into the kerfs and leave the back of the sewn sections smooth.

KERN.   (*Printing*) Any part of the face of a type letter which extends over the edge of the body and rests on the shoulder of the type adjacent to it, as *fi, fl*.

KERNED.   Said of a type letter which has part of the face projecting beyond the metal body on which it is cast.

KETTLE STITCH.   The stitch made at the head and tail of a book in hand sewing, by which the thread of one section is fastened to the thread of the one on each side. The term is frequently regarded as being a corruption of 'catch up stitch', but it may be derived from the German *Ketten-stich* (chain stitch) or *Kettel stich*, (the stitch that forms a little chain). Also called 'Catch stitch'.

KEY.   1. The block or forme in letterpress printing, and the plate or stone in lithography, which acts as a guide for position and registration of the other colours. Also called KEY PLATE (*q.v.*). 2. A binder's tool for securing the bands when sewing. 3. An explanation of the conventional signs or symbols used on a map or diagram.

KEY IN. The action of inserting a note in the margins of the type-script of a book to indicate the exact or approximate position where illustrations, or other items not incorporated in the text, are to appear.

KEY-LETTER-IN-CONTEXT. *See* KLIC.

KEY PLATE. 1. The plate of maximum detail in a set of colour plates to which other plates in the same set are registered during the printing process. 2. Any printing plate that is used to get others into register. Also called KEY (*q.v.*)

KEY TERM. *Synonymous with* KEYWORD (*q.v.*).

KEYBOARD. (*Verb*) To type (or otherwise record by depressing keys) data or information, usually for direct subsequent computer input and processing.

KEYBOARDING. Producing type, proofs, tape or film by manual operation of a keyboard machine.

KEYPUNCH. A manually operated mechanical device which punches holes in pre-determined positions to record information on punched cards used with an electric accounting machine system. The punching of such holes is called 'keypunching'. The checking of the correctness of such punching is performed on a machine known as a Keyverifier.

KEYS, LIBRARY. *See* LIBRARY KEYS.

KEYSORT. Trade name for a manual system of recording information in connexion with information retrieval; it consists of EDGE-NOTCHED CARDS (*q.v.*).

KEYVERIFIER. *See* KEYPUNCH.

KEYWORD. (*Information retrieval*) Grammatical element which conveys the significant meaning in a document. Word indicating a subject discussed in a document (*IBM*). In a PERMUTED TITLE INDEX (*q.v.*), the word considered to be most indicative of the title is to be used as an ACCESS POINT (*q.v.*), and therefore of the subject content of the document. *See also* CATCHWORD, KWAC.

KEYWORD-AND-CONTEXT. *See* KWAC.

KEYWORD-IN-CONTEXT. *See* KWIC.

KEYWORD-OUT-OF-TITLE. *See* KWOT.

KIER. The part of paper-making machinery used to boil the raw material (e.g. rags, esparto) especially under steam pressure. Also called 'Boiler'.

KILL. (*Printing*) Direction to the printer to melt down, or distribute, composed type matter which is no longer wanted. *See also* DEAD MATTER, LIVE MATTER.

KILLING. *(Printing)* Distributing set-up type after use so that it may be used again.

KINDERBOX. A box about 2 feet square and 8 inches deep, divided into four compartments and standing on short legs. It holds large-page books for young children and is placed in an adult lending library or a children's lending library. Called in the U.S.A. a 'Cart'. Some models accommodate larger books upright in narrow divisions below the floor of the box proper, i.e. at floor level.

KINETIC RELATION. *(Information retrieval)* A phase relation expressing motion, e.g. a person can move to, from, into, out of, through, off, onto, etc. *See also* PHASE.

KING REPORT. The report of a committee of which Dr. Gilbert W. King was chairman, set up in 1961 to survey the application of automatic devices to the work of the Library of Congress and other general research libraries. It specifically contemplates (a) that L. of C. catalogues may be so mechanized that they can be consulted electronically on viewing screens subject to the viewers' complete manipulation; (b) that the collections to which the catalogues refer will be so mechanized through photographic or electronic micro-reproduction as to place them within the individual user's electronic control. The Report *Automation and the Library of Congress: a survey sponsored by the Council on Library Resources, Inc.* was published by the Library of Congress in January 1963. The MARC (MAchine Readable Cataloguing) project was a result of this. *See* MARC.

KIRKUS SERVICE, THE. A periodical, started in January 1933 as *The New York Office* and known by several titles until the present one was adopted in 1967, containing book reviews which often appear before the books are published. It was originally designed to furnish advice to booksellers but is now aimed primarily at librarians.

KIS. Acronym for the Kirklees Information Service which was originally formed in 1959, as the Huddersfield and District Information Service (HADIS), and membership was confined to organizations in Huddersfield and its immediate vicinity. However, since local government reorganization in 1973, the service has been extended to cover the metropolitan district of Kirklees. Membership is open to public libraries, higher and further education institutions, and organizations and firms having libraries, which can usefully contribute to the provision of technical information. The aims of the Service are to: (a) promote the use of commercial, scientific and management information by making known the information resources within and available to the area, and teaching their use; (b) encourage co-operation in loans, supply of photocopies and information, and in the admission of readers; (c) collaborate in the provision of exceptional resources; (d) co-operate with other co-operative information services. The governing body of the association is a council which consists of one representative from each member organization. The administrative headquarters is the Kirklees Libraries and Museums Service, Huddersfield.

KIT. A combination of two or more media designed to be used as a unit for instructional purposes.

KLIC. Acronym of Key-Letter-In-Context, a method which was first developed by UKCIS (*q.v.*) for producing permuted term lists wherein all terms are sorted on each letter in every term with the balance of the term displayed. This method is useful for selecting truncation fragments.

KLISCHOGRAPH. A German electronic photoengraving machine for producing plastic, zinc, copper or magnesium half-tone plates. The original to be reproduced is placed face down on a glass plate on a table and a blank plate, face up, placed above it and clamped into position. A scanner under the table picks up reflected light by means of two electric cells and transmits impulses through amplifiers to the engraving head above the plate and thence to the V-shaped engraving needle which digs dots of a size and depth varying in relation to the brightness of the original. The engraving head is stationary, the plate and original being reciprocated under it, the scanner returning to its position as each line is completed ready for the next line. Blocks can be engraved for monochrome and for three- and four-colour printing. The machine was invented by Dr. Rudolph Hell of Kiel and is also known in Great Britain as the 'Clichograph'.

KNAPP FOUNDATION. The Knapp Foundation of North Carolina, Inc. and the Knapp Foundation of New York were established in 1929 by the late Joseph Palmer Knapp, prominent business leader, publisher, and for 50 years a director of the Metropolitan Life Insurance Company. These foundations have contributed substantial sums for many studies and projects for the advancement of health, welfare and education in America.

KNAPP SCHOOL LIBRARIES PROJECT. A demonstration project which was funded with a grant of $1,130,000 from the Knapp Foundation, Inc. It was in operation from 1st March 1963 until 29th February 1968 and had as its objects: (1) to demonstrate the educational value of school library programmes, services, and resources which fully meet the national standards for school libraries; (2) to promote improved understanding and use of library resources on the part of teachers and administrators, by relating the demonstration situations to teacher education programmes in nearby colleges; (3) to guide and encourage citizens, from as many communities as possible, in the development of their own library programmes through planned activities enabling them to study demonstration situations; (4) to increase interest and support for school library development among educators and citizens generally, by disseminating information about the demonstration programmes and evaluating their effectiveness in reaching the stated goals. The Project was organized and directed by the American Association of School Librarians, a Division of the American Library Association. In November 1967 the Foundation made the sum of $1,163,718 available for a second five-year project called the School Library Manpower Project; this 'is designed to attack three aspects of the problem of developing fully and using properly school library manpower – task and job analysis, education for school librarianship and recruitment from specific manpower pools'. This Project was extended into a sixth year Phase III summative evaluation study by an additional grant of $150,000 from the Knapp Foundation of North Carolina. Details are given in *School Media Quarterly*, 2 (1) Fall 1973 pp. 45–6.

KNIFE-FOLDER. A folding machine which has a blunt-edged knife parallel with and above the slot formed by two parallel and constantly revolving rollers. When a sheet of paper is placed above these with an edge against a stop the knife descends and presses the sheet between the rollers which carry it away, the fold being made where the knife made contact. *See also* BUCKLE-FOLDER.

KNOWLEDGE CLASSIFICATION. A classification used for any branch of knowledge, but which cannot be adapted for classifying books until a generalia class, form classes and divisions, a notation, and an index have been added.

KODAGRAPH. Trade name for an Eastman Kodax reader designed to take micro-opaques up to $14 \times 8\frac{1}{2}$ inches. It has a green filter on the surface of the reading screen to prevent reflections.

KOREAN LIBRARY ASSOCIATION. Founded on 16th April 1955 to contribute to cultural advancement and social improvement in Korea by accelerating the spread of libraries and the betterment of the library service. Its objects are: to study the principles of library organization and administration; to publish books and other materials about library services; to train library personnel and improve their working conditions; to provide guidance to any individual or organization in planning a library; to prepare selected lists of Korean books; to activate the national reading movement; to devise specifications for standard library furniture and equipment; to organize and operate a professional reference library; to co-operate with international organizations concerned with library services. Membership is open to libraries and also to individuals who have acquired more than eighteen academic credits in library science. Abbreviated KLA. Publishes *KLA Bulletin* (m.).

KRAFT PAPER. A strong calendered brown paper of medium colour and with prominent chain-lines (*see* LAID PAPER) used specially for wrapping purposes. It is sometimes strengthened with hessian or tar to make waterproof wrapping paper of great strength. *See also* BLEACHED KRAFT.

KRAFT ROTACOL. *See* ROTARY CARD FILE.

KURSIV. *See* CURSIVE.

KWAC. Acronym of Keyword-and-Context. An index of titles of documents permutated to bring each significant word to the beginning, in alphabetical order, followed by the remaining words which follow it in the title, and then followed by that part of the original title which came before the significant word. *See also* KWIC, KWOC.

KWIC. Acronym for Keyword-in-Context. 1. A method of PERMUTATION INDEXING (*q.v.*) which relies on mechanical means for selecting the terms. It was developed by Mr. H. P. Luhn of International Business Machines, and uses a computer to permute automatically words in periodical article titles, and to group titles in which the same words occur. An example of this kind of index is *Chemical Titles* published by the American Chemical Society since 5th January 1961. The system consists of a thesaurus of key words and associated words, coded and put on punched cards that operate a computer searching a magnetic tape. When search keywords and coded tape match, the computer prints out the keyword and the words following it, and the number of the document. When the index is printed, the keywords in each index line are printed at the middle of the type measure and thus, with a double space preceding each, appear under one another in alphabetical order in a column. The full measure of the line is filled by printing as much of the title immediately before and after the keyword as can be accommodated. 2. A listing, usually of titles, or significant sentences from an abstract, with the keywords put in a fixed position within the title or sentence and arranged in alphabetic order in a column (*IBM*). 3. An index based on the cyclic permutation of words; each 'substantive' term being brought to a predetermined position and alphabetized. *See also* Co-ORDINATE INDEXING, KWAC, KWOC, WADEX.

KWOC. Acronym for Keyword-Out-of-Context, a refinement of KWIC (*q.v.*). Titles are printed in full under as many Keywords as the indexer considers useful; these may be chosen from a thesaurus or list of standard headings as well as from the title, and there is no limit to the source of Keywords. The Keywords are separated from the title on a line of their own and act as subject headings. If the title is itself amended to give a concise but clear indication of the item's subject content it becomes a NOC (Notation of Content). *See also* WADEX.

KWOT. Acronym of Keyword-out-of-Title, a KWOC (*q.v.*) index, which is computer-produced by ABACUS (AB Atomic Energy Computerized User-oriented Services), the result of co-operation between the Royal Institute of Technology (Stockholm) and AB Atomenergi (Sweden).

KYLE CLASSIFICATION. *See* CLASSIFICATION FOR SOCIAL SCIENCES.

LANW. Library Association, North Western Branch. *See entry under* NORTH WESTERN BRANCH.

l.c. Abbreviation for lower case. *See* LOWER CASE LETTERS.

LCF. Acronym of Librarians' Christian Fellowship which was formed in 1974 in the U.K. Groups meet mainly for Bible study in different parts of the country. Publishes *Glow Worm*.

l.p. Abbreviation for LARGE PAPER COPY or EDITION (*q.v.*).

L.S. Abbreviation for LIBRARY SCHOOL (*q.v.*).

L.S. *See locus sigilli and* A.L.S.

LSCA. Library Services and Construction Act (American).

l.v. Abbreviation for *locis variis* (*Lat.* 'various places'). The revision of Chapter 6 of *AACR* (British Text) provides that, in a catalogue entry, *l.v.* be used when various places of publication are given in a series of related publications (as in a collection of pamphlets). Formerly *v.p.* was used.

LABEL. 1. A small strip of leather, usually of a different colour to that used for the binding of a book, placed on the spine and displaying one or more of the following: title, author's name, volume number, date. Also called 'Lettering pieces'. When two labels are used they are described as 'double lettering pieces'. Labels of paper were used on books bound in boards covered with paper. 2. (*Information retrieval*) In a machine-readable record, one or more characteristics which are written or attached to a set of data which contains information about the set, including its identification.

LABEL TITLE-PAGE. The title and author's name printed near the top of an otherwise blank page, or protecting leaf, at the beginning of a book. Often called 'label title', the name is given to the first form of title-page in early printed books (1470–1550). The earliest extant example is a Papal Bull of Pius II, printed in 1463 at Mainz, probably by Fust and Schöffer.

LABELLED NOTATION. The style of the notation used in the COLON CLASSIFICATION (q.v.). Each main class is labelled with a letter, and each facet is first symbolized by combining the main class letter with a facet indicator; simple terms are represented by numerals.

LABORATORY COLLECTION. *Synonymous with* DEPARTMENTAL LIBRARY (q.v.).

LACAP. Acronym for Latin America Co-operative Acquisitions Program. Organized in 1960 as a result of the extension of the FARMINGTON PLAN (q.v.) to Latin America and the organization of the SALALM (q.v.) which recommended its formation; it is a co-operative enterprise that provides its participants with a steady flow of the printed materials currently published in all the countries of Latin America. The University of Texas, the New York Public Library and Stechert-Hafner Inc. were the initiators of the scheme which was first called a 'Project'.

LACE BORDER. *See* LACEWORK 2.

LACED ON. ' *See* LACING-IN.

LACEWORK. 1. A border decoration on bindings, done by tooling, to represent lace. *See also* DENTELLE. 2. Borders framing whole-page illustrations in nineteenth-century French books, the border-decoration consisting of punching the pattern out of the paper as in paper doyleys.

LACING-IN. (*Binding*) Attaching the boards by the operation of passing the slips or cords on which the book is sewn, and after they have been splayed out and moistened with paste, through holes pierced in the boards.

LACIRS. *See* INCIRS.

LACUNA (*Pl.* LACUNAE). Gaps in the stock of a library, which await filling.

LADSIRLAC. Abbreviation for Liverpool and District Scientific, Industrial and Research Library Advisory Council which was sponsored by the Liverpool City Council in 1955 to provide extra-mural services to industry over and above the normal services offered through a public library. Membership is by payment of an annual subscription. LADSIRLAC is based on Liverpool City Library, the major reference library on Merseyside, which is a regional depository for publications issued by the UN, FAO, WHO, OECD, and EEC. The library also receives all HMSO publications and has the largest collection of British and foreign patents outside London. LADSIR-LAC answers enquiries for technical and commercial information by literature searches and by its contacts with research associations, government departments etc. Books and photocopies are posted to members. Publications include an Annual Report and monthly Technical and Commercial Bulletins.

LAID IN. Used in a note to a catalogue entry to indicate the inclusion in a gramophone record album or musical publication, of a leaflet or pamphlet relating to the music and its performance. *See also* ANALYTICAL BOOKLET.

LAID PAPER. Paper which, when held up to the light, shows thick and thin lines at right angles. They are caused by the weave of the dandy roll, or in hand-made paper by the mould having long thin wires placed very close together and fastened to thicker ones at intervals of about one inch. The horizontal thin ones are called 'wire-lines' or 'wire-marks' and the vertical thick ones 'chain-lines', 'chain-marks' or 'wide-lines'. To obtain the best impression when printing, the wire-lines should run across the page and the chain-lines down it. *See also* WATERMARK.

LAMBERT SCHOLARSHIP, NANCY STIRLING. Established by Blackwell's, the Oxford booksellers, to encourage the investigation of matters of common concern to libraries and the book trade. The Scholarship takes its name from the grandmother of Sir Basil Blackwell, President of the firm. She was married to Benjamin Harris Blackwell, the first City Librarian of Oxford, and virtually founded the business on her husband's death. The Scholarship is of £2,500 p.a. and is awarded to a graduate librarian to enable him to work for the University of Wales degree of Master of Librarianship, or for the Fellowship of the Library Association. It was first awarded, in 1974, to Alastair John Allan.

LAMBSKIN. A bookbinding leather with a smooth finish; it is similar in appearance to calf but less durable.

LAMINATED. A sheet of paper to which a sheet of clear plastic has been permanently adhered on one or both sides. Book jackets, leaves of books, or paper covers are treated in this way to strengthen them.

LAMINATION. A method of preserving frail papers or the thin or perishing leaves of books by placing them between two sheets of thin transparent thermo-plastic material which when subjected to heat under pressure protects the paper by making it impervious to atmospheric conditions. *See also* SILKING.

LAMPBLACK. Pure carbon deposit; formerly the most important black pigment used in manufacturing printing inks. It was produced by burning pitch resin in a vessel in a tent made of paper or sheepskins. The smoke was deposited on the inside of the tent which was then beaten to cause the black to fall on to the floor. Impurities were removed by heating it several times until red-hot in an iron box with a small aperture at the top.

LAMPOON. A satirical attack generally of a scurrilous but humorous character, upon a person, and written in prose or verse.

LAMSAC. Acronym of Local Authorities Managements Services and Computer Committee which was established in 1967 to help advise members of the Local Authority Associations and River Authorities in England, Scotland and Wales on the introduction and use of management services and computers. Much of the research work carried out for the benefit of local government is undertaken by various 'panels' but LAMSAC undertakes research through its staff and commissions work to be executed by other specialist organizations and local authorities. It organizes general appreciation and specialist training courses on management services and computer services. In 1972 it commenced a two-year ISORID research project into the staffing of public libraries in the U.K. *See also* ISORID.

LAND UTILIZATION SURVEY OF BRITAIN. Maps, the publication of which began in 1933, based on, and showing everything which appears on, the fourth edition of the 'Popular' series of Ordnance Survey maps, but showing in addition in contrasting colours the use to which land is put.

LANDSCAPE. A book or document that is wider than its height; one that is designed to be read with its longer edges towards the reader. More often called 'Oblong'.

LANDSCAPE BINDING. A type of binding which has landscape views on its covers, the landscape views being drawn freehand with Indian ink or acid and later coloured, or printed by some means. They date between 1777 and 1821.

LANDSCAPE PAGE. A page on which graphs, tables, illustrations, etc. are printed so that their foot is parallel to the fore-edge of the page. Also called 'Broadside page'. *See also* TURNED.

LANGUAGE NUMBER. A facet which may form part of a BOOK NUM-
BER (*q.v.*) in the Colon Classification. It is obtained by translating the
name of the language in which the book is written into appropriate
symbols in accordance with the language schedule given in Chapter 5
of the Schedules. *See also* ETHNIC NUMBERS.

LANGUAGE OF THE TEXT. The language in which the text of a
book is printed and which is not determinable from the title, e.g.
Faust. In such a case the cataloguer may (1) add a note, e.g. 'Text in
German and English'; (2) integrate a translator statement, e.g. 'Tr.
into English by . . .'; (3) augment the heading, e.g. 'Goethe, Johann
Wolfgang von. Faust. English.'

LANGUAGE SUB-DIVISION. (*Classification*) Sub-division of a subject according to the language in which it is written, or sub-division
of a language division in the philological class of a scheme of
classification.

LANSTON. *See* MONOTYPE.

LAPIDARY TYPE. A fount of capital letters similar to those on Roman
monumental inscriptions. Examples were cut by Erhard Ratdolt at
Augsburg in 1505. *See also* SQUARE CAPITALS.

LARC ASSOCIATION. Abbreviation for The Association for Library
Automation Research Communications (formerly Library Automation, Research and Consulting Association), an international non-
profit organization, established in July 1969 in California to promote
continuing education and training in library automation through
research, workshops, meetings and publications and to provide a
forum for the worldwide exchange of information about library
automation and related developments. Membership is open to any
person, library, or other organization. Financed through membership
dues. Publishes *The LARC Reports* (*q.*), *Network – International
Communications in Library Automation* (m.).

LARGE FOLIO. A general term to indicate a large-sized folio book.
See also FOLIO 3.

LARGE PAPER COPY, or EDITION. An impression of a book printed
on larger and better quality paper than the usual trade edition, thus
having wider margins. *See also* FINE PAPER COPY, LIMITED EDITION,
SMALL PAPER COPY.

LARGE POST. A sheet of printing paper measuring $16\frac{1}{2} \times 21$ inches.

LARGE ROYAL. A sheet of printing paper measuring 20×27
inches.

LASER. *See* LONDON & SOUTH EASTERN LIBRARY REGION.

LAST FOLD. *See* BOLT.

LATER CURSIVE. A Latin manuscript handwriting which came in sequence between UNCIAL and HALF UNCIAL (*qq.v.*). Its main characteristics are ligatures (joined letters) and the uneven height of the letters, some of which ascended or descended beyond the normal letter limits – which had not previously occurred. This distinction between tall and small letters marked the first stage in the development of minuscules (lower-case letters).

LATERAL FILING. Equipment which consists of pockets of tough paper, or linen, which are suspended (and usually move laterally within limits) from two rails placed one behind the other and running from left to right. They are made into fittings which will rest on shelves or as a complete filing cabinet the size of a book TIER (*q.v.*). The pockets usually have caption or heading holders on them, and there being no fronts or covers, the contents are immediately accessible. Filing capacity is much greater per cubic foot than in any other form of filing, whether vertical or in boxes on shelves. The specially-made cabinets have cupboard doors, roller, or spring blind fronts to keep out dust and provide security.

LATERALLY REVERSED. In documentary copying, reflecting the original as in a mirror. Also called 'Left-to-right-reversed'. *See also* RIGHT READING.

LATTICE. (*Information retrieval*) The network of inter-relationships between specific subjects (*IBM*). A partially ordered system in which any two elements have a greatest lower bound and a least upper bound. *See also* BOUND.

LATTICE STAMP. (*Binding*) A decorative ornament, the distinguishing feature of which is a central diamond formed of lattice or criss-cross work.

LATTICE STRUCTURE. (*Information retrieval*) The algebraic structure of an information file described as a network, or lattice, of units of information which are linked to each other and to document references.

LAURA INGALLS WILDER MEDAL. *See* WILDER MEDAL, LAURA INGALLS.

LAW BINDING. *See* LAW CALF.

LAW BOOKS, U.S.A. *See* BOOKS, U.S.A., INC.

LAW CALF. A leather binding using plain uncoloured calf or sheepskin. Mainly used for law books but now largely superseded by buckram cloth. Also called 'Fair calf', 'Law sheep'.

LAW OF SCATTERING. A 'law' deduced by Dr. S. C. Bradford (and later corrected by B. C. Vickery) who found that about a third of the articles on a subject are printed in the journals devoted to that subject, a further third appear in a larger number of journals devoted to related subjects, and the remaining third in an even larger number of journals in which such articles would not normally be expected to be published. According to the law of scattering, if Tx represents the number of journals having x references, T_{2x} the total number of journals having $2x$ references, and T_{3x} the total number of journals having $3x$ references, etc., then: $Tx : T_{2x} : T_{3x} = 1 : n : n^2$ where n may be any number depending on the value chosen for x.

LAW SHEEP. *Synonymous with* LAW CALF (*q.v.*).

LAY EDGES. The edges of a sheet of paper which are laid against the front and side lay gauges of a printing or folding machine. The front edge is known as the 'gripper edge'.

LAYOUT. 1. A plan, prepared for or by a printer, to show the arrangement of the matter, type faces, sizes of type, position of illustrations and captions, for a piece of printing. 2. The plan of an entire book.

LAYSTOOL. A stool on which white paper and printed sheets were laid close to the printing pressman's hand. By the nineteenth century a 'horse' with a sloping top had been evolved to take the paper and make it easier to pick sheets off the heap.

LE GASCON STYLE. Modified FANFARE bindings of the early seventeenth century, in which the strapwork is retained, the enclosed spaces differentiated by inlaid leather of different colours, and the sprays lighter. Fine dotted scrolls are frequently enclosed in the geometrical compartments and often extended into lines and curves of remarkable lustre and elegance. These scrolls and other ornaments are given dotted lines known as pointillé, instead of unbroken lines. Not practised after about 1660.

LEAD, TO. To insert leads between type or re-set on a larger body. A page of printed matter where the lines are well spaced out is said to be 'well leaded'.

LEAD MOULDING. A process for making electros or half-tone plates in which the base is lead instead of wax. Soft lead is forced into the forme under great (hydraulic) pressure and a mould of fine quality obtained. A copper shell is then deposited on the mould in the same manner as in wax moulding.

LEADED MATTER. (*Printing*) Having the lines of type separated by 'leads', or cast on a larger body, as 8 pt. type on 9 pt. body, to achieve the same effect. In the latter case, the type is called 'Long-bodied'. Type without 'leads' is said to be 'set solid'. 'Double-leaded' means a double space (usually 4 points) between lines of type. *See also* EM, LEADS, PICA, SOLID MATTER.

LEADER. 1. A short newspaper article expressing views or comments rather than (but often based on) news, and usually indicating the policy or editorial views of the proprietors of the paper. Fully, a leading article. 2. A portion of film at the beginning of a roll of film, and which is used for the threading of the film in a camera, processing machine, or projector. 3. (*Information retrieval*) A record which precedes a group of detail records; it gives information about the group which is not present on the detail records. 4. In machine-readable records, the part of the record which precedes the information content, and which carries data needed to manipulate, identify or locate the information content.

LEADER WRITER. The writer of newspaper editorials, or leaders.

LEADERETTE. A short editorial article in a newspaper or periodical.

LEADERS. A sequence of dots or hyphens to lead the eye from one word to another as in tabular work, or across a page as in a table of contents.

LEADING LINE. The top horizontal line on a standard ruled catalogue card; the one on which the author heading is entered.

LEADS. Thin strips of lead which are less than type high, used to separate lines of type or to space them further apart. Type set on a larger body, such as 8 point on a 9 point body to give the same effect without the use of separate leads between each line, is called *long-bodied type*. Leads are usually made 1, 1½ (thin), 2 (middle) which is the usual leading, 3 (thick), and 4 points – known as 'double leaded' thick when 6 and 12 point or more they are called 'clumps' and may be of wood or metal. When clumps are made of wood they are called 'reglets'. Spacing material of greater dimensions than 18 point is known as 'furniture'. *See also* LEADED MATTER, SOLID MATTER.

LEAF. A sheet of paper, printed, and folded once forms a section of two leaves or four pages, and is called folio; folded twice, it forms a section of four leaves or eight pages and is called quarto. A leaf consists of two pages, one on each side, either of which may or may not be printed on. Usually the recto has an odd number, and the verso the subsequent number, but in reprints this may not be the case. Books with unnumbered leaves or pages may be described in a catalogue or bibliographical entry as containing a specific number (ascertained by counting) of pages or leaves – preferably the latter if the book was published before pagination was general – in the form '320 l'. The revisions of the North American and British Texts of *AACR* provide for the recording of the number of leaves printed on both sides as 'pages', and those printed on one side only as 'leaves', and that the number of leaves should follow the number of pages. *See also* FOLDINGS, FOLIATION, PLATE, SECTION.

LEAFLET. A small sheet of paper folded once and printed on to make two to four pages following in the same sequence as in a book, but not stitched or bound. Often used to indicate a small, thin PAMPHLET (*q.v.*).

LEAGUE OF EUROPEAN RESEARCH LIBRARIES. *See* LIBER.

LEAN-FACE TYPE. Type, the stems and other strokes of which have not their full width.

LEAN MATTER. *See* MATTER.

LEARNING RESOURCES CENTER. Sometimes used in America in the late 1960s for a school library. Also called 'Instructional Materials Center'.

LEATHER. The cured and dyed hide of goat, pig or sheep. Used extensively for binding books.

LEATHER BOUND. A book bound in leather, either FULL, HALF, QUARTER, or THREE-QUARTER (*qq.v.*).

LEATHER JOINTS. Leather inner joints affixed (usually stuck in but sometimes sewn) to the endpapers of large hand-bound books to give greater strength. They were occasionally used in the seventeenth century in Europe; between 1750 and 1800 they were a fairly common feature of the best English morocco and russia bindings, and were usually heavily decorated with fillets, rolls and small tools.

LEATHERCLOTH. A fabric or plastic material which has been finished to simulate leather.

LEATHERETTE. Paper or cloth having a surface in imitation of leather.

LEAVES OF PLATES. *See* PLATE.

LECTERN. A sloped woodern ledge on which books were laid flat and chained, and at which they were consulted, in mediaeval libraries.

LECTURE SCRIPT. The text of a lecture.

LECTURE SERIES. The name given to a series of lectures delivered in connexion with lecture trusts such as the Bampton, Gifford, or Hibbert, and afterwards published.

LEDGER CATALOGUE. *Synonymous with* PAGE CATALOGUE (*q.v.*).

LEDGER CHARGING. An antiquated method of recording books on loan by entering book-numbers against names or ticket numbers in adjacent vertical columns on loose sheets or in a bound ledger.

LEDGER WEIGHT. (*Reprography*) Photographic paper of moderately heavy weight; used when greater body and mechanical durability are required. 'Duplex ledger' is coated on both sides for reproducing books; the paper used may have a wood, fibre or rag (linen ledger) base.

16

LEFT-TO-RIGHT REVERSED. *Synonymous with* LATERALLY RE-VERSED (*q.v.*).

LEGAL DEPOSIT. A method whereby certain libraries are entitled by law to receive one or more copies of every book or other publication which is printed or published in the country. Under English law the publisher must deliver to the British Museum within one month of publication, a copy of every book published, and the expression 'book' includes every part or division of a book, pamphlet, sheet of letterpress, sheet of music, map, plan, chart or table separately published, but not second and subsequent editions unless these contain additions or alterations in the letterpress or in the maps, prints or engravings. A copy must also be sent if requested in writing to the libraries of the universities of Oxford and Cambridge, to Trinity College, Dublin, to the National Library of Scotland (but law books to the Faculty of Advocates Library) and to the National Library of Wales (with certain classes of books excepted). Also called 'Copyright deposit', 'Copytax'. *See also* COPYRIGHT LIBRARY.

LEGAL FILE. A collection of material relating to law cases; it may include briefs, decisions, or histories of cases.

LEGEND. 1. The title or short description printed under an illustration or engraving, or on a coin or medal. Also called 'Caption' and 'Cutline'. 2. An explanation of symbols on a map or diagram. 3. A story based on tradition.

LEGISLATION. *See* PUBLIC LIBRARIES ACTS.

LEGISLATIVE HISTORY. A chronological account of the stages through which a particular bill has passed before enactment as a law. This would include all 'readings', committee debates and decisions, and 'floor' debates in both houses. The events leading to the bill, the efforts of organizations concerned in furthering it, any evidence given, and any history subsequent to enactment are also sometimes included.

LEMMA. The argument or subject written at the head of a literary composition.

LEMONNIER STYLE. A style of book decoration practised by Jean Christophe Henri Lemonnier, who worked for Count Hoym in France in the eighteenth century. It is characterized by pictorial mosaics of landscapes, bouquets, etc.

LENDING DEPARTMENT. The department of a library containing books for home-reading. Called a 'Circulation department' in America.

LENDING DESK. *See* CIRCULATION DESK.

LENDING LIBRARY. *Synonymous with* LENDING DEPARTMENT (*q.v.*).

LENIN STATE LIBRARY. One of the most important centres for library work and bibliography in the Soviet Union, it contains over 5,000,000 printed books which have been assembled since September 1922. Publishes *Novye knigi BSSR* (*New books in the Byelorussian SSR*) (m.). The Book Chamber of the Byelorussian S.S.R, a section of the Library, has become the republic's main centre for bibliographical work, recording and registering all printed material published in the republic. Publishes *Letopisi pecati BSSR* (*The Byelorussian SSR annual index of publications*) and a series of retrospective bibliographies. The Library's department for Byelorussian literature and bibliography has a unique collection of 200,000 books and periodicals published in Byelorussia since the beginning of the nineteenth century, and deals with a wide range of work on regional studies. The Library is the centre of an extensive network of public libraries, and takes an active part in improving library services in the republic, giving regular assistance to provincial and general libraries, and co-ordinating their activities.

LENSLESS COPYING. A general term for copying methods which do not use a camera. The apparatus used consists of a light-box with a ground-glass screen and pressure pad on top of it. Sensitized paper is placed in the closest possible contact with the original and exposed to light. If the original is translucent and has text on one side only it is placed next the light source with the sensitized surface of the copying paper against the back of the original: the light shines through the white paper of the original but does not pass through the text because the black print absorbs it. After development (which in many makes of copier is done in the copying machine) the result is a readable negative (i.e. white on black) which can be used as if it were a positive. This method is known as *direct copying* and sometimes, inadvisably because all non-camera methods rely on the closest contact between the original and the sensitized paper, as *contact copying*. When the original is opaque with text on both sides the REFLEX COPYING (*q.v.*) method is used, a normal white on black negative with the image in reverse being made. A black on white positive is made from this.

LET-IN NOTE. *Synonymous with* INCUT NOTE (*q.v.*).

LETTER BOOK. A book in which correspondence was copied by some means resulting in a facsimile copy. This was often done by writing the original letter with copying ink, placing it against a dampened sheet of thin paper (leaves of which comprised the book) and applying pressure. Such books were sometimes known as letterpress copybooks.

Also, a book of blank or ruled pages on which are written letters, either drafts written by the author or fair copies made by the author or by clerks. The term is also used for a book comprising copies of letters which are bound together, or of one into which such copies are pasted onto guards or pages.

LETTER-BY-LETTER. *See* ALPHABETIZATION.

LETTER SPACING. The insertion of spaces between the letters of a word or words to lengthen the MEASURE (*q.v.*), improve the appearance of the setting, or in special instances emphasize a word or sentence. This is letterspaced.

LETTER WRITER. 1. One who writes letters for illiterates. 2. A writer who has become famous for the letters he has written and possibly published.

LETTERA FONDA. *See* ANTIQUA.

LETTERED PROOF. The proof of an engraving in which the title and the names of the artist, engraver, printer, etc. are printed under the illustration.

LETTERING. The emplacement of the library CALL NUMBER (*q.v.*) on the spine of a book.

LETTERING ON THE SPINE. When the lettering on the spine of a book or bookjacket does not go across it, the direction may be up or down according to the choice of the publisher with consequent inconvenience to library users. In 1926 the Publishers Association and the Associated Booksellers of Great Britain and Ireland recommended that 'when a volume stands on the shelf the lettering reads from bottom to top', but in 1948 reversed their decision, recommending that the lettering should be downward so that the title can be easily read when the book lies flat, face upward. Librarians tend to prefer the earlier recommendation. *Periodicals of reference value* . . . (B.S. 2509:1959) recommends that the lettering of periodicals should be 'across the spine if the title is short enough; otherwise along the spine in such a way as to be readable when the publication is lying flat with the *front* cover uppermost.'

LETTERING PIECE. A piece of leather secured to the spine of a book to receive its title. *See also* LABEL.

LETTERPRESS. 1. The text of a book as distinguished from its illustrations. 2. Matter printed from type as distinct from plates. 3. A method of relief printing as opposed to intaglio or planographic.

LETTERPRESS COPYBOOK. *See* LETTER BOOK.

LETTERS CLOSE. Letter addressed usually by the sovereign to some individual or group of individuals and closed with a seal.

LETTERS PATENT. An open letter issued generally under the great seal of the sovereign or some other magnate as a guarantee to the person or corporation named therein.

LETTRE DE BATARDE. *See* GOTHIC TYPE.

LETTRE DE FORME. *See* GOTHIC TYPE.

LETTRE DE SOMME. *See* GOTHIC TYPE.

LETTRE RONDE. *See* ANTIQUA.

LEVANT. A high-grade Morocco leather used for binding books, and made from the skin of the Angora goat.

LEVEL. (*Classification*) A measure of the degree of complexity or generality of a concept, term or class. In the philosophy of 'integrative levels', terms are categorized according to the level of complexity and arranged in ascending order.

LEVEL SMALL CAPS. *Synonymous with* EVEN SMALL CAPS (*q.v.*).

LEVER PRESS. Any printing press on which the impression is made by moving a lever, but the term is usually applied to the type of press used for proofing, etc., in which the lever is pulled down.

LEVIGATION. The action of using the LEVIGATOR (*q.v.*).

LEVIGATOR. A heavy steel disc which is rotated by hand over a lithographic stone when preparing its surface, sand and water being used as the abrasive.

LEXEME. A word, particle or stem which denotes the meaning.

LEXICOGRAPHER. The compiler of a dictionary.

LEXICOGRAPHIST. A LEXICOGRAPHER (*q.v.*).

LEXICOGRAPHY. The act, or process, of compiling a dictionary.

LEXICOLOGY. The branch of knowledge which is concerned with words, their history, form and meaning.

LEXICON. A dictionary of the words of a language, the words being arranged in alphabetical order; especially one giving the meaning in another language. It is chiefly applied to a dictionary of Greek, Syriac, Arabic or Hebrew but is also used for encyclopaedias and subject dictionaries.

LIABILITY SLIP. A slip recording the loan of a book for use on the the library premises. It is cancelled, or returned to the reader, when the book is returned.

LIAISON OFFICER. A librarian who carries out duties calling for a personal link between a county librarian and local persons or bodies. The duties may include visiting branches and centres, advising local librarians, training branch staffs, attending local committee meetings, taking charge of branches in emergency, and undertaking other tasks requiring the presence of a senior member of the headquarters staff.

LIBER.   Acronym of Ligue des Bibliothèques Européennes de Recherche (League of European Research Libraries). This Association was founded in March 1971 by a steering group set up through the National and University Libraries Section of IFLA at the Council of Europe's headquarters in Strasbourg. Its purpose was to bring together the large libraries of Austria, Belgium, Cyprus, Denmark, Finland, France, the Federal Republic of Germany, Greece, Holy See, Iceland, Ireland, Italy, Luxemburg, Malta, Netherlands, Norway, Portugal, Spain, Sweden, Switzerland, Turkey and the U.K., and thereby to establish close co-operation between European research libraries particularly national and university libraries, and also to help in finding practical ways of improving the quality of the services these libraries provide. Also, to organize research into librarianship on a European scale, and set up working parties in well-defined and circumscribed subjects. It desires to facilitate international loans and exchange of publications and to find corresponding members in each country. Membership consists of European research libraries (mostly university libraries, some national libraries and other large research libraries) in Western Europe (at present). Financed by members' subscriptions with some assistance from the Council of Europe in respect of meetings. The Secretariat is at the Birmingham (England) University Library. Publishes *LIBER Bulletin* (2 p.a. free to members) and supplementary monographs.

LIBERATE ROLL.   A record of the writs authorizing delivery of money of out the Treasury. Chancery Liberate are rolls of letters issued, and the Exchequer series rolls of letters received; both are copied from the same originals.

LIBGIS 1.   *See* NATIONAL CENTER FOR EDUCATIONAL STATISTICS.

LIBRARIAN.   One who has the care of a library and its contents, selecting the books, documents and non-book materials which comprise its stock, and providing information and loan services to meet the needs of its users. As a result of the reorganization of local government in the United Kingdom (in Greater London in 1965; England and Wales outside Greater London in 1974; Scotland in 1975) with its consequent amalgamation of local authorities, many library services became amalgamated with other cultural, or with amenities or recreational, activities. The results have been that most librarians of public libraries have lost their chief officer status and have either had to serve under other officers who have had the management of libraries included in their responsibilities, or they have had to add these additional responsibilities to those of administering library services. *See also* LOCAL GOVERNMENT BOUNDARIES.

LIBRARIAN-IN-CHARGE. The librarian placed in charge of a particular department.

LIBRARIANS' CHRISTIAN FELLOWSHIP. *See* LCF.

LIBRARIANS OF INSTITUTES AND SCHOOLS OF EDUCATION. *See* LISE.

LIBRARIANSHIP. The profession of librarian.

LIBRARIES OF NORTH STAFFORDSHIRE IN CO-OPERATION. *See* LINOSCO.

LIBRARII. Used in mediaeval times to signify scribes.

LIBRARY. 1. A collection of books and other literary material kept for reading, study and consultation. 2. A place, building, room or rooms set apart for the keeping and use of a collection of books, etc. 3. A number of books issued by one publisher under a comprehensive title as the 'Loeb Classical Library', and usually having some general characteristic such as subject, binding, or typography. 4. A collection of films, photographs and other visual non-book materials, plastic or metal tapes and discs, computer tapes and programs. All of these, as well as printed and manuscript documents, may be provided in departments of one large library or they may be in collections restricted to one type of material. *See also* BRANCH LIBRARY, CENTRAL LIBRARY, CHILDREN'S LIBRARY, CIRCULATING LIBRARY, COLLEGE LIBRARY, DELIVERY STATION, DEPOSIT LIBRARY, DEPOSITORY LIBRARY, LENDING DEPARTMENT, REFERENCE DEPARTMENT, SCHOOL LIBRARY, SPECIAL LIBRARY, SUBSCRIPTION LIBRARY, UNIVERSITY LIBRARY.

LIBRARY ACCESS SYSTEM. 'A total library management system for monographic control' designed by IBM for large central libraries and networks. An on-line computer is used to improve the technical processing service for acquisitions, MARC cataloguing, circulation, and to assist the user with bibliographic search.

LIBRARY ACTS. *See* PUBLIC LIBRARIES ACTS.

LIBRARY ADMINISTRATION. The administration of a library is the force behind the machinery of its working routine. To oversee the work of a library in all its relations, and to plan for and promote its usefulness, is the work of the library administrator, and it embraces the supervision and development of the work of all departments and the solution of their various problems; library administration must of necessity begin where library organization ends.

LIBRARY ADMINISTRATION DIVISION. A Division of the American Library Association; it was established in 1957 'to guide and to conduct the activities of the ALA which pertain to library administration in general.' Has five sections. In January 1974 this Division took over the publication of *Library Technology Reports* (6 p.a.) which were issued under the Library Technology Program (*q.v.*). Abbreviated LAD. Publishes *LAD Newsletter* (q.).

LIBRARY ADVISORY COUNCILS. The formation of national advisory councils, one for England (excluding Monmouthshire) and the other for Wales and Monmouthshire, was provided for by Section 2 of the Public Libraries and Museums Act 1964. It is their duty 'to advise the Secretary of State upon such matters connected with the provision or use of library facilities whether under this Act or otherwise as they think fit, and upon any questions referred to them by him.' The Secretary of State appoints the members of the councils, their chairmen, and an officer of the Department of Education and Science as Secretary. *See also* LIBRARY AUTHORITY, LIBRARY REGION.

LIBRARY AGREEMENT. *See* NET BOOK AGREEMENT.

LIBRARY & INFORMATION SCIENCE ABSTRACTS. An extended and enlarged form of *LIBRARY SCIENCE ABSTRACTS* (*q.v.*); it commenced publication in January 1969 by the Library Association jointly with Aslib. A cumulative index covering the years 1969–1973 was published in 1975. Abbreviated *LISA.* Published bi-monthly.

LIBRARY AREA. The administrative area of a local authority acting as a library authority under the Public Libraries and Museums Act 1964: the administrative area of the authority, or, in the case of (a) a county council, so much of its administrative area as excludes the library area of any other library authority, (b) a joint board established under s.5 of the Act, the areas which, if the authorities constituting the board were library authorities, would form their library areas (s.4). Owing to local government boundary changes which took place in 1974 in England and Wales, and in 1975 in Scotland, the kinds of library authority empowered to provide libraries were altered. For the present position, *see* LOCAL GOVERNMENT BOUNDARIES. In Northern Ireland, the situation was altered owing to the prevailing conditions; *See also* JOINT BOARD, LIBRARY AUTHORITY.

LIBRARY ASSISTANTS' ASSOCIATION. *See* ASSOCIATION OF ASSISTANT LIBRARIANS.

LIBRARY ASSOCIATION. The British professional association for the examination and certification of librarians, for the regulation of the profession of librarianship, for the promotion of the better administration of libraries and the encouragement of bibliographical study and research and for the accumulation and dissemination of information concerning libraries. It was founded as the Library Association of the United Kingdom on 5th October 1877 at the conclusion of the First International Conference of Librarians, which was held at Brussels from 2–5 October under the presidency of Mr. John Winter Jones, the joint secretaries being E. W. B. Nicholson and H. R. Tedder. The *American Library Journal* was adopted as the official journal, the word 'American' being dropped. Publication of the *Monthly Notes* was commenced on 15th January 1880 and *The Library* was adopted as the official journal on 10th December 1880. On 30th January 1896 the name of the Association was changed to The Library Association, and the Association was granted its Royal Charter on 17th February 1898. The *Library Association Record* commenced publication as the official journal of the Association in January 1899. It became a wholly professional association in 1962 when new bye-laws came into operation. Members are automatically allocated to membership of one of twelve Branches according to their place of residence, and may become members of two Groups (more by paying a small annual subscription for each); the latter exist to further particular aspects of librarianship. The Association is controlled by a Council elected by the members. The Association's motto is *Ingenia hominum res publica* (The thoughts of men are the common wealth). The responsibility for the Association's library was transferred to THE BRITISH LIBRARY (*q.v.*) on the official formation of that Library on 1st April 1974. The Information Department continued to be wholly administered by the LA. For new groups, *see* LIBRARY EDUCATION GROUP, PUBLIC LIBRARIES GROUP. Abbreviated LA. Publishes *British Humanities Index* (q.), *British Technology Index* (m.), *Journal of Librarianship* (q.), *Library Association Record* (m.), *Proceedings of the Public Libraries Conference* (a.), *Radials Bulletin* (3 p.a.), books, pamphlets and booklists. Some of the groups and branches publish books, conference reports, a periodical and occasional reports and papers.

LIBRARY ASSOCIATION OF AUSTRALIA. Founded in 1949, being re-constituted from the Australian Institute of Librarians which had been founded in 1937. A Royal Charter of Incorporation was granted by Her Majesty the Queen on 29 January 1963; in this the objects of the Association are expressed as: '(a) to promote, establish and improve libraries and library services; (b) to improve the standard of librarianship and the status of the library profession; (c) to promote the association for the foregoing objects of persons engaged in or interested in libraries or library services'. The Association conducts examinations in librarianship and in archive administration, and confers on members proficient in librarianship the distinction of Fellow ('FLAA') or Associate ('ALAA') of the Library Association of Australia. The Association has Branches in the Australian States and Territories, and Sections devoted to special fields of library work. The Sections may haveDivisions in each State and in the Australian Capital Territory. The following sections have been formed: Archives, Cataloguers, Children's Libraries, Public Libraries, School Libraries, Special Libraries, University and College Libraries. Institutions engaged or interested in libraries or library services may become members; individuals may become 'private' or 'professional' members. The various sections issue free to members the publications mentioned: Public Libraries – *Australian Public Library Issues* (q.); Children's Libraries – *Newsletter* (*q.*); University and College Libraries – *Australian Academic and Research Libraries* (*q.*); Special Libraries – *Australian Special Library News*. (6 p.a.). Abbreviated LAA. Publishes *The Australian Library Journal* (11 p.a.).

LIBRARY ASSOCIATION OF CHINA. Founded in 1953 with the following aims: to help the Chinese Education Ministry to administer and direct the Summer Library Workshop; to publish the *Bulletin;* to constitute a collection of works for the use of librarians; to encourage the organization of book exhibitions; to carry out research on the libraries of China. Publishes *Bulletin* and books on librarianship.

LIBRARY ASSOCIATION OF IRELAND. Founded 1928, incorporated 1952. This Association represents the profession of librarianship in Eire; it provides postal tuition for, and conducts examinations for, the professional qualification (FLAI). Membership is open to all engaged in, or interested in, the profession of librarianship in Ireland or elsewhere. Abbreviated LAI. With the March 1972 issue (NS Vol. 1 No 1) of *An Leabharlann* (*q.*), it became the joint journal of the LAI and of the Northern Ireland Branch of the Library Association with the title *An Leabharlann. The Irish Library*. Conferences of the two bodies have been held since 1961, and there is a standing liaison committee between them. A successful joint fiction reserve scheme has been in operation for several years, and an agreed format for compiling Irish county bibliographies is in use.

LIBRARY ASSOCIATION OF MALAYSIA. Founded on 6th May 1960 to (a) unite all persons engaged in library work or interested in libraries in Malaysia; (b) promote the better administration of libraries; (c) encourage the establishment, development, and use of libraries in Malaysia; (d) encourage professional education and training for librarianship; (e) publish such information as will be of service to members; (f) undertake such activities, including the holding of meetings and conferences, as are appropriate to the attainments of the foregoing objects. Individual membership is open to all persons engaged in library work or interested in libraries in Malaysia; institutional membership is open to all libraries and other institutions which share the objects of the Association; honorary membership is conferred on persons who have distinguished themselves in library work. The Association was known as the Library Association of the Federation of Malaya from 6th May 1960 to 8th July 1964. Abbreviated PPM (Persatuan Perpustakaan Malaysia). Publishes *Perpustakaan* (semi-a.).

LIBRARY ASSOCIATION OF RHODESIA AND NYASALAND. Aims to unite all persons engaged in library work, improve standards in all aspects of librarianship, bibliography and documentation and act as an advisory body in these matters.

LIBRARY ASSOCIATION OF SINGAPORE. Founded in 1954 as the Malayan Library Group and successively known as: Library Association of Malaya & Singapore (from November 1958); Library Association of Singapore (1960); Library Association of Malaysia, Singapore Branch (from January 1965); Library Association of Singapore (since January 1966). The objects of the Association and membership conditions are similar to those of the LIBRARY ASSOCIA-TION OF MALAYSIA (*q.v.*). Abbreviated PPS (Persatuan Perpustakaan Singapura), LAS. Published *Majallah Perpustakaan Singapura* (three issues 1961–1964), *Perpustakaan Malaysia* 1965 (superseded *Malayan Library Journal* and *Majallah Perpustakaan Singapura*), *Perpustakaan* (1966).

LIBRARY AUTHORITY. In England, a library authority was any local council responsible for local government which had adopted the library acts, whether the council of an urban district, non-county borough, London borough, county borough, county or the Common Council of the City of London. Any other local authority which was a library authority immediately before 1 April 1965 when the Public Libraries and Museums Act 1964 came into operation, ceased to be a library authority. Under this Act, every library authority in England has the duty 'to provide a comprehensive and efficient library service' for all residents and non-resident employees and students, and for that purpose 'to provide and maintain such buildings and equipment, and such books and other materials, and to do such other things, as may be requisite.' In Ireland, the library authority in counties and rural districts was the county council; in incorporated boroughs, the council or the municipal commissioners; in towns, the town commissioners. In Scotland, the library authority in counties was the county education authority; and in burghs, the magistrates *and* the council. The reorganization of local authority areas in England and Wales, brought about by the Local Government Act 1972 (effective as from 1st April 1974) and in Scotland by the Local Government (Scotland) Act 1973 (effective as from 16th May 1975) altered considerably not only the geographical boundaries – and in a number of cases the names of the local authorities – but also the services which the various local authorities were able to provide. The number and variety of local authorities was reduced and the distribution of their functions rationalized. *In England and Wales* there are two tiers of authorities – Counties and Districts. In the urban areas they are known as Metropolitan Counties and Metropolitan Districts, and in the more rural areas as non-metropolitan counties and non-metropolitan districts. The Public Libraries and Museums Act 1964 is administered outside London by District Councils in the urban (or Metropolitan) Districts and by County Councils in the more rural (or non-metropolitan) counties. For the Greater London area, the London boroughs formed under the London Government Act 1963 are the library authorities. This Act established the Greater London Council, but this Council is not a library authority under the PUBLIC LIBRARIES AND MUSEUMS ACT 1964. In the City of London, the Common Council is the library authority.

In Wales they are (a) the council of a county, (b) the council of a district which has been constituted a library authority, (c) the joint board in the area which has been the subject of a joint board order. *In Scotland* there are local government areas known as Regions, each of which contains local government areas known as Districts; Orkney, Shetland and the Western Isles were designated island areas. For the purposes of the Public Library (Scotland) Acts 1887–1955 (which were in some respects superseded) the Islands and District Councils became the library authorities except that within the Highlands, Borders, and Dumfries and Galloway regions, the appropriate Regional Council became the library authority. School libraries became functions of the Regional Education Committees. *See also* PATERSON REPORT, SCHOOL LIBRARIES. In *Northern Ireland* Libraries are no longer a local authority responsibility. An Education and Libraries

Bill to establish education and library services in five areas, with a board having statutory responsibility for the local administration of library service, was presented to the Northern Ireland Parliament on 17th February 1972 and was given a second reading in the House of Commons on 15th March. But before the bill became law, direct rule from Westminster was introduced and the Northern Ireland Parliament was prorogued. The legislative proposals of the Education and Libraries Bill were, however, enshrined in the Education and Libraries (Northern Ireland) Order 1972. This Order repealed all library legislation dating back to the mid-nineteenth century; it became effective on 1st October 1973, and provided that one of the primary duties of a board is 'to provide a comprehensive and efficient library service'. Virtually, the librarians and their staffs immediately became civil servants. Whereas the HAWNT REPORT (*q.v.*) favoured the amalgamation of counties, the five new library areas ignored all long-standing county boundaries; each serves between a quarter and a half-million people. Under this Order, five area Education and Library Boards were established, each of which became the local education authority and library authority for its area. The areas are Belfast; South-Eastern (five districts); Southern (six districts); Western (five districts); North-Eastern (nine districts). The Order repealed the Public Libraries Acts (Northern Ireland) in so far as they relate to libraries. Those Acts and the Museums and Gymnasiums Act 1891 are still in force, however, in their application to museums and art galleries. For consideration of changes which have taken place in the provision of public libraries in England and Wales, and also in Scotland, due to the revision of local authority areas, *see* LOCAL GOVERNMENT BOUNDARIES. In consequence of the reorganization of local government, library authorities throughout the United Kingdom and Northern Ireland now have a *duty* to provide a comprehensive and efficient library service. The changes have resulted in the former 308 independent library authorities in England (excluding Greater London) being reduced to 75 (39 non-metropolitan counties and 36 Metropolitan Districts) and in Wales 36 independent authorities becoming 8 new county authorities. *See also* LIBRARY AREA, REVIEW DATE.

LIBRARY BINDING. A specially strong binding to enable library books to withstand considerable use. This is achieved by a number of means, but particularly by guarding sections, sewing the sections on tapes and using specially durable cloth.

LIBRARY BINDING INSTITUTE. An American non-profit trade

organization, founded in 1935 'to: (a) develop a spirit of mutual helpfulness and co-operation among those engaged in library binding and related industries; (b) encourage and direct activities leading to constructive co-operation between the industry and its customers . . .; (c) help sustain the highest possible standards of fair dealing between library binders, their customers, their employees and their competitors; (d) raise and sustain standards of craftsmanship and quality; (e) improve the methods of the industry and stimulate its progress through research and the exchange of experience; (f) give the fullest aid and support to the libraries of the nation and to the profession which makes them possible'. Membership is open to commercial library binders capable of doing work meeting the LBI standard, suppliers to library book binders, and those interested in the preservation of books and periodicals. Members' dues finance the Institute. Abbreviated LBI. Publishes *Library Scene* (q.) and various technical papers and brochures.

LIBRARY BOARD. *Synonymous with* BOARD OF LIBRARY TRUSTEES (*q.v.*).

LIBRARY CENTRE. *See* BRANCH LIBRARY.

LIBRARY CLERK. One who performs duties involving simple tasks related to library functions but limited to strict adherence to specific routines and procedures. The work is carried out under close supervision of a librarian or LIBRARY TECHNICAL ASSISTANT (*q.v.*). (American.)

LIBRARY COLLECTION. The total accumulation of material of all kinds assembled by a library for its clientele. Also called 'Library holdings', 'Library resources'.

LIBRARY COMMISSION. 1. An American organization created by an act of legislature, operating in one state but independent of the state library. It exists to promote library services by establishing, organizing and supervising public, and sometimes school, libraries, and by lending books and other material to communities which do not possess libraries. 'State Library Agency' is replacing this term. 2. Occasionally, a Board of Library Trustees.

LIBRARY COMMITTEE. The committee responsible for the provision of a library service.

LIBRARY CONSULTANT. An adviser to a librarian, a lay group or a body responsible for providing a library service.

LIBRARY CORNER. (*Binding*) The turning in of cloth at the corners of books so as to take up the excess in two diagonal folds, one under each turn-in. In this way the cloth is not cut, and the corner given additional strength. *See also* MITRED CORNER, SQUARE CORNER.

LIBRARY COUNCIL. England and Wales are divided into library regions, and each region has a library council consisting of persons representing each of the authorities in the region and such other persons as may be provided for by a scheme which is drawn up in respect of each library region by the Secretary of State after consulting the library authorities within the region. The library councils have 'a duty to make and supervise the working of arrangements for facilitating the co-operation of those authorities with one another and with other bodies within or outside the region having functions in relation to libraries.' The scheme referred to, provides (a) for the constitution, incorporation and functioning of the library council, and (b) for the observance by each of the authorities of any requirements made by the library council, including requirements as to the payment by the authority of contributions towards the expenses of the council. The scheme may also contain provisions directed to the promotion of inter-library co-operation within and outside the region as may appear to the Secretary of State to be expedient. The scheme is the subject of Section 3 of the Public Libraries and Museums Act 1964. Sub-section (5) of this section authorises the Secretary of State to require any library council to enter into and carry into effect arrangements with another such council or with any other body having functions in relation to libraries, with a view to improving the efficiency of the public library service or promoting its development. *See also* LIBRARY ADVISORY COUNCILS, LIBRARY AUTHORITY.

LIBRARY COUNCIL (of Ireland) – An Chomhairle Leabharlanna. A Republic of Ireland body with the status of a local authority; established by the Public Library Act 1947, it is the Agency for channelling central funds for the assistance and development of locally supported library services.

LIBRARY DISCOUNT. Discount on the cost of books purchased for a library.

LIBRARY DOCUMENTATION CENTRE. This Centre was established in November 1970 and is part of the Public Services Branch of the National Library of Canada in Ottawa. It serves as a collection centre for up-to-date documentation on library and information science in Canada for both the Library staff and the Canadian Library Community. It functions as Canada's national information transfer centre for ISORID (*q.v.*).

LIBRARY ECONOMY. The practical application of library science to the founding, organizing and administering of libraries.

LIBRARY EDITION. 1. A vague term indicating the edition of a book, series or set of books, often all the works of an author, in a substantial and uniform format to distinguish it from another less substantial edition, possibly in paper covers. Sometimes called 'Cabinet edition'. 2. An edition printed on good paper and in a specially strong binding for library use.

LIBRARY EDUCATION DIVISION. Established as a Division of the American Library Association on 21 June 1946. Has specific responsibility for continuous study and review of library education, conduct of activities and projects within its areas of responsibility. Abbreviated LED. Publishes *LED Newsletter* (q., free to membs.).

LIBRARY EDUCATION, GRADUATE. Library education for which post-baccalaureate library science credit is given by an institute of higher education. (American.)

LIBRARY EDUCATION GROUP. The formation of this Group was approved by the Council of the Library Association on 1st May 1970 to foster discussion in the field of library education by practising librarians, students and librarianship teachers. Publishes *LEG News* (2 p.a.).

LIBRARY EDUCATION, UNDERGRADUATE. Library education for which undergraduate credit is given by an institution of higher education. (American.)

LIBRARY EXTENSION. The provision of lectures, film shows, etc. in the library, arranging talks, book-displays, etc. outside the library buildings in order to draw attention to the library services and book stocks. In America, the promotion of libraries and the development of library services by state, regional or local agencies.

LIBRARY HAND. A handwriting used by librarians with the object of achieving uniformity and legibility in manuscript catalogues and other records. The formation of letters and the slope were determined with clarity in mind, and many librarians used this handwriting before the use of typewriters became common.

'LIBRARY HAS'. A note to a catalogue entry indicating a library's holdings of a serial publication.

'LIBRARY HAS' CARD. The card bearing the statement of a library's holdings of a SERIAL (*q.v.*); it is made on a separate card which is attached to the main entry card when there is more than one break in the continuity of the library's holdings.

'LIBRARY HAS' STATEMENT. A statement on a catalogue card, usually for a SERIAL (*q.v.*) which records the date of first publication, and to indicate what issues of the serial the library possesses in the form 'Library has . . .' These entries are made only when the library does not have a complete set, and appear only on the main entry card. *See also* 'LIBRARY HAS' CARD.

LIBRARY HISTORY GROUP. A Group of the Library Association, formed in 1962 to unite members interested in the history of libraries in order to further the aims set forth in the Charter of the LA, to encourage the discussion of, and promote interest in, all matters relating to library history, and encourage original work in the history of librarianship in the British Isles. Publishes *Library History* (2 p.a.).

LIBRARY HOLDINGS. *Synonymous with* LIBRARY COLLECTION (*q.v.*).

LIBRARY AND INFORMATION SERVICE FOR TEES-SIDE. *See* LIST.

LIBRARY KEYS. Said of the card catalogue, the circulation and information desks, the bibliographies and indexes to periodicals, etc., grouped together in what is called a 'Finding unit' in university libraries.

LIBRARY MANAGEMENT RESEARCH UNIT. Formed on 1st January 1969 to: (a) investigate in detail management problems in the organization and systems of university libraries and the use made of these libraries by readers; (b) develop and test management techniques which would assist academic librarians to obtain management information necessary to satisfy three objectives: 1. the efficient use of library resources, 2. the measurement of the effectiveness of existing services, 3. the planning of resources (including money, staff, materials and space) required in the future. Financed by OSTI (now the British Library Research and Development Department). Abbreviated LMRU. The Unit was based at the University of Cambridge until September 1976 when it moved to Loughborough University of Technology where, in addition it holds management courses for librarians. The Unit's papers and reports are mostly published in librarianship periodicals, mainly the *Journal of Librarianship*.

LIBRARY MATERIALS. Books, periodicals, pamphlets, reports, micro-forms, maps, MSS., gramophone records, tapes and all other audio-visual records.

LIBRARY OF CONGRESS.† The national and parliamentary library of the United States of America. Established on 24th April 1800 in Washington, it has become a library for government officers and also for the public. The stock totals 75 million pieces. *See also NATIONAL UNION CATALOG.*

LIBRARY OF CONGRESS CARD. A printed catalogue card on which a full catalogue entry is given, also notes, tracings, and Dewey and

L. of C. classification numbers. Such cards have been issued by the Library of Congress since 1901, and available for purchase. Each card bears a serial number which is used by libraries when ordering printed cards for their catalogues. These numbers are printed in the respective books if published in the U.S.A., usually on the back of the title-page. *See also* CATALOGUING IN PUBLICATION.

LIBRARY OF CONGRESS CLASSIFICATION. The scheme of classification used in the main national library of the U.S.A. The outline of the scheme, held to be the greatest and most modern of utilitarian schemes, was drawn up by Dr. Herbert Putnam, in 1897, and is based in some respects on the Dewey Decimal and Cutter's Expansive schemes, the schedules being worked out by specialists in the various subjects. The main tables have been published, each with its own relative index, as completed, and revised from time to time. The result is a series of special schedules of greater detail than any other scheme. The outline, which is purely arbitrary is as follows:

A   General Works. Polygraphy.
B   Philosophy. Religion.
C   Auxiliary Sciences of History.
D   Universal and Old World History [and Topography] (*except America*).
E–F   America.
G   Geography. Anthropology. Folk-lore. Manners and Customs. Sports and Games.
H   Social Sciences. Economics. Sociology.
J   Political Science.
L   Education.
M   Music.
N   Fine Arts.
P   Language and Literature.
PN–PZ Literary History. Literature.
Q   Science.
R   Medicine.
S   Agriculture. Plant and Animal Industry. Fish Culture and Fisheries. Hunting. Sports.
T   Technology.
U   Military Science.
V   Naval Science.
Z   Bibliography and Library Science.

The scheme does not conform to the theoretical rules for classification, being compiled to meet the needs of the library's huge collection of books. It typifies the enumerative method of classification and retains all powers of growth in the hands of the compiler. It is too detailed and complex for use in any but the largest library but the subject schedules are most useful for special and university libraries. There are no tables for sub-division by form or place which can be used in any part of the scheme. The notation is mixed, consisting of two letters and four figures used arithmetically, blanks being left in the alphabet and in the numbers for future insertions. The schedules are undergoing constant amendments and updating; these amendments are published in *LC Classification – additions and changes* and the schedules of whole classes are reprinted from time to time. In 1974 a task force on cataloguing, composed of head cataloguers of several Canadian university libraries, obtained a grant under the Canadian federal Local Initiatives Program (LIP) to compile the first general index to the classification, *An index to the Library of Congress Classification*, for publication by the Canadian Library Association.

LIBRARY OF DEPOSIT. Under the U.K. Copyright Act 1911, a library which is entitled to receive free copies of books published in the U.K. They are often referred to as a COPYRIGHT LIBRARY (*q.v.*) and wrongly as a DEPOSIT LIBRARY (*q.v.*).

LIBRARY OFFICER. As defined by the Public Libraries and Museums Act 1964, 'an officer of a local authority employed by the authority solely or mainly for the purposes of any functions exercisable by it in relation to the public library service'; 'officer' includes a servant (s.25).

LIBRARY ORGANIZATION. Library organization must obviously precede library administration. Decision upon the methods and lines along which the library is to be run, and getting these methods into working order is the basis of library organization. Plans for, and erection of, the library building, executive decisions with regard to selection, appointment and duties of the staff, the planning and putting into practice of a definite system upon which the work of the library is to be carried on – these are successive stages in library organization. Organization is the act or process of organizing; i.e. creating a systematic union of individuals in a body whose officials, agents and members work together for a common end. Administration is the act of administering such a union; i.e. directing an office, service, employment, etc. Organization creates the machine; administration runs it.

LIBRARY PRACTICE. A common method of carrying out a routine or providing a service in libraries.

LIBRARY PROCESSING.   *See* PROCESSING.

LIBRARY PUBLIC RELATIONS COUNCIL.   Founded in the U.S.A. in 1939 to investigate, discuss, and promote every phase of library public relations. Abbreviated LPRC.

LIBRARY RATE.   The amount of money per pound sterling of rateable value of a local authority area which is required to provide a public library service. A separate rate is not levied, the portion required for library purposes being raised as part of the general rate by the council of a local authority, i.e. of a county, London borough, county borough, non-county borough, or urban district.

LIBRARY REGION.   One of a number of areas into which England and Wales are divided to facilitate co-operation between library authorities. *See also* LIBRARY COUNCIL.

LIBRARY RESEARCH CENTER.   Established in 1961 at the University of Illinois to conduct applied research in the public library field. The scope of the Center has now been broadened to include school and academic libraries. Publishes annual reports. Its services are available on contract to individual libraries as well as national foundations, institutions, etc. A list of the research studies completed by the staff of the Center appears in *Information News and Sources*, November–December 1973. Abbreviated LRC. *See also* CENTER FOR RESEARCH LIBRARIES.

LIBRARY RESEARCH CIRCLE.   A group meeting under the auspices of the Indian Library Association to consider such matters as the elements of classification and the rationalization of terminology.

LIBRARY SCHOOL.   An organized course, or courses, in librarianship attended by full-time and/or part-time students. It may be a separately managed institution in its own building but is usually a department of an institution for further education, or a faculty within a university. Abbreviated LS.

LIBRARY SCIENCE.   The knowledge and skill concerned with the administration of libraries and their contents; library economy and bibliography.

LIBRARY SCIENCE ABSTRACTS.   A publication of the Library Association (quarterly since January 1950) giving abstracts of books and articles in periodicals on librarianship published throughout the world. Abbreviated *LSA*. Expanded in 1969 and renamed *Library & Information Science Abstracts* (*q.v.*).

LIBRARY SCIENCE CLASSIFICATION.   A fully faceted scheme, prepared in draft by members of the Classification Research Group and entitled *Classification of library science*, was published in 1965.

A later version with the title *A classification of library and information science* was published in 1975.

LIBRARY SERVICE. The facilities provided by a library for the use of books and the dissemination of information.

LIBRARY SERVICES ACT. An act passed by the Congress of the U.S.A. in 1956 authorising federal grants during five years to help bring public library services to rural areas of less than 10,000 population. It was extended in 1960 for a further period of five years, i.e. until 30 June 1966. The act is administered under the aegis of the Library Services Branch of the U.S. Office of Education. Funds may be used for salaries, books and other library materials, library equipment, and general operating expenses but may not be used for erecting buildings or purchasing land. *See also* LIBRARY SERVICES AND CONSTRUCTION ACT.

LIBRARY SERVICES AND CONSTRUCTION ACT. Passed in the U.S.A. in 1964, this act broadens the coverage of the LIBRARY SERVICES ACT (*q.v.*) by (1) making federal grants available for any urban or rural area without library services 'or with inadequate services', (2) authorizing federal grants for constructing library buildings where facilities are lacking. This Act has been amended several times since originally passed, and has been subsequently extended until 1982.

LIBRARY SHELVING. Shelving which is made to meet the special needs of libraries. This is usually made in standard shelf lengths of 3 feet (centre of upright to centre of upright) and the shelves should be easily adjustable.

LIBRARY SIGN. The sign consisting of a torch of learning with a red cartouche, bearing in white lettering the words 'Public Library', which is placed outside branches of English county, and many non-county, libraries, and on mobile library vehicles.

LIBRARY SOCIETY OF PUERTO RICO. Sociedad de Bibliotecarios de Puerto Rico. Founded to extol the position of the librarian and to promote a greater recognition of the profession in Puerto Rico; to obtain a better qualification from its associates, and to promote an interest in the profession with the object of drawing the best talent into it, and also to strive to get the authorities concerned to make available the means to offer courses in library science in the country; to work for a greater expansion of the library services in Puerto Rico, and to advocate for the establishment of public libraries in all the communities in the island; to stimulate a greater exchange among the librarians both local as well as from abroad. Publishes *Bulletin of the Library Society of Puerto Rico*.

LIBRARY STAMP. A rubber stamp bearing the name of the library; this is used to indicate the ownership of books, periodicals and other publications.

LIBRARY TECHNICAL ASSISTANT. One whose duties are based on skills required by a library clerk, but, in addition, possesses a proficiency developed in one or more functional areas or in certain limited phases of library services. Such an assistant works under the supervision of a librarian, and may supervise and direct library clerks or clerical staff. *See also* LIBRARY CLERK. (American.)

LIBRARY TECHNOLOGY PROGRAM. Established on 1st May 1959 by the American Library Association with a grant from the Council on Library Resources for a period of two years, and later extended for five years from 1st July 1961 and then annually. Until 1st July 1966 it was known as the Library Technology Project. Purpose: to explore ways and means by which modern technology and the principles of scientific management can be used to streamline library operations and improve services, and to disseminate the results of its studies and investigations in these areas to the library profession. In order to carry out these objects LTP (1) tests and evaluates library equipment, supplies, and systems, and conducts systems studies, (2) develops new or improved items of library equipment and promotes improvements in existing equipment by calling desirable modifications to the notice of manufacturers, (3) works to develop performance standards for library equipment and supplies, to improve the quality of library products, and to furnish purchasing guidelines to librarians, and (4) provides an individualized information service to the library profession so that the results of LTP research may be utilized as effectively and as widely as possible. In 1972 the Executive Board of the ALA adopted a budget which did not provide funds for a portion of the financial report required to enable LTP to continue its full range of activities. The result was that in 1973 there were only two major activities – the continued publication of the *Library Technology Reports* (6 p.a.) and book publication in which the results of some LTP research and commissioned scripts were published. The COUNCIL ON LIBRARY RESOURCES (*q.v.*) continued to support selected individual projects mainly concerned with library equipment, instead of direct operational support. Abbreviated LTP. Published *Library Technology Reports* (6 p.a.) until December 1973 when taken over by LAD.

LIBRARY TICKET. One indicating membership of a library and serving as the authority for borrowing books.

'THE LIBRARY WORLD' PUBLICITY AWARDS. These annual

Awards were first made in 1965. Publications submitted for adjudication must have been issued during the previous year. There are two groups: (1) libraries in Great Britain and Northern Ireland, and (2) libraries overseas. Each group is divided into three sections as follows: (a) annual reports; (b) booklists and other bibliographical publications; (c) library publicity generally or specially. The awards take the form of certificates which are awarded to the first three winners in each section and group. These Awards were discontinued in 1971–72.

LIBRARY TRUSTEES. *Synonymous with* BOARD OF LIBRARY TRUSTEES (*q.v.*).

LIBRETTIST. The author of the text of an opera or other extended choral composition.

LIBRETTO. The words to which an opera or other lengthy musical composition for voices is set.

LIBRI MANUSCRIPTI. Books written by hand, as were all books before the invention of printing.

LIBSKED. Abbreviation for Library Sort Key Edit, an expanded version of SKED (*q.v.*), which was developed co-operatively by the MARC Development Office and the Technical Processes Research Office of the Library of Congress. MARC records are used; these provide the information needed for the computer to arrange bibliographical entries according to very sophisticated and demanding filing rules. The new filing rules (*Filing arrangement in the Library of Congress Catalogs*) – *see* FILING CODE – have been implemented by LIBSKED and used for two regular LC publications: *Films and other materials for projection* (the Library's first computer-produced catalogue) and the 8th ed. of *Library of Congress subject headings*.

LIBTRAD. Abbreviation for the Working Party on Library and Book Trade Relations, a basically non-profit-making organization which was formed in London in 1965 to investigate and report on matters of common concern to publishers, booksellers and librarians. It is independent of the official associations connected with the world of books; membership is small, restricted by invitation to: large and small publishing firms, large and small bookselling firms, public and academic librarians, library suppliers, library school lecturers. Biennial conferences, known as 'Holborn' conferences (after the place where they are held), are organized to consider a problem area of general concern to libraries and the book trade. LIBTRAD is financed by the sale of conference papers.

LICENCE LEAF. *See* IMPRIMATUR.

LICHTDRUCK. A kind of COLLOTYPE (*q.v.*).

LIFTED MATTER. Type or blocks removed from the forme and put on one side for use in other pages or in another job.

LIGATURE. Two or more letters joined together, or differing in design from the separate letters, and cast on one type body, as st, ct, ffl, ff, fi, fl to save space, avoid the unsightly juxtaposition of st, ct, ffl, ff, fi, fl, and to reduce the risk of damage to kerned letters. The term also refers to the joining stroke which connects the characters. Also called 'Double letter', 'Tied letter'. *See also* LOGOTYPE.

LIGHT FACE. The weight of type-face which is lighter than medium – the ordinary book weight – having thinner strokes. The opposite of BOLD FACE (*q.v.*). Most type families are made in varying weights, usually called light, medium, bold, extra bold; but 'medium' is normally understood when referring to a type face and is therefore only expressed when it is essential to distinguish it from the other weights.

LIGHTWEIGHT PAPER. Sensitized photographic paper between 0·0044 and 0·0059 inches inclusive. *See also* PHOTOGRAPHIC PAPERS.

LIGUE DES BIBLIOTHÈQUES EUROPÉENNES DE RE-CHERCHE. *See* LIBER.

LIKENESS. The quality of similarity or alikeness which is used in classification in order to group together objects or ideas according to their likeness.

LILLIPUT EDITION. *See* MINIATURE BOOK.

LIMITATION NOTICE. The statement in a book published in a LIMITED EDITION (*q.v.*) indicating the number of copies printed which comprise the edition, or part of the edition. The statement would define the special character of the edition, such as printed on 'large paper' or hand-made paper, and provide for the number of the individual copy to be written in.

LIMITED CATALOGUING. A term used by the Library of Congress for the standard of descriptive cataloguing which began to be applied in 1951 by the Library of Congress to certain categories of books in order to speed up cataloguing processes. Limited cataloguing is practised in order to reduce the work and time involved in recording more details than are required to identify and locate works which are not of sufficient bibliographic and reference utility to compensate for the time expended. The following illustrate the kinds of categories which are subject to limited cataloguing: (1) trade publications in general: current fiction, biography, history, drama, poetry, religion, travel, juvenile books, etc.; (2) minor publications of governments, institutions and other corporate bodies, e.g. the miscellaneous pamphlets, leaflets, and informational literature issued by such organizations; (3) text books, technical manuals, handbooks, etc.; (4) translations from English into a foreign language. It will be noted that the scheme does not apply to music, maps and other non-textual materials. Details of the limitations are given on pages 74–5 of *Cataloguing Rules of the American Library Association and the Library of Congress. Additions and Changes, 1949–58.* Washington, Library of Congress, 1959. *See also* FULL CATALOGUING.

LIMITED EDITION.   An edition, printed on special paper and often with a special binding, which is printed in limited numbers (seldom more than 1,500, usually about 200 to 500, but often as few as ten) and sold at a higher price. Each copy bears a printed certificate (usually facing the title-page) indicating the size of the edition on which is written the actual copy number. Sometimes copies are signed by the author. Library of Congress catalogue cards usually bear details in a note, usually in quoted form, for editions of 500 copies or less, and numbered – and especially numbered and signed copies – are usually especially noted. Works in editions of 100 copies or less usually go to rare book collections, and fine limited editions which are not wanted in such collections are shelved in special locked collections for protection. *See also* LIMITATION NOTICE.

LIMITED EDITIONS CLUB.   An American subscription book club, founded in 1929 by George Macy, which produces well-designed and well-printed books.

LIMP BINDING.   Said of a book which is not bound in boards but with flexible cloth or leather.

LIMP CLOTH.   A term used to describe a style of publisher's binding. *See also* LIMP COVERS.

LIMP COVERS.   Thin flexible book covers made of plastic, or of other material, without boards and covered with cloth or leather.

LIMP LEATHER.   A full leather binding made without using stiff boards and therefore flexible. Often used for Bibles.

LINDISFARNE GOSPELS.   Written in Latin, this is the earliest and most beautiful extant manuscript in English half-uncials; it is supposed to have been written by Eadfrith, Bishop of Lindisfarne, about 700. Also known as the 'Durham Book'.

LINE.   1. The imaginary base-line of a piece of movable type, running set-wise on or about which all the characters are positioned. *See also* SET 2. 2. A row of printed or written characters extending across a column or page. *See also* MEASURE. 3. A FILLET (*q.v.*) used in book-binding. 4. Reproduction of a drawing which prints only solid areas and lines, there being no tones.

LINE BLOCK. A metal printing block made photographically direct from a black and white drawing without any intermediate tones other than tints, and mounted type-high for letterpress printing. *See also* ZINCOGRAPHY.

LINE-BY-LINE-INDEX. An entry in an index, with its page or other reference, which is printed on a single line. Also known as an 'Entry-a-Line-Index'. Where the entries consist of titles which are similarly confined to one line, it is known as a 'Title-a-line Index'.

LINE-CASTING MACHINE. A type-casting machine which casts a line of type in one slug. Intertype and Linotype are machines of this kind.

LINE COPY. A copy of a document which has no tone values. Also called 'Line reproduction'. *See also* LINE ORIGINAL.

LINE CUT. *Synonymous with* LINE ENGRAVING (*q.v.*).

LINE DIVISION MARK. A mark, usually a vertical or oblique line, used in bibliographical transcription to indicate the end of a line of type in the original.

LINE DRAWING. A black ink drawing made in line or stipple with indian ink, pencil, crayon, or brush, from which a line block may be made. An impression of grey is achieved by using a tint.

LINE END STROKE. *Synonymous with* LINE DIVISION MARK (*q.v.*).

LINE-ENDING. 1. Term used to indicate the last letter of a line of type when giving an exact bibliographical description of a title-page, the ending of each line being indicated by a vertical or oblique stroke or two such strokes. 2. An ornament (of which there are a great variety) filling the space at the end of a line in a mediaeval illuminated manuscript. Also called 'Line-filling'.

LINE ENGRAVING. 1. Engraving in which the effects are produced by lines of different width and proximity, cut into copper, steel, zinc or other similar material. 2. A plate produced by the line engraving process. 3. A picture printed from a line engraving.

LINE ETCHING. *Synonymous with* ETCHING (*q.v.*).

LINE-FILLING. *Synonymous with* LINE-ENDING (*q.v.*).

LINE ORIGINAL. An original document for copying, and having no tone values. A copy of such an original may be called a 'Line copy' or 'Line reproduction'.

LINE PRINTER. (*Information retrieval*) A device which prints out data from a computer one line at a time.

LINE REPRODUCTION. *Synonymous with* LINE COPY (*q.v.*). *See also* LINE ORIGINAL.

LINEALE. Styles of type face where the characters have no serifs. Such faces were formerly known as 'sans-serif'. They may be subdivided into GROTESQUE, NEO-GROTESQUE, GEOMETRIC and HUMANIST (*qq.v.*).

LINED. Said of a book which has a piece of material (strips of parchment which overlapped the joints and were pasted down under the endpapers of seventeenth- and eighteenth-century bindings) lining the spine to give it strength.

LINEN. A cloth made from flax for covering books.

LINEN FACED. Paper with a linen finish on one or both sides.

LINEN FINISH. Paper, the surface of which is made to resemble linen by placing it between plates of zinc and sheets of linen under pressure. *See also* CRASH FINISH.

LINEN-GRAINED. A book-cloth which is patterned to resemble linen.

LINEN PAPER. 1. Paper made from rags; originally from linen rags. 2. LINEN FACED (*q.v.*).

LINGUISTIC NUMBERS. *Synonymous with* ETHNIC NUMBERS (*q.v.*).

LINING. A piece of material, usually mull, placed in the spine of a book when binding it to give it strength. Also called 'Back lining'. *See also* FIRST LINING, SECOND LINING, TRIPLE LINING.

LINING, ORNAMENTAL INSIDE. *Synonymous with* DOUBLURE 1 (*q.v.*).

LINING FIGURES. (*Printing*) Arabic numerals which do not have ascenders or descenders, but which are the same size as capital letters, stretching from base-line to cap line thus: 1234567890. Also called 'Ranging figures'. *See also* HANGING FIGURES.

LINING PAPER. 1. That portion of an endpaper which is pasted down on the inner cover of a book. The other portion of the endpaper is known as the 'free endpaper'. *See also* ENDPAPER. 2. Coloured or marbled paper used as an ENDPAPER (*q.v.*).

LINING-UP TABLE. *Synonymous with* REGISTER TABLE (*q.v.*).

LINK LETTERS. *See* LINKS.

LINKED BOOKS. Separately bound books where the relationship between each other is indicated in various ways, such as collective or series title-pages; continuous paging, series or signatures; mention in contents or other preliminary leaves.

LINKS. In co-ordinate indexing, grouping devices; generally but not necessarily, symbols appended to item numbers. They show that terms are related. Also called 'Interfixes', 'Link letters', 'Punctuation', 'Association'.

LINOCUT. 1. A piece of linoleum engraved by hand, mounted on a wooden block at type height and printed from as if from a woodcut. Linocut blocks are very durable and can be electrotyped. Illustrations comprising broad flat masses and bold lettering are suitable for this method. 2. The impression made from a linocut block.

LINOFILM. A photo-composing machine built by the Mergenthaler Linotype Co., of New York and demonstrated in 1954. The machine has two units, a keyboard unit and a photographic unit. The standard typewriter keyboard unit has additional keys for hair-spacing, line erasing, quadding and fount selection; this punches a code into a paper strip and so specifies roman, italic, or bold in upper or lower case or small capitals, spaces and lines. Justification is achieved by a mechanical computer automatically punching into the strip. This strip is fed into the photographic unit which interprets electrically the specification of the punched strip and produces a positive with black letters on a clear base.

LINOLEUM BLOCK. An engraved piece of linoleum from which a Linocut (*q.v.*) is made.

LINOLEUM DRY-POINT. An impression made from a linoleum block on which the design has been made with a dry-point tool.

LINOSCO. Abbreviation for Libraries of North Staffordshire & South Cheshire in Co-operation. This scheme was begun in 1959 following several years of informal co-operation in the North Staffordshire area. Four public libraries, twelve university and college libraries and nine special libraries are members, and the organization is based on the Horace Banks Reference Library, City Central Library, Hanley, Stoke-on-Trent, Staffs., where a union list of periodical titles is maintained. Although the lending of books and periodicals between member libraries is the main purpose of LINOSCO, the committee has been concerned with the training of library assistants and has initiated the holding of classes. Meetings of the librarians of the co-operating libraries are held twice yearly at member libraries in rotation: at these, matters of national and local professional interest, as well as co-operation are discussed. *See also* MISLIC.

LINOTYPE. A typesetting machine casting a line of type in a slug. It was invented by Ottmar Mergenthaler (1854–99). The machine carries a large number of single matrices in a magazine; these are released as the keyboard is operated and assembled in sequence with double-wedge spaces separating the words. The spaces are used to justify the completed line as it is brought to the orifice of a mould, and there cast in a type-high slug. Linotype machines have been in use since 1890, and are the kind most used for printing newspapers.

LINOTYPE CALEDONIA. See TYPE FACE.

LINSON. The trade name for a particularly tough variety of paper used extensively for publisher's casing. It can be embossed to represent linen and is available in a wide variety of colours and finishes. It is used increasingly as an alternative to cloth, being much cheaper. It is one of a number of binder coverings made by Grange Fibre of Leicester.

LINT. Dust, or loose fibres, which separate from the raw material during paper-making.

LIPPINCOTT AWARD, JOSEPH W. Donated by Joseph W. Lippincott in 1937, and suspended between 1940 and 1947, this annual Award of $1,000 cash ($500 through 1959), a medal and a citation of achievement, is made to a librarian for distinguished service in the profession of librarianship, such service to include outstanding participation in the activities of professional library associations, notable published professional writing, or other significant activity on behalf of the profession and its aims. The Award is administered by the ALA Awards Committee, the selection being made by a jury of five appointed by the ALA Awards Committee. The first recipient was Mary U. Rothrock in 1938.

LISE. Acronym of Librarians of Institutes and Schools of Education. Formally inaugurated in 1954 to co-operate in the provision of library services and in bibliographic work in the field of education. Membership is granted at the discretion of the Group to librarians having an acknowledged function to provide a service to certain categories of reader requiring educational material. Maintains at the Birmingham School of Education a union catalogue of books. Publishes a *Union list of Periodicals held in Schools and Institutes of Education Libraries* and numerous other union lists.

LIST. 1. Acronym of Library and Information Service for Teesside. Formed in 1964 to provide access to information, and to inter-lend publications between members. Libraries, firms and organizations within the area are eligible for membership. The Scheme is operated from the Cleveland Central Library, Middlesbrough. 2. Acronym for *Library and Information Services To-day*, a key international source book for activities in progress in the fields of research and innovation in librarianship, documentation and information science being undertaken in governmental and academic institutions; industrial and research organizations, international associations, foundations, societies, etc. It commenced publication as an annual in 1971, being compiled as a library project of the University of Maryland, U.S.A. Vols. 1–3 had the title *Library and Information Science To-day*.

LIST, PUBLISHER'S.   A list of books published by one publisher and still in print.

LIST OF CONTENTS.   A contents-list or list of 'preliminaries'. *See* CONTENTS.

LIST OF ILLUSTRATIONS.   This follows the 'Table of Contents' and indicates the position in the book of the illustrations, both full-page and 'in the text'. *See also* PRELIMINARIES.

LIST OF SIGNATURES.   *See* REGISTER 2.

LIST PRICE.   The price of a book as quoted by the publisher in his catalogue.

LITERAL.   An error made in setting type, usually through confusion of similar letters or an unclear manuscript, and involving no more than a letter-for-letter correction, such as a full point for a comma, or a transposition.

LITERAL MNEMONICS.   *See* MNEMONICS.

LITERARY AGENT.   One who arranges the sale and publication of authors' work with publishers of books, newspapers and periodicals, and who negotiates subsidiary rights such as dramatic, broadcasting, and film rights. An agent also acts for publishers by arranging for the writing of scripts which they need. The author pays the agent on a commission basis for his services.

LITERARY GUILD.   One of the original American book clubs; it manufactured its own editions.

LITERARY MANUSCRIPT.   A record or document produced by hand and indicating literary rather than textual excellence. Also called 'Textual manuscript'. *See also* ARTISTIC MANUSCRIPT.

LITERARY PROPERTY.   The product of an author's creative effort in the form of manuscripts or published work which have an existing or potential financial value.

LITERARY WARRANT.   1. The volume of books which have been written on any topic. 2. (*Classification*) The quantity of expressed and embodied knowledge in any given field, waiting to be organized. 3. (*Information retrieval*) A subject which has appeared in the literature, is represented by the descriptors used in the retrieval system if it is desired to retrieve documents specifically relevant to that subject, and with minimum 'dilution' by other documents.

LITERARY WORK.   A work, other than a SACRED WORK (*q.v.*), written in a literary form, e.g. a poem, drama, novel, etc. and having outstanding qualities such as beauty of form, emotional or intuitive appeal.

LITERATURE REVIEW. A survey of progress in a particular aspect of science over a given period (e.g. one, five, or ten years); it may range from a bibliographical index or mere list of references, to a general critical review of original publications on the subjects covered.

LITERATURE SEARCH. A systematic and exhaustive search for published material on a specific subject, together with the preparation of annotated bibliographies or abstracts for the use of the researcher. This is an intermediate stage between reference work and research, and is differentiated from both. It is often the first step in a research project, patent search, or laboratory experiment and sometimes reveals that the proposed action is unnecessary, having been carried out previously by others; if this is not the case the search usually gives valuable information on similar or identical work previously undertaken. In some libraries a separate room called a 'search room' is set aside and equipped with appropriate bibliographical 'tools' such as volumes of abstracts, periodical indexes, etc. for the carrying out of searches.

LITERATURE SURVEY. 1. A bibliography relating to a specific subject and listing of material either in a given collection, or in more than one library, or of literature on the subject. 2. A listing, with full bibliographical references, of recently published books and articles on a given subject in current journals, prepared usually by librarians or information officers in industrial organizations or research associations for the information of members of, or users of, the organization. It serves to keep those to whom it is circulated up-to-date in the literature of the subjects with which they are concerned. Brief annotations are often provided. Also called 'Current publication survey'.

LITHO CRAYON. A special crayon for drawing on lithographic plates.

LITHO PAPERS. Papers made especially for lithographic printing. Made basically from esparto, they have dimensional stability to ensure correct register, and are usually placed the narrow way across the printing machines, for any stretch must be the narrow way of the sheet.

LITHOGRAPH. A print or illustration produced by LITHOGRAPHY (*q.v.*).

LITHOGRAPHIC PRESS. A press for printing from a lithographic stone or plate. It is similar in appearance to a stop-cylinder press used for bookwork, and operates in much the same way.

LITHOGRAPHIC PRINTING. A planographic printing process whereby the areas of the printing surface (the non-image areas) are hydrophic (i.e. have an affinity for water) and the printing (image) areas are hydrophobic (i.e. repel water and attract grease). *See also* LITHOGRAPHY.

LITHOGRAPHIC RIBBON.   A special ribbon used for typing direct on to lithographic plates.

LITHOGRAPHY.   The process of drawing designs on stone with a special greasy crayon, chalk, paint or ink, and of producing printed impressions therefrom; also any process based on the same principle in which a thin flexible metal plate or plastic is used instead of stone. The stone is saturated with water, the printing ink is then applied and adheres only to those portions covered by the crayon or other drawing medium. A separate drawing is required for each colour in the resulting print. In direct lithography the drawing is in reverse; in offset lithography the drawing is first made the right way round on transfer paper, printed on to a rubber-covered cylinder and 'offset' on to the paper. Lithography was invented by Aloys Senefelder, a Bavarian, in 1798. From the Greek 'Lithos' = stone. *See also* AUTO-LITHOGRAPHY, OFFSET LITHOGRAPHY, OFFSET PRINTING, PHOTO-LITHOGRAPHY, PHOTO-OFFSET.

LITHOGRAVURE.   A process of photo-engraving on stone.

LITHO-OFFSET.   *See* LITHOGRAPHY, OFFSET PRINTING.

LITHOPHOTOGRAPHY.   *Synonymous with* PHOTO-LITHOGRAPHY (*q.v.*).

LITHOPRINT.   *Synonymous with* OFFSET PRINTING (*q.v.*).

LITHOTINT.   An obsolete method of lithography by which the effect of a tinted drawing was produced. Also a picture so produced.

LITTERAE VENETIAE.   *Synonymous with* BOLOGNESE LETTERS (*q.v.*).

LIVE MATTER.   A forme of letterpress or illustrations, ready for printing, electrotyping or stereotyping. It may be held for future use. *See also* GOOD, MATTER, STANDING TYPE.

LIVERPOOL AND DISTRICT SCIENTIFIC, INDUSTRIAL AND RESEARCH LIBRARY ADVISORY COUNCIL.   *See* LADSIRLAC.

LIVRES À VIGNETTES.   Books printed in the eighteenth century which were illustrated by vignette copper-plate engravings. The kind of engraving used was a mixture of etching with some gravure work.

ll.   Abbreviation for leaves of a book, lines of type, *leges* (laws).

LOADED PAPER.   *See* COATED PAPER.

LOADING.   The adding of clay, chalk, or similar materials to STUFF (*q.v.*) when in the beater of a paper making machine, or flowed into the stock as it goes through the sluice-gate of the Fourdrinier machine. It fills the spaces between fibres and so imparts solidity to the paper and provides a better printing surface.

LOAN. 1. A large sum of money raised by the local authority and repayable within a specified time for local government developments such as the erection of libraries, purchase of furniture, etc. 2. A book, or a number of books, on loan to an individual, a group of persons, an institution or a library.

LOAN COLLECTION. A collection of books, prints or pictures which are available for use at home as distinct from a collection which may only be referred to on the premises.

LOAN DEPARTMENT. A department from which loans of books and other materials are made, or in which such materials are kept. *Synonymous with* LENDING DEPARTMENT (*q.v.*).

LOAN DESK. *See* CIRCULATION DESK.

LOAN FEE. A charge made for the use of library materials.

LOAN PERIOD. The period which is allowed for reading a book away from a library.

LOAN SANCTION. Authority given by the Minister of Housing and Local Government to local authorities permitting them to borrow money in order to discharge their statutory powers and duties.

loc cit. Abbreviation for *loco citato* (*Lat.* 'in the place already cited'). Used in a footnote reference to avoid using the title or short title of the periodical referred to. It should be used less sparingly than *op. cit.* (*q.v.*).

LOCAL AUTHORITIES MANAGEMENT SERVICES AND COMPUTER COMMITTEE. *See* LAMSAC.

LOCAL AUTHORITY. The unit of administration in Britain which is responsible for providing, either on its own behalf and as it is entitled to do by law, or on behalf of the central government, certain services within the area of its geographical boundaries. Not all of the various services may be provided by each kind of local authority. A local authority with power to provide public libraries is called a LIBRARY AUTHORITY (*q.v.*). *See also* LOCAL GOVERNMENT BOUNDARIES.

LOCAL BIBLIOGRAPHY. A bibliography of books and other forms of written record relating to a geographical area smaller than a county. It normally includes books by and about people born in, or who have resided in, the area, as well as books relating strictly to the geography natural history, architecture and social history of the area.

LOCAL COLLECTION. A collection of books, maps, prints, illustrations and other material relating to a specific locality, usually that in

17

which the library housing the collection is situated. *See also* LOCAL GOVERNMENT (RECORDS) ACT, 1962.

LOCAL DIRECTORY. A directory relating to a specified locality; it may be limited in scope in any way, e.g. to telephone addresses or businesses, but usually includes particulars of residents and businesses, the entries being arranged in street order with 'trade' entries in classified order in addition.

LOCAL GOVERNMENT BOUNDARIES. Under the Local Government Act 1972, the boundaries of most local authorities (excluding Greater London where local government was reorganized in 1965 – *See* LONDON BOROUGHS COMMITTEE) in England and Wales were changed on 1st April 1974. County Boroughs, Cities, Boroughs, Urban Districts and Rural Districts ceased to exist as such; they were all regrouped to form larger administrative units. Some counties were regrouped, at least one was absorbed, all were changed in some degree. There are now six Metropolitan Counties covering the main centres of population, and within these, thirty-six Metropolitan Districts. In the rest of England there are thirty-nine Counties and within these 296 Districts; in Wales, eight Counties and within these, thirty-seven Districts. The services provided by local authorities were re-allocated. Now, public library services outside the GLC area are provided *only* by the councils of the Counties, non-metropolitan counties and Metropolitan Districts. *In Scotland,* A somewhat similar re-arrangements of boundaries came into effect on 15th May 1975 under the provisions of the Local Government (Scotland) Act 1973. This was based on the White Paper of February 1971 which was itself based on the findings of a Royal Commission on Local Government in Scotland which had been appointed in 1966 at the same time as that for England and with similar terms of reference (*see* REDCLIFFE-MAUD REPORT). Lord Wheatley was appointed Chairman. The Report, known as the Wheatley Report, was published in September 1969 in 2 vols. In consequence of the passing of this Act, Scotland (other than Orkney, Shetland and the Western Isles which became three 'Island areas') was divided into nine Regions which in turn were subdivided into fifty-three Districts. On 16th May 1975 all 430 existing local government authorities (counties, cities of counties, large and small burghs, and districts) ceased to exist and were incorporated in the newly formed areas. Some of the fifty-three districts into which the Regions are sub-divided are identical in area, or almost identical, with the abolished counties, and in some cases they bear the same names. The provision of museums and art galleries is the responsibility of the Regional and District Councils. *See also* BAINS REPORT, LIBRARY AUTHORITY (for changes in the provision of public libraries in the United Kingdom and Northern Ireland), MAUD REPORT, REDCLIFFE-MAUD REPORT, WHEATLEY REPORT.

LOCAL GOVERNMENT (RECORDS) ACT, 1962. This Act amends the law relating to the functions of local authorities respecting records in written or other form. It (1) empowers local authorities to promote the adequate use of their records by allowing inspection, copying, indexing, publication, exhibition, etc.; (2) enables local authorities to acquire local records by gift or purchase – or accept on deposit – records which, or (in the case of a collection) the majority of which, appear to be of local interest, and may deposit them with itself or other authorities, (3) authorizes the appointment of sub-committees to deal with records, (4) provides funds for dealing with records of local interest whether under the authority's control or not. The clerk to the council is custodian 'subject to any direction which the council may give'.

LOCAL GOVERNMENT (SCOTLAND) ACT. *See* LOCAL GOVERN-MENT BOUNDARIES, LIBRARY AUTHORITY, WHEATLEY REPORT.

LOCAL LIBRARIAN. A voluntary worker at a village or other centre of a county library.

LOCAL LIST. 1. A list prepared by W. P. Cutter and appended to his *Expansive classification*, giving geographical and political divisions, with numbers, for use in arranging material geographically or to indicate relationship. 2. A list of places which may be used to permit subdivision by place in a scheme or classification. 3. A list of books relating to a particular locality.

LOCAL UNIT CARD. The basic catalogue entry, or UNIT CARD (*q.v.*), which is made at a library normally purchasing printed catalogue cards, in respect of a book which is not catalogued by the British National Bibliography, the Library of Congress, the H.W. Wilson Company or some other printed card issuing agency, or for a book which is to be catalogued locally, either temporarily until printed cards are received, or permanently. *See also* WILSON CARDS.

LOCATION. 1. The place on the shelves or elsewhere in which required material may be found. It is indicated on records, for example on catalogue entries, by the LOCATION MARK (*q.v.*). 2. That part of an index entry which enables the user to locate the document, or part of a document, to which the entry refers. It may be a book, line, column, page, abstract, patent, report, accession number, classification number, or a more or less complete bibliographic citation. It can be a component in a machine documentation system, hence a locative.

LOCATION INDEX.   A record used in county libraries for tracing the whereabouts of particular books. It consists of book cards bearing the names or numbers of the centres to which the books have been sent, and is arranged in alphabetical order.

LOCATION MARK.   A letter, word, group of words or symbols used on a catalogue entry, book list or bibliography, sometimes in conjunction with the CALL NUMBER (q.v.), to indicate the collection, library or position at which the book or item in question is shelved. Also called 'Location symbol'.

LOCATION REGISTER.   A collection, or list, of records of books, documents, or other items, which are arranged by the FIXED LOCATION (q.v.) method or in a CLOSED ACCESS (q.v.) library. The arrangement of the items on the register may be by author, title, or accession number.

LOCATION SYMBOL.   See LOCATION MARK.

LOCATIVE ABSTRACT.   See ABSTRACT.

LOCKING UP.   (Printing) Tightening up a forme of type matter in the metal frame known as a chase, preparatory to putting it on the press.

locus sigilli.   (Lat. 'the place of the seal'). Usually abbreviated L.S. and printed within a circle at the place for a signature on legal documents.

LOFT-DRIED.   Hand- or mould-made papers which are dried by suspension in a dry, airy loft.

LOG.   A registry of items, e.g. on an accession list (IBM).

LOGICAL ARRANGEMENT.   (Cataloguing) A departure from the normal alphabetical order so as to arrange entries by principles associated with the subject matter or type of the entries, e.g. chronological, hierarchical, numerical.

LOGICAL NOTATION.   One in which each symbol of a classification scheme may be divided without limit by a sequence of similar symbols, each having the same value but representing a further step in the subdivision of the subject as represented by the preceding symbol or group of symbols.

LOGICAL SEQUENCE.   (Cataloguing) A group of entries, in the filing of which, implicit rather than alphabetical criteria have been used. See also LOGICAL ARRANGEMENT.

LOGO.   Synonymous with MASTHEAD (q.v.).

LOGOGRAM.   An initial letter or number used as an abbreviation.

LOGOGRAPH.   A symbol that stands for a whole word.

LOGOGRAPHIC WRITING. The earliest form of picture writing in which a single symbol was used to represent an entire word.

LOGOGRAPHY. A method of casting logotypes. It was first patented by Henry Johnson in 1780 who had a fount of 3,500 words and syllables, but the idea never developed owing to opposition from compositors of the time.

LOGON. (*Information retrieval*) That which enables one new distinguished group or category to be added to a representation.

LOGOTYPE. Several letters, or a word, cast on one type, or as a single matrix. Used in the printing of directories or other works in which such combinations are frequently repeated. *See also* LIGATURE.

LOMBARDIC HANDWRITING. An offshoot of the Italian semi-cursive minuscule which was derived from the Roman cursive style used throughout Italy in the seventh to ninth centuries. *See also* CURSIVE, HANDWRITING.

LONDON AND HOME COUNTIES BRANCH. The largest and oldest Branch of the Library Association, having been formed in July 1923.

LONDON AND SOUTH EASTERN LIBRARY REGION (LASER). Formed early in 1969 by the amalgamation of the London Union Catalogue and the South Eastern Regional Library System (both of which were formed forty years earlier) consequent upon the reorganization of the London Borough boundaries in 1965. LASER operates in respect of forty-three public library systems and seven special libraries. Applications for printed materials on all subjects are handled; these include music scores, playsets, periodicals, etc., in addition to books. A valuable bibliographical collection is being built up to provide information needed by member libraries. The Region maintains schemes for the co-operative purchase and storage of books based on material listed in *BNB*; for the co-operative purchase and storage of fiction and playsets; and for several special subject collections, including books in a wide range of languages. Many of the libraries take part in the GLASS (*q.v.*) Scheme. A recent development has been the production of COM microfilms with locations recorded on them by ISBN for British and American material published from 1970 to date and by *BNB* numbers for material from 1950–69. These microfilms are available to subscribing libraries to enable direct interlending to take place.

LONDON BOROUGHS COMMITTEE. The committee on which are represented all the thirty-two London Boroughs (which were formed after the borough boundaries were revised, and the London County

Council and the Middlesex County Council ceased to exist, on 1st April 1965) plus the Common Council of the City of London. It performs similar functions to the Metropolitan Boroughs Standing Joint Committee which it superseded, viz. the co-ordination of local government services throughout Greater London.

LONDON EDUCATION CLASSIFICATION. A faceted classification scheme designed for use in the library of the University of London Institute for Education, where it has been used since 1962. The second edition, 1974, referred to as LEC 2, is a thesaurus/classification combining the advantages of faceted classification and thesauri and was used as the basis for the EUDISED Multilingual Thesaurus. The alphabetical index of LEC 2 is in the form of a thesaurus. Abbreviated LEC. *See also* EUDISED.

LONDON UNION CATALOGUE. The union catalogue of the (London) Metropolitan Public Libraries. From 1st November 1934 until the reorganization of the London boroughs on 1st April 1965 it was controlled by the Metropolitan Boroughs Standing Joint Committee which levied on all metropolitan libraries a like amount of money for its upkeep, and administered by the Association of Metropolitan Chief Librarians on behalf of the MBSJC. It was maintained at the premises of the National Central Library, and although not strictly a regional bureau, functioned as one, arranging for the loan of books between the London libraries and other libraries throughout the country. *See also* LONDON & SOUTH EASTERN LIBRARY REGION.

LONG. *See* BROAD, OBLONG.

LONG-BODIED TYPE. Type which is cast on bodies larger than usual, e.g. 10-point on 12-point. This avoids the use of LEADS (*q.v.*).

LONG DESCENDER. Letters g, j, p, q and y with extra long descenders; these are available as alternatives in some faces as, for example, Linotype Caledonia and Times Roman. *See also* ASCENDER, DESCENDER.

LONG ELEPHANT. *See* ELEPHANT.

LONG GRAIN. Paper in which the fibres lie in the longer direction of the sheet. *See also* GRAIN DIRECTION, SHORT GRAIN.

LONG INDEX. A very full index to a work in one or more volumes where the text is of such a nature that a very large number of entries and references is required.

LONG LETTER. A character, such as f, j or k, which has either ASCENDER or DESCENDER (*qq.v.*) or both. *See also* SHORT LETTER, which has neither.

LONG PAGE. A page of a book with more lines of type than most of the others. *See also* SHORT PAGE.

LONG PRIMER. An old name for a type size, about 10 point.

LONG REAM. 500 or 516 sheets of paper. *See also* REAM, SHORT REAM.

LOOK-THROUGH. The examination of paper by holding it up against strong light. By this means, the dispersion of fibres can be seen, and consequently the strength of the paper judged; it is also a means of seeing whether the paper is laid or wove, and if its texture is marred by impurities. *See also* WILD LOOK-THROUGH.

LOOSE. A book, the sections of which are badly loosened from the case, the sewing having broken.

LOOSE BACK. *Synonymous with* HOLLOW BACK (*q.v.*).

LOOSE LEAF BINDING. A binding which permits the immediate withdrawal and insertion of pages at any desired position, as in a loose leaf binder.

LOOSE LEAF CATALOGUE. A SHEAF CATALOGUE (*q.v.*).

LOOSE-LEAF SERVICE. A serial publication which is revised, supplemented, cumulated, and indexed by means of new replacement pages inserted in a loose-leaf binder; such publications are used where the latest statements and revisions of information are important, as with legal, political, social and scientific material. *See also* SERIAL SERVICE.

LOWER CASE LETTERS. Minuscules or 'small' letters such as a.b.c.; those other than capitals. The name originated from the fact that printers kept their type in two large cases, one above the other, each divided into sections containing one SORT (*q.v.*). The upper case contained the capital letters, majuscules, and the lower one the others. Abbreviated l.c. *See also* CAPITALS, SMALL CAPITALS, UPPER CASE LETTERS.

LOWER COVER. *Synonymous with* REVERSE COVER (*q.v.*).

LOWER EDGE. The TAIL (*q.v.*) of a book. Also called 'Bottom edge', 'Tail edge'.

LOWER MARGIN. *Synonymous with* TAIL MARGIN (*q.v.*).

LOXODROME. *See* PORTOLAN CHART.

LOZENGE. (*Binding*) A diamond-shaped figure, or a square figure, placed on one of its corners; it is usually decorated.

LUBETZKY CODE. A draft, issued in 1960, under the title of *Code of cataloguing rules, author and title entry*. This was written on entirely fresh lines (but firmly grounded in the Panizzi and Cutter traditions) under the direction of the (American) Catalog Code Revision Committee. In 1953, his critique of the second (1949) American edition of a code incorporating the Library of Congress rules, and superseding the A.A. Code, had been published under the title *Cataloging rules and principles.* Samuel Lubetzky was at the time the specialist in bibliographic and cataloguing policy at the Library of Congress.

LUDLOW. A machine which casts slugs for display work. Composing is done by hand, a special composing stick being used; when the characters are all in position, the stick is placed into the machine which casts a line as a slug. It is frequently used in conjunction with the Elrod machine which casts rules, leads, borders and plain slugs.

LULOP. *London Union List of Periodicals.* First issued in 1951, this publication records the periodicals available in the municipal and county libraries in Greater London. It gives the extent of the permanent files of periodicals processed, and also a guide to places where files or current issues only are available.

LUMBECKING. The PERFECT (*q.v.*), or flexible, method of binding whereby the separate sheets are not kept together by sewing but by adhesive only.

LUMINOTYPE. The original name for the UHERTYPE (*q.v.*) photocomposing machine.

LUMITYPE. A method of FILMSETTING (*q.v.*).

LUNDIA SHELVING. A patented design of adjustable shelving of Swedish origin made under licence in a number of countries. Two designs of wooden shelving are made. One is of traditional appearance and the other is cantilever shelving which gives the impression of unbroken rows of books. In the former the shelves are grooved at the ends to slide over rods the bent ends of which have been inserted into holes bored into uprights near the front and back edges. There are therefore no shelf supports on the underside of shelves to impede the shelving of books, and the shelves are quite rigid. Interlocking fixing bars enable the whole shelving, including uprights, top shelf and plinth to be assembled securely without using tools. The cantilever shelving consists of brackets (which may be of different lengths) placed in slotted metal uprights which are fixed to the wall. Some brackets are made so as to allow shelves to be placed at different angles, instead of at an angle of 90° to the upright, so as to permit books to be displayed flat or shelved flat. This is most suitable for large volumes which need to be shelved flat and for book and periodical displays, but as with most shelving of this type, book supports are essential if books are stood up on their bottom edges.

LUTHERAN CHURCH LIBRARY ASSOCIATION. Founded in 1958 in the U.S.A. 'to promote the growth of church libraries in Lutheran congregations by publishing a quarterly journal, *Lutheran Libraries*, furnishing booklists, assisting member libraries with technical problems, providing meetings for mutual encouragement, assistance and exchange of ideas among members'. Abbreviated LCLA.

LUTTRELL PSALTER. An English Psalter of the East Anglian School, illuminated (as was usual at the time) by mainly grotesque beasts and monkeys (babewyns) but also with agricultural scenes, games and sports, and also incidents from the lives of the saints. It was written about 1340 for Sir Geoffrey Louterell of Lincolnshire who is depicted on a charger, his wife and daughter being in the same group. It is in the British Museum.

LUX. As from 1st January 1969, the metric measurement of light value, one lumen or foot-candle being equal to 10.76 lux.

LUXURY BINDING. *Synonymous with* DE LUXE BINDING (*q.v.*).

LYONESE (LYONNAISE) STYLE. A style of binding with broad inter-laced geometrical strapwork usually painted, lacquered, or enamelled in different colours; so called because it appeared on books bound at Lyons in the latter part of the sixteenth century. Also a style in which the binding is decorated with large corner ornaments and with a prominent centre design, roughly lozenge shaped, the all-over back-ground being filled in with dots.

M. Roman figure for 1,000 used as an abbreviation by printers.

MAGB. Acronym for MICROFILM ASSOCIATION OF GREAT BRITAIN (*q.v.*).

M.F. (*Paper*) Abbreviation for MACHINE FINISH (*q.v.*).

M.G. (*Paper*) Abbreviation for MACHINE GLAZED (*q.v.*). *See also* PAPER FINISHES.

MACHINE COATED. (*Paper*) Paper which has been coated with clay or a similar substance during the actual making of the paper to give it a smooth printing surface. When the coating is applied as a separate and later operation, it is called 'brush coated'.

MACHINE COMPOSITION. Type setting by machine as distinct from setting by hand.

MACHINE DIRECTION. The direction in which paper travels through a paper-making machine. Most of the fibres lie in this direc-tion; therefore paper folds more easily along the machine direction (said to be 'with the grain'), and a sheet of paper when wetted expands mainly across this direction, with a corresponding shrinkage of the paper on drying. *See also* AGAINST THE GRAIN, GRAIN, GRAIN DIRECTION.

MACHINE-DRIED. *Synonymous with* CYLINDER DRIED (*q.v.*).

MACHINE FINISH. Paper which has been made smooth, but not glossy, by receiving the normal finish of a Fourdrinier paper-making machine: this passes the paper over heated drums and through steel calendering rollers. Abbreviated M.F. This is the normal paper for letterpress printing where half-tones are not to be used. *See also* PAPER FINISHES.

MACHINE GLAZED. Said of a paper in which the 'glaze' or polish is produced on the paper-making machine, and not by means of super-calenders or a glazing machine. The only paper-machine which glazes in the process of making is the single-cylinder machine or 'Yankee' in which the web of paper is dried on the one large steam-heated cylinder with a highly polished surface. Machine-glazed papers are identified by being glazed on only one side (the under), the other being in the rough condition in which it comes from the wet end of the machine. Papers made on such machines are very varied in character and uses, for example, manillas for envelopes; litho, poster, kraft and sulphite bag papers and cheap wrappings and tissues. Abbreviater. M.G.

MACHINE INDEXING. A process whereby the indexing processes are accomplished by mechanized means.

MACHINE LANGUAGE. Information in the physical form that a computer can handle, e.g. properly coded information punched on paper tape or cards, or in electrical or magnetic form on magnetic tape.

MACHINE-LANGUAGE CODING. 1. Linguistic or numerical patterns susceptible of being handled by data processing equipment. 2. A special type of notation used for a specific data processing machine. 3. Coding in the form in which instructions are executed by the computer. Contrasted to relative, symbolic and other non-machine-language coding (*IBM*).

MACHINE-MADE PAPER. The continuous web, or roll, of paper made on cylinder machines or on the Fourdrinier machine.

MACHINE PROOF. A proof taken when corrections which were marked on galley and page proofs have been made, and the forme is on the printing machine. This proof affords the last opportunity for correcting mistakes before machining takes place. Also called 'Press revise'.

MACHINE-READABLE. (*Information retrieval*) Relating to data (letters of the alphabet, symbols and/or numerals) which is capable of being identified, read or deciphered by a machine. The data can be recorded on punched paper tape, punched cards, magnetically encoded tape, disc and cards.

MACHINE-READABLE CATALOGUING. The preparation of cataloguing data in a form which can be handled by automatic data processing equipment.

MACHINE-READABLE RECORDS. Records, the information content of which is usually in code on such media as punched paper cards or tapes, or magnetic tapes, discs or drums. The coded information is retrievable only by machine.

MACHINE REVISE. A proof printed when the forme is on the printing machine, in order that a comprehensive revise may be made of the whole of the details of workmanship, including those which the reader has not had an opportunity of verifying. Also called 'Machine proof'.

MACHINE-SENSIBLE INFORMATION. (*Information retrieval*) Information which is in a form that can be read by an appropriate machine.

MACHINE SORTING. Sorting punched cards into a pre-determined order by machine.

MACHINE SYSTEM. A machine using the kind of electrical and electronic equipment that was designed initially for accounting and other data processing procedures; these are punched card or computer systems and capable of accepting a store of information appropriately coded, storing it until required, and then producing selected items in usable form. They can be used in information retrieval for recording full bibliographic information or for the indexing function only.

MACHINE TRANSLATION. Automatic translation from one representation to a different one. The translation may involve codes or other systems of representation. *See also* MECHANICAL TRANSLATION, TARGET LANGUAGE.

MACHINE WIRE. *Synonymous with* WIRE (*q.v.*).

MACHINING. (*Printing*) 1. That part of printing concerned with actually printing on the paper. The other major processes in producing a book are composition and binding. Called 'Press work' in America. 2. The actual process of printing by running the forme through the machine to give the paper an impression from the printing surface.

MACKLE. A printed sheet with a blurred impression, owing to some mechanical defect in the printing.

McMEEKING REPORT. *Report of the Advisory Committee on Further Education for Commerce, 1959.* Called McMeeking Report after the chairman, Mr. J. G. McMeeking.

MACRO-DOCUMENT. A book, treatise, or document embodying macro-thought. *See also* MACRO-THOUGHT, MICRO-DOCUMENT.

MACROFORM. A reproduction of a document which can be read with the unaided eye. *See also* MICROFORM.

MACROGRAPH. A photographic reproduction of an object that may be slightly reduced, or of natural size, or magnified up to about ten diameters.

MACRO-THOUGHT. (*Classification*) A subject of great extension, usually embodied in the form of a book. *See also* MACRO-DOCUMENT, MICRO-THOUGHT.

MADE-UP COPY. A book which has had imperfections made good by the insertion of portions from other copies of the same edition.

MADE-UP SET. A work in a number of volumes which is made up by assembling volumes of more than one edition. It is catalogued as a regular set except that the various editions are specified in a note unless they can be mentioned in the body of the entry.

MAGAZINE. 1. A periodical publication as distinct from a newspaper, separate issues being independently paginated and identified by date rather than by serial number. 2. A receptacle above the keyboard of a Linotype, or similar type-casting machine, for containing the matrices ready for assembling into lines of type or slugs. 3. A container for the automatic projection of photographic slides. 4. A container for roll microfilm which both protects the film and facilitates its loading into a reader.

MAGAZINE CASE. A cover for periodicals, usually having some contrivance for holding the magazine – cord, rod, etc. Also called 'Periodical case' and 'Reading case'.

MAGAZINE RACK. A fitting for displaying magazines.

MAGAZINE ROOM. A room used exclusively for the reading of periodicals. Sometimes called 'Periodical room'. *See also* NEWSROOM.

MAGNACARD. Trade name for a retrieval system developed by Magnavox in the U.S.A.; it has a magnetic information carrier system comprising a special rectangular card 25·4 × 76·2 mm with a magnetic coating. The storage capacity of the card is in excess of 5,000 bits – about 1,000 decimal digits. Cards are sorted at the rate of 6,000 cards a minute.

MAGNAPRINT. Trade name for a microfilm reader-printer made by the Recordak Corporation.

MAGNAVUE. Trade name for a mechanized storage and retrieval system using coded film chip storage media; made by the Magnavox Corporation.

MAGNETIC DISC (*Information retrieval*) A computer storage device in the form of a disc which has been magnetized in order to record sound; it provides fast direct access to items stored on the file. This is not considered to be a gramophone record, although it functions like one. Also called a 'Disc'.

MAGNETIC MASTER TRACK.   The track obtained from combining a number of separate sound tracks into a single magnetic track which is suitable for projection.

MAGNETIC STORAGE. (*Information retrieval*) A storage device that utilizes the magnetic properties of materials to store data, e.g. magnetic films, tapes, discs and cones.

MAGNETIC TAPE. (*Information retrieval*) Plastic tape coated with a magnetic material on which information can be recorded and identified by computers and other machines. It can hold more information than PAPER TAPE (*q.v.*) and may be used as an input medium for faster transfer of information than is possible with paper tape.

MAIN CARD.   The catalogue card bearing the MAIN ENTRY (*q.v.*).

MAIN CATALOGUE.   A colloquialism for what may be considered the most important catalogue in a library; it is usually the one with the most entries or the 'main entries'; it may be the classified catalogue without the author and subject indexes.

MAIN CLASS.   The principal division of a scheme of classification, e.g. in Brown's *Subject Classification*: Matter, Life, Mind, Record; or Dewey's General works, Philosophy, Religion, Social Sciences, Language, Pure science, Technology, The Arts, Literature, History. These are divided into 'Divisions' which are divided into 'Subdivisions' which are in turn divided into 'Sections', each division proceeding by gradual steps, and each new heading becoming more 'intense'.

MAIN ENTRY.   1. The basic catalogue entry; usually the entry under the author's name. The main entry has the fullest particulars for the complete identification of a work. In card catalogues – especially dictionary ones – the main entry bears the TRACING (*q.v.*). It may bear in addition the tracing of related references and a record of other pertinent official data concerning the work. For music, the entry under the composer's name. 2. The entry chosen for the basic entry, whether it be a personal or corporate name, or the title of an anonymous book, collection, composite work, periodical or serial, or a UNIFORM TITLE (*q.v.*).

MAIN HEADING. (*Indexing*) A description sometimes used (for a heading) in contradistinction to a subheading. (a) *Simple heading*. A heading consisting of a single word or a word with a hyphened prefix (e.g. anti-, co-, ex-, mid-, non-, pre-) which alone would either have no meaning or have a different meaning. (b) *Compound heading*. A heading comprising two or more elements (with or without connecting hyphen) of which at least the first element could stand alone with its own meaning, e.g.

air-sea rescue	John o'Groats
Henry VIII	Underwater-to-air missiles

(British Standard 3700:1964).

(*Cataloguing*) The first part of a composite heading which includes one or more subheadings. That part of a heading which precedes a subheading.

MAIN LIBRARY. *See* CENTRAL LIBRARY.

MAIN STROKE. The principal stroke, heavy line, or stem of a type letter.

MAIN SUBJECT. A book may treat of several subjects, or may be considered by classifier or cataloguer to need cross references from a subsidiary to the one most important subject. The subject which is given priority and to which references are made is the 'main subject'.

MAIN TITLE. That part of the title which precedes the SUB-TITLE (*q.v.*).

MAIN TITLE-PAGE. The title-page from which the details for a catalogue entry are taken. *See also* ADDED TITLE-PAGE, HALF TITLE-PAGE.

MAINZ PSALTER. In Latin, this famous masterpiece of printing was printed by Johann Fust and Peter Schoeffer in Mainz and is dated 14th August 1457. It is the first printed book to give the name of the printer and the date of printing. *See also* MAZARIN BIBLE.

MAIOLI STYLE. The style of book decoration executed for Thomasso Maioli or Mahieu, (actually Thomas Matthieu a Frenchman), a contemporary of Grolier, in the middle of the sixteenth century. A distinguishing characteristic is that the Arabic ornaments are frequently in outline, whereas those of Grolier are ajuré, and of Aldus, solid. The style is generally composed of a framework of shields or medallions, with a design of scrollwork flowing through it, portions of the design usually being studded with gold dots.

MAJUSCULE. Large letter whether capital (upper case) or UNCIAL (*q.v.*). *See also* MINUSCULE.

MAKE-READY (MAKING-READY). The process of preparing a forme ready for printing. Levelling up and lining up by patching with paper, or cutting away on the impression cyclinder or platen BED (*q.v.*) and by underlaying or interlaying the blocks so that the impression from type and blocks on paper will be clear, clean and of uniform colour. The amount and position of make-ready is determined by a trial pull. The time which this process takes is an important item in every printing bill. It is upon the care with which a job is made-ready that the quality of the printing depends. Make-ready is of paramount importance in colour and half-tone work. *See also* OVERLAY and UNDERLAY.

MAKE-UP. (*Printing*) 1. A general term for taking the type from the galleys, putting it into page form, insetting illustrative cuts, dividing the matter into page lengths, and adding running heads, titles of subdivisions, folios, footnotes, etc., and securing with page-cord. The pages of type are then ready for locking in the CHASE (*q.v.*). 2. Sometimes used instead of 'layout' to indicate the dummy showing the desired arrangement of letterpress and illustrations. 3. A list of the contents of a book supplied by the publisher to the binder to serve as an instruction as to the positioning of plates, plans, folded leaves, map endpapers, etc. 4. (Archives) The particular method and order in which the leaves, or membranes of a document are fastened together to constitute a complete volume or document, or the manner in which a single leaf or membrane is folded. *See also* MAKE-UP COPY, PUBLISHER'S BINDING.

MAKE-UP COPY. A set of folded sheets, plates, plans, etc. in correct order and sent by the publisher as an instruction to the binder. *See also* MAKE-UP.

MALIMET. Abbreviation for Master List of Medical Indexing Terms. A list of terms used in indexing; it is available on magnetic tape.

MANCHESTER TECHNICAL INFORMATION SERVICE. The information service provided by the Scientific and Technical Library and Information Service of the Manchester Public Libraries. The scheme began operation in 1948 and is not restricted either by geographical location or membership. There is no formal organization. Information is available to any firm or institution in the United Kingdom, and there is no membership subscription. Close co-operation exists between the Manchester College of Science and Technology and the Bureau of Industrial Liaison (formerly the Manchester Joint Research Council). No fees are charged for information, only the refunding postages on loans and payment for photocopies and publications. The service is often referred to as MANTIS but the scheme is usually referred to in full.

MANIÈRE CRIBLÉE. A fifteenth-century 'relief' method of producing illustrations by means of a plate of soft metal such as copper, pewter or zinc in which the drawing was made with a graver and which, being sunk below the level of the plate, would appear as white lines on a black ground when printed. Intermediate tones were produced by punching dots in the surface of the plate at more or less regular intervals. Also called 'Schrothlatt'.

MANILLA PAPER. A superfine tough quality of wrapping and label paper made from manilla hemp; also applied to cheap imitations made from wood pulp.

MANIPULABLE TEXT. The characters, markings, or other forms of record, which are used on punched cards, punched tape, magnetic tape or photographic film to record original text material in such a way that it can be identified and retrieved by machine.

MANIPULATIVE INDEX. An index in which manipulations other than turning pages, reading entries, following cross references, and locating documents are necessary. Mechanized indexes using punched cards, and the various co-ordinate indexing systems are examples (*IBM*).

MANN CITATION, MARGARET. Instituted in 1950, and administered by the Cataloging and Classification Section of the Resources and Technical Services Division of the American Library Association, this citation is made to a librarian in recognition of distinguished contributions to librarianship through publication of significant professional literature, participation in professional cataloguing associations, or valuable contributions to practice in individual libraries. The first recipient of the Citation was Miss Lucile M. Morsch in 1951.

MANORIAL COURTS. Administrative and legal courts concerned with matters affecting a particular manor. The *Court Customary* was principally concerned with the agricultural organization of the township, while the *Court Leet* had a minor criminal jurisdiction.

MANORIAL DOCUMENTS. Documents relating to manors and the management of estates. Manorial Documents Rules were made in 1926 (S.R. & O. 1926, No. 1310) to implement the provisions of the Law of Property Act, 1922, as amended, by which the Master of the Rolls has power to transfer manorial documents to the Public Record Office or a public library, museum, or historical or antiquarian society.

MANTIS. Abbreviation for Manchester Technical and Commercial Information Services. *See* MANCHESTER TECHNICAL INFORMATION SERVICE.

MANUAL. *Synonymous with* HANDBOOK (*q.v.*).

MANUAL INPUT. (*Information retrieval*) The insertion of data by hand into a machine or other device at the time of processing.

MANUALE. A case to protect a VOLUMEN (*q.v.*).

MANUSCRIPT. A document of any kind which is written by hand, or the text of a music or literary composition in hand-written or typescript form, and which, in that form, has not been reproduced in multiple copies. An *illuminated manuscript* is one which has been decorated as described under ILLUMINATED BOOK (*q.v.*). Abbreviated MS. (*Pl.* MSS.).

MANUSCRIPT CATALOGUE. One written by hand, or typed.

MANUSCRIPT LIBRARIAN. A librarian who has charge of a collection of manuscripts of all kinds, i.e. unprinted materials (whether written by hand or typed) other than books written by hand before the invention of printing (*libri manuscripti*).

MANUSCRIPT MUSIC BOOK. A book of MUSIC PAPER (*q.v.*).

MANUSCRIPT NOTE. A hand-written note in a book.

MANUSCRIPT SOCIETY, THE. An international organization of autograph collectors; founded in 1947, it aims to foster the greater use of original manuscript source material in the study, teaching, and writing of history; to facilitate the exchange of information and knowledge among researchers, scholars and collectors; to encourage the meeting of autograph collectors and stimulate and aid them in their various collecting specialities. Assistance is given to individuals and organizations in the matter of preservation and conservation, and in various other pertinent matters. A three-day meeting is held annually in an American city which is of interest to members because of manuscript resources. Membership is open to individuals and organizations and includes private collectors, dealers, librarians, historical societies, archivists, colleges and universities. Publishes *Manuscripts* (*q.*).

MANUSCRIPTS. The (American) Association of College and Research Libraries approved, in January 1974, Statements on (a) Access to Original Research Materials in Libraries, Archives, and Manuscript Repositories, and (b) the Reproduction of Manuscripts and Archives for Noncommercial Purposes. *Manuscripts*: a MARC *format* was published by the Library of Congress in 1973.

MAP. A plane representation of the earth's surface, or a part of same, indicating physical features, political boundaries, etc. *See also* MAPS. Also a similar representation of the heavens, showing the position of the stars, planets, etc. Also called an 'Astronomical map'. The first book to contain a printed map or diagram of the whole world was Isidore of Seville's *Etymologiarum sive Originum libri XX*, Augsburg, 19th November 1472. The earliest and most important maps to be printed from engraved copper plates in England were those of

Christopher Saxton, who issued county maps between 1574 and 1579. An 'early map' is considered to be one made before 1825.

MAP ENDPAPERS. Endpapers on which maps are printed. *See also* ENDPAPER.

MAP FILE. A sequence of sheet or folded maps arranged in classified order, or alphabetically by place name. Sheet maps are kept in shallow drawers, often with hinged fronts which fall down and so reduce wear when consulting the maps, or in specially made vertical cabinets. *See also* PLAN CABINET.

MAP PAPER. *See* PLAN PAPER.

MAP PROJECTION. The arrangement of parallels and meridians so as to enable part, or the whole, of the spheroidal surface of the earth to be represented on a plane-surface.

MAP ROOM. A room devoted to the storage and consultation of maps.

MAPS. For different kinds of maps, *see* ARTISTIC MAP, AVERAGE SLOPE MAP, ASTRONOMICAL MAP, CADASTRAL MAP, CARTOGRAM, CHOROCHROMATIC MAP, CHOROGRAPHIC MAP, CHOROPLETH MAP, CHOROSCHEMATIC MAP, DEMOPLETH MAP, DOT MAP, DYNAMIC MAP, FLOWLINE MAP, HYPSOMETRIC MAP, INTERNATIONAL MILLIONTH MAP, ISEPHODIC MAP, ISOCHRONIC MAP, ISOGONIC CHART, ISOPLETH MAP, RELATIVE RELIEF MAP.

MARBLED EDGES. The three edges of a book cut solid, and stained to resemble marble. *See also* EDGES, SPRINKLED EDGES, STAINED EDGES, STIPPLED EDGES.

MARBLED PAPER. Surface-coloured paper used by bookbinders. Marbling is done by floating white paper, or dipping the edges of a sewn book before inserting into the cover, on a bath of gum tragacanth, the surface of which has been sprinkled with various colours, and combed out to a desired pattern.

MARBLING. The process of colouring the endpapers and edges of a book in imitation of marble.

MARBLING UNDER GILT. Marbled edges of a book overlaid with gold. Usually the marbling is not very noticeable until the edges are fanned out. The style was first used in France in the seventeenth century, its invention being accredited to Le Gascon. Sometimes it is found in English bindings of the middle of the eighteenth century and later. *See also* GILT ON THE ROUGH, ROUGH GILT EDGES, SOLID GILT.

MARC. Abbreviation for MAchine Readable Catalogue Project. A system, initially developed in the United States by the Library of Congress with the purpose of organizing and disseminating in machine-readable form (and structured according to international cataloguing standards), bibliographic data for incorporation into national and local records for the purposes of documentation. Various applications have been developed in the United States, in Great Britain through the services of the *British National Bibliography*, on the continent of Europe, and in other countries throughout the world. Entries in U.S. MARC and U.K. MARC are based on the requirements of the Anglo-American Cataloguing Rules and contain subject information in the form of Decimal Classification numbers, Library of Congress Subject Headings and class numbers. U.K. MARC in association with PRECIS (*q.v.*) is used to provide the published record of the *British National Bibliography*, while U.K. and U.S. MARC serve to provide the total record on ultramicrofiche of 'Books in English'.

MARCIA C. NOYES AWARD. *See* NOYES AWARD, MARCIA C.

MARGARET MANN CITATION. *See* MANN CITATION, MARGARET.

MARGARET SCOGGIN SCHOLARSHIP. *See* SCOGGIN SCHOLARSHIP, MARGARET.

MARGIN. 1. The unprinted area between printed or written matter and the edges of a page. The proportional width of the margins is a very important element in a properly balanced book-page. A good ratio is: head (top) margin 2; fore-edge (outside) 3; tail, also called 'lower' or 'bottom' (bottom) 4; back (inside) $1\frac{1}{2}$. 2. The area of a map, drawing or print, between the line enclosing the information area and the edge of the paper. 3. On microfilm, the area of background between the line enclosing the information area and the edge of the film frame.

MARGINAL FIGURE. A figure printed in the margin of a book to indicate the number of a line of type for purposes of easy reference. *See also* RUNNERS.

MARGINAL HEADING. A heading printed at the side of the type area.

MARGINAL-HOLE PUNCHED CARDS. Cards which have rows of holes punched round the margins or over a large part of the card's area. These holes are notched or slotted to record information which is obtained, when required, by inserting needles, like knitting needles, in the holes and allowing cards on which the required information is recorded to fall away. They are also known as hand-sorted punched cards, edge-punched cards, edge-notched punched cards, Keysort cards, etc. In *direct* coding each marginal position is reserved for a specific piece of information or subject. In some designs of card, *combination* coding (the joint notching of two or more card positions) is possible. When the combination is such that the number of selection operations needed to isolate a subject is minimized, the coding scheme is called a 'Selector code'. *See also* DEQUEKER SYSTEM, EDGE-NOTCHED CARDS, SLOTTED CARDS.

MARGINAL NOTE.   A note or GLOSS (*q.v.*) written or printed on the margin of a page opposite the portion of text to which it refers. Notes are called *footnotes* when printed at the bottom of the page, and *Shoulder-notes* when printed at the top corner of the page. Also called 'Marginal Heading', 'Marginalia'. *Synonymous with* SIDE NOTE (*q.v.*).

MARGINALIA.   *Synonymous with* MARGINAL NOTES (*q.v.*).

MARINE LIBRARIANS' ASSOCIATION.   This British Association was formed in 1972 'to promote contact and co-operation between librarians and information officers in the marine field'. For the first few months of its existence it was named the Nautical Librarians' Association. Its scope includes fisheries, the marine sciences and technologies, ports and cargo handling, shipping, shipbuilding, marine engineering, and marine telecommunications. It produced, in conjunction with the Research, Special and Information Section of the Library Association, *Marine transport: a guide to libraries and resources of information in Great Britain* in 1974. The Association is financed by the fees of individual members and any surplus resulting from the annual conference. Membership is open to all who have a primary or substantial interest in the provision of literature or information in marine subjects.

MARK OF INTERROGATION.   *Synonymous with* INTERROGATION MARK (*q.v.*).

MARK-SENSE.   (*Information retrieval*) (*Verb*) To indicate a punch position by means of an electrically conductive pencil mark in such a way that a suitably designed machine can make the punch automatically (*IBM*).

MARKED PROOF.   *See* PROOF.

MARKER.   (*Information retrieval*) A symbol which is used to separate more than one independent subject description assigned to the same item in order to guard against FALSE COMBINATIONS (*q.v.*).

MARKERS.   1. In American libraries, members of the staff who process books by writing call numbers on the spines, insert book pockets, labels, etc. 2. Sensitized strips placed in books as part of a system to obviate their unauthorized removal from libraries.

MARKET LETTER.   A bulletin issued by a stockbroker or investment house at regular intervals.

MARKING.   1. The placing of call numbers on books and other library materials. 2. The placing of a mark of ownership, with a note about disposition, on each item of a serial publication, as each is checked.

MARKING-UP. In book-binding, dividing the spine into equal portions and marking the position of the cords.

MARKOV PROCESS. *See* STOCHASTIC PROCESS.

MARKS. *See* CODE.

MARKS OF OMISSION. *Synonymous with* OMISSION MARKS (*q.v.*).

MARKS OF REFERENCE. *See* REFERENCE MARKS.

MARLF. Acronym for Middle Atlantic Regional Library Federation which was formed in 1969 to encourage the development of co-operation between libraries in the states of Delaware, Maryland, New Jersey, New York, Pennsylvania and West Virginia.

MARLIS. Abbreviation for Multi-Aspect Relevance Linkage, an information system which consists basically of three units; (a) Intermediate File, (b) the Ultimate Store, and (c) the Homo. The Intermediate File is a store of records on each of which is inscribed (a) one or more addresses in the Ultimate Store, and (b) code symbols characterizing the items at these addresses. These code symbols relate to only a few characterizing features of the items in the Ultimate Store. Examples of features entered on the Intermediate File records are (1) words (descriptors) selected as descriptive of the subject content of the items characterized, (2) the authors of these items, (3) their titles, dates and physical size. The code symbols on the Intermediate File records permit linear arrangement according to usual sequences as alphabetical or numerical. The Ultimate Store may take various physical forms, but consists essentially of a collection of items which are called 'volumes' because of the large amount of information each contains. Each 'volume' (of whatever form) bears a symbol, which is its address, and by which it is identified in the Intermediate File. Homo is the almost human computing unit of the system.

MASKING. (*Printing*) The placement of an opaque cut-out overlay or a transparent overlay on which lines have been lightly drawn, over a photograph or drawing, or lines drawn on the back thereof, in order to indicate areas at the sides which are not to be reproduced.

MASS. Acronym of the MARC-based Automatic Serials System for recording and controlling serials by computer. It was developed by Loughborough University Library and the Birmingham Libraries Co-operative Mechanization Project. *See also* BLCMP.

MASS BOOK. *See* MISSAL.

MASTER. The plate, or stencil in duplicating processes, from which copies are made. In photocopying, the negative from which a positive print is made.

MASTER CARD. (*Information retrieval*) A card containing fixed or indicative information for a group of cards; it is usually the first card of the group.

MASTER CATALOGUE. A catalogue in which every main entry is a master card forming the official complete and up-to-date record of catalogued stock, and providing essential information for the cataloguers who maintain it. Being the union catalogue of the whole system it is usually kept in the cataloguing department or in the central library.

MASTER DATA CARD. *See* EAM CARD.

MASTER FILE. (*Information retrieval*) 1. A file containing relatively permanent information. 2. A main file of information.

MASTER FILM. Any film, but usually a negative, which is used for making further copies.

'MASTER' HOLE. An extra hole punched beside each group of holes representing a particular field in a punched card, the master hole being punched to the edge of the card only if any other hole in the field is so punched. This permits rapid selection or rejection of cards whether punched or not punched, in any field, without having to needle the field hole by hole.

MASTER MICROFILM CARD. An APERTURE CARD (*q.v.*) containing microfilm, usually a negative, which is used for making further copies.

MASTHEAD. The statement of the title, ownership, address and frequency of publication, printer's name and address, and sometimes postage and subscription rates of a periodical publication. It is usually on the last or the editorial page of a newspaper, and on the editorial or contents page of a magazine. Also called 'Flag' and 'Logo'.

MATCHING. In computer technology, the comparison of two sets of codes to ascertain their similarity or difference. It is the basic operation in selecting, sorting or collating.

MATERIAL BIBLIOGRAPHY. *See* HISTORICAL BIBLIOGRAPHY.

MATHEMATICAL ORDER. (*Classification*) Used by E. C. Richardson to indicate a possible order for terms in an ARRAY (*q.v.*) which forms a series of co-ordinate classes. Order by means of a NOTATION (q.v.). *Synonymous with* S. R. Ranganathan's CANONICAL ORDER (*q.v.*).

MATRIX (*Pl.* MATRICES). (*Printing*) 1. The mould from which a stereotype (stereo) or electrotype (electro) is made. The mould is made by placing wet flong (a material, about $\frac{1}{16}$ inch thick, made of alternate layers of tissue paper and blotting paper) over the type of which an impression is needed and then beating it with a stiff brush. It is then subjected to pressure, removed and dried. 2. A mould from which type is cast in a typesetting machine. 3. A copper mould which has been struck with a punch and from which individual type letters are cast. Also called a 'strike'. *See also* ELECTROTYPE, STEREOTYPE. (*Information retrieval*) A rectangular array of elements ... used to facilitate the study of problems in which the relation between these elements is fundamental.

MATT ART. *See* ART.

MATTER. 1. Type, whether in the process of setting up, or standing. It may be *live* matter (not yet printed from) or *dead* matter (awaiting distribution), *open* matter (leaded) or *solid* matter (without leads). The ancient terms, *fat* and *lean* matter, are still used to indicate the proportion of open spaces or break lines. The *fat*, of course, gives the compositor far less work to do than the *lean*. 2. Manuscript of copy to be printed. *See also* GOOD.

MAUD REPORT. The report of the Committee on the Management of Local Government which was set up by Sir Keith Joseph, when Minister of Housing and Local Government, on 3rd March 1964; so named after Sir John Maud, the Chairman. The terms of reference of the Committee were 'to consider in the light of modern condition show local government might best continue to attract and retain people (both elected representatives and principal officers) of the calibre necessary to ensure its maximum effectiveness'. The report itself occupies volume 1 of the 5 volumes the overall title of which is *Management of local government*; volumes 2–4 are enquiries carried out for the Committee and entitled *The local government councillor, The local government elector* and *Local government administration abroad.* Volumes 1–4 were published in May 1967; volume 5 *Local government administration in England and Wales,* comprising further research enquiries carried out for the Committee, was published in July 1967. Sir John Maud was created a life peer in 1967 and then took the title of Baron Redcliffe-Maud; the report became known as the Redcliffe-Maud Report.

MAYOR'S AUDITOR. *See* BOROUGH AUDITORS.

MAZARIN BIBLE. The 42-line Bible printed in Latin by Johann Gutenberg, Johann Fust and Peter Schoeffer at Mainz between 1450–5 and one of the earliest books to be printed from movable type. So called because the copy which first attracted the attention of bibliographers was discovered by Debure the French bookseller, in 1760, among the books of Cardinal Mazarin (1602–61) who was a well-known bibliophile. Mazarin's library is now in the Collège Mazarin, Paris. Forty-eight copies of this Bible are known, of which thirty-six

are printed on paper and twelve on vellum; twenty-one in all are perfect. The British Museum possesses one of each, both perfect. Also
known as the 'Gutenberg', or '42-line Bible'. *See also* MAINZ PSALTER.

MEAN LINE.   (*Printing*) An imaginary line running along the top of all
x-height letters, i.e. those without ascenders, a, c, e, etc. *See also*
ASCENDER LINE, BASE LINE, CAP LINE, SUPERIOR FIGURES (LETTERS).

MEANING.   (*Information retrieval*) The relation of formal equivalence
between symbols (codes).

MEARNE STYLE.   The style of book decoration used during the
seventeenth and early eighteenth centuries in England. This style is
named after Samuel Mearne, the stationer and binder to Charles II
and is a development of the Fanfare and Le Gascon styles. Red and
black inlay was used with great effect, and the centre panel was often
in the COTTAGE STYLE (*q.v.*). The ALL-OVER (*q.v.*) style was also often
used. Also called 'Restoration style'. *See also* RECTANGULAR STYLE.

MEASURE.   The width to which printed matter is set, i.e. the length of
line. It is usually counted in 12-point ems, e.g. the full measure of the
lines of type in this entry is 25 ems, i.e. $4\frac{1}{6} \div \cdot 166$ (or $\frac{1}{6}$) inches. *See
also* DIDOT SYSTEM, EM, POINT.

MECHANICAL BINDING.   A binding which uses a mechanical device
such as a spiral binding of metal or plastic to hold the pages together.

MECHANICAL OVERLAY.   *See* CHALK OVERLAY.

MECHANICAL PREPARATION.   The preparation of books and other
library materials for use. It includes rubber stamping and other
forms of ownership marks, pasting labels, book pockets, and, where
preparation is carried out in a cataloguing department, includes lettering books with class numbers and making out book-cards. (American.)
See also PROCESSING CENTER.

MECHANICAL SELECTION.   (*Information retrieval*) The retrieving,
or finding, of required information which has been recorded or indexed by machine punching or coding in such a way that when required no visual searching has to be done, but the records are scanned
and extracted by machine. Also called 'Automatic selection'.

MECHANICAL TINTS. Synonymous with TINT (*q.v.*).

MECHANICAL TRANSLATION.   A generic term for language translation by computer or some other mechanical means. *See also*
MACHINE TRANSLATION.

MECHANICAL WOOD.   The lowest grade of wood pulp used in the
manufacture of paper, and prepared by the purely mechanical process
of grinding. This method produces a higher yield than the chemical
process but the resulting pulp is less pure. It is suitable only for

newsprint: it has good printing qualities and is opaque but impermanent. Also called 'Groundwood pulp'. *See also* CHEMICAL WOOD.

MECHANICAL WOOD PULP. *Synonymous with* SEMI-CHEMICAL PULP (*q.v.*).

MECHANIZATION. Adding a notation to a classification schedule in order to mechanize the arrangement and re-arrangement.

MECHANIZED INDEXING. The accomplishment of indexing operations by mechanical means. This includes the preparation and compilation of indexes, and the sorting, assembling, duplication and interfiling of catalogue cards carrying index entries. *See also* AUTOMATIC INDEXING.

MECHANIZED LIBRARY. *See* VERAC.

MEDIA. 1. Abbreviation for Magnavox Electronic Data Image Apparatus, a unit system type of information retrieval. (*See* MICROFILM.) It is somewhat similar to, but less expensive than, the MINICARD (*q.v.*) system. Film chips are 16 × 32 mm and contain two pages of text as well as a number which is legible without magnification; this number can also be obtained in binary code form for machine retrieval of the chips. It is made by the Magnavox Corporation. 2. Printed and audio-visual forms of communication and any necessary equipment required to render them usable.

MEDIA AIDE. An individual engaged in clerical or secretarial duties in a MEDIA CENTRE (*q.v.*).

MEDIA CENTRE. Sometimes used in the late 1960s in America for a school library, or learning centre in a school, where a full range of print and audio-visual media, necessary equipment, and the services of a media specialist, are accessible to students and teachers.

MEDIA FILE. Information prepared for buyers of advertising space in newspapers and periodicals, and giving particulars of circulation, column and type sizes and rates.

MEDIA PROGRAMME. All the instructional and related services provided for students and teachers by a MEDIA CENTRE (*q.v.*) and its staff.

MEDIA RESOURCES. Collections of non-book MEDIA (*q.v.*).

MEDIA SPECIALIST. An individual who has broad professional preparation in educational media.

MEDIA STAFF. The personnel who carry out the work of a MEDIA CENTRE (*q.v.*) and its programme.

MEDIA TECHNICIAN. An individual who has training in the preparation of materials and the operation and maintenance of apparatus.

MEDIAAN SYSTEM. A Belgian system of line measurement used in conjunction with the Fournier system of measuring type bodies; 12-point equals 0·1649 inch or 4·18 mm.

MEDIAMOBILE. A motor coach fitted up with such audio-visual equipment as a puppet stage, indoor and outdoor film projection equipment, book shelving for about 2,500 paperbacks, filmstrip projectors, cassette player recorders, a microfilm and indoor-outdoor sound systems, art display panels, and shelves which swing down to form tables. Such a vehicle is used in Maryland, U.S.A., to provide educational and recreational facilities for the children of migrant workers passing through the State.

MEDICAL LIBRARY ASSISTANCE ACT. A 1965 amendment to the American Public Health Service Act, which expands the duties of the Board of Regents of the National Library of Medicine and the Surgeon General, provides 'a program of grants to assist in meeting the need for adequate medical services and facilities'. The programme, as outlined in the bill, will (1) assist in the construction of new, and the renovation, expansion, or rehabilitation, of existing medical library facilities; (2) help train medical librarians and other information specialists in the health sciences; (3) award special fellowships to physicians and scientists for the compilation of existing, and the creation of additional publications to facilitate the distribution and utilization of knowledge and information in the health sciences; (4) aid in research and investigations in medical library science and in the development of new techniques, systems, and equipment for information storage and retrieval; (5) help improve and expand the basic resources of medical libraries and related facilities; (6) aid in the development of a national system of regional medical libraries each of which would supplement the services of other medical libraries within the region served by it; and (7) provide financial support to biomedical scientific publications.

MEDICAL LIBRARY ASSOCIATION. Founded in the U.S.A. in 1898 to foster medical and allied scientific libraries, and exchange medical literature among its institutional members; to improve the professional qualifications and status of medical librarians; to organize efforts and resources for the furtherance of the purposes and objects of the Association. There are several subject groups and regional groups. Membership is of various categories (Active, Association, Student, Life, Institutional). A revised *Code for the certification of health sciences librarians and library technicians* was approved in 1975; changes are a requirement that all candidates for certification pass a

LIBRARIANS' GLOSSARY   539

years. Abbreviated MLA. Publishes *Bulletin of the Medical Library
Association* (q.), *MLA news* (q.), *Vital notes on medical periodicals*
(3 p.a.), *Directory of the Medical Library Association* (a.).

MEDICAL SECTION.   Formed on 24th September 1948 as a Section
of the Library Association. The aims of the Section are to unite
members of the Library Association working in, or interested in,
medical libraries (those whose *raison d'être* is primarily to meet the
needs of the medical, dental, pharmaceutical, veterinary and allied
professions), to discuss the problems of medical librarianship and to
promote the interests of medical librarians and medical libraries. The
Section has five sub-committees dealing with specific aspects of the
Section's work, and has organized annual week-end conferences
since 1952. It established the Cyril Barnard Memorial Prize. Publishes *Directory of medical libraries*, 4th ed., *Books and periodicals for
medical libraries.* 4th ed., *Reference citation: recommendations, Bulletin
of the Medical Section of the Library Association* (q.). *See also* BARNARD
MEMORIAL PRIZE, CYRIL.

MEDIUM.   1. The weight of type-face midway between light and bold.
This is the kind normally used for periodicals and book work. 2. An
alternative name for Ben Day tint. *See* BEN DAY PROCESS. 3. The
liquid, usually linseed oil, in which the pigment of printing ink is
dispersed and by means of which it leaves an impression on paper.
4. A standard size of printing paper, 18 × 23 inches. 5. A finish given
to paper that is neither highly calendered nor antique, but intermediate between the two extremes. Also called 'Medium finish'.
6. In music, the means (instrument/s or voice/s) by which musical
sounds are produced, as indicated in the score.

MEDIUM CATALOGUING.   Entries which are more complete than
in Short or Selective Cataloguing but not so complete as in Full
Cataloguing.

MEDIUM FACE.   The weight of type-face half-way between light and
bold. It is the kind that is normally used for periodicals and book work.
Also called 'Half-dark type'.

MEDIUM FINISH.   *See* MEDIUM 5.

MEDIUM WEIGHT PAPER.   Sensitized photographic paper between
0·0084 and 0·0111 inches inclusive. *See also* PHOTOGRAPHIC PAPERS.

MEDLARS.   Acronym for Medical Literature Analysis and Retrieval
System which is operated at the NATIONAL LIBRARY OF MEDICINE
(*q.v.*). It was initially a 2½-year project which was inaugurated to
initiate and develop an electronic data processing, information,

storage, and retrieval system in the field of medicine. The operation of this mechanized bibliographical system used the specially-designed Graphic Arts Composing Equipment (GRACE). MEDLARS is producing *Index Medicus* monthly and *Index Rheumatology* semi-monthly, recurring bibliographies and demand bibliographies. The Lending Division of the BRITISH LIBRARY (*q.v.*) is the U.K. centre for MEDLARS.

MEDLINE. A computerized service developed by the NATIONAL LIBRARY OF MEDICINE (*q.v.*) in 1971 for almost instantaneous bibliographic searching of current medical literature, in the MEDLARS data base in the NLM – hence the name, i.e. MEDLARS On-Line. The system is available to biomedical centres in the U.S.A. and abroad which have installed on-line terminals, and it enables a user to search the Medline files (citations to recent articles from approximately 1,100 biomedical journals in the Medlars data base). *See also* MEDLARS, NATIONAL LIBRARY OF MEDICINE.

MELA. Acronym of The Middle East Librarians' Association which was formed in the U.S.A. in November 1972 with the aim of increasing communication and co-operation among members, especially in acquisitions and in development of bibliographic controls. The group plans to compile and disseminate information about Middle East library collections and to improve the quality of area librarianship through the development of standards for the profession and the education of Middle East librarians. Membership is open to librarians and others interested in library activities which support the study and dissemination of information about the Middle East and North Africa since the rise of Islam. The Association proposes to meet at least annually, in conjunction with the Middle East Studies Association. All the officers are American librarians.

MELODY EDITION. *See* SCORE.

MELVIL DEWEY MEDAL. *See* DEWEY MEDAL, MELVIL.

MEMBERSHIP VOUCHER. An application voucher for membership of a lending library.

MEMBRANE. A single skin of parchment or vellum either forming part of a roll, or complete in itself. Skins of goats, sheep or calves are used; they are scraped free of hair and reduced in thickness, soaked, stretched, smoothed and dried. This produces a thin, smooth and white parchment, the flesh side being whiter and shinier than the hair side, which is known as the Dorse.

MEMOIR. 1. A biography of a person written by someone else. 2. A monograph, or dissertation, on some noteworthy subject.

MEMOIRS. 1. A narrative of events based on the observations, experiences and memories of the writer; an autobiographical record. 2. A collection of researches and accounts of experiments, or dissertations on a learned subject, published by a learned society, especially in the form of a record of proceedings or transactions.

MEMORIAL. 1. A written statement of views in the form of a petition for submission to an authoritative body. 2. Usually in pl., a chronicle or document containing a historical narrative.

MEMORIAL VOLUME. A publication, often consisting of contributions by several writers, in memory of a person or event. Also called 'Festschrift'.

MEMORIALIST. A person presenting, or signatory to, a memorial.

MEMORY. (*Information retrieval*) Often used synonymously with STORAGE (*q.v.*); whereas memory usually refers to a human function, storage refers to a machine function.

MENDING. Minor repairs to the leaves of a book not involving the replacement of any material or separation of the book from the cover. Not to be confused with REPAIRING (*q.v.*).

MENTEFACTS. (Classification) A group of 'artificial' entities, i.e. those which do not occur naturally, and which are abstract, e.g. systems of belief and products of the imagination. The other group is said to be ARTEFACTS (*q.v.*).

MERCATOR'S PROJECTION. A chart enabling a mariner to steer a course by compass in straight lines; invented by Gerardus Mercator, all the meridians are straight lines perpendicular to the equator and all the parallels are straight lines parallel to the equator. It was first used by Mercator in a world map in 1569, and made navigation by dead reckoning easier. Edward Wright made its use practicable by publishing a set of tables for constructing the network of charts, and this development has made it possible to use Mercator's projection for all nautical charts.

MERCURIUS INTELLIGENCE. *See* NEWSBOOK.

MERGE. (*Information retrieval*). (*Verb*) To combine two files, already in sequence, into a single file (*IBM*).

MEROVINGIAN HANDWRITING. The style of handwriting used in France from the sixth to the eighth centuries; a national style of cursive minuscule script which developed from the Latin cursive after the dissolution of the Roman Empire. *See also* CURSIVE, HANDWRITING.

MERRILL ALPHABETING NUMBERS. A scheme devised by Mr. W. S. Merrill for arranging books in rough alphabetical order. The table is reprinted in the Introduction to Brown's *Subject Classification* and consists of 100 numbers allocated as the following first sixteen from the table show:

01	A	09	Beno		
02	Agre	10	Bix		
03	Als	11	Bou	The numbers	
04	Ap	12	Brim	are applied	
05	Ash	13	Bum	fractionally.	
06	B	14	C		
07	Ban	15	Carr		
08	Bax	16	Chan		

MERRYTHOUGHT. (*Binding*) A finisher's stamp in the form of a merrythought, or wishbone, usually decorated with cusps or foliage ornament.

MeSH. Acronym for Medical Subject Headings, the 'vocabulary' of the (American) National Library of Medicine; it is used in connection with MEDLARS (*q.v.*), the Library's catalogue and the *Index Medicus*.

METABOLIC MAP. A map which shows the interrelations and correlations of biochemical reactions in metabolic sequences.

METAL FURNITURE. *See* FURNITURE.

METAL OXIDE. Magnetic material which is used to coat magnetic tape.

METALANGUAGE. A language that is used to specify another language. In documentation, this term is used in classification and indexing.

METALLOGRAPHY. A lithographic process in which metallic plates are used instead of stone.

METALWORK. (*Binding*) A decorative ornament which is obviously an imitation of wrought and curved ironwork.

METHODICAL CATALOGUE. *Synonymous with* SYSTEMATIC CATALOGUE (*q.v.*).

METONYMY. The use of an attribute of a thing instead of the thing, e.g. 'crown' for a king. Reversed metonymy, i.e. the use of a descriptor naming the thing to indicate the attributes of the thing, is common.

METRIC BOOK SIZES. The following are the metric book sizes recommended in *Page sizes for books* (BS 1413:1970).

	Trimmed sizes in mm	Untrimmed sizes in mm	'Quad' Paper sizes in mm
Metric Cr. 8vo.	186 × 123	192 × 126	768 × 1008
Metric Lge. Cr. 8vo.	198 × 129	204 × 132	816 × 1056
Metric Demy 8vo.	216 × 138	222 × 141	888 × 1128
Metric Royal 8vo.	234 × 156	240 × 159	960 × 1272
A5	210 × 148*	215 × 152.5	RA0860 × 1220*

The trimmed and untrimmed sizes of case-bound books are those of a folded sheet after and before trimming 3 mm from the edges of a page (head, tail and foredge). The measurements followed by a * are ISO sizes. The ISO sizes which are internationally recommended for general printing are not suitable for books and cannot, in practice, be used. The trimmed page size for a paperback should be 180 × 110 mm.

METRO. The New York Metropolitan Reference and Research Library Agency, Inc. is a part of the movement to develop research and reference in the State of New York. It was founded in 1964 as a result of the activities of a committee of librarians from public, academic and special libraries in Metropolitan New York City. METRO began to function in 1966. It was granted a charter by the New York State Board of Regents. Its principal purpose is 'to improve reference library services in the New York metropolitan area by promoting and facilitating the utilization of existing resources and by developing additional resources'. It sponsors studies of research library needs and encourages inter-library co-operation; over thirty libraries are involved.

METRON. A unit of metrical information which supplies one element (i.e. of evidence) for a pattern.

METROPOLITAN BOROUGH. The official term used to indicate a borough in the area of the former London County Council. These boroughs ceased to exist as such on 1st April 1965 when the Greater London Act came into operation; they then became known as 'London Boroughs'. The thirty-two boroughs in Greater London are known as London Boroughs and are so referred to in the Public Libraries and Museums Act 1964. *See also* BOROUGH COUNCIL, GREATER LONDON COUNCIL, LIBRARY AUTHORITY.

METROPOLITAN BOROUGH COUNCIL. A BOROUGH COUNCIL (*q.v.*) within the former Metropolitan area of London. These ceased to exist after 1st April 1965 owing to the re-organization of local government in London. *See also* ASSOCIATION OF METROPOLITAN CHIEF LIBRARIANS, LIBRARY AUTHORITY, METROPOLITAN BOROUGH.

MEZZOTINT. 1. A process of engraving on copper or steel in which the entire surface of the plate is slightly roughened, after which the drawing is traced and the plate smoothed in places by scraping, burnishing, etc., to produce the desired light and shade effect. 2. An engraving produced by the mezzotint process.

MICHEL STYLE. The style of book decoration practised during the nineteenth century by Marius Michel and his son in France. The designs are often based on natural forms and the ornament is generally expressed in colour, outlined in blind, and very often without the use of gold.

MICROBIBLIOGRAPHY. The production of subject bibliographies or indexes provided with supplements containing the full text in microprint of the material they list.

MICROCARD. 1. A term, trade-mark of the Microcard Corporation and covered by an American patent, which refers exclusively to 5 × 3 inch cards with images arranged in a specific manner. 2. The term is more generally used to indicate an opaque card of varying size on which microcopies have been reproduced photographically. A microcard resembles a MICROFICHE (*q.v.*) in that the microcopies are arranged in rows and catalogue details, readable with the naked eye, are at the top of the card. It differs from other microforms in that the prints are positive as well as being opaque, and cannot be directly reproduced. A microcard is not readable without optical aid in the form of a specially-made reader.

MICROCITE. Trade name for a retrieval system which provides micro images of documents to which separate indexes are keyed. It was developed by the (American) National Bureau of Standards.

MICROCOPY. A copy of a document, or image, the scale of which is greatly reduced (compared with the original) by means of an optical device, and which needs an enlarger to enable it to be legible to the unaided eye. Also called 'Microrecord'.

MICRODENSITOMETER. A densitometer designed to measure the density of very small areas of a photographic image.

MICRO-DOCUMENT. Communication on a specialized topic, and usually short, e.g. a periodical or newspaper article, news-cutting, separate, or pamphlet which embodies micro-thought. *See also* MACRO-DOCUMENT, MICRO-THOUGHT.

MICROFICHE. A flat sheet of photographic film standardized (B.S. 4187 : 1967 and ISO/R 193) at 105 × 148 mm (nominally 4 × 6 inches) and 75 × 125 mm (nominally 3 × 5 inches), displaying at the top a catalogue entry, or title, readable with the naked eye, and bearing in horizontal and vertical rows micro-images of the complete text of a publication. The standard size of a frame is 11·25 × 16 mm (single) and 23 × 16 mm (double). Where a document is too long to be recorded on one microfiche, each subsequent one is called a 'Trailer' microfiche. Microfiche can be (a) a positive copy printed from strips of microfilm, (b) an actual frame cut from microfilm (usually 77 mm film), or (c) made directly with a step-and-repeat camera. Such sheets may be stored vertically like catalogue cards but require envelopes to protect them from damage. Envelopes can be opaque, with details written on, or transparent in which case the transparencies do not have to be removed from the envelopes. They can be inserted in the reading machines which are needed to be able to make use of the sheets. The British Standard 4187 was revised in 1973 and published in two parts. *Part 1 : 60 frame format* is a revision of the 1967 edition; *Part 2 : 98 frame format* specifies a new frame size with ninety-eight images which allows a greater number of pages to be recorded on a single microfiche. This standard incorporates all the requirements of ISO 2707 : 1973 *Transparent AG size microfiche of uniform division – Image arrangements No 1 and No 2. See also* ULTRA-MICROFICHE.

MICROFILM. A microphotograph on cellulose film. It may be negative or positive and may be 16, 35 or even 70 mm wide and of any length, depending on the number of exposures thereon.

For information retrieval purposes the length of the film may vary from 100 to 2,000 feet long; in addition to the roll film form the material used may be a small chip of film, normally 16 or 35 mm wide and from one to three inches long and known as the *unit system*, or it may be the *matrix system* which is based on cut sheets of film bearing micro images in a two-dimensional array, the film sizes being in the general area of 6 × 6 to 8 × 8 inches. Within each of these categories the systems may be further sub-divided into the so-called '*address*' *systems*, in which each item of the collection bears a number or title, and retrieval of the document results from a request for that document by identification, and another type of system which provides documents on the basis of a general description of their contents. The *unit system*, which includes the Aperture or PEEPHOLE CARD (*q.v.*) lends itself to system designs which will retrieve material quicker than the roll film systems. The *matrix system* makes possible even quicker access to material providing it is used as an address system only.

For special purposes, e.g. copying newspapers, or engineering drawings, or the preparation of MICROFICHE (*q.v.*), film of 70 mm wide is used.

Microfilm should be stored in a relative humidity of below 60 per cent and violent heat variations should be avoided: air conditioning is therefore desirable. Cabinets can be obtained which incorporate chemical drying and humidifying agents, but with these there is a risk of damage to the film. Microfilm should be stored on its edge, in a small metal or cardboard canister if in spool form, and placed in cabinets consisting of shallow drawers, or if in strip form, in transparent sheaths. Machines are necessary for reading microfilm.

MICROFILM ASSOCIATION OF GREAT BRITAIN. Inaugurated as the Council for Microphotography and Document Reproduction in England in 1961, the name being changed in 1965. Aims: to (a) assist in the promotion of the effective use of microfilm and document reproduction in industry, business, local government, education and all spheres of private and public administration, (b) to raise the standard of microfilm and document reproduction techniques and applications, (c) encourage wider understanding of these subjects and contribute to the development of improved facilities, (d) maintain contact with other bodies, both national and international, with similar aims and objects, for the exchange of information, (e) represent and promote the interests of all those concerned with handling information in microfilm. Abbreviated MAGB. Publishes *Microdoc* (q.).

MICROFILM FLOW CAMERA. A flow camera for taking automatically microcopies of documents, usually on film. *See also* CONTINUOUS FLOW CAMERA, MICROCOPY.

MICROFILM JACKET. A transparent holder into which individual strips of film may be inserted for protection.

MICROFILM PRINT. An enlarged print made, normally on paper, from microfilm.

MICROFILM READER. An apparatus for the reading of microrecords by means of their enlarged projection on an opaque or transparent ground-glass screen, or white paper, or on a wall. It may be a machine for reading a microcopy on opaque material (microcard) in which light falls on the microcopy and is projected on to the screen by an optical system, or a machine for reading a microcopy on film (microfilm or microfiche).

MICROFILM READING GLASS. A magnifier for reading microcopies with or without artificial lighting equipment.

MICROFILM ROLL. A roll of MICROFILM (q.v.).

MICROFILM STRIP. A short length of MICROFILM (q.v.). *See also* FILMSTRIP, MICROSTRIP.

MICROFOLIO. A sheet of optically clear acetate that holds rows of microimages by a special adhesion process.

MICROFORM. A generic term indicating any form of micro record, whether on flat or roll film, paper or other material.

MICROGRAPH. 1. A graphic record of the image, formed by a microscope, of an object. 2. An instrument constructed for producing extremely small copies of writing, printing or engraving, or for executing minute writing or engraving.

MICROGRAPHICS. The science and technique of reproducing documents in so small a scale that enlargement is necessary to make them legible. *See also* NATIONAL MICROFILM ASSOCIATION.

MICROGROOVE. A disc on the surface of which the grooves are closely cut, thereby providing for longer recording and playing.

MICRO-IMAGE. *Synonymous with* MICROCOPY (*q.v.*).

MICROLEX. The trade name for readers, and for 6½ × 8½ inch opaque laminated microcards, which are produced photographically by the Microlex Corporation, New York. Sheet negatives are made by moving the sheet film automatically after each exposure to produce rows of micro-images. Positive prints are then produced and laminated back to back. Each side of the card contains 200 pages of text. The method is used for the publication of legal reports and journals.

MICRO-OPAQUE. A copy of the whole, or part, of a book or other document made by means of microphotography, the print being on opaque paper or card. May be made solely by photographic means or by a printing method. Also called 'Opaque microcopy'. *See also* MICROCARD, MICROFORM, MICROPRINT.

MICRO-OPAQUE READER. A device for reading a MICRO-OPAQUE (*q.v.*).

MICRO-OPAQUE TAPE. A form of microtext which can be stuck on index cards used as a filing medium.

MICROPHOTOGRAPHY. Photography on so reduced a scale that a visual aid is required to discern the features of the resulting microphotograph; 16 mm or 35 mm cellulose film is used, and the final form of the microcopy may be FILM STRIP, MICROFICHE, MICROFILM (*qq.v.*). The opposite of PHOTOMICROGRAPHY (*q.v.*).

MICROPRINT. A positive microphotograph size 9 × 6 inches and bearing a representation of 100 pages of a book. Reproduction is by a lithographic method on opaque paper. Microprint was invented by Mr. Albert Boni. *See also* MICROCARD, MICROFICHE, MICROFILM, MICROFORM, MICRO-OPAQUE, MICRORECORDING, MICROSLIDE, MICROSTRIP.

MICRORECORD. A copy of a document, the scale of which is reduced compared with the original, and which needs an enlarger to enable it to be legible. Also called 'Microcopy'.

MICRORECORDING. A form of photocopying in which the copy, either on film or paper, is reduced in size so much that it must be read in a 'reader' or by projection. The resultant copy may be made on roll film, sheet film or opaque paper, and is sometimes called 'Microtext'.

See also MICROCARD, MICROFICHE, MICROFORM, MICROSLIDE, MICROSTRIP.

MICROREPRODUCTION. 1. The process of making microcopies of documents, the images being too small to be read by the unaided eye, on either opaque or transparent materials. 2. The copies so produced.

MICROSCOPIC EDITION. *See* MINIATURE BOOK.

MICROSEAL. Trade name for the microfilm aperture cards made by Microseal Inc.

MICROSECOND. A millionth of a second; a unit of measurement used to determine the speed at which a computer operates. *See also* NANOSECOND.

MICRO-SKANER. Trade name for pocket-size reader for microcards. Batteries provide illumination and a 20x enlargement is given.

MICROSLIDE. A single frame of microfilm which has been mounted for use in a microfilm projector.

MICROSTRIP. 1. Micro-images made from 16 mm or 35 mm film on to a roll of gummed paper, cut into sections and stuck on to standard size cards. 2. A strip of microfilm about 8 inches long which has been cut from a roll of film. It usually contains ten pages of text together with a title sheet. (*Concepts* . . .) Also called 'Microfilm strip', 'Strip microfilm'. 3. Trade name for positive prints from microfilm on strips of printing paper specially made for the purpose, and having a backing paper that peels off to expose a sticky surface permitting it to adhere to a card. 'Microtape' is a trade name for similar material.

MICROTAPE. *See* MICROSTRIP.

MICROTEXT. *See* MICRORECORDING.

MICRO-THOUGHT. (*Classification*) A subject of small extension, and therefore of great intension, usually embodied in the form of an article in a periodical, or of a section or a paragraph in a book, or of a pamphlet. *See also* EXTENSION, MACRO-DOCUMENT, MACRO-THOUGHT.

MICROTRANSPARENCY. A microcopy, usually on a film base, which is read by light passing through the film on its way to the eye of the reader. It is usually in the form of MICROFICHE or MICROPRINT (*qq.v.*).

MICROXEROGRAPHY. The creation of micro-images by means of xerography. Negative as well as positive images are possible.

MIDDLE ATLANTIC REGIONAL LIBRARY FEDERATION. *See* MARLF.

MIDDLE EAST LIBRARIANS' ASSOCIATION. *See* MELA.

MIDDLE SPACE. *See* QUAD.

MIDLNET. Abbreviation for the (American) Midwest Regional Library Network, a consortium of university and state libraries and state library networks. It was formed at Chicago in April 1975.

MIDWAY. A publishing experiment conducted in 1973, in which Quartet Books Ltd. published, in association with another publisher, 'quality' paperbacks – new titles – at approximately half the hardback price simultaneously with the hardback editions.

MIDWEST INTER-LIBRARY CENTER. Founded on 4th March 1949 to (1) provide more adequate research materials for the needs of mid-western scholarship and research; (2) provide for economical and efficient utilization of resources to avoid needless duplication and expense. The Midwest Inter-Library Center which was formed to carry out these objectives operated over a central block of twelve mid-western states and had as its two initial activities: (1) the co-operative collecting and housing of little-used material for the use of the region as a whole; (2) the development of a programme for filling out and enriching the resources of the region. Over twenty libraries (mainly university) co-operated in this scheme. Abbreviated MILC. Its name was changed on 25th January 1965 to the CENTER FOR RESEARCH LIBRARIES (*q.v.*).

MIDWEST REGIONAL LIBRARY NETWORK. *See* MIDLNET.

MIEHLE. (*Printing*) The commonest type of TWO-REVOLUTION MACHINE (*q.v.*). Robert Miehle, a young Chicago machine-minder (d. 1932), made an important contribution to printing machine design by controlling the momentum of the bed (with the forme on it) at the instant of reversal by means of an enlarged star wheel and rack.

MILDRED L. BATCHELDER AWARD. *See* BATCHELDER AWARD, MILDRED L.

MILLBOARD. A kind of strong PASTEBOARD (*q.v.*) but made from old rope, sacking, wood pulp, and paper. Used for the covers of books which are heavy or have to stand hard wear. Also called 'Binder's board'.

MIMEOGRAPH. A trade name for a duplicator using wax stencils, and made by the A. B. Dick Co. of America. The term 'mimeographed' is incorrectly used for any form of duplication by means of wax stencils.

MINAFILE. Trade name for a type of vertical storage in which each unit consists of eight vertical drawers or containers, similar to steel transfer cases open at the top. The units can be built on to each other to any desired height, and will hold prints or photographs smaller than 15 × 10 inches in size.

MINIATURE. 1. A coloured initial letter or picture in an illuminated manuscript. 2. A greatly reduced copy of a document, but not so much as a MICROCOPY (*q.v.*), which is usually read or reproduced by means of optical aids. 3. A small highly-detailed drawing, painting, or portrait, especially on ivory or vellum.

MINIATURE BOOK. A very small book, generally 3 inches (10 cm) or less in height, conceived as a whole on a tiny scale, printed with small type on suitable paper, bound in a binding which is tooled delicately, and, if illustrated, having drawings or reproductions which are in keeping with the size of the book. Many distinguished printers and publishers have issued such books. They include Bibles, books of devotion, almanacs, the poets, the classics, books for children, etc. The height is recorded in a catalogue entry in millimetres, not centimetres. Also called 'Lilliput edition', 'Microscopic edition'.

MINIATURE-PAINTER. A painter of miniatures. Also called a 'MINIATURIST'.

MINIATURE SCORE. *See* SCORE.

MINIATURIST. *Synonymous with* MINIATURE-PAINTER (*q.v.*).

MINICARD. A microfilm system of information retrieval, worked out in 1954 by the Eastman Kodak Corporation, in which images and codes are recorded on microfilm. Each piece is 16 × 32 mm in size and can contain up to twelve images photographed up to a reduction of 1/60 as well as the coding. A machine sorter, working on the same principle as a punched card sorter directs the minicards in the appropriate storage magazine, and a machine selector scans the code field passing the required minicards into a special magazine. They can then be examined in a reader; enlarged prints can be made if required. A file of two million Minicards, equivalent to 1,000 normal filing cabinets full of documents, will occupy a cabinet about 15 × 30 × 50 inches in size. The large capital required to acquire the Minicard machinery suggests installation only for regional or national purposes.

MINICS. Abbreviation for the Minimal-Input Catalogue System which is being developed at Loughborough University of Technology. It is a multi-purpose local file structure that is simpler than MARC (*q.v.*) and which will enable (a) any kind of record to be catalogued; (b) accessions bulletins and other forms of current awareness bulletins to be produced; (c) information retrieval to be undertaken.

MINIM. 1. Single downstroke of a pen. 2. A sign in a musical score to indicate a note equal to two crochets or half a semi-breve.

MINIMAL-INPUT CATALOGUE SYSTEM. *See* MINICS.

MINIMATRIX SYSTEM. *See* TERMATREX SYSTEM.

MINION. An out-of-date name for a size of type equal to about 7 point.

MINISTER'S ACCOUNTS. Accounts rendered by stewards, bailiffs or other manorial officials to the lord of the Manor.

MINISTRY OF TECHNOLOGY. This Ministry is responsible for Government interest in applied science and technology and has general responsibility for guiding and stimulating a major national effort to bring advanced technical and new processes into British industry. It administers ten of the fifteen research stations of the former DEPARTMENT OF SCIENTIFIC AND INDUSTRIAL RESEARCH (*q.v.*), and took over that department's responsibilities towards government-aided research associations. It incorporates the Atomic Energy Authority and is responsible for the National Research Development Corporation. The Minister of Technology is advised by the Advisory Council on Technology.

MINITEXT EDITION. Microprint version of a document whose text layout has been arranged to fit a given size page (*IBM*).

MINT. A book which is in the same condition as when it came from the publisher.

MINUSCULE. 1. A small style of writing developed from cursive. 2. LOWER CASE LETTERS (*q.v.*).

MINUTE CLASSIFICATION. *Synonymous with* CLOSE CLASSIFICATION (*q.v.*).

MINUTE MARK. A printer's symbol ' to represent feet (measurement) and minutes; it is also placed after a syllable on which the stress falls.

MINUTES OF PROCEEDINGS OF THE HOUSE OF LORDS. *See* PARLIAMENTARY PAPERS.

MIRACODE. Abbreviation for Microfilm Information Retrieval Access Code, trade name for an Eastman Kodak Company system for searching information recorded on film the basic unit of which consists of a $4 \times 4 \times 1$ inch magazine containing 100 feet of 16 mm microfilm on which are recorded two types of image-reproducible images of documents, and adjacent to each, an identifying code pattern.

MISBOUND. A LEAF (*q.v.*), leaves or a SECTION (*q.v.*) which has been folded wrongly or misplaced by the binder.

MISCELLANEA. *Synonymous with* MISCELLANY (*q.v.*).

MISCELLANY. A collection of writings by various authors or on a variety of subjects. Also called 'Miscellanea'.

MISLEADING TITLE. One which does not indicate the subject-matter, or the form, of the work. In cataloguing when such a title is not clarified by the TRACING (*q.v.*), it can be amplified in the catalogue entry as: (a) *Doctor Zhivago, a novel;* (b) *A life of one's own* [autobiography]; or an explanatory note may be added.

MISLIC. Mid and South Staffordshire Libraries in Co-operation.

Established in 1963 and operating in parts of Staffordshire south of the LINOSCO (*q.v.*) scheme down to the environs of Birmingham; fifty-six organizations co-operate in the interlending of material, and in the purchase of costly books so as to avoid unnecessary duplication.

MISPRINT. A typographical error.

MISSAL. A book containing the service for the celebration of the mass throughout the year. Sometimes loosely used for any book of devotions. Before the invention of printing, the writing of missals was a branch of art which reached a high state of excellence in the monasteries. The books were written upon vellum in the most beautiful style of penmanship, and were adorned with the utmost magnificence. Also called 'Mass book'. *See also* BOOK OF HOURS.

MISSES. (*Information retrieval*) Relevant documents which were not retrieved in a search.

MISTLETOE TOOL. (*Binding*) A finisher's tool which appears to have been first used on Irish bindings in about 1766; it is particularly common on the panels of spines of Irish bindings about 1780. In some forms it is embossed, and seems to be a feather rather than a mistletoe leaf.

MITRED. (*Binding*) A junction of lines at an angle of 45 degrees such as is necessary at the turn-in of covering material on the inside of the covers. Lines, in finishing, which meet each other at right angles without over-running. The connexion at the angles of an outer FRAME 2 (*q.v.*) to an inner frame or PANEL 1 (*q.v.*) by the diagonal use of FILLETS 1 (*q.v.*) or a ROLL (*q.v.*).

MITRED CORNER. (*Binding*) Turning the covering material over the inside of the board in such a way, by cutting, that the turn-ins meet without overlapping. *See also* LIBRARY CORNER, SQUARE CORNER.

MIXED NOTATION. *See* NOTATION.

MIXED SUBJECT HEADING. (*Indexing*) A subject heading which, in addition to being followed by a number of entries or references, refers (by means of *see also* references) to other subject headings. *See also* INDIRECT SUBJECT HEADING.

MNEMONIC CHARACTERISTIC. The use of symbols in such a manner that they have a more or less constant meaning when applied anywhere in a classification scheme.

MNEMONICS. Symbols of the notation of a classification. When they are drawn from lists of divisions, tables or parts of schedules they are called by Ranganathan 'scheduled mnemonics'. Related ideas or 'associations' as used by Ranganathan in classifying, are called 'unscheduled mnemonics' or 'seminal mnemonics' to distinguish them from 'scheduled mnemonics'. Mnemonics may be *constant*, i.e. always denoting the same aspects or form wherever used throughout a scheme of classification, or *variable*, i.e. occasionally alternated or altered to suit the special needs of a specific subject. Dewey's common form divisions now called 'Standard subdivisions' are variable whereas the form marks of the Universal Decimal Classification are constant. *Systematic* mnemonics are those which reflect a consistent order; they are mainly a result of synthesis. *Literal* mnemonics depend on the use of letters in notation in such a way that the symbol for a class is the initial letter of the same class.

MOBILE BRANCH LIBRARY. *See* TRAVELLING LIBRARY.

MOBILE LIBRARIAN. A librarian whose duties are mainly carried out in a travelling or mobile library.

MOBILE LIBRARY. A vehicle devised, equipped and operated to provide, as far as reasonably practicable, a service comparable to a part-time branch library. The Lindsey County Library (now Lincolnshire) began in 1972 to use a helicopter flying out of Louth to take a library service to the North Sea Gas offshore platform east of Mablethorpe. *See also* CONTAINER LIBRARY SERVICE.

MOBILIBRARY. *Synonymous with* MOBILE LIBRARY (*q.v.*).

MODELLED INITIAL. In a mediaeval illuminated manuscript, an initial letter given a rounded or three-dimensional aspect.

MODERN FACE. Printers' types, French in origin dating from 1698; but not popular until after the Revolution when Didot (France), Bodoni (Italy), Figgins, Thorne and Fry (England) cut various versions. 'Moderns' were popular throughout the nineteenth century. They are characterized by vertical emphasis, there being a considerable difference between thick and thin strokes and curves thickened in the centre. The fine bracketed serifs are at right angles to the strokes. Examples are: Bodoni (most foundries); Walbaum (Monotype). The following is in 12 pt. Bodoni:

ABCGEFGHIJKLMNOPQRSTUVWXYZ
abcdefghijklmnopqrstuvwxyz   1234567890

For specimen alphabets of other faces, *see* TYPE FACE. It is characteristic of modern type faces that the numerals stand on the BASE LINE (*q.v.*), but in some type faces the numerals are available in both forms, e.g. Bookprint. The term 'Didone' has superseded 'Modern face' for this category of type faces. *See also* ARABIC FIGURES, OLD FACE, TRANSITIONAL.

MODIFICATION. (*Cataloguing*) Variation in the presentation of information in catalogue entries by, for example, inversion of the initials of a manufacturing firm to bring the last name to the front, the omission of the first part of a geographic name if it indicates a type of governmental administration, the use of a uniform title (perhaps a translation from an original 'foreign' form) to bring all entries for the same work together. (*Indexing*) A word or phrase(s) inserted after a heading to indicate an aspect or character of the information given in the text at the place referred to, to limit its meaning or subdivide the entries, e.g. Land, claims and cessions of, by the states, 319 *sq.*

MODIFIERS. *See* ROLES.

MODULANT. An INTERFIX (*q.v.*); a standardized suffix added to the root of a word (Ruby English) to bring out the different aspects of a word's basic meaning (U.S. Patent Office). *See also* ROLES, RUBY ENGLISH.

MODULAR CONSTRUCTION. A system of building construction introduced for libraries by A. S. Macdonald in 1945 whereby the cubage between the exterior walls, foundations and roof is divided into equal, rectangular prisms of space, bordered on bottom and top by floors and ceilings and on the vertical edges by structural columns. This enables the area of departments to be varied at will and makes it possible to provide stack rooms horizontally or vertically in close proximity to the departments, and to extend or contract them as desired. A modular library is one constructed on this principle.

MODULAR PLANNING. Planning a building so that it consists of a number of modules (units), having no permanent internal walls dividing the floor area into rooms. Each floor is supported by pillars at regular intervals and these pillars are often partly hollow to accommodate plumbing, electric wiring and air conditioning ducts. Except for core service areas (lifts, staircases, etc.) which are enclosed by permanent walls, the whole of the floor area can be sub-divided into rooms and departments by placing free-standing book cases, partitions and furniture where desired, and can be varied at will. Also called 'Unit construction'.

MODULATION OF TERMS. A phrase used to indicate the development of terms, or headings, of a classification. A term should modulate into the term following it.

MOHONK STATEMENT. A summary of an international conference on the Role of Books and other Educational Materials in meeting the educational and economic goals of developed and developing countries, held 10th–13th December 1972 at Mohonk Mountain House, New Paltz, New York. It is reproduced in *IFLA News*, No 43, March 1973.

MONK. An ink blot or splash on a printed sheet; the term originated in the days when formes were inked with ink balls. *See also* FRIAR.

MONOCHROME. Any illustration in one colour.

MONOGRAPH. A separate treatise on a single subject or class of subjects, or on one person, usually detailed in treatment but not extensive in scope and often containing extensive bibliographies. Frequently published in series. In cataloguing, any publication which is not a SERIAL (*q.v.*).

MONOGRAPH SERIES. A series of monographs with a series title as well as individual titles; often issued by a university or society. *See also* SERIES 3.

MONOGRAPHIC PUBLICATION. A non-serial publication, consisting of text and/or illustrations in eye-readable form, either complete in one volume or intended to be completed in a specified number of volumes.

MONOLINE. A type face in which all the strokes of the characters appear to be of the same thickness. Most LINEALE and SLAB SERIF (*qq.v.*) types are of this kind. *See also* GEOMETRIC.

MONOPHONIC. Relating to a sound transmission system in which, at some point only a single signal exists.

MONOPHOTO. Trade name for a photo-typesetting, or film-setting, machine manufactured by the Monotype Corporation which produces characters on film instead of metal. The machine is virtually a complex photographic enlarger; one image of a character can therefore be easily enlarged to a great number of sizes. These are related to the traditional typographic sizes which can be set from 6 point to 12 point in one point steps and from 12 point to 24 point in two points steps. The space between lines can be varied by as little as half a point, e.g. 10 point type can be set as if on a body of $10\frac{1}{2}$, 11, $11\frac{1}{2}$, 12, $12\frac{1}{2}$ points, and so on. *See also* FILMSETTING.

MONOTYPE. Separate paper-perforating and type-founding machines invented by Tolbert Lanston for composing and casting single types. Individual types are cast on the casting machine from paper rolls perforated on the perforating machine in which a keyboard is incorporated.

MONTAGE. The combination of several photographs, drawings, or parts of pictures, blended to form a single illustration for decorative, display or advertising purposes. *See also* PHOTO-MONTAGE.

MONTHLY. A periodical which appears once a month, with the possible exception of certain months, usually one during the summer.

MOOERS' LAW. 'An information retrieval system will tend *not* to be used wherever it is more painful and troublesome for a customer to have the information than for him not to have it.'

MOON TYPE.   A system of reading for the blind in which the letters are formed by raised lines based on a greatly modified form of Roman capital letters. It is more easily learned than Braille and is consequently used by adults who have become blind late in life and find it difficult to master Braille. It is named after Dr. William Moon, a blind clergyman who lived at Brighton.

MORDANT.   Acid or other corrosive, used in etching plates.

MORGUE.   A collection of obituary notices of famous living people kept up to date in newspaper offices.

MOROCCO.   1. Leather manufactured from the skins of goats and largely used in bookbinding. 'Niger' morocco is tanned with a vegetable tannin, and being durable, flexible and relatively thin, is suitable for bookbinding. 'Persian' morocco lacks strength and durability and is unsuitable for bookbinding. 2. Leather made from sheepskin and lambskin but finished to look like goatskin.

MORTICE (MORTISE).   An open space cut out of a printing plate or block so that type may be inserted in it. A block so prepared is said to be 'pierced'.

MOSAIC.   A book decoration formed by inlaying or onlaying small pieces of leather of various colours to form a pattern. The technique is particularly associated with the work of the eighteenth-century French binders Padeloup le Jeune and Le Monnier.

MOSAIC MAP.   A photographic representation of the earth's surface and the buildings, etc. thereon, made from two or more aerial photographs placed side by side.

MOTHER'S ROOM.   A room in a public library in which are kept books for mothers to take home to read to children who have not themselves learned to read, and also books on child psychology, child care and other subjects concerned with the upbringing of children.

MOTORISED SHELVES.   A form of compact shelving in which the bookcases are moved by electrical, or mechanical, power.

MOTTLED CALF.   A calf binding which has been mottled with colour or acid dabbed on with sponges or wads of cotton.

MOTTLED FINISH.   A paper with a variegated colour surface produced by mixing two slightly differently dyed shades of fibres, or by a drip of colour on the wet pulp.

MOULD.   (*Paper*) A rectangular wooden frame over which brass wires or wire cloth is stretched to serve as a sieve in order to permit water to drain away from the pulp fibres to form a sheet of paper. A wooden frame called a DECKLE (*q.v.*) fits round the edges of the mould and forms a tray with raised edges; this keeps the required thickness of pulp fibre on the wires until the excess water has drained away. (*Printing*) A device in two parts used for casting movable type.

MOULD-MADE PAPER. An imitation hand-made paper made from rag FURNISH (*q.v.*) on a machine.

MOUNT. A card or paper on to which something is pasted to protect, preserve, or display it.

MOUNTED. A cutting, print, photograph, page, or similar item which is pasted on a mount.

MOUNTED PLATE. An illustration printed on a separate sheet of paper and pasted to a page of a book.

MOVABLE LOCATION. *See* RELATIVE LOCATION.

MOVABLE TYPE. (*Printing*) Type cast as single units as distinct from slugs or blocks on which are a number of characters. It was the use of movable type towards the end of the fifteenth century, instead of engraved blocks, which led to the rapid development of printing. *See also* INCUNABULA, SLUG, XYLOGRAPHY.

MS. Abbreviation for MANUSCRIPT (*q.v.*).

MUDÉJAR BINDINGS. Spanish bindings in Cordovan leather, done between the thirteenth and fifteenth centuries by Moorish inhabitants of Spain known as mudéjares who were allowed religious freedom and to practise their crafts, of which bookbinding was one. The main design was a blind-tooled pattern of double outline interlacings with stamped strips of dots, curves, rings, etc. to form a background.

MUDGE CITATION, ISADORE GILBERT. Instituted in 1958, and administered by the Reference Services Division of the American Library Association, this Citation is given annually to a person who has made a distinguished contribution to reference librarianship. This contribution may take the form of an imaginative and constructive programme in a particular library, the writing of a significant book or articles in the reference field, creative and inspirational teaching or reference services, active participation in professional associations devoted to references services, or in other noteworthy activities which stimulate reference librarians to more distinguished performance. The first person to receive the Citation was Mary Neill Barton in 1959.

MULL. A thin loosely woven cotton cloth glued on to the backs of books to help hold the sections together. Known as 'super' in America.

MULTI-ASPECT INDEXING. Recording the various subjects a document deals with under the various subject headings (to which a card has been assigned), or by some other means. Usually punched cards are used because of the greater speed possible when retrieving information. *See also* CO-ORDINATE INDEXING.

MULTICOUNTY LIBRARY. A library established by the joint action of the governing bodies, or by vote of the residents, of the counties concerned, and governed by a single board of library directors. (American.)

MULTI-DIMENSIONAL CLASSIFICATION. The characterization of each document from more than one point of view. This can be accomplished for the physical placing of documents only when there are as many copies as there are classificatory points of view. When classification schemes also serve as guides to the physical collection of documents, as in a classified catalogue, copies of catalogue cards (each representing a document) are placed at the different numbers for each point of view. Although each catalogue card represents a single document, one such document may be represented by several cards. *See also* RIGID CLASSIFICATION.

MULTI-DIMENSIONAL RETRIEVAL. Bringing together references to any one concept or set of concepts on demand, on one card or other form of TALLY (*q.v.*). Edge-punched cards and tallies used in a variety of mechanical methods are used for this purpose.

MULTI-LAYER PAPER. *See* FURNISH LAYER.

MULTI-LEVEL ACCESS. (*Information retrieval*) A form of access to files in which entries or blocks of entries are arranged in a definite order of subject symbols. The symbols can arrange the entries systematically as effectively as in an alphabetical index, or as the notation of a classification can arrange the entries of a classified card catalogue.

MULTI-LEVEL INDEXING. The indexing of a document by the appropriate broader generic terms as well as the narrower term.

MULTIMEDIA. 1. A collection, or the record of a collection, of materials in various media, including non-book material, audio-visual material and non-print material, with or without books and other printed material. 2. Information presented through a combination of different communication techniques, either simultaneously or sequentially.

MULTIPLE APPROACH, PRINCIPLE OF. A fundamental fact that books may be approached from the points of view of author, title, subject, series, etc.; this always has to be borne in mind by cataloguers. *See also* CATALOGUING, PRINCIPLES OF.

MULTIPLE ENTRY. (*Information retrieval*) The filing of as many descriptors (terms, entries) in an ITEM ENTRY (q.v.) system as have been made in respect of a document.

MULTIPLE MEANING. *Synonymous with* POLYSEMIA (q.v.).

MULTIPLE REFERENCE. *Synonymous with* GENERAL REFERENCE (q.v.).

MULTI-PROGRAMMING. Computers which have large storage units and which can accommodate more than one program and the input information for them. Also called 'Dual programming'.

MULTI-TIER STACK. A self-supporting metal framework extending from basement to roof and designed to carry the weight of the deck floors and the book load. The columns are placed close together and permit the use of thin slab concrete or metal plate floors as well as shelf supports. Local bye-laws in many English towns do not permit this type of construction.

MULTIVALUED WORDS. (*Information retrieval*) Words which have different meanings in different contexts, whether they be homographs or homophones.

MULTI-VOLUME PUBLICATION. A non-serial publication issued in a number of physically separate parts known to have been conceived and published as an entity; the separate parts may have differing authorship and their individual titles as well as an inclusive title.

MUNICIPAL AUDIT. Borough councils may adopt in its entirety the system of district audit, or may choose to have professional audit which means that the accounts are audited by practising auditors whose qualifications are prescribed in the Act.* In practice, district audit and professional audit are the only two effective systems which are operated, but boroughs have additionally, the right to appoint three 'Borough auditors', two of whom are elected by the local government electors for the borough, and one is appointed by the mayor. This system is very little used except as a tradition in a few boroughs.

MUNICIPAL LIBRARY. A public library serving an urban area and financed, maintained, and administered by any local government authority other than a county or urban district council. The use of the word 'municipal' is becoming less common, and has no legal meaning or connexion. In America, one which may also be similarly provided by a village or school district. In Australia, a public library.

MUNIMENT ROOM. A room in which archives are kept.

MURRAY GOTTLIEB PRIZE. *See* GOTTLIEB PRIZE, MURRAY.

MUSEUM COMPUTER NETWORK, INC. Formed 1973, this non-profit Corporation provides for its members a full range of services

* The Local Government Act, 1933.

including records of fine art collections, artist biographies, documents and manuscripts, inscriptions, audio-visual materials, biological specimens, archaeological sites, and architecture. The Corporation developed from the Museum Computer Network which built up its records from a number of large U.S. museums. It is based on The Museum of Modern Art in New York.

MUSEUMS ASSOCIATION, THE. An organization comprising and representing museums and art galleries and those who work in them in both the British Isles and overseas. The main objects of the Association are to promote the establishment and better administration of museums and art galleries, and to improve the qualifications and status of members of museum staffs. The Diploma of the Association (AMA) is the recognized qualification in curatorship and is awarded to members who have the prescribed number of years' experience in a museum and passed the prescribed examinations. Suitably qualified Associates may be elected Fellows. Membership is also open to persons not professionally engaged in museum work but who are connected with or interested in museums. Publishes *The Museums Journal* (q.), *Bulletin* (m.), about twenty Information Sheets and about fourteen Handbooks for Museum Curators.

MUSIC. *See* BIBLIOGRAPHICAL INFORMATION IN PRINTED MUSIC.

MUSIC LIBRARY. One devoted to music.

MUSIC LIBRARY ASSOCIATION. Founded in the U.S.A. in 1931 to promote the development of music libraries, to encourage studies in the organization and administration of music in libraries. Abbreviated M.L.A. Publishes *Notes* (q.); *MLA Cataloguing Bulletin* (m.); *MLA Index Series* (irreg.); *MLA Newsletter* (irreg.).

MUSIC PAPER. Paper ruled with staves of five lines for the writing of music. When made up into a book it is called a manuscript music book.

MUSIC SCORE. *See* SCORE.

MUSICAL DESCRIPTION. A description of the separate parts for instruments or voices used *simultaneously* during a musical performance. To be distinguished from a BIBLIOGRAPHICAL DESCRIPTION (*q.v.*) which is only concerned with *successive* parts and/or volumes (i.e. the various editions) of a musical composition.

MUSICAL WORK. A composition to be played by one or more musical instruments or to be sung by one or more human voices.

MUSICOLOGY. The study of music as a branch of knowledge or field of research.

MUSIKRITER. A machine that will type music scores. It was invented by Miss Lily Pavey of Camberwell, London, and first manufactured by the Imperial Typewriter Co. in 1964.

MUTTON. *See* EM QUADRAT.

NACL. Acronym for NATIONAL ADVISORY COMMISSION ON LIBRARIES (*q.v.*).

NAEST. Acronym for National Archive for Electrical Science and Technology; formed in 1973 to ensure the collection and preservation of documentary and photographic material of historical interest relating to electrical science and technology in Britain, and to keep records of similar collections of materials elsewhere. The archive was formed and is maintained by the Institution of Electrical Engineers in London.

NBA. Acronym of the National Braille Association, a non-profit-making American organization founded in 1945, which exists to produce and distribute braille and large type publications and tape recordings for blind and partially sighted readers in the U.S.A., particularly students in elementary and secondary schools, colleges and universities. This material is produced by volunteers. The Association also operates the Braille Book Bank, the prime source of current college textbooks in Braille for blind students.

NBM. NON-BOOK MATERIALS (*q.v.*).

n.c. Abbreviation for 'not catalogued'; relates usually to a volume of miscellaneous pamphlets which are not individually catalogued.

NCALI. Acronym for National Clearinghouse for Alcohol Information which began operation in the U.S.A. in 1973 to gather, systematize, maintain and make widely available information on alcohol abuse and alcoholism. Publishes *Alcohol and Health Notes* (m.), *Alcohol Health and Research World* (q.).

NCET. Acronym of the National Council for Educational Technology which was set up in 1967 by the decision of the Secretary of State for Education and Science (Mr Antony Crosland) and following recommendations of the Brynmor Jones Report *Audio-visual aids in higher scientific education*, 1965. Aims to: (a) advise bodies including Government Departments, concerned with education and with training in industry and in the Services, on audio-visual aids and media and on the most appropriate and economical ways of using them; (b) survey work in educational technology and, in consultation with the bodies involved, to seek ways of improving co-ordination; (c) encourage research and development projects in educational technology; (d) collect and disseminate information about experience with existing audio-visual aids and media about new developments and research projects; (e) consider the training of staff who are concerned with audio-visual media and equipment and with the creation and use of audio-visual material; (f) . . . advise the Secretary of State for Education and Science and the Secretary of State for Scotland whether a National Centre for Educational Technology is required . . .' The Council co-operates with the Library Association. Publishes *British Journal of Educational Technology* (3 p.a.). *See also* HELPIS.

NCIC. Acronym for the National Cartographic Information Center which was established by the Department of the Interior of the US Geological Survey in July 1974. It provides a national information service to make cartographic data more easily accessible to the public and to federal, state and local agencies. Thirty federal agencies collect and prepare cartographic material of all kinds, including space photography and related data on the US and possessions and these form the basis of the Center's material resources numbering over 1.5 million maps, twenty million aerial and space photographs, and 1.5 million geodetic control points. The function of NCIC is not to obtain all of the cartographic data from the holders but to act as a central information agency by collecting and organizing descriptive information about the data and arrange for its availability. It is anticipated that NCIC will not form a network of information centres across the country but that local participating organizations will provide local users with direct access to NCIC information.

NCLIS. Acronym of National Commission on Libraries and Information Science, a permanent and independent agency within the Executive Branch, and established by Congress in July 1970; it has the primary responsibility for developing and recommending overall plans for providing library and information services adequate to meet the needs of the people of the U.S.A. Aims to: (a) ensure that all local communities are provided with basic, adequate library and information services; (b) provide adequate suitable services to special user constituencies; (c) strengthen existing statewide resources and systems; (d) develop the human resources required to implement a national programme; (e) co-ordinate existing federal library and information programmes; (f) make the private section a more active partner in the development of a national programme.

NCR. Abbreviation for No Carbon Required and also for the National Cash Register Company who have developed the type of paper indicated. It is used as business stationery and avoids the necessity of using carbons to make copies; the paper appears normal but is back-coated with a chemical which by contact with another paper through pressure causes an outline of the pressure to be reproduced. It is clean to handle.

NCRLC. Abbreviation for National Committee on Regional Library Co-operation. Formed in 1931. Functions: (a) to act as an advisory body on all matters concerning existing or potential regional areas, (b) to provide liaison between the various regional bureaux and the National Central Library. The Committee consists of representatives of the regions, the National Central Library, the Library Association, and the Association of University Teachers. The Committee was responsible for instituting the INTER-REGIONAL SUBJECT COVERAGE SCHEME and the PROVINCIAL JOINT FICTION RESERVE (*qq.v.*). *See also* JOINT FICTION RESERVE. Discontinued after incorporation of the NCL in the British Library.

n.d. *See* NO DATE.

NERC. Acronym of the (British) Natural Environment Research Council which was established by Royal Charter in 1965 under the Science and Technology Act with responsibility to encourage, plan and execute research in those physical and biological sciences which relate to man's natural environment and its resources. These researches are broadly grouped and defined as Solid Earth; Seas and Oceans; Inland Waters; Terrestrial Environments; and Atmosphere. The Council carries out research and training through its own institutes, grant-aided institutes, and by grants, fellowships and other post-graduate awards to universities and other institutions of higher education. The Council's institutes are: British Antarctic Survey; Culture Centre of Algae and Protozoa; Experimental Cartography Unit; Institute of Geological Sciences; Institute of Hydrology; Institute of Biochemistry, Institute for Marine Experimental Research, Institute of Oceanographic Sciences; Institute of Terrestrial Ecology; and the Unit of Invertebrate Virology. Grant-aided institutes are: Freshwater Biological Association, Marine Biological Association of the U.K., Scottish Marine Biological Association and Unit of Marine Invertebrate Biology, etc.

NFAIS. Acronym for NATIONAL FEDERATION OF ABSTRACTING AND INDEXING SERVICES (*q.v.*).

NIE. Acronym of NATIONAL INSTITUTE OF EDUCATION. The research development and dissemination arm of education in the U.S.A. federal government. Formed in 1972 and operating as a separate agency within the Department of Health, Education and Welfare (HEW), its functions are, for an initial period of three years, 'to conduct educational research, collect and disseminate the findings of educational research . . . assist and foster such research, collection, dissemination or training, through grants or technical assistance to, or jointly financed co-operative arrangements with, public or private organizations, institutions, agencies or individuals . . .' The NIE Educational Research Library began to function as the principal Federal Library in the field of education; it has been formed by the merger of the library of the Center for Urban Education in New York City and the education portion of the Office of Health, Education and Welfare Library.

NITCS. Acronym for National Information Transfer Centres. *See* ISORID.

NLA. Acronym of National Librarians Association which was formed in the U.S.A. in August 1975. It is a non-profit-making organization open for membership to 'all persons holding professional library degrees and who are practising librarians or library educators'.

NLL. Acronym for NATIONAL LENDING LIBRARY FOR SCIENCE AND TECHNOLOGY (*q.v.*).

NLL CARDS. An international card catalogue of published aerodynamic measurements first proposed by the National Lucht-en-ruim-tevaart Laboratorium at Amsterdam and now being issued regularly.

NLLST. Acronym for NATIONAL LENDING LIBRARY FOR SCIENCE AND TECHNOLOGY (*q.v.*).

n.p. 1. Abbreviation for no place of publication, no printer's name, no publisher's name. *See also* NO DATE. 2. Abbreviation for 'new paragraph'; an instruction to the compositor that a new paragraph is to be begun. It is indicated in a manuscript or proof by the letters 'n.p.' in the margin and [or // in the text before the first word of the new paragraph. 3. Also used in book reviews and elsewhere as an abbreviation for 'no price'.

NSRDS. Acronym of the National Standard Reference Data System which is intended to provide a basic service to the entire scientific and technical community of the United States, the technical scope of its activities being restricted to well-defined physical and chemical properties of substances which are well-characterized. The system began in 1963 when the Federal Council for Science and Technology asked the NATIONAL BUREAU OF STANDARDS (*q.v.*) to assume primary responsibility in the Federal Government for promoting and co-ordinating the critical evaluation of numerical data in the physical sciences. The NBS established the Office of Standard Reference Data

(OSRD) (*q.v.*) to manage the programme. The compilation and evaluation of data takes place in many widely separated groups of data centres and also by individual scientists; these groups form the components of the System.

NTBL. Abbreviation for Nuffield Talking Book Library for the Blind which was established in 1935 as the Talk Book Library for the Blind, the name being changed in 1954. In 1960 the Nuffield Foundation gave a grant to convert the information then on records on to tape. The Library is administered by the Royal National Institute for the Blind and St. Dunstan's through their joint Sound Recording Committee, and maintained by the funds of these two voluntary charities. Membership is free and open to blind persons over the age of 21 who are registered with their local Blind Welfare Authority. The 'books' are specially recorded in the Committee's own studio; they are mainly fiction but a number of recordings of biographies, travel books and other non-fiction subjects are also produced. The 'books' are lent free and played on special recording machines which are non-commercial and rented from the Library. Now known as the British Talking Book Service for the Blind.

NTIS. Acronym of National Technical Information Service which was formed in 1970 by the U.S. Department of Commerce to simplify and increase public access to federal publications and data files of interest to the business, scientific and technical communities. It is the American clearinghouse for the collection and dissemination of scientific, technical, and engineering information. Previously known as the Office of Technical Service (OTS), it is also a central source for the public sale of government-sponsored research, development and engineering reports and other analyses, information being brought together from hundreds of federal sources. It is also a central source for Federally-generated, machine-processable data files and programmes. The agency's on-line computer-based custom bibliographic search service NTISearch enables particulars of all Federally-sponsored research projects completed since 1964 (to which 200 new research reports are added daily) to obtain up-to-the-minute details from its information collection. In 1975 it was proposed that NTIS should become a constituent part of a SCIENCE AND TECHNOLOGY INFORMATION AND UTILIZATION CORPORATION (*q.v.*). *See also* CFSTI.

n.y.p. Abbreviation for 'not yet published'.

NAKED FORME. Pages of type secured by page-cord. *See also* DRESSED FORME, FORME.

NAME AUTHORITY FILE. The list of name headings used in a given catalogue, and the references made to them from other forms. *See also* AUTHORITY LIST, SUBJECT AUTHORITY FILE.

NAME CATALOGUE. A catalogue arranged alphabetically by names of persons or places, or both, whether used as authors or subjects.

NAME ENTRY. In indexing, an entry under the name of a person, place, or institution.

NAME INDEX. An index of names of authors or other persons.

NAME PALLET. *See* BINDER'S TICKET.

NAME REFERENCE. Where alternative forms of names are available, a reference to the one adopted for the heading in a catalogue.

NANCY STIRLING LAMBERT SCHOLARSHIP. *See* LAMBERT SCHOLARSHIP, NANCY STIRLING.

NANOSECOND. A billionth of a second, a unit of measurement used to determine the speed at which computers operate. *See also* MICRO-SECOND.

NANTIS. Acronym for Nottingham and Nottinghamshire Technical Information Service which was formed in 1962 to improve the existing co-operation between libraries and information services in the Nottinghamshire area, to speed the flow and interchange of books and information, and to strengthen the local resources of material available. Membership is open to any library, information service, research organization, trade organization, industrial or business firm in the Nottinghamshire area. The service is intended to be financially self-supporting; the amount of the subscription is nominal, members from outside the County of Nottinghamshire paying slightly more than those within the County. Although the scheme is centred on the Business, Science and Technology Library (at the Central Library, Nottingham) of the Nottinghamshire County Library, there is ready participation by all members in furthering the main aims of NANTIS. Publishes *NANTIS News* and other publications.

NARRATION. *Synonymous with* RELATION (*q.v.*).

NARROW. A book whose width is less than two thirds its height.

NARROWER TERM. (*Information retrieval*) A term which denotes a concept which is narrower than that of a term with a broader, more general, meaning, e.g. Chairs is narrower than Furniture. *See also* BROADER TERM, RELATED TERM.

NATIONAL ACADEMY OF ENGINEERING. The (U.S.) National Academy of Engineering was established in 1964 under the charter of the National Academy of Sciences. This Academy honours distinguished engineers through election to its membership, furthers the interests of engineering research and education, and collaborates with the National Academy of Sciences in advising the federal government on national policy issues involving science and technology through joint governance of the National Research Council. The Printing and Publishing Office of the corporate institution publishes seventy-five to one hundred monographs per year.

NATIONAL ACADEMY OF SCIENCES – NATIONAL RESEARCH COUNCIL. A private, non-profit organization of scientists, dedicated to the furtherance of science and to its use for the general welfare. The Academy was established in 1863 under a Congressional charter signed by President Lincoln, and is required to advise the Federal Government on scientific matters; it is not a governmental agency. The National Research Council was established by the Academy in 1916, at the request of President Wilson, to enable scientists generally to associate their efforts with those of the limited membership of the Academy in service to the nation, to society and to science in the U.S.A. and overseas. Income is received from both public and private sources, and by contributions, grant, or contract. Funds are used to stimulate research and its applications, to survey the broad possibilities of science, to promote effective utilization of the scientific and technical resources of the U.S.A., and to further the general interests of science. Abbreviated NAS–NRC. Publishes *Scientific and Technical Societies of the United States*, 9th ed., 1971.

NATIONAL ADVISORY COMMISSION ON LIBRARIES. Established in the U.S.A. by Executive Order of 2nd September 1966, and issued by President Johnson. The Commission was charged to make a comprehensive study and appraisal of the role of libraries as sources of scholarly pursuits or centres for the dissemination of knowledge, and make recommendations designed to ensure an effective and efficient library system for the nation. The report was submitted to President Johnson on 15th October 1968. It recommended that it be declared national policy, enunciated by the President and enacted into law by Congress, that the American people should be provided with library and informational services adequate to their needs, and that the Federal Government, in collaboration with State and local governments and private agencies, should exercise leadership assuring the provision of such services. Abbreviated NACL.

NATIONAL AGRICULTURAL LIBRARY. One of the three national libraries in the U.S.A., the others being the Library of Congress and the National Library of Medicine. It was formed as a result of the Organic Act of 1862 which placed upon the Department of Agriculture the duty of 'acquiring and preserving all information concerning agriculture', the nucleus of the library being the transfer of the book and journal collection amounting to 1,000 volumes from the Agricultural Division of the Patent Office. The library was designated the National Agricultural Library in 1962. Its services are provided to personnel of the Department of Agriculture in Washington, and the field, state agricultural agencies, agricultural colleges and universities, research institutions, industry, individual scientists, farmers and the general public in every part of the world. The stock numbers 1,300,000 volumes. In 1969 the library moved to a fifteen-storey building in Beltsville, Maryland. Abbreviated NAL.

NATIONAL ARCHIVE FOR ELECTRICAL SCIENCE AND TECHNOLOGY. *See* NAEST.

NATIONAL ARCHIVES AND RECORDS SERVICE. A grouping of five co-ordinate offices: the Office of Federal Records Centers, the Office of the Federal Register, the Office of the National Archives, the Office of Presidential Libraries, and the Office of Records Management. It supersedes the National Archives Establishment and is responsible to the Administrator of General Services of the U.S. government for promoting improved current records management and disposal practices in federal agencies; for selecting, preserving and making available to the government and the public the permanently valuable non-recurrent records of the federal government; for the preservation, publication and administration of the historical materials in the Franklin D. Roosevelt Library at Hyde Park, N.Y. The collection of the (U.S.) Public Documents Library of the Government Printing Office was transferred to the National Archives in 1974.

NATIONAL ART LIBRARY. The library of the Victoria and Albert Museum in South Kensington, London. One of the national libraries maintained by the British government.

NATIONAL AND LOCAL GOVERNMENT OFFICERS ASSOCIATION. The trade union to which most librarians and other officers employed by local authorities and 'utility' services (e.g. gas and electricity undertakings) and other services belong. It is the largest British trade union for 'black-coated' workers. Abbreviated NALGO.

NATIONAL BIBLIOGRAPHY. A bibliography which lists all the books and other publications published, or distributed in significant quantity, in a particular country. Sometimes the term is used in respect to the new publications published within a specific period, and sometimes in respect to all those published within a lengthy period of many years. It is also used to indicate a bibliography of publications about a country (whether written by its nationals or not) and those written in the language of the country as well as those published in it.

NATIONAL BIOGRAPHY. A publication containing biographies of nationals of one country, usually in alphabetical order.

NATIONAL BOOK AWARDS. Bestowed in the U.S.A. to honour books worthy of a distinguished role in general and cultural life. They are not intended for outstanding research, scholarship or scientific achievement in themselves, or to recognize works written for professional or otherwise specialized audiences, but rather to recognize distinction of thought and spirit, and their creative, literary expression. The $1,000 awards are presented annually for books written by American citizens and published in the United States in the preceding two calendar years. The prizes are contributed by six American book industry associations. From 1960 until 1974 the awards were administered by the NATIONAL BOOK COMMITTEE (*q.v.*). A twenty-member Awards Advisory Committee selects judges for each of the panels: arts and letters; children's literature; fiction; history and biography; poetry; translation; contemporary affairs; philosophy and religion, but when the NBC was unable to continue its activities, the National Institute of Arts and Letters took over the Awards Programme in 1975, reducing the prize categories to five: arts and letters; contemporary affairs; fiction; history and biography; and poetry. The Association of American Publishers' General Trade Division and other organizations including the Exxon, IBM, and Xerox corporations are financing the Awards. *See also* NATIONAL MEDAL FOR LITERATURE.

NATIONAL BOOK CENTRE. *See* BRITISH NATIONAL BOOK CENTRE, NATIONAL CENTRAL LIBRARY.

NATIONAL BOOK COMMITTEE. An American non-profit, educational society of citizens devoted to the use of books. Founded in 1954, its purpose is 'to keep books free, make them widely available, and encourage people to read them'. The two principal continuing projects were the NATIONAL BOOK AWARDS (*q.v.*) and the National Library Week Program. On 4th May 1965 it instituted the annual presentation of the NATIONAL MEDAL FOR LITERATURE (*q.v.*). In November 1974, the Chairman of the Committee announced that owing to increasing costs and sharply declining income it was no longer possible for the organization to continue functioning. The National Book Awards, consisting of 1,000 in each of ten categories, given annually to the authors of those books judged 'most distinguished', were to be made in 1975 under the auspices of the Committee on Awards policy, a sub-committee of the NBC. The National Library Week (which was only one of the programmes sponsored by NBC) was to be continued by its creator, the American Library Association. The annual National Medal for Literature is being sponsored by the National Institute of Arts and Letters.

NATIONAL BOOK COMMITTEE. Formed in August 1975 by the leading British organizations concerned with the printed word, for the purpose of furthering the production and use of books, particularly the resistance to the recent reduction of funds available to libraries for the purchase of books.

NATIONAL BOOK COUNCIL. An Australian organization, formed in 1973 'to bring together bodies and individuals who privately or professionally have an interest in or concern for books; to encourage the free flow of books, and for this purpose (inter alia): to (a) publish and circulate information about books and to encourage the ownership and use of books; (b) assist in the development of a healthy book industry in all aspects, including authorship, publishing, bookselling, and library use; (c) persuade Federal, State and Local Governments to give every support to the book trade and to ensure its freedom from undesirable imposts and restrictions; (d) generally do everything to increase the permeation of books, recreationally and educationally throughout Australia'. There are five categories of membership: corporate, institutional, book trade, associate, and individual. The Council is financed by membership fees and grants; it is known by the acronym NBC and has its office in Melbourne. Publishes *Newsletter* (m., membs. only) and occasional booklists.

NATIONAL BOOK DEVELOPMENT COUNCIL. At a series of regional meetings convened by Unesco, it was recommended that a council or similar body should be established by every nation with the following objectives: to (a) serve as an intermediary between the book professions and the government so as to ensure the integration of book production and distribution into overall economic and social plans; to act as spokesman for the industries in questions of finance, taxation, customs regulations involving the government; (b) initiate measures that would help prevent or correct conditions prejudicial to book development and to promote activities and plans for national book development; (c) encourage the formation of professional associations relating to reading material where none exist and to strengthen such as are already in being; (d) promote, assist, and, where necessary, co-ordinate plans for concerted action on such questions as the training of personnel; (e) establish suitable machinery for promoting the reading habit and conduct research essential to the full development of book industries; (f) provide information related to the book trade and practices which can serve the development of books and reading generally; (g) undertake such additional activities as would ensure the balanced production and distribution of books and reading materials. The Unesco Secretariat has drawn up a model constitution for such a council.

NATIONAL BOOK LEAGUE. A non-commercial body, the object of which is to promote books and reading. It is supported by the Arts Council of Great Britain, by publishers and booksellers as well as by libraries of various kinds; and by authors and private individuals. A Readers' Services Information Bureau is maintained at the head-quarters, 7 Albemarle Street, London W1X 4BB, where a restaurant, club and exhibition rooms are also provided. Lectures and exhibitions of books are held there, and some of the exhibitions are afterwards shown in other British towns and overseas countries. Booklists on a variety of subjects are published throughout the year. The National Book League developed from the National Book Council which was formed in 1924, the change of name and a new constitution occurring in 1944. A reference library of children's books containing all children's books published in the previous twelve months is main-tained at the headquarters. A Scottish office exists in Glasgow to cater for Scottish needs. Abbreviated NBL. Publishes *Booknews* (q.).

NATIONAL BOOK SALE. A plan which was introduced in 1955 by the British book trade to sell new copies of fairly recent publications for which there was reduced demand, at considerably reduced prices. The Sale is organized by a joint committee of the Publishers Associa-tion and of the Booksellers Association which fixes the date of the sale. No bookseller may sell at reduced prices before or after the agreed dates, and during the Sale may sell at any price but not higher than two-thirds of the published price.

NATIONAL BRAILLE ASSOCIATION. *See* NBA.

NATIONAL BUREAU OF STANDARDS. This organization serves as the focal point in the American Federal Government for assuring maximum application of the physical and engineering sciences to the advancement of technology in industry and commerce. The work of the Bureau is organized into four institutes (the Institute for Basic Standards, the Institute for Materials Research, the Institute for

Applied Technology, the Institute for Computer Sciences and Technology) and the Office for Information Programs. Abbreviated NBS. Publishes *Journal of Research*. A. *Physics and Chemistry* (6 p.a.). B. Mathematical Sciences (q.); *Dimensions/NBS* (formerly *Technical News Bulletin* (m.); *Journal of Physical and Chemical Reference Data* (q.); ten non-periodical publications, NBS inter-agency reports and many other publications.

NATIONAL CARTOGRAPHIC INFORMATION CENTER. *See* NCIC.

NATIONAL CATALOGUE. A list of books in a number of libraries in a country. *See also* NATIONAL BIBLIOGRAPHY.

NATIONAL CENTER FOR EDUCATION STATISTICS.† In the Education Amendments 1974, Congress removed this Center from the Office of Education and established it as a quasi-independent Agency within the office of the assistant secretary for education. The Center is concerned with the use of academic libraries; school libraries and media centres, and public libraries; it developed in 1974 a Library General Information Survey (LIBGIS 1) to provide uniform statistics nationwide on school library/media centres and public libraries. Abbreviated NCES.

NATIONAL CENTRAL LIBRARY. Formerly the Central Library for Students; the national centre for lending books for study, and the clearing house for loans of books and periodicals between public, university and special libraries of all types, working in co-operation with Regional Library Bureaux, and with special libraries known in this connexion as OUTLIER LIBRARIES (*q.v.*). The Library ceased to exist as an independent organization on its absorption into the Lending Division of the BRITISH LIBRARY (*q.v.*) in 1974, and thereby lost its identity. It was also the main centre for information about books, and the re-distribution of surplus books, at home and abroad, until the NCL was incorporated within the Lending Division of the BRITISH LIBRARY (*q.v.*); it had been carried out by the British National Book Centre. Abbreviated NCL. *See also* REGIONAL BUREAUX.

NATIONAL CLEARINGHOUSE FOR ALCOHOL INFORMATION. *See* NCALI.

NATIONAL COMMISSION ON LIBRARIES AND INFORMATION SCIENCE. *See* NCLIS.

NATIONAL COMMITTEE ON REGIONAL LIBRARY CO-OPERATION. *See* NCRLC.

NATIONAL COUNCIL FOR EDUCATIONAL TECHNOLOGY. *See* NCET.

NATIONAL DEFENSE EDUCATION ACT, TITLE III. This American Act of 1964 provides that the Federal government will pay 50 per cent of the cost of school books and audio-visual materials in science, mathematics, modern foreign languages, civics, English, geography, history, economics and reading; also the cost of full processing or for the cataloguing kits and minor re-modelling of existing facilities. The grants also apply to equipment in audio-visual libraries which are part of a school, an instructional materials centre, or a curriculum centre. Abbreviated NDEA.

NATIONAL FEDERATION OF ABSTRACTING AND INDEXING SERVICES. A confederation of major abstracting and indexing service organizations. Founded in the U.S.A. in 1922 and incorporated in January 1958 as the National Federation of Science Abstracting and Indexing Services to encourage and improve the documentation (abstracting, indexing, and analysing) of the world's scientific and technological literature so as to make it readily available to all scientists and technologists by: (a) encouraging the development of abstracting and indexing for the specialized subjects fields not covered by such services, and the further development of such services; (b) seeking greater uniformity in such matters as journal citations and abbreviations and transliteration of foreign titles; (c) co-operation, education, research, and the pursuit of mutually useful enterprises, to strive for the best possible research information services for science and technology in the U.S. and abroad. The scope of the Federation's activities was enlarged to include the social sciences and the humanities, and the word 'science' was consequently omitted from its name on 1st October 1972. In this year there were over thirty member services. The aims of the Federation are to help to improve members' services and operations and to advance their prestige nationally and internationally; to undertake specific projects on behalf of members that would be broadly useful to most of the member services but which they could not undertake alone; to act as a national spokesman for the member services. Address 3401 Market Street, Philadelphia, Pennsylvania, 19104; this is in the University City Science Center, a non-profit corporation sponsored by twenty-five academic institutions in the Delaware Valley. Abbreviated NFAIS. Publishes *nfais newsletter* (bi-m.) from Vol. 15, No. 1 February 1973 (formerly *News from Science Abstracting and Indexing Services*).

NATIONAL FILM ARCHIVE. Founded May 1935 to select, acquire, preserve and maintain a growing national collection of films and television programmes of artistic and historic significance whatever their source. Financed from a government grant awarded to the British Film Institute. A viewing service, production library and stills collection are provided. Catalogues of films in stock are published.

NATIONAL HANDWRITING. See HANDWRITING.

NATIONAL INFORMATION SYSTEMS. See NATIS.

NATIONAL INFORMATION TRANSFER CENTRES (NITCs). See ISORID.

NATIONAL INSTITUTE OF ARTS AND LETTERS. Chartered by Congress in 1898 'to further literature and the fine arts in the United States', this, the highest honour society of the arts in the U.S.A., now awards the NATIONAL MEDAL FOR LITERATURE (q.v.) and the NATIONAL BOOK AWARDS. (q.v.).

NATIONAL INSTITUTE OF EDUCATION. See NIE.

NATIONAL LENDING LIBRARY FOR SCIENCE AND TECHNO-LOGY. Founded (as a consequence of a recommendation in the *Eighth Annual Report* of the Advisory Council on Scientific Policy, 1955) in 1962 and based on the library of the Department of Scientific and Industrial Research with books and bound periodicals from the Science Museum Library and other sources. It aims to assemble a comprehensive collection of the world's literature (mainly periodicals and reports) of science and technology, including agriculture, and, to some extent, medicine, in all languages, and is strong in foreign, especially Russian, material in the original and in translation. The NLL took over the Book Loan Service from the Science Museum and lends material on request through university, technical, college, the larger public, and other libraries which have been appointed agents. Prepares and sells translations of technical articles and books in Russian. Answers enquiries about Russian technical literature, translations from the Russian, and the documents that were collected after World War II. Possesses 500,000 volumes. Subscribes to over 32,000 current serials of all kinds, including report literature, from all over the world. Situated at Boston Spa, Yorkshire. Abbreviated NLL and NLLST. This library ceased to function as an independent organization, and also lost its identity, on its absorption into the BRITISH LIBRARY (q.v.) in 1973, becoming a major part of the Lending Division of the British Library.

NATIONAL LIBRARIANS ASSOCIATION. See NLA.

NATIONAL LIBRARIES AUTHORITY. The name for the body which the *National Libraries Committee Report* recommended should be used for the administrative body responsible for the provision and administration of national libraries in the United Kingdom. *See also* DAINTON REPORT.

NATIONAL LIBRARIES COMMITTEE. *See* DAINTON REPORT.

NATIONAL LIBRARIES TASK FORCE. *See* U.S. NATIONAL LIBRARIES TASK FORCE ON CO-OPERATIVE ACTIVITIES.

NATIONAL LIBRARY. A library maintained out of government funds and serving the nation as a whole. Usually, books in such libraries are for reference only. They are usually copyright libraries. The function of such a library is to collect and preserve for posterity the books, periodicals and newspapers published in the country. This is best done by a law requiring publishers to deposit copies of all publications issued by them, and by purchasing books published in other countries. A copyright act normally has penalty clauses to enable the act to be enforced. *See also* COPYRIGHT, LEGAL DEPOSIT. The functions of national libraries vary considerably. They may compile union catalogues, produce a national bibliography, publish a retrospective national bibliography, or act as a national bibliographical centre. National libraries in the United Kingdom are: British Library, Imperial War Museum Library, National Art Library (situated at the Victoria and Albert Museum), Science Museum Library. These are in England. Additionally there are the National Library of Scotland and the National Library of Wales. For those which receive books under the Copyright Act, *see* COPYRIGHT LIBRARY. National libraries in the United States are: Library of Congress, National Agricultural Library (formerly the National Library for Agriculture) and National Library of Medicine.

NATIONAL LIBRARY FOR THE BLIND. The British library which makes books in raised characters available to blind persons, either directly through the post or through public libraries. It was founded in 1882 by Miss Arnold and Mrs. Dow and depends on subscriptions and legacies for most of its income. Abbreviated NLB.

NATIONAL LIBRARY OF AUSTRALIA. The National Library Act of 1960 (which created a statutory authority – the National Library Council – to manage the National Library which was then separated from the Parliamentary Library) was amended in 1973 in order to facilitate a major developmental programme and to create new library-based information services. The National Librarian was also redesignated Director-General and was nominated as the executive member of the Council. A new building was erected in Canberra on a site on which it was planned eventually to house 11,000,000 volumes and their related services.

NATIONAL LIBRARY OF CANADA. Established in 1953, this Library together with the Public Archives were accommodated in a new building in Ottawa in 1967. The Library is concerned mainly with material in social and behavioural sciences and the humanities, the sciences being served by the National Research Centre, the library of which was formerly known as the National Sciences Library but is now known as the Canada Institute for Scientific and Technical Information (CISTI *q.v.*). The Library operates an automated information retrieval system which regularly scans thousands of publications, searching for titles of interest to the system's subscribers. A union card catalogue of the accessions of over 300 Canadian libraries is maintained. In 1973 a Multilingual Biblioservice was established to select, purchase, catalogue and circulate books in all languages spoken in Canada other than English and French. A new National Library Act came into force on 1st September 1969; amongst other provisions, this assigned co-ordinating powers to the National Librarian and enabled him to provide active and effective leadership to the libraries of the federal government, it also provided for the appointment of a National Advisory Board to advise the National Librarian on the needs of Canadian libraries and their users.

NATIONAL LIBRARY OF IRELAND. Originally the library of the Royal Dublin Society, a semi-public, grant-aided institution; it became known as the National Library of Ireland in 1877. It benefits from Irish (but not English) legal deposit, and is controlled by the Irish government. It is the principal centre for research into Irish literature and history and contains 500,000 books, as well as collections of periodicals, newspapers, maps, prints, drawings, manuscripts, films and photographs, all relating to Ireland. It was the first library in the British Isles to adopt the Dewey classification.

NATIONAL LIBRARY OF MEDICINE. Founded in 1836 as the Library of the Surgeon General's Office, United States Army, re-named the Army Medical Library in 1922, again re-named the Armed Forces Medical Library in 1952 and finally re-named in 1956 when it became a part of the Public Health Service of the Department of Health, Education and Welfare. Situated in Bethesda, Md., it assists the advancement of medical and related sciences, and aids the dissemination and exchange of scientific and other information important to the progress of medicine and public health. Abbreviated NLM. Publishes: *Index Medicus* (m.). *The National Library of Medicine Classification* has been published. *See also* MEDLARS, MEDLINE.

NATIONAL LIBRARY OF QUEBEC. Formed in 1968, this Library performs all the modern functions of a national library, including legal deposit and the compilation of current and retrospective bibliographies relating to the Province of Quebec.

NATIONAL LIBRARY OF SCOTLAND. Founded as the Advocates' Library in 1682, it became the National Library of Scotland by Act of Parliament in 1925, when the Faculty of Advocates transferred to the nation all but its legal collection. The Library has held the British Copyright Privilege since 1710. Its collections of printed books and MSS., augmented by gift and purchase, are very large, and it has an unrivalled Scottish collection. A new building was opened in 1956. In 1974 the Scottish Central Library was incorporated to become Lending Services (NLSLS), and is the Scottish counterpart of the Lending Division of the British Library (*q.v.*). Abbreviated NLS. *See also* COPYRIGHT LIBRARY, DEPOSITORY LIBRARY.

NATIONAL LIBRARY OF WALES. A government-financed library which was founded in 1909 following the granting of a Royal Charter in 1907. It specializes in manuscripts and books relating to Wales and the Celtic peoples, and has a stock of nearly 2,000,000 printed books, 30,000 manuscripts, 3,500,000 deeds and documents, and numerous maps, prints and drawings. It is a Copyright Library in respect of books in the Welsh language or dealing with Wales.

NATIONAL LIBRARY WEEK. Sponsored by the (American) NATIONAL BOOK COMMITTEE AND THE AMERICAN LIBRARY ASSOCIATION (*qq.v.*) National Library Weeks have been held in the U.S.A. for seventeen years. Their object has been to attempt to reduce illiteracy and increase interest in books, reading and libraries but their effectiveness was dependent on the extent to which state library associations and agencies and individual libraries organized and developed programmes for their own purposes. From 1975 the (American) National Library Week is being organized by the American Library Association following the discontinuance of the BOOK WEEK, CHILDREN'S BOOK COUNCIL (*q.v.*) which had previously organized it. *See also* NATIONAL BOOK COMMITTEE. In 1966 and since, similar weeks have been organized in the U.K. but not annually; they have been planned by a national committee on which appropriate associations have been represented. In the early 1970s their character was broadened and the emphasis was on books rather than libraries. They were then organized as National Book Weeks.

NATIONAL MEDAL FOR LITERATURE. An award made annually to a living American author for the whole body of his or her

19

work; it was first presented to Thornton Wilder on 4th May 1965. The Medal, plus $5,000, is made possible by a grant from the Guinzburg Fund, honouring the late Harold K. Guinzburg, founder of the Viking Press, and was instituted by the NATIONAL BOOK COMMITTEE (q.v.). *See also* NATIONAL BOOK AWARDS.

NATIONAL MICROGRAPHICS ASSOCIATION. Founded in the United States in 1943 as the National Microfilm Association (the name being changed in 1975) to 'promote the lawful interests of the micro-reproduction industry in the direction of good business ethics, the liberal discussion of subjects pertaining to the industry; technological improvement and research; standardization; the methods of manufacturing and marketing; the education of the consumer in the use of microfilm and related technique'. The Association operates through Chapters in about twenty-five American states. In 1973 the Board of the Association approved a plan for the development of a Resource Center in the field of micrographics, the purpose of which is to provide access to all current and relative material to all interested persons. Abbreviated NMA. Publishes *Journal of Micrographics* (bi-m. to membs.), *Micro-news Bulletin* (bi-m. to membs.), *Proceedings of the Annual Convention* (a. to membs.).

NATIONAL PROGRAM FOR ACQUISITIONS AND CATALOGING. An acquisitions and cataloguing project initiated in the financial year 1966 and implemented in the following financial year, whereby the Library of Congress seeks to acquire abroad, catalogue immediately, and disseminate cataloguing data rapidly, all current monographs, as well as monographic series, of research value, in order to meet the current needs of American libraries through a national cataloguing effort. To avoid unnecessary duplication of cataloguing already accomplished in other countries, SHARED CATALOGUING (q.v.) techniques have been adopted wherever possible in co-operation with the producers of foreign national bibliographies. The House Appropriations Committee received a critical report from congressional staff investigators on this Program and on Shared Cataloguing in February 1974; this was reported in *American Libraries* 5, (8), Sept. 1974, pp. 406–7. Abbreviated NPAC.

NATIONAL REFERENCE LIBRARY OF SCIENCE AND INVENTION. Formed by amalgamating the Patent Office Library which was transferred to the British Museum in May 1966, with books on science in the British Museum in separate buildings apart from the British Museum, but under the control of the Trustees of the British Museum. A recommendation of this nature was made in the

Eighth Annual Report of the Advisory Council on Scientific Policy, 1955. It possesses the largest and most comprehensive collection of the world's technical literature in the U.K., and is primarily intended to serve science graduates, qualified engineers and technologists, research workers and patent agents. When the BRITISH LIBRARY (*q.v.*) was formed in 1973 this Library was denominated the Science Reference Library and became part of the Reference Division. Abbreviated NRLSI.

NATIONAL REFERRAL CENTER FOR SCIENCE AND TECHNO-LOGY. Usually referred to as the National Referral Center. Formed in 1963, and functioning at the Library of Congress as a clearing house to provide comprehensive, co-ordinated access to the U.S.A.'s resources of scientific and technical information. It has as its four major areas of responsibility: (1) the identification of all significant information resources in the fields of science and technology; (2) the acquisition, cataloguing, and correlation of substantive and procedural data defining the nature, scope, and capabilities of these resources; (3) the provision of advice and guidance about these resources to any organization or individual requiring access to them by responding to requests for referral assistance, and by publishing directories and guides in selected subject fields; and (4) the exploration, through actual operating experience, of the roles and relationships that exist or should exist among the many elements of the scientific and technical information complex. Between 1971 and 1974 four computer-produced directories of information sources were published, and later made available on tapes in the MARC Communications Format. Abbreviated NRC.

NATIONAL REGISTER OF ARCHIVES. Since 1945 the HISTORICAL MANUSCRIPTS COMMISSION (*q.v.*) has built up this collection of lists and related personal, subject and topographical indexes of non-official records in private custody and in libraries and record offices. The lists (in 1973 over 17,000) some summary, others detailed, cover a wide variety of accumulations from family and estate papers to the archives of institutions, political parties and businesses. The Register may be consulted without charge at the offices of the Historical Manuscripts Commission. The *Bulletin* (1–14, 1948–1967) is now discontinued; the *List of Accessions to Repositories* appears annually; and duplicated subject source lists are being issued.

NATIONAL REPROGRAPHIC CENTRE FOR DOCUMENTA-TION. Established January 1967 with a grant from OSTI. The Centre is attached to the Hatfield Polytechnic, Herts. Object: to promote and advise on the applications and technology of micrographic, reprographic and other new media for documentation. The Centre offers members (subscribers) information and advisory services, tests and evaluates equipment, organizes short courses and seminars, undertakes consultancy. Abbreviated NRCd. Publishes *NRCd Reprographics* (previously *NRCd Bulletin*), seminar proceedings, etc.

NATIONAL SCIENCE FOUNDATION. A United States federal agency established by Congress in 1950 'to promote the progress of science to advance the national health, prosperity and welfare; to secure the national defence; and for other purposes'. In carrying out these broad objectives, the Foundation supports research and education through grants and fellowships, fosters the exchange of scientific information among scientists in the U.S. and foreign countries, and surveys the nature and extent of scientific research and development activities in the U.S. Abbreviated NSF. *See also* OSIS.

NATIONAL SCIENCE LIBRARY (of Canada). The National Science Library (by name since 1966, and previously known from 1953 as the National Research Council Library) and the Technical Information Service of the NRC combined on 16th October 1974 to form the Canada Institute for Scientific and Technical Information. *See* CISTI. The NSL took responsibility in 1967 for providing the Health Sciences Research Centre, and in 1970 established an Information Exchange Centre for federally supported university research.

NATIONAL SERIALS DATA PROGRAM. Established on 17th April 1972 in the U.S.A. as Phase 3 of a co-ordinated effort to implement a system for identifying and controlling serial publications. Its immediate concern was to develop a corporate authority file (a serials data base) to take into consideration the various authorities used by the three National Libraries (Library of Congress, National Library of Medicine, National Agricultural Library); the assignment of ISSNs to prospective periodical titles published in the U.S.A. from 1971 onwards and listed in *New Serial Titles*, and assigning ISSNs to titles in science and technology mentioned in Bowker cumulations. Phase 1 resulted in the identification of data elements needed for the control of serials by machine methods and the development of the MARC (*q.v.*) serials format. Phase 2 was the creation of a machine-readable file of live serial titles in science and technology and the production of a variety of listings. In April 1972 it became the U.S. national centre for ISDS (*q.v.*), and assumed responsibility for allocating International Standard Serial Numbers. *See also* ISSN. Abbreviated NSDP.

NATIONAL STANDARD REFERENCE DATA SYSTEM. *See* NSRDS.

NATIONAL TECHNICAL INFORMATION SERVICE. *See* NTIS.

NATIONAL UNION CATALOG, THE. The National Union Catalog, *a cumulative author list* represents Library of Congress printed cards and titles reported by other American libraries. It commenced publication in 1948. The sequence of printed catalogues is as follows: *A catalog of books represented by Library of Congress printed cards issued to July 31, 1942* (167 vols.). *Supplement: cards issued August 1, 1942–December 31, 1947* (42 vols.), 1948. *Library of Congress author catalog; a cumulative list of works represented by Library of Congress printed cards, 1948–1952* (24 vols.), 1953. *Library of Congress catalog – books: authors, 1953–June 1956.* This was continued under the title *National union catalog: a cumulative author list representing Library of Congress printed cards and titles reported by other American libraries 1953–1957* (28 vols.), 1961. These volumes include one on music and phonorecords and one on motion pictures and film strips. This series was continued by one covering the years 1958–1962 and published in 1963; it comprised 54 volumes including two on music and two on motion pictures. This series is continuing with at least four volumes each year, being cumulations of monthly parts which are also cumulated quarterly. Meanwhile a series was published with the title *National union catalog, 1952–1955 imprints* (30 vols.), a similar author list, in 1961. The *National union catalog, pre-1956 imprints* began publication in 1968. The *Library of Congress catalog – books: subjects* began publication in 1950; 1950–1954 (20 vols., 1955); 1955–1959 (22 vols., 1960); 1960–1964 (25 vols., 1965); and then annually with a minimum of three volumes per annum. The publication of the *National union catalog of manuscript collections* was begun in 1959; these volumes contain descriptions of manuscript collections in over 660 archives, libraries and other institutions throughout the U.S.

NATIONAL UNION CATALOG OF MANUSCRIPT COLLEC-TIONS. A grant (the first of several) from the Council on Library Resources in 1959 enabled a commencement to be made on a large co-operative project to produce and bring together in a central file printed catalogue cards presenting uniform descriptions of some 24,000 manuscript collections in about ninety participating libraries and archives, and of some 3,000 collections in the Library of Congress.

Cards are available for purchase. The first volume covering the years 1959–61 was published in 1961 and the second covering 1962, in 1964; these consist of reproductions of cards published in the years mentioned. A cumulated index volume to the first and second volumes was also published in 1964. Abbreviated NUCMC.

NATIS. Abbreviation for National Information Systems, the formation of which in most countries is being encouraged; these encompass all services involved in the provision of information for all sectors of the community and for all categories of users. The objectives for the establishment of NATIS were discussed at the Intergovernmental Conference on the Planning of National Overall Documentation, Library and Archives Infrastructures which was attended by representatives from eighty-six countries in September 1974 when held in Paris. Its proposals were approved at the eighteenth session of the General Conference of Unesco held in Paris in October and November 1974 with a view to encouraging the creation, development or improvement of documentation, library and archives infrastructures in its Member States. The NATIS concept implies that national, state or local governments should maximize the availability of all relevant information through these services. At a meeting with FID, IFLA and ICA, held in April 1975, Unesco's Department of Documentation, Libraries and Archives asked these non-governmental organizations to make proposals for Unesco's long-term programme for NATIS, in consequence of which an *ad hoc* NATIS Working Group was formed.

NATURAL CLASSIFICATION. One in which qualities which are essential to the existence of the thing or things to be divided is adopted as the 'difference' (*see* PREDICABLES, FIVE) or characteristic of arrangement. One which exhibits the inherent properties of the things classified, and which groups or separates them according to their likeness or unlikeness. *See also* ARTIFICIAL CLASSIFICATION, CHARACTERISTIC OF A CLASSIFICATION.

NATURAL ENVIRONMENT RESEARCH COUNCIL. *See* NERC.

NATURAL LANGUAGE. (*Information retrieval. Indexing*). 1. A language the rules of which reflect current usage without being specifically prescribed. 2. The language of the documents indexed. *See also* ARTIFICIAL INDEXING LANGUAGE; INDEXING LANGUAGE.

NAUTICAL ALMANAC. A publication which tabulates the position of the sun, moon, planets and navigational stars for each date at any time of day or night.

NEAR PRINT. A general term for substitute printing processes, the basic techniques being typewriter composition and offset printing. *See also* JUSTOWRITER which is an example of this method.

NEAT LINE. A line, usually a GRID (*q.v.*) or GRATICULE (*q.v.*) bounding the borders of a map.

NEBITYPE. A slug-casting machine first made in 1958 in Italy for setting display matter. Linotype/Intertype and Ludlow matrices as well as Nebimats (the special Nebitype matrices) may be used to cast type from 6- to 72-point to a measure of 42 ems.

NECK. *Synonymous with* BEVEL (*q.v.*).

NEDERLANDS INSTITUUT VOOR DOCUMENTATIE EN REGISTRATUUR. *See* NIDER.

NEED TO KNOW. A basic principle of security which restricts access to classified documents and information to those whose duties make such access essential, no person being permitted to have access merely by virtue of rank or appointment.

NEEDLEWORK BINDING. *Synonymous with* EMBROIDERED BINDING (*q.v.*).

NEGATIVE. 1. In photographing with a camera, a negative image normally results when a film is developed; in this the tones are reversed black being white and vice versa. A positive print, in which the tones are again reversed and then seen as with the naked eye, can be produced from the negative either by contact or by enlargement. By reversal developing, positive pictures can be obtained direct; this principle is commonly used in colour photography. 2. A transparent photographic film on which the image and the light values are reversed. 3. In some forms of documentary reproduction negatives are made on paper, and positives (prints with normal image and light values) are made from these. In some cases the light values, but not the image, are in reverse; these 'white on black' prints are called 'readable negatives'. 4. In printing, reversed image and light values appear on half-tone blocks of illustrations, and these stand in the same relationship to the resulting print as do negatives in the ordinary photographic or documentary reproduction process.

NEGATIVE PROCESS. The opposite of POSITIVE PROCESS (*q.v.*). *See also* NEGATIVE.

NEGATIVE SELECTION. *Synonymous with* WEEDING (*q.v.*).

NEIGHBOURHOOD INFORMATION CENTERS. A project carried out between 1971 and 1974 at five major public library systems in the U.S.A. (Houston, Detroit, Cleveland, Atlanta and Queens Borough) and partly funded by a federal grant. Reports on the results indicate that the INFORMATION AND REFERRAL SERVICE (*q.v.*) which is the basis of the work is best carried out by libraries and that the demand for it is overwhelming. Abbreviated NIC.

NELINET. Abbreviation for New England Library Information Network, a computer-assisted centre for centralized technical processing. The initial collaborators were the university libraries of Connecticut, Maine, Massachusetts, New Hampshire, Rhode Island and Vermont.

NEMROC. Abbreviation for NEWCASTLE MEDIA RESOURCES ORGANIZING COMMITTEE (*q.v.*).

NEO-CAROLINE. *Synonymous with* HUMANISTIC HAND (*q.v.*).

NEO-GROTESQUE. A group of LINEALE (*q.v.*) type faces derived from the GROTESQUE (*q.v.*) group compared with which they have less contrast in the thickness of the strokes, and are more regular in design. The ends of the curved strokes are usually oblique and the g often has an open tail. Of such are Edeh/Wotan, Helvetica and Univers.

NET BOOK. One which is subject to the Standard Conditions of Sale of Net Books which are set out in the Net Book Agreement, 1957, which stipulates that a book shall not be sold at less than the 'net' price stated by the publisher other than in certain circumstances (e.g. to libraries) licensed by the Council of the Publishers Association.

NET BOOK AGREEMENT. An agreement drawn up in 1929 (and revised in 1957) between the Publishers Association, the Booksellers Association, and the Library Association, enabling rate-supported libraries and other libraries admitting the public without charge throughout the usual opening hours to receive a discount of 10 per cent on all new books purchased, provided the library applies for a licence. In consequence of the Library Association becoming a professional association it has discontinued its functions under the Library Licence Agreement, and handed them over to the authorities responsible for public libraries and for libraries in universities and colleges.

NETWORK.† A bookbinding design made of intersecting lines forming squares set lozengewise.

NEUTRALITY. In subject cataloguing, a situation in which user preference cannot influence one course over another because it is unascertainable or because it does not exist. Catalogues of general libraries are mostly neutral in this sense whereas those in special libraries may reflect the viewpoints of a homeogeneous clientele.

NEW-BOOK CARD. A temporary main entry catalogue card, made on a coloured card, and inserted in the catalogue until a permanent card is ready. This is often done when the regular entries are printed cards issued by a central cataloguing agency.

NEW-BOOK NUMBER. A temporary number assigned to a book which it is desired should be circulated before it is catalogued because it is in great demand or because of temporary shortage of staff. The number is from a special sequence, or preceded by some symbol, as: N.B., and the book is catalogued and finally processed subsequently. A temporary main entry is used in the catalogue.

NEW CLASSIFICATION SOCIETY. Formed in 1964 to study the principles of classification in its widest connotation, i.e. as applied to any subject, whether documentation, soil science, mathematics, etc.

NEW EDITION. An issue of a book in which misprints noticed in an earlier edition have been corrected. The BS 4719 : 1971 *Title leaves of a book* states that in current publishing practice, reprints which are made a substantial number of years after the original edition are regarded as new editions, and that a new edition is created when the type is re-set even if the text remains the same as in the earlier edition, but that such cases are best described as '2nd (etc.) edition re-set'. *See also* EDITION, FIRST EDITION, IMPRESSION, ISSUE, REPRINT, REVISED EDITION.

NEW ENGLAND DEPOSIT LIBRARY, INC. A storage library (1,500,000 volumes) opened on 2 March 1942, housing books in three types of rental storage: (a) material classed as permanent with books available on request, the largest depositor being Harvard University Library which sends part of its current additions to store, (b) temporary and (c) 'dead' stock; (b) and (c) are not available for general use. A union catalogue is maintained, and the books stored are available for loan to member libraries, and, with the permission of the owning library, to the inter-lending system. The large windowless storage warehouse is owned and operated by seven libraries – Massachusetts State Library, Massachusetts Institute of Technology, Massachusetts Historical Society, Boston Public Library, Boston Athenaeum, Boston University and Harvard University Library – each paying rent for the space occupied in order to cover operating costs. The scheme was proposed in 1937. Abbreviated NEDL.

NEW ENGLAND DOCUMENT CONSERVATION CENTER. Aims to administer and supervise a workshop having the necessary facilities and staff to restore, preserve and maintain the physical condition of documentary materials of historic, archival or cultural interest. The services and facilities of the Center are available to libraries and archival agencies of various kinds on an 'at cost' basis. The Center is operated by the co-operative action of a number of library organizations in New England, and is situated at North Andover, Massachusetts.

NEW ENGLAND LIBRARY INFORMATION NETWORK. *See* NELINET.

NEW IMPRESSION. *See* Impression.

NEW YORK TIMES INFORMATION BANK. An on-line inter-active information retrieval system; it was introduced to take over the work of the paper's morgue (a cuttings file of approximately 20 million items). In January 1968 *The Times Index* began computer-assisted production; all the indexing, abstracting, and editing continues to be done by trained personnel, but many arduous clerical and production functions were taken over by computers. The semi-monthly *Index*, cumulated annually, continues to be published.

NEW ZEALAND LIBRARY ASSOCIATION (INCORPORATED). A society incorporated by Act of Parliament in 1939 (The New Zealand Library Association Act 1939). Founded at a conference held in Dunedin in March 1910 as the Libraries Association of New Zealand. At a conference in 1935 the name was changed to New Zealand Library Association, and a new constitution adopted; this allowed among other things the formation of Branches and Sections. Abbreviated NZLA. Publishes *New Zealand Libraries* (6 p.a.), *Newsletter* (m. to membs.).

NEWARK CHARGING SYSTEM. An American method of recording book issues whereby the book cards are inscribed with the borrower's number and dated, so becoming the time record. The reader possesses a membership card which he retains whether he borrows books or not, and which enables him to borrow an unlimited number of books from any library in a system. *See also* DETROIT SELF-CHARGING SYSTEM.

NEWBERRY LIBRARY. A free reference library established in Chicago, Illinois, U.S.A., in 1887 and maintained by a moiety of the estate of Walter Loomis Newberry (1804–68), a Chicago merchant. This bequest is supplemented by subsequent gifts and by the continuing programme of the Newberry Library Associates. The stock totals 900,000 volumes on many subjects but mainly the humanities, certain subjects being relatively unrepresented by agreement with the Chicago Public Library and the John Crerar Library. The Library is particularly strong on Americana, American Indians, history of printing, Western Europe, Great Britain until the early twentieth century, Latin America, Portuguese discoveries and music, and there are treasures in each of the subject divisions. The first Librarian was William Frederick Poole (1887–95), compiler of *Poole's index to periodical literature, 1802–81*, 2 vols.

NEWBERY MEDAL. An Award instituted by Frederic G. Melcher, administered by the Children's Services Division of the American Library Association, and awarded annually to the author of the most distinguished contribution to American literature for children, but may be by an author of any nationality or race. Named after John Newbery (1713–67) the famous British publisher of St. Paul's Churchyard who was the first to publish books for children; he was part-author of some of the best of those he published. The medal was first awarded (in 1922) to Hendrik Willem Van Loon for *The story of mankind*.

NEWCASTLE MEDIA RESOURCES ORGANISING COMMITTEE. Founded in 1972 to foster local co-operation among librarians and educational technologists. An objective is the compilation of a data sheet to list all media resources. Abbreviated NEMROC.

NEWCOTT–CALDEBERRY LUNCHEON. A low-priced luncheon held during the American Library Association Midwinter meeting to raise funds to benefit deserving causes, enable those attending to have some fun and celebrate books not previously honoured. The Luncheon was first organized in 1972, taking place at Chicago; the Newcott Award went to Louise Fitzhugh for *Harriet the Spy* (Harper 1964) and the Caldeberry Award to Oliver Kirkpatrick for *Noja the Snake and Magnus the Mongoose: a Jamaican folktale* (Doubleday 1970). The awards (for the Newcott, a green notebook and pen, and for the Caldeberry, a cheque for the cost of the winner's lunch) were made on the basis of personal taste and experience with children.

NEWS BULLETIN. An announcement, or statement, of news, relating to the health of an important person, or of general and miscellaneous items of news. In a bibliothecal context, a digest of current news concerning or relating to the work of members or users of a special library's organization. It is usually prepared daily and is issued to key personnel, or, more generally, widely distributed.

NEWSBOOK. A publication printed in a small 4to volume of up to twenty-four pages, and containing news. Newsbooks were first published in 1622, being dated and numbered, and although calling themselves 'weekly', were published at irregular intervals and never on a fixed day of the week. They contained all kinds of news from all over the world but were strictly forbidden to print home news. They were not numbered until 1641 and dealt almost exclusively with the *Thirty Years War*. Their publication was considerably diminished after the outbreak of the Great Rebellion towards the end of 1641, and ceased in 1642. At first they comprised one sheet of quarto, and later two.

Variously called Diurnall, Mercurius Intelligence. *See also* CORANTO, RELATION.

NEWSLETTER. 1. A manuscript report of current happenings, written for special subscribers and issued irregularly or weekly in the sixteenth and seventeenth centuries. 2. A similar report published in the seventeenth century and sometimes set in scriptlike type and imitating the appearance of the earlier manuscript newsletter. 3. A brief publication conveying news. Frequently issued by societies or business organizations.

NEWSOM REPORT. *Half Our Future: a report of the Central Advisory Council for Education* 1963, so named after the Chairman, Mr. (later Sir) John Newsom. It was concerned with the education of children aged 13 to 16 years of age and of average, or less than average, ability.

NEWSPAPER. A publication issued periodically, usually daily or weekly, containing the most recent news. The word 'newspaper' was first used in 1670. Previously the word was CORANTO and later NEWSBOOK (*qq.v.*).

NEWSPAPER FILE. *See* STICK 2.

NEWSPAPER LIBRARY. A collection of reference books, pamphlets, reports, press cuttings and government publications provided to serve the needs of the staff of a daily newspaper.

NEWSPAPER RACK. A fitting for displaying newspapers. Also called 'Newspaper stand'.

NEWSPAPER ROD. *See* STICK 2.

NEWSPAPER STACK. Shelving designed to accommodate bound newspapers in which they lie flat.

NEWSPAPER STAND. A fitting on which one or more newspapers are displayed for consultation. Also called 'Newspaper rack'.

NEWSPAPER STICK. *See* STICK 2.

NEWSPRINT. The lowest grade of paper: it is made mostly from wood pulp and used for newspapers.

NEWSROOM. The department of a library in which current newspapers may be read. *See also* MAGAZINE ROOM.

NICK. The groove which is cut on the BELLY of a piece of movable type. Its purpose is to enable the compositor to set type the right way up without looking at the face of the type, and also (by reason of the position and number of nicks for each type size and face) to know immediately when a wrong SORT (*q.v.*) has come to hand. Also called 'Groove'. *See also* BODY.

NICKEL-FACED STEREO. A stereo which is given a facing of nickel in order to lengthen its effective life.

NICKELTYPE. An ELECTROTYPE (*q.v.*) which is faced with nickel instead of copper. (American.)

NICKNAME. A fanciful appellation given by others, in addition to, or in place of, a proper name, as, for example, Scaramouche to Tiberio Fiorella. Also called 'Byname,' 'Sobriquet'.

NICKNAME INDEX. A list of 'nicknames', or popular names, for places, persons, official reports, laws or organizations and giving the full, proper, or official names or titles. It is usually arranged alphabetically.

NIDER. Acronym for Nederlands Instituut voor Documentatie en Registratuur (Netherlands Institute for Documentation and Filing). Founded in the Netherlands in 1921 to promote documentation and co-operative action in its application, to disseminate knowledge about documentation, and to bring together all organizations and individuals concerned with this subject and to encourage their collaboration. It (a) works in close association with the Dutch Patent Office situated in the same building; (b) maintains a library covering documentation and related fields; (c) conducts an interlibrary loan service; (d) provides a documentary reproduction service; and (e) gives advice on library administration. Publishes *Tidjdschrift voor Efficientie en Documentatie* (m.) in association with the Nederlands Instituut voor Efficientie and Nederlandse Vereniging van Bedÿfsarchivarissen.

NIGER MOROCCO. Leather produced on the banks of the River Niger from native-tanned goatskin. Often abbreviated to 'Niger'.

NIGERIAN LIBRARY ASSOCIATION. Founded as the West African Library Association in August 1953 as an outgrowth of the Unesco Seminar on the Development of Public Libraries in Africa; it was superseded by the Ghana Library Association, and the Nigeria Library Association in 1963. Abbreviated NLA. Publishes *Nigerian Libraries* (3 a year), *NLA Newsletter* (membs. only).

nihil obstat. (*Lat.* 'nothing hinders'). Sanction for publication given by a Roman Catholic censor and usually found on the verso of the title-page or the following leaf.

NINETY-ONE RULES. A cataloguing code comprising ninety-one rules which was compiled at the instigation, and with the guidance, of Sir Anthony Panizzi, as a guide to cataloguing the printed books in the British Museum. It was the first major code for the consistent cataloguing of books, and set the pattern for good cataloguing practice. It was approved by the Trustees of the British Museum in 1839 and was published in 1841.

NIPPER.   *Synonymous with* BUMPER (*q.v.*).

No.   Abbreviation for number (*It.* 'numero.'). *Pl.* Nos.

'NO CONFLICT' POLICY.   The policy of adopting new cataloguing rules only when they do not conflict with existing headings in the catalogue. Also called 'Superimposition' policy.

NO DATE.   Abbreviation: n.d. Indicates that the date of publication is not known. If the book bears no indication of date of publication but this has been obtained from bibliographical or other sources, it is expressed in a bibliographical or catalogue entry within [ ]. The Chapter 6 revision to *AACR* (North American and British Texts) provides that an approximate date should be given within [ ]; also that if the place of publication is uncertain the probable place is given in [ ], but that if no probable place of publication can be given, the name of the country, state, province, or other jurisdiction may be given. If no place whatever can be given, the abbreviation [s.l.] (*sine loco*) is to be used. If the name of a publisher is unknown the abbreviation [s.n.] (*sine nomine*) is used.

NO MORE PUBLISHED.   A phrase used in a note to a catalogue entry for a work which was intended to be published in several volumes but the publication of which was not completed.

NO PLACE.   *See* NO DATE.

NO PUBLISHER.   *See* NO DATE.

NOC.   Abbreviation for Notation of Content. *See* KWOC.

NODIS CASTER.   A small, simple and versatile type-casting machine in which Monotype, Linotype and Intertype, as well as the Nodis, matrices may be used.

NOISE.   1. In information retrieval, items selected in a search which do not contain the information desired, or items delivered by a search through accidental code combinations (*Taube*). 2. An undesirable signal which disturbs the desired signal in a communication network (*IBM*). *See also* FALSE DROP.

NOM DE PLUME.   *Synonymous with* PSEUDONYM (*q.v.*).

NOMENCLATURE.   A system of names for a system of classes, or classification; its terms.

NON-BOOK MATERIALS.†   Those library materials which do not come within the definition of a book, periodical or pamphlet and which require special handling, e.g. audio-visual materials, vertical file materials and similar items, and are not individually cata-logued. *Non-book materials cataloguing rules: an integrated code of practice and draft revision of the Anglo-American Cataloguing Rules (British Text), Part III* – the LA/NCET rules – prepared by the

Media Cataloguing Rules Committee, was published in 1973 by the Library Association jointly with the National Council for Educational Technology as NCET Working Paper No. 11. This publication, which represented the first authoritative attempt in the U.K. to formulate integrated rules for the catalogue description of non-book materials currently in use, was subsequently submitted to the authors of the Anglo-American Cataloguing Rules Committee as a proposal for the reorganization of Part III of *AACR*. Abbreviated NBM. These rules are frequently referred to as LA/NCET Rules, sometimes as LANCET. *Nonbook materials: the organization of integrated collections*, prepared by a joint committee of the CLA/ALA/AECT/ EMAC/CAML, was published by the Canadian Library Association in 1973. It is known as the 'Canadian manual'. *See also* ISBD, NON-PRINT MATERIALS.

NON-COUNTY BOROUGH. Frequently used, when differentiating between the various forms of local government in England and Wales, to indicate boroughs which were not 'county boroughs'. In the Public Libraries and Museums Act of 1964, the councils of the London boroughs are referred to but these have the same local government powers as boroughs in respect of libraries but not in respect of education; previously boroughs in the area of the London County Council were known as 'Metropolitan boroughs'. *See also* BOROUGH COUNCIL, COUNTY BOROUGH COUNCIL, LIBRARY AUTHORITY, LOCAL GOVERNMENT BOUNDARIES.

NON-CURRENT RECORDS. (*Archives*) Those which are no longer required by current business and which can therefore be appraised for preservation in an archival depository, or destroyed.

NON-DISTINCTIVE TITLE. One that is common to many serials, e.g. *Bulletin, Journal, Proceedings, Transactions*.

NON-EXPRESSIVE NOTATION. *See* NOTATION.

NON-FICTION. Books that are not prose fiction.

NON-LINING FIGURES. (*Printing*) Arabic numerals which have ascenders and descenders. Also called 'Hanging figures', OLD STYLE FIGURES (*q.v.*).

NON NET. A book usually a school text, likely to be sold in large numbers at one time which is not subject to the minimum selling price of the Net Book Agreement. *See also* NET BOOK.

NON-PARLIAMENTARY PUBLICATIONS. Those published by HMSO but which are not PARLIAMENTARY PUBLICATIONS (*q.v.*). Prior to about 1925 when this heading began to be used in HMSO catalogues, such publications were known as 'Official Publications' or

'Stationery Office Publications'. These can be roughly grouped into (a) Statutory Instruments, (b) Reports, (c) other publications. Statutory Instruments are government orders or regulations made by a Minister under the authority of a specific Act of Parliament. They are numbered according to the calendar year in which they are made, a new sequence beginning each year. Prior to 1948 they were known as Statutory Rules and Orders. 'Reports' include a variety of departmental, committee and working party reports which are prepared for submission to, or for the information of, Parliament. 'Other publications' include the immense range of publications which are issued by HMSO.

NON-PERIODICAL. A publication which is published at one time, or at intervals, in complete, usually numbered, volumes, the total number of volumes being generally determined in advance.

NON-PRINT MATERIALS. *Standards for cataloguing non-print materials*, 3rd ed. 1972, was published by the (American) Association for Educational Communications and Technology (AECT) it having been prepared by the Information Science Committee of that body. The earlier standards were published in 1968 and 1971. *See also* NON-BOOK MATERIALS.

NON-RELIEF TYPE. Engraved or incised type in which the printing surface is not the character but the type-face around the incised character. This results in a white letter on a printed background.

NON-RESIDENT MEMBER. A person who is permitted to use a library in a district other than the one in which he resides, by paying a subscription, or because he owns property in, is employed in, or studies in, the district.

NON-SEMANTIC CODE. In information retrieval, one in which the notation does not carry meaningful information beyond that which is inherent in the spelling of the word in the source language for which it stands as the equivalent. *See also* SEMANTIC CODE.

non. seq. Abbreviation for *non sequitur* (*Lat.* 'it does not follow logically').

NON-STRUCTURAL NOTATION. *See* STRUCTURAL NOTATION.

NON-THESIS EDITION. A work published commercially as well as in thesis form. A catalogue entry has a note 'issued also as thesis' followed by the name of the university concerned.

NONESUCH PRESS. A publishing house founded in 1923 in London by Miss Vera Mendel with Francis Meynell to supervise book production and David Garnett to publish fine editions of scholarly works to be sold at modest prices through normal trade channels. After a period of inactivity during the Second World War production was resumed in 1953 with the Nonesuch Shakespeare in four volumes. Nearly all the books were machine set by various printers but were designed by Meynell. Many 'Monotype' matrices were specially designed for this Press. The press publishes its own books but does not do the actual printing.

NONET. A combination of nine singers or musicians; the music for same.

NONPAREIL. 1. An out-of-date name for a type size of about 6 point. 2. A 6-point lead.

NORDFORSK. Abbreviation for Nordiska Samarbetsorganisationen för Teknisk-Naturvetenskapelig Forening – Scandinavian Council for Applied Research (formerly referred to as SCAR). Founded jointly by Iceland, Denmark, Finland, Norway and Sweden on 4th June 1947 to promote and organize co-operation in the field of scientific and industrial research and in the utilization of research results in the five countries. Members: scientific and industrial research councils and academies of engineering sciences in the countries concerned. Has a special committee on technical information – Scandinavian Committee for Technical Information Services (NORDinfo) – which acts as a policy-formulating body. Publishes *Scandinavian Research Projects* (q.), *Scandinavian Research Information Notes* (2 p.a.), etc.

NORMAL FILE. (*Information retrieval*) A file in which each item relates to one document.

NORMAN TOMLINSON AWARD. *See* TOMLINSON AWARD, NORMAN.

NORTH MIDLAND LIBRARY ASSOCIATION. Formed in March 1890, and covering the counties of Nottingham, Derby, Leicester, Northampton and Lincoln. It became a Branch of the Library Association in 1929 and was known as the North Midland Branch of the Library Association until 1970 when it was changed to East Midland Branch.

NORTH WESTERN BRANCH. A Branch of the Library Association. Founded in 1896 at Manchester. The 'Librarians of the Mersey District' had been formed in 1887 but was disbanded in 1905 to become absorbed in the Branch. The aims of the Branch are the same as those of the LA which makes a capitation grant for expenses. Membership entitlement is residence or employment in the North Western geographical area, comprising Lancashire, Cheshire, the metropolitan counties of Merseyside and Greater Manchester, and the Isle of Man. Abbreviated LANW. Publishes *North Western Newsletter* (m.) and occasional books and booklets. *See also* C.N. AWARD.

NORTHERN BRANCH. A Branch of the Library Association, all members of which who live or work in the counties of Cleveland, Cumbria, Durham, Northumberland, and the Metropolitan County of Tyne and Wear, automatically become members.

NORTHERN IRELAND BRANCH. A branch of the LIBRARY ASSOCIATION (*q.v.*) formed in 1929. It is now associated with the LIBRARY ASSOCIATION OF IRELAND (*q.v.*) in the joint publication of *An Leabharlann* (q.).

NORTHERN LIBRARIES COLLOQUY. An international group of librarians, archivists and information specialists representing libraries and institutions of all kinds either located in the Arctic or Sub-Arctic or physically in milder latitudes but whose interests are wholly polar. Formed in June 1971, in which year the first of the annual colloquies was held; the organization publishes *Northern Libraries Bulletin* (2/3 p.a. free to members) and has published a *Directory of northern libraries*. Financed by the annual colloquy fees, and based on the Scott Polar Research Institute, Cambridge, England.

NORWEGIAN LIBRARY ASSOCIATION. (Norsk Bibliotekforening (NBF).) Originally founded in 1913, in 1972 the four Norwegian professional library associations combined to form one body which unites all types of library. Aims: to provide the Norwegian library system in general. Membership is open to individuals and institutions. The Association comprises four sections: 1. special and research librarians; 2. public librarians; 3. part-time librarians; 4. public and school librarians. Two groups exist, one for outreach activities, the other for work with children and young people.

NOT. A FINISH (*q.v.*) given to good quality rag papers – not glazed or hot pressed. Those with no finish are called 'rough'; 'not' is less rough but 'not-smooth'. *See also* HOT-PRESSED, MACHINE GLAZED, ROUGH.

NOTATION. 1. The symbols which stand for the divisions in a scheme of classification. The purposes of notation are (a) to mechanize the order of headings in a scheme of classification, (b) to serve as a shorthand sign for the easy arrangement of documents on shelves or in drawers or files, and also for entries in respect of them in catalogues and indexes (the alternative to which would possibly be cumbersome and not easy-to-remember sequences of words), and (c) to provide easily memorized links between catalogues and the storage position of documents. Symbols must be brief and easily extended. If the notation consists of two or more kinds of symbols it is called a 'mixed notation'; if of one kind only, a 'pure notation'. The notation may be expressive or non-expressive. Expressive notation reveals the hierarchical structure of the classification scheme, in addition to mechanizing the order of the headings. The notation must be (a) hospitable, i.e. enable symbols for additional subject to be added at any position, (b) easily comprehensible, i.e. consisting only of roman letters and/or arabic numbers, and (c) easily memorized, written and spoken. A 'flexible notation' is one which expands with the classification, and permits the insertion of new subjects without any dislocation. 2. In information retrieval, a symbolism which is not in natural language but humanly legible, as distinct from CODING (*q.v.*). 3. An arbitrary device to indicate the contents or location of a document (*IBM*). 4. In machine searching as part of information retrieval, the designation of a particular set of symbols used to represent a code; the physical representation of a code. *See Also* GRAPHIC LENGTH, HIERARCHICAL NOTATION, LABELLED NOTATION, PHONIC LENGTH, PRONOUNCEABLE NOTATION, STRUCTURAL NOTATION, SYLLABIC NOTATION.

NOTATIONAL PLANE. (*Classification*) The plane of symbols representing concepts.

NOTCHED CARDS. *Synonymous with* MARGINAL-HOLE PUNCHED CARDS (*q.v.*).

NOTE. 1. An explanation of the text of a book or additional matter, appearing usually with other notes at the foot of a page, at the end of a chapter or at the end of the book. Where numbers are not used to separate and distinguish the notes, REFERENCE MARKS (*q.v.*) are used in a recognized sequence. Also called FOOTNOTE (*q.v.*). 2. A concise statement, following particulars of collation in a catalogue or bibliographical entry, giving added information such as the name of the series, contents, or bibliographical information. The term is sometimes limited to the information which appears below the collation and the main body of an entry. Notes should only be made to supply significant additional data in order to amplify a catalogue entry or be helpful to a reader. *See also* FACET INDICATOR, FACETED NOTATION, FENCE, HIERARCHICAL NOTATION, INTERCALATION DEVICE, RETRO-ACTIVE NOTATION.

NOTHING BEFORE SOMETHING. Alphabetizing 'word by word', counting the space between one word and the next as 'nothing'. *See also* ALPHABETIZATION. A word files before another word having the same letters plus additional ones, these additional ones being considered 'something'.

NOTION. In co-ordinate indexing, an ENTITY (*q.v.*) or an ATTRIBUTE (*q.v.*).

NOTTINGHAM AND NOTTINGHAMSHIRE TECHNICAL SERVICE. *See* NANTIS.

NOUN ORDER. (*Information retrieval*) An order of nouns in a compound heading, the order being determined by one of several rules, e.g. concrete – process (*see* CONCRETES AND PROCESSES) by using OPERATORS (*q.v.*) or by using facet citation chains.

NOVEL. A long fictitious story of imaginary people and events.

NOVELA. A short prose narrative, generally with a structural centre represented by a surprising event. It requires a simple subject matter and disdains episodes.

NOVELETTE. A short novel.

NOVELIST. One who writes novels.

NOVELTY. (Copyright) The quality of a new INTELLECTUAL WORK (*q.v.*).

NOWELL AWARD. *See* C.N. AWARD.

NOYES AWARD, MARCIA C. This Award consists of a silver tray, and is given, not necessarily every year, to a medical librarian, anywhere in the world, for outstanding achievement in his chosen field. It was first awarded in 1953, to Mary Louise Marshall.

NUFFIELD TALKING BOOK LIBRARY FOR THE BLIND. *See* NTBL.

NUMBER. 1. A single numbered or dated issue of a periodical or serial publication. 2. One of the numbered fascicules of a literary, artistic or musical work issued in instalments, ordinarily in paper wrappers, and called 'number' by the publisher. 3. In extended vocal works such as cantatas, oratorios and operas (especially the latter), one of the distinct and separate sections into which the composition is divided, each of which is complete in itself and in a specific form, such as aria, duet, chorus. 4. Any item in the programme of a concert or other entertainment. *See also* OPUS NUMBER.

NUMBER BUILDING. (*Classification*) The process of making a number more specific by adding segments taken from other parts of the classification.

NUMBERED AND SIGNED EDITION. An edition of a work the copies of which are numbered, and signed by the author. *See also* LIMITED EDITION.

NUMBERED COLUMN. Where the text of a book is printed in two or more columns to a page, and these instead of the pages are numbered consecutively. Where this is done a note to this effect normally appears at the head of the index.

NUMBERED COPY. A copy of a limited edition of a book which bears the copy number, usually on the page facing the title-page.

NUMBERED ENTRY. One of the entries in a printed bibliography or catalogue in which the entries are numbered consecutively.

NUMBERING. Placing (a) the call number on the spine of, or (b) the charging symbol in, a library book.

NUMERAL. A graphic symbol or character to represent a number or a group of numbers. A figure. See also ARABIC FIGURES, HANGING FIGURES, RANGING FIGURES, ROMAN NUMERALS.

NUMERALS. The correct printer's term for the figures and fractions.

NUMERATION. (*Cataloguing*) A number, roman or arabic, appearing in a heading, indicating the sequence of the person (as e.g. monarchs bearing the same forename) or another element in the heading (e.g. chemical formulae), and so affecting the filing sequence. See also CHARACTER SIGNIFICANCE SEQUENCE, LOGICAL ARRANGEMENT.

NUT. See EN QUADRAT.

O.E. Abbreviation for OLD ENGLISH (*q.v.*).

OFR. Office for RESEARCH. A department of the AMERICAN LIBRARY ASSOCIATION (*q.v.*).

O.P. Abbreviation for OUT OF PRINT (*q.v.*).

O.S. Abbreviation for OUT OF STOCK (*q.v.*).

O.S. Abbreviation for ORDNANCE SURVEY (*q.v.*).

OSRD. Acronym of the (U.S.) Office for Standard Reference Data, which together with the Office of Technical Information and Publications are part of the Office for Information Programs under the NATIONAL BUREAU OF STANDARDS (*q.v.*). A primary goal of the OSRD is to establish continuing data centres in all the technical areas which fall within the scope of the Program.

OASIS. An area in a university or college library where selected students may read or undertake research. Less formal than a CARREL (*q.v.*) and more economic of space, it should be placed in a central and easily accessible position.

OBELISK. Alternative name for the dagger (†) reference mark. Similarly a double dagger (‡) is also called a 'Double obelisk'. See also REFERENCE MARKS.

OBERLY MEMORIAL AWARD, EUNICE ROCKWELL. Established in 1923, this Award consists of a citation and the biennial income (about $500) from the Eunice Rockwell Oberly Memorial Fund. The selection is made by the Oberly Memorial Award Committee of the A.C.R.L. Division of the American Library Association every two years to the American citizen who compiles the best bibliography in the field of agriculture or the related sciences in the two-year period preceding the year in which the Award is made. The Award was first made in 1925 to Max Meisel.

OBJECTIVE CLASSIFICATION. A classification of the sciences according to the attributes of the relative scientific subjects.

OBLONG. 1. Of a book that is wider than its height. Hence oblong folio, oblong quarto. This is the result of folding a sheet of paper across the long way (i.e. halving the short side). Also called 'Cabinet size', 'Landscape', 'Long'. The opposite of BROAD (*q.v.*). *See also* NARROW, SIZE, SQUARE. 2. Applies to a BROAD (*q.v.*) sheet of paper halved lengthways. A quarto size used with the longest dimension at the foot of the page, or sheet, is termed 'oblong quarto' and is the reverse of 'upright'.

OBVERSE COVER. The upper cover of a book. Also called 'Front cover'. 'Upper cover'. *See also* REVERSE COVER.

OCCUPATIONAL SAFETY AND HEALTH SCHEME. A scheme of classification compiled by D. J. Foskett for the Division of Occupational Safety and Health of the International Labour Office in Geneva and published in the *Proceedings of the International Study Conference on Classification for Information Retrieval*, 1957.

OCE. *See* AZOFLEX.

OCTAVE DEVICE. In classification, the name given by Ranganathan to a method of extending the decimal base of arabic numerals to infinity, by setting aside the figure 9 as an extender to bring in a further eight figures at the end of the first eight. The series thus reads: 1, 2, 3, 4, 5, 6, 7, 8, 91, 92, 93, 94, 95, 96, 97, 98, 991, 992, and so on, the figure 9 never being used unsupported. The figure 9 is known as the Octavizing Digit. This device, which was first used by Ranganathan in his *Colon Classification*, and adopted by the UNIVERSAL DECIMAL CLASSIFICATION (*q.v.*) in 1948, can be extended to letters, z (or any last letter of any other alphabet) being used in the same way. By this means the octave device provides hospitality in array.

OCTAVIZING DIGIT. *See* OCTAVE DEVICE.

OCTAVO (8vo). 1. A sheet of paper folded three times to form a section of eight leaves, or sixteen pages. The following size (in inches) of printing papers are usually used to produce an octavo page:

	Double	Quad	Size of 8vo
	Double	*Quad*	*Size of 8vo*
Foolscap	$13\frac{1}{2} \times 17$	17×27	27×34	$6\frac{3}{4} \times 4\frac{1}{4}$
Crown	15×20	20×30	30×40	$7\frac{1}{2} \times 5$
Large Post	$16\frac{1}{2} \times 21$	21×33	33×42	$8\frac{1}{4} \times 5\frac{1}{4}$
Demy	$17\frac{1}{2} \times 22\frac{1}{2}$	$22\frac{1}{2} \times 35$	35×45	$8\frac{3}{4} \times 5\frac{5}{8}$
Medium	18×23	23×36	36×46	$9 \times 5\frac{3}{4}$
Royal	20×25	25×40	40×50	$10 \times 6\frac{1}{4}$
Super Royal	$20\frac{1}{2} \times 27\frac{1}{2}$	$27\frac{1}{2} \times 41$	41×55	$10\frac{1}{4} \times 6\frac{7}{8}$
Imperial	22×30	30×44	44×60	$11 \times 7\frac{1}{2}$

2. A book having sections of eight leaves, or sixteen pages. 3. Any book whose height is between $6\frac{1}{4}$ and 10 inches. *See also* BOOK SIZES, PAPER SIZES.

OCTAVO EDITION. One issued in OCTAVO (*q.v.*) form.

OCTIFILM. Trademark of the Ozalid Corporation for a sheet of diazo film.

OCTODECIMO (18mo). *See* EIGHTEENMO.

ODD FOLIOS. The page-numbers which come on the first, or recto, side of each leaf, the right-hand of each OPENING (*q.v.*), 1, 3, 5, 7, 9, 11, etc.

ODD PAGE. The page of a publication bearing an odd number; the right-hand page of an OPENING (*q.v.*), and the recto of a LEAF (*q.v.*).

ODD PART. One part of a serial publication, or of a work published in a number of parts, which is separately issued and isolated from the others.

ODD SORTS. Characters not normally included in a standard fount of type. Also called 'Side sorts'. Such characters can be used on a machine which sets lines of type in SLUGS (*q.v.*) but the matrices from which they are cast must be inserted by hand in the correct position by the typesetter.

ODD VOLUME. One volume of a work in several volumes which is the only one possessed.

ODDMENTS. 1. The items of a printed book which precede and follow the text. These are known as the PRELIMINARIES (*q.v.*) and the END-MATTER (*q.v.*). 2. When the pages of a book make an exact multiple of sixteen (or thirty-two if the sections are of 32 pages) it is said to make an even working. If an odd eight pages or so are needed to complete the printing it is termed 'uneven working' and the additional pages are said to be oddments.

OESTERREICHISCHE ZEITSCHRIFT FÜR BUCH- UND BIBLIOTHEKSWESEN, DOKUMENTATION, BIBLIOGRA-PHIE UND BIBLIOPHILIE (Austrian Society for Documentation and Bibliography). Formed in 1951 to promote Librarianship, documentation, bibliography, etc. in Austria. Publishes *Biblos* (q.).

'OFF ITS FEET'. Type which has been cast in such a way that its base is not true, with the result that it does not stand firm in the galley.

OFF-LINE EQUIPMENT. (*Information retrieval*) The peripheral computer equipment, or devices, not in direct communication with a computer's central processing unit.

OFF-LINE OPERATION. (*Information retrieval*) The accomplishment of functions which are not a part of the main processing operations, such as the conversion from punched cards to magnetic tape on equipment primarily used for main processing. *See also* ON-LINE OPERATION.

OFFCUT. 1. That part of a sheet which has to be cut off after 'imposition', as in the case of a 12mo., so that the sheet may be correctly folded, the cut off piece being folded and inserted in the larger piece after folding. The cut off piece is then called an 'inset' and usually bears a signature mark to indicate its proper place in the gathering. 2. A piece cut off a sheet of paper to reduce it to the size required for a particular job. 3. Remainders of reams which have been cut down to a smaller size.

OFFICE COLLECTION. *Synonymous with* DEPARTMENTAL LIBRARY (*q.v.*).

OFFICE FOR LIBRARY EDUCATION. Set up within the American Library Association on 1st September 1966 to promote better co-ordination of the several programmes within the Association which are devoted to education for librarianship. The establishment of the Office was made possible by a grant of over $75,000 over six years (which will be matched by the ALA over the six years after which the ALA will assume complete support of the programme) from the H. W. Wilson Foundation, Inc., a charitable and educational foundation established by the late Mr. and Mrs. Halsey W. Wilson. Abbreviated OLE. This Office was abolished in 1973.

OFFICE FOR RESEARCH.† Became formally effective within the American Library Association on 1st September 1965, most of the cost of the Library Technology Project (which formed the nucleus of the Office but now discontinued), being provided by the Council on Library Resources, Inc. Abbreviated OFR.

OFFICE FOR SCIENTIFIC AND TECHNICAL INFORMATION. *See* OSTI.

OFFICE FOR STANDARD REFERENCE DATA. *See* OSRD.

OFFICE OF LIBRARIES AND LEARNING RESOURCES. One of the provisions of the (U.S.) Education Amendments of 1974 (HR 69) which became Public Law 93-380 on 21st August 1974 and amends and extends the existing Elementary and Secondary Education Act (ESEA), was the setting up of this office, the function of which is to administer all programmes related to 'libraries, information centers, and education technology'. The Office is within the U.S. Office of Education.

OFFICE OF RESEARCH IN LIBRARIANSHIP.† A non-profit-making international information service in librarianship, recording and disseminating particulars of research being undertaken. It is organized by Mr Edward R. Reid-Smith. Publishes *Research in librarianship* (irreg.).

OFFICE OF SCIENCE INFORMATION SERVICE. *See* OSIS.

OFFICE OF UNIVERSITY LIBRARY MANAGEMENT STUDIES. A major study, carried out by Booz, Allen and Hamilton for the (U.S.) Council on Library Resources, Inc., and published as *Problems in university management* in 1970, called for the creation of an office of University Library Management within the Association of Research Libraries. This was begun in 1970 with financial support from the CRL and is working with interested university libraries and by concentrating on the development of a policy or administrative manual on the use of policy as a management tool in large libraries. Abbreviated OULMS.

OFFICER. *See* LIBRARY OFFICER.

OFFICIAL CATALOGUE. A union catalogue for the use of library staff only, and usually kept in the cataloguing department.

OFFICIAL GAZETTE. A periodical publication issued by, or on behalf of, a government or university to convey official news, statements or decisions.

OFFICIAL NAME. The legal name of a corporate body, office or government department.

OFFICIAL PUBLICATION. One issued by a government or govern-ment department, it may be in a series or isolated. The Unesco Convention Concerning the Exchange of Official Publications and Government Documents between States, 1958, considered the following, when they are executed by the order and at the expense of any national governmental authority, to be official publications: parliamentary documents, reports and journals and other legislative papers; administrative publications and reports from central, federal and regional governmental bodies; national bibliographies,

State handbooks, bodies of law, decisions of the Courts of Justice; and other publications as may be agreed.

OFFICIAL TITLE. The title of a book appearing on the title-page, and which is accepted, either in whole or in part, by the cataloguer for purposes of cataloguing.

OFFPRINT. *Synonymous with* SEPARATE (*q.v.*).

OFFSET. 1. The printing process in which the impression is transferred from a litho stone or plate to a rubber-covered cylinder, and thence off-set by pressure on to the paper. *See also* OFFSET PRINTING. 2. Sometimes erroneously used to describe the unintentional transfer of ink from one sheet to another: this is correctly called 'set-off'. *See also* SLIP SHEET.

OFFSET FOIL. A printing plate used for making prints (copies of documents) by the offset process.

OFFSET LITHOGRAPHY. A method of printing in which a drawing is made on transfer paper the right way round, printed on to a rubber-covered cylinder and 'offset' on to paper. *See also* TRANSFER.

OFFSET PAPER. Paper especially made for use on an offset press. It should lie flat, be free from lint, and stretch as little as possible.

OFFSET-PHOTO-LITHOGRAPHY. *See* PHOTO-OFFSET.

OFFSET PRINTING. An adaptation of the principles of stone lithography, in which the design is drawn or reproduced upon a thin, flexible, metal plate which is curved to fit one of the revolving cylinders of the printing press; the design from this plate is transferred or 'offset' to the paper by means of a rubber blanket which runs over another cylinder and which has received its impression from the plate.

OGHAMIC CHARACTER. *See* RUNIC LETTERS.

OGHAMIC SCRIPTS. Inscriptions, peculiar to the Celtic population of the British Isles, usually found on wooden staves but sometimes also on shields or other hard material. They are also found on tombstones. Used for writing messages and letters. The alphabet consisted of twenty letters which were represented by straight or diagonal strokes varying from one to five in number and drawn, or cut, below, above or through, horizontal lines, or to the left, or right, of, or through, vertical lines.

OLA BOOKS. Books made in Ceylon from olas, or strips of young leaves of the Talipat or Palmyra palm which are soaked in hot water and pressed smooth. They are cut into strips about 3 inches wide and from 1 to 3 feet long. A cord is passed through holes pierced at the ends of each so as to secure the leaves between two lacquered wooden boards. Writing is done with an iron stylus, and the incisions made more easily readable by rubbing in a mixture of charcoal and oil. The aromatic and preservative nature of the oil is believed to have enabled the books to survive from pre-Christian days. Buddhist monks still make ola books in Ceylon. Also called 'olla books'.

OLD ENGLISH. An angular type of the black-letter group; abbreviated O.E. This is an example of Old English:

𝕿𝖍𝖎𝖘 𝖎𝖘 12 𝖕𝖔𝖎𝖓𝖙 𝕺𝖑𝖉 𝕰𝖓𝖌𝖑𝖎𝖘𝖍

OLD FACE. The majority of book types in England belong to this family of types. Its origin is generally attributed to Garamond (Paris, first half of sixteenth century) who modelled his design on the roman types of the Venetian printer Aldus Manutius which were actually cut in 1495 for Aldus by Francesco Griffo who also cut the famous Aldine italic. The Old Face group of letter is characterized by oblique emphasis, lightness of colour, comparatively small differences between thick and thin strokes and fairly substantial bracketed serifs. The capitals are slightly lower than the ascending lower case letters and the descenders are long. The modern versions of Old Face have a comparatively small X-Height (q.v.) and a narrow set. Examples are, Caslon Old Face (Stephenson Blake and others); Bembo, Fournier, Imprint, Plantin, Van Dijck (Monotype); Garamond (Monotype and Intertype). The figures of Old Face do not all stand on the line: 1234567890. The following is in 12-point Bembo:

This is BEMBO type face.

There is at present a revival of old faces, the most famous of recent years being Eric Gill's *Perpetua* which is effective and useful both as a book type, because it is narrow, (see example in TYPE FACE), and especially at titling. The term 'Garalde' has superseded 'Old face' for this category of type faces. *See also* ARABIC FIGURES, HANGING FIGURES, MODERN FACE, RANGING FIGURES, TRANSITIONAL.

OLD STYLE. A modification of OLD FACE (q.v.), the ascenders and descenders being shorter. Examples are: Old Style (Stephenson Blake); Old Style Antique (Miller & Richard); Bookprint (Linotype); Bookface (Intertype). This book is set in Plantin, an Old Face type. Old Style capitals, lower case letters and figures are as follows:
ABCDEFGHIJKLMNOPQRSTUVWXYZ
abcdefghijklmnopqrstuvwxyz 1234567890

OLD STYLE FIGURES. (*Printing*) Numerals, three of which are of x-height, the others having ascenders and descenders as in the specimen under OLD STYLE (q.v.). Also called 'Non-Lining figures'. *See also*, ARABIC FIGURES, MODERN FACE.

OLEOGRAPH. A reproduction of an oil painting, printed by lithography, mounted on canvas, sized and varnished, the irregularities of the oil painting and canvas being reproduced by an embossing process.

OLEOGRAPHY. The lithographic process used to produce an OLEO-GRAPH (*q.v.*).

OLIN BOOK NUMBER. An author number from a scheme devised by Charles R. Olin. The use of Olin Numbers enables collective biography to be separated yet to be brought into close relation at the same class number. They convert all authors' or compilers' surnames into A followed by figures, thus enabling collective biographies to be arranged before the individual biographies bearing Cutter Author Marks. The following is section S from the Table:

Sa	A77	Scr	A79	Sia	A82	Sq	A84
Sch	A78	Sea	A81	Sma	A83	Sva	A85

Strickland's *Queens of England* would be A84 (Olin number) and be arranged before a life of Queen Anne, An 7 (Cutter Author Mark). The Olin Book Numbers and the Biscoe Time Numbers were printed in the 11th, 12th and 13th editions of the Dewey Classifications.

OMISSIBLE. Something which may be omitted if required, necessary or desirable.

OMISSION MARKS. Three dots, thus . . . , used on the BASE LINE (*q.v.*) in quoted text, or a catalogue entry, to indicate that something in the original has been omitted. Also called 'Ellipsis'.

OMNIBUS BOOK. A volume containing reprints of short stories by various authors or of novels or other works by one or more authors.

OMNIBUS REVIEW. One which discusses a number of books of one type or field of literature.

ON APPROBATION. *Synonymous with* ON APPROVAL (*q.v.*).

ON APPROVAL. Applied to a transaction whereby a customer may have the opportunity of examining goods before deciding whether to purchase them, and to return same within a short specified time (for books usually three days) if he decides not to keep them. Abbreviated: on appro. 'On approbation' has the same meaning.

ON-LINE DEVICE. (*Information retrieval*) A device for data input/output directly connected to a computer.

ON-LINE EQUIPMENT. (*Information retrieval*) The peripheral computer equipment, or devices, in a system in which the operation of such equipment is under the control of the central processing unit, and in which information reflecting current activity is introduced into the data processing system as soon as it occurs; thus directly in line with the main flow of transaction processing, and receiving instructions from the computer.

ON-LINE OPERATION. (*Information retrieval*) The accomplishment of functions as part of the main processing operations. *See also* OFF-LINE OPERATION.

ON SALE. Books supplied to a bookseller under an agreement that they may be returned if unsold. Also known as 'On sale or return'. *See also* HALF SEE SAFE, SEE SAFE.

ONE PLACE INDEX. *See* SPECIFIC INDEX.

ONE PLACE THEORY. The classifying of material on various aspects of a subject at one place only.

ONE SHEET ON. *Synonymous with* ALL ALONG (*q.v.*).

ONE SHOT. 1. The reprinting in one issue of a periodical of the full text, or an abridgement, of a book, as distinct from a serialized reprint. 2. A magazine of which only one issue has been published. 3. Single issue rights, where the whole of a literary work or an abridgement of it, appears in a periodical.

ONE SIDE COLOURED. Paper or board which has been intentionally coloured during manufacture.

ONION SKIN. A thin, glazed, transparent paper.

ONLAY. A decorative panel of paper or other material glued to the cover of a book without preparing the cover to receive it. *See also* INLAY.

ONLAYING. *See* INLAY, INLAYING.

ONULP. Acronym for Ontario New Universities Library Project. A pioneer venture, initiated by the University of Toronto Library to purchase and process books centrally for five participating academic institutions.

ONYMOUS. The exact opposite of ANONYMOUS (*q.v.*).

op. cit. Abbreviation for *opere citato* (Lat. 'in the work cited'). Used in a footnote reference to avoid using the title or short title of the work referred to. It should not be used if there is more than one book by the author concerned, nor if it is over 1,000 words from the first citation, and preferably not if another book has been referred to since the first citation.

Op. no. Abbreviation for OPUS NUMBER (*q.v.*).

OPACITY. The quality of non-transparency in book papers. Creamy or off-white papers are more opaque than bright white ones, and a matt finish gives greater opacity than a glazed finish.

OPAQUE COPY. A copy of a document on opaque, or non-transparent, material.

OPAQUE MICROCOPY. A microcopy made on opaque, or non-transparent, material, usually paper or card. Also called 'Micro-opaque'.

OPAQUE PROJECTOR. A projector which can project small opaque printed images such as maps, post-cards, illustrations, photographs, pages of books, etc., but much enlarged on to screens or walls. *See also* BALOPTICON.

OPAQUING. Painting a negative with an opaque liquid to block out pin-holes and other defects, or render certain parts unprintable (*Verry*).

OPEN ACCESS. Applied to a library where readers are admitted to the shelves.

OPEN BACK. (*Binding*) *Synonymous with* HOLLOW BACK (*q.v.*).

OPEN-BACK CASE. *Synonymous with* SLIP CASE (q.v.).

OPEN BACK FILE. A box file for holding pamphlets and similar material, consisting of a five sided box the shape of a book. The sixth side (the back) is open to allow the easy insertion – and more easy removal – of material.

OPEN BAR SHELVING. Shelves consisting of a number of hollow steel bars about an inch square placed at intervals, one behind another, in place of a solid shelf. They are supported on cantilever type brackets fitting into slots, or are part of a rigid structure, and are suitable for very large and heavy volumes such as atlases and bound newspapers.

OPEN BIBLIOGRAPHY. *Synonymous with* CURRENT BIBLIOGRAPHY (*q.v.*).

OPEN EDGE. Any edge of a section of a book which is open and not enclosed by a BOLT (*q.v.*).

OPEN-ENDED. Being possessed of the quality by which the addition of new terms, subject headings, or classifications does not disturb the pre-existing system (*IBM*).

OPEN-ENDED TERM LIST. A list of terms to which, in contrast to a CONTROLLED TERM LIST (q.v.), terms may be added as required, provided that the terms in the existing list are not altered. Also called 'Open indexing system'. *See also* CLOSED INDEXING SYSTEM.

OPEN ENTRY. A catalogue entry which leaves room for the addition of information concerning a work which is in course of publication, or of which the library does not possess a complete copy or set, or concerning which complete information is lacking. Open entries usually occur in respect of serials still in course of publication, the date of the most recent issue and last volume number being omitted in the case of works in several volumes which are still in course of publication; or of living authors, in catalogues in which birth and death dates are given. Space may be left elsewhere than in the main part of the entry, e.g. in the notes, for particulars of publications or of the library's holdings. *See also* CLOSED ENTRY.

OPEN-LETTER PROOF. A proof of an engraving with the caption engraved in outline letters, whereas the finished engraving has solid letters.

OPEN LETTERS. Jobbing and display type which have the centres of the strokes of the characters incised, and so beyond the reach of the inkers; this gives the impression of white areas rather than black. Also called 'Outline letters'. *See also* INLINE LETTERS.

OPEN MATTER. Type which has been generously 'leaded'. *See also* LEADED MATTER.

OPEN ORDER. In book acquisition in North America, two types of order: (1) those made up of items listed individually, some or all of which have not been supplied, hence the orders are not closed or completed; (2) those which approximate to open requisitions, as they earmark sums of money with booksellers to be spent on a particular subject or category.

OPEN SCORE. The printed or written music for two or more voices or parts each of which is separately displayed one above another. Also called 'Extended score'. *See also* SCORE.

OPEN SHELF LIBRARY. *See* OPEN ACCESS.

OPENED. A book of which the top, fore, and sometimes bottom, edges have not been cut in manufacture but opened with a paper knife before being read.

OPENING. Two pages facing one another. *See also* CONJUGATE, DOUBLE-SPREAD.

OPERATION CODE. That part of an instruction in a computer programme designating the processing step to be performed (*IBM*).

OPERATORS. (*Classification*) Categories of relation, indicated by symbols, to mark steps of progression in analysing complex subjects. An analysis set down in this way is called an 'Analet'. *See also* RELATIONAL INDEXING (*q.v.*).

OPISTHOGRAPHIC. Applied to early-printed books printed on both sides of the paper and to manuscripts or parchments with writing on both sides. *See also* ANOPISTHOGRAPHIC PRINTING, BLOCK BOOK.

OPTICAL CHARACTER RECOGNITION. (*Information retrieval*) A technique for machine recognition of characters by their images, data being put into a computer, whereby printed characters are read directly by light-sensitive devices. Special forms of type have been designed for the purpose. Abbreviated OCR.

OPTICAL COINCIDENCE. *Synonymous with* UNITERM CONCEPT
CO-ORDINATION INDEXING (*q.v.*). *See also* BATTEN SYSTEM, CO-
ORDINATE INDEXING, PEEK-A-BOO, PEEPHOLE CARD.

OPTICAL COPYING. 1. Making a copy of a document on photographic material in the same scale, or one different from the original.
2. A print made by such a means may be called an 'optical copy'. 3. A
term used in REPROGRAPHY (*q.v.*) for a photograph made by means of
an optical system. *See also* CONTACT COPYING.

OPTICAL PHOTOCOPYING DEVICE. A machine for making 'optical copies' of an original, i.e. copies on photographic material of the
same, or a different, scale by means of an optical system.

OPTICAL PRINTER. A CONTINUOUS PRINTER (*q.v.*) for the production
of copies (prints) by optical means.

OPTICAL STENCIL CARD. A card used in information retrieval in
which holes are punched in certain positions to indicate files or documents containing particular information; a heading word is placed at
the top of the card, and is chosen from a thesaurus which is specially
compiled for the subject matter of the organization's material. Several
cards are placed together so that light can shine through the punched
holes and so indicate which files contain the information indicated by
their heading words. These cards are used in Uniterm systems. *See
also* PEEK-A-BOO, UNITERM CONCEPT CO-ORDINATION INDEXING.

OPTION. The privilege to buy rights in a manuscript or book if required.

OPTIONAL PROVISION. (*Classification*) In the Dewey Decimal
Classification, a variation from the preferred provision; it is offered
to users in the printed schedules and tables of the scheme, but not
used in centralized classification as supplied by the Library of
Congress.

OPUS ANGLICANUM. A form of split-stitch embroidery on satin;
used as a decorative binding in the fifteenth century. *See also* FABRIC
BINDING.

OPUS NUMBER. A number assigned to a musical work or collection of
works, usually in the order of composition. The numbers are assigned
by the composer or by the publisher. An opus number may refer to
one work or to a group of works of similar form and for the same
medium; each has a secondary number. Abbreviated Op. no.

OPUSCULE (*Pl.* Opuscula). 1. A lesser or minor literary or musical
work or composition. 2. A small book or treatise.

OR. Abbreviation for ORIGINAL (*q.v.*).

ORCHESTRAL MUSIC. Music in which most, if not all, of each of the instrumental parts are played by more than one performer. *See also* CHAMBER MUSIC.

ORCHESTRAL SCORE. *See* SCORE.

ORDER BOOK OF THE HOUSE OF COMMONS. *See* PARLIAMENTARY PAPERS.

ORDER CARD. The card used for recording orders placed, and later, the delivery of the material and payment for it: the official record of each individual order.

ORDER DEPARTMENT. The department of a library which deals with the ordering and sometimes processing of books and periodicals. *Also called* 'accession department', 'acquisition department'.

ORDER FILE. The file containing records of the books on order from booksellers.

ORDER INFORMATION. Data concerning the placing of orders for books and other library materials, and also of their receipt. It includes (1) entering an order, order number, date of order, name of supplier, and fund to which cost will be charged, and (2) after delivery of the goods, date of receipt, cost, and date of invoice.

ORDER LIBRARIAN. Assistant in an order department or division of a library in North America.

ORDER SECTION. *Synonymous with* ORDER DEPARTMENT (*q.v.*) except that it may be a section of another department, e.g. Cataloguing Department, rather than being an independent department.

ORDER SLIP. *See* ORDER CARD.

ORDERED FILE. (*Information Retrieval*) In mechanized systems, one in which the contents are arranged in a predetermined manner to facilitate reference.

ORDINAL NOTATION. (*Classification*) One which merely provides order and does not express hierarchical relations. *Also called* 'Non-expressive notation'. *See also* HIERARCHICAL NOTATION, NOTATION.

ORDNANCE SURVEY.† A department of the British government, founded 1791, which exists to make an accurate map survey of the British Isles. Maps of various kinds are published in scales varying from $\frac{1}{4}$ to 50 inches to a mile. Maps of Ireland were issued until April 1922, since when the governments of Eire and Northern Ireland have issued their own. Abbreviated O.S.

ORGAN-VOCAL SCORE. *See* SCORE.

ORGANIZATION FILE. A file of written or published material by or about the organization of which a special library is a part. It may include official minutes, proceedings, records and other archive material,

20

items prepared for the guidance or instruction of the staff, publicity material, information publications, etc. whether published for limited or for general distribution, periodical and newspaper articles about the organization, etc. Also called 'History file'.

ORIENT. (*Verb*) To write extracts in such a way as to meet the needs of a particular 'audience'.

ORIGINAL. 1. Finished art work (drawing, painting or photograph) as completed by the originator, and ready for reproduction. 2. In the author's own words or other original medium. 3. In the author's own language or as written by him. 4. A first copy. 5. A process block (half-tone or line) as distinct from a duplicate block (stereotype or electrotype). Abbreviated: Or. or Orig. 6. In documentary reproduction, an object, or document, to be reproduced.

ORIGINAL BINDING. The binding that was first put on a specific book.

ORIGINAL PARTS. A first edition of a work which appeared serially in a number of parts, each provided with a paper wrapper, and numbered.

ORIGINAL SOURCES. *See* PRIMARY SOURCES.

ORIGINAL WRIT. One issuing from the Chancery.

ORIGINALITY. (*Copyright*) The quality of an *intellectual* work which seems to be significantly different from any other work, either in form or in content. A work may possess originality even when not dealing with new material.

ORIHON. 1. A book composed of a continuous, folded, uncut sheet or, of small single sheets, folded but uncut. It is held together by cords laced through holes stabbed down one side. This form is used in China and Japan where the paper is so thin that it can only be printed on one side. 2. A 'stabbed binding' of Oriental origin. 3. A manuscript roll on which the text was written in columns running the short way of the paper; the roll was not cut but folded down the margins between the columns of text. *See also* FRENCH FOLD.

ORNAMENTAL INITIAL. *See* INITIAL LETTER.

ORNAMENTAL INSIDE LINING. *Synonymous with* DOUBLURE 1 (*q.v.*).

ORNAMENTS. Printers' ornaments are little designs used to decorate printed matter. They are often arranged as borders, head-pieces, tail-pieces, etc. Also called 'Printer's ornament'.

ORTHOGRAPHIC CODING. (*Information retrieval*) 1. A statistical analysis of the spelling of the descriptive headings used, as a device to increase the efficiency of single-field superimposed coding systems.

2. A superimposed coding system using pairs of letters in a single field.

ORTHOGRAPHY. Spelling correctly, or according to accepted usage.

OSBORNE COLLECTION. A collection of Early English Children's Books which was assembled by Mr E. Osborne, a former County Librarian of Lancashire. It is owned by the Toronto Public Libraries.

OSIS. Acronym of the Office of Science Information Service which operates within the (U.S.) NATIONAL SCIENCE FOUNDATION (*q.v.*). In 1976, following the reorganization of the NSF, OSIS was renamed the Division of Science Information. *See also* SCIENCE AND TECHNOLOGY INFORMATION AND UTILIZATION CORPORATION.

OSMOSIS, METHOD OF. The classification by a newly adopted scheme, of all literature received after a given date, and the reclassification of the older literature in stock, as and when able to do so.

OTHER TITLE. (*Cataloguing*) A title, other than the title proper, or a parallel title, which appears in a publication – e.g. a SUB-TITLE (*q.v.*), an ALTERNATIVE TITLE (*q.v.*).

OTHER TITLE INFORMATION. Any phrase (other than a title, a statement of authorship, or an edition statement) which appears in the PRELIMINARIES (*q.v.*) of a book, and which indicates the character or contents of the publication, or the motive for, or occasion of, its production.

OUSTINOFF SYSTEM. A method devised by Helen Oustinoff, Assistant Director of the University of Vermont Library, to reduce work and ensure accuracy in the ordering of books. By using a Polaroid CU–5 Close-up Land Camera, copies of bibliographical entries in books or catalogues, are made in 15 seconds; these are passed to ordering clerks for making up orders and subsequently filed with the orders. Such photographs of titles printed in characters which cannot be reproduced on a typewriter may be sent as orders to booksellers. Polaroid prints, after the addition of necessary 'local' information (headings, classification numbers, etc.) may be put through a copying machine to provide catalogue entries or other records.

OUT OF PRINT. A book is out of print when the publisher has no more copies for sale and no intention to reprint. Abbreviation: O.P.

OUT OF STOCK. Not available from the publisher (although in print) until his stock has been replenished. Abbreviated: O.S.

OUTER FORM. *See* FORM DIVISIONS.

OUTER FORME. The forme for the side to be printed first; it bears the SIGNATURE MARK (*q.v.*). *See also* INNER FORME.

OUTER INDENTION. *Synonymous with* FIRST INDENTION (*q.v.*).

OUTGUIDE. A form card on which is recorded the loan of material from a file, or the file itself. It is substituted for the material lent, and being large enough to project above the folder, immediately indicates material on loan and possibly overdue.

OUTLIER LIBRARY. A library of a research institution, or one devoted to a particular subject, which does not generally participate in the work of a regional bureau, but whose stock is available to other libraries through the NATIONAL CENTRAL LIBRARY (*q.v.*). *See also* REGIONAL BUREAUX.

OUTLINE. 1. Usually a popular treatment of an extensive subject, e.g. H. G. Wells *The outline of history.* 2. (*Printing*) A type face in which the shape of the character is outlined in a continuous line of more or less consistent width. *See also* INLINE LETTERS.

OUTLINE LETTERS. *Synonymous with* OPEN LETTERS (*q.v.*).

OUTPUT. (*Information retrieval*) The product of a process – that is, the information transferred from the internal storage of a computer to output devices for external storage (*IBM*).

OUTPUT DEVICE. (*Information retrieval*) Equipment whereby information required from a computer is transferred therefrom to a form in which it can be read by the human eye. Such a device may produce hard copy, e.g. a LINE PRINTER (*q.v.*), or microform (*see* COMPUTER OUTPUT MICROFILM), or it may display text or data on a screen.

OUTSERT. An extra double leaf placed round the outside of a printed section of a book, and forming part of it. *See also* WRAP ROUNDS.

OUTSIDE MARGIN. *Synonymous with* FORE-EDGE MARGIN (*q.v.*).

OUTSIDE SOURCE. An idiom used, often by special librarians, to indicate a source of information outside their own organization which may be drawn upon when the resources of the library are inadequate to deal with enquiry needs. Such sources are often listed in the catalogue under appropriate subject headings or in a separate SOURCE INDEX (*q.v.*).

OVAL HALF-TONE. *See* HALF-TONE.

OVALS, IN. A binding with an oval arabesque centrepiece impressed in the centre of the top and lower covers. A common style in the late sixteenth and early seventeenth centuries, and found both in gold and blind.

OVER MATTER. Matter set ready for printing but held over through lack of space.

OVER-RUN. (*Printing*) 1. To turn over words from one line to the next for several successive lines as necessary after an insertion or a deletion. 2. Copies printed in excess of the number ordered.

OVER-RUNNING. Re-adjusting a paragraph of type which has been set up, due to corrections affecting the length of a line or poor make-up, or to avoid a RIVER (*q.v.*) or the unsatisfactory division of words. Words set in one line are carried forward or backward to adjacent lines as necessary.

OVERCASTING. *Synonymous with* OVERSEWING (*q.v.*).

OVERDUE. Colloquialism for an overdue book and also for an OVERDUE NOTICE (*q.v.*).

OVERDUE BOOK. A library book which has been retained longer for home reading than the period allowed.

OVERDUE NOTICE. A request to a reader asking for the return of a book which has been kept out beyond the time allowed.

OVERHEAD PROJECTOR. A device for projecting images or transparent material of about nine inches square on to a screen in front of, or to one side of, the audience while the operator faces them. The transparency is known as an 'overhead transparency'. *See also* OVERLAY 2.

OVERLAY. 1. The placing of pieces of paper on the tympan or impression cylinder of a printing machine, by manipulation of which an even impression is obtained from the matter after it has been levelled as far as possible by UNDERLAY (*q.v.*). 2. A group of transparent or translucent prints or drawings which can be superimposed on one another to form a composite print or slide. This method is often used in overhead projectors. 3. (*Information retrieval*) A technique for bringing routines into high-speed storage from some other form of storage during processing so that several routines will occupy the same storage locations at different times. Overlay functions when the total storage requirements for instructions are in excess of the main storage which is available. 4. Also, a transparent sheet bearing additional or alternative information which registers over another sheet. *See also* ROUTINE.

OVERPLUS. (*Printing*) Additional sheets printed in excess of the number actually ordered to allow for getting exact position, testing colour, determining register and for spoilt sheets so that on completion of a job the number ordered is available. These are usually known as 'overs'. Bibliophiles also apply the term to limited editions, copies of which are numbered serially.

OVERPRINT. 1. To revise printed matter by blocking out unwanted matter and printing a revision above it. 2. To print over matter which has already been printed whether blocked out or not. 3. To add information in a space, or in a Box (*q.v.*), on something which has already been printed. This frequently occurs with circulars, catalogues and advertising leaflets where a name and address are inserted to give the impression that the printed matter appears to originate from this source. *See also* SEPARATE. 4. More copies printed than needed, or ordered. 5. In colour printing, to obtain required colours by printing with one colour superimposed over another.

OVERPRINTING. 1. Printing in a primary colour over printing already carried out in a different colour in order to obtain a compound shade. 2. Application of a varnish or lacquer to matter printed from type or by a litho process, by means of a brush, spray or roller. 3. In blockmaking, superimposing one negative over another on the coated metal plate before developing. *See also* OVERPRINT. 4. The printing of additional material, as e.g. the name and address of a retailer's name and address, on to a sheet or page that has already been printed.

OVERS. 1. Extra sheets issued from the paper warehouse to the printing room, to allow for make-ready, testing colour, and for spoilt sheets, so that on completion of a job the number ordered is available. 2. Sheets or copies of a work printed in excess of the number ordered to make up spoiled copies, and to provide review and presentation copies. Also called 'Overplus'.

OVERSEWING. The act or process of sewing over and over the leaves of a book, usually done when it consists of single leaves or when the paper is too poor or too heavy for normal sewing to be satisfactory. Called 'whip-stitching' in America.

OVERSIZE BOOK. One which is too large to be shelved in normal sequence.

OWNERSHIP MARK. A rubber-stamp impression, perforation, embossment, or other mark of ownership in a book.

OXFORD BIBLE. *Synonymous with* VINEGAR BIBLE (*q.v.*).

OXFORD CORNERS. In book finishing, border rules that cross and project beyond each other.

OXFORD DECIMAL SYSTEMS. A scheme of classification based on the Universal Decimal Classification. It was worked out at the School of Forestry of Oxford University and is restricted to the field of forestry.

OXFORD FOLIO. *See* VINEGAR BIBLE.

OXFORD HOLLOW. A tube-like lining which is flattened, and one side stuck to the folded and sewn sections of the book and the other to the inside of the spine of the cover.

OXFORD INDIA PAPER. An INDIA PAPER (*q.v.*) about 8 lb demy (480) used by the Oxford University Press mainly for Bibles and prayer books, and made from selected rag stock according to a secret formula at their Wolvercote Mill since 1857. It is similar to an India paper first brought to Oxford in 1841, being very thin and opaque (one thousand sheets making less than an inch in thickness), and is a proprietary article. *See also* BIBLE PAPER, CAMBRIDGE INDIA PAPER.

OXFORD RULE. A rule with one thick and one thin line running parallel with each other.

OXFORD UNIVERSITY SCHOOL OF FORESTRY. Has an extremely valuable collection of material on forestry, the catalogue of which has been microfilmed with a grant from the Ford Foundation. Produces *Centralised Title Service*, a current bibliography of forestry, on cards which are despatched to subscribers every two weeks.

OXIDATION. The action which occurs when air contacts the unprotected areas of a lithographic plate which has been inadequately gummed. *See also* GUMMING UP.

OZALID. Trade name for a document copying process which uses the diazo technique. *See also* DIAZOTYPE PROCESS.

OZARAPID. Trade name for a machine made by the Ozalid Company for copying by the 'soft diffusion process'. *See also* TRANSFER PROCESS.

p. Abbreviation for page; pp., pages.

P-SLIP. A slip of paper 5 × 3 inches. P-slips are often made up into pads. (American).

PCMI SYSTEM. The Photo-Chromic-Micro-Image system, developed by the National Cash Register Company for data recording. It was demonstrated at the New York World's Fair in 1964, and enables 1,245 pages to be recorded on a 2 × 2 inches film.

P.E. NOTES. In an attempt to speed up decisions on extensions to the Universal Decimal Classification the International Commission sends out *P.E. notes* (Projets d'extensions) which invite criticisms to be submitted within four months, and *P.P. notes* (projets provisoires) which are intimations of provisional 'revolutionary suggestions.'

PMEST FORMULA. Ranganathan's five FUNDAMENTAL CATEGORIES (*q.v.*) – Personality, Matter, Energy, Space, Time – or facets, which, in this order, are arranged by decreasing concreteness.

p.p. Abbreviation for PRIVATELY PRINTED (*q.v.*).

PACIFIC NORTHWEST BIBLIOGRAPHIC CENTER. An independent co-operative, non-profit research organization sponsored by the Pacific Northwest Library Association. It is situated at the University of Washington at Seattle and is supported by the subscriptions of participating libraries. It is concerned with research into union cataloguing of book and other printed materials in forty libraries in the N.W. states of the U.S.A. and British Columbia.

PACK. A collection of cards, commonly a complete set of cards, which have been punched for a definite service (*IBM*). Called in America a 'Deck'.

PACKAGE LIBRARY. A feature of American practice, especially in society libraries, whereby 'packages' of publications consisting of anything from a few reprints or 'tear-sheets' to sufficient to fill a box file are sent to members. The material is arranged by subject or form and is sometimes published in microform, in which case it is called a 'Desk-top library'. The 'library' usually includes indexes, and the whole is regularly updated.

PACKET DEVICE. The symbol used in building classification numbers to connect class numbers from two parts of the classification schedules, the second one being used to show an aspect of the subject indicated by the first number.

PACKET NOTATION. The use of a connecting symbol, e.g. in the Colon Classification a bracket, or in the Universal Decimal Classification square brackets, to divide an isolate number by a number drawn from another schedule. Such a digit can be used as an octavizing digit (*see* OCTAVE DEVICE) to extend the hospitality of an array.

PADDING. Blank leaves added at the back of a thin pamphlet when binding it to form a sizeable volume.

PADELOUP STYLE. A style of book decoration practised by the Padeloup family in France in the eighteenth century. It is mainly characterized by its inlays of coloured leathers of diapered simple geometrical form, devoid of any floreation.

PAGE. *See* LEAF.

PAGE BREAK. The point in the text of a book where one page ends and the next begins.

PAGE CATALOGUE. One in which only a few entries are made on a page at first, with spaces left for the insertion of subsequent entries in correct order. The catalogues in the Reading Room of the British Museum and in the Bodleian are of this variety. Also called 'Guard book catalogue', 'Ledger catalogue'.

PAGE CORD. A cord which withstands water, specially made for printers, and used to tie up pages of type prior to imposition or distribution.

PAGE HEADLINE. A summary of the contents of a page, or an OPEN-ING (*q.v.*), or of the main topic of a page or opening, appearing on both left- and right-hand pages, or on one side only in conjunction with a section headline on the other page. Also called 'Page head'. *See also* HEADLINE, RUNNING TITLE, SECTION HEADLINE.

PAGE-ON-GALLEY PROOF. A galley proof with the type already made up into pages. This is done to avoid the necessity for supplying page proofs after correcting galley proofs.

PAGE PROOF. *See* PROOF.

PAGE REFERENCE. In bibliographies, the number of the page on which the article, etc., indexed is to be found in a particular volume or volumes.

PAGINATION. 1. That part of a catalogue entry or bibliographical description specifying the number of pages in a book. 2. The system of numbers by which consecutive pages of a book or MS. are marked to indicate their order. Pagination is rare until 1500 and not really common until 1590.

PAINTED EDGES. *See* FORE-EDGE PAINTING.

PAIS. Acronym of Public Affairs Information Service, Inc., a non-profit association chartered by the regents of the University of the State of New York, the purpose of which is to issue a weekly *PAIS Bulletin* which lists by subject library material in the English language in the field of economics, social conditions and public administration. Publications of all kinds from all English-speaking countries are included as well as many printed in English in other countries. The *Foreign Language Index* (*q.*) which began publication in 1972 is a counterpart for the *PAIS Bulletin*; it covers a selection of the latest books, pamphlets, government publications, reports of public and private agencies, and articles in approximately 650 journals in French, German, Italian, Portuguese and Spanish in the same field of economics and public affairs.

PAISA LIBRARY SCHEME. A scheme which operated in Lahore in the early 1940s whereby children saved a paisa a day (less than a rupee, or ten U.S. cents, a month) and received a children's magazine and a children's book of from 72 to 112 pages each month. The scheme was discontinued, after more than fifty titles had been published, due to increasing costs caused by the war.

PAKISTAN ASSOCIATION OF SPECIAL LIBRARIES. Founded at Karachi in June 1968 and registered as the national organization of special libraries in the country. The (now defunct) Association was to promote the development of special libraries and information services.

PAKISTAN NATIONAL SCIENTIFIC AND TECHNICAL DOCU-
MENTATION CENTRE. This organization was established in
Karachi in 1957, with the technical assistance of Unesco. Abbrevi-
ated PANSDOC.

PALAEOGRAPHY. The study and description of ancient and mediaeval
manuscripts, documents and systems of writing, including the knowledge of the various characters used at different periods by the scribes
of different nations and languages, their usual abbreviations, etc.

PALIMPSEST. Manuscript in which a second writing has been superimposed upon the original text, which has been wholly or partially
obliterated.

PALLET. 1. A tool used to decorate the panels on the spine of a bound
book. Pallets are usually used to make straight lines (sometimes
decorative) but are also used to impress a whole word such as the
author's name or a title. 2. A bookbinder's typeholder.

PALM LEAF BOOK. Manuscript books consisting of strips of Palmyra
or Talipat palm leaf from 16 to 36 inches long and from $1\frac{1}{2}$ to 3 inches
broad. Writing was done by scratching with an iron stylus and ink prepared from oil and charcoal rubbed over the surface to fill the incisions.
The strips were then bound by piercing a hole in the middle of each
and stringing them on cords or a piece of twine, and attaching them
to a board. They were made in India, Burma and Ceylon. The
Palmyra and Talipat palm leaves which are thick but long and narrow,
were the only writing material for books in ancient Odra and other
parts of the Central Provinces of Southern India; they were also
used to some extent in Ceylon, Burma, Thailand and Northern India.
Sacred works were written on Talipat palm leaves in Thailand, the
edges of the leaves being gilded, or painted with vermilion, and the
leaves threaded on strings and folded like a fan.

PAMPHLET. A non-periodical publication of at least five but not more
than 48 pages, exclusive of the cover pages. (General Conference of
Unesco, 1964). See also BOOK. It usually has an independent entity,
not being a SERIAL (q.v.), but it may be one of a series of publications
having a similarity of format or subject matter.

PAMPHLET BINDING. 1. Binding done by, or for, a printer, in which
the sheets as they come from the press, are wire-stitched. The term
applies both to pamphlets and to magazines. 2. The manner in which
such publications are bound when they come from the publisher,
being WIRE-STITCHED, SIDE-STITCHED or SADDLE-STITCHED (qq.v.).

PAMPHLET BOX. A box, usually of cardboard covered with cloth, or
of steel, for holding pamphlets and other unbound material. See

also Box File, Solander Case, Transfer Box, Transfer File.

PAMPHLET-STYLE LIBRARY BINDING. A style of binding for a thin pamphlet or a group of thin pamphlets which are expected to be used infrequently. It is characterized by side stitching and a lightweight cover of plain boards, heavy paper, paper-covered boards or limp cloth, and an absence of gold lettering.

PAMPHLET VOLUME. A volume consisting of a number of pamphlets bound together with or without a title-page or table of contents.

PAN AMERICAN STANDARDS COMMISSION. *See* COPANT.

PANEL. 1. A compartment of the external cover of a book enclosed in a Border 2 (*q.v.*) or Frame 2 (*q.v.*). 2. The space between two bands on the back of a book. 3. The list of books 'by the same author' facing the title-page. This is more for bibliographical than for advertisting purposes and may therefore include out-of-print titles and those issued by other publishers.

PANEL BACK. In hand binding, a volume finished with panelled borders between the raised bands on the shelf-back.

PANEL STAMP. A large piece of metal, engraved intaglio, used for impressing a design on the sides of book covers. Some of the stamps used for the early leather bindings were of quarto and folio size, but often book covers of these sizes were impressed two, three, four or more times with small panel stamps. A popular form of ornamentation in the early sixteenth century. *See also* BLOCKING.

PANIZZI CLUB. Founded in 1914 (first honorary secretary, E. W. Hulme, Librarian of the Patent Office Library) 'to provide opportunities for social intercourse between the Senior Officers of Reference and Research Libraries and to promote all measures tending to their higher efficiency'. Librarians of all kinds of library were admitted to membership. It is not known when the Club ceased to function, but it was the foundation on which the CIRCLE OF STATE LIBRARIANS (*q.v.*) was built.

PANORAMIC CATALOGUE. The endless chain principle adapted for displaying catalogue entries.

PANTOGRAPH. An instrument for copying a drawing to a premeditated scale.

PANTONE. A photo-engraving method of printing from a flat (planographic) plate with letterpress equipment, having the advantage over letterpress half-tone in that it can print from a screen up to 400 lines on antique paper and other rough surfaces. It is based on the principle that a printing plate bearing an image that is not in relief can be made to repel ink in the bare parts by treating them with mercury, while the printing parts will take up ink.

PAPER. I. A fibrous material made by breaking down vegetable fibres, purifying them, interweaving them into a compact web and pressing them into thin sheets. Book papers are made from MECHANICAL WOOD (*q.v.*) pulp (used for the cheapest publications and newspapers), CHEMICAL WOOD (*q.v.*) pulp (for most books), ESPARTO (*q.v.*) or rags, which make the best quality hand-made papers (for fine books). 2. A brief, literary composition, especially one to be read at a public meeting. 3. Contraction for newspaper. 4. To insert the end papers and fly-leaves of a book before inserting in its cover.

PAPER-BACKED. *Synonymous with* PAPER-BOUND (*q.v.*).

PAPER BOARDS. *See* BOARDS.

PAPER-BOUND. Bound with a paper cover. Also called 'Paper backed'. A book so bound is called a PAPERBACK (*q.v.*).

PAPER COVERED. A pamphlet or small book which is not bound in boards, but covered with a stiff paper which is usually pasted on to the book or sewn through. If the paper covers are pasted down on to thin boards, cut flush at the head and tail, flaps turned over, the style is called 'Stiffened paper covers'.

PAPER FINISHES. *Antique:* a rough uneven surface. *Eggshell:* slightly finished surface, having the appearance of the shell of an egg. *Machine:* smoother than antique with a slight gloss, but not suitable for half-tone illustrations, excepting those of coarse-screen finish. *Smooth antique:* an antique slightly rolled. *Super-calendered:* smooth finish without lustre; this will print half-tone blocks up to 100-screen. *American:* a finish with medium gloss and suitable for half-tone illustrations up to 100-screen. *Enamel* or *coated:* has a very high gloss, being coated in the making with china-clay, satin white, and casein which fills in the pores. Takes illustrations of the finest screen. *Dull coated:* has the coating as on a coated paper, but is calendered for smoothness only, not for gloss. Thus it has a perfect surface of mellow softness for the finest cuts.

PAPER SIZES. The dimensions of a sheet of paper or board (generally rectangular shape) as supplied by the manufacturer, the width (the smaller dimension) being given first. The British Standards Specification for writing and printing paper is as follows:

	millimetres	*inches*
Foolscap	343 × 432	$13\frac{1}{2}$ × 17
Foolscap, Double	432 × 686	17 × 27
Foolscap, Oblong Double	343 × 864	$13\frac{1}{2}$ × 34
Foolscap, Quad	686 × 864	27 × 34

	millimetres	*inches*
Pinched Post	368 × 470	$14\frac{1}{2}$ × $18\frac{1}{2}$
Post	387 × 483	$15\frac{1}{4}$ × 19
Post, Double	483 × 775	19 × $30\frac{1}{2}$
Large Post	419 × 533	$16\frac{1}{2}$ × 21
Large Post, Double	533 × 838	21 × 33
Demy	445 × 572	$17\frac{1}{2}$ × $22\frac{1}{2}$
Demy, Double	572 × 890	$22\frac{1}{2}$ × 35
Demy, Quad	890 × 1144	35 × 45
Medium	457 × 584	18 × 23
Medium, Double	584 × 914	23 × 36
Medium, Quad	914 × 1168	36 × 46
Royal	508 × 635	20 × 25
Royal, Double	635 × 1016	25 × 40
Crown	391 × 508	15 × 20
Crown, Double	508 × 762★	20 × 30
Crown, Double Quad	1016 × 1524★	40 × 60
Crown, Quad	762 × 1016★	30 × 40
Imperial	559 × 762	22 × 30
Imperial, Double	762 × 1118	30 × 44

★ It is not expected that these sizes will be available after metrication. Other sizes are:

Pott	318 × 394	$12\frac{1}{2}$ × $15\frac{1}{2}$
Pott, Double	394 × 635	$15\frac{1}{2}$ × 25
Post, Small	400 × 495	$15\frac{3}{4}$ × $19\frac{1}{2}$
Royal, Large	508 × 686	20 × 27
Royal, Super	521 × 698	$20\frac{1}{2}$ × $27\frac{1}{2}$

A sheet of 'quad' gives four times the number of sections as a sheet of ordinary size, a 'double' sheet twice the number. Papers for other purposes differ in size. *See also* BOOK SIZES, OCTAVO.

The American practice is not to use names but to specify the size of paper by inches and its weight per ream. The ordinary sizes of book papers in the U.S.A. are:

22 × 32	28 × 44	34 × 44	44 × 56
24 × 36	29 × 52	35 × 45	44 × 64
25 × 38	$30\frac{1}{2}$ × 41	36 × 48	All the
26 × 39	32 × 44	38 × 50	above
26 × 40	33 × 44	41 × 51	measurements
28 × 42	33 × 46	42 × 56	are in inches.

The German DIN A series of paper sizes is widely used in Europe. DIN stands for Deutsche Industrie Normen, and indicates standards agreed by Deutscher Normenausschuss (Committee for Standards), a similar body to the British Standards Institution. The A is to distinguish this standard from others known as B and C which apply to related poster and envelope sizes. The chief features of the DIN A series are that they apply to all types of paper, and that the proportions of a sheet remain constant when it is cut or folded in half across the long side. The letters Ao indicate a basic size of 1 square metre. A sheet of paper half this size is indicated by A1, or half this size by A2 and so on. A larger sheet than Ao is indicated by a figure before the A; thus a sheet twice the size of Ao is indicated by 2A. The following table shows 7 trimmed sizes in the DIN A series which correspond to the British sizes from 8-demy to demy 8vo.

	Millimetres	*Inches (approx.)*	*Demy sizes*
2Ao	1189 × 1682	$46\frac{13}{16}$ × $66\frac{3}{16}$	45 × 70
Ao	841 × 1189	$33\frac{1}{8}$ × $46\frac{13}{16}$	35 × 45
A1	594 × 841	$23\frac{3}{8}$ × $33\frac{1}{8}$	$22\frac{1}{2}$ × 35
A2	420 × 594	$16\frac{9}{16}$ × $23\frac{3}{8}$	$17\frac{1}{2}$ × $22\frac{1}{2}$
A3	297 × 420	$11\frac{11}{16}$ × $16\frac{9}{16}$	$11\frac{1}{4}$ × $17\frac{1}{2}$
A4	210 × 297	$8\frac{1}{4}$ × $11\frac{11}{16}$	$8\frac{3}{4}$ × $11\frac{1}{4}$
A5	148 × 210	$5\frac{7}{8}$ × $8\frac{1}{4}$	$5\frac{5}{8}$ × $8\frac{3}{4}$
A6	105 × 148	$4\frac{1}{8}$ × $5\frac{7}{8}$	
A7	74 × 105	$2\frac{15}{16}$ × $4\frac{1}{8}$	
A8	52 × 74	$2\frac{1}{16}$ × $2\frac{15}{16}$	
A9	37 × 52	$1\frac{1}{2}$ × $2\frac{1}{16}$	
A10	26 × 37	1 × $1\frac{1}{2}$	

There is also a 4Ao size: 1682 and 2378 mm.
(Continental practice is to state the smaller dimensions first.)

Series B is intended for posters, wall charts and other large items, and C for envelopes, particularly where it is necessary for an envelope in the C series to fit into another envelope. The International Organization for Standardization (ISO) adopted the A series for trimmed sizes for administrative, commercial and technical uses, and printed matter such as forms, professional periodicals and catalogues; the sizes do not necessarily apply to newspapers, published books, posters, continuous stationery or other specialized items. These sizes are sometimes referred to as 'ISO-A' sizes. The B sizes have also been adopted by ISO and are sometimes referred to as 'ISO-B' sizes, but, unlike the A series, have not been adopted by the British Standards Institution. The ISO recommends that these sizes are intended for use in exceptional circumstances, when sizes are needed intermediate between any two adjacent sizes of the A series. The C sizes have not been adopted by the ISO. *See also* PERIODICAL, UNTRIMMED SIZE.

PAPER TAPE. (*Information retrieval*) A form of input medium for the computer; characters are indicated by holes punched in a strip of paper according to a code. *See also* MAGNETIC TAPE.

PAPER TAPE READER. (*Information retrieval*) Part of an input device, the input medium of which is PAPER TAPE (*q.v.*); it translates the information punched in code on paper tape into MACHINE LANGUAGE (*q.v.*) and transmits the data into a central processing unit.

PAPERBACK. A book bound in heavy paper covers trimmed to the size of the pages. A common term for novels of the late nineteenth century and also for contemporary books similarly bound. A new type of publishing venture was begun in 1935 when Allen Lane founded Penguin Books in England and began publishing large editions of paperback books to sell at a very low price – sixpence, which was about a twentieth of the price of a hardback edition.

PAPERS. (*Archives*) 1. An assemblage of personal and family material of miscellaneous nature as distinct from formal records. 2. A general term used to include more than one type of manuscript or typewritten material.

PAPYROLOGY. The study of ancient documents and literary manuscripts on papyrus.

PAPYRUS. 1. A giant water-reed from the stem of which the Egyptians made a writing material. 2. The material itself. 3. A manuscript written on papyrus.

PARADIGMS. In subject analysis, a term used by J. C. Gardin to indicate subjects which have a permanent relationship (e.g.

aluminium; polyethylene) whereas syntagmas are those in which subjects which are normally distinct are brought together to form a composite more specific than any of its elements considered separately.

PARAGRAPH INDENTION. (*Cataloguing*) *Synonymous with* SECOND INDENTION (*q.v.*). (*Printing*) Setting the first line of a paragraph one em or so in from the margin. Also called 'Paragraph indentation'. *See also* HANGING INDENTION.

PARAGRAPH MARK. 1. The reversed or 'blind' P sign (¶) used in a MS. or proof to indicate the commencement of a new paragraph. 2. The sixth reference mark for footnotes, coming after the parallel. *See also* REFERENCE MARKS.

PARALLEL. (*Information retrieval*) Pertaining to the simultaneous handling of all the elements in a group (*IBM*). *See also* SERIAL 3. (*Printing*) The printer's sign ‖; it is used as the fifth reference mark. *See also* REFERENCE MARKS.

PARALLEL ARRANGEMENT. Separating books of varying sizes to economize shelf space by arranging larger books by one of the following methods: (a) in a separate sequence on the bottom shelves of each tier; (b) in a separate sequence at the end of each class; (c) in a complete separate sequence of the whole classification.

PARALLEL CLASSIFICATION. Material classified by the same scheme is said to be placed in parallel classification when it is again divided by size, character, etc., e.g. there may be four perfectly classified sequences for octavos, folios, pamphlets and illustrations; thus giving four parallel classifications.

PARALLEL EDITION. A publication in which different texts of the same work are printed side by side, e.g. the Authorized and Revised versions of the Bible, or an original and a translation into another language, or two or more versions of a work.

PARALLEL MARK (‖). The fifth reference mark for footnotes, coming after the section mark. *See also* REFERENCE MARKS.

PARALLEL RULE. A RULE (*q.v.*) having two lines of the same thickness. *See also* DOUBLE RULE.

PARALLEL TEXT. *See* PARALLEL EDITION.

PARALLEL TITLE. The title proper, given in a publication, but in another language or in another script, than that used for the text. *See also* ADDED TITLE PAGE.

PARALLEL TRANSLATION. A text, with a translation into another language, both printed in parallel columns.

PARAPH. A mark or flourish after a signature, made often as a protection against forgery, and especially used by notaries. Also called a 'Flourish'.

PARAPHRASE. An arrangement, transcription or imitation of a vocal or instrumental work in a form for voices or instruments other than was originally intended.

PARCHMENT. 1. Sheepskin or goatskin dressed with alum and polished. It is not so strong as vellum (calfskin) which it resembles, and from which it can be distinguished by its grain. It is used for documents of a permanent nature and for binding large and heavy volumes. The term is now sometimes applied to fibrous imitations. 2. In the paper trade, wrapping paper with a high resistance to grease and atmospheric humidity. It is a tough, translucent, glossy paper resembling animal parchment and made by soaking ordinary unsized paper in cold dilute sulphuric acid, or in some instances zinc chloride. Such paper is impervious to air, water, moisture, fat or oil and is stronger wet than dry. It was first manufactured in France in 1846 by Poumarede and Le Figuier. This use of the word is an abbreviation for 'parchment-paper'. Also called 'Vegetable parchment', 'Imitation parchment', i.e. an imitation of parchment paper is made without treatment in sulphuric acid, the toughness being produced by long treatment in the beating engine. Such paper, although less impervious, is also suitable for wrapping greasy food, and similar products.

PARCHMENT-PAPER. *See* PARCHMENT 2.

PARENTHESES. Curved lines () used to include words inserted parenthetically. Used in cataloguing to enclose explanatory or qualifying words or phrases to set off some item in the entry, such as a series note. Also called 'Round brackets' or 'Curves'. *See also* SQUARE BRACKETS.

PARENTHESIS. A short explanatory clause inserted in a sentence, usually between parentheses. Abbreviated paren.

PARIS PRINCIPLES. (*Cataloguing*) The twelve principles on which an author/title entry should be based. So named as the International Conference on Cataloguing Principles (ICCP), at which they were drawn up, was held in Paris in October 1961. The Conference, which was organized by IFLA was intended to serve as a basis for international standardization in cataloguing. The principles apply only to the choice and form of headings and entry words in catalogues of printed books (and other library materials having similar characteristics) in which entries under authors' names, or the titles of works, are combined in one alphabetical sequence. The foregoing is a summary of part of the first Principle. The subject matter of the others are: (2) functions of the catalogue; (3) structure of the catalogue;

(4) kinds of entry; (5) use of multiple entries; (6) function of different kinds of entry; (7) choice of uniform heading; (8) single personal author; (9) entry under corporate bodies; (10) multiple authorship; (11) works entered under title; (12) entry word for personal names. *See also* ICCP. Since these principles were formulated, at least twenty cataloguing codes have been drawn up which have these principles as their common basis. Among these are cataloguing codes which are used internationally; one of these is the *Anglo-American Cataloguing Rules (AACR)*.

PARISH LIBRARY. One which was provided by a parish council.

PARLIAMENTARY PAPERS. A term which when used in the scholars' narrow sense means a particular group of Parliamentary Publications, e.g. (a) House of Lords Papers and Bills, (b) House of Commons Bills, (c) House of Commons Papers, (d) Command Papers, and not all the publications issued by Parliament and published by HMSO which alone has authority to publish on behalf of Parliament. *See also* PARLIAMENTARY PUBLICATIONS, SESSIONAL PAPERS.

PARLIAMENTARY PUBLICATIONS.

1. GENERAL DEFINITION. Papers printed for parliamentary purposes and placed on sale to the general public through HMSO. These comprise:

House of Lords Papers
    ,,   ,,   ,, Bills
    ,,   ,,   ,, Journals
    ,,   ,,   ,, Debates
    ,,   ,,   ,, Minutes of Proceedings
House of Commons Papers
    ,,   ,,   ,, Bills
    ,,   ,,   ,, Journals
    ,,   ,,   ,, Debates
    ,,   ,,   ,, Votes and Proceedings
Command Papers
Public General Acts
Local and Private Acts
Measures passed by the National Assembly of the Church
    of England.

2. 'HOUSE' PAPERS. Documents presented either to the House of Lords or to the House of Commons under statute or by order of the House and 'ordered to be printed'. The sessional number appears at the bottom left hand corner of the title-page. House of Lords Paper and

Bill numbers (in a common series) are printed in parentheses; House
of Commons Bill numbers are in square brackets; House of Commons
Paper numbers are not enclosed in brackets.

3. COMMAND PAPERS. Papers presented by a Minister to both Houses
of Parliament by Command of Her Majesty. Occasionally, a Paper has
been presented by Command to one House only, but with the exception of estimates (House of Commons Papers) the practice is now rare.
The series is limited to documents relating to matters likely to be the
subject of early legislation, or regarded as otherwise essential to
Members of Parliament to enable them to discharge their responsibilities.

They were first published as Appendices to the House of Commons
Journal but since 1836 have been numbered serially as follows:

1833–1869	[1]–[4222]
1870–1899	C.I.–C.9550
1900–1918	Cd.1–Cd.9239
1919–1956	Cmd.1–Cmd.9889
1956–	Cmnd.1–

4. 'HANSARD'. The official verbatim reports of the debates of both
Houses of Parliament. The debates of the House of Commons and of
the House of Lords (issued separately) are published daily while
Parliament is sitting. They are named after Luke Hansard (1752–1828)
and his descendants who printed these reports from 1811–1891. The
issue of an officially authorized edition began in 1892, and in 1909
HMSO assumed the responsibility for printing and publication.

5. VOTES AND PROCEEDINGS OF THE HOUSE OF COMMONS. These are
issued daily while the House is sitting and comprise six parts, each
separately paged. They are:

Proceedings of the previous day;
Private business;
Questions, notices of Motions, Orders of the day;
Papers delivered to the House, notices of sittings of Public Com-
    mittees;
Proposed amendments to Bills;
Proceedings in Standing Committees (each Committee's Pro-
    ceedings are paged separately);
Divisions.

In addition, a list of the Public Bills which have been introduced
during the Session, showing progress made, is circulated weekly with

the Votes and Proceedings, and a similar list of Private Bills is included periodically in the private business section.

6. MINUTES OF PROCEEDINGS OF THE HOUSE OF LORDS. These, also, are issued daily while the House is sitting and contain:

> The proceedings of the previous day;
> Notices of judicial business;
> Agenda for the day (including questions);
> Notices of future questions and business;
> Divisions;
> A list of Bills showing the stages reached.

7. THE JOURNALS OF THE HOUSE OF COMMONS AND OF THE HOUSE OF LORDS, containing a complete record of Parliamentary proceedings, are published separately at the end of each Session.

8. THE ORDER BOOK OF THE HOUSE OF COMMONS is a consolidation of the business appearing in the Votes and Proceedings. It is issued daily for the convenience of Members and is not generally available to the public.

See also GREEN PAPER, NON-PARLIAMENTARY PUBLICATIONS, PARLIAMENTARY PAPERS, WHITE PAPER. All parliamentary publications are published by HMSO.

PARLIAMENTARY SESSION. A parliamentary year which begins with the opening of Parliament and normally ends with its prorogation. It usually begins in the first week of November, immediately after the old session, and does not correspond either with the calendar year or with the government's financial year. Also called a 'Session'. *See also* SESSIONAL PAPERS.

PARRY REPORT. The *Report of the Committee on Libraries* (HMSO 1967) which was set up in 1963 by the University Grants Committee; so named after Dr. Thomas Parry, Principal of the University College of Wales, Aberystwyth, who was the chairman. It surveys libraries in British universities and makes recommendations on improving these and developing the British Museum Library as the chief functionary in the provision of library and bibliographical services.

PART. 1. A portion of a work in one or more volumes issued by a publisher as the work is completed for publication. Parts may be issued at frequent, regular intervals, as fortnightly, or at monthly, yearly, or irregular intervals, according to the nature of the work and its compilation. It usually has a separate title, half title, or cover title, and may have separate or continuous paging. It is distinguished from a FASCICLE (*q.v.*) by being a unit rather than a temporary portion of a unit. 2. A division of work (*see* WORK 1) according to its content (*IFLA*). 3. The music for any one of the participating voices or instruments of a musical composition. 4. The manuscript or printed copy of the music for such a participant. *See also* VOLUME. 5. A separately published number of a SERIAL (*q.v.*). Parts usually have paper covers bearing the title of the serial, the volume number (if any), issue number and date of issue. This information usually appears also on the first page of the text if the cover does not have textual matter on it, and nowadays often at the foot of each page in addition, the title usually being in an abbreviated form.

PART PUBLICATIONS. Long works which are issued in separate parts at regular intervals.

PART-TIME BRANCH. *See* BRANCH LIBRARY.

PART TITLE. *Synonymous with* DIVISIONAL TITLE (*q.v.*).

PARTIAL BIBLIOGRAPHY. One in which a mechanical limit has been put on the material included; e.g. periodicals only, books or articles of a certain period or in a certain country or library. *See also* SELECT BIBLIOGRAPHY.

PARTIAL CONTENTS NOTE. A note which gives only the more important items in the contents.

PARTIAL TITLE. One which consists of only a secondary part of the title as given in the title-page. It may be a CATCHWORD TITLE (*q.v.*), SUB-TITLE (*q.v.*) or ALTERNATIVE TITLE (*q.v.*).

PARTIAL TITLE ENTRY. A catalogue entry made under a PARTIAL TITLE (*q.v.*).

PASTE-DOWN. That part of an endpaper which is pasted down to the inner surface of the cover or boards of a book. Also called 'Board paper'. The free half of the endpaper forms a fly-leaf.

PASTE-DOWN ENDPAPER. *See* ENDPAPER.

PASTE-GRAIN. Split sheepskin hardened by coating with paste and given a highly polished surface.

PASTE-IN. 1. A correction or addition to the text supplied after the sheets have been printed, and tipped into the book opposite the place to which it refers. *See also* CORRIGENDA. 2. A separately printed illustration or map, cut to the size of the book, and the inner edge pasted into the text before gathering.

PASTE-UP. An arrangement on sheets of paper of proofs of a number of pages in order to plan the positioning of blocks, legends, illustrations and text. The use of a rubber adhesive simplifies re-arrangement.

PASTEBOARD. The material, made by pasting sheets of brown paper together, and lined on both sides with paper, which is used for printing and also for the covers of books. *See also* MILLBOARD, STRAWBOARD.

PASTICHE. A musical or artistic composition consisting of a medley of passages or parts from various sources, connected together.

PASTING DOWN. The action of attaching a sewn book to its case or cover.

PASTORAL. A book relating to the cure of souls.

PASTORAL LETTER. A letter from a spiritual pastor, especially from a bishop to the clergy or people of his diocese.

PATENT. 1. A specification concerning the design or manufacture of something which is protected by letters patent and secured for the exclusive profit of the designer or inventor for a limited number of years which varies in different countries from fifteen to twenty years. The department which controls the registration of patents is called a 'Patents office'. 2. A publication, issued by such an office, which gives details of designs and processes. 3. In the field of patents, a 'provisional specification' is a patent application which is merely to establish a date for disclosure of an inventive concept to the Patent Office. It does not include a claim to the monopoly sought; this is made in a 'complete specification' which describes at least one preferred way in which the invention may be performed, and which sets out a claim or claims for the protection sought.

PATENT BASE. A device for raising the level of the bed of a printing press so that the electrotypes or stereotypes need not be mounted on wood.

PATENT FILE. Patent specifications and drawings which may be arranged by country and number, name of patentee or subject, or an index of such material similarly arranged.

PATENT OF ADDITION. A patent which represents an improvement in, or modification of, the invention of another patent in the same name, and for which no renewal fees are necessary to keep it in force. It expires when the other patent expires. *See also* CONVENTION APPLICATION.

PATENT OFFICE LIBRARY. Founded in London in 1855 to stimulate developments in the field of invention by making relevant information on applied science freely and readily available to all. Since incorporation within the British Museum Library to form the NATIONAL REFERENCE LIBRARY OF SCIENCE AND INVENTION (*q.v.*), its scope has been widened to include developments and discoveries in any branch of the natural sciences and technology. Since incorporation within the Reference Division of the BRITISH LIBRARY (*q.v.*) in 1973, it has been known as the Science Reference Library.

PATENT ROLL. A parchment roll upon which royal letters patent were enrolled at the Chancery.

PATENTEE. The person or persons entered on the register of patents as grantee or proprietor of a patent according to the appropriate national procedure.

PATERSON REPORT. The report (of a working group appointed by the Scottish local authority associations and supported by the Secretary of State for Scotland). *The new Scottish local authorities: organization and management structures* (Edinburgh: HMSO 1973). The Chairman of the Steering Committee was J. F. Niven and of the Advisory Group, I. V. Paterson; the Report was published when the Local Government (Scotland) Bill had had its third reading in the House of Commons and was still under consideration in the House of Lords. The Report was prepared to enable those concerned with local government to study the new proposals and the principles of management involved.

PATRA. Abbreviation for the PRINTING, PACKAGING AND ALLIED TRADES RESEARCH ASSOCIATION *see* PRINTING AND ALLIED TRADES RESEARCH.

PATRISTICS. A publisher's series on the writings of the Fathers of the Christian Church, e.g. *The Library of Christian Classics* and *Ancient Christian Writers*.

PATTERN. A specimen volume, or rubbing, sent to a binder to indicate the style of lettering to be used.

PATTERN BOARD. A board maintained by a binder on which is mounted a specimen of the covering material to show titling lay-out, colour, size, etc., to ensure uniformity in the binding of a series.

PATTERN RECOGNITION. (*Information retrieval*) Machine-sensing or identification of visible patterns (shapes, forms and configurations).

PATTERN RUBBING. A rubbing made to ensure that subsequent volumes in a series are lettered in the same style. *See also* RUB.

PAY COLLECTION. *See* DUPLICATE PAY COLLECTION.

PAYNE STYLE. The style of book decoration practised by Roger Payne in England in the eighteenth century. It consisted of the repetition of small floral forms in borders or radiating corners, the background being formed with dots and circles.

PEACOCK ROLL. (*Binding*) A finisher's roll which includes a peacock in its ornamentation. It is characteristic of some English Restoration bindings, and also appears on eighteenth century Irish bindings.

PEARL. An out-of-date name for a size of type equivalent to 5 point.

PEAR TREE PRESS. A private printing press, begun in Essex in 1899 by James Guthrie. It moved to Flansham in 1907.

PEBBLING. *See* STIPPLING.

PEDESTRIAN WORK. (*Classification*) A work which is not a SACRED WORK (*q.v.*), a CLASSIC (*q.v.*) or a LITERARY WORK (*q.v.*), and is not treated as if it were a class or a subject in usage.

PEEK-A-BOO. A principle of punching ASPECT CARDS (*q.v.*) to record information which is represented by certain positions on the card. These positions may be numbered in columns (the punched cards which have been familiar in the U.K. for many years are of this kind), or, in the larger cards capable of having up to 10,000 positions on one side, be in numbered squares or grilles. Such cards are sorted by machine or are searched by placing several in front of the source of light, possibly in a light box. Wherever light shows through there is a coincidence of document-number punches and this identifies documents as possessing the aspects indicated by the position of the hole. The card represents an index unit and the holes stand for documents or parts of documents that have the particular index unit in common. The cards used in this system are also called 'Cordonnier cards' or 'Batten cards' after G. Cordonnier of France and W. E. Batten of Britain who were early exponents of the system. They are also called 'Optical coincidence cards'. *See also* BATTEN SYSTEM.

PEEPHOLE CARD. One with holes punched in it to represent information or characteristics possessed; it is used with a system of CO-ORDINATE INDEXING (*q.v.*). Also called 'Aperture card', 'Optical coincidence card'. It may also have an opening specifically prepared to mount one or more frames of a microfilm.

PELLET'S PROCESS. A blueprint process suitable only for the reproduction of line drawings whereby the prints have blue lines on an almost white background. It was introduced in 1877.

PEN-NAME. *Synonymous with* PSEUDONYM (*q.v.*).

PENCIL DATER. A combined rubber date stamp and pencil.

PENNY-DREADFUL. A thrilling story magazine for children sold at a very low price. A morbidly sensational story.

PERFECT. (*Binding*) A method of binding by which the folds of the sections forming the back of the book are cut away; the edges of the loose sheets so formed are then coated with a very flexible but strong adhesive and covered with paper, mull or other material. The book is then inserted into covers by ordinary methods employed when sections are not sewn on tapes. Also called 'Lumbecking'. *See also* CAOUT-CHOUC BINDING.

PERFECT COPY. A sheet of paper which has been printed on both sides from an 'inner forme' and also from an 'outer forme'.

PERFECTER. A printing machine which prints on both sides of the paper at the same time whereas stop-cylinder presses and two-revolution machines print on one side only. Also called a 'Perfecting machine' or 'Perfecting press'. The first machine of this kind was made in 1816 by Koenig and Bauer and was called by the maker a 'completing machine'.

PERFECTING. Printing the second side of a sheet. A perfecting press is one that prints both sides of a sheet in one operation. Also called 'Backing up'.

PERFECTING MACHINE. *See* PERFECTER.

PERFORATING STAMP. A punch or stamp which perforates a mark of ownership through the page of a book.

PERFORMANCE INDEX. A method of evaluating the service provided by a technical library; it is the ratio of (a) material supplied to (b) the material requested, the index being expressed as the percentage that (a) is of (b).

PERIOD BIBLIOGRAPHY. One limited to a certain period of time.

PERIOD DIVISION. 1. A division of a classification scheme for works covering a limited period of time. 2. A sub-division of a subject heading in a catalogue which indicates the period covered.

PERIOD PRINTING. Producing books in a style which is similar to that used when they were first published.

PERIODICAL. A publication with a distinctive title which appears at stated or regular intervals, generally oftener than once a year, without prior decision as to when the last issue shall appear. It contains articles, stories or other writings, by several contributors. *Newspapers,* whose chief function is to disseminate news, and the *memoirs, proceedings, journals,* etc. of societies are not considered periodicals under the cataloguing rules. *See also* SERIAL. At the General Conference of Unesco, held at Paris on 19th November 1964, it was agreed that a publication is a periodical 'if it constitutes one issue in a continuous series under the same title, published at regular or irregular intervals, over an indefinite period, individual issues in the series being numbered consecutively or each issue being dated'. In statistical records, a periodical publication with a single system of numeration whether or not the title has changed. Where a change of numeration occurs, a new sequence starting at one, irrespective of any change of title, is considered to be a separate unit.

PERIODICAL BIBLIOGRAPHY. One which is published in parts and revised or extended by the cumulative method. *See also* CLOSED BIBLIOGRAPHY, CURRENT BIBLIOGRAPHY.

PERIODICAL CASE. *Synonymous with* MAGAZINE CASE (*q.v.*).

PERIODICAL INDEX. 1. An index to one or more volumes of a periodical. 2. A subject index to a group of periodicals; usually issued at short intervals and cumulated.

PERIODICAL RACK. A fitting for accommodating current and possibly a few recent issues of periodicals, either horizontally or perpendicularly without displaying the covers. Each compartment has a label bearing the title of the periodical. Sometimes illogically called a 'Periodical stack'. *See also* PERIODICAL STAND.

PERIODICAL STAND. A piece of furniture for displaying periodicals so that much of the cover is visible. Sometimes the display fitting on which current issues are placed is constructed at an angle of 15 to 30° and is hinged to accommodate back numbers on a shelf immediately behind the slope. If merely hinged, this is inconvenient to use, even if a supporting stay is provided; a design which permits the slope to be slid back horizontally immediately below the shelf above is much more satisfactory. Slopes on which the periodicals rest should be between 15 and 25° to the perpendicular to prevent their falling forwards when not in periodical cases. Periodical racks accommodate current issues (and sometimes one or two of the most recent issues) horizontally without displaying their covers.

PERIODICALS COLLECTION. A library collection of periodicals, newspapers, and other serials whether bound, unbound, or in microform, treated like periodicals; usually kept as a collection and separate from other library materials.

PERIPHERALS (PERIPHERAL UNITS). (*Information retrieval*) A general term for the various input devices used with computers, and operating under computer control. They include input, output and storage devices.

PERMANENT PAPER. A term which is applied to pH neutral papers. Also called 'Durable paper'. *See also* pH VALUE.

PERMANENT RECORD FILM. Photographic material made and treated in such a way that both the image and the base will have the maximum archival quality when stored in ordinary room conditions.

PERMISSION. Authority from the owner of copyright to quote passages or reproduce illustrations from a work.

PERMISSIVE COMMITTEES. Committees which a local authority may appoint 'for any such general or special purpose as in the opinion of the local authority would be better managed by means of a committee', to quote the Local Government Act, 1933. *See also* STATUTORY COMMITTEES.

PERMUTATION INDEX. *Synonymous with* KWIC index. *See* KWIC.

PERMUTATION INDEXING. Indexing by selecting as entry headings words, phrases or sentences which the author has emphasized as important by using them in the title, introduction, section headings, conclusion, summary, etc. This method has been developed to become a technique of machine indexing; each entry in the index being a cyclic permutation of all the words in the original titles, each term being brought to a predetermined position for alphabetizing. So far this method has been used only for indexing by machine titles of technical documents. *See also* KWIC.

PERMUTED TITLE INDEX. The result of a method of indexing, which can be carried out by a machine, whereby entries are made for every important word in a title. The alphabetizing position of each entry is just to the right of the page centre and an unprinted area of one or two ems (*see* EM) appears immediately before the alphabeting word to make this obvious. When the right-hand limit of the title printing area is reached, the title is continued at the beginning of the MEASURE (*q.v.*) on the same line. The document identification code follows each entry. Types of such indexes are KWIC, KWOC and WADEX (*qq.v.*).

PERMUTED TITLE WORD INDEXING. Also called 'Keyword-in-Context (KWIC) Indexing', 'Permutation Indexing'. *See also* KWIC.

PERMUTERM. An indexing procedure which provides permitted pair combinations of all significant words within titles to form all possible pairs of terms. 'Permuterm' is a contraction of the phrase 'permuted terms'. The *Permuterm Subject Index* is generated from the computer data file of the *Science Citation Index* (*q.v.*).

PERPETUA. Eric Gill's most popular roman typeface, named after St. Perpetua, a female saint who was martyred at Carthage in A.D. 203 with a companion named Felicity. Cut in 1929, it is one of the most distinguished types, being not only used effectively for books, where dignity, repose and stateliness are required, but also for book jackets where the related Bold, and Bold Titling, are specially useful. The serifs are small, firmly pointed, sharply cut and horizontal. For a specimen alphabet, *see* TYPE FACE.

PERSIAN MOROCCO. A badly-tanned leather derived from Indian goat and sheep. It is an inferior leather unsuitable for binding books, being fairly strong but not durable.

PERSONAL AUTHORSHIP. Authorship of a work in which its

conception and execution is entirely the responsibility of an individual and carried out in his personal capacity, not by virtue of any paid or voluntary office held by him within a corporate body.

PERSONAL CATALOGUE. A catalogue in which entries are made under an individual's name for books both by him and about him. *See also* NAME CATALOGUE.

PERSONAL NAME. *Synonymous with* FORENAME (*q.v.*).

PERSONAL NAME ENTRY. An entry in a catalogue under the name of an individual.

PERSONAL PAPERS. (*Archives*) The private documents accumulated by, and belonging to, an individual, and subject to that person's disposition.

PERSONAL SUBJECT. The name of an author who is well known in connexion with one particular branch of knowledge, and which is used as a subject heading in selective cataloguing.

PERT. Acronym of Program Evaluation and Review Technique. A management term indicating a method, based on Henry L. Gantt's charting techniques, which produces charts using estimates of the time taken for producing each activity, in order to monitor the progress of a development project and in so doing focuses special attention on those parts which will cause the longest delay in progress.

pf. Abbreviation for portfolio.

pH VALUE. Measurement of the acid and alkaline content of paper, as recorded on a scale. pH7 is neutral; a figure lower than 7 indicates acid quality, higher than 7 indicates alkaline quality, the strengths being indicated by the respective distances from 7 and extending from 1 to 14. The measurement is determined by an electrical apparatus called an Ionometer. pH is an abbreviation for 'hydrogen-ions concentration'. The scale is logarithmic. *See also* PERMANENT PAPER.

PHASE. In classification, that part of a complex subject (i.e. a sub-class representing the interaction of an original subject on another separate subject, e.g. the influence of the Bible on English literature) derived from any one main class of knowledge: that part of a complex subject derived from one distinct field of knowledge: any one of two or more classes brought into relation to one another in a document. The interaction of two normally distinct subjects is called a Phase Relation. So far five kinds of phase-relation have been isolated. (1) Form phase (the method of presentation); (2) Bias phase (one subject presented for the requirements of another): (3) Influencing phase (one subject influenced by another); (4) Comparison phase (one subject compared with another); (5) Tool phase (one subject used as a method of expounding another). Ranganathan suggests that Form is not a phase relation, that it is more closely allied to the individual book than to the subject, and that it should accordingly be shown as part of the book number, not the class number. *See also* CLASSIFYING, FACET, FOCUS. Where relations occur between foci in the same facet, these are called 'Intrafacet relations'.

PHASE RELATION. *See* PHASE.

PHILOSOPHICAL CLASSIFICATION. *See* KNOWLEDGE CLASSIFI-CATION.

PHLOROGLUCIN. A chemical which is used in conjunction with hydrochloric acid and alcohol as a test solution to detect mechanical wood in paper, which it turns red.

PHOENIX SCHEDULE. (*Classification*) A completely new development of the schedule for a specific discipline. Unless by chance, only the basic number for the discipline remains the same as in earlier editions, all other numbers being freely re-used.

PHONETIC WRITING. A form of writing in which the signs or symbols represent sounds or groups of sounds, rather than objects or ideas as they did in earlier forms of writing such as ideography or pictography. Each element corresponds to a specific sound in the language represented. Phonetic writing may be syllabic or alphabetic, the latter being the more advanced of the two.

PHONIC LENGTH. A characteristic of the length of a sequence of notation symbols in a scheme of classification, whereby there is ability to remember them easily by reason of their pronounceability. *See also* GRAPHIC LENGTH.

PHONOGRAM. 1. A symbol used to express a sound or idea; it can represent a complete word, a syllable, or the sound which a syllable represents. 2. A speech record made by a phonograph, i.e. a gramophone.

PHONOGRAPH. An obsolete instrument for recording sounds on cylindrical wax records and reproducing them.

PHONOGRAPH RECORD. *Synonymous with* GRAMOPHONE RECORD (*q.v.*).

PHONORECORD. Any object on which sound has been recorded.

PHONOROLL. A perforated roll, usually of paper, which is used to activate a player-piano, or player-organ.

PHONOTAPE. *Synonymous with* AUDIOTAPE (*q.v.*).

PHOTOCHARGER. An electrical machine for recording the loan of books on microfilm.

PHOTOCHARGING. The recording of the loan of books by photographing on 35 mm film details of the book borrowed, the reader's identification card and a transaction card which is then placed in the book and taken by the reader.

PHOTOCHROMIC MICRO-IMAGE. *See* PCMI SYSTEM.

PHOTOCHROMIC SUBSTANCE. One which changes its colour when subjected to radiation from different light sources. Such substances are used in the PCMI SYSTEM (*q.v.*) of reprography.

PHOTOCLERK. The trade name for a well-known method of copying documents by a direct photocopying method; it employs an optical system for copying the original directly on to sensitized paper. On exposure, the camera lens with a mirror causes an image to be placed in readable form on the face of the sensitized paper. Chemical development, and drying, of the sensitized paper give a direct, negative copy of the original.

PHOTO-COMPOSING MACHINE. (*Printing*) A machine for setting solid text by photographic means, as distinct from metal-type composition. The following are makes of such machines: Fotosetter, Hadego, Highton, Huebner, Linofilm, Monophoto, Orotype, Photon, Rotofoto and Uhertype.

PHOTOCOMPOSITION. Setting type by means of a photo-composing machine, i.e. placing type images on photographic film or paper.

PHOTOCOPY. Strictly, a photographic copy made by a process which uses coatings of light-sensitive salts on the base material, but generally used to indicate any process, whether using light or other means of radiation, and with the aid of a camera or not. Dry-copying and all direct office copying methods are included. *See also* PHOTOSTAT, REFLEX COPYING.

PHOTO-ELECTROSTATIC REPRODUCTION. *Synonymous with* XEROGRAPHY (*q.v.*).

PHOTO-ENGRAVING. Any photo-mechanical process for reproducing pictures or the like in which the printing surface is in relief, as distinguished from photo-lithography and photo-gravure. It includes the half-tone process, zinc etching and other processes for making line cuts, the swelled-gelatine process, etc. *See also* ELECTRONIC PHOTO-ENGRAVING MACHINES.

PHOTO-GELATINE PROCESS. Any of the gelatine processes of photo-mechanical printing, as Collotype, Lichtdruck, Phototype, Albertype, Artotype, Heliotype, etc.

PHOTOGRAPHIC PAPERS. These are graded in thickness as follows:

Ultra thin (also called 'Extra lightweight')	between 0·0023 and 0·0031 inches inclusive				
Extra thin	„	0·0032	„	0·0037	„ „
Thin	„	0·0038	„	0·0043	„ „
Lightweight	„	0·0044	„	0·0059	„ „
Single weight	„	0·0060	„	0·0083	„ „
Medium „	„	0·0084	„	0·0111	„ „
Double „	„	0·0112	„	0·0190	„ „

PHOTOGRAPHIC PHOTOCOPYING. A documentary reproduction process using a base material on which light-sensitive silver salts have been coated. A copy so produced is called a 'Photographic photocopy'. *See also* PHOTOCOPY.

PHOTOGRAPHY. 1. A basic printing process in which the normal principles of photography are used at some stage, e.g. photo-engraving, photo-offset, photo-lithography. 2. In REPROGRAPHY (*q.v.*), all the processes which use light-radiation and base materials with coatings of light-sensitive silver salts. *See also* ELECTROPHOTOGRAPHY.

PHOTOGRAVURE. 1. Any of the various processes for producing prints from a plate prepared by photographic methods. Also called 'Heliogravure'. 2. A print so produced. *See also* ROTOGRAVURE.

PHOTO-LITHOGRAPHY. The process of reproducing a picture or design photographically on to metal for lithographic printing.

PHOTO-LITHO-OFFSET. *Synonymous with* PHOTO-OFFSET (*q.v.*).

PHOTOMACROGRAPH. 1. A photograph of an object which is the same size as the original, or slightly magnified (the upper limit being about ten diameters). A macrograph made by photography. 2. A photomicrograph of very low magnification.

PHOTOMAP. A map reproduced from a photomosaic to which names or other symbols have been added.

PHOTO-MECHANICAL PROCESS. *See* PROCESS ENGRAVING.

PHOTOMICROGRAPH. A photograph of a minute object, taken by means of a microscope in conjunction with a camera, i.e. by photomicrography which is not to be confused with microphotography – making minute photographs of large objects.

PHOTOMICROGRAPHY. Taking pictures by means of a microscope and a camera. The resulting photograph shows the original in greatly enlarged form. The opposite of MICROPHOTOGRAPHY (*q.v.*). *See also* PHOTOMACROGRAPH.

PHOTO-MONTAGE. A picture made by the combination of several

photographs or portions of photographs with a related interest into one large composite photograph, or parts of photographs cut out and pasted together to achieve a particular effect. Other methods are to make a number of exposures on the same negative, or to project a number of negatives to make a composite print.

PHOTOMOSAIC.   An assembly of parts of air photographs joined together to form a map.

PHOTO-OFFSET.   Offset printing in which the image is reproduced on a metal plate by photography. Also called 'Photo-litho-offset', and 'Offset-photo-lithography'.

PHOTON.   A photo-typesetting machine made in the U.S.A. by Photon Inc. and used since 1954. It consists of three major components, a standard Underwood electric typewriter, a telephone relay system, and a photographing unit. The operator using the keyboard selects the type style and type measure required to do a specific job and the machine automatically spaces and justifies the line. The mixing of styles and sizes is possible in the same line, thus allowing the operator greater flexibility. Photographic negatives or positives are produced and these may be used for lithography, gravure or to make letterpress blocks.

PHOTOSCOPE.   A small illustrated poster.

PHOTOSETTING.   (*Printing*) The setting of type by a photographic means. FOTOSETTER, LINOFILM, MONOPHOTO and PHOTON (*qq.v.*) are trade names of such methods and apparatus. *See also* FILM-SETTING.

PHOTOSTAT.   1. A trade name of a machine for reproducing photographically pages of printed, drawn or written matter, either the same size, or larger or smaller than the original, on sensitized paper without films or plates. 2. A copy made by such a machine; it is optical and right-reading. *See also* CAMERAGRAPH.

PHOTOTYPE.   A form of collotype, being a plate with a printing surface usually in relief, obtained from a photograph.

PHOTO-TYPOGRAPHY.   Any photo-mechanical process in which the printing surface is produced in relief so that it can be used with type.

PHOTO-ZINCOGRAPHY.   A method of reproducing pictures, drawings, etc., by using a zinc plate on which the design has been produced by photographic means.

PHRASE PSEUDONYM.   A pseudonym consisting of a phrase, as 'A Gentleman with a Duster'.

PHYLACTERY.   A narrow band or scroll on which a name or a speech was inscribed. Sometimes seen in block books, illuminated manuscripts or incunabula where they are drawn as if issuing from the mouths of characters, or held in the hand. They also appear in contemporary comics and comic strips as 'balloons' coming from the mouths of characters.

pi. (*Bibliography*) The Greek letter π used to denote an unsigned gathering or leaf which precedes signed gatherings, and in respect of which no signature can be inferred. *See also* CHI. (*Printing*) (*Verb*) To mix up type. (*Noun*) Type which has been mixed up. (American.) *See also* PIE.

PIANO-CONDUCTOR SCORE. *See* SCORE.

PIANO REDUCTION. An arrangement for piano of the voice parts of a work for unaccompanied voices for use as an accompaniment during rehearsal, such accompaniment not being intended by the composer for performance. Such music may be indicated by some such designation at the head of the score as 'Piano, for rehearsal only'.

PIANO SCORE. *See* SCORE.

PIANO-VOCAL SCORE. *Synonymous with* VOCAL SCORE. *See* SCORE.

PICA. 1. A standard of measurement, approximately $\frac{1}{6}$ inch; in the Point System ·166 inch, equal to 12 point. *See also* EM. 2. Pica type, the largest size ordinarily used for books; 12 point, six lines to an inch, as this.

PICK UP. Type which has been kept standing since first used, ready to be 'picked up' for further use when required.

PICTOGRAM. *See* PICTOGRAPHY.

PICTOGRAPH. A pictorial sign or simple illustration which tells a story instantaneously by representing an object or an idea. A primitive form of writing consisting of pictographs.

PICTOGRAPHY. The most primitive stage of true writing, in which a picture or sketch represents a thing, or a sequence of pictures drawings or symbols (each of which is termed a 'pictogram') tells a narrative. Pictography is a semantic representation, not a phonetic one. *See also* ALPHABETIC WRITING.

PICTORIAL MAP. A map which contains pictures indicating the distribution of physical and biological features, and social and economic characteristics, etc.

PICTURE BOOK. A (children's) book consisting wholly or mostly of pictures.

PICTURE COLLECTION. A collection of pictures, or of reproductions of pictures. *See also* ILLUSTRATIONS COLLECTION, PICTURE FILE.

PICTURE FILE. A collection of illustrations, prints, reproductions of pictures, and possibly cuttings; small enough to be filed rather than

21

needing to be displayed. They may be arranged by subject, artist, etc. This is American usage. *See also* ILLUSTRATIONS COLLECTION, PICTURE COLLECTION.

PICTURE-WRITING. *Synonymous with* PICTOGRAPHY (*q.v.*).

PIE. 1. A table, or collection, of ecclesiastical rules used before the Reformation in England to determine (from each of the 35 possible variations in the date of Easter) the proper service or office for the day. Also called 'Pye'. 2. An alphabetical index or catalogue, to count rolls and records (obsolete); usually called a 'pye book'.

PIE. (*Printing*) Type matter that has been mixed accidentally.

PIECE. (*Archives*) 1. The basic unit of archival arrangement and description which is produced from the repository as an entity under its own reference. For example, a file is a piece, but a single sheet on that file is not; however, a single document, once forming part of an original file would be a piece in this context. Also called 'Item'. 2. A fragment, or part, of a document, separated from the whole in any manner, such as cutting or detaching.

PIECE FRACTION. (*Printing*) A fraction that is made by using two or more pieces of type due to the fraction on one piece of type, as $\frac{3}{4}$, not being available. A SOLIDUS (*q.v.*) is used between the two groups of figures as 43/50.

PIERCED. *See* MORTICE.

PIERCY AWARD, ESTHER J. Established by the Resources and Technical Services Division of the American Library Association to honour the late editor of *Library Resources & Technical Services*. The Award is given annually 'to recognize the contribution to librarianship in the field of technical services by younger members of the profession', and consequently it is restricted to those with not more than ten years of professional experience. First awarded to Richard M. Dougherty in 1969.

PIERPOINT MORGAN LIBRARY. Assembled by John Pierpoint Morgan (1837–1913), inherited by his son J. P. Morgan, Jr. (1867–1943), who expanded it and in February 1924 conveyed it to six trustees to administer as a public reference library for the use of scholars. Subsequently the State of New York incorporated the collection and dedicated it to 'the advancement of knowledge and for the use of learned men of all countries.' The collection comprises about 55,000 books and manuscripts, and in addition, cuneiform tablets, drawings, prints, Italian medals, and Greek and Roman coins. The collection of mediaeval illuminated manuscripts is unique for its geographical and linguistic coverage.

PIGEONHOLE CLASSIFICATION. *Synonymous with* RIGID CLASSI-
FICATION (*q.v.*).

PIGSKIN. A strong leather made from the skin of a pig; it has good
lasting qualities and is used for covering large books.

PIN HOLES. 1. Minute and almost imperceptible pits in the surface of
art papers, due to frothy coating material. 2. Minute holes in paper,
caused by fine particles of sand, alum, etc., being crushed out during
the calendering process, leaving a hole. 3. Tiny transparent dots which
appear in a litho plate after development and which, unless covered
with an opaque medium, will appear in resulting prints.

PIN-MARK. A small depression on one side of the body of a piece of
movable type. It is made by the pin which ejects the types from the
moulds of certain casting machines and sometimes bears the number
of a body-size of the fount.

PIN SEAL. A binding leather from the skin of a very young, or baby,
seal, having much finer grain and a more lustrous finish than ordinary SEALSKIN (*q.v.*). Used for expensive bindings.

PINEAPPLE. (*Binding*) An ornament bearing some likeness to a conventional pineapple, and used in the same position as a FLEURON (*q.v.*).
See also TWISTED PINEAPPLES.

PIPE ROLL. A parchment roll upon which a record of the audit at the
exchequer was kept.

PIRA. Originally the Printing Industry Research Association. *See*
PRINTING AND ALLIED TRADES RESEARCH.

PIRACY. The publication in a foreign country of a literary work without
the permission of, or payment to, the author.

PIRATED EDITION. *See* UNAUTHORIZED EDITION.

PIVOTED BOOKCASE. *Synonymous with* SWINGING BOOKCASE (*q.v.*).

PIVOTED SHELVING. *See* SWINGING BOOKCASE.

pl. (*Pl.* pls.). Abbreviation for PLATE (*q.v.*) (illustration), also place.

PLACARD. A large, single, sheet of paper, usually printed, but sometimes written, on one side with an announcement or advertisement, for
display on a wall or notice board. Also called a 'Poster'.

PLACARD CATALOGUE. A list of books displayed on a large sheet,
or sheets, and hung up for consultation.

PLACE OF PRINTING. A bibliographer's or cataloguer's term for
the name of the town in which a book is printed. *See also* No
DATE.

PLACE OF PUBLICATION. A bibliographer's or cataloguer's term for
the name of the town or other locality in which the office of a publisher
who issues a book is situated. *See also* No DATE.

PLAGIARISM. To copy the writings of another person and publish the same as original work.

PLAIN TEXT. An edition of a classic without notes, or possibly even an introduction, and intended for study in a class or with a tutor.

PLAN. The representation of anything drawn on a plane, as a map or chart; the representation of a building or other structure, landscape design, arrangement of streets or buildings, or arrangement of furniture in a room or building, in horizontal plane.

PLAN. Acronym of the Public Library Automation Network which is funded by the American Library Services and Construction Act (LSCA); it seeks to indicate how users in different sizes and types of community benefit from a computerized system. The libraries participating are Los Angeles Public, Los Angeles County, Marin County, Orange County, San Francisco Public, Santa Clara County and Sutter County.

PLAN CABINET. A piece of furniture designed to accommodate plans, architectural drawings, or reproductions, either suspended or resting in a pocket vertically, or flat in shallow drawers. Also called 'Plan file'.

PLAN FILE. A container for filing plans and maps either vertically or horizontally. Also called 'Plan cabinet'.

PLAN PAPER. A thin, tough, paper which is made specially for printing maps, plans, etc. It is subject to much wear by constant handling and folding. Also called 'Map paper'. *See also* CHART PAPER.

PLANES. (*Classification*) In the Colon Classification these are three in number: Idea, Notation (or Notational) and Words (or Verbal); within which the designing or application of a scheme has to be done.

PLANETARY CAMERA. A camera used for photocopying in which the document being copied and the film are stationary during exposure. After each exposure the document is changed manually and the film is moved on one frame automatically. Also called a 'Flat-bed camera' or 'Stepwise operated camera'.

PLANOGRAPH. *Synonymous with* OFFSET PRINTING (*q.v.*).

PLANOGRAPHIC PRINTING. *See* PLANOGRAPHIC PROCESS.

PLANOGRAPHIC PROCESS. 1. A generic term for all printing which depends on chemical action, and in which the printing surface is a plane, merely transferring its image, as in lithography, collotype and offset. 2. The method of printing from flat surfaces, the parts to be printed accepting ink from the rollers while the non-printing areas reject it. The printing, or image, areas are greasy, the rest moist. Printing is by even pressure of a hand-roller or cylinder over the flat plate, or by offsetting the image from a curved plate on to a rubber

roller and so to the paper. It is one of the six basic principles of printing, the others being relief, intaglio, stencil, photography and xerography. Also called 'Surface printing'.

PLANOGRAPHY. Printing processes which are dependent on the anti-
pathy of oily ink and water, using methods of printing from flat
surfaces other than stone. The term replaces 'zincography' and
'aluminography'. *See also* PLANOGRAPHIC PROCESS.

PLANTIN. A type face designed by Christopher Plantin (1514–89) one
of the world's most distinguished printer-publishers, whose house and
printing equipment now form the Plantin – Moretus Museum at
Antwerp. This OLD FACE (*q.v.*) is characterized by the thickness, and
consequent black appearance, of all the strokes. For a specimen
alphabet, *see* TYPE FACE.

PLASTER OF PARIS MOULD. One made by placing a thin film of
plaster of Paris mixed with water to a fluid consistency on a sheet of
paper which is then transferred face downwards to the forme and
subjected to moderate pressure after several sheets of an absorbent
type of paper are placed on the paper-backed plaster of Paris. It is
used for reproducing illustrations by half-tone and three- and four-
colour half-tone processes.

PLASTIC BINDING. A type of binding used for pamphlets, commercial catalogues, etc. which are printed on unfolded leaves. These leaves
and the separate front and back covers are kept together by means of a
piece of curved synthetic plastic which has prongs, or combs, which
pass through slots punched near the binding edge of the leaves and
curled within the cylinder thus formed by the plastic. *See also* SPIRAL
BINDING.

PLASTICIZER. (*Archives*) A substance added to, for example, a
synthetic resin, to increase its flexibility. If the plasticizer is in some
measure chemically combined with the resin, it is said to be an 'internal' plasticizer.

PLASTICIZING. Putting a plastic cover or sleeve on to a book or BOOK
JACKET (*q.v.*), either by securing a loose cover or by laminating the
plastic by means of heat.

PLASTOCOWELL. A lithographic process introduced by W. S. Cowell,
Ltd., of Ipswich, in which a plastic sheet is used as a substitute for
stone or metal, and is easier and more convenient for the artist to work
than the ordinary forms of auto-lithography.

PLAT. A map or chart, such as a precise and detailed plan, showing the
actual or proposed divisions, special features, or uses of a piece of land,
e.g. a town or town site (American).

PLATE. 1. An illustration, often an engraving taken from a metal plate, printed separately from the text of the book with one side of the leaf blank, and often on different paper. Plates may be bound into a book or they may be loose in a portfolio. They are not generally included in the pagination. *See also* FIGURE. 2. A flat block of wood or metal, usually of copper, nickel or zinc, on the surface of which there is a design or reproduction of a type forme, to be used for printing, engraving, embossing, etc. The method of printing may be relief, intaglio, or planographic. 3. To make an electrotype or stereotype from printed matter. 4. *The Anglo-American cataloguing rules: British text* considers a plate to be a page containing illustrative matter and that it may also contain some text; it does not form part of the sequence of pages either physically or in enumeration. Plates may be distributed throughout the publication or gathered together; they may, or may not, be numbered; they are often printed on a different type of paper from that used for the text of the publication. The revisions of *AACR*, both North American and British Texts, provide for the recording of the number of pages (and/or leaves) of plates following the number of pages. *See also* ILLUSTRATIONS, LEAF.

PLATE CYLINDER. The roller of an offset printing machine which bears the printing plate. *See also* OFFSET PRINTING.

PLATE GUARDED AND HOOKED. An illustration printed on a separate piece of paper and stuck to a narrow strip of paper or linen to form a guard which is then placed around, or hooked-in, a section before sewing. *See also* HOOKED ON OWN GUARD.

PLATE LINE. *Synonymous with* PLATE MARK (*q.v.*).

PLATE MARK. A line marking the boundary edge of a plate used in making an engraving; it is caused by the pressure used to make the impression on the sheet of paper. The part of the paper on which the plate rested is depressed and more smooth than the surrounding portion.

PLATE NUMBER. One or more figures, or a combination of letters and figures, assigned serially to each musical composition on preparation for printing, being copied by the engraver at the bottom of each page and sometimes on the title-page also. If on the title-page only, it is better designated as 'Publisher's number'.

PLATE PAPER. A superfine soft rag paper of good substance, made for steel-plate or photogravure printing. Of recent years cheaper esparto qualities have been introduced.

PLATEN. The flat part of a printing press which presses the paper on to the forme. *See also* PLATEN PRESS. (*Reprography*) A mechanical device which holds the film in position in a camera, or copying apparatus, in the focal plane during exposure.

PLATEN PRESS. A printing press which has a flat impression, not a cylindrical one. The type is normally fixed on the bed in a vertical or almost vertical position, and the platen bearing the paper is swung up and pressed against the type. Such machines are usually used for jobbing work. *See also* CYLINDER PRESS.

PLATES VOLUME. In a work of several volumes, the one which consists of illustrations to the text, and has no printed matter other than that relating specifically to the illustrations.

PLATING. The process of pasting book plates and other labels in library books.

PLAQUETTE. A small metal relief, like a classical cameo, which is inlaid into Italian book bindings of the sixteenth century.

PLAYERTYPE. The REFLEX COPYING (*q.v.*) method used by J. Hart Player in 1896.

PLEA ROLL. A parchment roll on which a record of cases heard in the King's Courts was entered.

PLOUGH. The tool used for cutting the edges of a book, the book being secured in the lying press.

PLOWDEN REPORT. The Central Advisory Council for Education (England) was reconstituted in August 1963, under the chairmanship of Lady Plowden 'to consider primary education in all its aspects and the transition to secondary education'. The Council's Report was published in two volumes in January 1967 under the title *Children and their primary schools* (H.M.S.O.). The principal recommendation was for special assistance for schools in slum areas – designated 'education priority' areas – in the form of more teachers, additional finance for school-building, and more generous supplies of equipment.

POCHOIR. French for 'stencil'. A hand-coloured illustration process which, although dating from the eighteenth century, is still used in France, and is similar to SILK SCREEN (*q.v.*) except that paper, celluloid or metal stencils are used and the colour is dabbed through, rather than drawn across, the stencil. It is an expensive method, and is used for editions de luxe. 2. A method of reproducing gauche paintings. The design, necessarily simplified is preprinted by collotype and the ink applied with stencil and brush.

POCKET. A wallet-like receptacle made from linen or stiff paper inside a cover of a book (usually the back cover) to hold loose music parts, diagrams, or maps. Also called 'Cover pocket'. *See also* BOOK POCKET.

POCKET CARD CHARGING. The recording of loans of books by using a card kept in a corner pocket stuck to the inside of the cover of a book. The best-known method is the BROWNE BOOK CHARGING SYSTEM (*q.v.*).

POCKET EDITION. A small edition of a book, already printed in an octavo edition, of $6\frac{3}{4} \times 4\frac{1}{4}$ inches or less. Sometimes these are paper-bound but they are then usually called 'paperbacks'.

POCKET PART. A separate publication which is issued to bring a book up-to-date, and is usually kept in a pocket on the inside of the back cover.

POCKET SCORE. *See* SCORE.

POINT. 1. The unit of measure for printer's type: approximately 1/72 (0·013837) of an inch. Thus 12 point type is 12/72 or 1/6 of an inch in the body. One inch equals 72·25433 points and 72 points equal 0·9962 of an inch. Each body size is an exact multiplication of the point size. Type bodies are measured in points. The width of a line of type (or ('measure') is determined in pica (12-pt.) ems – called 'picas' in America. The depth of a page of type is similarly measured in ems or picas. After a fire at the typefoundry of Marder, Luse & Co. in Chicago in 1872, this firm began to supply type the bodies of which were multiples of 1/12 part of a typical Pica measuring 0·166 inch. The United States Type Founders' Association recommended this system to its members in 1886, and British typefounders conformed to the American point-system in 1898. The standard measurements according to the British-American Point System are:

5-point	0·0692 in.	14-point	0·1937 in.
6-point	0·0830 in.	16-point	0·2213 in.
7-point	0·0968 in.	18-point	0·2490 in.
8-point	0·1107 in.	24-point	0·3320 in.
9-point	0·1245 in.	30-point	0·4150 in.
10-point	0·1383 in.	36-point	0·4980 in.
11-point	0·1522 in.	48-point	0·6640 in.
12-point	0·1660 in.		

See also DIDOT SYSTEM 2. Any mark of punctuation. A full point (full stop).

POINT SYSTEM. *See* POINT.

POINTILLÉ. A binding decoration in gold done with tools with a dotted surface.

POINTS. 1. Small holes made in the sheets during the printing process which serve as guides in registering when the sheets are folded by machinery. 2. The bibliographical peculiarities of a printed book, the absence or presence of which determine whether the book is a first or other edition, or a particular issue of an edition, or a variant, etc.

POLAIRE. The leather case or satchel in which the ancient monks placed their books. Polaires were usually made without decoration unless for a wealthy man in which case they bore a design stamped in relief.

POLISH LIBRARY ASSOCIATION. Founded in 1917 as the Alliance of Polish Librarians – 'and Archivists' being added after the end of the Second World War until the archivists formed a separate organization in 1953, when the present name was adopted.

POLISH LIBRARY IN LONDON. The Lanckaroński Foundation Collection of Polonica amounting to some 3,000 books and over 500 etchings, drawings and engravings was received in 1969. This collection includes 16th- to 19th-century books, calendars, MSS., as well as more recent books, serials and pamphlets, and is the most outstanding of the bequests, gifts and legacies to be received by the Library from Poles all over the world. The Library originated in 1942 and functioned since 1943 as the Library of the Polish Government in London, its aim being to act as a central collection and bibliographical agency for Polish books published outside Poland since 1st September 1939 and also to acquire other material in Polish or in other languages concerning Poland and Polish affairs. From 1948 to 1953 it acted as the library of the Polish University College, and since then has concentrated on expanding its collection of books on Polish arts and humanities, and acting as a bibliographical centre for books in Polish or relating to Poland which are published outside that country. Of the Library's stock of about 100,000 volumes, 65% are in Polish. The Library has a reading room and lending library. Membership is free and is open to students and researchers.

POLONYM. A work by several authors.

POLYDECIMAL. A classification developed by L. Melot, which uses both letters and numbers in the notation.

POLYGLOT. A book giving versions of the same text in several languages, generally arranged in parallel columns. The first of the great Polyglot Bibles was the so-called COMPLUTENSIAN POLYGLOT (q.v.). The second of the famous polyglot Bibles was printed between 1569 and 1573 by Christopher Plantin, with the patronage of Philip II of Spain. It was in eight folio volumes, the text being in Hebrew, Greek,

Latin, Chaldaic, and Syriac. The Paris polyglot Bible, 1654, in nine volumes edited by G. Michel Le Jay and others added Arabic and also Samaritan to Plantin's text. The *Biblia sacra polyglotta* published in six volumes in London between 1655–7 was in nine languages.

POLYGRAPHIC.   Written by several authors.

POLYGRAPHY.   Books consisting of several works or extracts from works by one or a number of authors.

POLYHIERARCHIC.   (*Classification. Information retrieval*) Pertaining to an organizational pattern involving a multiplicity of facets or aspects.

POLYNOMIAL.   A work by several authors.

POLYONYMAL.   Having several, or different, names.

POLYONYMOUS.   Possessing many names.

POLYSEMIA.   The provision of instructions to an indexing machine as to how a significant word in a document is used in that document. Also called 'Multiple meaning'.

POLYSEMY.   (*Information retrieval*) The quality of a term having two or more independent or overlapping meanings.

POLYTERMS.   An extension of UNITERM CONCEPT CO-ORDINATION INDEXING (*q.v.*) whereby a group heading, instead of one simple basic idea, is used on each uniterm card. Also called 'Unit concepts'.

POLYTOPICAL.   Treating of several subjects.

POLYTYCH.   *See* CODEX.

POLYVALENT NOTATION.   A system of notation wherein each digit represents one of the characteristics of division. SEMAPHORE INDEXING (*q.v.*) is a polyvalent notation.

POMI.   A technique, developed by the National Cash Register Company's Electronic Division in California, U.S.A., for recording the contents of a 300-page book within one square-inch of film. The method is known as 'photochromic micro-images' and reduces printed material to microscopic size in a form that can be reproduced easily and inexpensively. It is not intended to replace conventional microfilm techniques; in fact the process consists of microfilming micro-film.

POPULAR COPYRIGHTS.   Used at the beginning of this century to denote books published by firms specializing in low-priced editions, who used, with the permission of the copyright owners, the plates made for the original editions.

POPULAR EDITION.   An edition of a book published on poorer paper, possibly without illustrations, and in a paper cover or a less substantial cloth binding than the normal edition, and sold at a cheaper price.

POPULAR LIBRARY.   In America, a department containing books of general interest for home-reading, those of special interest, or of an advanced character being placed in Subject Departments (*q.v.*). *See also* Browsing Room.

POPULAR NAME. An abbreviated, shortened, or simplified form of the name of a government department, society or other corporate body, by which it is usually known, e.g. Stationery Office; British Association.

PORCELAIN. A sheet of paper consisting of a sheet of blotting-paper pasted to one of coated stock. (American).

PORNOGRAPHY. Writings of an obscene or licentious character: originally applied only to treatises on prostitutes and prostitution. It comes from the Greek words meaning 'writing about harlots'. Many catalogues of old and rare books include such items under the term *Erotica*.

PORPHYRY, TREE OF. A device associated with the name of Porphyry, for abstracting the qualities of terms. It is, in a rough sense, a sub-dividing of the term Substance, by adding differences at different steps; thus Substance, by the addition of the difference Corporeality, divides into Corporeal and Incorporeal Substance; then (neglecting the Incorporeal), to corporeal is added the difference Body which results in Animate and Inanimate. This process is continued as the following Tree shows, until division reaches finality and a specific term (Plato) is reached.

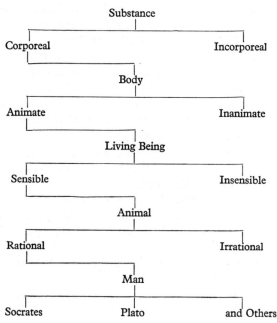

This method of division is known as bifurcate (or division in pairs, positive and negative). The Tree is used to illustrate the FIVE PREDICABLES.

port. (*Pl.* ports.) Abbreviation for PORTRAIT (*q.v.*).

PORTFOLIO. A case for holding loose paintings, drawings, illustrations, diagrams, papers or similar material. Usually made of two sheets of strawboard, covered with paper or cloth with a wide cloth joint to form the 'spine', often with cloth flaps attached at the edges of one board to turn in and so protect the papers, and with tapes at foreedges to secure the contents. Abbreviated pf.

PORTOLAN. *Synonymous with* PORTOLAN CHART (*q.v.*).

PORTOLAN CHART. An early type of chart produced, often in MS., between the thirteenth and seventeenth centuries to guide mariners in coastwise sailing. Such charts were based on estimated bearings and distances between the principal ports or capes. They are believed to have been first produced by the admirals and captains of the Genoese fleet during the second half of the thirteenth century, and are sometimes called 'Compass maps' or 'Loxo-dromes', but wrongly so, as they were used before compasses. Originally a harbour book or written sailing instructions, but the name has come to be used for a sea chart. In England a portolan became known as a 'ruttier' or 'rutter of the sea' (from 'route'). The portolan is much older than the sea-chart, and is known to have been made as early as the tenth and eleventh centuries. Also called 'Portolan', 'Portulan', 'Portolano'.

PORTOLANO. *Synonymous with* PORTOLAN CHART (*q.v.*).

PORTRAIT. 1. A representation of a person, made from life, especially a picture or representation of the face. 2. When portraits are a feature of a work they are indicated in the collation part of a catalogue entry as *ports*. Otherwise they are subsumed. *See also* ILLUSTRATIONS. 3. (*Publishing*) An illustration, or a book, is referred to as 'portrait' when its height is greater than its width. 4. (*Printing*) A table is said to be 'set portrait' when set upright on the page with the bottom of the table parallel with the bottom edge of the page. *See also* LANDSCAPE.

PORTULAN. *Synonymous with* PORTOLAN CHART (*q.v.*).

PORTWAY REPRINTS. A scheme arranged by the Library Association and Messrs Cedric Chivers for the reprinting of out-of-print books. This scheme was started in 1971 and is the successor to an arrangement made by the London and Home Counties Branch of the LA and Messrs Chivers.

POSITIVE. In photography and documentary reproduction, the film or print which has the same tones as the original. It is sometimes made from a NEGATIVE (*q.v.*) in which the image and the tones are in reverse compared with the original.

POSITIVE COPY.   In documentary reproduction, a copy prepared by a POSITIVE PROCESS (*q.v.*) and having the same tones and image as in the original. Also called 'Positive print'. *See also* NEGATIVE PROCESS.

POSITIVE MICROFILM.   A film bearing microcopies with tone values corresponding to those of the originals (*Concepts . . .*).

POSITIVE PRINT.   *Synonymous with* POSITIVE COPY (*q.v.*).

POSITIVE PROCESS.   A documentary reproduction, or copying, process, in which the tones and the image are the same as in the original. *See also* POSITIVE. The opposite of NEGATIVE PROCESS. *See also* NEGATIVE.

POST.   (*Information retrieval*) 1. To transfer an indicial notation from a parent or main entry to individual analytic entries – for example, to type the proper catalogue entry and number at the top of a group of catalogue cards. 2. In co-ordinate indexing, to put the accession number of a document under each entry representing a co-ordination term (*IBM*).

POST-CO-ORDINATE INDEXING SYSTEM.   One in which the indexer or cataloguer is concerned only with simple concepts as headings with a number of entries under each, providing a device or devices whereby the user can combine them to create the compound subjects in which he is interested. The BATTEN SYSTEM, PEEK-A-BOO and UNITERM (*q.v.*) systems are of this kind. *See also* PRE-CO-ORDINATE INDEXING SYSTEM.

POST-DATED. A book which bears a date of publication which is later than the actual date. The opposite of 'Ante-dated'.

POST OCTAVO.   A book size, 8 × 5 inches. *See also* BOOK SIZES.

POSTER.   *Synonymous with* PLACARD (*q.v.*).

POSTHUMOUS WORK.   One which is first published after the death of the author.

POSTING UP.   An indexing practice whereby terms describing the content of a document are also indexed by broader terms.

POSTINGS LIST.   (*Information retrieval*) An alphabetical list of descriptors with the identification numbers of documents using the descriptor posted against it.

POT CASSÉ DEVICE.   A device consisting of a broken jar, or urn, pierced by a wimble (Fr. *toret*) and usually accompanied by the motto 'non plus'. It was used by Geoffroy Tory the French printer on his title-pages. It was also used as part of the design for decorating book covers.

POTT. An obsolete name of a size of paper varying from 15 × 12½ inches to 17¼ × 14¼ inches, and being the smallest of the original (uncut) hand-made papers; the name is probably derived from a watermark design of a pot. *See also* PAPER SIZES.

POUNCE. (*Binding*) An adhesive used under gold or colours.

POWDER or SEMÉ (SEMÉE, SEMIS). (*Binding*) An heraldic term signifying a diaper design of small figures (sprays, flowers, leaves, etc.) frequently repeated by the use of one to three small tools at regular intervals over the greater part of a binding, producing a powdered effect. Sometimes there is a coat of arms, or some other vignette, in the centre, or even at each corner; there may be a lightly tooled fillet around the side of the cover.

POWER PRESS. A printing press in which the operation of the machine was done by some form of power other than the human being. It was introduced in the nineteenth century and superseded the HAND PRESS (*q.v.*) for rapid operation.

PRACTICAL BIBLIOGRAPHY. *See* BIBLIOGRAPHY 2.

PRACTILE. (*Information retrieval*) The percentage of useful documents retrieved per search.

PRAESES. The person or persons who open an academical disputation by propounding objections to some tenet or proposition, usually moral or philosophical, as distinguished from the RESPONDENT (*q.v.*) who defends it.

PREBOUND. *Synonymous with* PRE-LIBRARY BOUND (*q.v.*).

PRECATALOGUED BOOK. One which is accompanied by catalogue cards when supplied, the cards being obtained by purchase, contract, or agreement from a commercial supplier.

PRE-CATALOGUING. The bibliographic searching, usually done before ordering a book, to establish the correct entry and Library of Congress card order information. (American.)

PRECEDENT EPITHET. An epithet which both in common usage and in cataloguing practice precedes a person's forename(s), e.g. 'Mrs', 'Sir'.

PRECEPT. A demand on a RATING AUTHORITY (*q.v.*) specifying the amount required in the £ of rateable value, made by a PRECEPTING AUTHORITY (*q.v.*) to meet its financial requirements for providing services such as police, education and libraries in the area of the authority on which the precept is levied.

PRECEPTING AUTHORITY. One which administers local government services on behalf of other authorities but does not itself raise rates. County councils and the Metropolitan Police Force are precepting authorities. The monies required by precepting authorities must be provided by the respective rate-raising authorities.

PRECIS. Acronym of the PREserved Context Index System. A subject indexing system in which the initial string of terms, organized according to a scheme of role-indicating operators, is computer-manipulated so that selected words function in turn as the approach term. Entries are restructured at each step in such a way that the user can determine from the layout of the entry which terms set the appropriate term into its context and which terms are context-dependent on the approach term. This system was developed initially in the British National Bibliography and has been used in its publications since January 1971. It is also used by the *Australian National Bibliography* and by library services in Canada – *Derek Austin. See also* MARC.

PRECISION RATIO. (*Information retrieval*) The ratio of retrieved relevant documents to the total number of retrieved documents. *See also* RELEVANCE RATIO.

PRE-CO-ORDINATE INDEXING SYSTEM. (*Information retrieval*) A system by which terms are combined at the time of indexing a document, the combination of terms being shown in the entries. This is the system known as PRECIS (*q.v.*) and is used for the entries in the *British National Bibliography*. Such a system co-ordinates terms to form compound classes at the indexing stage, and is used with classification schemes, the classified catalogue and the alphabetical subject catalogue. *See also* POST-CO-ORDINATE INDEXING SYSTEM.

PREDICABLES, FIVE. A series of logical terms and notions, first explained by Porphyry in his treatise on Aristotle's *Topics*, and forming the basis of the science of classification. They are: 1. GENUS – a main class, or group of things, which may be divided into sub-groups called 2. SPECIES, the groups into which the genus is divided. 3. DIFFERENCE – a characteristic which enables a genus to be divided, e.g. add to the genus 'books' the difference 'method of production' and the species 'MS. books', and 'printed books' result. 4. PROPERTY – some quality of a thing or group of things which, although common, is not exclusive to them, e.g. 'jealousy' is common to 'human beings' and 'animals'. 5. ACCIDENT – a quality which is incidental to a class, which may or may not belong to it, and which has no effect on the other qualities of the class. *See also* PORPHYRY, TREE OF; BIFURCATION.

PREFACE. The author's reasons for writing, and his afterthoughts. It indicates the scope, history, and purpose of the book and the class of readers for whom it is intended, and expresses thanks to helpers. It is usually written by the author, follows the DEDICATION (*q.v.*), and precedes the INTRODUCTION (*q.v.*). It is usual to write a new preface to a new edition, outlining the extent of changes and additions. Sometimes called 'Foreword'.

PREFACE DATE. The date given at the beginning or end of the preface.

PREFERRED ORDER. The order in which the facets in a faceted classification schedule are arranged. Once this preferred order has been decided it is invariable. The purpose of preferred order is to display the relations between the terms to the best advantage.

PRE-LIBRARY BOUND. Books bound in a LIBRARY BINDING (*q.v.*) before being sold. Called 'prebound' for short.

PRELIMINARIES. Those parts of the book which precede the first page of the text. The order should be: half title, frontispiece, title, history of book (date of first publication, dates of subsequent reprints and revised editions) and imprint, dedication, acknowledgements, contents list, list of illustrations, list of abbreviations, foreword or preface, introduction, errata. All except the frontispiece, which faces the title-page, and the history and imprint which are on the verso of the title page, should begin on right-hand pages, but the errata may be placed on the left-hand or be printed on a separate slip and pasted in. They are usually printed last on a separate sheet or sheets, and paged separately, usually in Roman figures. Sometimes abbreviated to 'prelims'. When they are printed on leaves conjugate with leaves bearing part of the text, it is often an indication in very old books of an issue later than the first. Also called 'Front matter' in America, 'Preliminary matter'. The *Anglo-American cataloguing rules: British text. Chapter 6 revised* excludes all matter after the verso of the title-page from its definition, but the corresponding revision of the *North American Text* adds the cover and the spine to the definition in the British Text. *See also* SUBSIDIARIES.

PRELIMINARY CATALOGUING. The making of preliminary catalogue entries by typists utilizing data supplied by clerical officers or junior assistants who search the card catalogue for entries. These entries are examined with the books by the cataloguer, who is thus saved clerical work, being enabled to concentrate on professional work requiring judgment and decision. This system was devised by M. T. Franklin Currier, an American, in the 1920s. *See also* SEARCHING.

PRELIMINARY EDITION. An edition issued in advance of the ordinary edition. This is sometimes done in order to obtain criticisms of the text before the final edition is published. Also called 'Provisional edition'.

PRELIMINARY LEAF. One of the unnumbered leaves, printed on one or both sides, which appear before the numbered leaves at the beginning of a book.

PRELIMINARY PUFF. *See* PUFF.

PRELIMS. Abbreviation for PRELIMINARIES (*q.v.*).

PRE-NATAL CATALOGUING. *See* CATALOGUING-IN-PUBLICATION.

PRE-NATAL CLASSIFICATION. Classifying material before it is published. This is common in the U.S.A. where classification numbers (L.C. and Dewey) are printed on the back of the title-pages of books.

PRE-PRINT. A portion of a work printed and issued before the publication of the complete work. A paper submitted at a conference which is published prior to the holding of the conference.

PRE-PROCESSED BOOK. One which is delivered by the book supplier with all the necessary processing completed. (American.)

PRE-PUBLICATION. The practice of disseminating small numbers of duplicated copies of scientific or technical papers or documents, etc., prior to publication by normal routines in printed serial publications.

PRE-PUBLICATION CATALOGUING. Cataloguing books at a national library or national bibliographic centre from gathered and folded sections or review copies of books which are submitted for the purpose by the publishers. *See also* CATALOGUING-IN-PUBLICATION.

PRE-PUBLICATION PRICE. The price at which a book would be sold if ordered prior to a specified date (which is before the publication date) after which the book would cost substantially more.

PRESCRIBED BOOKS. Those which are prescribed for a course of reading.

PRESENTATION COPY. 1. A copy of a book bearing a presentation inscription, usually by the author. 2. A copy of a book presented by the publisher. Only a book that is spontaneously presented properly qualifies for this description; one that is merely autographed at the request of the owner should be called an 'inscribed copy'.

PRESERVATION. (*Archives*) 1. The primary function of an archive depository to provide adequate facilities for the care, protection and maintenance of the archives of whatever kind. 2. Specific individual and collective measures taken for the repair, restoration, protection and maintenance of the archives.

PRESERVED CONTEXT INDEX SYSTEM. *See* PRECIS.

PRESS. 1. A double-sided bookcase of not less than four tiers (i.e. two each side), called in America, a 'Range'. In America a single-sided bookcase with more than two tiers placed end to end; formerly, a 'Bookcase'. *See also* BOOK PRESS, BOOK STACK, BOOKCASE, DOUBLE-FACED SHELF, DOUBLE-SIDED STACK, TIER. 2. The machine, or apparatus, used to press the paper on to the type, plate, engraving or block. In printing there are three methods of imparting this pressure: (a) by the PLATEN PRESS; (b) by the FLAT-BED CYLINDER PRESS; (c) by the ROTARY PRESS (*qq.v.*). *See also* PRINTING PRESS. 3. A simple piece of machinery, possibly a 'screw press', used to keep a book or books in position under pressure to effect adhesion of pasted or glued surfaces, or for some other purpose, during the binding process. 4. A popular name for the trade, and craft, of writing for, and publishing, newspapers and periodicals.

PRESS A UN COUP. A hand printing press on which the operator could lower the platen on to the type in a single movement. It was invented by François Ambroise Didot (1720–1804), the elder son of François Didot (1689–1759).

PRESS AGENT. One who arranges for editorial publicity in the press (*see* PRESS 4) for individuals, institutions, etc.

PRESS BOOK. One issued by a private press.

PRESS COPY. *Synonymous with* REVIEW COPY (*q.v.*).

PRESS CUTTING. A piece cut from a newspaper or periodical. Also called 'Clipping' (American), 'Cutting'.

PRESS ERRORS. Errors made by a compositor when setting type. These are corrected at the printer's cost. Also called 'Printer's errors'.

PRESS MARK. The symbol given to a book to indicate its location. Used in old libraries to indicate the *press* in which the book is shelved, not the book's specific place. This is not so precise as the CALL NUMBER (*q.v.*). Press marks are usually written on the spine of a book (often on a label or tag), on the endpaper, on the front or back of the title-page and against the entry in the catalogue. *See also* CLASS MARK, CLASS NUMBER, FIXED LOCATION.

PRESS NOTICE. A short statement of specific information in a newspaper – including an 'obituary notice' – announcement of a death, notice of an engagement, birth or marriage, or a reference to, or a review of, a new book, or a criticism or commentary on an artistic performance of music, ballet, etc.

PRESS NUMBER. A small figure which in books printed between 1680 and 1823 often appears at the foot of a page, sometimes twice in a gathering (once on a page of the outer forme and once on a page of the inner), the page on which it appears being apparently a matter of indifference, though there is some tendency to avoid a page bearing an ordinary signature. The press number is believed to have been used to indicate on which press the sheet was printed.

PRESS PHOTOGRAPHER. One who takes and supplies photographs for publication in the press.

PRESS PROOF. The final proof passed by the author, editor, or publisher for printing.

PRESS QUERIES. Obscurities in a MS. referred to the author by the printer's proof reader.

PRESS-READY. Sometimes used as a synonym for MAKE-READY (*q.v.*) but also to indicate other machine preparations than that of the forme, such as of the inking, paper-feed, and paper delivery mechanisms.

PRESS RELEASE. An official statement giving information for publication in newspapers or periodicals.

PRESS REVISE. An extra proof taken from type in which corrections marked on earlier proofs have been made, and when machining is about to take place. The press revise is submitted to the machine reviser who finally passes it for press. Also called 'Machine proof'.

PRESS RUN. The number of copies to be printed rather than the number ordered: it is usually larger than the number ordered to allow for spoilage.

PRESSES. 1. In bookbinding, there are several kinds, namely, lying, cutting, standing, blocking and finishing. 2. In printing, the printing machines. In England, 'printing presses' refers to hand-operated apparatus, 'machines' to those operated by power. In America the term 'presses' refers to both. *See also* PRESS.

PRESSWORK. Making an impression on paper from matter set up in type; in modern usage, the care and attention devoted to this as indicated by the quality of the result. It includes the preparation of the printing surface for even printing and the control of inkflow during the running of the press. *See also* MACHINING.

PRESUMED AUTHOR. *Synonymous with* SUPPOSED AUTHOR (*q.v.*).

PRIMA. 1. The first word of the next page, sheet or slip being read, and printed (repeated) at the right hand of the measure immediately below the last line. 2. A mark made on copy where reading is to be resumed after interruption.

PRIMARY ACCESS. (*Information retrieval*) Access to a particular entry (or block of entries) in a file; it may be simultaneous, sequential, fractional or random access. *See also* SCANNING, SECONDARY ACCESS.

PRIMARY BIBLIOGRAPHY. 1. An original, 'extensive' or 'general' bibliography dealing with books unrelated in subject matter. 2. One which is the original record of the whole, or part of, a publication. *See also* SECONDARY BIBLIOGRAPHY. (American.)

PRIMARY BINDING. The style of binding used for a book when it is first published.

PRIMARY DISTRIBUTION. The initial despatch of a document from its originator, or publisher, to more than one destination, especially in accordance with a mailing or distribution list.

PRIMARY NAME HEADING. (*Cataloguing*) An author heading which is provided for an entry where one person or body has primary intellectual responsibility for the existence of a work.

PRIMARY PUBLICATION. A publication which contains mainly original (new) matter, e.g. papers describing the results of original research, as distinct from SECONDARY PUBLICATION (*q.v.*). Also called 'Primary Journal'.

PRIMARY SOURCES. Original manuscripts, contemporary records, or documents which are used by an author in writing a book or other literary compilation. Also called 'Source material' and sometimes 'Original sources'. *See also* SECONDARY SOURCES.

PRIMER. A simple introduction, of an elementary nature, to a subject, possibly intended as a school class book. *See also* INTRODUCTION 2.

PRINCETON FILE. A free-standing box file which is open at the top and back, and which has a front securing the upper parts only of the sides of the file deep enough to take a large label. Such files are used for containing pamphlets on the shelves. *See also* CUT CORNER PAMPHLET FILE.

PRINCIPLES OF CLASSIFICATION. The rules formulated by logicians and classifiers by which a scheme of classification is made.

PRINT. (*Noun*) A reproduction of a picture or drawing by any printing process. Generally applied to etchings, engravings, mezzotints, etc. (*Verb*) To apply ink and then paper to blocks, plates or type to make an 'impression' or a 'print' of the image.

PRINT COLLECTION. A collection of prints such as engravings, etchings, etc.

PRINT FILM. A fine grain, high resolution film which is used primarily for making contact film copies.

PRINT ROOM. A room in a large library in which the collection of prints is kept.

PRINT RUN. The number of copies printed.

PRINTED. Broadly, any representation of characters which are reproduced on any material by any method of mechanical impression, whatever it may be.

PRINTED AS MANUSCRIPT.   *See* PRINTED BUT NOT PUBLISHED.

PRINTED BOOK.   A book produced from type or by a similar process. (*IFLA*). *See also* BOOK, PUBLICATION.

PRINTED BUT NOT PUBLISHED.   Printed, but not put on sale, and therefore not published. This fact may be so noted on the title-page. Also called 'Printed as manuscript'.

PRINTED CATALOGUE.   A catalogue, printed and issued in book form as distinct from a card, or other, form of catalogue.

PRINTED EDGES.   Matter which is printed by means of rubber type on the cut edges of books. This is done on the fore-edge in order to aid speedy reference to the contents, but also here and on the top and bottom edges for the purposes of advertising.

PRINTED MATTER.   A literary composition in the sense of an intelligible, rather than a stylish, arrangement of words which has been set up in type and printed.

PRINTER.   The person or firm responsible for printing a book or other publication, as distinguished from the publisher or bookseller. Of considerable importance in old books. In cataloguing rare books, the printer statement, even when it includes a number of names, is given in the imprint. Added entries may be given under printers' names. When no publisher's name is given on the title page, the printer's may be given in the imprint.

PRINTER'S DEVICE.   *See* DEVICE.

PRINTER'S DEVIL.   An apprentice to the printing trade, especially to a compositor. The origin of the term is said to be that in 1561 a monk published a book called *The Anatomy of the Mass* (1561), and although it had only 172 pages, fifteen more were needed to correct the many typesetting mistakes. These were attributed to the special instigation of the devil, but they turned out to be the work of an apprentice learning the trade.

PRINTER'S ERRORS.   *Synonymous with* PRESS ERRORS (*q.v.*).

PRINTER'S FLOWER.   *See* FLOWER.

PRINTER'S IMPRINT.   *See* IMPRINT.

PRINTER'S KEEPSAKE.   *See* KEEPSAKE 3.

PRINTER'S MARK.   *See* DEVICE.

PRINTER'S ORNAMENT.   *See* ORNAMENT.

PRINTER'S PIE.   *See* PIE.

PRINTER'S READER.   *See* READER 1.

PRINTING.   *See* IMPRESSION.

PRINTING AND ALLIED TRADES RESEARCH.   The activities of the former British Paper and Board Industry Research Association (BPBIRA) and of the Printing, Packaging and Allied Trades Research Association (PATRA) are now undertaken by PIRA, the Research Association for the Paper and Board, Printing and Packaging Industries. Situated at Leatherhead, Surrey, PIRA is organized into four operating divisions – paper and board; printing; packaging; information, training and techno-economics. It provides technical enquiry, testing and consultancy services. Its worldwide monitoring of information and its computer-based data bank provide the basis for a number of services. A non-profit making organization, its sources of income are: membership subscriptions, government contracts and direct fee income from the sales of consultancies and services. Publishes *PIRA News* (m.), *Printing Abstracts* (m.), *Paper and Board Abstracts* (m.), *Packaging Abstracts* (m.), *PIRA Management and Marketing Abstracts* (m.), *Newsbrief* (for newspaper management (bi-w.).

PRINTING BLOCK.   A general term for any kind of BLOCK (*q.v.*) used in printing.

PRINTING HISTORICAL SOCIETY.   Founded in 1964 'to encourage the study of, and foster interest in, the history of printing; to encourage the preservation of historical equipment and printed matter; to promote meetings and exhibitions; to produce publications in connection with these aims'. Publishes *Journal* (a.).

PRINTING INDUSTRY RESEARCH ASSOCIATION.   The name by which the PRINTING, PACKAGING AND ALLIED TRADES RESEARCH ASSOCIATION (*qv.*) was known until 1930.

PRINTING PRESS.   A machine for making impressions from a plate, block or type which has been inked, on paper or some other material. *See also* CYLINDER PRESS, FLAT-BED PRESS, INTAGLIO, LETTERPRESS, LITHOGRAPHY, OFFSET, PLATEN PRESS, ROTARY PRESS.

PRINTINGS.   A general term for papers which are specially suitable for printing as distinct from other purposes.

PRINTOUT.   A statement printed automatically from data stored in a computer.

PRIORITY DATE.   The date when the basis of the claim was first disclosed to a patent office; it is usually the date on which a provisional or complete specification was filed, or a convention date. It is the date on which a patent claim relies if it is challenged. *See also* CONVENTION APPLICATION, PATENT OF ADDITION.

PRISON LIBRARY.   A library maintained in a prison for the use of prisoners. In many prisons in Great Britain the prison libraries are provided by the local authority, the Prison Commissioners contributing a fixed sum per prisoner towards the cost.

PRIVATE BILLS. Bills published by their promoters for submission in the House of Commons.

PRIVATE LIBRARIES ASSOCIATION. An international society of authors, publishers, booksellers, librarians and private book collectors – collectors of rare books, fine books, single authors, reference books on special subjects, and above all collectors of books generally for the simple pleasures of reading and ownership. Its functions include the organizing of lectures on subjects of bibliographical interest and visits to famous libraries, printing works, binderies, etc. running an Exchange Scheme enabling members to dispose of surplus material and advertise for desiderata; issuing publications of interest to members and running a Loans Library for members. An annual lecture is given. Publishes a Newsletter and Exchange List bi-monthly and *The Private Library* quarterly. Abbreviated PLA.

PRIVATE LIBRARY. One which is owned by a private individual. Also a library owned by a society, club or other organization, to which members of the public have no right of access.

PRIVATE MARK. Some indication of ownership, usually the name of the library impressed with a rubber stamp, which is always placed in a particular part of a library book.

PRIVATE PRESS. A printing establishment which undertakes only the work of the owner, or of publishing clubs who may be supporting it financially, or prints only those books (usually not first editions) which the proprietor fancies. Private presses are usually small establishments using hand presses or small letterpress machines, and producing well-printed books in limited editions on hand-made paper. Eric Gill, writing to the *Monotype Recorder* in 1933, said that such a press prints solely what it chooses and not what its customers demand of it, which is the case with a 'public' press, and that 'the distinction has nothing to do with the use of machinery or with questions of the artistic quality of the product'. Of such were the Kelmscott, Essex House, Doves, Vale, Gregynog, Ashendene, Cuala, Eragny, and Pear Tree.

PRIVATE PUBLISHER. One who has works printed by a commercial or private printer and publishes them himself, mainly to ensure the publication of work which might not otherwise be published and/or to achieve a high standard of physical production.

PRIVATELY PRINTED. This term is given to books printed for the author or a private individual, usually for distribution gratis. It is also applied to books printed on a PRIVATE PRESS (*q.v.*). When printed on a public press it is often described as being printed at the author's expense, or by private subscription. Abbreviated p.p.

PRIVILEGE ISSUE. Books issued at the close of a lecture to persons who do not present a borrower's ticket.

pro tem. Abbreviation for *pro tempore* (*Lat.* 'for the time being').

PROBABLE ASSOCIATION, PRINCIPLE OF. The principle that the heading chosen for a catalogue entry (whether for a person, subject, place, organization, etc.) should be the one most users of the library are likely to look under. *See also* CATALOGUING, PRINCIPLES OF.

PROCEDURE MANUAL. *Synonymous with* STAFF MANUAL (*q.v.*) except that in an American special library it may be more detailed, and personnel matters are omitted if they are contained in, as is usual in the case of corporations, the employee handbook. Also called 'Work manual'.

PROCEEDINGS. The published record of meetings of a society or institution, frequently accompanied by the papers read or submitted, or by abstracts or reports. *See also* TRANSACTIONS.

PROCESS. (*Verb*) 1. To manipulate data by mechanical means. 2. To prepare books and other documents for a collection, especially physical preparation such as labelling and giving marks of ownership.

PROCESS BLOCK. A metal printing surface produced with the aid of photography and a chemical or mechanical process.

PROCESS CAMERA. One used for the production of a photographic intermediate (usually film – either negative or positive) necessary for making an image on a material from which prints can be made, e.g. an offset-litho plate.

PROCESS COLOUR PRINTING. *See* COLOUR WORK.

PROCESS EMBOSSING. *Synonymous with* EMBOSSING (*q.v.*).

PROCESS ENGRAVING. Any of the processes for reproducing pictures, print, etc. that uses plates or blocks prepared by photographic, mechanical or chemical action rather than by hand. Also called 'Photomechanical process', and 'Process work'.

PROCESS PHOTOGRAPHY. The reproduction of line copy as distinct from continuous tone copy, e.g. a line drawing compared with a photograph. Materials of great contrast are used with this method.

PROCESS PUBLICATIONS. Those which are produced by a duplicating process other than ordinary printing. The output may be single sheets or complete books.

PROCESS RECORD. Usually a card record of a book or other item received at a library and in process of being added to library records.

PROCESS SLIP (ACCESSION SLIP, COPY SLIP, GUIDE SLIP, ROUTINE SLIP). A slip or card, usually the same size as a catalogue card, bearing author's name, title, imprint, collation, tracings, and allocations of copies to libraries or departments. It accompanies the book throughout the cataloguing department and is generally used as the copy for the typist or printer. Called also, in America, 'Rider slip'.

PROCESS STAMP. A rubber stamp impression on the back of the title-page of a book to give the library history of the book and to show which assistants were responsible for the various stages of its processing.

PROCESS WORK. *See* PROCESS ENGRAVING.

PROCESSES, DEPARTMENT OF TECHNICAL. *Synonymous with* PROCESSING DEPARTMENT (*q.v.*).

PROCESSING. 1. Strictly, the carrying out of the various routines such as stamping, labelling, numbering, etc., before a book is ready for the shelves, but it may include *all* the processes involved in so preparing a book. Also called 'Book preparation', 'Book processing'. In a technical information bureau or library, much more work may be done to enable information to be obtained readily ('retrieved') than is necessary in a general or public library. These processes may be grouped into three: library processing, bibliographic processing, and information processing. Library processing includes acquisition of materials; cataloguing; classification and filing of cards; physical processing as mentioned above, and the shelving of materials; notification of additions to stock. Bibliographic processing includes: bibliographic description; filing of cards in reference and bibliographic files; reproduction of cards; notification to individuals. Information processing includes: distribution of literature and documentation at the request of departments, members or others, or on standing order; notification of information, preparation of reference cards and filing in reference information file; preparation of abstracts; making of a translation; microfilming or photoreproduction; other forms of reproduction of materials; ordering of materials needed; assembling selections on particular topics. 2. In photography and documentary reproduction, the carrying out of such processes as are necessary after the projection of the image to be copied on to the sensitized material. *See also* MECHANICAL PREPARATION. 3. (*Archives*) The actions connected with the description, arrangement and preservation of archival material, and undertaken with a view to facilitating the use of the documents.

PROCESSING CENTER. In America, a building in which the processing of books for a number of libraries is carried out, thus releasing trained personnel for other work and reducing costs by various means. Such centers have developed by co-operation of librarians in adjoining areas, often being initiated under the provisions of the Library Services Act. Sometimes they operate from an existing public library, from a state library agency, as an entirely separate enterprise on a contract or other co-operative basis among a group of libraries, or as a commercial project.

PROCESSING DEPARTMENT. 1. A combined book-ordering (or acquisition) and cataloguing department. 2. In some libraries, a department in which the work of preparing books for circulation, other than cataloguing and classification, is carried out. *See also* CATALOGUING DEPARTMENT, TECHNICAL SERVICES DEPARTMENT.

PROCESSOR-CAMERA. A device which functions as a camera and film processor. *See also* CAMERA CARD.

PROCTOR ORDER. The system of classification of incunabula named after the order used by R. G. C. Proctor in his *Index of early printed books in the British Museum*, 1897–1903.

PROFESSIONAL ASSISTANT. In American libraries, a member of the professional staff performing work of a nature requiring training and skill in the theoretical or scientific parts of library work as distinct from its merely mechanical parts.

PROFESSIONAL AUDITOR. A person who is a member of an appropriate recognized body may be appointed as a professional auditor to audit the accounts of a borough or non-county borough council which are not subject to district audit. Professional auditors have no power of disallowance. In most county boroughs, accounts which are not required to be audited by the district auditor are audited by professional auditors. *See also* BOROUGH AUDITOR.

PROFILE. 1. A biographical account combined with a description and assessment of the subject's achievements. 2. (*Information retrieval*) A set of indexing terms which characterize the interests of an individual or a group using a selective dissemination of information service. Also called an INTEREST-PROFILE (*q.v.*), this is matched with the terms by which each document is indexed in the system.

PRO-FORMA INVOICE. An invoice received for checking and approval prior to receiving the formal invoice. It is used as a check list for periodical renewals and then returned for authorization for placing renewal orders, or as a request for confirmation of an order for an unexpectedly expensive item. It is never approved and forwarded for payment. (American.)

PROGRAM. (*Information retrieval*) (*Noun*) An outline giving the schedule of actions to be followed or the order and arrangement of such a schedule. A series of instructions expressed in symbols which a machine system can accept and understand (*IBM*). A sequence of steps or coded instructions to be executed by the computer to solve a given problem. (*Verb*) To determine the steps and plan the procedures necessary for the computer to solve the problem.

PROGRAM DISSERTATION. A dissertation accompanying a 'program' (i.e. announcement of a memorial exercise, lecture, etc.) published by a university or school, especially in Germany, Austria, Switzerland or one of the Scandinavian countries. (American.)

PROGRAMMER. A person who is skilled in the writing of computer programs.

PROGRAMMING LANGUAGE. A stylized method of writing instructions (a 'program') which instruct a computer what to do. All programming languages differ from natural language in being non-ambiguous.

PROGRESS, IN. *See* IN PROGRESS.

PROGRESSIVE PROOF. A proof showing the sequences and effect at each stage of a colour-printing process as each colour is added. *See also* FLAT PROOF.

PROJECT INTREX. A long range programme, established in January 1964 by the Massachusetts Institute of Technology, for the application of the principles and methods of information processing to library operation, with the specific object of establishing the bases upon which the technical library of the future may be modelled. Intrex stands for Information Transfer Exchange.

PROJECT LEER. A joint undertaking by the Books for the People Fund, Inc. and the Bro-Dart Foundation for the compilation and publication of annual lists of children's books and elementary reading materials for adults which are available in the Spanish language, and for the encouragement of the production and use of such reading materials. The project is being directed from the offices of the Organization of American States in Washington, D.C.

PROJECT LOC. A project, supported financially by the Andrew W. Mellon Foundation, for compiling a machine-readable union catalogue of pre-1801 books in the British Museum and in the university, college and departmental libraries of Oxford and Cambridge. The Report was published in 1974, 'for assessment and criticism'.

PROJECTED BOOKS. Microfilmed books intended for projecting on to a ceiling, wall or screen for the benefit of physically-handicapped people.

PROJECTION. The method used by a cartographer for representing on a plane the whole, or part, of the earth's surface, as Mercator's Projection.

PROJECTION PRINT. In documentary reproduction, a copy having a larger scale than the original: an enlargement. Also called a 'Blow-up'.

PROJECTION PRINTING. A method of obtaining a photographic copy by exposing a photosensitive surface by projecting an image through an optical system.

PROMPT BOOK. *Synonymous with* PROMPT COPY (*q.v.*).

PROMPT COPY. The copy of a play used by a prompter, showing action of a play, cues, movements of actors, properties, costumes, and scene and light plots.

PRONOUNCEABLE NOTATION. (*Classification*) A notation, which for ease of memorizing consists of letters which as a group can be pronounced. A scheme, the pronunciation of the symbols of which is recognized internationally, was designed by E. de Grolier; it uses only the letters A, E, I, K, L, M, N, O, P, S, T and U. Also called SYLLABIC NOTATION (*q.v.*).

PROOF. 1. In bookbinding: the rough edges of certain leaves left uncut by the plough are proof that the book is not cut down. 2. An impression made from type before being finally prepared for printing. Proofs are made on long sheets of normal page width (GALLEY or SLIP PROOF) for the author's inspection and correction but not until after a *First Proof* has been made, corrected by the printer's reader and returned to the compositor. When the printer has made the corrections the type is divided up into pages, the page numbers inserted, and a further proof submitted to the author. This third proof is called the *Page Proof*. A *Marked Proof* is one marked by the printer's reader, corrected by the author and again read by the printer's reader, and a *Revise* or *Revised Proof* is a further one embodying corrections made by the author/or reader to the first proof. *See also* AUTHOR'S PROOF, CLEAN PROOF. 3. A preliminary impression taken from an engraved plate or block, or a lithographic stone. Usually called 'Trial proof'. 4. An impression taken from a finished plate or block before the regular impression is published and usually before the title or other inscription is added. Also called 'Proof print' or 'Proof impression'.

PROOF BEFORE LETTERS. A proof of an engraving, etching or other illustration process made before the addition of title, artist's and engraver's name, date, dedication or other matter.

PROOF CORRECTIONS. Signs used by proof readers on printers' proofs to indicate corrections to be made in the typesetting. These have become established over the centuries and the British code is published in *British Standard* 5261: Part 2: 1976. The American Standard is Z 39.22–1974. A British Standard for colour printing was published in 1972 – BS 4785 : 1972 *Colour proof correction symbols.*

PROOF PRESS. A small or medium-sized press operated electrically or by hand on which proofs from type or other relief surfaces are made.

PROOF READER. A person who reads printers' proofs to discover errors in type, punctuation, statement and so forth, and marks the corrections on the proof while the 'copy' is read out to him by the copyholder.

PROOF READER'S MARKS. *Synonymous with* PROOF CORRECTIONS *(q.v.).*

PROOF READING. The process of reading a printer's proof and comparing it with the MS. or COPY *(q.v.)* in order to detect errors in typesetting. Errors are marked on the proof in accordance with generally accepted signs and the resulting 'corrected proof' is returned to the printer so that the necessary corrections may be carried out. *See also* PROOF, PROOF CORRECTIONS.

PROOF SHEET. A sheet of paper on which a proof of type-matter, plate, or block, is made by a printer. *See also* PROOF.

PROPER NAME. A name used as the designation of a single person, place or thing, e.g. Leonard, Wimbledon, Festival Hall, Loch Ness Monster.

PROPERTY. *See* PREDICABLES, FIVE.

PROPRIETARY INFORMATION. Information which is owned by reason of discovery or purchase, and is private or confidential to a specific firm or organization.

PROSPEC. The computer application, in association with INSPEC, by means of which the records of holdings at the Public Record Office will be recorded and reproduced for use of the public in place of the printed *Guides* formerly published.

PROSPECTUS. 1. A leaflet or pamphlet issued by a publisher and describing a new publication. 2. A publication written to inform, arouse interest in, and encourage the reader to take some action concerning, a book about to be published, a school or other education institution, or the issue of stock or shares of a company, etc.

PROTECTION. *(Copyright)* The legal guarantee of copyright in an INTELLECTUAL WORK *(q.v.)* which is given by the law of a country. This protection is usually given either from the date of its deposit with a national organization or its date of publication.

PROVENANCE. A record or indication of previous ownership of a book or manuscript. A special binding, book plate, or inscription may indicate previous owners, collections or libraries through which a particular book has passed. (*Archives*) 1. In archival theory, the principle that the archives of a given records creator must not be intermingled with those of different origin. 2. In general archival usage, the originating entity which created or accumulated the records; also the source of PERSONAL PAPERS (*q.v.*) and manuscript collections. 3. Information concerning the successive changes of ownership or custody of a particular document.

PROVINCIAL JOINT FICTION RESERVE. A national scheme for the co-operative preservation of books, similar to the scheme initiated by the former Association of Metropolitan Chief Librarians. It commenced to operate on 1st January 1962; each Regional Bureau outside London and the South East, which already had schemes, is responsible for a part of the alphabet. The scheme provides only for the purchase and retention of new publications and is not retrospective, although offers of older novels are sometimes made to the responsible library. Allocation by author amongst the regions is as follows:

A–C	North-Western	K–M	West Midlands
D–F	Northern	N–S	Yorkshire
G–J	East Midlands	T–Z	South-Western

PROVISIONAL EDITION. A book which is published in a small edition, possibly by some near-print process, and circulated to selected individuals or sold in the ordinary way, so that observations, criticisms and suggestions may be submitted and considered before a final edition is published. Also called 'Preliminary edition'.

PROVISIONAL SPECIFICATION. *See* PATENT, SPECIFICATION.

PRUDENTIAL COMMITTEE. *Synonymous with* ADMINISTRATIVE COUNCIL (*q.v.*).

PRUSSIAN INSTRUCTIONS. The German cataloguing code; an English translation was published by the University of Michigan Press in 1938.

PSALM-BOOK. A PSALTER (*q.v.*).

PSALTER. The Book of Psalms in which the Psalms are arranged as in the Book of Common Prayer for use in a religious service, whether to be spoken or sung; in the latter case they may be in a metrical version.

PSEUDANDRY. The use by a woman author of a masculine name as a pseudonym. *See also* PSEUDONYM.

PSEUDEPIGRAPHY. The attributing of false names to the authors of books.

PSEUDO ABSTRACT. An abstract that was written in anticipation that an article, or 'paper' would be written in the future, but has not been, and might never be, written. Such an abstract is written by a speaker invited to address a meeting of a professional association and is published prior to the delivery of the full 'paper' which may, in the event, be spoken extempore and never published or otherwise recorded.

PSEUDOGRAPH. A literary composition falsely attributed to a particular writer.

PSEUDOJYN. A man writing under a feminine pseudonym.

PSEUDONYM. A name used by an author, which is not his real name. Also called a 'Pen name' or 'Nom de plume'. *See also* SYNCOPISM, TELONISM, TITLONYM.

PSEUDONYMOUS WORKS. Those written by persons who have used a name other than their real name on the title-page in order to conceal their identity. *See also* PSEUDONYM.

PSEUDO-PHOTOGRAPHIC PHOTOCOPYING. Copying processes which are not photographic. Of such are THERMOFAX and XEROGRAPHY (*qq.v.*).

PSEUDO-WEEDING. *See* WEEDING.

PUBLIC AFFAIRS INFORMATION SERVICE, INC. *See* PAIS.

PUBLIC CATALOGUE. A catalogue issued for the use of the public as distinct from one issued for use by officials.

PUBLIC DOCUMENTS. The regular official publications of a government, containing reports, statistics, etc.

PUBLIC LENDING RIGHT.† A subsidy paid to authors in respect of books issued from public libraries. It has been in operation in Denmark, Sweden and Norway for many years and in Finland since 1961. Suggestions were made in 1951 that such a scheme should be adopted in Great Britain and in 1960 an 'Authors' and Publishers' Lending Right Association Committee' was formed to negotiate with the Library Association; no positive results were achieved. In the Scandinavian countries the subsidies are paid from government funds, either according to the books stocked in public libraries or according to the number of times copyright books are borrowed. The Society of Authors has continued its campaigning in Great Britain, and government spokesmen have stated that some form of subsidy should be paid from government funds. The Minister for the Arts stated in December 1974 that legislation on public lending right would be on the statute book by the Spring of 1975, but parliamentary time and the difficulties of determining satisfactory ways of measuring entitlement and the protracted investigations of the technical investigation group appointed by the Department of Education and Science did not make this possible. The Public Lending Right Bill was published on 19 March 1976; it confers on authors the right to payments in respect of loans from public libraries, and (apart from West Germany), the U.K. will be the first country to pass such legislation – in most other countries the right has been established by decree or regulation. In Australia, a scheme was introduced in 1974, similar to one adopted in New Zealand in 1973, whereby authors will receive 50c. (Aust.) a year for each copy of a title held by libraries (entitlement is determined by a minimum of fifty libraries holding a title). Payments are made for fifty years after a book's publication date. The publishers of the titles receive 12.5c. a year. The funds are being provided by the government. Abbreviated PLR.

PUBLIC LIBRARIES, STANDARDS FOR. *See* STANDARDS FOR PUBLIC LIBRARIES.

PUBLIC LIBRARIES ACTS. The 'adoptive' acts (i.e. those which apply only where they have been adopted by the appropriate authority) which govern the provision and management of libraries are: the Public Libraries Act, 1892; the Public Libraries (Amendment) Act, 1893; the Public Libraries Act, 1901; and the Public Libraries Act, 1919. Some provisions of the Local Government Act, 1933, also affect public libraries. *See also* LIBRARY AUTHORITY, LOCAL GOVERNMENT BOUNDARIES, LOCAL GOVERNMENT (RECORDS) ACT, 1962, PUBLIC LIBRARIES AND MUSEUMS BILL.

PUBLIC LIBRARIES AND MUSEUMS BILL. Introduced to the House of Commons on 24 January 1964, this bill provided a completely new legal basis for the public service, would repeal all existing library legislation by one comprehensive law for public library services in England and Wales. It would impose a statutory duty on local library authorities to provide a 'comprehensive and efficient public library service'. It would also give to the Minister of Education, for the first time, the responsibility 'to superintend and promote the development of the service and to secure the proper discharge by local authorities of their library functions, England and Wales would have their own National Advisory Councils to advise the Minister on library matters, and Regional Councils would be set up to make and supervise arrangements for co-operation within the region and with other bodies concerned with libraries. The Bill would take effect not earlier than 1 April 1965. It was based on the report of the two working parties set up in 1961 which resulted from the Roberts Committee Report of 1958. The resulting act was passed on 31 July 1964 and came into operation on 1st April 1965. *See also* BAKER REPORT, BOURDILLON REPORT, ROBERTS REPORT.

PUBLIC LIBRARIES GROUP. A Group of the Library Association. Formed in November 1974 'to establish an organization to unite members engaged or otherwise interested in public libraries with a view to increasing the effectiveness of Public Libraries and furthering the objects set forth in the Charter of the Library Association'. Membership is open to any member of the L.A., and also to duly nominated and approved representatives of those authorities in affiliated membership. The County Libraries Group ceased to function after December 1974 in order to combine its functions with those of the Public Library Group which will take over this former Group's publications programme and also its series of week-end schools.

PUBLIC LIBRARY. A library provided wholly or partly from public funds, and the use of which is not restricted to any class of persons in the community but is freely available to all. A major agency of enlightenment for adults, providing also for children the recorded experiences of others which will help them to grow into adulthood.

PUBLIC LIBRARY ASSOCIATION. A Division of the American Library Association under this name since 1958; originally organized in 1951, it is 'concerned with the improvement and expansion of public library services to users of all ages and in all types of communities, and with increasing professional awareness of the social responsibilities of the library to its public'. Abbreviated PLA. Publishes *PLA Newsletter* (4 p.a. to membs.)

PUBLIC LIBRARY AUTOMATION NETWORK. *See* PLAN.

PUBLIC LIBRARY MANIFESTO. A document published by Unesco first in 1949, revised in 1972 (text in *IFLA News*, No. 41, July 1972 and in the May–June 1972 issue of *Unesco Bulletin for Libraries*) and published in all the major languages of the world for wide distribution, particularly in developing countries. It sets out the basic services which public libraries should provide, how they should be provided, administered and financed. By July 1973, with the help of IFLA member associations and individuals, the Manifesto had been translated into thirty-five languages, and the U.S.S.R. was translating it into Russian and the fourteen major regional languages. It was expected that translations would be made into well over fifty languages.

PUBLIC RECORD OFFICE. The depository for British Official documents; it is situated in Chancery Lane, London, W.C.2., and contains

22

documents from the twelfth century to date. The Public Records Act 1958, much of which was based on the report of the Committee on Departmental Records (the 'Grigg Report') transferred the direction of the PRO from the Master of the Rolls to a Minister of the Crown, the Lord Chancellor, who now has a general responsibility for public records; he is authorized to appoint an Advisory Council on Public Records, of which the Master of the Rolls is the Statutory Chairman; this Council is particularly concerned with those aspects of the work of the PRO which affect members of the public making use of the facilities provided. The Act places on government departments a duty to select records for permanent preservation and to pass them to the PRO within thirty years of their creation. They were open to public inspection when they were fifty years old until 1 January 1968 when the period was reduced to thirty years. The Lord Chancellor has power to appoint for any class of records a special place of deposit; this enables public records accruing in local courts and offices to be kept in local repositories, and those of a technical character to be kept in appropriate specialist institutions. The 1958 Act declares that 'records' includes not only written records but those conveying information by any other means whatsoever.

PUBLIC RECORD OFFICE OF IRELAND. Founded by provisions of the Public Records (Ireland) Act 1867 in order to preserve and render readily accessible the non-recurrent records of Government and the courts, and other archival material of importance. The Office, which is situated in Dublin, is provided by Government and open to the public. Abbreviated PROI; often PROSPO (Public Record Office and State Paper Office). Publishes reports (annual) of the Deputy Keeper of Public Records. The Deputy Keeper of the PROI is also the Keeper of State Papers. The State Paper Office, which was established in 1706, aims to preserve and make accessible to researchers the state papers of Ireland, in particular the records of the Chief Secretary's Office; it is situated in Dublin Castle. The Reports of the Keeper appear as appendices to the Reports of the Deputy Keeper of Public Records, Ireland, 1–59 (1869–1962). Abbreviated SPOI.

PUBLIC RECORD OFFICE OF NORTHERN IRELAND. Formed in 1924 to provide for the reception and safe keeping of the records of the Northern Ireland Government, the Courts of Justice, the local authorities and other public bodies. The Office also encourages the depositing of documents by private individuals and institutions so that the public may have access to all material of social, economic and historical interest. Approximately 100,000,000 documents have been deposited. This office is provided by Government and is open to the public. Abbreviated PRONI. Publishes many calendars, facsimiles, books and Deputy Keeper's reports on accessions; these are available from H.M.S.O. bookshops.

PUBLIC RECORDS. Records made in the process of government and including those made by any means whatsoever, not only those which are written.

PUBLIC RECORDS ACT 1958. *See* PUBLIC RECORD OFFICE.

PUBLIC (SERVICE) AREA. That portion of the area of a library to which the public are admitted but which is occupied by fixed furniture used by both staff and public (staff enclosure, circulation desk, information, enquiries or registration desks, etc.), catalogues, exhibits and displays.

PUBLICATION. 1. A work (*see* WORK 1) issued to the public in the form of a document (*see* DOCUMENT 2) or book (*see* BOOK 4) (IFLA). 2. The act of issuing a book to the public (IFLA). 3. As defined in Article VI of the Universal Copyright Convention 1971, 'the reproduction in tangible form and the general distribution to the public of copies of a work from which it can be read or otherwise visually perceived'.

PUBLICATION DATE. *Synonymous with* DATE OF PUBLICATION (*q.v.*).

PUBLICATION DAY. 1. The day of the week or month on which a periodical is issued. 2. The first day on which a book may be sold to the public.

PUBLISH. 1. The action of a publisher in issuing and offering for sale to the public, a book or print produced on some kind of printing, copying or photographic reproducing machine. 2. The action of an author, artist, or composer of music, in creating something, and arranging for it to be reproduced in quantity and offered for sale.

PUBLISHED. A document which has been reproduced in a number of copies and made available to the public to whom it may be sold or distributed free of charge and whether or not it is intended to have a restricted readership such as to members of parliament, of a learned, professional or political organization.

PUBLISHED PRICE. The retail price at which a book is published.

PUBLISHER. A person, firm, or corporate body responsible for placing a book on the market, as distinguished from the printer. Publisher and printer may be the same, but in modern books usually is not. Relates also to publication of music, reproduction of works of art and of maps and photographs. A firm which undertakes publishing is sometimes referred to as a 'Publishing house' or 'Publishing firm'.

PUBLISHERS ASSOCIATION. A trade association which was founded in Britain in 1896. Membership is open to any publisher in the United Kingdom whose business, or an appreciable part of it, is publishing books. The original object of the Association was to maintain the prices of net books, and while this is still a matter of considerable interest, the Association is largely engaged in assisting its members to secure a greater, and more efficient, distribution of books, and in the education of publishers' staffs. It deals with problems which face publishers as a whole, regulates conditions of employment within the trade, supplies its members with information and advice on all matters of technical, economic and legal aspects of publishing, and represents publishers in discussions or negotiations with the government, local authorities, and public and trade bodies.

PUBLISHER'S BINDING. The binding in which a publisher issues a book.

PUBLISHER'S CASE. *Synonymous with* PUBLISHER'S COVER (*q.v.*).

PUBLISHER'S CATALOGUE. A list of books issued for sale by a publisher.

PUBLISHER'S CLOTH. Used to indicate a book as issued by the publisher in a cloth binding.

PUBLISHER'S COVER. The cover for a book that is provided by a publisher for the normal trade edition of a book. Also called 'Publisher's case'. *See also* CASE, EDITION BINDING.

PUBLISHER'S DEVICE. *See* DEVICE.

PUBLISHER'S DUMMY. A dummy book made up of the right number of sections of plain paper, and sometimes cased, to indicate the size of a proposed book.

PUBLISHER'S IMPRINT. *See* IMPRINT.

PUBLISHER'S INFORMATION CARD. A card bearing bibliographical details of a book. Such cards are distributed by publishers to libraries as a means of conveying accurate information in unit record form. Abbreviated PIC.

PUBLISHER'S LIST. A list of books published by one publisher and still in print.

PUBLISHER'S MARK. *See* DEVICE.

PUBLISHER'S NUMBER. *See* PLATE NUMBER.

PUBLISHER'S READER. One whose calling is the reading, judging and criticizing of manuscripts offered for publication.

PUBLISHER'S SERIES. The name given to a series of books which usually have been published previously, and comprising standard or current books on related or unrelated subjects, issued in a uniform style and at the same price, and bearing a series title such as *World's Classics*, or *Everyman's Library*. Each volume contains one or more distinct works, and some series include books published for the first time. Also called 'Trade series'. Series which comprise only books previously published are sometimes called 'Reprint series'.

PUBLISHING. The trade of publishing books; this includes negotiations with authors or their agents, design of books in conjunction with printers, book production, publicity and sales through book wholesalers and retailers. In addition to books it relates to music, reproduction of works of art and of photographs and maps.

PUFF. A term, in use since the seventeenth century, for exaggerated praise for a book, usually written by the author or publisher for use in advertisements and on the book's jacket. A 'Preliminary puff' is supplied to the publisher's travellers as pre-publication publicity. *See also* BLURB.

PUGILLARES. From two to eight small wooden writing tablets of ivory, wood, or metal and covered with wax on one side upon which writing could be scratched with a stylus. Sometimes the tablets were hinged together with rings or leather cords down one side to form a tablet book. Notebooks of this sort were known as *pugillaria*. *See also* CODEX.

PULL. A trial print taken from type or a block before an edition is printed.

PULLED. In bookbinding, a book the cover of which has been removed and all the sheets separated. *See also* TAKE DOWN.

PULLED TYPE. Type letters which have been pulled out of the forme by ink-balls.

PULLING. (*Binding*) Stripping the old covers off a book, separating the sections and removing any old glue prior to rebinding.

PULLOUT. (*Book production*) Synonymous *with* THROW OUT (*q.v.*).

PULP. The mechanically or chemically prepared mixture made from vegetable fibres which becomes paper when passed over the wire and dried. *See also* CHEMICAL WOOD, HAND-MADE PAPER, MECHANICAL WOOD. 2. A cheap magazine printed on newsprint.

PULP BOARD. Board manufactured in one thickness, or by bringing two or more thicknesses of board or paper together into a single structure on a multiple-wire machine, as distinct from boards made by laminations of paper pasted together and called 'Pasteboard'.

Sizes:

	inches
Imperial	22 × 30
Postal	22½ × 28½
Pulp Royal	20½ × 25

PULP MAGAZINE. A cheap magazine printed on newsprint and containing stories of adventure, mystery or love, usually of poor quality.

PUNCH. A piece of steel on which a type character is engraved. After hardening it is used as a die to strike the matrices from which type is cast.

PUNCH ENGRAVING. A method of book illustration which had previously been used by goldsmiths and ornament engravers. The tools used consisted of a dotting punch, a small pointed punch set in a wooden handle and used by hand pressure, and larger punches with either grained or plain striking surfaces intended for use with a hammer.

PUNCHED CARD. A lightweight card which has holes punched in certain positions either round the edges (edge-punched) or in the body of the card (body-punched) to represent specific pieces of information. Edge-punched cards are sorted manually with the aid of a 'needle' and body-punched cards usually by machine. They are used to record particulars of membership, book stock or classified material or information. Extensive use of them is made in connexion with information retrieval or document systems. Also called an 'EAM [electronic accounting machine] card'. *See also* DEQUEKER SYSTEM, EDGE-NOTCHED CARDS, MARGINAL-HOLE PUNCHED CARDS. Punched cards are also used in BOOKAMATIC, PHOTOCHARGING and PUNCHED CARD CHARGING (*qq.v.*) methods of recording the loan of books to avoid the manual sorting of, and searching for, transaction cards.

PUNCHED CARD CHARGING. A TRANSACTION CARD CHARGING (*q.v.*) system whereby a punching machine is used to punch two transaction cards simultaneously, to record book number, reader's number, main class number and date due for return. One card is placed in the book and is taken away by the reader; it has a readable date due for return stamped on it. The other is retained. *See also* CHARGING METHODS.

PUNCTUATION. *See* DASH, FILING CODE, LINKS, QUOTES.

PUNCTUATION SYMBOLS. A device used in co-ordinate indexing to associate terms or symbols in order to indicate relationship. For example, a double dot (. .) may be used before each associated set of words to indicate that they are to be considered together.

PURE BIBLIOGRAPHY. The type of bibliography which treats of the value of the contents of books, including textual criticism (*Maire*).

PURE NOTATION. *See* NOTATION.

PUSTAKA. A book consisting of long strips of the thin bark of trees or of a kind of paper made from tree bark; it may deal with magic medicine, domestic remedies, or 'the art' of destroying life. The Sanskrit word 'pustaka' is used for this kind of book in North Sumatra, Java and other countries, but in South Sumatra 'pustaha' is used; here such books were used as divination texts, for codes of law and for legends. Pustakas were written in a brilliant ink on long strips of writing material, folded concertina-fashion and tied together with a string of woven rushes.

PUT TO BED. *See* BED.

'PUTTING KNOWLEDGE TO WORK'. The slogan of the (American) SPECIAL LIBRARIES ASSOCIATION (*q.v.*).

PUTWITHS. Acknowledgements and other consequential papers such as corrigenda and addenda relating to documents already filed in a correspondence or similar file, and which in themselves are of no significance from a filing or indexing point of view.

PYE. An alternative spelling of PIE (*q.v.*).

PYE BOOK. *See* PIE 2.

PYES. A kind of ecclesiastical calendar.

q.v. Abbreviation for *quod vide* (*Lat.* 'which see'); *Pl.* qq.v. (*quae vide*)' Also for *quantum vis* (*Lat.* 'as much as you will').

QUAD. Abbreviation for QUADRAT. 1. A piece of metal, lower in height than type, and used for spacing.
An em quad (mutton), the square of the body.
An en quad (nut), $\frac{1}{2}$ the body or 2 to an em.
A thick space, $\frac{1}{3}$ the body or 3 to an em.
A middle space, $\frac{1}{4}$ the body or 4 to an em.
A thin space, $\frac{1}{5}$ the body or 5 to an em.
A hair space, $\frac{1}{12}$ the body approximately.
See also EM QUADRAT, EN QUADRAT, PAPER SIZES. 2. Prefix to standard paper-size names to indicate a sheet four times the size of a single and twice the size of a double, sheet. *See also* OCTAVO, PAPER SIZES.

QUAD MARK. *Synonymous with* BACK MARK, BLACK STEP, COLLATING MARK (*q.v.*).

QUADRAT. A term which is never used in its full form, but in the abbreviated version QUAD (*q.v.*).

QUADRATA. An early style of Latin manuscript writing; it was practised from the second to the fifth century A.D. and was characterized by a square capital letter based on formal inscriptions cut with a chisel in stone. Also called 'Square capital' hand.

QUADRIGESIMO-OCTAVO. *See* Forty-eightmo.

QUADRILLE. Paper ruled so as to form a very large number of small squares; it is used for graphs, etc.

QUALIFICATION. The addition of one or more words in parentheses to a subject heading, usually in dictionary catalogues, indicating the sense in which the heading is being used. Also used in indexes to the scheme of classification. Chiefly used to distinguish homonyms.

QUALIFIED HEADING. A heading followed by a qualifying term which is usually enclosed in parentheses, e.g. Composition (Art), Composition (Law) (*IBM*).

QUALIFIED LIST. Produced by deleting False and Unsought links of the chain (when using the chain procedure to produce subject index entries) and adding qualifiers to the remaining terms. It is the second stage of the conversion of a classification symbol to a verbal subject heading, the first being Basic Analysis (*q.v.*).

QUALIFIER. A sub-heading in a subject index which has been constructed by Chain Procedure (*q.v.*). (*Indexing*) A word, or words, added to a heading, after punctuation or within parentheses, in order (a) to distinguish it from identical headings which have different meanings, or (b) to identify the heading, e.g. by using an epithet or honorific title. *See also* Access point.

QUARTER BINDING. A binding in which the spine and a very small part of the sides is covered with a stronger material than the rest of the sides. 'Half binding' has the corners covered with the same material as the spine. In 'three-quarter binding' the material used on the spine extends up to three-quarters of the width of the sides.

QUARTER BOUND. *Synonymous with* Quarter Leather(*q.v.*).

QUARTER LEATHER. A term used to describe a book with a leather spine and cloth sides. *See also* Half Leather, Leather Bound, Three-quarter Leather.

QUARTERLY. A periodical published once every quarter.

QUARTERNION. Paper or vellum folded into a section of four leaves.

QUARTO. I. A sheet of paper folded twice to form a section of four leaves. The sheets given under the definition Octavo are folded twice to give the following quarto book sizes in inches. Double size sheets folded three times would give the same size sections but would be described bibliographically as octavos, not quartos.

Foolscap	$8\frac{1}{2} \times 6\frac{3}{4}$
Crown	$10 \times 7\frac{1}{2}$
Large Post	$10\frac{1}{2} \times 8\frac{1}{4}$
Demy	$11\frac{1}{4} \times 8\frac{3}{4}$
Medium	$11\frac{1}{2} \times 9$
Royal	$12\frac{1}{2} \times 10$
Large Royal	$13\frac{1}{2} \times 10$
Super Royal	$13\frac{1}{2} \times 10\frac{1}{4}$
Imperial	15×11

Abbreviated 4°, 4to. 2. A book having sections of four leaves, or eight pages. 3. A book over 10 and under 13 inches high. This is the popular, or book trade, definition.

QUARTO EDITION.   One issued in QUARTO (*q.v.*) form.

QUARTO SHELVING.   Shelves to accommodate quarto books.

QUASI-FACSIMILE BIBLIOGRAPHY.   One which attempts to reproduce the kind of type used in the original – roman, italic or gothic, etc.

QUERY.   The symbol ? written in the margin of a proof by the printer's reader to indicate to the author that he is required to check some detail. Sometimes 'Qv' is used.

QUESTION MARK.   *Synonymous with* INTERROGATION MARK (*q.v.*).

QUESTIONED DOCUMENT.   A document, the origin or authorship of which has been challenged and is in doubt.

QUICK-REFERENCE BOOKS.   Books which are essentially of a reference character, such as directories, dictionaries and gazetteers.

QUINTERNION.   A GATHERING (*q.v.*) of five sheets folded once to form ten leaves or twenty pages.

QUIRE.   1. 24 sheets of paper and one 'outside', making 25; the twentieth of a ream; 25 copies of a newspaper or periodical. 2. A gathering, section or signature, especially when unfolded. Books in sheets, unbound, are said to be 'in quires'. *See also* SECTION. For 'Cording quires', *see* CASSIE.

QUOINS.   Wedges of metal or wood, used to lock the matter in the CHASE (*q.v.*).

QUOTATION MARKS.   *See* QUOTES.

QUOTATIONS.   (*Printing*) Very large quads, used for filling up large areas of space in printed matter: they are usually hollow, simply four walls, sometimes strengthened by one or more internal girders. Also called 'Quotes'.

QUOTES.   The inverted commas " " placed at the beginning and end of quotations. *See also* QUOTATIONS.   Sometimes called 'Double quotes' to distinguish them from 'Single quotes': '. . .'. *See also* DOUBLE QUOTES, DUCK-FOOT QUOTES, SINGLE QUOTES, TURNED COMMA. In Germany and Austria they are printed thus „ . . .". although some German printers now prefer the French guillemets but pointing inwards (» . . . «). Spanish printers prefer the guillemets (« . . . ») pointing outwards.

RCA 'VIDEO FILE'.   A filing system, based on the manufacturer's video magnetic tape recording methods, employing television recording techniques to store pictorial data whether consisting of maps, charts, typewritten or handwritten matter, coloured or black and white. Coloured material is reproduced in black and white without half tones.

RLG.   Acronym of the Research Libraries Group which was formed in the U.S.A. in 1974 as a consortium of the research libraries of the New York Public Library, and of Yale, Harvard and Columbia universities. A grant of $750,000 (representing approximately 40% of the total amount budgeted for the first three years) was received from the Andrew W. Mellon Foundation. Other grants were made from the federal government and the participating institutions. The Group was established to improve availability of, and access to, recorded materials in member libraries, and among the first plans was the establishment of a bibliographic information centre at Yale to provide access to a combined collection of approximately 26,500,000 volumes. This was assisted by the establishment of a Bibliographic Data Center with a computer-based catalogue of holdings of periodicals and government documents, etc., in the co-operating libraries.

R.P.   Indicates that a book is not available from the publisher but is 'reprinting'. If R.P. is followed by a date as 'R.P. Jan.' it indicates when a reprint will be ready.

RRIS.   Acronym for Railroad Research Information Service which was formed, and became operative, in 1973. It is a computer-based service, developed within the U.S. National Research Council with financial support from the Federal Railroad Administration to give transportation administrators, engineers, and researchers rapid access to information about on-going and completed railroad-related research.

RACK.   A shelf, or group of shelves, or a case, usually built on to a wall or into a piece of furniture, for displaying books, magazines or periodicals, and distinguished as Book Rack, Magazine Rack, according to the special use of the fitting. The term is becoming out of fashion, 'case' or 'stand', being used now. *See also* BUTTERFLY PLAN.

RADIAL ROUTING.   *See* ROUTING. Also called 'controlled circulation'.

RADIATING STACKS. Island stacks arranged like a fan, the point being towards the staff enclosure thus enabling all readers on both sides of every stack to be visible from the enclosure.

RADIO SCRIPT. The text of an item for broadcasting.

RADIO TALKING LIBRARY. A radio programme provided in the U.S.A. for visually handicapped persons who are unable to read normal printed material or can only do so for short periods of time. The broadcasts consist of library materials comprising newspaper items, plays, short stories, novels, magazine features, shopping news, daily devotionals, news programmes, etc. Copyright laws may make it necessary for the service to be closed circuit, the listeners having special receivers and paying a subscription for the service.

RADIX NOTATION. The significance of digits in the representation of numeric data which is governed by their relative position with respect to 'period' (.).

RAG PAPER. Paper made from rags, especially cotton rags.

RAILROAD RESEARCH INFORMATION SERVICE. *See* RRIS.

RAISED BANDS. When the cords, on which the sections of a book are sewed, are not embedded in their backs and consequently show as ridges, they are called raised bands. The opposite of SUNK BANDS (*q.v.*).

RAISED-LETTER PRINTING. *Synonymous with* THERMOGRAPHY (*q.v.*).

RALPH R. SHAW MEMORIAL AWARD. *See* SHAW MEMORIAL AWARD, RALPH R.

RAMEAN TREE. *Synonymous with* the Tree of Porphyry. *See* PORPHYRY, TREE OF (*q.v.*).

RAMIE. China (Chinese) grass which has been used for paper making in China since the third century A.D. In Europe it is normally used only for textiles and banknotes.

RAMIFYING CLASSIFICATION. *Synonymous with* BRANCHING CLASSIFICATION (*q.v.*).

RANDOLPH J. CALDECOTT MEDAL. *See* CALDECOTT MEDAL, RANDOLPH J.

RANDOM ACCESS. (*Information retrieval*) A storage device not restricted to sequential scanning. Book indexes, card catalogues, magnetic drums and cards, magnetic or optical discs, and photographic strips are all of this kind. With this method, access to any location in the file is equally rapid; it is also quicker than sequential scanning. *See also* SCANNING.

RANDOM ACCESS STORAGE. A storage technique in which the time required to obtain information is independent of the location of the information – that is, items do not have to be processed in sequence (*IBM*). Also called 'Direct access'.

RANDOM FILE. A series of records on cards, or other material, which are not maintained in any recognisable sequence, but are 'mixed up'.

RANDTRIEVER. A system used at the University of Rotterdam since February 1971; it finds, conveys and shelves books electronically. It has three components: the stack area with robots between the shelves, the consoles at the service points which activate the whole system, and the conveyor belts between the stack area and the service consoles. Delivery time (one to two minutes) is much faster than conventional systems. Other advantages of the system are: stack attendants are not required, and more economic use is made of buildings as the stacks are more compact.

RANFURLY LIBRARY SERVICE. A service started by the Earl and Countess of Ranfurly in 1953 for collecting books from individuals and institutions in the U.K. and sending them to overseas countries in the fight against illiteracy and where there is an urgent need for English books. Books are sent to a central point in each country whence they are distributed to libraries and other institutions in over eighty countries. In addition to headquarters and branches in the U.K. there are donor libraries in Canada, Australia and New Zealand which distribute books within their own country and to adjacent territories.

RANGE. An American term for a bookcase, equivalent to the English PRESS (*q.v.*).

RANGING FIGURES. The numerals of modern type-faces which do not have ascenders or descenders but extend from the base line to the cap line, e.g. the Times New Roman figures 1234567890. Also called 'Lining figures'. *See also* HANGING FIGURES.

RANK. 1. (*Information retrieval*) A measure of the relative position in a series, group, classification or array (*IBM*). (*Classification*) 2. (*Noun*) A measure of the relative position of terms in a series, group, classification, or array. 3. (*Verb*) To arrange terms in an ascending or descending series according to importance.

RAPID COPYING. A speedy method of making copies of documents inexpensively. Used mainly in offices.

RAPID SELECTOR. A machine for document storage and retrieval. Documents are photographed on to 35 mm microfilm and alongside are placed digital dot codes indexing each frame. In searching, a reel of film is run past an optical scanner which reads the optical dot pattern. Documents selected are copied automatically from the reel of film (*IBM*). The original model was first conceived in 1939 by Vannevar Bush and developed by Ralph Shaw; it is one of the earliest retrieval systems and is of the roll film type. It has limited facilities for indexing the document content, and access to the material is by description rather than by address. A new Rapid Selector was later produced by the United States National Bureau of Standards under the sponsorship of the Bureau of Ships. This allowed searches to be made at the rate of 6,000 per minute (twelve times as fast), each reel containing 40,000 pages at an 8 : 1 reduction.

RARE BOOKS GROUP. A Group of the Library Association. It was formed (on the initiative of the then University and Research Section) in October 1967 'to unite librarians, who are concerned with the custody of collections of rare books and similar materials, and other members of the Library Association who are interested in rare books, and to promote the study and discussion of questions relating to the acquisition, maintenance and use of such collections'. A duplicated *Newsletter* began publication in March 1974.

RAS. Acronym of Readers Advisory Service. Formed at the end of 1973 by Science Associates International, Inc. and with the support of nearly 150 libraries and information centres throughout the U.S.A. and Canada. It collects and disseminates topical subject bibliographies, annotated reading lists, guides to the literature and booklists emanating from key academic, public, special and government libraries. Financed by members' subscriptions. Publishes *RAS Newsletter* (*q*).

RATE, LIBRARY. *See* LIBRARY RATE.

RATING AUTHORITY. The local authority responsible for levying and collecting rates; it is the council of the authority or the Common Council of the City of London.

RATTLE. The sound produced by shaking or snapping a sheet of paper; it is indicative of hardness (due to the degree of wetness or hydration) and, generally speaking, of quality. Called 'crackle' in the U.S.A. Linen rags will give a toughness and rattle to papers which is distinctive from those made from cotton.

RAW DATA. (*Information retrieval*) Data, in machine-sensible form or otherwise, which has not been processed.

RAW PAPER. *Synonymous with* BODY PAPER (*q.v.*).

READABLE NEGATIVE. *See* NEGATIVE 3.

READER. 1. A person employed by a printer to read through proofs with the 'copy' to make sure that corrections have been properly made. 2. A person who makes use of literary material in a library; a member of a lending library is frequently called a Borrower. *See also* PUB-LISHER'S READER. 3. In an American special library or information department, the member of staff who scans current publications to select articles, news items, etc., pertinent to the work of individuals and departments of the organization of which the library is a part, for subsequent dissemination. 4. In a newspaper library, the member of the library staff who scans the several editions of the paper and marks articles for cutting and filing. *See also* DISSEMINATION OF INFORMATION. 5. In reprography, a device for projecting a readable image of a microcopy on to a screen within the device or on to a separate portable screen or suitable surface which may be opaque or translucent. 6. In statistical records, an individual using a library who is counted once only. When he is counted separately on the occasion of each visit, this is recorded as a 'Reader-visit'. *See also* MICROFILM READER.

READER AREA.   That portion of the total floor space of a library which is allocated for use by readers.

READER FOR THE PRESS.   A printer's reader. *See* READER 1.

READER-INTEREST CLASSIFICATION.   A very simple and broad classification, intended to reflect the special interests of readers rather than the subject contents of books as such. It was developed in the Detroit Public Library.

READER-PRINTER.   In documentary reproduction, a microfilm reader which can also be used rapidly to make enlargements automatically.

READER VISIT.   *See* READER 6.

READERS' ADVISER.   An experienced, cultured and tactful member of the staff who is detailed for advising readers on their choice of books, interesting casual readers in more systematic reading, recording results of interviews, maintaining a close touch with local educational agencies and generally furthering the use of books.

READERS' ADVISORY SERVICE.   *See* RAS.

READER'S CARD.   The card issued to a reader when registering to use a library.

READER'S PROOF.   The first proof which is made from composed type; it is read by the printer's reader and sent to the compositor who makes any necessary alterations before the second proof is pulled and which is the first one sent to the author.

READERS' REGISTER.   A register, on cards or in a handwritten volume (usually the former) giving details of the members of a library.

READER'S SET. A set of proofs on which corrections are to be made, usually so marked on the proofs by the printer's reader.

READER'S TICKET. The ticket issued to a reader on joining a library.

READING CASE. *Synonymous with* MAGAZINE CASE (*q.v.*).

READING CIRCLE. A group of people who meet regularly in the library to read or study books.

READING COPY. A copy of a book offered for sale in poor condition the text being complete and legible. Also called 'Binding copy'.

READING FILE. (*Archives*) A file containing copies of documents arranged in chronological order. Also known as 'chronological file', 'Chronfile' and in Canada as a 'Continuity file'.

READING LIST. A list of recommended books and/or periodical articles in some special order and on a particular subject, often with guidance as to their purpose and features. It may be added to an encyclopaedia article or a chapter in a book in order to suggest matter for further study. *See also* SOURCE LIST.

READING MACHINE. Apparatus made for enlarging the image of microphotographic records (whether on film or paper) so that they can be read.

READING ROOM. A room set aside for the reading of periodicals or books.

READING SHELVES. Examining books to see that they are in correct order on the shelves. Also known as 'Shelf tidying', and in American practice as 'Shelf reading' and 'Revising shelves'.

READY REFERENCE. Reference work concerned with questions of a factual nature which can be answered readily, often from QUICK-REFERENCE BOOKS (*q.v.*) which in many libraries are shelved together with standard reference books, sometimes in a separate area reserved for dealing with questions of this nature.

REAL TIME. (*Information retrieval*) The technique of co-ordinating data processing with external related physical events on a time basis, thereby making possible the prompt reporting of conditions, such as the airline reservations system which can report reservation openings almost instantly.

REALIA. Three-dimensional objects such as museum materials, dioramas, models and samples which may be borrowed or purchased by a school library and used in connexion with class lessons.

REALIZATION. In music, the written expression, by an editor, on music staves of a full harmonization which is indicated by a figured bass on the original score. The realization may also be made in performance from the FIGURED BASS (*q.v.*).

REAM. A pack of 500 identical sheets of paper. A ream contains twenty quires. In the U.K., packs of 480 sheets for special classes of papers, such as wrapping papers and blotting paper, are recognized. A ream of hand-made and drawing papers may contain 472, 480 or 500 sheets. Originally a ream contained 516 sheets. A 'short ream' has 480 sheets, a 'long ream' 500 or 516 sheets.

REAR PROJECTION. The projection of an image on a transparent or opaque material through an appropriate type of projector on to a translucent screen from the side opposite to that from which the image is viewed.

RE-BACK. To repair a book by providing a new spine without re-covering the sides or re-sewing. *See also* BACKED.

RE-BOUND. Said of a book the original binding of which has been replaced with another, usually after resewing the sections.

REBUS. 1. A form of riddle, in which words or their syllables, names, mottoes, etc., are represented by objects or by a combination of objects, letters or words. 2. An enigmatical representation of a name, word or phrase by figures, pictures, arrangement of letters, etc., which resemble the intended words or syllables in sound.

RECALL. (*Verb*) To request the return to the library of a book or other item which is on loan. (*Noun*) The retrieval of a required document or reference from an information store.

RECALL NOTICE. A notice sent to a reader requesting the return of a book or other item which is overdue or required for use by someone else. *See also* OVERDUE NOTICE.

RECALL RATIO. In information retrieval, the number of documents actually recalled from an index in response to a question on a given theme, in proportion to the number of documents on that theme which are known to be indexed. Also called 'Sensitivity'. *See also* RELEVANCE RATIO.

RE-CASING. The re-insertion of a book into its original cover, with or without re-sewing.

RECEIVING DESK. *See* CIRCULATION DESK.

RECENSION. A revision. Used to indicate a scholarly edition of a work, for instance of a classic, in which the existing text is thoroughly re-edited, revised and re-examined by collation with all known sources of textual emendation. *See also* REDACTION.

RECESS PRINTING. Intaglio, photogravure and other processes whereby the ink is obtained from cavities or recesses in the printing plate or cylinder.

RECOMMENDATION CARD. *Synonymous with* SUGGESTION CARD.

RECOMMENDER. A ratepayer who recommends an applicant for membership of a lending library as being a fit and proper person to borrow books.

RECOMMENDING COMMITTEE. A (library) committee which recommends its proposals to the local council for approval.

RECON. Abbreviation for remote control.

RECORD. 1. A document preserving an account of fact in permanent form, irrespective of media or characteristics. 2. The data relating to a document on which a catalogue or other entry is based. 3. (*Information retrieval*) To preserve information in writing, typescript, or coded form. 4. A unit of information preserved in writing, typescript or coded form. A set of data elements forming a unit. Records are combined to form files. 5. In automatic data processing, a collection of related items of data, which for purpose of operating systems, is treated as representing a unit of information.

RECORD MARK. (*Information retrieval*) A character which is used to terminate each record within a machine-readable file. Also called 'Record terminator'.

RECORD OFFICE. An office in which contemporary official records concerning local government and also earlier records of all kinds relating to the respective area which have been obtained by purchase, gift, or on deposit, are preserved and made available to persons desiring to consult them. *See also* COUNTY RECORD OFFICE.

RECORDACALL. A proprietary installation for automatically receiving on a tape machine telephoned messages, for example the renewal of library books. Similar machines are ANSAPHONE and TEL-STOR (*qq.v.*).

RECORDS. All recorded information setting out facts or events, irrespective of media, characteristics or origin, which is maintained by an institution or organization in the transaction of its normal business or in pursuance of its legal obligations. Also referred to as 'Documents'. *See also* ARCHIVES.

RECORDS CENTRE. An institution or building providing accommodation for the inexpensive but efficient storage and further processing of records which are no longer frequently used but which must be preserved, and for the provision of a reference service.

RE-COVERING. The process of making a new book cover and affixing it to a volume without re-sewing the sections.

RECTANGULAR STYLE. Bindings executed for Charles II while Samuel Mearne was the Royal Bookbinder. Their design consists of a simple three-line gilt rectangular panel with a crown or similar emblem at each corner. Crimson morocco was mostly used.

RECTO. 1. The right-hand page of an open book or manuscript, usually bearing an odd page number. Sometimes called an uneven page. 2. The first side of a printed or ruled sheet of paper when folded and bound, as distinct from the 'verso' which is the reverse side. *See also* VERSO.

RED EDGES. The edges of a book cut, coloured red, and burnished.

RED OCHRE. A powder used by type casters to coat the inner surface of their moulds when casting very small sorts to make the metal flow more easily.

RED PRINTING. Printing in a second colour (usually red) for headings, capitals, etc. This is usually performed on a separate machine after the text has been printed.

RED UNDER GOLD EDGES. The three edges of a book cut, coloured red, and then gilt. *See also* EDGES.

REDACTION. 1. The editing, arranging, or revision for publication of a literary work which was left by the author incomplete or in a state unsuitable for publication. *See also* RECENSION. 2. A new, or revised, edition of a work.

REDCLIFFE-MAUD REPORT. The Report *Royal Commission on local government in England, 1966–69*, 3 vols., 1969. The Royal Commission was set up in 1966 'To consider the structure of local government in England outside Greater London . . . and to make recommendations for authorities and boundaries, and for functions and their division, having regard to the size and character of areas in which these can be most effectively exercised and the need to sustain a viable system of local democracy'. Sir John Maud was nominated as chairman and was created a Life Peer in 1967 when he chose the title Baron Redcliffe-Maud. A similar Commission on local government in Scotland was appointed at the same time under the chairmanship of Lord Wheatley. Its Report *Royal Commission on local government in Scotland, 1966–69* was published in 2 vols. in 1969. *See also* LIBRARY AUTHORITY (for changes in the provision of public libraries in Northern Ireland) and LOCAL GOVERNMENT BOUNDARIES, MAUD REPORT.

REDUCING. In documentary reproduction, the decrease of the DENSITY or CONTRAST of a negative or print (*Concepts . . .*).

REDUCTION. 1. In documentary reproduction, a copy the scale of which is reduced compared with the ORIGINAL (*q.v.*). 2. In music, an arrangement of a musical work for a smaller group of instruments than for which it was originally written.

REDUCTION OF NUMBERS. (*Classification*) Dropping by the classifier of one or more digits at the end of a notation number given in the schedules or tables. This results in a shorter number with a more inclusive meaning, and thus in broader classification. *See* BROAD CLASSIFICATION.

REDUCTION OF SCHEDULES. (*Classification*) Dropping by the editors of some or all of the previous subdivisions of a number in a classification scheme with resultant classification of these concepts in a higher number. This results in notation for the topic that is one or more digits shorter than it was in the immediately preceding edition.

REDUCTION RATIO. (*Reprography*) An expression of the number of times a copy or image is smaller in linear dimensions than the one from which it was made, e.g. 1 : 10 reduction.

REDUNDANCY. (*Information retrieval*) The use of more words or symbols than are necessary to convey a meaning (thought, word or idea). It may be planned repetition in order to overcome NOISE (*q.v.*) in the system.

REDUNDANT INDEXING. The use of more than one term, the meanings of which are not clearly distinguishable, for indexing the same information in a document.

RE-EDITION. A publication which is distinguished from previous editions by changes made in contents (revised edition) or layout (new edition). (*Unesco.*)

REEL FED. A printing press which prints on paper in a reel instead of single sheets.

REEL TO REEL. The playback or projection from one reel or spool of film or audiotape to a separate take-up reel or spool.

RE-ENLARGEMENT. An enlarged reproduction from a MICROCOPY (*q.v.*).

'REFER FROM' REFERENCE. An indication, in a list of subject headings, of the headings from which references should be made to the given heading; it is the reverse of the indication of a 'See' or 'See also' reference (*IBM*).

REFEREE. A scientist who assists the editor of a journal in evaluating the acceptability of contributions submitted for publication.

REFERENCE. (*Cataloguing*) 1. A direction from one heading to another. References may be *general* to indicate a class, giving an individual heading only as an example, as

> ANIMALS, *see also under the names of animals as* LION.

or *specific* by stating the exact heading to which reference must be made, as,

> ANIMALS, *see* LION.
> CLEMENS, S. L., *see* TWAIN, MARK.

They may be made between (a) synonymous headings – *see* references, and (b) related headings – *see also* references. 2. A partial registry of a book, omitting the imprint and collation, under subject or title, but referring to the main entry. 3. (*Information retrieval*) An indication referring to a document or passage (*IBM*). 4. An indication of where to find specific information, e.g. a page, column or other part of an entry in a book index, an author's name, classification number or other IDENTIFICATION (*q.v.*), mention of a document or of information contained in a document. *See also* COLLATERAL REFERENCE, CROSS-REFERENCES, DOWNWARD REFERENCE, UPWARD REFERENCE.

REFERENCE AND ADULT SERVICES DIVISION. A Division of the American Library Association; it was formed in 1972 by the amalgamation of the Adult Services Division and the Reference Services Division. The goal of the Division is to stimulate and support full access to library services which are user-oriented, concentrating on identifying and evaluating media and services which meet the educational, informational, recreational, research, and social needs of library users. Abbreviated RASD. Publishes *RQ* (q.)

REFERENCE ASSISTANT. An assistant librarian, working in a reference library.

REFERENCE BOOKS. 1. Books such as dictionaries, encyclopaedias, gazetteers, year books, directories, concordances, indexes, bibliographies and atlases, which are compiled to supply definite pieces of information of varying extent, and intended to be referred to rather than read through. 2. Books which are kept for reference only and are not allowed to be used outside the building.

REFERENCE CARD. A catalogue card bearing a cross reference. *See also* CROSS REFERENCES.

REFERENCE CENTRE. In the U.S.A., a scheme, which is stimulated through Library Service Act funds, whereby a number of small public libraries in a given geographical area contribute funds to a large library in the area having a good reference library which is willing to expand its resources and services to meet the reference and information needs of enquirers throughout the whole area. 'Information services' and 'bibliographic centres' undertake similar functions.

REFERENCE COLLECTION. A collection of books which may not be borrowed for use outside the library.

REFERENCE CORNER. The junction of the REFERENCE EDGES (*q.v.*), i.e. the bottom left-hand corner of a microcard or microfiche grid.

REFERENCE DEPARTMENT. The department of a library containing books which may not be taken away but are for consultation in the library only.

REFERENCE EDGES. The left-hand and bottom limits of a microfiche or microcard grid. In microcopying, the left-hand and bottom limits of a microfiche grid.

REFERENCE LIBRARIAN. A librarian in charge of, or undertaking the work of, a reference library.

REFERENCE LIBRARY. A library or department containing books which may not normally be used elsewhere than on the premises.

REFERENCE MARKS. 1. Printers' marks used to indicate references to other books or passages or to footnotes on the page. Where more than one reference is given on a page the order of the marks is as follows: * (asterisk or star), † (dagger or obelisk), ‡ (double dagger or double obelisk), § (section mark), ‖ (parallel mark), ¶ (paragraph mark). If more than six notes are required to a page, these signs are given first in single, then double and afterwards in treble sequence. Letter and figures in alphabetical or numerical order are more often used for the same purpose. 2. A set of suitable marks, usually fine line crosses, which provide reference points for registration in printing of art work, image location on printer-readers, etc.

REFERENCE MATERIAL. Books and other library materials which may not be borrowed for use out of the library, either because their nature is such that they are prepared for brief consultation rather than for continuous reading, or because they belong to a reference collection from which items may not be borrowed.

REFERENCE MATTER. *See* SUBSIDIARIES.

REFERENCE RETRIEVAL SYSTEM. One which provides a complete reference to a document in response to a general research request. A card catalogue or other index is such a system. An aspect of INFORMATION RETRIEVAL (*q.v.*).

REFERENCE ROOM. *Synonymous with* REFERENCE DEPARTMENT (*q.v.*).

REFERENCE SERVICE. The provision and organization by a library of REFERENCE WORK (*q.v.*).

REFERENCE SOURCE. Any publication which is used to obtain authoritative information.

REFERENCE, SPECIAL AND INFORMATION SECTION. A Group of the Library Association. It was formed on 6th October 1950 and has as its objects 'to unite members engaged or interested in the work of reference and special libraries and information departments, to foster their interests within the Library Association, and to increase the usefulness of all reference and special libraries and information departments'. There are seven Regional Groups of the Section, formed on a geographical basis. Abbreviated RSIS.

REFERENCE WORK. 1. That branch of the library's services which includes the assistance given to readers in their search for information on various subjects. 2. The work of the Reference Library. 3. A book, or work, compiled to be referred to rather than for continued reading. 4. Personal assistance given by the librarian to individual readers needing information.

REFERENCES. A list of publications to which an author has made specific reference; usually placed at the end of an article or chapter, or at the end of a book, sometimes in chapter order. The entries are usually arranged in number order, corresponding numbers appearing in the text. *Also called* 'Citations'.

REFERRAL CENTRE. An organization for directing researches for information and data to appropriate sources such as libraries, information evaluation centres, documents or documentation centres and individuals. A referral centre does not supply data or documents. *See also* DOCUMENT CENTRE, INFORMATION EVALUATION CENTRE.

REFLECTOGRAPHY. *Synonymous with* REFLEX COPYING (*q.v.*).

REFLEX COPY. In documentary reproduction, a reproduction of an ORIGINAL (*q.v.*), prepared by the reflection principle of exposure, using 'reflex' materials. (*Concepts* . . .). Also called 'Reflex print'. *See also* REFLEX COPYING.

REFLEX COPYING. A process for reproducing photographically copies of documents which are opaque or printed on both sides. The light-sensitive emulsion on the paper is placed against the document: light is passed through the sensitized paper and reflected back from the light parts of the document – not from the dark or printed parts. The reversed negative which results may then be used to print a positive by transmitted light on the same kind of paper. The apparatus used does not include either a camera or lenses. Many modern methods of documentary reproduction use the reflex principle of exposure but the term 'reflex' is reserved for the negative-positive method described. Stabilized machines which do away with the usual photographic washing and drying routines enable a copy to be produced in about ten seconds but the keeping qualities of such prints are doubtful. Makes of apparatus which enable documents to be copied by this method are Contoura, Copycat and Rutherstat. A print, or copy, made by this method may be called a 'Reflex copy'. Also called 'Reflectography', 'Reflex printing'. *See also* CONTACT PHOTOGRAPHY, PHOTOSTAT.

REFLEX PRINT. *Synonymous with* REFLEX COPY (*q.v.*).

REFLEX PRINTING. *Synonymous with* REFLEX COPYING (*q.v.*).

REGINA MEDAL. Established in 1959 by the (American) Catholic Library Association 'to dramatize its standards for the writing of good literature for children'. The award has been made possible through the generosity of an anonymous donor, and is given without regard to the recipient's religion, country, or birth, or the nature of the contribution (author, publisher, editor, illustrator, etc.) and in recognition of a lifetime contribution to the field of children's literature, which has been most representative of Walter de la Mare's philosophy 'Only the rarest kind of best in anything can be good enough for the young'. It was established in 1959 and was first awarded to Eleanor Farjeon.

REGION. (*County Libraries*) A part of the County Library area including branch libraries, centres, travelling libraries and other facilities administered from a REGIONAL HEADQUARTERS or REGIONAL BRANCH (*qq.v.*) as a library unit within the county library system.

REGIONAL BIBLIOGRAPHIC CENTRE. A clearing house for regional co-operation among library groups in the U.S.A., locating books required and facilitating their loan between libraries, directing research workers and students requiring materials on particular subjects and possibly compiling complete or partial union catalogues.

REGIONAL BIBLIOGRAPHY. *Synonymous with* NATIONAL BIBLIOGRAPHY (*q.v.*).

REGIONAL BRANCH. A library which, because of its larger size and greater resources, answers reference enquiries, supplies bibliographical information, display material, and books in bulk or individually, for a group of smaller libraries in a large county or urban system, as well as serving the public. Sometimes also called a 'Regional library'.

REGIONAL BUREAUX. The offices which act as clearing-houses for requests for particular books which are not in stock where asked for, and pass on the requests to other libraries in their own regional areas. If the books cannot be provided from within these areas, the bureaux forward the requests to the NATIONAL CENTRAL LIBRARY (*q.v.*). Each bureau usually compiles and maintains a catalogue of all the non-fiction books in the libraries within the region and forwards copies of the entries to the National Central Library where they are incorporated in the national union catalogue. The libraries in each bureau area, between them buy all new books appearing in *BNB*, and also as a whole undertake subject specialization in an agreed area of knowledge; since these arrangements became operative nationally, books appearing in *BNB* have not been included in union catalogues.

REGIONAL CATALOGUE. 1. A catalogue of the books in libraries situated in a given geographical region. 2. A catalogue of books relating to, or written by, people living in a given geographical region.

REGIONAL CLASSIFICATION. Classification by place rather than by subject.

REGIONAL HEADQUARTERS. Premises from which, in a county library system, are administered the library service points in its region but at which the public may or may not be served directly. It provides the control, bookstock, postal services and other facilities which are normally available from a county headquarters in a centralized system. *See also* AREA HEADQUARTERS.

REGIONAL LIBRARIAN. One who is responsible for the administration of a REGIONAL BRANCH library, and also the distribution of books to service points in a REGION (*q.v.*) centred on that branch.

REGIONAL LIBRARY. *Synonymous with* REGIONAL BRANCH (*q.v.*).

REGIONAL LIBRARY SYSTEM. *See* REGIONAL BUREAUX.

REGIONAL OFFICER. A librarian who is responsible for the development and administration of all aspects of a county library service throughout a REGION (*q.v.*), but not combining with this the functions of a Branch Librarian. *See also* REGIONAL LIBRARIAN.

REGISTER. 1. The ribbon attached to a volume to serve as a bookmarker. 2. A list of signatures attached to the end of early printed books, or printed above the colophon or on a separate leaf, for the guidance of the folder or binder. A 'registrum'. 3. In printing, a term used when the type area on the recto coincides exactly with that on the back of the verso. The adjustment of colour blocks so that the colours are superimposed with absolute accuracy. Register is of tremendous importance in multi-colour process work. When properly adjusted the work is said to be 'in register', when not, 'out of register'. 4. A catalogue or bibliography; particularly, an official list or enumeration.

REGISTER OF ELECTORS. A printed list of persons who are entitled to vote at a local government or parliamentary election. A new register is prepared each year and comes into force on 16th February. Also called 'Voter's list' and 'Electors' roll'.

REGISTER TABLE. A table with an opaque-glass top and a box-like interior fitted with lights and painted white. It is used to position negatives on positives together with any accompanying type matter, on a layout sheet. It is also used for other purposes, e.g. register work in colour printing. Also called a 'Lining-up Table', 'Shining-up Table'.

REGISTRATION. 1. The process of filing readers' application forms and making out membership tickets. This may be done at one library in a system (centralized registration) or at each library. 2. The entering of particulars of books added to a library in the ACCESSIONS REGISTER.

REGISTRATION CARD. A membership, or identity, card which is issued to members entitling them to use, or borrow books from, a library.

REGISTRATION DEPARTMENT. The unit which is concerned with maintaining records of membership and issuing membership tickets.

REGISTRATION MARKS. (*Printing*) Pairs of marks, usually in the form of a cross, to show the relative position and exact orientation of two pieces of artwork that are to be superimposed in printing.

REGISTRATION PERIOD. The period during which a REGISTERED READER is entitled to use library services before being required to re-register.

REGISTRUM. See REGISTER 2.

REGLET. A strip of wood, about the height of leads, used to separate lines of type, thus saving leads, lightening the forme and making it easier to handle. They are chiefly used in poster work. See also LEADS.

REGNAL NUMBERS. In Brown's classification, the first divisions of each block of numbers devoted to a country relate to the country's historical development, by reigning monarch or other ruler. These numbers provide for all royal biographies, State papers, histories and special monographs, or any event of a historical nature.

REGULAR FOLIO. See FOLIO.

REHEARSAL SCORE. See SCORE.

REIMPOSITION. The rearrangement of pages of type matter in a forme, consequent upon the addition of new matter to type already arranged in pages, or to the use of a different type of folding machine.

REINFORCED BINDING. Publisher's binding strengthened by a library bookbinder, usually by adding a cloth strip to the HINGE (*q.v.*) and resewing with strong thread.

REINFORCED UNION PAPER. UNION PAPER (*q.v.*) which has a lining between the two sheets of which it is made, in order to increase its mechanical strength.

REINFORCING-PIECE. (*Binding*) The paper or parchment, on which for greater strength, the backs of some or all of the sections are sewn, and part of which shows under the paste-downs. See also PASTE-DOWN.

RE-ISSUE. A re-publication at a different price, or in a different form, of an impression, or edition, which has already been issued, usually from standing type or plates.

REJECTION SLIP. A printed acknowledgement sent out by a publisher, or magazine editor, when returning a MS. to an author informing him that the MS. has not been accepted for publication.

REJECTS. Copies of printed matter which are rejected by publisher or customer because of inferiorities.

RELATED TERM. (*Information retrieval*) A term which is co-ordinate (i.e. equal in status or specificity) to another term, e.g. Blind person is related to Partially-sighted person. *See also* BROADER TERM, NARROWER TERM.

RELATED TITLE. A title which has a relationship to another by being a subsequent book in a series, or a commentary on, or a 'reply to' an earlier work. In the eighteenth century many anonymous pamphlets of this kind were published. Such books are catalogued under their title with an added entry under the title of another book included therein.

RELATED WORK. (*Cataloguing*) A work which has some relationship to another. It may be a continuation, supplement, index, concordance, manual, sequel, scenario, choreography, libretto, special number of a serial, collection of extracts from serials, a work produced by the editorial staff of a serial, or a work in a subseries.

RELATION. 1. A non-periodical pamphlet published in England and describing a battle or some other event. A forerunner of the newspaper. Also called a 'Discourse' or a 'Narration'. *See also* CORANTO, NEWSBOOK. 2. (*Information retrieval*) Relationship between two concepts or between class numbers of a classification. For different kinds of relationship, *see* EQUIVALENCE—, GENERIC—, HIERARCHICAL—, and SEMANTIC RELATION.

RELATION MARKS. Symbols used in an agreed order when building up the classification numbers of the UNIVERSAL DECIMAL CLASSIFICATION (*q.v.*) in order to separate the various parts and also to indicate their meaning.

RELATIONAL INDEXING. (*Information retrieval*). In facet analysis and indexing: 1. Any system which involves a formal statement of the relationship between terms and in particular one in which complex subjects are represented by terms connected by symbols indicating their notional relations. 2. Such a system in which the structure of complex subjects is represented by the interposition of symbols between terms to denote particular relations. The symbols are known as 'relational symbols' or 'operators'.

RELATIONAL SYMBOLS. *See* RELATIONAL INDEXING.

RELATIVE CLASSIFICATION. Classification which shows, as most modern schemes purport to do, the relationships between subjects.

RELATIVE INDEX. An alphabetic index to a classification scheme in which all relationships and aspects of the subject are brought together under each index entry (*IBM*). An index to a scheme of classification also translates a natural language term into a class number; this it does by putting the class number after the natural language term. Such an index is provided for the Dewey Decimal Classification. The indexes to the classification of Cutter and the Library of Congress, and to the *Encyclopaedia Britannica* are relative. *See also* SPECIFIC INDEX.

RELATIVE LOCATION. An arrangement of books according to their relation to each other and regardless of the shelves or rooms in which they are placed and allowing the insertion of new material in its proper relation to that already on the shelves. Also called 'Movable Location'. The opposite of FIXED LOCATION (*q.v.*).

RELATIVE RELIEF MAP. One which shows the relative height of land areas by colour or shading, but not the steepness of slope: this is shown by an AVERAGE SLOPE MAP (*q.v.*).

RELATIVITY. That property of the index to a scheme of classification which reverses the subordination of subject to discipline, thus bringing together from all disciplines the various aspects of individual subjects.

RELATOR. (*Cataloguing*) A word or words in a heading indicating the relationship of the person named in the heading to the work specified in the remainder of the entry, e.g. editor, illustrator.

RELEVANCE RATIO. In information retrieval, the number of documents which are actually wanted in proportion to the number of documents retrieved in response to a question on a given theme. *See also* RECALL RATIO. Later known as PRECISION RATIO (*q.v.*).

RELEVANT CHARACTERISTIC. *Synonymous with* 'essential characteristic'. *See* CHARACTERISTIC OF A CLASSIFICATION.

RELIEF. (*Binding*) Said of a finisher's tool which is made in such a way that the design, when impressed on the leather, appears in relief.

RELIEF MAP. One which represents elevations of the earth's surface by various methods.

RELIEF MODEL. (*Cartography*). A scaled representation in three dimensions of a section of the earth's crust or of another heavenly body. Usually the vertical scale is exaggerated compared with the horizontal in order to accentuate mountains and plateaus. Known in the U.S.A. as a 'terrain model'.

RELIEF PRINTING. Printing from characters or designs that are raised above their surrounding surface, such as type, plates, etc., as distinguished from INTAGLIO PRINTING (*q.v.*). It includes woodcuts, wood engravings, zinc etchings, and half-tones.

REMAINDERS. When books have ceased to sell well, the publisher's stock remaining is sold off by auction or at a price, to a wholesaler or bookseller. Such books are then known as remainders.

REMAKE. To re-page a book, either partly or completely. To re-arrange typographic elements in a page or publication.

REMARQUE PROOF. *See* ARTIST'S PROOF.

REMFLEX. A copying unit made by Remington Rand; it incorporates both the processing equipment and the light box in which the exposure is made.

REMOTE ACCESS. A console typewriter which is linked with a distant computer and is able to communicate directly with it.

REMOTE TERMINAL. An ON-LINE DEVICE (*q.v.*), e.g. a typewriter, which is directly connected to a computer but physically separated from it, the distance of separation being a few yards or many miles.

REMOVAL SLIP. A card inserted in a catalogue to indicate that an entry has been removed for alteration. It bears sufficient information for the book to be identified, and indicates the whereabouts of the permanent card.

REMOVES. Quotations, passages or notes set, usually at the foot of a page, and in smaller type than that of the text.

RENAISSANCE ORNAMENT. (*Binding*) Conventional decorative ornament, apparently suggested by columns, urns, vases, beasts, birds, garlands and foliage which appear in Renaissance architecture.

RENEW. To extend the period (a) for which a book or other item is on loan; (b) during which a library membership ticket is valid; (c) for supplying a periodical on subscription.

RENEWAL. 1. The extension of the time allowed to the same borrower for reading a book. 2. The re-registration of a reader at the expiry of a period of library membership.

RENEWAL SLIP. A form on which is recorded information necessary to renew a loan or a membership ticket.

RENTAL BOOK. A book which is in the stock of a DUPLICATE PAY COLLECTION (*q.v.*).

RENTAL CARD. 1. A membership card on which loans from a DUPLICATE PAY COLLECTION (*q.v.*) are issued. 2. A book card for a book in such a collection.

RENTAL COLLECTION. *Synonymous with* DUPLICATE PAY COLLECTION (*q.v.*).

RENTAL FEE.   A payment made to borrow a book from a DUPLICATE PAY COLLECTION (*q.v.*).

REPAIRING.   The repair of a worn binding including restoring the cover and reinforcing the joints. Not to be confused with MENDING (*q.v.*).

REPERTOIRE INTERNATIONALE DE LITTÉRATURE MUSICALE. *See* RILM.

REPERTORY CATALOGUE.   A catalogue of books in more than one library.

REPLACEMENT.   1. A book bought to take the place of a worn out copy of the same title. 2. The routine involved in substituting a volume for one which has been withdrawn.

REPLEVIN. (*Archives*) 1. The recovery of property such as archives, documents, manuscripts, by an institution or organization which claims ownership. 2. The writ and legal action by which a person or institution secures such property. *See also* ESTRAY.

REPLICA.   A copy or reproduction of a work of art, especially one made by the artist himself, and assumed to be of equal quality to the original. A doublette. A facsimile or nearly exact copy.

REPLIKA.   The trade name of a particular firm's photo-lithographic process.

REPORT.   A publication giving a formal or official record, as of the activities of a committee or corporate body, or of some special investigation, or the proceedings of a governmental body. *See also* TECHNICAL REPORT.

REPORT GENERATION. (*Information retrieval*) A technique for producing complete reports by machine from information which describes the INPUT (*q.v.*) file, the format and the content of the output report.

REPORT LITERATURE.   A general term which includes reports of all kinds, which give the results of research or development work, and which are associated with the name of the sponsor within a numbered sequence. The publications may include technical notes and memoranda, preprints, conference proceedings and papers, research and development reports, as well as formal reports.

REPORTING COMMITTEE.   A (library) committee which reports its actions (within the limit of the powers delegated to it – *see* DELEGATION OF POWERS) to the local council.

REPOSITORY.   1. A book store belonging to one library system, or a number of co-operating library systems prepared to inter-lend the books deposited therein. 2. A store for archives belonging to a RECORD OFFICE. (*q.v.*).

REPRESENTATIVE FRACTION. The ratio between distance measured on a map and the corresponding distance on the ground. Thus a map on the scale 1 inch to 1 mile has a representative fraction of 1 : 63,360 there being 63,360 inches in a mile.

REPRINT. 1. A copy of a book, made from the same type or stereotype as the original, with which it is identical except for possibly a new title-page and a note on the verso of the title-page of the number and date of reprinting and the correction of minor errors. *See also* EDITION, FACSIMILE REPRINT, FIRST EDITION, IMPRESSION, ISSUE, NEW EDITION, REVISED EDITION, SEPARATE. 2. Setting up type and printing again, using a previous printing as 'copy' as distinct from manuscript 'copy'. 3. A contribution to a periodical, afterwards issued separately, though not necessarily from the same type as the original. Sometimes called a SEPARATE (*q.v.*). 4. A British Standard (BS 4719 : 1971) defines a reprint as 'All those copies of an edition reproduced at an interval after the original printing of the edition. In current practice this term is frequently preferred to impression'. In recent years, arrangements have been made between publishers to print copies of out-of-print books which are in demand, but which the original publisher does not wish to reprint himself, or by firms specializing in the reproduction of very old and/or scarce books. Photographic reproduction methods are used, and the original text remains unchanged.

REPRINT SERIES. A series of books, which have been published previously by one or more publishers, in the same format by one publisher and bearing a series name. The books need not be related in either subject matter or treatment. *See also* PUBLISHER'S SERIES.

REPRINTED ARTICLE. One which has been reprinted, but with its own pagination. *See also* SEPARATE.

REPRODUCTION PROOF. A proof copy of a work of art, photograph, tabulation, etc., of the highest quality which may be used for reproduction purposes by means of a printing block or plate.

REPROGRAPHIC MARKING. The reprographic transfer of workshop drawings directly on to the materials, e.g. sheets of metal, to be fashioned (*Concepts . . .*).

REPROGRAPHIES. *Synonymous with* REPROGRAPHY (*q.v.*).

REPROGRAPHY. The reproduction in facsimile of documents of all kinds by any process using light, heat or electric radiation – photocopies, micro-copies, blueprints, electro-copies, thermo-copies, etc.; also reproduction by methods of duplicating and office printing.

REPUBLICATION. 1. The re-issuing of a publication by a publisher other than the original, without changes in the text. Sometimes used of reprints made in another country. 2. Broadly, re-issuing a work, with or without textual changes, or as a new edition.

REQUEST CARD. *Synonymous with* SUGGESTION CARD (*q.v.*).

REQUEST FORM. A form, or card distributed to the users of a special library to request information or material from the library. It can be so designed as to show the progress of steps taken to meet the request, record the borrowing of material from another library and record the loan of material to the user.

REQUISITION CARD. *Synonymous with* SUGGESTION CARD (*q.v.*).

REQUISITION FORM. *Synonymous with* CALL SLIP (*q.v.*).

RE-REGISTRATION. The re-registering (automatic or otherwise) of persons whose library tickets have expired.

RESEARCH AND DEVELOPMENT REPORT. A document which formally states the results of, or progress made with, a research and/or development instigation, which, where appropriate, draws conclusions and makes recommendations, and which is initially submitted to the person or body for whom the work was done. A report is usually one of a series and commonly carries a report number which identifies both the report and the producing, disseminating or sponsoring organization.

RESEARCH BOOK. In film studio research libraries, a scrapbook made up of sketches, abstracts, and other information relating to the settings, architecture, costumes, etc., which are gathered in advance of the production of a particular picture in order to ensure that the presentation is historically and artistically accurate.

RESEARCH CARREL. *Synonymous with* CARREL (*q.v.*).

RESEARCH LIBRARIAN. A title often used in respect of the librarian in a special library who undertakes the work of a RESEARCH SERVICE (*q.v.*) as distinct from one who undertakes the work normally carried out in a reference library. *See also* INFORMATION OFFICER.

RESEARCH LIBRARIES GROUP. *See* RLG.

RESEARCH LIBRARY. A library consisting of specialized documents, and providing facilities for undertaking exhaustive investigation. In the U.S.A. it may also provide referral services in support of studies in subject fields connected with development, tests, engineering and evaluation as well as research. *See also* CENTRE, REFERRAL CENTRE.

RESEARCH ROOM. *Synonymous with* SEARCH ROOM (*q.v.*).

RESEARCH SERVICE. A service rendered by special librarians by examining, appraising and summarizing information obtained from written sources and from individuals and organizations considered to be authorities in the appropriate fields. This implies giving the solutions to problems, providing statistics and other information as distinct from supplying publications from which the information may be obtained. The information assembled is usually presented in tabular, report or memorandum form. Also called 'Search service'. *See also* LITERATURE SEARCH.

RESEARCH STALL. *Synonymous with* CARREL (*q.v.*).

RESEARCH TICKET. *Synonymous with* SUPPLEMENTARY TICKET (*q.v.*).

RESERVATION. A request for a specific book or other item to be reserved for a reader as soon as it becomes available on completion of processing, or on its return from the binder or another reader.

RESERVE CARD (FORM, SLIP). A card on which borrowers enter particulars of books to be retained for them when available for borrowing.

RESERVE COLLECTION. 1. Library materials for which there is infrequent demand and which consequently is not kept on open shelves, but individual items of which are obtained on request. 2. In academic libraries, material which is in great demand because of being placed on reading lists and set on one side for very short limited periods, or for an academic term, and then only for use on the premises or overnight.

RESERVED BOOK. One which after having been returned by another reader is held on payment of any necessary fee for a certain length of time at a reader's request and until he can call and collect it for home reading. S.8 (2) of the Public Libraries and Museums Act, 1964 provides for the making of a charge for notifying readers that books and other articles reserved are available for borrowing.

RESERVOIR LIBRARY. *Synonymous with* STORAGE CENTRE (*q.v.*).

RE-SET EDITION. One printed from newly set type but without revision of the text.

RE-SETTING. Setting type again, because of corrections, additions, changes of layout, etc.

RESIST. A coating of glue, enamel or shellac used to protect a plate from acid corrosion during the etching process.

RESKA SHELVING. Trade name for a design of Danish bracket type shelving. Shelves are supported on brackets which fit into slots in wall uprights or the central pillars of island stacks. The brackets serve as book ends; book supports fit into the under sides of shelves and slide easily from one end to the other. Fittings are available to display periodicals, with or without storage for back numbers behind the current numbers.

RESOLUTION. In documentary reproduction, the measure of the ability of an emulsion to record fine line detail or of a lens to record minute lines or points clearly, distinctly and separately (*Concepts*). Also called 'Resolving power'. In photography, a measure of the sharpness or visibility of an image; it is usually measured in line pairs per mm.

RESOLVING POWER. *Synonymous with* RESOLUTION (*q.v.*).

RESOURCE CENTRES. Collections of books and non-book materials of all kinds, which are relevant sources of information and instruction in schools, colleges and institutions of higher education. They are developments of libraries in such centres of learning – a policy which the National Council for Educational Technology and the Schools Council have endorsed. The Library Association issued *School library resource centre : recommended standards for policy and provision* in 1970 and *A supplement on non-book materials* to this in 1972. Several policy statements on resource centres in colleges and universities were published between 1970 and 1973, and the Association also issued a general policy statement, followed by a short bibliography, in Libr. Ass. Rec., 75 (3) March 1973, p. 52. *See also* STANDARDS.

RESOURCES AND TECHNICAL SERVICES DIVISION. A Division of the American Library Association since 1957; it is responsible for these activities: acquisition, identification, cataloguing, classification and preservation of library materials in all types of institutions, and to the development and co-ordination of the country's library resources. Has several sections and discussion and regional groups. Abbreviated RTSD. Publishes *Library Resources and Technical Services* (q., free to membs.), *RTSD Newsletter* (q.).

'RESPECT DES FONDS'. (*Archives*) The cardinal principle to be followed in archival arrangement, namely that the original grouping of documents must be preserved so that there shall be no impairing of their archival value and significance.

RESPONDENT. The candidate for a degree who, in an academical disputation, defends a tenet or thesis against the objections proposed by the PRAESES (*q.v.*). The respondent is also called the defendant.

RESTORATION STYLE. *Synonymous with* MEARNE STYLE (*q.v.*).

RESTRICTED LOAN. A loan of library material with some form of limitation, as on period of loan, or number of volumes allowed at one time.

RET. The second side of a sheet of paper.

23

RETOUCHING. 1. Hand etching or improvements carried out to a photographic print or negative used in PROCESS ENGRAVING (q.v.). 2. The hand-correcting of colour separations used in the photo-engraving and photo-lithographic processes. Called 'Dot-etching' in America.

RETREE. Slightly defective sheets of paper. Derived from the French *retiré*, 'withdrawn'.

RETRIEVAL. 1. The act of finding again, recovery, retrospective searching and securing of documents. The act of going to a specific location or area and returning therefrom with an object or document (*IBM*). 2. The act and means of obtaining (a) facts and other information which is recorded and indexed in some way by subject, or (b) the documents containing the required facts. *See also* RETRIEVAL DEVICE.

RETRIEVAL DEVICE. A record of documents or information which is consulted in order to obtain what is needed and recorded as being in the STORE (q.v.). An abstracts journal, a text-book, a library catalogue, a mechanical selector or an electronic data processor used to select documentary information, are all retrieval devices.

RETRIEVAL SYSTEM. A sequence of actions which result in obtaining (retrieving) required information. The system requires such components as a SELECTOR (q.v.) which enables the information to be identified in the STORE (q.v.).

RETRO-ACTIVE NOTATION. (*Classification*) 1. A NOTATION (q.v.) in which FACET INDICATORS (q.v.) and intra-facet connectors are eliminated by using one species of characters indicating the construction of the notation (and thereby the subject matter of the material) in reverse order to the schedules. 2. A notation in which compounds are specified merely by adding earlier numbers to later ones. The notation to Dewey's Decimal Classification is of this kind, where, e.g. the form number 08 is used as a facet indicator to indicate the literary form in which a work is presented.

RETROSPEC. An experimental, supported by OSTI, project with a data base consisting of English language journal papers in computers and control engineering and specially selected from INSPEC *Computer & Control Abstracts*. The data base is in four broad subject divisions: systems and control theory; control technology; computer programming and applications; computer systems and equipment. *See also* INSPEC.

RETROSPECTIVE BIBLIOGRAPHY. A bibliography which lists books published in previous years as distinct from a 'current' bibliography which records books recently published. Also called a 'Closed bibliography'. *See also* BIBLIOGRAPHY.

RETROSPECTIVE CONVERSION. (*Information retrieval*) The partial or complete conversion of an existing catalogue into machine-readable form, as opposed to converting records created currently.

RETURN DESK. *See* CIRCULATION DESK.

RETURNS. Unsold publications which are returned by a bookseller to the publisher. Also called 'Crabs'.

RE-USE OF NUMBERS. (*Classification*) A total change in the meaning of a given number as between one edition and another.

rev. Abbreviation for revise, revised, revision. *See also* REVISED EDITION.

REVENUE STAMPS. Stamps which were stuck on English newspapers in accordance with the Stamp Act, 1712. The paper had to be stamped before printing. The duty was the same irrespective of the size of the newspaper, and the Act, which was repealed in 1855, consequently had the effect of increasing the size of newspapers.

REVERSAL MICROFILM. In documentary reproduction, sensitized material which gives by a reversal process a POSITIVE COPY (*q.v.*) only from a positive ORIGINAL (*q.v.*).

REVERSAL PROCESS. Developing in such a manner that the material exposed in the camera shows a positive instead of a negative image. Developing is carried out in the ordinary way until a negative silver image appears but instead of fixing this, the developed material is put into a bleaching bath which dissolves the silver reduced by the developer but leaves the silver bromide unchanged. The whole is then exposed to the light and again developed, only the silver bromide left after the first development being blackened. In this way a positive image is obtained. The reversal process is used extensively in colour photography, in amateur film photography, and for producing duplicate negatives.

REVERSE BROWNE. A method of issuing books which is similar to the BROWNE BOOK CHARGING SYSTEM (*q.v.*) but which uses a pocket book-card and a card ticket.

REVERSE COVER. The lower cover of a book, i.e. that nearest to the last leaf. Also called 'Back cover', 'Lower cover'. *See also* OBVERSE COVER.

REVERSE LEFT TO RIGHT. (*Printing*) To reverse a design, etc., so that it prints as if a mirror image.

REVERSE OUT. (*Printing*) When making a plate or block, reversing black to white so that the final appearance of the print is of white printed on black (or another colour) instead of the normal black on white.

REVIEW. 1. A periodical publication which is devoted largely to critical articles and reviews of new books. 2. An evaluation of a literary work published in a periodical or newspaper. *See also* OMNIBUS REVIEW.

REVIEW COPY. A copy of a book sent by the publisher to a newspaper or magazine for the favour of a review. Sometimes called 'Press copy'.

REVIEW DATE. The date of commencement of the Public Libraries and Museums Act 1964, i.e. 1 April 1965. This date, or a date falling within ten years thereof, or any subsequent review date regulates the period on or during which the Secretary of State may, under s. 6 of the Public Libraries and Museums Act 1964, provide by order that a non-county borough or an urban district with a population of less than 40,000, shall cease to be a library authority. *See also* LIBRARY AREA.

REVISE. *See* PROOF.

REVISED EDITION. A new edition of a book in which errors have been corrected, and possibly new material added. Sometimes wrongly called 'Enlarged edition'. *See also* EDITION, FIRST EDITION, IMPRESSION, ISSUE, NEW EDITION, REPRINT.

REVISED PROOF. *See* PROOF.

REVISING SHELVES. *Synonymous with* READING SHELVES (*q.v.*).

REVOLVING BOOKCASE. One having shelves on four sides; built around a central cylinder it rotates in either direction on a spindle.

RIBBON ARRANGEMENT. A method of arranging books in a public library with non-fiction on upper shelves and novels on lower shelves, or vice versa, or novels on middle shelves and non-fiction above and below, the object being to disperse the readers around the library and avoid congestion at the fiction shelves.

RICE PAPER. Paper made from the pith of a small tree, *Aralia* (also *Fatsia*) *papyrifera*, grown in Formosa.

RIDER. An additional MS. added to a proof.

RIDER SLIP. *Synonymous with* PROCESS SLIP (*q.v.*).

RIDGE. One of the two projections along the sides of a rounded and backed volume against which the board is fitted. Also called 'Flange' or 'Shoulder'. (American.) *See also* BINDING EDGE.

RIGHT. The printer often needs to know which is the right side of a sheet of paper owing to differences in surface, and the undesirable effect of using sheets laid one way mixed with those laid another way in the same publication. Flat papers are usually packed with the right side uppermost; if folded, the right side is outside. In hand-made papers, the right side touches the wire cover of the mould; the 'wire' side is therefore known as the right side. In blue and azure papers the right side is usually darker than the other. In machine-made papers, it is the upper side which is the right side, i.e. the one on which the couch roll acts and not the wire. A WATERMARK (*q.v.*), in both hand-made and machine-made paper is read from the right side. Thus, it can be taken that in hand-made papers, the 'wire' side is the right side, but in machine-made papers this is the wrong side.

RIGHT READING. (*Reprography*). An image which is legible in a normal reading position as opposed to being a mirror image, i.e. LATERALLY REVERSED (*q.v.*).

RIGHT TO READ. A programme inspired, introduced in the early 1970s and organized by Dr. Ruth Love Holloway in the U.S.A. with the object of eliminating illiteracy by 1980. It has been implemented by the public school systems in over forty states. Parents are admitted to classrooms as ancillary teachers, and help in the teaching of reading, writing and arithmetic.

RIGHTS. The privileges of entitlement to permit the publication, performance, or adaptation of authorship and receive payment for same. *Volume rights* give the publisher 'the exclusive rights to publish a work in volume form' within the territorial area for which he makes himself responsible. These include the right to reprint in paperback form, in book club or school editions, or to negotiate these on behalf of the author. Digest rights, ONE SHOT (*q.v.*) rights and anthology rights – are also included. *Subsidiary rights* include foreign publication, and film, TV, translation, serial, dramatic and mechanical reproduction rights; these may or may not be handled by the original publisher of the work.

RIGID CLASSIFICATION. 1. The classification of books relative to their positions on shelves rather than according to a scheme of book classification. Such methods of classification were used before the formation of modern schemes of bibliographical classification, and resulted in the allocation of numbers to books according to the shelf, in a given tier of a particular press, or alcove, in a specific room. Another form of rigid classification is the arrangement of books in broad subjects according to size and accession number. 2. The characterization of each document from a single point of view and thereby the allocation of only one classification symbol to it. When a document is shelved or stored, and only one copy is available, one single physical location must be provided: this is indicated by a symbol representing one point of view, usually the most important, or major, one. Sometimes called a 'Pigeonhole classification'. *See also* MULTI-DIMENSIONAL CLASSIFICATION.

RILM. Acronym of Repertoire Internationale de Littérature Musicale (International Repertory of Music Literature) which is a computer-indexed bibliography of significant literature on music. It was established in the summer of 1966 under the combined sponsorship of the International Musicological Society and the International Association of Music Librarians. Publishes *RILM Abstracts of Music Literature* (3 p.a.).

RINCO PROCESS. Trade name of a gravure printing process.

RISING SPACE. *Synonymous with* WORK UP (*q.v.*).

RISING TYPE. Type which rises up in the forme, usually in the centre, when locked up too tightly. Spaces and quads rise and print through poor justification or loose lock-up.

RIVER. What appears to be a streak of white running vertically or diagonally through printed matter. It is caused by spaces between words occurring almost one below the other in several lines of type. Rivers are avoided by re-setting the type and varying the spacing or placing a very short word on a line above or below.

ROAN. A thin sheepskin used for binding books.

ROBERTS COMMITTEE. *See* ROBERTS REPORT.

ROBERTS REPORT. Popular name for the Report of the 'Roberts Committee' which was set up by the Minister of Education in September 1957 under the chairmanship of Sir Sydney Roberts, 'to consider the structure of the Public Library Service in England and Wales, and to advise what changes, if any, should be made in the administrative arrangements, regard being had to the relation of public libraries to other libraries'. The Report is entitled *The Structure of the Public Library Service in England and Wales,* 1959. Cmnd. 660. This Report resulted in the setting up of working parties by the Minister of Education in 1961. *See also* BAKER REPORT, BOURDILLON REPORT, PUBLIC LIBRARIES AND MUSEUMS BILL, PUBLIC LIBRARIES AND MUSEUMS ACT 1964.

ROBINSON MEDAL. Awarded to firms and individuals – librarians or not – for originality shown in devising new and improved methods in library technology and any aspect of library administration. Funds for the award come from a bequest by the late Mr. Frederick Robinson, formerly Deputy Librarian at Colchester who left to the Library Association a trust fund from the proceeds of which a Medal and one hundred guineas are awarded at intervals. The Award was first made in 1969 to Mansell Information/Publishing Ltd. who have been responsible for the development of an automatic camera and associated techniques for use in producing book catalogues from library cards or other sequential material. The unique camera used was built to Mansell's specification by the Williamson Manufacturing Company Ltd. of Willesden, who had previously been responsible for the special cameras which had enabled Balding and Mansell to produce the 263-volume *British Museum general catalogue of printed books*. The experience gained with this publication and also with the *Union list of serials* was applied to the related problems of the Library of Congress *National union catalog: pre-1956 imprints* which forms a series of some 610 large volumes each of over 700 pages recording details that had previously existed only on $12\frac{3}{4}$ million cards.

ROCK MECHANICS INFORMATION SERVICE. Formed at the end of 1967 to supply technical information both within the Rock Mechanics Department and other departments at Imperial College, London (where it is situated), and also to individuals, companies and institutes involved in rock and soil mechanics throughout the world. Abbreviated RMIS. Publishes *Geomechanics Abstracts* (m.), incorporated into *International Journal of Rock Mechanics and Mining Sciences and Geomechanics Abstracts*.

ROLE DIRECTORS. *See* ROLES.

ROLE FACTORS. *See* ROLES.

ROLE INDICATORS. *See* ROLES.

ROLES. In CO-ORDINATE INDEXING (*q.v.*), generally but not necessarily, symbols appended to terms or term numbers and thereby narrowing the definition of the terms by designating the role of a word in its context. They describe the use of a term in its context, not how terms are related. Also called 'Modifiers', 'Modulants', 'Role factors', 'Role directors', 'Role indicators', 'Scope notes'.

ROLL. 1. A bookbinder's tool consisting of a brass wheel about 3 inches in diameter secured in a long handle which rests against the shoulder when being used. The edge of the wheel is engraved so as to impress a continuous line or repeating pattern as it revolves under pressure. Also called 'Fillet'. 2. The design impressed by the tool referred to. *See also* SCROLL, TOOLING.

ROLL CASSETTE. A light-proof container for roll film on a spool. Also called a 'Roll magazine'.

ROLL MAGAZINE. *Synonymous with* 'ROLL CASSETTE' (*q.v.*).

ROLL MICROFILM. Microcopies on roll film as distinct from those on sheet microfilm, as MICROFICHE (*q.v.*).

ROLLED EDGES. Edges of book covers decorated with a roll, or 'roulette', a finishing tool having a brass wheel with a design on its rim.

ROLLER SHELVES.   Deep shelves which rest on a series of rollers or ball bearings and are drawn out so that folio volumes such as bound volumes of newspapers can be lifted off instead of being dragged off with possible damage to the binding. Also a series of rollers placed horizontally behind one another and which support large books; they revolve on their spindles as the volumes are pushed on and off.

ROLLING BOOKCASE.   A metal bookcase secured to a framework on wheels, which runs on metal rails or wheels, and placed as close as possible to others side by side, so as to permit maximum storage in a book stack. The bookcases are rolled from one position to another to permit access to the books. *See also* COMPACT STORAGE, COMPACTUS.

ROLLING PRESS.   1. A bookcase suspended from overhead tracks or running on rails let into the floor enabling cases to be placed very close together and pulled out to permit consultation of the books. 2. A hand press, for printing from incised or etched plates. Power is applied by passing the plate and paper, covered by thick blankets, between oak rollers held in a rigid frame. The upper roller which is turned by a capstan, carries the plate through the press.

ROLSON.   *See* ROTARY CARD FILE.

ROL-STAR.   *See* ROTARY CARD FILE.

Rom.   Abbreviation for ROMAN (*q.v.*).

ROMAINS DU ROI.   A series of roman and italic types made for use in the Royal Printing Office of Louis XIV in the Palace of the Louvre, Paris, between 1694 and 1745. They were based on drawings which accompanied a report made to Louis XIV, and are characterized by being condensed letters with thin, flat, unbracketed serifs. Designed by Philippe Grandjean, they were first used in 1742 for *Médailles sur la événements du règne de Louis-le-Grand*.

ROMAN.   Ordinary type as distinct from italic, being vertical instead of sloping and having graduated thick and thin strokes and serifs. It is based on the Italian Humanistic or Neo-Caroline hand of the fifteenth century and was first used by Adolf Rusch in Strasbourg in 1464, and perfected by Johannes da Spira, a German who used roman type for the first book to be printed in Venice, in 1469, and by Nicholas Jenson, a Frenchman, also in Venice, 1470. The use of roman types was greatly expanded in Italy in the last quarter of the fifteenth century; they may be divided into three main groups, VENETIAN TYPE, OLD FACE and MODERN FACE (*qq.v.*). Written in full, or in its abbreviated form

'Rom', the word 'Roman' is used on printer's copy or on a proof to indicate that the matter is to be set up in Roman, i.e. not italic, type. This book is set in Roman. *See also* ANTIQUA, EGYPTIAN, ITALIC, ROMAN NUMERALS, TRANSITIONAL, TYPE FACE.

ROMAN À CLEF. A novel in which one or more characters are based on real people but are given fictitious names.

ROMAN INDEX. *See* INDEX LIBRORUM PROHIBITORUM.

ROMAN NUMERALS. Capital letters which are used as numbers in books for chapter headings and for the designation of part numbers, appendixes, on title-pages for date of publication, etc., and in lower-case italic form for the pagination of preliminary pages. The roman capitals most commonly in use as numerals are:

I	5	10	50	100	500	1000
I	V	X	L	C	D	M

A complete sequence to 20 in small capitals is: I, II, III, IV, V, VI, VII, VIII, IX, X, XI, XII, XIII, XIV, XV, XVI, XVII, XVIII, XIX, XX, and in tens from 30 to 100: XXX, XL, L, LX, LXX, LXXX, XC, C. The numerals from X to XX indicate the method of building numbers. Italic figures I to 20 are: *i, ii, iii, iv, v, vi, vii, viii, ix, x, xi, xii, xiii, xiv, xv, xvi, xvii, xviii, xix, xx*. Combinations of numbers are made up by addition and subtraction, e.g. XX = 20; XIX = 19; XXIV = 24; MCMLVII = 1957. 1000 was first represented by the Greek letter, *phi* Φ, which in lettering and in architectural inscription became CIꓛ; this soon became M. 500 was half a *phi*, a Iꓛ, and soon became D. 100 was represented by the symbol θ (*theta*) which became Ꜿ then C, and 50 by the Chalcidian form of the letter *chi* Ⴟ which became ⊥ and later L. The following table includes most of the known numerals.

B	300	Iꓛꓛ	5000
C	100	L	50
CIꓛ	1000	M	1000
CIꓛCIꓛ	2000	N	900
D	500	Q	500
E	250	R	80
F	40	T	160
G	400	V	5
H	200	X	10
I	1	Ⴟ	1000
Iꓛ	500	∞	1000

A bar or dash placed over a letter increases its value a thousand times.

Roman numerals were used by the earliest fifteenth-century printers because they had no arabic figures, and were normally used in early printed books. *See also* CHRONOGRAM.

ROMANIZATION. The representation of 'picture writing' characters, such as Chinese, Japanese and Korean in the Roman alphabet. *See also* TRANSLITERATION. British Standard in respect of Japanese characters was published in 1972 – BS 4812 : 1972 *The romanization of Japanese.* A BS on Chinese characters is being prepared (1975).

ROMANTIC STYLE. A bookbinding decoration with an informal, non-classical style in which fancy predominates.

RONDE. An upright angular form of script type. Being based on a French manuscript it has the appearance of upright handwriting.

RONEO, to. To duplicate, using a wax stencil on a machine with a rotating cylinder to which the stencil is attached. So named after the proprietary make of machine, RONEO.

ROTAPRINT. An offset lithographic printing and duplicating machine made by the Rotaprint Co.

ROTARY CAMERA. *Synonymous with* CONTINUOUS FLOW CAMERA (*q.v.*).

ROTARY CARD FILE. A filing cabinet in which cards are placed on their edges in a wheel- or drum-like container. The container revolves on an axle in the side of the drum in such a way that the cards are always on their edges, those in the lower half being prevented from falling out by a fixed retaining strap of webbing or other material. Up to four containers may be placed side by side in a cabinet. 'Rolson' and 'Rol-star' are trade names for files of this kind. Another type consists of large round trays which revolve on a pivot, each tray being divided up so as to provide several rows of cards side by side. Each fitting or cabinet will hold up to five such trays one above another. 'Kraft Rotacol' and 'Cardmaster' are trade names of units employing this principle.

ROTARY GRAVURE. *Synonymous with* ROTOGRAVURE (*q.v.*).

ROTARY PRESS. A style of press that prints from curved electrotype or stereotype plates held on a cylinder, the paper being fed from a continuous roll and passing between this cylinder and another one which makes the impression. It is used for printing newspapers, periodicals or large editions and occasionally for books of a large run. There are also 'sheet-fed rotary presses'. All printing presses are rotary in principle except the flat-bed press and the platen press which are largely used in letterpress work. Where printing is done from the original flat forme on an endless web of paper, this is called a 'flat-bed web press'. Also called a 'Web press' when the paper is fed from a continuous reel. *See also* CYLINDER PRESS, FLAT-BED PRESS, PLATEN PRESS.

ROTATED CATALOGUE. A classified catalogue in which entries are made under each integral part of the classification symbol, instead of making an entry under the class number with merely references from headings or parts comprising the composite symbol. Also called 'Cyclic classified catalogue'.

ROTATED ENTRY. An entry in an index to documents, or a classified catalogue, where full information and not merely a reference is given under each heading.

ROTATED INDEX. An index to a catalogue of documents classified by a faceted classification whereby entries are made under every heading and inverted heading which comprises part of the classification symbol. Also called 'Cyclic index'.

ROTATED INDEXING. The indexing of documents classified by a faceted classification whereby a full entry, and not a reference, is made under each heading representing, or being, a part of the classification symbol. Also called 'Cyclic indexing'.

ROTATIONAL INDEXING. The making of a CORRELATIVE INDEX (*q.v.*) wherein each term is 'rotated' so as to file in the first position (*IBM*).

ROTOFOTO PHOTO-TYPESETTING MACHINE. A British machine incorporating a standard Monotype keyboard. It was invented by George Westover of London and announced in 1948.

ROTOGRAVURE. 1. An intaglio or photogravure printing process for rotary presses, in which the impression is obtained from an etching made on a copper cylinder which is automatically inked as it revolves. 2. An illustration produced by this process.

ROTUNDA. *See* GOTHIC TYPE.

ROUGH. Rag paper that has not been given a finish. *See also* FINISH, HOT-PRESSED, NOT.

ROUGH CALF. A calf skin prepared with a nap similar to suede leather; used for bookbinding from the seventeenth century.

ROUGH EDGES. A widely used term to indicate paper with rough edges whether because they are UNCUT (*q.v.*) or a result of the way the paper was made. *See also* DECKLE EDGE.

ROUGH GILT EDGES. A book which has been 'cut rough' and the edges gilded, or which has been cut solid and gilded before sewing so that when the book is later sewn the edges are slightly uneven. This method has been widely used by English binders, specially by non-trade binders who dislike the solid-block-of-metal appearance of solid gilding. *See also* GILT ON THE ROUGH, MARBLING UNDER GILT, SOLID GILT.

ROUGH PULL. *Synonymous with* FLAT PULL (*q.v.*).

ROULETTE. *Synonymous with* FILLET (*q.v.*).

ROUND BACK. 1. The back of a thin booklet of which the folded sheets have been inserted inside each other and wire-stitched, sewn, or corded to the cover from the centre. 2. A book which has been rounded during the binding process and so given the familiar round back. The opposite of 'Flat back'. *See also* BACKING, FLAT BACK, ROUNDING.

ROUND BRACKETS. *Synonymous with* PARENTHESES (*q.v.*).

ROUND LETTER. *See* ANTIQUA.

ROUNDED CORNERS. In library bookbinding the sharp corners of the boards are sometimes cut and slightly rounded as a preventative against wear.

ROUNDEL. (*Binding*) A decoration consisting of a double ring, usually with a centre dot.

ROUNDING. The bookbinding process which gives the book a convex spine – and consequently concave fore-edges. It is achieved by a forwarder hammering the spine of a book, after it has been sewn and had its first coat of glue, with a round-headed hammer while gripped between backing boards at the same time as the book is backed. This operation can be done by machine. In Britain and America books are backed (to provide joints) as well as rounded. In most European countries backing is seldom done, with the result that there are no joints. *See also* BACKING, FLAT BACK, ROUND BACK.

ROUNDLET. A small circle in gold used by bookbinders' finishers as part of a book's decoration.

ROUTINE. (*Information retrieval*) A set of coded instructions arranged in proper sequence in order to direct the computer to perform a desired operation or sequence of operations. A subdivision of a programme consisting of two or more instructions that are related functionally – for this reason, a PROGRAMME (*q.v.*).

ROUTINE SLIP. *Synonymous with* PROCESS SLIP (*q.v.*).

ROUTING. (*Printing*) Cutting away mechanically the non-printing areas of a half-tone or line block.

ROUTING. The systematic circulation of periodicals or other printed material among the staff or officers of a library or organization in accordance with their interests in order to keep them informed of new developments. *Automatic routing* is the sending of each issue as soon as it is received to a pre-arranged list of persons. *Selective routing*, or *selective circulation*, is sending articles and publications individually selected by a reader (*see* READER 3) on the basis of an individual's known interests to the individual, usually with an ATTENTION NOTE (*q.v.*). *Circular routing* (also called *uncontrolled circulation*) is the sending of a periodical to all who need it before it is returned to the library: this is achieved by sticking to the cover a slip with the names of persons and/or departments for rapid perusal; such slips may bear a space for the insertion of the date of onward transmission. *Radial routing* (also called *controlled circulation*) ensures that the periodical is returned to the library by each reader before it is passed on to another reader. This method enables the librarian to keep better control of loans. *See also* ROUTING SLIP, SELECTIVE ROUTING.

ROUTING SLIP. A slip pasted on to the cover of a periodical and bearing the names of the persons (possibly with space for dates of sending) to whom it is to go. *See also* ATTENTION NOTE, ROUTING.

ROWE MEMORIAL AWARD, JOHN R. The new name of the EXHIBITS ROUND TABLE AWARD (*q.v.*).

ROXBURGHE BINDING. A book with plain black leather back, without raised bands, lettered in gold near the top within a border, having cloth or paper sides, and leaves gilt at top otherwise untrimmed. So named after the third Duke of Roxburghe (Scotland), a famous book collector who adopted this style for the books in his library.

ROYAL. A sheet of printing paper measuring 20 × 25 inches.

ROYAL COMMISSION ON HISTORICAL MANUSCRIPTS. *See* HISTORICAL MANUSCRIPTS COMMISSION.

ROYALTY. Payment made to an author by the publisher of a book, the basis being calculated as an agreed percentage of the retail price of the book, and paid half-yearly in respect of every copy of the book sold.

RUB. A representation of the back or sides of a book showing the lettering, bands, decoration, etc. It is done by firmly holding a piece of paper or tracing linen over the part of the binding of which an impression is to be made, and rubbing with a cobbler's heel-ball, lead pencil or soft crayon all over it until a recognizable copy of all details of the back or sides of the volume is obtained.

RUB-OFF. Printing ink which has rubbed on to the fingers from a printed sheet which has not dried sufficiently.

RUBBER BACK BINDING. A binding in which the folds of the sections are cut off and the spine dipped in rubber solution before insertion in the cover.

RUBBING. *See* RUB.

RUBRIC. 1. The heading of a chapter, section or other division of a book, and catchwords or marginal index words printed or written in red (the remainder of the text being in black), or otherwise distinguished in lettering, as a guide to the contents of pages. 2. A particular passage so marked.

RUBRICATED.   A book in which rubrics have been used.

RUBRICATION.   1. Underlining in red the filing entries on the tracings on standard printed catalogue cards or slips. Sometimes a red diagonal line leads from the upper left-hand corner to lead the eye to the underlining. 2. The carrying out of rubrics.

RUBRISHER.   One who carried out rubrication, or the plain painting of the large initial letters at the commencement of chapters of MSS. or early printed books, in red and blue. *See also* RUBRIC.

RULE.   A strip of metal used to print lines; it is of type height of varying thickness (hair, fine, medium, $1\frac{1}{2}$, 3, 4, 6, 12 point) with a face finished to a continuous line or lines. Rules which are placed at right angles to form frames or borders are said to be abutted or mitred according to whether the ends of the rules are square or mitred at an angle of 45°. A rule may also be designed to print dots or patterns. A SWELLED RULE is a line which is wide in the middle and tapers to a fine point at each end. *See also* DOTTED RULE, DOUBLE RULE.

18pt. R 121

12pt. R 95

6pt. R 71

6 pt. CB 862

1 pt. R 1

6 pt. CB 739

6 pt. 761

Dash D 69

Linotype 1028

Linotype 40

RULE BORDER.   (*Printing*) A frame, made up of rules, fitted around a page of type. Also called 'Rule frame'. *See also* BOX.

RULE FRAME.   *Synonymous with* RULE BORDER (*q.v.*).

RULES AND REGULATIONS.   Regulations are made by a local authority for the admission of the public to, and for the safety and use of, every library, museum and art gallery under its control. Regulations do not require confirmation by the Secretary of State for Education as do bye-laws, or by any other authority.

RULY ENGLISH. (*Information retrieval*) A modified form of English in which every word has one, and only one, conceptual meaning, and each concept has one and only one word to describe it. It is used by the U.S. Patent Office to develop certain index codes, and was proposed by S. Newman.

RUN. A machinist's term for a number of impressions taken from a forme, or plate, at one time. On completion, the job is said to be 'run-off'.

RUN-AROUND. Variation of length of lines of type to fit around blocks.

RUN ON. 1. A term, used in manuscripts and proof reading, to indicate to the printer that printed matter must be continuous and not broken up into paragraphs. This indication is marked by a line joining the end of one piece of matter to the beginning of the next and the writing of 'run on' in the margin. 2. To let a printing press continue to print sheets after the printing order has been completed. Sheets so printed 'run on cost' and involve little more than charges for paper and machine time.

RUN-ON CARD. A catalogue card which bears the continuation of an entry on the previous card. The heading is usually repeated on successive cards which are numbered 'Card 1', 'Card 2', etc. Also called 'Extension card'.

RUN-ON CHAPTERS. Chapters which do not start on a new page but run on at the end of the previous chapter. This is a style used in cheap bookwork.

RUN-ON STYLE. In book indexes, the typographical style which allows the subheadings to be printed continuously (with their relative page references) instead of being arranged under one another, and indented, under the heading to which they relate. Called in America 'Run-in Style'. *See also* INDENTED STYLE.

RUN OUT AND INDENTED. A style of typesetting where the first line is set to the full measure and the second and subsequent lines of the paragraph are indented as in this book.

RUN OVER. The continuation of matter on to another page.

RUN-UP GILT BOOK. In EXTRA BINDING (*q.v.*), used to describe the running of gold lines by a fillet so that the gilt panel lines are not mitred at each band. *See also* BANDS.

RUNES. 1. The earliest Scandinavian and Anglo-Saxon alphabet. Some letter forms continued in use in English documents until the seventeenth century and even later. A notable example is the 'y' form th, which has given rise to the pseudo-archaic form 'ye' for 'the'. 2. The name given to the characters which were cut or carved on metal, stone or wood by the ancient Teutons, usually as memorial inscriptions, but also for divination and for messages, and for carving the name of the artist or for the owner of weapons or ornaments. Runic characters were used for secular documents; amongst the more important runic manuscripts are: the old Danish legal MS., *Codex Runicus* (end 13th century), *Fasti Danici* (*c.* 1348), *Codex Leidensis* at Leyden, the *Codex Sangallensis* (878) at St. Gallen, and the *Codex Salisburgensis* (140). The old name of the Runic alphabet was 'futhark' or 'futhorc'.

RUNIC LETTERS. The 'national' writing of the ancient Germanic peoples; the characters have thorny, elongated and angular shapes.

RUNNERS. Figures or letters printed for reference purposes at regular intervals down the margins of a book and against lines of type to indicate the particular number or position of any given line. This is usually done in long poems or in school texts of plays or of texts in foreign languages.

RUNNING HEADLINE (RUNNING HEAD). *Synonymous with* RUNNING TITLE (*q.v.*).

RUNNING NUMBER. One, such as an accession number, which is given from a consecutive sequence to a book or other object.

RUNNING TITLE. The title that runs through a book or section of a book, repeated at the head of each page or at the top of the left-hand pages, with the chapter heading or the subject contents of both open pages on the right-hand page. Also called a 'Running head'. *See also* DROP-DOWN TITLE, HEADLINE, PAGE HEADLINE, SECTION HEADLINE.

RUSSELL COMMITTEE. The Committee of Inquiry appointed in February 1969 by the Secretary of State for Education and Science 'to assess the need for and to review the provision of non-vocational adult education in England and Wales; to consider the appropriateness of existing educational, administrative and financial policies; and to make recommendations . . .' The Committee is named after its Chairman, Sir E. Lionel Russell. The Committee's Report, *Adult education: a plan for development*, was published in 1973.

RUSSIA. A variety of calf leather used for bookbinding. It is specially tanned, and finished with birch oil which gives it a characteristic spicy odour. 'American Russia' is cowhide.

RUSTIC CAPITAL. 1. An upper case letter with a design engraved on the face, or an ornamentally designed letter. 2. The form of roman capital letters used by early scribes as a book hand between the second and sixth centuries A.D. The letters were less formal and not so heavy as the QUADRATA or SQUARE CAPITALS (*q.v.*) from which they were derived, giving a thinner, and more condensed appearance to the page. Also called 'Scriptura actuaria'.

RUSTICA. A freely-written, rather elegant fourth- and fifth-century writing used in Roman manuscripts. This style seems to have been influenced by Greek artistry and craftsmanship; it was displaced as a manuscript letter by the UNCIAL (*q.v.*), but used as initials or for emphasis in the line, in the same way that italics or small capitals are used by modern printers, in manuscripts until the eleventh century.

RUTHERSTAT. A trade name for a particular make of machine by means of which documents can be copied by reflex photography using silver halide paper. *See also* REFLEX COPYING.

RUTHVEN PRESS. An iron printing press, patented in 1813 by John Ruthven, an Edinburgh printer. In this, the bed which carried the type remained stationary while the platen was moved over it on a wheeled carriage. Springs kept the platen raised until the moment of impression, when power was applied through a series of levers which were worked by depressing a bar at the side of the press. It was not popular with the trade.

RUTLAND. Trade name for a fine-quality sheepskin used for bookbinding.

RUTTIER. *See* PORTOLAN.

RYLANDS LIBRARY, MANCHESTER, JOHN. *See* JOHN RYLANDS UNIVERSITY LIBRARY OF MANCHESTER.

s.a. Abbreviation in *Sears list of subject headings* for *see also* (*q.v.*).

SBN. Acronym for STANDARD BOOK NUMBER (*q.v.*).

SBN AGENCY. *See* STANDARD BOOK NUMBERING AGENCY.

s.c. Abbreviation for (1) small capitals; (2) super-calendered paper.

SD CLASSIFICATION. The scheme of classification, used by the U.S. government's Superintendent of Documents who is responsible for the centralized control and distribution of U.S. government documents. It is not a systematic scheme in that there is no visible subject relationship between the various parts. The notation consists of a combination of letters and numbers.

SDI. Abbreviation for Selective Dissemination of Information system which is an automated system of information retrieval utilizing a computer for disseminating relevant information to users. An interest profile depicting and defining each area of interest is compiled for each user; it consists of terms which are likely to appear in relevant documents. These profiles are stored on magnetic tape for computer processing. Key words representing documents are matched with these interest profiles. If, for any given document and user, the terms match, its abstract is sent to the user. *See also* CURRENT AWARENESS.

SDM. Abbreviation for selective dissemination of microfiche, a system whereby large-scale microfiche users regularly receive microfiche copies of documents in selected specified subject areas.

SDS. Acronym of the Space Documentation Service which is a part of the European Space Research Organization (ESRD), Europe's largest computerized information network containing information about most subjects within the natural and applied fields of science and technology. The SDS teledocumentation display terminal network encompasses research stations in at least nine European capitals, and supplies retrospective bibliographies on a number of national and international organizations for compiling and maintaining abstracts, indexes, files and data.

s.f. Abbreviation for *sub finem* (*Lat.* 'towards the end').

SfB. A classification system for trade literature, periodicals, and information concerning the building industry. The letters stand for the initials of the Swedish committee which originated it, Sanarbetskommittèn för Byttnadsfrågor.

SI UNITS. Abbreviation for units of the Système International d'Unités which are now normally used in science and mathematics books, and are receiving general acceptance. The basic SI units for physical quantity with their appropriate symbols are:
length: metre m
mass: kilogram kg
time: second s
electric current: ampere A
thermodynamic temperature: keloin K
luminous intensity: candela cd
amount of substance: mole mol

s.l. Abbreviation for *sine loco* (*Lat.* 'without a place'). Used in cataloguing entries when the probable place of publication cannot be ascertained.

s.n. Abbreviation for *sine nomine* (*Lat.* 'without a name'). Used in catalogue entries when the name of the publisher is unknown.

S.R. Abbreviation for the Register of the STATIONERS' COMPANY (*q.v.*).

SRC. Acronym of Subject-field Reference Code (taking the place of the name Broad System of Ordering BSO), a UNISIST (*q.v.*) project.

S.R.L. Science Reference Library, in Holborn, London, the former Patent Office Library and now part of the Reference Division of the British Library. *See also* BRITISH LIBRARY, NATIONAL REFERENCE LIBRARY OF SCIENCE AND INVENTION.

S/S. Abbreviation for same size; an instruction, written on the illustration, to the blockmaker to make a block the same size as the copy, and neither larger nor smaller.

s/t. Abbreviation for SMALL TYPE (*q.v.*).

STC. Abbreviation for *A short-title catalogue of books printed in England, Scotland, and Ireland, and of English books printed abroad, 1475–1640*, by A. W. Pollard and G. R. Redgrave, London, Bibliographical Society, 1926.

SVD. Schweizerische Vereinigung für Dokumentation/Association Suisse de Documentation. *See* ASD.

SAALIC. Abbreviation for Swindon Area Association of Libraries for Industry and Commerce, formed in 1961 and based on the Divisional Library, Regent Circus, Swindon, Wilts. The scheme arranges the inter-loan of books and periodicals, and the co-operative filing of periodicals, and deals with requests for information. There are no membership limitations.

SACAP. Acronym of Section, Acquisition, Cataloguing and Processing, which is a commercial cataloguing service provided by the ALANAR Book Processing Center of Bro-Dart Inc. It offers kits of processing materials, for the production of cards in customers' libraries.

SACRED WORK. A basic writing of a religion, such as the *Bible, Koran, Talmud, Upanishads*, etc., which is generally accepted as such by those who follow that religion. In classification, it is often treated as if it were a class or a subject.

SADDLE STITCHING. Binding a pamphlet by placing it on the saddle-shaped support of a stitching machine where it is automatically stitched with wire or thread through the centre of the fold. *See also* FLAT STITCHING, SIDE-STITCH.

SADSACT. Abbreviation for Self-Assigned Descriptors from Self and Cited Titles; statistical association techniques which have been used in the U.S.A. for small-scale experiments in machine indexing by members of the Information Technology Division (formerly Data Processing Systems Division) of the National Bureau of Standards.

SALALM. Acronym for Seminars on the Acquisition of Latin American Library Materials. The first Seminar was held in 1956 'to consider the problems involved in finding, buying and controlling library materials relating to Latin America'. A Seminar has been held each year since. Publishes *SALALM Newsletter* (2p.a.). *See also* LACAP.

SALLE. A well-lighted room in a paper-mill where the paper is examined sheet by sheet, sorted, counted and arranged in reams. Also called 'Finishing house' or 'Finishing room' in a machine paper mill.

SALTON'S MAGICAL AUTOMATIC RETRIEVER OF TEXTS. *See* SMART.

SAMPLE BACK. A strip of leather, cloth or other material made up to represent the back of a book and used as a sample for matching colour, material, lettering, etc.

SAMPLE PAGES. Selected pages of a proposed book, set by the printer as a specimen and model for the whole book.

SANDING. Rubbing down the edges of a book with sand-paper, or a sand-wheel machine, so as to remove as small an amount of paper as possible.

SANS SERIF. A type face without SERIFS (*q.v.*). The best known is 'Gill Sans' designed by Eric Gill; other well-known sans serif types are Futura and Vogue. The first sans serif type, designed by William Caslon, was named Egyptian; it was afterwards re-named Sanserif.

SARAH JOSEPHA HALE AWARD. *See* HALE AWARD, SARAH JOSEPHA.

SARBICA. Acronym for South-East Asian Regional Branch of the International Council on Archives; it was inaugurated in Kuala Lumpur in July 1968 as the first branch of the INTERNATIONAL COUNCIL ON ARCHIVES (*q.v.*). Its membership comprises the national archival institutions of six S.E.A. countries (Indonesia, Malaysia, the Philippines, Singapore, Thailand, and the Republic of Viet-Nam). Its aims, which are restricted to operations in the Region, are to: (a) establish and maintain relations between archivists of all countries and between all organizations concerned with the custody or administration of archives; (b) promote all measures for the preservation of archive material; (c) facilitate the use of archives; (d) promote, organize and co-ordinate activities in the field of archives; (e) sponsor the professional training of archivists; (f) co-operate with other organizations concerned with the documentation of human experience; (g) carry out the aims and objectives of the International Council on Archives. The Secretariat is provided by the National Archives of Malaysia, Pataling Jaya. Publishes *Southeast Asian Archives* (a.).

SARUM USE. In the fifteenth century, certain Parisian presses specialized in books of Hours of the Virgin (the layman's prayer book) which were similar in format but differed slightly according to the locality in which they were to be used. To prevent the printer and binder mixing the various editions, abbreviations such as 'Sar' for 'secundum usum Sarum' or 'Par' for 'secundum usum ecclesie Parisiensis' were placed after the signature letter. The version used mostly in England, particularly in the southern part, and in Scotland, was that of Salisbury or 'Sarum', the York use being confined to the north. Their use was discontinued after the Reformation. Sarum books were largely produced in Paris and Rouen.

SASLIC. Abbreviation for Surrey and Sussex Libraries in Co-operation, an organization which came into being formally in July 1969 following a year of preparatory investigation inspired by the Report of the Scientific Library Services Committee of the Library Association in 1968. The area covered comprises the counties of Surrey, East Sussex and West Sussex. Its aims are "to improve library resources and information services in science, technology, commerce and related subjects, by co-operative action, and to implement such recommendations of the Report mentioned 'as will contribute to that end'". Its functions are to: (a) prepare and maintain a published record of library resources and special materials available in the area, and to make them known to co-operating organizations; (b) ensure by co-operative purchase that the reference, bibliographical and other collections of special materials give full coverage to meet the information needs of the area; (c) commission the compilation and production of book lists, bibliographies, etc., which will further the work of the organizations; (d) encourage the provision of facilities for the training of librarians and information officers in the use of scientific and other relevant literature, and to encourage the provision of similar facilities for scientists, technologists and other users of libraries and information services. Membership is open to any organization in the area providing it is willing to participate in the exchange and provision of information (other than that which is confidential). Membership subscriptions, training course fees, and the proceeds from the sale of publications are the only sources of income. Over sixty public library authorities, the major academic institutions and special libraries of all kinds are in membership. Publishes SASLIC *Newsletter* (irreg.).

SATCOM. Abbreviation for the Committee on Scientific and Technical Communication which was set up in March 1966 at the suggestion of COSATI (*q.v.*) by the large U.S. learned academies, the National Academy of Sciences and the National Academy of Engineering, the object of which is to provide a focus for participation by scientists and engineers, through their societies, in planning a national network of information systems.

SAW CUTS. Grooves made in the back of a book with a saw to take the cords used in sewing.

SAWING-IN. Sawing grooves in the back of a book for the reception of the cord in sewing.

SAYERS MEMORIAL PRIZE. This Prize takes the form of professional books, and was created from the royalties of the *Sayers memorial volume*, and donated by the editors D. J. Foskett and B. I. Palmer. The volume was produced as a tribute to the late W. C. Berwick Sayers, Chief Librarian of the Croydon Public Libraries for many years, a former President of the Library Association, and particularly noted for his teaching and writing on classification. The Prize is awarded to the candidate gaining the highest mark in classification in the Final Examination of the Library Association. It was first awarded in 1965 to Henry Gilby.

sc. Abbreviation for *scilicet* (*Lat.* 'namely').

SCALE. The ratio of the distance on an architectural drawing, map, globe, model or vertical section, to the actual distances they represent.

SCALING. The process of calculating the area by which an illustration block must be altered to fit a given layout.

SCAMP. Abbreviation for the Scottish Association of Magazine Publishers which exists to promote the sale of the literary magazines receiving Scottish Arts Council grants along with any of their publications.

SCAN. To examine every reference or every entry in a file routinely as part of a retrieval scheme (*IBM*). To examine periodicals and other materials to determine the usefulness of the information contained to the library's users, especially to the interests and work of individuals served by a special library. This enables decisions to be made as to ROUTING (*q.v.*), the preparation of ABSTRACTS and ATTENTION NOTES (*qq.v.*), and how cataloguing and classifying should be carried out.

SCAN-COLUMN INDEX. A co-ordinate book-form index developed by J. O'Connor which provides for manual serial searching of terms arranged in columns (*IBM*). *See also* CO-ORDINATE INDEXING.

SCAN PLATES. A generic term for plates made by an electronic photo-engraving machine.

SCANDIA PLAN, THE. A system of voluntary co-operation between public, special and research libraries in Denmark, Finland, Norway and Sweden (where it originated) in the systematic acquisition of literature, implying a rational distribution of the obligation to purchase, exchange and store old and new materials in each subject in the broad field of the humanities which has been allocated, acts as a bibliographical centre, and lends freely. The initiative for the scheme was taken by the inter-Scandinavian federation, the Nordisk Vitenskapeliget Bibliotekarforbund; the expenses entailed by the numerous planning conferences are defrayed by the Nordic Cultural Commission, an inter-Scandinavian governmental organization for cultural affairs. None of the co-operating libraries receives any extra financial support to fulfil its special acquisitional commitments; each acts independently on its purchase and exchange policies; the allocation of special subject fields is made on the basis of the existing library collections and fields of interest. It is the only international scheme of its kind and has been operated since 1957. The practical development of the plan is promoted by the Scandinavian Association of Nordic Research Librarians. It is hoped that the Plan will be extended to more countries, reduce duplication, and move into the fields of science and social science. The responsibility for this plan was transferred in 1973 from the Scandinavian Association of Research Librarians to the newly organized Co-operation Committee of Scandinavian Research Libraries (Nordiska Forskningobiblioteks Samarketskommitté) which has been formed to co-ordinate Scandinavian co-operation projects in the library field, of which the Scandia Plan is one.

SCANDINAVIAN ASSOCIATION OF RESEARCH LIBRARIANS. Founded 1947 in Copenhagen to promote and facilitate contacts and co-operation between Scandinavian assistant librarians and their libraries. Associations in Denmark, Finland, Norway and Sweden are members. Abbreviated NVBF (Nordisk Videnskabeligt Bibliotekarieforbund).

SCANDINAVIAN COUNCIL FOR APPLIED RESEARCH. *See* NORDFORSK.

SCANDOC. Acronym of the Scandinavian Documentation Center, set up in Washington, D.C., by the Scandinavian Council for Applied Research (NORDFORSK, *q.v.*). Aims: to promote and organize co-operation in the field of scientific and industrial research and in the utilization of research results between the five Scandinavian countries which finance the Center. Publishes *Research Projects in Scandinavia* (2 p.a.), *Acta Polytechnica Scandinavica (irreg.)*, *Scandinavian Research Information Notes* (2 p.a.), and books, conference proceedings and research surveys. It also acts as a centre for Scandinavian research and industry in the U.S.A.

SCANNING. In information retrieval, the examination of tallies (records). This may be done (a) *sequentially*, in sequence one after another right through a file, (b) *simultaneously*, e.g. as a batch of edge-notched cards is needled, (c) *fractionally*, in a series of separate and intermittent consultations, e.g. as a catalogue is searched.

SCAR. *See* NORDFORSK.

SCARECROW PRESS AWARD FOR LIBRARY LITERATURE. Presented annually by the Scarecrow Press, this Award is $500 cash and a citation; it is administered by the ALA Awards Committee, the selection being made by a jury composed of one representative of each type-of-library division of the American Library Association. The first recipient (in 1960) was Mrs. Marjorie Fiske Lowenthal for *Book selection and censorship*.

SCATTER. The separation of entries in an index for the same topic or concept caused by entry under both singular and plural forms, or variant forms of name, or entry in one instance under a broad heading and in another under a specific heading, or by the imprecise use of terms, or by lack of control of synonymy. *See also* BIBLIOGRAPHICAL SCATTER.

SCATTERING. *See* LAW OF SCATTERING.

SCAUL. Acronym of the Standing Conference of African University Librarians. Founded 1964. Aims to support and develop academic library services in the area, and to promote interchange, contact and co-operation among academic libraries in Africa. Membership is open to institutions. Publishes SCAUL *Newsletter* (irreg.).

SCAULEA. Acronym of the Standing Conference of African University Libraries: Eastern Area, the first meeting of which was held from 10th–12th February 1971.

SCENARIO. 1. The outline of a film plot. 2. Any abbreviated presentation of the personages, plot, and outline of a dramatic work, such as a play, dramatic oratorio, cantata or opera. In cataloguing music, the term is also used for a ballet plot, directions for a dance composition, etc.

SCHEDULE. 1. A statement of the sub-divisions of a classification as set out on paper so as to show hierarchical relationship. *See also* SUMMUM GENUS. 2. A series of serial classifications, arranged in one series of co-ordinate classes, with sub-classes, if there are any, arranged in secondary series, or columns, indented to show the subordination. These secondary series may be sub-divided successively, resulting in tertiary and quaternary series. These forms are equivalent to TABULAR CLASSIFICATION (*q.v.*) of three or more dimensions. 3. In information retrieval, any list of terms used in constructing a file. *See also* FILE 3. 4. An appendix to an Act of Parliament or other document; an annex or supplement. 5. (*Archives*) A document attached to another document, especially in amplification.

SCHEDULED MNEMONICS. *See* MNEMONICS.

SCHEME. Provisions for inter-library co-operation in library regions in England and Wales and for the setting up of library councils in connexion therewith. *See also* LIBRARY COUNCIL.

SCHEME. *See* BILL OF TYPE.

SCHEME OF CLASSIFICATION. The schedules, index, and apparatus of a classification; the complete classification tables.

SCHOLISM. (*Pl.* Scholia.) An explanatory marginal note or comment, or interpretative remark, especially an annotation on a classical text by an ancient grammarian.

SCHOOL DISTRICT LIBRARY. A free public library established and financially supported by action of a school district for the use of residents of the district. Such a library is supervised by a local board of education or by a separate library board appointed by a board of education. (American.)

SCHOOL EDITION. An edition of a book especially prepared for use in school. It usually has no answers, or is in some other way less complete than the ordinary edition, it may be printed on poorer paper, or bound less substantially, and sold at a cheaper price.

SCHOOL LIBRARIES DEPARTMENT. A section of a public library service, or local education service, which administers a system of 'school libraries', comprising collections of books for home reading. Each collection, which varies in size according to the number of children to be served, and is made up from a large reservoir stock, is sent to each school at regular intervals, the exchange usually being made during school holidays.

SCHOOL LIBRARIES SECTION. A Section of the Library Association, the formation of which was agreed by the Council of the Association on 4th December 1936. It became a constituent part of the School Library Association when this was formed in 1937.

SCHOOL LIBRARY. An organized collection of books placed in a school for the use of teachers or pupils, but usually for pupils. It may comprise books of reference and/or books for home reading, and be in the care of a professional librarian, teacher, or teacher-librarian. Variously called in America in the later 1960s an *Instructional Materials Center*, a *Learning Resources Centre* or a *Media Centre*, due to the role of the centre being the housing and distributing of visual aids materials to teachers throughout a school. The provision of school libraries in Scotland was transferred, in May 1975, from the

County Councils (which had operated them for over fifty years in conjunction with the public library services in their areas) to the Education Committees of the Regional Authorities, due to the provisions of the Local Government (Scotland) Act 1973.

SCHOOL LIBRARY ASSOCIATION. Formally constituted on 23 January 1937, strengthened in 1945 by the adhesion of the former School Libraries Section of the Library Association, and incorporated in 1955. This Association aims to promote development of the school library as an instrument of education in schools of all kinds; to encourage efficient methods of administration and routine; and to provide opportunities for interchange of experience among school librarians and others interested in the aims of the Association. Corporate membership is open to any school, college, institute of education, or library; Personal membership is available to individuals, and Student membership to students. Abbreviated SLA. Publishes *The School Librarian* (4 p.a.) and books. *See also* INTERNATIONAL ASSOCIATION OF SCHOOL LIBRARIANSHIP.

SCHOOL LIBRARY ASSOCIATION IN SCOTLAND. Formed in 1953, this Association is an integral part of the SCHOOL LIBRARY ASSOCIATION (*q.v.*). Financed by the remission of a percentage of the membership fee from the SLA and a grant from the Scottish Education Department. Has branches in the largest Scottish cities.

SCHOOL LIBRARY MANPOWER PROJECT. *See* KNAPP SCHOOL LIBRARIES PROJECT.

SCHOOL LIBRARY SUPERVISOR. The American term for a librarian who supervises and co-ordinates the work of several other school librarians. The American Association of School Librarians recommends one for every system having five or more schools. Duties and responsibilities vary but usually include: consulting with school administrators, providing leadership, guidance and knowledge in school librarianship to stimulate improvement in the service. Also called 'Adviser', 'Consultant', 'Co-ordinator', 'Director', 'District-Librarian', 'Head Librarian', 'Specialist'.

SCHOOL OF LIBRARIANSHIP. *Synonymous with* LIBRARY SCHOOL (*q.v.*).

SCHOOL SYSTEM MATERIALS CENTER. A library located in the central office of a system of school libraries from which are circulated films, filmstrips, records, tapes and other audio-visual materials and equipment to the schools in the system.

SCHOOLS COUNCIL. In full, the Schools Council for Curriculum and Examinations; it is an independent body with a majority of teacher members. It was established in 1964 to undertake in England and Wales research and development work in curriculum, teaching methods and examinations in schools, and to advise the Secretary of State on matters of examinations policy. In all its work, it has regard to the general principle, expressed in its constitution, that each school should have the fullest possible measure of responsibility for its own curriculum and teaching methods based on the needs of its own pupils and evolved by its own staff. The Council is financed by equal contributions from local education authorities and the Department of Education and Science. The Council co-operates with the Library Association on matters of mutual interest.

SCHROTHLATT. *Synonymous with* MANIÈRE CRIBLÉE (*q.v.*).

SCHWABACHER. 1. An early variety of Gothic type used in Germany. 2. A type used in Germany today, based on early Gothic designs.

SCHWEIZERISCHE GESAMTKATALOG. The Swiss National Catalogue, which is housed at the National Library in Berne, lists all books published in Switzerland, and foreign books. Over 2,000,000 titles are entered on cards, and these are the basis of inter-library loans.

SCHWEIZERISCHE VEREINIGUNG FÜR DOKUMENTATION. The Association Suisse de Documentation. *See* ASD.

SCIENCE AND TECHNOLOGY INFORMATION AND UTILIZATION CORPORATION. In Title IV of the congressional bill (H.R. 4461), on which the (American) House of Representatives held hearings in 1975, it was proposed to combine NTIS, the Smithsonian Science Information Exchange and the OSIS to form a corporation with this name. The purposes of the Corporation would be 'to: (a) assure the widest possible dissemination of scientific and technological information to industry, labour, the academic community, state and local governments, and to the public at large; (b) co-ordinate, collate, publish, arrange, and manage such information so that it is readily available in effective form at the least feasible cost to the user'.

SCIENCE AND TECHNOLOGY POLICIES INFORMATION EXCHANGE SYSTEM. *See* SPINES.

SCIENCE CITATION INDEX. A printed index of books and periodical articles and all kinds of references to them in subsequent publications. Compiled and published by the Institute for Scientific Information, of Philadelphia, Pa., U.S.A., it is published quarterly, the fourth issue being a cumulation of the previous three issues.

SCIENCE FICTION. Imaginative fiction describing life and adventure in the future, life on other worlds, interplanetary travel, etc. It usually has a scientific or prophetic background.

SCIENCE REFERENCE LIBRARY. Part of the Reference Division of the BRITISH LIBRARY (q.v.). See also NATIONAL REFERENCE LIBRARY OF SCIENCE AND INVENTION, PATENT OFFICE LIBRARY. Abbreviated S.R.L.

SCIENCE-TECHNOLOGY DIVISION. A division of the (American) Special Libraries Association. Often abbreviated Sci-Tech.

SCIENTIFIC AND TECHNOLOGICAL INFORMATION SERVICES ENQUIRY COMMITTEE. See STISEC.

SCIENTIFIC DOCUMENTATION CENTRE LTD. Formed in 1962 as a non-profit-making research association to provide information services for scientists. Financed from subscriptions and payment for services provided; members are entitled to use certain types of service at reduced costs. Abbreviated SDC. Publishes SDC Bulletin (q.), which carries continuing bibliographies on information retrieval, spectrometric applications, bibliographies and reviews.

SCI-TECH. Abbreviation for the SCIENCE-TECHNOLOGY DIVISION (q.v.) of the Special Libraries Association.

SCOGGIN MEMORIAL COLLECTIONS. Begun in 1970, notable books of the year for children and young adults are selected by the Children's Service Division of the American Library Association and formed into collections. They were begun by the Children's Book Council, of NEW YORK CITY, to honour Margaret Scoggin, an authority on books for the young. They are a project of the U.S. Section of the INTERNATIONAL BOARD ON BOOKS FOR YOUNG PEOPLE (q.v.) and are presented each year to repositories in parts of the world where publishing either does not exist or is not fully developed; one collection also is given to the International Youth Library in Munich.

SCOGGIN SCHOLARSHIP, MARGARET. Offered by the Young Adult Services Division of the American Library Association to a librarian or prospective librarian working with youth. The Scholarship is offered to honour Margaret Clara Scoggin (1905–1968) who was Co-ordinator of Young Adult Services in the New York Public Library from 1952 until the end of 1967.

SCOLCAP. Abbreviation for Scottish Libraries Cataloguing Automation Project, which was initiated by the National Library of Scotland with a conference in June 1973. Other participating libraries are the universities of Stirling, Dundee and Glasgow and the public libraries of Glasgow and Edinburgh. The Project aims at achieving co-operative cataloguing in these six major Scottish libraries by 1977.

SCOLLUL. Acronym for Standing Conference of Librarians of the Libraries of the University of London which holds periodic meetings to consider aspects of co-operation between the libraries of the University.

SCOLMA. Acronym for Standing Conference on Library Materials on Africa. This organization was set up at a meeting held in Chatham House on 2 April 1962. Its aims are: to facilitate the acquisition and preservation of library materials needed for African studies; to assist in the recording and use of such materials. Membership is by invitation of the committee and is of three kinds, full membership which is limited to institutions in the United Kingdom actively acquiring materials on Africa and co-operating in the schemes promoted by the Conference, supporting membership which is open to other bodies interested in the aims of the organization, and personal membership. Publications: *African Research and Documentation* (3 p.a.), *The SCOLMA Directory of Libraries and Special Collections on Africa*, *U.K. Publications and theses on Africa* (a.).

SCONUL. Acronym for the Standing Conference of National and University Libraries; a British organization which is primarily concerned with co-operation. Founded in September 1950 'to promote the work of national and university libraries'. The main body of the organization meets twice a year, but much of its work is done by sub-committees which are formed as necessary to deal with specific matters; courses of instruction are arranged for members of library staffs, and exhibitions of foreign books are arranged. It is the equivalent of the (American) ASSOCIATION OF RESEARCH LIBRARIES (*q.v.*). A Library Design Award was instituted in 1975. The Award is made on the recommendation of the SCONUL Buildings Sub-committee, which makes a regular biennial review of recent buildings. No award is made in any two-year period if there is no outstanding building, but more than one award may be made if there is more than one outstanding building. The awards are offered to recognize outstanding functional efficiency of academic and national buildings, which have been in use for at least one year, rather than external aesthetics. The first award was made for an eight-storey extension to the British Library Lending Division building (formerly the National Lending Library for Science and Technology) at Boston Spa, Yorkshire, which was formally opened in April 1975.

SCOPAS. Acronym of the Standing Conference on Professional

Activities in Scotland which was formed about 1968 to co-ordinate activities in order to avoid possible date clashes when arranging meetings, etc.

SCOPE CARD. A comprehensive catalogue card indicating the extent of musical or other works possessed in one form or medium, or of an identical title by one author or composer.

SCOPE NOTE. 1. In information retrieval, a statement giving the range of meaning and scope of a subject heading or descriptor and usually referring to related or overlapping headings (*IBM*). 2. In co-ordinate indexing, a symbol appended to a term or term number to narrow the definition of the term rather than designate the role of a word in its context. *See also* ROLES.

SCORE. A printed or written version of a musical work in notational form which shows the parts for the participating voices or instruments on two or more staves ('staffs' in America), one above the other. The term is not usually applied to music for one performer. A *Full Score* shows the music for each participating voice or instrument on separate staves one above the other, with the music for each solo voice, each choral part and each instrument being set out on a separate stave one above another. The customary order in Europe is (reading from the top to the bottom) woodwind, brass, timpani, percussion, strings, solo instrumental parts (for concertos); additional orchestral parts such as harp(s) and organ, and choral parts, are normally placed between the percussion and strings. American scores usually place solo voices and chorus parts between the upper and lower strings, with organ at the bottom. A *Miniature Score* has the same music as a full score but is reduced considerably in size by photographic reproduction. Miniature scores are usually so described on the title-page, but if not, can be considered to be such if the music is smaller than normal and the page size is not more than 20 cms. An *Orchestral Score* is the full score of an orchestral work. A *Piano Score* is an orchestral or vocal work reduced to a piano version. A *Piano-Conductor Score* (violin-conductor score, etc.) is a piano (or violin etc.) part in a concerted work, with cues to indicate when vocal or instrumental performers 'come in', i.e. begin to perform. The pianist (or violinist etc.) performs and conducts (or attempts to) at the same time. A *Vocal Score* shows the music for voices on separate staves but the orchestral parts reduced to a piano version. This is the common version for members of choirs, of the music of cantatas, operas, and oratorios. Also called 'Piano-vocal score'. A *Close Score* has the music for more than one part or instrument on one stave. Also called 'Compressed score', 'Short score'. An *Open Score* has the music for each voice or part on a separate stave, each being placed above one another, as in a full score. Also called 'Extended score'. The term 'score' should not be used without qualification. A *Small full score* is a photographic reduction of a *Full score*. *Pocket score* is synonymous with *Miniature score*. A *Study score* is musically identical with a *Full score* and more than 20 cm. in height. A *Part* shows the individual instrumental or vocal lines and states the nature of the part, e.g. Chorus part, Tenor part, Violin part. A *Short Score* is one showing all the parts on the smallest possible number of staves; also called a 'Compressed Full Score'. A *Full Music Edition* is a fully harmonized version of a vocal work, especially a collection of hymns or of songs. A *Melody Edition* is the melody line only of a vocal work; it is used mainly of collections of songs and hymns. A *Chorus Score* is one showing all the chorus parts, with the accompaniment, if any, arranged for keyboard. *See also* REALIZATION REDUCTION *A Rehearsal Score* is a compressed version of a full score, in many respects similar to a 'Short Score' but with sufficient cues to be of practical use at rehearsals. An *Organ-vocal score* is a score of a work for chorus and/or solo voices and organ, the accompaniment being a reduction of the music originally composed for an instrumental ensemble. A *piano-vocal score* is a similar work to an organ-vocal score, but for piano instead of organ. *See also* TRANSCRIPTION.

SCORING.   Compressing the fibres of heavy paper along a line, to facilitate either folding or tearing. Scoring with a dull rule increases folding endurance. The use of a sharp rule however partially breaks the paper fibres and has a similar effect to perforating.

SCOTAPLL.   The Standing Conference of Theological and Philosophical Libraries in London. This Association was founded in 1948 to improve facilities for research in these subjects, and to interchange books between constituent libraries. It was merged with the Association of British Theological and Philosophical Libraries in 1964. *See also* ABTAPL.

SCOTTISH ASSOCIATION OF MAGAZINE PUBLISHERS.   *See* SCAMP.

SCOTTISH CENTRAL LIBRARY.   Now incorporated in the National Library of Scotland, it was the Scottish counterpart to the National Central Library; formed on 1st July 1952. It was founded in Dunfermline in 1921 as the Scottish Central Library for Students. As from 1st October 1953 it absorbed the Regional Library Bureau of Scotland (founded in 1945) and became responsible for the Scottish Union Catalogue from the same date. Abbreviated

SCL. On 1st May 1974 this Library was incorporated within the National Library of Scotland, becoming the NLS Lending Services (NLSLS).

SCOTTISH CHILDREN'S BOOK ASSOCIATION, THE. Founded 1973 to: (a) stimulate and encourage among children and others an interest in, and appreciation of, good literature for children; (b) encourage, or assist in promoting, the formation of groups of persons interested in children's books; (c) communicate information and advice about children's books; (d) promote discussion of all matters relating to children's books and their evaluation; (e) stimulate and encourage better provision of library facilities for children; (f) co-operate in furtherance of the Association's objects, with persons, institutions and organizations concerned with children. Membership is open to individuals, groups and institutions. Financed by members' subscriptions, donations and advertising in *Book Window* (3 p.a.).

SCOTTISH LIBRARIES CATALOGUING AUTOMATION PROJECT. *See* SCOLCAP.

SCOTTISH LIBRARY ASSOCIATION. A Branch of the Library Association. It was an independent association, having been formed in October 1908 at Edinburgh, until January 1931 when it was affiliated with the LA and incorporated as a Branch, its terminology being changed to Branch on the revision of the constitution of the Library Association in 1963. There are four regional branches each of which is represented on the SLA Council. Abbreviated SLA. Publishes *SLA News* (6 p.a.), *Proceedings* of the annual conferences (1950–), Annual Report of the Council (1909–), *Scottish Libraries* (reports on Scottish Library Studies – a series of books on Scottish libraries and librarianship).

SCOTTISH STYLE. An eighteenth-century style of book decoration resembling the HARLEIAN STYLE (*q.v.*), but which has for a centre-piece a straight stem from which short sprays branch at regular intervals on either side, or else consists mainly of a large wheel pattern.

SCRAPERBOARD. 1. A method of drawing for reproduction. It utilizes a 'board' coated with a chalk surface and covered with a black wash which the artist scrapes away to reveal the white lines and areas of his drawing. Black lines may be drawn in afterwards if desired. 2. A drawing made by this method. It is similar in appearance to a wood engraving.

SCRATCHBOARD. American term for paper coated with black ink which is scratched away to show the white paper underneath. The picture drawing so produced. A scraperboard.

SCREAMER.   The printer's term for exclamation marks used for display purposes.

SCREEN.   A grid of opaque lines cut in glass (used in making half-tone blocks) crossing at right angles, and producing transparent square apertures between the intersections which split up the image into dots; these dots are distinctive of the half-tone process. The number of lines to the inch varies from forty for a coarse screen for use with rough or poor quality paper to 250 for a fine screen for use with art paper. *See also* HALF-TONE.

SCREEN.   (*Reprography*) A surface of any material on to which, or if translucent, through which, an image is projected. (*Information retrieval*) To make a preliminary selection of information or documents with a view to reducing the number to be examined at a later date.

SCREW PRESS.   A press used by bookbinders to flatten paper or books in process of binding, especially after pasting or glueing. It is operated by turning a wheel or lever attached to the upper end of a large-dimension screw placed perpendicularly which has at its lower end a heavy iron plate below which, and on the bed of the press, are placed the papers or books to be pressed. *See also* PRESS.

SCRINIUM.   A cylinder-shaped container with movable lid used by the Romans to hold a number of scrolls.

SCRIPT.   1. A form of printer's cursive type resembling handwriting. 2. Any type face which is cut to resemble handwriting. 3. Handwriting, as opposed to printed characters. 4. A typescript, specially of a play, film scenario, or text of spoken matter for broadcasting.

This, Trafton Script, is an example of 1.

SCRIPT WRITING.   *Synonymous with* DISJOINED HAND (*q.v.*).

SCRIPTORES.   Writers who copied books by hand in Roman times.

SCRIPTORIUM.   The room in a mediaeval monastery or abbey which was set aside for the copying of manuscripts, and for writing and studying generally.

SCRIPTURA ACTUARIA.   *Synonymous with* RUSTIC CAPITAL (*q.v.*).

SCROLL.   1. A roll of paper or parchment, usually containing writing and rolled onto rollers. This was an early form of manuscript, called by the Romans *volumen* (roll) from which the word *volume* is derived. The scroll (or 'roll') comprised a number of sheets of papyrus or parchment glued together to form a 20- or 30-feet long strip which was wound on a cylinder with projecting ornaments or knobs in ivory or colours, and was finished with a coloured parchment cover, fastened

24

with laces and identified with a 'sittybus', or title label. The text was written in rather narrow columns on the recto of the material, where, if papyrus, the fibres run horizontally. 2. (*Binding*) A scroll-shaped stamp used for bearing an inscription, or an ornament of similar shape, and generally used between Flowers on a roll.

sculpt.   Abbreviation for *sculpsit* (*Lat.*). Indicates on an engraving the name of the engraver, and on sculpture the name of the sculptor. *See also* del., fecit.

SEAL.   Abbreviation for South East Area Libraries Information Service which was formed in 1968 and comprised the Municipal Borough of Dartford and the London Boroughs of Bexley and Greenwich. The area covered by the organization has been enlarged, and now extends along the South Bank of the Thames from London Bridge to Gravesend; it comprises the following local authorities: North West Kent (the Dartford and Gravesham Divisions of the Kent County Libraries), and the London Boroughs of Bexley, Greenwich, Lewisham and Southwark. The objects of the Service are to: (a) provide a reference and information service for industrial and commercial organizations within the area; (b) promote the rapid exchange of both written and verbal information; (c) broaden and strengthen the reference and information library facilities in the area by means of collaboration and co-operation between existing library services. Membership is open to public libraries; further educational institutions; industrial, commercial and research organizations; other interested bodies. Financed by subscription of the local authorities of the area in which the scheme operates.

SEAL PRINT.   A woodcut with blind embossing around the picture, the embossing being done after the printing. Practised in the fifteenth century. Also called 'Gypsographic print.'

SEALSKIN.   Binding leather made from the skin of the seal; it has a coarse grain, but is soft to the touch. *See also* PIN SEAL.

SEARCH RECORD.   A record which shows the publications, organizations, and individuals consulted in answering an enquiry or obtaining information. The completed memorandum, information statement, or report, may be inserted on the form or attached to it, or it may form a separate record kept in a JOB FILE (*q.v.*).

SEARCH ROOM.   1. A room associated with an archives or record centre in which people may carry out their searches in the documents. 2. A room in which volumes of indexes to periodicals, volumes of abstracts, and similar bibliographical and search tools are provided for users to conduct literature searches. *See also* ARCHIVES.

SEARCH SERVICE. *Synonymous with* RESEARCH SERVICE (*q.v.*).

SEARCH STRATEGY. (*Information retrieval*) The method selected in using a retrieval system for a particular search.

SEARCHER. A member of a library's staff who verifies the information available concerning a book it is proposed to purchase and then makes certain that the book is not already in stock.

SEARCHING. The act of checking a book against the catalogue to determine whether it is a duplicate, another edition of a book already in stock, or a new title (to be) added to the library. In PRELIMINARY CATALOGUING (*q.v.*), the searcher notes such descriptive and subject cataloguing details as may be helpful to the cataloguer. Often, searching slips are provided to standardize the operation. The term is also applied to the checking of titles for acquisition purposes.

SECOND GENERATION MICROFILM. *Synonymous with* FIRST REPRODUCTION MICROFILM (*q.v.*). *See also* GENERATION.

SECOND HALF-TITLE. A repetition of the title of a book between the preliminaries and the text.

SECOND INDENTION. The tenth typewriter space from the left edge of a catalogue card; the second, or inner, vertical line on a catalogue card ruled for handwriting. It is at this position that the title normally begins; if it runs over the line, it continues at the 'First indention', and is followed by particulars of edition and imprint. The *collation* also begins at the second indention, but without spacing between these two parts of the description. The collation is followed by a series note. The *notes* and the *contents* also begin at the second indention, but a 'blank line' is left between these and the previous parts of the description. Should either collation, notes or contents over-run the first line, subsequent lines begin at the first indention. Also called 'Title indention', 'Inner indention' and 'Paragraph indention'. *See also* FIRST INDENTION, INDENTION, SECOND VERTICAL, THIRD INDENTION.

SECOND LINING. A strip of brown paper the full size of the back of a book which is glued into position after the FIRST LINING (*q.v.*) has been affixed.

SECOND REPRODUCTION MICROFILM. A microfilm copy made from the FIRST REPRODUCTION MICROFILM (*q.v.*). Also called 'Third generation microfilm'. *See also* GENERATION.

SECOND VERTICAL. The second vertical line printed on a standard ruled catalogue card and serving as a guide to where the title should begin – at the SECOND INDENTION (*q.v.*). *See also* FIRST VERTICAL.

SECONDARY ACCESS. (*Information retrieval*) Access from one entry to related entries in a FILE (*q.v.*). *See also* PRIMARY ACCESS.

SECONDARY BIBLIOGRAPHY.   1. An 'intensive' or special bibliography dealing with books relating to one subject for the compilation
of which primary bibliographies have been used. 2. A bibliography in
which material is rearranged for convenience of research. (American.)
See also BIBLIOGRAPHY, PRIMARY BIBLIOGRAPHY.

SECONDARY ENTRY.   An entry in a catalogue other than the MAIN
ENTRY (*q.v.*): an ADDED ENTRY (*q.v.*). *See also* GENERAL SECONDARY.

SECONDARY FULLNESS.   The detail with which, in full cataloguing,
an author's name is given in all secondary entries, e.g. the Christian
name is given in full if there is only one, but initials if there are more
than one. Also called 'Subject fullness'.

SECONDARY PUBLICATION.   1. A document such as an abstract,
digest, index to periodicals, current awareness journal, or popularization, which is prepared in order to disseminate more widely information which has already appeared in another form, particularly in a
PRIMARY PUBLICATION (*q.v.*). 2. The act of publishing such material.

SECONDARY SERVICE.   *Synonymous with* ABSTRACTING SERVICE
(*q.v.*)

SECONDARY SOURCES.   Books or unpublished literary material in
the compilation of which PRIMARY SOURCES (*q.v.*) have been used.

SECONDARY TITLE.   An addition to the main title of a serial to
distinguish an independent section.

SECOND-HAND BOOK.   One which has previously been owned by
another person. A bookseller who deals in such books is called a
'Second-hand bookseller'. Librarians refer to such books when purchased for a library as 'Second-hand copies'.

SECOND-HAND CATALOGUE.   A list of second-hand books offered
for sale.

SECRET LITERATURE.   *Synonymous with* CLANDESTINE LITERATURE
(*q.v.*).

SECRET PRESS.   *See* CLANDESTINE PRESS.

SECTION.   1. The unit of paper which is printed, folded and sewn, and
which, together with other sections, goes to make up a printed book.
It usually consists of one sheet of paper, but may be one and a half
or two sheets, or even one sheet and an extra leaf pasted in. Also called
'Signature', 'Gathering', 'Quire', 'Stave'. Each section of a book bears
a different SIGNATURE (*q.v.*). *See also* FOLDINGS. 2. All the shelves
arranged between two uprights. *Synonymous with* TIER (*q.v.*). 3. A
sub-division of an administrative unit or department of a library, e.g.
'Processing section'. Sometimes called a 'Division' or 'Department'.
4. In the Dewey Classification a sub-division of a 'division'. 5. One of

the separately folded parts of an American newspaper, such as the 'Home section'. 6. A portion of a text of a book which can logically be divided into separate parts or sections. 7. A portion of the membership of the Library Association who were interested in a particular aspect of librarianship. Under the present bye-laws of the Association these are now mostly known as Groups although some still bear the former name of Section.

SECTION HEADLINE. One which consists of whatever subdivisions (chapters, books, parts, etc.) the book may have. *See also* HEADLINE, PAGE HEADLINE, RUNNING TITLE.

SECTION MARK. 1. The sign § used before a numeral thus: §6, to refer to a section. 2. The fourth reference mark for footnotes, coming after the double dagger. *See also* REFERENCE MARKS. It is sometimes also used in quantity for borders.

SECTION TITLE. A half title which introduces a section of a book.

SECTIONAL BRACE. *See* BRACE.

SECTIONALIZED INDEX. An index to a periodical split into sections such as (a) long articles of importance, (b) short paragraphs and brief news items, (c) literature abstracts, and similar well-defined groups.

SECTIONING. Microfilming a very large document in two or more parts in such a way as to permit mounting the film in the same number of aperture cards.

SECTIONS. *See* SECTION. For use in classification, *see* MAIN CLASS.

SECTOR DEVICE. The device of using a sectorizing digit, i.e. to form another sector or stretch of co-ordinate digits by adding to it the successive digits of the species and deeming the resulting double-digited numbers as if fused into a single digit, and repeating this process to form successive sectors. *See also* GROUP NOTATION DEVICE.

SECTORIZING DEVICE. A digit such as the OCTAVE DEVICE (*q.v.*) for extending the capacity of a numerical base in the Colon Classification.

SEDANOISE. The smallest size type of the early seventeenth century, designed by Jannon at Sedan. *See also* JANNON, JEAN.

See. (*Cataloguing*) A reference from a heading under which no entries are placed, to one or more which contain them. In *Sears list of subject headings*, 10th ed., 1972, a letter 'x' preceding a term indicates that a '*see*' reference should be made; such terms are never used as subject headings. When 'x x' is used, this indicates that a '*see also*' reference should be made from this term to the term under which it is placed.

See also. (*Cataloguing*) A reference often found in dictionary catalogues

– and sometimes in classified ones – from one heading with entries under it, to related ones. Abbreviated s.a. in *Sears list of subject headings*. For another abbreviation, look under *See*.

SEE COPY. An instruction written on a proof to a printer to refer to the 'copy' in order to correct a typesetting error.

SEE SAFE. Said of books bought from a publisher by a bookseller, and paid for, but with the understanding that at some future date the publisher may be asked to exchange unsold copies for copies of another title. *See also* HALF SEE SAFE, ON SALE.

SEGMENT. Part of a computer program which carries out a specific function.

SELECT BIBLIOGRAPHY. One which gives only a selection of the literature of a subject, the selection having been made with a view to excluding worthless material or to meeting the needs of a special class of people. Also called 'Selective bibliography'. *See also* BIBLIOGRAPHY I, CURRENT SELECTIVE BIBLIOGRAPHY, PARTIAL BIBLIOGRAPHY.

SELECT LIST. A reading list which includes a selection only of the books in the library on the subject of the list.

SELECT LIST OF REFERENCES. A partial list of references for material for further reading, the selection having eliminated items which for one reason or another are not particularly appropriate in the circumstances. The details included in the entries may be similar to those provided in a bibliography, although some items of a bibliographical nature may not be included, and the subject coverage would not be so great.

SELECTASINE. A process in silk screen printing; the term implies that one screen only is used for all the colours of a design.

SELECTED PUBLICATIONS IN EUROPEAN LANGUAGES. *See* SPEL.

SELECTED TERM CO-ORDINATION. (*Indexing*) The co-ordination of significant terms in titles with other selected title terms.

SELECTION SECTION. The division of a cataloguing, accessions, or order department, which deals with the selection of books.

SELECTIVE ABSTRACT. *See* ABSTRACT.

SELECTIVE ABSTRACT SERVICE. A service which abstracts only those publications and articles which are considered to be of use to a specific group of readers.

SELECTIVE BIBLIOGRAPHY. *Synonymous with* SELECT BIBLIOGRAPHY (*q.v.*).

SELECTIVE CATALOGUING. The omission of certain types of entry, or of entries for little-used books, or of parts of an entry (as for example some items of collations), in order to reduce the bulk and cost of a catalogue without impairing its efficiency.

SELECTIVE CHARGING. The practice of recording the loan of certain classes of books, usually non-fiction or particularly expensive books, while others are issued by a TOKEN CHARGING (*q.v.*) system.

SELECTIVE CIRCULATION. *See* ROUTING.

SELECTIVE CLASSIFICATION. The arrangement of large groups of little-used books either alphabetically or chronologically rather than by specific subject in order to save the expense of cataloguing and classifying.

SELECTIVE DISSEMINATION OF INFORMATION SYSTEM. *See* SDI.

SELECTIVE DISSEMINATION OF MICROFICHE. *See* SDM.

SELECTIVE LISTING IN COMBINATION. *See* SLIC INDEX.

SELECTIVE ROUTING. ROUTING (*q.v.*) to only a selection of the officers of a library or organization.

SELECTOR. The component in a RETRIEVAL SYSTEM (*q.v.*) which enables the information required to be identified in a STORE (*q.v.*). It may consist of, or comprise, recording media, code symbols or reading devices.

SELECTOR CODE. *See* MARGINAL-HOLE PUNCHED CARDS.

SELF-CHARGING SYSTEM. Any system for recording book loans in which the borrower makes part or all of the record.

SELF-COVER. A pamphlet in which the same paper is used for cover and text.

SELF-ENDS. Endpapers which are leaves forming part of the end sections of a book.

SELF POSITIVE. In documentary reproduction, a positive print which is prepared without the use of an intermediate negative. Also called 'Direct positive'.

SELF-WRAPPER. The paper cover of a pamphlet or book which is an integral part of the sheet or sheets comprising the publication. It may or may not be printed.

'SELFDEMARCATING' CODE. (*Information retrieval*) One of several systematic methods of abbreviating words.

SEMANTEME. The ultimate, smallest irreducible element or unit of meaning, such as a base or root which contains and represents the general meaning of a word or group of derivatives (*Pei*).

SEMANTIC CODE. 1. A linguistic system developed for use on machines designed to detect logically defined combinations; a symbol representing the concept of a word (*IBM*). 2. In information retrieval, one in which the notation carries meaningful information in addition to that which is carried by the source word. *See also* NON-SEMANTIC CODE.

SEMANTIC FACTOR. 1. In co-ordinate indexing, the separate unit of a code entry, representing one of a number of highly generic concepts. The semantic factors forming a code are arranged in alphabetical order. *See also* DESCRIPTOR. 2. A generalized concept used, with others, to construct a SEMANTIC CODE (*q.v.*).

SEMANTIC FACTORING. American term for FACET ANALYSIS (*q.v.*).

SEMANTIC RELATION. (*Information retrieval*) A general term used to indicate all types of relationship between language descriptors in a thesaurus. *See also* RELATION.

SEMANTICS. The study of the relations between linguistic symbols (words, expressions, phrases) and the objects or concepts to which they refer (*Pei*). Semantics relates a symbol to its meaning. *See also* SYNTAX.

SEMAPHORE INDEXING. A method of indexing with punched cards, each punch being shaped so as to indicate morphological changes in the subject; this is a POLYVALENT NOTATION (*q.v.*).

SEMÉ, SEMIS. *Synonymous with* POWDER (*q.v.*).

SEMI-ANNUAL. A periodical which is issued at six-monthly intervals. Also called 'Half yearly'.

SEMI-CHEMICAL PULP. The product of an intermediate process between Mechanical Wood Pulp (merely ground wood without the addition of chemicals or heat) and Chemical Wood Pulp which is obtained by the action of chemicals on wood chips. Also called 'Mechanical Wood pulp'.

SEMI-CURRENT RECORDS. (*Archives*) Records that are so infrequently required in the conduct of current business that they be moved to a holding area or to a RECORDS CENTRE (*q.v.*) (*American*).

SEMI-DRY PROCESS. A method of documentary reproduction in which copies are developed by a liquid but are nearly dry when they emerge from the copying machine. This method is used in some diazo processes and in ELECTROPHOTOGRAPHY (*q.v.*). The diazo compound is contained in the base and the coupler in a separate liquid developer. *See also* AMMONIA PROCESS, DIAZOTYPE PROCESS, DRY PROCESS.

SEMI-INDEXING. Listing a number of items to be indexed on one sheet of squared paper, either separate or bound into an exercise book, bearing the letters of the alphabet at the top to serve as guide-line headings. The entries commence on the lines having the corresponding initial letters entered at the top.

SEMI-MONTHLY. *Synonymous with* FORTNIGHTLY (*q.v.*).

SEMIOTICS. The science of signs; it is divided into three main sub-divisions: semantics, syntatics, and pragmatics, each of which (as can semiotics as a whole) can be pure, descriptive or applied. *Pure semiotic* elaborates a language to talk about signs, *descriptive semiotic* studies actual signs, *applied semiotic* utilizes knowledge about signs to accomplish various purposes.

SEMI-PULP. A term applied to the product of the grinding process in paper making, the ground wood still containing impurities and large fragments of wood.

SEMI-RAG. Paper made partly of rags.

SEMI-WEEKLY. A serial publication issued twice a week. Also called 'Twice weekly'. *See also* FORTNIGHTLY.

SEMINAR COLLECTION. *Synonymous with* DEPARTMENTAL LIBRARY (*q.v.*).

SENIOR ASSISTANT. An assistant librarian who has the supervision of the work of junior assistants but does not have the responsibility for a department.

SENIOR LIBRARIANS AWARD. A cash award of up to £800 (in 1973) is offered in alternate years to Chartered Librarians with at least seven years' experience since their election to the Register, who are past or present members of the London and Home Counties Branch. It is normally made for personal research into practical problems of librarianship or information work, or practical problems likely to result in improvement in library services over a wide area, either for staff or users. The award may be used for travel but not for assistance in preparing a thesis for a professional or academic qualification. It was first called a Mature Librarians' Award.

SENSING MARK. (*Reprography*) A mark on film or paper which activates an electrical device to carry out automatically a function such as cutting paper.

SENSITIVE PAPER. A paper which has been treated with light-sensitive chemicals for photographic purposes. *See also* SENSITIZED PAPER.

SENSITIVITY. *Synonymous with* RECALL RATIO (*q.v.*).

SENSITIZED PAPER. Paper used in documentary reproduction which is coated with an emulsion sensitive to light or heat as used in a thermographic process. *See also* SENSITIVE PAPER, THERMOGRAPHY.

SEPARATE. A copy of an article published in a periodical, specially reprinted for the author's use, but retaining the numbering of the issue from which it was taken. It may or may not have a title-page.

Sometimes called 'Extracted article', 'Off-print', 'Overprint' or 'Reprint'. *See also* REPRINTED ARTICLE.

SEPARATION NEGATIVES. Individual negatives for each colour used in colour reproductions. *See also* COLOUR SEPARATION.

SEPARATOR. (*Classification*) A symbol (e.g. a point, bracket, colon) used to separate parts of a lengthy notation.

SEPARATRIX. The diagonal stroke / , used in proof correction to mark and separate alterations.

SEPARATUM (*Pl.* Separata). A reprint of one of a series of papers. An offprint or SEPARATE (*q.v.*).

seq. (*Pl. Seqq.*). Abbreviation (in singular) of Latin *sequens* 'the following', *sequente* 'and in what follows', *sequitur* 'it follows' and (in plural) of *sequentes, -tia* 'the following', *sequentibus* 'in the following places'. *See also et seq.*

SEQUEL. A literary work, usually a novel, which is complete in itself, but continues an earlier work.

SEQUENCE OF SIGNS. The use of recognized signs in notes (*see* REFERENCE MARKS) and especially of 'Relation marks' in the UNIVERSAL DECIMAL CLASSIFICATION (*q.v.*) to separate the different components of a classification number and at the same time indicate their meaning.

SEQUENTIAL CAMERA. One which produces a sequence of images in column form on one film of suitable width from cards which are fed into the camera in a pre-determined sequence.

SERIAL. 1. Any publication issued in successive parts, appearing at intervals, usually regular ones, and, as a rule, intended to be continued indefinitely. The term includes periodicals, newspapers, annuals, numbered monographic series and the proceedings, transactions and memoirs of societies. Not to be confused with SERIES (*q.v.*). 2. A book consisting of parts or volumes published successively with a common title and intended to be continued indefinitely, not necessarily at regular intervals. (In the United States of America the term 'serial' is used to mean a periodical, regular or irregular) (*IFLA*). 3. (*Adj.*) The handling of data in a sequential fashion (*IBM*). *See also* PARALLEL. 4. A long story published in instalments. 5. As defined by the INTERNATIONAL SERIALS DATA SYSTEM (ISDS *q.v.*): for the purpose of allocating an INTERNATIONAL STANDARD SERIAL NUMBER (ISSN *q.v.*) 'a publication in print or in non-print form, issued in successive parts, usually having numerical or chronological designations, and intended to be continued indefinitely'. Serials may include periodicals, newspapers, annuals (reports, yearbooks, directories, etc.), the journals, memoirs, proceedings, transactions, etc., of societies and monographic series. A somewhat similar definition (taken from the *Anglo-American cataloguing rules: British text*, 1967) is given in BS 2509: 1970 *The presentation of serial publications, including periodicals*. The Standard deals with the form and presentation of periodicals of reference value only, and is designed primarily for the use of editors and publishers. It conforms in general to the principles contained in ISO/R 8 *Layout of periodicals* and ISO/R 215 *Presentation of contributions to periodicals*.

SERIAL CATALOGUE. An official, or a public, catalogue of serials in a library.

SERIAL CLASSIFICATION. A classification, the classes of which are in a series, or in an order of gradation.

SERIAL NUMBER. 1. The number indicating the order of publication in a series. 2. One of the consecutive numbers appearing in front of an entry in a bibliography or catalogue.

SERIAL PUBLICATION. *Synonymous with* SERIAL (*q.v.*).

SERIAL RECORD. A record of a library's holdings of serials.

SERIAL RIGHTS. An author's rights in the publication of his work by instalments.

SERIAL SECTION. A division of an order, or an acquisition, department that has charge of the acquisition of serials; or a subdivision of a preparation division where responsibility is taken for the cataloguing of serials.

SERIAL SERVICE. A serial publication which is revised, accumulated or indexed by means of new or replacement pages. *See also* LOOSE-LEAF SERVICE.

SERIALS DEPARTMENT. The administrative unit in charge of handling serials; this may include ordering, checking, cataloguing, preparation for binding, etc.

SERIALS LIBRARIAN. One who is responsible for the receipt of serials and for the maintenance of the relative records.

SERIES. 1. Volumes usually related to each other in subject matter, issued successively, sometimes at the same price, and generally by the same publisher, in a uniform style, and usually bearing a collective 'series title' on the HALF TITLE (*q.v.*) or the cover, or at the head of the TITLE-PAGE (*q.v.*). 2. Succeeding volumes of essays, etc., issued at intervals or in sequence. 3. A type of serial publication (*See* SERIAL 1) in which the parts (a) have, in addition to a constant title, a distinctive title for each part; (b) consist of a single work; (c) are not issued at predetermined intervals. The successive parts may, or may not, be given systematic or sequential numbering. This type of series is also called 'Monographic Series', 'Monograph Series'. 4. (*Archives*) A folder (*see* FOLDER 2) holding documents related to a particular subject or function, or documents arranged in accordance with a filing system. *See also* SERIAL. 5. A number of articles or stories of a similar nature or by the same author published in succession. *See also* PUBLISHER'S SERIES, REPRINT SERIES. 6. (*Classification*) A succession of classes, or terms, in some relation.

SERIES AUTHORITY FILE. A list of series entries used in a given catalogue together with the references made to them from other forms.

SERIES CARD. A catalogue card on which the SERIES ENTRY (*q.v.*) appears.

SERIES ENTRY. In a catalogue or bibliography, a brief entry under the name of the series to which the publication belongs. *See also* SERIES.

SERIES NOTE. In a bibliography or in a catalogue, a note following the collation, and giving, in parentheses, the name of the series to which a book belongs.

SERIES NUMBER. The number assigned by a publisher to an individual book or piece of music published in a series. The series may contain titles which are unrelated, or they may be related to one another by subject, musical form, medium of performance (musical), or the titles may be unrelated. *See also* PUBLISHER'S SERIES.

SERIES STATEMENT. 1. The information on a publication which names the series to which it belongs and gives the number, if any, of the publication in the series. 2. (*Cataloguing*) The statement in a catalogue entry, of the name of the series to which the document belongs, and the number, if any, of the publication in the series. This usually appears within curved brackets at the end of the entry.

SERIES TITLE. The title of a series to which a book belongs. It may appear on the half-title page, title-page, or a page following the title-page.

SERIF. A fine finishing stroke or grace, drawn at right angles to, or obliquely across, the ends of stems or arms of a letter. Letters without serifs are usually described as 'sans serif'.

SERIGRAPHY. *Synonymous with* SILK SCREEN PROCESS (*q.v.*).

SERIM. *Synonymous with* MULL (*q.v.*).

SERRATED SQUARE. (*Binding*) A stamp, more or less square with concave serrated sides, and usually a cruciform centre; often used in a group and giving the effect of a number of circles with serrated inner edges.

SERTAFILM. Trade name for a catalogue-card size device for holding short pieces of microfilm; the top third is of plain card stock on which identifying information is entered and to which a clear plastic sleeve for holding the microfilm is attached.

SERVICE AREA. *See* PUBLIC (SERVICE) AREA.

SERVICE BASIS. A method of determining prices for a publication or series of publications issued periodically and cumulated at regular intervals. The prices are scaled for individual libraries according to book expenditure, circulation and anticipated potential use to the subscriber. For periodical indexes, it is based on the number of indexed periodicals taken in a library.

SERVICE POINT. A place at which a library service is provided for all members of the public, including a major service such as a large branch, or a small service such as that at a training college or lighthouse, but excludes collections of books provided for limited periods for such groups as an adult class or a dramatic society.

SERVICE POINTS. (*County libraries*) Places at which the public are served. Include branches (inclusive of mobile branches and travelling libraries, each halt to count as a separate service point), centres, school libraries, hospital libraries, youth clubs, prisons, lighthouses, training colleges, military camps, etc. The characteristic denoting a Service Point is that provision is intended to be permanent and/or continuous, is of a relatively wide subject range, and is located at a definite place. Does not include the supply of collections of books to adult classes, choral and dramatic societies, and for other similar purposes where the use of the collection is intended to be limited in duration and where the books cover a relatively narrow subject range.

SESSION. *See* PARLIAMENTARY SESSION.

SESSIONAL PAPERS. Two series (*House of Commons Sessional Papers* and *House of Lords Sessional Papers*) of Parliamentary Papers arranged (and probably bound) in sessional sets. The *House of Commons Sessional Papers* consist of the *House of Commons Bills*, the *House of Commons Papers* and the *Command Papers*. The *House of Lords Sessional Papers* consist of the series called the *House of Lords Papers and Bills*.

SET. 1. series of publications associated by common publication or authorship, and which form one unit, being issued in a uniform style. They may be by one author, or on one subject, or they may be a file of periodicals or be unrelated but printed and bound uniformly. 2. (*Printing*) The distance between the left- and right-hand sides of a piece of movable type. Type is said to have a wide or narrow set according to the width of the BODY (*q.v.*); a figure is used to indicate the comparative width of a Monotype design, e.g. 12-point $10\frac{1}{2}$ set, is narrower than 12-point 12 set. 3. To compose type.

SET FLUSH. 1. An instruction to the typesetter to set the type right up to the left-hand margin, avoiding indentions at the beginning of paragraphs. 2. Matter so composed.

SET HAND. Writing which conforms to definite rules, such as set abbreviations. Not generally applied to hands later than the seventeenth century.

SET OF A FOUNT. (*Printing*) The measurement of the widest letter, described by the point-system as e.g. 12 point $11\frac{1}{4}$ set.

SET OF A LETTER. (*Printing*) The width of a piece of type across its shank (i.e. the piece of metal bearing the face, or printing-surface).

SET OF DOCUMENTS. Any collection of documents, large or small, restricted to an organization's research papers, or a collection of miscellaneous material, in many different languages, but homogeneous in that they will be indexed by one index. *See also* FEATURE CARD.

SET OF QUESTIONS. (*Information retrieval*) A number of questions that will be put to a single subject index.

SET-OFF. 1. The accidental transfer of ink from one printed sheet to another. 2. Any kind of paper placed between a sheet after printing to prevent the ink from one sheet soiling another. Also called 'Slip sheet'. *See also* OFFSET.

SET SOLID. Type matter with no leads between the lines.

SETTING RULE. *Synonymous with* COMPOSING RULE (*q.v.*).

SETTING TYPE. Composing type either by hand or by machine so that it is ready for printing.

SEVENSMA PRIZE, THE. A money prize awarded for an essay written on a prescribed subject to a member, under forty years of age, of any member-association of IFLA (*q.v.*). The Prize has a double purpose: honouring T. P. Sevensma, the Dutch librarian who was successively Director of the Public Library of Amsterdam, of the League of Nations Library, and of the University Library in Leyden. In 1929 he became Secretary of IFLA, and in 1939, on the occasion of his completing ten years in this honorary office, also on the occasion of his sixtieth birthday, the President of IFLA announced the establishment of the prize bearing Dr. Sevensma's name. The subject of the essay is set every two years and is on some aspect of libraries in their relation to practical life. The awards have been made as follows: 1948 to Mr. Valter Ahlstadt of Stockholm City Library 'Unit cataloguing', 1950 to Miss Olga S. Newman of Northallerton, England, 'A study in the field of rural library services'; 1952 to Mr. W. D. Richardson of Leeds, England, 'A study in the field of photographic reproduction in libraries'; 1955 Dr. E. Egger of the Swiss National

Library, Berne, 'Der Schweizerische Gesamtkatalog'; 1959 shared by Mr. H. Fairhurst of Salisbury, Southern Rhodesia, 'The information service in the library' and Miss Wanda Polaszewska of Poznan, Poland, 'The reference service in the library'; 1964 to Mr. P. W. Plumb, Lecturer at the School of Librarianship, North-Western Polytechnic, London, 'Central library storage of books'; 1968 to Miss M. J. Lewis, Lecturer at the same School, for 'Libraries for the handicapped'. In 1971 the award was made to Mr A. D. Burnett, an Assistant Librarian in the University Library, Durham, for 'Problems of comparing the library services of different countries'.

SEVENTY-TWOMO (72mo). A sheet of paper folded into seventy-two leaves, making 144 pages.

SEWED. In cataloguing a pamphlet stitched without covers.

SEWING. When the sections of a book have been gathered and collated, they are sewed together, one by one, with thread, usually by machinery. In job binding they are usually sewed by hand. As the art of sewing the sections and of attaching the covers to them was never reduced to a skilful practice until well on in the sixteenth century, books could not be stood on their bottom edges as they are now, but were laid flat on shelves or lecterns. This is why it was customary to decorate the top and back covers. *See also* ALL ALONG, STABBING, STITCHING, THREAD STITCHED, WIRE STITCHED.

SEWING FRAME. The frame on which cords or tapes are attached and stretched taut, and to which the sections of a book are sewn by hand.

SEWING ON TAPES. When the sections of a book are sewn together and two or more tapes are used to secure the book to the covers, some of the loops pass over the tapes thus also securing the sections to them. In LIBRARY BINDING (*q.v.*) and hand-sewing, each section is sewn to every tape.

SEWN. A book is said to be sewn when the sections are fastened together with linen threads passing round tapes or cords.

SEXAGESIMO-QUARTO. *Synonymous with* SIXTY-FOURMO (*q.v.*).

SEXTO (6to). A sheet of paper folded three times to form a section of six leaves or twelve pages; a half-sheet of twelves.

SEXTODECIMO (16mo). A sheet of paper folded four times to form a section of sixteen leaves (thirty-two pages); a half-sheet of thirty-two. Now called foolscap 8vo. Also called 'Sixteenmo'.

SHACKLETON REPORT. The *Report of the Committee on University Libraries*, 1966, so named after Mr R. Shackleton, the Chairman of the Committee which examined the structure of the three different types of library in Oxford: 1. direct grant libraries (Bodleian, Ashmolean and Taylorian); 2. libraries financed by the General Board (mainly faculty libraries); 3. college libraries. The report made many recommendations with regard to buildings, administration and services.

SHADED TOOLS. (*Binding*) Finisher's tools partly in outline and partly solid.

SHADOW. A type face which gives a three-dimensional effect.

SHAGREEN. A type of leather with a rough, granular surface. When used for bookbinding it is usually prepared from sharkskin.

SHAKEN. A cataloguing term used in the U.S.A. to describe copies of books which have loose leaves and/or binding.

SHANK. The rectangular body of a type letter, on which are the NICK, or nicks, PINMARK, BELLY and BACK (*qq.v.*). Also called BODY (*q.v.*) and STEM (*q.v.*). The piece of metal on which the shoulder bearing the FACE (*q.v.*) or printing surface of a type-letter is supported. *See also* SHOULDER.

SHAPE. Books which are not of normal proportions are described as 'oblong' or 'landscape' when the width of the page exceeds its height, 'narrow' when the width is less than $\frac{3}{5}$ of the height, and 'square' if more than $\frac{3}{4}$. *See also* SIZE.

SHARED AUTHORSHIP. A work which is produced by the collaboration of two authors, compilers, editors, translators, collectors, adapters, etc.

SHARED CATALOGUING. A form of cataloguing being undertaken by the Library of Congress and other agencies responsible for national bibliography. The L. of C., under the United States Higher Education Act, 1965 is charged with '(a) acquiring so far as possible, all library materials of value to scholarship currently published throughout the world; and (b) providing catalogue information, for such materials promptly after receipt . . .' and in order to achieve these objects has arranged with other national agencies to send catalogue entries for all works published in their country to the L. of C. Blanket-order suppliers acquire the works represented by the catalogue entries and send them together with the catalogue entries, to the L. of C. On their receipt, the L. of C. prints catalogue cards for each title and publishes entries in the *National Union Catalog*.

SHARPNESS. In photography, the density-gradient at an edge of an image.

SHAVED. A book which has been trimmed by the binder so closely that the lines of print have been grazed, without actually being cut into. *See also* CROPPED.

SHAW MEMORIAL AWARD, RALPH R. Established in 1974 by the University of Hawaii Foundation; it consists of monetary awards to individuals, particularly from Hawaii and the Pacific area, to provide further education through scholarships at accredited library schools, fellowships, conferences, institutes and workshops.

SHEAF BINDER. A case or binder to hold a sheaf of papers to form a loose-leaf catalogue or other record. The sheets of paper are punched with holes to go over posts which keep the sheets in position, and there is some form of locking device to keep the covers and the sheets securely in position.

SHEAF CATALOGUE. A catalogue made on slips of paper, as distinct from one made on cards, and fastened into a sheaf binder which permits the insertion of new material in correct order.

SHEAF HOLDER. *Synonymous with* SHEAF BINDER (*q.v.*).

SHEEPSKIN. The skin of a sheep prepared as a bookbinding material. Such skins have been used for bookbinding in the United Kingdom since about 1400. The boards they covered were usually of oak. *See also* ALASKA SEAL, LAW CALF, ROAN, RUTLAND, SKIVER, SMYRNA MOROCCO.

SHEET. 1. A large piece of paper as manufactured. Also used of the sheet after it has been printed and folded to form a section of a book or pamphlet; to avoid confusion, a folded sheet is best called a SECTION (*q.v.*). Sheets of paper bearing the same size name can be had in double ('double') or quadruple ('quad') size. *See also* OCTAVO, PAPER SIZES. 2. An individual map printed (usually) on one side of a sheet of paper. Also called 'Sheet map'.

SHEET-FEED. Said of a printing press which takes paper cut into sheets instead of paper in a continuous roll.

SHEET INDEX. (*Cartography*) An index, usually based on an outline map, showing the layout, numbering system, etc. of map sheets which cover an area.

SHEET MAP. A map printed on one side of a sheet of paper. Also called a 'Sheet'.

SHEET MUSIC. Printed music which a musician would use in learning a musical composition from memory, or in performance, which has not be bound into stiff covers. There is no limit on the number of pages. *See also* MINIATURE SCORE, SCORE.

SHEET STOCK. A stock of unbound printed sheets of a book which are kept in stock by the printer until the publisher orders them to be bound up. This method of binding books as required to meet orders, is done to spread the cost of production.

SHEET WORK. Printing one side of a sheet of paper from an 'inner forme' and the other from an 'outer forme'. Also called 'Work and back'. When both sides have been printed, the sheet is known as a 'Perfect copy'. By this method, one sheet is used to print one copy using two formes. *See also* HALF-SHEET WORK.

SHEETS. The printed pages of a book, either flat or folded, but unbound. *See also* IN SHEETS.

SHEETWISE. A method of printing in which a separate forme is used for printing each side of a sheet of paper. *See also* WORK AND TURN.

SHEFFIELD SCHEME. *See* SINTO.

SHELF. A flat piece of wood, steel or other material, which is placed horizontally between two uprights, or supported on brackets, to hold books. Metal shelves are usually turned down along back and front to form a flange and give strength. Shelves may be constructed of rollers to save wear on the binding of very heavy and large books. The normal length of shelves is 3 feet from centre to centre of the uprights supporting them.

SHELF-BACK. *Synonymous with* SPINE (*q.v.*).

SHELF CAPACITY. The capacity of a library for storing books on shelves; it is generally expressed by the total number of books which can be so accommodated or by the number of linear feet or metres available for housing books or other library materials.

SHELF CLASSIFICATION. A classification which is designed for use in arranging books on shelves rather than for minute precision in designating subject areas and relationships.

SHELF DEPARTMENT. The administrative unit of a library responsible for the care of books on the shelves, and sometimes for other work such as classification and shelf-listing.

SHELF DUMMY. A piece of wood or cardboard placed on a shelf to indicate a specific book which is shelved out of sequence.

SHELF GUIDE. A guide placed on the edge of a shelf to indicate its contents. Also called 'Shelf label'.

SHELF HEIGHT. The distance between two shelves.

SHELF LIFE. The length of time which sensitized materials used in photocopying or documentary reproduction may be kept before exposure without loss of efficiency.

SHELF LIST. A list of the books in a library, the entries being brief and arranged on cards or sheets in the order of the books on the shelves, and forming, in effect, in a classified library, a subject catalogue without added entries, analytics and cross-references.

SHELF MARK. *Synonymous with* SHELF NUMBER (*q.v.*).

SHELF NUMBER. With FIXED LOCATION (*q.v.*) a number given to a shelf to assist in the finding of books by indicating the one on which any individual book will be found. This number is incorporated in the BOOK NUMBER (*q.v.*). *See also* CALL NUMBER.

SHELF READING. *Synonymous with* READING SHELVES (*q.v.*).

SHELF REGISTER. *Synonymous with* SHELF LIST (*q.v.*).

SHELF SUPPORT. 1. The upright part of a book stack which holds the shelves, either directly or by means of a bracket. 2. The small fittings which fit into slots in the uprights and actually support the shelves. These may be pins, studs or brackets.

SHELF TIDYING. *Synonymous with* READING SHELVES (*q.v.*).

SHELL. (*Printing*) The electro plate before it is backed with metal.

SHELVING. 1. All the shelves in a library. For different kinds of shelving *see* ADJUSTABLE SHELVING, BRACKET SHELVING, CANTI-LEVER SHELVING, COMPACT STORAGE, 'LUNDIA' SHELVING, MULTI-TIER STACK, OPEN BAR SHELVING, 'RESKA' SHELVING, ROLLER SHELVES, ROLLING BOOKCASE, ROLLING PRESS, SLOTTED SHELVING, 'SPUR' SHELVING, STORAGE SHELVING, 'STOR-MOR' SHELVING. 2. The act of putting books away in their proper places on the shelves of a library.

SHINER. A mineral impurity in paper seen as a shining speck on the surface of the paper; sometimes it is due to mica in the china clay which is used as LOADING (*q.v.*) being compressed into a translucent spot during passage through the calenders. Hard, brittle materials fall out and leave 'pinholes'.

SHINING-UP TABLE. *Synonymous with* REGISTER TABLE (*q.v.*).

SHIPPING ROOM. The room of a library where parcels of books, etc., are unpacked and distributed to the various departments, and from which the outgoing material is despatched. (American.)

SHOES. (*Binding*) Metal attached to the edges only at the corners of the covers of books, and sometimes at the base of the spine, to protect the leather binding.

SHOOTING STICK. A tool of metal or hardened wood used to hammer wooden quoins into position against the side of a chase when locking up a forme.

SHOP LIBRARY. A library opened in a former shop, usually as a temporary measure and until permanent premises can be built. Some-times such accommodation is taken for a short time to test the best site for a permanent library.

SHORT AND. *See* AMPERSAND.

SHORT CATALOGUING. The style of cataloguing in which the entries give author, main title, and date only. *See also* FULL CATA-LOGUING.

SHORT DESCENDERS. Lower case letters with descenders (g, j, p, etc.) which are shorter than usual; these can be obtained with certain founts of type.

SHORT FILM. A term used by exhibitors for a 35 mm film of less than 3,000 feet in length; also three reels or less (33 minutes) of 16 mm film. *See also* FEATURE FILM.

SHORT FORM CATALOGUING. *See* SHORT CATALOGUING.

SHORT GRAIN. Paper in which the fibres lie in the shorter direction of the sheet. *See also* GRAIN DIRECTION, LONG GRAIN.

SHORT LETTER. A character, such as a, o, s, which has neither ascender nor descender. *See also* LONG LETTER.

SHORT PAGE. A page of type matter with fewer lines of type than there is room for, or than has been specified. In bookwork the space at the foot is left blank or it may be filled with a decorative piece. *See also* LONG PAGE, TYPE PAGE.

SHORT REAM. 480 sheets of paper. *See also* LONG REAM, REAM.

SHORT SCORE. *Synonymous with* CLOSE SCORE (*q.v.*). *See also* SCORE.

SHORT STORY. A complete story of from 1,000 to 8,000 words in length.

SHORT TITLE. 1. The abbreviated title by which an Act of Parliament is known and officially designated. 2. Enough of the title of a book to enable it to be identified in a catalogue or bibliography.

SHORT-TITLE SYSTEM. A system of bibliographical references in publications which uses a shortened form of the title of a book or periodical article after the first full mention.

SHORTS. 1. The copies of different sheets needed to complete an imperfect edition. 2. Books ordered from, but not delivered by, a bookseller owing to their not being in stock.

SHOULDER. The top of the shank of a piece of movable type. Its parts are the BEVEL (or neck), BEARD, LINE and SIDE BEARING (*q.v.*). The FACE (*q.v.*) is above the bevel.

SHOULDER-HEAD. A short descriptive heading, which precedes a paragraph; it is set in large or small capitals, or in italics, flush to the left-hand margin occupying a separate line and with a line of leading between it and the following paragraph. It marks the second division of text within the chapter, subsidiary to the CROSS HEAD (*q.v.*) and superior to the SIDE HEAD (*q.v.*). *See also* HEADING 4.

SHOULDER-NOTE. A note or sub-heading in the margin at the top outer, or fore-edge, corner of a page. *See also* MARGINAL NOTE.

SHOW THROUGH. Printed matter which shows through from the other side of a printed leaf, due to ink penetration because of the paper being insufficiently opaque or to improper pressure during machining. *See also* STRIKE THROUGH.

SIBMAS. Acronym of the Société Internationale des Bibliothèques – Musées des Arts du Spectacle; this international association was formed during the tenth international congress of the IFLA Section of Libraries and Museums of the Theatre Arts, held in Brussels in October 1972 during the annual IFLA Council when the former International Section for Performing Arts Libraries and Museums restructured itself in this way. *See also* INTERNATIONAL SOCIETY FOR PERFORMING ARTS LIBRARIES AND MUSEUMS.

sic. (*Lat.* 'so, thus, in this manner') Usually printed in [ ] to indicate that an exact reproduction of the original is being made.

SIDE. 1. The right hand or left hand of a piece of type when the printing surface is uppermost and facing the viewer. The front is called the 'belly' and the back the 'back'. 2. The front or back cover of a bound book.

SIDE BEARING. The amount of 'shoulder' on either side of a piece of movable type; it controls the amount of white space left between characters when composed into lines.

SIDE HEAD (SIDE HEADING). A short descriptive sub-heading dividing sections of a chapter, indented one em and usually printed in italics (but maybe in caps, large and small, or in bold), not occupying a separate line, and placed at the beginning of a paragraph with the matter running on. It is the third division of text within a chapter, subsidiary to the SHOULDER HEAD (*q.v.*). *See also* CROSS-HEAD, HEADING 4.

SIDE LETTERING. *Synonymous with* SIDE TITLE (*q.v.*).

SIDE NOTE. A marginal note outside the type page, and usually set in narrow measure in type several sizes smaller than the text of the page. *Synonymous with* MARGINAL NOTE (*q.v.*). Also called 'Hanging shoulder note'. Sometimes it is a substitute for a CROSS-HEAD (*q.v.*), but more usually provides a gloss on the text, or running commentary, which does not interrupt the argument; if read with continuity, side notes give an abstract of the whole book.

SIDE SEWING. *See* SIDE-STITCH.

SIDE SORTS. *Synonymous with* ODD SORTS (*q.v.*).

SIDE STICK. *See* CHASE.

SIDE-STITCH. (*Binding*) To stitch a booklet or pamphlet of two or more folded signatures from back to front through the leaves or sections (not through their folds), and near their binding edges, using thread or wire. Also called 'Flat stitching', 'Side sewing', 'Stab-stitch'.

When wire is used the process is called 'Wire-stabbing'. *See also* SADDLE STITCHING, SINGER SEWING.

SIDE TITLE. A title impressed on the front cover, or side, of a bound book.

SIDE-WIRE. To side-stitch a pamphlet with wire staples.

SIDEROGRAPHY. The process of producing steel engravings and making prints therefrom.

SIGIL. A chronological CODEN (*q.v.*) in which the first characters would represent the date of publication followed by those representing the title.

SIGILLOGRAPHY. The science or study of seals, being a branch of diplomatics. Also called 'SPHRAGISTICS'.

SIGLA. Symbols; it is sometimes printed at the head of a table of these.

SIG-LOGIS. Abbreviation for the Special Interest Group – Local Government Information Services which was formed at the April 1975 Week-end School of the Public Libraries Group of the Library Association. It was not immediately affiliated to any professional organization. Membership is open to anyone running or involved in planning a local authority information service, or who is employed as a librarian or information officer in a department of a local authority.

SIGN MANUAL. A signature written with the person's own hand, especially the signature of a sovereign or head of state, to give authority to a state document.

SIGNATURE. 1. A folded printed sheet, forming part of a book; a section. 2. The letter or number, or combination of letters and numbers, printed at the foot of the first page, and sometimes on subsequent leaves of a section, as a guide to the binder in arranging them in their correct order. These were written or stamped in until 1472 when Johann Koelhoff of Cologne, printed a signature as the last line of a text page. The binders of MSS. usually cut off the signature letters. Each section has a different signature and when letters are used, as is usual, they progress in alphabetical order, J, V and W usually being omitted to avoid confusion. There is also a historical reason for the omission of these letters: MSS. and early printed books were usually written in Latin, in which alphabet I stands for both I and J, and V for both U and V, and there is no W. When the alphabet has been used up a lower case sequence or a new sequence of double letters followed by one of treble letters, or sequences combining capital and lower case letters are used. If the same sequence is used again it is known as a duplicated or triplicated signature. Signatures are usually omitted in

American books. Also called 'Signature mark'. *See also* COLLATION, COLLATING MARK, DESIGNATION MARK, DIRECTION LINE, SECTION, TITLE SIGNATURE, VOLUME SIGNATURE. 3. The name or initials, written in a person's own hand to authenticate a document.

SIGNATURE AND CATCHWORD LINE. The line of type which in an old book bears both the signature and the catchword. It is usually below the lowest line of text. Also called 'Direction line'; should the signature and catchword be on separate lines, the lower is called the direction line.

SIGNATURE MARK. The letter or number, or a combination of both, placed at the left of the tail margin of the first page of each section of a book. *See also* SIGNATURE 2.

SIGNATURE TITLE. *Synonymous with* TITLE SIGNATURE (*q.v.*).

SIGNATURES, LIST OF. *See* REGISTER 2.

SIGNED EDITION. *Synonymous with* AUTOGRAPHED EDITION (*q.v.*). *See also* LIMITED EDITION.

SIGNED PAGE. The first page of a section – the one bearing the SIGNATURE (*q.v.*).

'SIGNIFICANT LETTER' CODE. (*Information retrieval*) One of several systematic methods of abbreviating words.

SIGNIFICANT PUNCTUATION. *See* FILING CODE.

SIGNIFICANT WORDS. In a PERMUTED TITLE INDEX (*q.v.*), words which are permitted to index by reason of their absence on a STOP LIST (*q.v.*).

SILHOUETTE. 1. To remove non-essential background from a half-tone block to produce an outline effect. 2. A print, illustration, draw-ing, or other form of artistic reproduction from which background has been removed.

SILK PAPER. Produced at Baghdad in the Middle Ages and famous throughout Persia. It was prepared from linen. The term is also used for papers containing a quantity of short, coloured silk fibres, or even one or more strands of silk or metal running through the sheet; this is used for bank notes, and is difficult to counterfeit.

SILK SCREEN. A stencil process for multiplying an original design and for lettering in colours which is used for posters and other jobs requiring short runs and for which lithography would be too expensive. Bolting silk, organdie, phosphor bronze or steel gauze are tightly stretched over a wooden frame. A stencil bearing the design is fixed to the underside of the silk or other material and paint is forced through the silk at the open parts of the stencil with a rubber squeegee on to the paper, silk, metal, glass, wood or other material to be printed.

SILKED.　A leaf of a book which has been repaired by backing it on both sides with transparent silk.

SILKING.　The application of silk chiffon to one or both sides of a sheet of paper as a means of repairing or preserving it. *See also* LAMINATION.

SILVER BOOK AWARD.　A little silver book mounted on a plaque; it is awarded by the (American) Library Binding Institute on the nomination of a Certified Library Binder to people who have made some significant or outstanding contribution to the field of library science.

SILVER HALIDE PAPER.　A paper used in lensless copying machines. It is necessary to use the traditional photographic developing processes of making negatives (i.e. developing, rinsing, fixing, washing, drying) before making positive copies.

SILVER PROCESSES.　A group of processes using silver halide sensitized materials for document copying. These include DIFFUSION TRANSFER (*q.v.*), Direct Positive (*see* LENSLESS COPYING), PHOTOSTAT, REFLEX (*qq.v.*). *See also* DRY SILVER TRANSFER PROCESS.

SILVERED.　The edges of a book which are treated with silver instead of gold.

SILVERFISH.　A small, quick-moving hexapod resembling a centipede. It flourishes in damp conditions, feeds on the glazed surface of photographs, the starchy content of paper, cardboard and paste, sometimes leaving narrow trenches where it has been feeding. D.D.T. or gammezane can be used as an exterminant.

SIMPLE HEADING.　*See* MAIN HEADING.

SIMPLEX.　A microcopying method using the width of the film for one set of pictures only (*Concepts . . .*).

SIMPLIFIED CATALOGUING.　The elimination of some of the information normally given in full catalogue entries to reduce the work involved in cataloguing and thereby the cost, or to make the catalogue simpler to use. *See also* FULL CATALOGUING, LIMITED CATALOGUING, SHORT CATALOGUING.

SIMULATOR.　A provision in some computers which allows the acceptance of a program written for a computer of a different type.

SIMULTANEOUS SCANNING.　(*Information retrieval*) A method of scanning a FILE (*q.v.*) e.g. needling a pack of hole-punched cards.

sine loco.　(*Lat.* 'without a place') used in a catalogue entry, in the abbreviated form [s.l.] for no place of publication. *See also* NO DATE.

sine nomine.　(*Lat.* 'without a name') used in a catalogue entry, in the abbreviated form [s.n.] for no known publisher. *See also* NO DATE.

SINGER SEWING.　Side-stitching with thread, the sewing extending the full length of the volume. *See also* SEWING, STABBING, THREAD STITCHED.

SINGLE LOOK-UP. An index to items embracing bibliographical references which give full bibliographical details, thus avoiding the need to refer to another section of the index.

SINGLE QUOTES. Superior commas used to indicate quoted matter already within quoted matter: '. . .'. So named to distinguish them from double quotes ". . .", the more common form of quotation mark. *See also* DOUBLE QUOTES.

SINGLE-REVOLUTION MACHINE. A letterpress printing machine in which the continuously running cylinder, having a diameter twice that of the TWO-REVOLUTION MACHINE (*q.v.*), runs at a constant speed. During the first half-rotation the bed moves forward and the impression is made; during the second half-rotation the bed returns. Some makes of this type of machine have varying speeds for the bed and/or cylinder.

SINGLE WEIGHT PAPER. Sensitized photographic paper between 0·0060 and 0·0083 inches inclusive. *See also* PHOTOGRAPHIC PAPERS.

SINKAGE. Space left at the top of a printed page in excess of the normal margin, as e.g. at the beginning of a new chapter.

SINTO. Abbreviation for Sheffield Interchange Organization. This is the earliest British scheme of local library co-operation, having been commenced in 1932 by J. P. Lamb. Membership is open to organizations with information/library units. There is a basic holdings requirement for periodicals taken. Its objects include the making known, and securing the greatest possible use of, the contents of members' libraries by means of interlending and by co-operation in solving problems of common professional interest. SINTO Headquarters is in the Commerce and Technology Division of the Sheffield City Libraries. A secretariat provides members with the following facilities and publications: *SINTO union list of periodicals*; *SINTO information resources directory and guide*; *SINTO news*; SINTO seminars on selected topics; periodicals exchange meetings; visits to relevant libraries, etc.; informal meetings both social and professional. The enquiry service at HQ library has special access lines for SINTO members. The World Metal Index is maintained in the HQ library. An extensive standards collection complements the general coverage afforded by the stock of HQ library. Sheffield is a patents deposit library, and issues the list of *Patent holdings in British public libraries*. Every effort is made to further the development of the information services of SINTO members' libraries.

SISO. A Dutch 'scheme for the classification of the subject catalogues in public libraries' which was published in 1958 by the Central Association of Public Libraries of Holland. It is basically Dr. Greve's 'Hague Scheme' first published in 1931; it has a decimal notation, and the schedules resemble the Universal Decimal Classification and Dewey, compared with which the arrangement of subjects shows improvements.

SITE LIBRARIAN. The librarian in charge of one of a number of libraries within a group but which does not include 'branch' or 'district' in its name, e.g., a library in one of a number of separate teaching units which are part of an educational institution such as a polytechnic or college.

SITTYBUS. A title label which identified papyrus rolls. *See also* SCROLL 1.

SIXTEENMO. *See* SEXTODECIMO.

SIXTY-FOURMO (64mo). A sheet of paper folded six times to form a section of sixty-four leaves, making 128 pages. Also called 'Sexagesimo-quarto'.

SIZE. 1. (*Cataloguing*) The size of a book is measured by its height; a book is called 'narrow' if the width of the cover is less than $\frac{3}{5}$ of the height; 'square' if more than $\frac{3}{4}$; and 'oblong' or 'landscape' if the width of the cover is greater than the height. Width is usually given only when unusual, or for old books. When both height and width are given, the height is given first. Measurements are usually given in centimetres in bibliographies and catalogues, although often in inches in the latter. The *Anglo-American Code* requires that size be given in centimetres to the nearest half centimetre. The fold symbol (e.g. f°, 4°, 8°, 12°) is often used as an indication of approximate size. *See also* BOOK SIZES, FOLD SYMBOL, FOLDINGS, TYPE SIZES. 2. (*Paper*) A mixture of gelatine, alum and formaldehyde through which paper is passed, after coming from the paper-making machine, in order to produce a better surface and to repel water. 3. (*Binding*) A bonding material placed between binding material and lettering.

SIZE COPY. A thickness or dummy copy. *See also* DUMMY 1.

SIZE LETTERS. The symbols (F, Q, O, D, etc.) used to indicate the size of books. *See also* FOLD SYMBOLS, FOLDINGS.

SIZE NOTATION. The method of indicating the size of a book: it may be by measurement in centimetres or inches, by FOLD SYMBOLS (*q.v.*) or by SIZE LETTERS (*q.v.*).

SIZE RULE. A rule graduated in inches and/or centimetres with fold symbols and corresponding size letters marked at the proper places; it is used for measuring books.

SIZED PAPER.   Paper which has been treated to make it less receptive to water. Blotting paper is unsized: writing paper is hard-sized. The treatment consists of adding resin to the stuff in the beater or to the surface of the paper or board (surface sizing) so that the finished paper will be non-absorbent. The suitability of resin for this purpose is said to have been discovered by Moritz Friedrich Illig of Darmstadt in 1806. Animal glue, starch or casein may be used as alternatives. *See also* SIZE (*Paper*).

SIZING.   1. The act of applying size. 2. (*Book Production*) Marking the reduction, or final, size on the original of an illustration as an instruction to the block maker. *See* SIZE 2, 3.

SKANDIA PLAN.   *See* SCANDIA PLAN.

SKED.   Abbreviation for Short Key Edit, a generalized computer programme, developed by the Library of Congress, for creating sort keys for MARC II records at the user's option. *See also* LIBSKED.

SKELETON.   The cross-bars which separate the pages of type in a forme, the 'furniture' (pieces of wood or metal) which form the page margins, and the running titles, which are left in position when the pages of type have been removed after printing for breaking up, ready for the emplacement of the next pages of the same volume.

SKELETON ABSTRACT.   (*Information retrieval*) An abbreviated stylized abstract commonly considered suitable for machine input and manipulation. *Synonymous with* 'telegraphic abstract' (*see* ABSTRACT 3).

SKELETON CATALOGUE CARD.   An outline catalogue card bearing the names of the parts of an entry to show a student of cataloguing the proper placing of the various parts.

SKETCH.   1. A drawing. 2. A brief description of a person or event. 3. A short musical or dramatic play.

SKINNER AWARD, CONSTANCE LINDSAY.   *See* WOMEN'S NATIONAL BOOK ASSOCIATION.

SKINNER DEVICE.   Any of a number of devices in mechanical teaching by teaching machines which provide a small space for the presentation of information, a small space for the student to write his response, and a mechanism to reveal the correct answer after he has responded.

SKIVER.   A leather made from the hair or grain side of split sheepskin; it is often embossed and finished in imitation of various leather grains.

SKIVER LABEL.   A paper-thin skiver used for a title panel on the spine of a book.

SLAB SERIF.   (*Printing*) A serif consisting of a plain horizontal stroke which is not bracketed to the upright stroke of a letter. **Rockwell, Clarendon and Playbill are faces of this kind.**

SLANTED ABSTRACT.   An abstract giving emphasis to a particular aspect of the contents of a document so as to cater for the interests of a particular group of readers.

SLEEVE.   1. A transparent, plastic jacket made to fit over a BOOK JACKET (*q.v.*) to protect the book from wear and at the same time preserve the information printed on the book jacket. 2. A plasticized, printed case made of thick card (*see* BOARDS 3) to slip over and so protect a gramophone record.

SLIC INDEX.   An index compiled on the principle of Selective Listing In Combination. It consists of deriving every combination of terms from the set of alphabetically ordered terms assigned by the indexer, selecting from these combinations only those which do not form the beginnings of longer combinations, and listing these selected groups in alphabetical order. Not more than five terms are assigned as a set, but these can be re-arranged so as to give a total of sixteen entries, or each can be transferred to a punched card.

SLICK.   A large-circulation consumer magazine printed on coated stock and usually characterized by articles chosen for popular appeal and fiction limited to formulized stories with happy endings. (Webster's *Third New International Dictionary*). The authors of the material published receive a higher rate than for the 'pulps'. Also called 'Slick paper'. *See also* PULP 2.

SLIDE.   A visual positive image on transparent material, usually film, mounted in rigid format designed for projection. This term is tending to be superseded by TRANSPARENCY (*q.v.*).

SLIDE BOX.   *Synonymous with* SLIP CASE (*q.v.*).

SLIDE CASE.   *Synonymous with* SLIP CASE (*q.v.*).

SLIDING SHELVES.   Large shelves for the flat storage of folios; designed so that they may be pulled out to facilitate handling and save wear and tear on the bindings.

SLIP.   (*Verb*) 1. To discharge a book. *See* BOOK CARD, DISCHARGING BOOKS.   2. To list books on separate slips of paper, one for each book. (*Noun*) A small piece of paper, usually of standard 5×3 inches size, used to record briefly author and title, etc., as part of the book-preparation processes, or for some temporary recording purpose. The master catalogue entry or the catalogue entry for a typist to copy, may be written on such a slip. *See also* P-SLIP, SLIPS.

SLIP CANCEL.   A small piece of paper bearing a printed correction and pasted over the incorrect matter in a printed book.

SLIP CASE.   1. A cardboard box made to fit one or more volumes published together, and open at the front to show the titles. Also called 'Open-back case', 'Slide box', Slide case', 'Slip-in case'. 2. (*Archives*) a box, usually open-fronted, sometimes with a soft fabric lining, used to protect a book or set of books.

SLIP CATALOGUE.   *Synonymous with* PAGE CATALOGUE (*q.v.*).

SLIP-IN CASE.   *Synonymous with* SLIP CASE (*q.v.*).

SLIP PROOF.   *See* PROOF.

SLIP SHEET.   A sheet of paper which is placed between sheets as they come from the printing machine to prevent offset. *See also* SET-OFF.

SLIPPING BOOKS.   The American term for DISCHARGING BOOKS (*q.v.*).

SLIPPING DESK.   *See* CIRCULATION DESK.

SLIPS.   1. The pieces of sewing cord or tape which project beyond the back of the book after it is sewn, and which are afterwards attached to the boards. Also called 'Tabs'. 2. The paper slips on which are written the instructions to the binder. 3. Applied to matter not set up into pages, but pulled as proofs, on long slips of paper called galley proofs. *See also* PROOF.

SLOPING SHELVES.   *Synonymous with* TILTED SHELVES (*q.v.*).

SLOTTED CARDS.   Cards which have had slots punched in them in rows. Information is recorded by punching out the space between two or three holes. The cards are kept in a cradle, and when cards recording particular information are required, needles are inserted through the holes which represent the wanted features and the cradle inverted. This causes the cards to fall out of position for examination, but not out of sequence. *See also* DEQUEKER SYSTEM, EDGE-NOTCHED CARDS, MARGINAL-HOLE PUNCHED CARDS.

SLOTTED SHELVING.   A form of adjustable steel shelving whereby the shelves slide into slots running through the uprights from back to front.

SLUG.   1. A line of type set solid on a composing machine. 2. A metal bar the length of a line of type characters, to print an entire line, having the appearance of a solid line of type and serving the same purpose.

SLUG-CASTING MACHINE.   A machine for setting up type in the form of cast lines or slugs. These include INTERTYPE, ITALTYPE, LINOTYPE, LUDLOW and TYPOGRAPH (*qq.v.*).

SLUGSET.   Type which has been set in slugs, e.g. lines of type cast in one piece.

SLUR. A letterpress machine printing fault caused by an irregular movement of the paper while the impression is being taken, and resulting in the distortion of dots in a half-tone or a double impression of the type characters.

SMALL CAPITALS. The smaller capital letters (as distinct from the full capitals) of which they are about ⅔ the size, thus: A, B, C; the same size as the X-HEIGHT (*q.v.*) of a letter. Indicated in a MS. or proof by two strokes underneath. Abbreviated s.c., s.cap., sm.cap., s.caps, small caps (*pl.*). *See also* CAPITALS, LOWER CASE LETTERS, UPPER CASE LETTERS.

SMALL DEMY. *See* DEMY.

SMALL FULL SCORE. *See* SCORE.

SMALL PAPER COPY. A copy, or an edition, of a book which is printed on paper of a smaller size than a LARGE PAPER COPY (*q.v.*) or large paper edition. Also called 'Small paper edition'.

SMALL PICA. An obsolete size of type, about 11 point.

SMALL TYPE. (*Printing*) Strictly, type which is intermediate in size between that used for the main text of a book and that used for the footnotes. Colloquially, type of any size except large. Abbreviated s/t.

SMALLER PUBLIC LIBRARIES GROUP. An association of the smaller public library authorities (in towns with a population of up to 50,000) which was formed in 1956 to (a) influence opinion and combat the views of individuals and organizations who considered that public library services could be provided more efficiently if such small libraries were incorporated into larger units and to maintain the right of efficient library authorities to continue to enjoy the powers they have under the Public Libraries Acts; and (b) to raise the standards of efficiency in the smaller library authorities. This controversy developed at the time the 'Roberts Committee' was collecting evidence on public library services for the guidance of the British Government. *See also* ROBERTS REPORT.

SMALT. A species of glass, usually deep blue through the use of oxide of cobalt, and finely pulverized for use as a colouring medium in paper making. It is usually used as a 'loading', and as it is resistant to acids alkalis, heat and moisture, it is a very permanent colouring material. As it has a low colouring power it is expensive, and is used mainly for hand-made and the better machine-made azures for writings. Having a high specific gravity, it usually sinks through the pulp and colours one side more than the other.

SMART. Acronym of Salton's Magical Automatic Retriever of Texts which was devised by Professor Gerard Salton of Cornell University in 1964. The system stores document text and matches the words and phrases in search queries to words in the text. In addition to being a retrieval system, it is a scientific instrument which, among other things, is able to compare the effectiveness of any retrieval method against that of any other.

SMASHER. *Synonymous with* BUMPER (*q.v.*).

SMASHING MACHINE. A machine used in binderies for compressing folded signatures to render them more compact for binding by expelling the air from between the pages.

SMITH & SON LITERARY AWARD, W. H. A cash award of £1,000 which has been offered by W. H. Smith & Son Ltd. annually since 1959 when Patrick White received it for *Voss*. The Award is made to the Commonwealth author whose book (originally written in English and published in the United Kingdom within the twenty-four months ending on 31st December preceding the year of the award) makes, in the opinion of the judges, the most outstanding contribution to literature. The composition of the panel of judges is at the discretion of W. H. Smith & Son Ltd. who submit a list of published books, for the information of the judges and also supply any books required, but are in no way consulted by the judges. The making of an award does not create any contractual or other rights.

SMOOTH ANTIQUE. *See* PAPER FINISHES.

SMYRNA MOROCCO. A sheepskin finished with a grain to imitate MOROCCO (*q.v.*). *See also* SHEEPSKIN.

SMYTH SEWING. Sewing through the sections of a book; done by a Smyth sewing machine. The usual kind of sewing in Edition binding (*q.v.*), usually without tapes. (American.) *See also* CASE.

SNAG. A book for which no record of loan can be found. (American.)

SNAG FILE. A file into which are placed items that will not fit into the organization of a main file, either because of certain weaknesses or deficiencies in the main file organization, or because the file system must perform a function which is not part of the original design.

SNOBEL. A PROGRAMMING LANGUAGE (*q.v.*) designed for dealing with sequences (strings) of alphanumeric characters of varying length, rather than for conventional scientific, mathematical, or business computer uses. It was developed at Bell Laboratories and implemented in a number of different versions for many different computer equipment configurations.

SOBRIQUET. A nickname: a fanciful appellation. As these names are usually better known than the real names, books by or about them are often entered in catalogues under the sobriquet. *See also* NICKNAME.

SOCIÉTÉ INTERNATIONALE DES BIBLIOTHÈQUES – MUSÉES DES ARTS DU SPECTACLE. *See* SIBMAS.

SOCIETY. A group or association of persons united under a set of regulations, conditions of membership, etc., for the promotion of common purposes or objects, such as politics, research, business, recreation, etc. For its distinction from an institution for purposes of cataloguing, see INSTITUTION.

SOCIETY OF AMERICAN ARCHIVISTS. Founded in 1936 to promote sound principles of archival economy, and to facilitate co-operation among archivists and archival agencies. Is concerned with the management of current records, archival administration, and the custody of historical manuscripts in government, business and semi-public institutions. Abbreviated SAA. Publishes *The American Archivist* (q.).

SOCIETY OF ARCHIVISTS. Founded in 1947 to foster the care and preservation of archives and to enable archivists to discuss common problems and interchange technical knowledge in Great Britiain and the Commonwealth. Publishes *Journal* . . . (two p.a.).

SOCIETY OF COUNTY LIBRARIANS, THE. First formed in 1954. It was re-formed in January 1966 by county librarians in England and Wales and has for its objects: 'to promote and facilitate discussion and exchange of views on matters affecting county libraries in England and Wales; to promote and safeguard the interests of the County Libraries of England and Wales; to take such action relating to the above objects as may be thought desirable'. The Society operates on a wide basis; it advises the Association of County Councils on library matters, collects information, supplies evidence, holds meetings and has its own officially appointed advisers. Membership is open to persons designated as County Librarians, Directors of County Library Services, Chief Librarians in charge of county library systems, or any variant terminology denoting similar responsibilities. Abbreviated S.C.L.

SOCIETY OF INDEXERS. Founded in London on 30th March 1957 with the aim of improving standards of book indexing and securing some measure of uniformity in its technique, advising publishers and editors on the qualification and remuneration of indexers, and safeguarding their interests. Publishes *The Indexer* (2 p.a.). *See also* INDEX, WHEATLEY MEDAL.

SOCIETY PUBLICATION. An official publication issued by, or under the auspices of, a society, institution or association.

SODA PULP. (*Papermaking*) Chemical wood pulp which is prepared by digesting the wood fibres under pressure with a solution of caustic soda. This process is usually applied to straw and soft or deciduous trees such as aspen, poplar, etc. which cannot be treated by the sulphite process (*see* SULPHITE PULP) usually confined to coniferous woods.

SOFT COVER. *Synonymous with* PAPERBACK and PAPER-BOUND (*qq.v.*).

SOFT GELATINE TRANSFER PROCESS. *See* TRANSFER PROCESS.

SOFT-GROUND ETCHING. One in which the ground commonly used is softened by mixing with tallow, the design being made with a pencil on a piece of fine-grained paper stretched over the ground. This, when etched with acid gives the effect of pencil or chalk lines in the printed impression. (*United Typothetæ*.)

SOFTWARE. (*Information retrieval*) Computer programs, procedures, rules and associated documentation concerned with the operation of a data processing system. *See also* HARDWARE. (*Reprography*) Microfilm, microfiche, aperture cards and similar material.

SOLANDER CASE. A book-shaped box for holding a book, prints, pamphlets or other material, named after its inventor, Daniel Charles Solander (1736–82). It may open at the side or front with hinges, or have two separate parts, one fitting over the other. Its most developed form has a rounded back, projecting SQUARES (*q.v.*) like a book, and possibly one or more spring catches. Also called 'Solander', 'Solander box', 'Solander cover'.

SOLID FILING. Synonymous with letter-by-letter filing. *See* ALPHABETIZATION.

SOLID GILT. A book the edges of which have been gilded 'in the round', i.e. after the book has undergone ROUNDING (*q.v.*). *See also* GILT ON THE ROUGH, MARBLING UNDER GILT, ROUGH GILT EDGES.

SOLID MATTER. Type which has been set without 'leads'. Matter so set is said to be 'Set solid'. *See also* LEADED MATTER, LEADS.

SOLIDUS. An oblique stroke used for various purposes, e.g. to indicate two or more adjoining premises in one occupancy, as: 14/18 Essex Road; to indicate line endings in a bibliographical description of a title-page, as: An/address/to the/ . . . Also called 'Virgule'.

SOLINET. Abbreviation for the Southeastern Library Network which is probably the largest (in terms of both membership and geographical area) of the U.S.A. groupings of libraries which have been formed to provide improved services by using combinations of electronic data processing and telecommunications. Ninety-nine academic and public libraries in ten southeastern states are members; the Network is non-profit-making and is incorporated under the laws of Louisiana.

25

The service began early in 1975. It has affiliated with the Southern Regional Education Board (SREB) from whose offices in Atlanta it operates.

SOMBRE. A binding with both BLIND (*q.v.*) and coloured TOOLING (*q.v.*).

SORORITY LIBRARY. A library in a sorority on an American college or university campus. It may be a circulating collection from the main library, or owned by the sorority, a girls' or women's club.

SORT. A single type-letter. The complete muster of sorts, made up in the correct proportion of characters, is called a 'fount'. Also called 'Character'. *See also* CODE, DIGIT, SPECIAL SORTS.

SORT OF SYMBOL. (*Information retrieval*) A constituent part of a symbol, e.g. in the symbol ABA 553 there are six digits but only four sorts or characters (A, B, 3 and 5).

SORTER. A machine which arranges punched cards in a pre-determined sequence according to the holes punched in the cards.

SOUND LIBRARY. A collection of audio records such as gramophone records, magnetic or other tape and sound film.

SOUND RECORDINGS GROUP. A Group of the Library Association which was formed in 1964. *See* AUDIO-VISUAL GROUP.

SOUNDEX. A coding system for names which groups together those which sound the same or tend to be confused when communication is blurred. Each name is represented by the first letter followed by three decimal digits. The latter are chosen according to the following rules: (1) double letters are treated as single letters, (2) A, E, I, O, U, W, H, Y are always ignored, (3) letters with similar sounds are then identified by the appropriate code number:

BFPV	1	L	4
CGJKQSXZ	2	MN	5
DT	3	R	6

(4) If there are less than three such consonants after the initial letter, zeros are added to produce the three-digit code.

Examples:	Name	Soundex code
	Kuckuck	K220
	Swinhart	S563
	Whiffen	W150
	Wullerwaber	W451

This system, perhaps the most popular of codes used in conjunction with large name files, permits filing and searching of large groups of names phonetically as well as alphabetically. It was developed by

Remington Rand, and, as with other such systems, can be used as an important element of a mechanized system.

SOURCE. 1. Any document which provides the users of libraries or of information services with the information sought. 2. Any document which provides information reproduced in another document. 3. The data or records providing the basis for an informational search.

SOURCE DOCUMENT. (*Information retrieval*) A document from which data is extracted. *See also* SOURCE.

SOURCE INDEX. A card, or other, index to sources of unusual and elusive information. This is usually built up in the process of dealing with enquiries.

SOURCE LANGUAGE. The natural language in which a document is originally written. *See also* CODE LANGUAGE.

SOURCE LIST. A list of references appended to a treatise to show the sources used by the author. *See also* READING LIST.

SOURCE MATERIAL. *See* PRIMARY SOURCES.

SOUTH AFRICAN LIBRARY ASSOCIATION. Founded on 5th July 1930 as a result of a conference held at Bloemfontein in 1928. Among its aims are: to unite all persons engaged in, or interested in, library work; to promote the better administration of libraries; to promote whatever may tend to the improvement of the position and qualifications of librarians; to promote the establishment of libraries for the use of the public; to watch any legislation affecting public libraries; to hold examinations in librarianship and to issue certificates of efficiency; to promote the fullest co-operation between libraries, public, governmental, institutional and private. Membership is open to libraries and other institutions and to librarians, bibliographers, members of library committees and other persons connected with the administration of libraries, or interested in the objects of the Association. Abbreviated SALA. Publishes *South African Libraries* (5 p.a.) and *Newsletter* (m.) A number of branches have been formed to function in geographical areas.

SOUTH EAST AREA LIBRARIES INFORMATION SERVICE. *See* SEAL.

SOUTH-EAST ASIAN REGIONAL BRANCH OF THE INTERNATIONAL COUNCIL ON ARCHIVES. *See* SARBICA.

SOUTHEASTERN LIBRARY NETWORK. *See* SOLINET.

SOUTH EASTERN REGIONAL LIBRARY SYSTEM. An interlending organization which was formed in 1933. Its member libraries were all the public urban and county libraries in South Eastern England excepting those of the Metropolitan boroughs (i.e. in the then London County Council) area – these functioned as a bureau under the name of the LONDON UNION CATALOGUE (*q.v.*). After the alteration of the local government boundaries which became operative in 1965, the System and the London Union Catalogue were combined to form the LONDON & SOUTH EASTERN LIBRARY REGION (LASER) (*q.v.*).

SPACE. (*Printing*) A small rectangular block of metal not bearing a character, which is used between letters or words to provide spacing. Spaces are less than type height, cast in point sizes and smaller than an em quad (mutton), the square of the body. The usual sizes are:

en quad (nut), $\frac{1}{2}$ body or two to the em;

thick space ($\frac{1}{3}$-em space), $\frac{1}{3}$ body or three to the em;

middle space ($\frac{1}{4}$-em space), $\frac{1}{4}$ body or four to the em;

thin space ($\frac{1}{5}$-em space), $\frac{1}{5}$ body or five to the em;

hair space ($\frac{1}{12}$-em space), $\frac{1}{12}$ body or twelve to the em.

SPACE. (*Information retrieval*) 1. A unit of area on a record, i.e. an area that may contain only one printed character. 2. To remove from one place to another according to a prescribed format (*see* FORMAT 3), e.g. to remove horizontally to the right, or vertically, on a printed page. 3. A place intended for the storage of data, e.g. on a location in a storage medium, or on a printed page.

SPACE DOCUMENTATION SERVICE. *See* SDS.

SPACE DOT. *Synonymous with* CENTRED DOT (*q.v.*).

SPACE LINES. Strips of brass which are often used in place of LEADS (*q.v.*).

SPACE TO FILL. Space left in a printing layout through insufficient COPY (*q.v.*) being provided.

SPACEBANDS. Wedge-shaped pieces of metal used in line-casting machines such as LINOTYPE and INTERTYPE (*qq.v.*) to separate words and at the same time automatically justify lines of type.

SPACING. The distribution of printed matter on a printed page or pair of pages so that it is aesthetically satisfactory. It relates to the space between letters, words, lines, and any decorative or illustrative matter.

SPANISH. The best grade of esparto grass. Cheaper grades grown in N. Africa are known as Tripoli.

SPANISH CALF. A light-coloured calf on which brilliant effects can be obtained by staining.

SPE CUSTOMER ORIENTED LANGUAGE. *See* SPECOL.

SPEC. Acronym of Systems and Procedures Exchange Center. *See* ASSOCIATION OF RESEARCH LIBRARIES.

SPECIAL BIBLIOGRAPHY. *See* BIBLIOGRAPHY 1.

SPECIAL CLASSIFICATION. A scheme of book classification which is applied to a section of knowledge; for example:

Barnard's *Classification for medical and veterinary libraries*,

Cutter's *Labor classification for the Baker Library, Harvard School of Business Administration*,

Dabagh's *Mnemonic classification for law libraries*,

Smith's *Classification of London literature*,

Classification scheme of agricultural science,

British catalogue of music classification

Schwerin, Kurt. *Classification for international law.*

Stein, Jay W. *A classification for communications materials.*

World Health Organization. *Manual of the international statistical classification of diseases, injuries, and causes of death.*

ASM-SLA. *Metallurgical literature classification.*

Commonwealth Agricultural Bureau. *The Oxford system of decimal classification for forestry.*

Vernon, K. D. C. and Lang, V. *The London classification of business studies.*

Moys, E. M. *A classification scheme for law books.*

Aitchison, J., Gomersall, A. and Ireland, R. (compilers). *Thesaurofacet: a thesaurus and faceted classification for engineering and related subjects.*

Field, B. J. *Inspec classification.*

SPECIAL COLLECTION. A collection of books connected with local history, celebrities, industries, etc., or on a certain subject or period, or gathered for some particular reason, in a library which is general in character.

SPECIAL EDITION. 1. An edition of a work or works, re-issued in a new format, sometimes with an introduction, appendix, or illustrations, and having a distinctive name. 2. An edition which differs from the normal edition by some distinctive feature, such as better paper and binding or the addition of illustrations. 3. An extra or enlarged number of a newspaper or periodical, such as an anniversary, Christmas, or souvenir number.

SPECIAL ESTIMATE. *See* ESTIMATES.

SPECIAL INTEREST GROUP – LOCAL GOVERNMENT INFORMATION SERVICE. *See* SIG–LOGIS.

SPECIAL ISSUE. 1. *Synonymous with* SPECIAL NUMBER (*q.v.*). 2. The loan of a book to a person who does not possess a membership ticket, or a loan for an unusual period.

SPECIAL LIBRARIAN. One who is in charge of, or is employed in, a special library; he should have a knowledge of the literature of the field covered by the library (not necessarily a special knowledge of the field itself) and also of the means of organizing it for use.

SPECIAL LIBRARIANSHIP. The branch of librarianship which is concerned with selecting, administering, and evaluating books and non-book materials in specific and limited fields of knowledge, and disseminating the information contained therein to meet the needs of the particular institution or its clientele.

SPECIAL LIBRARIES ASSOCIATION. Founded in the U.S.A. in 1909. A number of changes in the bylaws were made at the Annual Meeting held in 1974. The full name is now The Special Libraries Association, Inc., and the objectives of this 'not-for-profit corporation' were changed to: 'provide an association of individuals and organizations having a professional, scientific or technical interest in library and information science, especially as these are applied in the recording, retrieval and dissemination of knowledge and information in areas such as the physical, biological, technical and social sciences and the humanities; and to promote and improve the communication, dissemination and use of such information and knowledge for the benefit of libraries or other educational organizations.' It has as its slogan 'Putting knowledge to work'. The work of the Association is carried out through many subject divisions and geographical chapters. Abbreviated SLA. Publishes *Scientific Meetings* (4 p.a.), *Special Libraries* (11 p.a.), *Technical Book Review Index* (10 p.a.), *Information Science Abstracts* (bi–m.). *See also* DIVISION.

SPECIAL LIBRARY. 1. (a) A library or information centre, maintained by an individual, corporation, association, government agency or any other group; or, (b) a specialized or departmental collection within a library (*Special Libraries Association bylaws revision of 1974*). 2. A collection of books and other printed, graphic or record material dealing with a limited field of knowledge, and provided by a learned society, research organization, industrial or commercial undertaking, government department or educational institution. It may also be a special branch of a public library serving certain interests or occupational groups, such as a technical library; or a subject library meeting the needs of all enquirers on a given subject, such as a music library. A special library is broadly one which is neither academic, commercial, national nor public. It is intended to serve the needs of a portion of the community requiring detailed information respecting a limited subject field. Users of such libraries often require up-to-date information promptly and their requests may be for information rather than for a book or periodical known by the enquirer to contain the information required.

SPECIAL NUMBER. A special issue (usually enlarged in size) of a periodical devoted to a special subject or occasion. More routine occasions to which issues of periodicals are wholly or partly devoted are: (a) directory issue containing a directory of the trade or group served by the periodical; (b) membership list containing a list of members; (c) proceedings issue containing papers read at a conference, or a summary of the same; (d) an annual review, or annual report, issue surveying the past year and giving tables of statistics, possibly with forecasts relating to the following year; (e) yearbook (handbook, or almanac) issue combining any or all of the foregoing types, together with general data kept up to date by annual revisions. *See also* SPECIAL EDITION.

SPECIAL SORTS. Type characters which are not usually included in a FOUNT (*q.v.*), and are supplied on request, such as fractions, musical signs, superior and inferior letters and figures, etc.

SPECIAL TITLE-PAGE. A title-page, usually with imprint, preceding a single part of a larger work. Also one preceding the normal title-page of a complete work which is issued or re-issued as part of a collection, series, or serial publication.

SPECIALIST PUBLISHERS EXHIBITION. *See* SPEX.

SPECIES. 1. In classification, the groups into which a genus is divided. *See also* PREDICABLES, FIVE. 2. In computer coding, each conventional set of 'sorts' comprising a symbol. *See also* DIGIT.

SPECIFIC CLASSING. Allocating a book to the most specific or detailed place in a scheme of classification.

SPECIFIC CROSS-REFERENCE. A reference in a catalogue to a specific heading or headings.

SPECIFIC DIFFERENCES. (*Classification*) Differences which characterize some individuals as a *specific* sub-class within a more comprehensive *generic* class.

SPECIFIC ENTRY. An entry in a catalogue under the actual subject, as distinct from one under some broader heading embracing that subject. It should be as specific as, but not more specific than, the content of the document. This is the principle for entry of subjects in a dictionary, subject or classified catalogue. *See also* CATALOGUING, PRINCIPLES OF.

SPECIFIC INDEX. An index such as that to Brown's *Subject Classification*, which has one entry only to each subject. Also called 'One-place index'. *See also* RELATIVE INDEX.

SPECIFIC REFERENCE. (*Cataloguing*) One which states the exact heading to which reference must be made as (in a dictionary catalogue): AUTOMOBILES *see* MOTOR CARS, whereas a general reference would be: ANIMALS see also under the names of individual animals, as ANTELOPE. In the subject index to a classified catalogue references are usually specific as: RELIGION 200, METHODISTS 287. *See also* GENERAL REFERENCE.

SPECIFIC SUBJECT. (*Classification*) The most precise, and therefore least general, subject heading that is appropriate for a particular document. *See also* CLOSE CLASSIFICATION.

SPECIFICATION. 1. Instructions prepared for a binder, printer or builder setting out the details of work to be carried out. 2. (*Information retrieval*) The cataloguing, bibliographical, or similar description, of a document. *See also* UNIT RECORD. 3. (*Classification*) Definition by SPECIFIC DIFFERENCE (*q.v.*) in characters. 4. In the field of patents, a concise statement of a set of requirements to be satisfied by a product, a material or a process, indicating, whenever appropriate, the procedure by means of which it may be determined. A *provisional specification* is a specification field with a patent application merely to establish a date for disclosure of an inventive concept to the Patent Office; it does not include a claim to the monopoly sought. A *complete specification* is a patent specification which describes at least one preferred way in which the invention may be performed, and which sets out a claim or claims for the protection sought. 5. (*Book Production*) A book designer's specification listing typeface and size, style for headings, margins, illustration type and position, etc.

SPECIFICITY. (*Information retrieval*) In the testing of an information retrieval system, a measure expressing the ratio of the number of non-relevant documents not retrieved to the total number of non-relevant documents in a file.

SPECIFICITY RULE. (*Cataloguing*) This rule provides that an entry in a subject catalogue should be made under the specific subject of a document, not under a more general one which includes that specific subject.

SPECIMEN PAGES. Printed pages which are submitted by the printer to show the proposed style of setting. They usually number four and include a chapter opening with any sub-headings.

SPECKLED SAND EDGE. A bound book the top-, fore-, and bottom-edges of which have been rubbed down with sandpaper and sprinkled or sprayed with colour.

SPECOL. Abbreviation of SPE Customer Oriented Language, a

commercial software package for use with computers. It is used at Bath University Library in connection with catalogue compilation and book listing and by other departments for other purposes.

SPECTRUM.   Trade name for a make of periodical display rack which has sloping pieces of 'Perspex' projecting at an angle to a wall or backboard on which periodicals rest so as to display the whole of the front cover.

SPECULUM HUMANAE SALVATIONIS.   *See* BLOCK BOOKS.

SPEL.   Acronym of *Selected Publications in European Languages* which was first issued in February 1973 at the College of Librarianship Wales. It is a two-tier selective translating service. The first part is a bulletin appearing five times a year, drawing attention to articles and books published in European languages. The second part is a back-up service providing: 1. photocopies of the articles; 2. an oral run through of the contents of the primary material and/or a written summary; 3. a fuller translation if required.

SPEX.   Abbreviation for Specialist Publishers Exhibition. An organization which aims at publicizing the publications of small and specialist firms by means of holding an exhibition or 'book fair' annually in London; the first was held in 1971.

SPHRAGISTICS.   *Synonymous with* SIGILLOGRAPHY (*q.v.*).

SPINE.   The part of the cover of a book which conceals the folds of the sections. It normally bears the title, author and (when in a publisher's case) the publisher's name. Also called 'Back', 'Backbone', 'Shelfback', 'Backstrip'.

SPINE TITLE.   The title which appears on the spine of a book. It is often shorter than the title as given on the title-page.

SPINES.   Abbreviation for Science and Technology Policies Information Exchange System. Following the results of a feasibility study, it was agreed at the 18th Session of Unesco held in 1974 to authorize the Director-General to elaborate a programme for the international exchange of information on literature relating to science and technology policies. This programme included the preparation of a report and a resolution at the 19th Session on the establishment of SPINES and the publication of the English source version of the Unesco *SPINES thesaurus: controlled vocabulary covering science and technology policies.*

SPIRAL BINDING.   A type of binding used for pamphlets, art reproductions, commercial catalogues, and occasionally books, printed on separate leaves, usually of art paper. These leaves are drilled or slotted near the binding edge to take a spiral-twisted wire or strip of plastic, which is drawn through the apertures. A tendency for the wire to be torn through the holes makes this style unsuitable for publications likely to be subject to much, or to careless, handling. Also called 'Coil binding', 'Spirex binding'. *See also* PLASTIC BINDING.

SPIREX BINDING.	*See* SPIRAL BINDING.

SPIRIT DUPLICATOR.	A machine for duplicating copies of typed, written or drawn matter. A master copy is made by typing, writing or drawing on a piece of art paper which has a sheet of coloured hectograph carbon paper (black, purple, blue, green or red) underneath it. The carbon then adheres to the art paper where pressure has taken place and appears in reverse. Master copies may also be made by a thermal process. This is then placed on the drum of the duplicating machine and some of the carbon is transferred to the paper on which a copy is required as this passes into contact with the master copy and after having passed over a spirit-impregnated pad. *See also* HECTOGRAPH PROCESS.

SPLICE.	A join made by cementing or welding together two pieces of film or paper so that they will function as one when passing through a camera, processing machine, projector or other apparatus. Lap splices are those in which the two pieces overlap and are cemented together. Butt splices are those in which the two pieces are placed together without overlapping and welded.

SPLIT BOARDS.	The boards normally of MILLBOARD (*q.v.*) forming the covers of a book, which are split to receive the ends of the tapes on to which the sections are sewn.

SPLIT CATALOGUE.	A library catalogue in which the different varieties of entry – e.g. subject, author, title – are filed in separate alphabets (*IBM*). Sometimes called a 'Divided catalogue' (*q.v.*).

SPLIT FRACTIONS.	Type for setting fractions cast in two parts which when combined make the complete fraction. The upper half contains the upper figure and the lower half the dividing line and the lower figure. Fractions may be set horizontally, e.g. $\frac{3}{8}$ or diagonally, e.g. 3/8 or 3/8.

SPLIT LEATHER.	Leather which has been divided into two or more thicknesses.

SPOILED LETTER.	*Synonymous with* DAMAGED LETTER (*q.v.*).

SPOILED SHEETS.	Printed sheets which bear imperfections; it is to allow for such that additional sheets, called 'overs', are issued to the printer. Often called 'Spoils'.

SPOILS.	*See* SPOILED SHEETS.

SPONGY PAPER.	*Synonymous with* FEATHERWEIGHT PAPER (*q.v.*).

SPONSOR. A person or corporate body subsidizing or otherwise encouraging the production of a book (*IFLA*).

SPREAD. A pair of facing pages.

SPRINKLED EDGES. The three cut edges of a book which have been finely sprinkled with colour to prevent them becoming, or appearing to be, soiled. *See also* EDGES.

SPUR SHELVING. Trade name for particular designs of suspension and cantilever shelving.

SQUABBLE. A printing fault caused by one or more letters being pushed into an adjacent line.

SQUARE. Said of a book the width of the cover of which is more than three-quarters its height. *See also* NARROW, OBLONG.

SQUARE. (*Binding*). The boards of a book are cut slightly larger than the bound sections after trimming so as to leave an even projection over the HEAD, TAIL and FORE-EDGE (*qq.v.*). This projection of the boards is called the 'square'.

SQUARE BACK. *Synonymous with* FLAT BACK (*q.v.*).

SQUARE BRACKETS. Signs [ ] used in a catalogue or bibliographical entry to indicate that whatever appears within them does not appear in the original, but has been supplied by the copier. Not to be confused with PARENTHESES (*q.v.*).

SQUARE CAPITALS. The alphabet used as a book hand from the third to the fifth centuries, being adapted from the Roman lapidary capitals. The letters had square serifs instead of being sharply pointed as were those cut in stone. Also called 'Capitales quadrata' and 'Quadrata'. *See also* LAPIDARY TYPE, RUSTIC CAPITAL.

SQUARE CORNER. (*Binding*) Folding the covering material over the boards in such a way that after cutting a wedge-shaped piece at the corner, one turn-in may neatly overlap the other. *See also* LIBRARY CORNER, MITRED CORNER.

SQUARE UP. To trim, or adjust, illustrations so that all corners are right angles.

SQUARED-UP HALF-TONE. *See* HALF-TONE.

SQUARES. The portions of the boards of a bound book which project beyond the paper on which it is printed.

STAB MARKS. Punctures made in folded sheets of printed paper preparatory to sewing.

STAB-STITCH. *See* SIDE-STITCH.

STABBED. *See* STABBING.

STABBING. Binding together one or more sections of a book with wire or thread passed through holes stabbed through the back edge of the folded sheet. This method prevents the book from lying flat when open. A book so bound is said to be 'stabbed'. Piercing the boards with a bodkin for the slips to pass through is sometimes termed 'stabbing'. *See also* STITCHING.

STABILIZATION. A process which renders a photocopy on silver halide paper relatively stable to light, the stabilizer being used instead of the usual fixative and having the effect of rendering the unexposed and undeveloped silver salts colourless when applied to a print after development. A print made in this way will last several years if not exposed to light but is not considered to possess ARCHIVAL QUALITY (*q.v.*). *See also* TWIN-BATH STABILIZATION.

STACK. 1. A piece of furniture containing at least four tiers of shelves back to back. 2. The space equipped for the storage of books on one or more floors; more properly, the self-supporting structure of steel book cases, often extending for several floors, or decks, and independent of the walls of the building. For American terms used in connexion with book stack equipment, *see* COMPARTMENT, DECK, PRESS, RANGE, SECTION. 3. A stack room usually adjoining a public department, containing lesser-used books, and to which only the staff have access.

STACK ROOM. *See* STACK.

STAFF. American spelling for a STAVE (*q.v.*) in music. *Pl.* Staffs.

STAFF ENCLOSURE. That part of a public department of a library such as a junior, lending, or reference library, which is restricted to the use of the staff. Also called a 'Charging desk', 'Counter', or 'Desk'.

STAFF MANUAL. A guide book indicating the correct procedures and processes to be followed by the staff in the various departments or branches of a library system. Called in the U.S.A. a PROCEDURE MANUAL (*q.v.*).

STAFF ROOM. A room reserved for the use of the staff for purposes of rest, refreshment and recreation.

STAINED EDGES. The edges of a book which have been stained with colour. Where only the top edges have been stained the term 'stained top' is used. *See also* EDGES.

STAINED LABEL. A coloured panel painted or printed on the spine of a book as a background for lettering, and to simulate a leather label.

STAINED TOP. *See* STAINED EDGES.

STALLS. In old libraries, combined book shelves and reading desk, or LECTERN (*q.v.*), the books being stood upright on shelves (of which there were three) above the reading desk. The fore-edges of the books faced outwards, and the books were chained. This type of shelving was first used by Sir Thomas Bodley at the Bodleian Library, Oxford, and replaced the mediaeval lectern.

STAMP. *See* BLOCKING PANEL STAMP, TOOLING.

STAMP ACTS. Towards the end of the seventeenth century duties were imposed on certain legal documents, and paper, vellum and parchment. The Stamp Act of 1712 added to the list of dutiable articles, e.g. essay periodicals like the *Spectator*, and from time to time the list increased. The notorious Stamp Act of 1765 ordered a stamp to be applied to all legal documents in the colonies; it met with great opposition in N. America, and was repealed the following year. The subsequent history of the duties is of innumerable variations, generally increasing in the eighteenth, and declining in the nineteenth and twentieth centuries.

STANDARD AUTHOR. An author whose writings have sufficient literary merit to justify a place in the literature of the country, and which, it is hoped, will not become out of print.

STANDARD BOOK NUMBER. The use of a sequence of nine digits to individualize titles, editions or volumes. The digits comprising the first group are allocated to U.K. and Northern Ireland publishers, the remainder – except the last which is a check number to guard against mistakes when feeding into a computer – are allocated to identify individual titles, editions or volumes. The system was prepared by the Publishers Association of Great Britain so that identification and recording could be done by computers if desired, and came into operation on 1st January 1968. The numbers appear against entries in *The Bookseller*, in the *British National Bibliography* and in publishers' catalogues. The British Standard *Specification for book numbering* is BS 4762 : 1971, the American, Z39.21. *See also* STANDARD BOOK NUMBERING AGENCY. Early in 1969, at a meeting sponsored by ISO, this book numbering principle developed internationally with the result that the International Standard Book Number system was adopted, for which *see* ISBN. For the International Standard Serial Number for journals, *see* ISSN.

STANDARD BOOK NUMBERING AGENCY. A company which is formed in each participating country to operate the International Standard Book Number system. Its duties are to allocate where necessary, verify, record and publish International Standard Book Numbers and maintain master files which are kept on magnetic tape form for computer use. In the U.K., the Standard Book Numbering Agency Ltd. was jointly sponsored by J. Whitaker *&*

Sons Ltd., the Council of the British National Bibliography Ltd. (later incorporated within the Bibliographic Services Division of the British Library) and the Publishers Association. In the U.S.A. the R. R. Bowker Company performs this function. *See also* ISBN, STANDARD BOOK NUMBER.

STANDARD EDITION.   The edition of an author's books, so called by the publisher, to suggest a good quality of book production which is better than that used for a cheaper edition. It may contain notes and an introduction but need not be a CRITICAL EDITION nor a DEFINITIVE EDITION (*qq.v.*). *See also* UNIFORM EDITION.

STANDARD REFERENCE CODE.   A superstructure to be worked out by the Central Classification Committee of FID, primarily for the identification and location of information blocks or collections by the UNISIST network.

STANDARD SIZE CARD.   A card used for cataloguing and other purposes, of the internationally agreed size of 5 × 3 inches (7·5 × 12·5 centimetres in Continental countries). This is the size which is almost universally used for catalogues, although other standard sizes, particularly 6 × 8 inch cards are sometimes used. Tear-resistant card (weight 160–180 grammes per square metre) should be used. The American Standard (Z85.1–1969 U.S.A. Standard for Permanent and Durable Catalog Cards) gives 2.95 × 4.92 inches (75mm × 125mm) with a recommendation that the hole should be 5/16 in. (7.9mm) in diameter and that the lower edge of the hole should be 3/16 in. (4.8mm) from the bottom edge of the card. A note states that other dimensions may be used, but that as the size of the hole is reduced so there is less chance that the cards will fit the most numerous variety of card catalogue cabinets; it also points out the dangers of a small hole being too high or too low on the card. *See also* A7 LIBRARY CARD.

STANDARD STACK.   Name sometimes given to a steel bookcase made by manufacturers of high quality library shelving where good design and fine finish are of importance. Such shelving incorporates a continuous shelf-base supporting double sheet-steel uprights and a corniced cover plate.

STANDARD TITLE.   The title under which copies of a work, or musical composition, appearing under different titles, is entered in a catalogue. Also called 'Conventional title', 'Uniform title'.

STANDARD WORK.   A book recognized as of permanent value.

STANDARDS.   1. Objective, observable, and usually quantitative, measures of library service; these are usually drawn up by a body of practising librarians, bibliographers and information scientists, as being within the achievement of the average library or other service, and below which an individual service should not be allowed to fall. 2. In all countries, standards are drawn up for the manufacture of goods and provision of services with the object of trying to ensure the provision and maintenance of high qualities. These standards are produced by committees of representatives of professional and trade organizations working under the impetus and supervision of national standards organizations, each of which produces standards concerned with libraries and the materials libraries contain. They are affiliated with the INTERNATIONAL STANDARDS ORGANIZATION (ISO). *Standards for library service: an international survey* by F. N. Withers, Unesco Press, 1974, gives recommended standards for library services (national, university, college, special, public and school) in some twenty countries. *See also* NON-PRINT MATERIALS, RESOURCE CENTRES, STANDARDS FOR COLLEGE LIBRARIES, STANDARDS FOR PUBLIC LIBRARIES. *See also* ALPHABETICAL ARRANGEMENT, AMERICAN NATIONAL STANDARDS INSTITUTE, INC., ARCHIVES, BRITISH STANDARDS INSTITUTION, CEN, INTERNATIONAL STANDARDS, MANUSCRIPTS, NATIONAL BUREAU OF STANDARDS, PERIODICAL.

STANDARDS FOR COLLEGE LIBRARIES. A draft, designed as a complete revision of the existing standards for American college libraries and originally drawn up in 1959, was published with commentaries in *College and Research Libraries News*, December 1974. This twenty-one page document was the work of an ACRL *ad hoc* Committee. The 1975 *Standards* . . . was approved in July 1975 and published as a twenty-nine-page document in *College & Research Libraries News*, October 1975. It is a complete overhaul of, and replacement for, the 1959 *Standards* . . . and applies to libraries serving academic programmes at the bachelors and masters degree levels and to those serving universities granting fewer than ten doctoral degrees annually. In the same issues of *College and Research Libraries News* were respectively the draft (prepared by the ACRL Committee on Standards and Accreditation) and the approved policy statement 'Guidelines for Branch Libraries in Colleges and Universities'. The British recommendations, *College libraries: recommended standards of library provision in colleges of technology and other establishments of further education*, 2nd ed. (15pp) was published in 1971 by the Library Association. It was prepared by the Committee of the Colleges of Technology and Further Education Group of the Library Association, and supersedes the earlier report of 1957, *Standards for library service in Colleges of technology.* See also RESOURCE CENTRES, STANDARDS, STANDARDS FOR PUBLIC LIBRARIES.

STANDARDS FOR PUBLIC LIBRARIES. Prepared by the Public Libraries Section of IFLA, approved at the General Council Meeting in Budapest in 1972 and published in 1973 by Verlag Dokumentation of Munich, these Standards offer guidance as to the levels of provision needed to maintain efficient public library services. Standards are given for: (a) collections (including audio-visual materials); (b) special groups (including children and handicapped readers); (c) staff; (d) buildings. *See also* RESOURCE CENTRES, STANDARDS, STANDARDS FOR COLLEGE LIBRARIES.

STANDING COMMITTEES. Committees which local authorities may set up to carry out particular and continuing functions, or manage departments, or provide services. They are also known as 'Permissive' committees and some, according to their purpose, may be called 'Departmental' or 'Service'. *See also* STATUTORY COMMITTEES.

STANDING CONFERENCE OF AFRICAN UNIVERSITY LIBRARIES. *See* SCAUL.

STANDING CONFERENCE OF AFRICAN UNIVERSITY LIBRARIES: EASTERN AREA. *See* SCAULEA.

STANDING CONFERENCE OF CO-OPERATIVE LIBRARY AND INFORMATION SERVICES. Formerly the Standing Conference of Commercial and Technical Library Co-operative Services. Formed in 1964 to further co-operation between schemes of local library co-operation, to investigate the possibilities of procuring government grant-in-aid for the work of the schemes, and to further the dissemination of commercial and technical information by joint action where necessary. The Secretariat is at the Central Library of the Sheffield City Libraries. Abbreviated SCOCLIS.

STANDING CONFERENCE OF LIBRARIANS OF LIBRARIES OF THE UNIVERSITY OF LONDON. *See* SCOLLUL.

STANDING CONFERENCE OF NATIONAL AND UNIVERSITY LIBRARIES. *See* SCONUL.

STANDING CONFERENCE ON LIBRARY MATERIALS IN AFRICA. *See* SCOLMA.

STANDING CONFERENCE ON PROFESSIONAL ACTIVITIES IN SCOTLAND. *See* SCOPAS.

STANDING CONFERENCE ON THEOLOGICAL AND PHILO-SOPHICAL LIBRARIES IN LONDON. *See* SCOTAPLL.

STANDING FORMES. *See* Standing Type.

STANDING ORDER. 1. An order to supply each succeeding issue of a serial, periodical or annual publication, or subsequent volumes of a work published in a number of volumes issued intermittently. 2. One which is to be acted upon until countermanded. Also called 'Continuation order' and (in America) a 'Till-forbid order'.

STANDING PRESS.   A larger press than a BENCH PRESS (*q.v.*). It stands on the floor and is used to press cased books. Pressure is applied by a platen which is screwed down with a crow bar. *See also* BUILDING-IN MACHINE which dries and presses books in a few seconds.

STANDING TYPE.   The type from which a book has been printed and is kept 'standing' exactly as it came from the machine, to be used again if further copies are to be made. Also called 'Live matter', 'Standing formes'.

STANHOPE PRESS.   The first all-iron printing press introduced in 1800 by Charles Mahon, 3rd Earl Stanhope (1753–1816). The platen, which covered the whole forme, was operated by a screw which had several levers thus enabling a satisfactory impression to be obtained with less physical effort than with previous machines.

STAPLED.   A book or pamphlet the leaves or sections of which are held together by wire staples.

STAR.   *Synonymous with* ASTERISK (*q.v.*). *See also* REFERENCE MARKS.

STAR MAP.   A map of the heavens. Also called an 'Astronomical map'.

STAR SIGNATURE.   A signature indicating an off-cut (part of a sheet) and distinguished by an asterisk placed with the signature letter or figure of the main part of the sheet. This part of a section is usually placed inside the part bearing the plain signature.

STARCH.   The original material for sizing paper. It is now used in addition to other sizing agents as a loading agent in order to give a hard 'rattle' and an improved 'finish' to paper.

STARR.   A Hebrew deed, covenant, contract, or obligation, anciently required to be filed in the royal exchequer, and invalid unless so deposited. The name was applied to all agreements between Jews and Christians and, occasionally, to other Jewish documents before the expulsion of the Jews from England in 1290. Starrs were written in two languages, Latin or Norman-French, with an acknowledgement in Hebrew at the foot.

START.   Leaves of a book are said to 'start' when the sewing is defective, causing the leaves to become loose.

STARTER.   (*Classification*) The first curve, used in the Colon Classification to enclose the Subject Device Number. The second, or closing, curve is called the 'Arrester'. *See also* BRACKETS, CIRCULAR BRACKETS, CURVES.

STATE. An impression of an engraving taken from a plate at any stage in the perfecting process. Various states include *open letter proof* and *publication state*. An *early impression* is one of the first copies to be taken; it is consequently sought after by collectors as representing a print taken when the plate is in its best condition.

STATE DOCUMENT CENTRE. A library that has the responsibility of collecting, preserving and organizing as complete a file as possible of the public documents of the state in which it is situated. (American.)

STATE LIBRARY. In America, a library maintained by state funds, which preserves the state records and provides books for the use of state officials, books relating to the history of the state, books published by authors living in the state, and newspapers published in the state. In many states, all classes of books are purchased in order to supply any resident's needs for books or information. Books are sent by post or express to residents. *See also* NATIONAL LIBRARY.

STATE LIBRARY ADMINISTRATIVE AGENCY. A term used in the (American) Library Services Act, 1961, to mean the official State agency charged by State law with the extension and development of public library services throughout the State.

STATE LIBRARY AGENCY. An American state organization existing to extend and improve library services in the state. It should be free from partisan politics and political interference of all kinds, led by professional librarians, supported by law, and adequately financed. Amongst its functions are the planning of a state-wide public library service, promotion of the development of these libraries, supervising library provision with a view to improving services by formulating and enforcing minimum standards; providing a consulting and advisory service to librarians, boards of library trustees and citizen groups; administering a state system of grants-in-aid as well as federal grants-in-aid to libraries; providing supplementary services such as inter-library loans of books and non-book materials; travelling libraries; providing a centralized information and bibliographic service; centralized cataloguing; providing library services to schools, clubs and individuals where no public library services exist.

STATE OF THE ART. An exhaustive, systematic and sometimes critical, review of (mostly) published and unpublished material (largely periodical articles) on a specific subject.

STATE PAPER OFFICE OF IRELAND. *See* PUBLIC RECORD OFFICE OF IRELAND.

STATIONARII. Men commissioned by universities in mediaeval times to attend to the production and distribution of books.

STATIONER. From *Lat. stationarius* 'one who stands' (i.e. at a stall). One who sells stationery. Originally used to mean a bookseller.

STATIONERS' COMPANY. The authority which regulated and organized printing and the book trade in England. It was established by a Royal Charter from Queen Mary in 1557, created a livery company in 1560, and until the passing of the Copyright Act in 1842 had an absolute monopoly, as all apprentices to the printing trade were obliged to serve a member of the Company, and every publication was required to be 'Entered at Stationers' Hall' as proof of registration. The *Registers* which commenced in 1554 are of great value in the history of English literature.

STATISTICAL BIBLIOGRAPHY. 1. The assembling and interpretation of statistics relating to books and periodicals in order to: (a) demonstrate historical movements; (b) determine the national or universal research use of books and journals; (c) ascertain in many local situations the general use of books and journals. 2. To shed light on the processes of written communication and of the nature and course of development of a discipline by means of counting and analysing the various facets of written communication.

STATUTORY COMMITTEES. Committees which local authorities are required by law to set up in order to carry out certain functions. Finance, health, fire brigade and education committees, and library committees of Scottish burghs, are included amongst statutory committees. *See also* STANDING COMMITTEES.

STATUTORY INSTRUMENTS. Documents by which the power to make, confirm, or approve Orders, Regulations, or other subordinate legislation, conferred by an Act of Parliament on Her Majesty in Council or on a Minister of the Crown, is exercised. Prior to 1 January 1948, when the Statutory Instruments Act, 1946, came into operation, they were known as *Statutory Rules and Orders*. Although Statutory Instruments are frequently required to be laid before Parliament, they rank as Non-Parliamentary Publications.

STATUTORY REFERENCE. In the British patents field, a reference placed at the end of a patent specification as a Statutory act by the Comptroller to direct attention to another specification.

STAVE. The five horizontal lines on which musical notation is written or printed. Spelt 'staff' in America.

STAVE. *Synonymous with* SECTION 1 (*q.v.*).

STEEL ENGRAVING. *See* ENGRAVING.

STEM. 1. The outline of the design of a type letter; the bare lines apart from the serifs, which indicate most clearly the character and height of the letter. The main stroke of a letter. 2. The body of a type letter between the face and the foot. Also called the SHANK (*q.v.*) or BODY (*q.v.*).

STENCIL. 1. The basic principle of printing, in which a wax, silk or other stencil is used. The ink is applied to the back of the printing image carrier (i.e. the stencil) and reaches the front through the image areas which are porous and open. *See also* SILK SCREEN. 2. The 'master' or image area which carries the image, and by means of which the printing is done. 3. A thin cut metal plate which allows the transfer of a design, etc., to paper when an ink roller or brush is passed over its surface.

STENCIL DUPLICATING. A method of producing multiple copies from a specially prepared wax master. A particular kind of ink is forced through the cuts made by a typewriter in the stencil and transferred to the paper.

STEP-AND-REPEAT CAMERA. A microfilm camera which provides a series of latent image frames in a predetermined pattern on a single sheet of film.

STEP-AND-REPEAT MACHINE. A machine for multiple copying (on offset plates, etc.), with devices for the adjustment of each copy. Intended specially for reproduction in colour in which the printing plates for each colour must be superimposed precisely when printing.

STEPWISE OPERATED CAMERA. *Synonymous with* PLANETARY CAMERA (*q.v.*).

STEREO. *See* STEREOTYPE.

STEREOPHONIC. Relating to a sound transmission system in which is realized the illusion of auditory perspective.

STEREOPHONIC SOUND. A form of reproduction in which the apparent sources of sound are spread out.

STEREOSCOPIC SLIDE. A pair of positive photographic prints made from negatives taken from two slightly different viewpoints to give a 3-D effect when viewed through a specially made viewer. They have become familiar through the 'Viewmaster', a cheap viewer the slides for which can be purchased in many shops.

STEREOTOME. Trade name for a special container resembling a book, which can be stood upright on a shelf, and holds a set of stereo slides.

STEREOTYPE (STEREO). A metal printing plate carrying a printing surface in relief, made by pouring stereotype metal into a papier-mâché (called 'flong'), or plaster of paris, mould of the original type, line block or very coarse half-tone. Future printings are made from the resulting 'stereos'. The whole process is known as stereotyping.

Curved stereos are used on rotary presses for high-speed work, particularly newspaper printing. The process was patented in 1725 by William Ged, a Scottish printer, who was commissioned by Cambridge University to stereotype prayer-books and bibles. *See also* MATRIX.

STEREOTYPE METAL. An alloy of tin, antimony, and lead; used for casting stereos.

stet. (*Lat.* 'let the matter stand'.) Written in the margin of printer's copy or proof to denote the cancelling of any correction marked thereon. Dots under the words indicate the correction to which the 'stet' refers.

STEWARD. Agent and representative of the lord of a manor.

STEWART TRAVELLING BURSARY, J. D. Founded in 1958 as a testimonial to J. D. Stewart's outstanding and continuous service to the London and Home Counties Branch of the Library Association. It was awarded by the L&HCB to help a student-librarian visit an overseas country in order to study librarianship in that country and visit its libraries. At first, the award was £25; this was increased to £50 in 1961 and later to £100. The Bursary is now offered in alternate years, its value being £200. Applicants must be members of the LA and either current or former personal members of the L&HCB and also actively engaged in professional study, either full time or part time.

STICK. 1. The tool used by the compositor for setting or forming into lines the types as he picks them out of the CASE (*q.v.*). It usually contains about twenty lines of 8 point type. 2. A device like a small-diameter walking stick divided down its length, used for holding from one to about six copies of a newspaper. Also called 'Newspaper file', 'Newspaper rod', and 'Newspaper stick'.

STIFF BACK. *See* TIGHT BACK.

STIFFENED AND CUT FLUSH. *See* CUT FLUSH.

STIFFENED PAPER COVERS. *See* PAPER COVERED.

STIGMATYPY. The use of small type-units to design and print a picture or portrait.

STIGMONYM. Dots instead of the name of the author. Used on the title-page and elsewhere in a book. Where the authorship of such books cannot be traced, they are catalogued under their titles.

STIPPLE. A printing surface of a copper plate used for making illustrations; it consists of dots, instead of lines. The process is to cover the plate with ordinary etching ground, and through this to sketch the contours and lightly indicate the main shadows with dots by means of the etching needles and a roulette. The portions of the plate thus uncovered are bitten with acid, after which the drawing is completed and given brilliance by flicking or dotting directly on to the surface of the plate with a specially curved graver or roulette. The dots may be fine or coarse, to give effects of light and dark. Although this method was used by W. W. Ryland (1732–83) the Royal engraver, it was first made popular in the eighteenth century by Francesco Bartolozzi, an Italian painter and engraver who came to London in 1764 from Venice and worked for the publisher John Boydell. Half-tones are a kind of stipple engraving.

STIPPLED EDGES.   The edges of a book which have been spotted irregularly with colour to prevent them appearing to be soiled. *See also* EDGES, MARBLED EDGES, SPRINKLED EDGES, STAINED EDGES.

STIPPLING.   1. (*Paper*) A roughened finish, also called 'Pebbling'. 2. (*Printing* and *art*) A gradation of light and shade produced by dots.

STISEC.   Acronym of Scientific and Technological Information Services Enquiry Committee which was set up by the Council of the Australian National Library in 1971 to examine needs for scientific and technological information (STI) services and the existing facilities available in Australia, and make appropriate recommendations to enable identified needs to be met. The Committee's Report, published in two volumes in 1973, recommended that a scientific and technological information authority be established by the Australian Government to advise on an appropriate information policy and to promote the development of scientific and technological library and information services in Australia. *See also* ALBIS, ANSTEL.

STITCHING.   The operation of fastening a pamphlet consisting of a single section, with wire or thread passed through the centre of the fold. *See also* SEWING, STABBING, THREAD STITCHED.

STOCHASTIC PROCESS.   A system which produces a sequence of discrete symbols according to certain probabilities, as for example the sequence of letters which makes up a passage of printed English. If the probabilities depend on previous events in the series this is called a 'Markov process' after the Russian mathematician.

STOCK.   1. (*Printing*) Paper or other material for printing upon. 2. (*Paper*) The material (rags, waste-paper, esparto, ropes, etc.) used for making paper; the term is applied at any stage of manufacture, whether to untreated materials or the finished paper. *See also* HALF-STUFF, PULP, STUFF, WHOLE-STUFF. Also, the printing trade term for paper. 3. All the books and other items in a library. 4. All the books available for sale by a bookseller or publisher.

STOCK BOOK. *Synonymous with* ACCESSIONS REGISTER (*q.v.*).

STOCK EDITOR. A member of the staff of a library who is responsible for maintaining the book stock in good physical condition and up-to-date as well as for ensuring that the latest and most useful titles are available in adequate quantities.

STOCKHOLDING BOOKSELLER. A retail bookseller who keeps a varied and large stock of books on his shelves.

STOCKTAKING. The process of taking stock by checking records of books possessed with copies on the shelves or records of books on loan.

STONE. Usually a steel-top table (originally it was stone) on which the imposing work – that is, the assembling of the various parts of a printing job – is done. It is on the stone that the type, blocks, etc., are locked in the chase and levelled with mallet and planer. *See also* IMPOSITION.

STONE ENGRAVING. Engraving on blue or grey lithographic stone (fine-grained, compact limestone); a hand process which is used chiefly for script and line drawings in which sharpness and precision of line are more important than artistic expression. The outline is traced and then deeply scored with a steel or diamond pen. The process is used chiefly for script and line drawings of which relatively few copies are required. As the number of copies which can be made on a hand press is small, it is usual for a stone engraving to be made as an original for transferring to a plate for use on a printing press. Also used to indicate a print made from an engraved stone.

STONE PROOF. One made after the forme has been locked up for press, but before it has been put on the press.

STOP-CYLINDER PRESS. A type of printing machine in which a cylinder (which is placed over a reciprocating bed on which rests the forme) revolves once during which the impression is made on paper fed underneath the cylinder, and stops until the forme is again in position for printing the next sheet. Often called a 'Wharfedale' press. *See also* MIEHLE, PERFECTER, SINGLE-REVOLUTION MACHINE, TWO-REVOLUTION MACHINE.

STOP LIST. (*Indexing. Information retrieval*) A list of words or terms, or roots of words, which are considered to be meaningless or non-significant for purposes of information retrieval, and which are excluded from indexing. The opposite of GO LIST (*q.v.*).

STOPPING OUT. Painting with varnish such parts of an etching plate as are not to be further etched by acid during repeated dipping in the acid bath. In blockmaking, painting out of the screen or the negative, parts of the subject which are not required to be printed.

STORAGE. A source from which documents or information of specified descriptions may be supplied. A receptacle for information (*IBM*).

STORAGE AND RETRIEVAL. The recording of the holdings of library material of various kinds and of information recorded in such material, and the means of ascertaining the whereabouts of the material or information by means of catalogue cards, indexes, and particularly punched cards or other kinds of record which are used in high-speed sorting machines.

STORAGE AREA. That portion of the total floor area of a building which is allocated to the storage of materials, furniture, equipment and supplies not in current use. (American.)

STORAGE CENTRE. A library or library agency in which co-operating libraries store little-used library materials, and which are readily available on request. Also called 'Deposit library', 'Reservoir Library'. (American.)

STORAGE DEVICES. (*Information retrieval*) Equipment used to store both data and program instructions; it may be considered to have two categories: (a) the main memory, which is usually the internal store of the computer, i.e. immediate access store; (b) the backing store which is of larger capacity but offers slower access than the main memory.

STORAGE SHELVING. Shelving which is intended for accommodating little-used books or stores. It may consist of wooden slats or fixed steel shelves. If made of steel and the shelves are adjustable they are an integral part of the structure and can only be moved by unscrewing nuts and bolts; for this reason this kind of shelving is seldom used in libraries. *See also* ADJUSTABLE SHELVING, LIBRARY SHELVING.

STORE. 1. In information retrieval, the set of all codes which have been physically recorded in some medium (*Taube*). 2. A collection of books or other documentary information which are the subject of records: it may be a library but it may well be a single publication such as a text-book or abstracts journal. An index, or catalogue to a store, can be called a 'Retrieval device'.

STOR-MOR SHELVING. Trade name for a variety of compact book storage invented by Ingold, a Swiss engineer.

STORY HOUR. A definite period (which is usually about half an hour) set aside for telling stories to the youngest members of a junior library. The stories are told by members of the staff, particularly the children's librarians, and their friends.

STRAIGHT-GRAIN LEATHER. A leather that has been dampened

and rolled, or 'boarded', to make the grain run in straight lines. An innovation credited to Roger Paine.

STRAIGHT-GRAIN MOROCCO. Morocco leather in which the natural grain has been distorted by elongated lines or ridges all running in the same direction.

STRAIGHT MATTER. Text uninterrupted by illustrations, tables or any special settings.

STRAIGHTENING. The task (usually performed daily in a busy library) of arranging tidily books in correct classified order.

STRAP BINDER. A binder fitted with thin steel strips which pass through the staples of the periodicals.

STRAPWORK. (*Binding*) Interlaced double lines, usually forming a geometrical pattern.

STRAWBERRY HILL PRESS. The private press on which Sir Horace Walpole, fourth Earl of Orford, printed his own and other books. The Press functioned between 1757 and 1789, and the printers included successively William Robinson, Thomas Kirgate, Benjamin Williams, and others. The Press was situated at Walpole's estate at Strawberry Hill, Twickenham, Middlesex.

STRAWBOARD. A coarse yellow board, made from straw and used for the covers of books.

STREAMER. A printed poster used in shop or window advertising.

STREET INDEX. An index of streets in a town showing the number of houses and the number of persons therein who hold membership tickets for a public library. Also, an alphabetical list of streets in any given area.

STRESS. The thickened part of a curved stroke or letter.

STRIKE. *See* MATRIX 3.

STRIKE-ON COMPOSITION. The preparation of camera-ready copy on an electric typewriter or other machine operated by a similar principle.

STRIKE THROUGH. A fault in printing when ink printed on one side of a sheet penetrates to the other. *See also* SHOW THROUGH.

STRIP CARTOON. Small drawings, fewer than about eight or ten in number, about 2 inches square, appearing side by side in a row in a newspaper or periodical. They are usually serials and tell a continuing story or relate the adventures and experience of the characters.

STRIP FILM. A length of microfilm which is too short to be conveniently wound on a reel.

STRIP IN. To combine one photographic record with another, or others, or a photograph and lettering, preparatory to using all in making a printing plate. In lithography the operation of stripping is analogous to the operation of imposing in letterpress.

STRIP INDEX. A form of visible index in which entries are made on strips of card shallow enough to take only one line of typewriting. These strips are placed in a metal frame and the surface of the whole of each strip is visible and may be typed or written on.

STRIPED FILM. Cinematograph film edged with a narrow band of magnetic coating for carrying sound.

STRIPPING. The removal, and subsequent destruction, of documents, of no further importance from files which it is decided to preserve.

STRONG. (*Printing*) A term used by some printers to indicate a printed page with too many lines of type on it.

STRUCTERM. A term or descriptor having an appended role code indicating context in which the term is used (*IBM*).

STRUCTURAL NOTATION. A notation to a classification which indicates the hierarchy or structure of the scheme. A non-structural notation does not do this. *See also* HIERARCHICAL NOTATION.

STRUCTURED INDEXING LANGUAGE. The use of words in non-literary order to construct succinct meaningful subject headings (e.g. 'libraries, university', for university libraries; 'Greenhouses: heating, Natural gas-fired', for natural gas-fired heating of greenhouses). *See also* ARTIFICIAL INDEXING LANGUAGE, NATURAL LANGUAGE.

STUB. 1. The part of an original leaf which is left after most of it has been cut away to insert a correct one (*see* CANCEL). 2. A narrow strip of paper or linen sewn between sections of a book for attaching folded maps or other bulky items. *See also* COMPENSATION GUARD, GUARD.

STUDENTS' LIBRARY. A collection of books provided for the use of a particular group or category of students.

STUDENTS' SECTION. The department of a county library which sends (usually by post) non-fiction books specially requested by readers. It is usually accommodated at the County Library Headquarters.

STUDENT'S TICKET. *Synonymous with* SUPPLEMENTARY TICKET (*q.v.*).

STUDY ISSUE. Books issued to students in excess of the usual number and for a longer period than usual.

STUDY SCORE. A musical score, similar to a MINIATURE SCORE (*q.v.*) but of a somewhat larger size due to the work being fully scored, i.e. having music for so many instruments that it would be difficult to read if reduced to the normal miniature score size. *See also* SCORE.

STUFF.   The pulp in the paper-maker's vat prior to its being removed to the mould. *See also* HALF-STUFF, PULP, STOCK 2, WATER-LEAF, WHOLE-STUFF.

STYLE BOOK.   *Synonymous with* STYLE MANUAL (*q.v.*).

STYLE MANUAL.   A set of rules drawn up by a printing establishment for the guidance of its staff to ensure that details of typography, spelling, capitalization, punctuation and other matters about which opinions and customs differ, are in accordance with the prevailing practice of that establishment. Such rules are known as the 'style of the house'. *Rules for Compositors and Readers of the Oxford University Press* are a standard set followed by many printers and authors.

STYLE OF THE HOUSE.   (*Printing*) The practice of a printing establishment with regard to capitals, italics, spelling, punctuation, etc. It is called a 'Style manual' or 'Style book' when printed as a guide for use.

STYLE SHEET.   1. A guide to a printer's HOUSE STYLE. 2. A list of types and their sizes, style of setting, etc., proposed for a given publication. *See also* STYLE MANUAL, STYLE OF THE HOUSE.

STYLUS, STYLE.   A writing instrument, pointed at one end, which was used in ancient and mediaeval times for writing on wax or clay. *See also* ELECTRIC STYLUS.

SUBALTERN GENERA.   The intermediate classes of a classification between the SUMMUM GENUS (*q.v.*) and the INFIMA SPECIES (*q.v.*).

SUB-BRANCH.   A small branch library open a few hours each day. A part-time library. *See also* BRANCH LIBRARY. In America, a smaller book-circulating agency than a COMMUNITY LIBRARY (*q.v.*), having a minimum book collection with emphasis on popular reading. The population served would be not less than 10,000, and the library open on some part of five days a week.

SUB-COMMITTEE.   A committee formed from members of a larger committee to consider one or more matters on behalf of the larger committee to which it reports its deliberations.

SUBDIVISION.   1. The word commonly used to denote the process of dividing a scheme of classification into its parts. 2. The result of such subdivision.

SUB-ENTRY.   In indexing, the part of the entry following the entry-word or heading which is used to subdivide a large number of references into a group of related items, i.e. the whole entry minus the entry-word or heading.

SUB-HEAD.   *See* SUB-HEADING.

SUB-HEADING.   1. A secondary heading, used in the subdivision of a subject. In a verbal heading it is the second or subsequent word, separated from the preceding by punctuation. 2. A word or group of words added to a heading and designed to delimit a particular group of entries under the heading, or to designate a part of the entity named in the heading (*IFLA*). Sub-headings may be subjected to modification, and if there is more than one modification of a sub-heading, each of the modifications is then known as a sub-sub-heading. Each group of sub- and sub-sub-headings is indented in printing to make the meaning clear. The terms sub- and sub-sub-headings are often abbreviated to 'sub-head' and 'sub-sub-head'.

SUB-INDEX. An index within an index.

SUBINFEUDATION. The granting or sub-letting of lands by a feudal vassal to an undertenant on the same terms as he held them from his overlord. Abolished in England in 1290, but the principle still survives in Scotland.

SUBJECT. 1. The theme or themes of a book, whether stated in the title or not. 2. (*Indexing*) A unit concept found in, or derived from, manuscript or published literary material. It may be found, or expressed, as a theme, name, date, first line of a poem, title of a book, or be an expression coined to convey the gist of the material indexed, etc.

SUBJECT ANALYTIC. *See* ANALYTICAL ENTRY.

SUBJECT ARRANGEMENT. Books arranged in order of subject, either alphabetically or according to some scheme of classification.

SUBJECT AUTHORITY CARD. A card which, in addition to citing the authorities consulted in determining the choice of a given heading, also indicates the references made to and from related headings and synonymous terms (*IBM*).

SUBJECT AUTHORITY FILE. The list in a book, or on cards, of subject headings used in a given catalogue, and the references made to them. Also the entries made for the classified list of class symbols or numbers and the appropriate subject index entries made when first allocating a book to a particular position in the classification. An entry is made for each step taken when indexing by the chain indexing method. *See also* AUTHORITY CARD, AUTHORITY LIST, CHAIN INDEX, NAME AUTHORITY FILE.

SUBJECT BIBLIOGRAPHY. A list of material about a particular subject or individual.

SUBJECT CARD. A catalogue card bearing a subject entry.

SUBJECT CATALOGUE. Any catalogue arranged by subjects, whether in alphabetical or classified order, which directs users to the documents dealing with them. *See also* ALPHABETICO-SPECIFIC SUBJECT CATALOGUE, ALPHABETICO-CLASSED CATALOGUE.

SUBJECT CATALOGUING. 1. That part of cataloguing which involves the allocation of subject headings to entries for specific books or other documents. 2. The branch of cataloguing which is not concerned with DESCRIPTIVE CATALOGUING (*q.v.*) but with the provision of subject headings. In 1940 the Library of Congress adopted this term to cover both classification and subject heading; previously, subject headings had been assigned by the descriptive cataloguers, not the classifiers.

SUBJECT CLASSIFICATION. The scheme devised by J. D. Brown in 1906, in which the main classes are Matter and Force, Life, Mind, and Record. The notation is mixed (letter and figure) and does not permit of easy extension (as does Dewey's Decimal Classification by the use of decimal figures) although the CATEGORICAL TABLES (*q.v.*) enable a certain amount of subdivision. It is the best-known general scheme of British origin.

SUBJECT CONCEPTS. (*Classification*) The terms which result when a subject is divided by a single characteristic. The group of terms which so results is called a 'Facet'.

SUBJECT DEPARTMENT. A department in a large general library in which are shelved all the books on a particular subject, e.g. science, whether intended for reference or for home-reading. Where such departmentalization exists there is usually a POPULAR LIBRARY (*q.v.*) containing a selection of books of interest to the 'general reader'. Also called 'Departmentalized library'.

SUBJECT DEVICE. Ranganathan's term for the process of dividing by the whole classification. It is one of the distinctive principles of the Colon Classification for determining the sequence of subjects and is used in the Dewey Classification when a subject such as 016 Subject Bibliography is divided by the whole classification.

SUBJECT DEVICE NUMBER. In the Colon Classification, that part of an Isolate Number which is contributed by the SUBJECT DEVICE (*q.v.*).

SUBJECT ENTRY. 1. In a catalogue, an entry under the heading adopted to indicate a book's subject. In a subject catalogue it is the basic unit, and includes the description of the document, and its location. In the classified file of the CLASSIFIED CATALOGUE (*q.v.*) the heading may also be the LOCATION MARK (*q.v.*). Subject entries for music are entered under the medium of performance (*see* MEDIUM) or the form (*see* FORM 2) in which the music is written. They may also be given under the subject described in the music. 2. In an index, an entry relating to a subject as distinguished from one beginning with the name of a person.

SUBJECT-FIELD REFERENCE CODE. *See* UNISIST.

SUBJECT FULLNESS. *See* SECONDARY FULLNESS.

SUBJECT GUIDE. A guide to the shelves of a library, showing where books on particular subjects may be found. Also called 'Topic guide'.

SUBJECT HEADING.† The word or group of words under which books and other material on a subject are entered in a catalogue in which the entries are arranged in alphabetical order. The heading may include punctuation to which an arranging significance may be assigned. In a classified catalogue the subject heading consists of a classification symbol with or without its verbal meaning. It may also include entries for all material on the same subject in an index or bibliography, or arranged in a file. Lists of headings are used by some cataloguers to aid them in their choice of appropriate subject headings and to achieve uniformity. The two best-known are American. The 10th ed. of *Sears list of subject headings* ed. by Barbara M. Westby was published in 1972. A new edition (the 8th) of *Subject Headings used in the dictionary catalogs of the Library of Congress* (LCSH) was issued in 1975 with the title *Library of Congress Subject Headings*. This is a cumulation of the 7th edition and all the supplements issued through 1973.

SUBJECT HEADING LANGUAGE. The terms used as subject headings and under which entries are made, as well as those from which references are merely made to other subject terms.

SUBJECT INDEX ENTRY. An entry in the subject index of a classified catalogue which directs to the class number under which entries for books on the required subject will be found.

SUBJECT INDEX ILLUSION. The term used by H. E. Bliss for the alphabetical arrangement of subjects in a scheme of classification according to the first letter of the subject name, etc., e.g. Q Quartos, R Roman Antiquities, S Science, T Technology, U Unclassified. As subjects are subdivided similarly, an alphabetical index is essential to determine the position of any subject in the sequence, and Bliss wrote 'no index, however convenient or necessary, can convert an arbitrary or disordered arrangement into a systematic classification'.

SUBJECT LIBRARIES. *See* SUBJECT DEPARTMENT.

SUBJECT REFERENCE. A reference from one subject to another whether a synonym or a related heading.

SUBJECT SERIES. A number of books published in a named series by one publisher and dealing with different phases of a single subject or with a particular field of knowledge. The books are usually written by different authors, are not usually reprints, and are uniform in textual and physical characteristics. Similarly, a number of musical compositions dealing with different phases of music, media of performance, form, etc.

SUBJECT SPECIALIZATION. A scheme of co-operation whereby public libraries in a restricted geographical area purchase books on a specific subject. In some schemes the libraries act as depositories for preserving little-used books on their particular subject which might otherwise be discarded. For subject specialization in gramophone records, see GLASS. *See also* JOINT FICTION RESERVE.

SUBJECT STYLE. The use of red for headings in catalogue entries to indicate subjects. As an alternative (owing to the tendency of red ink or red typescript to fade) black capitals are sometimes used. *See also* AUTHOR STYLE.

SUBJECT-WORD ENTRY. Entry in a catalogue under a word of the title of a book indicative of its subject matter.

SUB-LIBRARIAN. *See* DEPUTY LIBRARIAN.

SUBORDINATION. The allocation of a subject term to its right place in the classification schedules; its order of precedence in the HIER-ARCHY (*q.v.*). In a FACETED CLASSIFICATION (*q.v.*) the placing of a term belonging to one FACET (*q.v.*) after a term belonging to another facet, in a CITATION ORDER (*q.v.*).

SUB-PROFESSIONAL ASSISTANT. In American libraries, one who undertakes, under the immediate supervision of professional staff members, work largely concerned with the lighter routine processes which are peculiar to library work and which require some knowledge of library procedure.

SUBSCRIBER. 1. A person who lives outside the municipal or county or other local authority boundary but who is permitted to use the public library on payment of an annual subscription. 2. A person who pays a subscription to receive a periodical as published, or to a society.

SUBSCRIBERS' EDITION. An edition prepared for circulation only to persons who have agreed to purchase on announcement and before publication. It may differ from the ordinary 'trade edition' by the inclusion of a list of subscribers, by being printed on hand-made or other special paper and having larger margins, or by being sumptuously bound.

SUBSCRIPT. 1. An indexing notation. 2. A small letter or figure put below the level of the foot of a full-size lower case character as in H_2O. Usually called an 'Inferior' character. *See also* SUPERSCRIPT.

SUBSCRIPTION AGENT. A firm or organization which arranges,

usually for a consideration, at the order of an individual or library, for the regular delivery of serials as published.

SUBSCRIPTION BOOKS.   1. Those published at intervals by societies and issued to subscribing members. 2. Individual books of limited appeal, the publication of which depends to some extent on subscriptions promised prior to publication, and the price of which is raised after publication.

SUBSCRIPTION EDITION.   One which is published after enough subscriptions have been received to ensure financial success.

SUBSCRIPTION LIBRARY.   A commercial lending library the members of which pay subscriptions entitling them to borrow books during the period of the validity of their subscription. They were first formed in England in the late seventeenth and early eighteenth centuries. *See also* CIRCULATING LIBRARY.

SUBSCRIPTION PRICE.   The price at which books are sometimes offered for sale before they are published. The price is usually lower than the after-publication price. This is done to give the publisher some guidance as to the potential sales of the book and therefore of the number to be printed.

SUBSERIES.   A series of publications, the title of which is distinctive and is dependent on the title of another series.

SUBSIDIARIES.   The parts of a book in addition to the text and including notes (whether placed in the pages or massed at the end of a book), bibliographies, appendices, glossaries, plates, indexes, imprint, colophon, blank leaves, end-papers and book jackets. Sometimes called 'Reference matter'. Also called 'End-matter', 'Back matter'. *See also* PRELIMINARIES.

SUBSIDIARY RIGHTS.   An author's rights to literary property other than the original one of first publication. These include dramatic, film, translation and serial rights.

SUBSIDY PUBLISHERS.   *Synonymous with* VANITY PUBLISHERS (*q.v.*).

SUBSTANCE.   The weight of paper expressed in terms of weight per ream of sheets of a given size; the weight of a ream of a particular size and number of sheets is known as the 'substance number'. The 'substance' of the paper is the product of the density, i.e. the degree of dilution of the stuff flowing on to the machine wire, and the speed at which it is permitted to flow, plus the speed of the machine wire.

SUBSTITUTION GENERIC.   In a HIERARCHICAL SEARCH (*q.v.*), a situation in which two headings in the alphabetico-specific subject catalogue, each with the same number of sub-headings, represent concepts in hierarchical relationship, i.e. the heading and the first sub-heading are identical, the second sub-heading being different. *See also* ALPHABETICAL COLLATERAL SEARCH, SYSTEMATIC COLLATERAL SEARCH.

SUB-SUB-HEADING. *See* SUB-HEADING.

SUB-TITLE. A secondary or subordinate title, usually explanatory, and often following a semicolon, 'or', 'an', or 'a'.

SUGGESTION CARD. A printed card which is filled in by a reader with particulars of a book suggested for addition to a library. All appropriate bibliographical information is entered, and in some libraries it subsequently serves as an ORDER CARD (*q.v.*). Also called 'Recommendation card', 'Request card', 'Requisition card', 'Suggestion slip'.

SULPHATE PULP. (*Papermaking*) Chemical wood pulp which has been prepared by cooking wood chips under pressure and high temperature in a solution consisting mainly of sulphate of soda (Glauber's salt). The resulting paper is strong, and is often used unbleached, but it can be bleached white. The process was introduced by Dahl in 1883–4. *See also* SODA PULP.

SULPHITE PULP. (*Papermaking*) Chemical wood pulp which has been prepared by submitting the wood fibres to the action of sulphurous acid and its acid salts (bisulphite of lime, magnesia, or soda) at high pressure and in closed vessels. The process was invented by B. C. and R. Tilghmann in 1863–6 and is usually used with coniferous woods. *See also* SODA PULP.

SUMMUM GENUS. The first, comprehensive class from which the division of a classification commences. The terminology of schedule construction, as used by Ranganathan is: *universe* (=*summum genus*) an aggregate of *entities* (things or ideas) under consideration which is *divided* by a succession or *train* of *characteristics* each of which gives rise to an *array* of classes. The *order* of a class is the number of characteristics used to divide it out of the universe; the *rank* of a class is its position in its array. A *chain* is a series of classes in successive subordination, each one being subordinate to the preceding one. *See also* INFIMA SPECIES, SUBALTERN GENERA.

SUNK BANDS. (*Binding*) Cords or bands (in old books, often of leather) which are placed in grooves sawn into the backs of sections of a book to give a smooth back or spine. The sewing of the sections passes round the bands. The opposite of RAISED BANDS (*q.v.*). Also called 'Sunk cords'.

SUPER. *See* MULL.

SUPER ROYAL. A sheet of printing paper measuring $20\frac{1}{2} \times 27\frac{1}{2}$ inches.

SUPER-CALENDER. A machine, separate from the paper-making machines, which consists of a stack of from five to sixteen rolls. Paper is passed through under pressure to be given a highly glazed finish; it is then known as 'Super-calendered'. *See also* CALENDERED PAPER.

SUPER-CALENDERED PAPER. Paper which is given an extra smooth, glossy surface by rolling between 'calenders' (metal rollers) in a super-calender machine.

SUPER-CASTER. An instrument for casting large sizes of type for hand-composition.

SUPERIMPOSED CODING. A system of coding which uses more than one code symbol per concept, the combination of code symbols being such that the number of random combinations is minimal.

'SUPERIMPOSITION' POLICY. *See* 'NO CONFLICT' POLICY.

SUPERINTENDENT OF BRANCHES. The liaison officer between the branch librarians of a large system and the chief librarian or his deputy. His duty is to make the units of the system smooth-working parts of a homogeneous whole.

SUPERINTENDENT OF THE READING ROOM. The librarian responsible for the service to readers in the reading room of a national, university or research library.

SUPERIOR FIGURES (LETTERS). Very small characters aligning with the top of the text type, usually as reference marks to footnotes or notes at the end of the chapter or text, or in a margin. They are cast on the mean line, and often on the same body as the type with which they appear. Also called 'Superiors,' 'Superscript'. *See also* INFERIOR CHARACTERS, MEAN LINE, REFERENCE MARKS.

SUPERORDINATE CLASS. (*Classification*) A class which is of more general extension or higher grade, or rank: a more general class. *See also* CO-ORDINATE CLASSES.

SUPERSCRIPT. (*Printing*) A small character aligning with the top of a full-size lower case character; superscripts are usually used as reference marks to footnotes or notes at the end of the chapter or text. Usually called 'Superior' characters. *See also* SUBSCRIPT, SUPERIOR FIGURES (LETTERS).

SUPPLEMENT. 1. Additional matter continuing, or adding new matter to that already published. It is usually issued separately. 2. An extra sheet, section, or number accompanying a normal issue of a newspaper or periodical. *See also* ADDENDUM.

SUPPLEMENTAL ESTIMATE. *See* ESTIMATES.

SUPPLEMENTARY PUBLICATION. *See* AUXILIARY PUBLICATION.

SUPPLEMENTARY TABLES. Additional tables, provided in the

fourteenth edition of Dewey's *Decimal Classification*, for extending the 'common subdivisions', of Viewpoints, and of Miscellaneous Signs of Relation.

SUPPLEMENTARY TICKET. A non-fiction ticket which is issued to students, teachers, the clergy and others in addition to the number usually allowed.

SUPPLIED TITLE. The title composed by the cataloguer to indicate the nature and scope of the monographic work under study (*IBM*).

SUPPOSED AUTHOR. One to whom is attributed by some authoritative source the authorship of a work published anonymously or of which the stated authorship is doubted. Also called 'Attributed author', 'Presumed author'. Such a book is catalogued under the name of the supposed author which phrase appears after the name to qualify it. The authority for the supposition is given in a note.

SUPPOSITITIOUS AUTHOR. One who is substituted for the genuine author with intent to defraud.

SUPPRESSED. 1. Withheld from publication or circulation by author, publisher, government, or ecclesiastical authority because of unreliability, inaccuracy or moral tone. 2. (*Bibliography*) Of a leaf which has been cancelled because of some inaccurate, imperfect, or objectionable feature.

supra (*Lat.* 'above'). Used in footnotes and sometimes in the text to refer to an item previously mentioned. *See also infra.*

SURFACE PAPER. *Synonymous with* COATED PAPER (*q.v.*).

SURFACE PRINTING. *Synonymous with* PLANOGRAPHIC PROCESS (*q.v.*).

SURFACE SIZING. The addition or resin or other materials to the surface of a sheet of paper or board to render it more resistant to liquids, especially writing ink. *See also* ENGINE-SIZING.

SURNAME. A family name which a person uses in conjunction with his personal names. He bears it in common with other members of a group who are related to him. It is used, often without his personal names, and sometimes in conjunction with a title of address, when referring to him outside the circle of his personal acquaintances. It is the name used as a heading for entries in a catalogue or bibliography.

SURNAME INDEXING. The allocation of symbols to surnames so that they may be arranged in order other than by strict alphabetization. *See also* SOUNDEX.

SURREY AND SUSSEX LIBRARIES IN CO-OPERATION. *See* SASLIC.

SURVEY. An account of some research, examination, or enquiry which has been done by a scientific or organized method.

SUSPENSION FILE. Loops of tough manila, the full width of a filing cabinet drawer, which are attached to, and suspended from, rigid metal or plastic bars which at their extreme ends rest on a cradle, or framework, contained in the drawer. Into these loops are placed files or wallets containing documents, papers, photographs, etc.

SUSPENSION SHELVING. Shelves affixed to, or between, shelf-ends having lugs which engage in slots in uprights fixed to the wall. No support other than the shelf end is provided at the front of the shelves. The shelf-ends are the full depth of the shelf and serve as book supports. Also called 'Bracket shelving'. *See also* CANTILEVER SHELVING.

SWASH LETTERS. Italic capitals and lower-case letters with tails and flourishes, as

B G N F A W P T Ro Ni

SWEDISH BINDING. *Synonymous with* CUT FLUSH (*q.v.*).

SWEDISH INSTITUTE FOR CHILDREN'S BOOKS. Opened in 1967; aims at acquiring literature which is unobtainable, or rarely found, in Swedish Libraries. It also serves as a documentary centre for children's books built up on an international basis; and to supply individuals and libraries with the information and material they need.

SWELLED RULE. *See* RULE.

SWINDON AREA ASSOCIATION OF LIBRARIES FOR INDUSTRY AND COMMERCE. *See* SAALIC.

SWINGING BOOKCASE. A form of compact book storage whereby two presses consisting of hinged three-foot tiers are placed one on each side of one fixed press. When the books on either side of the fixed press or on the inner sides of the two outside presses are to be consulted, the hinged tiers are swung out into the gangways. Also called 'Pivoted bookcase'.

SWUNG DASH. A curved dash ∼ similar to a TILDE (*q.v.*).

SYLLABIC NOTATION. A notation using the letters A–Z to produce pronounceable syllables, each of which signifies a CONCEPT. The three symbol letter notation is used in D. J. Foskett's London Education Classification, e.g. Jip = Assessment; Mob = Sciences; Ser = Further education. Such class marks are easy to say and remember. Also called PRONOUNCEABLE NOTATION (*q.v.*).

SYLLABIC WRITING. The middle stage in picture writing in which a symbol was used to represent each syllable or vowel when this constitutes a syllable in the spoken language; thus, a combination of signs representing a group of syllables conveys a spoken word. A syllabic form of writing is known as a syllabary. *See also* PHONETIC WRITING.

SYLLABICATION. *Synonymous with* SYLLABIFICATION (*q.v.*).

SYLLABIFICATION. The action or method of dividing words into syllables. Also called 'Syllabication'.

SYMBOL. A substitute or representation of characteristics, relationships, or transformations of ideas or things (*IBM*).

SYMPOSIUM. 1. A volume of the papers or addresses originally presented at a conference. 2. The conference itself. 3. A collection of articles specially written on a given theme.

SYNCHRONOUS. In user and citation studies, referring to changes that reflect the influence of age as shown in observations made on a single occasion. *See also* BIACHRONOUS.

SYNCOPISM. Applied to a pseudonym where dots take the place of certain letters. Such books are catalogued under their titles when the author's full name cannot be ascertained, with added entries under the leading initials of the syncopism. *See also* PSEUDONYM.

SYNDETIC. Having entries connected by cross references. In information retrieval, co-ordination of two or more related documents.

SYNDETIC CATALOGUE. A dictionary catalogue that connects entries by a scheme of cross-references to form a co-ordinated whole. References are made from broad subjects to those that are less broad, and from these to still more subordinate subjects, and sometimes *vice versa*.

SYNDETIC INDEX. An index in which relationships between headings are provided, e.g. by the indexing sequence (classified or other subject arrangements), the use of subheadings and cross-references.

SYNECDOCHE. A figure of speech in which a species is used for the whole genus (e.g. 'bread' for food in general) or the genus for a species. As applied by C. L. Bernier to information retrieval, the use of a GENERIC DESCRIPTOR (*q.v.*) to represent a set of included words.

SYNOPSIS. 1. A brief outline of the plot, setting, or important points of a play, book or serial. 2. A factual summary of an article or paper contributed to a learned journal, suitable for use as an abstract, published in accompaniment with the article, presumed to be prepared by the author of the article but in any case subjected to the same editorial scrutiny and correction which is given to the full article.

SYNOPTIC TABLE. A classification 'map' showing interconnections between terms.

SYNTACTICS. A theory dealing with the formal relations between signs or expressions and the formal properties of language, distinct from their meaning or interpreters.

SYNTAGMAS. *See* PARADIGMS.

SYNTAGMATICALLY ORIENTED LANGUAGE. A name sometimes used for the system of indexing in which terms are interconnected by relational symbols to express a complex concept, and known as SYNTOL (*q.v.*).

SYNTAX. Concerned with the relations between symbols without reference to their meanings. *See also* SEMANTICS.

SYNTHETIC CLASSIFICATION. *See* FACETED CLASSIFICATION.

SYNTHETIC INDEXING. *Synonymous with* CO-ORDINATE INDEXING (*q.v.*).

SYNTHETIC INDEXING LANGUAGE. A list of subject terms used as headings together with rules for the construction of headings for composite subjects. *See also* ENUMERATIVE INDEXING LANGUAGE.

SYNTOL. Abbreviation for Syntagmatic Organization Language, an artificial indexing and classification language adequate to represent written information and intended for manipulation by computing devices. It was devised by J. C. Gardin.

SYSTEM DESIGNER. One who is responsible for designing an information system. Also called a 'Systems analyst'.

SYSTEM MEDIA CENTRE. A centre provided by a school libraries system to provide supporting and supplementary services in individual schools in the system.

SYSTEMATIC AUXILIARY SCHEDULES. Twenty schedules provided in Bliss' *Bibliographic classification* to serve as tables of common subdivision. Only the first three – form divisions (*see* ANTERIOR NUMERICAL CLASSES), geographical subdivision, subdivision by language – are of general application throughout the scheme, the remainder being applicable to groups of classes, to single classes, or to sub-classes. Symbols from these schedules are added to those from the main tables of the classification which indicate subject matter. Auxiliary tables are also provided in the UNIVERSAL DECIMAL CLASSIFICATION (*q.v.*).

SYSTEMATIC BIBLIOGRAPHY. The enumeration and classification of books (*Besterman*). The assembling of bibliographical entries into logical and useful arrangements for study and reference.

SYSTEMATIC CATALOGUE. A classified catalogue. One in which the classes and subjects are arranged in a logical order according to some scheme of book classification.

SYSTEMATIC COLLATERAL SEARCH. An examination of entries

under headings which, in a scheme of classification, would be co-ordinate with, and stand next to, each of the headings covered in the HIERARCHICAL SEARCH (*q.v.*). *See also* ALPHABETIC COLLATERAL SEARCH, SUBSTITUTION GENERIC.

SYSTEMATIC FILE. *Synonymous with* CLASSIFIED FILE (*q.v.*).

SYSTEMATIC MNEMONICS. *See* MNEMONICS.

SYSTEMATIC SCHEDULES. *See* SYSTEMATIC AUXILIARY SCHEDULES.

SYSTEMS ANALYSIS. 1. A procedure, a systematic process which permits the judgement and experience of experts in numerous fields to be combined in order to yield results that transcend the contribution of any single discipline – *H. Borko*. 2. The examination of an activity, business, method, procedure or technique in order to determine the objective of the activity and the best way to attain it.

SYSTEMS AND PROCEDURES EXCHANGE CENTER. *See* ASSOCIATION OF RESEARCH LIBRARIES.

T-CARD CHARGING. Abbreviation for TRANSACTION CARD CHARGING (*q.v.*).

t.e.g. Abbreviation for top edge gilt. *See* GILT TOP.

T.L.S. *See* A.L.S.

TPI. Abbreviation for Title-page, Index. Used to refer to the separately published title-page and index to a volume of a serial which may often have to be separately ordered for insertion in a bound volume.

TRC. Acronym of the Technology Reports Centre of the (British) Department of Trade, a main source for providing scientific and technical reports. It is the Department's research and technical information centre, processing and making available for industry and research centres exploitable and unpublished research and development reports arising from U.K. Government programmes and those of overseas governments. Publishes *R & D Abstracts* (fortnightly).

T.S. Abbreviation for typescript and tub-sized. *See also* TUB-SIZING.

TTS. Abbreviation for TELETYPESETTING (*q.v.*).

TAB. (*Binding*) A small piece of paper, card, plastic or fabric attached to the outer edge of a card, or leaf of a book, and bearing one or more characters to serve as a guide or index.

TABBED. A GUIDE CARD (*q.v.*) which has tabs projecting from the upper edge. They are called 'three-, four- or five-tabbed' according to the portion of the card which projects. A 'three-tabbed' card is one, the tab of which is a third the length of the card.

TABLE. 1. An arrangement of written words, numbers or signs, or of combinations of them, in a series of separate lines or columns. 2. A synoptical statement or series of statements; a concise presentation of the details of a subject; a list of items. *Synonymous with* FILE 3 (*q.v.*).

TABLE BOOK.   1. An ancient writing book comprised of wax-covered tablets of metal, ivory or wood and fastened together at the back by rings or thongs of leather. The writing was done with a stylus. 2. An obsolete name for a note-book. 3. An elaborately decorated edition of a book, often covered in velvet or silk, for display on a drawing-room table. Popular in the nineteenth century.

TABLE OF CONTENTS.   *See* CONTENTS.

TABLE OF PRECEDENCE.   (*Classification*) A statement of the correct citation order under a subject that the schedules subdivide according to several characteristics.

TABLEDEX INDEX.   A co-ordinate book-form index developed by R. S. Ledley. Terms are arranged in tables with document numbers and associated term numbers in ascending number sequence (*IBM*). *See also* CO-ORDINATE INDEXING.

TABLET.   An ancient writing material made of clay (used when moist and afterwards baked), stone, lead, wood or ivory and covered with wax. Also called 'Tabula'. *Cum tabula* (*Lat.* 'with plates').

TABULAR CLASSIFICATION.   A classification or table consisting of several columns and several horizontal series, some of which may not be of equal numbers of terms. The terms need not recur as in cross-classifications. A tabular classification may be less regular and less complete than a cross-classification (*Bliss*). *See also* COLUMNAR, HORIZONTAL.

TABULAR WORK.   (*Printing*) Figures and other matter arranged vertically in columns, with or without rules.

TABULATED CODE.   In machine sorting as part of information retrieval, one that requires a code book or dictionary to provide code equivalents for source words and vice versa. Also called an 'Arbitrary code'. *See also* CODE.

TACHYGRAPHY.   A system of shorthand invented by Thomas Shelton and used by Samuel Pepys when writing his *Diary* (14th January 1660 – 31st May 1669).

TACK MARKS.   Small dots incorporated in imposing schemes for sheets printed by the WORK AND TURN (*q.v.*) method. One dot is used for the first side printed and two for the second.

TAG.   (*Information retrieval*) 1. A character or digit which attached to a record, or to a FIELD (*q.v.*) in a record, as a means of identification. 2. An identification label ('identifier') to signal to the computer what is coming next. 3. In a machine-readable record, one or more characters attached to a set of data that contains information about the set.

TAGGED (TAGGING). (*Cataloguing. Information retrieval*) 1. With Variable Field Coding (*see* FIXED FIELD CODING), the use of symbols to indicate what part of an entry is about to follow. 2. The attaching of characters or digits to a record, or to a field in a record, as a means of identification.

TAIL. The bottom or lower edge of a book. The term is applied both to the margin below the text and to the cover of the book.

TAIL. In typography, the lower portion of letter *g* and the projection on the *Q*.

TAIL EDGE. *Synonymous with* LOWER EDGE (*q.v.*).

TAIL FOLD. *See* BOLT.

TAIL MARGIN. The space below the bottom line of a page of type matter. Also called 'Lower margin'. *See also* MARGIN.

TAIL ORNAMENT. An ornament appearing at the foot of a page or the end of the matter occurring on it, especially at the end of a section, chapter or book. It is sometimes called a 'Tail piece'. *See also* HEAD ORNAMENT.

TAIL PIECE. *Synonymous with* TAIL ORNAMENT.

TAILBAND. A decorative band similar to a HEADBAND (*q.v.*) but placed at the tail of a book.

TAILCAP. The fold of leather at the foot of the spine of a book to protect the TAILBAND (*q.v.*).

TAILED LETTER. One which, appearing to be a digraph consisting of a letter and a full stop, gives the impression of being a letter with a horizontally tailed last stroke. *See also* SWASH LETTERS.

e m nt

TAKE. The amount of copy taken at one time by a compositor to set up in type. *See also* BREAK LINE, END A BREAK, END EVEN.

TAKE DOWN. (*Binding*) To take a book to pieces and reduce it to its original sections. *See also* PULLED.

TAKING OUT TURNS. Inserting the correct type character where the twin black footmarks (as ▌▐) on a galley proof indicate that the correct one was not available. *See also* TURNED SORT.

TALBOTYPE. *Synonymous with* CALOTYPE (*q.v.*).

TALIC. Abbreviation for Tyneside Association of Libraries for Industry and Commerce which was inaugurated in 1958; it is based on the Newcastle upon Tyne City Libraries' Commercial and Technical

Section. Its purpose is to co-ordinate library facilities on Tyneside in order to make information more readily available to industry and commerce, and especially to assist the smaller firms which have not the facilities to set up their own libraries. A union list of periodicals totalling 7,000 titles is maintained at Headquarters. No sub-scription is charged to members, and non-members may use the service.

TALKING BOOK. A book for the blind in the form of gramophone records, and played on a slowly revolving turntable. *See also* NTBL.

TALKING LIBRARY. *See* RADIO TALKING LIBRARY.

TALKING NEWSPAPERS. Cassettes containing news and short magazine articles; they are prepared locally and circulated amongst visually handicapped persons. First made early in 1974; within a year, thirty-five were being produced in the U.K. where there is a National Association of Talking Newspapers.

TALL COPY. A book that has lost nothing of its original height in binding.

TALLY. (*Information retrieval*) 1. The form of a record, or unit, on which may be made one or more entries. *See also* ENTRY 5, FILE 3. 2. Notched piece of wood used as a receipt for money or goods, both public and private, from the early Middle Ages until about the third decade of the nineteenth century.

TANN COLLECTION. A representative collection of children's books which is maintained by the Department of Education and Science, and is exhibited at teachers' courses and conferences.

TAPE. (*Data processing*) 1. A plastic strip coated or impregnated with magnetic or optically sensitive substances, used for data input, memory or output. 2. A paper or plastic strip with punches or other arbitrary signs representing alphabetic or numerical data and opera-tions (*IBM*).

TAPE MARK. (*Information retrieval*) A special configuration recorded on magnetic tape, to indicate the boundary between files and labels (*see* FILE and LABEL 5), and also between certain label groups.

TAPE READER. (*Information retrieval*) A device which senses infor-mation recorded on paper or magnetic tape.

TAPES. The pieces of tape to which the sections of a book are sewn, the ends being pasted to the boards or between the split boards which form the covers.

TAPE-SLIDE PRESENTATION. A co-ordinated and synchronized programme of transparencies and audiotape.

TARGET.   In microcopying, any document or chart containing identification information, coding or resolution test patterns.

TARGET LANGUAGE.   (*Information retrieval*) A language that is an output from a given automatic translation process. *See also* MACHINE TRANSLATION.

TARRED BROWN PAPER.   Wrapping paper consisting of one or more sheets of paper coated or impregnated with coal- or wood-tar or bitumen and so given some degree of waterproofing. *See also* UNION PAPER.

TAUBER REPORT.   A report, *Resources in Australian libraries*, written by Maurice F. Tauber, Melvil Dewey Professor of Library Service at Columbia University, New York, of a systematic survey of the total library resources of Australia. It was published in 1963.

TAXONOMY.   The science of classification. Also, the study of the names and naming of items in generic assemblies (*IBM*).

TAYLORISM.   The study of management and administration and the application of the results to the increase of production and economy. Named after Frederick W. Taylor who pioneered this field in the U.S.A.

TEACHER-LIBRARIAN.   A teacher who is also a school librarian. The Library Association, jointly with the School Library Association, sponsors examinations each year and awards a Certificate for Teacher-Librarians to successful candidates.

TEACHER'S BOOK.   An explanatory handbook issued with a series of textbooks or a single textbook for the use of teachers. It sometimes has a 'key' or answers to questions and problems.

TEAR SHEET.   A sheet of paper torn from a publication; when the item consists of more than one sheet, it is called a 'clipped article' or 'clipping'. *See also* CUTTING.

TECHNICAL ABSTRACT BULLETIN.   A periodical containing indicative and/or information abstracts of newly published or released technical literature. The abstracts are usually arranged in subject order, and alphabetical subject and/or author indexes are provided.

TECHNICAL INFORMATION CENTRE.   An organization for acquiring, processing and disseminating technical information. Such a centre usually has a library and a staff of scientists and engineers for extracting, evaluating and indexing technical literature.

TECHNICAL INFORMATION SYSTEM.   A network of information services providing facilities for the processing of information and data, and transmitting same to the enquirer.

TECHNICAL JOURNAL. A journal which is devoted to a particular branch of technology. Also called a 'Technical periodical'.

TECHNICAL LIBRARY. A library containing mostly books of a technical nature. When connected with a public library, it may be a section of the reference library, a separate department in the central building, or a separate building.

TECHNICAL PERIODICAL. Synonymous with TECHNICAL JOURNAL (q.v.).

TECHNICAL PROCESSES, DEPARTMENT OF. Synonymous with PROCESSING DEPARTMENT (q.v.).

TECHNICAL REPORT. A scientific paper, article, translation, probably recording the current position of scientific research and development, etc., whether security classified, unclassified or declassified.

TECHNICAL SERVICES. All the activities and processes concerned with obtaining, organizing and processing library material for use. (American.)

TECHNICAL SERVICES DEPARTMENT. A department of a library where the functions of book acquisition, cataloguing, classification and processing are carried out. Also called 'Technical services division'.

TECHNICAL STANDARDS FOR LIBRARY AUTOMATION. A committee of the Information Science and Automation Division of the American Library Association; it was formed in 1974 to serve as a clearinghouse for technical standards proposals with appropriate organizations such as the American National Standards Institute. Abbreviated TESLA.

TECHNILIB. A co-operatively owned centre providing technical services to public libraries in Victoria, Australia.

TECHNOLOGY REPORTS CENTRE (of the Department of Trade). See TRC.

TEES-SIDE, LIBRARY INFORMATION SERVICE FOR. See LIST.

TELEGRAPHIC ABSTRACT. 1. A special abbreviated style of abstract commonly considered suitable for machine input (*IBM*). See also ABSTRACT. 2. An essential part of the American Society of Metals (ASM) Documentation Service; it is made up of (1) significant words selected from the articles, (2) code symbols, called 'role indicators' which fit the selected words into context, and (3) punctuation symbols which separate and group the words and role indicators into various units in a somewhat similar way to conventional punctuation. A telegraphic abstract is prepared in addition to a conventional abstract and is an 'index' to be read, ultimately, by a machine.

TELEMARC. A cataloguing 'package' produced by Telecomputing, of Oxford. TeleMarc is an on-line library acquisitions and cataloguing system providing MARC (*q.v.*) handling facilities; it is able to provide a complete on-line transaction processing system into which further application routines may be added. A catalogue supplement consisting of the 1974 acquisitions into the Kent County public libraries was completed in six weeks and provides microfilm display units at all the major public lending libraries in the county.

TELEREFERENCE. A means of consulting catalogues from a remote location; it consists of a closed-circuit television system for viewing the catalogue, a relay for finding the portion of the catalogue to be examined, and mechanical equipment for moving the catalogue cards or pages.

TELESCOPED NOTATION. (*Classification*) The assignment of more than one facet to a single notation sequence, in an otherwise expressive notation.

TELETYPESETTING. The process of setting type with a teletype-setter apparatus, which automatically operates a keyboard slugcasting machine consisting essentially of a separate keyboard that perforates a tape which is fed into an attachment to the slug-casting machine, or into a sender that transmits electrical impulses telegraphically to any number of re-perforators, with the perforated tape causing the slug-casting machine to set type by automatic operation of the keyboard. Abbreviated TTS.

TELONISM. Terminal letters of an author's name used as a pseudonym, as N.S. (John Austis). *See also* TITLONYM.

TEL-STOR. Trade name for a telephone answering machine which records telephone conversations on tape, recording a conversation after the telephone has been replaced (if desirable), or acting as a separate dictating machine. Somewhat similar machines are ANSAPHONE and RECORDACALL (*qq.v.*).

TEMPORARY BRANCH. A service of books for home-reading provided in temporary quarters until it is determined whether there is sufficient demand to justify the erection of a permanent building, until the best site for a permanent building has been determined, or until authorization or finances permit the erection of a permanent building.

TEMPORARY CARD. A card, bearing brief particulars of a book, which is inserted in a catalogue in place of the usual card during its temporary removal for emendation. Also called 'Temporary slip'.

TEMPORARY SLIP.   *Synonymous with* TEMPORARY CARD (*q.v.*).

TERM.   (*Information retrieval*) In an index, the subject heading or DESCRIPTOR (*q.v.*) (*IBM*). *See also* FEATURE CARD, HEADING 2, ITEM. (*Indexing*) A heading consisting of the word(s) or symbol(s) selected from, or based on, an item in the text of a document, and used as an indexing unit, identifying an item in a classification scheme, or catalogue, or any form of information retrieval. *See also* HEADING 2, INDIRECT SUBJECT HEADING, MIXED SUBJECT HEADING. Also (in patents literature) a word, phrase or sentence (which is the officially recommended form of international systems of indexing patents material) which is descriptive of the subject-matter content, or part of the subject-matter content, of a document. *See also* AUTHORITY LIST 1, CONTROLLED TERM LIST, OPEN-ENDED TERM LIST.

TERM CARD.   *Synonymous with* ASPECT CARD, FEATURE CARD (*qq.v.*).

TERM ENTRY.   In information retrieval, the 'inverted' form of entry used by UNITERM (*q.v.*), peephole card, and other co-ordinate indexes, in which a TALLY (*q.v.*) is made and filed under a term chosen to describe a characteristic of information kept by the library or information centre, and on which are recorded symbols representing all the documents possessing this characteristic. Also called 'Aspect system'. *See also* ITEM ENTRY.

TERM INDEXING.   Choosing words used in the text as headings of the index to the text. *See also* CONCEPT INDEXING.

TERM PAPER.   An undergraduate-level research paper. It may be a report (a) which relates facts for the purpose of informing the reader or of showing progress over a period of time, or (b) based on the student's investigations, which analyses an event, a situation, or a period. It may also be a thesis (i.e. a dissertation presented by a candidate for an academic degree, usually the M.A. or M.S. degree) (a) which states and maintains by argument a position or a proposition, or (b) which presents and evaluates facts for the purpose of persuading or recommending (American).

TERMATREX SYSTEM.   A DATA PROCESSING (*q.v.*) system which uses the inverted mode, information retrieval being achieved by placing characteristic cards over a light source to reveal light spots which indicate the characteristics possessed. This is a commercial form of PEEK-A-BOO (*q.v.*) cards: each card represents an index unit (a piece of information) and has room for 10,000 punches, the position of each indicating a document number that has as one of its assigned index units the concept represented by the card. The Termatrex cards can be used with the 'Minimatrix' system; each of the record cards is photographed on film strip, the size of the record being reduced to $\frac{1}{2} \times \frac{1}{2}$ inch, and consulted in the Visual Minimatrex Recorder.

TERMINAL. (*Information retrieval*) Any physical point at which data may be input to, or output from, a data communications or computer system.

TERMINAL DIGIT POSTING. Arranging and recording serial numbers of documents on the basis of the last digit of the serial number.

TERMS. The headings – words or combinations of words – used in a scheme of classification for classes, divisions, subdivisions, or sections. The *names* of any subjects that may be included in the classification.

TERNION. Three sheets folded together in folio.

TERRAIN MODEL. *Synonymous with* RELIEF MODEL (*q.v.*).

TERRAPIN RESKA TRAVEL AWARD. First introduced in 1972, these annual awards are available only to students at the College of Librarianship Wales; they are designed to develop and further students' interest and knowledge of library systems, especially in Scandinavia.

TEST. The *Thesaurus of engineering and scientific terms* prepared and issued by the Engineer Joint Council. It is a controlled list of index terms, and uses five cross-reference terms: USE = use preferred term; UF = used for; BT = Broader Term; NT = Narrower Term; RT = Related Term.

TEST QUESTION. (*Information retrieval*) A 'proving' question, based on a document known to be in the collection, for testing the retrieval efficiency of a system.

TETRAEVANGELIUM. A book containing the four Gospels.

TETRALOGY. A set of four related dramatic or literary compositions, said especially of three Greek tragedies and a satyric comedy.

TEXT. 1. The body of a work following the PRELIMINARIES (*q.v.*). 2. The type matter on a page as distinct from the illustrations. 3. In the conservation of documents, that part of a sheet of paper or membrane of a document covered by writing, printing or drawing.

TEXT AREA. *Synonymous with* TYPE AREA (*q.v.*).

TEXT HAND. A style of writing employed for books, treatises and the headings of business documents from about 1100 to 1500.

TEXT TITLE. *Synonymous with* CAPTION TITLE (*q.v.*).

TEXT TYPE. Type used for setting the text of a book or periodical, or other large amounts of copy. It is seldom larger than 14 point.

TEXTBOOK. A book written specifically for use by those studying for an examination in any particular subject.

TEXTILE BINDING. An ornate style of binding using fabrics. It was popular in France and England during the Renaissance. Coloured satin and velvet, often embellished with many-coloured silk embroidery and gold and silver threads, was frequently used.

TEXTUAL BIBLIOGRAPHY. The study and comparison of texts and their transmission through different printings and editions.

TEXTUAL MANUSCRIPT. *See* LITERARY MANUSCRIPT.

TEXTUAL RECORDS. (*Archives*) Manuscript or typescript documents as distinct from cartographic, audiovisual, and machine-readable archives.

TEXTURA. *See* GOTHIC, or BLACK LETTER, TYPE.

THACKER SCHOLARSHIP, FRANCIS J. *See* WEST MIDLAND BRANCH.

THAMES BOARD. A British-made board much used in EDITION BINDING (*q.v.*). Each side is covered with brown kraft paper to give equal tension, and thus rigidity.

THEATRE LIBRARY ASSOCIATION. Founded in the U.S.A. in 1937 to further the interests of collecting, preserving and using theatre material (books, photographs, playbills, etc.) in libraries, museums and private collections. Publishes *Broadside* (irreg. to membs.).

THEATRE LIBRARY ASSOCIATION AWARD. Offered by the (U.S.) TLA for an outstanding book in the field of recorded performance (television, movies, etc.). It was first offered in 1975, and is in addition to the George Freedley Memorial Award, also offered by the Association.

THEMATIC CATALOGUE. One containing a list of one or more composers' works and the opening themes or passages of each composition, or for each section of lengthy musical compositions. Entries are usually arranged in chronological order, or by categories.

THEME. *Synonymous with* TOPIC (*q.v.*).

THEORY Y. A term often used in personnel management to denote a liberalized type of administrative philosophy based on a belief that employees are responsible workers more likely to be influenced by their own internal motivations than by the external threats and inducement of management. The possible adaptations of this theory to library operations are discussed by Donald J. Morton in *College & Research Libraries* 36 (4) July 1975 pp. 302–7.

THERMAL DIAZO PROCESS. A DIAZOTYPE PROCESS (*q.v.*) in which heat is used to release the neutralizing alkaline chemicals contained in the base with the acidic stabilizers.

THERMAL PROCESS. A process for copying documents without the use of liquid chemicals. Heat sensitive paper is used to make copies from an original having carbon or metallic writing or printing inks; some materials will not reproduce vegetable inks. THERMOFAX (*q.v.*) and Eichner Dry Copy are both thermal processes. Also called 'Heat copying', 'Thermography'. *See also* DIRECT CONTACT COPYING.

THERMIC COPYING. A documentary reproduction process which uses thermo-sensitive coatings on the base material. A copy made by this method may be called a 'Thermic copy'. *Synonymous with* THERMOGRAPHY. *See also* THERMAL PROCESS.

THERMOFAX. Trade name for a machine and method of copying documents; it is manufactured by the Minnesota Mining and Manufacturing Company. The method consists of passing a controlled beam of infra-red light across a sheet of heat-sensitive paper which is in contact with the document to be copied. The heat-sensitive material on the Thermofax paper is a non-transparent material which melts between 60° and 115°C. and then becomes transparent, revealing the colour of an infra-red transmitting material underneath. The print or other matter which is being copied converts the rays into heat, burns through the non-transparent material, exposes the colour of the material underneath and so produces a copy of the original.

THERMOGRAPHIC COPY. A copy of a document made by a THERMAL PROCESS (*q.v.*), or thermography. Also called 'Thermic copy'.

THERMOGRAPHY. 1. Any printing process which involves the use of heat; specifically that method of printing from ordinary type or plates on an ordinary press and in which a special ink is used, the type impression being sprinkled while still wet with a special powder and then subjected to a heating process which causes the particles to adhere to the printed surface and fuse together to give the printing a raised effect. Also called 'Raised-letter printing', 'Imitation embossing' and 'Virkotype process'. 2. The THERMAL PROCESS (*q.v.*) of document copying. *See also* DIRECT CONTACT COPYING.

THERMOPLASTIC BINDING. A method of binding a book without sewing. The folds are cut off, the edges roughened and glued and the covers stuck on.

THERMOPLASTIC PROCESS. A microfilming process whereby an electrostatic image is made to produce a permanent deformation of a plastic film layer. Recording can be made by optical projection, electron beams, or computer print-out devices. Thermoplastic systems also have a higher capacity than magnetic tape for carrying coded information for use with computers.

THESAURI (*Pl.*). *See* THESAURUS.

THESAUROFACET.   A faceted classification with a fully structural thesaurus as index. It was developed from the English Electric Company's faceted classification for engineering.

THESAURUS.   1. Literally, a storehouse, or treasury, of knowledge. A term which is best known through its use in the title *Thesaurus of English words and phrases* by P. M. Roget, first published in 1852 and frequently revised. 2. A lexicon, more especially where words are grouped by ideas; a grouping or classification of synonyms or near synonyms; a set of equivalence classes of terminology (*IBM*). 3. A compilation of groups of words, consisting of the links between words used in documents and words used as DESCRIPTORS (*q.v.*), prepared for consultation by a machine used in information retrieval. They display relations within the vocabulary based on semantics, not on orthography. A number of thesauri of the most commonly used terms in various fields have been published in order to achieve a unity of indexing terminology in their respective fields. 4. A thesaurus may be defined either in terms of its function or of its structure. In terms of function, it is a terminological control device used in translating from the natural language of documents . . . into a more constrained system language (documentation language, information language). In terms of structure, a thesaurus is a controlled and dynamic vocabulary of semantically and generically related terms which covers a specific domain of knowledge. 5. A list of descriptors. Also called 'Dictionary' or 'Words authority file'.

THESIS.   *Synonymous with* DISSERTATION (*q.v.*).

THICK SPACE.   (*Printing*) A space whose width is one-third of its own body.

THICKNESS COPY.   *Synonymous with* DUMMY (*q.v.*).

THIN PAPER.   Sensitized photographic paper between 0·0038 and 0·0043 inches inclusive. *See also* PHOTOGRAPHIC PAPERS.

THIN SPACE.   (*Printing*) A space whose width is one-fifth of its own body.

THIRD GENERATION MICROFILM.   *Synonymous with* SECOND REPRODUCTION MICROFILM (*q.v.*). *See also* GENERATION.

THIRD INDENTION.   The twelfth typewriter space from the left edge of a card, and the second space from the second or inner vertical line on a ruled card. The distance from the left-hand edge of a catalogue card at which certain parts of the description begin or continue. It is generally as far to the right of the SECOND INDENTION (*q.v.*) as this is from the FIRST INDENTION (*q.v.*). *See also* INDENTION.

THIRTY-SIXMO (36mo).   A sheet of paper folded to form thirty-six leaves, making seventy-two pages. Also called 'Trigesimo-sexto'.

THIRTY-TWOMO (32mo).   A sheet of paper folded five times to form a section of thirty-two leaves (sixty-four pages) each leaf being one thirty-second of the sheet. Also called 'Trigesimo-secundo'.

THOROUGH-BASS.   *Synonymous with* FIGURED-BASS (*q.v.*).

THREAD STITCHED.   A booklet that is fastened with thread through the section fold. *See also* SEWING, SIDE-STITCH, WIRE STITCHED.

THREE-COLOUR PROCESS.   Printing by photo-mechanical colour separation in half-tone, which will reproduce colour in the copy in three printings of yellow, red and blue. *See also* TWO-COLOUR PROCESS, TWO-COLOUR REPRODUCTION.

THREE-DECKER.   A novel published in three volumes during the latter half of the nineteenth century and sold at $1\frac{1}{2}$ guineas.

THREE DOTS.   Used on the type BASE LINE (*q.v.*) thus . . . in quoted text, or a catalogue entry, to indicate that some part of the original has been omitted. Called 'Omission marks'.

THREE-LAYER PAPER.   *See* FURNISH LAYER.

THREE NUMBER AUTHOR TABLE.   A table initiated by G. C. Makkar whereby numbers are allocated consecutively to sequences of not more than four letters of authors' names arranged alphabetically. The numbers serve to arrange books (which have been classified) or records of books alphabetically by authors' names. The table begins

	A	1
	Aa	11
	Aaa	111
	Aaaa	112
	Aaab	113
and continues to	Aaaz	139
	Aab	141
	Aaba	142
	Aabb	143
and continues to	Aac	171
	Aaca	172
	Aacb	173 and so on to
	Aazz	969
and then	Ab	11
	Aba	111
	Abaa	112
	Abab	113

The complete table was published for letter A in 1974 by Today &

Tomorrow's Printers and Publishers, New Delhi. The first two letters of the name are used before the number for the appropriate four letters, e.g. Ai 562 is for Ainsworth, the Table entry being Ains 562. The same numbers are used for the same sequence of letters; in this way the published tables can be used for any initial letter of a name; e.g. Binstead is Bi 562, Dinsdale is Di 562.

THREE-QUARTER BINDING.   *See* QUARTER BINDING.

THREE-QUARTER LEATHER.   A book bound similarly to one in HALF LEATHER (*q.v.*), but with the leather of the spine projecting across a third of the sides. *See also* LEATHER BOUND, QUARTER LEATHER.

THRILLER.   A novel of a sensational character, usually dealing with crime and criminals.

THROW OUT.   Maps, tables, or diagrams likely to be much consulted during the reading of a book, are sometimes 'thrown out' by the binder. This is done by making the 'guard' the size of the page, or printing the map on extra large paper, and pasting it at the end of a book or beyond the text which refers to it, so that the whole of the map, etc., when opened out, may remain in view during reading.

THUMB BOOK.   *Synonymous with* BIBELOT (*q.v.*).

THUMB INDEX.   A series of rounded notches cut into the fore-edges of a book, with or without tabs let in and bearing in progressive order from top to bottom the letters or words showing the arrangement. Usually provided for Bibles and dictionaries.

TICKLER SYSTEM.   Any method of recording or filing notes, enquiries, loans, material, publications 'in progress', etc., to ensure follow-up on a particular future date.

TIED DOWN.   (*Binding*) Where the fillets which flank the bands of the spine are carried on to meet at a point near the hinge.

TIED LETTER.   *Synonymous with* LIGATURE (*q.v.*).

TIED UP.   Said of type-matter that has been made up into pages and tied up with page-cord to secure it until imposition.

TIER.   A set of shelves one above another between two uprights and reaching from the floor to the top of the shelving: a section of a PRESS (*q.v.*). *See also* BOOK PRESS, BOOK STACK, BOOKCASE, DOUBLE-FACED SHELF, DOUBLE-SIDED STACK, PRESS.

TIER GUIDE.   A guide to the contents of a TIER (*q.v.*).

TIES.   1. Silk, leather, cord, tape, ribbon or other slips attached, usually in pairs, to the outer edges of boards of books for a decorative purpose, or to prevent sagging by holding the covers together. 2. Terminations to tooled lines on each side of projecting bands on the spine of a bound book and carried over on to the covers to form ornamental features.

TIGHE REPORT. A report, prepared largely by the late Mr. F. C. Tighe and based on a national survey of the conditions of service of assistant librarians in British public libraries. The *Recommendations on welfare and working conditions of public library staffs*, based on this report, were approved by the Council of the Association of Assistant Librarians and adopted by the Council of the Library Association in May 1953.

TIGHT BACK. A binding in which the cover of leather or other material is pasted or glued to the spine of the book, so that it does not become hollow when open. The pages do not lie flat when the book is open unless the paper used is thin and not stiff, as e.g. India paper. This is therefore a less satisfactory form of binding than either Flexible or Hollow. Also called 'Fast back', 'Stiff back'. *See also* FLEXIBLE SEWING, HOLLOW BACK.

TIGHT JOINT. *Synonymous with* CLOSED JOINT (*q.v.*).

TILDE. (*Printing*) An accent in the form of a wavy line as used over letters in Spanish and Portuguese: ñ; õ. Also used in mathematics.

TILL-FORBID ORDER. *Synonymous with* STANDING ORDER (*q.v.*).

TILTED SHELVES. The bottom or lower two or three shelves of a bookcase which are arranged in a sloping position to render the examination of titles easier.

TIME LAPSE CINEMATOGRAPH FILM. Cinematograph film exposed frame by frame over a considerable time interval in order to record motion or growth in an extremely accelerated form.

TIME NUMBERS. A series of numbers or letters designed to facilitate the arrangement of books in chronological instead of author or alphabetical order. *See also* BISCOE TIME NUMBERS, MERRILL ALPHABETING NUMBERS.

TIME-SCHEDULE. *See* TIME-SHEET.

TIME-SHARING. (*Information retrieval*) Being able to use a device for more than one purpose in the same time period. This process may be accomplished by interspersing different operations.

TIME-SHEET. A schedule showing the exact hours each day that each assistant is scheduled to be on duty. Also called 'Time-schedule'.

TIMES – EUROPA. A new type, designed by Walter Tracy for *The Times*, largely to replace TIMES NEW ROMAN (*q.v.*) which had been in use for forty years. Tracy was manager of the typographic department of the Linotype Co. and had designed five newspaper text faces: Jubilee (1954); Adsans (1958) a $4\frac{3}{4}$ pt. sans-serif face; Maximus; Linotype Modern (1961). It was first used by *The Times* on 9th October 1972.

TIMES NEW ROMAN. A type face designed under the direction of Stanley Morison by the Monotype Corporation for the *Times* newspaper in 1932 and later extensively used in book work. Usually called 'Times Roman'. For a specimen alphabet, *see* TYPE FACE.

TINT. (*Printing*) 1. A ready-made dotted, hachured or other pattern, available in various densities, which can be applied by a draughtsman, blockmaker or printer to an illustration in order to give an impression of grey to a line drawing. Usually called 'Mechanical tint'. 2. A solid panel in a second colour.

TIPPED IN. A single leaf, errata slip or illustration, inserted in a book at the inner edge with a narrow edge of paste against the following page.

TIPPING MACHINE. A bookbinding machine for the gluing of single plates and end-papers on to folded sheets or sewn sections. Some models also glue paper covers on to the folded and sewn sections.

TIPS. Very thin millboards used for book-binding.

TISSUE-PAPERS. Sheets of superfine thin paper placed in front of illustrations to protect them from set-off while the ink is fresh. These are often removed after the ink has dried, but sometimes they are to be found tipped-in, and they frequently bear a typographical description of the illustration.

TISSUED PLATE. An illustration in a book which has a thin tissue placed between it (either loose or pasted to the inner margin) and the text page to protect it from SET-OFF (*q.v.*). Sometimes the tissue bears the caption relating to the illustration or an appropriate quotation. *See also* INTERLEAF.

TITHE DOCUMENTS. Documents relating to tithes. The Tithe Act, 1936, as amended, provides that the Master of the Rolls may direct that sealed copies of tithe documents shall be transferred to the Public Record Office or to any public library or museum or historical or antiquarian society willing to receive them. On the transfer of such documents the governing body of the library, museum or society assumes responsibility for their proper preservation. The Tithe (Copies of Instruments of Apportionment) Rules were made in 1946 (S.R. & O., 1946, No. 2091) to implement the provisions of the Act.

TITLE. The word or words by which an intellectual work is designated on its title-page, and distinguished from any other work. In its fuller sense, it includes any sub-title, alternative title, or associated descriptive matter, but excludes the name of the author and/or editor, translator, etc. (unless the name forms a grammatically inseparable part of the title) and the edition, but not the imprint. In statistical records, the name of a document exclusive of any alternative title, subtitle or other associated descriptive matter on the title, which is catalogued separately. Thus a periodical which suffers a change of title is counted once under each; each monograph with an individual title is counted as well as any series title to which it belongs. *See also* BACK TITLE, BINDER'S TITLE, COLLECTIVE TITLE, COVER TITLE, SHORT TITLE, SPINE TITLE.

TITLE-A-LINE CATALOGUE. A catalogue in which the entries occupy only a single line of type.

TITLE-A-LINE INDEX. *See* LINE-BY-LINE INDEX.

TITLE ANALYTIC. *See* ANALYTICAL ENTRY.

TITLE AREA. (*Reprography*) The portion of a MICROFICHE (*q.v.*) which is specifically allotted for title and other bibliographical information.

TITLE BACKING. The material, or treatment, applied to the back of the title area (i.e. the area extending the full width of the film and above the micro-images) of a microfiche so that the title can be more easily read by reflected light. It is usually applied to a distribution MICROFICHE (*q.v.*) not intended to be used for the reproduction of additional microfiches.

TITLE CARD. A catalogue card bearing an entry under the title of a work.

TITLE CATALOGUE. A catalogue consisting only of title entries.

TITLE-CUT. *Synonymous with* FRAMED-CUT (*q.v.*).

TITLE ENTRY. A record in a catalogue, bibliography or index, usually under the first word of a title not an article. In practice such entries are limited to unusual or striking titles which are likely to be remembered, and are added entries, unless the authorship is unknown in which case the title entry may be the main entry.

TITLE INDENTION. *Synonymous with* SECOND INDENTION (*q.v.*).

TITLE INDEX. *Synonymous with* Key-word-in-context, or KWIC (*q.v.*) index.

TITLE LEAF. The leaf at the beginning of a book, the recto of which is the title-page. The verso usually bears bibliographical details of printer, copyright date, the ISBN (*q.v.*), etc. and any earlier editions. The BS 4719: 1971 *Title leaves of a book* defines title leaves as 'The initial printed leaves of a book. They normally consist of two leaves, the half-title leaf followed by the title leaf, but there may be only one leaf or more than two title leaves.' This BS is based on ISO Recommendation R 1086 *Title leaves of a book*, and lists fifteen items of bibliographical and other information which should be given on the title leaves. It incorporates recommendations for the dating of books which constituted Part 2 of BS 1413: 1947 *Book sizes and dating of books* (now superseded).

TITLE LIST.   A periodical publication in which important and relevant articles are selected from periodicals and listed by title and grouped in subject order.

TITLE OF HONOUR.   A title which denotes superior rank or station, or special distinction of any kind.

TITLE-PAGE.   Usually the recto of the second leaf which gives the title in full, sub-title (if any), author's name in full together with particulars of qualifications, degrees, etc., edition, publisher's name and address, and date of publication. The verso may give particulars of edition, printer's name and sometimes his address, binder's name, details of type and paper used in making the book, owner of copyright, and in the case of American books the Library of Congress catalogue card number. If there is more than one page giving particulars of the title, the title-page is that which gives the fullest information. The information which should be given on the title leaves of a book is given in BS 4719: 1971 *Title leaves of a book* and on the title page of printed music, in BS 4754: 1971 *The presentation of bibliographical information in printed music. See also* TITLE LEAF. The definition in *Anglo-American cataloguing code: British Text. Chapter 6 revised* provides that if no page bears 'the full title proper, another part of the publication bearing the full title proper is treated as the title-page. If the elements normally presented on the title-page are divided without repetition between two facing pages, the two pages together are regarded as the title-page'. *See also* DOUBLE TITLE-PAGE, ENGRAVED TITLE-PAGE, SECOND HALF-TITLE, SECTION TITLE, TITLE LEAF.

TITLE-PAGE BORDER.   A frame, at first a woodcut, and later made of heavy type ornaments, surrounding the matter on the title-page.

TITLE-PAGE TITLE.   The title of a book as it appears on the title-page. It is the authority for the correct reference to the book; other versions of the title as given on the spine, cover, half-title, top of the pages or jacket may vary slightly.

TITLE PIECE.   A leather label, sometimes coloured, pasted on the back of a binding, and bearing the title of the book.

TITLE PROPER.   The title appearing on the title-page, or elsewhere in a publication which does not possess a title-page, but which is obviously the chief title. It is the chief title of a publication and includes any ALTERNATIVE TITLE (*q.v.*) but excludes parallel titles and any other title.

TITLE SHEET. The first printed sheet of a book containing the title-page and other preliminary matter.

TITLE SIGNATURE. The title (often abbreviated to initial letters) placed on the signature line of signed pages to prevent the binder mixing up the sheets of various books. Also called 'Direction line'. *See also* SIGNATURE AND CATCHWORD LINE.

TITLE SPACE. The area specifically allotted on a microfiche or microcard for title information. *See also* TITLE BACKING.

TITLE STRIP. Wording at the beginning of a FILM STRIP (*q.v.*) or other sequence of microcopy frames giving the title or indicating their contents.

TITLE WRAP-AROUND. A feature of the KWIC (*q.v.*) index whereby unused space is filled by allowing the remainder of the imprinted title at the end of the type-line to appear at the beginning of the same line, providing space is available there. Also called 'Title recirculation', 'Title snap-back'.

TITLING. Capital letters of modern Roman type which are cast 'full face' on the BODY (*q.v.*); there are thus no BEARD (*q.v.*) or LOWER CASE letters (*q.v.*). They are used for headlines, titles, jackets, or posters.

TITLONYM. A quality or title used as a pseudonym, as 'A Barrister'. If the author's name cannot be determined, such books are catalogued as if they were anonymous, entry being made under the title. An added entry is made under the titlonym. *See also* TELONISM.

TOGGLE PRESS. The Albion press which was introduced in 1823 and allowed the platen to be lowered and given great pressure by means of a toggle-jointed lever instead of the screw method. A toggle-jointed lever is one with an elbow-shaped joint with two arms known as the chill and the wedge. When the joint is straightened so that chill and wedge form a straight line, great endwise pressure is produced.

TOKEN CHARGING. A system of issuing books whereby the borrower on entering the lending department of a library is given a token which he exchanges for a book as he leaves. It was first introduced at the Westminster Public Libraries in 1954.

TOME. A volume, or book, especially a heavy one.

TOMLINSON AWARD, NORMAN. Made first in 1969, in recognition of the work Mr. Tomlinson has done for the London and Home Counties Branch of the Library Association in connection with the Portway Reprints since 1963. It is intended to help personal research into practical problems which are likely to result in improved library services, over a wide area, either for readers or for staffs. Chartered librarians who have had a minimum of seven years' experience after their election to the Register are eligible, and the Award is confined to those thus qualified who are, or who have been previously personal members of the London and Home Counties Branch.

TONKS FITTINGS. The most generally used form of adjustable shelving fittings. They consist of slotted strips of metal into which small studs are placed to support book shelves (four for each shelf). Two strips are placed on one side of each upright, towards the back and front edges, so that each shelf rests on the four studs placed at the same level, one in each strip. These fittings are made by Tonks (Birmingham) Ltd.

TOOL PHASE. In classification, where one discipline is used to assist the investigation of another, the document is classified under the thing investigated, not under the tool of investigation. It is one of Ranganathan's three main 'phase relations', the other two are BIAS PHASE and INFLUENCE PHASE (qq.v.).

TOOLED EDGES. The edges of a book which have been impressed with designs. *See also* EDGES.

TOOLING. The impressing of designs – by means of finishing tools such as rolls – into a leather or cloth binding. The tools used may be 'embossed' in which case there is modelling on the top surface (i.e. the bottom of its impression), 'outline', 'shaded' or 'azured'. When this is done through gold leaf it is called 'gold tooling', when neither leaf nor pigment is used it is called 'blind tooling'. When the entire cover design is a single piece, it is called a 'stamp'. Gold tooling is believed to have been introduced by Thomas Berthelet, royal binder to Henry VIII. The tools used may be 'embossed' in which case there is modelling on the top surface, 'outline', 'shaded' or 'azured'. *See also* AZURE TOOLING, BLOCK 3, EDGE-ROLLED.

TOP EDGES GILT. The top edges of a book cut smooth and gilded. Abbreviated 't.e.g.' Also called 'Gilt top'.

TOP MARGIN. The space between the top line of type of a book or periodical, and the edge of the page. *See also* MARGIN.

TOP SIDE. *Synonymous with* FELT SIDE (q.v.).

TOPIC. In co-ordinate indexing, a group of terms describing a given subject. Also called 'Information item' and 'Theme'.

TOPIC GUIDE. A guide to a specific subject; it is usually a narrow block of wood or piece of cardboard bearing the subject and class number, placed on the shelf at the beginning of the books on the subject. Also called 'Subject guide'.

TOPICAL BIBLIOGRAPHY. A subject bibliography, consisting of

short lists of books or references placed at the ends of chapters.

TOPOGRAPHICAL CATALOGUE. A catalogue of books relating to places.

TOPOGRAPHICAL INDEX. An index of places arranged in alphabetical order.

TOPOGRAPHICAL MAP. One which shows physical or natural features of an area.

TORY STYLE. A style of binding executed in the sixteenth century for Geoffroy Tory the famous French printer, wood-engraver and designer. Distinguished by arabesque panels, borders and ornaments.

TOWN PLAN. A map of a town showing the organized arrangement of streets, open spaces, etc. *See also* PLAT.

TOXLINE DATA BANK. A rapid on-line data retrieval service provided by the NATIONAL LIBRARY OF MEDICINE (*q.v.*) to supply the needs of environmental and health scientists for information and data in the field of toxicology. It provides direct access to an extensive collection of citations, extracts, technical reports and data.

TOY LIBRARY. A collection of toys available on loan. The first, experimental, toy library, was organized by the National Association of Toy Libraries, a charity, and is provided at the Whitehawk Branch Library, Brighton, a library in the East Sussex Libraries system. Opened in December, 1973, it has been successful, and it is anticipated that the East Sussex Libraries will be responsible for operating it after the three-year pilot project is completed. A thousand toys have been obtained by purchase or gift, and are arranged on open shelves, grouped according to whether they are games, puzzles, puppets, dolls or educational. Members range in age from nine months to fifteen years. The Library is open daily and is staffed by a whole-time supervisor (whose salary is paid by the Association) and volunteers. Toys are issued for a week at a time. A number of similar toy libraries have since been opened in other towns.

Tr. (trans.). Abbreviation for Transactions (*q.v.*), translated, TRANSLATION (*q.v.*), TRANSLATOR (*q.v.*).

TRACING. An indication on the front or back of a main entry catalogue card showing under what additional headings added entries appear. Also, the record (on the main entry card, or on an authority card) of all the related references made. Specially important in a dictionary catalogue in order to ensure that in case of change, correction or removal, all the cards referring to a given book may be traced and the change applied to all of them. In co-ordinate indexing, a list of the descriptors, Uniterms, etc., applied to a specific document.

TRACING PAPER. Paper treated with a coating of Canada balsam in turpentine, or a solution of castor oil or linseed oil in alcohol. The papers chosen for this treatment must have excellent transparency, high tearing strength, and be resistant to erasure; they must contain no loading and be engine-sized. Tracing papers cockle readily on absorbing moisture from the atmosphere and must therefore be wrapped in waxed or other waterproof paper.

TRACT. 1. A pamphlet containing a short propagandist discourse, especially on a religious, political or social subject. 2. A pamphlet printed on a single sheet and imposed in pages.

TRADE BIBLIOGRAPHY. *See* BIBLIOGRAPHY 1, TRADE CATALOGUE 1.

TRADE BINDING. 1. The binding in which a publisher issues a book. Also called 'Publisher's binding'. 2. Plain calf or sheep bindings which were used in England by publishers from the fifteenth–eighteenth centuries; only rarely did they carry lettering on the spines. Until the nineteenth century, purchasers usually bought books unbound or enclosed in wrappers, and had them bound to order.

TRADE BOOK. A common U.S. publishing term for a book intended for general readership. It is neither a children's book, a textbook, nor a technical treatise, but a book which would interest anybody, and be published by a commercial publisher as distinct from one published by a society, institution, governmental agency or other non-commercial group.

TRADE CATALOGUE. 1. A list of the books in print published in a country, and frequently of books published abroad, for which the home publishers are agents. 2. A publication containing particulars of goods manufactured by, or sold by, a firm; frequently illustrated and containing prices.

TRADE DIRECTORY. A DIRECTORY (*q.v.*) which is concerned with one trade or a group of related trades.

TRADE EDITION. Copies of a book which are regularly printed and supplied to booksellers by publishers at the appropriate wholesale rates. *See also* LARGE PAPER EDITION, SUBSCRIBERS' EDITION, especially such an edition contrasted with a de luxe, paperback, library-bound, or book club edition.

TRADE INFORMATION. *Synonymous with* BIBLIOGRAPHIC INFORMATION (*q.v.*).

TRADE JOURNAL. A periodical restricted to the interests of a trade or industry and including all or some of the following: news items, articles and descriptions of goods, products and manufactured articles, lists of new publications, statistical data, patents, personal notes, legislative activities, etc. Also called 'Trade paper'.

TRADE LIST. A list of publications in print, which is issued by a publisher for the information of the bookselling trade, often providing space for ordering the various titles and giving particulars of the terms under which the books are sold to booksellers.

TRADE PAPER. *Synonymous with* TRADE JOURNAL (*q.v.*).

TRADE SERIES. *See* PUBLISHER'S SERIES.

TRADE TERMS. The provision of facilities for retailers to obtain goods at a discount for re-sale to the public. In the book trade, the discounts may vary according to the kind of book (general, children's, educational, technical, etc.) but they are fairly standard. Export terms are usually different from those for the home market.

TRADITIONAL ABSTRACT. *See* ABSTRACT.

TRADITIONAL FORMAT. The format of oriental books, consisting of double leaves with folds at the fore-edge and with free edges sewn together to make a fascicle. Usually several fascicles are contained in a cloth-covered case.

TRAILER. A portion of developed but unexposed copying material, such as film strip, at the end of a sequence of exposures, which is not cut off; it serves to protect the exposed portion and assists projection.

TRAILER CARD. A microfiche card which follows another, and is provided to give additional data, information or pages of a document.

TRAILER MICROFILM. *See* MICROFICHE.

TRAILER RECORD. A record which follows a group of similar records and contains pertinent data related to the group of records.

TRAINING COLLEGES AND INSTITUTE OF EDUCATION, SUB-SECTION. Subsequently the Colleges, Institutes and Schools of Education Sub-Section of the UNIVERSITY, COLLEGE AND RESEARCH SECTION (*q.v.*), but now an independent Group, of the Library Association.

TRANSACTION CARD. A card which is inserted in a book, the loan of which is recorded by a TRANSACTION CARD CHARGING (*q.v.*) method.

TRANSACTION CARD CHARGING. Book issue methods in which the records of loans are kept in the order in which they are made, transactions being given numbers in consecutive order. At the time of recording the loan a numbered 'transaction card' is inserted in the book and remains there until the book is returned to the library when it is withdrawn. Transaction cards for all returned books are then put into number order, any missing ones indicating overdue books. The transaction cards usually have the date the books are due for return stamped on them. Photo-charging, AUDIO-CHARGING (*q.v.*) and PUNCHED CARD CHARGING (*q.v.*) and the BOOKAMATIC (*q.v.*) systems are transaction card charging methods. Abbreviated T-card charging.

TRANSACTION ROOM.   A room to which books issued by a method using transaction cards are taken on their return by readers, for examination, checking with lists of reserved books, or sorting for shelving. The manual sorting of transaction cards may also be done here, punched transaction cards being sent to the machine sorter.

TRANSACTIONS.   The published papers read at meetings of a society or institution, or abstracts of the same. *Also sometimes synonymous with* PROCEEDINGS (*q.v.*). A general distinction made between Transactions and Proceedings is that the Transactions are the papers presented and the Proceedings the records of meetings.

TRANSCRIBE.   (*Information retrieval*) To copy from one external storage medium to another.

TRANSCRIPT.   1. A copy made from an original, particularly of a legal document. 2. Also, a written record of words usually spoken, e.g. of court proceedings, or of a broadcast. In the archives field, an exact reproduction, so far as the resources of script or typography allow, of an original document, with the single exception that abbreviations may be extended providing their interpretation is unquestionable.

TRANSCRIPTION.   1. An expression in one notation that is equivalent to an expression in another. 2. In music, the arrangement for one musical medium of music originally composed for another, e.g. an organ piece from an orchestral overture. 3. An arrangement in which some liberty is taken by way of modification or embellishment. *See also* VERSION.

TRANSFER.   A chemically prepared paper for transferring drawings direct on to lithographic stone or a rubber-covered cylinder used in offset lithography.

TRANSFER BOX.   A box, somewhat similar to a PAMPHLET BOX (*q.v.*) but of less durable construction and serving to store lesser used pamphlet material which is transferred from the current sequence.

TRANSFER FILE.   1. A container of some kind (box-like or folder) of a less sturdy type and cheaper, to contain older material which must be filed but which is seldom referred to and encumbers current files. 2. The material itself which is removed from current files.

TRANSFER PRINTING.   *See* DECALCOMANIA.

TRANSFER PROCESS.   A method of making copies of documents. The 'soft gelatine transfer process' involves the mechanical transference of the image; in this the negative material consists of paper coated with a gelatine emulsion containing silver halide – a light-sensitive compound, a tanning, or non-diffusing, developer, and a dye-forming agent. After exposure the paper is put in an alkali solution known as an activator, in which the dye is formed and the exposed portions of the image hardened, leaving the unexposed portions soft. A sheet of plain white paper is placed in contact with the negative and the two sheets pressed firmly together by a roller; this transfers the dye from the negative to the white paper. The two are peeled apart, the image having been transferred to the white paper which is almost dry. Up to three copies can usually be made from the same negative which is placed in the activator for each printing: if the negative is contrasty and the correct exposure made, it might be possible to make six copies. The other transfer process, called the 'diffusion transfer process', involves a chemical transference of the image. This process requires two gelatine emulsion-coated papers, the negative one being coated with a silver halide emulsion which is sensitive to light, the positive one being coated with a non-light-sensitive layer containing colloidal silver. After exposure the negative paper is placed in contact with the positive (emulsion side to emulsion side) and they are inserted in adjacent slots in a developing machine where they pass through a weak alkaline developing solution and are then pressed firmly together by a pair of rollers. Soon after they emerge from the machine they are peeled apart. Only one positive can be made from each negative unless a multi-copy paper is used for the master, but a transfer can be made on to translucent paper and this can be used for printing diazo copies.

TRANSFORMER.   In information retrieval, the selector which searches the DESCRIPTOR FILE (*q.v.*).

TRANSITIONAL.   A name sometimes given to the type face designed about 1760 by John Baskerville, and those based on it. Transitional types retain the bracketed serifs of old face and suggest by their precision the engraved quality of modern face types. The faces are more angular, with sharper contrast between the thick and thin strokes. *See also* EGYPTIAN, MODERN FACE, OLD FACE, TYPE FACE.

The following is in 12 point BASKERVILLE:

ABCDEFGHIJKLMNOPQRSTUVWXYZ

abcdefghijklmnopqrstuvwxyz   1234567890

This sentence is set in Bell which is a 'transitional' type face, as are also Fournier, Caledonia and Columbia.

TRANSITIONAL FACE.   *See* TRANSITIONAL.

TRANSLATED TITLE LIST. A periodically issued bulletin which lists, usually in a systematic order, the translated titles of periodical articles and documents which are likely to be of interest to its readers.

TRANSLATION. 1. The act of turning a literary composition from one language into another. 2. The work so produced.

TRANSLATION POOL. A centrally held collection of translations acquired from a variety of sources, and available for use on a co-operative basis.

TRANSLATION RIGHTS. The right to allow or refuse the publication of any literary production in another language is a part of COPYRIGHT (*q.v.*).

TRANSLATOR. One who translates from one language into another.

TRANSLITERATION. The representation of the ordinary characters of a language by those of another, as from Russian, Arabic, Cyrillic, Irish or Greek into Roman, each digit or letter being transcribed independently of the others. British Standards for transliteration are: BS 2979 : 1958 *Transliteration of Cyrillic and Greek characters* and BS 4280 : 1968 *Transliteration of Arabic characters. See also* ROMANIZATION.

TRANSLUCENT COPY. In documentary reproduction, a copy on translucent material.

TRANSLUCENT SCREEN. A sheet of glass treated in some way (ground, opal, coated, etc.), or of plastic, on to which an image is projected in a microfilm reader.

TRANSMISSION COPYING. In documentary reproduction, making a photocopy by passing light through a one-sided original which is in contact with sensitized paper. Included in this method are blue-print and Diazo or dyeline processes and the use of silver halide paper in contact with a single-sided document which is thin enough to permit light to pass through it.

TRANSMISSION PRINT. A copy of a document made by TRANS-MISSION PRINTING (*q.v.*).

TRANSMISSION PRINTING. The making of contact prints by passing light through the original and on to the material of reproduction. *See also* CONTACT COPYING, TRANSMISSION COPYING.

TRANSPARENCY. An image, in black and white or colour, on transparent base-stock, usually film, which may be viewed by transmitted light, usually with the aid of a projector.

TRANSPARENT VELLUM. A method (patented in 1785) used by Edwards of Halifax which rendered the vellum to be used in bookbinding transparent. A painting or drawing was done on the underside and the whole then lined with white paper.

TRANSPOSE. To change over the positions of letters, words or lines of type. This is marked on a proof by putting a loop round the characters to be changed and writing 'trs.' in the margin.

TRANSPOSING INSTRUMENT. A musical instrument for which the music is written in a key or in an octave other than its actual sound, but which (mechanically and without thought on the part of the player) transposes the music to a higher or lower pitch.

TRAVELLING CARD. A catalogue card on which subsequent issues of annuals or other serial publications (see CONTINUATION 3) are entered and which is passed to each department or library in turn for the appropriate addition to be made to the catalogue entry. On completion of the addition to all the catalogues, this card is filed in the official catalogue, or in a special sequence, to await subsequent publications when the process is repeated.

TRAVELLING LIBRARY. A large motor vehicle equipped with shelves and a staff enclosure, which visits districts where there is no other library service at specified times on a certain day or days of the week. The public may choose their books from the shelves. In British county libraries there is a tendency to describe such a vehicle as a 'Mobile Branch Library' or 'Mobile Library' and to use the term 'Travelling Library' for a small vehicle which is shelved or otherwise equipped to provide a service to villages, and isolated farms and houses, with short stops for issuing books. See also DELIVERY VAN, EXHIBITION VAN, MOBILE LIBRARY. In America, the term also refers to a small collection of selected books sent by a central library agency for the use of a branch, group or community, during a limited period.

TRAVELLING MOULD. See WIRE.

TRAY LABEL. A label inserted in the holder provided on the front of a catalogue drawer to indicate its contents.

TREADLE LATCHES. Latches to release wickets which are worked with the foot.

TREATMENT OF CORRESPONDENCE. See CORRESPONDENCE MANAGEMENT.

TREE CALF. A calf binding which has had acid poured on it in such a way as to form stains resembling a tree-like pattern.

TREE OF PORPHYRY. See PORPHYRY, TREE OF.

TREND REPORT. *Committee of enquiry into the organization of civil science* (Cmnd. 2171), the report of the committee appointed by the Prime Minister (then Mr. Harold Macmillian) in March 1962 and

27

under the chairmanship of Sir Burke Trend, to consider whether any changes were desirable in the existing functions of the various scientific agencies and research organizations. The report was published on 30th October 1963 and led to the dissolution of the Department of Scientific and Industrial Research and the formation of a system of independent research councils.

TRIAL BINDING. A sample of the proposed cover for a book submitted by the binder or casemaker to the publisher.

TRIAL ISSUE. A few copies of a book printed for circulation to critical friends prior to the printing of the edition for publication which was printed without re-setting of the type. If re-setting occurred then the preliminary edition was known as a 'trial edition'.

TRIAL PROOF. *See* PROOF.

TRIGESIMO-SECUNDO (32mo). A sheet of paper folded five times to form a section of thirty-two leaves (sixty-four pages). Also called 'Thirty-twomo'.

TRIGESIMO-SEXTO. *Synonymous with* THIRTY-SIXMO (*q.v.*).

TRILOGY. A set of three related dramatic or literary compositions.

TRIMMED. 1. Paper which has been trimmed on one or more sides to ensure exactness of corner angles and to reduce to the size required. 2. (*Binding*) The top edge untouched, and only the inequalities removed from the others, the folds not being opened. *See also* EDGES.

TRIMMED PAGE SIZE. The size of a sheet after folding and trimming.

TRIMMED SIZE. The final dimensions of a sheet of paper. British papermakers may interpret this term as 'guillotine trimmed'. *See also* PAPER SIZES, UNTRIMMED SIZE.

TRINITY COLLEGE LIBRARY, DUBLIN. The oldest library in Ireland; it was established by Royal Charter in 1592 and in 1801 was granted the right to receive a copy of every publication issued in the United Kingdom. It is rich in manuscripts, its best-known treasure being the *Book of Kells*.

TRIPLE LINING. A method of LINING (*q.v.*) used to give added strength. It is used in better-quality cased books and consists of providing a strip of crêpe manila lining, with head-and-tailbands if desired. All the lining processes used in this instance number seven and can be carried out mechanically.

TRIPLEX PAPER. *See* DUPLEX PAPER.

TRIPOLI. The cheaper grades of esparto grass, grown in N. Africa. *See also* ESPARTO.

TRIPPER. (*Reprography*) A device, operated mechanically or

electronically, to control lights, film advance, or the beginning or end of the operation.

TRIPTYCH. *See* CODEX.

TROY TYPE. A type cut by William Morris in 1892; it was an 18-point Gothic type based on the early types of Schoeffer, Mentelin and Zainer. *See also* CHAUCER TYPE, GOLDEN TYPE.

trs. Abbreviation for transpose; in proof correcting it is written in the margin to indicate that the position of the words, letters or lines around which a loop is drawn are to be exchanged.

TRUE ANONYMA. Books which would be catalogued as Type A, i.e. under the author's name if their authors were known. These are catalogued in the Library of Congress and some other libraries with the author line left blank so that it can be entered without re-typing the whole entry should the authorship be discovered. This method is known as 'hanging indention'. *See also* FORMAL ANONYMA.

TRUE SIDED. Reflecting a document or object to be reproduced without the aid of a mirror.

TRUNCATION. The process of shortening or cutting off part of a keyword or a title in a PERMUTED TITLE INDEX (*q.v.*). A truncated title lacks one or more words or syllables at the beginning or end.

TUB-SIZING. Dipping sheets of WATERLEAF (*q.v.*) into a tub of animal glue, gelatine, a prepared starch, or a combination of these, drying on cow-hair ropes or hessian, and then glazing them. Tub-sized paper (abbreviated 'T.S.') is strong and has a high resistance to moisture. Also called 'Animal Tub-sized' (abbreviated 'A.T.S.'). *See also* ENGINE-SIZING.

TUMBLER SCHEME. The method of perfecting sheets to be printed from a form imposed in the oblong, or landscape, manner. In order to obtain correct page sequence, the sheet must be turned or tumbled, in its short direction. *See also* WORK AND TURN.

TURN-IN. 1. That portion of the material covering the boards of a book which overlaps the head, tail and fore-edges of the boards and is turned-in over these edges of the boards. 2. To make use of type matter which is already set. 3. The turned-over end of a book jacket which is folded around the cover.

TURN OVER. 1. Printed matter extending beyond the allotted space. 2. The part of an article continued from a preceding page. Also called RUN OVER (*q.v.*). 3. The second and subsequent lines of a paragraph.

TURNED. (*Printing*) A printed impression of a graph, table or illustration, etc., which is turned at right angles so that its foot is parallel to the fore-edge of the page. *See also* LANDSCAPE PAGE.

TURNED COMMA. A comma which is used upside down and in a superior position, i.e. on the MEAN LINE (*q.v.*); it is used at the beginning of quoted matter '. . .' and in the abbreviation of the Scottish 'Mac', as in M'Gregor.

TURNED LETTER. A letter used upside down such as a 'u' for an 'n'.

TURNED SORT. A type letter used foot uppermost for one not known or not available, thus: ▓. This is very conspicuous in galley proof. When turned sorts are replaced with the correct letters, the process is called 'taking out turns'.

TURNOVER LINES. The second or subsequent lines of type in a paragraph. Called 'Run-in lines' in America.

TURNS. *See* TAKING OUT TURNS.

TUTOR LIBRARIAN. A librarian of an adult education institution who gives lectures to students on the library and how to make the best use of it, and sometimes on academic subjects, as well as having some responsibility for the administration or functioning of the library.

TWELVEMO. *See* DUODECIMO.

TWENTY-FOURMO (24mo). A sheet of paper folded to form a section of twenty-four leaves (forty-eight pages). Also called 'Vicesimo-quarto'.

TWENTYMO (20mo). A sheet of paper folded into twenty leaves, making 40 pages.

TWICE WEEKLY. A periodical which is published twice a week. Also called 'Semi-weekly'. *See also* FORTNIGHTLY.

TWIN-BATH STABILIZATION. A reprography process which employs two solutions for processing – a developer or activator and a stabilizer. Transfer of the exposed material from one solution to the other is usually automatic. *See also* STABILIZATION.

TWIN WIRE PAPER. A DUPLEX PAPER (*q.v.*) made by bringing the two wet webs together, WIRE SIDES (*q.v.*) innermost, to form a single sheet with two top or FELT SIDES (*q.v.*) and no wire side or 'under-side'. Such paper is particularly suitable for offset printing. *See also* RIGHT.

TWISTED PINEAPPLES. (*Binding*) The form of ornament used on a number of English and French finishers' rolls, and consisting of twisted stems with conventional pineapples at intervals. *See also* PINE-APPLE.

TWO-COLOUR HALF-TONES. Two half-tone plates in which one of the plates is made with the line of the screen as in a one-colour half-tone, and the other with lines at a different angle, usually about 30°. The colours tend to blend into one another in different tones.

TWO-COLOUR PRESS. A machine which prints in two colours at one operation. The principle is applicable to letterpress, lithographies and offset machines. Most offset printing is carried out on two-colour presses.

TWO-COLOUR PROCESS. A photo-mechanical process in which the printing is done in two colours.

TWO-COLOUR REPRODUCTION. Printing in two colours instead of the more usual three. The colours used are normally green or blue, and orange; subjects have to be carefully chosen or the resulting prints may be not true to the original, or they may be crude.

TWO-COMPONENT DIAZOTYPE MATERIALS. Diazotype materials having in the layer, the diazo compounds as well as the coupling components (two component paper) (*Concepts* . . .). *See also* DIAZO-TYPE PROCESS.

TWO-LAYER PAPER. *See* FURNISH LAYER.

TWO-LINE LETTER. (*Printing*) A capital letter having a depth of body (or height of letter on the printed page) equal to double that of the size specified, as 'two-line pica'. Three- and four-line letters are used similarly. They are often used as the initial letter for the first word of a chapter.

TWO ON. Printing two sheets, jobs, page, etc., at the same time. The printing of small jobs in duplicate is done to facilitate the work and economize in time and costs.

TWO-PAGE SPREAD. *Synonymous with* DOUBLE SPREAD (*q.v.*).

TWO-REVOLUTION MACHINE. A printing machine in which the cylinder, over which the paper is fed, does not stop after traversing the forme but continues to revolve, rising slightly during its second revolution so that it cannot come into contact with the type, and descending when the form is again in position for printing. During its second revolution, the bed with the forme returns and the sheet is delivered. The earliest machine of this kind was made by Koenig in 1814. *See also* MIEHLE, PERFECTER, SINGLE-REVOLUTION MACHINE, STANHOPE PRESS, STOP-CYLINDER PRESS.

TWO SHEETS (SECTIONS) ON. The method of sewing books when two sections are treated as one. In hand-sewing two sheets at a time are placed on the sewing-frame; the thread is passed from the kettle stitch of the lower section, and brought out at the first tape or cord, when it is inserted in the upper section, and so on. Thus, two sections receive only the same number of stitches one would do by the ALL ALONG method (*q.v.*). Although a weaker method than the 'all along', it helps to reduce the swelling in the back in the case of very thin books.

TWO SIDES COLOURED. Paper or board both sides of which have been coloured intentionally during manufacture.

TWO-UP. 1. Printing two texts, or duplicate stereos made from the same forme, side by side on the same sheet of paper. It is an economical way of machining short runs. 2. The processing of two books as a single unit from the forme through all the binding processes until they are separated by the trimmer. A method which is sometimes used for mass-producing PAPERBACKS (*q.v.*).

TWO-WAY PAGING. The system of page numbering used for a book with the texts in two languages, one of which reads from left to right (as English) and the other from right to left (as Hebrew or Arabic); the texts being in two sections with page sequences from opposite ends of the book.

TWOPENNY LIBRARY. A circulating library, usually in shop premises, for which the charge for borrowing a book was twopence a week. The charge became much greater but the name persisted.

TYING-UP. The tying of a volume after the cover has been drawn on, so as to make the leather adhere better to the sides of the bands; also for setting the headband.

TYMPAN. A kind of leaf consisting of a thin frame of metal over which is stretched parchment or cambric, and which is hinged to the carriage bearing the forme of a printing press in such a way that it places the paper resting on it in the exact position for printing.

TYNESIDE ASSOCIATION OF LIBRARIES FOR INDUSTRY AND COMMERCE. *See* TALIC.

TYPE. (*Classification*) *See* CHARACTERISTIC. (*Printing*) A small rectangular block of metal or wood, having on its upper end a raised letter, figure, or other character, for use in letterpress printing. Also, a number of such characters. *See also* TYPE FACE, TYPE SIZES. For purposes of nomenclature, a single movable type character has always been considered as a human being standing erect, and having a BODY (but no head), a FACE, BEARD, NECK, SHOULDER, BACK, BELLY, FEET. Type letters are formed within three imaginary lines: the 'base line' on which the bases of capitals rest, the 'mean line' running along the top of the lower-case letters which are without ascenders, the 'cap line' which runs across the top of the capital letters. *See also* BODY, X-HEIGHT.

TYPE A CATALOGUE ENTRY. An entry, being the main entry,

made under the personal name of the author, even if there is an editor, translator or subordinate editor.

TYPE AREA. The area, or part, of a page of a book, periodical or other publication which will be, or has been, filled with printed matter.

TYPE C CATALOGUE ENTRY. An entry which is used for a book which, because a corporate body is responsible for its existence, has its main entry under the name of the corporate body. A *Type CG entry* is one in which the corporate name, or a formalized version of it, is added to a geographic base, e.g. Manchester, Chamber of Commerce. A *Type CGG entry* is one in which the name of a government body, or office, is added to a geographic base, e.g. Great Britain, War Office.

TYPE-CASTING MACHINE. Originally, one which cast single type units which were then set up in a stick by hand. Modern machines such as *Monotype*, *Linotype* and *Intertype* both set and cast.

TYPE CG CATALOGUE ENTRY. *See* TYPE C CATALOGUE ENTRY.

TYPE CGG CATALOGUE ENTRY. *See* TYPE C CATALOGUE ENTRY.

TYPE F CATALOGUE ENTRY. An entry, being the main entry, for six classes of work, which, although usually treated by the codes with corporate entries, are virtually in the same category as conventional title entries. The six classes are: charters; constitutions; constitutional conventions; laws, statutes, etc.; ordinances, etc.; treaties, etc.

TYPE FACE. 1. The printing surface of the upper end of a piece of type which bears the character to be printed. 2. The style, or design, of characters on a set of pieces of type, comprising all the sizes in which the particular design is made. There are four classes of type face: ABSTRACT, CURSIVE, DECORATIVE, ROMAN (*qq.v.*), and they may also be divided in the following nine categories: HUMANIST, GARALDE, TRANSITIONAL, DIDONE, SLAB-SERIF, LINEALE, GLYPHIC, SCRIPT and GRAPHIC. The following is a selection of type faces (nearly all in 12-point):

12 pt Antique
ABCDEFGHIJKLMNOPQRSTUVWXYZ -
abcdefghijklmnopqrstuvwxyz - 1234567890

12 pt. Baskerville
ABCDEFGHIJKLMNOPQRSTUVWXYZ – abcd
efghijklmnopqrstuvwxyz–1234567890 –1234567890
*ABCDEFGHIJKLMNOPQRSTUVWXYZ – abcdefg
hijklmnopqrstuvwxyz–*

12 pt. Bell
ABCDEFGHIJKLMNOPQRSTUVWXYZ–abcdefg
hijklmnopqrstuvwxyz – 1234567890 –*ABCDEFGHI
JKLMNOPQRSTUVWXYZ – abcdefghijklmnopqrst
uvwxyz*

12 pt. Bembo
ABCDEFGHIJKLMNOPQRSTUV WXYZ – abcdefghijk
lmnopqrstuvwxyz – 1234567890–*ABCDEFGHIJKLMNO
PQRSTUVWXYZ – abcdefghijklmnopqrstuvwxyz*

12 pt. Poliphilus & Blado
ABCDEFGHIJKLMNOPQRSTUVWXYZ – abcde
fghijklmnopqrstuvwxyz – 1234567890–*ABCDEFGHIJK
LMNOPQRSTUVWXYZ – abcdefghijklmnopqrstuvwxyz*

12 pt. Bodoni
ABCDEFGHIJKLMNOPQRSTUVWXYZ – abcde
fghijklmnopqrstuvwxyz – 1234567890 –*ABCDEFG
HIJKLMNOPQRSTUVWXYZ – abcdefghijklmno
pqrstuvwxyz*

12 pt. Bookprint
ABCDEFGHIJKLMNOPQRSTUVWXYZ– abc
defghijklmnopqrstuvwxyz– 1234567890– 1234567
890 –*ABCDEFGHIJKLMNOPQRSTUVWXYZ
-- abcdefghijklmnopqrstuvwxyz*

12 pt. Caslon
ABCDEFGHIJKLMNOPQRSTUVWXYZ – abcde
fghijklmnopqrstuvwxyz – 1234567890 –*ABCDEFGH
IJKLMNOPQRSTUVWXYZ – abcdefghijklmnopqrstu
vwxyz*

12 pt. Centaur
ABCDEFGHIJKLMNOPQRSTUVWXYZ – abcdefghijkl
mnopqrstuvwxyz – 1234567890 –*ABCDEFGHIJKLMNOPQ
RSTUVWXYZ – abcdefghijklmnopqrstuvwxyz – 1234567890*

12 pt. Clarendon
ABCDEFGHIJKLMNOPQRSTUVWXYZ – ab
cdefghijklmnopqrstuvwxyz – 1234567890

12 pt. Cochin
ABCDEFGHIJKLMNOPQRSTUVWXYZ –
abcdefghijklmnopqrstuvwxyz – 1234567890 – *ABCD*
EFGHIJKLMNOPQRSTUVWXYZ – abcdefghijk
lmnopqrstuvwxyz

10 pt. Cornell
ABCDEFGHIJKLMNOPQRSTUVWXYZ – abcdefghijklmn
opqrstuvwxyz – 1234567890 – *ABCDEFGHIJKLMNOPQR*
STUVWXYZ – abcdefghijklmnopqrstuvwxyz

12 pt Egmont
ABCDEFGHIJKLMNOPQRSTUVWXYZ—abc
defghijklmnopqrstuvwxyz—1234567890
ABCDEFGHIJKLMNOPQRSTUVWXYZ—abc
defghijklmnopqrstuvwxyz—

12 pt. Ehrhardt
ABCDEFGHIJKLMNOPQRSTUVWXYX – abcdefg
hijklmnopqrstuvwxyz–1234567890 –1234567890 –*ABCD*
EFGHIJKLMNOPQRSTUVWXYZ – abcdefghijklmno
pqrstuvwxyz

12 pt. Fournier
ABCDEFGHIJKLMNOPQRSTUVWXYZ – abcdefghijk
lmnopqrstuvwxyz – 1234567890 – *ABCDEFGHIJKLMN*
OPQRSTUVWXYZ – abcdefghijklmnopqrstuvwxyz

12 pt. Garamond
ABCDEFGHIJKLMNOPQRSTUVWXYZ – abcdef
ghijklmnopqrstuvwxyz–1234567890 –*ABCDEFGHI*
JKLMNOPQRSTUVWXYZ – abcdefghijklmnopqrstuv
wxyz

12 pt. Georgian
ABCDEFGHIJKLMNOPQRSTUVWXYZ – abcdefg
hijklmnopqrstuvwxyz – 1234567890 – 1234567890 – *A*
BCDEFGHIJKLMNOPQRSTUVWXYZ – abcdefghi
jklmnopqrstuvwxyz

12 pt. Gill
ABCDEFGHIJKLMNOPQRSTUVWXYZ – abcdefghij
klmnopqrstuvwxyz – 1234567890 – *ABCDEFGHIJKLM*
NOPQRSTUVWXYZ – abcdefghijklmnopqrstuvwxyz

12 pt. Goudy
ABCDEFGHIJKLMNOPQRSTUVWXYZ - abcde
fghijklmnopqrstuvwxyz - 1234567890 - *ABCDEF*
GHIJKLMNOPQRSTUVWXYZ - abcdefghijklmn
opqrstuvwxyz

12 pt. Granjon
ABCDEFGHIJKLMNOPQRSTUVWXYZ — abcdefghi
jklmnopqrstuvwxyz — 1234567890 — *ABCDEFGHIJKL*
MNOPQRSTUVWXYZ — abcdefghijklmnopqrstuvwxyz

11 pt. Grotesque 215   (12 pt. not cut)
ABCDEFGHIJKLMNOPQRSTUVWXYZ – abcdefghij
klmnopqrstuvwxyz – 1234567890 – *ABCDEFGHIJKLMN*
OPQRSTUVWXYZ – abcdefghijklmnopqrstuvwxyz

12 pt. Imprint
ABCDEFGHIJKLMNOPQRSTUVWXYZ – abcd
efghijklmnopqrstuvwxyz – 1234567890–*ABCDEFG*
HIJKLMNOPQRSTUVWXYZ - abcdefghijklmnop
qrstuvwxyz

12 pt. Juliana
ABCDEFGHIJKLMNOPQRSTUVWXYZ – abcdefghij
klmnopqrstuvwxyz–1234567890 – ABCDEFGHIJKLM
NOPQRSTUVWXYZ–*abcdefghijklmnopqrstuvwxyz*

12 pt. Modern
ABCDEFGHIJKLMNOPQRSTUVWXYZ – abcd
efghijklmnopqrstuvwxyz–1234567890–*ABCDEF*
GHIJKLMNOPQRSTUVWXYZ – abcdefghijklm
nopqrstuvwxyz

11pt Pastonchi
ABCDEFGHIJKLMNOPQRSTUVWXYZ ⸱ abcdefghijklmno
pqrstuvwxyz ⸱ 1234567890 ⸱ *ABCDEFGHIJKLMNOPQRST*
UVWXYZ ⸱ abcdefghijklmnopqrstuvwxyz

12 pt. Perpetua
ABCDEFGHIJKLMNOPQRSTUVWXYZ — abcdefghijklmn
opqrstuvwxyz—1234567890 — *ABCDEFGHIJKLMNOPQRST*
UVWXYZ—abcdefghijklmnopqrstvwxyz–

12 pt. Pilgrim
ABCDEFGHIJKLMNOPQRSTUVWXYZ – abcdefghijkl
mnopqrstuvwxyz – 1234567890 – *ABCDEFGHIJKLM*
NOPQRSTUVWXYZ – abcdefghijklmnopqrstuvwxyz

12 pt. Plantin
ABCDEFGHIJKLMNOPQRSTUVWXYZ – abcd
efghijklmnopqrstuvwxyz-1234567890-*ABCDEFGH*
IJKLMNOPQRSTUVWXYZ – abcdefghijklmnopqrs
tuvwxyz

12 pt. Rockwell
ABCDEFGHIJKLMNOPQRSTUVWXYZ – abcdef
ghijklmnopqrstuvwxyz – 1234567890 – *ABCDEF*
GHIJKLMNOPQRSTUVWXYZ–abcdefghijklmno
pqrstuvwxyz

12 pt. Scotch
ABCDEFGHIJKLMNOPQRSTUVWXYZ–abcd
efghijklmnopqrstuvwxyz – 1234567890 – *A BCDE*
FGHIJKLMNOPQRSTUVWXYZ – abcdefghijk
lmnopqrstuvwxyz

12 pt. Times
ABCDEFGHIJKLMNOPQRSTUVWXYZ–abcd
efghijklmnopqrstuvwxyz–1234567890–*ABCDEFG*
HIJKLMNOPQRSTUVWXYZ– abcdefghijklmnop
qrstuvwxyz

12pt. Van Dijck
ABCDEFGHIJKLMNOPQRSTUVWXYZ– abcdefghijklmno
pqrstuvwxyz-1234567890-*ABCDEFGHIJKLMNOPQRSTU*
VWXYZ – abcdefghijklmnopqrstuvwxyz

11D on 12 pt. Walbaum
ABCDEFGHIJKLMNOPQRSTUVWXYZ – abcdefghijklm
nopqrstuvwxyz – 1234567890 – *ABCDEFGHIJKLMNOP*
QRSTUVWXYZ – abcdefghijklmnopqrstuvwxyz

The type suppliers providing the above faces are as follows:
INTERTYPE:
 Cornell
 Egmont

LINOTYPE:
  Bookprint
  Georgian
  Granjon
  Pilgrim

MONOTYPE:
  Baskerville
  Bell
  Bembo
  Blado
  Bodoni
  Caslon
  Centaur
  Cochin
  Ehrhardt
  Fournier
  Garamond
  Gill Sans Serif
  Goudy
  Grotesque
  Imprint
  Juliana
  Modern
  Pastonchi
  Perpetua
  Plantin
  Poliphilus
  Rockwell
  Scotch
  Times New Roman
  Van Dijck
  Walbaum

TYPE FOUNDERS:
  Antique
  Clarendon

TYPE FACSIMILE. A reprint in which a printed original is copied exactly.

TYPE FLOWERS. Conventional designs cast in type metal of type height and used to decorate a book as an alternative to using blocks. *See also* FLOWERS.

TYPE GAUGE.   A rule marked off in ems, points and inches and used for measuring width of type, page depths, etc.

TYPE HEIGHT.   1. The standard height to which type bodies are cast. In the U.K. and the U.S.A. this is 0·918 of an inch from the feet, on which the type rests, to the printing surface, except for the Oxford University Press which works to 0·9395 inches. On the continent of Europe the standard height is 'Didot Normal' (0·9278 inches). 2. The height to which a printing plate is mounted for use in letterpress work; it must be the same height as the letterpress.

TYPE-HIGH.   A printing block or plate which has been mounted on wood or metal to the same height as type for use on a printing machine.

TYPE M CATALOGUE ENTRY.   An entry for a work of joint authorship where one of several alternative headings (for individuals, a corporate body, or a form) can be chosen with equal correctness and clarity.

TYPE METAL.   (*Printing*) An alloy of tin, lead, antimony and sometimes copper which is used for casting type.

TYPE ORNAMENTS.   Conventional designs cast in type metal, being larger than TYPE FLOWERS (*q.v.*) and used to ornament chapter heads and tails, and title-pages.

TYPE PAGE.   The part of a page that is printed upon; i.e. the type area, the margins being excluded.

TYPE SIZE.   The measure of the dimensions of type, taken from the body of the individual type rather than the actual printing area. Also called 'Body size'. The following are the type sizes normally used in book-work:

	Old name:
5 point	Pearl
6 point	Nonpareil
7 point	Minion
8 point	Brevier
9 point	Bourgeois
10 point	Long Primer
11 point	Small Pica
12 point	Pica
14 point	English
16 point	Columbian
18 point	Great Primer
22 point	Double Pica

Larger sizes exist, but these are used for display and not book work. Other, mostly discarded, sizes with their names, are:

	Old name:
3½ point	Minikin (or Brilliant)
4 point	Brilliant
4 point	Gem
4½ point	Diamond
5½ point	Ruby (or Agate)
6½ point	Emerald
16 point	Two-line Brevier
20 point	Paragon
24 point	Two-line Pica
28 point	Two-line English
36 point	Two-line Great Primer
40 point	Two-line Paragon
44 point	Two line Double Pica
48 point	Four-line Pica (or Canon)
60 point	Five-line Pica
72 point	Six-line Pica.

British Standard 4786 : 1972 *Metric typographic measurement* describes a system employing the conventional millimetric scale, intended first as a viable alternative to present systems and later as a replacement. It recommends a basic unit of 0.5 mm having twenty sub-multiples of 0.025 mm for calculation of character width, the expression of line length in millimetres, and interlinear spacing in multiples of 0.25 mm. It recommends the measurement of lettering from BASE LINE (*q.v.*) to base line; this is already the film-setting practice.

TYPE T CATALOGUE ENTRY.   A main catalogue entry, made under the title of the work. There are four main classes of Type T main entry: (1) for a strictly anonymous book; (2) where the cataloguing code prefers to put the entry under the title on technical grounds, e.g. (a) for a work of joint authorship where four or more authors are involved, (b) for a work normally cited under its title, (c) for a work whose only clue to authorship consists of initials, a non-descriptive phrase as 'A Lady of Leisure', a typographical device, (d) for a work the authorship of which is indicated by a statement 'By the Author of' another anonymous work; (3) for certain anonymous works which are frequently reprinted and the wording of the titles of which can vary from one edition to another so that the entries would be scattered in the catalogue unless brought together under a common entry; (4) periodicals other than serials, e.g. annual reports, which go under a corporate name.

TYPESCRIPT. Typewritten matter; a typed manuscript. Abbreviated T.S.

TYPESETTER. One who sets type; a compositor.

TYPESETTING. The arrangement of printing types in order for printing, including the operation of Intertype, Linotype, Ludlow or Monotype machines.

TYPE-SETTING MACHINE. A machine for selecting, assembling and spacing typefounders' letterpress printing types which are arranged in channels instead of cases. *See also* TYPE-CASTING MACHINE.

TYPEWRITER SETTING. Typesetting by means of a typewriter made specially for the purpose, such as an IBM composer, Justowriter or Varityper; such machines enable word spacing to be varied and justifying to be achieved.

TYPICAL CHARACTERISTIC. *See* CHARACTERISTIC OF A CLASSIFICATION.

TYPICAL CLASS. *See* CHARACTERISTIC OF A CLASSIFICATION.

TYPOGRAPH. Trade name for a typecasting, setting and distributing machine which casts a slug or line of type, similar to the LINOTYPE (*q.v.*) machine.

TYPOGRAPHER. One who is responsible for the lay-out and appearance of printed matter.

TYPOGRAPHICAL ERROR. A mistake made by the typesetter.

TYPOGRAPHY. 1. Printing, or taking impressions from movable letter-units or 'types'. The art of printing. The opposite of XYLOGRAPHY (*q.v.*). 2. The character and appearance of printed matter.

TYPOMETER. A gauge for measuring the body and thickness of type and comparing them with a standard.

UBC. Acronym of Universal Bibliographic Control; it was a proposal made in 1973 by IFLA that Unesco should adopt as a major policy objective the promotion of a worldwide system for the control and exchange of bibliographic information. The International Office for Universal Bibliographic Control was established in July 1974 and absorbed the former IFLA Cataloguing Secretariat which was housed at the British Museum Library. The purpose of the system is to make universally and promptly available, in a machine-readable form that is internationally acceptable, basic bibliographic data on all publications issued in all countries; and the guiding principle is that the information should be produced as completely and correctly as possible at the earliest date, as near to the source as possible. The concept of UBC presupposes the creation of a network made up of component national parts, each covering a wide range of publishing and library activities, and all integrated at the international level to form the total system.

UCRS. *See* UNIVERSITY, COLLEGE AND RESEARCH SECTION.

US NATIONAL LIBRARIES TASK FORCE ON CO-OPERATIVE ACTIVITIES. Established in 1967 by the three Directors of the Library of Congress, the National Library of Medicine and the National Agricultural Library to 'improve access to the world's literature in all areas of human concern and scholarship, so that comprehensive access to the materials of learning can be afforded to all citizens of the United States'. In 1972 the Task Force membership was expanded, a structural reorganization implemented, and formal operating procedures adopted. The principal areas for investigation were also identified as: (a) the relationship of the national libraries to the national information system; (b) co-operation in and co-ordination of public service functions . . .; (c) co-operation in and co-ordination of technical service functions . . . and co-operation in the NATIONAL SERIALS DATA PROGRAM (*q.v.*).

USA STANDARDS INSTITUTE. *See* AMERICAN NATIONAL STANDARDS INSTITUTE, INC.

USASI. Abbreviation for United States of America Standards Institute, now the AMERICAN NATIONAL STANDARDS INSTITUTE, INC. (*q.v.*).

UFOD. Acronym for Union Française des Organismes de Documentation (French Union of Documentary Organizations). Provides professional training for assistants in documentation services. Publishes *Informations UFOD* (irr.), *Documentation en France* (6 p.a.), *l'Aide-Mémoire du Documentaliste*.

ÜHERTYPE. A photo-composing machine built in 1928 by Edmund Üher, a Hungarian. It was first called Luminotype.

UKCIS. Acronym of the United Kingdom Chemical Information Service which came into operation in August 1969 having previously operated as a research unit under the title The Chemical Society Research Unit in Information Dissemination and Retrieval which had been set up in August 1966 with assistance from OSTI to investigate the scope and viability of computer-based information service in chemistry in a U.K. environment. The Research Unit became the Research and Development Department of the UKCIS when this superseded the Unit. Aims: primarily, to disseminate scientific information to the community, also, to promote research into the usage and handling of large files of information or data. Financed by the sale of its products and services; it also receives grants from national and international bodies to carry out research on a contractual basis. By agreement with the American Chemical Society, UKCIS has the sole right to sell in the U.K. all printed microform and computer-readable products of the Chemical Abstracts Service. Abbreviated UKCIS (pronounced 'you kiss'). Centred on Nottingham University. *See also* BIS.

ult. Abbreviation for *ultimo* (*Lat.* 'last'). Used for 'last month'. *See also* inst.

ULTIMATE CLASS. The class of the smallest extension admitted by the scheme of classification, into which a document can be placed.

ULTIMATE STORE. *See* MARLIS.

ULTRA-MICROFICHE. A MICROFICHE (*q.v.*) with such small images that 3,000 page-images can be accommodated on one 4×6 inch fiche.

ULTRA THIN PAPER. Sensitized photographic paper between 0·0023 and 0·0031 inches inclusive. Also called 'Extra lightweight'. *See also* PHOTOGRAPHIC PAPERS.

ULVERSCROFT SERIES. A series of books printed in large type (18 pt.) and published by Mr. F. A. Thorpe, of Ulverscroft, with whom the Library Association has cooperated in the selection of titles for this venture which has proved very successful. The volumes are available to public libraries, welfare organizations and blind agencies direct, and not through the book trade.

UNAUTHORIZED EDITION. An edition issued without the consent of the author, his representative or the original publisher. The responsibility to the author would be moral, not legal. A *pirated edition* is an unauthorized reprint involving an infringement of copyright.

UNBACKED. Printed on only one side of the paper.

UNBLEACHED PAPER. Special paper made from unbleached STUFF (*q.v.*). Such papers do not usually have a good colour; they retain the colour of the original white rags, no bleaching during the process of manufacture having taken place. The paper is consequently stronger, as bleaching weakens the pulp.

UNBOUND. A publication the leaves or sections of which have not been fastened together.

UNCIAL. Style of majuscule writing, resembling capitals in some letter forms, but with rounder curves. This was a more flowing, cursive form of Latin manuscript handwriting and was used for commercial and everyday writing. In use generally from the fourth to the eighth centuries.

UNCUT. A book is described as being 'uncut' when the edges have not been trimmed or cut by a guillotine, thus leaving 'bolts' which have to be opened with a paper knife. Until this has been done the book is described as being unopened. Also called 'Unploughed', 'Untrimmed'. *See also* EDGES.

UNDERGROUND LITERATURE. *Synonymous with* CLANDESTINE LITERATURE (*q.v.*).

UNDERGROUND PRESS. A printing press which secretly prints leaflets, pamphlets, periodicals or books which have as their object the overthrow of the government, or of authority, or the propagation of subversive or generally unacceptable political views.

UNDERLAY. Work done on the printing machine by placing paper, thin card, etc., under the matter in the forme so as to level it up as much as possible for printing, before the final touches are put on by means of OVERLAY (*q.v.*).

UNDERLINE. A line or series of lines placed under parts of 'copy' or proof to indicate style of type to be used: a single line indicates italic; a double line, small capitals; a treble line, capitals; a wavy line (which can be placed under any of the forementioned) bold face. Called 'Underscore' in America. *See also* CAPTION 2.

UNDERRUN. A shortage in the number of copies printed.

UNDERSCORE. *Synonymous with* UNDERLINE (*q.v.*).

UNDIFFERENTIATED ENTRIES. In a PERMUTED TITLE INDEX (*q.v.*), a series of similar entries with no discriminating features.

UNDIS. Acronym of the United Nations Documentation Information System, the computer-based information storage and retrieval system developed and operated by the United Nations Library to facilitate access to information on official documents and publications of the United Nations.

UNESCO. Abbreviation for United Nations Educational, Scientific and Cultural Organization, an international body which exists to further the development of emerging nations in the fields mentioned. Constituted 16th November 1945 in London by representatives of forty-four governments; an agreement between the United Nations and Unesco was approved by the General Assembly of the U.N. in New York at its October-December 1946 session. It is financed by Member States of the U.N. who are all eligible for membership. There is a division of libraries, documentation and archives which operates as part of the cultural programme. Many books and periodicals have been published; among the latter are the *Bibliography, documentation and terminology* (bi-monthly), *Museum* (q.) and *Unesco bulletin for libraries* (bi-monthly). The Unesco Press was established in 1974 to continue the publishing and distribution functions of the former Office of Publications. *See also* PUBLIC LIBRARY MANIFESTO.

UNESCO COUPONS. A form of international currency enabling foreign payments to be made for education, scientific and cultural materials without the tedious and time-consuming procedures of making payments through the normal machinery of banks, and the involvement of currency control regulations. The government of a country wishing to use Unesco coupons nominates a body to distribute the coupons against local currency payment to organizations or individuals who send them to suppliers of goods who then obtain cash for them. The denominations of the coupons, in equivalents of U.S. dollars, are $1, $3, $10, $30, $100, $1,000. They are used extensively for purchasing books.

UNEVEN PAGES. Those which bear the odd page-numbers. The right-hand, or recto, pages.

UNEVEN WORKING. *See* EVEN WORKING.

UNEXPURGATED EDITION. An edition of a work in which the full text is given, including any objectionable material which normally would be omitted. *See also* EXPURGATED EDITION.

UNGATHERED. The printed sheets of a book which have not been gathered, or collected, into order.

UNIDO. Acronym for United Nations Industrial Development Organization. Established 1st January 1967 to promote industrial development by encouraging the mobilization of national and international resources to assist in, promote and accelerate the industrialization of the developing countries, with particular emphasis on the manufacturing sector. The Organization advises and assists governments of developing countries to formulate industrial development programmes, form and strengthen industrial support institutions and prepare specific industrial projects. Membership open to all members of the U.N., of the specialized Agencies and of the International Atomic Energy Agency (IAEA). Publishes *Bulletin on Industrialization and Productivity*, *Industrial Research and Development News* (q.), *UNIDO Newsletter*, *Industrial Development Abstracts*.

UNIFORM EDITION. The individual works of an author published in an identical format and binding. *See also* STANDARD EDITION.

UNIFORM HEADING. The form of a heading adopted for use in the catalogue for an author (personal or corporate), title, or for any other heading (IFLA).

UNIFORM TITLE.   The distinctive title by which a work, which has appeared under varying titles and in various versions, is most generally known, and under which catalogue entries are made. Also called 'Conventional title', 'Filing title', 'Standard title'.

UNION CATALOGUE.   A catalogue of the various departments of a library, or of a number of libraries, indicating their location. It may be an author or a subject catalogue of all the books, or of a selection of them, and may be limited by subject or type of material. *See also* CENTRALIZED CATALOGUING, CO-OPERATIVE CATALOGUING.

UNION FINDING LIST.   American term for a complete record of the holdings of a given group of libraries. It may be of materials of a given type, in a particular field, or on a particular subject.

UNION FRANÇAISE DES ORGANISMES DE DOCUMENTATION.   *See* UFOD.

UNION LIST.   A complete record, usually printed, of holdings of material in a certain field, on a particular subject, or of a given type such as of periodicals or annuals, for a group of libraries.

UNION OF INTERNATIONAL ASSOCIATIONS.   Founded in Brussels in 1907 as the Central Office of International Associations and became a federation under its present name at the first World Congress of International Organizations in 1910. Serves as a documentation centre on international governmental and non-governmental organizations, their activities and meetings; undertakes and promotes research on legal, administrative and technical problems common to international non-governmental organizations, publicizes their work and encourages their mutual contacts, and secures understanding of the necessity for maintaining a balance at the international level between the governmental and the private non-governmental sectors.

UNION PAPER.   Two sheets of wrapping paper stuck together with tar, bitumen, or some similar material with a waterproofing property. *See also* REINFORCED UNION PAPER, TARRED BROWN PAPER.

UNIQUE ENTRY, PRINCIPLE OF.   (*Cataloguing*) The entry for a book under a heading chosen (from more than one alternative) for person, subject, organization, place, etc., cross-references being provided from the other words which might have been used as alternatives. *See also* CATALOGUING, PRINCIPLES OF.

UNISIST.   Abbreviation for United Nations World Science Information System, resulting from a feasibility study undertaken by Unesco and the International Council of Scientific Unions (ICSU), and approved by the 17th session of the General Conference of Unesco in November 1972. It comprises five main objectives: '(a) improving tools of systems interconnection; (b) improving information transfer; (c) developing specialized information manpower; (d) developing science information policy and national networks; (e) special assistance to developing countries.' UNISIST's most embracing and far-reaching activity is the establishment of a standardization programme for all phases of information handling, the ultimate goal being the evolution of a worldwide science information system. UNISIST National Committees have been formed in many Member States and governmental agencies nominated to act as national focal points for questions relating to the UNISIST programme. The focal point for the U.K. is at the BRITISH LIBRARY (*q.v.*); for the U.S.A., at the Office of Science Information Service, National Science Foundation, Washington, D.C.; for Canada at the National Library of Canada, Ottawa; for India at the Department of Science and Technology, New Delhi; and for Ireland at the National Science Council, Dublin. Publishes *UNISIST Newsletter*. (q.). *See also* BSO, INFOTERM, ISDS, ISSN.

UNIT ABSTRACT CARD.   A card, or other record, bearing an abstract prepared for use in a selective dissemination of information, or other current awareness, system. *See also* SDI.

UNIT BIBLIOGRAPHY.   A bibliography of different editions of a book with the same title.

UNIT CARD.   A basic catalogue card, in the form of a main entry, a duplicate of which may be used as a unit wherever an entry for that particular book is required in any catalogue, after the addition of any heading which may be necessary. The Library of Congress catalogue cards are the most-used form of unit cards, although several American organizations are now issuing printed cards, usually for subject groups or form groups of literature. Entries which appear in the *British National Bibliography* (*q.v.*) are issued on cards and on sheaf paper. *See also* LOCAL UNIT CARD, WILSON CARDS.

UNIT CARD SYSTEM.   (*Information retrieval*) A TERM ENTRY (*q.v.*) system which uses machine-sorted punched cards each of which bears a single term and a single document number. It was developed by G. L. Peakes.

UNIT CONCEPT CO-ORDINATE INDEXING.   (*Information retrieval*) A system based on a combination of the Colon Classification structure with the techniques of the Uniterm system. It was devised by J. Waddington.

UNIT CONCEPTS.   *Synonymous with* POLYTERMS (*q.v.*).

UNIT CONSTRUCTION. *See* MODULAR PLANNING.

UNIT ENTRY. A basic catalogue entry which gives the fullest information – a MAIN ENTRY (*q.v.*) – and which, being reproduced by printing or other duplication method, is used for all ADDED ENTRIES (*q.v.*), usually with the addition above the entry of appropriate headings (subject, author, title, series, editor, illustrator, translator, etc.). The suppression of appropriate headings may also enable it to be used for other entries.

UNIT RECORD. The records comprising a descriptor file. Each consists of (a) descriptors (e.g. subject headings or class numbers) appropriate to the subject of the documents, (b) specifications of the documents (e.g. author, title, publisher, date, pagination, etc., plus possibly an annotation or abstract), (c) a document address, i.e. class number, call number, shelf number, file number, accession number or other indication of its whereabouts in the STORE (*q.v.*). Each card, or punched card, contains only one complete record.

UNIT SYSTEM. *See* MICROFILM.

L'UNITÉ. A system for analysing abstracts and coding them without using human agency. 'L'Unité-cards' are finally punched and these are machine sorted to retrieve the information required.

UNITED KINGDOM CHEMICAL INFORMATION SERVICE. *See* UKCIS.

UNITED KINGDOM READING ASSOCIATION. A non-profit-making professional organization which was founded in 1964 to: (a) encourage the study of reading problems at all educational levels; (b) stimulate and promote research in reading; (c) study the various factors that influence progress in reading; (d) publish the results of pertinent and significant investigations and practices; (e) assist in the development of teacher-training programmes; (f) act as a clearing-house for information relating to reading; (g) disseminate knowledge helpful in the solution of problems relating to reading; (h) sponsor conferences and meetings planned to implement the purposes of the Association. Membership is open to anyone interested in the teaching of reading. There are four categories of membership – Individual, Student, Institutional, Overseas. Publishes *Newsletter* (3 p.a.); *Reading* (3 p.a.). Affiliated to the parent body, The International Reading Association. Abbreviated UKRA.

UNITED NATIONS DOCUMENTATION INFORMATION SYSTEM. *See* UNDIS.

UNITED NATIONS INDUSTRIAL DEVELOPMENT ORGANIZATION. *See* UNIDO.

UNITED NATIONS INFORMATION SYSTEM IN SCIENCE AND TECHNOLOGY. *See* UNISIST.

UNITED STATES BOOK EXCHANGE, INC. *See* USBE.

UNITED STATES GOVERNMENT PRINTING OFFICE. Created by a Congressional Joint Resolution on 23rd June 1860, the Government Printing Office executes orders for printing and binding placed by Congress and the departments, independent establishments, and agencies of the federal government; it distributes government publications as required by law, and maintains necessary catalogues and a library of these publications; it also prints for sale to the public, documents which are of a non-controversial nature. It has the largest printing plant in the world.

UNITED STATES INFORMATION AGENCY. Abbreviated USIA. An arm of U.S. foreign policy which receives its foreign policy guidance from the President of the U.S. and the Department of State. It has public information missions in 106 countries, libraries or information centres in eighty-six, and seventy reading rooms in thirty-four countries. The responsibilities of USIA include explaining those activities of American domestic agencies which have significance in the foreign field. The functions of USIA are (a) to explain abroad U.S. foreign policies and programmes; (b) to disseminate accurate information about the U.S.; (c) to counter and correct Communist propaganda distortions and lies about U.S. policies and intentions; (d) to administer cultural and educational exchanges and programmes as the cultural and educational arm of the Department of State. Gives financial assistance in the publishing of American books in foreign languages, arranges for such translation to be undertaken; publishes books in English overseas; arranges with U.S. publishers to publish books in paperback and simplified editions for distribution overseas; supplies books to USIS libraries, to foreign libraries, bi-national centres, schools and other institutions.

UNITED STATES INFORMATION SERVICE. *See* USIS, UNITED STATES INFORMATION AGENCY.

UNITED STATES OF AMERICA STANDARDS INSTITUTE. *See* AMERICAN NATIONAL STANDARDS INSTITUTE, INC.

UNITERM CONCEPT CO-ORDINATION INDEXING. With this system, invented by Mortimer Taube in 1953, periodical articles or other documents to be indexed are scanned to see their subject contents. Aspects of the subject, called 'concepts', are expressed in one or two simple basic words called 'keywords' (which are to be found in the *Thesaurus* (*q.v.*) containing all the keywords likely to be used in the literature of the subject) and the accession number of the document recorded (by punching holes in numbered squares) on cards on which are entered as headings the 'keywords' or 'uniterms', sometimes called 'descriptors'. The cards are arranged in alphabetical order of uniterms, and the information is retrieved by placing the cards several at a time (for a separate card is punched for each aspect of the document's subject) over an illuminated glazed frame so that the light shines through the holes; alternatively the numbers may be written in columns according to the last digit and the numbers on each card visually examined to discover identical numbers. Sometimes instead of punching holes the 'accession' number is written in the appropriate column (each column being reserved in numerical sequence for the last unit figure) of each selected keyword card. This involves reading the numbers and comparing them on each card to discover which documents are entered on *each* of the chosen cards and therefore which document has all the qualities needed. Light shining through holes on the punched card reveals the same information. The use of a uniterm system is an attempt to replace traditional schemes of classification by a method based on an alphabetical arrangement of 'aspects' of the subject-matter covered by the material to be indexed. It also has the merit of being a method which can be carried out by persons untrained in classifying. 'Uniterm' is a trademark of the developer of the system, Documentation, Inc., Washington, D.C., and is the abbreviation for Uniterm Concept Co-ordination System. *See also* COMAC, CO-ORDINATE INDEXING.

UNITERM INDEX. A method of indexing which involves the selection of 'key words' from graphic records. Keywords represent the content of the record or document that is being indexed. It is not necessary to create or maintain a list of approved headings since a list is compiled as the work proceeds. The keywords must be predicted when analysing a question in order to provide searching clues.

UNITIZE. The separation of a roll of microfilm into separate frames for use individually.

UNITYPER. A modified Remington Electric typewriter which is equipped with electronic circuits and will record pulse patterns on magnetic tape.

UNIVERSAL BIBLIOGRAPHIC CONTROL. *See* UBC.

UNIVERSAL BIBLIOGRAPHY. A bibliography of the world's books. None exists at present, but an attempt has been made by the Fédération Internationale de Documentation (formerly the Institut International de Documentation and the Institut International de Bibliographie). *See also* INTERNATIONAL FEDERATION FOR DOCUMENTATION.

UNIVERSAL COPYRIGHT CONVENTION. *See* COPYRIGHT, INTERNATIONAL.

UNIVERSAL DECIMAL CLASSIFICATION (UDC). French abbreviation: CDU; German: DK. A general scheme of classification covering the whole field of knowledge. It is an elaborate expansion of the Dewey Decimal Classification which was first suggested by Senator Henri La Fontaine and Paul Otlet at the first International Conference of Librarians held at Brussels in 1895, and carried out by the Institut International de Bibliographie, now called the Fédération (formerly Institut) Internationale de Documentation. It has been called the International Classification, is constantly under revision, and is extremely flexible. In application, the three-figure notation of Dewey is simplified where possible (usually by the omission of 'unit') and, when both occur, 'tens' (noughts), and auxiliary signs or Relation Marks sometimes called 'Common auxiliaries' which are recommended to be filed in the following 'Standard' order:

SYNOPSIS OF AUXILIARIES (IN ORDER OF FILING)

a. Aggregation signs + and / (*preceding the simple class number*)
b. Relation signs : and [ ]
c. Language auxiliaries = . . .
d. Form and presentation auxiliaries (0 . . .)
e. Place, region, country auxiliaries (1/9)
f. Race, people, nationality auxiliaries (= . . .)
g. Time, date, period auxiliaries '. . .' (alternatively before e.)
h. Alphabetical and numerical (non-UDC) auxiliaries A/Z, No. 1 to . . .
i. Point of view subdivisions .00. . .
k. Special auxiliaries –. . . and .0. . .

These are called 'Common auxiliaries'.

The object of the scheme is to arrange and individualize, by the use of the subdivisions tabulated above, the entries in a great general catalogue or bibliography, or the written or printed material, however detailed, in a specialized library, in order that users may, to some extent, judge the material without actually handling it. The U.D.C. is used by several hundred libraries, abstracting services and individuals in Great Britain. It has been adopted by the International Organization for Standardization (ISO) which has recommended it for adoption by the national standards bodies which are members of ISO for the classification of their published standards. It has therefore become the most widely used of all classification systems. Full editions of the whole, or of sections, have been published in French, English, German, Japanese, Spanish, Polish and Portuguese. The publication of the English translation of the complete edition (BS 1000), in sections, has almost been completed. It incorporates all authorized extensions and modifications up to the date of publication. The third English abridged edition was published in 1961 (BS. 1000A), (F.I.D. No. 289) and is the shortest abridgement suitable for practical classification. It contains some new sections, and some thoroughly revised ones; the detailed alphabetical index has been extended accordingly. A *Guide to the Universal Decimal Classification* (*UDC*) was published in 1963 – BS. 1000C: 1963. The first section of this publication, by Mr. J. Mills, outlines the modern theory of classification and examines the practical problems of classifying by means of the U.D.C. This is followed by an outline of the U.D.C. tables. Since 1968 the programme of publishing subject sections of the schedules in English has been continued – a list of published schedules (number SL 35) is available from the British Standards Institution, 101, Pentonville Road, London, N1 9ND – and others are being prepared. Versions in other languages are constantly being published. *See also* CCC, INTERNATIONAL COUNCIL FOR BUILDING RESEARCH STUDIES AND DOCUMENTATION.

UNIVERSAL INFORMATION SYSTEM IN SCIENCE AND TECHNOLOGY. *See* UNISIST.

UNIVERSAL SERIALS AND BOOK EXCHANGE, INC. *See* USBE.

UNIVERSITY AND RESEARCH SECTION. Former name for the UNIVERSITY, COLLEGE AND RESEARCH SECTION (*q.v.*) of the Library Association.

UNIVERSITY, COLLEGE AND RESEARCH SECTION. A section of the Library Association; formerly the University and Research Section. It was the first 'section' of the Library Association to be formed (in 1927). The objects of the Section are to increase the usefulness of national, university, and other academic libraries serving research. There are several regional groups and sub-sections. Abbreviated UC & RS. The Scottish Group publishes *Bibliotheck*.

UNIVERSITY LIBRARY. A library or group of libraries established, maintained, and administered by a university to meet the needs of its students and members of the academic staff. *See also* LIBRARY MANAGEMENT RESEARCH UNIT.

UNJUSTIFIED. (*Printing*) Type which is set with equal word spacing resulting in text lines of different lengths. *See also* JUSTIFYING.

UNLETTERED. A book without the title or the author's name on the spine.

UNOPENED. When the 'bolts' or folded edges of the sections of a book, have not been opened with a paper-knife. Not to be confused with UNCUT (*q.v.*).

UNPAGED. Pages of a book which do not bear page numbers. These usually occur amongst the PRELIMINARIES (*q.v.*), if referred to in a catalogue or bibliography, the total number, or the page numbers which the individual pages would have been given, are entered within [ ].

UNPROCESSED PAPER (OR BOARD). Paper or board in sheets or reels as supplied to the printer or stationer.

UNSCHEDULED MNEMONICS. *See* MNEMONICS.

UNSCHEDULED RECORDS. (*Archives*) Those for which no final decision has been made as to their disposition.

UNSEWN BINDING. *Synonymous with* PERFECT (*q.v.*).

UNSIGNED. A book, the sections of which bear no signature letters or figures, and are therefore 'unsigned'.

UNSOUGHT LINK. (*Classification*) In chain indexing, a step in a notational hierarchy which is unwanted for indexing purposes, either because no enquirer is likely to search under the appropriate verbal term, or because of faulty subordination in the classification scheme itself. *See also* CHAIN INDEX, FALSE LINK, SUBORDINATION.

UNTRIMMED PAGE SIZE. The size of a sheet after folding and before trimming – BS. 1413: 1970.

UNTRIMMED SIZE. The dimensions of a sheet of paper, untrimmed and not specially squared, sufficiently large to allow a trimmed size to be obtained from it as required. British papermakers may interpret this term as 'not guillotine trimmed'. *See also* PAPER SIZES, PERIODICAL, TRIMMED SIZE.

UPDATED VERSION. A DERIVATE WORK (*q.v.*) resulting in modifying an INTELLECTUAL WORK (*q.v.*) by removing items of information and substituting for them, or adding, new or more up-to-date knowledge.

UPPER CASE LETTERS. Capital letters, i.e. those contained in the upper of the two cases of printer's type. The 'terms' in this glossary are printed in capitals. Their use is indicated in a MS. or proof by underlining with three lines. Abbreviation: u.c. *See also* CAPITALS, LOWER CASE LETTERS, SMALL CAPITALS.

UPPER COVER. *Synonymous with* OBVERSE COVER (*q.v.*).

UPRIGHT. 1. A book that is taller than its width. 2. A sample of print, or a printing job, that is set to an upright size. *See also* BROAD.

UPWARD REFERENCE. A direction from a less to a more comprehensive subject heading in an alphabetico-specific subject catalogue. The reverse of DOWNWARD REFERENCE (*q.v.*).

URBAN AND REGIONAL INFORMATION SYSTEMS ASSOCIATION. *See* URISA.

URBAN DISTRICT COUNCIL. A statutory local authority which provided local government services within its geographical area. It was entitled to provide public library services under the Public Libraries Act 1892. Councils which had not adopted this act by the time the Act of 1919 became operative lost their power to become library authorities. Abbreviated UDC. *See also* LOCAL GOVERNMENT BOUNDARIES.

URBAN LIBRARY. A public library provided by a local authority other than a county council, to serve an urban area.

URBANDOC. An American project to control the vast literature of urban planning and renewal by developing a computerized system for the retrieval of information. The name URBANDOC was first used in 1964 although the scheme had its origins at a Special Library Association Convention at Denver in 1963.

URISA. Acronym of the Urban and Regional Information Systems Association. Founded 1964 to advance information capabilities relating to urban areas. Membership is open to individuals interested in all phases of information systems. Operates from Claremont Men's College, Claremont, Calif. Publishes *Newsletter* (bi-m.), *Journal* (q.), *Proceedings* (a).

USBE. Acronym for Universal Serials and Book Exchange, Inc., which until the Fall of 1975 was known as the UNITED STATES BOOK EXCHANGE, INC. A private, non-profit making, self-supporting library service organization centred at Washington, D.C., sponsored by national, state, and international library bodies, which took over the stock of the American Book Center for War Devastated Libraries and began its present activities on 1 January 1949. Its function is to transfer publications obtained on exchange from libraries in the United States and other countries, and as gifts from professional organizations, individuals and publishers in the United States, to libraries where they will be useful. These materials are stored in a depository until needed. United States libraries and libraries all over the world are thus able to complete runs of periodicals which are not readily available through commercial channels. About 85 per cent of the exchange members are U.S. and Canadian institutions. A reservoir of four million periodical items and 100,000 books in research fields received from libraries and other agencies is maintained. Publishes *USBE News* (m.).

USER-PROFILE. *Synonymous with* INTEREST-PROFILE (*q.v.*).

USER RELEVANCE. The appropriateness of information retrieved for a user even if it is not exactly what was requested.

USIS. Abbreviation for the United States Information Service which provides libraries in overseas countries as part of the work of the UNITED STATES INFORMATION AGENCY (*q.v.*).

ut infra. (*Lat.* 'as below'.)

ut sup. Abbreviation for *ut supra* (*Lat.* 'as above').

v. Abbreviation for verse, *versus* (against), *vide* (see), *vice* (in place of), *violino* (violin), *voce* (voice) and VOLUME (*q.v.*).

v.d. Abbreviation for VARIOUS DATES (*q.v.*).

v.p. Abbreviation for 'various places' or 'various publishers'. *See also* l.v.

VSC FORMULA. A method of calculating the total desirable floor space for public libraries. It was enunciated by Wheeler and Githens in *The American Public Library Building* and is as follows:

V = number of volumes the building is to contain,

S = number of seats for readers,

C = circulation (loans) per annum (for central libraries the figure for the whole system, for a branch library the figure for the branch only).

Average relations of the above to square footage of area, based on a study of American buildings, gives 10 volumes per square foot, 40 square feet per seat, one square foot of space for loans of 40 volumes per annum; these convert into the formula $\dfrac{V}{10} + 40\,S + \dfrac{C}{40}$ to give the required area of a library in square feet. This formula is affected by the type of plan and particularly by the relative extent of the basement. Wheeler records that this formula applied to his own library at Baltimore approximates to the actual size of the library, but Anthony Thompson in *Library Buildings of Britain and Europe* records that when it was tested out on two branch libraries it gave an area two or three times greater than the buildings actually occupy.

VADE-MECUM. A guide, handbook, or manual which can be conveniently carried for reference.

VALIDATION ROUTINE. *See* DATA VALIDATION ROUTINE.

VAN GELDER PAPER. A brand of good-quality paper which is produced in Holland and used mainly for fine paper copies. A variety with an ANTIQUE FINISH (*q.v.*) is used by artists for drawings, sketches and water-colour paintings. Also called 'Dutch paper'.

VANITY PUBLISHERS. Firms who publish and market books at authors' risk and expense. Also called 'Subsidy' or 'Co-operative' Publishers.

VARIABLE FIELD CODING. (*Cataloguing. Information retrieval*) *See* FIXED FIELD CODING.

VARIABLE MNEMONICS. *See* MNEMONICS.

VARIANT. A term given to corrections inserted in later printings of a book. These are frequent in hand-printed books and are accounted for by the fact that mistakes were noticed and the type altered during printing, the sheets already printed remaining untouched.

VARIANT EDITION. The edition of a work which gives the author's variations, textual changes and alterations in the text of his work possibly from their first composition to their final appearance in a DEFINITIVE EDITION (*q.v.*).

VARIORUM. Abbreviation of the Latin *cum notis variorum* 'with notes by various editors'.

VARIORUM EDITION. An edition of a work composed from a comparison of various texts which have been published previously, variations being given in footnotes, and including the notes of various commentators. In the U.S.A., publishers tend to use this term for Definitive Edition, Textual Variant or Variant Edition.

VARIOUS DATES. Used to describe a volume containing several works of different date or a work consisting of several volumes published at different dates. Abbreviated v.d.

VARITYPER. An electric typewriter (formerly the Hammond) which enables characters additional to normal roman ones to be typed. This is possible by the use of shuttles, of which there are several hundred different ones, bearing the particular type face required. The shuttles, which are semi-circular bands of metal, can be exchanged quickly; an alternative set of type can be brought into action without stopping the machine.

VARNISHING. A process applied to book jackets to give them a shiny appearance.

VAT. The tank containing beaten pulp from which hand-made sheets of paper are made.

VAT PAPER. Another name for HAND-MADE PAPER (*q.v.*).

VAT-SIZED. Said of paper when the size is added to the pulp before the pulp is used to form a sheet.

VATICAN CODE. The Vatican Library's *Rules for the Catalog of*

Printed Books (A.L.A. 1931. 2nd ed., 1948, tr. from the 2nd Italian ed. publ. in 1938) were drawn up to provide a new general catalogue of the Library.

VEGETABLE PARCHMENT. A partially transparent wrapping paper. *See* PARCHMENT 2.

VELLUM. Calf skin dressed with alum and polished, and not tanned like leather. A smooth, fine parchment.

VELLUM PARCHMENT. A very strong hand-made vellum paper, similar in appearance to animal parchment, but almost indestructible and not as easily affected by heat, mildew and insects as are skins. Called 'art parchment' in the U.S.A.

'VENDOR-SPECS-MICROFILE'. A service, designated V-S-V-F, which offers, on microfilm, vendors' catalogues and manufacturers' specifications by industry groups. A Recordak Reader-Printer enables immediate enlargements of selected pages to be made.

VENETIAN TYPE. A roman type which is characterized by heavy slab serifs, thick main strokes, and a slightly oblique calligraphic emphasis in the round forms. The bar of the small 'e' is tilted. The roman types of Nicholas Jenson (for specimen, *see* TYPE FACE) are the finest examples of this kind of type. *See also* HUMANISTIC HAND.

VENN DIAGRAMS. Graphic methods of sorting out the simple logical relationships between objects or classes of objects. They are named after the English logician John Venn (1834–1923).

VERAC. A matrix microfilm storage system (*see* MICROFILM) which was originally known as 'The Mechanized Library'. Information is stored on sheets of film approximately 8 × 8 inches in size. Reduction is between seventy and 140 times. This system has an impressive retrieval speed whereby any one of a million pages can be produced in approximately one second.

verbatim et literatum. (*Lat.* 'word for word' or 'letter for letter'). A literal translation or transcription.

VERBATIM REPORT. A word for word version of a speech, lecture, or debate.

VERIFAX. Trade name for a Kodak copying machine using the soft gelatine transfer process. After the negative sheet (matrix) is made it can be used to transfer six or more images to uncoated paper, each copy becoming progressively fainter. A RAPID COPYING (*q.v.*) process. *See also* GELATIN-DYE-TRANSFER, TRANSFER PROCESS.

VERIFICATION. (*Information retrieval*) The process of checking the original punching of data into an input medium for the computer.

VERNACULAR. The language of a country. When it is directed that a name shall be given in the vernacular, it means the form which is customary in the country concerned.

VERSION. 1. A rendering in graphic art form, or sequence of words, of a record, publication, or document, especially a translation of the Bible. 2. One of several intellectual forms taken by the same work. (These may be an original text and its translation, or various texts in one language based on the same original work) (IFLA). 3. In music, a TRANSCRIPTION (*q.v.*) in which the original work is so changed as to be virtually a new work, either in the same or in a different medium.

VERSO. The left-hand page of an open book or manuscript, usually bearing an even page number. The reverse, or second, side of a sheet of paper to be printed. *See also* RECTO.

VERTICAL FILE. 1. A drawer, or number of drawers, in a case, in which papers or similar material may be filed on their edges. 2. A collection of pamphlets, cuttings, correspondence, or similar material arranged on their edges in a drawer or box.

VERTICAL FILING CABINET. A cabinet of two, three or four drawers, each of which is wide enough to take quarto or foolscap files resting on their spines.

VERTICAL INTEGRATION. The opening of a library for use after all chairs and tables had been removed and serving patrons only on a stand-up check-out basis. This occurred in the Southern States of the U.S.A. during the period, in the early 1960's, of developing racial equality, and followed a few months when some all-white or all-Negro libraries were closed for a period and subsequently opened upon court orders.

VERTICAL PRESS. A printing press in which the flat forme moves up and down instead of to and fro horizontally.

VESICULAR FILM. Film which has the light-sensitive element suspended in a plastic layer and which, upon exposure, creates strains within the layer in the form of a latent image. Heating the plastic layer releases the strains and the image becomes visible; it becomes permanent when the layer cools and the film has received a second exposure which acts as a fixation process.

VESICULAR PROCESS. A photographic process in which nitrogen released during exposure expands on subsequent heating to form minute vesicule bubbles which produce an image by light scattering.

VIBANK. A computerized information retrieval system on mechanical vibration; started in early 1970 under the sponsorship of the National Science Library of Canada, it is based on the Université Laval, Quebec, Canada.

VICESIMO-QUARTO (24mo). *Synonymous with* TWENTY-FOURMO (*q.v.*).

vid. Abbreviation for *vide* (*Lat.* 'see').

vide ante. (*Lat.* 'see before'). ⎱

vide infra. (*Lat.* 'see below'). ⎰ Used in footnotes to refer to an item

vide post. (*Lat.* 'see below'). ⎰ mentioned elsewhere.

vide supra. (*Lat.* 'see above'). ⎰

VIDEOCOMP. A computer filmsetting device which is marketed by RCA.

VIDEOFORM. A textual or graphic image recorded on magnetic tape for transmission by electronic means.

VIDEOTAPE RECORDING. An electronic recording of sound and vision on magnetic tape.

VIGNETTE. A small illustration or ornament used principally in book production at the beginning and ends of chapters, not having a definite border but the edges shading off gradually.

VIGNETTED HALF-TONE. *See* HALF-TONE.

VINCULUM. In mathematics a straight, horizontal line placed over two or more numbers of a compound quality to join them. An old name for a BRACE (*q.v.*).

VINEGAR BIBLE. A Bible printed in two volumes at Oxford by John Baskett, the King's Printer, in 1716–17; so-called from one of its misprints, the 'Parable of the vineyard' in Luke XX being rendered the 'Parable of the vinegar'. Although the production was excellent, it was so full of errors that it became known as a 'Basket(t) full of Printers' Errors'. It was also known as the 'Oxford Folio'.

VINITI. Vsesoyuznyi Institut Nauchnoi i Tekhnicheskoi Informatsii. (All-Union Institute of Scientific and Technical Information). Viniti is subordinate to the U.S.S.R. State Committee for the Co-ordination of Scientific Research, Moscow and to the U.S.S.R. Academy of Sciences, Moscow. It was established in 1952 and is the most important of the organizations concerned with scientific information in the Soviet Union, and has as its main tasks: (a) the preparation of abstracts in the natural and applied sciences, excluding architecture, building, medicine and agriculture; (b) the organization of instruction in scientific information in universities and institutes at undergraduate and postgraduate levels; (c) the organization and co-ordination of research into the rational organization of information activities, and the mechanical and automatic means of processing and retrieving scientific information. Publishes *Referativnyi Zhurnal* (the basic Viniti publication; it is issued in twenty-four series representing various individual branches of the natural and technical sciences excluding building and architecture; over a third of the world's output of scientific and technical periodicals and a great quantity of other literature being processed, and providing the most comprehensive abstracting service in the world), *Scientific and Technical Information* (m.), *Achievements of Science* (a.), *World Scientific and Technical Periodicals*, an annotated index is in process of being published in ten to twelve volumes.

VIRGULE. An oblique stroke, /, used typographically for a number of purposes, e.g. 14/18 as an alternative to 14–18; and/or; in bibliographical descriptions to indicate line-endings. Usually called 'Solidus'.

VIRKOTYPE PROCESS. *Synonymous with* THERMOGRAPHY (*q.v.*).

VISIBLE CLOTH JOINT. A cloth joint used to fasten the sections of a sewn book to its covers, and visible when the book is bound.

VISIBLE INDEX. 1. A frame, or series of frames, usually of metal, for holding cards or strips of card, on which records are entered. They are made so that all the headings contained in the frame are visible at the same time and so that entries may be added or extracted at will whilst maintaining the alphabetical, or other, sequence. *See also* BLIND INDEX. 2. A record, as of periodicals or a list of subjects, contained in such a device.

VISIGOTHIC HANDWRITING. A Spanish form of handwriting, being a national adaptation of the Latin cursive after the dissolution of the Roman Empire. It was used in Spain in the eighth and ninth centuries, and also spread to Italy. *See also* CURSIVE, HANDWRITING.

*VISI*SCAN. *See* BRISCH-VISTEM SYSTEM.

VISUAL AIDS. Film strips, films, lantern slides and other illustrative material used as an adjunct to teaching or lecturing.

VISUAL DISPLAY UNIT. (*Information retrieval*) A terminal consisting of a cathode ray tube; it is used to display data, visually read, from the main memory of the computer. Also incorporated are facilities to key-in inquiries, so that computer files can be interrogated from remote locations. Abbreviated VDU.

VISUAL PUNCHED CARD. Cards which are punched in positions to represent specifically numbered documents, each card being named according to a list of keywords, or thesaurus, and so reserved to represent a particular aspect of information. *See also* UNITERM CONCEPT CO-ORDINATION INDEXING. A card punched to record specific information.

viz. Abbreviation for *videlicet* (*Lat.* 'namely').

VOCABULARY. *See* INDEX LANGUAGE.

VOCAL MUSIC. Music written to be sung by one or more persons: if for many people, it is known as choral music, and in its larger concerted forms of cantata, oratorio, or opera is accompanied by an orchestra, otherwise it may be unaccompanied, or a piano or organ used.

VOCAL SCORE. *See* SCORE.

VOCATIONAL EDUCATION ACT. Passed in 1963, this Act provides for the payment of librarians' salaries, books and other materials for libraries in American vocational and technical high schools.

vol. (*Pl.* vols.). Abbreviation for VOLUME (*q.v.*).

VOLLANS REPORT. *Library Co-operation in Great Britain*, 1952, the report on the working of the National inter-lending system which R. F. Vollans wrote at the request of the joint working party set up by the National Central Library in 1949. The recommendations, together with other proposals were incorporated in a joint memorandum, *Recommendations on library co-operation*, was issued by the joint working party in 1954, and measures to implement them were taken by the National Committee on Regional Library Co-operation.

VOLUME. 1. A book distinguished from other books or from other volumes of the same work by having its own title-page, half-title, cover title or portfolio title, and usually independent pagination, foliation, or register. It may be designated 'part' by the publisher, and it may have various title-pages, paginations, or include separate works or portfolios, etc. The volume may be as originally issued or as bound subsequently; in this sense 'volume' as a physical, or material, unit, may not be the same as 'volume' as a bibliographical unit. A volume of music may consist of a score, of loose parts, or of a score with loose parts in pockets. 2. Whatever is contained in one binding. 3. A document (*see* DOCUMENT 2) or part of a document bound or intended to be bound in one cover and, normally, having its own title-page (IFLA). 4. For library statistical purposes, any book, pamphlet, or document, in whatever form it exists which has been separately published and is separately catalogued and accessioned. 5. A collection of items forming part of the Ultimate Store of information recorded as part of the information retrieval system known as MARLIS (*q.v.*). In a catalogue entry the statement of the number of volumes relates to the physical, not the bibliographical, number, e.g. 1 *vol in* 2; 2 *v. in* 1; 8 *vols. in* 6. The abbreviation for volume is optional.

VOLUME CAPACITY. *Synonymous with* SHELF CAPACITY (*q.v.*).

VOLUME NUMBER. A number used to distinguish certain volumes of a work, set or series.

VOLUME RIGHTS. *See* RIGHTS.

VOLUME SIGNATURE. The number of the volume, as 'Vol. I,' or simply 'I,' or a letter, placed on the same line as the signature (*see* SIGNATURE 2) to prevent the binder mixing the sections of various volumes.

VOLUMEN (*Lat.* 'a thing rolled up'). The papyrus roll used in ancient Egypt, Greece and Rome, which was written on one side in ink with a reed pen, the text being in columns, the lines of which ran parallel with the length of the roll. The last sheet of the papyrus was rolled round a stick which had knobbed ends and served as a handle. The rolls were kept in boxes or on shelves, and for purposes of distinction when placed in this position had a vellum label attached to the end of the roll. This label bore the title of the work, and was sometimes coloured. A wooden case (*Manuale*) was sometimes used to protect the edges of the roll from being frayed by the owner's toga or cloak.

VOLUMINOUS AUTHOR. An author under whose name many titles are entered in a catalogue, whether for different books or for books the various editions of which have different titles. (American.)

VOLUNTARY CENTRE. A library service point which is staffed by unpaid workers – usually in a county library system.

VOLUNTARY OVERSEAS LIBRARIES SERVICE. Formed in conjunction with the Voluntary Overseas Service Association, the organization aims to create libraries in communities that have no official assistance for the buying of books, hoping to supply a need where no other grant is available. British volunteers working in developing countries are asked to gauge demand and to advise on the subject matters of the books required, to ensure that all books are housed safely and accessibly, and that libraries will be maintained after their departure. Abbreviated VOLS.

VOLUTE. (*Binding*) An ornament consisting of a large curl in the form of a Corinthian volute, and at the opposite end a small curl turning the other way. Found in pairs in sixteenth-century finishers' rolls of the heads-in-medallions type.

VOTERS' LIST. *Synonymous with* REGISTER OF ELECTORS (*q.v.*).

VOTES AND PROCEEDINGS OF THE HOUSE OF COMMONS. *See* PARLIAMENTARY PAPERS.

VOUCHER. *See* APPLICATION FORM.

VOWEL-LIGATURES. The ligatures æ or œ are used in Old English and French words (Ælfric, Cædmon, hors d'œuvre, etc.), but the combinations *ae* and *oe* are printed as two letters in Latin, Greek and English words (Aetua, Boeotia, larvae, etc.).

VULGATE. The Latin Bible translated by St. Jerome in the fourth century and authorized by the Roman Catholic Church.

w.a.f. With all faults. An abbreviation used in booksellers' and auctioneers' catalogues to indicate that a book is, or may be, faulty and is offered for sale in this condition and therefore not subject to return because of defects.

w.f. See WRONG FOUNT.

WADEX. Abbreviation for Word and Author Index. A computerized indexing system which uses authors' names as well as titles, printing authors and significant words from titles on the left-hand margin, using them as headings and following them with the full author and title. See also KWIC, KWOC.

WAITRO. Acronym of World Association of Industrial and Technological Research Organizations which is an association of eighty-six independent, non-profit-making technological research organizations in developing and advanced countries. Founded October 1970 to provide mutual assistance among its members and to act as a referral centre and source of technological information and technical assistance to developing countries. Financed by members' dues fixed by the General Assembly, members' contributions, grants from supporting agencies, foundations and industrial organizations, and from the sale of publications. Operates from Vancouver, Canada. Publishes *WAITRO Communique* (q.).

WALIC. Abbreviation for Wiltshire Association of Libraries of Industry and Commerce which was founded in 1961 to develop co-operation between the colleges of further education and the County Library in the matter of improving the supply of, and facilities for access to, technical literature. Lending between libraries is on a voluntary basis; a location list of publications is maintained centrally; the librarians meet regularly to confer about the purchase of books and effect co-operation. The organization is based on the Headquarters of the Wiltshire Library and Museum Service which provides administrative facilities and maintains a union catalogue of the Association's holdings of books and periodicals.

WALL SHELVING. Shelving placed against walls.

WALNUT. Trade name for a mechanized storage and retrieval system which uses photographic and computer techniques. Made by the I.B.M. Corporation.

WALTER PRESS. A rotary press which was first used in 1866 for printing *The Times*. It was constructed by J. C. MacDonald and J. Calverlye for J. Walter, owner of *The Times*. By 1880 this kind of press was in use throughout Europe.

WANDPETLS. Wandsworth Public, Educational and Technical Library Services; a co-operative organization formed as a result of librarians meeting over National Library Week, 1966. Most of the members are attached to educational institutions in Wandsworth. Aims are to provide better facilities for students by exchanging bibliographies, pooling information, co-operatively purchasing special periodicals and books, and making known the resources of individual libraries by means of visits and talks.

WANDSWORTH PUBLIC, EDUCATIONAL AND TECHNICAL LIBRARY SERVICES. *See* WANDPETLS.

WANTING. This word when followed by details of parts or volumes of a publication in a catalogue entry, indicates that those items are not possessed.

WANTS LIST. A list of books wanted, which is issued by a librarian or second-hand bookseller.

WASH DRAWING. An illustration, usually in sepia or black and white, done with a brush.

WASHING. When developing photographic negatives, or making prints on sensitized paper, the materials are thoroughly washed in clean running water after they have been in the fixing solution so as to remove all traces of the developing or fixing solutions.

WASHINGTON PRESS. The American counterpart of the ALBION PRESS (*q.v.*). It was invented in 1827.

WATERLEAF. Hand-made paper in its initial stage of manufacture, consisting of pulp spread and evened by shaking in the hand mould, and pressed between felts. It is semi-absorbent, being unsized, and must be sized before it is suitable for use as writing paper. *See also* ENGINE-SIZING, TUB-SIZING.

WATERLEAF PAPER. BODY PAPER (*q.v.*) which has been prepared for surface sizing or impregnation.

WATERMARK. A paper-maker's device which can be seen on any sheet of good paper when held up to the light. In handmade paper this is caused by twisting or soldering wire into the mould on which the paper is made; in machine-made paper, by a special roller called a 'dandy', which revolves over the moving pulp on the mould, impressing the mark at every revolution. The watermark is usually placed in the centre of one-half of the sheet. *See also* COUNTERMARK, IMPRESSED WATERMARK.

WATERMARKED PAPER. Paper containing a watermark.

WATTS-VERNON TEST. A test devised by Dr. A. F. Watts and Professor P. E. Vernon for determining a person's reading ability. It consists of thirty-five questions of increasing difficulty and has a time limit of ten minutes. For each question the examinee has to select the right answer from five given words. The range varies from the average reading and comprehension ability of an eleven-year-old to that of a grammar school fifteen-year-old. The test is used in national surveys of reading standards.

WAVE-BORDER. (*Binding*) An eighteenth-century finisher's roll border incorporating an undulating line with other conventional ornament. Found in both English and Irish bindings.

WAVY LINE. A line placed underneath words in 'copy' or proof to indicate that bold-faced type is to be used.

WAX ENGRAVING. A method of making electros from which to print maps in letterpress work. The outline is drawn on a wax mould and the lettering impressed by hand. On this a copper shell is then deposited.

WEB. A large roll of paper which is fed into a printing machine.

WEB FED. A printing machine which receives paper from a reel instead of loose sheets.

WEB PERFECTING PRESS. A rotary press which prints consecutively on both sides of a reel of paper.

WEB PRESS. A printing machine on which the paper is fed from a continuous reel. A 'web perfecting press' prints consecutively on both sides of a continuous reel of paper. Also called 'Web machine'.

WEEDING. Discarding from stock books which it is considered are of no further use in the library. PSEUDO-WEEDING is transferring from one department to another, from stack to shelf and *vice versa*, or from files to bound form. Also, examining documents in an archives depository in order to discard items which appear to lack permanent value. *See also* STRIPPING.

WEEKLY. A newspaper or periodical published once a week.

WEIGHT. 'The degree of blackness of a typeface'. (BS. 2961: 1967.) The types in a FAMILY (*q.v.*) vary in weight from extra-light to ultra bold.

WEIGHT OF FACE. Comparative colour value of type faces when printed, as light, medium, bold.

WEIGHT OF TYPE. Four square inches of solid type weigh approximately one pound.

WEIGHTING DESCRIPTORS. (*Information retrieval*) Giving a

measure of relevance to a particular document or question when assigning descriptors to documents and formulating research questions. The weight 'increases' from 1/8 for 'barely relevant' to 8/8 for a 'major subject' when the term is highly specific and covers an entire major subject of the document.

WELSH LIBRARY ASSOCIATION. A Branch of the Library Association formed in 1931; until 1971, it was called the Wales and Monmouthshire Branch. All members of the LA who live or work in Wales are automatically members.

WESLINK. Abbreviation for the West Midlands Library and Information Network, a scheme inaugurated by the Birmingham Public Libraries early in 1975 to promote co-operation among all types of library in the fields of science and technology; to encourage public libraries to be concerned with the problems of small special libraries, and to use the potential of the collective membership to provide improved enquiry and referral services. The area covered is most of the West Midlands Metropolitan County plus the area south of the areas covered by MISLIC and CADIG (qq.v.).

WEST AFRICAN LIBRARY ASSOCIATION. See NIGERIAN LIBRARY ASSOCIATION.

WEST GERMAN SCHEME. A scheme for the co-operative acquisition of foreign books and periodicals which has operated since 1949 and benefits from a state subsidy from the Deutsche Forschungsgemeinschaft (German Research Association). Thirty-six participating research libraries have been given assistance in purchasing foreign books of a scholarly standard in their allotted subject fields, and over 7,000 foreign periodicals have been distributed. All such materials are available to German researchers.

WEST LONDON COMMERCIAL AND TECHNICAL LIBRARY SERVICE. See CICRIS.

WEST MIDLAND BRANCH. A Branch of The Library Association; it operates in the area of the counties of Hereford and Worcester, Salop, Staffordshire, Warwickshire and the Metropolitan County of the West Midlands. The Branch awards the Francis J. Thacker Scholarship every other year for the best essay on a subject connected with librarianship; the prize is £40 to be spent on an approved project in connexion with the winner's studies; entrants must be members of the Branch. The award is financed from funds contributed on the death in 1933 of F. J. Thacker who had been Reference Librarian of the Birmingham Public Libraries and a leading member of the Branch, having been Treasurer and Secretary, 1920–33, of the

Birmingham Branch (afterwards the Birmingham and District Library Association, then the Birmingham and District Branch and finally the West Midland Branch). The scholarship was first awarded in 1934 to Mr Wilfred Pearson. Abbreviated WMBLA. Several publications have been issued in addition to *Open Access* (3 p.a.).

WEST MIDLANDS LIBRARY AND INFORMATION NETWORK. *See* WESLINK.

WESTERN. An adventure story set in the 'Wild West' of America.

WET END. The part of the paper-making machine where the wet pulp is formed into a web of paper, up to the first drier. The other end is known as the 'Dry end'.

WET FLONG. *See* FLONG.

WHARFEDALE. *See* STOP-CYLINDER PRESS.

WHATMAN PAPER. A brand of fine grade English hand-made wove drawing paper which was originally made by James Whatman from *c.* 1770 at Turkey Mill near Maidstone, Kent. Sometimes used for limited editions and privately-printed books.

WHEATLEY MEDAL. An award offered annually for an outstanding index first published in the U.K. The Medal, which is named after Henry B. Wheatley (author of *How to make an index*, 1902) is awarded on the recommendation of a joint panel of the Library Association and of the Society of Indexers. The first award was made in 1962 to Michael Maclagan for his index to *Clemency Canning*.

WHEATLEY REPORT. *The Report of the Royal Commission on Local Government in Scotland* 1966–1969, 2 vols. (H.M.S.O. 1969). The Commission is named after Lord Wheatley who was its Chairman; it was set up on 9th June 1966 'to consider the structure of local government in Scotland in relation to its existing functions and to make recommendations for authorities and boundaries . . . and the need to sustain a viable system of local democracy', and was the basis of the Local Government (Scotland) Act 1973. *See also* LOCAL GOVERNMENT BOUNDARIES.

WHIG BIBLE. *See* GENEVA BIBLE.

WHIP-STITCHING. The American term for OVERSEWING (*q.v.*).

WHITE BOOK. An official report published by the German government, so-called because issued in a white paper cover. *See also* BLUE BOOK.

WHITE EDGES. Edges of books which have been cut but not coloured or gilded. *See also* EDGES.

WHITE LETTER. 'Roman' type as opposed to BLACK LETTER or GOTHIC TYPE (*qq.v.*). This book is printed in roman type.

29

WHITE LINE. (*Printing*) A line of space of the same depth as a line of printed characters.

WHITE-LINE METHOD. *See* WOOD ENGRAVING.

WHITE-OUT. To space out composed matter, as in displayed or advertisement work.

WHITE PAPER. A term often used to denote a Report, Account or other Paper ordered by the House of Commons to be printed, or prepared primarily for debate in the House, and printed in the parliamentary series of official publications. There is a growing tendency, however, to apply the term to similar official publications not required by Parliament and published accordingly in the non-parliamentary series. *See also* BLUE BOOK, PARLIAMENTARY PUBLICATIONS.

WHITE PRINT. A print made by the DIAZOTYPE PROCESS (*q.v.*).

WHOLE BOUND. Books bound entirely in leather.

WHOLE NUMBER. The number given by a publisher to an issue of a periodical or serial publication, and continuing from the first issue. It is distinguished from the numbers assigned for volume and part of volume, and from those assigned for series and volume.

WHOLE-STUFF. The pulp used in making paper after it has been thoroughly beaten and bleached, and is ready for the VAT (*q.v.*) or the paper machine. *See also* HALF-STUFF.

WHO'S WHO FILE. *Synonymous with* BIOGRAPHY FILE (*q.v.*).

WICKERSHAM QUOINS. Expanding steel QUOINS (*q.v.*) which are inserted with FURNITURE (*q.v.*) at the side and foot of a CHASE (*q.v.*). They are adjusted with a key to lock and unlock pages of type in the chase.

WICKETS. The hinged gates fixed at both sides of the staff enclosure to control the entrance and exit of readers.

WIDE. Any material, such as a map or illustration that is wider than the type pages.

WIDE LINES. *Synonymous with* CHAIN-LINES. *See* LAID PAPER.

WIDENER LIBRARY. Collected by Harry Elkins Widener (1885–1912) who lost his life in the steamship *Titanic* in 1912. The books, which are all 'rare', are placed in a special room in the building which was given to Harvard University in 1913 by his mother as a memorial to her son; the building, known as the Harry Elkins Widener Memorial Library, also houses the college library.

WIDOW. An incomplete line of type at the top of a column or page, usually the last line of a paragraph, and avoided in good typography because of its unsightliness.

WIDTH. Type faces are of varying widths in the same FAMILY (*q.v.*), and are distinguished by the following (in progressive order): ultra-condensed, extra-condensed, condensed, semi-condensed, medium, semi-expanded, expanded, extra-expanded, ultra-expanded. 'Medium' is the width usually used and indicates the width which the manufacturer determines is the one representing the design and from which variants in the family have been, or may be, derived. *See also* FOUNT, TYPE FACE 2, WEIGHT.

WILD LOOK-THROUGH. LOOK-THROUGH (*q.v.*) which is irregular and cloudy.

WILDER MEDAL, LAURA INGALLS. A bronze medal designed by Garth Williams, awarded by the Children's Services Division of the American Library Association, to an author or illustrator whose books, published in the U.S., have over a period of years made a substantial and lasting contribution to children's literature. It was first awarded (to Laura Ingalls Wilder) in 1954, and beginning in 1960 was awarded every five years. The selection is made by a special committee of The Children's Services Division.

WILLIAM L. CLEMENTS LIBRARY. *See* CLEMENTS LIBRARY, WILLIAM L.

WILLIAMS AND WILKINS v. THE UNITED STATES.† A lawsuit brought by periodical publishers Williams and Wilkins in 1968 and amended in 1970, alleging that copyright had been infringed by the National Institute of Health and the National Library of Medicine, both U.S. government libraries, in the photo-copying of eight articles in four copyright registered journals twenty-one to twenty-four months old (*Medicine*; *Pharmacological Review*; *Journal of Immunology* and *Gastroenterology*) published by Williams and Wilkins. On 16th February 1972, Commissioner James F. Davis of the U.S. Court of Claims rendered his opinion and recommended decision that Williams and Wilkins was entitled to recover reasonable and entire compensation for infringement of copyright. The propriety of this opinion was strenuously contested in the Court of Claims by the federal government, the American Library Association, the Association of Research Libraries, the Medical Library Association and a number of other educational groups. A panel of the full Court of Claims, on 27th November 1973 overruled by four votes to three Commissioner Davis's opinion. An appeal was filed on 20th February 1974 to the Supreme Court and on 25th February 1975 this appeal failed, the justices voting four to four and one abstaining.

WILLOW. A machine consisting mainly of two rotating drums inside which spikes are fixed to tear out the raw material (rags, esparto, waste paper, etc.) for paper-making. Also called a 'Devil'. Often combined with a 'duster' which removes unwanted dust from the material.

WILSON CARDS. Catalogue cards printed by the H. W. Wilson Company which can be purchased for use in library catalogues. They are specially useful for school or 'popular' libraries, using a simpler form of cataloguing than the Library of Congress. Entries have annotations, and the cards may, if desired, be purchased with class marks, subject headings and added entry headings printed on the top of the cards ready for filing. These were discontinued in 1975.

WILSON COMPANY LIBRARY PERIODICAL AWARD, H. W. A cash award of $250 and a certificate offered annually by the H. W. Wilson Company in respect of a periodical published by a local, state, or regional library, library group, or library association in the United States or Canada which has made an outstanding contribution to librarianship. Publications of the ALA, CLA, and their divisions are excluded. The Award is administered by the ALA Awards Committee, the selection being made by a jury of 3, including an editor of a national library periodical and a member of the Library Periodicals Round Table. The first periodical to receive the Award (in 1961) was *The California Librarian*, the journal of the California Library Association which was then edited by William R. Eshelman. All issues for the calendar year prior to the presentation of the Award are judged on the basis of sustained excellence in both format and content, with consideration being given to purpose and budget.

WILSON LIBRARY RECRUITMENT AWARD, HALSEY W. A cash award of $1000 made by the H. W. Wilson Company annually, and administered by the ALA Awards Committee. It is given to any local, state, or regional library association, any library school, or any other appropriate group concerned with recruitment to the profession. The Award is made for the development of a sustained programme of recruitment for librarianship based on a total continuing programme, not limited to one year's activity. The money comprising the Award is to be used for the continuation and further development of a recruitment programme. The first recipient (in 1966) was the Pennsylvania State Library, Harrisburg.

WILTSHIRE ASSOCIATION OF LIBRARIES OF INDUSTRY AND COMMERCE. *See* WALIC.

WINDOW. (*Archives*) An opening made in repair paper or parchment to expose a small portion of text.

'WINDOW' COPY. Printed pages pasted up on sheets of paper cut to expose the type area so that both sides of each printed page are visible.

WIPO. Acronym of the World Intellectual Property Organization, located in Geneva; it was established in Stockholm in July 1967 and became operative in April 1970 when it continued the work of the United International Bureaux for the Protection of Intellectual Property (BIRPI). Aims to: (a) promote the protection of intellectual property throughout the world through co-operation among States and, where appropriate, in collaboration with any other international organization; (b) ensure administrative co-operation between the Unions created by certain international conventions or agreements dealing with various subjects of intellectual property. WIPO is the only intergovernmental organization specializing in all subjects of intellectual property. It administers the six intergovernmental Unions, the most important of which are the International Union for the Protection of Industrial Property created in 1883 at the Paris Convention, and the International Union of the Protection of Literary and Artistic Works (including scientific works) created in 1886 at the Berne Convention. This last is basically concerned with copyright and works jointly with the IGC (*q.v.*). The Secretariat of WIPO, called the International Bureau of Intellectual Property, functions also as the secretariat of the various organs of the Union. WIPO is not only the administrative centre but also the international organization responsible for the promotion of such property throughout the world through co-operation between the States. The special organ for this purpose is its 'Conference' consisting of all States party to the WIPO Convention. *See also* BERNE COPYRIGHT UNION, COPYRIGHT INTERNATIONAL, IGC.

WIRE. The endless band of plain brass or bronze, tinned or leaded, or of nickel or stainless steel wires, which forms the moulding unit of a paper-making machine and carries the pulp from the breast box to the couching rolls and so felting it into a sheet, or web of paper. The mesh of the wire varies from fifty to ninety wires per inch according to the quality of paper made. Also called 'Machine wire', 'Wire-cloth', 'Wire-gauze' or 'Travelling mould'.

WIRE-CLOTH. *See* WIRE.

WIRE-GAUGE. *See* WIRE.

WIRE LINES. *See* LAID PAPER.

WIRE MARK. *See* LAID PAPER.

WIRE SEWING. Sewing the sections of a book with wire staples driven through the folds of the sections and through tapes, canvas or muslin to which the staples are clinched. Also called 'Wire stitching'. *See also* SADDLE STITCHING, SEWING, STITCHING, THREAD STITCHED.

WIRE SIDE. The side of a sheet of paper which has come in contact with the WIRE of the paper-making machine during the course of manufacture. *See also* FELT SIDE, RIGHT, TWIN WIRE PAPER.

WIRE STABBING. Securing a number of leaves or sections by inserting one or more wire staples, usually from back to front (i.e. not through the fold of sections). This work is done on a stapling machine. Also called 'Side-stitching'. *See also* SADDLE STITCHING.

WIRE STITCHED. The fastening of a single section with wire driven through the centre of the fold and clinched (saddle stitched) or through the inner margin of the section (side stitched).

WIRED. *Synonymous with* WIRE STITCHED (*q.v.*).

WISI. Acronym of World Information System on Informatics, which was set up following a report issued by the Intergovernmental Bureau for Informatics (IBI) in 1972. Developed in direct response to UNISIST Recommendation 1, and financed by Unesco, its long-term objectives are: the comprehensive collection of world information in the fields of computer science, operations research, mathematics, statistics, software and hardware in related areas, dissemination of information in the form of current awareness services (SDI services); dissemination of information in the form of abstracting and indexing services (continuing bibliographical services); distribution of published documents in both hardcopy and microform; special search, reference and referral services; investigation of compatibility of existing information systems and media including standardization of existing formats.

WITH THE GRAIN. Said of paper which has been folded in the direction in which the fibres tend to lie. *See also* AGAINST THE GRAIN.

WITHDRAWAL. The process of altering or cancelling records in respect of books which have been withdrawn from the stock of a library.

WITHDRAWALS REGISTER. A record (in book form or on cards) which gives particulars of all books withdrawn from the stock of a library.

WOMEN'S NATIONAL BOOK ASSOCIATION. The only professional organization in the book trade that covers a national cross-section of women engaged in all phases of the American book industry. Founded in 1917. Membership is open to all women in the world of books – booksellers, critics, editors, librarians, literary agents, writers, illustrators, those engaged in publishing, book production or other activities allied to the book trade. There are ten chapters in the U.S.A., and affiliated groups in Japan and India. It offers the Constance Lindsay Skinner Award, as a tribute to an author and editor who was for a long time active in the affairs of the Association, to a woman for distinguished contributions to the book world. It was first awarded in 1940 to Anna Carroll Moore, and in 1973 to Mary Virginia Gaver, a former President of the American Library Association. Abbreviated WNBA. Publishes *The Bookwoman* (2 p.a.).

WOOD BLOCK. A block of wood, usually box, on which a design for printing from has been cut in relief.

WOOD ENGRAVING. 1. The art or process of cutting designs with a graver or burin upon the end-grain of a block of box-wood, leaving the designs in intaglio for printing. The resulting print appears as white lines or masses on a dark background; this has caused the process to be known as the 'white-line' method. This technique was introduced by Thomas Bewick. 2. A print from a wood engraving.

WOOD LETTER. A large type-letter of wood; used in poster printing.

WOOD PULP. Wood reduced to a pulp by mechanical or chemical means for subsequent paper-making.

WOOD TYPE. Wood letters above 72-point used in poster work, because they are lighter and cheaper than metal.

WOODCUT. An illustration made by pressing a sheet of dampened paper on a block of soft wood such as beech or sycamore which has been cut away to leave a design at the surface, so that when the block is inked an impression will be left on the paper, the cut-away parts showing white. The side-grain of a block of softer wood such as pear or sycamore, is used for woodcuts than for wood engravings, and the design is executed with a knife whereas a variety of gravers are used for wood engravings. The design of a woodcut is of black lines or masses on a white background whereas that of a wood engraving is the reverse; woodcutting is therefore known as a *black-line* method whereas wood engraving is a *white-line* method. Before the invention of movable type, books (text and illustrations) were printed in this way; these are called BLOCK BOOKS (*q.v.*). When movable type came into use, only borders, capitals and illustrations were printed from wooden blocks. *See also* FLORENTINE WOODCUTS.

WOODCUT TITLE-PAGE WITH PANEL. *Synonymous with* FRAMED CUT (*q.v.*).

WOODEN BOARDS. Said of books made before the sixteenth century which had covers made of thick wooden boards. By 1550 they had been replaced almost completely by pasteboards in England, although these had been used in the East for centuries. Leather was stretched over the boards and secured.

WOODSON BOOK AWARD, CARTER G. Offered by the (American) National Council for the Social Studies for the most distinguished social science book appropriate for young readers which depicts ethnicity in the U.S.A.; the purpose of this award is to encourage the writing, publishing, and dissemination of outstanding social science books for young readers which treat topics related to ethnic minorities and race relations sensitively and accurately. Dr. Woodson was a distinguished black social scientist, historian and educator who wrote books for adults and young people which told the story of the black man in the U.S.A. The Award takes the form of a plaque and was first presented in November 1974 to Eloise Greenfield for *Rosa Parks*, the 'mother of the civil rights movement', published by Thomas Y. Crowell of New York.

WORD. In information retrieval, a spoken or written symbol of an idea (*Pei*). In computer terminology, the contents of a storage location. *See also* FILING CODE.

WORD-BOOK. A lexicon, or dictionary.

WORD BREAK. (*Printing*) Splitting a word at the end of a line.

'WORD BY WORD'. *See* ALPHABETIZATION.

WORD INDEX. An index which is based on the choice of words used in a document without considering synonyms and more generic concepts related to the word selected as a heading, or term.

WORD INDEXING. A form of indexing which is the simplest to apply as it assumes on the part of the indexer a minimum knowledge of the subject-matter background and the least amount of technical skill. Such a type of indexing can be performed with precision by machines. *See also* CONCORDANCE, KWIC, PERMUTATION INDEXING and UNITERM INDEX which are of this kind, and CONTROLLED INDEXING, INDEX, UNITERM CONCEPT CO-ORDINATION INDEXING.

WORD RECOGNITION TEST. Usually a standardized test of the ability to read single words aloud. The words are graded in difficulty and the tests yield scores which can be converted into reading ages (the measure most commonly employed when standards of reading are being discussed).

WORDLESS BOOKS. Collections of pictures specially drawn; usually for children, and bound up without words into hard covers.

WORDS AUTHORITY FILE. *Synonymous with* THESAURUS (*q.v.*).

WORK. Any expression of thought in language, signs or symbols, or other media for record and communication [i.e. a work before printing or other publication]. After publication it becomes a 'published work'. *See also* DOCUMENT. A work is now generally taken to mean a published DOCUMENT (*q.v.*) varying in extent from a single paper (*see* PAPER 2) or ARTICLE (*q.v.*) to a contribution to knowledge written by one or more persons and published in several volumes, or even all the published writings by one person. It is also used to include a series of related but separate series (*see* SERIES 1, 2, 3) or PERIODICALS (*q.v.*).

WORK AND BACK. *See* SHEET WORK.

WORK AND TUMBLE. The method of printing the second side of a sheet of paper by turning it over in its narrow direction and feeding it into a printing machine to print the reverse side.

WORK AND TURN. To print from a forme in which the pages have been so imposed that when a sheet has been printed on both sides and cut in half it will provide two copies. *See also* SHEETWISE, TUMBLER SCHEME.

WORK AREA. That portion of a library's total floor space which is allocated for use as working space for the staff. It includes space for desks, furniture and equipment as well as rooms set aside for the exclusive use of staff members.

WORK BOOK. A departmental log book which sets out the duties for the staff each day.

WORK CARD. A card used to record the results of bibliographical searching and checking prior to ordering a book. The SUGGESTION CARD (*q.v.*) sometimes serves for this purpose.

WORK MANUAL. *Synonymous with* PROCEDURE MANUAL (*q.v.*).

WORK MARK. A letter indicating the title, edition, etc., of a work. This is added to the normal author mark to distinguish several books by one author on the same subject, and to give each a definite location. It usually consists of the letter of the first word not an article of the title, plus, in the case of later editions, the edition number, and/or in the case of other titles beginning with the same letter and having the same class number, a figure (consecutively for each title). *See also* AUTHOR MARK, BOOK NUMBER, CALL NUMBER, VOLUME NUMBER.

WORK OFF. To print the paper; to finish printing.

WORK RESPONSIBILITY SCHEDULE. A schedule concerned with the special work assigned to each member of the staff as his own individual responsibility. (American.)

WORK ROOM. A room not open to the public in which any of the technical library routines or manual processes are carried out.

WORK SLIP. A card, or other form of record, that accompanies a document throughout the cataloguing and preparation processes and on which the cataloguer notes directions and information necessary to prepare full catalogue entries, cross-references, etc.

WORK SPACE. The part of a book stack which is allotted to assistants to carry out routine duties, including the space for necessary furniture or apparatus. This space is included in calculations of floor areas and cubic capacity.

WORK UP. A smudge or mark on a printed page caused by a letter or piece of spacing material in an improperly locked forme working up into a printing position during a press run. Also called 'Black', 'Rising space'.

WORKARD. Trade name for the microfilm card made by the Microseal Corporation.

WORKING PARTY ON LIBRARY AND BOOK TRADE RELATIONS. See LIBTRAD.

'WORKING WITH FIGURES'. See PRESS NUMBER.

WORLD ASSOCIATION OF INDUSTRIAL AND TECHNICAL RESEARCH ORGANIZATIONS. See WAITRO.

WORLD BIBLIOGRAPHY. Synonymous with UNIVERSAL BIBLIOGRAPHY (q.v.).

WORLD INFORMATION SYSTEM ON INFORMATICS. See WISI.

WORLD INTELLECTUAL PROPERTY ORGANIZATION. See WIPO.

WORM-BORE (WORMHOLE). A hole or series of holes bored into, or through, a book by a book worm. A book containing such holes is said to be 'wormed'.

WOVE PAPER. Paper which, when held up to the light, shows a faint network of diamonds. This is caused by the weave of an ordinary DANDY ROLL (q.v.) (machine-made paper) or mould (hand-made paper). James Whatman was probably the first manufacturer of wove paper, and it was first used by John Baskerville in 1757 when he printed his Virgil on it. Not to be confused with LAID PAPER (q.v.).

WRAP. Writing and Reading Aids for the Paralysed. This is a subcommittee of the Polio Research Fund; it was responsible for the Samaritan Microfilm Reader which is used by those unable to hold a book or to turn its pages.

WRAP-AROUND GATHERING. A book in which one or more leaves at one end are printed on paper forming part of a section at the other end. This practice was used most in the late seventeenth and eighteenth centuries.

WRAP ROUNDS. Units of four pages of illustrations, or multiples of four, wrapped around a section of a book and sewn with it. Also called 'Outserts'.

WRAPPER. *Synonymous with* BOOK JACKET (*q.v.*).

WRENCH TRAVELLING FELLOWSHIP FOR LIBRARIANS, THE SIR EVELYN. Originally set up in 1965 by the founder of the English-Speaking Union, this Fellowship is now run jointly by the Library Association and the ESU which is an independent organization founded to foster good relations between the U.S.A. and the Commonwealth by a programme of educational exchanges. The aims of the Fellowship are: (1) to enable the librarian chosen to enrich his professional knowledge by visiting American libraries noted for their achievements in his special field(s) of interest, and (2) to give him an insight into, and understanding of, the American way of life. It is open to librarians who are British subjects aged twenty-five to thirty-five who have at least five years' library experience after admission to the Register of Chartered Librarians. Each year the Fellowship finances one award-winner on a month-long tour of American libraries. Although the main emphasis is on American libraries, a proportion of visits may also be made in Canada. The Fellowship covers the cost of all travel and accommodation, and there is also a generous expenses grant. The award-winner himself selects the libraries he (or she) wishes to visit. On his return, he is asked to write a report of professional standard on experiences and impressions received.

WRIT. King's precept in writing under seal commanding an official to perform or abstain from some action.

WRITING MASTERS. In the fifteenth century professional writers, no longer needed for literary works because of the invention of printing, became writing masters. The increase of reading led to a general demand to learn the art of writing, and these masters found employment in the universities, schools, Courts, and houses of the wealthy. 'Writing Masters' Books' giving examples of the various hands, appeared in the sixteenth century.

WRONG FOUNT. A letter of a different face or size from the rest of the text. This is caused in hand-set printing by placing type in a wrong case of type when 'distributing' after a printing job. Abbreviated w.f.

WRONG SIDE. (*Printing*) There is a wrong side and a right side to paper and this is important for many printing purposes. *See* RIGHT.

x. Abbreviation used in *Sears list of subject headings*, 10th ed., 1972, to indicate to the cataloguer under which headings a '*see*' reference is to be made. Similarly, 'xx' indicates that a '*see also*' reference is required.

X-HEIGHT. The height of that part of a lower case letter between the

ASCENDER (*q.v.*) and the DESCENDER (*q.v.*), i.e. the height of a lower case x. Used to describe the apparent height of a type which may vary within the same point size according to the design of the type face, e.g. in 12-point type from 0·056 to 0·08 inches. Centaur, Egmont, Perpetua and Walbaum have small x-heights, Plantin and Times Old Roman have big.

XEROCOPIES. Books reproduced by XEROGRAPHY (*q.v.*).

XERODUPLICATING. The taking of duplicate copies of a document by the Xerox process.

XEROGRAPHY. A method of making copies by the use of light and an electrostatically charged plate. It was invented by Chester F. Carlson, patented by him in 1937 and developed in the Graphic Arts Research Laboratory at the Battelle Memorial Institute. Rank-Xerox Limited., a joint company formed by the Haloid Company and Rank Organization (Rank-Xerox), exploits this process throughout the world. It is used for 5% of the reprographic market and 30% of the office copying market in the United States. Smaller and larger copies than the original can be made, as also can offset plates on a paper base. This is a dry method of positive reproduction of drawn or written material (whether in ink, pencil or colour) and of printed or typewritten matter, or the representation of objects, directly on to ordinary paper which does not need a coated or emulsified surface. The process depends on the ability of static electricity to attract particles of black powder to un-exposed areas of the image. A selenium-coated surface is given a positive electrostatic charge and the image is then exposed to it through a camera. Where light is reflected, the charge will be dissi-pated, leaving a positive charge in the image areas. When a negatively-charged black resinous powder is cascaded over the selenium it is attracted to the charged area. Paper which is then placed over the selenium and charged positively will have the powder image trans-ferred to it, and the image is fused permanently to the paper by the application of heat. The process is automatic and speedy. Books can be copied by using the Copyflo machine. Microfilm can be copied on to rolls of paper or card (giving a normal-sized image) which can be cut to a standard size afterwards. The machines doing this work operate automatically at great speeds.

XERORADIOGRAPHY. The xerographic process used with X-rays. *See also* XEROGRAPHY.

XEROX. Trade name for machines produced by the Haloid Company, Rochester, New York, and available in the U.K. from Rank-Xerox, Ltd., which use the xerographic method of copying. They are being used extensively for copying records, catalogue cards and books. *See also* XEROGRAPHY.

XEROXED BOOK. A copy of a book made by a XEROGRAPHY (*q.v.*) method.

XYLOGRAPH. 1. A block book. 2. A wood engraving.

XYLOGRAPHIC BOOK. *See* BLOCK BOOKS.

XYLOGRAPHICA. Block books.

XYLOGRAPHY. The art or process of engraving on wood. (*United Typothetae*). *See also* WOODCUT, WOOD ENGRAVING.

XYLOTYPE. Wood engraving, or a print from a wood engraving.

YANKEE MACHINE. A machine on which machine-glazed papers are made. Its chief characteristic is one large steam-heated cylinder with a highly polished surface in place of the usual drying rolls. Machine-glazed papers are glazed on only one (the under) side, the other being in the (rough) condition in which it comes from the WET END (*q.v.*) of the machine.

YAPP EDGES. *Synonymous with* CIRCUIT EDGES (*q.v.*).

YEAR BOOK. A volume often called an annual, containing current information of a variable nature, in brief descriptive and/or statistical form, which is published once every year. Often year books review the events of a year.

YEAR NUMBER. A symbol used to represent the year in which a book was published. This may form part of the BOOK NUMBER (*q.v.*), as used with the Colon Classification, and is obtained by translating the year of publication into the appropriate symbols in accordance with the Scheme's Time Schedule.

YELLOW BOOK. An official report published by the French government, so called because issued in a yellow paper cover. *See also* BLUE BOOK.

YELLOW PRESS. A popular name for sensational newspapers and periodicals.

YELLOWBACK. A cheap popular novel, usually not of the first quality. So named from the fact that such books were published in shiny yellow paper covers with a picture on the front.

YORKSHIRE AND HUMBERSIDE JOINT LIBRARIES' COM-MITTEE. An organization which operates (as from 1st April 1974 when changes in local authority boundaries took place) as one of a number of joint services, an inter-library lending system covering the four Metropolitan Districts in South Yorkshire, the five Metropolitan Districts in West Yorkshire, and the Counties of North Yorkshire and Humberside. It supersedes the Yorkshire Regional Library System.

YOUNG ADULT BOOK. One intended for adults but suitable for adolescents.

YOUNG ADULT SERVICES DIVISION. Established as a Division of the American Library Association on 1st January 1957. It is interested in the improvement and extension of services to young people in all types of library, and has specific responsibility for the evaluation and selection of books and non-book materials and the interpretation and use of materials for young adults, except when such materials are designed for only one type of library. Abbreviated YASD. Publishes *Top of the News* (q.), jointly with the Children's Services Division.

YOUNG PEOPLE'S DEPARTMENT. *Synonymous with* CHILDREN'S LIBRARY (*q.v.*).

YOUNG READER'S CHOICE. An award bestowed on the author of a children's book. It takes the form of a parchment presented by Harry Hartman, a Seattle bookseller, and was first awarded in 1940 to Dell McCormick for *Paul Bunyan swings his axe*. Except for three years, it has been awarded annually; the Work with Children & Young People Division of the Pacific Northwest Library Association makes the award.

YOUTH LIBRARIES GROUP. A Group of the Library Association; it exists to bring together all those interested in encouraging children and young people to use and enjoy books. There are ten Branches of the Group. It was founded as the Work with Young People Section in 1946 and changed its name when the present constitution of the Library Association came into operation in 1963. Publishes *YLG News* (3 p.a.) (publication suspended with the Spring/Summer 1975 issue), booklists and a series of handbooks.

Z39. Abbreviation for Standards Committee Z39, a committee of the American National Standards Institute, which represents, in an organized and official channel, the progress of the library profession towards standards for concepts, definitions, terminology, letters and signs, practices and methods in the field of library work, in the preparation and utilization of documents, and in those aspects of publishing that affect library methods and use. It has been sponsored and administered by the Council of National Library Associations since 1951. Standards published include: Z39.1-1967 *Periodicals format and arrangement* Z39.4-1968 *Basic criteria for indexes*; Z39.5-1969 *Abbreviation of titles of periodicals*; Z39.7-1968 *Library statistics*; Z39.10-1971 *Directories of libraries and information centers*; Z39.11-1972 *System for the romanization of Japanese*;

Z39.12–1972 *System for the romanization of Arabic*;

Z39.13–1971 *Advertising of books*;

Z39.14–1971 *Writing abstracts*;

Z39.15–1971 *Title leaves of a book*;

Z39.18–1974 *Guidelines for format and production of scientific and technical reports*;

Z39.19–1974 *Guidelines for thesaurus structure, construction and use*;

Z39.21–1973 *Book numbering*;

Z39.22–1974 *Proof corrections*;

Z39.23–1974 *Standard technical report number*,

It is anticipated that the standard on the *Transliteration of Slavic Cyrillic characters* will be approved shortly.

ZATOCODING. A punched card system for the mechanical selection of information. It uses cards with marginal perforations for notching and was invented by Calvin N. Mooers. A card is used for each document and its subject content is indicated by the notches in the edges of the cards; these permit a mechanical sorter (a Zator '800' Selector) to scan the cards and select those required.

ZATOR. Trade name for a notched-card system of recording information in connexion with information retrieval. A list of subjects must be developed for a specific application, then the coding is done; this consists of a pattern of notches for each subject, all of them overlapping one another. The system can only be used under contract with the Zator Co.

ZIG-ZAG FOLD. *Synonymous with* CONCERTINA FOLD (*q.v.*).

ZINC ETCHING. *Synonymous with* ZINCOGRAPHY (*q.v.*).

ZINC OXIDE. A photo-conductive material used in an electrophotographic process such as ELECTROFAX (*q.v.*).

ZINCO. 1. Abbreviation for ZINCOGRAPH (*q.v.*). 2. A block made of zinc and used as an alternative to a BINDER'S BRASS (*q.v.*). It is less durable, and the impression made with it lacks sharpness.

ZINCOGRAPH. 1. A zinc plate which is etched and mounted for use as a line block for printing book illustrations and diagrams in black and white. The printing method is known as Zincography. 2. A print or design made from such a block. Abbreviated 'zinco'.

ZINCOGRAPHY. A photo-mechanical method of printing whereby designs or line drawings are produced in black and white. It is a relief method, zinc being used for the blocks, although copper is used for specially fine work.

ZINCPLATE LITHO. *See* LITHOGRAPHY.

ZONE LIBRARIAN. One who has charge of a group of branch libraries, one of which provides a full range of materials (books for adults and children, a small collection of reference books, gramophone records, tapes and cassettes), the others being three or four smaller branches providing fewer or smaller services.

ZONE LIBRARY.   A library providing a full library service, but from which smaller near-by libraries, which provide a restricted service within the same system, are supervised and from which their resources are supplemented.

ZONE OF CONVENIENCE.   An area for shelving which is a suitable height for readers. (American.)

ZOOMORPHIC INITIAL.   In a mediaeval illuminated manuscript, an initial letter formed by the bodies of beasts.

ZURICH INDEX.   *See* CONCILIUM BIBLIOGRAPHICUM.

Supplement

This Supplement consists of some entries for organizations or terms which complement others in the main sequence, but consists mainly of recent changes or new developments which have taken place since the main work was prepared for the printer.

AGLINET. Agricultural Libraries Information Network. *See entry under* AGLINET.

AGRIS. International Information System for the Agricultural Sciences and Technology. *See entry under* AGRIS.

ANHUL. Australian National Humanities Library. *See entry under* ANHUL.

BANSDOC. Bangladesh National Scientific and Technical Documentation Centre. *See entry under* BANSDOC.

BASIC. Beginners' All Purpose Symbolic Instruction Code. *See entry under* BASIC.

BSD. Bibliographic Services Division (of the BRITISH LIBRARY).

CARIS. Current Agricultural Research Information System. *See entry under* CARIS.

ChLA. Children's Literature Association.

CID. Centre for Information and Documentation. *See* EURATOM.

CONTU. National Commission on New Technological Uses of Copyrighted Works. *See entry under* CONTU.

EPC. Editorial Processing Centre.

FORTRAN. FORmula TRANslator. *See entry under* FORTRAN.

GLASS. Greater London Audio Specialisation Scheme. *See entry under* GLASS (main sequence).

IBC. International Book Committee (main sequence).

IPRC. Information Privacy Research Center. *See entry under* IPRC.

ISA. Irish Society for Archives.

LIBGIS. Library General Information Survey. *See entry under* LIBGIS.

MERLIN. MachinE Readable Library INformation. *See entry under* MERLIN.

NCIC.   National Cartographic Information Center. *See entry under* NCIC (main sequence).

OCLC.   Ohio College Library Center. *See entry under* OCLC.

OIP.   Office for Information Programs. *See entry under* OIP.

SCOPE.   Systematic   Computerized   Processing   in   Cataloguing. Systematic Control of Periodicals. *See entries under* SCOPE.

STI.   Scientific and Technical Information.*

SWALCAP.   South West Academic Libraries Co-operative Automation Project. *See entry under* SWALCAP.

TOXICON.   Toxicology Information Conversation On-Line Network. *See entry under* TOXICON.

URBIN.   Urban Information Network in New York. *See entry under* URBIN.

DEFINITIONS

ACRILIS.   Acronym of the Australian Centre for Research in Library and Information Science which has been established to pool the resources of documents, reports, theses, expertise and international contacts available at the Information Resources Centre and the Department of Library and Information Science at the Riverina College of Advanced Education at Wagga Wagga and the Office of Research in Librarianship in the U.K., and to collect research reports worldwide with the objects of making them available throughout Australia, promoting research, maintaining indexes to research methodology and abstracts, etc. *See also* PRINTING AND ALLIED TRADES RESEARCH, OFFICE FOR RESEARCH, OFFICE OF RESEARCH IN LIBRARIANSHIP (all main sequence).

ADVISORY GROUP ON NATIONAL BIBLIOGRAPHIC CONTROL.   Established in the U.S.A. through the joint effort of the National Science Foundation, the National Commission on Libraries and Information Science (NCLIS) and the Council on Library Resources (CLR), with the responsibility of advising the sponsoring agencies on how best to co-ordinate their programmes and recommending priorities for action.

AGLINET.   Abbreviation for Agricultural Libraries Information Network which was established within the framework of the International Association of Agricultural Librarians and Documentalists (IAALD), for the purpose of organizing at regional and international levels cooperation among agricultural libraries.

AGRICULTURAL LIBRARIES INFORMATION NETWORK. *See* AGLINET.

AGRIS. Abbreviation for International Information System for the Agricultural Sciences and Technology which was adopted in November 1971 at the 16th Conference of the Food and Agricultural Organization (FAO) of the United Nations. It is in process of organization at two levels: (1) a co-operative, comprehensive and rapid current awareness service covering all the subject fields of FAO's interests; (2) the formation of a network of services, including specialized information services, data banks and data analysis services. An experimental issue of *AGRINDEX* was made in August 1973 in implementation of the Level 1 activity; this began publication monthly in 1975 and is an index of bibliographical material – journal articles, reports, monographs, conference proceedings – in forty national information centres.

ANGLO-AMERICAN CODE. The A.L.A. published in 1976 a revision of AACR North American Text Chapter 12 following consultations in 1972 with the Library of Congress and the Joint Advisory Committee on Non-book Materials. Films, filmstrips, slides and transparencies are included as well as other media not previously covered anywhere in the *Rules*. *See also* ANGLO-AMERICAN CODE and ISBD (both main sequence).

ANHUL. Abbreviation for the Australian National Humanities Library which has been established by the Australian National Library to monitor library resources and library-based information services in the humanities and the arts, to identify gaps and encourage relevant institutions to fill gaps within the appropriate networks of traditional, computer-based, referral and consultancy services. It will also develop networks for films, MSS, rare books, pictorial material, music and sound recordings and maps.

AUSTRALIAN NATIONAL HUMANITIES LIBRARY. *See* ANHUL.

BANGLADESH NATIONAL SCIENTIFIC AND TECHNICAL DOCUMENTATION CENTRE. *See* BANSDOC.

BANSDOC. Abbreviation for the Bangladesh National Scientific and Technical Documentation Centre which developed in Dacca from the East Pakistan branch office of PANSDOC and is now a part of the Bangladesh Council of Scientific and Industrial Research (BCSIR). BANSDOC operates from the premises of the Bangladesh Council of Scientific and Industrial Research, based in Dacca, and functions 'to serve as an infrastructure for an effective research and development programme as a part of the overall development of the country'.

BASIC. Acronym of Beginners' All Purpose Symbolic Instruction Code which is one of the simplest programming languages in common use; it was developed at Dartmouth College.

BEGINNERS' ALL PURPOSE SYMBOLIC INSTRUCTION CODE. *See* BASIC.

BRITISH NATIONAL BIBLIOGRAPHY. From early in 1977, *BNB* entries included records of items catalogued in advance of publication (CIP).

BRITISH STANDARDS INSTITUTION. Further standards of interest:

5332 : 1976 *Data elements essential to the interchange of serials records.*

5374 : 1976 *Codes for the representation of names of countries*

CARIS. Acronym of Current Agricultural Research Information System, a pilot project covering West Africa.

CHILDREN'S LITERATURE ASSOCIATION. Essentially a university-oriented organization, formed in the U.S.A. to advance the scholarly and critical teaching of children's literature, especially at college level. Works in conjunction with other organizations, with publishers and with the public to disseminate information about children's literature. Membership is open to anyone interested in children's books. Abbreviated ChLA. Publishes a quarterly newsletter (members only) and an annual journal *Children's Literature: the Great Excluded.*

CLASSIFICATION SOCIETY, THE. Founded in 1964 as an international body to promote co-operation and interchange of views arising from the inter-disciplinary interest in the principles and practice of classification. Membership is open to persons concerned with a variety of disciplines (various branches of science, linguistics, etc.) as well as classificationists and those concerned with information retrieval in its various forms. Two branches – European, and North American – were formed in 1968. Symposia and discussion meetings are organized. Publishes *Bulletin* (a).

CONSER. A grant from the Council on Library Resources has enabled the Ohio College Library Centre (*q.v.*) to integrate the functions of CONSER with other technical processing activities to form the library's national bibliographic service.

CONTU. Abbreviation for the National Commission on New Technological Uses of Copyrighted Works which is charged with recommending to the President and the Congress changes in copyright law and procedures necessary both to assure access to copyrighted works and to provide recognition of the rights of copyright owners in works reproduced by modern technological systems. CONTU prepared guidelines and submitted them to the House and Senate Judiciary Committees when the copyright bill (S 22) was under consideration.

COPYRIGHT, U.S.A. On 30 September 1976 a bill (S 22) was approved by Congress as Title 1 General Revision of Copyright Law which provided the first general overhaul of the nation's copyright provisions since 1909. It raised royalties paid to song-writers by record-makers and extended new protections to periodical and book writers. For the first time, it imposed copyright liability upon three industries (public broadcasters, cable and television systems and jukebox operators) that were heavy users of copyright material. To bring U.S.A. laws into conformity with international law it extended the duration of copyright from the maximum term of 56 years to the lifetime of the author plus 50 years but for existing copyrighted works, duration was extended for 75 years. The bill limited the photocopying of protected works by schools and libraries, and for the first time codified the judicial doctrine of 'fair use' – the free use of portions of copyrighted material for such purposes as quotation in other works, teaching, news reporting, parody, legal or legislative proceedings and reproduction of damaged literary works. Specifically, *inter alia*, S 22 defined the criteria for copyright protection as 'original works of authorship fixed in any tangible medium of expression', including but not limited to: (a) literary works; (b) musical works, including accompanying words; (c) dramatic works, including accompanying music; (d) pantomimes and choreographic works; (e) pictorial, graphic and sculptural works; (f) motion pictures and audio-visual works; (g) sound recordings. It included among protected works 'compilations and derivative works' such as anthologies, but stipulated that protection extended only to new material added by the author and not to pre-existing material copyrighted or in the public domain. It also protected all unpublished works of foreign origin and published works which met one of the four following conditions: (a) the author was a resident or domiciliary of the U.S.A. or of a country which had a copyright treaty with the U.S.A.; (b) the work was first published in the U.S.A. or in a country party to the Universal Copyright Convention; (c) the work was first published by the United Nations or the Organization of American States; (d) the work was covered by presidential proclamation extending copyright protection to works originating in a country that extended the same protections to U.S.A. works as to its own. U.S.A. Government works are precluded from protection, but the Government is allowed to own copyrights on works transferred to it by bequest, assignment or otherwise. The NTIS (*q.v.*) is claiming copyright under the Universal Copyright Convention. The law takes effect on 1 January 1978 except for the provision relating to works by Americans first published abroad which becomes effective in 1982. *Information Hotline*, November 1976, gives the text of the law and information on the provisions of bill S 22 and the action preceding them.

CURRENT AGRICULTURAL RESEARCH INFORMATION SYSTEM. *See* CARIS.

DEFENSE DOCUMENTATION CENTER. DDC's present organizations are the Headquarters Defense Supply Agency and the Office of the Director, Defense Research and Engineering, Department of Defense; the Center is responsible for the interchange of Department of Defense (DoD) scientific, technical, and management information. The oldest and largest of the four major collections in the DDC depository is the Technical Report collection which was established after World War II. DDC provides paper and microform copies of classified and unclassified/limited-distribution reports from this collection and bibliographic data by manual transfer methods and via an automated on-line retrieval system. The National Technical Information Service (NTIS), Department of Commerce, provides copies of the unclassified/unlimited portion of the Defense collection to the Federal R & D community and to the general public. The other three data collections consist of summaries of management information concerning current DoD and contractually performed research projects at the work unit level, planned research at the project and task level, and current research being performed independently in industrial organizations. Data from these three bases are selectively made available from DDC to authorized users.

DOCUMENTATION CENTRE FOR EDUCATION IN EUROPE. Founded as a tool for inter-governmental co-operation in education, it is financed by the Council of Europe. Publishes *News-letter* (6 p.a.), *Information Bulletin* (3 p.a.), surveys and studies (all dealing with aspects of education in Europe) and also publications of the European Documentation and Information System for Education – except the *Thesaurus* referred to under EUDISED – and are distributed free.

EDITORIAL PROCESSING CENTRE. Facilities provided for a group of societies through co-operative journal publishing by using innovative computer technology as well as the preparation and tracking down of MSS and all the normal manual functions involved in periodical production and distribution.

ENTITY. The name of a country, dependency, or other area of special geopolitical interest (BS 5374 : 1976 ISO 3166 – 1974 *Codes for the representation of names of countries.*

EURATOM. Abbreviation for Communauté Européenne de l'Energie Atomique (CEEA), European Atomic Energy Community. Established on 1 January 1958 in consequence of the Rome Treaty signed on 25 March 1957. Aims to (a) establish the conditions necessary for the formation and growth of the nuclear industries of Member States; (b) develop nuclear research; (c) establish safety standards for health protection, etc. Publishes: *Bulletin of the European Communities* (m.), *Journal Officiel*; *Euro Spectra* (q.) EURATOM was combined with the two other European Communities – the European Coal and Steel Community (ECSC) and the European Economic Community (EEC) – to form the Commission of European Communities (CEC), and Euratom's Centre for Information and Documentation (CID) in Luxembourg assumed operational responsibility for all Commission activities related to documentation and information. *See also* FORATOM (main sequence).

EURONET. Abbreviation for the European Information Network, a community-wide telecommunications network giving on-line access to a number of major scientific and technical data-bases including INSPEC's own files which is being investigated by INSPEC under a contract. EURONET was set up by the Commission of European Communities (CEC) which accepted the Action Plan of its Committee for Information and Documentation in Science and Technology (CIDST) for (a) the further development of sectoral information systems; (b) the development of a joint data transmission network, to be known as EURONET; (c) technical support for information programmes, including training, research, standardization, etc.

FACSIMILE REPRINT. The revision of Chapter 6 of *AACR* provides that facsimile reprints, including the name of the reprint publisher and the date of the reprint should be recorded in the imprint area of a catalogue entry.

FAIR COPYING DECLARATION, 'FAIR DEALING'. *See* FAIR USE.

FAIR USE. The WILLIAMS AND WILKINS v. THE UNITED STATES case (*q.v.*) brought attention and emphasis to the words 'fair use' and, for the first time, they are given statutory recognition. In S 107 of the 1976 General Review of Copyright Law it was stated that it is not an infringement of copyright to reproduce copies 'for purposes such as criticism, comment, news, reporting, teaching (including multiple copies for classroom use), scholarship or research'. Factors for determining whether the use made of a work in any particular case is a fair use are specified, and detailed guidelines are included. *Information Hotline*, November 1976, gives the text of the law and information on the provisions of the bill S 22 and the action preceding them. *See also* GENTLEMEN'S AGREEMENT (main sequence).

FOLIO. 6. One sheet of MS (which should be written, typed or printed on one side only) supplied to a printer's compositor for setting. Folios are numbered consecutively from 1 with arabic numerals to indicate correct sequence, and bear no relation to subsequent page numbering of the resultant print.

FORTRAN. Abbreviation for FORmula TRANslator, a language which is designed for the description of algorithmic processes but is probably the most widely used programming language, having as its main purpose conveying directions from a programmer to a computer.

GENTLEMEN'S AGREEMENT. *See* FAIR USE.

IPRC. Acronym of Information Privacy Research Center which operates from Purdue University to provide industry, government, education, universities and other organizations that share a common concern for information privacy with objective, impartial data and insight into some of the major questions surrounding the current situation.

ISBD. *See* ANGLO-AMERICAN CODE. (Supplement and main sequence).

INFORMATION SCIENCE ABSTRACTS. A ten-year cumulative index covering extracts which have appeared in the years 1966–1975 of this bi-monthly publication (which is sponsored by the American Society for Information Science, the Division of Chemical Information of the American Chemical Society, and the Special Libraries Association); covers more than 28,000 publications in information science, library science and related fields, and was published in 1977. It is the equivalent of 700 closely-packed printed pages but is available only as a 16mm microfilm at 24X reduction.

INTERNATIONAL FEDERATION OF LIBRARY ASSOCIATIONS. At the 1976 General Council, held in Lausanne, 'and Institutions' was added to its name but the acronym IFLA was retained. The purposes of IFLA were revised to 'be an independent international non-governmental association, without profit motive, whose purposes shall be to promote international understanding, co-operation, discussion, research and development in fields of library activity, including bibliography, information services and the education of personnel, and to provide a body through which librarianship can be represented in matters of international interest. In pursuance of these objectives the Federation shall undertake such tasks and enterprises as may be determined appropriate and desirable, and notably: undertake, support and co-ordinate research and studies; collect, collate and otherwise disseminate information relating to library, bibliography, information and training activity; organize general and specialized meetings and conferences; collaborate with international organizations in the fields of information, documentation and archives; set up offices and carry out specific tasks; and shall undertake such other activities as will promote fulfillment of theoretical and practical objectives in every field of library activity.' Membership of IFLA is to be expanded considerably, and there is much work to be done on the detailed implementation of the new constitution. Final decisions concerning the international communications format for the exchange of bibliographical data, UNIMARC, will be taken in April 1977 and publication should follow in July.

INTERNATIONAL INFORMATION SYSTEM FOR AGRICULTURAL SCIENCE AND TECHNOLOGY. *See* AGRIS.

IRISH SOCIETY FOR ARCHIVES (CUMANN CARTLANNA-IOCHTA EIRANN). Founded in December 1970 'to stimulate, encourage and co-ordinate the work of the many individuals, authorities and societies interested in the conservation and use of archives in Ireland.' Membership is available to students, individuals and organizations. Financed by members' subscriptions. Abbreviated ISA. Publishes *Irish Archives Bulletin* (a.).

ISSUE DATE. 1. The date on which a publication was issued to a reader. 2. (Publishing) The specified day, date, month or period by which the date of publication of a particular issue of a serial may be identified.

ITEK PLATE. An offset-litho plate which is created by the Kodak Itek process.

LAMSAC REPORT. *The staffing of public libraries* 3 vols. 1976, published by the Department of Education and Science as No. 7 in their Library Information Series. It has been welcomed by the L.A. as a positive step forward in the assessment of staffing needs now and in the future. *See also* LAMSAC (main sequence).

LA/NCET (LANCET) RULES. *See* NON-BOOK MATERIALS (main sequence).

LEER. Acronym for Libros Elementales, Educativos y Recreativos, an organization formed to evaluate and review recreational and educational materials in Spanish for children and adults; train librarians and teachers in the selection of materials for the Spanish-speaking; and co-operate with libraries, schools, etc. to make available the materials and information. Financed by the Ford Foundation and other foundation grants.

LIBGIS. Abbreviation for Library General Information Survey which carries out detailed surveys on the expenditure, stock and use in groups of library services in school library/media centres, public libraries, and college and university libraries. The first of the surveys (for 1974) was published in 1976. LIBGIS is part of the National Center for Education Statistics.

LIBRARY GENERAL INFORMATION SURVEY. *See* LIBGIS.

LIBRARY OF CONGRESS. In 1976 a grant was received from the CLR to support the systems design and programming required to integrate the functions of the Conversion of Serials Project (*see* CONSER) with other technical processing activities making up the library's projected national bibliographic service. The Library proposes to assume responsibility for managing and maintaining permanently the national serials data base and for distributing the resulting products; it expects to complete absorbing the functions of CONSER by the end of 1977.

LOCAS. Abbreviation for the Local Catalogue Service which the British Library provides for organizations which do not have access to a computer but nevertheless wish to implement an automated cataloguing system.

MACHINE READABLE LIBRARY INFORMATION. *See* MERLIN.

MANUSCRIPTS. The Committee on Manuscripts Collections of the Rare Books and Manuscripts Section of the American Association of College and Research Libraries has revised the 'Statement on the Reproduction of Manuscripts and Archives for Non-commercial Purposes' and the 'Statement on Access to Original Research Materials in Libraries, Archives and Manuscript Repositories.' Both have been approved as policy by the ACRL, and the texts reproduced in *College and Research Libraries News*, November 1976. In the same issue, the Committee's proposed revision of the 'Draft Statement on the Reproduction of Manuscripts and Archives for Commercial Purposes' is printed for submission to the Board of Directors of the ACRL in 1977.

MEDIAMOBILE. A vehicle which carries various forms of media, in addition to books, for loan to the public.

MERLIN. Abbreviation for MachinE Readable Library INformation, an integrated computer system which is being developed by the Computer Services Office of the British Library's Bibliographical Services Division. It is concerned with the existing cataloguing systems which produce the *BNB* and the PRECIS subject indexes and microfilm or microfiche catalogues for BL departments and many outside libraries, and will also develop more advanced techniques and services centred on a data base which will consist of all catalogue records for all users stored in one computer file. It is expected to be available for general on-line use in 1979.

MINISTRY OF TECHNOLOGY. Since the discontinuance of this Ministry, central responsibility for basic civil sciences has rested with the Secretary of State for Education and Science who is advised by the Advisory Board for the Research Councils of which there are five – Science, Medical, Agricultural, Natural Environment and Social Science. Responsibility for technology rests mainly with the Secretary of State for Industry. Other government departments are responsible for research and development related to their executive responsibilities. Several of the government research establishments are the responsibility of the Department of the Environment. A number of research associations are assisted financially by government to carry out industrial research co-operatively. *See also* ACRILIS, PRINTING AND ALLIED TRADES RESEARCH, OFFICE FOR RESEARCH, OFFICE OF RESEARCH IN LIBRARIANSHIP (Supplement and main sequence).

NATIONAL CENTER FOR EDUCATION STATISTICS. The first survey on expenditure on schools libraries and media centres to be made since 1962 was obtained for 1974 by LIBGIS (*q.v.*) and published in 1976. Data for the same year was obtained in respect of expenditure, stock and use of public libraries for 1974 and was also published in 1976. Data relating to college and university libraries remains to be published. Surveys in each of these three fields are to be made annually.

NATIONAL COMMISSION ON NEW TECHNOLOGICAL USES OF COPYRIGHTED WORKS. *See* CONTU.

NETWORK. In the field of information retrieval, inter-connected groups of computer systems (Central Processing Units [CPUs] and peripheral devices or remote terminals) which share resources such as data, software and hardware, thus enabling users to eliminate the duplication of computers and communication facilities. Sometimes these networks are referred to as 'distributed intelligence networks' or 'resources sharing networks'. The major objectives for networking, or linking different computer-based systems together, are to: (a) make scientific and/or bibliographical information more readily accessible; (b) exploit available technology and information resources; (c) increase the productivity of manpower.

NON-BOOK MATERIALS. *See* ANGLO-AMERICAN CODE.

OCLC. Acronym for the Ohio College Library Center, the largest on-line library network at present in existence – in mid-1975 it was serving more than 600 libraries with a rapidly growing data base. Originally set up to serve only college and university libraries in Ohio (it has now extended its services to public libraries and other networks in other States), this computerized bibliographic data exchange system is becoming a national organization via various regional library networks such as NELINET and SOLINET (*qq.v.* main sequence). It provides on-line union cataloguing and SHARED CATALOGUING (*q.v.* main sequence) and has potential for serials control, technical processing system (acquisitions control), interlibrary loan communication, remote catalogue access and circulation control, and retrieval by subject.

OIP. Acronym of Office for Information Programs, a constituent part of the National Bureau of Standards. Aims to promote: (a) optimum dissemination and accessibility of scientific information generated within the NBS and other agencies of the Federal Government; (b) the development of the National Standard Reference Data System and a system of information analysis centres dealing with the broader aspects of the National Measurement System. *See also* NSRDS, OSRD (main sequence).

OFFICE FOR INFORMATION PROGRAMS. *See* OIP.

OFFICE FOR RESEARCH. An 'Office' of the A.L.A., which focuses on the research needs of the profession, surveys existing activity and, in co-operation with units of the Association, universities and other agencies engaged in library research, translates unmet needs into active programmes.

OFFICE OF RESEARCH IN LIBRARIANSHIP. *See* ACRILIS.

OHIO COLLEGE LIBRARY CENTER. *See* OCLC.

ORDNANCE SURVEY. The metric 1 : 50,000 series of maps was issued in 1976.

PLENUM PUBLISHING CORPORATION AWARD. Offered by the Corporation 'to a member of the Special Libraries Association for an outstanding original paper, not previously published or presented, covering any aspect of special libraries or special librarianship.'

The Award consists of $1,000 and a certificate; the Corporation also provides the travel costs for the winner to attend the annual conference of the SLA for the presentation ceremony at the Awards Luncheon. The Award was first made in 1977.

PUBLIC LENDING RIGHT. The Bill was discussed at the committee stage in the House of Commons in November 1976 but not approved. Neither was it included in the Queen's Speech the same month for consideration during the next session of Parliament.

PUBLIC LIBRARY RESEARCH GROUP. Formed as a Group of the London and Home Counties Branch of the Library Association in 1971, in the first instance to consider the question of output measurement and the related area of aims and objectives. It became an independent body in 1974 with an L. & H.C.B. representative on its organizing committee.

RANGANATHAN AWARD FOR CLASSIFICATION RESEARCH. This Award is offered by the Committee on Classification Research of the International Federation for Documentation (FID) in honour of Dr. R. S. Ranganathan, the Indian classificationist. It is made every two years for an outstanding contribution in the field of classification, and was first awarded in 1976 to Derek Austin in recognition of his achievement in designing PRECIS.

RESOURCES SCHOLARSHIP AWARD. An award first offered in 1976 by the Resources Section of the Resources and Technical Services Division of the American Library Association 'to honour the author or authors of a monograph, published article, or original paper on acquisitions pertaining to college and university libraries'. It is a $1,000 scholarship, donated by the National Library Service, Inc., to the U.S.A. or Canadian library school of the winning author's choice, which will select a library science student concentrating in the area of acquisitions or collection development to receive the scholarship money. It was first awarded to Hendrik Edelman, Carol Nemeyer and Sandra Paul for a jointly-written article.

SCATT. Acronym of a proposed national network known as National Scientific Communication and Technology Transfer system which was developed by a team at the Busch Center of the Wharton School, University of Pennsylvania, under a grant from the (American) National Science Foundation, and presented in 1976 to groups of potential participants and users for evaluation and suggestions. Details are in *Information Hotline*, October 1976.

SCOCLIS. Acronym of the STANDING CONFERENCE OF CO-OPERATIVE LIBRARY AND INFORMATION SERVICES (*q.v.* main sequence).

SCOPE. 1. Abbreviation for the Systematic Computerized Processing in Cataloguing system which is an automated system for the catalogue department of a university library. It is an economic system which produces spine labels, pocket labels, book cards for the circulation system, catalogue cards including shelf list, main entry, subject and added entry cards, statistics, an updated master file in machine-readable form, and an accessions file. It was developed at the University of Guelph Library, Canada. 2. Abbreviation for Systematic Control of Periodicals, a system implemented by the Technical Information Department of Pfizer, Inc. at the Medical Research Laboratories in Groton, Connecticut, and is used for a computerized serials record system.

SOUTH WEST ACADEMIC LIBRARIES CO-OPERATIVE AUTOMATION PROJECT. See SWALCAP.

SUBJECT HEADING. There will henceforth be annual supplements to the 8th edition of *Library of Congress Subject Headings*, published in 1975, listing all subsequent additions and changes.

SWALCAP. Acronym of the South West Academic Libraries Co-operative Automation Project. It is a new on-line computerized system (centred on the Bristol University Library) for circulation control and for the tracing of books within libraries. It became operative late in 1976 between Bristol and Exeter Universities and University College Cardiff.

SYSTEMATIC COMPUTERIZED PROCESSING IN CATALOGUING. See SCOPE.

SYSTEMATIC CONTROL OF PERIODICALS. See SCOPE.

THESAURUS. 6. A terminological control device used in translating from the natural language of documents, indexers or users into a more constrained 'system language'. It is a controlled and dynamic vocabulary of semantically and generically related terms which covers a specific domain of knowledge. (Adopted by Unesco and published in *Guidelines for the establishment and development of monolingual thesauri*.)

TOXICOLOGY INFORMATION CONVERSATION ON-LINE NETWORK. See TOXICON.

TOXICON. Acronym for Toxicology Information Conversation On-Line Network which provides a data-base of bibliographic information on toxicology. Access to it is provided by the National Library of Medicine's on-line system TOXLINE. See also TOXLINE DATA BANK (main sequence).

UNIMARC. A system for the international communications format for the exchange of bibliographic data. It was proposed by IFLA and became operative in 1977.

URBAN INFORMATION NETWORK IN NEW YORK. *See* URBIN.

URBIN. Abbreviation for Urban Information Network in New York, an informal local level group of urban affairs librarians who, through personal contacts, are learning the expertise and resources of each other and their libraries.

WILLIAMS AND WILKINS v. THE UNITED STATES. *See* FAIR USE.

Z39. Further standards of the American National Standards Institute:

Z39. 25 – 1975 *Romanization of Hebrew.*

Z39. 27 – 1976 *Structure for the representation of names of countries of the world for information exchange.*